D1173431

THE
OXFORD SPANISH
MINIDICTIONARY

Spanish-English
English-Spanish

Español-Inglés
Inglés-Español

CHRISTINE LEA

Oxford   New York
OXFORD UNIVERSITY PRESS

Oxford University Press, Walton Street, Oxford OX2 6DP

Oxford New York

Athens Auckland Bangkok Bombay
Calcutta Cape Town Dar es Salaam Delhi
Florence Hong Kong Istanbul Karachi
Kuala Lumpur Madras Madrid Melbourne
Mexico City Nairobi Paris Singapore
Taipei Tokyo Toronto
and associated companies in
Berlin Ibadan

Oxford is a trade mark of Oxford University Press

British Library Cataloguing in Publication Data

Lea, Christine
The Oxford Spanish minidictionary Spanish-English.
English-Spanish.—(Oxford minidictionaries).
1. Spanish language—Dictionaries—English.
2. English language—Dictionaries—Spanish.
I. Title
453cu   PC1640

Library of Congress Cataloging in Publication Data

The Oxford Spanish minidictionary
1. Spanish language—Dictionaries—English.
2. English language—Dictionaries—Spanish.
I. Lea, Christine.
PC1640.09   1986   453v.21   86-12453
ISBN 0-19-864156-7 (pbk)

9 10 8

Printed in Great Britain by
Charles Letts (Scotland) Ltd., Dalkeith, Scotland

Contents · Índice

Preface · Prefacio .... iv · v

Introduction · Introducción .... vi · vii

Pronunciation · Pronunciación .... viii · x
  Spanish · española .... viii · ix
  English · inglesa x

Abbreviations · Abreviaturas .... xi · xii

Spanish-English · Español-Inglés .... 1 · 277

English-Spanish · Inglés-Español ...... 279 · 628

Numbers · Números .... 629 · 630

Spanish verbs · Verbos españoles .... 631 · 638

Verbos irregulares ingleses .... 639 · 643

Preface

The Oxford Spanish Minidictionary has been written with speakers of both English and Spanish in mind and contains the most useful words and expressions of the English and Spanish languages of today. Wide coverage of culinary and motoring terms has been included to help the tourist.

Common abbreviations, names of countries, and other useful geographical names are included.

English pronunciation is given by means of the International Phonetic Alphabet. It is shown for all headwords and for those derived words whose pronunciation is not easily deduced from that of a headword. The rules for pronunciation of Spanish are given on page viii.

I should like to thank particularly Mary-Carmen Beaven whose comments have been invaluable. I would also like to acknowledge the help given me unwittingly by Dr M. Janes and Mrs J. Andrews whose French and Italian Minidictionaries have served as models for the present work.

C.A.L.

November 1992

Prefacio

Este minidiccionario de Oxford se escribió tanto para los hispanohablantes como para los anglo-parlantes y contiene las palabras y frases más corrientes de ambas lenguas de hoy. Se incluyen muchos términos culinarios y de automovilismo que pueden servir al turista.

Las abreviaturas más corrientes, los nombres de países, y otros términos geográficos figuran en este diccionario.

La pronunciación inglesa sigue el Alfabeto Fonético Internacional. Se incluye para cada palabra clave y todas las derivadas cuya pronunciación no es fácil de deducir a partir de la palabra clave. Las reglas de la pronunciación española se encuentran en la página viii.

Quisiera reconocer la ayuda de Mary-Carmen Beaven cuyas observaciones me han sido muy valiosas. También quiero agradecerles al Dr. M. Janes y a la Sra. J. Andrews cuyos minidiccionarios del francés y del italiano me han servido de modelo para el presente.

C.A.L.

Noviembre 1992

Introduction

The swung dash (~) is used to replace a headword or that part of a headword preceding the vertical bar (|). In both English and Spanish only irregular plurals are given. Normally Spanish nouns and adjectives ending in an unstressed vowel form the plural by adding *s* (e.g. *libro, libros*). Nouns and adjectives ending in a stressed vowel or a consonant add *es* (e.g. *rubí, rubíes; pared, paredes*). An accent on the final syllable is not required when *es* is added (e.g. *nación, naciones*). Final *z* becomes *ces* (e.g. *vez, veces*). Spanish nouns and adjectives ending in *o* form the feminine by changing the final *o* to *a* (e.g. *hermano, hermana*). Most Spanish nouns and adjectives ending in anything other than final *o* do not have a separate feminine form with the exception of those denoting nationality etc; these add *a* to the masculine singular form (e.g. *español, española*). An accent on the final syllable is then not required (e.g. *inglés, inglesa*). Adjectives ending in *án, ón,* or *or* behave like those denoting nationality with the following exceptions: *inferior, mayor, mejor, menor, peor, superior* where the feminine has the same form as the masculine. Spanish verb tables will be found in the appendix.

The Spanish alphabet

In Spanish *ch, ll* and *ñ* are considered separate letters and in the Spanish-English section, therefore, they will be found after *cu, lu* and *ny* respectively.

Introducción

La tilde (∼) se emplea para substituir a la palabra cabeza de artículo o aquella parte de tal palabra que precede a la barra vertical (|). Tanto en inglés como en español se dan los plurales solamente si son irregulares. Para formar el plural regular en inglés se añade la letra *s* al sustantivo singular, pero se añade *es* cuando se trata de una palabra que termina en *ch, sh, s, ss, us, x, o z* (p.ej. *sash, sashes*). En el caso de una palabra que termina en *y* precedida por una consonante, la *y* se cambia en *ies* (p.ej. *baby, babies*). Para formar el tiempo pasado y el participio pasado se añade *ed* al infinitivo de los verbos regulares ingleses (p.ej. *last, lasted*). En el caso de los verbos ingleses que terminan en *e* muda se añade sólo la *d* (p.ej. *move, moved*). En el caso de los verbos ingleses que terminan en *y* hay que cambiar la *y* en *ied* (p.ej. *carry, carried*). Los verbos irregulares se encuentran en el diccionario por orden alfabético remitidos al infinitivo, y también en la lista en el apéndice.

Pronunciation of Spanish

Vowels:

a	is between pronunciation of *a* in English *cat* and *arm*
e	is like *e* in English *bed*
i	is like *ee* in English *see* but a little shorter
o	is like *o* in English *hot* but a little longer
u	is like *oo* in English *too*
y	when a vowel is as Spanish **i**

Consonants:

b	1) in initial position or after nasal consonant is like English *b*
	2) in other positions is between English *b* and English *v*
c	1) before **e** or **i** is like *th* in English *thin*
	2) in other positions is like *c* in English *cat*
ch	is like *ch* in English *chip*
d	1) in initial position, after nasal consonants and after **l** is like English *d*
	2) in other positions is like *th* in English *this*
f	is like English *f*
g	1) before **e** or **i** is like *ch* in Scottish *loch*
	2) in initial position is like *g* in English *get*
	3) in other positions is like 2) but a little softer
h	is silent in Spanish but see also **ch**
j	is like *ch* in Scottish *loch*
k	is like English *k*
l	is like English *l* but see also **ll**
ll	is like *lli* in English *million*
m	is like English *m*
n	is like English *n*
ñ	is like *ni* in English *opinion*

p	is like English *p*
q	is like English *k*
r	is rolled or trilled
s	is like *s* in English *sit*
t	is like English *t*
v	1) in initial position or after nasal consonant is like English *b*
	2) in other positions is between English *b* and English *v*
w	is like Spanish **b** or **v**
x	is like English *x*
y	is like English *y*
z	is like *th* in English *thin*

Proprietary terms

This dictionary includes some words which are, or are asserted to be, proprietary names or trade marks. Their inclusion does not imply that they have acquired for legal purposes a non-proprietary or general significance, nor is any other judgement implied concerning their legal status. In cases where the editor has some evidence that a word is used as a proprietary name or trade mark this is indicated by the letter (P), but no judgement concerning the legal status of such words is made or implied thereby.

Marcas registradas

Este diccionario incluye algunas palabras que son o pretenden ser marcas registradas. No debe atribuirse ningún valor jurídico ni a la presencia ni a la ausencia de tal designación.

Pronunciación Inglesa

Símbolos fonéticos

Vocales y diptongos

iː	see	ə	ago
ɪ	sit	eɪ	page
e	ten	əʊ	home
æ	hat	aɪ	five
ɑː	arm	aɪə	fire
ɒ	got	aʊ	now
ɔː	saw	aʊə	flour
ʊ	put	ɔɪ	join
uː	too	ɪə	near
ʌ	cup	eə	hair
ɜː	fur	ʊə	poor

Consonantes

p	pen	s	so
b	bad	z	zoo
t	tea	ʃ	she
d	dip	ʒ	measure
k	cat	h	how
g	got	m	man
tʃ	chin	n	no
dʒ	June	ŋ	sing
f	fall	l	leg
v	voice	r	red
θ	thin	j	yes
ð	then	w	wet

Abbreviations · Abreviaturas

adjective	*a*	adjetivo
abbreviation	*abbr/abrev*	abreviatura
administration	*admin*	administración
adverb	*adv*	adverbio
American	*Amer*	americano
anatomy	*anat*	anatomía
architecture	*archit/arquit*	arquitectura
definite article	*art def*	artículo definido
indefinite article	*art indef*	artículo indefinido
astrology	*astr*	astrología
motoring	*auto*	automóvil
auxiliary	*aux*	auxiliar
aviation	*aviat/aviac*	aviación
biology	*biol*	biología
botany	*bot*	botánica
commerce	*com*	comercio
conjunction	*conj*	conjunción
cookery	*culin*	cocina
electricity	*elec*	electricidad
school	*escol*	enseñanza
Spain	*Esp*	España
feminine	*f*	femenino
familiar	*fam*	familiar
figurative	*fig*	figurado
philosophy	*fil*	filosofía
photography	*foto*	fotografía
geography	*geog*	geografía
geology	*geol*	geología
grammar	*gram*	gramática
humorous	*hum*	humorístico
interjection	*int*	interjección
interrogative	*inter*	interrogativo
invariable	*invar*	invariable
legal, law	*jurid*	jurídico
Latin American	*LAm*	latinoamericano
language	*lang*	lengua(je)
masculine	*m*	masculino
mathematics	*mat(h)*	matemáticas
mechanics	*mec*	mecánica
medicine	*med*	medicina

military	*mil*	militar
music	*mus*	música
mythology	*myth*	mitología
noun	*n*	nombre
nautical	*naut*	náutica
oneself	*o.s.*	uno mismo, se
proprietary term	*P*	marca registrada
pejorative	*pej*	peyorativo
philosophy	*phil*	filosofía
photography	*photo*	fotografía
plural	*pl*	plural
politics	*pol*	política
possessive	*poss*	posesivo
past participle	*pp*	participio de pretérito
prefix	*pref*	prefijo
preposition	*prep*	preposición
present participle	*pres p*	participio de presente
pronoun	*pron*	pronombre
psychology	*psych*	psicología
past tense	*pt*	tiempo pasado
railway	*rail*	ferrocarril
relative	*rel*	relativo
religion	*relig*	religión
school	*schol*	enseñanza
singular	*sing*	singular
slang	*sl*	argot
someone	*s.o.*	alguien
something	*sth*	algo
technical	*tec*	técnico
television	*TV*	televisión
university	*univ*	universidad
auxiliary verb	*v aux*	verbo auxiliar
verb	*vb*	verbo
intransitive verb	*vi*	verbo intransitivo
pronominal verb	*vpr*	verbo pronominal
transitive verb	*vt*	verbo transitivo
transitive & intransitive verb	*vti*	verbo transitivo e intransitivo

ESPAÑOL-INGLÉS
SPANISH—ENGLISH

A

a *prep* in, at; (*dirección*) to; (*tiempo*) at; (*hasta*) to, until; (*fecha*) on; (*más tarde*) later; (*medio*) by; (*precio*) for, at. ~ 5 km 5 km away. ¿~ cuántos estamos? what's the date? ~l día siguiente the next day. ~ la francesa in the French fashion. ~ las 2 at 2 o'clock. ~ los 25 años (*edad*) at the age of 25; (*después de*) after 25 years. ~ no ser por but for. ~ que I bet. ~ 28 de febrero on the 28th of February

ábaco *m* abacus

abad *m* abbot

abadejo *m* (*pez*) cod

abad|esa *f* abbess. ~ía *f* abbey

abajo *adv* (down) below; (*dirección*) down(wards); (*en casa*) downstairs. —*int* down with. **calle** ~ down the street. **el** ~ **firmante** the undersigned. **escaleras** ~ downstairs. **la parte de** ~ the bottom part. **los de** ~ those at the bottom. **más** ~ below.

abalanzarse [10] *vpr* rush towards

abalorio *m* glass bead

abanderado *m* standard-bearer

abandon|ado *adj* abandoned; (*descuidado*) neglected; (*personas*) untidy. ~**ar** *vt* leave (*un lugar*); abandon (*personas*, *cosas*). —*vi* give up. ~**arse** *vpr* give in; (*descuidarse*) let o.s. go. ~**o** *m* abandonment; (*estado*) abandon

abani|car [7] *vt* fan. ~**co** *m* fan. ~**queo** *m* fanning

abarat|amiento *m* reduction in price. ~**r** *vt* reduce. ~**rse** *vpr* (*precios*) come down

abarca *f* sandal

abarcar [7] *vt* put one's arms around, embrace; (*comprender*) embrace; (*LAm*, *acaparar*) monopolize

abarquillar *vt* warp. ~**se** *vpr* warp

abarrotar *vt* overfill, pack full

abarrotes *mpl* (*LAm*) groceries

abast|ecer [11] *vt* supply. ~**ecimiento** *m* supply; (*acción*) supplying. ~**o** *m* supply. **dar** ~**o** supply

abati|do *a* depressed. ~**miento** *m* depression. ~**r** *vt* knock down, demolish; (*fig*, *humillar*) humiliate. ~**rse** *vpr* swoop (**sobre** on); (*ponerse abatido*) get depressed

abdica|ción *f* abdication. ~**r** [7] *vt* give up. —*vi* abdicate

abdom|en *m* abdomen. ~**inal** *a* abdominal

abecé *m* (*fam*) alphabet, ABC. ~**edario** *m* alphabet

abedul *m* birch (tree)

abej|a *f* bee. **∼arrón** *m* bumble-bee. **∼ón** *m* drone. **∼orro** *m* bumble-bee; (*insecto coleóptero*) cockchafer

aberración *f* aberration

abertura *f* opening

abet|al *m* fir wood. **∼o** *m* fir (tree)

abierto *pp* *véase* **abrir**. —*a* open

abigarra|do *a* multi-coloured; (*fig, mezclado*) mixed. **∼miento** *m* variegation

abigeato *m* (*Mex*) rustling

abism|al *a* abysmal; (*profundo*) deep. **∼ar** *vt* throw into an abyss; (*fig, abatir*) humble. **∼arse** *vpr* be absorbed (**en** in), be lost (**en** in). **∼o** *m* abyss; (*fig, diferencia*) world of difference

abizcochado *a* spongy

abjura|ción *f* abjuration. **∼r** *vt* forswear. —*vi.* **∼r de** forswear

abланда|miento *m* softening. **∼r** *vt* soften. **∼rse** *vpr* soften

ablución *f* ablution

abnega|ción *f* self-sacrifice. **∼do** *a* self-sacrificing

aboba|do *a* silly. **∼miento** *m* silliness

aboca|do *a* (*vino*) medium. **∼r** [7] *vt* pour out

abocetar *vt* sketch

abocinado *a* trumpet-shaped

abochornar *vt* suffocate; (*fig, avergonzar*) embarrass. **∼se** *vpr* feel embarrassed; (*plantas*) wilt

abofetear *vt* slap

aboga|cía *f* legal profession. **∼do** *m* lawyer; (*notario*) solicitor; (*en el tribunal*) barrister, attorney (*Amer*). **∼r** [12] *vi* plead

abolengo *m* ancestry

aboli|ción *f* abolition. **∼cionismo** *m* abolitionism. **∼cionista** *m & f* abolitionist. **∼r** [24] *vt* abolish

abolsado *a* baggy

abolla|dura *f* dent. **∼r** *vt* dent

abomba|do *a* convex; (*Arg, borracho*) drunk. **∼r** *vt* make

convex. **∼rse** *vpr* (*LAm, corromperse*) start to rot, go bad

aomina|ble *a* abominable. **∼ción** *f* abomination. **∼r** *vt* detest. —*vi.* **∼r de** detest

abona|ble *a* payable. **∼do** *a* paid. —*m* subscriber

abonanzar *vi* (*tormenta*) abate; (*tiempo*) improve

abon|ar *vt* pay; (*en agricultura*) fertilize. **∼aré** *m* promissory note. **∼arse** *vpr* subscribe. **∼o** *m* payment; (*estiércol*) fertilizer; (*a un periódico*) subscription

aborda|ble *a* reasonable; (*persona*) approachable. **∼je** *m* boarding. **∼r** *vt* tackle (*un asunto*); approach (*una persona*); (*naut*) come alongside

aborigen *a & m* native

aborrascarse *vpr* get stormy

aborrec|er [11] *vt* hate; (*exasperar*) annoy. **∼ible** *a* loathsome. **∼ido** *a* hated. **∼imiento** *m* hatred

aborregado *a* (*cielo*) mackerel

abort|ar *vi* have a miscarriage. **∼ivo** *a* abortive. **∼o** *m* miscarriage; (*voluntario*) abortion; (*fig, monstruo*) abortion. **hacerse ∼ar** have an abortion

abotaga|miento *m* swelling. **∼rse** [12] *vpr* swell up

abotonar *vt* button (up)

abóveda|do *a* vaulted. **∼r** *vt* vault

abra *f* cove

abracadabra *m* abracadabra

abrasa|dor *a* burning. **∼r** *vt* burn; (*fig, consumir*) consume. **∼rse** *vpr* burn

abrasi|ón *f* abrasion; (*geología*) erosion. **∼vo** *a* abrasive

abraz|adera *f* bracket. **∼ar** *vt* [10] embrace; (*encerrar*) enclose. **∼arse** *vpr* embrace. **∼o** *m* hug. **un fuerte ∼o de** (*en una carta*) with best wishes from

abrecartas *m* paper-knife

ábrego *m* south wind

abrelatas *m invar* tin opener (*Brit*), can opener

abreva|**dero** *m* watering place. **~r** *vt* water (*animales*). **~rse** *vpr* (*animales*) drink

abrevia|**ción** *f* abbreviation; (*texto abreviado*) abridged text. **~do** *a* brief; (*texto*) abridged. **~r** *vt* abbreviate; abridge (*texto*); cut short (*viaje etc*). **~vi** be brief. **~tura** *f* abbreviation

abrig|**ada** *f* shelter. **~adero** *m* shelter. **~ado** *a* (*lugar*) sheltered; (*personas*) well wrapped up. **~ar** [12] *vt* shelter; cherish (*esperanza*); harbour (*duda, sospecha*). **~arse** *vpr* (take) shelter; (*con ropa*) wrap up. **~o** *m* (over)coat; (*lugar*) shelter

abril *m* April. **~eño** *a* April

abrillantar *vt* polish

abrir [*pp* **abierto**] *vt/i* open. **~se** *vpr* open; (*extenderse*) open out; (*el tiempo*) clear

abrocha|**dor** *m* buttonhook. **~r** *vt* do up; (*con botones*) button up

abrojo *m* thistle

abroncar [7] *vt* (*fam*) tell off; (*abuchear*) boo; (*avergonzar*) shame. **~se** *vpr* be ashamed; (*enfadarse*) get annoyed

abroquelarse *vpr* shield o.s.

abruma|**dor** *a* overwhelming. **~r** *vt* overwhelm

abrupto *a* steep; (*áspero*) harsh

abrutado *a* brutish

absceso *m* abscess

absentismo *m* absenteeism

ábside *m* apse

absintio *m* absinthe

absolución *f* (*relig*) absolution; (*jurid*) acquittal

absolut|**amente** *adv* absolutely, completely. **~ismo** *m* absolutism. **~ista** *a & m & f* absolutist. **~o** *a* absolute. **en ~o** *orio* of acquittal. **en ~o** (*de manera absoluta*) absolutely; (*con sentido negativo*) (not) at all

absolver [2, *pp* **absuelto**] *vt* (*relig*) absolve; (*jurid*) acquit

absor|**bente** *a* absorbent; (*fig, interesante*) absorbing. **~ber** *vt* absorb. **~ción** *f* absorption. **~to** *a* absorbed

abstemio *a* teetotal. **—m** teetotaller

absten|**ción** *f* abstention. **~erse** [40] *vpr* abstain, refrain (*de* from)

abstinen|**cia** *f* abstinence. **~te** *a* abstinent

abstrac|**ción** *f* abstraction. **~cto** *a* abstract. **~er** [41] *vt* abstract. **~erse** *vpr* be lost in thought. **~ído** *a* absent-minded

abstruso *a* abstruse

absuelto *a* (*relig*) absolved; (*jurid*) acquitted

absurdo *a* absurd. **—m** absurd thing

abuche|**ar** *vt* boo. **~o** *m* booing

abuel|**a** *f* grandmother. **~o** *m* grandfather. **~os** *mpl* grandparents

abulia *f* lack of willpower. **~úlico** *a* weak-willed

abulta|**do** *a* bulky. **~miento** *m* bulkiness. **~r** *vt* enlarge; (*hinchar*) swell; (*fig, exagerar*) exagerate. **~vi** be bulky

abunda|**ncia** *f* abundance. **~nte** *a* abundant, plentiful. **~r** *vi* be plentiful. **nadar en la ~ncia** be rolling in money

aburguesa|**miento** *m* conversion to a middle-class way of life. **~rse** *vpr* become middle-class

aburri|**do** *a* (*con estar*) bored; (*con ser*) boring. **~miento** *m* boredom; (*cosa pesada*) bore. **~r** *vt* bore. **~rse** *vpr* be bored, get bored

abus|**ar** *vi* take advantage. **~ar de la bebida** drink too much.

~ivo *a* excessive. ~o *m* abuse. ~ón *a* (*fam*) selfish

abyec|ción *f* wretchedness. ~to *a* abject

acá *adv* here; (*hasta ahora*) until now. ~ y allá here and there. de ~ para allá to and fro. de ayer ~ since yesterday

acaba|do *a* finished; (*perfecto*) perfect; (*agotado*) worn out. —*m* finish. ~miento *m* finishing; (*fin*) end. ~r *vt/i* finish. ~rse *vpr* finish; (*agotarse*) run out; (*morirse*) die. ~r con put an end to. ~r de (+ *infinitivo*) have just (+ *pp*). ~ de llegar he has just arrived. ~r por (+ *infinitivo*) end up (+ *gerundio*). ¡se acabó! that's it!

acabóse *m*. ser el ~ be the end, be the limit

acacia *f* acacia

acad|emia *f* academy. ~émico *a* academic

acaec|er [11] *vi* happen. ~imiento *m* occurrence

acalora|damente *adv* heatedly. ~do *a* heated. ~miento *m* heat. ~r *vt* warm up; (*fig, excitar*) excite. ~rse *vpr* get hot; (*fig, excitarse*) get excited

acallar *vt* silence

acampanado *a* bell-shaped

acampar *vi* camp

acanala|do *a* grooved. ~dura *f* groove. ~r *vt* groove

acantilado *a* steep. —*m* cliff

acanto *m* acanthus

acapara|r *vt* hoard; (*monopolizar*) monopolize. ~miento *m* hoarding; (*monopolio*) monopolizing

acaracolado *a* spiral

acaricia|dor *a* caressing. ~r *vt* caress; (*rozar*) brush; (*proyectos etc*) have in mind

ácaro *m* mite

acarre|ar *vt* transport; (*desgracias etc*) cause. ~o *m* transport

acartona|do *a* (*persona*) wizened. ~rse *vpr* (*ponerse rígido*) go stiff; (*persona*) become wizened

acaso maybe, perhaps. —*m* chance. ~ llueva mañana perhaps it will rain tomorrow. al ~ at random. por si ~ in case

acata|miento *m* respect (a for). ~r *vt* respect

acatarrarse *vpr* catch a cold, get a cold

acaudalado *a* well off

acaudillar *vt* lead

acceder *vi* agree; (*tener acceso*) have access

acces|ibilidad *f* accessibility. ~ible *a* accessible; (*persona*) approachable. ~o *m* access, entry; (*med, ataque*) attack; (*llegada*) approach

accesorio *a & m* accessory

accidenta|do *a* (*terreno*) uneven; (*agitado*) troubled; (*persona*) injured

accidental *a* accidental. ~arse *vpr* have an accident. ~e *m* accident

acci|ón *f* (*incl jurid*) action; (*hecho*) deed. ~onar *vt* work. — *vi* gesticulate. ~onista *m & f* shareholder

acebo *m* holly (tree)

acebuche *m* wild olive tree

acecina|r *vt* cure (*carne*). ~se *vpr* become wizened

acech|ar *vt* spy on; (*aguardar*) lie in wait for. ~o *m* spying. al ~o on the look-out

acedera *f* sorrel

acedía *f* (*pez*) plaice; (*acidez*) heartburn

aceit|ar *vt* oil; (*culin*) add oil to. ~e *m* oil; (*de oliva*) olive oil. ~era *f* oil bottle; (*para engrasar*) oilcan. ~ero *a* oil. ~oso *a* oily

aceituna *f* olive. ~ado *a* olive. ~o *m* olive tree

acelera|ción f acceleration. **~damente** adv quickly. **~dor** m accelerator. **~r** vt accelerate; (fig) speed up, quicken

acelga f chard

ac|émila f mule; (como insulto) ass (fam). **~emilero** m muleteer

acendra|do a pure. **~r** vt purify; refine (metales)

acensuar vt tax

acento m accent; (énfasis) stress. **~uación** f accentuation. **~uar** [21] vt stress; (fig) emphasize. **~uarse** vpr become noticeable

aceña f water-mill

acepción f meaning, sense

acepta|ble a acceptable. **~ción** f acceptance; (aprobación) approval. **~r** vt accept

acequia f irrigation channel

acera f pavement (Brit), sidewalk (Amer)

acerado a steel; (fig, mordaz) sharp

acerca de prep about

acerca|miento m approach; (fig) reconciliation. **~r** [7] vt bring near. **~rse** vpr approach

acería f steelworks

acerico m pincushion

acero m steel. **~ inoxidable** stainless steel

acérrimo a (fig) staunch

acert|ado a right, correct; (apropiado) appropriate. **~ar** [1] vt hit (el blanco); (adivinar) get right, guess. **~vi** get right. **~ar a** happen to. **~ar con** hit on. **~ijo** m riddle

acervo m pile; (bienes) common property

acetato m acetate

acético a acetic

acetileno m acetylene

acetona m acetone

aciago a unlucky

aciano m cornflower

acíbar m aloes; (planta) aloe; (fig, amargura) bitterness. **~ibarar** vt add aloes to; (fig, amargar) embitter

acicala|do a dressed up, overdressed. **~r** vt dress up. **~rse** vpr get dressed up

acicate m spur

acid|ez f acidity. **~ificar** [7] vt acidify. **~ificarse** vpr acidify

ácido a sour. —m acid

acierto m success; (idea) good idea; (habilidad) skill

aclama|ción f acclaim; (aplausos) applause. **~r** vt acclaim; (aplaudir) applaud

aclara|ción f explanation. **~r** vt lighten (colores); (explicar) clarify; (enjuagar) rinse. **—vi** (el tiempo) brighten up. **~rse** vpr become clear. **~torio** a explanatory

aclimata|ción f acclimatization, acclimation (Amer). **~r** vt acclimatize, acclimate (Amer). **~rse** vpr become acclimatized, become acclimated (Amer)

acné m acne

acobardar vt intimidate. **~se** vpr get frightened

acocil m (Mex) freshwater shrimp

acod|ado a bent. **~ar** vt (doblar) bend; (agricultura) layer. **~arse** vpr lean on (en on). **~o** m layer

acog|edor a welcoming; (ambiente) friendly. **~er** [14] vt welcome; (proteger) shelter; (recibir) receive. **~erse** vpr take refuge; (fig) take refuge. **~ida** f welcome; (refugio) refuge

acogollar vi bud. **~se** vpr bud

acolchado a quilted. **~r** vt quilt, pad

acólito m acolyte; (monaguillo) altar boy

acomet|edor a aggressive; (emprendedor) enterprising.

~er *vt* attack; (*emprender*) undertake; (*llenar*) fill. ~ida *f* attack. ~ividad *f* aggression; (*iniciativa*) enterprise

acomodable *a* adaptable. ~adizo *a* accommodating. ~ado *a* well off. ~ador *m* usher. ~adora *f* usherette. ~amiento *m* suitability. ~ar *vt* arrange; (*adaptar*) adjust. —*vi* be suitable. ~arse *vpr* settle down; (*adaptarse*) conform. ~aticio *a* accommodating. ~o *m* position

acompaña|do *a* accompanied; (*concurrido*) busy. ~miento *m* accompaniment. ~nta *f* companion. ~nte *m* companion; (*mus*) accompanist. ~r *vt* accompany; (*adjuntar*) enclose. ~rse *vpr* (*mus*) accompany o.s.

acompasa|do *a* rhythmic. ~r *vt* keep in time; (*fig, ajustar*) adjust

acondiciona|do *a* equipped. ~miento *m* conditioning. ~r *vt* fit out; (*preparar*) prepare

acongojar *vt* distress. ~se *vpr* get upset

acónito *m* aconite

aconseja|ble *a* advisable. ~do *a* advised. ~r *vt* advise. ~rse *vpr* take advice. ~rse con consult

aconsonantar *vt/i* rhyme

acontec|er [11] *vi* happen. ~imiento *m* event

acopiar *vt* collect. ~o *m* store

acopla|do *a* coordinated. ~miento *m* coupling; (*elec*) connection. ~r *vt* fit; (*elec*) connect; (*rail*) couple

acoquina|miento *m* intimidation. ~r *vt* intimidate. ~rse *vpr* be intimidated

acoraza|do *a* armour-plated. —*m* battleship. ~r [10] *vt* armour

acorazonado *a* heart-shaped

acorchar|se *vpr* (*esponja*) go spongy; (*parte del cuerpo*) go to sleep

acord|ado *a* agreed. ~ar [2] *vt* agree (upon); (*decidir*) decide; (*recordar*) remind. ~e *a* in agreement; (*mus*) harmonious. —*m* chord

acorde|ón *m* accordion. ~onista *m* & *f* accordionist

acordona|do *a* (*lugar*) cordoned off. ~miento *m* cordoning off. ~r *vt* tie, lace; (*rodear*) surround, cordon off

acorrala|miento *m* (*de animales*) rounding up; (*de personas*) cornering. ~r *vt* round up (*animales*); corner (*personas*)

acorta|miento *m* shortening. ~r *vt* shorten; (*fig*) cut down

acos|ar *vt* hound; (*fig*) pester. ~o *m* pursuit; (*fig*) pestering

acostar [2] *vt* put to bed; (*naut*) bring alongside. —*vi* (*naut*) reach land. ~se *vpr* go to bed; (*echarse*) lie down; (*Mex, parir*) give birth

acostumbra|do *a* (*habitual*) usual. ~do a used to, accustomed to. ~r *vt* get used. me ha acostumbrado a levantarme por la noche he's got me used to getting up at night. —*vi.* ~ (a) be accustomed to. acostumbro comer a la una I usually have lunch at one o'clock. ~rse *vpr* become accustomed, get used

acota|ción *f* (*nota*) marginal note; (*en el teatro*) stage direction; (*cota*) elevation mark. ~do *a* enclosed. ~r *vt* mark out (*terreno*); (*anotar*) annotate

ácrata *a* anarchistic. —*m* & *f* anarchist

acre *m* acre. —*a* (*color*) pungent; (*sabor*) sharp, bitter

acrecenta|miento *m* increase. ~r [1] *vt* increase. ~rse *vpr* increase

acrec|er [11] *vt* increase. **∼imiento** *m* increase

acredita|do *a* reputable; (*pol*) accredited. **∼r** *vt* prove; accredit ‹*representante diplomático*›; (*garantizar*) guarantee; (*autorizar*) authorize. **∼rse** *vpr* make one's name

acreedor *a* worthy (**a** of). —*m* creditor

acribillar *vt* (*a balazos*) riddle (**a** with); (*a picotazos*) cover (**a** with); (*fig, a preguntas etc*) pester (**a** with)

acrimonia *f* (*de sabor*) sharpness; (*de olor*) pungency; (*fig*) bitterness

acrónimo *m* acronym

acrisola|do *a* pure; (*fig*) proven. **∼r** *vt* purify; (*confirmar*) prove

acritud *f* (*de sabor*) sharpness; (*de olor*) pungency; (*fig*) bitterness

acr|obacia *f* acrobatics. **∼obacias aéreas** aerobatics. **∼óbata** *m & f* acrobat. **∼obático** *a* acrobatic. **∼obatismo** *m* acrobatics

acrónimo *m* acronym

acróstico *a & m* acrostic

acta *f* minutes; (*certificado*) certificate

actinia *f* sea anemone

actitud *f* posture, position; (*fig*) attitude, position

activ|ación *f* speed-up. **∼amente** *adv* actively. **∼ar** *vt* activate; (*acelerar*) speed up. **∼idad** *f* activity. **∼o** *a* active. —*m* assets

acto *m* act; (*ceremonia*) ceremony. **en el ∼** immediately

act|or *m* actor. **∼riz** *f* actress

actuación *f* action; (*conducta*) behaviour; (*theat*) performance

actual *a* present; (*asunto*) topical. **∼idad** *f* present. **∼idades** *fpl* current affairs. **∼ización** *f* modernization. **∼izar** [10] *vt* modernize. **∼mente** *adv* now,

at the present time. **en la ∼idad** nowadays

actuar [21] *vt* work. —*vi* act. **∼ como**, **∼ de** act as

actuario *m* clerk of the court. **∼ (de seguros)** actuary

acuarel|a *f* watercolour. **∼ista** *m & f* watercolourist

acuario *m* aquarium. **A∼** Aquarius

acuartela|do *a* quartered. **∼miento** *m* quartering. **∼r** *vt* quarter, billet; (*mantener en cuartel*) confine to barracks

acuático *a* aquatic

acucl|ador *a* pressing. **∼ar** *vt* urge on; (*dar prisa a*) hasten. **∼oso** *a* keen

acuclillarse *vpr* crouch down, squat down

acuchilla|do *a* slashed; (*persona*) stabbed. **∼r** *vt* slash; stab ‹*persona*›; (*alisar*) smooth

acudir *vi* **∼ a** go to, attend; keep ‹*una cita*›; (*en auxilio*) go to help

acueducto *m* aqueduct

acuerdo *m* agreement. —*vb véase* **acordar**. **¡de ∼!** OK! **de ∼ con** in accordance with. **estar de ∼** agree. **ponerse de ∼** agree

acuesto *vb véase* **acostar**

acuidad *f* acuity, sharpness

acumula|ción *f* accumulation. **∼dor** *a* accumulative. —*m* accumulator. **∼r** *vt* accumulate. **∼rse** *vpr* accumulate

acunar *vt* rock

acuña|ción *f* minting, coining. **∼r** *vt* mint, coin

acuos|idad *f* wateriness. **∼o** *a* watery

acupuntura *f* acupuncture

acurrucarse [7] *vpr* curl up

acusa|ción *f* accusation. **∼do** *a* accused; (*destacado*) marked. —*m* accused. **∼dor** *a* accusing. —*m* accuser. **∼r** *vt* accuse; (*mostrar*) show; (*denunciar*) denounce. **∼rse** *vpr* confess;

(*notarse*) become marked. ~**torio** *a* accusatory

acuse *m*. ~ **de recibo** acknowledgement of receipt

acus|ica *m & f* (*fam*) telltale. ~**ón** *a & m* telltale

acústic|a *f* acoustics. ~**o** *a* acoustic

achacar [7] *vt* attribute

achacoso *a* sickly

achaflanar *vt* bevel

achantar *vt* (*fam*) intimidate. ~**se** *vpr* hide; (*fig*) back down

achaparrado *a* stocky

achaque *m* ailment

achares *mpl* (*fam*). **dar** ~ make jealous

achata|miento *m* flattening. ~**r** *vt* flatten

achica|do *a* childish. ~**r** [7] *vt* make smaller; (*fig, empequeñecer, fam*) belittle; (*naut*) bale out. ~**rse** *vpr* become smaller; (*humillarse*) be humiliated

achicopalado *a* (*Mex*) depressed

achicoria *f* chicory

achicharra|dero *m* inferno. ~**nte** *a* sweltering. ~**r** *vt* burn; (*fig*) pester. ~**rse** *vpr* burn

achispa|do *a* tipsy. ~**rse** *vpr* get tipsy

achocolatado *a* (chocolate-) brown

achuch|ado *a* (*fam*) hard. ~**ar** *vt* jostle, push. ~**ón** *m* shove, push

achulado *a* cocky

adagio *m* adage, proverb; (*mus*) adagio

adalid *m* leader

adamascado *a* damask

adapta|ble *a* adaptable. ~**ción** *f* adaptation. ~**dor** *m* adapter. ~**r** *vt* adapt; (*ajustar*) fit. ~**rse** *vpr* adapt o.s.

adecentar *vt* clean up. ~**se** *vpr* tidy o.s. up

adecua|ción *f* suitability. ~**damente** *adv* suitably. ~**do** *a* suitable. ~**r** *vt* adapt, make suitable

adelant|ado *a* advanced; (*niño*) precocious; (*reloj*) fast. ~**amiento** *m* advance(ment); (*auto*) overtaking. ~**ar** *vt* advance, move forward; (*acelerar*) speed up; put forward (*reloj*); (*auto*) overtake. —*vi* advance, go forward; (*reloj*) gain, be fast. ~**arse** *vpr* advance, move forward; (*reloj*) gain; (*auto*) overtake. ~**e** *adv* forward. —*int* come in!; (*¡siga!*) carry on! ~**e** *m* advance; (*progreso*) progress. **más** ~**e** (*lugar*) further on; (*tiempo*) later on. **pagar por** ~**ado** pay in advance

adelfa *f* oleander

adelgaza|dor *a* slimming. ~**miento** *m* slimming. ~**r** [10] *vt* make thin. —*vi* lose weight; (*adrede*) slim. ~**rse** *vpr* lose weight; (*adrede*) slim

ademán *m* gesture. **ademanes** *mpl* (*modales*) manners. **en** ~ **de** as if to

además *adv* besides; (*también*) also. ~ **de** besides

adentr|arse *vpr*. ~ **en** penetrate into; study thoroughly (*tema etc*). ~**o** *adv* in(side). **mar** ~**o** out at sea. **tierra** ~**o** inland

adepto *m* supporter

aderez|ar [10] *vt* flavour (*bebidas*); (*condimentar*) season; dress (*ensalada*). ~**o** *m* flavouring; (*con condimentos*) seasoning; (*para ensalada*) dressing

adeud|ar *vt* owe. ~**o** *m* debit

adhe|rencia *f* adhesion; (*fig*) adherence. ~**rente** *a* adherent. ~**rir** [4] *vi* stick on. —*vi* stick. ~**rirse** *vpr* stick; (*fig*) follow. ~**sión** *f* adhesion; (*fig*) support. ~**sivo** *a & m* adhesive

adici|ón *f* addition. ~**onal** *a* additional. ~**onar** *vt* add

adicto *a* devoted. —*m* follower

adiestra|do *a* trained. **~miento** *m* training. **~r** *vt* train. **~rse** *vpr* practise

adinerado *a* wealthy

adiós *int* goodbye!; *(al cruzarse con alguien)* hello!

adit|amento *m* addition; *(accesorio)* accessory. **~ivo** *m* additive

adivin|ación *f* divination; *(por conjeturas)* guessing. **~ador** *m* fortune-teller. **~anza** *f* riddle. **~ar** *vt* foretell; *(acertar)* guess. **~o** *m* fortune-teller

adjetivo *a* adjectival. —*m* adjective

adjudica|ción *f* award. **~r** [7] *vt* award. **~rse** *vpr* appropriate. **~tario** *m* winner of an award

adjunt|ar *vt* enclose. **~o** *a* enclosed; *(auxiliar)* assistant. — *m* assistant

adminículo *m* thing, gadget

administra|ción *f* administration; *(gestión)* management. **~dor** *m* administrator; *(gerente)* manager. **~dora** *f* administrator; manageress. **~r** *vt* administer. **~tivo** *a* administrative

admira|ble *a* admirable. **~ción** *f* admiration. **~dor** *m* admirer. **~r** *vt* admire; *(asombrar)* astonish. **~rse** *vpr* be astonished. **~tivo** *a* admiring

admi|sibilidad *f* admissibility. **~sible** *a* acceptable. **~sión** *f* admission; *(aceptación)* acceptance. **~tir** *vt* admit; *(aceptar)* accept

adobar *vt* *(culin)* pickle; *(fig)* twist

adobe *m* sun-dried brick. **~ra** *f* mould for making (sun-dried) bricks

adobo *m* pickle

adocena|do *a* common. **~rse** *vpr* become common

adoctrinamiento *m* indoctrination

adolecer [11] *vi* be ill. **~ de** suffer with

adolescen|cia *f* adolescent. **~te** *a & m & f* adolescent

adonde *conj* where

adónde *adv* where?

adop|ción *f* adoption. **~tar** *vt* adopt. **~tivo** *a* adoptive; *(patria)* of adoption

adoquín *m* paving stone; *(imbécil)* idiot. **~inado** *m* paving. **~inar** *vt* pave

adora|ble *a* adorable. **~ción** *f* adoration. **~dor** *a* adoring. —*m* worshipper. **~r** *vt* adore

adormec|edor *a* soporific; *(droga)* sedative. **~er** [11] *vt* send to sleep; *(fig, calmar)* calm, soothe. **~erse** *vpr* fall asleep; *(un miembro)* go to sleep. **~ido** *a* asleep; *(un miembro)* numb. **~imiento** *m* sleepiness; *(de un miembro)* numbness

adormidera *f* opium poppy

adormilarse *vpr* doze

adorn|ar *vt* adorn (**con, de** with). **~o** *m* decoration

adosar *vt* lean (**a** against)

adqui|rido *a* acquired. **~rir** [4] *vt* acquire; *(comprar)* buy. **~sición** *f* acquisition; *(compra)* purchase. **~sitivo** *a* acquisitive. **poder** *m* **~sitivo** purchasing power

adrede *adv* on purpose

adrenalina *f* adrenalin

adscribir [*pp* **adscrito**] *vt* appoint

aduan|a *f* customs. **~ero** *a* customs. —*m* customs officer

aducir [47] *vt* allege

adueñarse *vpr* take possession

adul|ación *f* flattery. **~ador** *a* flattering. —*m* flatterer. **~ar** *vt* flatter

ad|ulteración *f* adulteration. **~ulterar** *vt* adulterate. —*vi* commit adultery. ∼**ulterino** *a* adulterous. ∼**ulterio** *m* adultery. ∼**últera** *f* adulteress. ∼**últero** *a* adulterous. ∼*m* adulterer

adulto *a & m* adult, grown-up

adusto *a* severe, harsh

advenedizo *a & m* upstart

advenimiento *m* advent, arrival; (*subida al trono*) accession

adventicio *a* accidental

adverbi|**al** *a* adverbial. ∼**o** *m* adverb

advers|**ario** *m* adversary. ∼**idad** *f* adversity. ∼**o** *a* adverse, unfavourable

advert|**encia** *f* warning; (*prólogo*) foreword. ∼**ido** *a* informed. ∼**ir** [4] *vt* warn; (*notar*) notice

adviento *m* Advent

advocación *f* dedication

adyacente *a* adjacent

aéreo *a* air; (*photo*) aerial; (*ferrocarril*) overhead; (*fig*) flimsy

aeróbica *a* aerobics

aerodeslizador *m* hovercraft

aerodinámic|**a** *f* aerodynamics. ∼**o** *a* aerodynamic

aeródromo *m* aerodrome, airdrome (*Amer*)

aero|**espacial** *a* aerospace. ∼**faro** *m* beacon. ∼**lito** *m* meteorite. ∼**nauta** *m & f* aeronaut. ∼**náutica** *f* aeronautics. ∼**náutico** *a* aeronautical. ∼**nave** *f* airship. ∼**puerto** *m* airport. ∼**sol** *m* aerosol

afab|**ilidad** *f* affability. ∼**le** *a* affable

afamado *a* famous

af|**án** *m* hard work; (*deseo*) desire. ∼**anar** *vt* (*fam*) pinch. ∼**anarse** *vpr* strive (**en, por** to). ∼**anoso** *a* laborious

afea|**miento** *m* disfigurement. ∼**r** *vt* disfigure, make ugly; (*censurar*) censure

afección *f* disease

afecta|**ción** *f* affectation. ∼**do** *a* affected. ∼**r** *vt* affect

afect|**ísimo** *a* affectionate. ∼**ísimo amigo** (*en cartas*) my dear friend. ∼**ividad** *f* emotional nature. ∼**ivo** *a* sensitive. ∼**o** *m* (*cariño*) affection. ∼*a.* ∼**o** *a* attached to. ∼**uosidad** *f* affection. ∼**uoso** *a* affectionate. **con un** ∼**uoso saludo** (*en cartas*) with kind regards. **suyo** ∼**ísimo** (*en cartas*) yours sincerely

afeita|**do** *m* shave. ∼**dora** *f* electric razor. ∼**r** *vt* shave. ∼**rse** *vpr* (have a) shave

afelpado *a* velvety

afemina|**do** *a* effeminate. ∼*m* effeminate person. ∼**miento** *m* effeminacy. ∼**rse** *vpr* become effeminate

aferrar [1] *vt* grasp

afgano *a & m* Afghan

afianza|**miento** *m* (*reforzar*) strengthening; (*garantía*) guarantee. ∼**rse** [10] *vpr* become established

afici|**ón** *f* liking; (*conjunto de aficionados*) fans. ∼**onado** *a* keen (**a** on), fond (**a** of). ∼*m* fan. ∼**onar** *vt* make fond. ∼**onarse** *vpr* take a liking to. **por** ∼**ón** as a hobby

afila|**do** *a* sharp. ∼**dor** *m* knifegrinder. ∼**dura** *f* sharpening. ∼**r** *vt* sharpen. ∼**rse** *vpr* get sharp; (*ponerse flaco*) grow thin

afilia|**ción** *f* affiliation. ∼**do** *a* affiliated. ∼**rse** *vpr* become a member (**a** of)

afiligranado *a* filigreed; (*fig*) delicate

afín *a* similar; (*próximo*) adjacent; (*personas*) related

afina|**ción** *f* refining; (*auto, mus*) tuning. ∼**do** *a* finished; (*mus*) in tune. ∼**r** *vt* refine; (*afilar*) sharpen; (*acabar*) finish; (*auto,* *mus*) tune. —*vi* be in tune. ∼**rse** *upr* become more refined

afincarse [7] *upr* settle

afinidad *f* affinity; (*parentesco*) relationship

afirma|ción *f* affirmation. ∼**r** *vt* make firm; (*asentir*) affirm. ∼**rse** *upr* steady o.s.; (*confirmar*) confirm. ∼**tivo** *a* affirmative

aflic|ción *f* affliction. ∼**tivo** *a* distressing

afligi|do *a* distressed. —*m* afflicted. ∼**r** [14] *vt* distress. ∼**rse** *upr* grieve

afloja|miento *m* loosening. ∼**r** *vt* loosen; (*relajar*) ease. —*vi* let up

aflora|miento *m* outcrop. ∼**r** *vi* appear on the surface

aflu|encia *f* flow. ∼**ente** *a* flowing. —*m* tributary. ∼**ir** [17] *vi* flow (**a** into)

afonía *f* hoarseness. ∼**ónico** *a* hoarse

aforismo *m* aphorism

aforo *m* capacity

afortunado *a* fortunate, lucky

afrancesado *a* francophile

afrent|a *f* insult; (*vergüenza*) disgrace. ∼**ar** *vt* insult. ∼**oso** *a* insulting

África *f* Africa. ∼ **del Sur** South Africa

africano *a* & *m* African

afrodisíaco *a* & *m*, **afrodisiaco** *a* & *m* aphrodisiac

afrontar *vt* bring face to face; (*enfrentar*) face, confront

afuera *adv* out(side). **∼!** out of the way! ∼**s** *fpl* outskirts

agachar *vt* lower. ∼**se** *upr* bend over

agalla *f* (*de los peces*) gill. ∼**s** *fpl* (*fig*) guts

agarrada *f* row

agarrader|a *f* (*LAm*) handle. ∼**o** *m* handle. **tener** ∼**as** (*LAm*), **tener** ∼**os** have influence

agarr|ado *a* (*fig, fam*) mean. ∼**ador** *a* (*Arg*) (*bebida*) strong. ∼**ar** *vt* grasp; (*esp LAm*) take, catch. —*vi* (*plantas*) take root. ∼**arse** *upr* hold on; (*reñirse, fam*) fight. ∼**ón** *m* tug; (*LAm, riña*) row

agarrota|miento *m* tightening; (*auto*) seizing up. ∼**r** *vt* tie tightly; (*el frío*) stiffen; garotte (*un reo*). ∼**rse** *upr* go stiff; (*auto*) seize up

agasaj|ado *m* guest of honour. ∼**ar** *vt* look after well. ∼**o** *m* good treatment

ágata *f* agate

agavilla|dora *f* (*máquina*) binder. ∼**r** *vt* bind

agazaparse *upr* hide

agencia *f* agency. ∼ **de viajes** travel agency. ∼ **inmobiliaria** estate agency (*Brit*), real estate agency (*Amer*). ∼**r** *vt* find. ∼**rse** *upr* find (out) for o.s.

agenda *f* notebook

agente *m* agent; (*de policía*) policeman. ∼ **de aduanas** customs officer. ∼ **de bolsa** stockbroker

ágil *a* agile

agilidad *f* agility

agita|ción *f* waving; (*de un líquido*) stirring; (*de un mar*) rough; (*fig*) stir up. ∼**se** *upr* wave; (*el mar*) get rough; (*fig*) get excited

agitanado *a* gypsy-like

agitar *vt* wave; shake (*botellas etc*); stir (*líquidos*); (*fig*) stir up. ∼**se** *upr* wave; (*el mar*) get rough; (*fig*) get excited

aglomera|ción *f* agglomeration; (*de tráfico*) traffic jam. ∼**r** *vt* amass. ∼**rse** *upr* form a crowd

agn|osticismo *m* agnosticism. ∼**óstico** *a* & *m* agnostic

agobi|ador *a* (*trabajo*) exhausting; (*calor*) oppressive. ∼**ante** *a* (*trabajo*) exhausting; (*calor*) oppressive. ~**ar** *vt* weigh down; (*fig, abrumar*) overwhelm. ~**o** *m* weight; (*cansancio*) exhaustion; (*opresión*) oppression

agolpa|miento *m* (*de gente*) crowd; (*de cosas*) pile. ~**rse** *vpr* crowd together

agon|ía *f* death throes; (*fig*) agony. ~**izante** *a* dying; (*luz*) failing. ~**izar** [10] *vi* be dying

agor|ar [16] *vt* prophesy. ~**ero** *a* of ill omen. ~**m** soothsayer

agostar *vt* wither

agosto *m* August. **hacer su** ~ feather one's nest

agota|do *a* exhausted; (*libro*) out of print. ~**dor** *a* exhausting. ~**miento** *m* exhaustion. ~**r** *vt* exhaust. ~**rse** *vpr* be exhausted; (*libro*) go out of print

agracia|ble *a* attractive; (*que tiene suerte*) lucky. ~**r** make attractive

agrada|ble *a* pleasant, nice. ~**r** *vi* please. **esto me** ~ I like this

agradec|er [11] *vt* thank (*persona*); be grateful for (*cosa*). ~**ido** *a* grateful. ~**imiento** *m* gratitude. ¡**muy** ~**ido!** thanks a lot!

agrado *m* pleasure; (*amabilidad*) friendliness

agrandar *vt* enlarge; (*fig*) exaggerate. ~**se** *vpr* get bigger

agrario *a* agrarian, land; (*política*) agricultural

agrava|miento *m* worsening. ~**nte** *a* aggravating. ~*f* additional problem. ~**r** *vt* aggravate; (*aumentar el peso*) make heavier. ~**rse** *vpr* get worse

agravi|ar *vt* offend; (*perjudicar*) wrong. ~**arse** *vpr* be offended. ~**o** *m* offence

agraz *m*. **en** ~ prematurely

agredir [24] *vt* attack. ~ **de palabra** insult

agrega|do *m* aggregate; (*funcionario diplomático*) attaché.

~**r** [12] *vt* add; (*unir*) join; appoint (*persona*)

agremiar *vt* form into a union. ~**se** *vpr* form a union

agres|ión *f* aggression; (*ataque*) attack. ~**ividad** *f* aggressiveness. ~**ivo** *a* aggressive. ~**or** *m* aggressor

agreste *a* country

agria|do *a* (*fig*) embittered. ~**r** [*regular, o raramente* 20] *vt* sour. ~**rse** *vpr* turn sour; (*fig*) become embittered

agr|ícola *a* agricultural. ~**icultor** *a* agricultural. —*m* farmer. ~**icultura** *f* agriculture, farming

agridulce *a* bitter-sweet; (*culin*) sweet-and-sour

agriera *f* (*LAm*) heartburn

agrietar *vt* crack. ~**se** *vpr* crack; (*piel*) chap

agrimens|or *m* surveyor. ~**ura** *f* surveying

agrio *a* sour; (*fig*) sharp. ~**s** *mpl* citrus fruits

agronomía *f* agronomy

agropecuario *a* farming

agrupa|ción *f* group; (*acción*) grouping. ~**r** *vt* group. ~**rse** *vpr* form a group

agua *f* water; (*lluvia*) rain; (*marea*) tide; (*vertiente del tejado*) slope. ~ **abajo** downstream. ~ **arriba** upstream. ~ **bendita** holy water. ~ **caliente** hot water. **estar entre dos** ~**s** sit on the fence. **hacer** ~ (*naut*) leak. **nadar entre dos** ~**s** sit on the fence

aguacate *m* avocado pear; (*árbol*) avocado pear tree

aguacero *m* downpour, heavy shower

agua f corriente running water

aguachinarse *vpr* (*Mex*) (*cultivos*) be flooded

aguada *f* watering place; (*naut*) drinking water; (*acuarela*) water-colour

agua *f* **de colonia** eau-de-Cologne

aguad|o *a* watery. **~ucho** *m* refreshment kiosk

agua: **~ dulce** fresh water. **~fiestas** *m & f invar* spoil-sport, wet blanket. **~ fría** cold water. **~fuerte** *m* etching

aguaje *m* spring tide

agua: **~mala** *f*, **~mar** *m* jellyfish

aguamarina *f* aquamarine

agua: **~miel** *f* mead. **~ mineral con gas** fizzy mineral water. **~ mineral sin gas** still mineral water. **~nieve** *f* sleet

aguanoso *a* watery; *(tierra)* waterlogged

aguant|able *a* bearable. **~aderas** *fpl* patience. **~ar** *vt* put up with, bear; *(sostener)* support. — *vi* hold out. **~arse** *vpr* restrain o.s. **~e** *m* patience; *(resistencia)* endurance

agua: **~pié** *m* watery wine. **~ potable** drinking water. **~r** [15] *vt* water down. **~ salada** salt water.

aguardar *vt* wait for. —*vi* wait

agua: **~rdiente** *m* (cheap) brandy. **~rrás** *m* turpentine, turps *(fam)*. **~turma** *f* Jerusalem artichoke. **~zal** *m* puddle

agud|eza *f* sharpness; *(fig, perspicacia)* insight; *(fig, ingenio)* wit. **~izar** [10] *vt* sharpen. **~izarse** *vpr* *(enfermedad)* get worse. **~o** *a* sharp; *(ángulo, enfermedad)* acute; *(voz)* high-pitched

agüero *m* omen. **ser de buen ~** augur well

aguij|ada *f* goad. **~ar** *vt* *(incl fig)* goad. **~ón** *m* point of a goad. **~onazo** *m* prick. **~onear** *vt* goad

águila *f* eagle; *(persona perspicaz)* astute person

aguileña *f* columbine

aguil|eño *a* aquiline. **~ucho** *m* eaglet

aguinaldo *m* Christmas box

aguja *f* needle; *(del reloj)* hand; *(arquit)* steeple. **~s** *fpl* *(rail)* points

agujer|ear *vt* make holes in. **~o** *m* hole

agujetas *fpl* stiffness. **tener ~** be stiff

agujón *m* hairpin

agusanado *a* full of maggots

agutí *m* *(LAm)* guinea pig

aguza|do *a* sharp. **~miento** *m* sharpening. **~r** [10] *vt* sharpen

ah *int* ah!, oh!

aherrojar *vt* *(fig)* oppress

ahí *adv* there. **de ~ que** so that. **por ~** over there; *(aproximadamente)* thereabouts

ahija|da *f* goddaughter, godchild. **~do** *m* godson, godchild. **~r** *vt* adopt

ahínco *m* enthusiasm; *(empeño)* insistence

ahíto *a* full up

ahoga|do *a* *(en el agua)* drowned; *(asfixiado)* suffocated. **~ar** [12] *vt* *(en el agua)* drown; *(asfixiar)* suffocate; put out *(fuego)*. **~arse** *vpr* *(en el agua)* drown; *(asfixiarse)* suffocate. **~o** *m* breathlessness; *(fig, angustia)* distress; *(apuro)* financial trouble

ahond|ar *vt* deepen. —*vi* go deep. **~ en** *(fig)* examine in depth. **~arse** *vpr* get deeper

ahora *adv* now; *(hace muy poco)* just now; *(dentro de poco)* very soon. **~ bien** but. **~ mismo** right now. **de ~ en adelante** from now on, in future. **por ~** for the time being

ahorca|dura *f* hanging. **~r** [7] *vt* hang. **~rse** *vpr* hang o.s.

ahorita *adv* *(fam)* now. **~ mismo** right now

ahorquillar *vt* shape like a fork

ahorr|ador a thrifty. ∼**ar** vt save. ∼**arse** vpr save o.s. ∼**o** m saving; (cantidad ahorrada) savings. ∼**os** mpl savings

ahuecar [7] vt hollow; fluff up ⟨colchón⟩; deepen ⟨la voz⟩; (marcharse, fam) clear off (fam)

ahuizote m (Mex) bore

ahulado m (LAm) oilskin

ahuma|do a (culin) smoked; (de colores) smoky. ∼**r** vt (culin) smoke; (llenar de humo) fill with smoke. —vi smoke. ∼**rse** vpr become smoky; ⟨comida⟩ acquire a smoky taste; (emborracharse, fam) get drunk

ahusa|do a tapering. ∼**rse** vpr taper

ahuyentar vt drive away; banish ⟨pensamientos etc⟩

airado a annoyed

aire m air; ⟨viento⟩ breeze; ⟨corriente⟩ draught; ⟨aspecto⟩ appearance; (mus) tune, air. ∼**ación** f ventilation. ∼ **acondicionado** air-conditioned. ∼**ar** vt air; (ventilar) ventilate; (fig, publicar) make public. ∼**arse** vpr. **salir para** ∼**arse** go out for some fresh air. **al** ∼ **libre** in the open air. **darse** ∼**s** give o.s. airs

airón m heron

airosa|mente adv gracefully. ∼**o** a draughty; (fig) elegant

aisla|do a isolated; (elec) insulated. ∼**dor** a (elec) insulating. —m (elec) insulator. ∼**miento** m isolation; (elec) insulation. ∼**nte** a insulating. ∼**r** [23] vt isolate; (elec) insulate

ajajá int good! splendid!

ajar vt crumple; (estropear) spoil

ajedre|cista m & f chess-player. ∼**z** m chess. ∼**zado** a chequered, checked

ajenjo m absinthe

ajeno a (de otro) someone else's; (de otros) other people's; (extraño) alien

ajetre|arse vpr be busy. ∼**o** m bustle

ají m (LAm) chilli; (salsa) chilli sauce

aj|iaceite m garlic sauce. ∼**ilimójili** m piquant garlic sauce. ∼**illo** m garlic. **al** ∼**illo** cooked with garlic. ∼**o** m garlic. ∼**o-arriero** m cod in garlic sauce

ajorca f bracelet

ajuar m furnishings; (de novia) trousseau

ajuma|do a (fam) drunk. ∼**rse** vpr (fam) get drunk

ajust|ado a right; (vestido) tight. ∼**ador** m fitting; (adaptación) adjustment; (acuerdo) agreement; (de una cuenta) settlement. ∼**ar** vt fit; (adaptar) adapt; (acordar) agree; settle ⟨una cuenta⟩; (apretar) tighten. —vi fit. ∼**arse** vpr fit; (adaptarse) adapt o.s.; (acordarse) come to an agreement. ∼**e** m fitting; (adaptación) f adjustment; (acuerdo) agreement; (de una cuenta) settlement

ajusticiar vt execute

al = **a** + **el**

ala f wing; (de sombrero) brim; (deportes) winger

alaba|ncioso a boastful. ∼**nza** f praise. ∼**r** vt praise. ∼**rse** vpr boast

alabastro m alabaster

álabe m (paleta) paddle; (diente) cog

alabe|ar vt warp. ∼**arse** vpr warp. ∼**o** m warping

alacena f cupboard (Brit), closet (Amer)

alacrán m scorpion

alacridad f alacrity

alado a winged

alambi|cado a distilled; (fig) subtle. ∼**camiento** m distillation; (fig) subtlety. ∼**car** [7] vt distil. ∼**que** m still

alambr|ada f wire fence; (de alambre de espinas) barbed wire fence. **~ar** vt fence. **~e** m wire. **~e de espinas** barbed wire. **~era** f fireguard

alameda f avenue; (plantío de álamos) poplar grove

álamo m poplar. **~ temblón** aspen

alano m mastiff

alarde m show. **~ar** vi boast

alarg|adera f extension. **~do** a long. **~dor** m extension. **~miento** m lengthening. **~r** [12] vt lengthen; stretch out (mano etc); (dar) give, pass. **~rse** vpr lengthen, get longer

alarido m shriek

alarm|a f alarm. **~ante** a alarming. **~ar** vt alarm, frighten. **~arse** vpr be alarmed. **~ista** m & f alarmist

alba f dawn

albacea m executor. **—f** executrix

albacora (culin) tuna(-fish)

albahaca f basil

albanés a & m Albanian

Albania f Albania

albañal m sewer, drain

albañil m bricklayer. **~ería** f (arte) bricklaying

albarán m delivery note

albarda f packsaddle; (Mex) saddle. **~r** vt saddle

albaricoque m apricot. **~ro** m apricot tree

albatros m albatross

albedrío m will. **libre ~** free will

albéitar m veterinary surgeon (Brit), veterinarian (Amer), vet (fam)

alberca f tank, reservoir

alberg|ar [12] vt (alojar) put up; (viviendas) house; (dar asilo) shelter. **~arse** vpr stay; (refugiarse) shelter. **~ue** m accommodation; (refugio) shelter. **~ue de juventud** youth hostel

albóndiga f meatball, rissole

albor m dawn. **~ada** f dawn; (mus) dawn song. **~ear** vi dawn

albornoz m (de los moros) burnous; (para el baño) bathrobe

alborot|adizo a excitable. **~ado** a excited; (aturdido) hasty. **~ador** a rowdy. **—m** troublemaker. **~ar** vt disturb, upset. **—vi** make a racket. **~arse** vpr get excited; (el mar) get rough. **~o** m row, uproar

alboroz|ado a overjoyed. **~ar** [10] vt make laugh; (regocijar) make happy. **~arse** vpr be overjoyed. **~o** m joy

albufera f lagoon

álbum m (pl ~es o ~s) album

alcachofa f artichoke

alcalde m mayor. **~esa** f mayoress. **~ía** f mayoralty; (oficina) mayor's office

álcali m alkali

alcalino a alkaline

alcance m reach; (de arma, telescopio etc) range; (déficit) deficit

alcancía f money-box

alcantarilla f sewer; (boca) drain

alcanzar [10] vt (llegar a) catch up; (coger) reach; catch (un autobús); (bala etc) strike, hit. **—vi** reach; (ser suficiente) be enough. **~ a manage**

alcaparra f caper

alcaucil m artichoke

alcayata f hook

alcazaba f fortress

alcázar m fortress

alcoba f bedroom

alcohol m alcohol. **~ol desnaturalizado** methylated spirits, meths (fam). **~ólico** a & m alcoholic. **~olímetro** m breathalyser (Brit). **~olismo** m alcoholism. **~olizarse** [10] vpr become an alcoholic

Alcorán m Koran

alcornoque m cork-oak; (*persona torpe*) idiot

alcuza f (olive) oil bottle

aldaba f door-knocker. ~**da** f knock at the door

aldea f village. ~**ano** a village; (*campesino*) rustic, country. ~**huela** f hamlet

aleación f alloy. ~**r** vt alloy

aleatorio a uncertain

aleccionador a instructive. ~**miento** m instruction. ~**r** vt instruct

aledaños mpl outskirts

alegación f allegation; (*Arg, Mex, disputa*) argument. ~**r** [12] vt claim; (*jurid*) allege. —vi (*LAm*) argue. ~**to** m plea

alegoría f allegory. ~**órico** a allegorical

alegrar vt make happy; (*avivar*) brighten up. ~**arse** vpr be happy; (*emborracharse*) get merry; (*achispado*) merry, tight. ~**emente** adv happily. ~**ía** f happiness. ~**ón** m sudden joy, great happiness

alejado a distant. ~**miento** m removal; (*entre personas*) estrangement; (*distancia*) distance. ~**r** vt remove; (*ahuyentar*) get rid of; (*fig, apartar*) separate. ~**rse** vpr move away

alelado a stupid. ~**r** vt stupefy. ~**rse** vpr be stupefied

aleluya m & f alleluia

alemán a & m German

Alemania f Germany. ~ **Occidental** (*historia*) West Germany. ~ **Oriental** (*historia*) East Germany

alentador a encouraging. ~**r** [1] vt encourage. —vi breathe

alerce m larch

alergia f allergy. ~**érgico** a allergic

alero m (*del tejado*) eaves

alerón m aileron

alerta adv alert, on the alert. ¡~! look out! ~**r** vt alert

aleta f wing; (*de pez*) fin

aletargado a lethargic. ~**miento** m lethargy. ~**r** [12] vt make lethargic. ~**rse** vpr become lethargic

aletazo m (*de un ave*) flap of the wings; (*de pez*) flick of the fin. ~**ear** vi flap its wings, flutter. ~**eo** m flapping (of the wings)

aleve a treacherous

alevín m young fish

alevosía f treachery. ~**o** a treacherous

alfabético a alphabetical. ~**etizar** [10] vt alphabetize; teach to read and write ‹a uno›. ~**eto** m alphabet. ~**eto Morse** Morse code

alfalfa f lucerne (*Brit*), alfalfa (*Amer*)

alfar m pottery. ~**ería** f pottery. ~**ero** m potter

alféizar m window-sill

alferecía f epilepsy

alférez m second lieutenant

alfil m (*en ajedrez*) bishop

alfiler m pin. ~**razo** m pinprick. ~**tero** m pin-case

alfombra f (*grande*) carpet; (*pequeña*) rug, mat. ~**ar** vt carpet. ~**illa** f rug, mat; (*med*) German measles

alforja f saddle-bag

algas fpl seaweed

algarabía f (*fig, fam*) gibberish, nonsense

algarada f uproar

algarroba f carob bean. ~**o** m carob tree

algazara f uproar

álgebra f algebra

algebraico a algebraic

álgido a (*fig*) decisive

algo pron something; (*en frases interrogativas*) anything. —adv rather. ¿~ **más**? is there anything else? ¿quieres tomar

algo? (de beber) would you like a drink?; (de comer) would you like something to eat?

algod|ón m cotton. ~**ón de azúcar** cotton floss (Brit), cotton candy (Amer). ~**onero** a cotton. —m cotton plant. ~**ón hidrófilo** cotton wool

alguacil m bailiff

alguien pron someone, somebody; (en frases interrogativas) anyone, anybody

alguno a (delante de nombres masculinos en singular **algún**) some; (en frases interrogativas) any; (pospuesto al nombre en frases negativas) at all. **no tiene idea alguna** he hasn't any idea at all. —pron one; (en plural) some; (alguien) someone. **alguna que otra vez** from time to time. **algunas veces, alguna vez** sometimes

alhaja f piece of jewellery; (fig) treasure. ~**r** vt deck with jewels; (amueblar) furnish

alharaca f fuss

alhelí m wallflower

alheña f privet

alhucema f lavender

alia|do a allied. —m ally. ~**nza** f alliance; (anillo) wedding ring. ~**r** [20] vt combine. ~**rse** vpr be combined; (formar una alianza) form an alliance

alias adv & m alias

alicaído a (fig, débil) weak; (fig, abatido) depressed

alicates mpl pliers

aliciente m incentive; (de un lugar) attraction

alien|ado a mentally ill. ~**ista** m & f psychiatrist

aliento m breath; (ánimo) courage

aligera|miento m lightening; (alivio) alleviation. ~**r** vt make lighter; (aliviar) alleviate, ease; (apresurar) quicken

alij|ar vt (descargar) unload; smuggle ⟨contrabando⟩. ~**o** m unloading; (contrabando) contraband

alimaña f vicious animal

aliment|ación f food; (acción) feeding. ~**ar** vt feed; (nutrir) nourish. —vi be nourishing. ~**arse** vpr feed (con, de on). ~**icio** a nourishing. ~**o** m food. ~**os** mpl (jurid) alimony. **productos** mpl ~**icios** foodstuffs

alimón. al ~ adv jointly

aline|ación f alignment; (en deportes) line-up. ~**r** vt align, line up

aliñ|ar vt (culin) season. ~**o** m seasoning

alioli m garlic sauce

alisar vt smooth

alisios apl. **vientos** mpl ~ trade winds

aliso m alder (tree)

alista|miento m enrolment. ~**r** vt put on a list; (mil) enlist. ~**rse** vpr enrol; (mil) enlist

aliteración f alliteration

alivi|ador a comforting. ~**ar** vt lighten; relieve ⟨dolor, etc⟩; (hurtar, fam) steal, pinch (fam). ~**arse** vpr ⟨dolor⟩ diminish; ⟨persona⟩ get better. ~**o** m relief

aljibe m tank

alma f soul; (habitante) inhabitant

almac|én m warehouse; (LAm, tienda) grocer's shop; (de un arma) magazine. ~**enes** mpl department store. ~**enaje** m storage; (derechos) storage charges. ~**enamiento** m storage; (mercancías almacenadas) stock. ~**enar** vt store; stock up with ⟨provisiones⟩. ~**enero** m (Arg) shopkeeper. ~**enista** m & f shopkeeper

almádena f sledge-hammer

almanaque m almanac

almeja f clam

almendr|a f almond. **~ado** a almond-shaped. **~o** m almond tree

almiar m haystack

alm|íbar m syrup. **~ibarado** a syrupy. **~ibarar** vt cover in syrup

almid|ón m starch. **~onado** a starched; (fig, estirado) starchy

alminar m minaret

almirant|azgo m admiralty. **~e** m admiral

almirez m mortar

almizcle m musk

almohad|a f cushion; (de la cama) pillow; (funda) pillowcase. **~illa** f small cushion; (acerico) pincushion. **~ón** m large pillow, bolster. **consultar con la ~** a sleep on it

almorranas fpl haemorrhoids, piles

alm|orzar [2 & 10] vt (a mediodía) have for lunch; (desayunar) have for breakfast. —vi (a mediodía) have lunch; (desayunar) have breakfast. **~uerzo** m (a mediodía) lunch; (desayuno) breakfast

alocado a scatter-brained

alocución f address, speech

aloja|do m (Mex) lodger, guest. **~miento** m accommodation. **~r** vt put up. **~rse** vpr stay

alondra f lark

alpaca f alpaca

alpargat|a f canvas shoe, espadrille. **~ería** f shoe shop

Alpes mpl Alps

alpin|ismo m mountaineering, climbing. **~ista** m & f mountaineer, climber. **~o** a Alpine

alpiste m birdseed

alquil|ar vt (tomar en alquiler) hire ⟨vehículo⟩, rent ⟨piso, casa⟩; (dar en alquiler) let, rent ⟨piso, casa⟩, rent (out) ⟨vehículo⟩, rent (out) ⟨piso, casa⟩. **~arse** vpr ⟨casa⟩ be let; ⟨vehículo⟩ be on hire. **se alquila** to let (Brit), for rent (Amer). **~er** m (acción de alquilar un piso etc) renting; (acción de alquilar un vehículo) hiring; (precio por el que se alquila un piso etc) rent; (precio por el que se alquila un vehículo) hire charge. **de ~er** for hire

alquimi|a f alchemy. **~sta** m alchemist

alquitara f still. **~r** vt distil

alquitr|án m tar. **~anar** vt tar

alrededor adv around. **~ de** around; (con números) about. **~es** mpl surroundings; (de una ciudad) outskirts

alta f discharge

altamente adv highly

altaner|ía f (orgullo) pride. **~o** a proud, haughty

altar m altar

altavoz m loudspeaker

altera|bilidad f changeability. **~ble** a changeable. **~ción** f change, alteration. **~do** a changed, altered; (perturbado) disturbed. **~r** vt change, alter; (perturbar) disturb; (enfadar) anger, irritate. **~rse** vpr change, alter; (agitarse) get upset; (enfadarse) get angry; (comida) go off

alterca|do m argument. **~r** [7] vi argue

altern|ado a alternate. **~ador** m alternator. **~ante** a alternating. **~ar** vt/i alternate. **~arse** vpr take turns. **~ativa** f alternative. **~ativo** a alternating. **~o** a alternate

alteza f height. **A~** (título) Highness

altibajos mpl (de terreno) unevenness; (fig) ups and downs

altiplanicie f high plateau

altísimo a very high. —m. **el A~** the Almighty

altisonante a, **altísono** a pompous

altitud f height; ⟨aviat, geog⟩ altitude

altiv|ez f arrogance. **~o** a arrogant

alto a high; ⟨persona⟩ tall; ⟨voz⟩ loud; ⟨fig, elevado⟩ lofty; ⟨mus⟩ ⟨nota⟩ high(-pitched); ⟨mus⟩ ⟨voz, instrumento⟩ alto; ⟨horas⟩ early. **tiene 3 metros de ~** it is 3 metres high. —adv high; ⟨de sonidos⟩ loud(ly). —m height; ⟨de un edificio⟩ high floor; ⟨viola⟩ viola; ⟨voz⟩ alto; ⟨parada⟩ stop. —int halt!, stop! **en lo ~ de** on the top of

altoparlante m ⟨esp LAm⟩ loudspeaker

altruis|mo m altruism. **~ta** a altruistic. —m & f altruist

altura f height; ⟨altitud⟩ altitude; ⟨de agua⟩ depth; ⟨fig, cielo⟩ sky. **a estas ~s** at this stage. **tiene 3 metros de ~** it is 3 metres high

alubia f French bean

alucinación f hallucination

alud m avalanche

aludi|do a in question. **darse por ~do** take it personally. **no darse por ~do** turn a deaf ear. **~r** vi mention

alumbra|do a lit; ⟨achispado, fam⟩ tipsy. —m lighting. **~miento** m lighting; ⟨parto⟩ childbirth. **~r** vt light. —vi give birth. **~rse** vpr ⟨emborracharse⟩ get tipsy

aluminio m aluminium ⟨Brit⟩, aluminum ⟨Amer⟩

alumno m pupil; ⟨univ⟩ student

aluniza|je m landing on the moon. **~r** [10] vi land on the moon

alusi|ón f allusion. **~vo** a allusive

alverja f vetch; ⟨LAm, guisante⟩ pea

alza f rise. **~cuello** m clerical collar, dog-collar ⟨fam⟩. **~da** f ⟨de caballo⟩ height; ⟨jurid⟩

appeal. **~do** a raised; ⟨persona⟩ fraudulently bankrupt; ⟨Mex, soberbio⟩ vain; ⟨precio⟩ fixed. **~miento** m raising; ⟨aumento⟩ rise, increase; ⟨pol⟩ revolt. **~r** [10] vt raise, lift (up); raise ⟨precios⟩. **~rse** vpr ⟨ponerse en pie⟩ stand up; ⟨pol⟩ revolt; ⟨quebrar⟩ go fraudulently bankrupt; ⟨apelar⟩ appeal

allá adv there. **¡~ él!** that's his business. **~ fuera** out there. **~ por el 1970** around about 1970. **el más ~** the beyond. **más ~** further on. **más ~ de** beyond. **por ~** over there

allana|miento m levelling; ⟨de obstáculos⟩ removal. **~miento de morada** burglary. **~r** vt level; remove ⟨obstáculos⟩; ⟨fig⟩ iron out ⟨dificultades etc⟩; burgle ⟨una casa⟩. **~rse** vpr level off; ⟨hundirse⟩ fall down; ⟨ceder⟩ submit (a to)

allega|do a close. —m relation. **~r** [12] vt collect

allí adv there; ⟨tiempo⟩ then. **~ donde** wherever. **~ fuera** out there, over there. **por ~** over there

ama f lady of the house. **~ de casa** housewife. **~ de cría** wet-nurse. **~ de llaves** housekeeper

amab|ilidad f kindness. **~le** a kind; ⟨simpático⟩ nice

amado a dear. **~r** m lover

amaestra|do a trained; ⟨en circo⟩ performing. **~miento** m training. **~r** vt train

amag|ar [12] vt ⟨amenazar⟩ threaten; ⟨mostrar intención de⟩ show signs of. —vi threaten; ⟨algo bueno⟩ be in the offing. **~o** m threat; ⟨señal⟩ sign; ⟨med⟩ symptom

amalgama f amalgam. **~r** vt amalgamate

amamantar vt breast-feed

amancebarse vpr live together

amanecer m dawn. —vi dawn; ⟨persona⟩ wake up. **al ~** at dawn, at daybreak

amanera|do a affected. **~miento** m affectation. **~rse** vpr become affected

amanezca f (Mex) dawn

amansa|dor m tamer. **~miento** m taming. **~r** vt tame; break in ⟨un caballo⟩; soothe ⟨dolor etc⟩. **~rse** vpr calm down

amante a fond. —m & f lover

amañar vt arrange. **~o** m scheme

amapola f poppy

amar vt love

amara|je m landing on the sea; ⟨de astronave⟩ splash-down. **~r** vt land on the sea; ⟨astronave⟩ splash down

amarg|ado a embittered. **~ar** [12] vt make bitter; embitter ⟨persona⟩. **~arse** vpr get bitter. **~o** a bitter. —m bitterness. **~ura** f bitterness

amariconado a effeminate

amarill|ear vi go yellow. **~ento** a yellowish; ⟨tez⟩ sallow. **~ez** f yellow; ⟨de una persona⟩ paleness. **~o** a & m yellow

amarra f mooring rope. **~s** fpl ⟨fig, fam⟩ influence. **~do** a ⟨LAm⟩ mean. **~r** vt moor; ⟨atar⟩ tie. **~r** vi ⟨empollar, fam⟩ study hard, swot ⟨fam⟩

amartillar vt cock ⟨arma de fuego⟩

amas|ar vt knead; ⟨fig, tramar, fam⟩ concoct, cook up ⟨fam⟩. **~ijo** m dough; ⟨acción⟩ kneading; ⟨fig, mezcla, fam⟩ hotchpotch

amate m ⟨Mex⟩ fig tree

amateur a & m & f amateur

amatista f amethyst

amazona f Amazon; ⟨mujer varonil⟩ mannish woman; ⟨que monta a caballo⟩ horsewoman

Amazonas m. **el río ~** the Amazon

ambages mpl circumlocutions. **sin ~** in plain language

ámbar m amber

ambarino a amber

ambici|ón f ambition. **~onar** vt strive after. **~onar ser** have an ambition to be. **~oso** a ambitious. —m ambitious person

ambidextro a ambidextrous. —m ambidextrous person

ambient|ar vt give an atmosphere to. **~arse** vpr adapt o.s. **~e** m atmosphere; ⟨medio⟩ environment

ambig|uamente adv ambiguously. **~üedad** f ambiguity. **~uo** a ambiguous; ⟨fig, afeminado, fam⟩ effeminate

ámbito m ambit

ambos a & pron both. **~ a dos** both (of them)

ambulancia f ambulance; ⟨hospital móvil⟩ field hospital

ambulante a travelling

ambulatorio m out-patients' department

amedrentar vt frighten, scare. **~se** vpr be frightened

amén m amen. —int amen! **en un decir ~** in an instant

amenaza f threat. **~dor** a, **~nte** a threatening. **~r** [10] vt threaten

amen|idad f pleasantness. **~izar** [10] vt brighten up. **~o** a pleasant

América f America. **~ Central** Central America. **~ del Norte** North America. **~ del Sur** South America. **~ Latina** Latin America

american|a f jacket. **~ismo** m Americanism. **~ista** m & f Americanist. **~o** a American

amerindio a & m & f Amerindian, American Indian

ameriza|je *m* landing on the sea; *(de astronave)* splash-down. **~r** [10] *vt* land on the sea; *(astronave)* splash down

ametralla|dora *f* machine-gun. **~r** *vt* machine-gun

amianto *m* asbestos

amig|a *f* friend; *(novia)* girlfriend; *(amante)* lover. **~able** *a* friendly. **~ablemente** *adv* amicably. **~rse** [12] *vpr* live together

amígdala *f* tonsil. **~igdalitis** *f* tonsillitis

amigo *a* friendly. **—m** friend; *(novio)* boy-friend; *(amante)* lover. **ser ~ de** to be fond of. **ser muy ~s** to be good friends

amilanar *vt* frighten, scare. **~se** *vpr* be frightened

aminorar *vt* lessen; slow down *(velocidad)*

amist|ad *f* friendship. **~ades** *mpl* friends. **~osamente** *adv* amicably. **~oso** *a* friendly

amnesia *f* amnesia

amnist|ía *f* amnesty. **~iar** [20] *vt* grant an amnesty to

amo *m* master; *(dueño)* owner; *(jefe)* boss; *(cabeza de familia)* head of the family

amodorra|miento *m* sleepiness. **~rse** *vpr* get sleepy

amojonar *vt* mark out

amola|dor *m* knife-grinder. **~r** [2] *vt* sharpen; *(molestar, fam)* annoy

amoldar *vt* mould; *(acomodar)* fit

amonedar *vt* coin, mint

amonesta|ción *f* rebuke, reprimand; *(de una boda)* banns. **~r** *vt* rebuke, reprimand; *(anunciar la boda)* publish the banns

amoniaco *m*, **amoníaco** *m* ammonia

amontillado *m* Amontillado, pale dry sherry

amontona|damente *adv* in a heap. **~miento** *m* piling up. **~r** *vt* pile up; *(fig, acumular)* accumulate. **~rse** *vpr* pile up; *(gente)* crowd together; *(amancebarse, fam)* live together

amor *m* love. **~es** *mpl* *(relaciones amorosas)* love affairs. **con mil ~es, de mil ~es** with (the greatest of) pleasure. **hacer el ~** make love. **por (el) ~ de Dios** for God's sake

amorata|do *a* purple; *(de frío)* blue. **~rse** *vpr* go black and blue

amorcillo *m* Cupid

amordazar [10] *vt* gag; *(fig)* silence

amorfo *a* amorphous, shapeless

amor: ~ío *m* affair. **~oso** *a* loving; *(cartas)* love

amortajar *vt* shroud

amortigua|dor *a* deadening. **—m** *(auto)* shock absorber. **~miento** *m* deadening; *(de la luz)* dimming. **~r** [15] *vt* deaden *(ruido)*; dim *(luz)*; cushion *(golpe)*; tone down *(color)*

amortiza|ble *a* redeemable. **~ción** *f* *(de una deuda)* repayment; *(recuperación)* redemption. **~r** [10] *vt* repay *(una deuda)*

amoscarse [7] *vpr* *(fam)* get cross, get irritated

amostazarse [10] *vpr* get cross

amotina|do *a* & *m* insurgent, rebellious. **~miento** *m* riot; *(mil)* mutiny. **~r** *vt* incite to riot. **~rse** *vpr* rebel; *(mil)* mutiny

amparar *vt* help; *(proteger)* protect. **~rse** *vpr* seek protection; *(de la lluvia)* shelter. **~o** *m* protection; *(de la lluvia)* shelter. **al ~o de** under the protection of

amperio *m* ampere, amp *(fam)*

amplia|ción *f* extension; *(photo)* enlargement. **~r** [20] *vt* enlarge, extend; *(photo)* enlarge

amplifica|ción f amplification. **~dor** m amplifier. **~r** [7] amplify

ampli|o a wide; (*espacioso*) spacious; (*ropa*) loose-fitting. **~tud** f extent; (*espaciosidad*) spaciousness; (*espacio*) space

ampolla f (*med*) blister; (*frasco*) flask; (*de medicamento*) ampoule, phial

ampuloso a pompous

amputa|ción f amputation; (*fig*) deletion. **~r** vt amputate; (*fig*) delete

amueblar vt furnish

amuinar vt (*Mex*) annoy

amuralla|do a walled. **~r** vt build a wall around

anacardo m (*fruto*) cashew nut

anaconda f anaconda

anacr|ónico a anachronistic. **~onismo** m anachronism

ánade m & f duck

anagrama m anagram

anales mpl annals

analfabet|ismo m illiteracy. **~o** a & m illiterate

analgésico a & m analgesic, pain-killer

an|álisis m invar analysis. **~álisis de sangre** blood test. **~alista** m & f analyst. **~alítico** a analytical. **~alizar** [10] vt analyze

an|alogía f analogy. **~álogo** a analogous

ananás m pineapple

anaquel m shelf

anaranjado a orange

an|arquía f anarchy. **~árquico** a anarchic. **~arquismo** m anarchism. **~arquista** a anarchistic. **~m & f** anarchist

anatema m anathema

anat|omía f anatomy. **~ómico** a anatomical

anca f haunch; (*parte superior*) rump; (*nalgas*, *fam*) bottom. **~s** fpl **de rana** frogs' legs

ancestral a ancestral

anciano a elderly, old. **—m** elderly man, old man; (*relig*) elder. **los ~s** old people

ancla f anchor. **~dero** m anchorage. **~r** vi anchor, drop anchor. **echar ~s** anchor. **levar ~s** weigh anchor

áncora f anchor; (*fig*) refuge

ancho a wide; (*ropa*) loose-fitting; (*fig*) relieved; (*demasiado grande*) too big; (*ufano*) smug. **—m** width; (*rail*) gauge. **a mis anchas**, **a sus anchas etc** comfortable, relaxed. **quedarse tan ancho** behave as if nothing has happened. **tiene 3 metros de ~** it is 3 metres wide

anchoa f anchovy

anchura f width; (*medida*) measurement

andaderas fpl baby-walker

andad|or a good at walking. **—m** baby-walker. **~ura** f walking; (*manera de andar*) walk

Andalucía f Andalusia

andaluz a & m Andalusian

andamio m platform. **~s** mpl scaffolding

andar [25] vt (*recorrer*) cover, go. **—vi** walk; (*máquina*) go, work; (*estar*) be; (*moverse*) move. **—m** walk. **¡anda!** go on! come on! **~iego** a fond of walking; (*itinerante*) wandering. **~ por** be about. **~se** vpr (*marcharse*) go away

andén m platform; (*en un muelle*) quayside; (*LAm*, *acera*) pavement (*Brit*), sidewalk (*Amer*)

Andes mpl Andes

andino a Andean

Andorra f Andorra

andrajo m rag. **~so** a ragged

andurriales mpl (*fam*) out-of-the-way place

anduve vb *véase* **andar**

anécdota f anecdote

anega|dizo *a* subject to flooding. **~r** [12] *vt* flood. **~rse** *vpr* be flooded, flood

anejo *a* attached. —*m* annexe; (*de libro etc*) appendix

an|emia *f* anaemia. **~émico** *a* anaemic

anest|esia *f* anaesthesia. **~ésico** *a & m* anaesthetic. **~esista** *m & f* anaesthetist

anex|ión *f* annexation. **~ionar** *vt* annex. **~o** *a* attached. —*m* annexe

anfibio *a* amphibious. —*m* amphibian

anfiteatro *m* amphitheatre; (*en un teatro*) upper circle

anfitri|ón *m* host. **~ona** *f* hostess

ángel *m* angel; (*encanto*) charm

angelical *a*, **angélico** *a* angelic

angina *f*. **~ de pecho** angina (pectoris). **tener ~s** have tonsillitis

anglicano *a & m* Anglican

anglicismo *m* Anglicism

anglófilo *a & m* Anglophile

anglo|hispánico *a* Anglo-Spanish. **~sajón** *a & m* Anglo-Saxon

angosto *a* narrow

anguila *f* eel

angula *f* elver, baby eel

angular *a* angular

ángulo *m* angle; (*rincón, esquina*) corner; (*curva*) bend

anguloso *a* angular

angusti|a *f* anguish. **~ar** *vt* distress; (*inquietar*) worry. **~arse** *vpr* get distressed; (*inquietarse*) get worried. **~oso** *a* anguished; (*que causa angustia*) distressing

anhel|ante *a* panting; (*deseoso*) longing. **~ar** *vt* (+ *nombre*) long for; (+ *verbo*) long to. —*vi* pant. **~o** *m* (*fig*) yearning. **~oso** *a* panting; (*fig*) eager

anidar *vi* nest

anill|a *f* ring. **~o** *m* ring. **~o de boda** wedding ring

ánima *f* soul

anima|ción *f* (*de personas*) life; (*de cosas*) liveliness; (*bullicio*) bustle; (*en el cine*) animation. **~do** *a* lively; (*sitio etc*) busy. **~dor** *m* compère, host

animadversión *f* ill will

animal *a* animal; (*fig, torpe, fam*) stupid. —*m* animal; (*fig, idiota, fam*) idiot; (*fig, bruto, fam*) brute

animar *vt* give life to; (*dar ánimo*) encourage; (*dar vivacidad*) liven up. **~se** *vpr* (*decidirse*) decide; (*ponerse alegre*) cheer up. **¿te animas a venir al cine?** do you fancy coming to the cinema?

ánimo *m* soul; (*mente*) mind; (*valor*) courage; (*intención*) intention. **¡~!** come on!, cheer up! **dar ~s** encourage

animosidad *f* animosity

animoso *a* brave; (*resuelto*) determined

aniquila|ción *f* annihilation. **~miento** *m* annihilation. **~r** *vt* annihilate; (*acabar con*) ruin. **~rse** *vpr* deteriorate

anís *m* aniseed; (*licor*) anisette

aniversario *m* anniversary

ano *m* anus

anoche *adv* last night, yesterday evening

anochecer [11] *vi* get dark; (*persona*) be at dusk. **anochecí en Madrid** I was in Madrid at dusk. —*m* nightfall, dusk. **al ~** at nightfall

anodino *a* indifferent

an|omalía *f* anomaly. **~ómalo** *a* anomalous

an|onimato *m* anonymity. **~ónimo** *a* anonymous; (*sociedad*) limited. —*m* anonymity; (*carta*) anonymous letter

anormal *a* abnormal; (*fam*) stupid, silly. **~idad** *f* abnormality

anota|ción f noting; (*acción de poner notas*) annotation; (*nota*) note. **~r** vt (*poner nota*) annotate; (*apuntar*) make a note of

anquilosa|miento m paralysis. **~r** vt paralyze. **~rse** vpr become paralyzed

ansi|a f anxiety, worry; (*anhelo*) yearning. **~ar** [20 o *regular*] vt long for. **~edad** f anxiety. **~oso** a anxious; (*deseoso*) eager

antag|ónico a antagonistic. **~onismo** m antagonism. **~onista** a & f antagonist

antaño adv in days gone by

antártico a & m Antarctic

ante prep in front of, before; (*en comparación con*) compared with; (*frente a peligro, enemigo*) in the face of; (*en vista de*) in view of. —m (*piel*) suede. **~anoche** adv the night before last. **~ayer** adv the day before yesterday. **~brazo** m forearm

ante... pref ante...

antece|dente a previous. —m antecedent. **~dentes** mpl history, background. **~dentes penales** criminal record. **~der** vt precede. **~sor** m predecessor; (*antepasado*) ancestor

antedicho a aforesaid

antela|ción f advance. con **~** in advance

antemano adv. de **~** beforehand

antena f antenna; (*radio, TV*) aerial

anteojeras fpl blinkers

anteojo m telescope. **~s** mpl (*gemelos*) opera glasses; (*prismáticos*) binoculars; (*LAm, gafas*) glasses, spectacles

ante|pasados mpl forebears, ancestors. **~pecho** m rail; (*de ventana*) sill. **~poner** [34] vt put in front (a of); (*fig*) put before, prefer. **~proyecto** m preliminary sketch; (*fig*) blueprint. **~puesto** a put before

anterior a previous; (*delantero*) front, fore. **~idad** f. con **~idad** previously. **~mente** adv previously

antes adv before; (*antiguamente*) in days gone by; (*mejor*) rather; (*primero*) first. **~** de before. **~ de ayer** the day before yesterday. **~ de que** + subj before. **~ de que llegue** before he arrives. **cuanto ~**, **lo ~ posible** as soon as possible

antesala f anteroom; (*sala de espera*) waiting-room. **hacer ~** wait (to be received)

anti... pref anti...

anti|: ~aéreo a anti-aircraft. **~biótico** a & m antibiotic. **~ciclón** m anticyclone

anticipa|ción f anticipation. **~ción** in advance. con media hora de **~ción** half an hour early. **~adamente** adv in advance. **~ado** a. por **~ado** in advance. **~ar** vt bring forward; advance (*dinero*). **~arse** vpr be early. **~o** m (*dinero*) advance; (*fig*) foretaste

anti|: ~concepcional a & m contraceptive. **~conceptivo** a & m contraceptive. **~congelante** m antifreeze

anticua|do a old-fashioned. **~rio** m antique dealer. **~rse** vpr go out of date

anticuerpo m antibody

antídoto m antidote

anti|: ~estético a ugly. **~faz** m mask. **~gás** a invar. **careta ~gás** gas mask

antig|ualla f old relic. **~uamente** adv formerly; (*hace mucho tiempo*) long ago. **~üedad** f antiquity; (*objeto*) antique; (*en un empleo*) length of service. **~uo** a old, ancient. **chapado a la ~ua** old-fashioned

antílope m antelope

Antillas fpl West Indies

antinatural *a* unnatural

antip|**atía** *f* dislike; *(cualidad de antipático)* unpleasantness. ~**ático** *a* unpleasant, unfriendly

anti: ~**semita** *m & f* anti-Semite. ~**semítico** *a* anti-Semitic. ~**semitismo** *m* anti-Semitism. ~**séptico** *a & m* antiseptic. ~**social** *a* antisocial

antítesis *f invar* antithesis

antoj|**adizo** *a* capricious. ~**arse** *vpr* fancy. **se le** ~**a un caramelo** he fancies a sweet. ~**o** *m* whim; *(de embarazada)* craving

antología *f* anthology

antorcha *f* torch

antro *m* cavern; *(fig)* dump, hole. ~ **de perversión** den of iniquity

antropófago *m* cannibal

antrop|**ología** *f* anthropology. ~**ólogo** *m & f* anthropologist

anual *a* annual. ~**lidad** *f* annuity. ~**lmente** *adv* yearly. ~**rio** *m* yearbook

anudar *vt* tie, knot; *(fig, iniciar)* begin; *(fig, continuar)* resume. ~**se** *vpr* get into knots. ~**se la voz** get a lump in one's throat

anula|**ción** *f* annulment, cancellation. ~*vt* annul, cancel. — *a (dedo)* ring. —*m* ring finger

Anunciación *f* Annunciation

anunci|**ante** *m & f* advertiser. ~**ar** *vt* announce; advertise *(producto comercial)*; *(presagiar)* be a sign of. ~**arse** *vpr* promise to be. ~**o** *m* announcement; *(para vender algo)* advertisement, advert *(fam)*; *(cartel)* poster

anzuelo *m* (fish)hook; *(fig)* bait. **tragar el** ~ be taken in, fall for

añadi|**do** *a* added. ~**dura** *f* addition. ~**r** *vt* add. **por** ~**dura** besides

añejo *a (vino)* mature; *(jamón etc)* cured

añicos *mpl* bits. **hacer** ~ *(romper)* smash (to pieces); *(dejar cansado)* wear out

añil *m* indigo

año *m* year. ~ **bisiesto** leap year. ~ **nuevo** new year. **al** ~ per year, a year. **¿cuántos** ~**s tiene? tiene 5** ~**s** how old is he? he's 5 (years old). **el** ~ **pasado** last year. **el** ~ **que viene** next year. **entrado en** ~**s** elderly. **los** ~**s** 60 the sixties

añora|**nza** *f* nostalgia. ~**r** *vt* miss. —*vi* pine

apabullar *vt* crush; *(fig)* intimidate

apacentar [1] *vt* graze. ~**se** *vpr* graze

apacib|**ilidad** *f* gentleness; *(calma)* peacefulness. ~**le** *a* gentle; *(tiempo)* mild

apacigua|**dor** *a* pacifying. ~**miento** *m* appeasement. ~**r** [15] *vt* pacify; *(calmar)* calm; relieve *(dolor etc)*. ~**rse** *vpr* calm down

apadrina|**miento** *m* sponsorship. ~**r** *vt* sponsor; be godfather to *(a un niño)*; *(en una boda)* be best man for

apaga|**dizo** *a* slow to burn. ~**do** *a* extinguished; *(color)* dull; *(aparato eléctrico)* off; *(persona)* lifeless; *(sonido)* muffled. ~**r** [12] *vt* put out *(fuego, incendio)*; turn off, switch off *(aparato eléctrico)*; quench *(sed)*; muffle *(sonido)*. ~**rse** *vpr (fuego)* go out; *(luz)* go out; *(sonido)* die away; *(fig)* pass away

apagón *m* blackout

apalabrar *vt* make a verbal agreement; *(contratar)* engage. ~**se** *vpr* come to a verbal agreement

apalanca|**miento** *m* leverage. ~**r** [7] *vt (levantar)* lever up; *(abrir)* lever open

apalea|**miento** *m (de grano)* winnowing; *(de alfombras,* *frutos, personas*) beating. ~r *vt* winnow ⟨*grano*⟩; beat ⟨*alfombras, frutos, personas*⟩; (*fig*) be rolling in ⟨*dinero*⟩

apantallado *a* (*Mex*) stupid

apañ|ado *a* handy. ~ar *vt* (*arreglar*) fix; (*remendar*) mend; (*agarrar*) grasp, take hold of. ~arse *vpr* get along, manage. ¡estoy ~ado! that's all I need!

aparador *m* sideboard

aparato *m* apparatus; (*máquina*) machine; (*teléfono*) telephone; (*rad, TV*) set; (*ostentación*) show, pomp. ~samente *adv* ostentatiously; (*impresionante*) spectacularly. ~sidad *f* ostentation. ~so *a* showy, ostentatious; (*caída*) spectacular

aparca|miento *m* car park (*Brit*), parking lot (*Amer*). ~r [7] *vt/i* park

aparea|miento *m* pairing off. ~r *vt* pair off; mate ⟨*animales*⟩. ~rse *vpr* match ⟨*animales*⟩ mate

aparecer [11] *vi* appear. ~se *vpr* appear

aparej|ado *a* ready; (*adecuado*) fitting. **llevar** ~ado, **traer** ~ado mean, entail. ~o *m* preparation; (*avíos*) equipment

aparent|ar *vt* (*afectar*) feign; (*parecer*) look. —*vi* show off. ~a **20 años** she looks like 20. ~e *a* apparent; (*adecuado, fam*) suitable

apari|ción *f* appearance; (*visión*) apparition. ~encia *f* appearance; (*fig*) show. **cubrir las** ~encias keep up appearances

apartad|ero *m* lay-by; (*rail*) siding. ~o *a* separated; (*aislado*) isolated. —*m* (*en un texto*) section. ~o **(de correos)** post-office box, PO box

apartamento *m* flat (*Brit*), apartment

apart|amiento *m* separation; (*LAm, piso*) flat (*Brit*), apartment; (*aislamiento*) seclusion. ~ar *vt* separate; (*quitar*) remove. ~arse *vpr* leave; abandon ⟨*creencia*⟩; (*quitarse de en medio*) get out of the way; (*aislarse*) cut o.s. off. ~e *adv* apart; (*por separado*) separately; (*además*) besides. —*m* aside; (*párrafo*) new paragraph. ~e de apart from. **dejar** ~e leave aside. **eso** ~e apart from that

apasiona|do *a* passionate; (*entusiasta*) enthusiastic; (*falto de objetividad*) biassed. —*m* lover (**de** of). ~miento *m* passion. ~r *vt* excite. ~rse *vpr* get excited (**de, por** about), be mad (**de, por** about); (*ser parcial*) become biassed

apat|ía *f* apathy. ~ático *a* apathetic

apea|dero *m* (*rail*) halt. ~r *vt* fell ⟨*árbol*⟩; (*disuadir*) dissuade; overcome ⟨*dificultad*⟩; sort out ⟨*problema*⟩. ~rse *vpr* (*de un vehículo*) get off

apechugar [12] *vi* push (with one's chest). ~ **con** put up with

apedrear *vt* stone

apeg|ado *a* attached. ~o *m* (*fam*) affection. **tener** ~o a be fond of

apela|ción *f* appeal. ~r *vt* appeal; (*recurrir*) resort (**a** to)

apelmazar [10] *vt* compress

apellid|ar *vt* call. ~arse *vpr* be called. **¿cómo te apellidas?** what's your surname? ~o *m* surname

apenar *vt* pain. ~se *vpr* grieve

apenas *adv* hardly, scarcely; (*enseguida que*) as soon as. ~ **si** (*fam*) hardly

ap|éndice *m* (*med*) appendix; (*fig*) appendage; (*de un libro*) appendix. ~endicitis *f* appendicitis

apercibi|miento *m* warning. **~r** *vt* warn (de of, about); (*amenazar*) threaten. **~rse** *vpr* prepare; (*percatarse*) provide o.s. (de with)

apergaminado *a* ⟨piel⟩ wrinkled

aperitivo *m* ⟨bebida⟩ aperitif; ⟨comida⟩ appetizer

aperos *mpl* agricultural equipment

apertura *f* opening

apesadumbrar *vt* upset. **~se** *vpr* be upset

apestar *vt* stink out; (*fastidiar*) pester. **—***vi* stink (a of)

apet|ecer [11] *vt* long for; (*interesar*) appeal to. ¿te **~ece una copa?** do you fancy a drink? do you feel like a drink?. **—***vi* be welcome. **~ecible** *a* attractive. **~ito** *m* appetite; (*fig*) desire. **~itoso** *a* tempting

apiadarse *vpr* feel sorry (de for)

ápice *m* ⟨nada, en frases negativas⟩ anything. **no ceder un ~** not give an inch

apicult|or *m* bee-keeper. **~ura** *f* bee-keeping

apilar *vt* pile up

apiñar *vt* pack in. **~se** *vpr* ⟨personas⟩ crowd together; ⟨cosas⟩ be packed tight

apio *m* celery

apisonadora *f* steamroller

aplacar [7] *vt* placate; relieve ⟨dolor⟩

aplanar *vt* smooth. **~se** *vpr* become smooth; ⟨persona⟩ lose heart

aplasta|nte *a* overwhelming. **~r** *vt* crush. **~rse** *vpr* flatten o.s.

aplatanarse *vpr* become lethargic

aplau|dir *vt* clap, applaud; (*fig*) applaud. **~so** *m* applause; (*fig*) praise

aplaza|miento *m* postponement. **~r** [10] *vt* postpone; defer ⟨pago⟩

aplebeyarse *vpr* lower o.s.

aplica|ble *a* applicable. **~ción** *f* application. **~do** *a* ⟨persona⟩ diligent. **~r** [7] *vt* apply; ⟨fijar⟩ attach. **~rse** *vpr* apply o.s.

aplomado *a* self-confident; (*vertical*) vertical. **~o** *m* (self-) confidence, aplomb; (*verticalidad*) verticality

apocado *a* timid

Apocalipsis *f* Apocalypse

apocalíptico *a* apocalyptic

apoca|miento *m* diffidence. **~r** [7] *vt* belittle ⟨persona⟩. **~rse** *vpr* feel small

apodar *vt* nickname

apodera|do *m* representative. **~r** *vt* authorize. **~rse** *vpr* seize

apodo *m* nickname

apogeo *m* (*fig*) height

apolilla|do *a* moth-eaten. **~rse** *vpr* get moth-eaten

apolítico *a* non-political

apología *f* defence

apoltronarse *vpr* get lazy

apoplejía *f* stroke

apoquinar *vt/i* (*fam*) fork out

aporrear *vt* hit, thump; beat up ⟨persona⟩

aporta|ción *f* contribution. **~r** *vt* contribute

aposent|ar *vt* put up, lodge. **~o** *m* room, lodgings

apósito *m* dressing

aposta *adv* on purpose

apostar[1] [2] *vt/i* bet

apostar[2] *vt* station. **~se** *vpr* station o.s.

apostilla *f* note. **~r** *vt* add notes to

apóstol *m* apostle

apóstrofo *m* apostrophe

apoy|ar *vt* lean (en against); ⟨descansar⟩ rest; ⟨asentar⟩ base; ⟨reforzar⟩ support. **~arse** *vpr* lean, rest. **~o** *m* support

apreci|able *a* appreciable; ⟨digno de estima⟩ worthy.

~ación f appreciation; (*valoración*) appraisal. **~ar** vt value; (*estimar*) appreciate. **~ativo** a appreciative. **~o** m appraisal; (*fig*) esteem

aprehensión f capture

apremi|ante a urgent, pressing. **~ar** vt urge; (*obligar*) compel; (*dar prisa a*) hurry up. —vi be urgent. **~o** m urgency; (*obligación*) obligation

aprender vt/i learn. **~se** vpr learn (by heart)

aprendiz m apprentice. **~aje** m apprenticeship

aprensi|ón f apprehension; (*miedo*) fear. **~vo** a apprehensive, fearful

apresa|dor m captor. **~miento** m capture. **~r** vt seize; (*prender*) capture

aprestar vt prepare. **~se** vpr prepare

apresura|damente adv hurriedly, in a hurry. **~do** a in a hurry; (*hecho con prisa*) hurried. **~miento** m hurry. **~r** vt hurry. **~rse** vpr hurry

apret|ado a tight; (*difícil*) difficult; (*tacaño*) stingy, mean. **~ar** [1] vt tighten; press (*botón*); squeeze (*persona*); (*comprimir*) press down. —vi be too tight. **~arse** vpr crowd together. **~ón** m squeeze. **~ón de manos** handshake

aprieto m difficulty. **verse en un ~** be in a tight spot

aprisa adv quickly

aprisionar vt imprison

aproba|ción f approval. **~r** [2] vt approve (of); pass (*examen*). —vi pass

apropia|do a appropriate. **~rse** vpr. **~rse de** appropriate, take

aprovecha|ble a usable. **~do** a (*aplicado*) diligent; (*ingenioso*) resourceful; (*egoísta*) selfish; (*económico*) thrifty. **~miento** m

advantage; (*uso*) use. **~r** vt take advantage of; (*utilizar*) make use of. —vi be useful. **~rse** vpr make the most of it. **~rse de** take advantage of. **¡que aproveche!** enjoy your meal!

aprovisionar vt supply (**con, de** with)

aproxima|ción f approximation; (*proximidad*) closeness; (*en la lotería*) consolation prize. **~damente** adv roughly, approximately. **~do** a approximate, rough. **~r** vt bring near; (*fig*) bring together (*personas*). **~rse** vpr come closer, approach

aptitud f suitability; (*capacidad*) ability. **~o** a (*capaz*) capable; (*adecuado*) suitable

apuesta f bet

apuesto m smart. —vb véase **apostar**

apunta|ción f note. **~do** a sharp. **~dor** m prompter

apuntalar vt shore up

apunt|amiento m aiming; (*nota*) note. **~ar** vt aim (*arma*); (*señalar*) point at; (*anotar*) make a note of, note down; (*sacar punta*) sharpen; (*en el teatro*) prompt. **~arse** vpr put one's name down; score (*triunfo, tanto etc*). **~e** m note; (*bosquejo*) sketch. **tomar ~s** take notes

apuñalar vt stab

apur|adamente adv with difficulty. **~ado** a difficult; (*sin dinero*) hard up; (*agotado*) exhausted; (*exacto*) precise, carefully done. **~ar** vt exhaust; (*acabar*) finish; drain (*vaso etc*); (*fastidiar*) annoy; (*causar vergüenza*) embarrass. **~arse** vpr worry; (*esp LAm, apresurarse*) hurry up. **~o** m tight spot, difficult situation; (*vergüenza*) embarrassment; (*estrechez*) hardship, want; (*esp LAm, prisa*) hurry

aquejar *vt* trouble

aquel *a* (*f* **aquella**, *mpl* **aquellos**, *fpl* **aquellas**) that; (*en plural*) those; (*primero de dos*) former

aquél *pron* (*f* **aquélla**, *mpl* **aquéllos**, *fpl* **aquéllas**) that one; (*en plural*) those; (*primero de dos*) the former

aquello *pron* that; (*asunto*) that business

aquí *adv* here. **de ~** from here. **de ~ a 15 días** in a fortnight's time. **de ~ para allí** to and fro. **de ~ que** so that. **hasta ~** until now. **por ~** around here

aquiescencia *f* acquiescence

aquietar *vt* calm (down)

aquí: ~ fuera out here. **~ mismo** right here

árabe *a* & *m* & *f* Arab; (*lengua*) Arabic

Arabia *f* Arabia. **~ saudita**, **~ saudí** Saudi Arabia

arábigo *a* Arabic

arado *m* plough. **~r** *m* ploughman

Aragón *m* Aragon

aragonés *a* & *m* Aragonese

arancel *m* tariff. **~ario** *a* tariff

arandela *f* washer

araña *f* spider; (*lámpara*) chandelier

arañar *vt* scratch

arar *vt* plough

arbitra|je *m* arbitration; (*en deportes*) refereeing. **~r** *vt/i* arbitrate; (*en fútbol etc*) referee; (*en tenis etc*) umpire

arbitr|ariedad *f* arbitrariness. **~ario** *a* arbitrary. **~io** *m* (free) will; (*jurid*) decision, judgement

árbitro *m* arbitrator; (*en fútbol etc*) referee; (*en tenis etc*) umpire

árbol *m* tree; (*eje*) axle; (*palo*) mast

arbol|ado *m* trees. **~adura** *f* rigging. **~eda** *f* wood

árbol: ~ genealógico family tree. **~ de navidad** Christmas tree

arbusto *m* bush

arca *f* (*caja*) chest. **~ de Noé** Noah's ark

arcada *f* arcade; (*de un puente*) arches; (*náuseas*) retching

arca|ico *a* archaic. **~ísmo** *m* archaism

arcángel *m* archangel

arcano *m* mystery. —*a* mysterious, secret

arce *m* maple (tree)

arcén *m* (*de autopista*) hard shoulder; (*de carretera*) verge

arcilla *f* clay

arco *m* arch; (*de curva*) arc; (*arma, mus*) bow. **~ iris** *m* rainbow

archipiélago *m* archipelago

archiv|ador *m* filing cabinet. **~ar** *vt* file (away). **~o** *m* file; (*de documentos históricos*) archives

arder *vt/i* burn; (*fig, de ira*) seethe. **~se** *vpr* burn (up). **estar que arde** be very tense. **y va que arde** and that's enough

ardid *m* trick, scheme

ardiente *a* burning. **~mente** *adv* passionately

ardilla *f* squirrel

ardor *m* heat; (*fig*) ardour. **~ del estómago** *m* heartburn. **~oso** *a* burning

arduo *a* arduous

área *f* area

arena *f* sand; (*en deportes*) arena; (*en los toros*) (bull)ring. **~l** *m* sandy area

arenga *f* harangue. **~r** [12] *vt* harangue

aren|isca *f* sandstone. **~isco** *a*, **~oso** *a* sandy

arenque *m* herring. **~ ahumado** kipper

argamasa *f* mortar

Argel *m* Algiers. **~ia** *f* Algeria

argelino *a* & *m* Algerian

argentado *a* silver-plated

Argentina *f.* **la** ∼ Argentina

argentin|**ismo** *m* Argentinism. ∼**o** *a* silvery; (*de la Argentina*) Argentinian, Argentine. —*m* Argentinian

argolla *f* ring

argot *m* slang

argucia *f* sophism

argüir [19] *vt* (*deducir*) deduce; (*probar*) prove, show; (*argumentar*) argue; (*echar en cara*) reproach. —*vi* argue

argument|**ación** *f* argument. ∼**ador** *a* argumentative. ∼**ar** *vt*/*i* argue. ∼**o** *m* argument; (*de libro, película etc*) story, plot; (*resumen*) synopsis

aria *f* aria

aridez *f* aridity, dryness

árido *a* arid, dry. —*m.* ∼**s** *mpl* dry goods

Aries *m* Aries

arisco *a* (*persona*) unsociable; ⟨*animal*⟩ vicious

arist|**ocracia** *f* aristocracy. ∼**ócrata** *m* & *f* aristocrat. ∼**ocrático** *a* aristocratic

aritmética *f* arithmetic

arma *f* arm, weapon; (*sección*) section. ∼**da** *f* navy; (*flota*) fleet. ∼ **de fuego** firearm. ∼**do** *a* armed (**de** with). ∼**dura** *f* armour; (*de gafas etc*) frame; (*tec*) framework. ∼**mento** *m* arms, armaments; (*acción de armar*) armament. ∼**r** *vt* arm (**de** with); (*montar*) put together. ∼**r un lío** kick up a fuss. **La A**∼**da Invencible** the Armada

armario *m* cupboard; (*para ropa*) wardrobe. ∼ **ropero** wardrobe

armatoste *m* monstrosity, hulk (*fam*)

armazón *m* & *f* frame(work)

armer|**ía** *f* gunsmith's shop; (*museo*) war museum. ∼**o** *m* gunsmith

armiño *m* ermine

armisticio *m* armistice

armonía *f* harmony

armónica *f* harmonica, mouth organ

armoni|**oso** harmonious. ∼**zación** *f* harmonizing. ∼**zar** [10] *vt* harmonize. —*vi* harmonize; (*personas*) get on well (**con** with); (*colores*) go well (**con** with)

arnés *m* armour. **arneses** *mpl* harness

aro *m* ring, hoop; (*Arg, pendiente*) ear-ring

arom|**a** *m* aroma; (*de vino*) bouquet. ∼**ático** *a* aromatic. ∼**atizar** [10] *vt* perfume; (*culin*) flavour

arpa *f* harp

arpado *a* serrated

arpía *f* harpy; (*fig*) hag

arpillera *f* sackcloth, sacking

arpista *m* & *f* harpist

arp|**ón** *m* harpoon. ∼**onar** *vt*, ∼**onear** *vt* harpoon

arque|**ar** *vt* arch, bend. ∼**arse** *vpr* arch, bend. ∼**o** *m* arching, bending

arque|**ología** *f* archaeology. ∼**ológico** *a* archaeological. ∼**ólogo** *m* archaeologist

arquería *f* arcade

arquero *m* archer; (*com*) cashier

arqueta *f* chest

arquetipo *m* archetype; (*prototipo*) prototype

arquitect|**o** *m* architect. ∼**ónico** *a* architectural. ∼**ura** *f* architecture

arrabal *m* suburb; (*LAm, tugurio*) slum. ∼**es** *mpl* outskirts. ∼**ero** *a* suburban; (*de modales groseros*) common

arracima|**do** *a* in a bunch; (*apiñado*) bunched together. ∼**rse** *vpr* bunch together

arraiga|**damente** *adv* firmly. ∼**r** [12] *vi* take root. ∼**rse** *vpr* take root; (*fig*) settle

arran|cada *f* sudden start. **~car** [7] *vt* pull up ⟨*planta*⟩; extract ⟨*diente*⟩; ⟨*arrebatar*⟩ snatch; ⟨*auto*⟩ start. —*vi* start. **~carse** *upr* start. **~que** *m* sudden start; ⟨*auto*⟩ start; ⟨*de emoción*⟩ outburst

arras *fpl* security

arrasa|dor *a* overwhelming, devastating. **~r** *vt* level, smooth; raze to the ground ⟨*edificio etc*⟩; ⟨*llenar*⟩ fill to the brim. —*vi* ⟨*el cielo*⟩ clear. **~se** *upr* ⟨*el cielo*⟩ clear; ⟨*los ojos*⟩ fill with tears; ⟨*triunfar*⟩ triumph

arrastr|ado *a* ⟨*penoso*⟩ wretched. **~ar** *vt* pull; ⟨*rozar contra el suelo*⟩ drag (along); give rise to ⟨*consecuencias*⟩. —*vi* trail on the ground. **~arse** *upr* crawl; ⟨*humillarse*⟩ grovel. **~e** *m* dragging; ⟨*transporte*⟩ haulage. **estar para el ~e** ⟨*fam*⟩ have had it, be worn out. **ir ~ado** be hard up

arrayán *m* myrtle

arre *int* gee up! **~ar** *vt* urge on; give ⟨*golpe*⟩

arrebañar *vt* scrape together; scrape clean ⟨*plato etc*⟩

arrebat|ado *a* enraged; ⟨*irreflexivo*⟩ impetuous; ⟨*cara*⟩ flushed. **~ar** *vt* snatch (away); ⟨*el viento*⟩ blow away; ⟨*fig*⟩ win (over); captivate ⟨*corazón etc*⟩. **~arse** *upr* get carried away. **~o** *m* ⟨*de cólera etc*⟩ fit; ⟨*éxtasis*⟩ extasy

arrebol *m* red glow

arreciar *vi* get worse, increase

arrecife *m* reef

arregl|ado *a* neat; ⟨*bien vestido*⟩ well-dressed; ⟨*moderado*⟩ moderate. **~ar** *vt* arrange; ⟨*poner en orden*⟩ tidy up; sort out ⟨*asunto, problema etc*⟩; ⟨*reparar*⟩ mend. **~arse** *upr* ⟨*ponerse bien*⟩ improve; ⟨*prepararse*⟩ get ready; ⟨*apañarse*⟩ manage, make do; ⟨*ponerse de acuerdo*⟩ come to an agreement. **~árselas** manage, get by. **~o** *m* ⟨*incl mus*⟩ arrangement; ⟨*acción de reparar*⟩ repair; ⟨*acuerdo*⟩ agreement; ⟨*orden*⟩ order. **con ~o a** according to

arrellanarse *upr* lounge, sit back

arremangar [12] *vt* roll up ⟨*mangas*⟩; tuck up ⟨*falda*⟩. **~se** *upr* roll up one's sleeves

arremet|er *vt/i* attack. **~ida** *f* attack

arremolinarse *upr* mill about

arrenda|dor *m* ⟨*que da en alquiler*⟩ landlord; ⟨*que toma en alquiler*⟩ tenant. **~miento** *m* renting; ⟨*contrato*⟩ lease; ⟨*precio*⟩ rent. **~r** [1] *vt* ⟨*dar casa en alquiler*⟩ let; ⟨*dar cosa en alquiler*⟩ hire out; ⟨*tomar en alquiler*⟩ rent. **~tario** *m* tenant

arreos *mpl* harness

arrepenti|miento *m* repentance, regret. **~rse** [4] *upr*. **~rse de** be sorry, regret; repent ⟨*pecados*⟩

arrest|ar *vt* arrest, detain; ⟨*encarcelar*⟩ imprison. **~o** *m* arrest; ⟨*encarcelamiento*⟩ imprisonment

arriar [20] *vt* lower ⟨*bandera, vela*⟩; ⟨*aflojar*⟩ loosen; ⟨*inundar*⟩ flood. **~se** *upr* be flooded

arriba *adv* ⟨*up*⟩ above; ⟨*dirección*⟩ up(wards); ⟨*en casa*⟩ upstairs. —*int* up with; ⟨*¡levántate!*⟩ up you get!; ⟨*¡ánimo!*⟩ come on! **¡~ España!** long live Spain! **~ mencionado** aforementioned. **calle ~** up the street. **de ~ abajo** from top to bottom. **de 100 pesetas para ~** more than 100 pesetas. **escaleras ~** upstairs. **la parte de ~** the top part. **los de ~** those at the top. **más ~** above

arribar *vi* ⟨*barco*⟩ reach port; ⟨*esp LAm, llegar*⟩ arrive

arribista *m & f* self-seeking person, arriviste

arribo *m* (*esp LAm*) arrival

arriero *m* muleteer

arriesga|do *a* risky. ~**r** [12] *vt* risk; (*aventurar*) venture. ~**rse** *vpr* take a risk

arrim|ar *vt* bring close(r); (*apartar*) move out of the way ‹*cosa*›, (*apartar*) push aside ‹*persona*›. ~**arse** *vpr* come closer, approach; (*apoyarse*) lean (**a** on). ~**o** *m* support. **al** ~**o de** with the support of

arrinconaldo *a* forgotten. ~**rse** *vt* put in a corner; (*perseguir*) corner; (*arrumbar*) put aside; (*apartar a uno*) leave out, ignore. ~**rse** *vpr* become a recluse

arriscado *a* ‹*terreno*› uneven

arrobar *vt* entrance. ~**se** *vpr* be enraptured

arrocero *a* rice

arrodillarse *vpr* kneel (down)

arrogan|cia *f* arrogance; (*orgullo*) pride. ~**te** *a* arrogant; (*orgulloso*) proud

arrogarse [12] *vpr* assume

arroj|ado *a* brave. ~**ar** *vt* throw; (*dejar caer*) drop; (*emitir*) give off, throw out; (*producir*) produce. —*vi* (*esp LAm, vomitar*) be sick. ~**arse** *vpr* throw o.s. ~**o** *m* courage

arrolla|dor *a* overwhelming. ~**r** *vt* roll (up); (*atropellar*) run over; (*ejército*) crush; (*agua*) sweep away; (*tratar sin respeto*) have no respect for

arropar *vt* wrap up; (*en la cama*) tuck up; (*fig, amparar*) protect. ~**se** *vpr* wrap up (o.s.) up

arroyo *m* stream; (*de una calle*) gutter; (*fig, de lágrimas*) flood; (*fig, de sangre*) pool. **poner en el** ~**o** throw into the street. ~**uelo** *m* small stream

arroz *m* rice. ~**al** *m* rice field. ~ **con leche** rice pudding

arruga *f* (*en la piel*) wrinkle, line; (*en tela*) crease. ~**r** [12] *vt* wrinkle; crumple ‹*papel*›; crease ‹*tela*›. ~**rse** *vpr* ‹*la piel*› wrinkle, get wrinkled; ‹*tela*› crease, get creased

arruinar *vt* ruin; (*destruir*) destroy. ~**se** *vpr* ‹*persona*› be ruined; ‹*edificio*› fall into ruins

arrullar *vt* lull to sleep. —*vi* ‹*palomas*› coo. ~**se** *vpr* bill and coo

arrumaco *m* caress; (*zalamería*) flattery

arrumbar *vt* put aside

arsenal *m* (*astillero*) shipyard; (*de armas*) arsenal; (*fig*) store

arsénico *m* arsenic

arte *m en singular, f en plural* art; (*habilidad*) skill; (*astucia*) cunning. **bellas** ~**s** fine arts. **con** ~ skilfully. **malas** ~**s** trickery. **por amor al** ~ for nothing, for love

artefacto *m* device

arter|amente *adv* artfully. ~**ia** *f* cunning

arteria *f* artery; (*fig, calle*) main road

artero *a* cunning

artesan|al *a* craft. ~**ía** *f* handicrafts. ~**o** *m* artisan, craftsman. **objeto** *m* **de** ~**ía** hand-made article

ártico *a & m* Arctic

articula|ción *f* joint; (*pronunciación*) articulation. ~**damente** *adv* articulately. ~**do** *a* articulated; ‹*lenguaje*› articulate. ~**r** *vt* articulate

articulista *m & f* columnist

artículo *m* article. ~**s** *mpl* (*géneros*) goods. ~ **de exportación** export commodity. ~ **de fondo** editorial, leader

artificial *a* artificial

artificiero *m* bomb-disposal expert

artificio m (habilidad) skill; (dispositivo) device; (engaño) trick. **~so** a clever; (astuto) artful

artilugio m gadget

artillería f artillery. **~o** m artilleryman, gunner

artimaña f trap

artista m & f artist; (en espectáculos) artiste. **~ísticamente** adv artistically. **~ístico** a artistic

artrítico a arthritic. **~itis** f arthritis

arveja f vetch; (LAm, guisante) pea

arzobispo m archbishop

as m ace

asa f handle

asado a roast(ed). —m roast (meat), joint. **~o a la parrilla** grilled. **~o al horno** (sin grasa) baked; (con grasa) roast. **~or** m spit. **~ura** f offal

asalariado a salaried. —m employee

asaltante m attacker; (de un banco) robber. **~ar** vt storm (fortaleza); attack (persona); raid (banco etc); (fig) (duda) assail; (fig) (idea etc) cross one's mind. **~o** m attack; (en boxeo) round

asamblea f assembly; (reunión) meeting; (congreso) conference. **~ísta** m & f member of an assembly

asapán m (Mex) flying squirrel

asar vt roast; (fig, acosar) pester (a with). **~se** vpr be very hot. **~ a la parrilla** grill. **~ al horno** (sin grasa) bake; (con grasa) roast

asbesto m asbestos

ascendencia f descent

ascendente a ascending. **~er** [1] vt promote. —vi go up, ascend; (cuenta etc) come to, amount to; (ser ascendido) be promoted. **~iente** m & f ancestor; (influencia) influence

ascensión f ascent; (de grado) promotion. **~ional** a upward. **~o** m ascent; (de grado) promotion. **día** m **de la A~ión** Ascension Day

ascensor m lift (Brit), elevator (Amer). **~ista** m & f lift attendant (Brit), elevator operator (Amer)

asceta m & f ascetic. **~ético** a ascetic

asco m disgust. **dar ~** be disgusting; (fig, causar enfado) be infuriating. **estar hecho un ~** be disgusting. **hacer ~s de algo** turn up one's nose at sth. **me da ~ el ajo** I can't stand garlic. **¡qué ~!** how disgusting! **ser un ~** be a disgrace

ascua f ember. **estar en ~s** be on tenterhooks

aseadamente adv cleanly. **~do** a clean; (arreglado) neat. **~r** vt (lavar) wash; (limpiar) clean; (arreglar) tidy up

asediar vt besiege; (fig) pester. **~o** m siege

asegurado a & m insured. **~dor** m insurer. **~r** vt secure, make safe; (decir) assure; (concertar un seguro) insure; (preservar) safeguard. **~rse** vpr make sure

asemejarse vpr be alike

asentada f. **de una ~da** at a sitting. **~do** a situated; (arraigado) established. **~r** [1] vt place; (asegurar) settle; (anotar) note down. —vi be suitable. **~rse** vpr settle; (estar situado) be situated

asentimiento m consent. **~r** [4] vi agree (a to). **~r con la cabeza** nod

aseo m cleanliness. **~s** mpl toilets

asequible a obtainable; (precio) reasonable; (persona) approachable

asesin|ar *vt* murder; (*pol*) assassinate. **~ato** *m* murder; (*pol*) assassination. **~o** *m* murderer; (*pol*) assassin

asesor *m* adviser, consultant. **~amiento** *m* advice. **~ar** *vt* advise. **~arse** *vpr* **con/de** consult. **~ía** *f* consultancy; (*oficina*) consultant's office

asestar *vt* aim ⟨*arma*⟩; strike ⟨*golpe etc*⟩; (*disparar*) fire

aseveración *f* assertion. **~r** *vt* assert

asfalt|ado *a* asphalt. **~ar** *vt* asphalt. **~o** *m* asphalt

asfixia *f* suffocation. **~nte** *a* suffocating. **~r** *vt* suffocate. **~rse** *vpr* suffocate

así *adv* so; (*de esta manera*) like this, like that. —*a* such. **~ ~, ~ asá, ~ asado** so-so. **~ como** just as. **~... como** both... and. **~ pues** so. **~ que** so; (*enseguida*) as soon as. **~ sea** so be it. **~ y todo** even so. **aun ~** even so. **¿no es ~?** isn't that right? **y ~ (sucesivamente)** and so on

Asia *f* Asia

asiático *a* & *m* Asian

asidero *m* handle; (*fig, pretexto*) excuse

asidu|amente *adv* regularly. **~idad** *f* regularity. **~o** *a* & *m* regular

asiento *m* seat; (*situación*) site. **~ delantero** front seat. **~ trasero** back seat. **tome Vd ~** please take a seat

asignación *f* assignment; (*sueldo*) salary. **~r** *vt* assign; allot ⟨*porción, tiempo etc*⟩

asignatura *f* subject. **~ pendiente** (*escol*) failed subject; (*fig*) matter still to be resolved

asil|ado *m* inmate. **~ado político** refugee. **~o** *m* asylum; (*fig*) shelter; (*de ancianos etc*) home. **~o de huérfanos** orphanage. **pedir ~o político** ask for political asylum

asimétrico *a* asymmetrical

asimila|ción *f* assimilation. **~r** *vt* assimilate. **~rse** *vpr* be assimilated. **~rse a** resemble

asimismo *adv* in the same way, likewise

asir [45] *vt* grasp. **~se** *vpr* grab hold (**a, de** of)

asist|encia *f* attendance; (*gente*) people (present); (*en un teatro etc*) audience; (*ayuda*) assistance. **~encia médica** medical care. **~enta** *f* assistant; (*mujer de la limpieza*) charwoman. **~ente** *m* assistant. **~ente social** social worker. **~ido** *a* assisted. **~ir** *vt* assist, help; ⟨*un médico*⟩ treat. —*vi*. **~ir a** attend, be present at

asm|a *f* asthma. **~ático** *a* & *m* asthmatic

asn|ada *f* (*fig*) silly thing. **~o** *m* donkey; (*fig*) ass

asocia|ción *f* association; (*com*) partnership. **~do** *a* associated; ⟨*miembro etc*⟩ associate. **~m** associate. **~r** *vt* associate; (*com*) take into partnership. **~rse** *vpr* associate; (*com*) become a partner

asolador *a* destructive

asolar¹ [1] *vt* destroy. **~se** *vpr* be destroyed

asolar² *vt* dry up ⟨*plantas*⟩

asoma|da *f* brief appearance. **~r** *vt* show. —*vi* appear, show. **~rse** *vpr* ⟨*persona*⟩ lean out (**a, por** of); ⟨*cosa*⟩ appear

asombr|adizo *a* easily frightened. **~ar** *vt* (*pasmar*) amaze; (*sorprender*) surprise. **~arse** *vpr* be amazed; (*sorprenderse*) be surprised. **~o** *m* amazement, surprise. **~osamente** *adv* amazingly. **~oso** *a* amazing, astonishing

asomo *m* sign. **ni por ~** by no means

asonada *f* mob; (*motín*) riot

aspa f cross, X-shape; (de molino) (windmill) sail. **~do** a X-shaped

aspaviento m show, fuss. **~s** mpl gestures. **hacer ~s** make a big fuss

aspecto m look, appearance; (fig) aspect

aspereza f roughness; (de sabor etc) sourness

áspero a rough; (sabor etc) bitter

aspersión f sprinkling

aspiración f breath; (deseo) ambition

aspirador a suction. **~a** f vacuum cleaner

aspira|nte m candidate. **~r** vt breathe in; (máquina) suck up. —vi breathe in; (máquina) suck. **~r a** aspire to

aspirina f aspirin

asquear vt sicken. —vi be sickening. **~se** vpr be disgusted

asqueros|amente adv disgustingly. **~idad** f filthiness. **~o** a disgusting

asta f spear; (de la bandera) flagpole; (mango) handle; (cuerno) horn. **a media ~** at half-mast. **~do** a horned

asterisco m asterisk

astilla f splinter. **~s** fpl firewood. **~r** vt splinter. **hacer ~s** smash. **hacerse ~s** shatter

astillero m shipyard

astringente a & m astringent

astro m star

astr|ología f astrology. **~ólogo** m astrologer

astronauta m & f astronaut. **~ve** f spaceship

astr|onomía f astronomy. **~onómico** a astronomical. **~ónomo** m astronomer

astu|cia f cleverness; (ardid) cunning. **~to** a astute; (taimado) cunning

asturiano a & m Asturian

Asturias fpl Asturias

asueto m time off, holiday

asumir vt assume

asunción f assumption. **A~** Assumption

asunto m subject; (cuestión) matter; (de una novela) plot; (negocio) business. **~s** mpl exteriores foreign affairs. **el ~ es que** the fact is that

asusta|dizo a easily frightened. **~r** vt frighten. **~rse** vpr be frightened

ataca|nte m & f attacker. **~r** [7] vt attack

atad|ero m rope; (cierre) fastening; (gancho) hook. **~ijo** m bundle. **~o** a tied; (fig) timid. —m bundle. **~ura** f tying; (cuerda) string

ataj|ar vi take a short cut. **~o** m short cut; (grupo) bunch. **echar por el ~o** take the easy way out

atalaya f watch-tower; (fig) vantage point

atañer [22] vt concern

ataque m attack; (med) fit, attack. **~ al corazón** heart attack. **~ de nervios** hysterics

atar vt tie (up). **~se** vpr get tied up

atardecer [11] vi get dark. —m dusk. **al ~** at dusk

atarea|do a busy. **~rse** vpr work hard

atasc|adero m stumbling block. **~ar** [7] vt block; (fig) hinder. **~arse** vpr get stuck; (tubo etc) block. **~o** m obstruction; (auto) traffic jam

ataúd m coffin

atav|iar [20] vt dress up. **~iarse** vpr dress up, get dressed up. **~ío** m dress, attire

atemorizar [10] vt frighten. **~se** vpr be frightened

Atenas fpl Athens

atenazar [10] vt (fig) torture; (duda, miedo) grip

atención f attention; (cortesía) courtesy, kindness; (interés) interest. ¡~! look out! — **a beware of. llamar la ~** attract attention, catch the eye. **pre-star ~** pay attention

atender [1] *vt* attend to; heed *(consejo etc)*; *(cuidar)* look after. —*vi* pay attention

atenerse [40] *vpr* abide (**a** by)

atentado *m* offence; *(ataque)* attack. **~ contra la vida de uno** attempt on s.o.'s life

atentamente *adv* attentively; *(con cortesía)* politely; *(con amabilidad)* kindly. **le saluda ~** *(en cartas)* yours faithfully

atentar *vi* commit an offence. **~ contra la vida de uno** make an attempt on s.o.'s life

atento *a* attentive; *(cortés)* polite; *(amable)* kind

atenua|nte *a* extenuating. —*f* extenuating circumstance. **~r** [21] *vt* attenuate; *(hacer menor)* diminish, lessen. **~rse** *vpr* weaken

ateo *a* atheistic. —*m* atheist

aterciopelado *a* velvety

aterido *a* frozen (stiff), numb (with cold)

aterra|dor *a* terrifying. **~r** *vt* terrify. **~rse** *vpr* be terrified

aterrizaje *m* landing. **~je forzoso** emergency landing. **~r** [10] *vt* land

aterrorizar [10] *vt* terrify

atesorar *vt* hoard

atesta|do *a* packed, full up. —*m* sworn statement. **~r** *vt* fill up, pack; *(jurid)* testify. **~rse** *vpr* stuff o.s.

atestiguar [15] *vt* testify to; *(fig)* prove

atiborrar *vt* fill, stuff. **~se** *vpr* stuff o.s.

ático *m* attic

atilda|do *a* elegant, neat. **~r** *vt* put a tilde over; *(arreglar)* tidy up. **~rse** *vpr* smarten o.s. up

atina|damente *adv* rightly. **~do** *a* right; *(juicioso)* wise, sensible.

~r *vt/i* hit upon; *(acertar)* guess right

atípico *a* exceptional

atiplado *a* high-pitched

atirantar *vt* tighten

atisb|ar *vt* spy on; *(vislumbrar)* make out. **~o** *m* spying; *(indicio)* hint, sign

atizar [10] *vt* poke; give *(golpe)*; *(fig)* stir up; arouse, excite *(pasión etc)*

atlántico *a* Atlantic. **el (océano) A~** the Atlantic (Ocean)

atlas *m* atlas

atl|eta *m* & *f* athlete. **~ético** *a* athletic. **~etismo** *m* athletics

atm|ósfera *f* atmosphere. **~osférico** *a* atmospheric

atolondra|do *a* scatter-brained; *(aturdido)* bewildered. **~miento** *m* bewilderment; *(irreflexión)* thoughtlessness. **~r** *vt* bewilder; *(pasmar)* stun. **~rse** *vpr* be bewildered

atolladero *m* bog; *(fig)* tight corner

at|ómico *a* atomic. **~omizador** *m* atomizer. **~omizar** [10] *vt* atomize

átomo *m* atom

atónito *a* amazed

atonta|do *a* bewildered; *(tonto)* stupid. **~r** *vt* stun. **~rse** *vpr* get confused

atormenta|dor *a* tormenting. —*m* tormentor. **~r** *vt* torture. **~rse** *vpr* worry, torment o.s.

atornillar *vt* screw on

atosigar [12] *vt* pester

atracadero *m* quay

atracador *m* bandit

atracar [7] *vt* *(amarrar)* tie up; *(arrimar)* bring alongside; rob *(banco, persona)*. —*vi* *(barco)* tie up; *(astronave)* dock. **~se** *vpr* stuff o.s. (**de** with)

atracci|ón *f* attraction. **~ones** *fpl* entertainment, amusements

atrac|o *m* hold-up, robbery. **∼ón** *m.* darse un **∼ón** stuff o.s.

atractivo *a* attractive. **—m** attraction; *(encanto)* charm

atraer [41] *vt* attract

atragantarse *vpr* choke (con on). **la historia se me atraganta** I can't stand history

atranc|ar [7] *vt* bolt *(puerta)*; block up *(tubo etc)*. **∼arse** *vpr* get stuck; *(tubo)* get blocked. **∼o** *m* difficulty

atrapar *vt* trap; *(fig)* land *(empleo etc)*; catch *(resfriado)*

atrás *adv* behind; *(dirección)* back(wards); *(tiempo)* previously, before. **—int** back! dar un paso **∼**, para **∼** backwards

atras|ado *a* behind; *(reloj)* slow; *(con deudas)* in arrears; *(país)* backward. **llegar ∼ado** arrive late. **∼ar** *vt* slow down; *(retrasar)* put back; *(demorar)* delay, postpone. **—vi** be slow. **∼arse** *vpr* be late; *(reloj)* be slow; *(quedarse atrás)* be behind. **∼o** *m* delay; *(de un reloj)* slowness; *(de un país)* backwardness. **∼os** *mpl* arrears

atraves|ado *a* lying across; *(bizco)* cross-eyed; *(fig, malo)* wicked. **∼r** [1] *vt* cross; *(traspasar)* go through; *(poner transversalmente)* put across. **∼rse** *vpr* lie across; *(en la garganta)* get stuck, stick; *(entrometerse)* interfere

atrayente *a* attractive

atrev|erse *vpr* dare. **∼erse con** tackle. **∼ido** *a* daring, bold; *(insolente)* insolent. **∼imiento** *m* daring, boldness; *(descaro)* insolence

atribución *f* attribution. **atribuciones** *fpl* authority

atribuir [17] *vt* attribute; confer *(función)*. **∼se** *vpr* take the credit for

atribular *vt* afflict. **∼se** *vpr* be distressed

atribut|ivo *a* attributive. **∼o** *m* attribute; *(símbolo)* symbol

atril *m* lectern; *(mus)* music stand

atrincherar *vt* fortify with trenches. **∼se** *vpr* entrench (o.s.)

atrocidad *f* atrocity. **decir ∼es** make silly remarks. **¡qué ∼!** how terrible!

atrochar *vi* take a short cut

atrojarse *vpr* (Mex) be cornered

atrona|dor *a* deafening. **∼r** [2] *vt* deafen

atropell|adamente *adv* hurriedly. **∼ado** *a* hasty. **∼ar** *vt* knock down, run over; *(empujar)* push aside; *(maltratar)* bully; *(fig)* outrage, insult. **∼arse** *vpr* rush. **∼o** *m* *(auto)* accident; *(fig)* outrage

atroz *a* atrocious; *(fam)* huge. **∼mente** *adv* atrociously, awfully

atuendo *m* dress, attire

atufar *vt* choke; *(fig)* irritate. **∼se** *vpr* be overcome; *(enfadarse)* get cross

atún *m* tuna (fish)

aturdi|do *a* bewildered; *(irreflexivo)* thoughtless. **∼r** *vt* bewilder, stun; *(ruido)* deafen. **∼rse** *vpr* be stunned; *(intentar olvidar)* try to forget

atur(r)ullar *vt* bewilder

atusar *vt* smooth; trim *(pelo)*

auda|cia *f* boldness, audacity. **∼z** *a* bold

audib|ilidad *f* audibility. **∼le** *a* audible

audición *f* hearing; *(concierto)* concert

audiencia *f* audience; *(tribunal)* court

auditor *m* judge-advocate; *(de cuentas)* auditor

auditorio *m* audience; *(sala)* auditorium

auge *m* peak; *(com)* boom

augurar *vt* predict; *(cosas)* augur. **~io** *m* omen. **~ios** *mpl*. **con nuestros ~ios para** with our best wishes for

augusto *a* august

aula *f* class-room; *(univ)* lecture room

aulaga *f* gorse

aullar [23] *vi* howl. **~ido** *m* howl

aumentar *vt* increase; put up *(precios)*; magnify *(imagen)*; step up *(producción, voltaje)*. —*vi* increase. **~arse** *vpr* increase. **~ativo** *a* & *m* augmentative. **~o** *m* increase; *(de sueldo)* rise

aun *adv* even. **~ así** even so. **~ cuando** although. **más ~** even more. **ni ~** not even

aún *adv* still, yet. **~ no ha llegado** it still hasn't arrived, it hasn't arrived yet

aunar [23] *vt* join. **~se** *vpr* join together

aunque *conj* although, (even) though

aúpa *int* up! **de ~** wonderful

aureola *f* halo

auricular *m* *(de teléfono)* receiver. **~es** *mpl* headphones

aurora *f* dawn

ausencia *f* absence. **~tarse** *vpr* leave. **~te** *a* absent. —*m* & *f* absentee; *(jurid)* missing person. **en ~ de** in the absence of

auspicio *m* omen. **bajo los ~s de** sponsored by

austeridad *f* austerity. **~o** *a* austere

austral *a* southern. —*m* *(unidad monetaria argentina)* austral

Australia *m* Australia

australiano *a* & *m* Australian

Austria *f* Austria

austriaco, **austríaco** *a* & *m* Austrian

autenticar [7] authenticate. **~enticidad** *f* authenticity. **~éntico** *a* authentic

auto *m* sentence; *(auto, fam)* car. **~s** *mpl* proceedings

auto... *pref* auto...

autoayuda *f* self-help. **~biografía** *f* autobiography. **~biográfico** *a* autobiographical. **~bombo** *m* self-glorification

autobús *m* bus. **en ~** by bus

autocar *m* coach *(Brit)*, (long-distance) bus *(Amer)*

autocracia *f* autocracy. **~ócrata** *m* & *f* autocrat. **~ocrático** *a* autocratic

autóctono *a* autochthonous

auto: ~determinación *f* self-determination. **~defensa** *f* self-defence. **~didacto** *a* self-taught. —*m* autodidact. **~escuela** *f* driving school. **~giro** *m* autogiro

autógrafo *m* autograph

automación *f* automation

autómata *m* robot

automático *a* automatic. —*m* press-stud. **~atización** *f* automation. **~atizar** [10] *vt* automate

automotor *a* (*f* **automotriz**) self-propelled. —*m* diesel train

automóvil *a* self-propelled. —*m* car. **~ovilismo** *m* motoring. **~ovilista** *m* & *f* driver, motorist

autonomía *f* autonomy. **~onómico** *a*, **~ónomo** *a* autonomous

autopista *f* motorway *(Brit)*, freeway *(Amer)*

autopsia *f* autopsy

autor *m* author. **~a** *f* author(ess)

autoridad *f* authority. **~tario** *a* authoritarian. **~tarismo** *m* authoritarianism

autorización *f* authorization. **~damente** *adv* officially. **~do** *a* authorized, offical; *(opinión etc)* authoritative. ~r [10] *vt* authorize

auto: ~rretrato *m* self-portrait. ~servicio *m* self-service restaurant. ~stop *m* hitch-hiking. hacer ~stop hitch-hike

autosuficien|cia *f* self-sufficiency. ~te *a* self-sufficient

autovia *f* dual carriageway

auxili|ar *a* assistant; *(servicios)* auxiliary. —*m* assistant. —*vt* help. ~o *m* help. ¡~o! help! ~os espirituales last rites. en ~o de in aid of. pedir ~o shout for help. primeros ~os first aid

Av. *abrev (Avenida)* Ave, Avenue

aval *m* guarantee

avalancha *f* avalanche

avalar *vt* guarantee

avalorar *vt* enhance; *(fig)* encourage

avance *m* advance; *(en el cine)* trailer; *(balance)* balance; *(de noticias)* early news bulletin. ~ informativo publicity handout

avante *adv (esp LAm)* forward

avanza|do *a* advanced. ~r [10] *vt* move forward. —*vi* advance

avar|icia *f* avarice. ~icioso *a*, ~iento *a* greedy; *(tacaño)* miserly. ~o *a* miserly. —*m* miser

avasalla|dor *a* overwhelming. ~r *vt* dominate

Avda. *abrev (Avenida)* Ave, Avenue

ave *f* bird. ~ de paso *(incl fig)* bird of passage. ~ de presa, ~ de rapiña bird of prey

avecinarse *vpr* approach

avecindarse *vpr* settle

avejentarse *vpr* age

avellan|a *f* hazel-nut. ~o *m* hazel (tree)

avemaría *f* Hail Mary. al ~ at dusk

avena *f* oats

avenar *vt* drain

avenida *f (calle)* avenue; *(de río)* flood

avenir [53] *vt* reconcile. ~se *vpr* come to an agreement

aventaja|do *a* outstanding. ~r *vt* surpass

aventar [1] *vt* fan; winnow *(grano etc)*; *(viento)* blow away

aventur|a *f* adventure; *(riesgo)* risk. ~a amorosa love affair. ~ado *a* risky. ~ar *vt* risk. ~arse *vpr* dare. ~a sentimental love affair. ~ero *a* adventurous. —*m* adventurer

avergonza|do *a* ashamed; *(embarazado)* embarrassed. ~r [10 & 16] *vt* shame; *(embarazar)* embarrass. ~rse *vpr* be ashamed; *(embarazarse)* be embarrassed

aver|ía *f (auto)* breakdown; *(daño)* damage. ~iado *a* broken down; *(fruta)* damaged, spoilt. ~iar [20] *vt* damage. ~iarse *vpr* get damaged; *(coche)* break down

averigua|ble *a* verifiable. ~ción *f* verification; *(investigación)* investigation; *(Mex, disputa)* argument. ~dor *m* investigator. ~r [15] *vt* verify; *(enterarse de)* find out; *(investigar)* investigate. —*vi (Mex)* quarrel

aversión *f* aversion (a, hacia, por)

avestruz *m* ostrich

aviación *f* aviation; *(mil)* air force

aviado *a (Arg)* well off. estar ~ be in a mess

aviador *m (aviat)* member of the crew; *(piloto)* pilot; *(Arg, prestamista)* money-lender; *(Arg, de minas)* mining speculator

aviar [20] *vt* get ready, prepare; *(arreglar)* tidy; *(reparar)* repair; *(LAm, prestar dinero)* lend money; *(dar prisa)* hurry up.

~se *vpr* get ready. **¡avíate!** hurry up!

avícula *a* poultry. **~icultor** *m* poultry farmer. **~icultura** *f* poultry farming

avidez *f* eagerness, greed

ávido *a* eager, greedy

avieso *a* (*maligno*) wicked

avinagra|do *a* sour. **~r** *vt* sour; (*fig*) embitter. **~rse** *vpr* go sour; (*fig*) become embittered

avío *m* preparation. **~s** *mpl* provisions; (*utensilios*) equipment

avi|ón *m* aeroplane (*Brit*), airplane (*Amer*). **~oneta** *f* light aircraft

avis|ado *a* wise. **~ar** *vt* warn; (*informar*) notify, inform; call (*médico etc*). **~o** *m* warning; (*anuncio*) notice. **estar sobre ~o** be on the alert. **mal ~ado** ill-advised. **sin previo ~o** without notice

avisp|a *f* wasp. **~ado** *a* sharp. **~ero** *m* wasps' nest; (*fig*) mess. **~ón** *m* hornet

avistar *vt* catch sight of

avitualla|miento *m* supplying. **~r** *vt* provision

avivar *vt* stoke up (*fuego*); brighten up (*color*); arouse (*interés*, *pasión*); intensify (*dolor*). **~se** *vpr* revive; (*animarse*) cheer up

axila *f* axilla, armpit

axiom|a *m* axiom. **~ático** *a* axiomatic

ay *int* (*de dolor*) ouch!; (*de susto*) oh!; (*de pena*) oh dear! **~ de poor.** **¡~ de tí!** poor you!

aya *f* governess, child's nurse

ayer *adv* yesterday. —*m* past. **antes de ~** the day before yesterday. **~ por la mañana** yesterday morning. **~ (por la) noche** last night

ayo *m* tutor

ayote *m* (*Mex*) pumpkin

ayuda *f* help, aid. **~ de cámara** valet. **~nta** *f*, **~nte** *m* assistant; (*mil*) adjutant. **~nte técnico sanitario (ATS)** nurse. **~r** *vt* help

ayun|ar *vi* fast. **~as** *fpl*. **estar en ~as** have had no breakfast; (*fig*, *fam*) be in the dark. **~o** *m* fasting

ayuntamiento *m* town council, city council; (*edificio*) town hall

azabache *m* jet

azad|a *f* hoe. **~ón** *m* (large) hoe

azafata *f* air hostess

azafrán *m* saffron

azahar *m* orange blossom

azar *m* chance; (*desgracia*) misfortune. **al ~** at random. **por ~** by chance

azararse *vpr* go wrong; (*fig*) get flustered

azaros|amente *adv* hazardously. **~o** *a* hazardous, risky; (*persona*) unlucky

azoga|do *a* restless. **~rse** [12] *vpr* be restless

azolve *m* (*Mex*) obstruction

azora|do *a* flustered, excited, alarmed. **~miento** *m* confusion, embarrassment. **~r** *vt* embarrass; (*aturdir*) alarm. **~rse** *vpr* get flustered, be alarmed

Azores *fpl* Azores

azot|aina *f* beating. **~ar** *vt* whip, beat. **~e** *m* whip; (*golpe*) smack; (*fig*, *calamidad*) calamity

azotea *f* flat roof. **estar mal de la ~** be mad

azteca *a & m & f* Aztec

az|úcar *m & f* sugar. **~ucarado** *a* sweet. **~ucarar** *vt* sweeten. **~ucarero** *m* sugar bowl

azucena *f* (white) lily

azufre *m* sulphur

azul *a & m* blue. **~ado** *a* bluish. **~ de lavar** (washing) blue. **~ marino** navy blue

azulejo *m* tile

azuzar *vt* urge on, incite

B

bab|a f spittle. **~ear** vi drool, slobber; ⟨niño⟩ dribble. **caerse la ~a** be delighted
babel f bedlam
babe|o m drooling; ⟨de un niño⟩ dribbling. **~ro** m bib
Babia f. **estar en ~** have one's head in the clouds
babieca a stupid. —m & f simpleton
babor m port. **a ~** to port, on the port side
babosa f slug
babosada f (Mex) silly remark
babos|ear vt slobber over; ⟨niño⟩ dribble over. **~eo** m drooling; ⟨de niño⟩ dribbling. **~o** a slimy; (LAm, tonto) silly
babucha f slipper
babuino m baboon
baca f luggage rack
bacaladilla f small cod
bacalao m cod
bacon m bacon
bacteria f bacterium
bache m hole; (fig) bad patch
bachillerato m school-leaving examination
badaj|azo m stroke (of a bell). **~o** m clapper; (persona) chatterbox
bagaje m baggage; (animal) beast of burden; (fig) knowledge
bagatela f trifle
Bahamas fpl Bahamas
bahía f bay
bail|able a dance. **~ador** a dancing. —m dancer. **~aor** m Flamenco dancer. **~ar** vt/i dance. **~arín** dancer. **~arina** f dancer; ⟨de baile clásico⟩ ballerina. **~e** m dance. **~e de etiqueta** ball. **ir a ~ar** go dancing
baja f drop, fall; (mil) casualty. **~ por maternidad** maternity leave. **~da** f slope; ⟨acto de bajar⟩ descent. **~mar** m low

tide. **~r** vt lower; ⟨llevar abajo⟩ get down; bow ⟨la cabeza⟩. **~r la escalera** go downstairs. —vi go down; ⟨temperatura, precio⟩ fall. **~rse** vpr bend down. **~r(se) de** get out of ⟨coche⟩; get off ⟨autobús, caballo, tren, bicicleta⟩. **dar(se) de ~** take sick leave
bajeza f vile deed
bajío m sandbank
bajo a low; ⟨de estatura⟩ short, small; ⟨cabeza, ojos⟩ lowered; ⟨humilde⟩ humble, low; ⟨vil⟩ vile, low; ⟨color⟩ pale; ⟨voz⟩ low; ⟨mus⟩ deep. —m lowland; ⟨bajío⟩ sandbank; ⟨mus⟩ bass. —adv quietly; ⟨volar⟩ low. —prep under; ⟨temperatura⟩ below. **~ la lluvia** in the rain. **los ~s fondos** the low district. **por lo ~** under one's breath; (fig) in secret
bajón m drop; ⟨de salud⟩ decline; ⟨com⟩ slump
bala f bullet; ⟨de algodón etc⟩ bale. **~ perdida** stray bullet. **como una ~** like a shot
balada f ballad
baladí a trivial
baladrón a boastful
baladron|ada f boast. **~ear** vi boast
balan|ce m swinging; ⟨de una cuenta⟩ balance; ⟨documento⟩ balance sheet. **~cear** vt balance. —vi hesitate. **~cearse** vpr swing; ⟨vacilar⟩ hesitate. **~ceo** m swinging. **~za** f scales; ⟨com⟩ balance
balar vi bleat
balaustrada f balustrade, railing(s); ⟨de escalera⟩ banisters
balay m (LAm) wicker basket
balazo m ⟨disparo⟩ shot; ⟨herida⟩ bullet wound
balboa f ⟨unidad monetaria panameña⟩ balboa
balbuc|ear vt/i stammer; ⟨niño⟩ babble. **~eo** m stammering; ⟨de

niño) babbling. **~iente** *a* stammering; *(niño)* babbling. **~ir** [24] *vt/i* stammer; *(niño)* babble

balc|ón *m* balcony. **~onada** *f* row of balconies. **~onaje** *m* row of balconies

balda *f* shelf

baldado *a* disabled, crippled; *(rendido)* shattered. **—***m* disabled person, cripple

baldaquín *m*, **baldaquino** *m* canopy

baldar *vt* cripple

balde *m* bucket. **de ~** free (of charge). **en ~** in vain. **~ar** *vt* wash down

baldío *a* *(terreno)* waste; *(fig)* useless

baldosa *f* (floor) tile; *(losa)* flagstone

balduque *m* *(incl fig)* red tape

balear *a* Balearic. **—***m* native of the Balearic Islands. **las Islas** *fpl* **B~es** the Balearics, the Balearic Islands

baleo *m* *(LAm, tiroteo)* shooting; *(Mex, abanico)* fan

balido *m* bleat; *(varios sonidos)* bleating

bal|ín *m* small bullet. **~ines** *mpl* shot

balística *f* ballistics

baliza *f* *(naut)* buoy; *(aviat)* beacon

balneario *m* spa; *(con playa)* seaside resort. **—***a*. **estación** *f* **balnearia** spa; *(con playa)* seaside resort

balompié *m* football *(Brit)*, soccer

bal|ón *m* ball, football. **~oncesto** *m* basketball. **~onmano** *m* handball. **~volea** *m* volleyball

balotaje *m* *(LAm)* voting

balsa *f* *(de agua)* pool; *(plataforma flotante)* raft

bálsamo *m* balsam; *(fig)* balm

balsón *m* *(Mex)* stagnant water

baluarte *m* *(incl fig)* bastion

balumba *f* mass, mountain

ballena *f* whale

ballesta *f* crossbow

ballet /ba'le/ *(pl* **ballets** /ba'le/) *m* ballet

bambole|ar *vi* sway; *(mesa etc)* wobble. **~arse** *vpr* sway; *(mesa etc)* wobble. **~o** *m* swaying; *(de mesa etc)* wobbling

bambú *m* *(pl* **bambúes)** bamboo

banal *a* banal. **~idad** *f* banality

banan|a *f* *(esp LAm)* banana. **~o** *m* *(LAm)* banana tree

banasta *f* large basket. **~o** *m* large round basket

banc|a *f* banking; *(en juegos)* bank; *(LAm, asiento)* bench. **~ario** *a* bank, banking. **~arrota** *f* bankruptcy. **~o** *m* *(asiento)* bench; *(com)* bank; *(bajío)* sandbank. **hacer ~arrota, ir a la ~arrota** go bankrupt

banda *f* *(incl mus, radio)* band; *(grupo)* gang, group; *(lado)* side. **~da** *f* *(de aves)* flock; *(de peces)* shoal. **~ de sonido, ~ sonora** sound-track

bandeja *f* tray; *(LAm, plato)* serving dish. **servir algo en ~ a uno** hand sth to s.o. on a plate

bandera *f* flag; *(estandarte)* banner, standard

banderill|a *f* banderilla. **~ear** *vt* stick the banderillas in. **~ero** *m* banderillero

banderín *m* pennant, small flag, banner

bandido *m* bandit

bando *m* edict, proclamation; *(partido)* faction. **~s** *mpl* banns. **pasarse al otro ~** go over to the other side

bandolero *m* bandit

bandolina *f* mandolin

bandoneón *m* large accordion

banjo *m* banjo

banquero *m* banker

banqueta *f* stool; (*LAm*, *acera*) pavement (*Brit*), sidewalk (*Amer*)

banquete *m* banquet; (*de boda*) wedding reception. ~**ar** *vt/i* banquet

banquillo *m* bench; (*jurid*) dock; (*taburete*) footstool

bañ\|ado *m* (*LAm*) swamp. ~**ador** *m* (*de mujer*) swimming costume; (*de hombre*) swimming trunks. ~**ar** *vt* bathe, immerse; bath (*niño*); (*culin*, *recubrir*) coat. ~**arse** *vpr* go swimming, have a swim; (*en casa*) have a bath. ~**era** *f* bath, bath-tub. ~**ero** *m* life-guard. ~**ista** *m & f* bather. ~**o** *m* bath; (*en piscina*, *mar etc*) swim; (*bañera*) bath, bath-tub; (*capa*) coat(ing)

baptisterio *m* baptistery; (*pila*) font

baquet\|a *f* (*de fusil*) ramrod; (*de tambor*) drumstick. ~**ear** *vt* bother. ~**eo** *m* nuisance, bore

bar *m* bar

barahúnda *f* uproar

baraja *f* pack of cards. ~**r** *vt* shuffle; juggle, massage (*cifras etc*). —*vi* argue (**con** with); (*enemistarse*) fall out (**con** with). ~**s** *fpl* argument. **jugar a la** ~ play cards. **jugar a dos** ~**s**, **jugar con dos** ~**s** be deceitful, indulge in double-dealing

baranda *f*, **barandal** *m*, **barandilla** *f* handrail; (*de escalera*) banisters

barat\|a *f* (*Mex*) sale. ~**ija** *f* trinket. ~**illo** *m* junk shop; (*géneros*) cheap goods. ~**o** *a* cheap. —*m* sale. —*adv* cheap(ly). ~**ura** *f* cheapness

baraúnda *f* uproar

barba *f* chin; (*pelo*) beard. ~**do** *a* bearded

barbacoa *f* barbecue; (*Mex*, *carne*) barbecued meat

bárbaramente *adv* savagely; (*fig*) tremendously

barbari\|dad *f* barbarity; (*fig*) outrage; (*mucho*, *fam*) awful lot (*fam*). **¡qué ~dad!** how awful! ~**e** *f* barbarity; (*fig*) ignorance. ~**smo** *m* barbarism

bárbaro *a* barbaric, cruel; (*bruto*) uncouth; (*estupendo*, *fam*) terrific (*fam*). —*m* barbarian. **¡qué ~!** how marvellous!

barbear *vt* (*afeitar*) shave; (*Mex*, *lisonjear*) fawn on

barbecho *m* fallow

barber\|ía *f* barber's (shop). ~**o** *m* barber; (*Mex*, *adulador*) flatterer

barbi\|lampiño *a* beardless; (*fig*) inexperienced, green. ~**lindo** *m* dandy

barbilla *f* chin

barbitúrico *m* barbiturate

barbo *m* barbel. ~ **de mar** red mullet

barbot\|ar *vt/i* mumble. ~**ear** *vt/i* mumble. ~**eo** *m* mumbling

barbudo *a* bearded

barbullar *vi* jabber

barca *f* (small) boat. ~ **de pasaje** ferry. ~**r** *m* fare. ~**za** *f* barge

Barcelona *f* Barcelona

barcelonés *a* of Barcelona, from Barcelona. —*m* native of Barcelona

barco *m* boat; (*navío*) ship. ~ **cisterna** tanker. ~ **de vapor** steamer. ~ **de vela** sailing boat. **ir en** ~ go by boat

bario *m* barium

baritono *m* baritone

barman *m* (*pl* **barmans**) barman

barniz *m* varnish; (*para loza etc*) glaze; (*fig*) veneer. ~**ar** [10] *vt* varnish; glaze (*loza etc*)

baro\|métrico *a* barometric. ~**ómetro** *m* barometer

bar\|ón *m* baron. ~**onesa** *f* baroness

barquero *m* boatman

barra *f* bar; (*pan*) French bread; (*de oro o plata*) ingot; (*palanca*) lever. **~ de labios** lipstick. **no pararse en ~s** stop at nothing

barrabasada *f* mischief, prank

barraca *f* hut; (*vivienda pobre*) shack, shanty

barranco *m* ravine, gully; (*despeñadero*) cliff, precipice

barre|dera *f* road-sweeper. **~dura** *f* rubbish. **~minas** *m invar* mine-sweeper

barren|a *f* drill, bit. **~ar** *vt* drill. **~o** *m* large (mechanical) drill. **entrar en ~a** (*avión*) go into a spin

barrer *vt* sweep; (*quitar*) sweep aside

barrera *f* barrier. **~ del sonido** sound barrier

barriada *f* district

barrica *f* barrel

barricada *f* barricade

barrido *m* sweeping

barrig|a *f* (pot-)belly. **~ón** *a*, **~udo** *a* pot-bellied

barril *m* barrel. **~ete** *m* keg, small barrel

barrio *m* district, area. **~bajero** *a* vulgar, common. **~s bajos** poor quarter, poor area. **el otro ~** (*fig, fam*) the other world

barro *m* mud; (*arcilla*) clay; (*arcilla cocida*) earthenware

barroco *a* Baroque. *—m* Baroque style

barrote *m* heavy bar

barrunt|ar *vt* sense, have a feeling. **~e** *m*, **~o** *m* sign; (*presentimiento*) feeling

bartola *f*. **tenderse a la ~, tumbarse a la ~** take it easy

bártulos *mpl* things. **liar los ~** pack one's bags

barullo *m* uproar; (*confusión*) confusion. **a ~** galore

basa *f*, **basamento** *m* base; (*fig*) basis

basar *vt* base. **~se** *vpr*. **~se en** be based on

basca *f* crowd. **~as** *fpl* nausea. **~osidad** *f* filth. **la ~a** the gang

báscula *f* scales

bascular *vi* tilt

base *f* base; (*fig*) basis, foundation. **a ~ de** thanks to; (*mediante*) by means of; (*en una receta*) as the basic ingredient(s). **a ~ de bien** very well. **partiendo de la ~ de, tomando como ~** on the basis of

básico *a* basic

basílica *f* basilica

basilisco *m* basilisk. **hecho un ~** furious

basta *f* tack, tacking stitch

bastante *a* enough; (*varios*) quite a few, quite a lot of. *—adv* rather, fairly; (*mucho tiempo*) long enough; (*suficiente*) enough; (*Mex, muy*) very

bastar *vi* be enough. **¡basta!** that's enough! **basta decir que** suffice it to say that. **basta y sobra** that's more than enough

bastardilla *f* italics. **poner en ~** italicize

bastardo *m* bastard; (*fig, vil*) mean, base

bastidor *m* frame; (*auto*) chassis. **~es** *mpl* (*en el teatro*) wings. **entre ~es** behind the scenes

bastión *f* (*incl fig*) bastion

basto *a* coarse. **~s** *mpl* (*naipes*) clubs

bastón *m* walking stick. **empuñar el ~ón** take command. **~onazo** *m* blow with a stick

basura *f* rubbish, garbage (*Amer*); (*en la calle*) litter. **~ero** *m* dustman (*Brit*), garbage collector (*Amer*); (*sitio*) rubbish dump; (*recipiente*) dustbin (*Brit*), garbage can (*Amer*). **cubo** *m* **de la ~a** dustbin (*Brit*), garbage can (*Amer*)

bata f dressing-gown; (de médico etc) white coat. ~ **de cola** Flamenco dress

batall|a f battle. ~**a campal** pitched battle. ~**ador** a fighting. —m fighter. ~**ar** vi battle, fight. ~**ón** m battalion. —a. **cuestión** **a batallona** vexed question. **de** ~**a** everyday

batata f sweet potato

bate m bat. ~**ador** m batter; (cricket) batsman

batería f battery; (mus) percussion. ~ **de cocina** kitchen utensils, pots and pans

batido a beaten; (nata) whipped. —m batter; (bebida) milk shake. ~**ra** f beater. ~**ra eléctrica** mixer

batín m dressing-gown

batir vt beat; (martillar) hammer; mint (monedas); whip (nata); (derribar) knock down. ~ **el récord** break the record. ~ **palmas** clap. ~**se** vpr fight

batuta f baton. **llevar la** ~ be in command, be the boss

baúl m trunk; (LAm, auto) boot (Brit), trunk (Amer)

bauti|smal a baptismal. ~**smo** m baptism, christening. ~**sta** a & m & f Baptist. ~**zar** [10] vt baptize, christen

baya f berry

bayeta f (floor-)cloth

bayoneta f bayonet. ~**zo** m (golpe) bayonet thrust; (herida) bayonet wound

baza f (naipes) trick; (fig) advantage. **meter** ~ interfere

bazar m bazaar

bazofia f leftovers; (basura) rubbish

beat|itud f (fig) bliss. ~**o** a blessed; (de religiosidad afectada) sanctimonious

bebé m baby

beb|edero m drinking trough; (sitio) watering place. ~**edizo** a

drinkable. —m potion; (veneno) poison. ~**edor** a drinking. —m heavy drinker. ~**er** vt/i drink. **dar de** ~**er a uno** give s.o. a drink. ~**ida** f drink. ~**ido** a tipsy, drunk

beca f grant, scholarship. ~**rio** m scholarship holder, scholar

becerro m calf

befa f jeer, taunt. ~**r** vt scoff at. ~**rse** vpr. ~**rse de** scoff at. **hacer** ~ **de** scoff at

beige /beis, bes/ a & m beige

béisbol m baseball

beldad f beauty

belén m crib, nativity scene; (barullo) confusion

belga a & m & f Belgian

Bélgica f Belgium

bélico a, **belicoso** a warlike

beligerante a belligerent

bella|co a wicked. —m rogue. ~**quear** vi cheat. ~**quería** f dirty trick

bell|eza f beauty. ~**o** a beautiful. ~**as artes** fpl fine arts

bellota f acorn

bemol m flat. **tener (muchos)** ~**es** be difficult

bencina f (Arg, gasolina) petrol (Brit), gasoline (Amer)

bend|ecir [46 pero imperativo **bendice**, futuro, condicional y pp regulares] vt bless. ~**ición** f blessing. ~**ito** a blessed, holy; (que tiene suerte) lucky; (feliz) happy

benefactor m benefactor. ~**a** f benefactress

benefic|encia f (organización pública) charity. ~**iar** vt benefit. ~**iarse** vpr benefit. ~**iario** m beneficiary; (de un cheque etc) payee. ~**io** m benefit; (ventaja) advantage; (ganancia) profit, gain. ~**ioso** a beneficial, advantageous

benéfico a beneficial; (de beneficencia) charitable

benemérito *a* worthy

beneplácito *m* approval

ben evolencia *f* benevolence. **∼évolo** *a* benevolent

bengala *f* flare. **luz** *f* **de B∼** flare

benign idad *f* kindness; *(falta de gravedad)* mildness. **∼o** *a* kind; *(moderado)* gentle, mild; *(tumor)* benign

beodo *a* drunk

berberecho *m* cockle

berenjena *f* aubergine (*Brit*), egg-plant. **∼l** *m* (*fig*) mess

bermejo *a* red

berr ear *vi* *(animales)* low, bellow; *(niño)* howl; *(cantar mal)* screech. **∼ido** *m* bellow; *(de niño)* howl; *(de cantante)* screech

berrinche *m* temper; *(de un niño)* tantrum

berro *m* watercress

berza *f* cabbage

besamel(a) *f* white sauce

bes ar *vt* kiss; *(rozar)* brush against. **∼arse** *vpr* kiss (each other); *(tocarse)* touch each other. **∼o** *m* kiss

bestia *f* beast; *(bruto)* brute; *(idiota)* idiot. **∼ de carga** beast of burden. **∼l** *a* bestial, animal; *(fig, fam)* terrific. **∼lidad** *f* bestiality; *(acción brutal)* horrid thing

besugo *m* sea-bream. **ser un ∼** be stupid

besuquear *vt* cover with kisses

betún *m* bitumen; *(para el calzado)* shoe polish

biberón *m* feeding-bottle

Biblia *f* Bible

bíblico *a* biblical

bibliografía *f* bibliography

biblioteca *f* library; *(librería)* bookcase. **∼ de consulta** reference library. **∼ de préstamo** lending library. **∼rio** *m* librarian

bicarbonato *m* bicarbonate. **∼ sódico** bicarbonate of soda

bici *f* (*fam*) bicycle, bike (*fam*). **∼cleta** *f* bicycle. **ir en ∼cleta** go by bicycle, cycle. **montar en ∼cleta** ride a bicycle

bicolor *a* two-colour

bicultural *a* bicultural

bicho *m* *(animal)* small animal, creature; *(insecto)* insect. **∼ raro** odd sort. **cualquier ∼ viviente, todo ∼ viviente** everyone

bidé *m*, **bidet** *m* bidet

bidón *m* drum, can

bien *adv* (**mejor**) well; *(muy)* very, quite; *(correctamente)* right; *(de buena gana)* willingly. **—m** good; *(efectos)* property; *(provecho)* advantage, benefit. **¡∼!** fine!, OK!, good! **∼...(o)** ∼ either... or; **∼ que** although. **¡está ∼!** fine! alright! **más ∼** rather. **¡muy ∼!** good! **no ∼** as soon as. **¡qué ∼!** marvellous!, great! (*fam*). **si ∼** although

bienal *a* biennial

bien: ∼aventurado *a* fortunate. **∼estar** *m* well-being. **∼hablado** *a* well-spoken. **∼hechor** *m* benefactor. **∼hechora** *f* benefactress. **∼intencionado** *a* well-meaning

bienio *m* two years, two year-period

bien: ∼quistar *vt* reconcile. **∼quistarse** *vpr* become reconciled. **∼quisto** *a* well-liked

bienvenid a *f* welcome. **∼o** *a* welcome. **¡∼o!** welcome! **dar la ∼a a uno** welcome s.o.

bife *m* (*Arg*), **biftek** *m* steak

bifurca ción *f* fork, junction. **∼rse** [7] *vpr* fork

b igamia *f* bigamy. **∼ígamo** *a* bigamous. **—m & f** bigamist

bigote *m* moustache. **∼udo** *a* with a big moustache

bikini *m* bikini; *(culin)* toasted cheese and ham sandwich

bilingüe *a* bilingual

billar m billiards

billete m ticket; (de banco) note (Brit), bill (Amer). ~ **de banco** banknote. ~ **de ida y vuelta** return ticket (Brit), round-trip ticket (Amer). ~ **sencillo** single ticket (Brit), one-way ticket (Amer). ~**ro** m, ~**ra** f wallet, billfold (Amer)

billón m billion (Brit), trillion (Amer)

bimbalete m (Mex) swing

bi|**mensual** a fortnightly, twice-monthly. ~**mestral** a two-monthly. ~**motor** a twin-engined. —m twin-engined plane

binocular a binocular. ~**es** mpl binoculars

biodegradable a biodegradable

bio|**grafía** f biography. ~**ográfico** a biographical. ~**ógrafo** m biographer

bio|**logía** f biology. ~**ológico** a biological. ~**ólogo** m biologist

biombo m folding screen

biopsia f biopsy

bioquímic|**a** f biochemistry; (persona) biochemist. ~**o** m biochemist

bípedo m biped

biplano m biplane

biquini m bikini

birlar vt (fam) steal, pinch (fam)

birlibirloque m. **por arte de** ~ (as if) by magic

Birmania f Burma

birmano a & m Burmese

biromen m (Arg) ball-point pen

bis m encore. ¡~**!** encore! **vivo en el 3** ~ I live at 3A

bisabuel|**a** f great-grandmother. ~**o** m great-grandfather. ~**os** mpl great-grandparents

bisagra f hinge

bisar vt encore

bisbise|**ar** vt whisper. ~**o** m whisper(ing)

bisemanal a twice-weekly

bisiesto a leap. **año** m ~ leap year

bisniet|**a** f great-granddaughter. ~**o** m great-grandson. ~**os** mpl great-grandchildren

bisonte m bison

bisté m, **bistec** m steak

bisturí m scalpel

bisutería f imitation jewellery, costume jewellery

bizco a cross-eyed. **quedarse** ~ be dumbfounded

bizcocho m sponge (cake); (Mex, galleta) biscuit

bizquear vi squint

blanc|**a** f white woman; (mus) minim. ~**o** a white; (tez) fair. —m white; (persona) white man; (intervalo) interval; (espacio) blank; (objetivo) target. ~**o de huevo** white of egg, egg-white. **dar en el** ~**o** hit the mark. **dejar en** ~**o** leave blank. **pasar la noche en** ~**o** have a sleepless night. ~**o y negro** black and white. ~**ura** f whiteness. ~**uzco** a whitish

blandir [24] vt brandish

bland|**o** a soft; (carácter) weak; (cobarde) cowardly; (palabras) gentle, tender. ~**ura** f softness. ~**uzco** a softish

blanque|**ar** vt whiten; white-wash (paredes); bleach (tela). —vi turn white; (presentarse blanco) look white. ~**cino** a whitish. ~**o** m whitening

blasfem|**ador** a blasphemous. —m blasphemer. ~**ar** vi blaspheme. ~**ia** f blasphemy. ~**o** a blasphemous. —m blasphemer

blasón m coat of arms; (fig,) honour, glory. ~**onar** vt emblazon. —vi boast (**de** of, about)

bledo m nothing. **me importa un** ~, **no se me da un** ~ I couldn't care less

blindaje *m* armour. **~r** *vt* armour

bloc *m* (*pl* **blocs**) pad

bloque *m* block; (*pol*) bloc. **~ar** *vt* block; (*mil*) blockade; (*com*) freeze. **~o** *m* blockade; (*com*) freezing. **en ~** en bloc

blusa *f* blouse

boato *m* show, ostentation

bob|ada *f* silly thing. **~alicón** *a* stupid. **~ería** *f* silly thing. **decir ~adas** talk nonsense

bobina *f* bobbin, reel; (*foto*) spool; (*elec*) coil

bobo *a* silly, stupid. —*m* idiot, fool

boca *f* mouth; (*fig*, *entrada*) entrance; (*de cañón*) muzzle; (*agujero*) hole. **~ abajo** face down. **~ arriba** face up. **a ~ de jarro** point-blank. **con la ~ abierta** dumbfounded

bocacalle *f* junction. **la primera ~ a la derecha** the first turning on the right

bocad|illo *m* sandwich; (*comida ligera*, *fam*) snack. **~o** *m* mouthful; (*mordisco*) bite; (*de caballo*) bit

boca: **~jarro. a ~jarro** point-blank. **~manga** *f* cuff

bocanada *f* puff; (*de vino etc*) mouthful

bocaza *f invar*, **bocazas** *f invar* big-mouth

boceto *m* outline, sketch

bocina *f* horn. **~zo** *m* toot, blast. **tocar la ~** sound one's horn

bock *m* beer mug

bocha *f* bowl. **~s** *fpl* bowls

bochinche *m* uproar

bochorno *m* sultry weather; (*fig*, *vergüenza*) embarrassment. **~so** *a* oppressive; (*fig*) embarrassing. **¡qué ~!** how embarrassing!

boda *f* marriage; (*ceremonia*) wedding

bodega *f* cellar; (*de vino*) wine cellar; (*almacén*) warehouse; (*de un barco*) hold. **~ón** *m* cheap restaurant; (*pintura*) still life

bodoque *m* pellet; (*tonto*, *fam*) thickhead

bofes *mpl* lights. **echar los ~** slog away

bofet|ada *f* slap; (*fig*) blow. **dar una ~ada a uno** slap s.o. in the face. **darse de ~adas** clash. **~ón** *m* punch

boga *m & f* rower; (*hombre*) oarsman; (*mujer*) oarswoman; (*moda*) fashion. **estar en ~** be in fashion, be in vogue. **~da** *f* stroke (of the oar). **~dor** rower, oarsman. **~r** [12] *vt* row. **~vante** *m* (*crustáceo*) lobster

Bogotá *f* Bogotá

bogotano *a* from Bogotá. —*m* native of Bogotá

bohemio *a & m* Bohemian

bohío *m* (*LAm*) hut

boicot *m* (*pl* **boicots**) boycott. **~ear** *vt* boycott. **~eo** *m* boycott. **hacer el ~** boycott

boina *f* beret

boîte /bwat/ *m* night-club

bola *f* ball; (*canica*) marble; (*naipes*) slam; (*betún*) shoe polish; (*mentira*) fib; (*Mex*, *reunión desordenada*) rowdy party. **~ del mundo** (*fam*) globe. **contar ~s** tell fibs. **dejar que ruede la ~** let things take their course. **meter ~s** tell fibs

bolas *fpl* (*LAm*) bolas

boleada *f* (*Mex*) polishing of shoes

boleadoras (*LAm*) *fpl* bolas

bolera *f* bowling alley

bolero *m* (*baile*, *chaquetilla*) bolero; (*fig*, *mentiroso*, *fam*) liar; (*Mex*, *limpiabotas*) bootblack

boletín *m* bulletin; (*publicación periódica*) journal; (*escolar*) report. **~ de noticias** news bulletin. **~ de precios** price list. **~**

informativo news bulletin. ~ **meteorológico** weather forecast

boleto m (esp LAm) ticket

boli m (fam) Biro (P), ball-point pen

boliche m (juego) bowls; (bolera) bowling alley

bolígrafo m Biro (P), ball-point pen

bolillo m bobbin; (Mex, panecillo) (bread) roll

bolívar m (unidad monetaria venezolana) bolívar

Bolivia f Bolivia

boliviano a Bolivian. —m Bolivian; (unidad monetaria de Bolivia) boliviano

bolo m skittle

bolsa f bag; (monedero) purse; (LAm, bolsillo) pocket; (com) stock exchange; (cavidad) cavity. ~ **de agua caliente** hot-water bottle

bolsillo m pocket; (monedero) purse. **de** ~ pocket

bolsista m & f stockbroker

bolso m (de mujer) handbag

bollería f baker's shop. ~**ero** m baker. ~**o** m roll; (con azúcar) bun; (abolladura) dent; (chichón) lump; (fig, jaleo, fam) fuss

bomba f bomb; (máquina) pump; (noticia) bombshell. ~ **de aceite** (auto) oil pump. ~ **de agua** (auto) water pump. ~ **de incendios** fire-engine. **pasarlo** ~ have a marvellous time

bombacha fpl (LAm) knickers, pants. ~**o** m (esp Mex) baggy trousers, baggy pants (Amer)

bombardear vt bombard; (mil) bomb. ~**o** m bombardment; (mil) bombing. ~**ro** m (avión) bomber

bombazo m explosion

bombear vt pump; (mil) bomb

bombero m fireman. **cuerpo** m **de** ~**s** fire brigade (Brit), fire department (Amer)

bombilla f (light) bulb; (LAm, para maté) pipe for drinking maté; (Mex, cucharón) ladle

bombín m pump; (sombrero, fam) bowler (hat), derby (Amer)

bombo m (tambor) bass drum. **a** ~ **y platillos** with a lot of fuss

bombón m chocolate. **ser un** ~**ón** be a peach. ~**ona** f container. ~**onera** f chocolate box

bonachón a easygoing; (bueno) good-natured

bonaerense a from Buenos Aires. —m native of Buenos Aires

bonanza f (naut) fair weather; (prosperidad) prosperity. **ir en** ~ (naut) have fair weather; (fig) go well

bondad f goodness; (amabilidad) kindness. **tenga la** ~ **de** would you be kind enough to. ~**osamente** adv kindly. ~**oso** a kind

bongo m (LAm) canoe

boniato m sweet potato

bonito a nice; (mono) pretty. **¡muy** ~**!, ¡qué** ~**!** that's nice!, very nice!. ~m bonito

bono m voucher; (título) bond. ~ **del Tesoro** government bond

boqueada f gasp. **dar las** ~**s** be dying

boquerón m anchovy

boquete m hole; (brecha) breach

boquiabierto a open-mouthed; (fig) amazed, dumbfounded. **quedarse** ~ be amazed

boquilla f mouthpiece; (para cigarillos) cigarette-holder; (filtro de cigarillo) tip

borbollar vi bubble. ~**ón** m bubble. **hablar a** ~**ones** gabble. **salir a** ~**ones** gush out

borbotar vt bubble. ~**ón** m bubble. **hablar a** ~**ones** gabble. **salir a** ~**ones** gush out

bordado *a* embroidered. —*m* embroidery. **quedar ~, salir ~** come out very well

bordante *m* (*Mex*) lodger

bordar *vt* embroider; (*fig, fam*) do very well

borde *m* edge; (*de carretera*) side; (*de plato etc*) rim; (*de un vestido*) hem. **~ear** *vt* go round the edge of; (*fig*) border on. **~illo** *m* kerb. **al ~de** on the edge of; (*fig*) on the brink of

bordo *m* board. **a ~** on board

borinqueño *a* & *m* Puerto Rican

borla *f* tassel

borra *f* flock; (*pelusa*) fluff; (*sedimento*) sediment

borrach|**era** *f* drunkenness. **~ín** *m* drunkard. **~o** *a* drunk. —*m* drunkard; (*temporalmente*) drunk. **estar ~o** be drunk. **ni ~o** never in a million years. **ser ~o** be a drunkard

borrador *m* rough copy; (*libro*) rough notebook

borradura *f* crossing-out

borrajear *vt/i* scribble

borrar *vt* rub out; (*tachar*) cross out

borrasc|**a** *f* storm. **~oso** *a* stormy

borreg|**o** *m* year-old lamb; (*fig*) simpleton; (*Mex, noticia falsa*) hoax. **~uil** *a* meek

borric|**ada** *f* silly thing. **~o** *m* donkey; (*fig, fam*) ass

borrón *m* smudge; (*fig, imperfección*) blemish; (*de una pintura*) sketch. **~ y cuenta nueva** let's forget about it!

borroso *a* blurred; (*fig*) vague

bos|**caje** *m* thicket. **~coso** *a* wooded. **~que** *m* wood, forest. **~quecillo** *m* copse

bosquej|**ar** *vt* sketch. **~o** *m* sketch

bosta *f* dung

bostez|**ar** [10] *vi* yawn. **~o** *m* yawn

bota *f* boot; (*recipiente*) leather wine bottle

botadero *m* (*Mex*) ford

botánic|**a** *f* botany. **~o** *a* botanical. —*m* botanist

botar *vt* launch. —*vi* bounce. **estar que bota** be hopping mad

botarat|**ada** *f* silly thing. **~e** *m* idiot

bote *m* bounce; (*golpe*) blow; (*salto*) jump; (*sacudida*) jolt; (*lata*) tin, can; (*vasija*) jar; (*en un bar*) jar for tips; (*barca*) boat. **~ salvavidas** lifeboat. **de ~ en ~** packed

botella *f* bottle. **~ita** *f* small bottle

botica *f* chemist's (shop) (*Brit*), drugstore (*Amer*). **~rio** *m* chemist (*Brit*), druggist (*Amer*)

botija *f*, **botijo** *m* earthenware jug

botín *m* half boot; (*despojos*) booty; (*LAm, calcetín*) sock

botiquín *m* medicine chest; (*de primeros auxilios*) first aid kit

bot|**ón** *m* button; (*yema*) bud. **~onadura** *f* buttons. **~ón de oro** buttercup. **~ones** *m invar* bellboy (*Brit*), bellhop (*Amer*)

botulismo *m* botulism

boutique /bu'tik/ *m* boutique

bóveda *f* vault

boxe|**ador** *m* boxer. **~ar** *vi* box. **~o** *m* boxing

boya *f* buoy; (*corcho*) float. **~nte** *a* buoyant

bozal *m* (*de perro etc*) muzzle; (*de caballo*) halter

bracear *vi* wave one's arms; (*nadar*) swim, crawl

bracero *m* labourer. **de ~** (*fam*) arm in arm

braga *f* underpants, knickers; (*cuerda*) rope. **~dura** *f* crotch. **~s** *fpl* knickers, pants. **~zas** *m invar* (*fam*) henpecked man

bragueta *f* flies

braille /breil/ *m* Braille

bram|ar *vi* roar; *(vaca)* moo; *(viento)* howl. **~ido** *m* roar

branquia *f* gill

bras|a *f* hot coal. **a la ~a** grilled. **~ero** *m* brazier; *(LAm, hogar)* hearth

Brasil *m*. **el ~** Brazil

brasile|ño *a* & *m* Brazilian. **~ro** *a* & *m* *(LAm)* Brazilian

bravata *f* boast

bravío *a* wild; *(persona)* coarse, uncouth

bravo *a* brave; *(animales)* wild; *(mar)* rough. **¡~!** *int* well done! bravo! **~ura** *f* ferocity; *(valor)* courage

braza *f* fathom. **nadar a ~a** do the breast-stroke. **~ada** *f* waving of the arms; *(en natación)* stroke; *(cantidad)* armful. **~ado** *m* armful. **~al** *m* arm-band. **~alete** *m* bracelet; *(brazal)* arm-band. **~o** *m* arm; *(de animales)* foreleg; *(rama)* branch. **~o derecho** right-hand man. **a ~o** by hand. **del ~o** arm in arm

brea *f* tar, pitch

brear *vt* ill-treat

brécol *m* broccoli

brecha *f* gap; *(mil)* breach; *(med)* gash. **estar en la ~** be in the thick of it

brega *f* struggle. **~r** [12] *vi* struggle, *(trabajar mucho)* work hard, slog away. **andar a la ~** work hard

breña *f*, **breñal** *m* scrub

Bretaña *f* Brittany. **Gran ~** Great Britain

breve *a* short. **~dad** *f* shortness. **en ~** soon, shortly. **en ~s momentos** soon

brezal *m* moor. **~o** *m* heather

brib|ón *m* rogue, rascal. **~onada** *f*, **~onería** *f* dirty trick

brida *f* bridle. **a toda ~** at full speed

bridge /britʃ/ *m* bridge

brigada *f* squad; *(mil)* brigade. **general de ~** brigadier *(Brit)*, brigadier-general *(Amer)*

brill|ante *a* brilliant. **—m** diamond. **~antez** *f* brilliance. **~ar** *vi* shine; *(centellear)* sparkle. **~o** *m* shine; *(brillantez)* brilliance; *(centelleo)* sparkle. **dar ~o, sacar ~o** polish

brinc|ar [7] *vi* jump up and down. **~o** *m* jump. **dar un ~o** jump. **estar que brinca** be hopping mad. **pegar un ~o** jump

brind|ar *vt* offer. **—vi. ~ar por** toast, drink a toast to. **~is** *m* toast

brío *m* energy; *(decisión)* determination. **~ioso** *a* spirited; *(garboso)* elegant

brisa *f* breeze

británico *a* British. **—m** Briton, British person

brocado *m* brocade

bróculi *m* broccoli

brocha *f* paintbrush; *(para afeitarse)* shaving-brush

broche *m* clasp, fastener; *(joya)* brooch; *(Arg, sujetapapeles)* paper-clip

brocheta *f* skewer

brom|a *f* joke. **~a pesada** practical joke. **~ear** *vi* joke. **~ista** *a* fun-loving. **—m** & *f* joker. **de ~a, en ~a** in fun. **ni de ~a** never in a million years

bronca *f* row; *(reprensión)* telling-off

bronce *m* bronze. **~ado** *a* bronze; *(por el sol)* tanned, sunburnt. **~ar** *vt* tan *(piel)*. **~arse** *vpr* get a suntan

bronco *a* rough

bronquitis *f* bronchitis

broqueta *f* skewer

brot|ar *vi* *(plantas)* bud, sprout; *(med)* break out; *(líquido)* gush forth; *(lágrimas)* well up. **~e** *m* bud, shoot; *(med)* outbreak; *(de* *líquido*) gushing; (*de lágrimas*) welling-up

bruces *mpl.* de ∼ face down(wards). **caer de ∼** fall on one's face

bruj|a *f* witch. —*a* (*Mex*) penniless. ∼**ear** *vi* practise witchcraft. ∼**ería** *f* witchcraft. ∼**o** *m* wizard, magician; (*LAm*) medicine man

brújula *f* compass

brum|a *f* mist; (*fig*) confusion. ∼**oso** *a* misty, foggy

bruñi|do *m* polish. ∼**r** [22] *vt* polish

brusco *a* (*repentino*) sudden; (*persona*) brusque

Bruselas *fpl* Brussels

brusquedad *f* abruptness

brut|al *a* brutal. ∼**alidad** *f* brutality; (*estupidez*) stupidity. ∼**o** *a* (*estúpido*) stupid; (*tosco*) rough, uncouth; (*peso, sueldo*) gross

bucal *a* oral

buce|ar *vi* dive; (*fig*) explore. ∼**o** *m* diving

bucle *m* curl

budín *m* pudding

budis|mo *m* Buddhism. ∼**ta** *m & f* Buddhist

buen *véase* **bueno**

buenamente *adv* easily; (*voluntariamente*) willingly

buenaventura *f* good luck; (*adivinación*) fortune. **decir la ∼ a uno, echar la ∼ a uno** tell s.o.'s fortune

bueno *a* (*delante de nombre masculino en singular* **buen**) good; (*apropiado*) fit; (*amable*) kind; (*tiempo*) fine. —*int* well!; (*de acuerdo*) OK!, very well! ¡**buena la has hecho!** you've gone and done it now! ¡**buenas noches!** good night! ¡**buenas tardes!** (*antes del atardecer*) good afternoon!; (*después del atardecer*) good evening! ¡∼**s días!** good

morning! **estar de buenas** be in a good mood. **por las buenas** willingly

Buenos Aires *m* Buenos Aires

buey *m* ox

búfalo *m* buffalo

bufanda *f* scarf

bufar *vi* snort. **estar que bufa** be hopping mad

bufete *m* (*mesa*) writing-desk; (*despacho*) lawyer's office

bufido *m* snort; (*de ira*) outburst

bufo *a* comic. ∼**ón** *a* comical. — *m* buffoon. ∼**onada** *f* joke

bugle *m* bugle

buharda *f*, **buhardilla** *f* attic; (*ventana*) dormer window

búho *m* owl

buhoner|ía *f* pedlar's wares. ∼**o** *m* pedlar

buitre *m* vulture

bujía *f* candle; (*auto*) spark(ing)-plug

bula *f* bull

bulbo *m* bulb

bulevar *m* avenue, boulevard

Bulgaria *f* Bulgaria

búlgaro *a & m* Bulgarian

bulo *m* hoax

bulto *m* (*volumen*) volume; (*tamaño*) size; (*forma*) shape; (*paquete*) package; (*protuberancia*) lump. **a ∼** roughly

bulla *f* uproar; (*muchedumbre*) crowd

bullicio *m* hubbub; (*movimiento*) bustle. ∼**so** *a* bustling; (*ruidoso*) noisy

bullir [22] *vt* stir, move. —*vi* boil; (*burbujear*) bubble; (*fig*) bustle

buñuelo *m* doughnut; (*fig*) mess

BUP *abrev* (*Bachillerato Unificado Polivalente*) secondary school education

buque *m* ship, boat

burbuj|a *f* bubble. ∼**ear** *vi* bubble; (*vino*) sparkle. ∼**eo** *m* bubbling

burdel *m* brothel

burdo *a* rough, coarse; *(excusa)* clumsy

burgués *a* middle-class, bourgeois. —*m* middle-class person. **~esía** *f* middle class, bourgeoisie

burla *f* taunt; *(broma)* joke; *(engaño)* trick. **~dor** *a* mocking. —*m* seducer. **~r** *vt* trick, deceive; *(seducir)* seduce. **~rse** *vpr*. **~rse de** mock, make fun of

burlesco *a* funny

burlón *a* mocking

buro|cracia *f* civil service. **~ócrata** *m & f* civil servant. **~ocrático** *a* bureaucratic

burro *m* donkey; *(fig)* ass

bursátil *a* stock-exchange

bus *m (fam)* bus

busca *f* search. **a la ~ de** in search of. **en ~ de** in search of

busca: **~pié** *m* feeler. **~pleitos** *m invar (LAm)* trouble-maker

buscar [7] *vt* look for. —*vi* look. **buscársela** for it. **ir a ~ a uno** fetch s.o.

busca|ruidos *m invar* trouble-maker

buscona *f* prostitute

busilis *m* snag

búsqueda *f* search

busto *m* bust

butaca *f* armchair; *(en el teatro etc)* seat

butano *m* butane

buzo *m* diver

buzón *m* postbox *(Brit)*, mailbox *(Amer)*

C

C/ *abrev (Calle)* St, Street, Rd, Road

cabal *a* exact; *(completo)* complete. **no estar en sus ~es** not be in one's right mind

cabalga|dura *f* mount, horse. **~r** [12] *vi* ride. —*vi* ride, go riding. **~ta** *f* ride; *(desfile)* procession

cabalmente *adv* completely; *(exactamente)* exactly

caballa *f* mackerel

caballada *f (LAm)* stupid thing

caballeresco *a* gentlemanly. **literatura *f* caballeresca** books of chivalry

caballer|ía *f* mount, horse. **~iza** *f* stable. **~izo** *m* groom

caballero *m* gentleman; *(de orden de caballería)* knight; *(tratamiento)* sir. **~samente** *adv* like a gentleman. **~so** *a* gentlemanly

caballete *m (del tejado)* ridge; *(de la nariz)* bridge; *(de pintor)* easel

caballito *m* pony. **~ del diablo** dragonfly. **~ de mar** sea-horse. **los ~s** *(tiovivo)* merry-go-round

caballo *m* horse; *(del ajedrez)* knight; *(de la baraja española)* queen. **~ de vapor** horsepower. **a ~** on horseback

cabaña *f* hut

cabaret /kaba're/ *m (pl* **cabarets** /kaba're/) night-club

cabece|ar *vi* nod; *(para negar)* shake one's head. **~o** *m* nodding, nod; *(acción de negar)* shake of the head

cabecera *f (de la cama, de la mesa)* head; *(en un impreso)* heading

cabecilla *m* leader

cabell|o *m* hair. **~os** *mpl* hair. **~udo** *a* hairy

caber [28] *vi* fit **(en** into). **los libros no caben en la caja** the books won't fit in the box. **no cabe duda** there's no doubt

cabestr|illo *m* sling. **~o** *m* halter

cabeza *f* head; *(fig, inteligencia)* intelligence. **~da** *f* butt; *(golpe recibido)* blow; *(saludo, al dormirse)* nod; *(en fút-bol)* header. **andar de ~** have a lot to do. **dar una ~da** nod off

cabida f capacity; (*extensión*) area. **dar ~ a** leave room for, leave space for

cabina f (*de avión*) cabin, cockpit; (*electoral*) booth; (*de camión*) cab. **~ telefónica** telephone box (*Brit*), telephone booth (*Amer*)

cabizbajo a crestfallen

cable m cable

cabo m end; (*trozo*) bit; (*mil*) corporal; (*mango*) handle; (*geog*) cape; (*naut*) rope. **al ~** eventually. **al ~ de una hora** after an hour. **de ~ a rabo** from beginning to end. **llevar(se) a ~** carry out

cabr|**a** f goat. **~a montesa** f mountain goat. **~iola** f jump, skip. **~itilla** f kid. **~ito** m kid

cabrón m cuckold

cabuya (*LAm*) pita, agave

cacahuate m (*Mex*), **cacahuete** m peanut

cacao m (*planta y semillas*) cacao; (*polvo*) cocoa; (*fig*) confusion

cacare|**ar** vt boast about. *—vi* (*gallo*) crow; (*gallina*) cluck. **~o** m (*incl fig*) crowing; (*de gallina*) clucking

cacería f hunt

cacerola f casserole, saucepan

caciqu|**e** m cacique, Indian chief; (*pol*) cacique, local political boss. **~il** a despotic. **~ismo** m caciquism, despotism

caco m pickpocket, thief

cacof|**onía** f cacophony. **~ónico** a cacophonous

cacto m cactus

cacumen m acumen

cacharro m earthenware pot; (*para flores*) vase; (*coche estropeado*) wreck; (*cosa inútil*) piece of junk; (*chisme*) thing. **~s** mpl pots and pans

cachear vt frisk

cachemir m, **cachemira** f cashmere

cacheo m frisking

cachetada f (*LAm*), **cachete** m slap

cachimba f pipe

cachiporra f club, truncheon. **~zo** m blow with a club

cachivache m thing, piece of junk

cacho m bit, piece; (*LAm, cuerno*) horn; (*miga*) crumb

cachondeo m (*fam*) joking, joke

cachorro m (*perrito*) puppy; (*de otros animales*) young

cada a invar each, every. **~ uno** each one, everyone. **uno de ~ cinco** one in five

cadalso m scaffold

cadáver m corpse. **ingresar ~** be dead on arrival

cadena f chain; (*TV*) channel. **~ de fabricación** production line. **~ de montañas** mountain range. **~ perpetua** life imprisonment

cadencia f cadence, rhythm

cadera f hip

cadete m cadet

caduc|**ar** [7] vi expire. **~idad** f. **fecha** f **de caducidad** sell-by date. **~o** a decrepit

caedizo a unsteady. **~r** [29] vi fall. **~rse** vpr fall (over). **dejar ~r** drop. **estar al ~r** be about to happen. **este vestido no me ~ bien** this dress doesn't suit me. **hacer ~r** knock over. **Juan me ~ bien** I get on well with Juan. **su cumpleaños cayó en Martes** his birthday fell on a Tuesday

café m coffee; (*cafetería*) café. *—a.* **color ~** coffee-coloured. **~ con leche** white coffee. **~ cortado** coffee with a little milk. **~ (solo)** black coffee

cafe|**ína** f caffeine. **~tal** m coffee plantation. **~tera** f coffee-pot. **~tería** f café. **~tero** a coffee

caíd|a f fall; (*disminución*) drop; (*pendiente*) slope. **~o** a fallen; (*abatido*) dejected. **~m** fallen

caigo vb *véase* **caer**

caimán m cayman, alligator

caj|a f box; (*grande*) case; (*de caudales*) safe; (*donde se efectúan los pagos*) cash desk; (*en supermercado*) check-out. **~a de ahorros** savings bank. **~a de caudales, ~a fuerte** safe. **~a postal de ahorros** post office savings bank. **~a registradora** till. **~ero** m cashier. **~etilla** f packet. **~ita** f small box. **~ón** m large box; (*de mueble*) drawer; (*puesto de mercado*) stall. **ser de ~ón** be a matter of course

cal m lime

cala f cove

calaba|cín m marrow; (*fig, idiota, fam*) idiot. **~za** f pumpkin; (*fig, idiota, fam*) idiot

calabozo m prison; (*celda*) cell

calado a soaked. **~m** (*naut*) draught. **estar ~ hasta los huesos** be soaked to the skin

calamar m squid

calambre m cramp

calami|dad f calamity, disaster. **~toso** a calamitous, disastrous

calar vt soak; (*penetrar*) pierce; (*fig, penetrar*) see through; sample (*fruta*). **~se** vpr get soaked; (*zapatos*) leak; (*auto*) stall

calavera f skull

calcar [7] vt trace; (*fig*) copy

calceta f. **hacer ~** knit

calcetín m sock

calcinar vt burn

calcio m calcium

calco m tracing. **~manía** f transfer. **papel** m **de ~** tracing-paper

calcula|dor a calculating. **~dora** f calculator. **~dora de bolsillo** pocket calculator. **~r** vt calculate; (*suponer*) reckon, think

cálculo m calculation; (*fig*) reckoning

caldea|miento m heating. **~r** vt heat, warm. **~rse** vpr get hot

calder|a f boiler; (*Arg, para café*) coffee-pot; (*Arg, para té*) teapot. **~eta** f small boiler

calderilla f small change, coppers

calder|o m small boiler. **~ón** m large boiler

caldo m stock; (*sopa*) soup, broth. **poner a ~ a uno** give s.o. a dressing-down

calefacción f heating. **~ central** central heating

caleidoscopio m kaleidoscope

calendario m calendar

caléndula f marigold

calenta|dor m heater. **~miento** m heating; (*en deportes*) warmup. **~r** [1] vt heat, warm. **~rse** vpr get hot, warm up

calentur|a f fever, (high) temperature. **~iento** a feverish

calibr|ar vt calibrate; (*fig*) measure. **~e** m calibre; (*diámetro*) diameter; (*fig*) importance

calidad f quality; (*función*) capacity. **en ~ de** as

cálido a warm

calidoscopio m kaleidoscope

caliente a hot, warm; (*fig, enfadado*) angry

califica|ción f qualification; (*evaluación*) assessment; (*nota*) mark. **~r** [7] vt qualify; (*evaluar*) assess; mark (*examen etc*). **~r de** describe as, label. **~tivo** a qualifying. **~m** epithet

caliza f limestone. **~o** a lime

calma f calm. **¡~!** calm down! **~ante** a & m sedative. **~ar** vt calm, soothe. **~vi** (*viento*) abate. **~arse** vpr calm down; (*viento*) abate. **~oso** a calm; (*flemático, fam*) phlegmatic. **en ~a** calm. **perder la ~a** lose one's composure

calor *m* heat, warmth. **hace ~** it's hot. **tener ~** be hot

caloría *f* calorie

calorífero *m* heater

calumni|a *f* calumny; (*oral*) slander; (*escrita*) libel. **~ar** *vt* slander; (*por escrito*) libel. **~oso** *a* slanderous; (*cosa escrita*) libellous

caluros|amente *adv* warmly. **~o** *a* warm

calv|a *f* bald patch. **~ero** *m* clearing. **~icie** *f* baldness. **~o** *a* bald; (*terreno*) barren

calza *f* (*fam*) stocking; (*cuña*) wedge

calzada *f* road

calza|do *a* wearing shoes. **—***m* footwear. **~dor** *m* shoehorn. **~r** [10] *vt* put shoes on; (*llevar*) wear. **—***vi* wear shoes. **—***vpr* put on. **¿qué número calza Vd?** what size shoe do you take?

calz|ón *m* shorts; (*ropa interior*) knickers, pants. **~ones** *mpl* shorts. **~oncillos** *mpl* underpants

calla|do *a* quiet. **~r** *vt* silence; keep (*secreto*); hush up (*asunto*). **—***vi* be quiet, keep quiet, shut up (*fam*). **~rse** *vpr* be quiet, keep quiet, shut up (*fam*). **¡cállate!** be quiet! shut up! (*fam*)

calle *f* street, road; (*en deportes, en autopista*) lane. **~ de dirección única** one-way street. **~ mayor** high street, main street. **abrir ~** make way

calleja *f* narrow street. **~ear** *vi* wander about the streets. **~ero** *a* street. **—***m* street plan. **~ón** *m* alley. **~uela** *f* back street, side street. **~ón sin salida** cul-de-sac

call|ista *m & f* chiropodist. **~o** *m* corn, callus. **~os** *mpl* tripe. **~oso** *a* hard, rough

cama *f* bed. **~ de matrimonio** double bed. **~ individual** single bed. **caer en la ~** fall ill. **guardar ~** be confined to bed

camada *f* litter; (*fig, de ladrones*) gang

camafeo *m* cameo

camaleón *m* chameleon

cámara *f* room; (*de reyes*) royal chamber; (*fotográfica*) camera; (*de armas, pol*) chamber. **~ fotográfica** camera. **a ~ lenta** in slow motion

camarada *f* colleague; (*amigo*) companion

camarer|a *f* chambermaid; (*de restaurante etc*) waitress; (*en casa*) maid. **~o** *m* waiter

camarín *m* dressing-room; (*naut*) cabin

camarón *m* shrimp

camarote *m* cabin

cambi|able *a* changeable; (*com etc*) exchangeable. **~ante** *a* variable. **~ar** *vt* change; (*trocar*) exchange. **—***vi* change. **~ar de idea** change one's mind. **~arse** *vpr* change. **~o** *m* change; (*com*) exchange rate; (*moneda menuda*) (small) change. **~sta** *m & f* money-changer. **en ~** on the other hand

camelia *f* camellia

camello *m* camel

camilla *f* stretcher; (*sofá*) couch

camina|nte *m* traveller. **~r** *vt* cover. **—***vi* travel; (*andar*) walk; (*río, astros etc*) move. **~ta** *f* long walk

camino *m* road; (*sendero*) path, track; (*dirección, medio*) way. **~ de** towards, on the way to. **abrir ~** make way. **a medio ~, a la mitad del ~** half-way. **de ~** on the way. **ponerse en ~** set out

cami|ón *m* lorry; (*Mex, autobús*) bus. **~onero** *m* lorry-driver. **~oneta** *f* van

camis|a *f* shirt; (*de un fruto*) skin. **~a de dormir** nightdress. **~a de fuerza** strait-jacket. **~ería** *f* shirt shop. ~eta f T-shirt; (ropa interior) vest. ~ón m nightdress

camorra f (fam) row. buscar ~ look for trouble, pick a quarrel

camote m (LAm) sweet potato

campamento m camp

campana f bell. ~ada f stroke of a bell; (de reloj) striking. ~ario m bell tower, belfry. ~eo m peal of bells. ~illa f bell. ~udo a bell-shaped; (estilo) bombastic

campaña f countryside; (mil, pol) campaign. de ~ (mil) field

campe|ón a & m champion. ~onato m championship

campes|ino a country. —m peasant. ~tre a country

camping /'kampiŋ/ m (pl **campings** /'kampiŋ/) camping; (lugar) campsite. hacer ~ go camping

campiña f countryside

campo m country; (agricultura, fig) field; (de tenis) court; (de fútbol) pitch; (de golf) course. ~santo m cemetery

camufla|do a camouflaged. ~je m camouflage. ~r vt camouflage

cana f grey hair, white hair. echar una ~ al aire have a fling. peinar ~s be getting old

Canadá m. el ~ Canada

canadiense a & m Canadian

canal m (incl TV) channel; (artificial) canal; (del tejado) gutter. ~ de la Mancha English Channel. ~ de Panamá Panama Canal. ~ón m (horizontal) gutter; (vertical) drain-pipe

canalla f rabble. —m (fig, fam) swine. ~da f dirty trick

canapé m sofa, couch; (culin) canapé

Canarias fpl. (las islas) the Canary Islands, the Canaries

canario a of the Canary Islands. —m native of the Canary Islands; (pájaro) canary

canast|a f (large) basket. ~illa f small basket; (para un bebé) layette. ~illo m small basket. ~o m (large) basket

cancela f gate

cancela|ción f cancellation. ~r vt cancel; write off (deuda); (fig) forget

cáncer m cancer. C~ Cancer

canciller m chancellor; (LAm, ministro de asuntos exteriores) Minister of Foreign Affairs

canci|ón f song. ~ón de cuna lullaby. ~onero m song-book. ¡siempre la misma ~ón! always the same old story!

cancha f (de fútbol) pitch, ground; (de tenis) court

candado m padlock

candel|a f candle. ~ero m candlestick. ~illa f candle

candente a (rojo) red-hot; (blanco) white-hot; (fig) burning

candidato m candidate

candidez f innocence; (ingenuidad) naïvety

cándido a naïve

candil m oil-lamp; (Mex, araña) chandelier. ~ejas fpl footlights

candinga m (Mex) devil

candor m innocence; (ingenuidad) naïvety. ~oso a innocent; (ingenuo) naïve

canela f cinnamon. ser ~ be beautiful

cangrejo m crab. ~ de río crayfish

canguro m kangaroo; (persona) baby-sitter

can|íbal a & m cannibal. ~ibalismo m cannibalism

canica f marble

canijo m weak

canino a canine. —m canine (tooth)

canje m exchange. ~ar vt exchange

cano a grey-haired

canoa f canoe; (con motor) motor boat

canon m canon

can|ónigo m canon. **~onizar** [10] vt canonize

canoso a grey-haired

cansa|do a tired. **~ncio** m tiredness. **~r** vt tire; (aburrir) bore. —vi be tiring; (aburrir) get boring. **~rse** vpr get tired

cantábrico a Cantabrian. **el mar ~** the Bay of Biscay

canta|nte a singing. —m singer; (en óperas) opera singer. **~or** m Flamenco singer. **~r** vt/i sing. —m singing; (canción) song; (poema) poem. **~rlas claras** speak frankly

cántar|a f pitcher. **~o** m pitcher. **llover a ~os** pour down

cante m folk song. **~ flamenco, ~ jondo** Flamenco singing

cantera f quarry

cantidad f quantity; (número) number; (de dinero) sum. **una ~ de** lots of

cantilena f, **cantinela** f song

cantimplora f water-bottle

cantina f canteen; (rail) buffet

canto m singing; (canción) song; (borde) edge; (de un cuchillo) blunt edge; (esquina) corner; (piedra) pebble. **~ rodado** boulder. **de ~** on edge

cantonés a Cantonese

cantor a singing. —m singer

cantur|ear vt/i hum. **~o** m humming

canuto m tube

caña f stalk, stem; (planta) reed; (vaso) glass; (de la pierna) shin. **~ de azúcar** sugar-cane. **~ de pescar** fishing-rod

cañada f ravine; (camino) track

cáñamo m hemp. **~ índio** cannabis

cañer|ía f pipe; (tubería) piping. **~o** m pipe, tube; (de fuente) jet. **~ón** m pipe, tube; (de órgano)

pipe; (de chimenea) flue; (arma de fuego) cannon; (desfiladero) canyon. **~onazo** m gunshot. **~onera** f gunboat

caoba f mahogany

ca|os m chaos. **~ótico** a chaotic

capa f cloak; (de pintura) coat; (culin) coating; (geol) stratum, layer

capacidad f capacity; (fig) ability

capacitar vt qualify, enable; (instruir) train

caparazón m shell

capataz m foreman

capaz a capable, able; (espacioso) roomy. **~ para** which holds, with a capacity of

capazo m large basket

capcioso a sly, insidious

capellán m chaplain

caperuza f hood; (de pluma) cap

capilla f chapel; (mus) choir

capita f small cloak, cape

capital a capital, very important. —m (dinero) capital. —f (ciudad) capital; (LAm, letra) capital (letter). **~ de provincia** county town

capital|ismo m capitalism. **~sta** a & m & f capitalist. **~zar** [10] vt capitalize

capit|án m captain. **~anear** vt lead, command; (un equipo) captain

capitel m (arquit) capital

capitulaci|ón f surrender; (acuerdo) agreement. **~ones** fpl marriage contract

capítulo m chapter. **~s matrimoniales** marriage contract

capó m bonnet (Brit), hood (Amer)

capón m (pollo) capon

caporal m chief, leader

capota f (de mujer) bonnet; (auto) folding top, sliding roof

capote m cape

Capricornio m Capricorn

capricho *m* whim. ∼**so** *a* capricious, whimsical. **a** ∼ capriciously

cápsula *f* capsule

captar *vt* harness ‹agua›; grasp ‹sentido›; hold ‹atención›; win ‹confianza›; (radio) pick up

captura *f* capture. ∼**r** *vt* capture

capucha *f* hood

capullo *m* bud; (de insecto) cocoon

caqui *m* khaki

cara *f* face; (de una moneda) obverse; (de un objeto) side; (aspecto) look, appearance; (descaro) cheek. ∼ **a** towards; (frente a) facing. ∼ **a** ∼ face to face. ∼ **o cruz** heads or tails. **dar la** ∼ face up to. **hacer** ∼ **a** face. **no volver la** ∼ **atrás** not look back. **tener** ∼ **de** look, seem to be. **tener** ∼ **para** have the face to. **tener mala** ∼ look ill. **volver la** ∼ look the other way

carabela *f* caravel, small light ship

carabina *f* rifle; (fig, señora, fam) chaperone

Caracas *m* Caracas

caracol *m* snail; (de pelo) curl. **¡**∼**es!** Good Heavens! **escalera** *f* **de** ∼ spiral staircase

carácter *m* (pl **caracteres**) character. **con** ∼ **de, por su** ∼ **de** as

característica *f* characteristic; (LAm, teléfonos) dialling code. ∼**o** *a* characteristic, typical

caracteriza|**do** *a* characterized; (prestigioso) distinguished. ∼**r** [10] *vt* characterize

cara: ∼ **dura** cheek, nerve. ∼**dura** *m & f* cheeky person, rotter (fam)

caramba *int* good heavens!, goodness me!

carámbano *m* icicle

caramelo *m* sweet (Brit), candy (Amer); (azúcar fundido) caramel

carancho *m* (Arg) vulture

carapacho *m* shell

caraqueño *a* from Caracas. —*m* native of Caracas

carátula *f* mask; (fig, teatro) theatre; (Mex, esfera del reloj) face

caravana *f* caravan; (fig, grupo) group; (auto) long line, traffic jam

caray *int* (fam) good heavens!, goodness me!

carbón *m* coal; (papel) carbon (paper); (para dibujar) charcoal. ∼**oncillo** *m* charcoal. ∼**onero** *a* coal. —*m* coal-merchant. ∼**onizar** [10] *vt* (fig) burn (to a cinder). ∼**ono** *m* carbon

carburador *m* carburettor

carcajada *f* burst of laughter. **reírse a** ∼**s** roar with laughter. **soltar una** ∼ burst out laughing

cárcel *m* prison, jail; (en carpintería) clamp

carcel|**ario** *a* prison. ∼**ero** *a* prison. —*m* prison officer

carcom|**a** *f* woodworm. ∼**er** *vt* eat away; (fig) undermine. ∼**erse** *vpr* be eaten away; (fig) waste away

cardenal *m* cardinal; (contusión) bruise

cárdeno *a* purple

cardiaco, cardíaco *a* cardiac, heart. —*m* heart patient

cardinal *a* cardinal

cardiólogo *m* cardiologist, heart specialist

cardo *m* thistle

carear *vt* bring face to face ‹personas›; compare ‹cosas›

carecer [11] *vi* ∼ **de** lack. ∼ **de sentido** not to make sense

caren|**cia** *f* lack. ∼**te** *a* lacking

carero *a* expensive

carestía *f* (precio elevado) high price; (escasez) shortage

careta *f* mask

carey *m* tortoiseshell

carga *f* load; *(fig)* burden; *(acción)* loading; *(de barco)* cargo; *(obligación)* obligation. **∼do** a loaded; *(fig)* burdened; *(tiempo)* heavy; *(hilo)* live; *(pila)* charged. **∼mento** *m* load; *(acción)* loading; *(de un barco)* cargo. **∼nte** a demanding. **∼r** [12] *vt* load; *(fig)* burden; *(mil, elec)* charge; fill *(pluma etc)*; *(fig, molestar, fam)* annoy. **∼vi** load. **∼r con pico** up. **∼rse** *vpr (llenarse)* fill; *(cielo)* become overcast; *(enfadarse, fam)* get cross. **llevar la ∼ de algo** be responsible for sth

cargo *m* load; *(fig)* burden; *(puesto)* post; *(acusación)* accusation, charge; *(responsabilidad)* charge. **a ∼ de** in the charge of. **hacerse ∼ de** take responsibility for. **tener a su ∼** be in charge of

carguero *m (Arg)* beast of burden; *(naut)* cargo ship

cari *m (LAm)* grey

cariacontecido a crestfallen

caria|do a decayed. **∼rse** *vpr* decay

caribe a Caribbean. **el mar** *m* **C∼** the Caribbean (Sea)

caricatura *f* caricature

caricia *f* caress

caridad *f* charity. **¡por ∼!** for goodness sake!

caries *f invar* (dental) decay

carilampiño a clean-shaven

cariño *m* affection; *(caricia)* caress. **∼ mío** my darling. **∼samente** *adv* tenderly, lovingly; *(en carta)* with love from. **∼so** a affectionate **con mucho ∼** *(en carta)* with love from. **tener ∼ a** be fond of. **tomar ∼ a** take a liking to. **un ∼** *(en carta)* with love from

carism|a *m* charisma. **∼ático** a charismatic

caritativo a charitable

cariz *m* look

carlinga *f* cockpit

carmesí a & *m* crimson

carmín *m (de labios)* lipstick; *(color)* red

carnal a carnal; *(pariente)* blood, full. **primo ∼** first cousin

carnaval *m* carnival. **∼esco** a carnival. **martes** *m* **de ∼** Shrove Tuesday

carne *f (incl de frutos)* flesh; *(para comer)* meat. **∼ de cerdo** pork. **∼ de cordero** lamb. **∼ de gallina** goose-flesh. **∼ picada** mince. **∼ de ternera** veal. **∼ de vaca** beef. **me pone la ∼ de gallina** it gives me the creeps. **ser de ∼ y hueso** be only human

carné *m* card; *(cuaderno)* notebook. **∼ de conducir** driving licence *(Brit)*, driver's license *(Amer)*. **∼ de identidad** identity card.

carnero *m* sheep; *(culin)* lamb

carnet /kar'ne/ *m* card; *(cuaderno)* notebook. **∼ de conducir** driving licence *(Brit)*, driver's license *(Amer)*. **∼ de identidad** identity card

carnicer|ía *f* butcher's (shop); *(fig)* massacre. **∼o** a carnivorous; *(fig, cruel)* cruel, savage. —*m* butcher; *(animal)* carnivore

carnívoro a carnivorous. —*m* carnivore

carnoso a fleshy

caro a dear. —*adv* dear, dearly. **costar ∼ a uno** cost s.o. dear

carpa *f* carp; *(tienda)* tent

carpeta *f* folder. **∼zo** *m*. **dar ∼zo a** shelve, put on one side

carpinter|ía *f* carpentry. **∼o** *m* carpenter, joiner

carraspe|ar *vi* clear one's throat. **∼ra** *f*. **tener ∼ra** have a frog in one's throat

carrera f run; (prisa) rush; (concurso) race; (recorrido, estudios) course; (profesión) profession, career

carreta f cart. **~da** f cart-load

carrete m reel; (película) 35mm film

carretera f road. **~ de circunvalación** bypass, ring road. **~ nacional** A road (Brit), highway (Amer). **~ secundaria** B road (Brit), secondary road (Amer)

carret|illa f trolley; (de una rueda) wheelbarrow; (de bebé) baby-walker. **~ón** m small cart

carril m rut; (rail) rail; (de autopista etc) lane

carrillo m cheek; (polea) pulley

carrizo m reed

carro m cart; (LAm, coche) car. **~ de asalto, ~ de combate** tank

carrocería f (auto) bodywork; (taller) car repairer's

carroña f carrion

carroza f coach, carriage; (en desfile de fiesta) float

carruaje m carriage

carrusel m merry-go-round

carta f letter; (documento) document; (lista de platos) menu; (lista de vinos) list; (geog) map; (naipe) card. **~ blanca** free hand. **~ de crédito** credit card

cartearse vpr correspond

cartel m poster; (de escuela etc) wall-chart. **~era** f hoarding; (en periódico) entertainments. **~ito** m notice. **de ~** celebrated. **tener ~** be a hit, be successful

cartera f wallet; (de colegial) satchel; (para documentos) briefcase

cartería f sorting office

carterista m & f pickpocket

cartero m postman, mailman (Amer)

cartílago m cartilage

cartilla f first reading book. **~ de ahorros** savings book. **leerle la ~ a uno** tell s.o. off

cartón m cardboard

cartucho m cartridge

cartulina f thin cardboard

casa f house; (hogar) home; (empresa) firm; (edificio) building. **~ de correos** post office. **~ de huéspedes** boarding-house. **~ de socorro** first aid post. **amigo** m **de la ~** family friend. **ir a ~** go home. **salir de ~** go out

casad|a f married woman. **~o a** married. **—m** married man. **los recién ~os** the newly-weds

casamentero m matchmaker

casa|miento m marriage; (ceremonia) wedding. **~r** vt marry. **—vi** get married. **~rse** vpr get married

cascabel m small bell. **~eo** m jingling

cascada f waterfall

cascado a broken; (voz) harsh

cascanueces m invar nutcrackers

cascar [7] vt break; crack (frutos secos); (pegar) beat. **—vi** (fig, fam) chatter, natter (fam). **~se** vpr crack

cáscara f (de huevo, frutos secos) shell; (de naranja) peel; (de plátano) skin

casco m helmet; (de cerámica etc) piece, fragment; (cabeza) head; (de barco) hull; (envase) empty bottle; (de caballo) hoof; (de una ciudad) part, area

cascote m rubble

caserío m country house; (conjunto de casas) hamlet

casero a home-made; (doméstico) domestic, household; (amante del hogar) home-loving; (reunión) family. **—m** owner; (vigilante) caretaker

caseta *f* small house, cottage. ~ **de baño** bathing hut

caset(t)e *m* & *f* cassette

casi *adv* almost, nearly; (*en frases negativas*) hardly. ~ ~ very nearly. ~ **nada** hardly any. ¡~ **nada!** is that all! ~ **nunca** hardly ever

casilla *f* small house; (*cabaña*) hut; (*de mercado*) stall; (*en ajedrez etc*) square; (*departamento de casillero*) pigeon-hole

casillero *m* pigeon-holes

casimir *m* cashmere

casino *m* casino; (*sociedad*) club

caso *m* case; (*atención*) notice. ~ **perdido** hopeless case. ~ **urgente** emergency. **darse el** ~ **(de) que** happen. **el** ~ **es que** the fact is that. **en** ~ **de** in the event of. **en cualquier** ~ in any case, whatever happens. **en ese** ~ in that case. **en todo** ~ in any case. **en último** ~ as a last resort. **hacer** ~ **de** take notice of. **poner por** ~ suppose

caspa *f* dandruff

cáspita *int* good heavens!, goodness me!

casquivano *a* scatter-brained

cassette *m* & *f* cassette

casta *f* (*de animal*) breed; (*de persona*) descent

castaña *f* chestnut

castañet.a *f* click of the fingers. ~**ear** *vi* (*dientes*) chatter

castaño *a* chestnut, brown. —*m* chestnut (tree)

castañuela *f* castanet

castellano *a* Castilian. —*m* (*persona*) Castilian; (*lengua*) Castilian, Spanish. ~**parlante** *a* Castilian-speaking, Spanish-speaking. ¿**habla Vd** ~? do you speak Spanish?

castidad *f* chastity

castigar [12] *vt* punish; (*en deportes*) penalize. ~**o** *m* punishment; (*en deportes*) penalty

castillo *m* castle

cast.izo *a* true; (*lengua*) pure. ~**o** *a* pure

castor *m* beaver

castración *f* castration. ~**r** *vt* castrate

castrense *m* military

casual *a* chance, accidental. ~**idad** *f* chance, coincidence. ~**mente** *adv* by chance. **la** ~**idad** happen. **de** ~**idad**, **por** ~**idad** by chance. ¡**qué** ~**idad!** what a coincidence!

cataclismo *m* cataclysm

catador *m* taster; (*fig*) connoisseur

catalán *a* & *m* Catalan

catalejo *m* telescope

catalizador *m* catalyst

cat.alogar [12] *vt* catalogue; (*fig*) classify. ~**álogo** *m* catalogue

Cataluña *f* Catalonia

catamarán *m* catamaran

cataplúm *int* crash! bang!

catapulta *f* catapult

catar *vt* taste, try

catarata *f* waterfall, falls; (*med*) cataract

catarro *m* cold

cat.ástrofe *m* catastrophe. ~**astrófico** *a* catastrophic

catecismo *m* catechism

catedral *f* cathedral

catedrático *m* professor; (*de instituto*) teacher, head of department

categ.oría *f* category; (*clase*) class. ~**órico** *a* categorical. ~**oría** important. **de primera** ~**oría** first-class

catinga *f* (*LAm*) bad smell

catita *f* (*Arg*) parrot

catoche *m* (*Mex*) bad mood

cat.olicismo *m* catholicism. ~**ólico** *a* (Roman) Catholic. —*m* (Roman) Catholic

catorce *a* & *m* fourteen

cauce *m* river bed; (*fig, artificial*) channel

caución *f* caution; (*jurid*) guarantee

caucho *m* rubber

caudal *m* (*de río*) flow; (*riqueza*) wealth. **~oso** *a* (*río*) large

caudillo *m* leader, caudillo

causa *f* cause; (*motivo*) reason; (*jurid*) lawsuit. **~r** *vt* cause. **a ~ de, por ~ de** because of

cáustico *a* caustic

cautela *f* caution. **~arse** *vpr* guard against. **~osamente** *adv* warily, cautiously. **~oso** *a* cautious, wary

cauterizar [10] *vt* cauterize; (*fig*) apply drastic measures to

cautiv|**ar** *vt* capture; (*fig, fascinar*) captivate. **~erio** *m*, **~idad** *f* captivity. **~o** *a* & *m* captive

cauto *a* cautious

cavar *vt/i* dig

caverna *f* cave, cavern

caviar *m* caviare

cavidad *f* cavity

cavil|**ar** *vi* ponder, consider. **~oso** *a* worried

cayado *m* (*de pastor*) crook; (*de obispo*) crozier

caza *f* hunting; (*una expedición*) hunt; (*animales*) game. —*m* fighter. **~dor** *m* hunter. **~dora** *f* jacket. **~ mayor** big game hunting. **~ menor** small game hunting. **~r** [10] *vt* hunt; (*fig*) track down; (*obtener*) catch, get. **andar a (la) ~ de** be in search of. **dar ~** chase, go after

cazo *m* saucepan; (*cucharón*) ladle. **~leta** *f* (small) saucepan

cazuela *f* casserole

cebada *f* barley

ceb|**ar** *vt* fatten (up); (*con trampa*) bait; prime (*arma de fuego*). **~o** *m* bait; (*de arma de fuego*) charge

cebolla *f* onion. **~ana** *f* chive. **~eta** *f* spring onion. **~ino** *m* chive

cebra *f* zebra

cece|**ar** *vi* lisp. **~o** *m* lisp

cedazo *m* sieve

ceder *vt* give up. —*vi* give in; (*disminuir*) ease off; (*fallar*) give way, collapse. **ceda el paso** give way

cedilla *f* cedilla

cedro *m* cedar

cédula *f* document; (*ficha*) index card

CE(E) *abrev* (*Comunidad (Económica) Europea*) E(E)C, European (Economic) Community

cefalea *f* severe headache

ceg|**ador** *a* blinding. **~ar** [1 & 12] *vt* blind; (*tapar*) block up. **~ar** *vpr* be blinded (**de** by). **~ato** *a* short-sighted. **~uera** *f* blindness

ceja *f* eyebrow

cejar *vi* move back; (*fig*) give way

celada *f* ambush; (*fig*) trap

cela|**dor** *m* (*de niños*) monitor; (*de cárcel*) prison warder; (*de museo etc*) attendant. **~r** *vt* watch

celda *f* cell

celebra|**ción** *f* celebration. **~r** *vt* celebrate; (*alabar*) praise. **~rse** *vpr* take place

célebre *a* famous; (*fig, gracioso*) funny

celebridad *f* fame; (*persona*) celebrity

celeridad *f* speed

celest|**e** *a* heavenly. **~ial** *a* heavenly. **azul ~e** sky-blue

celibato *m* celibacy

célibe *a* celibate

celo *m* zeal. **~s** *mpl* jealousy. **dar ~s** make jealous. **papel** *m* **~** adhesive tape, Sellotape (P). **tener ~s** be jealous

celofán *m* cellophane

celoso *a* enthusiastic; *(que tiene celos)* jealous

celta *a* Celtic. —*m & f* Celt

céltico *a* Celtic

célula *f* cell

celular *a* cellular

celuloide *m* celluloid

celulosa *f* cellulose

cellisca *f* sleetstorm

cementerio *m* cemetery

cemento *m* cement; *(hormigón)* concrete; *(LAm, cola)* glue

cena *f* dinner; *(comida ligera)* supper. **~duría** *f (Mex)* restaurant

cenagal *m* marsh, bog; *(fig)* tight spot. **~oso** *a* muddy

cenar *vt* have for dinner; *(en cena ligera)* have for supper. —*vi* have dinner; *(tomar cena ligera)* have supper

cenicero *m* ashtray

cenit *m* zenith

ceniza *f* ash. **~o** *a* ashen. —*m* jinx

censo *m* census. **~ electoral** electoral roll

censura *f* censure; *(de prensa etc)* censorship. **~r** *vt* censure; censor *(prensa etc)*

centavo *a & m* hundredth; *(moneda)* centavo

centella *f* flash; *(chispa)* spark. **~ar** *vi,* **~ear** *vi* sparkle. **~eo** *m* sparkle, sparkling

centena *f* hundred. **~r** *m* hundred. **a ~res** by the hundred

centenario *a* centenary; *(persona)* centenarian. —*m* centenary; *(persona)* centenarian

centeno *m* rye

centésim|**a** *f* hundredth. **~o** *a* hundredth; *(moneda)* centésimo

centígrado *a* centigrade, Celsius. **~igramo** *m* centigram. **~ilitro** *m* centilitre. **~ímetro** *m* centimetre

céntimo *a* hundredth. —*m* cent

centinela *f* sentry

centolla *f,* **centollo** *m* spider crab

central *a* central. —*f* head office. **~ de correos** general post office. **~ eléctrica** power station. **~ nuclear** nuclear power station. **~ telefónica** telephone exchange. **~ismo** *m* centralism. **~ita** *f* switchboard

centraliza|**ción** *f* centralization. **~r** [10] *vt* centralize

centrar *vt* centre

céntrico *a* central

centrífugo *a* centrifugal

centro *m* centre. **~ comercial** shopping centre

Centroamérica *f* Central America

centroamericano *a & m* Central American

centuplicar [7] *vt* increase a hundredfold

ceñi|**do** *a* tight. **~r** [5 & 22] *vt* surround, encircle; *(vestido)* be a tight fit. **~rse** *vpr* limit o.s. (**a** to)

ceño *m* frown. **~udo** *a* frowning. **fruncir el ~o** frown

cepill|**ar** *vt* brush; *(en carpintería)* plane. **~o** *m* brush; *(en carpintería)* plane. **~o de dientes** toothbrush

cera *f* wax

cerámic|**a** *f* ceramics; *(materia)* pottery; *(objeto)* piece of pottery. **~o** *a* ceramic

cerca *f* fence. —*adv* near, close. **~s** *mpl* foreground. **~ de** *prep* near; *(con números, con tiempo)* nearly. **de ~** from close up, closely

cercado *m* enclosure

cercan|**ía** *f* nearness, proximity. **~ías** *fpl* outskirts. **tren** *m* **de ~ías** local train. **~o** *a* near, close. **C~o Oriente** *m* Near East

cercar [7] *vt* fence in, enclose; *(gente)* surround, crowd round; *(asediar)* besiege

cerciorar *vt* convince. **~se** *vpr* make sure, find out

cerco *m* (*grupo*) circle; (*cercado*) enclosure; (*asedio*) siege

Cerdeña *f* Sardinia

cerdo *m* pig; (*carne*) pork

cereal *m* cereal

cerebr|al *a* cerebral. **~o** *m* brain; (*fig, inteligencia*) intelligence, brains

ceremoni|a *f* ceremony. **~al** *a* ceremonial. **~oso** *a* ceremonious, stiff

céreo *a* wax

cerez|a *f* cherry. **~o** *m* cherry tree

cerill|a *f* match. **~o** *m* (*Mex*) match

cern|er [1] *vt* sieve. **~erse** *vpr* hover; (*fig, amenazar*) hang over. **~idor** *m* sieve

cero *m* nought, zero; (*fútbol*) nil (*Brit*), zero (*Amer*); (*tenis*) love; (*persona*) nonentity. **partir de ~** start from scratch

cerquillo *m* (*LAm, flequillo*) fringe

cerquita *adv* very near

cerra|do *a* shut, closed; (*espacio*) shut in, enclosed; (*cielo*) overcast; (*curva*) sharp. **~dura** *f* lock; (*acción de cerrar*) shutting, closing. **~jero** *m* locksmith. **~r** [1] *vt* shut, close; (*con llave*) lock; (*con cerrojo*) bolt; (*cercar*) enclose; turn off (*grifo*); block up (*agujero etc*). **—vi** shut, close. **~rse** *vpr* shut, close; (*herida*) heal. **~r con llave** lock

cerro *m* hill. **irse por los ~s de Úbeda** ramble on

cerrojo *m* bolt. **echar el ~** bolt

certamen *m* competition, contest

certero *a* accurate

certeza *f*, **certidumbre** *f* certainty

certifica|do *a* (*carta etc*) registered. **—m** certificate;

(*carta*) registered letter. **~r** [7] *vt* certify; register (*carta etc*)

certitud *f* certainty

cervato *m* fawn

cerve|cería *f* beerhouse, bar; (*fábrica*) brewery. **~za** *f* beer. **~za de barril** draught beer. **~za de botella** bottled beer

cesa|ción *f* cessation, suspension. **~nte** *a* out of work. **~r** *vt* stop. **—vi** stop, cease; (*dejar un empleo*) give up. **sin ~r** incessantly

cesáreo *a* Caesarian. **operación** *f* **cesárea** Caesarian section

cese *m* cessation; (*de un empleo*) dismissal

césped *m* grass, lawn

cest|a *f* basket. **~ada** *f* basketful. **~o** *m* basket. **~o de los papeles** waste-paper basket

cetro *m* sceptre; (*fig*) power

ciánuro *m* cyanide

ciática *f* sciatica

cibernética *f* cibernetics

cicatriz *f* scar. **~ación** *f* healing. **~ar** [10] *vt/i* heal. **~arse** *vpr* heal

ciclamino *m* cyclamen

cíclico *a* cyclic(al)

ciclis|mo *m* cycling. **~ta** *m & f* cyclist

ciclo *m* cycle; (*LAm, curso*) course

ciclomotor *m* moped

ciclón *m* cyclone

ciclostilo *m* cyclostyle, duplicating machine

ciego *a* blind. **—m** blind man, blind person. **a ciegas** in the dark

cielo *m* sky; (*relig*) heaven; (*persona*) darling. **¡~s!** good heavens!, goodness me!

ciempiés *m invar* centipede

cien *a* a hundred. **~ por ~** (*fam*) completely, one hundred per cent. **me pone a ~** it drives me mad

ciénaga *f* bog, swamp

ciencia *f* science; *(fig)* knowledge. **~s** *fpl (univ etc)* science. **~s empresariales** business studies. **saber a** **~ cierta** know for a fact, know for certain

cieno *m* mud

científico *a* scientific. —*m* scientist

ciento *a & m (delante de nombres, y numerales a los que multiplica* **cien)** a hundred, one hundred. **por ~** per cent

cierne *m* blossoming. **en ~** in blossom; *(fig)* in its infancy

cierre *m* fastener; *(acción de cerrar)* shutting, closing. **~ de cremallera** zip, zipper *(Amer)*

cierro *vb véase* **cerrar**

cierto *a* certain; *(verdad)* true. **estar en lo ~** be right. **lo ~ es que** the fact is that. **no es ~** that's not true. **¿no es ~?** right? **por ~** certainly, by the way. **si bien es ~ que** although

ciervo *m* deer

cifra *f* figure, number; *(cantidad)* sum. **~do a** coded. **~r** *vt* code; *(resumir)* summarize. **en ~** in code, in code

cigala *f* (Norway) lobster

cigarra *f* cicada

cigarr|illo *m* cigarette. **~o** *m (cigarillo)* cigarette; *(puro)* cigar

cigüeña *f* stork

cil|índrico *a* cylindrical. **~indro** *m* cylinder; *(Mex, organillo)* barrel organ

cima *f* top; *(fig)* summit

címbalo *m* cymbal

cimbrear *vt* shake. **~se** *vpr* sway

cimentar [1] *vt* lay the foundations of; *(fig, reforzar)* strengthen

cimer|a *f* crest. **~o** *a* highest

cimiento *m* foundations; *(fig)* source. **desde los ~s** from the very beginning

cinc *m* zinc

cincel *m* chisel. **~ar** *vt* chisel

cinco *a & m* five

cincuenta *a & m* fifty; *(quincuagésimo)* fiftieth. **~ón** *a* about fifty

cine *m* cinema. **~matografiar** [20] *vt* film

cinético *a* kinetic

cínico *a* cynical; *(desvergonzado)* shameless. —*m* cynic

cinismo *m* cynicism; *(desvergüenza)* shamelessness

cinta *f* band; *(adorno de pelo etc)* ribbon; *(película)* film; *(magnética)* tape; *(de máquina de escribir etc)* ribbon. **~ aisladora, ~ aislante** insulating tape. **~ magnetofónica** magnetic tape. **~ métrica** tape measure

cintur|a *f* waist. **~ón** *m* belt. **~ón de seguridad** safety belt. **~ón salvavidas** lifebelt

ciprés *m* cypress (tree)

circo *m* circus

circuito *m* circuit; *(viaje)* tour. **~ cerrado** closed circuit. **corto ~** short circuit

circula|ción *f* circulation; *(vehículos)* traffic. **~r** *a* circular. —*vt* circulate. —*vi* circulate; *(líquidos)* flow; *(conducir)* drive; *(autobús etc)* run

círculo *m* circle. **~ vicioso** vicious circle. **en ~** in a circle

circunci|dar *vt* circumcise. **~sión** *f* circumcision

circunda|nte *a* surrounding. **~r** *vt* surround

circunferencia *f* circumference

circunflejo *m* circumflex

circunscri|bir [*pp* **circunscrito**] *vt* confine. **~pción** *f (distrito)* district. **~pción electoral** constituency

circunspecto *a* wary, circumspect

circunstancia f circumstance. **~te** a surrounding. **—m** bystander. **los ~tes** those present

circunvalación f. **carretera** f **de ~** bypass, ring road

cirio m candle

ciruela f plum. **~ claudia** greengage. **~ damascena** damson

cirugía f surgery. **~jano** m surgeon

cisne m swan

cisterna f tank, cistern

cita f appointment; (entre chico y chica) date; (referencia) quotation. **~ción** f quotation; (jurid) summons. **~do** a aforementioned. **~r** vt make an appointment with; (mencionar) quote; (jurid) summons. **~rse** vpr arrange to meet

cítara f zither

ciudad f town; (grande) city. **~anía** f citizenship; (habitantes) citizens. **~ano** a civic **—m** citizen, inhabitant; (habitante de ciudad) city dweller

cívico a civic

civil a civil. **—m** civil guard. **~idad** f politeness

civilización f civilization. **~r** [10] vt civilize. **~rse** vpr become civilized

civismo m community spirit

cizaña f (fig) discord

clam|ar vi cry out, clamour. **~or** m cry; (griterío) noise, clamour; (protesta) outcry. **~oroso** a noisy

clandestin|idad f secrecy. **~o** a clandestine, secret

clara f (de huevo) egg white

claraboya f skylight

clarear vi dawn; (aclarar) brighten up. **~se** vpr be transparent

clarete m rosé

claridad f clarity; (luz) light

clarificación f clarification. **~r** [7] vt clarify

clarín m bugle

clarinet|e m clarinet; (músico) clarinettist. **~ista** m & f clarinettist

clarividen|cia f clairvoyance; (fig) far-sightedness. **~te** a clairvoyant; (fig) far-sighted

claro a (con mucha luz) bright; (transparente, evidente) clear; (colores) light; (líquido) thin. **—m** (en bosque etc) clearing; (espacio) gap. **—adv** clearly. **—int** of course! **~ de luna** moonlight. **¡~ que sí!** yes of course! **¡~ que no!** of course not!

clase f class; (aula) classroom. **~ media** middle class. **~ obrera** working class. **~ social** social class. **dar ~s** teach. **toda ~ de** all sorts of

clásico a classical; (fig) classic. **—m** classic

clasificación f classification; (deportes) league. **~r** [7] vt classify; (seleccionar) sort

claudia f greengage

claudicar [7] (ceder) give in; (cojear) limp

claustro m cloister; (univ) staff

claustrofobia f claustrophobia. **~óbico** a claustrophobic

cláusula f clause

clausura f closure; (ceremonia) closing ceremony. **~r** vt close

clav|ado a fixed; (con clavo) nailed. **~r** vt knock in (clavo); (introducir a mano) stick; (fijar) fix; (juntar) nail together. **es ~do a su padre** he's the spitting image of his father

clave f key; (mus) clef; (clavicémbalo) harpsichord

clavel m carnation

clavicémbalo m harpsichord

clavícula f collar bone, clavicle

clavija f peg; (elec) plug

clavo m nail; (culin) clove

claxon *m* (*pl* **claxons** /'klakson/)
horn

clemen|cia *f* clemency, mercy.
~te *a* clement, merciful

clementina *f* tangerine

cleptómano *m* kleptomaniac

cler|ecía *f* priesthood. **~ical** *a*
clerical

clérigo *m* priest

clero *m* clergy

cliché *m* cliché; (*foto*) negative

cliente *m & f* client, customer;
(*de médico*) patient. **~la** *f* clientele, customers; (*de médico*)
patients, practice

clim|a *m* climate. **~ático** *a* cli-
matic. **~atizado** *a* air-
conditioned. **~atológico** *a*
climatological

clínic|a *f* clinic. **~o** *a* clinical.
—*m* clinician

clip *m* (*pl* **clips**) clip

clo *m* cluck. **hacer ~ ~** cluck

cloaca *f* drain, sewer

cloque|ar *vi* cluck. **~o** *m*
clucking

cloro *m* chlorine

club *m* (*pl* **clubs** *o* **clubes**) club

coacci|ón *f* coercion, compul-
sion. **~onar** *vt* coerce, compel

coagular *vt* coagulate; clot (*sangre*); curdle (*leche*). **~se** *vpr*
coagulate; (*sangre*) clot; (*leche*)
curdle

coalición *f* coalition

coartada *f* alibi

coartar *vt* hinder; restrict (*libertad etc*)

cobard|e *a* cowardly. —*m*
coward. **~ía** *f* cowardice

cobaya *f*, **cobayo** *m* guinea pig

cobert|era *f* (*tapadera*) lid. **~izo**
m lean-to, shelter. **~or** *m* bedspread; (*manta*) blanket. **~ura** *f*
covering

cobij|a *f* (*LAm, ropa de cama*)
bedclothes; (*Mex, manta*) blanket. **~ar** *vt* shelter. **~arse** *vpr*

shelter, take shelter. **~o** *m*
shelter

cobra *f* cobra

cobra|dor *m* conductor. **~dora** *f*
conductress. **~r** *vt* collect;
(*ganar*) earn; charge (*precio*);
cash (*cheque*); (*recuperar*)
recover. —*vi* be paid. **~rse** *vpr*
recover

cobre *m* copper; (*mus*) brass
(instruments)

cobro *m* collection; (*de cheque*)
cashing; (*pago*) payment.
ponerse en ~ go into hiding.
presentar al ~ cash

cocada *f* (*LAm*) sweet coconut

cocaína *f* cocaine

cocción *f* cooking; (*tec*) baking,
firing

cocear *vt/i* kick

coc|er [2 & 9] *vt/i* cook; (*hervir*)
boil; (*en horno*) bake. **~ido** *a*
cooked. **~** *m* stew

cociente *m* quotient. **~ intelectual** intelligence quotient, IQ

cocin|a *f* kitchen; (*arte de coci-
nar*) cookery, cuisine; (*aparato*)
cooker. **~a de gas** gas cooker.
~a eléctrica electric cooker.
~ar *vt/i* cook. **~ero** *m* cook

coco *m* coconut; (*árbol*) coconut
palm; (*cabeza*) head; (*duende*)
bogeyman. **comerse el ~** think
hard

cocodrilo *m* crocodile

cocotero *m* coconut palm

cóctel *m* (*pl* **cócteles** *o* **cócteles**)
cocktail; (*reunión*) cocktail
party

coche *m* car (*Brit*), motor car
(*Brit*), automobile (*Amer*); (*de
tren*) coach, carriage. **~-cama**
sleeper. **~ fúnebre** hearse. **~ra**
f garage; (*de autobuses*) depot. **~
restaurante** dining-car. **~s de
choque** dodgems

cochin|ada *f* dirty thing. **~o** *a*
dirty, filthy. —*m* pig

cod|azo m nudge (with one's elbow); (Mex, aviso secreto) tip-off. ~**ear** vt/i elbow, nudge

codici|a f greed. ~**ado** a coveted, sought after. ~**ar** vt covet. ~**oso** a greedy (**de** for)

código m code. ~ **de la circulación** Highway Code

codo m elbow; (dobladura) bend. **hablar por los** ~**s** talk too much. **hasta los** ~**s** up to one's neck

codorniz f quail

coeducación f coeducation

coerción f coercion

coetáneo a contemporary

coexist|encia f coexistence. ~**ir** vi coexist

cofradía f brotherhood

cofre m chest

coger [14] vt (España) take; catch (tren, autobús, pelota, catarro); (agarrar) take hold of; (del suelo) pick up; pick (frutos etc). —vi (caber) fit. ~**se** upr trap, catch

cogollo m (de lechuga etc) heart; (fig, lo mejor) cream; (fig, núcleo) centre

cogote m back of the neck

cohech|ar vt bribe. ~**o** m bribery

coherente a coherent

cohesión f cohesion

cohete m rocket; (Mex, pistola) pistol

cohibi|ción f inhibition. ~**r** vt restrict; inhibit (persona). ~**rse** upr feel inhibited; (contenerse) restrain o.s.

coincid|encia f coincidence. ~**ente** a coincidental. ~**ir** vi coincide. **dar la** ~**encia** happen

coje|ar vt limp; (mueble) wobble. ~**ra** f lameness

coj|ín m cushion. ~**inete** m small cushion. ~**inete de bolas** ball bearing

cojo a lame; (mueble) wobbly. —m lame person

col f cabbage. ~**es de Bruselas** Brussel sprouts

cola f tail; (fila) queue; (para pegar) glue. **a la** ~ at the end. **hacer** ~ queue (up). **tener** ~, **traer** ~ have serious consequences

colabora|ción f collaboration. ~**dor** m collaborator. ~**r** vi collaborate

colada f washing. **hacer la** ~ do the washing

colador m strainer

colapso m collapse; (fig) stoppage

colar [2] vt strain (líquidos); (lavar) wash; pass (moneda falsa etc). —vi (líquido) seep through; (fig) be believed, wash (fam). ~**se** upr slip; (no hacer caso de la cola) jump the queue; (en fiesta) gatecrash; (meter la pata) put one's foot in it

colcha f bedspread. ~**ón** m mattress. ~**oneta** f mattress

colear vi wag its tail; (asunto) not be resolved. **vivito y coleando** alive and kicking

colec|ción f collection; (fig, gran número de) a lot of. ~**onar** vt collect. ~**onista** m & f collector

colecta f collection

colectiv|idad f community. ~**o** a collective. —m (Arg) minibus

colector m (en las alcantarillas) main sewer

colega m & f colleague

colegi|al m schoolboy. ~**ala** f schoolgirl. ~**o** m private school; (de ciertas profesiones) college. ~**o mayor** hall of residence

colegir [5 & 14] vt gather

cólera f cholera; (ira) anger, fury. **descargar su** ~ vent one's anger. **montar en** ~ fly into a rage

colérico a furious, irate

colesterol m cholesterol

coleta f pigtail

colga|nte *a* hanging. —*m* pendant. ~**r** [2 & 12] *vt* hang; hang out ⟨*colada*⟩; hang up ⟨*abrigo etc*⟩. —*vi* hang; ⟨*teléfono*⟩ hang up, ring off. ~**rse** *vpr* hang o.s. **dejar a uno** ~**do** let s.o. down

cólico *m* colic

coliflor *m* cauliflower

colilla *f* cigarette end

colina *f* hill

colinda|nte *a* adjacent. ~**r** *vt* border (**con** on)

colisión *f* collision, crash; (*fig*) clash

colmar *vt* fill to overflowing; (*fig*) fulfill. ~ **a uno de amabilidad** overwhelm s.o. with kindness

colmena *f* beehive, hive

colmillo *m* eye tooth, canine (tooth); (*de elefante*) tusk; (*de otros animales*) fang

colmo *m* height. **ser el** ~ be the limit, be the last straw

coloca|ción *f* positioning; (*empleo*) job, position. ~**r** [7] *vt* put, place; (*buscar empleo*) find work for. ~**rse** *vpr* find a job

Colombia *f* Colombia

colombiano *a* & *m* Colombian

colon *m* colon

colón *m* (*unidad monetaria de Costa Rica y El Salvador*) colón

Colonia *f* Cologne

coloni|a *f* colony; (*agua de colonia*) eau-de-Cologne; (*LAm, barrio*) suburb. ~**a de verano** holiday camp. ~**al** *a* colonial. ~**ales** *mpl* overseas foodstuffs; (*comestibles en general*) groceries. ~**alista** *m* & *f* colonialist. ~**zación** *f* colonization. ~**zar** [10] colonize

coloqui|al *a* colloquial. ~**o** *m* conversation; (*congreso*) conference

color *m* colour. ~**ado** *a* (*rojo*) red. ~**ante** *m* colouring. ~**ar** *vt* colour. ~**ear** *vt/i* colour. ~**ete**

m rouge. ~**ido** *m* colour. **de** ~ colour. **en** ~ (*fotos, película*) colour

colosal *a* colossal; (*fig, magnífico, fam*) terrific

columna *f* column; (*fig, apoyo*) support

columpi|ar *vt* swing. ~**arse** *vpr* swing. ~**o** *m* swing

collar *m* necklace; (*de perro etc*) collar

coma *f* comma. —*m* (*med*) coma

comadre *f* midwife; (*madrina*) godmother; (*vecina*) neighbour. ~**ar** *vi* gossip

comadreja *f* weasel

comadrona *f* midwife

comand|ancia *f* command. ~**ante** *m* commander. ~**o** *m* command; (*soldado*) commando

comarca *f* area, region

comba *f* bend; (*juguete*) skipping-rope. ~**r** *vt* bend. ~**rse** *vpr* bend. **saltar a la** ~ skip

combat|e *m* fight; (*fig*) struggle. ~**iente** *m* fighter. ~**ir** *vt/i* fight

combina|ción *f* combination; (*bebida*) cocktail; (*arreglo*) plan, scheme; (*prenda*) slip. ~**r** *vt* combine; (*arreglar*) arrange; (*armonizar*) match, go well with. ~**rse** *vpr* combine; (*ponerse de acuerdo*) agree (**para** to)

combustible *m* fuel

comedia *f* comedy; (*cualquier obra de teatro*) play. **hacer la** ~ pretend

comedi|do *a* reserved. ~**rse** [5] *vpr* be restrained

comedor *m* dining-room; (*restaurante*) restaurant; (*persona*) glutton. **ser buen** ~ have a good appetite

comensal *m* companion at table, fellow diner

comentar *vt* comment on; (*anotar*) annotate. **~io** *m* commentary; (*observación*) comment; (*fam*) gossip. **~ista** *m & f* commentator

comenzar [1 & 10] *vt/i* begin, start

comer *vt* eat; (*a mediodía*) have for lunch; (*corroer*) eat away; (*en ajedrez*) take. — *vi* eat; (*a mediodía*) have lunch. **~se** *vpr* eat (up). **dar de ~ a** feed

comercial *a* commercial. **~ante** *m* trader; (*de tienda*) shopkeeper. **~ar** *vt* trade (con, en in); (*con otra persona*) do business. **~o** *m* commerce; (*actividad*) trade; (*tienda*) shop; (*negocio*) business

comestible *a* edible. **~s** *mpl* food. **tienda de ~s** grocer's (shop) (*Brit*), grocery (*Amer*)

cometa *m* comet. —*f* kite

comet|er *vt* commit; make (*falta*). **~ido** *m* task

comezón *m* itch

comicastro *m* poor actor, ham (*fam*)

comicios *mpl* elections

cómico *a* comic(al). —*m* comic actor; (*cualquier actor*) actor

comida *f* food; (*a mediodía*) lunch. **hacer la ~** prepare the meals

comidilla *f* topic of conversation. **ser la ~ del pueblo** be the talk of the town

comienzo *m* beginning, start. **a ~s de** at the beginning of

comilón *a* greedy. **~ona** *f* feast

comillas *fpl* inverted commas

comino *m* cumin. **(no) me importa un ~** I couldn't care less

comisar|ía *f* police station. **~io** *m* commissioner; (*deportes*) steward. **~io de policía** police superintendent

comisión *f* assignment; (*comité*) commission, committee; (*com*) commission

comisura *f* corner. **~ de los labios** corner of the mouth

comité *m* committee

como *adv* as. —*conj* as; (*en cuanto*) as soon as. **~ quieras** as you like. **~ sabes** as you know. **~ si** as if

cómo *a* how? ¿~? I beg your pardon? ¿~ está Vd? how are you? ¡~ no! (*esp LAm*) of course! ¿~ son? what are they like? ¿~ te llamas? what's your name? ¡y ~! and how!

cómoda *f* chest of drawers

comodidad *f* comfort. **a su ~** at your convenience

cómodo *a* comfortable; (*útil*) handy

comoquiera *conj.* **~ que** since. **~ que sea** however it may be

compacto *a* compact; (*denso*) dense; (*líneas etc*) close

compadecer [11] *vt* feel sorry for. **~se** *vpr.* **~se de** feel sorry for

compadre *m* godfather; (*amigo*) friend

compañ|ero *m* companion; (*de trabajo*) colleague; (*amigo*) friend. **~ía** *f* company. **en ~ía de** with

comparable *a* comparable. **~ción** *f* comparison. **~r** *vt* compare. **~tivo** *a & m* comparative. **en ~ción con** in comparison with, compared with

comparecer [11] *vi* appear

comparsa *f* group; (*en el teatro*) extra

compartimiento *m* compartment

compartir *vt* share

compás *m* (*instrumento*) (pair of) compasses; (*ritmo*) rhythm; (*división*) bar (*Brit*), measure

(*Amer*); (*naut*) compass. **a ~ in time**

compasión *f* compassion, pity. **tener ~ón de** feel sorry for. **~vo a** compassionate

compatibilidad *f* compatibility. **~le a** compatible

compatriota *m & f* compatriot

compeler *vt* compel, force

compendiar *vt* summarize. **~o** *m* summary

compenetración *f* mutual understanding

compensación *f* compensation. **~ción por despido** redundancy payment. **~r** *vt* compensate

competencia *f* competition; (*capacidad*) competence; (*terreno*) field, scope. **~te a** competent; (*apropiado*) appropriate, suitable

competición *f* competition. **~dor** *m* competitor. **~r** [5] *vi* compete

compilar *vt* compile

compinche *m* accomplice; (*amigo, fam*) friend, mate (*fam*)

complacencia *f* pleasure; (*indulgencia*) indulgence. **~er** [32] *vt* please; (*prestar servicio*) help. **~erse** *vpr* have pleasure, be pleased. **~iente** *a* helpful; (*marido*) complaisant

complejidad *f* complexity. **~o** *a* & *m* complex

complementario *a* complementary. **~o** *m* complement; (*gram*) object, complement

completar *vt* complete. **~o** *a* complete; (*lleno*) full; (*perfecto*) perfect

complexión *f* disposition; (*constitución*) constitution

complicación *f* complication. **~r** [7] *vt* complicate; involve (*persona*). **~rse** *vpr* become complicated

cómplice *m* accomplice

complot *m* (*pl* **complots**) plot

componente *a* component. **—m** component; (*culin*) ingredient; (*miembro*) member. **~er** [34] *vt* make up; (*mus, literatura etc*) write, compose; (*reparar*) mend; (*culin*) prepare; (*arreglar*) restore; settle (*estómago*); reconcile (*diferencias*). **~erse** *vpr* be made up; (*arreglarse*) get ready. **~érselas** manage

comportamiento *m* behaviour. **~r** *vt* involve. **~rse** *vpr* behave. **~rse como es debido** behave properly. **~rse mal** misbehave

composición *f* composition. **~tor** *m* composer

compostelano *a* from Santiago de Compostela. **—m** native of Santiago de Compostela

compostura *f* composition; (*arreglo*) repair; (*culin*) condiment; (*comedimiento*) composure

compota *f* stewed fruit

compra *f* purchase. **~ a plazos** hire purchase. **~dor** *m* buyer; (*en una tienda*) customer. **~r** *vt* buy. **~venta** *f* dealing. **hacer la ~, ir a la ~, ir de ~s** do the shopping, go shopping. **negocio** *m* **de ~venta** second-hand shop

comprender *vt* understand; (*incluir*) include. **~sible** *a* understandable. **~sión** *f* understanding. **~sivo** *a* understanding; (*que incluye*) comprehensive

compresa *f* compress; (*de mujer*) sanitary towel

compresión *f* compression. **~imido** *a* compressed. **—m** pill, tablet. **~imir** *vt* compress; keep back (*lágrimas*), (*fig*) restrain

comprobante *m* (*recibo*) receipt. **~r** *vt* check; (*confirmar*) confirm

comprometer *vt* compromise; (*arriesgar*) endanger. **~erse** *vpr* compromise o.s.; (*obligarse*) agree to. **~ido** *a* (*situación*) awkward, embarrassing

compromiso *m* obligation; (*apuro*) predicament; (*cita*) appointment; (*acuerdo*) agreement. **sin ~** without obligation

compuesto *a* compound; (*persona*) smart. **—** *m* compound

compungido *a* sad, sorry

computador *m*, **computadora** *f* computer

computar *vt* calculate

cómputo *m* calculation

comulgar [12] *vi* take Communion

común *a* common. **—** *m* community. **en ~** in common. **por lo ~** generally

comunal *a* municipal, communal

comunica|ción *f* communication. **~do** *m* communiqué. **~do a la prensa** press release. **~r** [7] *vt/i* communicate; pass on (*enfermedad, información*). **~rse** *vpr* communicate; (*enfermedad*) spread. **~tivo** *a* communicative. **está ~ndo** (*al teléfono*) it's engaged, the line's engaged

comunidad *f* community. **~ de vecinos** residents' association. **C~ (Económica) Europea** European (Economic) Community. **en ~** together

comunión *f* communion; (*relig*) (Holy) Communion

comunis|mo *m* communism. **~ta** *a & m & f* communist

comúnmente *adv* generally, usually

con *prep* with; (*a pesar de*) in spite of; (+ *infinitivo*) by. **~ decir la verdad** by telling the truth. **~ que** so. **~ tal que** as long as

conato *m* attempt

concatenación *f* chain, linking

cóncavo *a* concave

concebir [5] *vt/i* conceive

conceder *vt* concede, grant; award (*premio*); (*admitir*) admit

concejal *m* councillor. **~o** *m* town council

concentra|ción *f* concentration. **~do** *m* concentrated. **~r** *vt* concentrate. **~rse** *vpr* concentrate

concep|ción *f* conception. **~to** *m* concept; (*opinión*) opinion. **bajo ningún ~to** in no way. **en mi ~to** in my view. **por ningún ~to** in no way

concerniente *a* concerning. **en lo ~ a** with regard to

concertar [1] *vt* (*mus*) harmonize; (*coordinar*) coordinate; (*poner de acuerdo*) agree. **—***vi* be in tune; (*fig*) agree. **~se** *vpr* agree

concertina *f* concertina

concesión *f* concession

conciencia *f* conscience; (*conocimiento*) consciousness. **~ción** *f* awareness. **~ limpia** clear conscience. **~ sucia** guilty conscience. **a ~ de que** fully aware that. **en ~** honestly. **tener ~ de** be aware of. **tomar ~ de** become aware of

concienzudo *a* conscientious

concierto *m* concert; (*acuerdo*) agreement; (*mus, composición*) concerto

concilia|ble *a* reconcilable. **~ción** *f* reconciliation. **~r** *vt* reconcile. **~r el sueño** get to sleep. **~rse** *vpr* gain

concilio *m* council

conciso *m* concise

conciudadano *m* fellow citizen

conclu|ir [17] *vt* finish; (*deducir*) conclude. **—***vi* finish, end. **~irse** *vpr* finish, end. **~sión** *f* conclusion. **~yente** *a* conclusive

concord|ancia *f* agreement. **~ar** [2] *vt* reconcile. **—***vi* agree. **~e** *a* in agreement. **~ia** *f* harmony

concret|amente *adv* specifically, to be exact. **~ar** *vt* make specific. **~arse** *vpr* become definite; (*limitarse*) confine o.s. **~o** *a* concrete; (*determinado*) specific, particular. **—m** (*LAm, hormigón*) concrete. **en ~o** definite; (*concretamente*) to be exact; (*en resumen*) in short

concurr|encia *f* coincidence; (*reunión*) crowd, audience. **~ido** *a* crowded, busy. **~ir** *vi* meet; (*asistir*) attend; (*coincidir*) coincide; (*contribuir*) contribute; (*en concurso*) compete

concurs|ante *m & f* competitor, contestant. **~ar** *vi* compete, take part. **~o** *m* competition; (*concurrencia*) crowd; (*ayuda*) help

concha *f* shell; (*carey*) tortoiseshell

condado *m* county

conde *m* earl, count

condena *f* sentence. **~ción** *f* condemnation. **~do** *m* convict. **~r** *vt* condemn; (*jurid*) convict

condensa|ción *f* condensation. **~r** *vt* condense. **~rse** *vpr* condense

condesa *f* countess

condescende|ncia *f* condescension; (*tolerancia*) indulgence. **~r** [1] *vi* agree; (*dignarse*) condescend

condici|ón *f* condition; (*naturaleza*) nature. **~onado** *a*, **~onal** *a* conditional. **~onar** *vt* condition. **a ~ón de (que)** on the condition that

condiment|ar *vt* season. **~o** *m* condiment

condolencia *f* condolence

condominio *m* joint ownership

condón *m* condom

condonar *vt* (*perdonar*) reprieve; cancel (*deuda*)

conducir [47] *vt* drive (*vehículo*); carry (*electricidad, gas, agua*

etc). **—vi** drive; (*fig, llevar*) lead. **~se** *vpr* behave. **¿a qué conduce?** what's the point?

conducta *f* behaviour

conducto *m* pipe, tube; (*anat*) duct. **por ~ de** through

conductor *m* driver; (*jefe*) leader; (*elec*) conductor

conduzco *vb véase* **conducir**

conectar *vt/i* connect; (*enchufar*) plug in

conejo *m* rabbit

conexión *f* connection

confabularse *vpr* plot

confecci|ón *f* making; (*prenda*) ready-made garment. **~ones** *fpl* clothing, clothes. **~onado** *a* ready-made. **~onar** *vt* make

confederación *f* confederation

conferencia *f* conference; (*al teléfono*) long-distance call; (*univ etc*) lecture. **~ cumbre, ~ en la cima, ~ en la cumbre** summit conference. **~nte** *m & f* lecturer

conferir [4] *vt* confer; award (*premio*)

confes|ar [1] *vt/i* confess. **~arse** *vpr* confess. **~ión** *f* confession. **~ional** *a* confessional. **~ionario** *m* confessional. **~or** *m* confessor

confeti *m* confetti

confia|do *a* trusting; (*seguro de sí mismo*) confident. **~nza** *f* trust; (*en sí mismo*) confidence; (*intimidad*) familiarity. **~r** [20] *vt* entrust. **—vi** trust. **~rse** *vpr* put one's trust in

confiden|cia *f* confidence, secret. **~cial** *a* confidential. **~te** *m & f* close friend; (*de policía*) informer

configuración *f* configuration, shape

confín *m* border. **~ar** *vt* confine; (*desterrar*) banish. **—vi** border (**con** on). **~ines** *mpl* outermost parts

confirma|ción f confirmation. **~r** vt confirm.

confiscar [7] vt confiscate

confit|ería f sweet-shop (Brit), candy store (Amer). **~ura** f jam

conflagración f conflagration

conflicto m conflict

confluencia f confluence

conforma|ción f conformation, shape. **~r** vt (acomodar) adjust. **—vi** agree. **~rse** upr conform

conform|e a in agreement; (contento) happy, satisfied; (según) according (**con** to). **—conj** as. **—int** OK! **~e a** in accordance with, according to. **~idad** f agreement; (tolerancia) resignation. **~ista** m & f conformist

conforta|ble a comfortable. **~nte** a comforting. **~r** vt comfort

confronta|ción f confrontation; (comparación) comparison. **~r** vt confront; (comparar) compare

confu|ndir vt blur; (equivocar) mistake, confuse; (perder) lose; (mezclar) mix up, confuse. **~ndirse** upr become confused; (equivocarse) make a mistake. **~sión** f confusion; (vergüenza) embarrassment. **~so** a confused; (avergonzado) embarrassed

congela|do a frozen. **~dor** m freezer. **~r** vt freeze

congeniar vi get on

congesti|ón f congestion. **~onado** a congested. **~onar** vt congest. **~onarse** upr become congested

congoja f distress

congraciar vt win over. **~se** upr ingratiate o.s.

congratular vt congratulate

congrega|ción f gathering; (relig) congregation. **~rse** [12] upr gather, assemble

congres|ista m & f delegate, member of a congress. **~o** m congress, conference. **C~o de los Diputados** House of Commons

cónico a conical

conífer|a f conifer. **~o** a coniferous

conjetura f conjecture, guess. **~r** vt conjecture, guess

conjuga|ción f conjugation. **~r** [12] vt conjugate

conjunción f conjunction

conjunto a joint. **—m** collection; (mus) band; (ropa) suit, outfit. **en ~** altogether

conjura f, **conjuración** f conspiracy

conjurar vt plot, conspire

conmemora|ción f commemoration. **~r** vt commemorate. **~tivo** a commemorative

conmigo pron with me

conminar vt threaten; (avisar) warn

conmiseración f commiseration

conmo|ción f shock; (tumulto) upheaval; (terremoto) earthquake. **~cionar** vt shock. **~ cerebral** concussion. **~ver** [2] vt shake; (emocionar) move

conmuta|dor m switch. **~r** vt exchange

connivencia f connivance

connota|ción f connotation. **~r** vt connote

cono m cone

conoc|edor a & m expert. **~er** [11] vt know; (por primera vez) meet; (reconocer) recognize, know. **~erse** upr know o.s.; (dos personas) know each other; (notarse) be obvious. **dar a ~er** make known. **darse a ~er** make o.s. known. **~ido** a well-known. **—m** acquaintance. **~imiento** m knowledge; (sentido) consciousness; (*conocido*) acquaintance. **perder el ~imiento** faint. **se ~e que** apparently. **tener ~imiento de** know about

conozco *vb véase* **conocer**

conque *conj* so

conquense *a* from Cuenca. —*m* native of Cuenca

conquista *f* conquest. **~dor** *a* conquering. —*m* conqueror; (*de América*) conquistador; (*fig*) lady-killer. **~r** *vt* conquer, win

consabido *a* well-known

consagra|ción *f* consecration. **~r** *vt* consecrate; (*fig*) devote. **~rse** *vpr* devote o.s.

consanguíneo *m* blood relation

consciente *a* conscious

consecución *f* acquisition; (*de un deseo*) realization

consecuen|cia *f* consequence; (*firmeza*) consistency. **~te** *a* consistent. **a ~cia de** as a result of. **en ~cia, por ~cia** consequently

consecutivo *a* consecutive

conseguir [5 & 13] *vt* get, obtain; (*lograr*) manage; achieve *⟨objetivo⟩*

conseja *f* story, fable

consej|ero *m* adviser; (*miembro de consejo*) member. **~o** *m* advice; (*pol*) council. **~o de ministros** cabinet

consenso *m* assent, consent

consenti|do *a* *⟨niño⟩* spoilt. **~miento** *m* consent. **~r** [4] *vt* allow. —*vi* consent. **~rse** *vpr* break

conserje *m* porter, caretaker. **~ría** *f* porter's office

conserva *f* preserves; (*mermelada*) jam, preserve; (*en lata*) tinned food. **~ción** *f* conservation; (*de alimentos*) preservation; (*de edificio*) maintenance. **en ~** preserved

conservador *a & m* (*pol*) conservative

conservar *vt* keep; preserve *⟨alimentos⟩*. **~se** *vpr* keep; (*costumbre etc*) survive

conservatorio *m* conservatory

considera|ble *a* considerable. **~ción** *f* consideration; (*respeto*) respect. **~do** *a* considered; (*amable*) considerate; (*respetado*) respected. **~r** *vt* consider; (*respetar*) respect. **de ~ción** considerable. **de su ~ción** (*en cartas*) yours faithfully. **tomar en ~ción** take into consideration

consigna *f* order; (*rail*) left luggage office (*Brit*), baggage room (*Amer*); (*eslogan*) slogan

consigo *pron* (*él*) with him; (*ella*) with her; (*Ud, Uds*) with you; (*uno mismo*) with o.s.

consiguiente *a* consequent. **por ~** consequently

consist|encia *f* consistency. **~ente** *a* consisting (*en* of); (*firme*) solid. **~ir** *vi* consist (*en* of); (*deberse*) be due (*en* to)

consola|ción *f* consolation. **~r** [2] *vt* console, comfort

consolidar *vt* consolidate. **~se** *vpr* consolidate

consomé *m* clear soup, consommé

consonan|cia *f* consonance. **~te** *a* consonant. —*f* consonant

consorcio *m* consortium

consorte *m & f* consort

conspicuo *a* eminent; (*visible*) visible

conspira|ción *f* conspiracy. **~dor** *m* conspirator. **~r** *vi* conspire

constan|cia *f* constancy. **~te** *a* constant

constar *vi* be clear; (*figurar*) appear, figure; (*componerse*) consist. **hacer ~** point out. **me consta que** I'm sure that. **que conste que** believe me

constatar *vt* check; *(confirmar)* confirm

constelación *f* constellation

consternación *f* consternation

constipa|**do** *m* cold. —*a.* estar **~do** have a cold. **~rse** *vpr* catch a cold

constitu|**ción** *f* constitution; *(establecimiento)* setting up. **~cional** *a* constitutional. **~ir** [17] *vt* constitute; *(formar)* form; *(crear)* set up, establish. **~irse** *vpr* set o.s. up (en as); *(presentarse)* appear. **~tivo** *a*, **~yente** *a* constituent

constreñir [5 & 22] *vt* force, oblige; *(restringir)* restrain

constricción *f* constriction

constru|**cción** *f* construction. **~ctor** *m* builder. **~ir** [17] *vt* construct; build *(edificio)*

consuelo *m* consolation, comfort

consuetudinario *a* customary

cónsul *m* consul

consula|**do** *m* consulate. **~r** *a* consular

consult|**a** *f* consultation. **~ar** *vt* consult. **~orio** *m* surgery. **~orio sentimental** problem page. **horas** *fpl* **de ~a** surgery hours. **obra** *f* **de ~a** reference book

consumar *vt* complete; commit *(crimen)*; consummate *(matrimonio)*

consum|**ición** *f* consumption; *(bebida)* drink; *(comida)* food. **~ido** *a* *(persona)* skinny, wasted; *(frutas)* shrivelled. **~idor** *m* consumer. **~ir** *vt* consume. **~irse** *vpr* *(persona)* waste away; *(cosa)* wear out; *(quedarse seco)* dry up. **~ismo** *m* consumerism. **~o** *m* consumption

contab|**ilidad** *f* book-keeping; *(profesión)* accountancy. **~le** *m* & *f* accountant

contacto *m* contact. **ponerse en ~ con** get in touch with

contado *a* counted. **~s** *apl* few. **~r** *m* meter; *(LAm, contable)* accountant. **al ~** cash

contagi|**ar** *vt* infect *(persona)*; pass on *(enfermedd)*; *(fig)* contaminate. **~o** *m* infection. **~oso** *a* infectious

contamina|**ción** *f* contamination, pollution. **~r** *vt* contaminate, pollute

contante a. dinero ~ cash

contar [2] *vt* count; tell *(relato)*. —*vi* count. **~ con** rely on, count on. **~se** *vpr* be included *(entre* among); *(decirse)* be said

contempla|**ción** *f* contemplation. **~r** *vt* look at; *(fig)* contemplate. **sin ~ciones** unceremoniously

contemporáneo *a & m* contemporary

contend|**er** [1] *vi* compete. **~iente** *m & f* competitor

conten|**er** [40] *vt* contain; *(restringir)* restrain. **~erse** *vpr* restrain o.s. **~ido** *a* contained. —*m* contents

content|**ar** *vt* please. **~arse** *vpr*. **~arse de** be satisfied with, be pleased with. **~o** *a* *(alegre)* happy; *(satisfecho)* pleased

contesta|**ción** *f* answer. **~dor** *m*. **~ automático** answering machine. **~r** *vt/i* answer; *(replicar)* answer back

contexto *m* context

contienda *f* struggle

contigo *pron* with you

contiguo *a* adjacent

continen|**cia** *f* continence. **~tal** *a* continental. **~te** *m* continent

contingen|**cia** *f* contingency. **~te** *a* contingent. —*m* contingent; *(cuota)* quota

continu|**ación** *f* continuation. **~ar** [21] *vt* continue, resume.

~*ví* continue. ~**ará** (*en revista, TV etc*) to be continued. ~**idad** *f* continuity. ~**o** *a* continuous; (*muy frecuente*) continual. **co-rriente** *f* ~**a** direct current

contorno *m* outline; (*geog*) contour. ~**s** *mpl* surrounding area

contorsión *f* contortion

contra *adv & prep* against. —*m* cons. **en** ~ against

contralmirante *m* rear-admiral

contraata|**car** [7] *vt/i* counter-attack. ~**que** *m* counter-attack

contrabajo *m* double-bass; (*persona*) double-bass player

contrabalancear *vt* counter-balance

contraband|**ista** *m & f* smuggler. ~**o** *m* contraband

contracción *f* contraction

contrachapado *m* plywood

contrad|**ecir** [46] *vt* contradict. ~**icción** *f* contradiction. ~**ictorio** *a* contradictory

contraer [41] *vt* contract. ~**matrimonio** marry. ~**se** *vpr* contract; (*limitarse*) limit o.s.

contrafuerte *m* buttress

contragolpe *m* backlash

contrahecho *a* fake; (*moneda*) counterfeit; (*persona*) hunch-backed

contraindicación *f* contra-indication

contralto *m* alto. —*f* contralto

contramano. a ~ in the wrong direction

contrapartida *f* compensation

contrapelo. a ~ the wrong way

contrapes|**ar** *vt* counterbalance. ~**o** *m* counterbalance

contraponer [34] oppose; (*comparar*) compare

contraproducente *a* counter-productive

contrari|**ar** [20] *vt* oppose; (*molestar*) annoy. ~**edad** *f* obstacle; (*disgusto*) annoyance. ~**o**

a contrary; (*dirección*) opposite; (*persona*) opposed. **al** ~**o** on the contrary. **al** ~**o de** contrary to. **de lo** ~**o** otherwise. **en** ~**o** against. **llevar la** ~**a** contradict. **por el** ~**o** on the contrary

contrarrestar *vt* counteract

contrasentido *m* contradiction

contraseña *f* secret mark; (*palabra*) password

contrast|**ar** *vt* check, verify. —*vi* contrast. ~**e** *m* contrast; (*en oro, plata etc*) hallmark

contratar *vt* sign a contract for; engage (*empleados*)

contratiempo *m* setback; (*accidente*) accident

contrat|**ista** *m & f* contractor. ~**o** *m* contract

contraven|**ción** *f* contravention. ~**ir** [53] *vi.* ~**ir a** contravene

contraventana *f* shutter

contribu|**ción** *f* contribution; (*tributo*) tax. ~**ir** [17] *vt/i* contribute. ~**yente** *m & f* contributor; (*que paga impuestos*) taxpayer

contrincante *m* rival, opponent

contrito *a* contrite

control *m* control; (*inspección*) check. ~**ar** *vt* control; (*examinar*) check

controversia *f* controversy

contundente *a* (*arma*) blunt; (*argumento etc*) convincing

conturbar *vt* perturb

contusión *f* bruise

convalec|**encia** *f* convalescence. ~**er** [11] *vi* convalesce. ~**iente** *a & m & f* convalescent

convalidar *vt* confirm; recognize (*título*)

convenc|**er** [9] *vt* convince. ~**imiento** *m* conviction

convenci|**ón** *f* convention. ~**onal** *a* conventional

conveni|**encia** *f* convenience; (*aptitud*) suitability. ~**encias** (**sociales**) conventions. ~**ente**

a suitable; (*aconsejable*) advisable; (*provechoso*) useful, advantageous. **~o** *m* agreement. **~r** [53] *vt* agree. —*vi* agree; (*ser conveniente*) be convenient for, suit; (*ser aconsejable*) be advisable

convento *m* (*de monjes*) monastery; (*de monjas*) convent

convergente *a* converging

converger [14] *vi*, **convergir** [14] *vi* converge

conversa|ción *f* conversation. **~r** *vi* converse, talk

conver|sión *f* conversion. **~so** *a* converted. —*m* convert. **~tible** *a* convertible. **~tir** [4] *vt* convert. **~tirse** *vpr* be converted

convexo *a* convex

convic|ción *f* conviction. **~to** *a* convicted

convidar *vt* invite. **te convido a un helado** I'll treat you to an ice-cream

convincente *a* convincing

convite *m* invitation; (*banquete*) banquet

conviv|encia *f* coexistence. **~ir** *vi* live together

convocar [7] *vt* convene (*reunión*); summon (*personas*)

convoy *m* convoy; (*rail*) train; (*vinagrera*) cruet

convulsión *f* convulsion; (*fig*) upheaval

conyugal *a* conjugal; (*vida*) married

cónyuge *m* spouse. **~s** *mpl* (married) couple

coñac *m* (*pl* **coñacs**) brandy

coopera|ción *f* co-operation. **~r** *vi* co-operate. **~tiva** *f* co-operative. **~tivo** *a* co-operative

coord|enada *f* coordinate. **~inación** *f* co-ordination. **~inar** *vt* co-ordinate

copa *f* glass; (*deportes*, *fig*) cup. **~s** *fpl* (*naipes*) hearts. **tomar una ~** have a drink

copia *f* copy. **~ en limpio** fair copy. **~r** *vt* copy. **sacar una ~** make a copy

copioso *a* copious; (*lluvia*, *nevada etc*) heavy

copla *f* verse; (*canción*) song

copo *m* flake. **~ de nieve** snow-flake. **~s de maíz** cornflakes

coquet|a *f* flirt; (*mueble*) dressing-table. **~ear** *vi* flirt. **~eo** *m* flirtation. **~o** *a* flirtatious

coraje *m* courage; (*rabia*) anger. **dar ~** make mad, make furious

coral *a* choral. —*m* (*materia*, *animal*) coral

Corán *m* Koran

coraza *f* (*naut*) armour-plating; (*de tortuga*) shell

coraz|ón *m* heart; (*persona*) darling. **~onada** *f* hunch; (*impulso*) impulse. **sin ~ón** heartless. **tener buen ~ón** be good-hearted

corbata *f* tie, necktie (*esp Amer*). **~ de lazo** bow tie

corcova *f* hump. **~do** *a* hunchbacked

corchea *f* quaver

corchete *m* fastener, hook and eye; (*gancho*) hook; (*paréntesis*) square bracket

corcho *m* cork

cordel *m* cord, thin rope

cordero *m* lamb

cordial *a* cordial, friendly. —*m* tonic. **~idad** *f* cordiality, warmth

cordillera *f* mountain range

córdoba *m* (*unidad monetaria de Nicaragua*) córdoba

Córdoba *f* Cordova

cordón *m* string; (*de zapatos*) lace; (*cable*) flex; (*fig*) cordon. **~ umbilical** umbilical cord

corear *vt* chant

coreografía *f* choreography

corista *m* & *f* member of the chorus. —*f* (*bailarina*) chorus girl

cornet|a f bugle. **~ín** m cornet

Cornualles m Cornwall

cornucopia f cornucopia

cornudo a horned. **—m** cuckold

coro m chorus; (*relig*) choir

corona f crown; (*de flores*) wreath, garland. **~ción** f coronation. **~r** vt crown

coronel m colonel

coronilla f crown. **estar hasta la ~** be fed up

corporación f corporation

corporal a corporal

corpulento a stout

corpúsculo m corpuscle

corral m pen. **aves** fpl **de ~** poultry

correa f strap; (*de perro*) lead; (*cinturón*) belt

correc|**ción** f correction; (*reprensión*) rebuke; (*cortesía*) good manners. **~to** a correct; (*cortés*) polite

corre|**dizo** a running. **nudo ~dizo** slip knot. **puerta** f **~diza** sliding door. **~dor** m runner; (*pasillo*) corridor; (*agente*) agent, broker. **~dor automovilista** racing driver

corregir [5 & 14] vt correct; (*reprender*) rebuke

correlación f correlation. **~onar** vt correlate

correo m courier; (*correos*) post, mail; (*tren*) mail train. **~s** mpl post office. **echar al ~** post

correr vt run; (*viajar*) travel; draw (*cortinas*). **—vi** run; (*agua, electricidad etc*) flow; (*tiempo*) pass. **~se** vpr (*apartarse*) move along; (*pasarse*) go too far; (*colores*) run. **~se una juerga** have a ball

correspond|**encia** f correspondence. **~er** vi correspond; (*ser adecuado*) be fitting; (*contestar*) reply; (*pertenecer*) belong; (*incumbir*) fall to. **~erse** vpr (*amarse*) love one

another. **~iente** a corresponding

corresponsal m correspondent

corrida f run. **~a de toros** bullfight. **~o** a (*peso*) good; (*continuo*) continuous; (*avergonzado*) embarrassed. **de ~a** from memory

corriente a (*agua*) running; (*monedas, publicación, cuenta, año etc*) current; (*ordinario*) ordinary. **—f** current; (*de aire*) draught; (*fig*) tendency. **—m** current month. **al ~** (*al día*) up-to-date; (*enterado*) aware

corr|**illo** m small group, circle. **~o** m circle

corroborar vt corroborate

corroer [24 & 37] vt corrode; (*geol*) erode; (*fig*) eat away. **~se** vpr corrode

corromper vt rot (*madera*); turn bad (*alimentos*); (*fig*) corrupt. **—vi** (*fam*) stink. **~se** vpr (*madera*) rot; (*alimentos*) go bad; (*fig*) be corrupted

corrosi|**ón** f corrosion. **~vo** a corrosive

corrupción f (*de madera etc*) rot; (*soborno*) bribery; (*fig*) corruption

corsé m corset

cortacésped m invar lawnmower

corta|**do** a cut; (*leche*) sour; (*avergonzado*) embarrassed; (*confuso*) confused. **—m** coffee with a little milk. **~ura** f cut

corta|**nte** a sharp; (*viento*) biting; (*frío*) bitter. **~r** vt cut; (*recortar*) cut out; (*aislar, detener*) cut off; (*interrumpir*) cut in. **—vi** cut. **~rse** vpr cut o.s.; (*leche etc*) curdle; (*al teléfono*) be cut off; (*fig*) be embarrassed, become tongue-tied. **~rse el pelo** have one's hair cut. **~rse las uñas** cut one's nails

cortauñas m invar nail-clippers

corte m cutting; (de instrumento cortante) cutting edge; (de corriente) cut; (de prendas de vestir) cut; (de tela) length. —f court. ~ **de luz** power cut. ~ **y confección** dressmaking. **hacer la** ~ court. **las C~s** the Spanish parliament

cortej|ar vt court. **~o** m (de rey etc) entourage. **~o fúnebre** cortège, funeral procession. **~o nupcial** wedding procession

cortés a polite

cortesan|a f courtesan. **~o** m courtier

cortesía f courtesy

corteza f bark; (de naranja etc) peel, rind; (de pan) crust

cortijo m farm; (casa) farmhouse

cortina f curtain

corto a short; (escaso) scanty; (apocado) shy. **~circuito** m short circuit. ~ **de alcances** dim, thick. ~ **de oído** hard of hearing. ~ **de vista** short-sighted. **a la corta o a la larga** sooner or later. **quedarse** ~ fall short; (miscalcular) under-estimate

Coruña f. **La** ~ Corunna

corvo a bent

cosa f thing; (asunto) business; (idea) idea. ~ **de** about. **como si tal** ~ just like that; (como si no hubiera pasado nada) as if nothing had happened. **decirle a uno cuatro** ~**s** tell s.o. a thing or two. **lo que son las** ~**s** much to my surprise

cosaco a & m Cossack

cosech|a f harvest; (de vino) vintage. **~ar** vt harvest. **~ero** m harvester

coser vt/i sew. **~se** vpr stick to s.o. **eso es** ~ **y cantar** it's as easy as pie

cosmético a & m cosmetic

cósmico a cosmic

cosmonauta m & f cosmonaut

cosmopolita a & m & f cosmopolitan

cosmos m cosmos

cosquillas fpl ticklishness. **buscar a uno las** ~ provoke s.o. **hacer** ~ tickle. **tener** ~ be ticklish

costa f coast. **a** ~ **de** at the expense of. **a toda** ~ at any cost

costado m side

costal m sack

costar [2] vt/i cost. ~ **caro** be expensive. **cueste lo que cueste** at any cost

Costa Rica f Costa Rica

costarricense a & m, **costarriqueño** a & m Costa Rican

coste m cost. **~ar** vt pay for; (naut) sail along the coast

costero a coastal

costilla f rib; (chuleta) chop

costo m cost. **~so** a expensive

costumbre f custom, habit. **de** ~ a usual. —adv usually

costur|a f sewing; (línea) seam; (confección) dressmaking. **~era** f dressmaker. **~ero** m sewing box

cotejar vt compare

cotidiano a daily

cotill|ear vt gossip. **~o** m gossip

cotiza|ción f quotation, price. **~r** [10] vt (en la bolsa) quote. —vi pay one's subscription. **~rse** vpr fetch; (en la bolsa) stand at; (fig) be valued

coto m enclosure; (de caza) preserve. ~ **de caza** game preserve

cotorr|a f parrot; (urraca) magpie; (fig) chatterbox. **~ear** vi chatter

coyuntura f joint; (oportunidad) opportunity; (situación) situation; (circunstancia) occasion, juncture

coz f kick

cráneo m skull

cráter m crater

crea|**ción** f creation. **~dor** a creative. **—m** creator. **~r** vt create

crec|**er** [11] vi grow; (*aumentar*) increase. **~ida** f (*de río*) flood. **~ido** a (*persona*) grown-up; (*número*) large, considerable; (*plantas*) fully-grown. **~iente** a growing; (*luna*) crescent. **~imiento** m growth

credencial a credential. **~es** fpl credentials

credibilidad f credibility

crédito m credit. **digno de ~** reliable, trustworthy

credo m creed. **en un ~** in a flash

crédulo a credulous

crea|**encia** f belief. **~er** [18] believe; (*pensar*) think. **~o que no** I don't think so, I think not. **~o que sí** I think so. **—vi** believe. **~erse** vpr consider o.s. **no me lo ~o** I don't believe it. **~ible** a credible. **¡ya lo ~o!** I should think so!

crema f cream; (*culin*) custard. **~ bronceadora** sun-tan cream

cremación f cremation; (*de basura*) incineration

cremallera f zip, zipper (*Amer*)

crematorio m crematorium; (*de basura*) incinerator

crepitar vi crackle

crepúsculo m twilight

crescendo m crescendo

crespo a frizzy. **~ón** m crêpe

cresta f crest; (*tupé*) toupee; (*geog*) ridge

Creta f Crete

cretino m cretin

creyente m believer

cría f breeding; (*animal*) baby animal

cria|**da** f maid, servant. **~dero** m nursery. **~do** a brought up. **—m** servant. **~dor** m breeder. **~nza** f breeding. **~r** [20] vt suckle; grow (*plantas*); breed (*animales*); (*educar*) bring up. **~rse** vpr grow up

criatura f creature; (*niño*) baby

crim|**en** m crime. **~inal** a & m & f criminal

crin m mane; (*relleno*) horsehair

crinolina f crinoline

crío m child

criollo a & m Creole

cripta f crypt

crisantemo m chrysanthemum

crisis f crisis

crisol m melting-pot

crispar vt twitch; (*irritar, fam*) annoy. **~ los nervios a uno** get on s.o.'s nerves

cristal m crystal; (*vidrio*) glass; (*de una ventana*) pane of glass. **~ de aumento** magnifying glass. **~ino** a crystalline; (*fig*) crystal-clear. **~izar** [10] crystallize. **limpiar los ~es** clean the windows

cristian|**amente** adv in a Christian way. **~dad** f Christianity. **~ismo** m Christianity. **~o** a & m Christian

Cristo m Christ

cristo m crucifix

criterio m criterion; (*opinión*) opinion

crítica f criticism; (*reseña*) review. **~iticar** [7] vt criticize. **~ítico** a critical. **—m** critic

croar vi croak

crom|**ado** a chromium-plated. **~o** m chromium, chrome

cromosoma m chromosome

crónica f chronicle; (*de periódico*) news. **~o** a chronic

cronista m & f reporter

cronología f chronology. **~ógico** a chronological

cron|**ometraje** m timing. **~ometrar** vt time. **~ómetro** m chronometer; (*en deportes*) stop-watch

croquet /'kroket/ m croquet

croqueta f croquette

cruce m crossing; (*de calles, de carreteras*) crossroads; (*de peatones*) (pedestrian) crossing

crucial *a* cross-shaped; *(fig)* crucial

crucificar [7] *vt* crucify. **~jo** *m* crucifix. **~xión** *f* crucifiction

crucigrama *m* crossword (puzzle)

crudo *a* raw; *(fig)* crude. **petróleo** *m* ~ crude oil

cruel *a* cruel. **~dad** *f* cruelty

crujido *m* *(de seda, de hojas secas etc)* rustle; *(de muebles etc)* creak. **~r** *vi* *(seda, hojas secas etc)* rustle; *(muebles etc)* creak

cruz *f* cross; *(de moneda)* tails. ~ **gamada** swastika. **la C~ Roja** the Red Cross

cruzada *f* crusade

cruzar [10] *vt* cross; *(poner de un lado a otro)* lay across. **~se** *vpr* cross; *(pasar en la calle)* pass

cuaderno *m* exercise book; *(para apuntes)* notebook

cuadra *f* *(caballeriza)* stable; *(LAm, manzana)* block

cuadrado *a* & *m* square

cuadragésimo *a* fortieth

cuadrar *vt* square. —*vi* suit; *(estar de acuerdo)* agree. **~se** *vpr* *(mil)* stand to attention; *(fig)* dig one's heels in. **~ilátero** *a* quadrilateral. —*m* quadrilateral; *(boxeo)* ring

cuadrilla *f* group; *(pandilla)* gang

cuadro *m* square; *(pintura)* painting; *(de obra de teatro, escena)* scene; *(de jardín)* bed; *(de números)* table; *(de mando etc)* panel; *(conjunto del personal)* staff. ~ **de distribución** switchboard. **a ~s, de ~s** check. **en ~** in a square. **¡qué ~!**, **¡vaya un ~!** what a sight!

cuadrúpedo *m* quadruped

cuádruple *a* & *m* quadruple

cuajar *vt* thicken; clot *(sangre)*; curdle *(leche)*; *(llenar)* fill up. —*vi* *(nieve)* settle; *(fig, fam)* work out. **cuajado de** full of.

~se *vpr* coagulate; *(sangre)* clot; *(leche)* curdle. **~ón** *m* clot

cual *pron*. **el ~, la ~** etc *(animales y cosas)* that, which; *(personas, sujeto)* who, that; *(personas, objeto)* whom. —*a* as, like. —*a* such as. ~ **si** as if. **~... tal** like... like. **cada ~** everyone. **por lo ~** because of which

cuál *pron* which

cualidad *f* quality; *(propiedad)* property

cualquiera *a* *(delante de nombres* **cualquier**, *pl* **cualesquiera)** any. —*pron* *(pl* **cualesquiera)** anyone, anybody; *(cosas)* whatever, whichever. **un ~** a nobody

cuando *adv* when. —*conj* when; *(aunque)* even if. ~ **más** at the most. ~ **menos** at the least. ~ **no** if not alone. —*aun* even if. **de ~ en** ~ from time to time

cuándo *adv* & *conj* when. **¿de ~ acá?**, **¿desde ~?** since when?

cuantía *f* quantity; *(extensión)* extent. **~ioso** *a* abundant

cuanto *a* as much... as, as many... as. —*pron* as much as, as many as. —*adv* as much as. ~ **más, mejor** the more the merrier. **en ~** as soon as. **en ~ a** as for. **por ~** since. **unos ~s** a few, some

cuánto *a* *(interrogativo)* how much?; *(interrogativo en plural)* how many?; *(exclamativo)* what a lot of! *(como* how much?; *(en plural)* how many? —*adv* how much. *¿~* **tiempo?** how long? **¡~ tiempo sin verte!** it's been a long time! **¿a ~?** how much? **¿a ~s estamos?** what's the date today? **un Sr. no sé ~s** Mr So-and-So

cuáquero *m* Quaker

cuarenta *a* & *m* forty; *(cuadragésimo)* fortieth. **~ena** *f* (about) forty; (*med*) quarantine. **~ón** *a* about forty

cuaresma *f* Lent

cuarta *f* (*palmo*) span

cuartear *vt* quarter, divide into four; (*zigzaguear*) zigzag. **~se** *vpr* crack

cuartel *m* (*mil*) barracks. **~ general** headquarters. **no dar ~** show no mercy

cuarteto *m* quartet

cuarto *a* fourth. —*m* quarter; (*habitación*) room. **~ de baño** bathroom. **~ de estar** living room. **~ de hora** quarter of an hour. **estar sin un ~** be broke. **menos ~** (a) quarter to. **y ~** (a) quarter past

cuarzo *m* quartz

cuatro *a & m* four. **~cientos** *a & m* four hundred

Cuba *f* Cuba

cuba: **~libre** *m* rum and Coke (P). **~no** *a & m* Cuban

cúbico *a* cubic

cubículo *m* cubicle

cubiert|a *f* cover, covering; (*de la cama*) bedspread; (*techo*) roof; (*neumático*) tyre; (*naut*) deck. **~o** *a* covered; (*cielo*) overcast. —*m* place setting, cutlery; (*comida*) meal. **a ~o** under cover. **a ~o de** safe from

cubis|mo *m* cubism. **~ta** *a & m & f* cubist

cubil *m* den, lair. **~ete** *m* bowl; (*molde*) mould; (*para echar los dados*) cup

cubo *m* bucket; (*en geometría y matemáticas*) cube

cubrecama *m* bedspread

cubrir *vt* [*pp* **cubierto**] cover; (*sonido*) drown; fill (*vacante*). **~se** *vpr* cover o.s.; (*ponerse el sombrero*) put on one's hat; (*el cielo*) cloud over, become overcast

cucaracha *f* cockroach

cuclillas. **en ~** *adv* squatting

cuclillo *m* cuckoo

cuco *a* shrewd; (*mono*) pretty, nice. —*m* cuckoo; (*insecto*) grub

cucurucho *m* cornet

cuchar|a *f* spoon. **~ada** *f* spoonful. **~adita** *f* teaspoonful. **~illa** *f*, **~ita** *f* teaspoon. **~ón** *m* ladle

cuchiche|ar *vi* whisper. **~o** *m* whispering

cuchill|a *f* large knife; (*de carnicero*) cleaver; (*hoja de afeitar*) razor blade. **~ada** *f* slash; (*herida*) knife wound. **~o** *m* knife

cuchitril *m* pigsty; (*fig*) hovel

cuello *m* neck; (*de camisa*) collar. **cortar el ~ a uno** cut s.o.'s throat

cuenc|a *f* hollow; (*del ojo*) (eye) socket; (*geog*) basin. **~o** *m* hollow; (*vasija*) bowl

cuenta *f* count; (*acción de contar*) counting; (*factura*) bill; (*en banco, relato*) account; (*asunto*) affair; (*de collar etc*) bead. **~ corriente** current account, checking account (*Amer*). **ajustar las ~s** settle accounts. **caer en la ~ de que** realize that. **darse ~ de** realize. **en resumidas ~s** in short. **por mi ~** for myself. **tener en ~, tomar en ~** bear in mind

cuentakilómetros *m invar* milometer

cuent|ista *m & f* story-writer; (*de mentiras*) fibber. **~o** *m* story; (*mentira*) fib, tall story. —*vb véase* **contar**

cuerda *f* rope; (*más fina*) string; (*mus*) string. **~ floja** tightrope. **dar ~ a** wind up (*un reloj*)

cuerdo *a* (*persona*) sane; (*acción*) sensible

cuern|a *f* horns. **~o** *m* horn

cuero *m* leather; (*piel*) skin; (*del grifo*) washer. **~ cabelludo** scalp. **en ~s (vivos)** stark naked

cuerpo *m* body

cuervo m crow

cuesta f slope, hill. ~ **abajo** downhill. ~ **arriba** uphill. **a ~s** on one's back

cuesti|ón f matter; (*altercado*) quarrel; (*dificultad*) trouble. **~onario** m questionnaire

cueva f cave; (*sótano*) cellar

cuida|do m care; (*preocupación*) worry; (*asunto*) affair. **¡~do!** (be) careful! **~doso** a careful. **~dosamente** adv carefully. ~r vt look after. —vi. ~r **de** look after. **~rse** vpr look after o.s. **~rse de** be careful to. **tener ~rse de** be careful to. **tener ~do** be careful

culata f (*de arma de fuego*) butt; (*auto*) cylinder head. **~zo** m recoil

culebra f snake

culebrón m (*LAm*) soap opera

culinario a culinary

culmina|ción f culmination. ~r vi culminate

culo m (*fam*) bottom. **ir de ~** go downhill

culpa f fault; (*jurid*) guilt. **~bilidad** f guilt. **~ble** a guilty. —m culprit. ~r vt blame (de for). **echar la ~** blame. **por ~ de** because of. **tener la ~** de be to blame for

cultiv|ar vt farm; grow (*plantas*); (*fig*) cultivate. **~o** m farming; (*de plantas*) growing

cult|o a (*tierra etc*) cultivated; (*persona*) educated. —m cult; (*homenaje*) worship. **~ura** f culture. **~ural** a cultural

culturismo m body-building

cumbre f summit; (*fig*) height

cumpleaños m invar birthday

cumplido a perfect; (*grande*) large; (*cortés*) polite. —m compliment. ~r a reliable. **de ~** courtesy. **por ~** out of politeness

cumplim|entar vt carry out; (*saludar*) pay a courtesy call to;

(*felicitar*) congratulate. **~iento** m carrying out, execution

cumplir vt carry out; observe (*ley*); serve (*condena*); reach (*años*); keep (*promesa*). —vi do one's duty. **~se** vpr expire; (*realizarse*) be fulfilled. **hoy cumple 3 años** he's 3 (years old) today. **por ~** as a mere formality

cumulativo a cumulative

cúmulo m pile, heap

cuna f cradle; (*fig, nacimiento*) birthplace

cundir vi spread; (*rendir*) go a long way

cuneta f gutter

cuña f wedge

cuñad|a f sister-in-law. **~o** m brother-in-law

cuño m stamp. **de nuevo ~** new

cuota f quota; (*de sociedad etc*) subscription, fees

cupe vb véase **caber**

cupé m coupé

Cupido m Cupid

cupo m cuota

cupón m coupon

cúpula f dome

cura f cure; (*tratamiento*) treatment. —m priest. **~ble** a curable. **~ción** f healing. **~ndero** m faith-healer. ~r vt (*incl culin*) cure; dress (*herida*); (*tratar*) treat; (*fig*) remedy; tan (*pieles*). —vi (*persona*) get better; (*herida*) heal; (*fig*) be cured. **~rse** vpr get better

curios|ear vi pry; (*mirar*) browse. **~idad** f curiosity; (*limpieza*) cleanliness. **~o** a curious; (*raro*) odd, unusual; (*limpio*) clean

curriculum vitae m curriculum vitae

cursar vt send; (*estudiar*) study

cursi a pretentious, showy. —m affected person

cursillo m short course

cursiva f italics

curso m course; (univ etc) year. **en ~** under way; (año etc) current
curtir vt tan; (fig) harden. **~se** vpr become tanned; (fig) become hardened
curv|a f curve; (de carretera) bend. **~o a** curved
cúspide f peak
custodi|a f care, safe-keeping. **~ar** vt take care of. **~o a & m** guardian
cutáneo a skin. **enfermedad** f **cutánea** skin disease
cutícula f cuticle
cutis m skin, complexion
cuyo pron (de persona) whose, of whom; (de cosa) whose, of which. **en ~ caso** in which case

CH

chabacano a common; (chiste etc) vulgar. —m (Mex, albaricoque) apricot
chabola f shack. **~s** fpl shanty town
chacal m jackal
chacota f fun. **echar a ~** make fun of
chacra f (LAm) farm
cháchara f chatter
chacharear vt (Mex) sell. —vi chatter
chafar vt crush. **quedar chafado** be nonplussed
chal m shawl
chalado a (fam) crazy
chalé m house (with a garden), villa
chaleco m waistcoat, vest (Amer). **~ salvavidas** life-jacket
chalequear vt (Arg, Mex) trick
chalet m (pl **chalets**) house (with a garden), villa
chalón m (LAm) shawl

chalote m shallot
chalupa f boat
chamac|a f (esp Mex) girl. **~o** m (esp Mex) boy
chamagoso a (Mex) filthy
chamarr|a f sheepskin jacket. **~o** m (LAm) coarse blanket
chamba f (fam) fluke; (Mex, empleo) job. **por ~** by fluke
champán m, **champaña** m champagne
champiñón m mushroom
champú m (pl **champúes** o **champús**) shampoo
chamuscar [7] vt scorch; (Mex, vender) sell cheaply
chance m (esp LAm) chance
chanclo m clog; (de caucho) rubber overshoe
chancho m (LAm) pig
chanchullo m swindle, fiddle (fam)
chandal m tracksuit
chanquete m whitebait
chantaj|e m blackmail. **~ista** m & f blackmailer
chanza f joke
chapa f plate, sheet; (de madera) plywood; (de botella) metal top. **~do a** plated. **~do a la antigua** old-fashioned. **~do de oro** gold-plated
chaparrón m downpour. **llover a chaparrones** pour (down), rain cats and dogs
chapotear vi splash
chapuce|ar vt botch; (Mex, engañar) deceive. **~ro a** (persona) careless; (cosas) shoddy. —m careless worker
chapurrar vt, **chapurrear** vt speak badly, speak a little; mix (licores)
chapuza f botched job, mess; (de poca importancia) odd job
chaqueta f jacket. **cambiar la ~** change sides
chaquetero m turncoat
charada f charade

charca f pond, pool. **~o** m puddle, pool. **cruzar el ~o** cross the water; (*ir a América*) cross the Atlantic

charla f chat; (*conferencia*) talk. **~dor** a talkative. **~r** vi (*fam*) chat

charlatán a talkative. —m chatterbox; (*curandero*) charlatan

charol m varnish; (*cuero*) patent leather

chárter a charter

chascar [7] vt crack (*látigo*); click (*lengua*); snap (*dedos*). —vi (*látigo*) crack; (*con la lengua*) click one's tongue; (*los dedos*) snap

chascarrillo m joke, funny story

chasco m disappointment; (*broma*) joke; (*engaño*) trick

chasis m (*auto*) chassis

chasqu|ear vt crack (*látigo*); click (*lengua*); snap (*dedos*). —vi (*látigo*) crack; (*con la lengua*) click one's tongue; (*los dedos*) snap. **~ido** m crack; (*de la lengua*) click; (*de los dedos*) snap

chatarra f scrap iron; (*fig*) scrap

chato a (*nariz*) snub; (*persona*) snub-nosed; (*objetos*) flat. —m wine glass; (*niño, mujer, fam*) dear, darling; (*hombre, fam*) mate (*fam*)

chaval m (*fam*) boy, lad. **~a** f girl, lass

che int (*Arg*) listen!, hey!

checo a & m Czech. **la república f Checa** the Czech Republic

checoslovaco a & m (*history*) Czechoslovak

Checoslovaquia f (*history*) Czechoslovakia

chelín m shilling

chelo a (*Mex, rubio*) fair

cheque m cheque. **~ de viaje** traveller's cheque. **~ra** f cheque-book

chica f girl; (*criada*) maid, servant

chicano a & m Chicano, Mexican-American

chicle m chewing-gum

chico a (*fam*) small. —m boy. **~s** mpl children

chicoleo m compliment

chicoria f chicory

chicharra f cicada; (*fig*) chatterbox

chicharrón m (*de cerdo*) crackling; (*fig*) sunburnt person

chichón m bump, lump

chifla|do a (*fam*) crazy, daft. **~r** vt (*fam*) drive crazy. **~rse** vpr be mad (*por* about). **le tiene chiflado el chocolate** he's mad about chocolate. **se ha chiflado esa chica** he's crazy about that girl

Chile m Chile

chile m chilli

chileno a & m Chilean

chill|ar vi scream, shriek; (*gato*) howl; (*ratón*) squeak; (*cerdo*) squeal. **~ido** m scream, screech; (*de gato etc*) howl. **~ón** a noisy; (*colores*) loud; (*sonido*) shrill

chimenea f chimney; (*hogar*) fireplace

chimpancé m chimpanzee

China f China

chinch|ar vt (*fam*) annoy, pester. **~e** m drawing-pin (*Brit*), thumbtack (*Amer*); (*insecto*) bedbug; (*fig*) nuisance. **~eta** f drawing-pin (*Brit*), thumbtack (*Amer*)

chinela f slipper

chino a & m Chinese

Chipre m Cyprus

chipriota a & m & f Cypriot

chiquillo a childish. —m child, kid (*fam*)

chiquito a small, tiny. —m child, kid (*fam*)

chiribita f spark. **estar que echa ~s** be furious

chirimoya f custard apple

chiripa f fluke. **por ~** by fluke

chirivía f parsnip

chirri|ar vi creak; ⟨pájaro⟩ chirp. **~do** m creaking; ⟨al freír⟩ sizzling; ⟨de pájaros⟩ chirping

chis int sh!, hush!; ⟨para llamar a uno, fam⟩ hey!, psst!

chism|e m gadget, thingumajig ⟨fam⟩; ⟨chismorreo⟩ piece of gossip. **~es** mpl things, bits and pieces. **~orreo** m gossip. **~oso** a gossipy. —m gossip

chispa f spark; ⟨gota⟩ drop; ⟨gracia⟩ wit; ⟨fig⟩ sparkle. **estar que echa ~(s)** be furious

chispea|nte a sparkling. **~r** vi spark; ⟨lloviznar⟩ drizzle; ⟨fig⟩ sparkle

chisporrotear vt throw out sparks; ⟨fuego⟩ crackle; ⟨aceite⟩ sizzle

chistar vi speak. **sin ~** without saying a word

chiste m joke, funny story. **hacer ~ de** make fun of. **tener ~** be funny

chistera f ⟨fam⟩ top hat, topper ⟨fam⟩

chistoso a funny

chiva|r vi inform ⟨policía⟩; ⟨niño⟩ tell. **~tazo** m tip-off. **~to** m informer; ⟨niño⟩ telltale

chivo m kid, young goat

choca|nte a surprising; ⟨persona⟩ odd. **~r** [7] vt clink ⟨vasos⟩; shake ⟨la mano⟩. —vi collide, hit. **~r con**, **~r contra** crash into. **lo ~nte es que** the surprising thing is that

chocolate m chocolate. **tableta** f **de ~** bar of chocolate

choch|ear vi be senile. **~o** a senile; ⟨fig⟩ soft

chófer m chauffeur; ⟨conductor⟩ driver

cholo a & m ⟨LAm⟩ half-breed

chopo m poplar

choque m collision; ⟨fig⟩ clash; ⟨eléctrico⟩ shock; ⟨auto, rail etc⟩ crash, accident; ⟨sacudida⟩ jolt

chorizo m salami

chorr|ear vi gush forth; ⟨fig⟩ be dripping. **~o** m jet, stream; ⟨caudal pequeño⟩ trickle; ⟨fig⟩ stream. **a ~os** ⟨fig⟩ in abundance. **hablar a ~os** jabber

chovinis|mo m chauvinism. **~ta** a chauvinistic. **—m & f** chauvinist

choza f hut

chubas|co m squall, heavy shower; ⟨fig⟩ bad patch. **~quero** m raincoat, anorak

chuchería f trinket; ⟨culin⟩ sweet

chufa f tiger nut

chuleta f chop

chulo a insolent; ⟨vistoso⟩ showy. **—m** ruffian; ⟨rufián⟩ pimp

chumbo m prickly pear; ⟨fam⟩ bump. **higo** m **~** prickly pear

chup|ada f suck; ⟨al cigarro etc⟩ puff. **~ado** a skinny; ⟨fácil, fam⟩ very easy. **~ar** vt suck, lick; puff at ⟨cigarro etc⟩; ⟨absorber⟩ absorb. **~arse** vpr lose weight. **~ete** m dummy ⟨Brit⟩, pacifier ⟨Amer⟩

churro m fritter; ⟨fam⟩ mess. **me salió un ~** I made a mess of it

chusco a funny

chusma f riff-raff

chutar vi shoot. **¡va que chuta!** it's going well!

D

dactilógrafo m typist

dado m dice. **—a** given; ⟨hora⟩ gone. **~ que** since, given that

dalia f dahlia

daltoniano a colour-blind

dama f lady; ⟨en la corte⟩ lady-in-waiting. **~s** fpl draughts ⟨Brit⟩, checkers ⟨Amer⟩

damasco m damask

danés *a* Danish. —*m* Dane; *(idioma)* Danish

danza *f* dance; *(acción)* dancing; *(enredo)* affair. ~**r** [10] *vt/i* dance

dañ|ado *a* damaged. ~**ar** *vt* damage; harm *(persona)*. ~**ino** *a* harmful. ~**o** *m* damage; *(a una persona)* harm. ~**oso** *a* harmful. ~**os y perjuicios** damages. **hacer** ~**o a** harm; hurt *(persona)*. **hacerse** ~**o** hurt o.s.

dar [26] *vt* give; *(producir)* yield; strike *(la hora)*. —*vi* give. **da igual** it doesn't matter. **¡dale!** go on! **da lo mismo** it doesn't matter. ~ **a** *(ventana)* look on to; *(edificio)* face. ~ **a la luz** give birth. ~ **con** meet *(persona)*; find *(cosa)*; ~ **de cabeza** fall flat on one's face. ~ **por** assume; (+ *infinitivo)* decide. ~**se** *vpr* give o.s. up; *(suceder)* happen. **dárselas de** make o.s. out to be. ~**se por** consider o.s. **¿qué más da?** it doesn't matter!

dardo *m* dart

dársena *f* dock

datar *vt* date. —*vi*. ~ **de** date from

dátil *m* date

dato *m* fact. ~**s** *mpl* data, information

de *prep* of; *(procedencia)* from; *(suposición)* if. ~ **día** by day. ~ **dos en dos** two by two. ~ **haberlo sabido** if I (you, he etc) had known. ~ **niño** as a child. **el libro** ~ **mi amigo** my friend's book. **las 2** ~ **la madrugada** 2 (o'clock) in the morning. **un puente** ~ **hierro** an iron bridge. **soy** ~ **Loughborough** I'm from Loughborough

deambular *vi* stroll

debajo *adv* underneath. ~ **de** underneath, under. **el de** ~ the one underneath. **por** ~ underneath. **por** ~ **de** below

debat|e *m* debate. ~**ir** *vt* debate

deber *vt* owe. —*vi* have to, must. —*m* duty. ~**es** *mpl* homework. ~**se** *vpr*. ~**se a** be due to. **debo marcharme** I must go, I have to go

debido *a* due; *(correcto)* proper. ~ **a** due to. **como es** ~ as is proper. **con el respeto** ~ with due respect

débil *a* weak; *(ruido)* faint; *(luz)* dim

debili|dad *f* weakness. ~**tar** *vt* weaken. ~**tarse** *vpr* weaken, get weak

débito *m* debit; *(deuda)* debt

debutar *vi* make one's debut

década *f* decade

deca|dencia *f* decline. ~**dente** *a* decadent. ~**er** [29] *vi* decline; *(debilitarse)* weaken. ~**ído** *a* depressed. ~**imiento** *m* decline, weakening

decano *m* dean; *(miembro más antiguo)* senior member

decantar *vt* decant *(vino etc)*

decapitar *vt* behead

decena *f* ten; *(aproximadamente)* about ten

decencia *f* decency, honesty

decenio *m* decade

decente *a* *(persona)* respectable, honest; *(cosas)* modest; *(limpio)* clean, tidy

decepci|ón *f* disappointment. ~**onar** *vt* disappoint

decibelio *m* decibel

decid|ido *a* decided; *(persona)* determined, resolute. ~**r** *vt* decide; settle *(cuestión etc)*. —*vi* decide. ~**rse** *vpr* make up one's mind

decimal *a & m* decimal

décimo *a & m* tenth. —*m* *(de lotería)* tenth part of a lottery ticket

decimo: ~**ctavo** *a & m* eighteenth. ~**cuarto** *a & m* fourteenth. ~**nono** *a & m* nineteenth. ~**noveno** *a & m* nineteenth. ~**quinto** *a & m* fifteenth. ~**séptimo** *a & m* seventeenth. ~**sexto** *a & m* sixteenth. ~**tercero** *a & m,* ~**cio** *a & m* thirteenth

decir [46] *vt* say; (*contar*) tell. —*m* saying. ~**se** *upr* be said. ~ **que** no say no. ~ **que sí** say yes. **dicho de otro modo** in other words. **dicho y hecho** no sooner said than done. ¿**dígame?** can I help you? ¡**dígame!** (*al teléfono*) hello **digamos** let's say. **es** ~ that is to say. **mejor dicho** rather. ¡**no me digas!** you don't say!, really! **por así** ~, **por** ~**lo así** so to speak, as it were. **querer** ~ mean. **se dice que** it is said that, they say that

decisión *f* decision. ~**vo** *a* decisive

declamar *vt* declaim

declaración *f* statement. ~**ción de renta** income tax return. ~**r** *vt*/*i* declare. ~**rse** *upr* declare o.s.; (*epidemia etc*) break out

declinación *f* (*gram*) declension. ~**r** *vt*/*i* decline; (*salud*) deteriorate

declive *m* slope; (*fig*) decline. en ~ sloping

decolorar *vt* discolour, fade. ~**se** *upr* become discoloured, fade

decoración *f* decoration. ~**do** *m* (*en el teatro*) set. ~**dor** *m* decorator. ~**r** *vt* decorate. ~**tivo** *a* decorative

decoro *m* decorum; (*respeto*) respect. ~**so** *a* proper; (*modesto*) modest; (*profesión*) honourable

decrecer [11] *vi* decrease, diminish; (*aguas*) subside

decrépito *a* decrepit

decretar *vt* decree. ~**o** *m* decree

dedal *m* thimble

dedicación *f* dedication. ~**r** [7] *vt* dedicate; devote (*tiempo*). ~**toria** *f* dedication, inscription

dedil *m* finger-stall. ~**illo** *m*. **al** ~**illo** at one's fingertips. ~**o** *m* finger; (*del pie*) toe. ~**o anular** ring finger. ~**o corazón** middle finger. ~**o gordo** thumb. ~**o índice** index finger. ~**o meñique** little finger. ~**o pulgar** thumb

deducción *f* deduction. ~**ir** [47] *vt* deduce; (*descontar*) deduct

defecto *m* fault, defect. ~**uoso** *a* defective

defender [1] *vt* defend. ~**sa** *f* defence. ~**sivo** *a* defensive. ~**sor** *m* defender. **abogado** *m* ~**sor** defence counsel

deferencia *f* deference. ~**te** *a* deferential

deficiencia *f* deficiency. ~**cia mental** mental handicap. ~**te** *a* deficient; (*imperfecto*) defective. ~**te mental** mentally handicapped

déficit *m invar* deficit

definición *f* definition. ~**do** *a* defined. ~**r** *vt* define; (*aclarar*) clarify. ~**tivo** *a* definitive. **en** ~**tiva** (*en resumen*) in short

deflación *f* deflation

deformación *f* deformation; (*TV etc*) distortion. ~**ar** *vt* deform; (*TV etc*) distort. ~**arse** *upr* go out of shape. ~**e** *a* deformed; (*feo*) ugly

defraudar *vt* cheat; (*decepcionar*) disappoint; evade (*impuestos etc*)

defunción *f* death

degeneración *f* degeneration; (*moral*) degeneracy. ~**do** *a* degenerate. ~**r** *vi* degenerate

deglutir *vt*/*i* swallow

degollar [16] *vt* cut s.o.'s throat; (*fig, arruinar*) ruin

degradar *vt* degrade. ~**se** *upr* lower o.s.

degustación *f* tasting. ~**r** *vt* taste

dehesa *f* pasture

dei|dad *f* deity. ∼**ficar** [7] *vt* deify

deja|ción *f* surrender. ∼**dez** *f* abandon; (*pereza*) laziness. ∼**do** *a* negligent. ∼**r** *vt* leave; (*abandonar*) abandon; (*prestar*) lend; (*permitir*) let. ∼**r aparte**, ∼**r a un lado** leave aside. ∼**r de** stop. **no** ∼**r de** not fail to

dejo *m* aftertaste; (*tonillo*) accent

del = de + el

delantal *m* apron

delante *adv* in front; (*enfrente*) opposite. ∼ **de** in front of. **de** ∼ front

delanter|a *f* front; (*de teatro etc*) front row; (*ventaja*) advantage. **coger la** ∼**a** get ahead. ∼**o** *a* front. —*m* forward. **llevar la** ∼**a** be ahead

delat|ar *vt* denounce. ∼**or** *m* informer

delega|ción *f* delegation; (*sucursal*) branch. ∼**do** *m* delegate; (*com*) agent, representative. ∼**r** [12] *vt* delegate

deleit|ar *vt* delight. ∼**e** *m* delight

deletéreo *a* deleterious

deletre|ar *vt* spell (out). ∼**o** *m* spelling

deleznable *a* brittle, crumbly; (*argumento etc*) weak

delfín *m* dolphin

delgad|ez *f* thinness. ∼**o** *a* thin; (*esbelto*) slim. ∼**ucho** *a* skinny

delibera|ción *f* deliberation. ∼**r** *vt* discuss, decide. —*vi* deliberate

delicad|eza *f* delicacy; (*fragilidad*) frailty; (*tacto*) tact. ∼**o** *a* delicate; (*sensible*) sensitive; (*discreto*) tactful, discreet. **falta de** ∼**eza** tactlessness

delici|a *f* delight. ∼**oso** *a* delightful; (*sabor etc*) delicious; (*gracioso, fam*) funny

delimitar *vt* delimit

delincuen|cia *f* delinquency. ∼**te** *a & m* delinquent

delinea|nte *m* draughtsman. ∼**r** *vt* outline; (*dibujar*) draw

delinquir [8] *vi* commit an offence

delir|ante *a* delirious. ∼**ar** *vi* be delirious; (*fig*) talk nonsense. ∼**io** *m* delirium; (*fig*) frenzy

delito *m* crime, offence

delta *f* delta

demacrado *a* emaciated

demagogo *m* demagogue

demand|a *f*. **en** ∼ asking for; (*en busca de*) in search of. ∼**nte** *m & f* (*jurid*) plaintiff. ∼**r** *vt* (*jurid*) bring an action against

demarca|ción *f* demarcation. ∼**r** [7] *vt* demarcate

demás *a* rest of the, other. —*pron* rest, others. **lo** ∼ the rest. **por** ∼ useless; (*muy*) very. **por lo** ∼ otherwise

demasía *f* excess; (*abuso*) outrage; (*atrevimiento*) insolence. **en** ∼ too much

demasiado *a* too much; (*en plural*) too many. —*adv* too much; (*con adjetivo*) too

demen|cia *f* madness. ∼**te** *a* demented, mad

dem|ocracia *f* democracy. ∼**ócrata** *m & f* democrat. ∼**ocrático** *a* democratic

demol|er [2] *vt* demolish. ∼**ición** *f* demolition

demonio *m* devil, demon. ¡∼**s!** hell! **¿cómo** ∼**s?** how the hell? **¡qué** ∼**s!** what the hell!

demor|a *f* delay. ∼**r** *vt* delay. —*vi* stay on. ∼**rse** *vpr* be a long time

demostra|ción *f* demonstration, show. ∼**r** [2] *vt* demonstrate; (*mostrar*) show; (*probar*) prove. ∼**tivo** *a* demonstrative

denegar [1 & 12] *vt* refuse

deng|oso *a* affected, finicky. ∼**ue** *m* affectation

denigrar *vt* denigrate

denomina|ción *f* denomination. ∼**do** *a* called. ∼**dor** *m* denominator. ∼**r** *vt* name

denotar vt denote

dens|idad f density. **~o** a dense, thick

denta|dura f teeth. **~dura post-iza** denture, false teeth. **~l** a dental

dentera f. **dar ~ a uno** set s.o.'s teeth on edge; (dar envidia) make s.o. green with envy

dentífrico m toothpaste

dentista m & f dentist

dentro adv inside; (de un edificio) indoors. **~ de** in. **~ de poco** soon. **por ~** inside

denuncia f report; (acusación) accusation. **~r** vt report (a crime); (periódico etc) denounce; (indicar) indicate

departamento m department; (Arg, piso) flat (Brit), apartment (Amer)

dependencia f dependence; (sección) section; (sucursal) branch

depender vi depend (**de** on)

dependient|a f shop assistant. **~e** a dependent (**de** on). —m employee; (de oficina) clerk; (de tienda) shop assistant

depila|ción f depilation. **~r** vt depilate. **~torio** a depilatory

deplora|ble a deplorable. **~r** vt deplore, regret

deponer [34] vt remove from office. —vi give evidence

deporta|ción f deportation. **~r** vt deport

deport|e m sport. **~ista** m sportsman. —f sportswoman. **~ivo** a sports. —m sports car. **hacer ~e** take part in sports

deposición f deposition; (de un empleo) removal from office

dep|ositador m depositor. **~ositante** m & f depositor. **~ositar** vt deposit; (poner) put, place. **~ósito** m deposit; (conjunto de cosas) store; (almacén) warehouse; (mil) depot; (de líquidos) tank

deprava|ción f depravity. **~do** a depraved. **~r** vt deprave. **~rse** vpr become depraved

deprecia|ción f depreciation. **~r** vt depreciate. **~rse** vpr depreciate

depresión f depression

deprim|ente a depressing. **~ido** a depressed. **~ir** vt depress. **~irse** vpr get depressed

depura|ción f purification; (pol) purging. **~r** vt purify; (pol) purge

derech|a f (mano) right hand; (lado) right. **~ista** a a right-wing. —m & f right-winger. **~o** a right; (vertical) upright; (recto) straight. —adv straight. —m right; (ley) law; (lado) right side. **~os** mpl dues. **~os de autor** royalties. **a la ~a** on the right; (hacia el lado derecho) to the right. **todo ~o** straight on

deriva f drift. **a la ~a** drifting, adrift

deriva|ción f derivation; (cambio) diversion. **~do** a derived. —m derivative, by-product. **~r** vt derive; (cambiar la dirección de) divert. —vi. **~r de** derive from, be derived from. **~rse** vpr be derived

derram|amiento m spilling. **~amiento de sangre** blood-shed. **~ar** vt spill; (verter) pour; shed (lágrimas). **~arse** vpr spill. **~e** m spilling; (pérdida) leakage; (cantidad perdida) spillage; (med) discharge (med, de sangre) haemorrhage

derretir [5] vt melt. **~se** vpr melt; (enamorarse) fall in love (**por** with)

derriba|do a fallen down. **~r** vt knock down; bring down, over-throw (gobierno etc). **~rse** vpr fall down

derrocar [7] vt bring down, over-throw (gobierno etc)

derroch|ar vt squander. **~e** m waste

derrot|a f defeat; (rumbo) course. **~ar** vt defeat. **~ado** a defeated; (vestido) shabby. **~ero** m course

derrumba|miento m collapse. **~r** vt (derribar) knock down. **~rse** vpr collapse

desaborido a tasteless; (persona) dull

desabotonar vt unbutton, undo. —vi bloom. **~se** vpr come undone

desabrido a tasteless; (tiempo) unpleasant; (persona) surly

desabrochar vt undo. **~se** vpr come undone

desacat|ar vt have no respect for. **~o** m disrespect

desac|ertado a ill-advised; (erróneo) wrong. **~ertar** [1] vt be wrong. **~ierto** m mistake

desaconseja|ble a inadvisable. **~do** a unwise, ill-advised. **~r** vt advise against, dissuade

desacorde a discordant

desacostumbrado a unusual. **~r** vt give up

desacreditar vt discredit

desactivar vt defuse

desacuerdo m disagreement

desafiar [20] vt challenge; (afrontar) defy

desafilado a blunt

desafina|do a out of tune. **~r** vi be out of tune. **~rse** vpr go out of tune

desafío m challenge; (combate) duel

desaforado a (comportamiento) outrageous; (desmedido) excessive; (sonido) loud; (enorme) huge

desafortunad|amente adv unfortunately. **~o** a unfortunate

desagrada|ble a unpleasant. **~r** vt displease. —vi be unpleasant.

me **~** el sabor I don't like the taste

desagradecido a ungrateful

desagrado m displeasure. **con ~** unwillingly

desagravi|ar vt make amends to. **~o** m amends; (expiación) atonement

desagregar [12] vt break up. **~se** vpr disintegrate

desagüe m drain; (acción) drainage. **tubo** m **de ~** drain-pipe

desaguisado a illegal. —m offence; (fam) disaster

desahog|ado a roomy; (adinerado) well-off; (fig, descarado, fam) impudent. **~ar** [12] vt relieve; vent (ira). **~arse** vpr (desfogarse) let off steam. **~o** m comfort; (alivio) relief

desahuci|ar vt deprive of hope; give up hope for (enfermo); evict (inquilino). **~o** m eviction

desair|ado a humiliating; (persona) humiliated, spurned. **~ar** vt snub (persona); disregard (cosa). **~e** m rebuff

desajuste m maladjustment; (avería) breakdown

desal|entador a disheartening. **~entar** [1] vt (fig) discourage. **~iento** m discouragement

desaliño m untidiness, scruffiness

desalmado a wicked

desalojar vt eject (persona); evacuate (sitio). —vi move (house)

desampar|ado a helpless; (abandonado) abandoned. **~ar** vt abandon. **~o** m helplessness; (abandono) abandonment

desangelado a insipid, dull

desangrar vt bleed. **~se** vpr bleed

desanima|do a down-hearted. **~r** vt discourage. **~rse** vpr lose heart

desánimo m discouragement

desanudar *vt* untie

desapacible *a* unpleasant; ⟨*sonido*⟩ harsh

desapar|ecer [11] *vi* disappear; ⟨*efecto*⟩ wear off. ~**ecido** *a* disappeared. —*m* missing person. ~**ecidos** *mpl* missing. ~**ición** *f* disappearance

desapasionado *a* dispassionate

desapego *m* indifference

desapercebido *a* unnoticed

desaplicado *a* lazy

desaprensi|ón *f* unscrupulousness. ~**vo** *a* unscrupulous

desaproba|ción *f* disapproval. ~**r** [2] *vt* disapprove of; ⟨*rechazar*⟩ reject.

desaprovecha|do *a* wasted; ⟨*alumno*⟩ lazy. ~**r** *vt* waste

desarm|ar *vt* disarm; ⟨*desmontar*⟩ take to pieces. ~**e** *m* disarmament

desarraig|ado *a* rootless. ~**ar** [12] *vt* uproot; ⟨*fig, erradicar*⟩ wipe out. ~**o** *m* uprooting; ⟨*fig*⟩ eradication

desarregl|ado *a* untidy; ⟨*desordenado*⟩ disorderly. ~**ar** *vt* mess up; ⟨*deshacer el orden*⟩ make untidy. ~**o** *m* disorder; ⟨*de persona*⟩ untidiness

desarroll|ado *a* (well-) developed. ~**ar** *vt* develop; ⟨*desenrollar*⟩ unroll, unfold. ~**arse** *vpr* ⟨*incl foto*⟩ develop; ⟨*desenrollarse*⟩ unroll; ⟨*suceso*⟩ take place. ~**o** *m* development

desarrugar [12] *vt* smooth out

desarticular *vt* dislocate ⟨*hueso*⟩; ⟨*fig*⟩ break up

desaseado *a* dirty; ⟨*desordenado*⟩ untidy

desasirse [45] *vpr* let go (**de** of)

desasos|egar [1 & 12] *vt* disturb. ~**egarse** *vpr* get uneasy. ~**iego** *m* anxiety; ⟨*intranquilidad*⟩ restlessness

desastr|ado *a* scruffy. ~**e** *m* disaster. ~**oso** *a* disastrous

desata|do *a* untied; ⟨*fig*⟩ wild. ~**r** *vt* untie; ⟨*fig, soltar*⟩ unleash. ~**rse** *vpr* come undone

desatascar [7] *vt* pull out of the mud; unblock ⟨*tubo etc*⟩

desaten|ción *f* inattention; ⟨*descortesía*⟩ discourtesy. ~**der** [1] *vt* not pay attention to; neglect ⟨*deber etc*⟩. ~**to** *a* inattentive; ⟨*descortés*⟩ discourteous

desatin|ado *a* silly. ~**o** *m* silliness; ⟨*error*⟩ mistake

desatornillar *vt* unscrew

desatracar [7] *vt/i* cast off

desautorizar [10] *vt* declare unauthorized; ⟨*desmentir*⟩ deny

desavenencia *f* disagreement

desayun|ar *vt* have for breakfast. —*vi* have breakfast. ~**o** *m* breakfast

desazón *m* ⟨*fig*⟩ anxiety

desbandarse *vpr* ⟨*mil*⟩ disband; ⟨*dispersarse*⟩ disperse

desbarajust|ar *vt* throw into confusion. ~**e** *m* confusion

desbaratar *vt* spoil

desbloquear *vt* unfreeze

desbocado *a* ⟨*vasija etc*⟩ chipped; ⟨*caballo*⟩ runaway; ⟨*persona*⟩ foul-mouthed

desborda|nte *a* overflowing. ~**r** *vt* go beyond; ⟨*exceder*⟩ exceed. —*vi* overflow. ~**rse** *vpr* overflow

descabalgar [12] *vi* dismount

descabellado *a* crazy

descabezar [10] *vt* behead

descafeinado *a* decaffeinated. —*m* decaffeinated coffee

descalabr|ar *vt* injure in the head; ⟨*fig*⟩ damage. ~**o** *m* disaster

descalificar [7] *vt* disqualify; ⟨*desacreditar*⟩ discredit

descalz|ar [10] *vt* take off ⟨*zapato*⟩. ~**o** *a* barefoot

descaminar *vt* misdirect; ⟨*fig*⟩ lead astray

descamisado *a* shirtless; (*fig*) shabby

descampado *a* open. —*m* open ground

descansado *a* rested; (*trabajo*) easy. ~**apiés** *m* footrest. ~**ar** *vt/i* rest. ~**illo** *m* landing. ~**o** *m* rest; (*descansillo*) landing; (*en deportes*) half-time; (*en el teatro etc*) interval

descapotable *a* convertible

descarado *a* insolent, cheeky; (*sin vergüenza*) shameless

descarga *f* unloading; (*mil, elec*) discharge. ~**ar** [12] *vt* unload; (*mil, elec*) discharge, shock; deal (*golpe etc*). —*vi* flow into. ~**o** *m* unloading; (*recibo*) receipt; (*jurid*) evidence

descarnado *a* scrawny, lean; (*fig*) bare

descaro *m* insolence, cheek; (*cinismo*) nerve, effrontery

descarriar [20] *vt* misdirect; (*fig*) lead astray. ~**se** *vpr* go the wrong way; (*res*) stray; (*fig*) go astray

descarrilamiento *m* derailment. ~**r** *vi* be derailed. ~**se** *vpr* be derailed

descartar *vt* discard; (*rechazar*) reject. ~**se** *vpr* discard

descascarar *vt* shell

descendencia *f* descent; (*personas*) descendants. ~**dente** *a* descending. ~**der** [1] *vt* lower, get down; go down (*escalera etc*). —*vi* go down; (*provenir*) be descended (*de* from). ~**diente** *m & f* descendent. ~**so** *m* descent; (*de temperatura, fiebre etc*) fall, drop

descentralizar [10] *vt* decentralize

descifrar *vt* decipher; decode (*clave*)

descolgar [2 & 12] *vt* take down; pick up (*el teléfono*). ~**se** *vpr* let o.s. down; (*fig, fam*) turn up

descolorar *vt* discolour, fade

descolorido *a* discoloured, faded; (*persona*) pale. ~**r** *vt* discolour, fade

descomedido *a* rude; (*excesivo*) excessive, extreme

descompás *m* disproportion. ~**asado** *a* disproportionate

descomponer [34] *vt* break down; decompose (*substancia*); distort (*rasgos*); (*estropear*) break; (*desarreglar*) disturb, spoil. ~**onerse** *vpr* decompose; (*persona*) lose one's temper. ~**osición** *f* decomposition; (*med*) diarrhoea. ~**ostura** *f* breaking; (*de un motor*) breakdown; (*desorden*) disorder. ~**uesto** *a* broken; (*podrido*) decomposed; (*encolerizado*) angry. **estar** ~**uesto** have diarrhoea

descomunal *a* (*fam*) enormous

desconcertante *a* disconcerting. ~**ertar** [1] *vt* disconcert; (*dejar perplejo*) puzzle. ~**ertarse** *vpr* be put out; (*mecanismo*) break down. ~**ierto** *m* confusion

desconectar *vt* disconnect

desconfiado *a* distrustful. ~**nza** *f* distrust, suspicion. ~**r** [20] *vi*. ~**r** de not trust; (*no creer*) doubt

descongelar *vt* defrost; (*com*) unfreeze

desconocer [11] *vt* not know, not recognize. ~**ido** *a* unknown; (*cambiado*) unrecognizable. —*m* stranger. ~**imiento** *m* ignorance

desconsideración *f* lack of consideration. ~**do** *a* inconsiderate

desconsolado *a* distressed. ~**olar** [2] *vt* distress. ~**olarse** *vpr* despair. ~**uelo** *m* distress; (*tristeza*) sadness

descontado *a*. **dar por** ~**do** take for granted. **por** ~**do** of course. ~**r** [2] *vt* discount

descontent|adizo *a* hard to please. **~ar** *vt* displease. **~o** *a* unhappy (**de** about), discontented (**de** with). **—m** discontent

descontrolado *a* uncontrolled

descorazonar *vt* discourage. **~se** *vpr* lose heart

descorchar *vt* uncork

descorrer *vt* draw ⟨*cortina*⟩. **~ el cerrojo** unbolt the door

descort|és *a* rude, discourteous. **~esía** *f* rudeness

descos|er *vt* unpick. **~erse** *vpr* come undone. **~ido** *a* unstitched; (*fig*) disjointed. **como un ~ido** a lot

descoyuntar *vt* dislocate

descrédito *m* disrepute. **ir en ~ de** damage the reputation of

descreído *a* unbelieving

descremar *vt* skim

descri|bir [*pp* **descrito**] *vt* describe. **~pción** *f* description. **~ptivo** *a* descriptive

descuartizar [10] *vt* cut up

descubierto *a* disvovered; (*no cubierto*) uncovered; (*expuesto*) exposed; ⟨*cielo*⟩ clear; (*sin sombrero*) bareheaded. **—m** overdraft; (*déficit*) deficit. **poner al ~** expose

descubri|miento *m* discovery. **~r** [*pp* **descubierto**] *vt* discover; (*quitar lo que cubre*) uncover; (*revelar*) reveal; unveil ⟨*estatua*⟩. **~rse** *vpr* be discovered; ⟨*cielo*⟩ clear; (*quitarse el sombrero*) take off one's hat

descuento *m* discount

descuid|ado *a* careless; ⟨*aspecto etc*⟩ untidy; (*desprevenido*) unprepared. **~ar** *vt* neglect. **—vi** not worry. **~arse** *vpr* be careless; (*no preocuparse*) not worry. **¡~a!** don't worry! **~o** *m* carelessness; (*negligencia*) negligence. **al ~** nonchalantly.

estar ~ado not worry, rest assured

desde *prep* (*lugar etc*) from; (*tiempo*) since, from. **~ hace poco** for a short time. **~ hace un mes** for a month. **~ luego** of course. **~ Madrid hasta Barcelona** from Madrid to Barcelona. **~ niño** since childhood

desdecir [46, *pero imperativo* **desdice**, *futuro y condicional regulares*] *vi.* **~ de** be unworthy of; (*no armonizar*) not match. **~se** *vpr.* **~ de** take back ⟨*palabras etc*⟩; go back on ⟨*promesa*⟩

desd|én *m* scorn. **~eñable** *a* contemptible. **~eñar** *vt* scorn. **~eñoso** *a* scornful

desdicha *f* misfortune. **~do** *a* unfortunate. **por ~** unfortunately

desdoblar *vt* straighten; (*desplegar*) unfold

dese|able *a* desirable. **~r** *vt* want; wish ⟨*algo a uno*⟩. **de ~r** desirable. **le deseo un buen viaje** I hope you have a good journey. **¿qué desea Vd?** can I help you?

desecar [7] *vt* dry up

desech|ar *vt* throw out. **~o** *m* rubbish

desembalar *vt* unpack

desembarazar [10] *vt* clear. **~se** *vpr* free o.s.

desembarca|dero *m* landing stage. **~r** [7] *vt* unload. **—vi** disembark

desemboca|dura *f* (*de río*) mouth; (*de calle*) opening. **~r** [7] *vi.* **~r en** ⟨*río*⟩ flow into; ⟨*calle*⟩ join; (*fig*) lead to, end in

desembols|ar *vt* pay. **~o** *m* payment

desembragar [12] *vi* declutch

desembrollar *vt* unravel

desembuchar *vi* tell, reveal a secret

desemejan|te *a* unlike, dissim-
ilar. **~za** *f* dissimilarity

desempapelar *vt* unwrap

desempaquetar *vt* unpack,
unwrap

desempat|ar *vi* break a tie. **~e** *m*
tie-breaker

desempeñ|ar *vt* redeem; play
⟨*papel*⟩; hold ⟨*cargo*⟩; perform,
carry out ⟨*deber etc*⟩. **~arse** *vpr*
get out of debt. **~o** *m* redemp-
tion; ⟨*de un papel, de un cargo*⟩
performance

desemple|ado *a* unemployed.
~m unemployed person. **~o** *m*
unemployment. **los ~ados** *mpl*
the unemployed

desempolvar *vt* dust; ⟨*fig*⟩
unearth

desencadenar *vt* unchain; ⟨*fig*⟩
unleash. **~se** *vpr* break loose;
⟨*guerra etc*⟩ break out

desencajar *vt* dislocate;
⟨*desconectar*⟩ disconnect. **~se**
vpr become distorted

desencant|ar *vt* disillusion. **~o**
m disillusionment

desenchufar *vt* unplug

desenfad|ado *a* uninhibited.
~ar *vt* calm down. **~arse** *vpr*
calm down. **~o** *m* openness;
⟨*desenvoltura*⟩ assurance

desenfocado *a* out of focus

desenfren|ado *a* unrestrained.
~arse *vpr* rage. **~o** *m*
licentiousness

desenganchar *vt* unhook

desengañ|ar *vt* disillusion.
~arse *vpr* be disillusioned;
⟨*darse cuenta*⟩ realize. **~o** *m* disillusionment, disappointment

desengrasar *vt* remove the
grease from. **~vi** lose weight

desenla|ce *m* outcome. **~zar** [10]
vt undo; solve ⟨*problema*⟩

desenmarañar *vt* unravel

desenmascarar *vt* unmask

desenojar *vt* calm down. **~se**
vpr calm down

desenred|ar *vt* unravel. **~arse**
vpr extricate o.s. **~o** *m*
denouement

desenrollar *vt* unroll, unwind

desenroscar [7] *vt* unscrew

desentenderse [1] *vpr* want
nothing to do with; ⟨*afectar igno-
rancia*⟩ pretend not to know.
hacerse el desentendido ⟨*fingir no oir*⟩ pretend not to hear

desenterrar [1] *vt* exhume; ⟨*fig*⟩
unearth

desenton|ar *vi* be out of tune; ⟨*co-
lores*⟩ clash. **~o** *m* rudeness

desentrañar *vt* work out

desenvoltura *f* ease; ⟨*falta de
timidez*⟩ confidence; ⟨*descaro*⟩
insolence

desenvolver [2, *pp* **desenvuelto**] *vt* unwrap; expound
⟨*idea etc*⟩. **~se** *vpr* act with
confidence

deseo *m* wish, desire. **~so** *a*
desirous. **arder en ~s de** long
for. **buen ~** good intentions.
estar ~so de be eager to

desequilibr|ado *a* unbalanced.
~io *m* imbalance

des|erción *f* desertion; ⟨*pol*⟩
defection. **~ertar** *vt* desert. **~ér-
tico** *a* desert-like. **~ertor** *m*
deserter

desespera|ción *f* despair. **~do** *a*
desperate. **~nte** *a* infuriating.
~r *vt* drive to despair. **—vi** despair.
—rse *vpr* despair

desestimar *vt* ⟨*rechazar*⟩ reject

desfachat|ado *a* brazen, impud-
ent. **~ez** *f* impudence

desfalc|ar [7] *vt* embezzle. **~o** *m*
embezzlement

desfalle|cer [11] *vt* weaken. **—vi**
get weak; ⟨*desmayarse*⟩ faint.
~imiento *m* weakness

desfas|ado *a* ⟨*persona*⟩ out of
place, out of step; ⟨*máquina etc*⟩
out of phase. **~e** *m* jet-lag. **estar
~ado** have jet-lag

desfavor|**able** *a* unfavourable. **~ecer** [11] *vt* (*ropa*) not suit

desfigurar *vt* disfigure; (*desdibujar*) blur; (*fig*) distort

desfiladero *m* pass

desfil|**ar** *vi* march (past). **~e** *m* procession, parade. **~e de modelos** fashion show

desfogar [12] *vt* vent (**en, con** on). **~se** *vpr* let off steam

desgajar *vt* tear off; (*fig*) uproot (*persona*). **~se** *vpr* come off

desgana *f* (*falta de apetito*) lack of appetite; (*med*) weakness, faintness; (*fig*) unwillingness

desgarr|**ador** *a* heart-rending. **~ar** *vt* tear; (*fig*) break (*corazón*). **~o** *m* tear, rip; (*descaro*) insolence. **~ón** *m* tear

desgast|**ar** *vt* wear away; wear out (*ropa*). **~arse** *vpr* wear away; (*ropa*) be worn out; (*persona*) wear o.s. out. **~e** *m* wear

desgracia *f* misfortune; (*accidente*) accident; (*mala suerte*) bad luck. **~damente** *adv* unfortunately. **~do** *a* unlucky; (*pobre*) poor; (*desagradable*) unpleasant. —*m* unfortunate person, poor devil (*fam*). **~r** *vt* spoil. **caer en ~** fall from favour. **estar en ~** be unfortunate. **por ~** unfortunately. **¡qué ~!** what a shame!

desgranar *vt* shell (*guisantes etc*)

desgreñado *a* ruffled, dishevelled

desgua|**ce** *m* scrapyard. **~zar** [10] *vt* scrap

deshabitado *a* uninhabited

deshabituarse [21] *vpr* get out of the habit

deshacer [31] *vt* undo; strip (*cama*); unpack (*maleta*); (*desmontar*) take to pieces; break (*trato*); (*derretir*) melt; (*en agua*) dissolve; (*destruir*) destroy; (*estropear*) spoil; (*derrotar*) defeat.

~se *vpr* come undone; (*descomponerse*) fall to pieces; (*derretirse*) melt. **~se de algo** get rid of sth. **~se en lágrimas** burst into tears. **~se por hacer algo** go out of one's way to do sth

deshelar [1] *vt* thaw. **~se** *vpr* thaw

desheredar *vt* disinherit

deshidratar *vt* dehydrate. **~se** *vpr* become dehydrated

deshielo *m* thaw

deshilachado *a* frayed

deshincha|**do** *a* (*neumático*) flat. **~r** *vt* deflate. **~rse** *vpr* go down

deshollina|**dor** *m* (chimney-) sweep. **~r** *vt* sweep (*chimenea*)

deshon|**esto** *a* dishonest; (*obsceno*) indecent. **~or** *m*, **~ra** *f* disgrace. **~rar** *vt* dishonour

deshora: *f.* **a ~** (*a hora desacostumbrada*) at an unusual time; (*a hora inoportuna*) at an inconvenient time; (*a hora avanzada*) very late

deshuesar *vt* bone (*carne*); stone (*fruta*)

desidia *f* laziness

desierto *a* deserted. —*m* desert

designa|**ción** *f* designation. **~r** *vt* designate; (*fijar*) fix

desigual *a* unequal; (*terreno*) uneven; (*distinto*) different. **~dad** *f* inequality

desilusi|**ón** *f* disappointment; (*pérdida de ilusiones*) disillusionment. **~onar** *vt* disappoint; (*quitar las ilusiones*) disillusion. **~onarse** *vpr* become disillusioned

desinfecta|**nte** *m* disinfectant. **~r** *vt* disinfect

desinfestar *vt* decontaminate

desinflar *vt* deflate. **~se** *vpr* go down

desinhibido *a* uninhibited

desintegra|**ción** *f* disintegration. **~r** *vt* disintegrate. **~rse** *vpr* disintegrate

desinterés m impartiality; (*generosidad*) generosity. ~**esado** a impartial; (*liberal*) generous

desistir vi. ~ **de** give up

desleal a disloyal. ~**tad** f disloyalty

desleír [51] vt thin down, dilute

deslenguado a foul-mouthed

desligar [12] vt untie; (*separar*) separate; (*fig, librar*) free. ~**se** vpr break away; (*de un compromiso*) free o.s.

deslizar [10] vt slide, slip. ~**se** vpr slide, slip; (*tiempo*) slide by, pass; (*fluir*) flow

deslucido a tarnished; (*gastado*) worn out; (*fig*) undistinguished

deslumbrar vt dazzle

deslustrar vt tarnish

desmadr|ado a unruly. ~**arse** vpr get out of control. ~**e** m excess

desmán m outrage

desmandarse vpr get out of control

desmantelar vt dismantle; (*despojar*) strip

desmañado a clumsy

desmaquillador m make-up remover

desmay|ado a unconscious. ~**ar** vi lose heart. ~**arse** vpr faint. ~**o** m faint; (*estado*) unconsciousness; (*fig*) depression

desmedido a excessive

desmedrarse vpr waste away

desmejorarse vpr deteriorate

desmelenado a dishevelled

desmembrar vt (*fig*) divide up

desmemoriado a forgetful

desmentir [4] vt deny. ~**se** vpr contradict o.s.; (*desdecirse*) go back on one's word

desmenuzar [10] vt crumble; chop (*carne etc*)

desmerecer [11] vt be unworthy of. —vi deteriorate

desmesurado a excessive; (*enorme*) enormous

desmigajar vt, **desmigar** [12] vt crumble

desmonta|ble a collapsible. ~**r** vt (*quitar*) remove; (*desarmar*) take to pieces; (*derribar*) knock down; (*allanar*) level. —vi dismount

desmoralizar [10] vt demoralize

desmoronar vt wear away; (*fig*) make inroads into. ~**se** vpr crumble

desmovilizar [10] vt/i demobilize

desnatar vt skim

desnivel m unevenness; (*fig*) difference, inequality

desnud|ar vt strip; undress, strip (*persona*). ~**arse** vpr get undressed. ~**ez** f nudity. ~**o** a naked; (*fig*) bare. —m nude

desnutri|ción f malnutrition. ~**do** a undernourished

desobed|ecer [11] vt disobey. ~**iencia** f disobedience. ~**iente** a disobedient

desocupa|do a (*asiento etc*) vacant, free; (*sin trabajo*) unemployed; (*ocioso*) idle. ~**r** vt vacate

desodorante m deodorant

desoír [50] vt take no notice of

desola|ción f desolation; (*fig*) distress. ~**do** a desolate; (*persona*) sorry, sad. ~**r** vt ruin; (*desconsolar*) distress

desollar vt skin; (*fig, criticar*) criticize; (*fig, hacer pagar demasiado, fam*) fleece

desorbitante a excessive

desorden m disorder, untidiness; (*confusión*) confusion. ~**ado** a untidy. ~**ar** vt disarrange, make a mess of

desorganizar [10] vt disorganize; (*trastornar*) disturb

desorienta|do a confused. ~**r** vt disorientate. ~**rse** vpr lose one's bearings

desovar *vi* ⟨*pez*⟩ spawn; ⟨*insecto*⟩ lay eggs

despabila|do *a* wide awake; ⟨*listo*⟩ quick. **~r** *vt* ⟨*despertar*⟩ wake up; ⟨*avivar*⟩ brighten up. **~rse** *vpr* wake up; ⟨*avivarse*⟩ brighten up. ¡**despabílate**! get a move on!

despacio *adv* slowly. —*int* easy does it! **~to** *adv* slowly

despach|ar *vt* finish; ⟨*tratar con*⟩ deal with; ⟨*vender*⟩ sell; ⟨*enviar*⟩ send; ⟨*despedir*⟩ send away; issue ⟨*billete*⟩. —*vi* hurry up. **~arse** *vpr* get rid; ⟨*terminar*⟩ finish. **~o** *m* dispatch; ⟨*oficina*⟩ office; ⟨*venta*⟩ sale; ⟨*del teatro*⟩ box office

despampanante *a* stunning

desparejado *a* odd

desparpajo *m* confidence; ⟨*descaro*⟩ impudence

desparramar *vt* scatter; spill ⟨*líquidos*⟩; squander ⟨*fortuna*⟩

despavorido *a* terrified

despectivo *a* disparaging; ⟨*sentido etc*⟩ pejorative

despecho *m* spite. **a ~ de** in spite of. **por ~** out of spite

despedazar [10] *vt* tear to pieces

despedi|da *f* goodbye, farewell. **~da de soltero** stag-party. **~r** [5] *vt* say goodbye, see off; dismiss ⟨*empleado*⟩; evict ⟨*inquilino*⟩; ⟨*arrojar*⟩ throw; give off ⟨*olor etc*⟩. **~rse** *vpr*. **~rse de** say goodbye to

despeg|ado *a* cold, indifferent. **~ar** [12] *vt* unstick. —*vi* ⟨*avión*⟩ take off. **~o** *m* indifference. **~ue** *m* take-off

despeinar *vt* ruffle the hair of

despej|ado *a* clear; ⟨*persona*⟩ wide awake. **~r** *vt* clear; ⟨*aclarar*⟩ clarify. —*vi* clear. **~rse** *vpr* ⟨*aclararse*⟩ become clear; ⟨*cielo*⟩ clear; ⟨*tiempo*⟩ clear up; ⟨*persona*⟩ liven up

despellejar *vt* skin

despensa *f* pantry, larder

despeñadero *m* cliff

desperdici|ar *vt* waste. **~o** *m* waste. **~os** *mpl* rubbish. **no tener ~o** be good all the way through

desperezarse [10] *vpr* stretch

desperfecto *m* flaw

desperta|dor *m* alarm clock. **~r** [1] *vt* wake up; ⟨*fig*⟩ awaken. **~rse** *vpr* wake up

despiadado *a* merciless

despido *m* dismissal

despierto *a* awake; ⟨*listo*⟩ bright

despilfarr|ar *vt* waste. **~o** *m* squandering; ⟨*gasto innecesario*⟩ extravagance

despista|do *a* ⟨*con estar*⟩ confused; ⟨*con ser*⟩ absent-minded. **~r** *vt* throw off the scent; ⟨*fig*⟩ mislead. **~rse** *vpr* go wrong; ⟨*fig*⟩ get confused

despiste *m* swerve; ⟨*error*⟩ mistake; ⟨*confusión*⟩ muddle

desplaza|do *a* out of place. **~miento** *m* displacement; ⟨*de opinión etc*⟩ swing, shift. **~r** [10] *vt* displace. **~rse** *vpr* travel

despl|egar [1 & 12] *vt* open out; spread ⟨*alas*⟩; ⟨*fig*⟩ show. **~iegue** *m* opening; ⟨*fig*⟩ show

desplomarse *vpr* lean; ⟨*caerse*⟩ collapse

desplumar *vt* pluck; ⟨*fig, fam*⟩ fleece

despobla|do *m* deserted area. **~r** [2] *vt* depopulate

despoj|ar *vt* deprive ⟨*persona*⟩; strip ⟨*cosa*⟩. **~o** *m* plundering; ⟨*botín*⟩ booty. **~os** *mpl* left-overs; ⟨*de res*⟩ offal; ⟨*de ave*⟩ giblets

desposado *a* & *m* newly-wed

déspota *m* & *f* despot

despreci|able *a* despicable; ⟨*cantidad*⟩ negligible. **~ar** *vt* despise; ⟨*rechazar*⟩ scorn. **~o** *m* contempt

desprend|er vt remove; give off ⟨olor⟩. **~erse** vpr fall off; (fig) part with; (deducirse) follow. **~imiento** m loosening; (generosidad) generosity

despreocupa|ción f carelessness. **~do** a unconcerned; (descuidado) careless. **~rse** vpr not worry

desprestigiar vt discredit

desprevenido a unprepared. **coger a uno** ~ catch s.o. unawares

desproporci|ón f disproportion. **~onado** a disproportionate

despropósito m irrelevant remark

desprovisto a. ~ **de** lacking, without

después adv after, afterwards; (más tarde) later; (a continuación) then. ~ **de** after. ~ **de comer** after eating. ~ **de todo** after all. ~ **que** after. **poco** ~ soon after. **una semana** ~ a week later

desquiciar vt (fig) disturb

desquit|ar vt compensate. **~arse** vpr make up for; (vengarse) take revenge. **~e** m compensation; (venganza) revenge

destaca|do a outstanding. **~r** [7] vt emphasize. —vi stand out. **~rse** vpr stand out

destajo m piece-work. **hablar a** ~ talk nineteen to the dozen

destap|ar vt uncover; open ⟨botella⟩. **~arse** vpr reveal one's true self. **~e** m (fig) permissiveness

destartalado a ⟨habitación⟩ untidy; ⟨casa⟩ rambling

destell|ar vi sparkle. **~o** m sparkle; (de estrella) twinkle; (fig) glimmer

destemplado a out of tune; (agrio) harsh; ⟨tiempo⟩ unsettled; ⟨persona⟩ out of sorts

desteñir [5 & 22] vt fade; (manchar) discolour. —vi fade. **~se** vpr fade; (color) run

desterra|do m exile. **~r** [1] vt banish

destetar vt wean

destiempo m. **a** ~ at the wrong moment

destierro m exile

destil|ación f distillation. **~ar** vt distil. **~ería** f distillery

destin|ar vt destine; (nombrar) appoint. **~atario** m addressee. **~o** m (uso) use, function; (lugar) destination; (empleo) position; (suerte) destiny. **con** ~**o a** going to, bound for. **dar** ~**o a** find a use for

destitu|ción f dismissal. **~ir** [17] vt dismiss

destornilla|dor m screwdriver. **~r** vt unscrew

destreza f skill

destripar vt rip open

destroz|ar [10] vt ruin; (fig) shatter. **~o** m destruction. **causar** ~**os, hacer** ~**os** ruin

destru|cción f destruction. **~ctivo** a destructive. **~ir** [17] vt destroy; demolish ⟨edificio⟩

desunir vt separate

desus|ado a old-fashioned; (insólito) unusual. **~o** m disuse. **caer en** ~**o** become obsolete

desvaído a pale; (borroso) blurred; ⟨persona⟩ dull

desvalido a needy, destitute

desvalijar vt rob; burgle ⟨casa⟩

desvalorizar [10] vt devalue

desván m loft

desvanec|er [11] vt make disappear; tone down ⟨colores⟩; (borrar) blur; (fig) dispel. **~erse** vpr disappear; (desmayarse) faint. **~imiento** m (med) fainting fit

desvariar [20] vi be delirious; (fig) talk nonsense

desvel|ar vt keep awake. **~arse** vpr stay awake, have a sleepless night. **~o** m insomnia, sleeplessness

desvencijar vt break; (agotar) exhaust

desventaja f disadvantage

desventura f misfortune. **~do** a unfortunate

desverg|onzado a impudent, cheeky. **~üenza** f impudence, cheek

desvestirse [5] vpr undress

desvi|ación f deviation; (auto) diversion. **~iar** [20] vt deflect, turn aside. **~iarse** vpr be deflected; (del camino) make a detour; (del tema) stray. **~ío** m diversion; (frialdad) f indifference

desvivirse vpr long (por for); (afanarse) strive, do one's utmost

detall|ar vt relate in detail. **~e** m detail; (fig) gesture. **~ista** m & f retailer. **al ~e** in detail; (al por menor) retail. **con todo ~e** in great detail. **en ~es** in detail. **¡qué ~e!** how thoughtful!

detect|ar vt detect. **~ive** m detective

deten|ción f stopping; (jurid) arrest; (en la cárcel) detention. **~er** [40] vt stop; (jurid) arrest; (encarcelar) detain; (retrasar) delay. **~erse** vpr stop; (entretenerse) spend a lot of time. **~idamente** adv carefully. **~ido** a (jurid) under arrest; (minucioso) detailed. **—** m prisoner

detergente a & m detergent

deterior|ar vt damage, spoil. **~arse** vpr deteriorate. **~o** m damage

determina|ción f determination; (decisión) decison. **~nte** a decisive. **~r** vt determine; (decidir) decide; (fijar) fix. **tomar una ~ción** make a decision

detestar vt detest

detonar vi explode

detrás adv behind; (en la parte posterior) on the back. **~ de** behind. **por ~** on the back; (detrás de) behind

detrimento m detriment. **en ~ de** to the detriment of

detrito m debris

deud|a f debt. **~or** m debtor

devalua|ción f devaluation. **~r** [21] vt devalue

devanar vt wind

devasta|dor a devastating. **~r** vt devastate

devoción f devotion

devol|ución f return; (com) repayment, refund. **~ver** [5] (pp **devuelto**) vt return; (com) repay, refund; restore (edificio etc). **—vi** be sick

devorar vt devour

devoto a devout; (amigo etc) devoted. **—m** enthusiast

di vb véase **dar**

día m day. **~ de fiesta** (public) holiday. **~ del santo** saint's day. **~ festivo** (public) holiday. **~ hábil, ~ laborable** working day. **al ~** up to date. **al ~ siguiente** (on) the following day. **¡buenos ~s!** good morning! **dar los buenos ~s** say good morning. **de ~** by day. **el ~ de hoy** today. **el ~ de mañana** tomorrow. **en pleno ~** in broad daylight. **en su ~** in due course. **todo el santo ~** all day long. **un ~ de estos** one of these days. **un ~ sí y otro no** every other day. **vivir al ~** live from hand to mouth

diab|etes f diabetes. **~ético** a diabetic

diab|lo m devil. **~lura** f mischief. **~ólico** a diabolical

diácono m deacon

diadema f diadem

diáfano a diaphanous

diafragma m diaphragm

diagnosis f diagnosis. **~osticar** [7] vt diagnose. **~óstico** a diagnostic

diagonal a & f diagonal

diagrama m diagram

dialecto m dialect

diálisis f dialysis

dialogar [12] vi talk. **~álogo** m dialogue

diamante m diamond

diámetro m diameter

diana f reveille; (blanco) bull's-eye

diapasón m (para afinar) tuning fork

diapositiva f slide, transparency

diariamente adv every day. **~o** a daily. —m newspaper; (libro) diary. **a ~o** daily. **~o hablado** (en la radio) news bulletin. **de ~o** everyday, ordinary

diarrea f diarrhoea

diatriba f diatribe

dibujar [12] vt draw. **~o** m drawing. **~os animados** cartoon (film)

diccionario m dictionary

diciembre m December

dictado m dictation

dictador m dictator. **~ura** f dictatorship

dictamen m opinion; (informe) report

dictar vt dictate; pronounce (sentencia etc)

dicha f happiness. **~o** a said; (susodicho) aforementioned. —m saying. **~oso** a happy; (afortunado) fortunate. **~o y hecho** no sooner said than done. **mejor ~o** rather. **por ~a** fortunately

didáctico a didactic

diecinueve a & m nineteen. **~ocho** a & m eighteen. **~séis** a & m sixteen. **~siete** a & m seventeen

diente m tooth; (de tenedor) prong; (de ajo) clove. **~ de león**

dandelion. **hablar entre ~s** mumble

diesel /'disel/ a diesel

diestra f right hand. **~o** a (derecho) right; (hábil) skillful

dieta f diet

diez a & m ten

diezmar vt decimate

difamación f (con palabras) slander; (por escrito) libel. **~r** vt (hablando) slander; (por escrito) libel

diferencia f difference; (desacuerdo) disagreement. **~ciar** vt differentiate between. —vi differ. **~ciarse** vpr differ. **~te** a different

diferido a (TV etc) recorded. **~ir** [4] vt postpone, defer. —vi differ

difícil a difficult. **~cultad** f difficulty; (problema) problem. **~icultar** vt make difficult

difteria f diphtheria

difundir vt spread; (TV etc) broadcast. **~se** vpr spread

difunto a late, deceased. —m deceased

difusión f spreading

digerir [4] vt digest. **~stión** f digestion. **~stivo** a digestive

digital a digital; (de los dedos) finger

dignarse vpr deign. **dígnese Vd** be so kind as

dignatario m dignitary. **~idad** f dignity; (empleo) office. **~o** a worthy; (apropiado) appropriate

digo vb véase **decir**

digresión f digression

dije vb véase **decir**

dilación f delay. **~tación** f dilation, expansion. **~tado** a extensive; (tiempo) long. **~tar** vt expand; (med) dilate; (prolongar) prolong. **~tarse** vpr expand; (med) dilate; (extenderse) extend. **sin ~ción** immediately

dilema *m* dilemma

diligen|cia *f* diligence; (*gestión*) job; (*historia*) stagecoach. **~te** *a* diligent

dilucidar *vt* explain; solve (*misterio*)

diluir [17] *vt* dilute

diluvio *m* flood

dimensión *f* dimension; (*tamaño*) size

diminut|ivo *a* & *m* diminutive. **~o** *a* minute

dimi|sión *f* resignation. **~tir** *vt/i* resign

Dinamarca *f* Denmark

dinamarqués *a* Danish. **—***m* Dane

din|ámica *f* dynamics. **~ámico** *a* dynamic. **~amismo** *m* dynamism

dinamita *f* dynamite

dínamo *m*, **dinamo** *m* dynamo

dinastía *f* dynasty

dineral *m* fortune

dinero *m* money. **~** **efectivo** cash. **~** **suelto** change

dinosaurio *m* dinosaur

diócesis *f* diocese

dios *m* god. **~a** *f* goddess. **¡D~ mío!** good heavens! **¡gracias a D~!** thank God! **¡válgame D~!** bless my soul!

diploma *m* diploma

diplomacia *f* diplomacy

diplomado *a* qualified

diplomático *a* diplomatic. **—***m* diplomat

diptongo *m* diphthong

diputa|ción *f* delegation. **~ción provincial** county council. **~do** *m* delegate; (*pol, en España*) member of the Cortes; (*pol, en Inglaterra*) Member of Parliament; (*pol, en Estados Unidos*) congressman

dique *m* dike

direc|ción *f* direction; (*señas*) address; (*los que dirigen*) management; (*pol*) leadership.

~ción prohibida no entry. **~ción única** one-way. **~ta** *f* (*auto*) top gear. **~tiva** *f* directive, guideline. **~tivo** *m* executive. **~to** *a* direct; (*línea*) straight; (*tren*) through. **~tor** *m* director; (*mus*) conductor; (*de escuela etc*) headmaster; (*de periódico*) editor; (*gerente*) manager. **~tora** *f* (*de escuela etc*) headmistress. **en ~to** (*TV etc*) live. **llevar la ~ción de** direct

dirig|ente *a* ruling. **—***m* & *f* leader; (*de empresa*) manager. **~ible** *a* & *m* dirigible. **~ir** [14] *vt* direct; (*mus*) conduct; run (*empresa etc*); address (*carta etc*). **~irse** *vpr* make one's way; (*hablar*) address

discernir [1] *vt* distinguish

disciplina *f* discipline. **~r** *vt* discipline. **~rio** *a* disciplinary

discípulo *m* disciple; (*alumno*) pupil

disco *m* disc; (*mus*) record; (*deportes*) discus; (*de teléfono*) dial; (*auto*) lights; (*rail*) signal

disconforme *a* not in agreement

discontinuo *a* discontinuous

discord|ante *a* discordant. **~e** *a* discordant. **~ia** *f* discord

discoteca *f* discothèque, disco (*fam*); (*colección de discos*) record library

discreción *f* discretion

discrepa|ncia *f* discrepancy; (*desacuerdo*) disagreement. **~r** *vi* differ

discreto *a* discreet; (*moderado*) moderate; (*color*) subdued

discrimina|ción *f* discrimination. **~r** *vt* (*distinguir*) discriminate between; (*tratar injustamente*) discriminate against

disculpa *f* apology; (*excusa*) excuse. **~r** *vt* excuse, forgive. **~rse** *vpr* apologize. **dar ~s**

make excuses. **pedir** ~s apologize

discurrir *vt* think up. —*vi* think (en about); *(tiempo)* pass

discurs|ante *m* speaker. ~**ar** *vi* speak (**sobre** about). ~**o** *m* speech

discusión *f* discussion; *(riña)* argument. **eso no se admite** ~ there can be no argument about that

discuti|ble *a* debatable. ~**r** *vt* discuss; *(argumentar)* argue about; *(contradecir)* contradict. —*vi* discuss; *(argumentar)* argue

disec|ar [7] *vt* dissect; stuff *(animal muerto)*. ~**ción** *f* dissection

disemina|ción *f* dissemination. ~**r** *vt* disseminate, spread

disentería *f* dysentery

disenti|miento *m* dissent, disagreement. ~**r** [4] *vi* disagree (**de** with) (**en** on)

diseñ|ador *m* designer. ~**ar** *vt* design. ~**o** *m* design; *(fig)* sketch

disertación *f* dissertation

disfraz *m* disguise; *(vestido)* fancy dress. ~**ar** [10] *vt* disguise. ~**arse** *vpr*. ~**arse de** disguise o.s. as

disfrutar *vt* enjoy. —*vi* enjoy o.s. ~ **de** enjoy

disgregar [12] *vt* disintegrate

disgust|ar *vt* displease; *(molestar)* annoy. ~**arse** *vpr* get annoyed, get upset; *(dos personas)* fall out. ~**o** *m* annoyance; *(problema)* trouble; *(repugnancia)* disgust; *(riña)* quarrel; *(dolor)* sorrow, grief

disiden|cia *f* disagreement, dissent. ~**te** *a* & *m* & *f* dissident

disímil *a* *(LAm)* dissimilar

disimular *vt* conceal. —*vi* pretend

disipa|ción *f* dissipation; *(de dinero)* squandering. ~**r** *vt* dissipate; *(derrochar)* squander

diskette *m* floppy disk

dislocarse [7] *vpr* dislocate

disminu|ción *f* decrease. ~**ir** [17] *vi* diminish

disociar *vt* dissociate

disolver [2, *pp* **disuelto**] *vt* dissolve. ~**se** *vpr* dissolve

disonante *a* dissonant

dispar *a* different

disparar *vt* fire. —*vi* shoot (**contra** at)

disparat|ado *a* absurd. ~**ar** *vi* talk nonsense. ~**e** *m* silly thing; *(error)* mistake. **decir** ~**es** talk nonsense. **¡qué** ~**e!** how ridiculous! **un** ~**e** *(mucho, fam)* a lot, an awful lot *(fam)*

disparidad *f* disparity

disparo *m* *(acción)* firing; *(tiro)* shot

dispensar *vt* distribute; *(disculpar)* excuse. **¡Vd dispense!** forgive me

dispers|ar *vt* scatter, disperse. ~**arse** *vpr* scatter, disperse. ~**ión** *f* dispersion. ~**o** *a* scattered

dispon|er [34] *vt* arrange; *(preparar)* prepare. —*vi*. ~**er de** have; *(vender etc)* dispose of. ~**erse** *vpr* get ready. ~**ibilidad** *f* availability. ~**ible** *a* available

disposición *f* arrangement; *(aptitud)* talent; *(disponibilidad)* disposal; *(jurid)* order, decree. ~ **de ánimo** frame of mind. **a la** ~ **de** at the disposal of. **a su** ~ at your service

dispositivo *m* device

dispuesto *a* ready; *(hábil)* clever; *(inclinado)* disposed; *(servicial)* helpful

disputa *f* dispute. ~**r** *vt* dispute. —*vi*. ~**r por** argue about; *(competir para)* compete for. **sin** ~ undoubtedly

distan|cia *f* distance. ~**ciar** *vt* space out; *(en deportes)* outdistance. ~**ciarse** *vpr* *(dos personas)* fall out. ~**te** *a* distant. **a**

~cia from a distance. **guardar las** ~cias keep one's distance
distar *vi* be away; (*fig*) be far.
dista 5 kilómetros it's 5 kilometres away
distin|ción *f* distinction. ~**guido** *a* distinguished; (*en cartas*) Honoured. ~**guir** [13] *vt/i* distinguish. ~**guirse** *vpr* distinguish o.s.; (*diferenciarse*) differ; (*verse*) be visible. ~**tivo** *a* distinctive. —*m* badge. ~**to** *a* different; (*claro*) distinct
distorsión *f* distortion; (*med*) sprain
distra|cción *f* amusement; (*descuido*) absent-mindedness, inattention. ~**er** [41] *vt* distract; (*divertir*) amuse; embezzle (*fondos*). —*vi* be entertaining. ~**erse** *vpr* amuse o.s.; (*descuidarse*) not pay attention. ~**ído** *a* amusing; (*desatento*) absent-minded
distribu|ción *f* distribution. ~**idor** *m* distributor, agent. ~**idor automático** vending machine. ~**ir** [17] *vt* distribute
distrito *m* district
disturbio *m* disturbance
disuadir *vt* dissuade
diurético *a & m* diuretic
diurno *a* daytime
divagar [12] *vi* (*al hablar*) digress
diván *m* settee, sofa
diverg|encia *f* divergence. ~**ente** *a* divergent. ~**ir** [14] *vi* diverge
diversidad *f* diversity
diversificar [7] *vt* diversify
diversión *f* amusement, entertainment; (*pasatiempo*) pastime
diverso *a* different
diverti|do *a* amusing; (*que tiene gracia*) funny; (*agradable*) enjoyable. ~**r** [4] *vt* amuse, entertain. ~**rse** *vpr* enjoy o.s.
dividir *vt* divide; (*repartir*) share out

divin|idad *f* divinity. ~**o** *a* divine
divisa *f* emblem. ~**s** *fpl* foreign exchange
divisar *vt* make out
divis|ión *f* division. ~**or** *m* divisor. ~**orio** *a* dividing
divorci|ado *a* divorced. —*m* divorcee. ~**ar** *vt* divorce. ~**arse** *vpr* get divorced. ~**o** *m* divorce
divulgar [12] *vt* divulge; (*propagar*) spread. ~**se** *vpr* become known
do *m* C; (*solfa*) doh
dobl|adillo *m* hem; (*de pantalón*) turn-up (*Brit*), cuff (*Amer*). ~**ado** *a* double; (*plegado*) folded; (*película*) dubbed. ~**ar** *vt* double; (*plegar*) fold; (*torcer*) bend; turn (*esquina*); dub (*película*). —*vi* turn; (*campana*) toll. ~**arse** *vpr* double; (*encorvarse*) bend; (*ceder*) give in. ~**e** *a* double. —*m* double; (*pliegue*) fold. ~**egar** [12] *vt* (*fig*) force to give in. ~**egarse** *vpr* give in. **el** ~**e** twice as much
doce *a & m* twelve. ~**na** *f* dozen. ~**no** *a* twelfth
docente *a* teaching. —*m & f* teacher
dócil *a* obedient
doct|o *a* learned. ~**or** *m* doctor. ~**orado** *m* doctorate. ~**rina** *f* doctrine
document|ación *f* documentation, papers. ~**al** *a & m* documentary. ~**ar** *vt* document. ~**arse** *vpr* gather information. ~**o** *m* document. **D~o Nacional de Identidad** national identity card
dogm|a *m* dogma. ~**ático** *a* dogmatic
dólar *m* dollar
dol|er [2] *vi* hurt, ache; (*fig*) grieve. **me duele la cabeza** my head hurts. **le duele el estómago** he has a pain in his stomach. ~**erse** *vpr* regret; (*quejarse*)

complain. **~or** m pain; (*sordo*) ache; (*fig*) sorrow. **~oroso** a painful. **~or de cabeza** headache. **~or de muelas** toothache

domar vt tame; break in (*caballo*)

dom esticar [7] vt domesticate. **~éstico** a domestic. **—m** servant

domicilio m home. **a ~** at home. **servicio a ~** home delivery service

domina ción f domination. **~nte** a dominant; (*persona*) domineering. **~r** vt dominate; (*contener*) control; (*conocer*) have a good knowledge of. **—vi** dominate; (*destacarse*) stand out. **~rse** vpr control o.s.

domin go m Sunday. **~guero** a Sunday. **~ical** a Sunday

dominio m authority; (*territorio*) domain; (*fig*) good knowledge

dominó m (*juego*) dominoes

don m talent, gift; (*en un sobre*) Mr. **~ Pedro** Pedro. **tener ~ de lenguas** have a gift for languages. **tener ~ de gentes** have a way with people

donación f donation

donaire m grace, charm

dona nte m (*de sangre*) donor. **~r** vt donate

doncella f (*criada*) maid

donde adv where

dónde adv where? **¿hasta ~?** how far? **¿por ~?** whereabouts? (*¿por qué camino?*) which way? **¿a ~ vas?** where are you going? **¿de ~ eres?** where are you from?

dondequiera adv anywhere; (*en todas partes*) everywhere. **~ que** wherever. **por ~** everywhere

doña f (*en un sobre*) Mrs. **~ María** María

dora do a golden; (*cubierto de oro*) gilt. **~dura** f gilding. **~r** vt gilt; (*culin*) brown

dormi lón m sleepyhead. **—a** lazy. **~r** [6] vt send to sleep. **—vi** sleep. **~rse** vpr go to sleep. **~tar** vi doze. **~torio** m bedroom. **~r la siesta** have an afternoon nap, have a siesta. **echarse a dormir** go to bed

dorsal a back. **—m** (*en deportes*) number. **~o** m back

dos a & m two. **~cientos** a & m two hundred. **cada ~ por tres** every five minutes. **de ~ en ~** in twos, in pairs. **en un ~ por tres** in no time. **los dos, las dos** both (of them)

dosi ficar [7] vt dose; (*fig*) measure out. **~s** f dose

dot ado a gifted. **~ar** vt give a dowry; (*proveer*) endow (**de** with). **~e** m dowry

doy vb véase **dar**

dragar [12] vt dredge

drago m dragon tree

dragón m dragon

dram a m drama; (*obra de teatro*) play. **~ático** a dramatic. **~atizar** [10] vt dramatize. **~aturgo** m playwright

drástico a drastic

droga f drug. **~dicto** m drug addict. **~do** a drugged. **—m** drug addict. **~r** [12] vt drug. **~rse** vpr take drugs. **~ta** m & f (*fam*) drug addict

droguería f hardware shop (*Brit*), hardware store (*Amer*)

dromedario m dromedary

ducha f shower. **~rse** vpr have a shower

dud a f doubt. **~ar** vt/i doubt. **~oso** a doubtful; (*sospechoso*) dubious. **poner en ~a** question. **sin ~a (alguna)** without a doubt

duelo m duel; (*luto*) mourning

duende m imp

dueñ a f owner, proprietress; (*de una pensión*) landlady. **~o** m owner, proprietor; (de una pensión) landlord

duermo vb véase **dormir**

dul|ce a sweet; (agua) fresh; (suave) soft, gentle. —m sweet. ~**zura** f sweetness; (fig) gentleness

duna f dune

dúo m duet, duo

duodécimo a & m twelfth

duplica|do a in duplicate. —m duplicate. ~**r** [7] vt duplicate. ~**rse** vpr double

duque m duke. ~**sa** f duchess

dura|ción f duration, length. ~**dero** a lasting

durante prep during, in; (medida de tiempo) for. ~ **todo el año** all year round

durar vi last

durazno m (LAm, fruta) peach

dureza f hardness, toughness; (med) hard patch

durmiente a sleeping

duro a hard; (culin) tough; (fig) harsh. —adv hard. —m fivepeseta coin. **ser ~ de oído** be hard of hearing

E

e conj and

ebanista m & f cabinet-maker

ébano m ebony

ebri|edad f drunkenness. ~**o** a drunk

ebullición f boiling

eccema m eczema

eclesiástico a ecclesiastical. —m clergyman

eclipse m eclipse

eco m echo. **hacer(se)** ~ echo

ecolog|ía f ecology. ~**ista** m & f ecologist

economato m cooperative store

econom|ía f economy; (ciencia) economics. ~**ómicamente** adv

economically. ~**ómico** a economic(al); (no caro) inexpensive. ~**omista** m & f economist. ~**omizar** [10] vt/i economize

ecuación f equation

ecuador m equator. **el E~** Ecuador

ecuánime a level-headed; (imparcial) impartial

ecuanimidad f equanimity

ecuatoriano a & m Ecuadorian

ecuestre a equestrian

echar vt throw; post (carta); give off (olor); pour (líquido); sprout (hojas etc); (despedir) throw out; dismiss (empleado); (poner) put on; put out (raíces); show (película). ~**se** vpr throw o.s.; (tumbarse) lie down. ~ **a** start. ~ **a perder** spoil. ~ **de menos** miss. ~**se atrás** (fig) back down. **echárselas de** feign

edad f age. ~ **avanzada** old age. **E~ de Piedra** Stone Age. **E~ Media** Middle Ages. **¿qué ~ tiene?** how old is he?

edición f edition; (publicación) publication

edicto m edict

edific|ación f building. ~**ante** a edifying. ~**ar** [7] vt build; (fig) edify. ~**io** m building; (fig) structure

Edimburgo m Edinburgh

edit|ar vt publish. ~**or** a publishing. —m publisher. ~**orial** a editorial. —m leading article. —f publishing house

edredón m eiderdown

educa|ción f upbringing; (modales) (good) manners; (enseñanza) education. ~**do** a polite. ~**dor** m teacher. ~**r** [7] vt bring up; (enseñar) educate. ~**tivo** a educational. **bien ~do** polite. **falta de ~ción** rudeness, bad manners. **mal ~do** rude

edulcorante m sweetener

EE.UU. *abrev* (*Estados Unidos*) USA, New York (of America)

efectivamente *adv* really; (*por supuesto*) indeed. (*por lo efectivo*) real; (*empleo*) permanent. *—m* cash. **∼o** *m* effect; (*impresión*) impression. **∼os** *mpl* belongings; (*com*) goods. **∼uar** [21] *vt* carry out, effect; make *⟨viaje, compras etc⟩*. **en ∼o** in fact; (*por supuesto*) indeed

efervescente *a* effervescent; *⟨bebidas⟩* fizzy

eficacia *f* effectiveness; (*de persona*) efficiency. **∼z** *a* effective; (*persona*) efficient

eficiencia *f* efficiency. **∼te** *a* efficient

efigie *f* effigy

efímero *a* ephemeral

efluvio *m* outflow

efusión *n* effusion. **∼vo** *a* effusive; *⟨gracias⟩* warm

Egeo *m*. **mar ∼** Aegean Sea

égida *f* aegis

egipcio *a & m* Egyptian

Egipto *m* Egypt

egocéntrico *a* egocentric. *—m* egocentric person. **∼ísmo** *m* selfishness. **∼ísta** *a* selfish. *—m* selfish person

egregio *a* eminent

egresar *vi* (*LAm*) leave; (*univ*) graduate

eje *m* axis; (*tec*) axle

ejecución *f* execution; (*mus etc*) performance. **∼tante** *m & f* executor; (*mus etc*) performer. **∼tar** *vt* carry out; (*mus etc*) perform; (*matar*) execute

ejecutivo *m* director, manager

ejemplar *a* exemplary. *—m* (*ejemplo*) example, specimen; (*libro*) copy; (*revista*) issue, number. **∼ificar** [7] *vt* exemplify. **∼o** *m* example. **dar ∼o** set an example. **por ∼o** for example. **sin ∼** unprecedented

ejercer [9] *vt* exercise; practise *⟨profesión⟩*; exert *⟨influencia⟩*. *—vi* practise. **∼icio** *m* exercise; (*de una profesión*) practice. **∼itar** *vt* exercise. **∼itarse** *vpr* exercise. **hacer ∼icios** take exercise

ejército *m* army

el *art def m* (*pl* **los**) the. *—pron* (*pl* **los**) the one. **∼ de Antonio** Antonio's. **∼ que** whoever, the one

él *pron* (*persona*) he; (*persona con prep*) him; (*cosa*) it. **el libro de ∼** his book

elaboración *f* processing; (*fabricación*) manufacture. **∼r** *vt* process; manufacture (*producto*); (*producir*) produce

elasticidad *f* elasticity. **∼ástico** *a & m* elastic

elección *f* choice; (*de político etc*) election. **∼ciones** *fpl* (*pol*) election. **∼tor** *m* voter. **∼torado** *m* electorate. **∼toral** *a* electoral

electricidad *f* electricity. **∼sta** *m & f* electrician

eléctrico *a* electric; (*de la electricidad*) electrical

electrificar [7] *vt*, **electrizar** [10] *vt* electrify

electrocutar *vt* electrocute

electrodo *m* electrode

electrodoméstico *a* electrical household. **∼s** *mpl* electrical household appliances

electrólisis *f* electrolysis

electrón *m* electron

electrónica *f* electronics. **∼o** *a* electronic

elefante *m* elephant

elegancia *f* elegance. **∼te** *a* elegant

elegía *f* elegy

elegible *a* eligible. **∼do** *a* chosen. **∼r** [5 & 14] *vt* choose; (*por votación*) elect

elemental *a* elementary. **∼o** *m* element; (*persona*) person, bloke *(fam).* ~**os** *mpl (nociones)* basic principles

elenco *m (en el teatro)* cast

eleva|ción *f* elevation; *(de precios)* rise, increase; *(acción)* raising. ~**dor** *m (LAm)* lift. ~**r** *vt* raise; *(promover)* promote

elimina|ción *f* elimination. ~**r** *vt* eliminate. ~**toria** *f* preliminary heat

el|ipse *f* ellipse. ~**íptico** *a* elliptical

élite /e'lit, e'lite/ *f* elite

elixir *m* elixir

elocución *f* elocution

elocuen|cia *f* eloquence. ~**te** *a* eloquent

elogi|ar *vt* praise. ~**o** *m* praise

elote *m (Mex)* corn on the cob

eludir *vt* avoid, elude

ella *pron (persona)* she; *(persona con prep)* her; *(cosa)* it. ~**s** *pron pl* they; *(con prep)* them. **el libro de** ~ her book. **el libro de** ~**s** their book

ello *pron* it

ellos *pron pl* they; *(con prep)* them. **el libro de** ~ their book

emaciado *a* emaciated

emana|ción *f* emanation. ~**r** *vi* emanate *(de* from); *(originarse)* originate *(de* from, in)

emancipa|ción *f* emancipation. ~**do** *a* emancipated. ~**r** *vt* emancipate. ~**rse** *vpr* become emancipated

embadurnar *vt* smear

embajad|a *f* embassy. ~**or** *m* ambassador

embalar *vt* pack

embaldosar *vt* tile

embalsamar *vt* embalm

embalse *m* dam; *(pantano)* reservoir

embaraz|ada *a* pregnant. ~*f* pregnant woman. ~**ar** [10] *vt* hinder. ~**o** *m* hindrance; *(de mujer)* pregnancy. ~**oso** *a* awkward, embarrassing

embar|cación *f* boat. ~**cadero** *m* jetty, pier. ~**car** [7] *vt* embark *(personas)*; ship *(mercancías).* ~**carse** *vpr* embark. ~**carse en** *(fig)* embark upon

embargo *m* embargo; *(jurid)* seizure. **sin** ~ however

embarque *m* loading

embarullar *vt* muddle

embaucar [7] *vt* deceive

embeber *vt* absorb; *(empapar)* soak. —*vi* shrink. ~**se** *vpr* be absorbed

embelesar *vt* delight. ~**se** *vpr* be delighted

embellecer [11] *vt* embellish

embesti|da *f* attack. ~**r** [5] *vt/i* attack

emblema *m* emblem

embobar *vt* amaze

embobecer [11] *vt* make silly. ~**se** *vpr* go silly

embocadura *f (de un río)* mouth

emboquillado *a* tipped

embolsar *vt* pocket

emborrachar *vt* get drunk. ~**se** *vpr* get drunk

emborrascarse *vpr* get stormy

emborronar *vt* blot

embosca|da *f* ambush. ~**rse** [7] *vpr* lie in wait

embotar *vt* blunt; *(fig)* dull

embotella|miento *m (de vehículos)* traffic jam. ~**r** *vt* bottle

embrague *m* clutch

embriag|ar [12] *vt* get drunk; *(fig)* intoxicate; *(fig, enajenar)* enrapture. ~**arse** *vpr* get drunk. ~**uez** *f* drunkenness; *(fig)* intoxication

embrión *m* embryo

embroll|ar *vt* mix up; involve *(personas).* ~**arse** *vpr* get into a muddle; *(en un asunto)* get involved. ~**o** *m* tangle; *(fig)* muddle. ~**ón** *m* troublemaker

embromar *vt* make fun of; *(engañar)* fool

embruja|do a bewitched; ⟨casa etc⟩ haunted. **~r** vt bewitch

embrutecer [11] vt brutalize

embuchar vt wolf ⟨comida⟩

embudo m funnel

embuste m lie. **~ro** a deceitful. —m liar

embuti|do m ⟨culin⟩ sausage. **~r** vt stuff

emergencia f emergency; ⟨acción de emerger⟩ emergency. **en caso de ~** in case of emergency

emerger [14] vi appear, emerge; ⟨submarino⟩ surface

emigra|ción f emigration. **~nte** m & f emigrant. **~r** vi emigrate

eminen|cia f eminence. **~te** a eminent

emisario m emissary

emis|ión f emission; ⟨de dinero⟩ issue; ⟨TV etc⟩ broadcast. **~or** a issuing; ⟨TV etc⟩ broadcasting. **~ora** f radio station

emitir vt emit; let out ⟨grito⟩; ⟨TV etc⟩ broadcast; ⟨expresar⟩ express; ⟨poner en circulación⟩ issue

emoci|ón f emotion; ⟨excitación⟩ excitement. **~onado** a moved. **~onante** a exciting; ⟨conmovedor⟩ moving. **~onar** vt excite; ⟨conmover⟩ move. **~onarse** vpr get excited; ⟨conmoverse⟩ be moved. **¡qué ~ón!** how exciting!

emotivo a emotional; ⟨conmovedor⟩ moving

empacar [7] vt ⟨LAm⟩ pack

empacho m indigestion; ⟨vergüenza⟩ embarrassment

empadronar vt register. **~se** vpr register

empalagoso a sickly; ⟨demasiado amable⟩ ingratiating; ⟨demasiado sentimental⟩ mawkish

empalizada f fence

empalm|ar vt connect, join. —vi meet. **~e** m junction; ⟨de trenes⟩ connection

empanad|a f ⟨savoury⟩ pie. **~illa** f ⟨small⟩ pie. **~o** a fried in breadcrumbs

empanizado a ⟨Mex⟩ fried in breadcrumbs

empantanar vt flood. **~se** vpr become flooded; ⟨fig⟩ get bogged down

empañar vt mist; dull ⟨metales etc⟩; ⟨fig⟩ tarnish. **~se** vpr ⟨cristales⟩ steam up

empapar vt soak; ⟨absorber⟩ soak up. **~se** vpr be soaked

empapela|do m wallpaper. **~r** vt paper; ⟨envolver⟩ wrap ⟨in paper⟩

empaquetar vt package; pack together ⟨personas⟩

emparedado m sandwich

emparejar vt match; ⟨nivelar⟩ make level. **~se** vpr pair off

empast|ar vt fill ⟨muela⟩. **~e** m filling

empat|ar vi draw. **~e** m draw

empedernido a inveterate; ⟨insensible⟩ hard

empedrar [1] vt pave

empeine m instep

empeñ|ado a in debt; ⟨decidido⟩ determined; ⟨acalorado⟩ heated. **~ar** vt pawn; pledge ⟨palabras⟩; ⟨principiar⟩ start. **~arse** vpr ⟨endeudarse⟩ get into debt; ⟨meterse⟩ get involved; ⟨estar decidido a⟩ insist ⟨en on⟩. **~o** m pledge; ⟨resolución⟩ determination. **casa de ~s** pawnshop

empeorar vt make worse. —vi get worse. **~se** vpr get worse

empequeñecer [11] vt dwarf; ⟨fig⟩ belittle

empera|dor m emperor. **~triz** f empress

empezar [1 & 10] vt/i start, begin. **para ~** to begin with

empina|do *a* upright; ‹*cuesta*›
steep. **~r** *vt* raise. **~rse** ‹*persona*› stand on tiptoe; ‹*animal*›
rear

empírico *a* empirical

emplasto *m* plaster

emplaza|miento *m* (*jurid*) summons; (*lugar*) site. **~r** [10] *vt*
summon; (*situar*) site

emple|ado *m* employee. **~ar** *vt*
use; employ ‹*persona*›; spend ‹*tiempo*›. **~arse** *vpr* be used; ‹*persona*› be employed. **~o** *m* use; (*trabajo*) employment; (*puesto*)
job

empobrecer [11] *vt* impoverish.
~se *vpr* become poor

empolvar *vt* powder

empoll|ar *vt* incubate ‹*huevos*›; (*estudiar, fam*) swot up (*Brit*),
grind away at (*Amer*). —*vi* ‹*ave*›
sit; ‹*estudiante*› swot (*Brit*),
grind away (*Amer*). **~ón** *m* swot

emponzoñar *vt* poison

emporio *m* emporium; (*LAm, almacén*) department store

empotra|do *a* built-in, fitted. **~r**
vt fit

emprendedor *a* enterprising

emprender *vt* undertake; set out
on ‹*viaje etc*›. **~la con uno** pick
a fight with s.o.

empresa *f* undertaking; (*com*)
company, firm. **~rio** *m* impresario; (*com*) contractor

empréstito *m* loan

empuj|ar *vt* push; press ‹*botón*›.
~e *m* push, shove; (*fig*) drive.
~ón *m* push, shove

empuñar *vt* grasp; take up
‹*pluma, espada*›

emular *vt* emulate

emulsión *f* emulsion

en *prep* in; (*sobre*) on; (*dentro*)
inside, in; (*con dirección*)
into, in; (*medio de transporte*) by. **~ casa**
at home. **~ coche** by car. **~ 10
días** in 10 days. **de pueblo ~
pueblo** from town to town

enagua *f* petticoat

enajena|ción *f* alienation; (*éxtasis*) rapture. **~r** *vt* alienate; (*volver loco*) drive mad; (*fig, extasiar*) enrapture. **~ción
mental** insanity

enamora|do *a* in love. —*m* lover.
~r *vt* win the love of. **~rse** *vpr*
fall in love (**de** with)

enan|ito *m* dwarf. **~o** *a & m*
dwarf

enardecer [11] *vt* inflame. **~se**
vpr get excited (**por** about)

encabeza|miento *m* heading;
(*de periódico*) headline. **~r** [10]
vt introduce ‹*escrito*›; (*poner título a*) entitle; head ‹*una lista*›;
lead ‹*revolución etc*›; (*empadronar*) register

encadenar *vt* chain; (*fig*) tie
down

encaj|ar *vt* fit; fit together ‹*varias
piezas*›. —*vi* fit; (*estar de
acuerdo*) tally. **~arse** *vpr*
squeeze into. **~e** *m* lace; (*acción
de encajar*) fitting

encajonar *vt* box; (*en sitio estrecho*) squeeze in

encalar *vt* whitewash

encallar *vt* run aground; (*fig*) get
bogged down

encaminar *vt* direct. **~se** *vpr*
make one's way

encandilar *vt* (*pasmar*) bewilder; (*estimular*) stimulate

encanecer [11] *vi* go grey

encant|ado *a* enchanted; (*hechizado*) bewitched; (*casa etc*)
haunted. **~ador** *a* charming.
—*m* magician. **~amiento**
magic. **~ar** *vt* bewitch; (*fig*)
charm, delight. **~o** *m* magic;
(*fig*) delight. **¡~ado!** pleased to
meet you! **me ~a la leche** I love
milk

encapotado *a* ‹*cielo*› overcast

encapricharse *vpr*. **~ con** take
a fancy to

encarar *vt* face. **~se** *vpr*. **~se con** face

encarcelar *vt* imprison

encarecer [11] *vt* put up the price of; (*alabar*) praise. —*vi* go up

encarg|ado *a* in charge. —*m* manager, attendant, person in charge. **~ar** [12] *vt* entrust; (*pedir*) order. **~arse** vpr take charge (**de** of). **~o** *m* job; (*com*) order; (*recado*) errand. **hecho de ~o** made to measure

encariñarse *vpr*. **~ con** take to, become fond of

encarna|ción *f* incarnation. **~do** *a* incarnate; (*rojo*) red. —*m* red

encarnizado *a* bitter

encarpetar *vt* file; (*LAm, dar carpetazo*) shelve

encarrilar *vt* put back on the rails; (*fig*) direct, put on the right road

encasillar *vt* pigeonhole

encastillarse *vpr*. **~ en** (*fig*) stick to

encauzar [10] *vt* channel

encend|edor *m* lighter. **~er** [1] *vt* light; (*pegar fuego a*) set fire to; switch on, turn on (*aparato eléctrico*); (*fig*) arouse. **~erse** *vpr* light; (*prender fuego*) catch fire; (*excitarse*) get excited; (*ruborizarse*) blush. **~ido** *a* lit; (*aparato eléctrico*) on; (*rojo*) bright red. —*m* (*auto*) ignition

encera|do *a* waxed. —*m* (*pizarra*) blackboard. **~r** *vt* wax

encerr|ar [1] *vt* shut in; (*con llave*) lock up; (*fig, contener*) contain. **~ona** *f* trap

encía *f* gum

encíclica *f* encyclical

enciclop|edia *f* encyclopaedia. **~édico** *a* encyclopaedic

encierro *m* confinement; (*cárcel*) prison

encima *adv* on top; (*arriba*) above. **~ de** on, on top of; (*sobre*) over; (*además de*) besides, as well as. **por ~** on top; (*a la ligera*) superficially. **por ~ de todo** above all

encina *f* holm oak

encinta *a* pregnant

enclave *m* enclave

enclenque *a* weak; (*enfermizo*) sickly

encog|er [14] *vt* shrink; (*contraer*) contract. **~erse** *vpr* shrink. **~erse de hombros** shrug one's shoulders. **~ido** *a* (*fig, tímido*) timid

encolar *vt* glue; (*pegar*) stick

encolerizar [10] *vt* make angry. **~se** *vpr* get angry, lose one's temper

encomendar [1] *vt* entrust

encomi|ar *vt* praise. **~o** *m* praise

encono *m* bitterness, ill will

encontra|do *a* contrary, conflicting. **~r** [2] *vt* find; (*tropezar con*) meet. **~rse** *vpr* meet; (*hallarse*) be. **no ~rse** feel uncomfortable

encorvar *vt* bend, curve. **~se** *vpr* stoop

encrespado (*pelo*) curly; (*mar*) rough

encrucijada *f* crossroads

encuaderna|ción *f* binding. **~dor** *m* bookbinder. **~r** *vt* bind

encuadrar *vt* frame

encubi|erto *a* hidden. **~rir** [*pp* **encubierto**] *vt* hide, conceal; shelter (*delincuente*)

encuentro *m* meeting; (*colisión*) crash; (*en deportes*) match; (*mil*) skirmish

encuesta *f* survey; (*investigación*) inquiry

encumbra|do *a* eminent. **~r** *vt* (*fig, elevar*) exalt. **~rse** *vpr* rise

encurtidos *mpl* pickles

encharcar [7] *vt* flood. **~se** *vpr* be flooded

enchuf|ado *a* switched on. **~ar** *vt* plug in; fit together (*tubos etc*).

~e *m* socket; (*clavija*) plug; (*de tubos etc*) joint; (*fig, empleo, fam*) cushy job; (*influencia, fam*) influence. **tener** ~**e** have friends in the right places

endeble *a* weak

endemoniado *a* possessed; (*malo*) wicked

enderezar [10] *vt* straighten out; (*poner vertical*) put upright (again); (*fig, arreglar*) put right, sort out; (*dirigir*) direct. ~**se** *vpr* straighten out

endeudarse *vpr* get into debt

endiablado *a* possessed; (*malo*) wicked

endomingarse [12] *vpr* dress up

endosar *vt* endorse (*cheque etc*); (*fig, fam*) lumber

endrogarse [12] *vpr* (*Mex*) get into debt

endulzar [10] *vt* sweeten; (*fig*) soften

endurecer [11] *vt* harden. ~**se** *vpr* harden; (*fig*) become hardened

enema *m* enema

enemi|go *a* hostile. —*m* enemy. ~**stad** *f* enmity. ~**star** *vt* make an enemy of. ~**starse** *vpr* fall out (**con** with)

en|ergía *f* energy. ~**érgico** *a* (*persona*) lively; (*decisión*) forceful

energúmeno *m* madman

enero *m* January

enervar *vt* enervate

enésimo *a* nth, umpteenth (*fam*)

enfad|adizo *a* irritable. ~**ado** *a* cross, angry. ~**ar** *vt* make cross, anger; (*molestar*) annoy. ~**arse** *vpr* get cross. ~**o** *m* anger; (*molestia*) annoyance

énfasis *m invar* emphasis, stress. **poner** ~ stress, emphasize

enfático *a* emphatic

enferm|ar *vi* fall ill. ~**edad** *f* illness. ~**era** *f* nurse. ~**ería** *f* sick

bay. ~**ero** *m* (male) nurse. ~**izo** *a* sickly. ~**o** *a* ill. —*m* patient

enflaquecer [11] *vt* make thin. —*vi* lose weight

enfo|car [7] *vt* shine on; focus (*lente etc*); (*fig*) consider. ~**que** *m* focus; (*fig*) point of view

enfrascarse [7] *vpr* (*fig*) be absorbed

enfrentar *vt* face, confront; (*poner frente a frente*) bring face to face. ~**se** *vpr*. ~**se con** confront; (*en deportes*) meet

enfrente *adv* opposite. ~ **de** opposite. **de** ~ opposite

enfria|miento *m* cooling; (*catarro*) cold. ~**r** [20] *vt* cool (down); (*fig*) cool down. ~**rse** *vpr* go cold; (*fig*) cool off

enfurecer [11] *vt* infuriate. ~**se** *vpr* lose one's temper; (*mar*) become rough

enfurruñarse *vpr* sulk

engalanar *vt* adorn. ~**se** *vpr* dress up

enganchar *vt* hook; hang up (*ropa*). ~**se** *vpr* get caught; (*mil*) enlist

engañ|ar *vt* deceive, trick; (*ser infiel*) be unfaithful. ~**arse** *vpr* be wrong, be mistaken; (*no admitir la verdad*) deceive o.s. ~**o** *m* deceit, trickery; (*error*) mistake. ~**oso** *a* deceptive; (*persona*) deceitful

engarzar [10] *vt* string (*cuentas*); set (*joyas*); (*fig*) link

engatusar *vt* (*fam*) coax

engendr|ar *vt* breed; (*fig*) produce. ~**o** *m* (*monstruo*) monster; (*fig*) brainchild

englobar *vt* include

engomar *vt* glue

engordar *vt* fatten. —*vi* get fatter, put on weight

engorro *m* nuisance

engranaje *m* (*auto*) gear

engrandecer [11] *vt* (*enaltecer*) exalt, raise

engrasar vt grease; (con aceite) oil; (ensuciar) make greasy

engreído a arrogant

engrosar [2] vt swell. —vi (persona) get fatter; (río) swell

engullir [22] vt gulp down

enharinar vt sprinkle with flour

enhebrar vt thread

enhorabuena f congratulations. **dar la** ~ congratulate

enigm|a m enigma. ~ático a enigmatic

enjabonar vt soap; (fig, fam) butter up

enjalbegar vt whitewash

enjambre m swarm

enjaular vt put in a cage

enjuag|ar [12] vt rinse (out). ~atorio m mouthwash. ~ue m rinsing; (para la boca) mouthwash

enjugar [12] vt dry; (limpiar) wipe; cancel (deuda)

enjuiciar vt pass judgement on

enjuto a (persona) skinny

enlace m connection; (matrimonial) wedding

enlatar vt tin, can

enlazar [10] vt tie together; (fig) relate, connect

enlodar vt, **enlodazar** [10] vt cover in mud

enloquecer [11] vt drive mad. —vi go mad. ~se vpr go mad

enlosar vt (con losas) pave; (con baldosas) tile

enlucir [11] vt plaster

enluta|do a in mourning. ~r vt dress in mourning; (fig) sadden

enmarañar vt tangle (up), entangle; (confundir) confuse. ~se vpr get into a tangle; (confundirse) get confused

enmarcar [7] vt frame

enmascarar vt mask. ~se vpr masquerade as

enm|endar vt correct. ~endarse vpr mend one's way.

~ienda f correction; (de ley etc) amendment

enmohecerse [11] vpr (con óxido) go rusty; (con hongos) go mouldy

enmudecer [11] vi be dumbstruck; (callar) say nothing

ennegrecer [11] vt blacken

ennoblecer [11] vt ennoble; (fig) add style to

enoj|adizo a irritable. ~ado a angry, cross. ~ar vt make cross, anger; (molestar) annoy. ~arse vpr get cross. ~o m anger; (molestia) annoyance. ~oso a annoying

enorgullecerse [11] vpr be proud

enorm|e a enormous; (malo) wicked. ~emente adv enormously. ~idad f immensity; (atrocidad) enormity. **me gusta una** ~idad I like it enormously

enrabiar vt infuriate

enraizar [10 & 20] vi take root

enrarecido a rarefied

enrasar vt make level

enred|adera f creeper. ~adero a climbing. ~ar vt tangle (up), entangle; (confundir) confuse; (comprometer a uno) involve, implicate; (sembrar la discordia) cause trouble between. —vi get up to mischief. ~ar con fiddle with, play with. ~arse vpr get into a tangle; (confundirse) get confused; (persona) get involved. ~o m tangle; (fig) muddle, mess

enrejado m bars

enrevesado a complicated

enriquecer [11] vt make rich; (fig) enrich. ~se vpr get rich

enrojecer [11] vt turn red, redden. ~se vpr (persona) go red, blush

enrolar vt enlist

enrollar vt roll (up); wind (hilo etc)

enroscar [7] *vt* coil; (*atornillar*) screw in

ensalad|a *f* salad. **~era** *f* salad bowl. **~illa** *f* Russian salad. **armar una ~a** make a mess

ensalzar [10] *vt* praise; (*enaltecer*) exalt

ensambladura *f*, **ensamblaje** *m* (*acción*) assembling; (*efecto*) joint

ensamblar *vt* join

ensanch|ar *vt* widen; (*agrandar*) enlarge. **~arse** *vpr* get wider. **~e** *m* widening; (*de ciudad*) new district

ensangrentar [1] *vt* stain with blood

ensañarse *vpr*. **~ con** treat cruelly

ensartar *vt* string (*cuentas etc*)

ensay|ar *vt* test; rehearse (*obra de teatro etc*). **~arse** *vpr* rehearse. **~o** *m* test, trial; (*composición literaria*) essay

ensenada *f* inlet, cove

enseña|nza *f* education; (*acción de enseñar*) teaching. **~nza media** secondary education. **~r** *vt* teach; (*mostrar*) show

enseñorearse *vpr* take over

enseres *mpl* equipment

ensillar *vt* saddle

ensimismarse *vpr* be lost in thought

ensoberbecerse [11] *vpr* become conceited

ensombrecer [11] *vt* darken

ensordecer [11] *vt* deafen. **~vi** go deaf

ensortijar *vt* curl (*pelo etc*)

ensuciar *vt* dirty. **~se** *vpr* get dirty

ensueño *m* dream

entablar *vt* (*empezar*) start

entablillar *vt* put in a splint

entalegar [12] *vt* put into a bag; (*fig*) hoard

entallar *vt* fit (*un vestido*). **~vi** fit

entarimado *m* parquet

ente *m* entity, being; (*persona rara*, *fam*) odd person; (*com*) firm, company

entend|er [1] *vt* understand; (*opinar*) believe, think; (*querer decir*) mean. **~vi** understand. **~erse** *vpr* make o.s. understood; (*comprenderse*) be understood. **~er de** know all about. **~erse con** get on with. **~ido** *a* understood; (*enterado*) well-informed. **~interj** agreed!, OK! (*fam*). **~imiento** *m* understanding. **a mi ~er** in my opinion. **dar a ~er** hint. **no darse por ~ido** pretend not to understand, turn a deaf ear

entenebrecer [11] *vt* darken. **~se** *vpr* get dark

enterado *a* well-informed; (*que sabe*) aware. **no darse por ~** pretend not to understand, turn a deaf ear

enteramente *adv* entirely, completely

enterar *vt* inform. **~se** *vpr*. **~se de** find out about, hear of. **¡entérate!** listen! **¿te enteras?** do you understand?

entereza *f* (*carácter*) strength of character

enternecer [11] *vt* (*fig*) move, touch. **~se** *vpr* be moved, be touched

entero *a* entire, whole; (*firme*) firm. **por ~** entirely, completely

enterra|dor *m* gravedigger. **~r** [1] *vt* bury

entibiar *vt* cool. **~se** *vpr* cool down; (*fig*) cool off

entidad *f* entity; (*organización*) organization; (*com*) company

entierro *m* burial; (*ceremonia*) funeral

entona|ción *f* intonation; (*fig*) arrogance. **~r** *vt* intone. **~vi** (*mus*) be in tune; (*colores*) match. **~rse** *vpr* (*fortalecerse*) tone o.s. up; (*engreírse*) be arrogant

entonces *adv* then. **en aquel ~, por aquel ~** at that time, then

entontecer [11] *vt* make silly. **~se** *vpr* get silly

entornar *vt* half close; leave ajar (*puerta*)

entorpecer [11] *vt* (*frío etc*) numb; (*dificultar*) hinder

entra|da *f* entrance; (*acceso*) admission, entry; (*billete*) ticket; (*de datos, tec*) input. **~do** *a*. **~do en años** elderly. **ya ~da la noche** late at night. **~nte** *a* next, coming. **dar ~da a** (*admitir*) admit. **de ~da** right away.

entraña *f* (*fig*) heart. **~s** *fpl* entrails; (*fig*) heart. **~ble** *a* (*cariño etc*) deep; (*amigo*) close. **~r** *vt* involve

entrar *vt* put; (*traer*) bring. —*vi* go in, enter; (*venir*) come in, enter; (*empezar*) start, begin. **no ~ ni salir en** have nothing to do with

entre *prep* (*de dos personas o cosas*) between; (*más de dos*) among(st)

entreabi|erto *a* half-open. **~rir** [*pp* **entreabierto**] *vt* half open

entreacto *m* interval

entrecano *a* (*pelo*) greying; (*persona*) who is going grey

entrecejo *m* forehead. **arrugar el ~, fruncir el ~** frown

entrecerrar [1] *vt* (*Amer*) half close

entrecortado *a* (*voz*) faltering; (*respiración*) laboured

entrecruzar [10] *vt* intertwine

entrega *f* handing over; (*de mercancías etc*) delivery; (*de novela etc*) instalment; (*dedicación*) commitment. **~r** [12] *vt* hand over, deliver, give. **~rse** *vpr* surrender, give o.s. up; (*dedicarse*) devote o.s. (**a** to)

entrelazar [10] *vt* intertwine

entremés *m* hors-d'oeuvre; (*en el teatro*) short comedy

entremeter *vt* insert. **~erse** *vpr* interfere. **~ido** *a* interfering

entremezclar *vt* intermingle

entrena|dor *m* trainer. **~miento** *m* training. **~r** *vt* train. **~rse** *vpr* train

entrepierna *f* crotch

entresacar [7] *vt* pick out

entresuelo *m* mezzanine

entretanto *adv* meanwhile

entretejer *vt* interweave

entreten|er [40] *vt* entertain, amuse; (*detener*) delay, keep; (*mantener*) keep alive, keep going. **~erse** *vpr* amuse o.s.; (*tardar*) delay, linger. **~ido** *a* entertaining. **~imiento** *m* entertainment; (*mantenimiento*) upkeep

entrever [43] *vt* make out, glimpse

entrevista *f* interview; (*reunión*) meeting. **~rse** *vpr* have an interview

entristecer [11] *vt* sadden, make sad. **~se** *vpr* be sad

entromet|erse *vpr* interfere. **~ido** *a* interfering

entroncar [7] *vi* be related

entruchada *f*, **entruchado** *m* (*fam*) plot

entumece|rse [11] *vpr* go numb. **~ido** *a* numb

enturbiar *vt* cloud

entusias|mar *vt* fill with enthusiasm; (*gustar mucho*) delight. **~marse** *vpr*. **~marse con** get enthusiastic about; (*ser aficionado a*) be mad about, love. **~asmo** *m* enthusiasm. **~asta** *a* enthusiastic. —*m & f* enthusiast. **~ástico** *a* enthusiastic

enumera|ción *f* count, reckoning. **~r** *vt* enumerate

enuncia|ción *f* enunciation. **~r** *vt* enunciate

envainar vt sheathe

envalentonar vt encourage. **~se** upr be brave, pluck up courage

envanecer [11] vt make conceited. **~se** upr be conceited

envas|ado a tinned. —m packaging. **~ar** vt package; (en latas) tin, can; (en botellas) bottle. **~e** m packing; (lata) tin, can; (botella) bottle

envejec|er [11] vt make old. —vi get old, grow old. **~erse** upr get old, grow old. **~ido** a aged, old

envenenar vt poison

envergadura f (alcance) scope

envés m wrong side

envia|do a sent. —m representative; (de la prensa) correspondent. **~r** vt send

enviciar vt corrupt

envidi|a f envy; (celos) jealousy. **~able** a enviable. **~ar** vt envy, be envious of. **~oso** a envious. **tener ~a** a envy

envilecer [11] vt degrade

envío m sending, dispatch; (de mercancías) consignment; (de dinero) remittance. **~ contra reembolso** cash on delivery. **gastos** mpl **de envío** postage and packing (costs)

enviudar vi (mujer) become a widow, be widowed; (hombre) become a widower, be widowed

env|oltura f wrapping. **~olver** [2, pp envuelto] vt wrap; (cubrir) cover; (fig, acorralar) corner; (fig, enredar) involve; (mil) surround. **~olvimiento** m involvement. **~uelto** a wrapped (up)

enyesar vt plaster; (med) put in plaster

enzima f enzyme

épica f epic

epicentro m epicentre

épico a epic

epid|emia f epidemic. **~émico** a epidemic

epil|epsia f epilepsy. **~éptico** a epileptic

epílogo m epilogue

episodio m episode

epístola f epistle

epitafio m epitaph

epíteto m epithet

epítome m epitome

época f age; (período) period. **hacer ~** make history, be epoch-making

equidad f equity

equilátero a equilateral

equilibr|ar vt balance. **~io** m balance; (de balanza) equilibrium. **~ista** m & f tightrope walker

equino a horse, equine

equinoccio m equinox

equipaje m luggage (esp Brit), baggage (esp Amer); (de barco) crew

equipar vt equip; (de ropa) fit out

equiparar vt make equal; (comparar) compare

equipo m equipment; (en deportes) team

equitación f riding

equivale|ncia f equivalence. **~nte** a equivalent. **~r** [42] vi be equivalent; (significar) mean

equivoca|ción f mistake, error. **~do** a wrong. **~r** [7] vt mistake. **~rse** upr be mistaken, be wrong, make a mistake. **~rse de** be wrong about. **~rse de número** dial the wrong number. **si no me equivoco** if I'm not mistaken

equívoco a equivocal; (sospechoso) suspicious. —m ambiguity; (juego de palabras) pun; (doble sentido) double meaning

era f era. —vb véase **ser**

erario m treasury

erección f erection; (fig) establishment

eremita *m* hermit

eres *vb véase* **ser**

erguir [48] *vt* raise. ~ **la cabeza** hold one's head high. ~**se** *vpr* straighten up

erigir [14] *vt* erect. ~**se** *vpr* set o.s. up (**en as**)

eriza|do *a* prickly. ~**rse** [10] *vpr* stand on end

erizo *m* hedgehog; (*de mar*) sea urchin. ~ **de mar**, ~ **marino** sea urchin

ermita *f* hermitage. ~**ño** *m* hermit

erosi|ón *f* erosion. ~**onar** *vt* erode

er|ótico *a* erotic. ~**otismo** *m* eroticism

errar [1, *la* **i** *inicial se escribe* **y**] *vt* miss. —*vi* wander; (*equivocarse*) make a mistake, be wrong

errata *f* misprint

erróneo *a* erroneous, wrong

error *m* error, mistake. **estar en un** ~ be wrong, be mistaken

eructar *vi* belch

erudi|ción *f* learning, erudition. ~**to** *a* learned

erupción *f* eruption; (*med*) rash

es *vb véase* **ser**

esa *a véase* **ese**

ésa *pron véase* **ése**

esbelto *a* slender, slim

esboz|ar [10] *vt* sketch, outline. ~**o** *m* sketch, outline

escabeche *m* pickle. **en** ~ pickled

escabroso *a* ⟨*terreno*⟩ rough; ⟨*asunto*⟩ difficult; ⟨*atrevido*⟩ crude

escabullirse [22] *vpr* slip away

escafandra *f*, **escafandro** *m* diving-suit

escala *f* scale; (*escalera de mano*) ladder; (*de avión*) stopover. ~**da** *f* climbing; (*pol*) escalation. ~**r** *vt* scale; break into ⟨*una casa*⟩. —*vi* (*pol*) escalate. **hacer** ~ **en**

stop at. **vuelo sin** ~**s** non-stop flight

escaldar *vt* scald

escalera *f* staircase, stairs; (*de mano*) ladder. ~ **de caracol** spiral staircase. ~ **de incendios** fire escape. ~ **mecánica** escalator. ~ **plegable** stepladder

escalfa|do *a* poached. ~**r** *vt* poach

escalinata *f* flight of steps

escalofrío *m* shiver

escal|ón *m* step; (*de escalera interior*) stair; (*de escala*) rung. ~**onar** *vt* spread out

escalope *m* escalope

escam|a *f* scale; (*de jabón*) flake; (*fig*) suspicion. ~**oso** *a* scaly

escamotear *vt* make disappear; ⟨*robar*⟩ steal, pinch (*fam*); disregard (*dificultad*)

escampar *vi* stop raining

esc|andalizar [10] *vt* scandalize, shock. ~**andalizarse** *vpr* be shocked. ~**ándalo** *m* scandal; (*alboroto*) uproar. ~**andaloso** *a* scandalous; (*alborotado*) noisy

Escandinavia *f* Scandinavia

escandinavo *a* & *m* Scandinavian

escaño *m* bench; (*pol*) seat

escapa|da *f* escape; (*visita*) flying visit. ~**do** *a* in a hurry. ~**r** *vi* escape. ~**rse** *vpr* escape; ⟨*líquido, gas*⟩ leak. **dejar** ~**r** let out

escaparate *m* (shop) window. **ir de** ~**s** go window-shopping

escapatoria *f* (*fig, fam*) way out

escape *m* (*de gas, de líquido*) leak; (*fuga*) escape; (*auto*) exhaust

escarabajo *m* beetle

escaramuza *f* skirmish

escarbar *vt* scratch; pick ⟨*dientes, herida etc*⟩; (*fig, escudriñar*) delve (**en** into)

escarcha *f* frost. ~**do** *a* ⟨*fruta*⟩ crystallized

escarlat|**a** *a invar* scarlet. **~ina** *f* scarlet fever

escarm|**entar** [1] *vt* punish severely. —*vi* learn one's lesson. **~iento** *m* punishment; (*lección*) lesson

escarn|**ecer** [11] *vt* mock. **~io** *m* ridicule

escarola *f* endive

escarpa *f* slope. **~do** *a* steep

escas|**ear** *vi* be scarce. **~ez** *f* scarcity, shortage; (*pobreza*) poverty. **~o** *a* scarce; (*poco*) little; (*insuficiente*) short; (*muy justo*) barely

escatimar *vt* be sparing with

escayola *f* plaster. **~r** *vt* put in plaster

escena *f* scene; (*escenario*) stage. **~rio** *m* stage; (*en el cine*) scenario; (*fig*) scene

escénico *a* scenic

escenografía *f* scenery

esc|**epticismo** *m* scepticism. **~éptico** *a* sceptical. —*m* sceptic

esclarecer [11] *vt* (*fig*) throw light on, clarify

esclavina *f* cape

esclav|**itud** *f* slavery. **~izar** [10] *vt* enslave. **~o** *m* slave

esclerosis *f* sclerosis

esclusa *f* lock

escoba *f* broom

escocer [2 & 9] *vt* hurt. —*vi* sting

escocés *a* Scottish. —*m* Scotsman

Escocia *f* Scotland

escog|**er** [14] *vt* choose, select. **~ido** *a* chosen; (*de buena calidad*) choice

escolar *a* school. —*m* schoolboy. —*f* schoolgirl. **~idad** *f* schooling

escolta *f* escort

escombros *mpl* rubble

escond|**er** *vt* hide. **~erse** *vpr* hide. **~idas. a ~idas** secretly. **~ite** *m* hiding place; (*juego*)

hide-and-seek. **~rijo** *m* hiding place

escopeta *f* shotgun. **~zo** *m* shot

escoplo *m* chisel

escoria *f* slag; (*fig*) dregs

Escorpión *m* Scorpio

escorpión *m* scorpion

escot|**ado** *a* low-cut. **~adura** *f* low neckline. **~ar** *vt* cut out. —*vi* pay one's share. **~e** *m* low neckline. **ir a ~e, pagar a ~e** share the expenses

escozor *m* pain

escri|**bano** *m* clerk. **~biente** *m* clerk. **~bir** [*pp* escrito] *vt/i* write. **~bir a máquina** type. **~birse** *vpr* write to each other; (*deletrearse*) be spelt. **~to** *a* written. —*m* writing; (*documento*) document. **~tor** *m* writer. **~torio** *m* desk; (*oficina*) office. **~tura** *f* (hand)writing; (*documento*) document; (*jurid*) deed. **¿cómo se escribe...?** how do you spell...? **poner por ~to** put into writing

escr|**úpulo** *m* scruple; (*escrupulosidad*) care, scrupulousness. **~uloso** *a* scrupulous

escrut|**ar** *vt* scrutinize; count (*votos*). **~inio** *m* count. **hacer el ~inio** count the votes

escuadr|**a** *f* (*instrumento*) square; (*mil*) squad; (*naut*) fleet. **~ón** *m* squadron

escuálido *a* skinny; (*sucio*) squalid

escuchar *vt* listen to. —*vi* listen

escudilla *f* bowl

escudo *m* shield. **~ de armas** coat of arms

escudriñar *vt* examine

escuela *f* school. **~ normal** teachers' training college

escueto *a* simple

escuincle *m* (*Mex, perro*) stray dog; (*Mex, muchacho, fam*) child, kid (*fam*)

escul|pir vt sculpture. **~tor** m sculptor. **~tora** f sculptress. **~tura** f sculpture; (*en madera*) carving

escupir vt/i spit

escurr|eplatos m invar plate-rack. **~idizo** a slippery. **~ir** vt drain; wring out (*ropa*). —vi drip; (*ser resbaladizo*) be slippery. **~irse** vpr slip

ese a (f **esa**, mpl **esos**, fpl **esas**) that; (*en plural*) those

ése pron (f **ésa**, mpl **ésos**, fpl **ésas**) that one; (*en plural*) those; (*primero de dos*) the former. **ni por ésas** on no account

esencia f essence. **~l** a essential. **lo ~l** the main thing

esf|era f sphere; (*de reloj*) face. **~érico** a spherical

esfinge f sphinx

esf|orzarse [2 & 10] vpr make an effort. **~uerzo** m effort

esfumarse vpr fade away; (*persona*) vanish

esgrim|a f fencing. **~ir** vt brandish; (*fig*) use

esguince m swerve; (*med*) sprain

eslab|ón m link. **~onar** vt link (together)

eslavo a Slav, Slavonic

eslogan m slogan

esmalt|ar vt enamel; varnish (*uñas*); (*fig*) adorn. **~e** m enamel. **~e de uñas**, **~e para las uñas** nail varnish (*Brit*), nail polish (*Amer*)

esmerado a careful

esmeralda f emerald

esmerarse vpr take care (**en** over)

esmeril m emery

esmero m care

esmoquin m dinner jacket, tuxedo (*Amer*)

esnob a invar snobbish. —m & f (pl **esnobs**) snob. **~ismo** m snobbery

esnórkel m snorkel

eso pron that. **¡~ es!** that's it! **~ mismo** exactly. **¡~ no!** certainly not! **¡~ sí!** of course. **a ~ de** about. **en ~** at that moment. **¿no es ~?** isn't that right? **por ~** therefore. **y ~ que** although

esos a pl véase **ese**

ésos pron pl véase **ése**

espabila|do a bright. **~r** vt snuff (*vela*); (*avivar*) brighten up; (*despertar*) wake up. **~rse** vpr wake up; (*apresurarse*) hurry up

espaci|al a space. **~ar** vt space out. **~o** m space. **~oso** a spacious

espada f sword. **~s** fpl (*en naipes*) spades

espagueti m spaghetti

espald|a f back. **~illa** f shoulder-blade. **a ~as de uno** behind s.o.'s back. **a las ~as** on one's back. **tener las ~as anchas** be broad-shouldered. **volver la ~a a uno, volver las ~as a uno** give s.o. the cold shoulder

espant|ada f stampede. **~adizo** a timid, timorous. **~ajo** m, **~apájaros** m inv scarecrow. **~ar** vt frighten; (*ahuyentar*) frighten away. **~arse** vpr be frightened; (*ahuyentarse*) be frightened away. **~o** m terror; (*horror*) horror. **~oso** a frightening; (*muy grande*) terrible. **¡qué ~ajo!** what a sight!

España f Spain

español a Spanish. —m (*persona*) Spaniard; (*lengua*) Spanish. **los ~es** the Spanish. **~izado** a Hispanicized

esparadrapo m sticking-plaster, plaster (*Brit*)

esparci|do a scattered; (*fig*) widespread. **~r** [9] vt scatter; (*difundir*) spread. **~rse** vpr be scattered; (*difundirse*) spread; (*divertirse*) enjoy o.s.

espárrago m asparagus

esparto *m* esparto (grass)

espasmo *m* spasm. **~ódico** *a* spasmodic

espátula *f* spatula; (*en pintura*) palette knife

especia *f* spice

especial *a* special. **~idad** *f* speciality (*Brit*), specialty (*Amer*). **~ista** *a* & *m* & *f* specialist. **~ización** *f* specialization. **~izar** [10] *vt* specialize. **~izarse** *upr* specialize. **~mente** *adv* especially. **en ~** especially

especie *f* kind, sort; (*en biología*) species; (*noticia*) piece of news. **en ~** in kind

especificación *f* specification. **~r** [7] *vt* specify

específico *a* specific

espectáculo *m* sight; (*diversión*) entertainment, show. **~ador** *m* & *f* spectator. **~acular** *a* spectacular

espectro *m* spectre; (*en física*) spectrum

especulación *f* speculation. **~dor** *m* speculator. **~r** *vi* speculate. **~tivo** *a* speculative

espejismo *m* mirage. **~o** *m* mirror. **~o retrovisor** (*auto*) rearview mirror

espeleólogo *m* potholer

espeluznante *a* horrifying

espera *f* wait. **sala** *f* **de ~** waiting room

esperanza *f* hope. **~r** *vt* hope; (*aguardar*) wait for; (*creer*) expect. —*vi* hope; (*aguardar*) wait. **~r en** trust in s.o. **en ~ de** awaiting. **espero que no** I hope not. **espero que sí** I hope so

esperma *f* sperm

esperpento *m* fright; (*disparate*) nonsense

espesar *vt* thicken. **~arse** *upr* thicken. **~o** *a* thick; (*pasta etc*) stiff. **~or** *m*, **~ura** *f* thickness; (*bot*) thicket

espetón *m* spit

espía *f* spy. **~iar** [20] *vt* spy on. —*vi* spy

espiga *f* (*de trigo etc*) ear

espina *f* thorn; (*de pez*) bone; (*dorsal*) spine; (*astilla*) splinter; (*fig, dificultad*) difficulty. **~ dorsal** spine

espinaca *f* spinach

espinazo *m* spine

espinilla *f* shin; (*med*) blackhead

espino *m* hawthorn. **~ artificial** barbed wire. **~so** *a* thorny; (*pez*) bony; (*fig*) difficult

espionaje *m* espionage

espiral *a* & *f* spiral

espirar *vt/i* breathe out

espiritismo *m* spiritualism. **~iritoso** *a* spirited. **~iritista** *m* & *f* spiritualist. **~iritu** *m* spirit; (*mente*) mind; (*inteligencia*) intelligence. **~iritual** *a* spiritual. **~iritualismo** *m* spiritualism

espita *f* tap, faucet (*Amer*)

espléndido *a* splendid; (*persona*) generous. **~endor** *m* splendour

espliego *m* lavender

espolear *vt* (*fig*) spur on

espoleta *f* fuse

espolvorear *vt* sprinkle

esponja *f* sponge; (*tejido*) towelling. **~oso** *a* spongy. **pasar la ~a** forget about it

espontaneidad *f* spontaneity. **~áneo** *a* spontaneous

esporádico *a* sporadic

esposa *f* wife. **~as** *fpl* handcuffs. **~ar** *vt* handcuff. **~o** *m* husband. **los ~os** the couple

espuela *f* spur; (*fig*) incentive. **dar de ~s** spur on

espuma *f* foam; (*en bebidas*) froth; (*de jabón*) lather. **~ar** *vt* skim. —*vi* foam; (*bebidas*) froth; (*jabón*) lather. **~oso** *a* (*vino*) sparkling. **echar ~a** foam, froth

esqueleto *m* skeleton

esquema m outline. **~ático** a sketchy

esquí m (pl **esquís**) ski; (el deporte) skiing. **~iador** m skier. **~iar** [20] vi ski

esquilar vt shear

esquimal a & m Eskimo

esquina f corner

esquirol m blackleg

esquivar vt avoid. **~o** a aloof

esquizofrénico a & m schizophrenic

esta a véase **este**

ésta pron véase **éste**

estabilidad f stability. **~ilizador** m stabilizer. **~ilizar** [10] vt stabilize. **~le** a stable

establecer [11] vt establish. **~erse** vpr settle; (com) start a business. **~imiento** m establishment

establo m cowshed

estaca f stake; (para apalear) stick. **~da** f (cerca) fence

estación f station; (del año) season; (de vacaciones) resort. **~ de servicio** service station

estacionamiento m parking. **~r** vt station; (auto) park. **~rio** a stationary

estadio m stadium; (fase) stage

estadista m statesman. **~f** stateswoman

estadística f statistics. **~o** a statistical

estado m state. **~ civil** marital status. **~ de ánimo** frame of mind. **~ de cuenta** bank statement. **~ mayor** (mil) staff. **en buen ~** in good condition. **en ~ (interesante)** pregnant

Estados Unidos mpl United States

estadounidense a American, United States. **—m & f** American

estafa f swindle. **~r** vt swindle

estafeta f (oficina de correos) (sub-)post office

estalactita f stalactite. **~gmita** f stalagmite

estallar vi explode; (olas) break; (guerra, epidemia etc) break out; (fig) burst. **~ar en llanto** burst into tears. **~ar de risa** burst out laughing. **~ido** m explosion; (de guerra, epidemia etc) outbreak; (de risa etc) outburst

estampa f print; (aspecto) appearance. **~ado** a printed. **—m** printing; (tela) cotton print. **~ar** vt stamp; (imprimir) print. **dar a la ~a** (imprimir) print; (publicar) publish. **la viva ~a** the image

estampía. de **~ía** suddenly

estampido m explosion

estampilla f stamp; (Mex) (postage) stamp

estancado a stagnant. **~miento** m stagnation. **~r** [7] vt stem; (com) turn into a monopoly

estancia f stay; (Arg, finca) ranch, farm; (cuarto) room. **~ero** m (Arg) farmer

estanco a watertight. **—m** tobacconist's (shop)

estandarte m standard, banner

estanque m lake; (depósito de agua) reservoir

estanquero m tobacconist

estante m shelf. **~ría** f shelves; (para libros) bookcase

estaño m tin. **~adura** f tinplating

estar [27] vi be; (quedarse) stay; (estar en casa) be in. **¿estamos?** alright? **estamos a 29 de noviembre** it's the 29th of November. **~ para** be about to. **~ por** remain to be; (con ganas de) be tempted to; (ser partidario de) be in favour of. **~se** vpr stay. **¿cómo está Vd?, ¿cómo estás?** how are you?

estarcir [9] vt stencil

estatal a state

estático *a* static; *(pasmado)* dumbfounded

estatua *f* statue

estatura *f* height

estatutario *a* statutory. ∼o *m* statute

este *m* east; *(viento)* east wind. — *a* (*f* esta, *mpl* estos, *fpl* estas) this; *(en plural)* these. —*int* (*LAm*) well, er

éste *pron* (*f* ésta, *mpl* éstos, *fpl* éstas) this one, *(en plural)* these; *(segundo de dos)* the latter

estela *f* wake; *(arquit)* carved stone

estera *f* mat; *(tejido)* matting

estéreo *a* stereo. ∼reofónico *a* stereo, stereophonic

esterilla *f* mat

estereotipado *a* stereotyped. ∼o *m* stereotype

estéril *a* sterile; *(mujer)* infertile; *(terreno)* barren. ∼erilidad *f* sterility; *(de mujer)* infertility; *(de terreno)* barrenness

esterlina *a* sterling. libra *f* ∼ pound sterling

estético *a* aesthetic

estevado *a* bow-legged

estiércol *m* dung; *(abono)* manure

estigma *m* stigma. ∼s *mpl* *(relig)* stigmata

estilarse *vpr* be used

estilista *m* & *f* stylist. ∼izar [10] *vt* stylize. ∼o *m* style. por el ∼o of that sort

estilográfica *f* fountain pen

estima *f* esteem. ∼do *a* esteemed. ∼do señor *(en cartas)* Dear Sir. ∼r *vt* esteem; have great respect for *(persona)*; *(valorar)* value; *(juzgar)* think

estimulante *a* stimulating. —*m* stimulant. ∼imular *vt* stimulate; *(incitar)* incite. ∼ímulo *m* stimulus

estipular *vt* stipulate

estirado *a* stretched; *(persona)* haughty. ∼ar *vt* stretch; *(fig)* stretch out. ∼ón *m* pull, tug; *(crecimiento)* sudden growth

estirpe *m* stock

estival *a* summer

esto *pron* *neutro* this; *(este asunto)* this business. en ∼ at this point. en ∼ de in this business of. por ∼ therefore

estofa *f* class. de baja ∼ *(gente)* low-class

estofado *a* stewed. —*m* stew. ∼r *vt* stew

estoicismo *m* stoicism. ∼o *a* stoical. —*m* stoic

estómago *m* stomach. dolor *m* de ∼ stomach-ache

estorbar *vt* hinder, obstruct; *(molestar)* bother, annoy. ∼ar *vi* be in the way. ∼o *m* hindrance; *(molestia)* nuisance

estornino *m* starling

estornudar *vi* sneeze. ∼vi be in the way. ∼o *m* sneeze

estos *a* *mpl véase* este

éstos *pron mpl véase* éste

estoy *vb véase* estar

estrabismo *m* squint

estrado *m* stage; *(mus)* bandstand

estrafalario *a* outlandish

estragar [12] *vt* devastate. ∼o *m* devastation. hacer ∼os devastate

estragón *m* tarragon

estrambótico *a* outlandish

estrangulación *f* strangulation. ∼dor *m* strangler; *(auto)* choke. ∼miento *m* blockage; *(auto)* bottleneck. ∼r *vt* strangle

estraperlo *m* black market. comprar algo de ∼ buy sth on the black market

estratagema *f* stratagem

estratega *m* & *f* strategist. ∼ia *f* strategy

estratégic|amente *adv* strategically. **∼o** *a* strategic

estrato *m* stratum

estratosfera *f* stratosphere

estrech|ar *vt* make narrower; take in *(vestido)*; *(apretar)* squeeze; hug *(persona)*. **∼ar la mano a uno** shake hands with s.o. **∼arse** *vpr* become narrower; *(apretarse)* squeeze up. **∼ez** *f* narrowness; *(apuro)* tight spot; *(falta de dinero)* want. **∼o** *a* narrow; *(vestido etc)* tight; *(fig, íntimo)* close. —*m* straits. **∼o de miras, de miras ∼as** narrow-minded

estregar [1 & 12] *vt* rub

estrella *f* star. **∼ de mar**, **∼mar** *m* starfish

estrellar *vt* smash; fry *(huevos)*. **∼se** *vpr* smash; *(fracasar)* fail. **∼se contra** crash into

estremec|er [11] *vt* shake. **∼erse** *vpr* tremble (**de** with). **∼imiento** *m* shaking

estren|ar *vt* use for the first time; wear for the first time *(vestido etc)*; show for the first time *(película)*. **∼arse** *vpr* make one's début; *(película)* have its première; *(obra de teatro)* open. **∼o** *m* first use; *(de película)* première; *(de obra de teatro)* first night

estreñido *a* constipated. **∼miento** *m* constipation

estr|épito *m* din. **∼epitoso** *a* noisy; *(fig)* resounding

estreptomicina *f* streptomycin

estrés *m* stress

estría *f* groove

estribar *vt* rest (**en** on); *(consistir)* lie (**en** in)

estribillo *m* refrain; *(muletilla)* catchphrase

estribo *m* stirrup; *(de vehículo)* step; *(contrafuerte)* buttress. **perder los ∼s** lose one's temper

estribor *m* starboard

estricto *a* strict

estridente *a* strident, raucous

estrofa *f* strophe

estropajo *m* scourer. **∼so** *a* *(carne etc)* tough; *(persona)* slovenly

estropear *vt* spoil; *(romper)* break. **∼se** *vpr* be damaged; *(fruta etc)* go bad; *(fracasar)* fail

estructura *f* structure. **∼l** *a* structural

estruendo *m* din; *(de mucha gente)* uproar. **∼so** *a* deafening

estrujar *vt* squeeze; *(fig)* drain

estuario *m* estuary

estuco *m* stucco

estuche *m* case

estudi|ante *m & f* student. **∼antil** *a* student. **∼ar** *vt* study. **∼o** *m* study; *(de artista)* studio. **∼oso** *a* studious

estufa *f* heater; *(LAm)* cooker

estupefac|ción *f* astonishment. **∼iente** *a* astonishing. —*m* narcotic. **∼to** *a* astonished

estupendo *a* marvellous; *(hermoso)* beautiful

est|upidez *f* stupidity; *(acto)* stupid thing. **∼úpido** *a* stupid

estupor *m* amazement

esturión *m* sturgeon

estuve *vb véase* **estar**

etapa *f* stage. **hacer ∼ en** break the journey at. **por ∼s** in stages

etc *abrev (etcétera)* etc

etcétera *adv* et cetera

éter *m* ether

etéreo *a* ethereal

etern|amente *adv* eternally. **∼idad** *f* eternity. **∼izar** [10] *vt* drag out. **∼izarse** *vpr* be interminable. **∼o** *a* eternal

étic|a *f* ethics. **∼o** *a* ethical

etimología *f* etymology

etiqueta *f* ticket, tag; *(ceremonial)* etiquette. **de ∼** formal

étnico *a* ethnic

eucalipto *m* eucalyptus

eufemismo *m* euphemism

euforia *f* euphoria

Europa f Europe

europeo a & m European. ∼**izar** [10] vt Europeanize

eutanasia f euthanasia

evacua|**ción** f evacuation. ∼**r** [21 o *regular*] vt evacuate

evadir vt avoid. ∼**se** vpr escape

evaluar [21] vt evaluate

evang|**élico** a evangelical. ∼**elio** m gospel. ∼**elista** m & f evangelist

evapora|**ción** f evaporation. ∼**r** vi evaporate. ∼**rse** vpr evaporate; (*fig*) disappear

evasi|**ón** f evasion; (*fuga*) escape. ∼**vo** a evasive

evento m event. **a todo** ∼ at all events

eventual a possible. ∼**idad** f eventuality

eviden|**cia** f evidence. ∼**ciar** vt show. ∼**ciarse** vpr be obvious. ∼**te** a obvious. ∼**temente** adv obviously. **poner en** ∼**cia** show; (*fig*) make a fool of

evitar vt avoid; (*ahorrar*) spare

evocar [7] vt evoke

evoluci|**ón** f evolution. ∼**onado** a fully-developed. ∼**onar** vi evolve; (*mil*) manoeuvre

ex pref ex-, former

exacerbar vt exacerbate

exact|**amente** adv exactly. ∼**itud** f exactness. ∼**o** a exact; (*preciso*) accurate; (*puntual*) punctual. ¡∼**!** exactly!. **con** ∼**itud** exactly

exagera|**ción** f exaggeration. ∼**do** a exaggerated. ∼**r** vt/i exaggerate

exalta|**do** a exalted; (*fanático*) fanatical. ∼**r** vt exalt. ∼**rse** vpr get excited

exam|**en** m examination; (*escol, univ*) exam(ination). ∼**inador** m examiner. ∼**inar** vt examine. ∼**inarse** vpr take an exam

exánime a lifeless

exaspera|**ción** f exasperation. ∼**r** vt exasperate. ∼**rse** vpr get exasperated

excava|**ción** f excavation. ∼**dora** f digger. ∼**r** vt excavate

excede|**ncia** f leave of absence. ∼**nte** a & m surplus. ∼**r** vi exceed. ∼**rse** vpr go too far. ∼**rse a sí mismo** excel o.s.

excelen|**cia** f excellence; (*tratamiento*) Excellency. ∼**te** a excellent

exc|**entricidad** f eccentricity. ∼**éntrico** a & m eccentric

excepci|**ón** f exception. ∼**onal** a exceptional. **a** ∼**ón de, con** ∼**ón de** except (for)

excepto prep except (for). ∼**uar** [21] vt except

exces|**ivo** a excessive. ∼**o** m excess. ∼**o de equipaje** excess luggage (*esp Brit*), excess baggage (*esp Amer*)

excita|**ble** a excitable. ∼**ción** f excitement. ∼**nte** a exciting. —m stimulant. ∼**r** vt excite; (*incitar*) incite. ∼**rse** vpr get excited

exclama|**ción** f exclamation. ∼**r** vi exclaim

exclu|**ir** [17] vt exclude. ∼**sión** f exclusion. ∼**siva** f sole right; (*en la prensa* exclusive (story). ∼**sive** adv exclusive; (*exclusivamente*) exclusively. ∼**sivo** a exclusive

excomu|**lgar** [12] vt excommunicate. ∼**nión** f excommunication

excremento m excrement

exculpar vt exonerate; (*jurid*) acquit

excursi|**ón** f excursion, trip. ∼**onista** m & f day-tripper. **ir de** ∼**ón** go on an excursion

excusa f excuse; (*disculpa*) apology. ∼**r** vt excuse. **presentar sus** ∼**s** apologize

execra|ble *a* loathsome. **~r** *vt* loathe

exento *a* exempt; (*libre*) free

exequias *fpl* funeral rites

exhala|ción *f* shooting star. **~r** *vt* exhale, breath out; give off ⟨*olor etc*⟩. **~rse** *vpr* hurry. **como una ~ción** at top speed

exhaust|ivo *a* exhaustive. **~o** *a* exhausted

exhibi|ción *f* exhibition. **~cionista** *m & f* exhibitionist. **~r** *vt* exhibit

exhortar *vt* exhort (**a** to)

exhumar *vt* exhume; (*fig*) dig up

exig|encia *f* demand. **~ente** *a* demanding. **~ir** [14] *vt* demand. **tener muchas ~encias** be very demanding

exiguo *a* meagre

exil|(i)ado *a* exiled. —*m* exile. **~(i)arse** *vpr* go into exile. **~io** *m* exile

eximio *a* distinguished

eximir *vt* exempt; (*liberar*) free

existencia *f* existence. **~s** *fpl* stock

existencial *a* existential. **~ismo** *m* existentialism

exist|ente *a* existing. **~ir** *vi* exist

éxito *m* success. **no tener ~** fail. **tener ~** be successful

exitoso *a* successful

éxodo *m* exodus

exonerar *vt* (*de un empleo*) dismiss; (*de un honor etc*) strip

exorbitante *a* exorbitant

exorci|smo *m* exorcism. **~zar** [10] *vt* exorcise

exótico *a* exotic

expan|dir *vt* expand; (*fig*) spread. **~dirse** *vpr* expand. **~sión** *f* expansion. **~sivo** *a* expansive

expatria|do *a & m* expatriate. **~r** *vt* banish. **~rse** *vpr* emigrate; (*exiliarse*) go into exile

expectativa *f*. **estar a la ~** be on the lookout

expedición *f* dispatch; (*cosa expedida*) shipment; (*mil, científico etc*) expedition

expediente *m* expedient; (*jurid*) proceedings; (*documentos*) record, file

expedi|r [5] *vt* dispatch, send; issue ⟨*documento*⟩. **~to** *a* clear

expeler *vt* expel

expende|dor *m* dealer. **~dor automático** vending machine. **~duría** *f* shop; (*de billetes*) ticket office. **~r** *vt* sell

expensas *fpl*. **a ~ de** at the expense of. **a mis ~** at my expense

experiencia *f* experience

experiment|al *a* experimental. **~ar** *vt* test, experiment with; (*sentir*) experience. **~o** *m* experiment

experto *a & m* expert

expiar [20] *vt* atone for

expirar *vi* expire; (*morir*) die

explana|da *f* levelled area; (*paseo*) esplanade. **~r** *vt* level

explayar *vt* extend. **~se** *vpr* spread out, extend; (*hablar*) be long-winded; (*confiarse*) confide (**a** in)

expletivo *m* expletive

explica|ción *f* explanation. **~r** [7] *vt* explain. **~rse** *vpr* understand; (*hacerse comprender*) explain o.s. **no me lo explico** I can't understand it

explícito *a* explicit

explora|ción *f* exploration. **~dor** *m* explorer; (*muchacho*) boy scout. **~r** *vt* explore. **~torio** *a* exploratory

explosi|ón *f* explosion; (*fig*) outburst. **~onar** *vt* blow up. **~vo** *a & m* explosive

explota|ción *f* working; (*abuso*) exploitation. **~r** *vt* work ⟨*mina*⟩; farm ⟨*tierra*⟩; (*abusar*) exploit. —*vi* explode

exponente *m* exponent. **~r** [34] *vt* expose; display ⟨*mercancías*⟩; ⟨*explicar*⟩ expound; exhibit ⟨*cuadros etc*⟩; ⟨*arriesgar*⟩ risk. —*vi* hold an exhibition. **~rse** *vpr* run the risk (**a** of)

exporta|ción *f* export. **~dor** *m* exporter. **~r** *vt* export

exposi|ción *f* exposure; ⟨*de cuadros etc*⟩ exhibition; ⟨*en escaparate etc*⟩ display; ⟨*explicación*⟩ exposition, explanation

expresamente *adv* specifically

expres|ar *vt* express. **~arse** *vpr* express o.s. **~ión** *f* expression. **~ivo** *a* expressive; ⟨*cariñoso*⟩ affectionate

expreso *a* express. —*m* express messenger; ⟨*tren*⟩ express

exprimi|dor *m* squeezer. **~r** *vt* squeeze; ⟨*explotar*⟩ exploit

expropiar *vt* expropriate

expuesto *a* on display; ⟨*lugar etc*⟩ exposed; ⟨*peligroso*⟩ dangerous. **estar ~ a** be liable to

expuls|ar *vt* expel; throw out ⟨*persona*⟩; send off ⟨*jugador*⟩. **~ión** *f* expulsion

expurgar [12] *vt* expurgate

exquisit|o *a* exquisite. **~amente** *adv* exquisitely

extasiar [20] *vt* enrapture

éxtasis *m invar* ecstasy

extático *a* ecstatic

extend|er [1] *vt* spread (out); draw up ⟨*documento*⟩. **~erse** *vpr* spread; ⟨*paisaje etc*⟩ extend, stretch; ⟨*tenderse*⟩ stretch out. **~ido** *a* spread out; ⟨*generalizado*⟩ widespread; ⟨*brazos*⟩ outstretched

extens|amente *adv* widely; ⟨*detalladamente*⟩ in full. **~ión** *f* extension; ⟨*amplitud*⟩ expanse; ⟨*mus*⟩ range. **~o** *a* extensive

extenuar [21] *vt* exhaust

exterior *a* external, exterior; ⟨*del extranjero*⟩ foreign; ⟨*aspecto etc*⟩ outward. —*m* exterior;

⟨*países extranjeros*⟩ abroad. **~izar** [10] *vt* show

extermin|ación *f* extermination. **~ar** *vt* exterminate. **~io** *m* extermination

externo *a* external; ⟨*signo etc*⟩ outward. —*m* day pupil

extin|ción *f* extinction. **~guir** [13] *vt* extinguish. **~guirse** *vpr* die out; ⟨*fuego*⟩ go out. **~to** *a* extinguished; ⟨*raza etc*⟩ extinct. **~tor** *m* fire extinguisher

extirpar *vt* uproot; extract ⟨*muela etc*⟩; remove ⟨*tumor*⟩. **~ción** *f* (*fig*) eradication

extorsi|ón *f* (*fig*) inconvenience. **~onar** *vt* inconvenience

extra *a invar* extra; ⟨*de buena calidad*⟩ good-quality; ⟨*huevos*⟩ large. **paga** *f* **~** bonus

extrac|ción *f* extraction; ⟨*de lotería*⟩ draw. **~to** *m* extract

extradición *f* extradition

extraer [41] *vt* extract

extranjero *a* foreign. —*m* foreigner; ⟨*países*⟩ foreign countries. **del ~** from abroad. **en el ~, por el ~** abroad

extrañ|ar *vt* surprise; ⟨*encontrar extraño*⟩ find strange; ⟨*LAm, echar de menos*⟩ miss; ⟨*desterrar*⟩ banish. **~arse** *vpr* be surprised (**de** at); ⟨*2 personas*⟩ grow apart. **~eza** *f* strangeness; ⟨*asombro*⟩ surprise. **~o** *a* strange. —*m* stranger

extraoficial *a* unofficial

extraordinario *a* extraordinary. —*m* ⟨*correo*⟩ special delivery; ⟨*plato*⟩ extra dish; ⟨*de periódico etc*⟩ special edition. **horas** *fpl* **extraordinarias** overtime

extrarradio *m* suburbs

extrasensible *a* extra-sensory

extraterrestre *a* extraterrestrial. —*m* alien

extravagan|cia *f* oddness, eccentricity. **~te** *a* odd, eccentric

extravertido *a & m* extrovert

extrav|iado *a* lost; ⟨*lugar*⟩ isolated. **~iar** [20] *vt* lose. **~iarse** *vpr* get lost; ⟨*objetos*⟩ be missing. **~ío** *m* loss

extremar *vt* overdo. **~se** *vpr* make every effort

extremeño *a* from Extremadura. **—m** person from Extremadura

extrem|idad *f* extremity. **~idades** *fpl* extremities. **~ista** *a & m & f* extremist. **~o** *a* extreme. **—m** end; ⟨*colmo*⟩ extreme. **en ~o** extremely. **en último ~o** as a last resort

extrovertido *a & m* extrovert

exuberan|cia *f* exuberance. **~te** *a* exuberant

exulta|ción *f* exultation. **~r** *vi* exult

eyacular *vt/i* ejaculate

F

fa *m* F; ⟨*solfa*⟩ fah

fabada *f* Asturian stew

fábrica *f* factory. **marca** *f* **de ~** trade mark

fabrica|ción *f* manufacture. **~ción en serie** mass production. **~nte** *m & f* manufacturer. **~r** [7] *vt* manufacture; ⟨*inventar*⟩ fabricate

fábula *f* fable; ⟨*mentira*⟩ story, lie; ⟨*chisme*⟩ gossip

fabuloso *a* fabulous

facci|ón *f* faction. **~ones** *fpl* ⟨*de la cara*⟩ features

faceta *f* facet

fácil *a* easy; ⟨*probable*⟩ likely; ⟨*persona*⟩ easygoing

facili|dad *f* ease; ⟨*disposición*⟩ aptitude. **~dades** *fpl* facilities. **~tar** *vt* facilitate; ⟨*proporcionar*⟩ provide

fácilmente *adv* easily

facistol *m* lectern

facón *m* ⟨*Arg*⟩ gaucho knife

facsímil(e) *m* facsimile

factible *a* feasible

factor *m* factor

factoría *f* agency; ⟨*esp LAm, fábrica*⟩ factory

factura *f* bill, invoice; ⟨*hechura*⟩ manufacture. **~r** *vt* ⟨*hacer la factura*⟩ invoice; ⟨*cobrar*⟩ charge; ⟨*en ferrocarril*⟩ register ⟨*Brit*⟩, check ⟨*Amer*⟩

faculta|d *f* faculty; ⟨*capacidad*⟩ ability; ⟨*poder*⟩ power. **~tivo** *a* optional

facha *f* ⟨*aspecto, fam*⟩ look

fachada *f* façade; ⟨*fig, apariencia*⟩ show

faena *f* job. **~s domésticas** housework

fagot *m* bassoon; ⟨*músico*⟩ bassoonist

faisán *m* pheasant

faja *f* ⟨*de tierra*⟩ strip; ⟨*corsé*⟩ corset; ⟨*mil etc*⟩ sash

fajo *m* bundle; ⟨*de billetes*⟩ wad

falange *f* ⟨*política española*⟩ Falange. **~ista** *m & f* Falangist

falda *f* skirt; ⟨*de montaña*⟩ side

fálico *a* phallic

fals|ear *vt* falsify, distort. **~edad** *f* falseness; ⟨*mentira*⟩ lie, falsehood. **~ificación** *f* forgery. **~ificador** *m* forger. **~ificar** [7] *vt* forge. **~o** *a* false; ⟨*equivocado*⟩ wrong; ⟨*falsificado*⟩ fake

falta *f* lack; ⟨*ausencia*⟩ absence; ⟨*escasez*⟩ shortage; ⟨*defecto*⟩ fault, defect; ⟨*culpa*⟩ fault; ⟨*error*⟩ mistake; ⟨*en fútbol etc*⟩ foul; ⟨*en tenis*⟩ fault. **~ar** *vi* be lacking; ⟨*estar ausente*⟩ be absent. **~o** *a* lacking (de in). **~a de** for lack of. **echar en ~a** miss. **hacer ~a** be necessary. **me hace ~a** I need. **¡no ~aba más!** don't mention it! ⟨*naturalmente*⟩ of course! **sacar ~as** find fault

falla f (incl geol) fault. ∼r vi fail; (romperse) break, give way; (motor, tiro etc) miss. **sin ∼r** without fail

fallec|er [11] vi die. ∼**ido** a late. —m deceased

fallido a vain; (fracasado) unsuccessful

fallo m failure; (defecto) fault; (jurid) sentence

fama f fame; (reputación) reputation. **de mala ∼** of ill repute. **tener ∼ de** have the reputation of

famélico a starving

famili|a f family. **∼ numerosa** large family. ∼**r** a familiar; (de la familia) family; (sin ceremonia) informal. ∼**ridad** f familiarity. ∼**rizarse** [10] vpr become familiar (**con** with)

famoso a famous

fanático a fanatical. —m fanatic

fanfarr|ón a boastful. —m braggart. ∼**onada** f boasting; (dicho) boast. ∼**onear** vi show off

fango m mud. ∼**so** a muddy

fantas|ear vi daydream; (imaginar) fantasize. ∼**ía** f fantasy. **de ∼** fancy

fantasma m ghost

fantástico a fantastic

fantoche m puppet

faringe f pharynx

fardo m bundle

farfullar vi jabber, gabble

farmac|éutico a pharmaceutical. —m chemist (Brit), pharmacist, druggist (Amer). ∼**ia** f (ciencia) pharmacy; (tienda) chemist's (shop) (Brit), pharmacy, drugstore (Amer)

faro m lighthouse; (aviac) beacon; (auto) headlight

farol m lantern; (de la calle) street lamp. ∼**a** f street lamp. ∼**ita** f small street lamp

farsa f farce

fas adv. **por ∼ o por nefas** rightly or wrongly

fascículo m instalment

fascina|ción f fascination. ∼**r** vt fascinate

fasci|smo m fascism. ∼**ta** a & m & f fascist

fase f phase

fastidi|ar vt annoy; (estropear) spoil. ∼**arse** vpr (aguantarse) put up with it; (hacerse daño) hurt o.s. ∼**o** m nuisance; (aburrimiento) boredom. ∼**oso** a annoying. **¡para que te ∼es!** so there! **¡qué ∼o!** what a nuisance!

fatal a fateful; (mortal) fatal; (pésimo, fam) terrible. ∼**idad** f fate; (desgracia) misfortune. ∼**ista** m & f fatalist

fatig|a f fatigue. ∼**as** fpl troubles. ∼**ar** [12] vt tire. ∼**arse** vpr get tired. ∼**oso** a tiring

fatuo a fatuous

fauna f fauna

fausto a lucky

favor m favour. ∼**able** a favourable. **a ∼ de, en ∼ de** in favour of. **haga el ∼ de** would you be so kind as to, please. **por ∼** please

favorec|edor a flattering. ∼**er** [11] vt favour; (vestido, peinado etc) suit. ∼**ido** a favoured

favorit|ismo m favouritism. ∼**o** a & m favourite

faz f face

fe f faith. **dar ∼ de** certify. **de buena ∼** in good faith

fealdad f ugliness

febrero m February

febril a feverish

fecund|ación f fertilization. ∼**ación artificial** artificial insemination. ∼**ar** vt fertilize. ∼**o** a fertile; (fig) prolific

fecha f date. ∼**r** vt date. **a estas ∼s** now; (todavía) still. **hasta la ∼** so far. **poner la ∼** date

fechoría f misdeed

federa|ción f federation. **∼l** a federal

feísimo a hideous

felici|dad f happiness. **∼dades** fpl best wishes; (congratulaciones) congratulations. **∼tación** f congratulation. **∼tar** vt congratulate. **∼tarse** vpr be glad

feligr|és m parishioner. **∼esía** f parish

felino a & m feline

feliz a happy; (afortunado) lucky. **¡Felices Pascuas!** Happy Christmas! **¡F∼ Año Nuevo!** Happy New Year!

felpudo a plush. **—m** doormat

femeni|l a feminine. **∼no** a feminine; (biol, bot) female. **—m** feminine. **∼nidad** f femeninity. **∼sta** a & m & f feminist

fen|omenal a phenomenal. **∼ómeno** m phenomenon; (monstruo) freak

feo a ugly; (desagradable) nasty; (malo) bad

féretro a coffin

feria f fair; (verbena) carnival; (descanso) holiday; (Mex, cambio) change. **∼do** a. **día ∼do** holiday

ferment|ación f fermentation. **∼ar** vt/i ferment. **∼o** m ferment

fero|cidad f ferocity. **∼z** a fierce; (persona) savage

férreo a iron. **vía férrea** railway (Brit), railroad (Amer)

ferreter|ía f ironmonger's (shop) (Brit), hardware store (Amer). **∼o** m ironmonger (Brit), hardware dealer (Amer)

ferro|bús m local train. **∼carril** m railway (Brit), railroad (Amer). **∼viario** a rail. **—m** railwayman (Brit), railroad worker (Amer)

fértil a fertile

fertili|dad f fertility. **∼zante** m fertilizer. **∼zar** [10] vt fertilize

férvido a fervent

ferv|iente a fervent. **∼or** m fervour

festej|ar vt celebrate; entertain (persona); court (novia etc); (Mex, golpear) beat. **∼o** m entertainment; (celebración) celebration

festival m festival. **∼idad** f festivity. **∼o** a festive; (humorístico) humorous. **día ∼o** feast day, holiday

festonear vt festoon

fétido a stinking

feto m foetus

feudal a feudal

fiado m. **al ∼** on credit. **∼r** m fastener; (jurid) guarantor

fiambre m cold meat

fianza f (dinero) deposit; (objeto) surety. **bajo ∼** on bail. **dar ∼** pay a deposit

fiar [20] vt guarantee; (vender) sell on credit; (confiar) confide. **–vi** trust. **∼se** vpr. **∼se de** trust

fiasco m fiasco

fibra f fibre; (fig) energy. **∼ de vidrio** fibreglass

fic|ción f fiction. **∼ticio** a fictitious; (falso) false

fich|a f token; (tarjeta) index card; (en los juegos) counter. **∼ar** vt file. **∼ero** m card index. **estar ∼ado** have a (police) record

fidedigno a reliable

fidelidad f faithfulness. **alta ∼** hi-fi (fam), high fidelity

fideos mpl noodles

fiebre f fever. **∼ del heno** hay fever. **tener ∼** have a temperature

fiel a faithful; (memoria, relato etc) reliable. **—m** believer; (de balanza) needle. **los ∼es** the faithful

fieltro m felt

fiera f wild animal; (*persona*) brute. ~**o** a fierce; (*cruel*) cruel. **estar hecho una** ~**a** be furious

fierro m (*LAm*) iron

fiesta f party; (*día festivo*) holiday. ~**s** fpl celebrations. ~ **nacional** bank holiday (*Brit*), national holiday

figura f figure; (*forma*) shape; (*en obra de teatro*) character; (*en naipes*) court-card. ~**r** vt feign; (*representar*) represent. —vi figure; (*ser importante*) be important. ~**rse** vpr imagine. **¡figúrate!** just imagine! ~**tivo** a figurative

fij|ación f fixing. ~**ar** vt fix; stick (*sello*); post (*cartel*). ~**arse** vpr settle; (*fig, poner atención*) notice. **¡fíjate!** just imagine! ~**o** a fixed; (*firme*) stable; (*persona*) settled. **de** ~**o** certainly

fila f line; (*de soldados etc*) file; (*en el teatro, cine etc*) row; (*cola*) queue. **ponerse en** ~ line up

filamento m filament

fil|antropía f philanthropy. ~**antrópico** a philanthropic. ~**ántropo** m philanthropist

filarmónico a philharmonic

filat|elia f stamp collecting, philately. ~**élico** a philatelic. —m stamp collector, philatelist

filete m fillet

filfa f (*fam*) hoax

filial a filial. —f subsidiary

filigrana f filigree (work); (*en papel*) watermark

Filipinas fpl. **las (islas)** ~ the Philippines

filipino a Philippine, Filipino

filmar vt film

filo m edge; (*de hoja*) cutting edge; (*Mex, hambre*) hunger. **al** ~ **de las doce** at exactly twelve o'clock. **dar** ~ **a**, **sacar** ~ **a** sharpen

filología f philology

filón m vein; (*fig*) gold-mine

fil|osofía f philosophy. ~**osófico** a philosophical. ~**ósofo** m philosopher

filtr|ar vt filter. ~**arse** vpr filter; (*dinero*) disappear. ~**o** m filter; (*bebida*) philtre

fin m end; (*objetivo*) aim. ~ **de semana** weekend. **a** ~ **de** in order to. **a** ~ **de cuentas** all things considered. **a** ~ **de que** in order that. **a** ~**es de** at the end of. **al** ~ finally. **al** ~ **y al cabo** after all. **dar** ~ **a** end. **en** ~ in short. **poner** ~ **a** end. **por** ~ finally. **sin** ~ endless

final a final, last. —m end. —f final. ~**idad** f aim. ~**ista** m & f finalist. ~**izar** [10] vt/i end. ~**mente** adv finally

financi|ar vt finance. ~**ero** a financial. —m financier

finca f property; (*tierras*) estate; (*LAm, granja*) farm

finés a Finnish. —m Finn; (*lengua*) Finnish

fingi|do a false. ~**r** [14] vt feign; (*simular*) simulate. —vi pretend. ~**rse** vpr pretend to be

finito a finite

finlandés a Finnish. —m (*persona*) Finn; (*lengua*) Finnish

Finlandia f Finland

fin|o a fine; (*delgado*) slender; (*astuto*) shrewd; (*sentido*) keen; (*cortés*) polite; (*jerez*) dry. ~**ura** f fineness; (*astucia*) shrewdness; (*de sentido*) keenness; (*cortesía*) politeness

fiordo m fiord

firma f signature; (*empresa*) firm

firmamento m firmament

firmar vt sign

firme a firm; (*estable*) stable, steady; (*persona*) steadfast. —m (*pavimento*) (road) surface. —adv hard. ~**za** f firmness. **de** ~ hard. **en** ~ firm, definite

fisc|al a fiscal. —m & f public prosecutor. ~**o** m treasury

fisg|ar [12] *vt* pry into ⟨*asunto*⟩; spy on ⟨*persona*⟩. —*vi* pry. ~**ón** *a* prying. —*m* busybody

físic|a *f* physics. ~**o** *a* physical. —*m* physique; ⟨*persona*⟩ physicist

fisi|ología *f* physiology. ~**ológico** *a* physiological. ~**ólogo** *m* physiologist

fisioterap|euta *m* & *f* physiotherapist. ~**ia** *f* physiotherapy. ~**ista** *m* & *f* ⟨*fam*⟩ physiotherapist

fisonom|ía *f* physiognomy, face. ~**ista** *m* & *f*. **ser buen ~ista** be good at remembering faces

fisura *f* ⟨*Med*⟩ fracture

fláccido *a* flabby

flaco *a* thin, skinny; ⟨*débil*⟩ weak

flagelo *m* scourge

flagrante *a* flagrant. **en ~** red-handed

flamante *a* splendid; ⟨*nuevo*⟩ brand-new

flamenco *a* flamenco; ⟨*de Flandes*⟩ Flemish. —*m* ⟨*música etc*⟩ flamenco

flan *m* crème caramel

flaqueza *f* thinness; ⟨*debilidad*⟩ weakness

flash *m* flash

flato *m*, **flatulencia** *f* flatulence

flaut|a *f* flute. —*m* & *f* ⟨*músico*⟩ flautist, flutist ⟨*Amer*⟩. ~**ín** *m* piccolo. ~**ista** *m* & *f* flautist, flutist ⟨*Amer*⟩

fleco *m* fringe

flecha *f* arrow

flem|a *f* phlegm. ~**ático** *a* phlegmatic

flequillo *m* fringe

fletar *vt* charter

flexib|ilidad *f* flexibility. ~**le** *a* flexible. —*m* flex, cable

flirte|ar *vi* flirt. ~**o** *m* flirting

floj|ear *vi* ease up. ~**o** *a* loose; ⟨*poco fuerte*⟩ weak; ⟨*viento*⟩ light; ⟨*perezoso*⟩ lazy

flor *f* flower; ⟨*fig*⟩ cream. ~**a** *f* flora. ~**al** *a* floral. ~**ecer** [11] *vi*

flower, bloom; ⟨*fig*⟩ flourish. ~**eciente** *a* ⟨*fig*⟩ flourishing. ~**ero** *m* flower vase. ~**ido** *a* flowery; ⟨*selecto*⟩ select; ⟨*lenguaje*⟩ florid. ~**ista** *m* & *f* florist

flota *f* fleet

flot|ador *m* float. ~**ar** *vi* float. ~**e** *m*. **a ~e** afloat

flotilla *f* flotilla

fluctua|ción *f* fluctuation. ~**r** [21] *vi* fluctuate

flu|idez *f* fluidity; ⟨*fig*⟩ fluency. ~**ido** *a* fluid; ⟨*fig*⟩ fluent. —*m* fluid. ~**ir** [17] *vi* flow. ~**jo** *m* flow. ~**o y reflujo** ebb and flow

fluorescente *a* fluorescent

fluoruro *m* fluoride

fluvial *a* river

fobia *f* phobia

foca *f* seal

foc|al *a* focal. ~**o** *m* focus; ⟨*lámpara*⟩ floodlight; ⟨*LAm, bombilla*⟩ light bulb

fogón *m* ⟨*cocina*⟩ cooker

fogoso *a* spirited

folio *m* leaf

folk|lore *m* folklore. ~**órico** *a* folk

follaje *m* foliage

follet|ín *m* newspaper serial. ~**o** *m* pamphlet

follón *m* ⟨*lío*⟩ mess; ⟨*alboroto*⟩ row

fomentar *vt* foment, stir up

fonda *f* ⟨*pensión*⟩ boarding-house

fondo *m* bottom; ⟨*parte más lejana*⟩ bottom, end; ⟨*de escenario, pintura etc*⟩ background; ⟨*profundidad*⟩ depth. ~**s** *mpl* funds, money. **a ~** thoroughly. **en el ~** deep down

fonética *f* phonetics. ~**o** *a* phonetic

fono *m* ⟨*LAm, del teléfono*⟩ earpiece

fontaner|ía *f* plumbing. ~**o** *m* plumber

footing /ˈfutin/ *m* jogging

forastero *a* alien. —*m* stranger

forceje|ar *vi* struggle. **~o** *m* struggle

fórceps *m invar* forceps

forense *a* forensic

forjar *vt* forge

forma *f* form, shape; (*horma*) mould; (*modo*) way; (*de zapatero*) last. **~s** *fpl* conventions. **~ción** *f* formation; (*educación*) training. **dar ~** a shape; (*expresar*) formulate. **de ~ que** so (that). **de todas ~s** anyway. **estar en ~** be in good form. **guardar ~s** keep up appearances

formal *a* formal; (*de fiar*) reliable; (*serio*) serious. **~idad** *f* formality; (*fiabilidad*) reliability; (*seriedad*) seriousness

formar *vt* form; (*hacer*) make; (*enseñar*) train. **~se** *vpr* form; (*desarrollarse*) develop

formato *m* format

formidable *a* formidable; (*muy grande*) enormous; (*muy bueno, fam*) marvellous

fórmula *f* formula; (*receta*) recipe

formular *vt* formulate; make (*queja etc*); (*expresar*) express

fornido *a* well-built

forraje *m* fodder. **~ar** *vt/i* forage

forr|ar *vt* (*en el interior*) line; (*en el exterior*) cover. **~o** *m* lining; (*cubierta*) cover. **~o del freno** brake lining

fortale|cer [11] *vt* strengthen; **~za** *f* strength; (*mil*) fortress; (*fuerza moral*) fortitude

fortificar [7] *vt* fortify

fortuito *a* fortuitous. **encuentro ~** *m* chance meeting

fortuna *f* fortune; (*suerte*) luck. **por ~** fortunately

forz|ado *a* hard. **~ar** [2 & 10] *vt* force. **~osamente** *adv* necessarily. **~oso** *a* inevitable; (*necesario*) necessary

fosa *f* grave

fosfato *m* phosphate

fósforo *m* phosphorus; (*cerilla*) match

fósil *a & m* fossil

fosilizarse [10] *vpr* fossilize

foso *m* ditch

foto *f* photo, photograph. **sacar ~s** take photographs

fotocopia *f* photocopy. **~dora** *f* photocopier. **~r** *vt* photocopy

fotogénico *a* photogenic

fot|ografía *f* photography; (*foto*) photograph. **~ografiar** [20] *vt* photograph. **~ográfico** *a* photographic. **~ógrafo** *m* photographer. **sacar ~ografías** take photographs

foyer *m* foyer

frac *m* (*pl* **fraques** *o* **fracs**) tails

fracas|ar *vi* fail. **~o** *m* failure

fracción *f* fraction; (*pol*) faction

fractura *f* fracture. **~r** *vt* fracture, break. **~rse** *vpr* fracture, break

fragan|cia *f* fragrance. **~te** *a* fragrant

fragata *f* frigate

frá|gil *a* fragile; (*débil*) weak. **~agilidad** *f* fragility; (*debilidad*) weakness

fragment|ario *a* fragmentary. **~o** *m* fragment

fragor *m* din

fragoso *a* rough

fragua *f* forge. **~r** [15] *vt* forge; (*fig*) concoct. **—***vi* harden

fraile *m* friar; (*monje*) monk

frambuesa *f* raspberry

francés *a* French. **—***m* (*persona*) Frenchman; (*lengua*) French

Francia *f* France

franco *a* frank; (*com*) free. **—***m* (*moneda*) franc

francotirador *m* sniper

franela *f* flannel

franja *f* border; (*fleco*) fringe

franquear *vt* clear; stamp (*carta*); overcome (*obstáculo*). **~o** *m* stamping; (*cantidad*) postage

franqueza f frankness; (*familiaridad*) familiarity

franquismo m General Franco's regime; (*política*) Franco's policy. **~ta** a pro-Franco

frasco m small bottle

frase f phrase; (*oración*) sentence. **~ hecha** set phrase

fraternal a fraternal. **~idad** f fraternity

fraude m fraud. **~ulento** a fraudulent

fray m brother, friar

frecuencia f frequency. **~tar** vt frequent. **~te** a frequent. **con ~cia** frequently

fregadero m sink. **~r** [1 & 12] vt scrub; wash up ‹los platos›; mop ‹el suelo›; (*LAm, fig, molestar, fam*) annoy

freír [51, pp frito] vt fry; (*fig, molestar, fam*) annoy. **~se** vpr fry; (*persona*) be very hot, be boiling (*fam*)

frenar vt brake; (*fig*) check

frenesí m frenzy. **~ético** a frenzied

freno m (*de caballería*) bit; (*auto*) brake; (*fig*) check

frente m front. —f forehead. **~ a** opposite; (*en contra de*) opposed to. **~ por** opposite; (*en un choque*) head-on. **al ~** at the head; (*hacia delante*) forward. **arrugar la ~** frown. **de ~** forward. **hacer ~ a** face ‹cosa›; stand up to ‹persona›

fresa f strawberry

fresca f fresh air. **~o** a (*frío*) cool; (*nuevo*) fresh; (*descarado*) cheeky. —m fresh air; (*frescor*) coolness; (*mural*) fresco; (*persona*) impudent person. **~or** m coolness. **~ura** f freshness; (*frío*) coolness; (*descaro*) cheek. **al ~o** in the open air. **hacer ~o** be cool. **tomar el ~o** get some fresh air

fresno m ash (tree)

friable a friable

frialdad f coldness; (*fig*) indifference

fricción f rubbing; (*fig, tec*) friction; (*masaje*) massage. **~onar** vt rub

frigidez f coldness; (*fig*) frigidity

frígido a frigid

frigorífico m refrigerator, fridge (*fam*)

frijol m bean. **~es refritos** (*Mex*) purée of black beans

frío a & m cold. **coger ~** catch cold. **hacer ~** be cold

frisar vi. **~ en** be getting on for, be about

frito a fried; (*exasperado*) exasperated. **me tiene ~** I'm sick of him

frivolidad f frivolity. **~ívolo** a frivolous

fronda f foliage

frontera f frontier; (*fig*) limit. **~izo** a frontier. **~o** a opposite

frontón m pelota court

frotar vt rub; strike ‹cerilla›

fructífero a fruitful

frugal a frugal

fruncir [9] vt gather ‹tela›; wrinkle ‹piel›

fruslería f trifle

frustración f frustration. **~r** vt frustrate. **~rse** vpr (*fracasar*) fail. **quedar ~do** be disappointed

fruta f fruit. **~ería** f fruit shop. **~ero** a fruit. —m fruiterer; (*recipiente*) fruit bowl. **~icultura** f fruit-growing. **~illa** f (*LAm*) strawberry. **~o** m fruit

fucsia f fuchsia

fuego m fire. **~s artificiales** fireworks. **a ~ lento** on a low heat. **tener ~** have a light

fuente f fountain; (*manantial*) spring; (*plato*) serving dish; (*fig*) source

fuera *adv* out; *(al exterior)* outside; *(en otra parte)* away; *(en el extranjero)* abroad; *–vb véase* ir y ser.~ **de** outside; *(excepto)* except for, besides. **por** ~ on the outside

fuerte *a* strong; *(color)* bright; *(sonido)* loud; *(dolor)* severe; *(duro)* hard; *(grande)* large; *(lluvia, nevada)* heavy. *—m* fort; *(fig)* strong point. *—adv* hard; *(con hablar etc)* loudly; *(mucho)* a lot

fuerza *f* strength; *(poder)* power; *(en física)* force; *(mil)* forces. ~ **de voluntad** will-power. **a** ~ **de** by dint of, by means of. **a la** ~ by necessity. **por** ~ by force; *(por necesidad)* by necessity. **tener** ~**s para** to have the strength to

fuese *vb véase* ir y ser

fug|**a** *f* flight, escape; *(de gas etc)* leak; *(mus)* fugue. ~**arse** [12] *vpr* flee, escape. ~**az** *a* fleeting. ~**itivo** *a & m* fugitive. **ponerse en** ~**a** take to flight

fui *vb véase* ir y ser

fulano *m* so-and-so. ~, **mengano y zutano** Tom, Dick and Harry

fulgor *m* brilliance; *(fig)* splendour

fulminar *vt* strike by lightning; *(fig, mirar)* look daggers at

fuma|**dor** *m* smoking. *—m* smoker. ~**r** *vt/i* smoke. ~**rse** *vpr* smoke; *(fig, gastar)* squander. ~**rada** *f* puff of smoke. ~**r en pipa** smoke a pipe. **prohibido** ~**r** no smoking

funámbulo *m* tightrope walker

funci|**ón** *f* function; *(de un cargo etc)* duties; *(de teatro)* show, performance. ~**onal** *a* functional. ~**onar** *vi* work, function. ~**onario** *m* civil servant. **no** ~**ona** out of order

funda *f* cover. ~ **de almohada** pillowcase

funda|**ción** *f* foundation. ~**mental** *a* fundamental. ~**mentar** *vt* lay the foundations of; *(fig)* base. ~**mento** *m* foundation. ~**r** *vt* found; *(fig)* base. ~**rse** *vpr* be based

fundi|**ción** *f* melting; *(de metales)* smelting; *(taller)* foundry. ~**r** *vt* melt; smelt *(metales)*; cast *(objeto)*; blend *(colores)*; *(fusionar)* merge. ~**rse** *vpr* melt; *(unirse)* merge

fúnebre *a* funeral; *(sombrío)* gloomy

funeral *a* funeral. *—m* funeral. ~**es** *mpl* funeral

funicular *a & m* funicular

furg|**ón** *m* van. ~**oneta** *f* van

furi|**a** *f* fury; *(violencia)* violence. ~**ibundo** *a* furious. ~**ioso** *a* furious. ~**or** *m* fury

furtivo *a* furtive

furúnculo *m* boil

fuselaje *m* fuselage

fusible *m* fuse

fusil *m* gun. ~**ar** *vt* shoot

fusión *f* melting; *(unión)* fusion; *(com)* merger

fútbol *m* football

futbolista *m* footballer

fútil *a* futile

futur|**ista** *a* futuristic. *—m & f* futurist. ~**o** *a & m* future

G

gabán *m* overcoat

gabardina *f* raincoat; *(tela)* gabardine

gabinete *m* *(pol)* cabinet; *(en museo etc)* room; *(de dentista, médico etc)* consulting room

gacela *f* gazelle

gaceta *f* gazette

gachas *fpl* porridge

gacho *a* drooping

gaélico *a* Gaelic

gafa f hook. **~s** fpl glasses, spectacles. **~s de sol** sun-glasses

gaf|ar vt hook; (fam) bring bad luck to. **~e** m jinx

gaita f bagpipes

gajo m (de naranja, nuez etc) segment

gala|s fpl finery, best clothes. **estar de ~** be dressed up. **hacer ~ de** show off

galán m (en el teatro) male lead; (enamorado) lover

galante a gallant. **~ar** vt court. **~ría** f gallantry

galápago m turtle

galardón m reward

galaxia f galaxy

galeón m galleon

galera f galley

galería f gallery

Gales m Wales. **país de ~** Wales

gal|és a Welsh. —m Welshman; (lengua) Welsh. **~esa** f Welshwoman

galgo m greyhound

Galicia f Galicia

galimatías m invar (fam) gibberish

galón m gallon; (cinta) braid; (mil) stripe

galop|ar vi gallop. **~e** m gallop

galvanizar [10] vt galvanize

gallard|ía f elegance. **~o** a elegant

gallego a & m Galician

galleta f biscuit, (Brit), cookie (Amer)

gall|ina f hen, chicken; (fig, fam) coward. **~o** m cock

gama f scale; (fig) range

gamba f prawn (Brit), shrimp (Amer)

gamberro m hooligan

gamuza f (piel) chamois leather

gana f wish, desire; (apetito) appetite. **de buena ~** willingly. **de mala ~** reluctantly. **no me da la ~** I don't feel like it. **tener**

~s de (+ infinitivo) feel like (+ gerundio)

ganad|ería f cattle raising; (ganado) livestock. **~o** m livestock. **~o de cerda** pigs. **~o lanar** sheep. **~o vacuno** cattle

ganar vt earn; (en concurso, juego etc) win; (alcanzar) reach; (aventajar) beat. —vi (vencer) win; (mejorar) improve. **~se la vida** earn a living. **salir ganando** come out better off

ganch|illo m crochet. **~o** m hook. **~oso** a, **~udo** a hooked. **echar el ~ a** hook. **hacer ~illo** crochet. **tener ~o** be very attractive

gandul a & m & f good-for-nothing

ganga f bargain; (buena situación) easy job, cushy job (fam)

gangrena f gangrene

gans|ada f silly thing. **~o** m goose

gañi|do m yelping. **~r** [22] vi yelp

garabat|ear vt/i (garrapatear) scribble. **~o** m (garrapato) scribble

garaj|e m garage. **~ista** m & f garage attendant

garant|e m & f guarantor. **~ía** f guarantee. **~ir** [24] vt (esp LAm), **~izar** [10] vt guarantee

garapiñado a. **almendras** fpl **garapiñadas** sugared almonds

garbanzo m chick-pea

garbo m poise; (de escrito) style. **~so** a elegant

garfio m hook

garganta f throat; (desfiladero) gorge; (de botella) neck

gárgaras fpl. **hacer ~** gargle

gargarismo m gargle

gárgola f gargoyle

garita f hut; (de centinela) sentry box

garito m gambling den

garra f (de animal) claw; (de ave) talon

garrafa f carafe

garrapata f tick

garrapat|ear vi scribble. ~o m scribble

garrote m club, cudgel; (tormento) garrotte

gárrulo a garrulous

garúa f (LAm) drizzle

garza f heron

gas m gas. **con** ~ fizzy. **sin** ~ still

gasa f gauze

gaseosa f lemonade

gasfitero m (Arg) plumber

gas|óleo m diesel. ~**olina** f petrol (Brit), gasoline (Amer), gas (Amer). ~**olinera** f petrol station (Brit), gas station (Amer); (lancha) motor boat. ~**ómetro** m gasometer

gast|ado a spent; (vestido etc) worn out. ~**ador** m spendthrift. ~**ar** vt spend; (consumir) use; (malgastar) waste; wear (vestido etc); crack (broma). —vi spend. ~**arse** vpr wear out. ~o m expense; (acción de gastar) spending

gástrico a gastric

gastronomía f gastronomy

gat|a f cat. **a** ~**as** on all fours. ~**ear** vi crawl

gatillo m trigger; (de dentista) (dental) forceps

gat|ito m kitten. ~o m cat. **dar** ~o **por liebre** take s.o. in

gaucho a & m Gaucho

gaveta f drawer

gavilla f sheaf; (de personas) band, gang

gaviota f seagull

gazpacho m gazpacho, cold soup

géiser m geyser

gelatina f gelatine; (jalea) jelly

gelignita f gelignite

gema f gem

gemelo m twin. ~**s** mpl (anteojos) binoculars; (de camisa) cuff-links. **G**~**s** Gemini

gemido m groan

Géminis mpl Gemini

gemir [5] vi groan; (animal) whine, howl

gen m, **gene** m gene

geneal|ogía f genealogy. ~**ógico** a genealogical. **árbol** m ~**ógico** family tree

generación f generation

general a general; (corriente) common. —m general. ~**ísimo** m generalíssimo, supreme commander. ~**ización** f generalization. ~**izar** [10] vt/i generalize. ~**mente** adv generally. **en** ~ in general. **por lo** ~ generally

generar vt generate

género m type, sort; (biol) genus; (gram) gender; (producto) product. ~**s de punto** knitwear. ~ **humano** mankind

generos|idad f generosity. ~o a generous; (vino) full-bodied

génesis m genesis

genética f genetics. ~o a genetic

genial a brilliant; (agradable) pleasant

genio m temper; (carácter) nature; (talento, persona) genius

genital a genital. ~**es** mpl genitals

gente f people; (nación) nation; (familia, fam) family; (Mex, persona) person

gentil a charming; (pagano) pagan. ~**eza** f elegance; (encanto) charm; (amabilidad) kindness

gentío m crowd

genuflexión f genuflection

genuino a genuine

ge|ografía f geography. ~**ográfico** a geographical. ~**ógrafo** m geographer

ge|ología f geology. ~**ólogo** m geologist

geom|etría f geometry. ~**étrico** a geometrical

geranio m geranium

geren|cia f management. **~te** m manager

geriatría f geriatrics

germánico a & m Germanic

germen m germ

germicida f germicide

germinar vi germinate

gestación f gestation

gesticula|ción f gesticulation. **~r** vi gesticulate; (*hacer muecas*) grimace

gestión f step; (*administración*) management. **~onar** vt take steps to arrange; (*dirigir*) manage

gesto m expression; (*ademán*) gesture; (*mueca*) grimace

Gibraltar m Gibraltar

gibraltareño a & m Gibraltarian

gigante a gigantic. —m giant. **~sco** a gigantic

gimn|asia f gymnastics. **~asio** m gymnasium, gym (*fam*). **~asta** m & f gymnast. **~ástica** f gymnastics

gimotear vi whine

ginebra f gin

Ginebra f Geneva

ginec|ología f gynaecology. **~ólogo** m gynaecologist

gira f excursion; (*a varios sitios*) tour

girar vt spin; (*por giro postal*) transfer. —ví rotate, go round; ‹*camino etc*› turn

girasol m sunflower

gir|atorio a revolving. **~o** m turn; (*com*) draft; (*locución*) expression. **~o postal** postal order

giroscopio m gyroscope

gis m chalk

gitano a & m gypsy

glaciala l a icy. **~r** m glacier

gladiador m gladiator

glándula f gland

glasear vt glaze; (*culin*) ice

glicerina f glycerine

glicina f wisteria

glob|al a global; (*fig*) overall. **~o** m globe; (*aeróstato, juguete*) balloon

glóbulo m globule; (*med*) corpuscle

gloria f glory. **~rse** vpr boast (**de** about)

glorieta f bower; (*auto*) roundabout (*Brit*), (traffic) circle (*Amer*)

glorificar [7] vt glorify

glorioso a glorious

glosario m glossary

glot|ón a gluttonous. —m glutton. **~onería** f gluttony

glucosa f glucose

gnomo /'nomo/ m gnome

gob|ernación f government. **~ernador** a governing. —m governor. **~ernante** a governing. **~ernar** [1] vt govern; (*dirigir*) manage, direct. **~ierno** m government; (*dirección*) management, direction. **~ierno de la casa** housekeeping. **Ministerio** m **de la G~ernación** Home Office (*Brit*), Department of the Interior (*Amer*)

goce m enjoyment

gol m goal

golf m golf

golfo m gulf; (*niño*) urchin; (*holgazán*) layabout

golondrina f swallow

golos|ina f titbit; (*dulce*) sweet. **~o** a fond of sweets

golpe m blow; (*puñetazo*) punch; (*choque*) bump; (*de emoción*) shock; (*acceso*) fit; (*en fútbol*) shot; (*en golf, en tenis, de remo*) stroke. **~ar** vt hit; (*dar varios golpes*) beat; (*con mucho ruido*) bang; (*con el puño*) punch. —vi knock. **~ de estado** coup d'etat. **~ de fortuna** stroke of luck. **~ de mano** raid. **~ de vista** glance. **~ militar** military coup. **de** ~ suddenly. **de un** ~ at one go

goma a *f* rubber; (*para pegar*) glue; (*anillo*) rubber band; (*elástico*) elastic. ~**a de borrar** rubber. ~**a de pegar** glue. ~**a espuma** foam rubber. ~**ita** *f* rubber band

gongo *m* gong

gord a *f* (*Mex*) thick tortilla. ~**iflón** *m* (*fam*), ~**inflón** *m* (*fam*) fatty. ~**o** *a* (*persona*) fat; (*carne*) fatty; (*grande*) large, big. —*m* first prize. ~**ura** *f* fatness; (*grasa*) fat

gorila *f* gorilla

gorje ar *vi* chirp. ~**o** *m* chirping

gorra *f* cap

gorrión *m* sparrow

gorro *m* cap; (*de niño*) bonnet

got a *f* drop; (*med*) gout. ~**ear** *vi* drip. ~**eo** *m* dripping. ~**era** *f* leak. **ni** ~**a** nothing

gótico *a* Gothic

gozar [10] *vt* enjoy. —*vi*. ~ **de** enjoy. ~**se** *vpr* enjoy

gozne *m* hinge

gozo *m* pleasure; (*alegría*) joy. ~**so** *a* delighted

graba ción *f* recording. ~**do** *m* engraving, print; (*en libro*) illustration. ~**r** *vt* engrave; record (*discos etc*)

gracejo *m* wit

graci a *f* grace; (*favor*) favour; (*humor*) wit. ~**as** *fpl* thanks. ¡~**as**! thank you!, thanks! ~**oso** *a* funny. —*m* fool, comic character. **dar las** ~**as** thank. **hacer** ~**a** amuse; (*gustar*) please. ¡**muchas** ~**as**! thank you very much! **tener** ~**a** be funny

grad a *f* step; (*línea*) row; (*de anfiteatro*) tier. ~**ación** *f* gradation. ~**o** *m* degree; (*escol*) year (*Brit*), grade (*Amer*); (*voluntad*) willingness

gradua ción *f* graduation; (*de alcohol*) proof. ~**do** *m* graduate.

~**l** *a* gradual. ~**r** [21] *vt* graduate; (*medir*) measure; (*univ*) confer a degree on. ~**rse** *vpr* graduate

gráfic a *f* graph. ~**o** *a* graphic. —*m* graph

grajo *m* rook

gram ática *f* grammar. ~**atical** *a* grammatical

gramo *m* gram, gramme (*Brit*)

gramófono *m* record-player, gramophone (*Brit*), phonograph (*Amer*)

gran *a véase* **grande**

grana *f* (*color*) scarlet

granada *f* pomegranate; (*mil*) grenade

granate *m* garnet

Gran Bretaña *f* Great Britain

grande *a* (*delante de nombre en singular* **gran**) big, large; (*alto*) tall; (*fig*) great. —*m* grandee. ~**za** *f* greatness

grandioso *a* magnificent

granel *m*. **a** ~ **in** bulk; (*suelto*) loose; (*fig*) in abundance

granero *m* barn

granito *m* granite; (*grano*) small grain

graniz ado *m* iced drink. ~**ar** [10] *vi* hail. ~**o** *m* hail

granj a *f* farm. ~**ero** *m* farmer

grano *m* grain; (*semilla*) seed; (*de café*) bean; (*med*) spot. ~**s** *mpl* cereals

granuja *m* & *f* rogue

gránulo *m* granule

grapa *f* staple

gras a *f* grease; (*culin*) fat. ~**iento** *a* greasy

gratifica ción *f* (*propina*) tip; (*de sueldo*) bonus. ~**r** [7] *vt* (*dar propina*) tip

gratis *adv* free

gratitud *f* gratitude

grato *a* pleasant; (*bienvenido*) welcome

gratuito *a* free; (*fig*) uncalled for

grava *f* gravel

grava|men m obligation. ~**r** vt tax; (cargar) burden

grave a serious; (pesado) heavy; (sonido) low; (acento) grave. ~**dad** f gravity

gravilla f gravel

gravita|ción f gravitation. ~**r** vi gravitate; (apoyarse) rest (**sobre** on); (fig, pesar) weigh (**sobre** on)

gravoso a onerous; (costoso) expensive

graznar vi (cuervo) caw; (pato) quack

Grecia f Greece

gregario a gregarious

greguería f uproar

gremio m union

greña f mop of hair. ~**udo** a unkempt

gresca f uproar; (riña) quarrel

griego a & m Greek

grieta f crack

grifo m tap, faucet (Amer); (animal fantástico) griffin

grilletes mpl shackles

grillo m cricket; (bot) shoot. ~**s** mpl shackles

grima f. **dar** ~ annoy

gringo m (LAm) Yankee (fam), American

gripe f flu (fam), influenza

gris a grey. ~**m** grey; (policía, fam) policeman

grit|ar vt shout (for); (como protesta) boo. ~vi shout. ~**ería** f, ~**erío** m uproar. ~**o** m shout; (de dolor, sorpresa) cry; (chillido) scream. **dar** ~**s** shout

grosella f redcurrant. ~ **negra** blackcurrant

groser|ía f coarseness; (palabras etc) coarse remark. ~**o** a coarse; (descortés) rude

grosor m thickness

grotesco a grotesque

grúa f crane

gruesa f gross. ~**o** a thick; (persona) fat, stout. ~**m** thickness; (fig) main body

grulla f crane

grumo m clot; (de leche) curd

gruñi|do m grunt; (fig) grumble. ~**r** [22] vi grunt; (perro) growl; (refunfuñar) grumble

grupa f hindquarters

grupo m group

gruta f grotto

guacamole m (Mex) avocado purée

guadaña f scythe

guagua f trifle; (esp LAm, autobús, fam) bus

guante m glove

guapo a good-looking; (chica) pretty; (elegante) smart

guarapo m (LAm) sugar cane liquor

guarda m & f guard; (de parque etc) keeper. ~**f** protection. ~**ba-rros** m invar mudguard. ~**bos-que** m gamekeeper. ~**costas** m invar coastguard vessel. ~**dor** a careful. ~**m** keeper. ~**espaldas** m invar bodyguard. ~**meta** m invar goalkeeper. ~**r** vt keep; (vigilar) guard; (proteger) protect; (reservar) save, keep. ~**rse** vpr be on one's guard. ~**rse de** (+ infinitivo) avoid (+ gerundio). ~**rropa** m wardrobe; (en local público) cloakroom. ~**vallas** m invar (LAm) goalkeeper

guardería f nursery

guardia f guard; (custodia) care. ~**f** guard. **G~** **Civil** Civil Guard. ~ **municipal** police-man. ~ **de tráfico** traffic police-man. **estar de** ~ be on duty. **estar en** ~ be on one's guard. **montar la** ~ mount guard

guardián m guardian; (de parque etc) keeper; (de edificio) caretaker

guardilla f attic

guar|ecer [11] (albergar) give shelter to. ~**ecerse** vpr take shelter. **~ida** f den, lair; (de personas) hideout

guarnec|er [11] vt provide; (adornar) decorate; (culin) garnish. **~ición** m decoration; (de caballo) harness; (culin) garnish; (mil) garrison; (de piedra preciosa) setting

guarro m pig

guasa f joke; (ironía) irony

guaso a (Arg) coarse

guasón a humorous. —m joker

Guatemala f Guatemala

guatemalteco a from Guatemala. —m person from Guatemala

guateque m party

guayaba f guava; (dulce) guava jelly

guayabera f (Mex) shirt

gubernamental a, **gubernativo** a governmental

güero a (Mex) fair

guerr|a f war; (método) warfare. **~a civil** civil war. **~ear** vi wage war. **~ero** a war; (belicoso) fighting. —m warrior. **~illa** f band of guerillas. **~illero** m guerilla. **dar ~a** annoy

guía m & f guide. —f guidebook; (de teléfonos) directory; (de ferrocarriles) timetable

guiar [20] vt guide; (llevar) lead; (auto) drive. **~se** vpr be guided (por)

guij|arro m pebble. **~o** m gravel

guillotina f guillotine

guind|a f morello cherry. **~illa** f chilli

guiñapo m rag; (fig, persona) reprobate

guiñ|ar vt/i wink. **~o** m wink. **hacer ~os** wink

gui|ón m hyphen, dash; (de película etc) script. **~onista** m & f scriptwriter

guirnalda f garland

güiro m (LAm) gourd

guisa f manner, way. **a ~ de** as. **de tal ~** in such a way

guisado m stew

guisante m pea. **~ de olor** sweet pea

guis|ar vt/i cook. **~o** m dish

güisqui m whisky

guitarr|a f guitar. **~ista** m & f guitarist

gula f gluttony

gusano m worm; (larva de mosca) maggot

gustar vt taste. —vi please. **¿te gusta?** do you like it? **me gusta el vino** I like wine

gusto m taste; (placer) pleasure. **~so** a tasty; (agradable) pleasant. **a ~** comfortable. **a mi ~** to my liking. **buen ~** (good) taste. **con mucho ~** with pleasure. **dar ~** please. **mucho ~** pleased to meet you

gutural a guttural

H

ha vb véase **haber**

haba f broad bean; (de café etc) bean

Habana f. **la ~** Havana

haban|era f habanera, Cuban dance. **~ero** a from Havana. —m person from Havana. **~o** m (puro) Havana

haber v aux [30] have. —v impersonal (presente s & pl **hay**, imperfecto s & pl **había**, pretérito s & pl **hubo**) be. **hay 5 bancos en la plaza** there are 5 banks in the square. **hay que hacerlo** it must be done, you have to do it. **he aquí** here is, here are. **no hay de qué** don't mention it, not at all. **¿qué hay?** (¿qué pasa?) what's the matter?; (¿qué tal?) how are you?

habichuela f bean

hábil a skilful; (*listo*) clever; (*adecuado*) suitable

habilidad f skill; (*astucia*) cleverness

habilita|ción f qualification. ∼r vt qualify

habita|ble a habitable. ∼ción f room; (*casa etc*) dwelling; (*cuarto de dormir*) bedroom; (*en biología*) habitat. ∼ción de matrimonio, ∼ción doble double room. ∼ción individual , ∼ción sencilla single room. ∼do a inhabited. ∼nte m inhabitant. ∼r vt live in. —vi live

hábito m habit

habitual a usual, habitual; (*cliente*) regular. ∼mente adv usually

habituar [21] vt accustom. ∼se vpr. ∼se a get used to

habla f speech; (*idioma*) language; (*dialecto*) dialect. al ∼ (*al teléfono*) speaking. ponerse al ∼ con get in touch with. ∼dor a talkative. —m chatterbox. ∼duría f rumour. ∼durías fpl gossip. ∼nte a speaking. —m & f speaker. ∼r vt speak. —vi speak, talk (con to). ∼rse vpr speak. ¡ni ∼r! out of the question! se ∼ español Spanish spoken

hacedor m creator, maker

hacendado m landowner; (*LAm*) farmer

hacendoso a hard-working

hacer [31] vt do; (*fabricar, producir etc*) make; (*en matemáticas*) make, be. —v impersonal (*con expresiones meteorológicas*) be; (*con determinado período de tiempo*) ago. ∼se vpr become; (*acostumbrarse*) get used (a to); (*estar hecho*) be made. ∼ de act as. ∼se a la mar put to sea. ∼se el sordo pretend to be deaf. hace buen tiempo it's fine weather.

hace calor it's hot. **hace frío** it's cold. **hace poco** recently. **hace 7 años** 7 years ago. **hace sol** it's sunny. **hace viento** it's windy. **¿qué le vamos a ∼?** what are we going to do?

hacia prep towards; (*cerca de*) near; (*con tiempo*) at about. ∼ abajo down(wards). ∼ arriba up(wards). ∼ las dos at about two o'clock

hacienda f country estate; (*en LAm*) ranch; (*LAm, ganado*) livestock; (*pública*) treasury. Ministerio m de H∼ Ministry of Finance; (*en Gran Bretaña*) Exchequer; (*en Estados Unidos*) Treasury. ministro m de H∼ Minister of Finance; (*en Gran Bretaña*) Chancellor of the Exchequer; (*en Estados Unidos*) Secretary of the Treasury

hacinar vt stack

hacha f axe; (*antorcha*) torch

hachís m hashish

hada f fairy. **cuento** m **de** ∼s fairy tale

hado m fate

hago vb véase **hacer**

Haití m Haiti

halag|ar [12] vt flatter. ∼üeño a flattering

halcón m falcon

hálito m breath

halo m halo

hall /xol/ m hall

hallar vt find; (*descubrir*) discover. ∼rse vpr be. ∼zgo m discovery

hamaca f hammock; (*asiento*) deck-chair

hambr|e f hunger; (*de muchos*) famine. ∼iento a starving. **tener** ∼ be hungry

Hamburgo m Hamburg

hamburguesa f hamburger

hampa f underworld. ∼ón m thug

handicap /'xandikap/ *m* handicap

hangar *m* hangar

haragán *a* lazy, idle. —*m* layabout

harap|**iento** *a* in rags. **~o** *m* rag

harina *f* flour

harpa *f* harp

hart|**ar** *vt* satisfy; (*fastidiar*) annoy. **~arse** *vpr* (*comer*) eat one's fill; (*cansarse*) get fed up (**de** with). **~azgo** *m* surfeit. **~o** *a* full; (*cansado*) tired; (*fastidiado*) fed up (**de** with). —*adv* enough; (*muy*) very. **~ura** *f* surfeit; (*abundancia*) plenty; (*de deseo*) satisfaction

hasta *prep* as far as; (*con tiempo*) until, till; (*Mex*) not until. —*adv* even. ¡**~ la vista!** goodbye!, see you! (*fam*) ¡**~ luego!** see you later! ¡**~ mañana!** see you tomorrow! ¡**~ pronto!** see you soon!

hast|**iar** [20] *vt* annoy; (*cansar*) weary, tire; (*aburrir*) bore. **~iarse** *vpr* get fed up (**de** with). **~ío** *m* weariness; (*aburrimiento*) boredom; (*asco*) disgust

hat|**illo** *m* bundle (of belongings); (*ganado*) small flock. **~o** *m* belongings; (*ganado*) flock, herd

haya *f* beech (tree). —*vb véase* **haber**

Haya *f.* **la ~** the Hague

haz *m* bundle; (*de trigo*) sheaf; (*de rayos*) beam

hazaña *f* exploit

hazmerreír *m* laughing-stock

he *vb véase* **haber**

hebdomadario *a* weekly

hebilla *f* buckle

hebra *f* thread; (*fibra*) fibre

hebreo *a* Hebrew; (*actualmente*) Jewish. —*m* Hebrew; (*actualmente*) Jew; (*lengua*) Hebrew

hecatombe *f* (*fig*) disaster

hechi|**cera** *f* witch. **~cería** *f* witchcraft. **~cero** *a* magic. —*m* wizard. **~zar** [10] *vt* cast a spell on; (*fig*) fascinate. **~zo** *m* witchcraft; (*un acto de brujería*) spell; (*fig*) fascination

hecho *pp de* **hacer**. —*a* mature; (*terminado*) finished; (*vestidos etc*) ready-made; (*culin*) done. —*m* fact; (*acto*) deed; (*cuestión*) matter; (*suceso*) event. **~ura** *f* making; (*forma*) form; (*del cuerpo*) build; (*calidad de fabricación*) workmanship. **de ~o** *a* fact

hed|**er** [1] *vi* stink. **~iondez** *f* stench. **~iondo** *a* stinking, smelly. **~or** *m* stench

hela|**da** *f* freeze; (*escarcha*) frost. **~dera** *f* (*LAm*) refrigerator, fridge (*Brit, fam*). **~dería** *f* ice-cream shop. **~do** *a* frozen; (*muy frío*) very cold. —*m* ice-cream. **~dora** *f* freezer. **~r** [1] *vt* freeze. **~rse** *vpr* freeze

helecho *m* fern

hélice *f* spiral; (*propulsor*) propeller

heli|**cóptero** *m* helicopter. **~puerto** *m* heliport

hembra *f* female; (*mujer*) woman

hemisferio *m* hemisphere

hemorragia *f* haemorrhage

hemorroides *fpl* haemorrhoids, piles

henchir [5] *vt* fill. **~se** *vpr* stuff o.s.

hend|**er** [1] *vt* split. **~idura** *f* crack, split; (*geol*) fissure

heno *m* hay

heráldica *f* heraldry

herb|**áceo** *a* herbaceous. **~olario** *m* herbalist. **~oso** *a* grassy

hered|**ad** *f* country estate. **~ar** *vt/i* inherit. **~era** *f* heiress. **~ero** *m* heir. **~itario** *a* hereditary

hereje *m* heretic. **~ía** *f* heresy

herencia f inheritance; (fig) heritage

heri|da f injury. **~do** a injured, wounded. **—m** injured person. **~r** [4] vt injure, wound; (fig) hurt. **~rse** vpr hurt o.s. an **~dos** the injured; (cantidad) the number of injured

herman|a f sister. **~a política** sister-in-law. **~astra** f stepsister. **~astro** m stepbrother. **~dad** f brotherhood. **~o** m brother. **~o político** brother-in-law. **~os gemelos** twins

hermético a hermetic; (fig) watertight

hermos|o a beautiful; (esplén-dido) splendid; (hombre) handsome. **~ura** f beauty

hernia f hernia

héroe m hero

hero|ico a heroic. **~ína** f heroine; (droga) heroin. **~ísmo** m heroism

herr|adura f horseshoe. **~amienta** f tool. **~ería** f smithy. **~ero** m blacksmith. **~umbre** f rust

herv|idero m (manantial) spring; (fig) hotbed; (multitud) throng. **~ir** [4] vt/i boil. **~or** m boiling; (fig) ardour

heterogéneo a heterogeneous

heterosexual a & m & f heterosexual

hex|agonal a hexagonal. **~ágono** m hexagon

hiato m hiatus

hiberna|ción f hibernation. **~r** vi hibernate

hibisco m hibiscus

híbrido a & m hybrid

hice vb véase **hacer**

hidalgo m nobleman

hidrata|nte a moisturizing. **~r** vt hydrate; (crema etc) moisturize. **crema** f **~nte** moisturizing cream

hidráulico a hydraulic

hidroavión m seaplane

hidroeléctrico a hydroelectric

hidrófilo a absorbent

hidr|ofobia f rabies. **~ófobo** a rabid

hidrógeno m hydrogen

hidroplano m seaplane

hiedra f ivy

hiel f (fig) bitterness

hielo m ice; (escarcha) frost; (fig) coldness

hiena f hyena; (fig) brute

hierba f grass; (culin, med) herb. **~buena** f mint. **mala ~** weed; (gente) bad people, evil people

hierro m iron

hígado m liver

higi|ene f hygiene. **~énico** a hygienic

higo m fig. **~uera** f fig tree

hij|a f daughter. **~a política** daughter-in-law. **~astra** f stepdaughter. **~astro** m stepson. **~o** m son. **~o político** son-in-law. **~s** mpl sons; (chicos y chicas) children

hilar vt spin. **~ delgado** split hairs

hilaridad f laughter, hilarity

hilera f row; (mil) file

hilo m thread; (elec) wire; (de líquido) trickle; (lino) linen

hilv|án m tacking. **~anar** vt tack; (fig, bosquejar) outline

himno m hymn. **~ nacional** anthem

hincapié m. **hacer ~ en** stress, insist on

hincar [7] vt drive in. **~se** vpr sink into. **~se de rodillas** kneel down

hincha f (fam) grudge; (aficionado, fam) fan

hincha|do a inflated; (med) swollen; (persona) arrogant. **~r** vt inflate, blow up. **~rse** vpr swell up; (fig, comer mucho, fam) gorge o.s. **~zón** f swelling; (fig) arrogance

hindi *m* Hindi
hindú *a* Hindu
hiniesta *f* (*bot*) broom
hinojo *m* fennel
hiper... *pref* hyper...
hiper|mercado *m* hypermarket. ∼sensible *a* hypersensitive. ∼tensión *f* high blood pressure
hípico *a* horse
hipn|osis *f* hypnosis. ∼ótico *a* hypnotic. ∼otismo *m* hypnotism. ∼otizador *m* hypnotist. ∼otizar [10] *vt* hypnotize
hipo *m* hiccup. tener ∼ have hiccups
hipocondríaco *a & m* hypochondriac
hip|ocresía *f* hypocrisy. ∼ócrita *a* hypocritical. —*m & f* hypocrite
hipodérmico *a* hypodermic
hipódromo *m* racecourse
hipopótamo *m* hippopotamus
hipoteca *f* mortgage. ∼r [7] *vt* mortgage
hip|ótesis *f invar* hypothesis. ∼otético *a* hypothetical
hiriente *a* offensive, wounding
hirsuto *a* shaggy
hirviente *a* boiling
hispánico *a* Hispanic
hispano... *pref* Spanish
Hispanoamérica *f* Spanish America
hispano|americano *a* Spanish American. ∼hablante *a*, ∼parlante *a* Spanish-speaking
hist|eria *f* hysteria. ∼érico *a* hysterical. ∼erismo *m* hysteria
hist|oria *f* history; (*cuento*) story. ∼oriador *m* historian. ∼órico *a* historical. ∼orieta *f* tale; (*con dibujos*) strip cartoon. pasar a la ∼oria go down in history
hito *m* milestone
hizo *vb véase* hacer
hocico *m* snout; (*fig, de enfado*) grimace

hockey *m* hockey. ∼ sobre hielo ice hockey
hogar *m* hearth; (*fig*) home. ∼eño *a* home; (*persona*) home-loving
hogaza *f* large loaf
hoguera *f* bonfire
hoja *f* leaf; (*de papel, metal etc*) sheet; (*de cuchillo, espada etc*) blade. ∼ de afeitar razor blade. ∼lata *f* tin. ∼latería *f* tinware. ∼latero *m* tinsmith
hojaldre *m* puff pastry, flaky pastry
hojear *vt* leaf through; (*leer superficialmente*) glance through
hola *int* hello!
Holanda *f* Holland
holand|és *a* Dutch. —*m* Dutchman; (*lengua*) Dutch. ∼esa *f* Dutchwoman
holg|ado *a* loose; (*fig*) comfortable. ∼ar [2 & 12] *vt* (*no trabajar*) not work, have a day off; (*sobrar*) be unnecessary. ∼azán *a* lazy. —*m* idler. ∼ura *f* looseness; (*fig*) comfort; (*en mecánica*) play. huelga decir que needless to say
holocausto *m* holocaust
hollín *m* soot
hombre *m* man; (*especie humana*) man(kind). —*int* Good Heavens!; (*de duda*) well. ∼ de estado statesman. ∼ de negocios businessman. ∼ rana frogman. el ∼ de la calle the man in the street
hombr|era *f* epaulette; (*almohadilla*) shoulder pad. ∼o *m* shoulder
hombruno *a* masculine
homenaje *m* homage; (*fig*) tribute. rendir ∼ a pay tribute to
home|ópata *m* homoeopath. ∼opatía *f* homoeopathy. ∼opático *a* homoeopathic

homicid|**a** a murderous. —m & f murderer. **~io** m murder

homogéneo a homogeneous

homosexual a & m & f homosexual. **~idad** f homosexuality

hond|**o** a deep. **~onada** f hollow. **~ura** f depth

Honduras fpl Honduras

hondureño a & m Honduran

honest|**idad** f decency. **~o** a proper

hongo m fungus; (culin) mushroom; (venenoso) toadstool

hon|**or** m honour. **~orable** a honourable. **~orario** a honorary. **~orarios** mpl fees. **~ra** f honour; (buena fama) good name. **~radez** f honesty. **~rado** a honest. **~rar** vt honour. **~rarse** vpr be honoured

hora f hour; (momento determinado, momento oportuno) time. **~ avanzada** late hour. **~ punta** rush hour. **~s fijo de trabajo** working hours. **~s fpl extraordinarias** overtime. **a estas ~s** now. **¿a qué ~?** at what time? when? **de ~ en ~** hourly. **de última ~** lastminute. **en buena ~** at the right time. **media ~** half an hour. **¿qué ~ es?** what time is it? **¿tiene Vd ~?** can you tell me the time?

horario a time; (cada hora) hourly. —m timetable. **a ~** (LAm) on time

horca f gallows

horcajadas. **a ~** astride

horchata f tiger-nut milk

horda f horde

horizont|**al** a & f horizontal. —m horizon

horma f mould; (para fabricar calzado) last; (para conservar forma del calzado) shoe-tree

hormiga f ant

hormigón m concrete

hormigue|**ar** vt tingle; (bullir) swarm. **me ~a la mano** I've got pins and needles in my hand. **~o** m tingling; (fig) anxiety

hormiguero m anthill; (de gente) swarm

hormona f hormone

horn|**ada** f batch. **~ero** m baker. **~illo** m cooker. **~o** m oven; (para ladrillos, cerámica etc) kiln; (tec) furnace

horóscopo m horoscope

horquilla f pitchfork; (para el pelo) hairpin

horr|**endo** a awful. **~ible** a horrible. **~ipilante** a terrifying. **~or** m horror; (atrocidad) atrocity. **~orizar** [10] vt horrify. **~orizarse** vpr be horrified. **~oroso** a horrifying. **¡qué ~or!** how awful!

hort|**aliza** f vegetable. **~elano** m market gardener. **~icultura** f horticulture

hosco a surly; (lugar) gloomy

hospeda|**je** m lodging. **~r** vt put up. **~rse** vpr lodge

hospital m hospital

hospital|**ario** m hospitable. **~idad** f hospitality

hostal m boarding-house

hostería f inn

hostia f (relig) host; (golpe, fam) punch

hostigar [12] vt whip; (fig, excitar) urge; (fig, molestar) pester

hostil a hostile. **~idad** f hostility

hotel m hotel. **~ero** a hotel. —m hotelier

hoy adv today. **~ (en) día** nowadays. **~ mismo** this very day. **~ por ~** for the time being. **de ~ en adelante** from now on

hoya f hole; (sepultura) grave. **~o** m hole; (sepultura) grave. **~uelo** m dimple

hoz f sickle; (desfiladero) pass

hube vb véase **haber**

hucha f money box

hueco a hollow; (*vacío*) empty; (*esponjoso*) spongy; (*resonante*) resonant. —*m* hollow

huelg|**a** *f* strike. **~a de brazos caídos** sit-down strike. **~a de celo** work-to-rule. **~a de hambre** hunger strike. **~uista** *m & f* striker. **declarar la ~a, declararse en ~a** come out on strike

huelo *vb véase* **oler**

huella *f* footprint; (*de animal, vehículo etc*) track. **~ dactilar, ~ digital** fingerprint

huérfano a orphaned. —*m* orphan. **~ de** without

huero a empty

huert|**a** *f* market garden (*Brit*), truck farm (*Amer*); (*terreno de regadío*) irrigated plain. **~o** *m* vegetable garden; (*de árboles frutales*) orchard

huesa *f* grave

hueso *m* bone; (*de fruta*) stone. **~so** a bony

huésped *m* guest; (*que paga*) lodger; (*animal*) host

huesudo a bony

huev|**a** *f* roe. **~era** *f* eggcup. **~o** *m* egg. **~o duro** hard-boiled egg. **~o escalfado** poached egg. **~o estrellado, ~o frito** fried egg. **~o pasado por agua** boiled egg. **~os revueltos** scrambled eggs

hui|**da** *f* flight, escape. **~dizo** a (*tímido*) shy; (*fugaz*) fleeting. **~r** [17] *vt/i* flee, run away; (*evitar*) avoid

huipil *m* (*Mex*) embroidered smock

huitlacoche *m* (*Mex*) edible black fungus

hule *m* oilcloth, oilskin

human|**idad** *f* mankind; (*fig*) humanity. **~idades** *fpl* humanities. **~ismo** *m* humanism. **~ista** *m & f* humanist. **~itario** a humanitarian. **~o** a human;

(*benévolo*) humane. —*m* human (being)

hum|**areda** *f* cloud of smoke. **~ear** *vi* smoke; (*echar vapor*) steam

humed|**ad** *f* dampness (*en meteorología*) humidity. **~ecer** [11] *vt* moisten. **~ecerse** *vpr* become moist

húmedo a damp; ‹*clima*› humid; ‹*mojado*› wet

humil|**dad** *f* humility. **~lde** a humble. **~llación** *f* humiliation. **~llar** *vt* humiliate. **~llarse** *vpr* humble o.s.

humo *m* smoke; (*vapor*) steam; (*gas nocivo*) fumes. **~s** *mpl* conceit

humor *m* mood, temper; (*gracia*) humour. **~ismo** *m* humour. **~ista** *m & f* humorist. **~ístico** a humorous. **estar de mal ~** be in a bad mood

hundi|**do** a sunken. **~miento** *m* sinking. **~r** *vt* sink; destroy ‹*edificio*›. **~rse** *vpr* sink; ‹*edificio*› collapse

húngaro a & *m* Hungarian

Hungría *f* Hungary

huracán *m* hurricane

huraño a unsociable

hurg|**ar** [12] *vt* poke; (*fig*) stir up. **~ón** *m* poker

hurón *m* ferret. —a unsociable

hurra *int* hurray!

hurtadillas. a ~ stealthily

hurt|**ar** *vt* steal. **~o** *m* theft; (*cosa robada*) stolen object

husmear *vt* sniff out; (*fig*) pry into

huyo *vb véase* **huir**

I

Iberia *f* Iberia

ibérico a Iberian

ibero *a* & *m* Iberian

ibice *m* ibex, mountain goat

Ibiza *f* Ibiza

iceberg /i6'ber/ *m* iceberg

icono *m* icon

ictericia *f* jaundice

ida *f* outward journey; (*salida*) departure. **de ~ y vuelta** return (*Brit*), round-trip (*Amer*)

idea *f* idea; (*opinión*) opinion. **cambiar de ~** change one's mind. **no tener la más remota ~, no tener la menor ~** not have the slightest idea, not have a clue (*fam*)

ideal *a* ideal; (*imaginario*) imaginary. —*m* ideal. **~ista** *m* & *f* idealist. **~izar** [10] *vt* idealize

idear *vt* think up, conceive; (*inventar*) invent

ídem *pron* & *adv* the same

idéntico *a* identical

identi|dad *f* identity. **~ficación** *f* identification. **~ficar** [7] *vt* identify. **~ficarse** *vpr*. **~ficarse con** identify with

ideo|logía *f* ideology. **~ógico** *a* ideological

idílico *a* idyllic

idilio *m* idyll

idioma *m* language. **~ático** *a* idiomatic

idiosincrasia *f* idiosyncrasy

idiot|a *a* idiotic. —*m* & *f* idiot. **~ez** *f* idiocy

idiotismo *m* idiom

idolatrar *vt* worship; (*fig*) idolize

ídolo *m* idol

idóneo *a* suitable (**para** for)

iglesia *f* church

iglú *m* igloo

ignición *f* ignition

ignominia *f* ignominy, disgrace. **~oso** *a* ignominious

ignora|ncia *f* ignorance. **~nte** *a* ignorant. —*m* ignoramus. **~r** *vt* not know, be unaware of

igual *a* equal; (*mismo*) the same; (*similar*) like; (*llano*) even; (*liso*)

smooth. —*adv* easily. —*m* equal. **~ que** (the same as). **al ~ que** the same as. **da ~, es ~** it doesn't matter

igual|ar *vt* make equal; (*ser igual*) equal; (*allanar*) level. **~arse** *vpr* be equal. **~dad** *f* equality. **~mente** *adv* equally; (*también*) also, likewise; (*respuesta de cortesía*) the same to you

ijada *f* flank

ilegal *a* illegal

ilegible *a* illegible

ilegítimo *a* illegitimate

ileso *a* unhurt

ilícito *a* illicit

ilimitado *a* unlimited

ilógico *a* illogical

ilumina|ción *f* illumination; (*alumbrado*) lighting; (*fig*) enlightenment. **~r** *vt* light (up); (*fig*) enlighten. **~rse** *vpr* light up

ilusi|ón *f* illusion; (*sueño*) dream; (*alegría*) joy. **~onado** *a* excited. **~onar** *vt* give false hope. **~onarse** *vpr* have false hopes. **hacerse ~ones** build up one's hopes. **me hace ~ón** I'm thrilled; I'm looking forward to (*algo en el futuro*)

ilusionis|mo *m* conjuring. **~ta** *m* & *f* conjurer

iluso *a* easily deceived. —*m* dreamer. **~rio** *a* illusory

ilustra|ción *f* learning; (*dibujo*) illustration. **~do** *a* learned; (*con dibujos*) illustrated. **~r** *vt* explain; (*instruir*) instruct; (*añadir dibujos etc*) illustrate. **~rse** *vpr* acquire knowledge. **~tivo** *a* illustrative

ilustre *a* illustrious

imagen *f* image; (*TV etc*) picture

imagina|ble *a* imaginable. **~ción** *f* imagination. **~r** *vt* imagine. **~rse** *vpr* imagine. **~rio** *m* imaginary. **~tivo** *a* imaginative

imán *m* magnet

imantar *vt* magnetize
imbécil *a* stupid. —*m & f* imbecile, idiot
imborrable *a* indelible; ‹*recuerdo etc*› unforgettable
imbuir [17] *vt* imbue (**de** with)
imita|ción *f* imitation. **~r** *vt* imitate
impacien|cia *f* impatience. **~tarse** *vpr* lose one's patience. **~te** *a* impatient; (*intranquilo*) anxious
impacto *m* impact
impar *a* odd
imparcial *a* impartial. **~idad** *f* impartiality
impartir *vt* impart
impasible *a* impassive
impávido *a* fearless; (*impasible*) impassive
impecable *a* impeccable
impedi|do *a* disabled. **~menta** *f* (*esp mil*) baggage. **~mento** *m* hindrance. **~r** [5] *vt* prevent; (*obstruir*) hinder
impeler *vt* drive
impenetrable *a* impenetrable
impenitente *a* unrepentant
impensa|ble *a* unthinkable. **~do** *a* unexpected
imperar *vi* reign
imperativo *a* imperative; ‹*persona*› imperious
imperceptible *a* imperceptible
imperdible *m* safety pin
imperdonable *a* unforgivable
imperfec|ción *f* imperfection. **~to** *a* imperfect
imperial *a* imperial. —*f* upper deck. **~ismo** *m* imperialism
imperio *m* empire; (*poder*) rule; (*fig*) pride. **~so** *a* imperious
impermeable *a* waterproof. —*m* raincoat
impersonal *a* impersonal
impertérrito *a* undaunted
impertinen|cia *f* impertinence. **~te** *a* impertinent
imperturbable *a* imperturbable

ímpetu *m* impetus; (*impulso*) impulse; (*impetuosidad*) impetuosity
impetuos|idad *f* impetuosity; (*violencia*) violence. **~o** *a* impetuous; (*violento*) violent
impío *a* ungodly; ‹*acción*› irreverent
implacable *a* implacable
implantar *vt* introduce
implica|ción *f* implication. **~r** [7] *vt* implicate; (*significar*) imply
implícito *a* implicit
implora|ción *f* entreaty. **~r** *vt* implore
imponderable *a* imponderable; (*inapreciable*) invaluable
impon|ente *a* imposing; (*fam*) terrific. **~er** [34] *vt* impose; (*requerir*) demand; deposit ‹*dinero*›. **~erse** *vpr* be imposed; (*hacerse obedecer*) assert o.s.; (*hacerse respetar*) command respect. **~ible** *a* taxable
impopular *a* unpopular. **~idad** *f* unpopularity
importa|ción *f* import; (*artículo*) import. **~dor** *a* importing. —*m* importer
importa|ncia *f* importance; (*tamaño*) size. **~nte** *a* important; (*en cantidad*) considerable. **~r** *vt* import; (*valer*) cost. —*vi* be important, matter. **importa...?** would you mind...? **no ~** it doesn't matter
importe *m* price; (*total*) amount
importun|ar *vt* bother. **~o** *a* troublesome; (*inoportuno*) inopportune
imposib|ilidad *f* impossibility. **~le** *a* impossible. **hacer lo ~le** do all one can
imposición *f* imposition; (*impuesto*) tax
impostor *m & f* impostor
impotable *a* undrinkable

impoten|cia f impotence. **∼te** a powerless, impotent

impracticable a impracticable; (*intransitable*) unpassable

impreca|ción f curse. **∼r** [7] vt curse

imprecis|ión f vagueness. **∼o** a imprecise

impregnar vt impregnate; (*empapar*) soak; (*fig*) cover

imprenta f printing; (*taller*) printing house, printer's

imprescindible a indispensable, essential

impresi|ón f impression; (*acción de imprimir*) printing; (*tirada*) edition; (*huella*) imprint. **∼onable** a impressionable. **∼onante** a impressive; (*espantoso*) frightening. **∼onar** vt impress; (*conmover*) move; (*foto*) expose. **∼onarse** vpr be impressed; (*conmover*) be moved

impresionis|mo m impressionism. **∼ta** a & m & f impressionist

impreso a printed. —m printed paper, printed matter. **∼ra** f printer

imprevis|ible a unforeseeable. **∼to** a unforeseen

imprimir [pp **impreso**] vt impress; print (*libro etc*)

improbab|ilidad f improbability. **∼le** a unlikely, improbable

improcedente a unsuitable

improductivo a unproductive

improperio m insult. **∼s** mpl abuse

impropio a improper

improvis|ación f improvisation. **∼adamente** adv suddenly. **∼ado** a improvised. **∼ar** vt improvise. **∼o** a. **de ∼o** suddenly

impruden|cia f imprudence. **∼te** a imprudent

impuden|cia f impudence. **∼te** a impudent

imp|údico a immodest; (*desvergonzado*) shameless. **∼udor** m immodesty; (*desvergüenza*) shamelessness

impuesto a imposed. —m tax. **∼ sobre el valor añadido** VAT, value added tax

impugnar vt contest; (*refutar*) refute

impulsar vt impel

impuls|ividad f impulsiveness. **∼ivo** a impulsive. **∼o** m impulse

impune a unpunished. **∼idad** f impunity

impur|eza f impurity. **∼o** a impure

imputa|ción f charge. **∼r** vt attribute; (*acusar*) charge

inacabable a interminable

inaccesible a inaccessible

inaceptable a unacceptable

inacostumbrado a unaccustomed

inactiv|idad f inactivity. **∼o** a inactive

inadaptado a maladjusted

inadecuado a inadequate; (*inapropiado*) unsuitable

inadmisible a inadmissible; (*intolerable*) intolerable

inadvert|ido a unnoticed. **∼encia** f inadvertence

inagotable a inexhaustible

inaguantable a unbearable; (*persona*) insufferable

inalterable a unchangeable; (*color*) fast; (*carácter*) calm. **∼do** a unchanged

inanimado a inanimate

inaplicable a inapplicable

inapreciable a imperceptible

inapropiado a inappropriate

inarticulado a inarticulate

inasequible a out of reach

inaudito a unheard-of

inaugura|ción f inauguration. **∼l** a inaugural. **∼r** vt inaugurate

inca a Incan. —m & f Inca. ~**ico** a Incan

incalculable a incalculable

incandecen|cia f incandescence. ~**te** a incandescent

incansable a tireless

incapa|cidad f incapacity. ~**ci-tar** vt incapacitate. ~**z** a incapable

incauto a unwary; (fácil de engañar) gullible

incendi|ar vt set fire to. ~**arse** vpr catch fire. ~**ario** a incendiary. —m arsonist. ~**o** m fire

incentivo m incentive

incertidumbre f uncertainty

incesante a incessant

incest|o m incest. ~**uoso** a incestuous

inciden|cia f incidence; (incidente) incident. ~**tal** a incidental. ~**te** m incident

incidir vi fall; (influir) influence

incienso m incense

incierto a uncertain

incinera|ción f incineration; (de cadáveres) cremation. ~**dor** m incinerator. ~**r** vt incinerate; cremate (cadáver)

incipiente a incipient

incisión f incision

incisivo a incisive. —m incisor

incitar vt incite

incivil a rude

inclemen|cia f harshness. ~**te** a harsh

inclina|ción f slope; (de la cabeza) nod; (fig) inclination. ~**r** vt incline. ~**rse** vpr lean; (encorvarse) stoop; (en saludo) bow; (fig) be inclined. ~**rse** a (parecerse) resemble

inclu|ido a included; (precio) inclusive; (en cartas) enclosed. ~**ir** [17] vt include; (en cartas) enclose. ~**sión** f inclusion. ~**sive** adv inclusive. **hasta el lunes** ~**sive** up to and including Monday. ~**so** a included; (en

cartas) enclosed. —adv including; (hasta) even

incógnito a unknown. **de** ~ incognito

incoheren|cia f incoherence. ~**te** a incoherent

incoloro a colourless

incólume a unharmed

incomestible a, **incomible** a uneatable, inedible

incomodar vt inconvenience; (molestar) bother. ~**se** vpr trouble o.s.; (enfadarse) get angry

incómodo a uncomfortable; (inoportuno) inconvenient

incomparable a incomparable

incompatib|ilidad f incompatibility. ~**le** a incompatible

incompeten|cia f incompetence. ~**te** a incompetent

incompleto a incomplete

incompren|dido a misunderstood. ~**sible** a incomprehensible. ~**sión** f incomprehension

incomunicado a isolated; (preso) in solitary confinement

inconcebible a inconceivable

inconciliable a irreconcilable

inconcluso a unfinished

incondicional a unconditional

inconfundible a unmistakable

incongruente a incongruous

inconmensurable a (fam) enormous

inconscien|cia f unconsciousness; (irreflexión) recklessness. ~**te** a unconscious; (irreflexivo) reckless

inconsecuente a inconsistent

inconsiderado a inconsiderate

inconsistente a insubstantial

inconsolable a unconsolable

inconstan|cia f inconstancy. ~**te** a changeable; (persona) fickle

incontable a countless

incontaminado *a* uncontaminated

incontenible *a* irrepressible

incontestable *a* indisputable

incontinen|cia *f* incontinence. ~te *a* incontinent

inconvenien|cia *f* disadvantage. ~te *a* inconvenient; (*inapropiado*) inappropriate; (*incorrecto*) improper. —*m* difficulty; (*desventaja*) drawback

incorpora|ción *f* incorporation. ~r *vt* incorporate; (*culin*) mix. ~rse *vpr* sit up; join (*sociedad, regimiento etc*)

incorrecto *a* incorrect; (*acción*) improper; (*descortés*) discourteous

incorregible *a* incorrigible

incorruptible *a* incorruptible

incrédulo *a* incredulous

increíble *a* incredible

increment|ar *vt* increase. ~o *m* increase

incriminar *vt* incriminate

incrustar *vt* encrust

incuba|ción *f* incubation. ~dora *f* incubator. ~r *vt* incubate; (*fig*) hatch

incuestionable *a* unquestionable

inculcar [7] *vt* inculcate

inculpar *vt* accuse; (*culpar*) blame

inculto *a* uncultivated; (*persona*) uneducated

incumplimiento *m* nonfulfilment; (*de un contrato*) breach

incurable *a* incurable

incurrir *vi*. ~ en incur; fall into (*error*); commit (*crimen*)

incursión *f* raid

indaga|ción *f* investigation. ~r [12] *vt* investigate

indebido *a* undue

indecen|cia *f* indecency. ~te *a* indecent

indecible *a* inexpressible

indecis|ión *f* indecision. ~o *a* undecided

indefenso *a* defenceless

indefini|ble *a* indefinable. ~do *a* indefinite

indeleble *a* indelible

indelicad|eza *f* indelicacy. ~o *a* indelicate; (*falto de escrúpulo*) unscrupulous

indemne *a* undamaged; (*persona*) unhurt. ~idad *f* indemnity. ~izar [10] *vt* indemnify, compensate

independ|encia *f* independence. ~iente *a* independent

independizarse [10] *vpr* become independent

indescifrable *a* indecipherable, incomprehensible

indescriptible *a* indescribable

indeseable *a* undesirable

indestructible *a* indestructible

indetermina|ble *a* indeterminable. ~do *a* indeterminate

India *f*. la ~ India. las ~s *fpl* the Indies

indica|ción *f* indication; (*sugerencia*) suggestion. ~ciones *fpl* directions. ~dor *m* indicator; (*tec*) gauge. ~r [7] *vt* show, indicate; (*apuntar*) point at; (*hacer saber*) point out; (*aconsejar*) advise. ~tivo *a* indicative. —*m* indicative; (*al teléfono*) dialling code

índice *m* indication; (*dedo*) index finger; (*de libro*) index; (*catálogo*) catalogue; (*aguja*) pointer

indicio *m* indication, sign; (*vestigio*) trace

indiferen|cia *f* indifference. ~te *a* indifferent. me es ~te it's all the same to me

indígena *a* indigenous. —*m & f* native

indigen|cia *f* poverty. ~te *a* needy

indigestión f indigestion. ~o a undigested; (difícil de digerir) indigestible

indignación f indignation. ~ado a indignant. ~ar vt make indignant. ~arse vpr be indignant. ~o a unworthy; (despreciable) contemptible

indio a & m Indian

indirecta f hint. ~o a indirect

indisciplina f lack of discipline. ~do a undisciplined

indiscreción f indiscretion. ~to a indiscreet

indiscutible a unquestionable

indisoluble a indissoluble

indispensable a indispensable

indisponer [34] vt (enemistar) set against. ~onerse vpr fall out; (ponerse enfermo) fall ill. ~osición f indisposition. ~uesto a indisposed

indistinto a indistinct

individual a individual; (cama) single. ~alidad f individuality. ~alista m & f individualist. ~alizar [10] vt individualize. ~o a & m individual

índole f nature; (clase) type

indolencia f indolence. ~te a indolent

indoloro a painless

indomable a untameable

indómito a indomitable

Indonesia f Indonesia

inducir [47] vt induce; (deducir) infer

indudable a undoubted. ~mente adv undoubtedly

indulgencia f indulgence. ~te a indulgent

indultar vt pardon; exempt (de un pago etc). ~o m pardon

industria f industry. ~l a industrial. —m industrialist. ~lización f industrialization. ~lizar [10] vt industrialize

industriarse vpr do one's best

industrioso a industrious

inédito a unpublished; (fig) unknown

ineducado a impolite

inefable a inexpressible

ineficaz a ineffective

ineficiente a inefficient

inelegible a ineligible

ineludible a inescapable, unavoidable

ineptitud f ineptitude. ~o a inept

inequívoco a unequivocal

inercia f inertia

inerme a unarmed; (fig) defenceless

inerte a inert

inesperado a unexpected

inestable a unstable

inestimable a inestimable

inevitable a inevitable

inexacto a inaccurate; (incorrecto) incorrect; (falso) untrue

inexistente a non-existent

inexorable a inexorable

inexperiencia f inexperience. ~to a inexperienced

inexplicable a inexplicable

infalible a infallible

infamar vt defame. ~atorio a defamatory. ~e a infamous; (fig, muy malo, fam) awful. ~ia f infamy

infancia f infancy

infanta f infanta, princess. ~e m infante, prince; (mil) infantryman. ~ería f infantry. ~il a (de niño) child's; (como un niño) infantile

infarto m coronary (thrombosis)

infatigable a untiring

infatuación f conceit. ~rse vpr get conceited

infausto a unlucky

infección f infection. ~cioso a infectious. ~tar vt infect. ~tarse vpr become infected. ~to a infected; (fig) disgusting

infecundo a infertile

infeli|cidad f unhappiness. **~z a** unhappy

inferior a inferior. —m & f inferior. **~idad** f lower; (calidad) inferiority

inferir [4] vt infer; (causar) cause

infernal a infernal, hellish

infestar vt infest; (fig) inundate

infi|delidad f unfaithfulness. **~el a** unfaithful

infierno m hell

infiltra|ción f infiltration. **~rse** vpr infiltrate

ínfimo a lowest

infini|dad f infinity. **~tivo** m infinitive. **~to a** infinite. —m infinite; (en matemáticas) infinity. **una ~dad de** countless

inflación f inflation; (fig) conceit

inflama|ble a (in)flammable. **~ción** f inflammation. **~r** vt set on fire; (fig, med) inflame. **~rse** vpr catch fire; (med) become inflamed

inflar vt inflate; (fig, exagerar) exaggerate

inflexi|ble a inflexible. **~ón** f inflexion

infligir [14] vt inflict

influ|encia f influence. **~enza f** flu (fam), influenza. **~ir** [17] vt/i influence. **~jo** m influence. **~yente** a influential

informa|ción f information. **~ciones** fpl (noticias) news; (de teléfonos) directory enquiries. **~dor** m informant

informal a informal; (incorrecto) incorrect

inform|ante m & f informant. **~ar** vt/i inform. **~arse** vpr find out. **~ática** f information technology. **~ativo** a informative

informe a shapeless. —m report; (información) information

infortun|ado a unfortunate. **~io** m misfortune

infracción f infringement

infraestructura f infrastructure

infranqueable a impassable; (fig) insuperable

infrarrojo a infrared

infrecuente a infrequent

infringir [14] vt infringe

infructuoso a fruitless

infundado a unfounded

infu|ndir vt instil. **~sión** f infusion

ingeniar vt invent

ingenier|ía f engineering. **~o m** engineer

ingenio m ingenuity; (agudeza) wit; (LAm, de azúcar) refinery. **~so a** ingenious

ingenu|idad f ingenuousness. **~o a** ingenuous

ingerir [4] vt swallow

Inglaterra f England

ingle f groin

ingl|és a English. —m Englishman; (lengua) English. **~esa** f Englishwoman

ingrat|itud f ingratitude. **~o** a ungrateful; (desagradable) thankless

ingrediente m ingredient

ingres|ar vt deposit. —vi. **~ar en** come in, enter; join (sociedad). **~o** m entry; (en sociedad, hospital etc) admission. **~os** mpl income

inh|ábil a unskillful; (no apto) unfit. **~abilidad** f unskillfulness

inhabitable a uninhabitable

inhala|ción f inhalation. **~dor** m inhaler. **~r** vt inhale

inherente a inherent

inhibi|ción f inhibition. **~r** vt inhibit

inhospitalario a, **inhóspito** a inhospitable

inhumano a inhuman

inicia|ción f beginning. **~l a & f** initial. **~r** vt initiate; (comenzar) begin, start. **~tiva** f initiative

inicio *m* beginning
inicuo *a* iniquitous
igualado *a* unequalled
ininterrumpido *a* continuous
injer encia *f* interference. **~ir**
[4] *vt* insert. **~irse** *vpr* interfere
injertar *vt* graft. **~to** *m* graft
injuria *f* insult; (*ofensa*) offence.
~ar *vt* insult; **~oso** *a* offensive
injust icia *f* injustice. **~o** *a*
unjust
inmaculado *a* immaculate
inmaduro *a* unripe; (*persona*)
immature
inmediaciones *fpl* neighbour-
hood
inmediat amente *adv* immediately. **~o** *a* immediate; (*contiguo*) next
inmejorable *a* excellent
inmemorable *a* immemorial
inmens idad *f* immensity. **~o** *a*
immense
inmerecido *a* undeserved
inmersión *f* immersion
inmigra ción *f* immigration.
~nte *a & m* immigrant. **~r** *vt*
immigrate
inminen cia *f* imminence. **~te** *a*
imminent
inmiscuirse [17] *vpr* interfere
inmobiliario *a* property
inmoderado *a* immoderate
inmodesto *a* immodest
inmolar *vt* sacrifice
inmoral *a* immoral. **~idad** *f*
immorality
inmortal *a* immortal. **~izar** [10]
vt immortalize
inmóvil *a* immobile
inmueble *a*. **bienes ~s** property
inmund icia *f* filth. **~icias** *fpl*
rubbish. **~o** *a* filthy
inmun e *a* immune. **~idad** *f*
immunity. **~ización** *f* immu-
nization. **~izar** [10] *vt* immunize
inmuta ble *a* unchangeable.
~rse *vpr* turn pale
innato *a* innate

innecesario *a* unnecessary
innegable *a* undeniable
innoble *a* ignoble
innova ción *f* innovation. **~r**
vt/i innovate
innumerable *a* innumerable
inocen cia *f* innocence. **~tada** *f*
practical joke. **~te** *a* innocent.
~tón *a* naïve
inocuo *a* innocuous
inodoro *a* odourless. **—m** toilet
inofensivo *a* inoffensive
inolvidable *a* unforgettable
inoperable *a* inoperable
inopinado *a* unexpected
inoportuno *a* untimely; (*incómodo*) inconvenient
inorgánico *a* inorganic
inoxidable *a* stainless
inquebrantable *a* unbreakable
inquiet ar *vt* worry. **~arse** *vpr*
get worried. **~o** *a* worried; (*agitado*) restless. **~ud** *f* anxiety
inquilino *m* tenant
inquirir [4] *vt* enquire into,
investigate
insaciable *a* insatiable
insalubre *a* unhealthy
insanable *a* incurable
insatisfecho *a* unsatisfied;
(*descontento*) dissatisfied
inscri bir [pp **inscrito**] *vt*
inscribe; (*en registro etc*) enrol,
register. **~birse** *vpr* register.
~pción *f* inscription; (*registro*)
registration
insect icida *m* insecticide. **~o** *m*
insect
insegur idad *f* insecurity. **~o** *a*
insecure; (*dudoso*) uncertain
insemina ción *f* insemination.
~r *vt* inseminate
insensato *a* senseless
insensible *a* insensitive; (*med*)
insensible; (*imperceptible*)
imperceptible
inseparable *a* inseparable
insertar *vt* insert
insidia *f* trap. **~oso** *a* insidious

insigne a famous
insignia f badge; (bandera) flag
insignificante a insignificant
insincero a insincere
insinua|ción f insinuation.
~**nte** a insinuating. ~**r** [21] vt
insinuate. ~**rse** upr ingratiate
o.s. ~**rse en** creep into
insípido a insipid
insist|encia f insistence. ~**ente**
a insistent. ~**ir** vi insist; (hacer
hincapié) stress
insolación f sunstroke
insolen|cia f rudeness, insol-
ence. ~**te** a rude, insolent
insólito a unusual
insoluble a insoluble
insolven|cia f insolvency. ~**te** a
& m & f insolvent
insomn|e a sleepless. ~**io** m
insomnia
insondable a unfathomable
insoportable a unbearable
insospechado a unexpected
insostenible a untenable
inspec|ción f inspection.
~**cionar** vt inspect. ~**tor** m
inspector
inspira|ción f inspiration. ~**r** vt
inspire. ~**rse** upr be inspired
instala|ción f installation. ~**r** vt
install. ~**rse** upr settle
instancia f request
instant|ánea f snapshot. ~**áneo**
a instantaneous; (café etc)
instant. ~**e** m instant. **a cada**
~**e** constantly. **al** ~**e**
immediately
instar vt urge
instaura|ción f establishment.
~**r** vt establish
instiga|ción f instigation. ~**dor**
m instigator. ~**r** [12] vt instigate;
(incitar) incite
instint|ivo a instinctive. ~**o** m
instinct
institu|ción f institution.
~**cional** a institutional. ~**ir** [17]
vt establish. ~**to** m institute;

(escol) (secondary) school. ~**triz**
f governess
instru|cción f instruction.
~**ctivo** a instructive. ~**ctor** m
instructor. ~**ir** [17] vt instruct;
(enseñar) teach
instrument|ación f instru-
mentation. ~**al** a instrumental.
~**o** m instrument; (herramienta)
tool
insubordina|ción f insub-
ordination. ~**r** vt stir up. ~**rse**
upr rebel
insuficien|cia f insufficiency;
(inadecuación) inadequacy. ~**te**
a insufficient
insufrible a insufferable
insular a insular
insulina f insulin
insulso a tasteless; (fig) insipid
insult|ar vt insult. ~**o** m insult
insuperable a insuperable;
(excelente) excellent
insurgente a insurgent
insurrec|ción f insurrection.
~**to** a insurgent
intacto a intact
intachable a irreproachable
intangible a intangible
integra|ción f integration. ~**l** a
integral; (completo) complete;
(pan) wholemeal (Brit), wholewheat (Amer). ~**r** vt make up
integridad f integrity; (entereza)
wholeness
íntegro a complete; (fig) upright
intelect|o m intellect. ~**ual** a &
m & f intellectual
inteligen|cia f intelligence. ~**te**
a intelligent
inteligible a intelligible
intemperancia f intemperance
intemperie f bad weather. **a la**
~ in the open
intempestivo a untimely
intención f intention. ~**onado**
a deliberate. ~**onal** a inten-
tional. **bien** ~**onado** well-
meaning. **mal** ~**onado** malicious. **segunda** ~**ón** duplicity

intens|idad f intensity. **~ificar** [7] vt intensify. **~ivo** a intensive. **~o** a intense

intent|ar vt try. **~o** m intent; (tentativa) attempt. **de ~o** intentionally

intercalar vt insert

intercambio m exchange

interceder vi intercede

interceptar vt intercept

intercesión f intercession

interdicto m ban

inter|és m interest; (egoísmo) self-interest. **~esado** a interested; (parcial) biassed; (egoísta) selfish. **~esante** a interesting. **~esar** vt interest; (afectar) concern. **—vi** be of interest. **~esarse** vpr take an interest (**por** in)

interfer|encia f interference. **~ir** [4] vi interfere

interino a temporary; (persona) acting. **—m** stand-in; (médico) locum

interior a interior. **—m** inside. **Ministerio** m **del I~** Home Office (Brit), Department of the Interior (Amer)

interjección f interjection

interlocutor m speaker

interludio m interlude

intermediario a & m intermediary

intermedio a intermediate. **—m** interval

interminable a interminable

intermitente a intermittent. **—m** indicator

internacional a international

intern|ado m (escol) boarding-school. **~ar** vt intern; (en manicomio) commit. **~arse** vpr penetrate. **~o** a internal; (escol) boarding. **—m** (escol) boarder

interpelar vt appeal

interponer [34] vt interpose. **~se** vpr intervene

interpretación f interpretation. **~erpretar** vt interpret. **~érprete** m interpreter; (mus) performer

interroga|ción f question; (acción) interrogation; (signo) question mark. **~r** [12] vt question. **~tivo** a interrogative

interru|mpir vt interrupt; (suspender) stop. **~pción** f interruption. **~ptor** m switch

intersección f intersection

interurbano a inter-city; (conferencia) long-distance

intervalo m interval; (espacio) space. **a ~s** at intervals

interven|ir [53] vt control; (med) operate on. **—vi** intervene; (participar) take part. **~tor** m inspector; (com) auditor

intestino m intestine

intim|ar vi become friendly. **~idad** f intimacy

intimidar vt intimidate

íntimo a intimate. **—m** close friend

intitular vt entitle

intolera|ble a intolerable. **~nte** a intolerant

intoxicar [7] vt poison

intranquil|izar [10] vt worry. **~o** a worried

intransigente a intransigent

intransitable a impassable

intransitivo a intransitive

intratable a intractable

intrépido a intrepid

intriga f intrigue. **~nte** a intriguing. **~r** [12] vt/i intrigue

intrincado a intricate

intrínseco a intrinsic

introduc|ción f introduction. **~ir** [47] vt introduce; (meter) insert. **~irse** vpr get into; (entrometerse) interfere

intromisión f interference

introvertido a & m introvert

intrus|ión f intrusion. **~o** a intrusive. **—m** intruder

intui|ción f intuition. **~r** [17] vt sense. **~tivo** a intuitive

inunda|ción f flooding. **~r** vt flood

inusitado a unusual

in|útil a useless; (vano) futile. **~utilidad** f uselessness

invadir vt invade

inv|alidez f invalidity; (med) disability. **~álido** a & m invalid

invaria|ble a invariable. **~do** a unchanged

invas|ión f invasion. **~or** a invading. —m invader

invectiva f invective

invencible a invincible

inven|ción f invention. **~tar** vt invent

inventario m inventory

invent|iva f inventiveness. **~ivo** a inventive. **~or** m inventor

invernadero m greenhouse

invernal a winter

inverosímil a improbable

inversión f inversion; (com) investment

inverso a inverse; (contrario) opposite. **a la inversa** the other way round

invertebrado a & m invertebrate

inverti|do a inverted; (homosexual) homosexual. —m homosexual. **~r** [4] vt reverse; (volcar) turn upside down; (com) invest; spend (tiempo)

investidura f investiture

investiga|ción f investigation; (univ) research. **~dor** m investigator. **~r** [12] vt investigate

investir [5] vt invest

inveterado a inveterate

invicto a unbeaten

invierno m winter

inviolable a inviolable

invisib|ilidad f invisibility. **~le** a invisible

invita|ción f invitation. **~do** m guest. **~r** vt invite. **te invito a una copa** I'll buy you a drink

invoca|ción f invocation. **~r** [7] vt invoke

involuntario a involuntary

invulnerable a invulnerable

inyec|ción f injection. **~tar** vt inject

ion m ion

ir [49] vi go; (ropa) (convenir) suit. —m going. **~se** vpr go away. **~ a hacer** be going to do. **~ a pie** walk. **~ en coche** go by car. **no me va ni me viene** it's all the same to me. **no vaya a ser que** in case. **¡qué va!** nonsense! **va mejorando** it's gradually getting better. **¡vamos!**, **¡vámonos!** come on! let's go! **¡vaya** fancy that! **¡vete a saber!** who knows? **¡ya voy!** I'm coming!

ira f anger. **~cundo** a irascible

Irak m Iraq

Irán m Iran

iraní a & m & f Iranian

iraquí a & m & f Iraqi

iris m (anat) iris; (arco iris) rainbow

Irlanda f Ireland

irland|és a Irish. —m Irishman; (lengua) Irish. **~esa** f Irishwoman

ir|onía f irony. **~ónico** a ironic

irracional a irrational

irradiar vt/i radiate

irrazonable a unreasonable

irreal a unreal. **~idad** f unreality

irrealizable a unattainable

irreconciliable a irreconcilable

irreconocible a unrecognizable

irrecuperable a irretrievable

irreducible a irreducible

irreflexión f impetuosity

irrefutable a irrefutable

irregular a irregular. **~idad** f irregularity

irreparable a irreparable

irreprimible a irrepressible

irreprochable a irreproachable

irresistible *a* irresistible
irresoluto *a* irresolute
irrespetuoso *a* disrespectful
irresponsable *a* irresponsible
irrevocable *a* irrevocable
irriga|ción *f* irrigation. **~r** [12] *vt* irrigate
irrisorio *a* derisive; (*insignificante*) ridiculous
irrita|ble *a* irritable. **~ción** *f* irritation. **~r** *vt* irritate. **~rse** *upr* get annoyed
irrumpir *vi* burst (**en** in)
irrupción *f* irruption
isla *f* island. **las I~s Británicas** the British Isles
Islam *m* Islam
islámico *a* Islamic
islandés *a* Icelandic. **—m** Icelander; (*lengua*) Icelandic
Islandia *f* Iceland
isleño *a* island. **—m** islander
Israel *m* Israel
israelí *a & m* Israeli
istmo /'ismo/ *m* isthmus
Italia *f* Italy
italiano *a & m* Italian
itinerario *a* itinerary
IVA *abrev* (*impuesto sobre el valor añadido*) VAT, value added tax
izar [10] *vt* hoist
izquierd|a *f* left(-hand); (*pol*) left(-wing). **~ista** *m & f* leftist. **~o** *a* left. **a la ~a** on the left; (*con movimiento*) to the left

J

ja *int* ha!
jabalí *m* wild boar
jabalina *f* javelin
jab|ón *m* soap. **~onar** *vt* soap. **~onoso** *a* soapy
jaca *f* pony
jacinto *m* hyacinth

jacta|ncia *f* boastfulness; (*acción*) boasting. **~rse** *upr* boast
jadea|nte *a* panting. **~r** *vi* pant
jaez *m* harness
jaguar *m* jaguar
jalea *f* jelly
jaleo *m* row, uproar. **armar un ~** kick up a fuss
jalón *m* (*LAm, tirón*) pull; (*Mex, trago*) drink
Jamaica *f* Jamaica
jamás *adv* never; (*en frases afirmativas*) ever
jamelgo *m* nag
jamón *m* ham. **~ de York** boiled ham. **~ serrano** cured ham
Japón *m*. **el ~** Japan
japonés *a & m* Japanese
jaque *m* check. **~ mate** checkmate
jaqueca *f* migraine. **dar ~** bother
jarabe *m* syrup
jardín *m* garden. **~ de la infancia** kindergarten, nursery school
jardiner|a *f* gardening. **~o** *m* gardener
jarocho *a* (*Mex*) from Veracruz
jarr|a *f* jug. **~o** *m* jug. **echar un ~o de agua fría** a throw cold water on. **en ~as** with hands on hips
jaula *f* cage
jauría *f* pack of hounds
jazmín *m* jasmine
jef|a *f* boss. **~atura** *f* leadership; (*sede*) headquarters. **~e** *m* boss; (*pol etc*) leader. **~e de camareros** head waiter. **~e de estación** stationmaster. **~e de ventas** sales manager
jengibre *m* ginger
jeque *m* sheikh
jer|arquía *f* hierarchy. **~árquico** *a* hierarchical
jerez *m* sherry. **al ~** with sherry

jerga f coarse cloth; (*argot*) jargon

jerigonza f jargon; (*galimatías*) gibberish

jeringa f syringe; (*LAm, molestia*) nuisance. **~r** [12] *vt* (*fig, molestar, fam*) annoy

jeroglífico m hieroglyph(ic)

jersey m (*pl* jerseys) jersey

Jerusalén m Jerusalem

Jesucristo m Jesus Christ. **antes de ~** BC, before Christ

jesuita a & m & f Jesuit

Jesús m Jesus. —*int* good heavens!; (*al estornudar*) bless you!

jícara f small cup

jilguero m goldfinch

jinete m rider, horseman

jipijapa f straw hat

jirafa f giraffe

jirón m shred, tatter

jitomate m (*Mex*) tomato

jocoso a funny, humorous

jorna|da f working day; (*viaje*) journey; (*etapa*) stage. **~l** m day's wage; (*trabajo*) day's work. **~lero** m day labourer

joroba f hump. **~do** a hunchbacked. —m hunchback. **~r** vt annoy

jota f letter J; (*danza*) jota, popular dance; (*fig*) iota. **ni ~** nothing

joven (*pl* jóvenes) a young. —m young man, youth. —f young woman, girl

jovial a jovial

joya f jewel. **~as** fpl jewellery. **~ería** f jeweller's (shop). **~ero** m jeweller; (*estuche*) jewellery box

juanete m bunion

jubil|ación f retirement. **~ado** a retired. **~ar** vt pension off. **~arse** vpr retire. **~eo** m jubilee

júbilo m joy

jubiloso a jubilant

judaísmo m Judaism

judía f Jewish woman; (*alubia*) bean. **~ blanca** haricot bean. **~ escarlata** runner bean. **~ verde** French bean

judicial a judicial

judío a Jewish. —m Jewish man

judo m judo

juego m game; (*de niños, tec*) play; (*de azar*) gambling; (*conjunto*) set. —*vb véase* jugar. **estar en ~** be at stake. **estar fuera de ~** be offside. **hacer ~** match

juerga f spree

jueves m Thursday

juez m judge. **~ de instrucción** examining magistrate. **~ de línea** linesman

juga|dor m player; (*en juegos de azar*) gambler. **~r** [3] vt play. —*vi* play; (*a juegos de azar*) gamble; (*apostar*) bet. **~rse** vpr risk. **~r al fútbol** play football

juglar m minstrel

jugo m juice; (*de carne*) gravy; (*fig*) substance. **~so** a juicy; (*fig*) substantial

juguet|e m toy. **~ear** vi play. **~ón** a playful

juicio m judgement; (*opinión*) opinion; (*razón*) reason. **~so** a wise. **a mi ~** in my opinion

juliana f vegetable soup

julio m July

junco m rush, reed

jungla f jungle

junio m June

junt|a f meeting; (*consejo*) board, committee; (*pol*) junta; (*tec*) joint. **~ar** vt join; (*reunir*) collect. **~arse** vpr join; (*gente*) meet. **~o** a joined; (*en plural*) together. **~o a** next to. **~ura** f joint. **por ~o** all together

jura|do a sworn. —m jury; (*miembro de jurado*) juror. **~mento** m oath. **~r** vt/i swear. **~r en falso** commit perjury. **jurárselas a uno** have it in for s.o. **prestar** ∼**mento** take the oath

jurel *m* (type of) mackerel

jurídico *a* legal

juris|dicción *f* jurisdiction. ∼**prudencia** *f* jurisprudence

justamente *a* exactly; *(con justicia)* fairly

justicia *f* justice

justifica|ción *f* justification. ∼**r** [7] *vt* justify

justo *a* fair, just; *(exacto)* exact; *(ropa)* tight. *—adv* just. ∼ **a tiempo** just in time

juven|il *a* youthful. ∼**tud** *f* youth; *(gente joven)* young people

juzga|do *m (tribunal)* court. ∼**r** [12] *vt* judge. **a** ∼**r por** judging by

K

kilo *m*, **kilogramo** *m* kilo, kilogram

kil|ometraje *m* distance in kilometres, mileage. ∼**ométrico** *a (fam)* endless. ∼**ómetro** *m* kilometre. ∼**ómetro cuadrado** square kilometre

kilovatio *m* kilowatt

kiosco *m* kiosk

L

la *m* A; *(solfa)* lah. *—art def f* the. *—pron (ella)* her; *(Vd)* you; *(ello)* it. ∼ **de** the one. ∼ **de Vd** your one, yours. ∼ **que** whoever, the one

laberinto *m* labyrinth, maze

labia *f* glibness

labio *m* lip

labor *f* work; *(tarea)* job. ∼**able** *a* working. ∼**ar** *vi* work. ∼**es** *fpl*

de aguja needlework. ∼**es** *fpl* **de ganchillo** crochet. ∼**es** *fpl* **de punto** knitting. ∼**es** *fpl* **domésticas** housework

laboratorio *m* laboratory

laborioso *a* laborious

laborista *a* Labour. *—m & f* member of the Labour Party

labra|do *a* worked; *(madera)* carved; *(metal)* wrought; *(tierra)* ploughed. ∼**dor** *m* farmer; *(obrero)* labourer. ∼**nza** *f* farming. ∼**r** *vt* work; carve *(madera)*; cut *(piedra)*; till *(la tierra)*; *(fig, causar)* cause

labriego *m* peasant

laca *f* lacquer

lacayo *m* lackey

lacerar *vt* lacerate

lacero *m* lassoer; *(cazador)* poacher

lacio *a* straight; *(flojo)* limp

lacón *m* shoulder of pork

lacónico *a* laconic

lacra *f* scar

lacr|ar *vt* seal. ∼**e** *m* sealing wax

lactante *a* breast-fed

lácteo *a* milky. **productos** *mpl* ∼**s** dairy products

ladear *vt/i* tilt. ∼**se** *vpr* lean

ladera *f* slope

ladino *a* astute

lado *m* side. **al** ∼ near. **al** ∼ **de** at the side of, beside. **los de al** ∼ the next door neighbours. **por otro** ∼ on the other hand. **por todos** ∼**s** on all sides. **por un** ∼ on the one hand

ladr|ar *vi* bark. ∼**ido** *m* bark

ladrillo *m* brick; *(de chocolate)* block

ladrón *a* thieving. *—m* thief

lagart|ija *f (small)* lizard. ∼**o** *m* lizard

lago *m* lake

lágrima *f* tear

lagrimoso *a* tearful

laguna *f* small lake; *(fig, omisión)* gap

laico *a* lay

lamé *m* lamé

lamedura *f* lick

lament|able *a* lamentable, pitiful. **~ar** *vt* be sorry about. **~arse** *vpr* lament; (*quejarse*) complain. **~o** *m* moan

lamer *vt* lick; (*olas etc*) lap

lámina *f* sheet; (*foto*) plate; (*dibujo*) picture

lamina|do *a* laminated. **~r** *vt* laminate

lámpara *f* lamp; (*bombilla*) bulb; (*lamparón*) grease stain. **~ de pie** standard lamp

lamparón *m* grease stain

lampiño *a* clean-shaven, beardless

lana *f* wool. **~r** *a*. **ganado** *m* **~r** sheep. **de ~** wool(len)

lanceta *f* lancet

lancha *f* boat. **~ motora** *f* motor boat. **~ salvavidas** lifeboat

lanero *a* wool(len)

langost|a *f* (*crustáceo marino*) lobster; (*insecto*) locust. **~ino** *m* prawn

languide|cer [11] *vi* languish. **~z** *f* languor

lánguido *a* languid; (*decaído*) listless

lanilla *f* nap; (*tela fina*) flannel

lanudo *a* woolly

lanza *f* lance, spear

lanza|llamas *m invar* flame-thrower. **~miento** *m* throw; (*acción de lanzar*) throwing; (*de proyectil, de producto*) launch. **~r** [10] *vt* throw; (*de un avión*) drop; launch (*proyectil, producto*). **~rse** *vpr* fling o.s.

lapicero *m* (propelling) pencil

lápida *f* memorial tablet. **~ sepulcral** tombstone

lapidar *vt* stone

lápiz *m* pencil; (*grafito*) lead. **~ de labios** lipstick

Laponia *f* Lapland

lapso *m* lapse

larg|a *f*. **a la ~a** in the long run. **dar ~as** put off. **~ar** [12] *vt* slacken; (*dar, fam*) give; (*fam*) deal (*bofetada etc*). **~arse** *vpr* (*fam*) go away, clear off (*fam*). **~o** *a* long; (*demasiado*) too long. **—m** length. **¡~o!** go away! **~ueza** *f* generosity. **a lo ~o** lengthwise. **a lo ~o de** along. **tener 100 metros de ~o** be 100 metres long

laringe *f* larynx. **~itis** *f* laryngitis

larva *f* larva

las *art def fpl* the. **—pron** them. **~ de** those, the ones. **~ de Vd** your ones, yours. **~ que** whoever, the ones

lascivo *a* lascivious

láser *m* laser

lástima *f* pity; (*queja*) complaint. **dar ~** be pitiful. **ella me da ~** I feel sorry for her. **¡qué ~!** what a pity!

lastim|ado *a* hurt. **~ar** *vt* hurt. **~arse** *vpr* hurt o.s. **~ero** *a* doleful. **~oso** *a* pitiful

lastre *m* ballast

lata *f* tinplate; (*envase*) tin (*esp Brit*), can; (*molestia, fam*) nuisance. **dar la ~** be a nuisance. **¡qué ~!** what a nuisance!

latente *a* latent

lateral *a* side, lateral

latido *m* beating; (*cada golpe*) beat

latifundio *m* large estate

latigazo *m* (*golpe*) lash; (*chasquido*) crack

látigo *m* whip

latín *m* Latin. **saber ~** (*fam*) not be stupid

latino *a* Latin. **L~américa** *f* Latin America. **~americano** *a* & *m* Latin American

latir *vi* beat; (*herida*) throb

latitud *f* latitude

latón *m* brass

latoso a annoying; (*pesado*) boring

laucha f (*Arg*) mouse

laúd m lute

laudable a laudable

laureado a honoured; (*premiado*) prize-winning

laurel m laurel; (*culin*) bay

lava f lava

lava|ble a washable. ∼**bo** m wash-basin; (*retrete*) toilet. ∼**dero** m sink, wash-basin. ∼**do** m washing. ∼**do de cerebro** brainwashing. ∼**do en seco** dry-cleaning. ∼**dora** f washing machine. ∼**ndería** f laundry. ∼**ndería automática** launderette, laundromat (*esp Amer*). ∼**parabrisas** m invar windscreen washer (*Brit*), windshield washer (*Amer*). ∼**platos** m & f invar dishwasher; (*Mex, fregadero*) sink. ∼**r** vt wash. ∼**r en seco** dry-clean. ∼**rse** vpr have a wash. ∼**rse las manos** (*incl fig*) wash one's hands. ∼**tiva** f enema. ∼**vajillas** m & f inv dishwasher

lax|ante a & m laxative. ∼**o** a loose

laz|ada f bow. ∼**o** m knot; (*lazada*) bow; (*fig, vínculo*) tie; (*cuerda con nudo corredizo*) lasso; (*trampa*) trap

le pron (*acusativo, él*) him; (*acusativo, Vd*) you; (*dativo, él*) (to) him; (*dativo, ella*) (to) her; (*dativo, ello*) (to) it; (*dativo, Vd*) (to) you

leal a loyal; (*fiel*) faithful. ∼**tad** f loyalty; (*fidelidad*) faithfulness

lebrel m greyhound

lección f lesson; (*univ*) lecture

lect|or m reader; (*univ*) language assistant. ∼**ura** f reading

leche f milk; (*golpe*) bash. ∼ **condensada** condensed milk. ∼ **desnatada** skimmed milk. ∼ **en polvo** powdered milk. ∼**ra** f

(*vasija*) milk jug. ∼**ría** f dairy. ∼**ro** a milk, dairy. —m milkman. ∼ **sin desnatar** whole milk. **tener mala** ∼ be spiteful

lecho m bed

lechoso a milky

lechuga f lettuce

lechuza f owl

leer [18] vt/i read

legación f legation

legado m legacy; (*enviado*) legate

legajo m bundle, file

legal a legal. ∼**idad** f legality. ∼**izar** [10] vt legalize; (*certificar*) authenticate. ∼**mente** adv legally

legar [12] vt bequeath

legendario a legendary

legible a legible

legi|ón f legion. ∼**onario** m legionary

legisla|ción f legislation. ∼**dor** m legislator. ∼**r** vi legislate. ∼**tura** f legislature

legitim|idad f legitimacy. ∼**ítimo** a legitimate; (*verdadero*) real

lego a lay; (*ignorante*) ignorant. —m layman

legua f league

legumbre f vegetable

lejan|ía f distance. ∼**o** a distant

lejía f bleach

lejos adv far. ∼ **de** far from. **a lo** ∼ in the distance. **desde** ∼ from a distance, from afar

lelo a stupid

lema m motto

lencería f linen; (*de mujer*) lingerie

lengua f tongue; (*idioma*) language. **irse de la** ∼ talk too much. **morderse la** ∼ hold one's tongue. **tener mala** ∼ have a vicious tongue

lenguado m sole

lenguaje m language

lengüeta f (*de zapato*) tongue

lengüetada f, **lengüetazo** m lick

lente f lens. **~s** mpl glasses. **~s de contacto** contact lenses

lenteja f lentil. **~uela** f sequin

lentilla f contact lens

lent|itud f slowness. **~o** a slow

leña f firewood. **~ador** m woodcutter. **~o** m log

Leo m Leo

le|ón m lion. **León** Leo. **~ona** f lioness

leopardo m leopard

leotardo m thick tights

lepr|a f leprosy. **~oso** m leper

lerdo a dim; (torpe) clumsy

les pron (acusativo) them; (acusativo, Vds) you; (dativo) (to) them; (dativo, Vds) (to) you

lesbia(na) f lesbian

lesbiano a, **lesbio** a lesbian

lesi|ón f wound. **~onado** a injured. **~onar** vt injure; (dañar) damage

letal a lethal

letanía f litany

let|árgico a lethargic. **~argo** m lethargy

letr|a f letter; (escritura) handwriting; (de una canción) words, lyrics. **~a de cambio** bill of exchange. **~a de imprenta** print. **~ado** a learned. **~ero** m notice; (cartel) poster

letrina f latrine

leucemia f leukaemia

levadizo a. **puente** m **~** drawbridge

levadura f yeast. **~ en polvo** baking powder

levanta|miento m lifting; (sublevación) uprising. **~r** vt raise, lift; (construir) build; (recoger) pick up; (separar) take off. **~rse** vpr get up; (ponerse de pie) stand up; (erguirse, sublevarse) rise up

levante m east; (viento) east wind. **L~** Levant

levar vt weigh ⟨ancla⟩. **—vi** set sail

leve a light; ⟨enfermedad etc⟩ slight; (de poca importancia) trivial. **~dad** f lightness; (fig) slightness

léxico m vocabulary

lexicografía f lexicography

ley f law; (parlamentaria) act. **plata f de ~** sterling silver

leyenda f legend

liar [20] vt tie; (envolver) wrap up; roll ⟨cigarillo⟩; (fig, confundir) confuse; (fig, enredar) involve. **~se** vpr get involved

libanés a & m Lebanese

Líbano m. **el ~** Lebanon

libel|ista m & f satirist. **~o** m satire

libélula f dragonfly

libera|ción f liberation. **~dor** a liberating. **—m** liberator

liberal a & m & f liberal. **~idad** f liberality. **~mente** adv liberally

liber|ar vt free. **~tad** f freedom. **~tad de cultos** freedom of worship. **~tad de imprenta** freedom of the press. **~tad provisional** bail. **~tar** vt free. **en ~tad** free

libertino m libertine

Libia f Libya

libido f libido

libio a & m Libyan

libra f pound. **~ esterlina** pound sterling

Libra f Libra

libra|dor m (com) drawer. **~r** vt free; (de un peligro) rescue. **~rse** vpr free o.s. **~rse de** get rid of

libre a free; ⟨aire⟩ open; (en natación) freestyle. **~ de impuestos** tax-free. **—m** (Mex) taxi

librea f livery

libr|ería f bookshop (Brit), bookstore (Amer); (mueble) bookcase. **~ero** m bookseller. **~eta** f notebook. **~o** m book. **~o de a bordo** logbook. **~o de bolsillo** paperback. **~o de ejercicios**

exercise book. **~o de recla-maciones** complaints book

licencia f permission; (*documento*) licence. **~do** m graduate. **~ para manejar** (*LAm*) driving licence. **~r** vt (*mil*) discharge; (*echar*) dismiss. **~tura** f degree

licencioso a licentious

liceo m (*esp LAm*) (secondary) school

licita|dor m bidder. **~r** vt bid for

lícito a legal; (*permisible*) permissible

licor m liquid; (*alcohólico*) liqueur

licua|dora f liquidizer. **~r** [21] liquefy

lid f fight. **en buena ~** by fair means

líder m leader

liderato m, **liderazgo** m leadership

lidia f bullfighting; (*lucha*) fight; (*LAm, molestia*) nuisance. **~r** vt/i fight

liebre f hare

lienzo m linen; (*del pintor*) canvas; (*muro, pared*) wall

liga f garter; (*alianza*) league; (*mezcla*) mixture. **~dura** f bond; (*mus*) slur; (*med*) ligature. **~mento** m ligament. **~r** [12] vt tie; (*fig*) join; (*mus*) slur. **—ví** mix. **~r con** (*fig*) pick up. **~rse** vpr (*fig*) commit o.s.

liger|eza f lightness; (*agilidad*) agility; (*rapidez*) swiftness; (*de carácter*) fickleness. **~o** a light; (*rápido*) quick; (*ágil*) agile; (*superficial*) superficial; (*de poca importancia*) slight. **—adv** quickly. **a la ~a** lightly, superficially

liguero m suspender belt

lija f dogfish; (*papel de lija*) sandpaper. **~r** vt sand

lila f lilac

Lima f Lima

lima f file; (*fruta*) lime. **~duras** fpl filings. **~r** vt file (down)

limbo m limbo

limita|ción f limitation. **~do** a limited. **~r** vt limit. **~r con** border on. **~tivo** a limiting

límite m limit. **~ de velocidad** speed limit

limítrofe a bordering

limo m mud

limón m lemon. **~onada** f lemonade

limosn|a f alms. **~ear** vi beg. **pedir ~a** beg

limpia f cleaning. **~botas** m invar bootblack. **~parabrisas** m inv windscreen wiper (*Brit*), windshield wiper (*Amer*). **~pipas** m invar pipe-cleaner. **~r** vt clean; (*enjugar*) wipe

limpi|eza f cleanliness; (*acción de limpiar*) cleaning. **~eza en seco** dry-cleaning. **~o** a clean; (*cielo*) clear; (*fig, honrado*) honest. **—adv** fairly. **en ~o** (*com*) net. **jugar ~o** play fair

linaje m lineage; (*fig, clase*) kind

lince m lynx

linchar vt lynch

lind|ante a bordering (**con** on). **~ar** vi border (**con** on). **~e** f boundary. **~ero** m border

lindo a pretty, lovely. **de lo ~** (*fam*) a lot

línea f line. **en ~s generales** in broad outline. **guardar la ~** watch one's figure

lingote m ingot

lingü|ista m & f linguist. **~ística** f linguistics; **~ístico** a linguistic

lino m flax; (*tela*) linen

linóleo m, **linóleum** m lino, linoleum

linterna f lantern; (*de bolsillo*) torch, flashlight (*Amer*)

lío m bundle; (*jaleo*) fuss; (*embrollo*) muddle; (*amorío*) affair

liquen m lichen

liquida|ción f liquidation; (*venta especial*) (clearance) sale. ~r vt liquify; (*com*) liquidate; settle ⟨*cuenta*⟩

líquido a liquid; (*com*) net. —m liquid

lira f lyre; (*moneda italiana*) lira

líric|a f lyric poetry. ~o a lyric(al)

lirio m iris. ~ **de los valles** lily of the valley

lirón m dormouse; (*fig*) sleepyhead. **dormir como un** ~ sleep like a log

Lisboa f Lisbon

lisia|do a disabled. ~r vt disable; (*herir*) injure

liso a smooth; (*pelo*) straight; (*tierra*) flat; (*sencillo*) plain

lisonj|a f flattery. ~eador a flattering. —m flatterer. ~ear vt flatter. ~ero a flattering

lista f stripe; (*enumeración*) list; (*de platos*) menu. ~ **de correos** poste restante. ~do a striped. a ~s striped

listo a clever; (*preparado*) ready

listón m ribbon; (*de madera*) strip

lisura f smoothness

litera f (*en barco*) berth; (*en tren*) sleeper; (*en habitación*) bunk bed

literal a literal

litera|rio a literary. ~tura f literature

litig|ar [12] vi dispute; (*jurid*) litigate. ~io m dispute; (*jurid*) litigation

litografía f (*arte*) lithography; (*cuadro*) lithograph

litoral a coastal. —m coast

litro m litre

lituano a & m Lithuanian

liturgia f liturgy

liviano a fickle, inconstant

lívido a livid

lizo m warp thread

lo art def neutro. ~ **importante** what is important, the important thing. —pron (*él*) him; (*ello*) it. ~ **que** what(ever), that which

loa f praise. ~**ble** a praiseworthy. ~r vt praise

lobo m wolf

lóbrego a gloomy

lóbulo m lobe

local a local. —m premises; (*lugar*) place. ~**idad** f locality; (*de un espectáculo*) seat; (*entrada*) ticket. ~**izar** [10] vt localize; (*encontrar*) find, locate

loción f lotion

loco a mad; (*fig*) foolish. —m lunatic. ~ **de alegría** mad with joy. **estar** ~ **por** be crazy about. **volverse** ~ go mad

locomo|ción f locomotion. ~**tora** f locomotive

locuaz a talkative

locución f expression

locura f madness; (*acto*) crazy thing. **con** ~ madly

locutor m announcer

locutorio m (*de teléfono*) telephone booth

lodazal m quagmire. ~o m mud

logaritmo m logarithm, log

lógic|a f logic. ~o a logical

logística f logistics

logr|ar vt get; win ⟨*premio*⟩. ~ **hacer** manage to do. ~o m achievement; (*de premio*) winning; (*éxito*) success

loma f small hill

lombriz f worm

lomo m back; (*de libro*) spine; (*doblez*) fold. ~ **de cerdo** loin of pork

lona f canvas

loncha f slice; (*de tocino*) rasher

londinense a from London. —m Londoner

Londres m London

loneta f thin canvas

longánimo a magnanimous

longaniza f sausage

longev|idad f longevity. **~o** a long-lived

longitud f length; (geog) longitude

lonja f slice; (de tocino) rasher; (com) market

lord m (pl **lores**) lord

loro m parrot

los art def mpl the. —pron them. **~ de Antonio** Antonio's. **~ que** whoever, the ones

losa f slab; (baldosa) flagstone. **~ sepulcral** tombstone

lote m share

lotería f lottery

loto m lotus

loza f crockery

lozano a fresh; (vegetación) lush; (persona) lively

lubri(fi)ca|nte a lubricating. —m lubricant. **~r** [7] vt lubricate

lucero m (estrella) bright star; (planeta) Venus

lucid|ez f lucidity. **~o** a splendid

lúcido a lucid

luciérnaga f glow-worm

lucimiento m brilliance

lucir [11] vt (fig) show off. —vi shine; (lámpara) give off light; (joya) sparkle. **~se** vpr (fig) shine, excel

lucr|ativo a lucrative. **~o** m gain

lucha f fight. **~dor** m fighter. **~r** vi fight

luego adv then; (más tarde) later. —conj therefore. **~ que** as soon as. **desde ~** of course

lugar m place. **~ común** cliché. **~eño** a village. **dar ~ a** give rise to. **en ~ de** instead of. **en primer ~** in the first place. **hacer ~** make room. **tener ~** take place

lugarteniente m deputy

lúgubre a gloomy

lujo m luxury. **~so** a luxurious. **de ~** de luxe

lujuria f lust

lumbago m lumbago

lumbre f fire; (luz) light. ¿**tienes ~?** have you got a light?

luminoso a luminous; (fig) brilliant

luna f moon; (de escaparate) window; (espejo) mirror. **~ de miel** honeymoon. **~r** a lunar. —m mole. **claro de ~** moonlight. **estar en la ~** be miles away

lunes m Monday. **cada ~ y cada martes** day in, day out

lupa f magnifying glass

lúpulo m hop

lustr|abotas m inv (LAm) bootblack. **~ar** vt shine, polish. **~e** m shine; (fig, esplendor) splendour. **~oso** a shining. **dar ~e a, sacar ~e a** polish

luto m mourning. **estar de ~** be in mourning

luxación f dislocation

Luxemburgo m Luxemburg

luz f light; (electricidad) electricity. **luces** fpl intelligence. **~ antiniebla** (auto) fog light. **a la ~ de** in the light of. **a todas luces** obviously. **dar a ~** give birth. **hacer la ~ sobre** shed light on. **sacar a la ~** bring to light

LL

llaga f wound; (úlcera) ulcer

llama f flame; (animal) llama

llamada f call; (golpe) knock; (señal) sign

llama|do a known as. **~miento** m call. **~r** vt call; (por teléfono) ring (up). —vi call; (golpear en la puerta) knock; (tocar el timbre) ring. **~rse** vpr be called. **~r por teléfono** ring (up), telephone. ¿**cómo te ~s?** what's your name?

llamarada f blaze; (fig) blush; (fig, de pasión etc) outburst

llamativo *a* loud, gaudy

llamear *vi* blaze

llan|eza *f* simplicity. **~o** *a* flat, level; (*persona*) natural; (*sencillo*) plain. —*m* plain

llanta *f* (*auto*) (wheel) rim; (*LAm, neumático*) tyre

llanto *m* weeping

llanura *f* plain

llave *f* key; (*para tuercas*) spanner; (*grifo*) tap (*Brit*), faucet (*Amer*); (*elec*) switch. **~ inglesa** monkey wrench. **~ro** *m* key-ring. **cerrar con ~** lock. **echar la ~** lock up

llega|da *f* arrival. **~r** [12] *vi* arrive, come; (*alcanzar*) reach; (*bastar*) be enough. **~rse** *vpr* come near; (*ir*) go (round). **~r a** (*conseguir*) manage to. **~r a saber** find out. **~r a ser** become

llen|ar *vt* fill (up); (*rellenar*) fill in. **~o** *a* full. —*m* (*en el teatro etc*) full house. **de ~** completely

lleva|dero *a* tolerable. **~r** *vt* carry; (*inducir, conducir*) lead; (*acompañar*) take; wear (*ropa*); (*traer*) bring. **~rse** *vpr* run off with (*cosa*). **~rse bien** get on well together. **¿cuánto tiempo ~s aquí?** how long have you been here? **llevo 3 años estudiando inglés** I've been studying English for 3 years

llor|ar *vi* cry; (*ojos*) water. **~iquear** *vi* whine. **~iqueo** *m* whining. **~o** *m* crying. **~ón** *a* whining. —*m* cry-baby. **~oso** *a* tearful

llov|er [2] *vi* rain. **~izna** *f* drizzle. **~iznar** *vi* drizzle

llueve *vb* véase **llover**

lluvi|a *f* rain; (*fig*) shower. **~oso** *a* rainy; (*clima*) wet

M

maca *f* defect; (*en fruta*) bruise

macabro *a* macabre

macaco *a* (*LAm*) ugly. —*m* macaque (monkey)

macadam *m*, **macadán** *m* Tarmac (*P*)

macanudo *a* (*fam*) great

macarrón *m* macaroon. **~es** *mpl* macaroni

macerar *vt* macerate

maceta *f* mallet; (*tiesto*) flowerpot

macilento *a* wan

macizo *a* solid. —*m* mass; (*de plantas*) bed

macrobiótico *a* macrobiotic

mácula *f* stain

macuto *m* knapsack

mach /mak/ *m*. **(número de) Mach** (number)

machac|ar [7] *vt* crush. —*vi* go on (*en* about). **~ón** *a* boring. —*m* bore

machamartillo. a ~ *adv* firmly

machaqueo *m* crushing

machet|azo *m* blow with a machete; (*herida*) wound from a machete. **~e** *m* machete

mach|ista *m* male chauvinist. **~o** *a* male; (*varonil*) macho

machón *m* buttress

machucar [7] *vt* crush; (*estropear*) damage

madeja *f* skein

madera *f* (*vino*) Madeira. —*f* wood; (*naturaleza*) nature. **~ble** *a* yielding timber. **~je** *m*, **~men** *m* woodwork

madero *m* log; (*de construcción*) timber

madona *f* Madonna

madr|astra *f* stepmother. **~e** *f* mother. **~eperla** *f* mother-of-pearl. **~eselva** *f* honeysuckle

madrigal *m* madrigal

madriguera *f* den; (*de liebre*) burrow

madrileño *a* of Madrid. —*m* person from Madrid

madrina f godmother; (en una boda) chief bridesmaid

madroño m strawberry-tree

madrugada f dawn. ~ador a who gets up early. —m early riser. ~ar [12] vi get up early. ~ón m. darse un ~ón get up very early

maduración f maturing; (de fruta) ripening. ~ar vt/i mature; (fruta) ripen. ~ez f maturity; (de fruta) ripeness. ~o a mature; (fruta) ripe

maestr|a f teacher. ~ía f skill. ~o m master. ~a, ~o (de escuela) schoolteacher

mafia f Mafia

magdalena f madeleine, small sponge cake

magia f magic

mágico a magic; (maravilloso) magical

magín m (fam) imagination

magisterio m teaching (profession); (conjunto de maestros) teachers

magistrado m magistrate; (juez) judge

magistral a teaching; (bien hecho) masterly; (lenguaje) pedantic

magistratura f magistracy

magn|animidad f magnanimity. ~ánimo a magnanimous

magnate m magnate

magnesia f magnesia. ~ efervescente milk of magnesia

magnético a magnetic

magneti|smo m magnetism. ~zar [10] vt magnetize

magnetofón m, **magnetófono** m tape recorder

magnificencia f magnificence

magnífico a magnificent

magnitud f magnitude

magnolia f magnolia

mago m magician. los (tres) reyes ~s the Magi

magr|a f slice of ham. ~o a lean; (tierra) poor; (persona) thin

magulla|dura f bruise. ~r vt bruise

mahometano a & m Muhammadan

maíz m maize, corn (Amer)

majada f sheepfold; (estiércol) manure; (LAm) flock of sheep

majader|ía f silly thing. ~o m idiot; (mano del mortero) pestle. —a stupid

majador m crusher

majagranzas m idiot

majar vt crush; (molestar) bother

majest|ad f majesty. ~uoso a majestic

majo a nice

mal adv badly; (poco) poorly; (difícilmente) hardly; (equivocadamente) wrongly. —a see **malo**. —m evil; (daño) harm; (enfermedad) illness. ~ que bien somehow (or other). de ~ en peor worse and worse. hacer ~ en be wrong to. ¡menos ~! thank goodness!

malabar a. juegos ~es juggling. ~ismo m juggling. ~ista m & f juggler

malaconsejado a ill-advised

malacostumbrado a with bad habits

malagueño a of Málaga. —m person from Málaga

malamente adv badly; (fam) hardly enough

malandanza f misfortune

malapata m & f nuisance

malaria f malaria

Malasia f Malaysia

malasombra m & f clumsy person

malavenido a incompatible

malaventura f misfortune. ~do a unfortunate

malayo a Malay(an)

malbaratar vt sell off cheap; (malgastar) squander

malcarado *a* ugly

malcasado *a* unhappily married; (*infiel*) unfaithful

malcomer *vi* eat poorly

malcriad|eza *f* (*LAm*) bad manners. **~o** *a* (*niño*) spoilt

maldad *f* evil; (*acción*) wicked thing

maldecir [46 *pero imperativo* **maldice**, *futuro y condicional regulares, pp* **maldecido** *o* **maldito**] *vt* curse; —*vi* speak ill (**de** of); (*quejarse*) complain (**de** about)

maldici|ente *a* backbiting; (*que blasfema*) foul-mouthed. **~ón** *f* curse

maldit|a *f* tongue. **¡~a sea!** damn it! **~o** *a* damned. —*m* (*en el teatro*) extra

maleab|ilidad *f* malleability. **~le** *a* malleable

malea|nte *a* wicked. —*m* vagrant. **~r** *vt* damage; (*pervertir*) corrupt. **~rse** *vpr* be spoilt; (*pervertirse*) be corrupted

malecón *m* breakwater; (*rail*) embankment; (*para atracar*) jetty

maledicencia *f* slander

maleficio *m* curse

maléfico *a* evil

malestar *m* indisposition; (*fig*) uneasiness

malet|a *f* (*suit*)case; (*auto*) boot, trunk (*Amer*); (*LAm, lío de ropa*) bundle; (*LAm, de bicicleta*) saddlebag. **hacer la ~a** pack one's bags. —*m & f* (*fam*) bungler. **~ero** *m* porter; (*auto*) boot, trunk (*Amer*). **~ín** *m* small case

malevolencia *f* malevolence

malévolo *a* malevolent

maleza *f* weeds; (*matorral*) undergrowth

malgasta|dor *a* wasteful. —*m* spendthrift. **~r** *vt* waste

malgeniado *a* (*LAm*) bad-tempered

malhablado *a* foul-mouthed

malhadado *a* unfortunate

malhechor *m* criminal

malhumorado *a* bad-tempered

malici|a *f* malice. **~arse** *vpr* suspect. **~as** *fpl* (*fam*) suspicions. **~oso** *a* malicious

malign|idad *f* malice; (*med*) malignancy. **~o** *a* malignant; (*persona*) malicious

malintencionado *a* malicious

malmandado *a* disobedient

malmirado *a* (*con estar*) disliked; (*con ser*) inconsiderate

malo *a* (*delante de nombre masculino en singular* **mal**) bad; (*enfermo*) ill. **~ de** difficult. **estar de malas** be out of luck; (*malhumorado*) be in a bad mood. **lo ~ es que** the trouble is that. **ponerse a malas con uno** fall out with s.o. **por las malas** by force

malogr|ar *vt* waste; (*estropear*) spoil. **~arse** *vpr* fall through. **~o** *m* failure

maloliente *a* smelly

malparto *m* miscarriage

malpensado *a* nasty, malicious

malquerencia *f* dislike

malquist|ar *vt* set against. **~arse** *vpr* fall out. **~o** *a* disliked

malsano *a* unhealthy; (*enfermizo*) sickly

malsonante *a* ill-sounding; (*grosero*) offensive

malta *f* malt; (*cerveza*) beer

maltés *a & m* Maltese

maltratar *vt* ill-treat

maltrecho *a* battered

malucho *a* (*fam*) poorly

malva *f* mallow. **(color de) ~** *a invar* mauve

malvado *a* wicked

malvavisco *m* marshmallow

malvender *vt* sell off cheap

malversa|ción f embezzlement. **~dor** a embezzling. —m embezzler. **~r** vt embezzle

Malvinas fpl. **las islas ~** the Falkland Islands

malla f mesh. **cota de ~** coat of mail

mallo m mallet

Mallor|ca f Majorca. **~quín** a & m Majorcan

mama f teat; (de mujer) breast

mamá f mum(my)

mama|da f sucking. **~r** vt suck; (fig) grow up with; (engullir) gobble

mamario a mammary

mamarrach|adas fpl nonsense. **~o** m clown; (cosa ridícula) (ridiculous) sight

mameluco a Brazilian half-breed; (necio) idiot

mamífero a mammalian. —m mammal

mamola f. **hacer la ~** chuck (under the chin); (fig) make fun of

mamotreto m notebook; (libro voluminoso) big book

mampara f screen

mamporro m blow

mampostería f masonry

mamut m mammoth

maná m manna

manada f herd; (de lobos) pack. **en ~** in crowds

manager /'manaʒer/ m manager

mana|ntial m spring; (fig) source. **~r** vi flow; (fig) abound. —vt run with

manaza f big hand; (sucia) dirty hand. **ser un ~s** be clumsy

manceb|a f concubine. **~ía** f brothel. **~o** m youth; (soltero) bachelor

mancera f plough handle

mancilla f stain. **~r** vt stain

manco a (de una mano) one-handed; (de las dos manos) hand-less; (de un brazo) one-armed; (de los dos brazos) armless

mancomún adv. **de ~** jointly

mancomun|adamente adv jointly. **~ar** vt unite; (jurid) make jointly liable. **~arse** vpr unite. **~idad** f union

mancha f stain

Mancha f. **la ~** la Mancha (region of Spain). **el canal de la ~** the English Channel

mancha|do a dirty; (animal) spotted. **~r** vt stain. **~rse** vpr get dirty

manchego a of la Mancha. —m person from la Mancha

manchón m large stain

manda f legacy

manda|dero m messenger. **~miento** m order; (relig) commandment. **~r** vt order; (enviar) send; (gobernar) rule. —vi be in command. **¿mande?** (esp LAm) pardon?

mandarín m mandarin

mandarin|a f (naranja) mandarin; (lengua) Mandarin. **~o** m mandarin tree

mandat|ario m attorney. **~o** m order; (jurid) power of attorney

mandíbula f jaw

mandil m apron

mandioca f cassava

mando m command; (pol) term of office. **~ a distancia** remote control. **los ~s** the leaders

mandolina f mandolin

mandón a bossy

manducar [7] vt (fam) stuff oneself with

manecilla f needle; (de reloj) hand

manej|able a manageable. **~ar** vt handle; (fig) manage; (LAm, conducir) drive. **~arse** vpr behave. **~o** m handling; (intriga) intrigue

manera f way. **~s** fpl manners. **de ~ que** so (that). **de ninguna ~** not at all. **de otra ~** otherwise. **de todas ~s** anyway

manga f sleeve; (*tubo de goma*) hose(pipe); (*red*) net; (*para colar*) filter

mangante m beggar; (*fam*) scrounger

mangle m mangrove

mango m handle; (*fruta*) mango

mangonear vt boss about. —vi (*entrometerse*) interfere

manguera f hose(pipe)

manguito m muff

manía f mania; (*antipatía*) dislike

maniaco a, **maníaco** a maniac(al). —m maniac

maniatar vt tie s.o.'s hands

maniático a maniac(al); (*fig*) crazy

manicomio m lunatic asylum

manicura f manicure; (*mujer*) manicurist

manido a stale; (*carne*) high

manifestación f manifestation; (*pol*) demonstration. **~nte** m demonstrator. **~r** [1] vi manifest; (*pol*) state. **~rse** vpr show; (*pol*) demonstrate

manifiesto a clear; (*error*) obvious; (*verdad*) manifest. —m manifesto

manilargo a light-fingered

manilla f bracelet; (*de hierro*) handcuffs

manillar m handlebar(s)

maniobra f manoeuvring; (*rail*) shunting; (*fig*) manoeuvre. **~r** vt operate; (*rail*) shunt. —vi manoeuvre. **~s** fpl (*mil*) manoeuvres

manipulación f manipulation. **~r** vt manipulate

maniquí m dummy. —f model

manirroto a extravagant. —m spendthrift

manita f little hand

manivela f crank

manjar m (*special*) dish

mano f hand; (*de animales*) front foot; (*de perros, gatos*) front paw. **~ de obra** work force. **¡~s**

arriba! hands up! **a ~** by hand; (*próximo*) handy. **de segunda ~** second hand. **echar una ~** lend a hand. **tener buena ~ para** be good at

manojo m bunch

manosear vt handle; (*fig*) overwork. **~o** m handling

manotada f, **manotazo** m slap

manotear vi gesticulate. **~o** m gesticulation

mansalva. a ~ adv without risk

mansarda f attic

mansedumbre f gentleness; (*de animal*) tameness

mansión f stately home

manso a gentle; (*animal*) tame

manta f blanket. **~ eléctrica** electric blanket. **a ~ (de Dios)** a lot

manteca f fat; (*LAm*) butter. **~ado** m bun; (*helado*) ice-cream. **~oso** a greasy

mantel m tablecloth; (*del altar*) altar cloth. **~ería** f table linen

mantener [40] vt support; (*conservar*) keep; (*sostener*) maintain. **~erse** vpr remain. **~de/con** live off. **~imiento** m maintenance

mantequera f butter churn. **~ería** f dairy. **~illa** f butter

mantilla f mantilla

manto m cloak

mantón m shawl

manual a & m manual

manubrio m crank

manufactura f manufacture; (*fábrica*) factory

manuscrito a handwritten. —m manuscript

manutención f maintenance

manzana f apple. **~r** m (*apple*) orchard

manzanilla f camomile tea; (*vino*) manzanilla, pale dry sherry

manzano m apple tree

maña f skill. **~s** fpl cunning

mañan|a *f* morning; (*el día siguiente*) tomorrow. —*m* future. —*adv* tomorrow. ~**ero** *a* who gets up early. —*m* early riser. ~**a por la** ~**a** tomorrow morning. **pasado** ~**a** the day after tomorrow. **por la** ~**a** in the morning

mañoso *a* clever; (*astuto*) crafty

mapa *m* map. ~**mundi** *m* map of the world

mapache *m* racoon

mapurite *m* skunk

maqueta *f* scale model

maquiavélico *a* machiavellian

maquilla|**je** *m* make-up. ~**r** *vt* make up. ~**rse** *vpr* make up

máquina *f* machine; (*rail*) engine. ~ **de escribir** typewriter. ~ **fotográfica** camera

maquin|**ación** *f* machination. ~**al** *a* mechanical. ~**aria** *f* machinery. ~**ista** *m & f* operator; (*rail*) engine driver

mar *m & f* sea. **alta** ~ high seas. **la** ~ **de** (*fam*) lots of

maraña *f* thicket; (*enredo*) tangle; (*embrollo*) muddle

maravedí *m* (*pl* **maravedís**, **maravedises**) maravedi, old Spanish coin

maravill|**a** *f* wonder. ~**ar** *vt* astonish. ~**arse** *vpr* be astonished (**con** at). ~**oso** *a* marvellous, wonderful. **a** ~**a**, **a las mil** ~**as** marvellously. **contar/decir** ~**as de** speak wonderfully of. **hacer** ~**as** work wonders

marbete *m* label

marca *f* mark; (*de fábrica*) trademark; (*deportes*) record. ~**do** *a* marked. ~**dor** *m* marker; (*deportes*) scoreboard. ~**r** [7] *vt* mark; (*señalar*) show; (*anotar*) note down; score ⟨*un gol*⟩; dial ⟨*número de teléfono*⟩. —*vi* score. **de** ~ brand name; (*fig*) excellent. **de** ~ **mayor** (*fam*) first-class

marcial *a* martial

marciano *a & m* Martian

marco *m* frame; (*moneda alemana*) mark; (*deportes*) goalposts

marcha *f* (*incl mus*) march; (*auto*) gear; (*curso*) course. **a toda** ~ at full speed. **dar/hacer** ~ **atrás** put into reverse. **poner en** ~ start; (*fig*) set in motion

marchante *m* (*f* **marchanta**) dealer; (*LAm*, *parroquiano*) client

marchar *vi* go; (*funcionar*) work, go. ~**se** *vpr* go away, leave

marchit|**ar** *vt* wither. ~**arse** *vpr* wither. ~**o** *a* withered

marea *f* tide. ~**do** *a* sick; (*en el mar*) seasick; (*aturdido*) dizzy; (*borracho*) drunk. ~**r** *vt* sail, navigate; (*baquetear*) annoy. ~**rse** *vpr* feel sick; (*en un barco*) be seasick; (*estar aturdido*) feel dizzy; (*irse la cabeza*) feel faint; (*emborracharse*) get slightly drunk

marejada *f* swell; (*fig*) wave

maremagno *m* (*de cosas*) sea; (*de gente*) (noisy) crowd

mareo *m* sickness; (*en el mar*) seasickness; (*aturdimiento*) dizziness; (*fig*, *molestia*) nuisance

marfil *m* ivory. ~**eño** *a* ivory. **torre** *f* **de** ~ ivory tower

margarina *f* margarine

margarita *f* pearl; (*bot*) daisy

marg|**en** *m* margin; (*borde*) edge, border; (*de un río*) bank; (*de un camino*) side; (*nota marginal*) marginal note. ~**inado** *a* on the edge. —*m* outcast. ~**inal** *a* marginal. ~**inar** *vt* (*excluir*) exclude; (*dejar márgenes*) leave margins; (*poner notas*) write notes in the margin. **al** ~**en** (*fig*) outside

mariachi (*Mex*) *m* (*música popular de Jalisco*) Mariachi; (*conjunto popular*) Mariachi band

mariano a Marian

marica f (hombre afeminado) sissy; (urraca) magpie

maricón m homosexual, queer (sl)

maridaje m married life; (fig) harmony. ~o m husband

mariguana f, **marihuana** f marijuana

marimacho m mannish woman

marimandona f bossy woman

marimba f (type of) drum; (LAm, especie de xilofón) marimba

marimorena f (fam) row

marina f coast; (cuadro) seascape; (conjunto de barcos) navy; (arte de navegar) seamanship. ~era f seamanship; (conjunto de marineros) crew. ~ero a marine; (barco) seaworthy. ~m sailor. ~o a marine. ~a de guerra navy. ~a mercante merchant navy. a la ~era in tomato and garlic sauce. azul ~o navy blue

marioneta f puppet. ~s fpl puppet show

mariposa f butterfly. ~ear vi be fickle; (galantear) flirt. ~n m flirt. ~a nocturna moth

mariquita f ladybird, ladybug (Amer)

marisabidilla f know-all

mariscador m shell-fisher

mariscal m marshal

marisco m seafood, shellfish. ~quero m (persona que pesca mariscos) seafood fisherman; (persona que vende mariscos) seafood seller

marital a marital

marítimo a maritime; (ciudad etc) coastal, seaside

maritornes f uncouth servant

marmita f pot. ~ón m kitchen boy

mármol m marble

marmolera f marblework, marbles. ~ista m & f marble worker

marmóreo a marble

marmota f marmot

maroma f rope; (LAm, función de volatines) tightrope walking

marqués m marquess. ~esa f marchioness. ~esina f glass canopy

marquetería f marquetry

marrajo a (toro) vicious; (persona) cunning. ~m shark

marrana f sow. ~ada f filthy thing; (cochinada) dirty trick. ~o a filthy. ~m hog

marrar vt (errar) miss; (fallar) fail

marrón a & m brown

marroquí a & m & f Moroccan. ~m (tafilete) morocco

marrubio m (bot) horehound

Marruecos m Morocco

marrullería f cajolery. ~o a cajoling. ~m cajoler

marsopa f porpoise

marsupial a & m marsupial

marta f marten

Marte m Mars

martes m Tuesday

martillada f blow with a hammer. ~ar vt hammer. ~azo m blow with a hammer. ~ear vt hammer. ~eo m hammering. ~o m hammer

martín m **pescador** kingfisher

martinete m (macillo del piano) hammer; (mazo) drop hammer

martingala f (ardid) trick

mártir m & f martyr

martirio m martyrdom. ~izar [10] vt martyr; (fig) torment, torture. ~ologio m martyrology

marxismo m Marxism. ~ta a & m & f Marxist

marzo m March

más adv & a (comparativo) more; (superlativo) most. ~ caro dearer. ~ curioso more curious. el ~ caro the dearest; (de dos) the dearer. el ~ curioso the most curious; (de dos) the more curious. —conj and, plus. ~m plus (sign). ~ bien rather. ~ de (cantidad indeterminada) more than. ~ o menos more or less. ~ que more than. ~ y ~ more and more. a lo ~ at (the) most. de ~ too many. es ~ moreover. no ~ no more

masa f dough; (cantidad) mass; (física) mass. en ~ en masse

masacre f massacre

masaje m massage. ~ista m masseur. —f masseuse

mascada f (LAm) plug of tobacco. ~dura f chewing. ~r [7] vt chew

máscara f mask; (persona) masked figure/person

mascarada f masquerade. ~illa f mask. ~ón m (large) mask

mascota f mascot

masculinidad f masculinity. ~o a masculine; (sexo) male. —m masculine

mascullar [3] vt mumble

masilla f putty

masivo a massive, large-scale

masón m (free)mason. ~onería f (free)masonry. ~ónico a masonic

masoquismo m masochism. ~ta a masochistic. —m & f masochist

mastate m (Mex) loincloth

mastelero m topmast

masticación f chewing. ~r [7] vt chew; (fig) chew over

mástil m mast; (palo) pole; (en instrumentos de cuerda) neck

mastín m mastiff

mastitis f mastitis

mastodonte m mastodon

mastoides a & f mastoid

mastuerzo m cress

masturbación f masturbation. ~rse vpr masturbate

mata f grove; (arbusto) bush

matadero m slaughterhouse. ~or a killing. —m killer; (torero) matador

matadura f sore

matamoscas m invar fly swatter

matanza f killing. ~r vt kill (personas); slaughter (reses). ~rife m butcher. ~rse vpr commit suicide; (en un accidente) be killed. estar a ~r con uno be deadly enemies with s.o.

matarratas m invar cheap liquor

matasanos m invar quack

matasellos m invar postmark

match m match

mate a matt, dull; (sonido) dull. —m (ajedrez) (check)mate; (LAm, bebida) maté

matemáticas fpl mathematics, maths (fam), math (Amer, fam). ~o a mathematical. ~ mathematician

materia f matter; (material) material. ~ prima raw material. en ~ de on the question of

material a & m material. ~idad f material nature. ~ismo m materialism. ~ista a materialistic. —m & f materialist. ~izar [10] vt materialize. ~izarse vpr materialize. ~mente adv materially; (absolutamente) absolutely

maternal a maternal; (como de madre) motherly. ~idad f motherhood; (casa de maternidad) maternity home. ~o a motherly; (lengua) mother

matinal a morning. ~ée m matinée

matiz m shade. ~ación f combination of colours. ~ar [10] vt blend (colores); (introducir variedad) vary; (teñir) tinge (de with)

matojo m bush

matón m bully. ~onismo m bullying

matorral *m* scrub; (*conjunto de matas*) thicket

matra|ca *f* rattle. **~quear** *vt* rattle; (*dar matraca*) pester. **dar ~ca** pester. **ser un(a) ~ca** be a nuisance

matraz *m* flask

matriarca|do *m* matriarchy. **~l** *a* matriarchal

matrícula *f* (*lista*) register, list; (*acto de matricularse*) registration; (*auto*) registration number. **~icular** *vt* register. **~icularse** *vpr* enrol, register

matrimoni|al *a* matrimonial. **~o** *m* marriage; (*pareja*) married couple

matritense *a* from Madrid

matriz *f* matrix; (*anat*) womb, uterus

matrona *f* matron; (*partera*) midwife

Matusalén *m* Methuselah. **más viejo que ~** as old as Methuselah

matute *m* smuggling. **~ro** *m* smuggler

matutino *a* morning

maula *f* piece of junk

maull|ar *vi* miaow. **~ido** *m* miaow

mauritano *a* & *m* Mauritanian

mausoleo *m* mausoleum

maxilar *a* maxillary. **hueso ~** jaw(bone)

máxima *f* maxim

máxime *adv* especially

máximo *a* maximum; (*más alto*) highest. **—m** maximum

maya *f* daisy; (*persona*) Maya Indian

mayestático *a* majestic

mayo *m* May; (*palo*) maypole

mayólica *f* majolica

mayonesa *f* mayonnaise

mayor *a* (*más grande, comparativo*) bigger; (*más grande, superlativo*) biggest; (*de edad, comparativo*) older; (*de edad,*

superlativo) oldest; (*adulto*) grown-up; (*principal*) main, major; (*mus*) major. **—m & f** boss; (*adulto*) adult. **~al** *m* foreman; (*pastor*) head shepherd. **~azgo** *m* entailed estate. **al por ~** wholesale

mayordomo *m* butler

mayor|ía *f* majority. **~ista** *m & f* wholesaler. **~mente** *adv* especially

mayúscul|a *f* capital (letter). **~o** *a* capital; (*fig, grande*) big

maza *f* mace

mazacote *m* hard mass

mazapán *m* marzipan

mazmorra *f* dungeon

mazo *m* mallet; (*manojo*) bunch

mazorca *f*. **~ de maíz** corn on the cob

me *pron* (*acusativo*) me; (*dativo*) (to) me; (*reflexivo*) (to) myself

meandro *m* meander

mecánic|a *f* mechanics. **~o** *a* mechanical. **—m** mechanic

mecani|smo *m* mechanism. **~zación** *f* mechanization. **~zar** [10] *vt* mechanize

mecanograf|ía *f* typing. **~iado** *a* typed, typewritten. **~iar** [20] *vt* type

mecanógrafo *m* typist

mecate *m* (*LAm*) (*pita*) rope

mecedora *f* rocking chair

mecenazgo *m* patronage

mecer [9] *vt* rock; swing (*columpio*). **~se** *vpr* rock; (*en un columpio*) swing

mecha *f* (*de vela*) wick; (*de mina*) fuse

mechar *vt* stuff, lard

mechero *m* (*cigarette*) lighter

mechón *m* (*de pelo*) lock

medall|a *f* medal. **~ón** *m* medallion; (*relicario*) locket

media *f* stocking; (*promedio*) average

mediación *f* mediation

mediado a half full; ⟨trabajo etc⟩ halfway through. **~s de marzo** in the middle of March

mediador m mediator

medialuna f croissant

median|amente adv fairly. **~era** f party wall. **~ero** a ⟨muro⟩ party. **~a** f average circumstances. **~o** a average, medium; ⟨mediocre⟩ mediocre

medianoche f midnight; ⟨culin⟩ small sandwich

mediante prep through, by means of

mediar vi mediate; ⟨llegar a la mitad⟩ be halfway (en through)

mediatizar [10] vt annex

medic|ación f medication. **~amento** m medicine. **~ina** f medicine. **~inal** a medicinal. **~inar** vt administer medicine

medición f measurement

médico a medical. —m doctor. **~ de cabecera** GP, general practitioner

medid|a f measurement; ⟨unidad⟩ measure; ⟨disposición⟩ measure, step; ⟨prudencia⟩ moderation. **~or** m (LAm) meter. **a la ~a** made to measure. **a ~a que** as. **en cierta ~a** to a certain point

mediero m share-cropper

medieval a medieval. **~ista** m & f medievalist

medio a half (a); ⟨mediano⟩ average. **~ litro** half a litre. —m middle; ⟨manera⟩ means; ⟨en deportes⟩ half-back). **en ~** in the middle (**de** of). **por ~** de through

mediocr|e a ⟨mediano⟩ average; ⟨de escaso mérito⟩ mediocre. **~idad** f mediocrity

mediodía m midday, noon; ⟨sur⟩ south

medioevo m Middle Ages

Medio Oriente m Middle East

medir [5] vt medir; weigh up ⟨palabras etc⟩. —vi measure, be. **~se** vpr ⟨moderarse⟩ be moderate

medita|bundo a thoughtful. **~ción** f meditation. **~r** vt think about. —vi meditate

Mediterráneo m Mediterranean

mediterráneo a Mediterranean

médium m & f medium

medrar vi thrive

medroso a ⟨con estar⟩ frightened; ⟨con ser⟩ fearful

médula f marrow

medusa f jellyfish

mefítico a noxious

mega... pref mega...

megáfono m megaphone

megal|ítico a megalithic. **~ito** m megalith

megal|omanía f megalomania. **~ómano** m megalomaniac

mejicano a & m Mexican

Méjico m Mexico

mejido a ⟨huevo⟩ beaten

mejilla f cheek

mejillón m mussel

mejor a & adv ⟨comparativo⟩ better; ⟨superlativo⟩ best. **~a** f improvement. **~able** a improvable. **~amiento** m improvement. **~ dicho** rather. **a lo ~** perhaps. **tanto ~** so much the better

mejorana f marjoram

mejorar vt improve, better. —vi get better

mejunje m mixture

melanc|olía f melancholy. **~ólico** a melancholic

melaza f molasses, treacle (Amer)

melen|a f long hair; ⟨de león⟩ mane. **~udo** a long-haired

melifluo a mellifluous

melillense a of/from Melilla. —m person from Melilla

melindre m (*mazapán*) sugared marzipan cake; (*masa frita con miel*) honey fritter. ∼**oso** *a* affected

melocot|**ón** m peach. ∼**onero** m peach tree

mel|**odía** f melody. ∼**ódico** *a* melodic. ∼**odioso** *a* melodious

melodram|**a** m melodrama. ∼**áticamente** *adv* melodramatically. ∼**ático** *a* melodramatic

melómano m music lover

mel|**ón** m melon; (*bobo*) fool. ∼**onada** f something stupid

meloncillo m (*animal*) mongoose

melos|**idad** f sweetness. ∼**o** *a* sweet

mella f notch. ∼**do** *a* jagged. ∼**r** vt notch

mellizo *a* & m twin

membran|**a** f membrane. ∼**oso** *a* membranous

membrete m letterhead

membrill|**ero** m quince tree. ∼**o** m quince

membrudo *a* burly

memez f something silly

memo *a* stupid. —*m* idiot

memorable *a* memorable

memorando m, **memorándum** m notebook; (*nota*) memorandum

memoria f memory; (*informe*) report; (*tesis*) thesis. ∼**s** fpl (*recuerdos personales*) memoirs. **de** ∼ from memory

memorial m memorial. ∼**ista** m amanuensis

memor|**ión** m good memory. ∼**ista** *a* having a good memory. ∼**ístico** *a* memory

mena f ore

menaje m furnishings

menci|**ón** f mention. ∼**onado** *a* aforementioned. ∼**onar** vt mention

menda|**cidad** f mendacity. ∼**z** *a* lying

mendi|**cante** *a* & m mendicant. ∼**cidad** f begging. ∼**gar** [12] vt beg (for). —*vi* beg. ∼**go** m beggar

mendrugo m (*pan*) hard crust; (*zoquete*) blockhead

mene|**ar** vt move, shake. ∼**arse** vpr move, shake. ∼**o** m movement, shake

menester m need. ∼**oso** *a* needy. **ser** ∼ be necessary

menestra f stew

menestral m artesan

mengano m so-and-so

mengua f decrease; (*falta*) lack; (*descrédito*) discredit. ∼**do** *a* miserable; (*falto de carácter*) spineless. ∼**nte** *a* decreasing; (*luna*) waning; (*marea*) ebb. —f (*del mar*) ebb tide; (*de un río*) low water. ∼**r** [15] vt/i decrease, diminish

meningitis f meningitis

menisco m meniscus

menjurje m mixture

menopausia f menopause

menor *a* (*más pequeño, comparativo*) smaller; (*más pequeño, superlativo*) smallest; (*más joven, comparativo*) younger; (*más joven*) youngest; (*mus*) minor. —m & f (*menor de edad*) minor. **al por** ∼ retail

Menorca f Minorca

menorquín *a* & m Minorcan

menos *a* (*comparativo*) less; (*comparativo, con plural*) fewer; (*superlativo*) least; (*superlativo, con plural*) fewest. —*adv* (*comparativo*) less; (*superlativo*) least. —*prep* except. ∼**cabar** vt lessen; (*fig, estropear*) damage. ∼**cabo** m lessening. ∼**preciable** *a* contemptible. ∼**preciar** vt despise. ∼**precio** m contempt. **a** ∼ **que** unless. **al** ∼ at least. **ni mucho** ∼ far from it. **por lo** ∼ at least

mensaje *m* message. **~ro** *m* messenger

menso *a* (*Mex*) stupid

menstru|ación *f* menstruation. **~al** *a* menstrual. **~ar** [21] *vi* menstruate. **~o** *m* menstruation

mensual *a* monthly. **~idad** *f* monthly pay

ménsula *f* bracket

mensurable *a* measurable

menta *f* mint

mental *a* mental. **~idad** *f* mentality. **~mente** *adv* mentally

mentar [1] *vt* mention, name

mente *f* mind

mentecato *a* stupid. —*m* idiot

mentir [4] *vi* lie. **~a** *f* lie. **~oso** *a* lying. —*m* liar. **de ~ijillas** for a joke

mentís *m* invar denial

mentol *m* menthol

mentor *m* mentor

menú *m* menu

menudear *vi* happen frequently

menudencia *f* trifle

menudeo *m* retail trade

menudillos *mpl* giblets

menudo *a* tiny; ⟨*lluvia*⟩ fine; (*insignificante*) insignificant. **~s** *mpl* giblets. **a ~** often

meñique *a* ⟨*dedo*⟩ little. —*m* little finger

meollo *m* brain; (*médula*) marrow; (*parte blanda*) soft part; (*fig, inteligencia*) brains

meramente *adv* merely

mercachifle *m* hawker; (*fig*) profiteer

mercader *m* (*LAm*) merchant

mercado *m* market. **M~ Común** Common Market. **~ negro** black market

mercan|cía *f* article. **~cías** *fpl* goods, merchandise. **~te** *a & m* merchant. **~til** *a* mercantile, commercial. **~tilismo** *m* mercantilism

mercar [7] *vt* buy

merced *f* favour. **su/vuestra ~** your honour

mercenario *a & m* mercenary

mercer|ía *f* haberdashery, notions (*Amer*). **~o** *m* haberdasher

mercurial *a* mercurial

Mercurio *m* Mercury

mercurio *m* mercury

merece|dor *a* deserving. **~er** [11] *vt* deserve. —*vi* be deserving. **~idamente** *adv* deservedly. **~ido** *a* well deserved. **~imiento** *m* (*mérito*) merit

merendar [1]. *vt* have as an afternoon snack. —*vi* have an afternoon snack. **~ero** *m* snack bar; (*lugar*) picnic area

merengue *m* meringue

meretriz *f* prostitute

mergo *m* cormorant

meridian|a *f* ⟨*diván*⟩ couch. **~o** *a* midday; (*fig*) dazzling. —*m* meridian

meridional *a* southern. —*m* southerner

merienda *f* afternoon snack

merino *a* merino

mérito *m* merit; (*valor*) worth

meritorio *a* meritorious. —*m* unpaid trainee

merlo *m* black wrasse

merluza *f* hake

merma *f* decrease. **~r** *vt/i* decrease, reduce

mermelada *f* jam

mero *a* mere; (*Mex, verdadero*) real. —*adv* (*Mex, precisamente*) exactly; (*Mex, verdaderamente*) really. —*m* grouper

merode|ador *a* marauding. —*m* marauder. **~ar** *vi* maraud. **~o** *m* marauding

merovingio *a & m* Merovingian

mes *m* month; (*mensualidad*) monthly pay

mesa *f* table; (*para escribir o estudiar*) desk. **poner la ~** lay the table

mesana f (palo) mizen-mast

mesarse vpr tear at one's hair

mesenterio m mesentery

meseta f plateau; (descansillo) landing

mesiánico a Messianic

Mesías m Messiah

mesilla f small table. ~ de noche bedside table

mesón m inn

mesoner|a f landlady. ~o m landlord

mestiz|aje m crossbreeding. ~o a (persona) half-caste; (animal) cross-bred. —m (persona) half-caste; (animal) cross-breed

mesura f moderation. ~do a moderate

meta f goal; (de una carrera) finish

metabolismo m metabolism

metacarpiano m metacarpal

metafísic|a f metaphysics. ~o a metaphysical

met|áfora f metaphor. ~afórico a metaphorical

met|al m metal; (instrumentos de latón) brass; (de la voz) timbre. ~álico a (objeto) metal; (sonido) metallic. ~alizarse** [10] vpr (fig) become mercenary

metal|urgia f metallurgy. ~úrgico a metallurgical

metam|órfico a metamorphic. ~orfosear** vt transform. ~orfosis** f metamorphosis

metano m methane

metatarsiano m metatarsal

metátesis f invar metathesis

metedura f. ~ de pata blunder

mete|órico a meteoric. ~orito** m meteorite. ~oro** m meteor. ~orología** f meteorology. ~orológico** a meteorological. ~orólogo** m meteorologist

meter vt put, place; (ingresar) deposit; score (un gol); (enredar) involve; (causar) make. ~se** vpr

get; (entrometerse) meddle. ~se con uno pick a quarrel with s.o.

meticulos|idad f meticulousness. ~o a meticulous

metido m reprimand. —a. ~ en años getting on. estar muy ~ con uno be well in with s.o.

metilo m methyl

metódico a methodical

metodis|mo m Methodism. ~ta a & m & f Methodist

método m method

metodología f methodology

metomentodo m busybody

metraje m length. de largo ~ (película) feature

metrall|a f shrapnel. ~eta** f submachine gun

métric|a f metrics. ~o a metric; (verso) metrical

metro m metre; (tren) underground, subway (Amer). ~ cuadrado cubic metre

metrónomo m metronome

metr|ópoli f metropolis. ~opolitano** a metropolitan. —m metropolitan; (tren) underground, subway (Amer)

mexicano a & m (LAm) Mexican

México m (LAm) Mexico. ~ D. F.** Mexico City

mezcal m (Mex) (type of) brandy

mezc|la f (acción) mixing; (substancia) mixture; (argamasa) mortar. ~lador** m mixer. ~lar** vt mix; shuffle (los naipes). ~larse** vpr mix; (intervenir) interfere. ~olanza** f mixture

mezquin|dad f meanness. ~o a mean; (escaso) meagre. —m mean person

mezquita f mosque

mi a my. —m (mus) E; (solfa) mi

mí pron me

miaja f crumb

miasma m miasma

miau m miaow

mica f (silicato) mica; (Mex, embriaguez) drunkenness

mico *m* (long-tailed) monkey

micro... *pref* micro...

microbio *m* microbe

micro: ~**biología** *f* microbiology. ~**cosmo** *m* microcosm. ~**film(e)** *m* microfilm

micrófono *m* microphone

micrómetro *m* micrometer

microonda *f* microwave. **horno** *m* **de** ~**s** microwave oven

microordenador *m* microcomputer

microscópico *a* microscopic. ~**opio** *m* microscope

micro: ~**surco** *m* long-playing record. ~**taxi** *m* minicab

miedo *m* fear. ~**so** *a* fearful. **dar** ~ frighten. **morirse de** ~ be scared to death. **tener** ~ be frightened

miel *f* honey

mielga *f* lucerne, alfalfa (*Amer*)

miembro *m* limb; (*persona*) member

mientras *conj* while. —*adv* meanwhile. ~ **que** whereas. ~ **tanto** in the meantime

miércoles *m* Wednesday. ~ **de ceniza** Ash Wednesday

mierda *f* (*vulgar*) shit

mies *f* corn, grain (*Amer*)

miga *f* crumb; (*fig, meollo*) essence. ~**jas** *fpl* crumbs. ~**r** [12] *vt* crumble

migra|ción *f* migration. ~**torio** *a* migratory

mijo *m* millet

mil *a* & *m* a/one thousand. ~**es de** thousands of. ~ **novecientos noventa y dos** nineteen ninety-two. ~ **pesetas** a thousand pesetas

milagro *m* miracle. ~**so** *a* miraculous

milano *m* kite

mildeu *m*, **mildiu** *m* mildew

milen|ario *a* millenial. ~**io** *m* millennium

milenrama *f* milfoil

milésimo *a* & *m* thousandth

mili *f* (*fam*) military service

milicia *f* soldiering; (*gente armada*) militia

mili|gramo *m* milligram. ~**litro** *m* millilitre

milímetro *m* millimetre

militante *a* militant

militar *a* military. —*m* soldier. ~**ismo** *m* militarism. ~**ista** *a* militaristic. —*m* & *f* militarist. ~**izar** [10] *vt* militarize

milonga *f* (*Arg, canción*) popular song; (*Arg, baile*) popular dance

milord *m*. **vivir como un** ~ live like a lord

milpies *m invar* woodlouse

milla *f* mile

millar *m* thousand. **a** ~**es** by the thousand

mill|ón *m* million. ~**onada** *f* fortune. ~**onario** *m* millionaire. ~**onésimo** *a* & *m* millionth. **un** ~**n de libros** a million books

mimar *vt* spoil

mimbre *m* & *f* wicker. ~**arse** *vpr* sway. ~**ra** *f* osier. ~**ral** *m* osier-bed

mimetismo *m* mimicry

mímica *f* mime. ~**o** *a* mimic

mimo *m* mime; (*a un niño*) spoiling; (*caricia*) caress

mimosa *f* mimosa

mina *f* mine. ~**r** *vt* mine; (*fig*) undermine

minarete *m* minaret

mineral *m* mineral; (*mena*) ore. ~**ogía** *f* mineralogy. ~**ogista** *m* & *f* mineralogist

miner|ía *f* mining. ~**o** *a* mining. —*m* miner

mini... *pref* mini...

miniar *vt* paint in miniature

miniatura *f* miniature

minifundio *m* smallholding

minimizar [10] *vt* minimize

mínimo *a* & *m* minimum. ~**um** *m* minimum

minino *m* (*fam*) cat, puss (*fam*)

minio *m* red lead

minist|erial *a* ministerial. **~erio** *m* ministry. **~ro** *m* minister

minor|ación *f* diminution. **~a** *f* minority. **~idad** *f* minority. **~ista** *m* & *f* retailer

minuci|a *f* trifle. **~osidad** *f* thoroughness. **~oso** *a* thorough; (*con muchos detalles*) detailed

minué *m* minuet

minúscul|a *f* small letter, lower case letter. **~o** *a* tiny

minuta *f* draft; (*menú*) menu

minut|ero *m* minute hand. **~o** *m* minute

mío *a* & *pron* mine. **un amigo ~** a friend of mine

miop|e *a* short-sighted. **—***m* & *f* short-sighted person. **~ía** *f* short-sightedness

mira *f* sight; (*fig, intención*) aim. **~da** *f* look. **~do** *a* thought of; (*comedido*) considerate; (*cirunspecto*) circumspect. **~dor** *m* windowed balcony; (*lugar*) viewpoint. **~miento** *m* consideration. **~r** *vt* look at; (*observar*) watch; (*considerar*) consider. **~r fijamente a** stare at. **—***vi* look; (*edificio etc*) face. **~rse** *vpr* (*personas*) look at each other. **la ~ on** the lookout for. **con ~s a** with a view to. **echar una ~da a** glance at

mirilla *f* peephole

miriñaque *m* crinoline

mirlo *m* blackbird

mirón *a* nosey. **—***m* nosey-parker; (*espectador*) onlooker

mirra *f* myrrh

mirto *m* myrtle

misa *f* mass

misal *m* missal

mis|antropía *f* misanthropy. **~antrópico** *a* misanthropic. **~ántropo** *m* misanthropist

miscelánea *f* miscellany; (*Mex, tienda*) corner shop

miser|able *a* very poor; (*lastimoso*) miserable; (*tacaño*) mean. **~ia** *f* extreme poverty; (*suciedad*) squalor

misericordi|a *f* pity; (*piedad*) mercy. **~oso** *a* merciful

misero *a* very poor; (*lastimoso*) miserable; (*tacaño*) mean

misil *m* missile

misi|ón *f* mission. **~onal** *a* missionary. **~onero** *m* missionary

misiva *f* missive

mism|amente *adv* just. **~ísimo** *a* very same. **~o** *a* same; (*después de pronombre personal*) myself, yourself, himself, herself, itself, ourselves, yourselves, themselves; (*enfático*) very. **—***adv* right. **ahora ~** right now. **aquí ~** right here

mis|oginia *f* misogyny. **~ógino** *m* misogynist

misterio *m* mystery. **~so** *a* mysterious

mística *f* mysticism. **~o** *a* mystical

mistifica|ción *f* falsification; (*engaño*) trick. **~r** [7] *vt* falsify; (*engañar*) deceive

mitad *f* half; (*centro*) middle

mítico *a* mythical

mitiga|ción *f* mitigation. **~r** [12] *vt* mitigate; quench (*sed*); relieve (*dolor etc*)

mitin *m* meeting

mito *m* myth. **~logía** *f* mythology. **~lógico** *a* mythological

mitón *m* mitten

mitote *m* (*LAm*) Indian dance

mitra *f* mitre. **~do** *m* prelate

mixteca *f* (*Mex*) southern Mexico

mixt|o *a* mixed. **—***m* passenger and goods train; (*cerilla*) match. **~ura** *f* mixture

mnemotécnica *f* mnemonics. **~o** *a* mnemonic

moaré *m* moiré

mobiliario *m* furniture

moblaje *m* furniture

moca *f* mocha

moce|dad *f* youth. **~ro** *m* young people. **~tón** *m* strapping lad

moción *f* motion

moco *m* mucus

mochales *a invar.* **estar ~ be** round the bend

mochila *f* rucksack

mocho *a* blunt. —*m* butt end

mochuelo *m* little owl

moda *f* fashion. **~l** *a* modal. **~les** *mpl* manners. **~lidad** *f* kind. de **~** in fashion

model|ado *m* modelling. **~ador** *m* modeller. **~ar** *vt* model; (*fig*, *configurar*) form. **~o** *m* model

modera|ción *f* moderation. **~do** *a* moderate. **~r** *vt* moderate; reduce (*velocidad*). **~rse** *vpr* control oneself

modern|amente *adv* recently. **~idad** *f* modernity. **~ismo** *m* modernism. **~ista** *m & f* modernist. **~izar** [10] *vt* modernize. **~o** *a* modern

modest|ia *f* modesty. **~o** *a* modest

modicidad *f* reasonableness

módico *a* moderate

modifica|ción *f* modification. **~r** [7] *vt* modify

modismo *m* idiom

modist|a *f* dressmaker. **~o** *m & f* designer

modo *m* manner, way; (*gram*) mood; (*mus*) mode. **~ de ser** character. **de ~ que** so that. de ningún **~** certainly not. de todos **~s** anyhow

modorr|a *f* drowsiness. **~o** *a* drowsy

modoso *a* well-behaved

modula|ción *f* modulation. **~dor** *m* modulator. **~r** *vt* modulate

módulo *m* module

mofa *f* mockery. **~rse** *vpr.* **~rse de** make fun of

mofeta *f* skunk

moflet|e *m* chubby cheek. **~udo** *a* with chubby cheeks

mogol *m* Mongol. **el Gran M~** the Great Mogul

moh|ín *m* grimace. **~ino** *a* sulky. **hacer un ~ín** pull a face

moho *m* mould; (*óxido*) rust. **~so** *a* mouldy; (*metales*) rusty

moisés *m* Moses basket

mojado *a* damp, wet

mojama *f* salted tuna

mojar *vt* wet; (*empapar*) soak; (*humedecer*) moisten, dampen. —*vi.* **~ en** get involved in

mojicón *m* blow in the face; (*bizcocho*) sponge cake

mojiganga *f* masked ball; (*en el teatro*) farce

mojigat|ería *f* hypocrisy. **~o** *m* hypocrite

mojón *m* boundary post; (*señal*) signpost

molar *m* molar

mold|e *m* mould; (*aguja*) knitting needle. **~ear** *vt* mould, shape; (*fig*) form. **~ura** *f* moulding

mole *f* mass, bulk. —*m* (*Mex, guisado*) (Mexican) stew with chili sauce

mol|écula *f* molecule. **~ecular** *a* molecular

mole|dor *a* grinding. —*m* grinder; (*persona*) bore. **~r** [2] grind; (*hacer polvo*) pulverize

molest|ar *vt* annoy; (*incomodar*) bother. **¿le ~a que fume?** do you mind if I smoke? **no ~ar** do not disturb. —*vi* be a nuisance. **~arse** *vpr* bother; (*ofenderse*) take offence. **~ia** *f* bother, nuisance; (*inconveniente*) inconvenience; (*incomodidad*) discomfort. **~o** *a* annoying; (*inconveniente*) inconvenient; (*ofendido*) offended

molicie *f* softness; (*excesiva comodidad*) easy life

molido a ground; (fig, muy cansado) worn out

molienda f grinding

molin|**ero** m miller. ~**ete** m toy windmill. ~**illo** m mill; (juguete) toy windmill. ~**o** m (water) mill. ~**o de viento** windmill

molusco m mollusc

mollar a soft

molleja f gizzard

mollera f (de la cabeza) crown; (fig, sesera) brains

moment|**áneamente** adv momentarily; (por el momento) right now. ~**áneo** a momentary. ~**o** m moment; (mecánica) momentum

momi|**a** f mummy. ~**ficación** f mummification. ~**ficar** [7] vt mummify. ~**ficarse** vpr become mummified

momio a lean. —m bargain; (trabajo) cushy job

monaca|**l** a monastic. ~**to** m monasticism

monada f beautiful thing; (de un niño) charming way; (acción tonta) silliness

monaguillo m altar boy

mon|**arca** m & f monarch. ~**quía** f monarchy. ~**árquico** a monarchic(al). ~**arquismo** m monarchism

mon|**asterio** m monastery. ~**ástico** a monastic

monda f pruning; (peladura) peel

mond|**adientes** m invar toothpick. ~**adura** f pruning; (peladura) peel. ~**ar** vt peel (fruta etc); dredge (un río). ~**o** a (sin pelo) bald; (sin dinero) broke; (sencillo) plain

mondongo m innards

moned|**a** f coin; (de un país) currency. ~**ero** m minter; (portamonedas) purse

monetario a monetary

mongol a & m Mongolian

mongolismo m Down's syndrome

monigote m weak character; (muñeca) rag doll; (dibujo) doodle

monises mpl money, dough (fam)

monitor m monitor

monj|**a** f nun. ~**e** m monk. ~**il** a nun's; (como de monja) like a nun

mono a (monkey; (sobretodo) overalls. —a pretty

mono... pref mono...

monocromo a & m monochrome

monóculo m monocle

mon|**ogamia** f monogamy. ~**ógamo** a monogamous

monografía f monograph

monograma m monogram

monol|**ítico** a monolithic. ~**ito** m monolith

mon|**ologar** [12] vi soliloquize. ~**ólogo** m monologue

monoman|**ía** f monomania. ~**íaco** a monomaniac

monoplano m monoplane

monopoli|**o** m monopoly. ~**zar** [10] vt monopolize

monos|**ilábico** a monosyllabic. ~**ílabo** m monosyllable

monoteís|**mo** m monotheism. ~**ta** a monotheistic. —m & f monotheist

mon|**otonía** f monotony. ~**ótono** a monotonous

monseñor m monsignor

monserga f boring talk

monstruo m monster. ~**sidad** f monstrosity. ~**so** a monstrous

monta f mounting; (valor) value

montacargas m invar service lift

monta|**do** a mounted. ~**dor** m fitter. ~**je** m assembly; (cine) montage; (teatro) staging, production

montañ|**a** f mountain. ~**ero** a mountaineer. ~**és** a mountain. —m highlander. ~**ismo** m mountaineering. ~oso *a* mountainous. ~a rusa big dipper

montaplatos *m invar* service lift

montar *vt* ride; (*subirse*) get on; (*ensamblar*) assemble; cock (*arma*); set up (*una casa, un negocio*). —*vi* ride; (*subirse a*) mount. ~ a caballo ride a horse

montaraz *a* (*animales*) wild; (*personas*) mountain

monte *m* (*montaña*) mountain; (*terreno inculto*) scrub; (*bosque*) forest. ~ de piedad pawn-shop. ingeniero *m* de ~s forestry expert

montepío *m* charitable fund for dependents

montera *f* cloth cap. ~o *m* hunter

montés *a* wild

Montevideo *m* Montevideo

montevideano *a* & *m* Montevidean

montículo *m* hillock

montón *m* heap, pile. a montones in abundance, lots of

montuoso *a* hilly

montura *f* mount; (*silla*) saddle

monumental *a* monumental; (*fig, muy grande*) enormous. ~o *m* monument

monzón *m* & *f* monsoon

moña *f* hair ribbon. ~o *m* bun

moque|o *m* runny nose. ~ro *m* handkerchief

moqueta *f* fitted carpet

moquillo *m* distemper

mora *f* mulberry; (*zarzamora*) blackberry

morada *f* dwelling

morado *a* purple

morador *m* inhabitant

moral *m* mulberry tree. —*f* morals. —*a* moral. ~eja *f* moral. ~idad *f* morality. ~ista *m* & *f* moralist. ~izador *a* moralizing. —*m* moralist. ~izar [10] *vt* moralize

morapio *m* (*fam*) cheap red wine

morar *vi* live

moratoria *f* moratorium

morbidez *f* softness

mórbido *a* soft; (*malsano*) morbid

morbo *m* illness. ~sidad *f* morbidity. ~so *a* unhealthy

morcilla *f* black pudding

morda|cidad *f* bite. ~z *a* biting

mordaza *f* gag

mordazmente *adv* bitingly

morde|dura *f* bite. ~r [2] *vt* bite; (*fig, quitar porciones a*) eat into; (*denigrar*) gossip about. —*vi* bite

mordis|car [7] *vt* nibble (at). —*vi* nibble. ~co *m* bite. ~quear *vt* nibble (at)

morelense *a* (*Mex*) from Morelos. —*m* & *f* person from Morelos

morena *f* (*geol*) moraine

moreno *a* dark; (*de pelo obscuro*) dark-haired; (*de raza negra*) negro

morera *f* mulberry tree

morería *f* Moorish lands; (*barrio*) Moorish quarter

moretón *m* bruise

morfema *m* morpheme

morfin|a *f* morphine. ~ómano *a* morphine. —*m* morphine addict

morfolog|ía *f* morphology. ~ógico *a* morphological

moribundo *a* moribund

morillo *m* andiron

morir [6] (*pp* muerto) *vi* die; (*fig, extinguirse*) die away; (*fig, terminar*) end. ~se *vpr* die. ~se de hambre starve to death; (*fig*) be starving. se muere por una flauta she's dying to have a flute

moris|co *a* Moorish. —*m* Moor. ~ma *f* Moors

morm|ón *m* & *f* Mormon. ~ónico *a* Mormon. ~onismo *m* Mormonism

moro *a* Moorish. —*m* Moor

moros|idad *f* dilatoriness. ~o *a* dilatory

morrada *f* butt; *(puñetazo)* punch
morral *m (mochila)* rucksack; *(del cazador)* gamebag; *(para caballos)* nosebag
morralla *f* rubbish
morrillo *m* nape of the neck
morriña *f* homesickness
morro *m* snout
morrocotudo *a (esp Mex) (fam)* terrific *(fam)*
morsa *f* walrus
mortaja *f* shroud
mortal *a & m & f* mortal. **∼idad** *f* mortality. **∼mente** *adv* mortally
mortandad *f* death toll
mortecino *f* a failing; *(color)* faded
mortero *m* mortar
mortífero *a* deadly
mortifica|ción *f* mortification. **∼r** [7] *vt (med)* damage; *(atormentar)* plague; *(humillar)* humiliate. **∼rse** *vpr (Mex)* feel embarrassed
mortuorio *a* death
morueco *m* ram
moruno *a* Moorish
mosaico *a* of Moses, Mosaic. *—m* mosaic
mosca *f* fly. **∼rda** *f* blowfly. **∼rdón** *m* botfly; *(mosca de cuerpo azul)* bluebottle
moscatel *a* muscatel
moscón *m* botfly; *(mosca de cuerpo azul)* bluebottle
moscovita *a & m & f* Muscovite
Moscú *m* Moscow
mosque|arse *vpr* get cross. **∼o** *m* resentment
mosquete *m* musket. **∼ro** *m* musketeer
mosquit|ero *m* mosquito net. **∼o** *m* mosquito; *(mosca pequeña)* fly, gnat
mostacho *m* moustache
mostachón *m* macaroon
mostaza *f* mustard

mosto *m* must
mostrador *m* counter
mostrar [2] *vt* show. **∼se** *vpr* (show oneself to) be. **se mostró muy amable** he was very kind
mostrenco *a* ownerless; *(animal)* stray; *(torpe)* thick; *(gordo)* fat
mota *f* spot, speck
mote *m* nickname; *(lema)* motto
motea|do *a* speckled. **∼r** *vt* speckle
motejar *vt* call
motel *m* motel
motete *m* motet
motín *m* riot; *(rebelión)* uprising; *(de tropas)* mutiny
motiv|ación *f* motivation. **∼ar** *vt* motivate; *(explicar)* explain. **∼o** *m* reason. **con ∼o de** because of
motocicl|eta *f* motor cycle, motor bike *(fam)*. **∼ista** *m & f* motor-cyclist
motón *m* pulley
motonave *f* motor boat
motor *a* motor. *—m* motor, engine. **∼a** *f* motor boat. **∼ de arranque** starter motor
motoris|mo *m* motorcycling. **∼ta** *m* *f* motorist; *(de una moto)* motorcyclist
motorizar [10] *vt* motorize
motriz *af* motive, driving
move|dizo *a* movable; *(poco firme)* unstable; *(persona)* fickle. **∼r** [2] *vt* move; shake *(la cabeza)*; *(provocar)* cause. **∼rse** *vpr* move; *(darse prisa)* hurry up. **arenas** *fpl* **∼dizas** quicksand
movi|ble *a* movable. **∼do** *a* moved; *(foto)* blurred; *(inquieto)* fidgety
móvil *a* movable. *—m* motive
movili|dad *f* mobility. **∼zación** *f* mobilization. **∼zar** [10] *vt* mobilize
movimiento *m* movement, motion; *(agitación)* bustle

moza f girl; (*sirvienta*) servant, maid. **~lbete** m young lad

mozárabe a Mozarabic. **—m &** f Mozarab

moz|o m boy, lad. **~uela** f young girl. **~uelo** m young boy/lad

muaré m moiré

mucam|a f (*Arg*) servant. **~o** m (*Arg*) servant

mucos|idad f mucus. **~o** a mucous

muchach|a f girl; (*sirvienta*) servant, maid. **~o** m boy, lad; (*criado*) servant

muchedumbre f crowd

muchísimo a very much. **—adv** a lot

mucho a much (*pl* **many**), a lot of. **—pron** a lot; (*personas*) many (people). **—adv** a lot, very much; (*de tiempo*) long, a long time. **ni ~ menos** by no means. **por ~ que** however much

muda f change of clothing; (*de animales*) moult. **~ble** a changeable; (*personas*) fickle. **~nza** f change; (*de casa*) removal. **~r** vt/i change. **~rse** (*de ropa*) change one's clothes; (*de casa*) move (house)

mudéjar a & m & f Mudéjar

mud|ez f dumbness. **~o** a dumb; (*callado*) silent

mueble a movable. **—m** piece of furniture

mueca f grimace, face. **hacer una ~** pull a face

muela f (*diente*) tooth; (*diente molar*) molar; (*piedra de afilar*) grindstone; (*piedra de molino*) millstone

muelle a soft. **—m** spring; (*naut*) wharf; (*malecón*) jetty

muérdago m mistletoe

muero vb véase **morir**

muert|e f death; (*homicidio*) murder. **~o** a dead; (*matado*, *fam*) killed; (*colores*) pale. **—m**

dead person; (*cadáver*) body, corpse

muesca f nick; (*ranura*) slot

muestra f sample; (*prueba*) proof; (*modelo*) model; (*seal*) sign. **~rio** m collection of samples

muestro vb véase **mostrar**

muevo vb véase **mover**

mugi|do m moo. **~r** [14] vi moo; (*fig*) roar

mugr|e m dirt. **~iento** a dirty, filthy

mugrón m sucker

muguete m lily of the valley

mujer f woman; (*esposa*) wife. **—int** my dear! **~iego** a (*hombre*) fond of the women. **~il** a womanly. **~ío** m (crowd of) women. **~zuela** f prostitute

mújol m mullet

mula f mule; (*Mex*) unsaleable goods. **~da** f drove of mules

mulato a & m mulatto

mulero m muleteer

mulet|a f crutch; (*fig*) support; (*toreo*) stick with a red flag

mulo m mule

multa f fine. **~r** vt fine

multi... pref multi...

multicolor a multicolour(ed)

multicopista m copying machine

multiforme a multiform

multilateral a multilateral

multilingüe a multilingual

multimillonario m multimillionaire

múltiple a multiple

multiplic|ación f multiplication. **~ar** [7] vt multiply. **~arse** vpr multiply; (*fig*) go out of one's way. **~idad** f multiplicity

múltiplo a & m multiple

multitud f multitude, crowd. **~inario** a multitudinous

mulli|do a soft. **—m** stuffing. **~r** [22] vt soften

mund|ano a wordly; (*de la sociedad elegante*) society. —*m* socialite. ~**ial** a world-wide. **la segunda guerra** ~**ial** the Second World War. ~**illo** m world, circles. ~**o** m world. ~**ología** f worldly wisdom. **todo el** ~ everybody

munición f ammunition; (*provisiones*) supplies

municip|al a municipal. ~**alidad** f municipality. ~**io** m municipality; (*ayuntamiento*) town council

mun|ificencia f munificence. ~**ífico** a munificent

muñe|ca f (*anat*) wrist; (*juguete*) doll; (*maniquí*) dummy. ~**co** m boy doll. ~**quera** f wristband

muñón m stump

mura|l a mural, wall. —*m* mural. ~**lla** f (*city*) wall. ~**r** vt wall

murciélago m bat

murga f street band; (*lata*) bore, nuisance. **dar la** ~ bother, be a pain (*fam*)

murmullo m (*de personas*) whisper(ing), murmur(ing); (*del agua*) rippling; (*del viento*) sighing, rustle

murmura|ción f gossip. ~**dor** a gossiping. —*m* gossip. —*r* vi murmur; (*hablar en voz baja*) whisper; (*quejarse en voz baja*) mutter; (*criticar*) gossip

muro m wall

murri|a f depression. ~**o** a depressed

mus m card game

musa f muse

musaraña f shrew

muscula|r a muscular. ~**tura** f muscles

músculo m muscle

musculoso a muscular

muselina f muslin

museo m museum. ~ **de arte** art gallery

musgaño m shrew

musgo m moss. ~**so** a mossy

música f music

musical a & m musical

músico a musical. —*m* musician

music|ología f musicology. ~**ólogo** m musicologist

musitar vt/i mumble

muslímico a Muslim

muslo m thigh

mustela a weasel

musti|arse vpr wither, wilt. ~**o** a (*plantas*) withered; (*cosas*) faded; (*personas*) gloomy; (*Mex, hipócrita*) hypocritical

musulmán a & m Muslim

muta|bilidad f mutability. ~**ción** f change; (*en biología*) mutation

mutila|ción f mutilation. ~**do** a crippled. —*m* cripple. ~**r** vt mutilate; cripple, maim (*persona*)

mutis m (*en el teatro*) exit. ~**mo** m silence

mutu|alidad f mutuality; (*asociación*) friendly society. ~**amente** adv mutually. ~**o** a mutual

muy adv very; (*demasiado*) too

N

nab|a f swede. ~**o** m turnip

nácar m mother-of-pearl

nac|er [11] vi be born; (*huevo*) hatch; (*planta*) sprout. ~**ido** a born. ~**iente** a (*sol*) rising. ~**imiento** m birth; (*de río*) source; (*belén*) crib. **dar** ~**imiento a** give rise to. **lugar** m **de** ~**imiento** place of birth. **recien** ~**ido** newborn. **volver a** ~**er** have a narrow escape

naci|ón f nation. ~**onal** a national. ~**onalidad** f nationality. ~**onalismo** m nationalism. ~**onalista** m & f

nationalist. **~onalizar** [10] *vt*
nationalize. **~onalizarse** *vpr*
become naturalized

nada *pron* nothing, not
anything. —*adv* not at all. **¡~ de
eso!** nothing of the sort! **antes
de ~** first of all. **¡de ~!** (*después
de 'gracias'*) don't mention it!
para ~ (not) at all. **por ~ del
mundo** not for anything in the
world

nada|dor *m* swimmer. **~r** *vi*
swim

nadería *f* trifle

nadie *pron* no one, nobody

nado *adv.* **a ~** swimming

nafta *f* (*LAm, gasolina*) petrol,
(*Brit*), gas (*Amer*)

nailon *m* nylon

naipe *m* (playing) card. **juegos
mpl de ~s** card games

nalga *f* buttock. **~s** *fpl* bottom

nana *f* lullaby

Nápoles *m* Naples

naranj|a *a & m* orange. **~ada** *f*
orangeade. **~al** *m* orange grove.
~o *m* orange tree

narcótico *a & m* narcotic

nariz *f* nose; (*orificio de la nariz*)
nostril. **¡narices!** rubbish!

narra|ción *f* narration. **~dor** *m*
narrator. **~r** *vt* tell. **~tivo** *a*
narrative

nasal *a* nasal

nata *f* cream

natación *f* swimming

natal *a* birth; (*pueblo etc*) home.
~idad *f* birth rate

natillas *fpl* custard

natividad *f* nativity

nativo *a & m* native

nato *a* born

natural *a* natural. —*m* native.
~eza *f* nature; (*nacionalidad*)
nationality; (*ciudadanía*) natur-
alization. **~eza muerta** still
life. **~idad** *f* naturalness. **~ista**
m & f naturalist. **~izar** [10] *vt*
naturalize. **~izarse** *vpr* become

naturalized. **~mente** *adv* naturally. —*int* of course!

naufrag|ar [12] *vi* (*barco*) sink;
(*persona*) be shipwrecked; (*fig*)
fail. **~io** *m* shipwreck

náufrago *a* shipwrecked. —*m*
shipwrecked person

náusea *f* nausea. **dar ~s a uno**
make s.o. feel sick. **sentir ~s**
feel sick

nauseabundo *a* sickening

náutico *a* nautical

navaja *f* penknife; (*de afeitar*)
razor. **~zo** *m* slash

naval *a* naval

Navarra *f* Navarre

nave *f* ship; (*de iglesia*) nave. **~
espacial** spaceship. **quemar
las ~s** burn one's boats

navega|ble *a* navigable; (*barco*)
seaworthy. **~ción** *f* navigation.
~nte *m & f* navigator. **~r** [12] *vi*
sail; (*avión*) fly

Navid|ad *f* Christmas. **~eño** *a*
Christmas. **en ~ades** at Christmas. **¡feliz ~ad!** Happy Christmas! **por ~ad** at Christmas

navío *m* ship

nazi *a & m & f* Nazi

neblina *f* mist

nebuloso *a* misty; (*fig*) vague

necedad *f* foolishness. **decir ~es**
talk nonsense. **hacer una ~** do
sth stupid

necesari|amente *adv* neces-
sarily. **~o** *a* necessary

necesi|dad *f* necessity; (*pobreza*)
poverty. **~dades** *fpl* hardships.
por ~dad (out) of necessity.
~tado *a* in need (de of); (*pobre*)
needy. **~tar** *vt* need. —*vi.* **~tar
de** need

necio *a* silly. —*m* idiot

necrología *f* obituary column

néctar *m* nectar

nectarina *f* nectarine

nefasto *a* unfortunate, ominous

nega|ción *f* negation; (*desmen-
timiento*) denial; (*gram*) negative. **~do** *a* incompetent. **~r** [1 &**

12] *vt* deny; *(rehusar)* refuse.
~**rse** *vpr.* ~**rse a** refuse. ~**tiva** *f*
negative; *(acción)* denial; *(acción
de rehusar)* refusal. ~**tivo a** & *m*
negative

negligen|cia *f* negligence. ~**te** *a*
negligent

negoci|able *a* negotiable.
~**ación** *f* negotiation. ~**ante** *m*
& *f* dealer. ~**ar** *vt/i* negotiate.
~**ar en** trade in. ~**o** *m* business;
(com, trato) deal. ~**os** *mpl* business. **hombre de** ~**os**
businessman

negr|a *f* Negress; *(mus)* crotchet.
~**o** *a* black; *(persona)* Negro.
—*m* *(color)* black; *(persona)*
Negro. ~**ura** *f* blackness.
~**uzco** *a* blackish

nene *m* & *f* baby, child

nenúfar *m* water lily

neo... *pref* neo...

neocelandés *a* from New
Zealand. — *m* New Zealander

neolítico *a* Neolithic

neón *m* neon

nepotismo *m* nepotism

nervio *m* nerve; *(tendón)* sinew;
(bot) vein. ~**sidad** *f*, ~**sismo** *m*
nervousness; *(impaciencia)* im-
patience. ~**so** *a* nervous; *(de
temperamento)* highly-strung.
crispar los ~**s a uno** *(fam)* get
on s.o.'s nerves. **ponerse** ~**so**
get excited

neto *a* clear; *(verdad)* simple;
(com) net

neumático *a* pneumatic. —*m*
tyre

neumonía *f* pneumonia

neuralgia *f* neuralgia

neur|ología *f* neurolgy. ~**ólogo**
m neurologist

neur|osis *f* neurosis. ~**ótico** *a*
neurotic

neutr|al *a* neutral. ~**alidad** *f*
neutrality. ~**alizar** [10] *vt* neut-
ralize. ~**o** *a* neutral; *(gram)*
neuter

neutrón *m* neutron

neva|da *f* snowfall. ~**r** [1] *vi*
snow. ~**sca** *f* blizzard

nevera *f* fridge *(Brit, fam)*,
refrigerator

nevisca *f* light snowfall. ~**r** [7] *vi*
snow lightly

nexo *m* link

ni *conj* nor, neither; *(ni siquiera)*
not even. ~**...** ~ neither... nor. ~
que as if. ~ **siquiera** not even

Nicaragua *f* Nicaragua

nicaragüense *a* & *m* & *f*
Nicaraguan

nicotina *f* nicotine

nicho *m* niche

nido *m* nest; *(de ladrones)* den;
(escondrijo) hiding-place

niebla *f* fog; *(neblina)* mist. **hay**
~ it's foggy

niet|a *f* granddaughter. ~**o** *m*
grandson. ~**os** *mpl* grand-
children

nieve *f* snow; *(LAm, helado)*
ice-cream

Nigeria *f* Nigeria. ~**no** *a* Ni-
gerian

niki *m* T-shirt

nilón *m* nylon

nimbo *m* halo

nim|iedad *f* triviality. ~**o** *a*
insignificant

ninfa *f* nymph

ninfea *f* water lily

ningún *véase* **ninguno**

ninguno *a (delante de nombre
masculino en singular* ningún)
no, not any. —*pron* none; *(persona)* no-one, nobody; *(de dos)*
neither. **de ninguna manera,
de ningún modo** by no means.
en ninguna parte nowhere

niñ|a *f (little)* girl. ~**ada** *f* child-
ish thing. ~**era** *f* nanny. ~**ería** *f*
childish thing. ~**ez** *f* childhood.
~**o** *a* childish. —*m (little)* boy.
de ~**o** as a child. **desde** ~**o** from
childhood

níquel *m* nickel

níspero *m* medlar

nitidez *f* clearness

nítido *a* clear; *(foto)* sharp

nitrato *m* nitrate

nítrico *a* nitric

nitrógeno *m* nitrogen

nivel *m* level; *(fig)* standard. **~ar** *vt* level. **~arse** *vpr* become level. **~ de vida** standard of living

no *adv* not; *(como respuesta)* no. ¿~? isn't it? **~ más** only. **¡a que ~!** I bet you don't! **¡cómo ~!** of course! **Felipe ~ tiene hijos** Felipe has no children. **¡que ~!** certainly not!

nobil·iario *a* noble. **~le** *a* & *m* & *f* noble. **~leza** *f* nobility

noción *f* notion. **nociones** *fpl* rudiments

nocivo *a* harmful

nocturno *a* nocturnal; *(clase)* evening; *(tren etc)* night. **—m** nocturne

noche *f* night. **~ vieja** New Year's Eve. **de ~** at night. **hacer ~** spend the night. **media ~** midnight. **por la ~** at night

Nochebuena *f* Christmas Eve

nodo *m (Esp, película)* newsreel

nodriza *f* nanny

nódulo *m* nodule

nogal *m* walnut(-tree)

nómada *a* nomadic. **—m** & *f* nomad

nombr·adía *f* fame. **~ado** *a* famous; *(susodicho)* aforementioned. **~amiento** *m* appointment. **~ar** *vt* appoint; *(citar)* mention. **~e** *m* name; *(gram)* noun; *(fama)* renown. **~e de pila** Christian name. **en ~e de** in the name of. **no tener ~e** be unspeakable. **poner de ~e** call

nomeolvides *m* *invar* forget-me-not

nómina *f* payroll

nominal *a* nominal. **~tivo** *a* & *m* nominative. **~tivo a** *(cheque etc)* made out to

non *a* odd. **—m** odd number

nonada *f* trifle

nono *a* ninth

nordeste *a* *(región)* northeastern; *(viento)* northeasterly. **—m** north-east

nórdico *a* northern. **—m** northerner

noria *f* water-wheel; *(en una feria)* ferris wheel

norma *f* rule

normal *a* normal. **—f** teachers' training college. **~idad** *f* normality *(Brit)*, normalcy *(Amer)*. **~izar** [10] *vt* normalize. **~mente** *adv* normally, usually

Normandía *f* Normandy

noroeste *a* *(región)* northwestern; *(viento)* northwesterly. **—m** north-west

norte *m* north; *(viento)* north wind; *(fig, meta)* aim

Norteamérica *f* (North) America

norteamericano *a* & *m* (North) American

norteño *a* northern. **—m** northerner

Noruega *f* Norway

noruego *a* & *m* Norwegian

nos *pron (acusativo)* us; *(dativo)* (to) us; *(reflexivo)* (to) ourselves; *(recíproco)* (to) each other

nosotros *pron* we; *(con prep)* us

nostalg·ia *f* nostalgia; *(de casa, de patria)* homesickness. **~álgico** *a* nostalgic

nota *f* note; *(de examen etc)* mark. **~ble** *a* notable. **~ción** *f* notation. **~r** *vt* notice; *(apuntar)* note down. **de mala ~** notorious. **de ~** famous. **digno de ~** notable. **es de ~r** it should be noted. **hacerse ~r** stand out

notario *m* notary

notici·a *f* (piece of) news. **~as** *fpl* news. **~ario** *m* news. **~ero** *a* news. **atrasado de ~as** behind the times. **tener ~as de** hear from

notifica|ción f notification. **~r** [7] vt notify

notori|edad f notoriety. **~o** a well-known; (*evidente*) obvious

novato m novice

novecientos a & m nine hundred

noved|ad f newness; (*noticia*) news; (*cambio*) change; (*moda*) latest fashion. **~oso** a (LAm) novel. **sin ~ad** no news

novel|a f novel. **~ista** m & f novelist

noveno a ninth

novent|a a & m ninety; (*nonagésimo*) ninetieth. **~ón** a & m ninety-year-old

novia f girlfriend; (*prometida*) fiancée; (*en boda*) bride. **~zgo** m engagement

novicio m novice

noviembre m November

novilunio m new moon

novill|a f heifer. **~o** m bullock. **hacer ~os** play truant

novio m boyfriend; (*prometido*) fiancé; (*en boda*) bridegroom. **los ~s** the bride and groom

novísimo a very new

nub|arrón m large dark cloud. **~e** f cloud; (*de insectos etc*) swarm. **~lado** a cloudy, overcast. **—m** cloud. **~lar** vt cloud. **~larse** vpr become cloudy. **~loso** a cloudy

nuca f back of the neck

nuclear a nuclear

núcleo m nucleus

nudillo m knuckle

nudis|mo m nudism. **~ta** m & f nudist

nudo m knot; (*de asunto etc*) crux. **~so** a knotty. **tener un ~ en la garganta** have a lump in one's throat

nuera f daughter-in-law

nuestro a our; (*pospuesto al sustantivo*) of ours. **—pron** ours. **~**

nueva f (piece of) news. **~s** fpl news. **~mente** adv newly; (*de nuevo*) again

Nueva York f New York

Nueva Zelanda f, **Nueva Zelandia** f (LAm) New Zealand

nueve a & m nine

nuevo a new. **de ~** again

nuez f nut; (*del nogal*) walnut; (*anat*) Adam's apple. **~ de Adán** Adam's apple. **~ moscada** nutmeg

nul|idad f incompetence; (*persona, fam*) nonentity. **~o** a useless; (*jurid*) null and void

numera|ción f numbering. **~eral** a & m numeral. **~erar** vt number. **~érico** a numerical

número m number; (*arábigo, romano*) numeral; (*de zapatos etc*) size. **sin ~** countless

numeroso a numerous

nunca adv never, not ever. **~ (ja)más** never again. **casi ~** hardly ever. **más que ~** more than ever

nupcia|l a nuptial. **~s** fpl wedding. **banquete ~l** wedding breakfast

nutria f otter

nutri|ción f nutrition. **~do** a nourished, fed; (*fig*) large; (*aplausos*) loud; (*fuego*) heavy. **~r** vt nourish, feed; (*fig*) feed. **~tivo** a nutritious. **valor ~tivo** nutritional value

nylon m nylon

Ñ

ña f (LAm, fam) Mrs

ñacanina f (Arg) poisonous snake

ñame *m* yam

ñapindá *m* (*Arg*) mimosa

ñato (*LAm*) snub-nosed

ño *m* (*LAm*, *fam*) Mr

ñoñ|ería *f*, ~ez *f* insipidity. ~o *a* insipid; (*tímido*) bashful; (*quisquilloso*) prudish

ñu *m* gnu

O

o *conj* or. ~ bien rather. ~... ~ either... or. ~ sea in other words

oasis *m invar* oasis

obcecar [7] *vt* blind

obed|ecer [11] *vt/i* obey. ~iencia *f* obedience. ~iente *a* obedient

obelisco *m* obelisk

obertura *f* overture

obes|idad *f* obesity. ~o *a* obese

obispo *m* bishop

obje|ción *f* objection. ~tar *vt/i* object

objetiv|idad *f* objectivity. ~o *a* objective. —*m* objective; (*foto etc*) lens

objeto *m* object

objetor *m* objector. ~ de conciencia conscientious objector

oblicuo *a* oblique; (*mirada*) sidelong

obliga|ción *f* obligation; (*com*) bond. ~do *a* obliged; (*forzoso*) obligatory; ~r [12] *vt* force, oblige. ~rse *vpr*. ~rse a undertake to. ~torio *a* obligatory

oboe *m* oboe; (*músico*) oboist

obra *f* work; (*de teatro*) play; (*construcción*) building. ~ maestra masterpiece. en ~s under construction. por ~ de thanks to. ~r *vt* do; (*construir*) build

obrero *a* labour; (*clase*) working. —*m* workman; (*en fábrica*) worker

obscen|idad *f* obscenity. ~o *a* obscene

obscu... *véase* oscu...

obsequi|ar *vt* lavish attention on. ~ar con give, present with. ~o *m* gift, present; (*agasajo*) attention. ~oso *a* obliging. en ~o de in honour of

observa|ción *f* observation; (*objeción*) objection. ~dor *m* observer. ~ncia *f* observance. ~nte *a* observant. ~r *vt* observe; (*notar*) notice. ~rse *vpr* be noted. ~torio *m* observatory. hacer una ~ción make a remark

obses|ión *f* obsession. ~ionar *vt* obsess. ~ivo *a* obsessive. ~o *a* obsessed

obst|aculizar [10] *vt* hinder. ~áculo *m* obstacle

obstante. no ~ *adv* however, nevertheless. —*prep* in spite of

obstar *vi*. ~ para prevent

obstétrico *a* obstetric

obstina|ción *f* obstinacy. ~do *a* obstinate. ~rse *vpr* be obstinate. ~rse en (+ *infinitivo*) persist in (+ *gerundio*)

obstru|cción *f* obstruction. ~ir [17] *vt* obstruct

obtener [40] *vt* get, obtain

obtura|dor *m* (*foto*) shutter. ~r *vt* plug; fill (*muela etc*)

obtuso *a* obtuse

obviar *vt* remove

obvio *a* obvious

oca *f* goose

ocasi|ón *f* occasion; (*oportunidad*) opportunity; (*motivo*) cause. ~onal *a* chance. ~onar *vt* cause. aprovechar la ~ón take the opportunity. con ~ón de on the occasion of. de ~ón bargain; (*usado*) second-hand. en ~ones sometimes. perder una ~ón miss a chance

ocaso *m* sunset; (*fig*) decline

occident|al *a* western. —*m & f* westerner. ~e *m* west

océano *m* ocean

ocio m idleness; (*tiempo libre*) leisure time. **~sidad** f idleness. **~so** a idle; (*inútil*) pointless

oclusión f occlusion

octano m octane. **índice** m de **~** octane number, octane rating

octav|a f octave. **~o** a & m eighth

octogenario a & m octogenarian, eighty-year-old

oct|ogonal a octagonal. **~ógono** m octagon

octubre m October

oculista m & f oculist, optician

ocular a eye

ocult|ar vt hide. **~arse** vpr hide. **~o** a hidden; (*secreto*) secret

ocupa|ción f occupation. **~do** a occupied; (*persona*) busy. **~nte** m occupant. **~r** vt occupy. **~rse** vpr look after

ocurr|encia f occurrence, event; (*idea*) idea; (*que tiene gracia*) witty remark. **~ir** vi happen. **~irse** vpr occur. **¿qué ~e?** what's the matter? **se me ~e que** it occurs to me that

ochent|a a & m eighty. **~ón** a & m eighty-year-old

ocho a & m eight. **~cientos** a & m eight hundred

oda f ode

odi|ar vt hate. **~o** m hatred. **~oso** a hateful

odisea f odyssey

oeste m west; (*viento*) west wind

ofen|der vt offend; (*insultar*) insult. **~derse** vpr take offence. **~sa** f offence. **~siva** f offensive. **~sivo** a offensive

oferta f offer; (*en subasta*) bid; (*regalo*) gift. **~s de empleo** situations vacant. **en ~** on (special) offer

oficial a official. —m skilled worker; (*funcionario*) civil servant; (*mil*) officer. **~a** f skilled (woman) worker

oficin|a f office. **~a de colocación** employment office. **~a**

de Estado government office. **~a de turismo** tourist office. **~ista** m & f office worker. **horas** fpl de **~a** business hours

oficio m job; (*profesión*) profession; (*puesto*) post. **~so** a (*no oficial*) unofficial

ofrec|er [11] vt offer; give (*fiesta, banquete etc*); (*prometer*) promise. **~erse** vpr (*persona*) volunteer; (*cosa*) occur. **~imiento** m offer

ofrenda f offering. **~r** vt offer

ofusca|ción f blindness; (*confusión*) confusion. **~r** [7] vt blind; (*confundir*) confuse. **~rse** vpr be dazzled

ogro m ogre

oí|ble a audible. **~da** f hearing. **~do** m hearing; (*anat*) ear. **al ~do** in one's ear. **de ~das** by hearsay. **de ~do** by ear. **duro de ~do** hard of hearing

oigo vb véase **oír**

oír [50] vt hear. **~ misa** go to mass. **¡oiga!** listen!; (*al teléfono*) hello!

ojal m buttonhole

ojalá int I hope so! —conj if only

ojea|da f glance. **~r** vt eye; (*para inspeccionar*) see; (*ahuyentar*) scare away. **dar una ~da a**, **echar una ~da a** glance at

ojeras fpl (*del ojo*) bags

ojeriza f ill will. **tener ~ a** have a grudge against

ojete m eyelet

ojo m eye; (*de cerradura*) keyhole; (*de un puente*) span. **¡~!** careful!

ola f wave

olé int bravo!

olea|da f wave. **~je** m swell

óleo m oil; (*cuadro*) oil painting

oleoducto m oil pipeline

oler [2, *las formas que empezarían por* ue *se escriben* hue] vt smell; (*curiosear*) pry into;

(*descubrir*) discover. —*vi* smell
(a of)

olfat ear *vt* smell, sniff; (*fig*) sniff
out. ~**o** *m* (sense of) smell; (*fig*)
intuition

olimpiada *f*, **olimpíada** *f* Olympic games, Olympics

olímpico *a* (*juegos*) Olympic

oliv a *f* olive; (*olivo*) olive tree.
~**ar** *m* olive grove. ~**o** *m* olive
tree

olmo *m* elm (tree)

olor *m* smell. ~**oso** *a*
sweet-smelling

olvid adizo *a* forgetful. ~**ar** *vt*
forget. ~**arse** *vpr* forget; (*estar
olvidado*) be forgotten. ~**o** *m*
oblivion; (*acción de olvidar*) for-
getfulness. **se me** ~**ó** I forgot

olla *f* pot, casserole; (*guisado*)
stew. ~ **a/de presión**, ~
exprés pressure cooker. ~ **po-
drida** Spanish stew

ombligo *m* navel

ominoso *a* awful, abominable

omi sión *f* omission; (*olvido*) for-
getfulness. ~**tir** *vt* omit

ómnibus *a* omnibus

omnipotente *a* omnipotent

omóplato *m*, **omoplato** *m*
shoulder blade

once *a* & *m* eleven

ond a *f* wave. ~**a corta** short
wave. ~**a larga** long wave.
~**ear** *vi* wave; (*agua*) ripple.
~**ulación** *f* undulation; (*del
pelo*) wave. ~**ular** *vi* wave. **longitud** *f* **de** ~**a** wavelength

oneroso *a* onerous

ónice *m* onyx

onomástico *a*. **día** ~, **fiesta
onomástica** name-day

ONU *abrev* (*Organización de las
Naciones Unidas*) UN, United
Nations

onza *f* ounce

opa *a* (*LAm*) stupid

opaco *a* opaque; (*fig*) dull

ópalo *m* opal

opción *f* option

ópera *f* opera

opera ción *f* operation; (*com*)
transaction. ~**dor** *m* operator;
(*cirujano*) surgeon; (*TV*) cam-
eraman. ~**r** *vt* operate on; work
(*milagro* etc). —*vi* operate; (*com*)
deal. ~**rse** *vpr* occur; (*med*) have
an operation. ~**torio** *a* operative

opereta *f* operetta

opin ar *vi* think. ~**ión** *f* opinion.
la ~**ión pública** public opinion

opio *m* opium

opone nte *a* opposing. —*m* & *f*
opponent. ~**r** *vt* oppose; offer (*resistencia*); raise (*objeción*). ~**rse**
vpr be opposed; (*dos personas*)
oppose each other

oporto *m* port (wine)

oportun idad *f* opportunity;
(*cualidad de oportuno*) time-
liness. ~**ista** *m* & *f* opportunist.
~**o** *a* opportune; (*apropiado*)
suitable

oposi ción *f* opposition. ~**ciones**
fpl competition, public examination. ~**tor** *m* candidate

opres ión *f* oppression; (*ahogo*)
difficulty in breathing. ~**ivo** *a*
oppressive. ~**o** *a* oppressed.
~**or** *m* oppressor

oprimir *vt* squeeze; press (*botón
etc*); (*ropa*) be too tight for; (*fig*)
oppress

oprobio *m* disgrace

optar *vi* choose. ~ **por** opt for

ópti ca *f* optics; (*tienda*)
optician's (shop). ~**o** *a*
optic(al). —*m* optician

optimis mo *m* optimism. ~**ta** *a*
optimistic. —*m* & *f* optimist

opuesto *a* opposite; (*enemigo*)
opposed

opulen cia *f* opulence. ~**to** *a*
opulent

oración *f* prayer; (*discurso*)
speech; (*gram*) sentence

oráculo *m* oracle

orador *m* speaker

oral *a* oral

orar *vi* pray

oratoria *f* oratory. **∼o** *a* oratorical. —*m* (*mus*) oratorio

orbe *m* orb

órbita *f* orbit

orden *m & f* order; (*Mex, porción*) portion. **∼ado** *a* tidy. **∼ del día** agenda. **órdenes** *fpl* **sagradas** Holy Orders. **a sus órdenes** (*esp Mex*) can I help you? **en ∼** in order. **por ∼** in turn

ordenador *m* computer

ordenanza *f* order. —*m* (*mil*) orderly. **∼r** *vt* put in order; (*mandar*) order; (*relig*) ordain

ordeñar *vt* milk

ordinal *a & m* ordinal

ordinario *a* ordinary; (*grosero*) common

orear *vt* air

orégano *m* oregano

oreja *f* ear

orfanato *m* orphanage

orfebre *m* goldsmith, silversmith

orfeón *m* choral society

orgánico *a* organic

organigrama *m* flow chart

organillo *m* barrel-organ

organismo *m* organism

organista *m & f* organist

organización *f* organization. **∼dor** *m* organizer. **∼r** [10] *vt* organize. **∼rse** *vpr* get organized

órgano *m* organ

orgasmo *m* orgasm

orgía *f* orgy

orgullo *m* pride. **∼so** *a* proud

orientación *f* direction

oriental *a & m & f* oriental

orientar *vt* position. **∼se** *vpr* point; (*persona*) find one's bearings

oriente *m* east. **O∼ Medio** Middle East

orificio *m* hole

origen *m* origin. **∼inal** *a* original; (*excéntrico*) odd. **∼inalidad** *f* originality. **∼inar** *vt* give rise to. **∼inario** *a* original; (*nativo*) native. **dar ∼en a** give rise to. **ser ∼inario de** come from

orilla *f* (*del mar*) shore; (*de río*) bank; (*borde*) edge

orín *m* rust

orina *f* urine. **∼l** *m* chamber-pot. **∼r** *vi* urinate

oriundo *a*. **∼ de** (*persona*) (originating) from; (*animal etc*) native to

orla *f* border

ornamental *a* ornamental

ornitología *f* ornithology

oro *m* gold. **∼s** *mpl* Spanish card suit. **∼ de ley** 9 carat gold. **hacerse de ∼** make a fortune. **prometer el ∼ y el moro** promise the moon

oropel *m* tinsel

orquesta *f* orchestra. **∼l** *a* orchestral. **∼r** *vt* orchestrate

orquídea *f* orchid

ortiga *f* nettle

ortodoxia *f* orthodoxy. **∼o** *a* orthodox

ortografía *f* spelling

ortopedia *f* orthopaedics. **∼édico** *a* orthopaedic

oruga *f* caterpillar

orzuelo *m* sty

os *pron* (*acusativo*) you; (*dativo*) (to) you; (*reflexivo*) (to) yourselves; (*recíproco*) (to) each other

osadía *f* boldness. **∼o** *a* bold

oscilación *f* swinging; (*de precios*) fluctuation; (*tec*) oscillation. **∼r** *vi* swing; (*precio*) fluctuate; (*tec*) oscillate; (*fig, vacilar*) hesitate

oscurecer [11] *vi* darken; (*fig*) obscure. **∼ecerse** *vpr* grow dark; (*nublarse*) cloud over. **∼idad** *f* darkness; (*fig*) obscurity. **∼o** *a* dark; (*fig*) obscure. **a ∼as** in the dark

óseo a bony

oso m bear. ~ **de felpa**, ~ **de peluche** teddy bear

ostensible a obvious

ostent|ación f ostentation. ~**ar** vt show off; (mostrar) show. ~**oso** a ostentatious

osteoartritis f osteoarthritis

oste|ópata m & f osteopath. ~**opatía** f osteopathy

ostión m (esp Mex) oyster

ostra f oyster

ostracismo m ostracism

Otan abrev (Organización del Tratado del Atlántico Norte) NATO, North Atlantic Treaty Organization

otear vt observe; (escudriñar) scan, survey

otitis f inflammation of the ear

otoño m autumn (Brit), fall (Amer)

otorga|miento m granting; (documento) authorization. ~**r** [12] vt give; (jurid) draw up

otorrinolaringólogo m ear, nose and throat specialist

otro a other; (uno más) another. —pron another (one); (en plural) others; (otra persona) someone else. **el** ~ **lo** the other. **el uno al** ~ one another, each other

ovación f ovation

oval a oval

óvalo m oval

ovario m ovary

oveja f sheep; (hembra) ewe

overol m (LAm) overalls

ovino a sheep

ovillo m ball. **hacerse un** ~ curl up

OVNI abrev (objeto volante no identificado) UFO, unidentified flying object

ovulación f ovulation

oxida|ción f rusting. ~**r** vi rust. ~**rse** vpr go rusty

óxido m oxide

oxígeno m oxygen

oye vb véase **oír**

oyente a listening. —m & f listener

ozono m ozone

P

pabellón m bell tent; (edificio) building; (de instrumento) bell; (bandera) flag

pabilo m wick

paceño a from La Paz. —m person from La Paz

pacer [11] vi graze

pacien|cia f patience. ~**te** a & m & f patient

pacificar [7] vt pacify; reconcile (dos personas). ~**se** vpr calm down

pacífico a peaceful. **el (Océano m)P** ~ the Pacific (Ocean)

pacifis|mo m pacifism. ~**ta** a & m & f pacifist

pact|ar vi agree, make a pact. ~**o** m pact, agreement

pachucho a (fruta) overripe; (persona) poorly

padec|er [11] vt/i suffer (de from); (soportar) bear. ~**imiento** m suffering; (enfermedad) ailment

padrastro m stepfather

padre a (fam) great. —m father. ~**s** mpl parents

padrino m godfather; (en boda) best man

padrón m census

paella f paella

paga f pay, wages. ~**ble** a, ~**dero** a payable

pagano a & m pagan

pagar [12] vt pay; pay for (compras). —vi pay. ~**é** m IOU

página f page

pago m payment

pagoda f pagoda

país _m_ country; (_región_) region. ~ **natal** native land. **el P~ Vasco** the Basque Country. **los P~es Bajos** the Low Countries

paisa|**je** _m_ countryside. ~**no** _a_ of the same country. —_m_ compatriot

paja _f_ straw; (_fig_) nonsense

pajarera _f_ aviary

pájaro _m_ bird. ~ **carpintero** woodpecker

paje _m_ page

Pakistán _m._ **el** ~ Pakistan

pala _f_ shovel; (_laya_) spade; (_en deportes_) bat; (_de tenis_) racquet

palabr|**a** _f_ word; (_habla_) speech. ~**ota** _f_ swear-word. **decir** ~**otas** swear. **pedir la** ~**a** ask to speak. **soltar** ~**otas** swear. **tomar la** ~**a** (begin to) speak

palacio _m_ palace; (_casa grande_) mansion

paladar _m_ palate

paladino _a_ clear; (_público_) public

palanca _f_ lever; (_fig_) influence. ~ **de cambio** (**de velocidades**) gear lever (_Brit_), gear shift (_Amer_)

palangana _f_ wash-basin

palco _m_ (_en el teatro_) box

Palestina _f_ Palestine

palestino _a_ & _m_ Palestinian

palestra _f_ (_fig_) arena

paleta _f_ (_de pintor_) palette; (_de albañil_) trowel

paleto _m_ yokel

paliativo _a_ & _m_ palliative

palide|**cer** [11] _vi_ turn pale. ~**z** _f_ paleness

pálido _a_ pale

palillo _m_ small stick; (_de dientes_) toothpick

palique _m._ **estar de** ~ be chatting

paliza _f_ beating

palizada _f_ fence; (_recinto_) enclosure

palma _f_ (_de la mano_) palm; (_árbol_) palm (tree); (_de dátiles_) date palm. ~**s** _fpl_ applause. ~**da** _f_ slap. ~**das** _fpl_ applause. **dar** ~(**da**)**s** clap. **tocar las** ~**s** clap

palmera _f_ date palm

palmo _m_ span; (_fig, pequeña cantidad_) small amount. ~ **a** ~ inch by inch

palmote|**ar** _vi_ clap, applaud. ~**o** _m_ clapping, applause

palo _m_ stick; (_del teléfono etc_) pole; (_mango_) handle; (_de golf_) club; (_golpe_) blow; (_de naipes_) suit; (_mástil_) mast

paloma _f_ pigeon, dove

palomitas _fpl_ popcorn

palpa|**ble** _a_ palpable. ~**r** _vt_ feel

palpita|**ción** _f_ palpitation. ~**nte** _a_ throbbing. ~**r** _vi_ throb; (_latir_) beat

palta _f_ (_LAm_) avocado pear

pal|**údico** _a_ marshy; (_de paludismo_) malarial. ~**udismo** _m_ malaria

pampa _f_ pampas. ~**ear** _vi_ (_LAm_) travel across the pampas. ~**ero** _a_ of the pampas

pan _m_ bread; (_barra_) loaf. ~ **integral** wholemeal bread (_Brit_), wholewheat bread (_Amer_). ~ **tostado** toast. ~ **rallado** breadcrumbs. **ganarse el** ~ earn one's living

pana _f_ corduroy

panacea _f_ panacea

panader|**ía** _f_ bakery; (_tienda_) baker's (shop). ~**o** _m_ baker

panal _m_ honeycomb

Panamá _m_ Panama

panameño _a_ & _m_ Panamanian

pancarta _f_ placard

panda _m_ panda; (_pandilla_) gang

pander|**eta** _f_ (small) tambourine. ~**o** _m_ tambourine

pandilla _f_ gang

panecillo _m_ (bread) roll

panel _m_ panel

panfleto _m_ pamphlet

pánico m panic

panorama m panorama. **~ámico** a panoramic

panqué m (LAm) pancake

pantaletas fpl (LAm) underpants, knickers

pantal|**ón** m trousers. **~ones** mpl trousers. **~ón corto** shorts. **~ón tejano**, **~ón vaquero** jeans

pantalla f screen; (de lámpara) (lamp)shade

pantano m marsh; (embalse) reservoir. **~so** a boggy

pantera f panther

pantomima f pantomime

pantorrilla f calf

pantufla f slipper

panucho m (Mex) stuffed tortilla

panz|**a** f belly. **~ada** f (hartazgo, fam) bellyful; (golpe, fam) blow in the belly. **~udo** a fat, pot-bellied

pañal m nappy (Brit), diaper (Amer)

pañ|**ería** f draper's (shop). **~o** m material; (de lana) woollen cloth; (trapo) cloth. **~o de cocina** dishcloth; (para secar) tea towel. **~o higiénico** sanitary towel. **en ~os menores** in one's underclothes

pañuelo m handkerchief; (de cabeza) scarf

papa m pope. —f (esp LAm) potato. **~s francesas** (LAm) chips

papá m dad(dy). **~s** mpl parents. **P~ Noel** Father Christmas

papada f (de persona) double chin

papado m papacy

papagayo m parrot

papal a papal

papanatas m inv simpleton

paparrucha f (tontería) silly thing

papaya f pawpaw

papel m paper; (en el teatro etc) role. **~ carbón** carbon paper. **~ celofán** celophane paper. **~ de calcar** carbon paper. **~ de embalar**, **~ de envolver** wrapping paper. **~ de plata** silver paper. **~ de seda** tissue paper. **~era** f waste-paper basket. **~ería** f stationer's (shop). **~eta** f ticket; (para votar) paper. **~ higiénico** toilet paper. **~ pintado** wallpaper. **~ secante** blotting paper. **blanco como el ~** as white as a sheet. **desempeñar un ~**, **hacer un ~** play a role

paperas fpl mumps

paquebote m packet (boat)

paquete m packet; (paquebote) packet (boat); (Mex, asunto difícil) difficult job. **~ postal** parcel

paquistaní a & m Pakistani

par a equal; ⟨número⟩ even. —m couple; ⟨dos cosas iguales⟩ pair; (igual) equal; (título) peer. **a la ~** at the same time; ⟨monedas⟩ at par. **al ~ que** at the same time. **a ~es** two by two. **de ~ en ~** wide open. **sin ~** without equal

para prep for; (hacia) towards; (antes del infinitivo) (in order) to. **~ con** to(wards). ¿**~ qué**? why? **~ que** so that

parabienes mpl congratulations

parábola f (narración) parable

parabrisas m inv windscreen (Brit), windshield (Amer)

paraca f (LAm) strong wind (from the Pacific)

paraca|**ídas** m inv parachute. **~idista** m & f parachutist; (mil) paratrooper

parachoques m inv bumper (Brit), fender (Amer); (rail) buffer

parad|**a** f (acción) stopping; (sitio) stop; (de taxis) rank; (mil) parade. **~ero** m whereabouts;

(alojamiento) lodging. **~o** *a* stationary; *(obrero)* unemployed; *(lento)* slow. **dejar ~o** confuse. **tener mal ~ero** come to a sticky end

paradoja *f* paradox

parador *m* state-owned hotel

parafina *f* paraffin

parafrasear *vt* paraphrase. **~áfrasis** *f inv* paraphrase

paraguas *m inv* umbrella

Paraguay *m* Paraguay

paraguayo *a & m* Paraguayan

paraíso *m* paradise; *(en el teatro)* gallery

paralel|a *f* parallel (line). **~as** *fpl* parallel bars. **~o** *a & m* parallel

par|álisis *f inv* paralysis. **~alítico** *a* paralytic. **~alizar** [10] *vt* paralyse

paramilitar *a* paramilitary

páramo *m* barren plain

parang|ón *m* comparison. **~onar** *vt* compare

paraninfo *m* hall

paranoi|a *f* paranoia. **~co** *a* paranoiac

parapeto *m* parapet; *(fig)* barricade

parapléjico *a & m* paraplegic

parar *vt/i* stop. **~se** *vpr* stop. **sin ~** continuously

pararrayos *m inv* lightning conductor

parásito *a* parasitic. —*m* parasite

parasol *m* parasol

parcela *f* plot. **~r** *vt* divide into plots

parcial *a* partial. **~idad** *f* prejudice; *(pol)* faction. **a tiempo ~** part-time

parco *a* sparing, frugal

parche *m* patch

pardo *a* brown

parear *vt* pair off

parec|er *m* opinion; *(aspecto)* appearance. —*vi* [11] seem; *(asemejarse)* look like; *(aparecer)*

appear. **~erse** *vpr* resemble, look like. **~ido** *a* similar. —*m* similarity. **al ~er** apparently. **a mi ~er** in my opinion. **bien ~ido** good-looking. **me ~e** I think. **¿qué te parece?** what do you think? **según ~e** apparently

pared *f* wall. **~ón** *m* thick wall; *(de ruinas)* standing wall. **~ por medio** next door. **llevar al ~ón** shoot

parej|a *f* pair; *(hombre y mujer)* couple; *(la otra persona)* partner. **~o** *a* alike, the same; *(liso)* smooth

parentela *f* relations. **~sco** *m* relationship

paréntesis *m inv* parenthesis; *(signo ortográfico)* bracket. **entre ~** *(fig)* by the way

paria *m & f* outcast

paridad *f* equality

pariente *m & f* relation, relative

parihuela *f*, **parihuelas** *fpl* stretcher

parir *vt* give birth to. —*vi* have a baby, give birth

París *m* Paris

parisiense *a & m & f*, **parisino** *a & m* Parisian

parking /'parkin/ *m* car park *(Brit)*, parking lot *(Amer)*

parlament|ar *vi* discuss. **~ario** *a* parliamentary. —*m* member of parliament *(Brit)*, congressman *(Amer)*. **~o** *m* parliament

parlanchín *a* talkative. —*m* chatterbox

parmesano *a* Parmesan

paro *m* stoppage; *(desempleo)* unemployment; *(pájaro)* tit

parodia *f* parody. **~r** *vt* parody

parpadear *vi* blink; *(luz)* flicker; *(estrella)* twinkle

párpado *m* eyelid

parque *m* park. ~ **de atrac-**
ciones funfair. ~ **infantil** children's playground. ~ **zoológico**
zoo, zoological gardens

parqué *m* parquet

parquedad *f* frugality; *(mode-*
eración) moderation

parra *f* grapevine

párrafo *m* paragraph

parrilla *f* grill; *(LAm, auto)* radiator grill. ~**da** *f* grill. **a la** ~
grilled

párroco *m* parish priest

parroquia *f* parish; *(iglesia)* parish church. ~**no** *m* parishioner;
(cliente) customer

parsimoni|**a** *f* thrift. ~**oso** *a*
thrifty

parte *m* message; *(informe)*
report. —*f* part; *(porción)* share;
(lado) side; *(jurid)* party. **dar** ~
report. **de mi** ~ for me. **de** ~ **de**
from. **¿de** ~ **de quién?** *(al telé-*
fono) who's speaking? **en**
cualquier ~ anywhere. **en**
gran ~ largely. **en** ~ partly. **en**
todas ~**s** everywhere. **la**
mayor ~ the majority. **nin-**
guna ~ nowhere. **por otra** ~ on
the other hand. **por todas** ~**s**
everywhere

partera *f* midwife

partición *f* sharing out

participa|**ción** *f* participation;
(noticia) notice; *(de lotería)* lottery ticket. ~**nte** *a* parti-
cipating. —*m & f* participant. ~**r**
vt notify. —*vi* take part

participio *m* participle

partícula *f* particle

particular *a* particular; *(clase)*
private. —*m* matter. ~**idad** *f*
peculiarity. ~**izar** [10] *vt* distinguish; *(detallar)* give details
about. **en** ~ in particular. **nada**
de ~ nothing special

partida *f* departure; *(en registro)*
entry; *(documento)* certificate;

(juego) game; *(de gente)* group.
mala ~ dirty trick

partidario *a & m* partisan. ~ **de**
keen on

partido *a* divided. —*m* *(pol)*
party; *(encuentro)* match, game;
(equipo) team. ~**r** *vt* divide;
(romper) break; *(repartir)* share;
crack *(nueces)*. —*vi* leave; *(empe-*
zar) start. ~**rse** *vpr* *(romperse)*
break; *(dividirse)* split. **a** ~**r de**
(starting) from

partitura *f* *(mus)* score

parto *m* birth; *(fig)* creation.
estar de ~ be in labour

párvulo *m*. **colegio de** ~**s**
nursery school

pasa *f* raisin. ~ **de Corinto** currant. ~ **de Esmirna** sultana

pasa|**ble** *a* passable. ~**da** *f* pass-
ing; *(de puntos)* row. ~**dero** *a*
passable. ~**dizo** *m* passage. ~**do**
a past; *(día, mes etc)* last; *(antic-*
uado) old-fashioned; *(comida)*
bad, off. ~**do mañana** the day
after tomorrow. ~**dor** *m* bolt;
(de pelo) hair-slide; *(culin)*
strainer. **de** ~**da** in passing. **el**
lunes ~**do** last Monday

pasaje *m* passage; *(naut)* crossing; *(viajeros)* passengers. ~**ro** *a*
passing. —*m* passenger

pasamano(s) *m* handrail; *(bar-*
andilla de escalera) banister(s)

pasamontañas *m inv* Balaclava
(helmet)

pasaporte *m* passport

pasar *vt* pass; *(poner)* put; *(fil-*
trar) strain; spend *(tiempo)*; *(tra-*
gar) swallow; show *(película)*;
(tolerar) tolerate, overlook; give
(mensaje, enfermedad). —*vi*
pass; *(suceder)* happen; *(ir)* go;
(venir) come; *(tiempo)* go by. ~
de have no interest in. ~**se** *vpr*
(pasar) be over; *(flo-*
res) wither; *(comida)* go bad;
spend *(tiempo)*; *(excederse)* go
too far. ~**lo bien** have a good

time. ~ **por alto** leave out. **como si no hubiese pasado nada** as if nothing had happened. **lo que pasa es que** the fact is that. **pase lo que pase** whatever happens. **¡pase Vd!** come in!, go in! **¡que lo pases bien!** have a good time! **¿qué pasa?** what's the matter?, what's happening?

pasarela *f* footbridge; (*naut*) gangway

pasatiempo *m* hobby, pastime

pascua *f* (*fiesta de los hebreos*) Passover; (*de Resurrección*) Easter; (*Navidad*) Christmas. ~**s** *fpl* Christmas. **hacer la ~ a uno** mess things up for s.o. **¡y santas ~s!** and that's that!

pase *m* pass

pase|ante *m & f* passer-by. ~**ar** *vt* take for a walk; (*exhibir*) show off. —*vi* go for a walk; (*en coche etc*) go for a ride. ~**arse** *vpr* go for a walk; (*en coche etc*) go for a ride. ~**o** *m* walk; (*en coche etc*) ride; (*calle*) avenue. ~**o marítimo** promenade. **dar un ~o** go for a walk. **¡vete a ~o!** (*fam*) go away!, get lost! (*fam*)

pasillo *m* passage

pasión *f* passion

pasiv|idad *f* passiveness. ~**o** *a* passive

pasm|ar *vt* astonish. ~**arse** *vpr* be astonished. ~**o** *m* astonishment. ~**oso** *a* astonishing

paso *a* (*fruta*) dried —*m* step; (*acción de pasar*) passing; (*huella*) footprint; (*manera de andar*) walk; (*camino*) way through; (*entre montañas*) pass; (*estrecho*) strait(s). ~ **a nivel** level crossing (*Brit*), grade crossing (*Amer*). ~ **de cebra** Zebra crossing. ~ **de peatones** pedestrian crossing. ~ **elevado** flyover. **a cada** ~ at every turn. **a dos** ~**s** very near. **al** ~ **que** at the same time as. **a** ~ **lento** slowly. **ceda el** ~ give way. **de** ~ in passing. **de** ~ **por** on the way through. **prohibido el** ~ no entry

pasodoble *m* (*baile*) pasodoble

pasota *m & f* drop-out

pasta *f* paste; (*masa*) dough; (*dinero*, *fam*) money. ~**s** *fpl* pasta; (*pasteles*) pastries. ~ **de dientes**, ~ **dentífrica** toothpaste

pastar *vt/i* graze

pastel *m* cake; (*empanada*) pie; (*lápiz*) pastel. ~**ería** *f* cakes; (*tienda*) cake shop, confectioner's

paste(u)rizar [10] *vt* pasteurize

pastiche *m* pastiche

pastilla *f* pastille; (*de jabón*) bar; (*de chocolate*) piece

pastinaca *f* parsnip

pasto *m* pasture; (*hierba*) grass; (*Mex*, *césped*) lawn. ~**r** *m* shepherd; (*relig*) minister. ~**ral** *a* pastoral

pata *f* leg; (*pie*) paw, foot. ~**s** *fpl* legs. **a cuatro** ~**s** on all fours. **meter la** ~ put one's foot in it. **tener mala** ~ have bad luck

pataca *f* Jerusalem artichoke

pata|da *f* kick. ~**lear** *vt* stamp; (*niño pequeño*) kick

pataplum *int* crash!

patata *f* potato. ~**s fritas** chips (*Brit*), French fries (*Amer*). ~**s fritas (a la inglesa)** (potato) crisps (*Brit*), potato chips (*Amer*)

patent|ar *vt* patent. ~**e** *a* obvious. —*f* licence. ~**e de invención** patent

patern|al *a* paternal; (*cariño etc*) fatherly. ~**idad** *f* paternity. ~**o** *a* paternal; (*cariño etc*) fatherly

patético *a* moving

patillas *fpl* sideburns

patín *m* skate; (*juguete*) scooter

pátina *f* patina

patina|dero *m* skating rink. **∼je** *m* skating. **∼r** *vi* skate; (*deslizarse*) slide. **∼zo** *m* skid; (*fig, fam*) blunder

patio *m* patio. **∼ de butacas** stalls (*Brit*), orchestra (*Amer*)

pato *m* duck

patol|ogía *f* pathology. **∼ógico** *a* pathological

patoso *a* clumsy

patraña *f* hoax

patria *f* native land

patriarca *m* patriarch

patrimonio *m* inheritance; (*fig*) heritage

patri|ota *a* patriotic. **—***m* & *f* patriot. **∼ótico** *a* patriotic. **∼otismo** *m* patriotism

patrocin|ar *vt* sponsor. **∼io** *m* sponsorship

patr|ón *m* patron; (*jefe*) boss; (*de pensión etc*) landlord; (*modelo*) pattern. **∼onato** *m* patronage; (*fundación*) trust, foundation

patrulla *f* patrol; (*fig, cuadrilla*) group. **∼r** *vt/i* patrol

paulatinamente *adv* slowly

pausa *f* pause. **∼do** *a* slow

pauta *f* guideline

pavimen|tar *vt* pave. **∼o** *m* pavement

pavo *m* turkey. **∼ real** peacock

pavor *m* terror. **∼oso** *a* terrifying

payas|ada *f* buffoonery. **∼o** *m* clown

paz *f* peace. **La P∼** La Paz

peaje *m* toll

peatón *m* pedestrian

pebet|a *f* (*LAm*) little girl. **∼e** *m* little boy

peca *f* freckle

peca|do *m* sin; (*defecto*) fault. **∼dor** *m* sinner. **∼minoso** *a* sinful. **∼r** [7] *vi* sin

pecoso *a* freckled

pectoral *a* pectoral; (*para la tos*) cough

peculiar *a* peculiar, particular. **∼idad** *f* peculiarity

pech|era *f* front. **∼ero** *m* bib. **∼o** *m* chest; (*de mujer*) breast; (*fig, corazón*) heart. **∼uga** *f* breast. **dar el ∼o** breast-feed *(a un niño)*; (*afrontar*) confront. **tomar a ∼o** take to heart

pedagogo *m* teacher

pedal *m* pedal. **∼ear** *vi* pedal

pedante *a* pedantic

pedazo *m* piece, bit. **a ∼s** in pieces. **hacer ∼s** break to pieces. **hacerse ∼s** fall to pieces

pedernal *m* flint

pedestal *m* pedestal

pedestre *a* pedestrian

pediatra *m & f* paediatrician

pedicuro *m* chiropodist

pedi|do *m* order. **∼r** [5] *vt* ask (for); (*com, en restaurante*) order. **—***vi* ask. **∼r prestado** borrow

pegadizo *a* sticky; (*mus*) catchy

pegajoso *a* sticky

pega|r [12] *vt* stick (on); (*coser*) sew on; give *(enfermedad etc)*; (*juntar*) join; (*golpear*) hit; (*dar*) give. **—***vi* stick. **∼rse** *vpr* stick; (*pelearse*) hit each other. **∼r fuego a** set fire to. **∼tina** *f* sticker

pein|ado *m* hairstyle. **∼ar** *vt* comb. **∼arse** *vpr* comb one's hair. **∼e** *m* comb. **∼eta** *f* ornamental comb

p.ej. *abrev* (*por ejemplo*) e.g., for example

pela|do *a* (*fruta*) peeled; (*cabeza*) bald; (*número*) exactly; (*terreno*) barren. **—***m* bare patch. **∼dura** *f* (*acción*) peeling; (*mondadura*) peelings

pela|je *m* (*de animal*) fur; (*fig, aspecto*) appearance. **∼mbre** *m* (*de animal*) fur; (*de persona*) thick hair

pelar *vt* cut the hair; (*mondar*) peel; (*quitar el pellejo*) skin

peldaño *m* step; *(de escalera de mano)* rung

pelea *f* fight; *(discusión)* quarrel. **~r** *vi* fight. **~rse** *vpr* fight

peletería *f* fur shop

peliagudo *a* difficult, tricky

pelícano *m*, **pelicano** *m* pelican

película *f* film *(esp Brit)*, movie *(Amer)*. **~ de dibujos** (animados) cartoon (film). **~ en colores** colour film

peligro *m* danger; *(riesgo)* risk. **~so** *a* dangerous. **poner en ~** endanger

pelirrojo *a* red-haired

pelma *m* & *f*, **pelmazo** *m* bore, nuisance

pelo *m* hair; *(de barba o bigote)* whisker. **~ón** *a* bald; *(rapado)* with very short hair. **no tener ~os en la lengua** be outspoken. **tomar el ~o a uno** pull s.o.'s leg

pelota *f* ball; *(juego vasco)* pelota. **~ vasca** pelota. **en ~(s)** naked

pelotera *f* squabble

pelotilla *f*. **hacer la ~ a** ingratiate o.s. with

peluca *f* wig

peludo *a* hairy

peluquer|ía *f* *(de mujer)* hairdresser's; *(de hombre)* barber's. **~o** *m* *(de mujer)* hairdresser; *(de hombre)* barber

pelusa *f* down; *(celos, fam)* jealousy

pelvis *f* pelvis

pella *f* lump

pelleja *f*, **pellejo** *m* skin

pellizc|ar [7] *vt* pinch. **~o** *m* pinch

pena *f* sadness; *(dificultad)* difficulty. **~ de muerte** death penalty. **a duras ~s** with difficulty. **da ~ que** it's a pity that. **me da ~ que** I'm sorry that. **merecer la ~** be worthwhile. **¡qué ~!** what a pity! **valer la ~** be worthwhile

penacho *m* tuft; *(fig)* plume

penal *a* penal; *(criminal)* criminal. **—** *m* prison. **~idad** *f* suffering; *(jurid)* penalty. **~izar** [10] *vt* penalize

penalty *m* penalty

penar *vt* punish. **—** *vi* suffer. **~ por** long for

pend|er *vi* hang. **~iente** *a* hanging; *(terreno)* sloping; *(cuenta)* outstanding; *(fig)* *(asunto etc)* pending. **—** *m* earring. **—** *f* slope

pendón *m* banner

péndulo *a* hanging. **—** *m* pendulum

pene *m* penis

penetra|nte *a* penetrating; *(sonido)* piercing; *(herida)* deep. **~r** *vt* penetrate; *(fig)* pierce; *(entender)* understand. **—** *vi* penetrate; *(entrar)* go into

penicilina *f* penicillin

pen|ínsula *f* peninsula. **~ínsula Ibérica** Iberian Peninsula. **~insular** *a* peninsular

penique *m* penny

peniten|cia *f* penitence; *(castigo)* penance. **~te** *a* & *m* & *f* penitent

penoso *a* painful; *(difícil)* difficult

pensa|do *a* thought. **~dor** *m* thinker. **~miento** *m* thought. **~r** [1] *vt* think; *(considerar)* consider. **—** *vi* think. **~r en** think about. **~tivo** *a* thoughtful. **bien ~do** all things considered. **cuando menos se piensa** when least expected. **menos ~do** least expected. **¡ni ~rlo!** certainly not! **pienso que sí** I think so

pensi|ón *f* pension; *(casa de huéspedes)* guest-house. **~ón completa** full board. **~onista** *m* & *f* pensioner; *(huésped)* lodger; *(escol)* boarder

pentágono *m* pentagon

pentagrama *m* stave

Pentecostés *m* Whitsun; *(fiesta judía)* Pentecost

penúltimo *a* & *m* penultimate, last but one

penumbra *f* half-light

penuria *f* shortage

peña *f* rock; *(de amigos)* group; *(club)* club. **~ón** *m* rock. **el peñón de Gibraltar** The Rock (of Gibraltar)

peón *m* labourer; *(en ajedrez)* pawn; *(en damas)* piece; *(juguete)* (spinning) top

peonía *f* peony

peonza *f* (spinning) top

peor *a* *(comparativo)* worse; *(superlativo)* worst. —*adv* worse. **~ que** ~ worse and worse. **lo** ~ the worst thing. **tanto** ~ so much the worse

pepinillo *m* gherkin. **~o** *m* cucumber. **(no) me importa un** ~**o** I couldn't care less

pepita *f* pip

pepitoria *f* fricassee

pequeñez *f* smallness; *(minucia)* trifle. **~ito** *a* very small, tiny. **~o** *a* small, little. **de** ~**o** as a child. **en** ~**o** in miniature

pequinés *m* *(perro)* Pekingese

pera *f* *(fruta)* pear. **~l** *m* pear (tree)

percance *m* setback

percatarse *vpr*. ~ **de** notice

percepción *f* perception. **~ptible** *a* perceptible. **~ptivo** *a* perceptive. **~ibir** *vt* perceive; earn *(dinero)*

percusión *f* percussion

percutir *vt* tap

percha *f* hanger; *(de aves)* perch. **de** ~ off the peg

perdedor *a* losing. —*m* loser. **~r** [1] *vt* lose; *(malgastar)* waste; miss *(tren etc)*. —*vi* lose; *(tela)* fade. **~rse** *vpr* get lost; *(desaparecer)* disappear; *(despedirse)* be wasted; *(estropearse)* be spoilt. **echar(se) a** ~**r** spoil

pérdida *f* loss; *(de líquido)* leak; *(de tiempo)* waste

perdido *a* lost

perdiz *f* partridge

perdón *m* pardon, forgiveness. —*int* sorry! **~onar** *vt* excuse, forgive; *(jurid)* pardon. **¡~one (Vd)!** sorry! **pedir** ~ apologize

perdurable *a* lasting. **~r** *vi* last

perecedero *a* perishable. **~r** [11] *vi* perish

peregrinación *f* pilgrimage. **~ar** *vi* go on a pilgrimage; *(fig, fam)* travel. **~o** *a* strange. —*m* pilgrim

perejil *m* parsley

perengano *m* so-and-so

perenne *a* everlasting; *(bot)* perennial

perentorio *a* peremptory

pereza *f* laziness. **~oso** *a* lazy

perfección *f* perfection. **~cionamiento** *m* perfection; *(mejora)* improvement. **~cionar** *vt* perfect; *(mejorar)* improve. **~cionista** *m* & *f* perfectionist. **~tamente** *adv* perfectly. —*int* of course! **~to** *a* perfect; *(completo)* complete. **a la ~ción** perfectly, to perfection

perfidia *f* treachery

pérfido *a* treacherous

perfil *m* profile; *(contorno)* outline; **~es** *mpl* *(fig, rasgos)* features. **~ado** *a* *(bien terminado)* well-finished. **~ar** *vt* draw in profile; *(fig)* put the finishing touches to

perforación *f* perforation. **~do** *m* perforation. **~dora** *f* punch. **~r** *vt* pierce, perforate; punch *(papel, tarjeta etc)*

perfumar *vt* perfume. **~arse** *vpr* put perfume on. **~e** *m* perfume, scent. **~ería** *f* perfumery

pergamino *m* parchment

pericia *f* expertise

pericón *m* popular Argentinian dance

perif|eria *f* (*de población*) outskirts. **~érico** *a* peripheral

perilla *f* (*barba*) goatee

perímetro *m* perimeter

periódico *a* periodic(al). —*m* newspaper

periodis|mo *m* journalism. **~ta** *m* & *f* journalist

período *m*, **periodo** *m* period

periquito *m* budgerigar

periscopio *m* periscope

perito *a* & *m* expert

perju|dicar [7] *vt* harm; (*desfavorecer*) not suit. **~dicial** *a* harmful. **~icio** *m* harm. **en ~icio de** to the detriment of

perjur|ar *vi* perjure o.s. **~io** *m* perjury

perla *f* pearl. **de ~s** *adv* very well. —*a* excellent

permane|cer [11] *vi* remain. **~ncia** *f* permanence; (*estancia*) stay. **~nte** *a* permanent. —*f* perm

permeable *a* permeable

permi|sible *a* permissible. **~sivo** *a* permissive. **~so** *m* permission; (*documento*) licence; (*mil etc*) leave. **~so de conducción**, **~so de conducir** (*Brit*), driver's license (*Amer*). **~tir** *vt* allow, permit. **~tirse** *vpr* be allowed. **con ~so** excuse me. *¿me ~te?* may I?

permutación *f* exchange; (*math*) permutation

pernicioso *a* pernicious; (*persona*) wicked

pernio *m* hinge

perno *m* bolt

pero *conj* but. —*m* fault; (*objeción*) objection

perogrullada *f* platitude

perol *m* pan

peronista *m* & *f* follower of Juan Perón

perorar *vi* make a speech

perpendicular *a* & *f* perpendicular

perpetrar *vt* perpetrate

perpetu|ar [21] *vt* perpetuate. **~o** *a* perpetual

perplej|idad *f* perplexity. **~o** *a* perplexed

perr|a *f* (*animal*) bitch; (*moneda*) coin, penny (*Brit*), cent (*Amer*); (*rabieta*) tantrum. **~era** *f* kennel. **~ería** *f* (*mala jugada*) dirty trick; (*palabra*) harsh word. **~o** *a* awful. —*m* dog. **~o corredor** hound. **~o de aguas** spaniel. **~o del hortelano** dog in the manger. **~o galgo** greyhound. **de ~os** awful. **estar sin una ~a** be broke

persa *a* & *m* & *f* Persian

perse|cución *f* pursuit; (*tormento*) persecution. **~guir** [5 & 13] *vt* pursue; (*atormentar*) persecute

persevera|ncia *f* perseverance. **~nte** *a* persevering. **~r** *vi* persevere

persiana *f* (Venetian) blind

persist|encia *f* persistence. **~ente** *a* persistent. **~ir** *vi* persist

person|a *f* person. **~as** *fpl* people. **~aje** *m* (*persona importante*) important person; (*de obra literaria*) character. **~al** *a* personal; (*para una persona*) single. —*m* staff. **~alidad** *f* personality. **~arse** *vpr* appear in person. **~ificar** [7] *vt* personify. **~ificación** *f* personification

perspectiva *f* perspective

perspica|cia *f* shrewdness; (*de vista*) keen eye-sight. **~z** *a* shrewd; (*vista*) keen

persua|dir *vt* persuade. **~sión** *f* persuasion. **~sivo** *a* persuasive

pertenecer [11] *vi* belong

pertinaz *a* persistent

pertinente *a* relevant

perturba|ción f disturbance. **~r** vt perturb

Perú m. **el ~** Peru

peruano a & m Peruvian

perver|sión f perversion. **~so** a perverse. **—m** pervert. **~tir** [4] vt pervert

pervivir vi live on

pesa f weight. **~dez** f weight; (de cabeza etc) heaviness; (lentitud) sluggishness; (cualidad de fastidioso) tediousness; (cosa fastidiosa) bore, nuisance

pesadilla f nightmare

pesad|o a heavy; (lento) slow; (duro) hard; (aburrido) boring, tedious. **~umbre** f (pena) sorrow

pésame m sympathy, condolences

pesar vt/i weigh. **—m** sorrow; (remordimiento) regret. **a ~ de (que)** in spite of. **me pesa que** I'm sorry that. **pese a (que)** in spite of

pesario m pessary

pesca f fishing; (peces) fish; (pescado) catch. **~da** f hake. **~dería** f fish shop. **~dilla** f whiting. **~do** m fish. **~dor** a fishing. **—m** fisherman. **~r** [7] vt catch. **—vi** fish. **ir de ~** go fishing

pescuezo m neck

pesebre m manger

pesero m (Mex) minibus taxi

peseta f peseta; (Mex) twenty-five centavos

pesim|ismo m pessimism. **~ta** a pessimistic. **—m & f** pessimist

pésimo a very bad, awful

peso m weight; (moneda) peso. **~ bruto** gross weight. **~ neto** net weight. **a ~** by weight. **de ~** influential

pesquero a fishing

pesquisa f inquiry

pestañ|a f eyelash. **~ear** vi blink. **sin ~ear** without batting an eyelid

pest|e f plague; (hedor) stench. **~icida** m pesticide. **~ilencia** f pestilence; (hedor) stench

pestillo m bolt

pestiño m pancake with honey

petaca f tobacco case; (LAm, maleta) suitcase

pétalo m petal

petardo m firework

petición f request; (escrito) petition. **a ~ de** at the request of

petirrojo m robin

petrificar [7] vt petrify

petr|óleo m oil. **~olero** a oil. **—m** oil tanker. **~olífero** a oil-bearing

petulante a arrogant

peyorativo a pejorative

pez f fish; (substancia negruzca) pitch. **~ espada** swordfish

pezón m nipple; (bot) stalk

pezuña f hoof

piada f chirp

piadoso a compassionate; (devoto) devout

pian|ista m & f pianist. **~o** m piano. **~o de cola** grand piano

piar [20] vi chirp

pib|a f (LAm) little girl. **~e** m (LAm) little boy

picad|illo m mince; (guiso) stew. **~o** a perforated; (carne) minced; (ofendido) offended; (mar) choppy; (diente) bad. **~ura** f bite, sting; (de polilla) moth hole

picante a hot; (palabras etc) cutting

picaporte m door-handle; (aldaba) knocker

picar [7] vt prick, pierce; (ave) peck; (insecto, pez) bite; (avispa) sting; (comer poco) pick at; mince (carne). **—vi** prick; (ave) peck; (insecto, pez) bite; (sol) scorch; (sabor fuerte) be hot. **~ alto** aim high

picard|ear vt corrupt. **~ía** f wickedness; (travesura) naughty thing

picaresco *a* roguish; ⟨*literatura*⟩ picaresque

pícaro *a* villainous; ⟨*niño*⟩ mischievous. —*m* rogue

picatoste *m* toast; ⟨*frito*⟩ fried bread

picazón *f* itch

pico *m* beak; ⟨*punta*⟩ corner; ⟨*herramienta*⟩ pickaxe; ⟨*cima*⟩ peak. ~**tear** *vt* peck; ⟨*comer, fam*⟩ pick at. **y** ~ ⟨*con tiempo*⟩ a little after; ⟨*con cantidad*⟩ a little more than

picudo *a* pointed

pichona *f* (*fig*) darling; ~**ón** *m* pigeon

pido *vb véase* **pedir**

pie *m* foot; ⟨*bot, de vaso*⟩ stem. ~ **cuadrado** square foot. **a cuatro** ~**s** on all fours. **al** ~ **de la letra** literally. **a** ~ on foot. **a** ~(**s**) **juntillas** (*fig*) firmly. **buscarle tres** ~**s al gato** split hairs. **de** ~ standing (up). **de** ~**s a cabeza** from head to foot. **en** ~ standing (up). **ponerse de/en** ~ stand up

piedad *f* pity; ⟨*relig*⟩ piety

piedra *f* stone; ⟨*de mechero*⟩ flint; ⟨*granizo*⟩ hailstone

piel *f* skin; ⟨*cuero*⟩ leather. **artículos de** ~ leather goods

pienso *vb véase* **pensar**

pierdo *vb véase* **perder**

pierna *f* leg. **estirar las** ~**s** stretch one's legs

pieza *f* piece; ⟨*parte*⟩ part; ⟨*obra teatral*⟩ play; ⟨*moneda*⟩ coin; ⟨*habitación*⟩ room. ~ **de recambio** spare part

pífano *m* fife

pigmentación *f* pigmentation. ~**o** *m* pigment

pigmeo *a* & *m* pygmy

pijama *m* pyjamas

pila *f* ⟨*montón*⟩ pile; ⟨*recipiente*⟩ basin; ⟨*eléctrica*⟩ battery. ~ **bautismal** font

píldora *f* pill

pilotar *vt* pilot. ~**o** *m* pilot

pillaje *m* pillage. ~**r** *vt* pillage; ⟨*alcanzar, agarrar*⟩ catch; ⟨*atropellar*⟩ run over

pillo *a* wicked. —*m* rogue

pimentero *m* ⟨*vasija*⟩ pepperpot. ~**entón** *m* paprika, cayenne pepper. ~**ienta** *f* pepper. ~**iento** *m* pepper. **grano** *m* **de** ~**ienta** peppercorn

pináculo *m* pinnacle

pinar *m* pine forest

pincel *m* paintbrush. ~**ada** *f* brush-stroke. **la última** ~**ada** (*fig*) the finishing touch

pinchar *vt* pierce, prick; puncture ⟨*neumático*⟩; (*fig, incitar*) push; ⟨*med, fam*⟩ give an injection to. ~**azo** *m* prick; ⟨*en neumático*⟩ puncture. ~**itos** *mpl* kebab(s); ⟨*tapas*⟩ savoury snacks. ~**o** *m* point

pingajo *m* rag. ~**o** *m* rag

ping-pong *m* table tennis, ping-pong

pingüino *m* penguin

pino *m* pine (tree)

pinta *f* spot; (*fig, aspecto*) appearance. ~**ada** *f* graffiti. ~**ar** *vt* paint. ~**arse** *vpr* put on make-up. ~**or** *m* painter. ~**or de brocha gorda** painter and decorator. ~**oresco** *a* picturesque. ~**ura** *f* painting. **no** ~**a nada** (*fig*) it doesn't count. **tener** ~**a de** look like

pinza *f* (clothes-)peg ⟨*Brit*⟩; (clothes-)pin ⟨*Amer*⟩; ⟨*de cangrejo etc*⟩ claw. ~**s** *fpl* tweezers

pinzón *m* chaffinch

piña *f* pine cone; ⟨*ananás*⟩ pineapple; (*fig, grupo*) group. ~**ón** *m* ⟨*semilla*⟩ pine nut

pío *a* pious; ⟨*caballo*⟩ piebald. —*m* chirp. **no decir (ni)** ~ not say a word

piocha *f* pickaxe

piojo *m* louse

pionero *m* pioneer

pipa f pipe; (semilla) seed; (de girasol) sunflower seed

pipián m (LAm) stew

pique m resentment; (rivalidad) rivalry. **irse a ~** sink

piqueta f pickaxe

piquete m picket

piragua f canoe

pirámide f pyramid

pirata m & f pirate

Pirineos mpl Pyrenees

piropo m (fam) compliment

piruet|a f pirouette. **~ear** vi pirouette

pirulí m lollipop

pisa|da f footstep; (huella) footprint. **~papeles** m invar paperweight. **~r** vt tread on; (apretar) press; (fig) walk over. —vi tread. **no ~r el césped** keep off the grass

piscina f swimming pool; (para peces) fish-pond

Piscis m Pisces

piso m floor; (vivienda) flat (Brit), apartment (Amer); (de zapato) sole

pisotear vt trample (on)

pista f track; (fig, indicio) clue. **~ de aterrizaje** runway. **~ de baile** dance floor. **~ de hielo** skating-rink. **~ de tenis** tennis court

pistacho m pistachio (nut)

pisto m fried vegetables

pistol|a f pistol. **~era** f holster. **~ero** m gunman

pistón m piston

pit|ar vt whistle at. —vi blow a whistle; (auto) sound one's horn. **~ido** m whistle

pitill|era f cigarette case. **~o** m cigarette

pito m whistle; (auto) horn

pitón m python

pitorre|arse vpr. **~arse de** make fun of. **~o** m teasing

pitorro m spout

pivote m pivot

pizarr|a f slate; (encerrado) blackboard. **~ón** m (LAm) blackboard

pizca f (fam) tiny piece; (de sal) pinch. **ni ~** not at all

pizz|a f pizza. **~ería** f pizzeria

placa f plate; (conmemorativa) plaque; (distintivo) badge

pláceme m congratulations

place|ntero a pleasant. **~r** [32] vt please. **me ~** I like. —m pleasure

plácido a placid

plaga f plague; (fig, calamidad) disaster; (fig, abundancia) glut. **~r** [12] vt fill

plagi|ar vt plagiarize. **~o** m plagiarism

plan m plan; (med) course of treatment. **a todo ~** on a grand scale. **en ~ de** as

plana f (llanura) plain; (página) page. **en primera ~** on the front page

plancha f iron; (lámina) sheet. **~do** m ironing. **~r** vt/i iron. **a la ~** grilled. **tirarse una ~** put one's foot in it

planeador m glider

planear vt plan. —vi glide

planeta m planet. **~rio** a planetary. —m planetarium

planicie f plain

planifica|ción f planning. **~r** [7] vt plan

planilla f (LAm) list

plano a flat. —m plane; (de ciudad) plan. **primer ~** foreground; (foto) close-up

planta f (anat) sole; (bot, fábrica) plant; (plano) ground plan; (piso) floor. **~ baja** ground floor (Brit), first floor (Amer)

planta|ción f plantation. **~do** a planted. **~r** vt plant; deal (golpe). **~r en la calle** throw out. **~rse** vpr stand; (fig) stand firm. **bien ~do** good-looking

plantear vt (exponer) expound; (causar) create; raise (cuestión)

plantilla f insole; (*modelo*) pattern; (*personal*) personnel

plaqué m plate

plasma m plasma

plástico a & m plastic

plata f silver; (*fig, dinero, fam*) money. ~ **de ley** sterling silver. ~ **alemana** nickel silver

plataforma f platform

plátano m plane (tree); (*fruta*) banana; (*platanar*) banana tree

platea f stalls (*Brit*), orchestra (*Amer*)

plateado a silver-plated; (*color de plata*) silver

pl|ática f chat, talk. ~**aticar** [7] vi chat, talk

platija f plaice

platillo m saucer; (*mus*) cymbal. ~ **volante** flying saucer

platino m platinum. ~**s** mpl (*auto*) points

plato m plate; (*comida*) dish; (*parte de una comida*) course

platónico a platonic

plausible a plausible; (*loable*) praiseworthy

playa f beach; (*fig*) seaside

plaza f square; (*mercado*) market; (*sitio*) place; (*empleo*) job. ~ **de toros** bullring

plazco vb véase **placer**

plazo m period; (*pago*) instalment; (*fecha*) date. **comprar a ~s** buy on hire purchase (*Brit*), buy on the installment plan (*Amer*)

plazuela f little square

pleamar f high tide

plebe f common people. ~**yo** a & m plebeian

plebiscito m plebiscite

plectro m plectrum

plega|ble a pliable; (*silla etc*) folding. ~**r** [1 & 12] vt fold. ~**rse** vpr bend; (*fig*) give way

pleito m (court) case; (*fig*) dispute

plenilunio m full moon

plen|itud f fullness; (*fig*) height. ~**o** a full. **en ~o día** in broad daylight. **en ~o verano** at the height of the summer

pleuresía f pleuresy

plieg|o m sheet. ~**ue** m fold; (*en ropa*) pleat

plinto m plinth

plisar vt pleat

plom|ero m (*esp LAm*) plumber. ~**o** m lead; (*elec*) fuse. **de ~o** lead

pluma f feather; (*para escribir*) pen. ~ **estilográfica** fountain pen. ~**je** m plumage

plúmbeo a leaden

plum|ero m feather duster; (*para plumas, lapices etc*) pencil-case. ~**ón** m down

plural a & m plural. ~**idad** f plurality; (*mayoría*) majority. **en ~** in the plural

pluriempleo m having more than one job

plus m bonus

pluscuamperfecto m pluperfect

plusvalía f appreciation

plut|ocracia f plutocracy. ~**ócrata** m & f plutocrat. ~**ocrático** a plutocratic

plutonio m plutonium

pluvial a rain

pobla|ción f population; (*ciudad*) city, town; (*pueblo*) village. ~**do** a populated. —m village. ~**r** [2] vt populate; (*habitar*) inhabit. ~**rse** vpr get crowded

pobre a poor. —m & f poor person; (*fig*) poor thing. **¡~cito!** poor (little) thing! **¡~ de mí!** poor (old) me! ~**za** f poverty

pocilga f pigsty

poción f potion

poco a not much, little; (*en plural*) few; (*unos*) a few. —m (a) little. —adv little, not much; (*con adjetivo*) not very; (*poco tiempo*) not long. ~ **a** little by little, gradually. **a ~ de** soon after.

dentro de ~ soon. hace ~ not long ago. poca cosa nothing much. por ~ (fam) nearly

podar vt prune

poder [33] vi be able. no pudo venir he couldn't come. ¿puedo hacer algo? can I do anything? ¿puedo pasar? may I come in? —m power. ~es mpl públicos authorities. ~oso a powerful. en el ~ in power. no ~ con not be able to cope with; (no aguantar) not be able to stand. no ~ más be exhausted; (estar harto de algo) not be able to manage any more. no ~ menos que not be able to help. puede que it is possible that. puede ser it is possible. ¿se puede ...? may I ...?

podrido a rotten

po|ema m poem. ~esía f poetry; (poema) poem. ~eta m poet. ~ético a poetic

polaco a Polish. —m Pole; (lengua) Polish

polar a polar. estrella ~ polestar

polarizar [10] vt polarize

polca f polka

polea f pulley

pol|émica f controversy. ~émico a polemic(al). ~emizar [10] vi argue

polen m pollen

policía f police (force); (persona) policewoman. —m policeman. ~co a police; (novela etc) detective

policlínica f clinic, hospital

policromo, policromo a polychrome

polideportivo m sports centre

poliéster m polyester

poliestireno m polystyrene

polietileno m polythene

pol|igamia f polygamy. ~ígamo a polygamous

polígloto m & f polyglot

polígono m polygon

polilla f moth

polio(mielitis) f polio(myelitis)

pólipo m polyp

politécnic|a f polytechnic. ~o a polytechnic

polític|a f politics. ~o a political; (pariente) -in-law. —m politician. padre m ~o father-in-law

póliza f document; (de seguros) policy

polo m pole; (helado) ice lolly (Brit); (juego) polo. ~ helado ice lolly (Brit). ~ norte North Pole

Polonia f Poland

poltrona f armchair

polución f (contaminación) pollution

polv|areda f cloud of dust; (fig, escándalo) scandal. ~era f compact. ~o m powder; (suciedad) dust. ~os mpl powder. en ~o powdered. estar hecho ~o be exhausted. quitar el ~ dust

pólvora f gunpowder; (fuegos artificiales) fireworks

polvor|iento a dusty. ~ón m Spanish Christmas shortcake

poll|ada f brood. ~era f (para niños) baby-walker; (LAm, falda) skirt. ~ería f poultry shop. ~o m chicken; (gallo joven) chick

pomada f ointment

pomelo m grapefruit

pómez a. piedra f ~ pumice stone

pomp|a f bubble; (esplendor) pomp. ~as fúnebres funeral. ~oso a pompous; (espléndido) splendid

pómulo m cheek; (hueso) cheekbone

poncha|do a (Mex) punctured, flat. ~r vt (Mex) puncture

ponche m punch

poncho m poncho

ponderar vt (alabar) speak highly of

poner [34] *vt* put; put on ‹*ropa, obra de teatro, TV etc*›; (*suponer*) suppose; lay ‹*la mesa, un huevo*›; (*hacer*) make; (*contribuir*) contribute; give ‹*nombre*›; show ‹*película, interés*›; open ‹*una tienda*›; equip ‹*una casa*›. **~vi** lay. **~se** *vpr* put o.s.; (*volverse*) get; put on ‹*ropa*›; ‹*sol*› set. **~ con** (*al teléfono*) put through to. **~ en claro** clarify. **~ por escrito** put into writing. **~ una multa** fine. **~se** a start to. **~se a mal con uno** fall out with s.o.

pongamos let's suppose

pongo *vb véase* **poner**

poniente *m* west; (*viento*) west wind

pont|ificado *m* pontificate. **~ifical** *a* pontifical. **~ificar** [7] *vi* pontificate. **~ífice** *m* pontiff

pontón *m* pontoon

popa *f* stern

popelín *m* poplin

popul|acho *m* masses. **~ar** *a* popular; ‹*lenguaje*› colloquial. **~aridad** *f* popularity. **~arizar** [10] *vt* popularize. **~oso** *a* populous

póquer *m* poker

poquito *m* a little bit. —*adv* a little

por *prep* for; (*para*) (in order) to; (*a través de*) through; (*a causa de*) because of; (*como agente*) by; (*en matemática*) times; (*como función*) as; (*en lugar de*) instead of. **~ la calle** along the street. **~ mí** as for me, for my part. **~ si** in case. **~ todo el país** throughout the country. **50 kilómetros ~ hora** 50 kilometres per hour

porcelana *f* china

porcentaje *m* percentage

porcino *a* pig. —*m* small pig

porción *f* portion; (*de chocolate*) piece

pordiosero *m* beggar

porfía *f* persistence; (*disputa*) dispute. **~iado** *a* persistent. **~iar** [20] *vi* insist. **a ~ía** in competition

pormenor *m* detail

pornograf|ía *f* pornography. **~áfico** *a* pornographic

poro *m* pore. **~so** *a* porous

poroto *m* (*LAm, judía*) bean

porque *conj* because; (*para que*) so that

porqué *m* reason

porquer|ía *f* filth; (*basura*) rubbish; (*grosería*) dirty trick

porra *f* club; (*culin*) fritter

porrón *m* wine jug (with a long spout)

portaaviones *m invar* aircraft-carrier

portada *f* façade; (*de libro*) title page

portador *m* bearer

porta|equipaje(s) *m invar* boot (*Brit*), trunk (*Amer*); (*encima del coche*) roof-rack. **~estandarte** *m* standard-bearer

portal *m* hall; (*puerta principal*) main entrance; (*soportal*) porch

porta|lámparas *m invar* socket. **~ligas** *m invar* suspender belt. **~monedas** *m invar* purse

portarse *vpr* behave

portátil *a* portable

portavoz *m* megaphone; (*fig, persona*) spokesman

portazgo *m* toll

portazo *m* bang. **dar un ~** slam the door

porte *m* transport; (*precio*) carriage. **~ador** *m* carrier

portento *m* marvel

porteño *a* (*de Buenos Aires*) from Buenos Aires. —*m* person from Buenos Aires

porter|ía *f* caretaker's lodge, porter's lodge; (*en deportes*) goal. **~o** *m* caretaker, porter; (*en deportes*) goalkeeper. **~o automático** intercom (*fam*)

portezuela *f* small door; *(auto)* door

pórtico *m* portico

portill|a *f* gate; *(en barco)* port-hole. **~o** *m* opening

portorriqueño *a* Puerto Rican

Portugal *m* Portugal

portugués *a & m* Portuguese

porvenir *m* future

posada *f* guest house; *(mesón)* inn

posaderas *fpl (fam)* bottom

posar *vt* put. **—***vi (pájaro)* perch; *(modelo)* sit. **~se** *vpr* settle

posdata *f* postscript

pose|**edor** *m* owner. **~er** [18] *vt* have, own; *(saber)* know well. **~ído** *a* possessed. **~sión** *f* possession. **~sionar** *vt.* **~sionar de** hand over. **~sionarse** *vpr.* **~sionarse de** take possession of. **~sivo** *a* possessive

posfechar *vt* postdate

posguerra *f* post-war years

posib|**ilidad** *f* possibility. **~le** *a* possible. **de ser ~le** if possible. **en lo ~le** as far as possible. **hacer todo lo ~le para** do everything possible to. **si es ~le** if possible

posición *f* position

positivo *a* positive

poso *m* sediment

posponer [34] *vt* put after; *(diferir)* postpone

posta *f.* **a ~** on purpose

postal *a* postal. **—***f* postcard

poste *m* pole

postergar [12] *vt* pass over; *(diferir)* postpone

posteri|**dad** *f* posterity. **~or** *a* back; *(ulterior)* later. **~ormente** *adv* later

postigo *m* door; *(contraventana)* shutter

postizo *a* false, artificial. **—***m* hairpiece

postra|**do** *a* prostrate. **~r** *vt* prostrate. **~rse** *vpr* prostrate o.s.

postre *m* dessert, sweet *(Brit).* **de ~** for dessert

postular *vt* postulate; collect *(dinero)*

póstumo *a* posthumous

postura *f* position, stance

potable *a* drinkable; *(agua)* drinking

potaje *m* vegetable stew

potasio *m* potassium

pote *m* jar

poten|**cia** *f* power. **~cial** *a & m* potential. **~te** *a* powerful. **en ~cia** potential

potingue *m (fam)* concoction

potr|**a** *f* filly. **~o** *m* colt; *(en gimnasia)* horse. **tener ~a** be lucky

pozo *m* well; *(hoyo seco)* pit; *(de mina)* shaft

pozole *m (Mex)* stew

práctica *f* practice; *(destreza)* skill. **en la ~** in practice. **poner en ~** put into practice

practica|**ble** *a* practicable. **~nte** *m & f* nurse. **~r** [7] *vt* practise; play *(deportes)*; *(ejecutar)* carry out

práctico *a* practical; *(diestro)* skilled. **—***m* practitioner

prad|**era** *f* meadow; *(terreno grande)* prairie. **~o** *m* meadow

pragmático *a* pragmatic

preámbulo *m* preamble

precario *a* precarious

precaución *f* precaution; *(cautela)* caution. **con ~** cautiously

precaver *vt* guard against

prece|**dencia** *f* precedence; *(prioridad)* priority. **~nte** *a* preceding. **—***m* precedent. **~r** *vt/i* precede

precepto *m* precept. **~r** *m* tutor

precia|**do** *a* valuable; *(estimado)* esteemed. **~rse** *vpr* boast

precinto *m* seal

precio *m* price. **~ de venta al público** retail price. **al ~ de** at the cost of. **no tener ~** be priceless. **¿qué ~ tiene?** how much is it?

precios|idad f value; (*cosa preciosa*) beautiful thing. ~**o** a a precious; (*bonito*) beautiful. **¡es una ~idad!** it's beautiful!

precipicio m precipice

precipita|ción f precipitation. ~**damente** adv hastily. ~**do** a hasty. ~**r** vt hurl; (*acelerar*) accelerate; (*apresurar*) hasten. ~**rse** upr throw o.s.; (*correr*) rush; (*actuar sin reflexionar*) act rashly

precis|amente a exactly. ~**ar** vt require; (*determinar*) determine. ~**ión** f precision; (*necesidad*) need. ~**o** a precise; (*necesario*) necessary

preconcebido a preconceived

precoz a early; (*niño*) precocious

precursor m forerunner

predecesor m predecessor

predecir [46]; o [46, *pero imperativo* **predice**, *futuro y condicional regulares*] vt foretell

predestina|ción f predestination. ~**r** vt predestine

prédica f sermon

predicamento m influence

predicar [7] vt/i preach

predic|ción f prediction; (*del tiempo*) forecast

predilec|ción f predilection. ~**to** a favourite

predisponer [34] vt predispose

predomin|ante a predominant. ~**ar** vt dominate. —vi predominate. ~**io** m predominance

preeminente a pre-eminent

prefabricado a prefabricated

prefacio m preface

prefect|o m prefect. ~**ura** f prefecture

prefer|encia f preference. ~**ente** a preferential. ~**ible** a preferable. ~**ido** a favourite. ~**ir** [4] vt prefer. **de ~encia** preferably

prefigurar vt foreshadow

prefij|ar vt fix beforehand; (*gram*) prefix. ~**o** m prefix; (*telefónico*) dialling code

pregón m announcement. ~**onar** vt announce

pregunta f question. ~**r** vt/i ask. ~**rse** upr wonder. **hacer ~s** ask questions

prehistórico a prehistoric

preju|icio m prejudice. ~**zgar** [12] vt prejudge

prelado m prelate

preliminar a & m preliminary

preludio m prelude

premarital a, **prematrimonial** a premarital

prematuro a premature

premedita|ción f premeditation. ~**r** vt premeditate

premi|ar vt give a prize to; (*recompensar*) reward. ~**o** m prize; (*recompensa*) reward; (*com*) premium. ~**o gordo** first prize

premonición f premonition

premura f urgency; (*falta*) lack

prenatal a antenatal

prenda f pledge; (*de vestir*) article of clothing, garment; (*de cama etc*) linen. ~**s** fpl (*cualidades*) talents; (*juego*) forfeits. ~**r** vt captivate. ~**rse** upr be captivated (**de** by); (*enamorarse*) fall in love (**de** with)

prender vt capture; (*sujetar*) fasten. —vi catch; (*arraigar*) take root. ~**se** upr (*encenderse*) catch fire

prensa f press. ~**r** vt press

preñado a pregnant; (*fig*) full

preocupa|ción f worry. ~**do** a worried. ~**r** vt worry. ~**rse** upr worry. ~**rse de** look after. **¡no te preocupes!** don't worry!

prepara|ción f preparation. ~**do** a prepared. —m preparation. ~**r** vt prepare. ~**rse** upr get ready. ~**tivo** a preparatory. —

m preparation. **∼torio** *a* preparatory

preponderancia *f* preponderance

preposición *f* preposition

prepotente *a* powerful; *(fig)* presumptious

prerrogativa *f* prerogative

presa *f* (*acción*) capture; (*cosa*) catch; (*embalse*) dam

presagi|ar *vt* presage. **∼o** *m* omen; (*premonición*) premonition

présbita *a* long-sighted

presbi|teriano *a* & *m* Presbyterian. **∼iterio** *m* presbytery. **∼ítero** *m* priest

prescindir *vi.* **∼ de** do without; (*deshacerse de*) dispense with

prescri|bir (*pp* **prescrito**) *vt* prescribe. **∼pción** *f* prescription

presencia *f* presence; (*aspecto*) appearance. **∼r** *vt* be present at; (*ver*) witness. **en ∼ de** in the presence of

presenta|ble *a* presentable. **∼ción** *f* presentation; (*aspecto*) appearance; (*de una persona a otra*) introduction. **∼dor** *m* presenter. **∼r** *vt* present; (*ofrecer*) offer; (*hacer conocer*) introduce; show (*película*). **∼rse** *vpr* present o.s.; (*hacerse conocer*) introduce o.s.; (*aparecer*) turn up

presente *a* present; (*este*) this. **—**m present. **los ∼s** those present. **tener ∼** remember

presenti|miento *m* presentiment; (*de algo malo*) foreboding. **∼r** [4] *vt* have a presentiment of

preserva|ción *f* preservation. **∼r** *vt* preserve. **∼tivo** *m* condom

presiden|cia *f* presidency; (*de asamblea*) chairmanship. **∼cial** *a* presidential. **∼ta** *f* (woman) president. **∼te** *m* president; (*de*

asamblea) chairman. **∼te del gobierno** leader of the government, prime minister

presidi|ario *m* convict. **∼o** *m* prison

presidir *vt* preside over

presilla *f* fastener

presi|ón *f* pressure. **∼onar** *vt* press; *(fig)* put pressure on. **a ∼ón** under pressure. **hacer ∼ón** press

preso *a* under arrest; *(fig)* stricken. **—**m prisoner

presta|do *a* (*a uno*) lent; (*de uno*) borrowed. **∼mista** *m* & *f* moneylender. **pedir ∼do** borrow

préstamo *m* loan; (*acción de pedir prestado*) borrowing

prestar *vt* lend; give (*ayuda etc*); pay (*atención*). **—**vi lend

prestidigita|ción *f* conjuring. **∼dor** *m* magician

prestigio *m* prestige. **∼so** *a* prestigious

presu|mido *a* presumptuous. **∼mir** *vt* presume. **—**vi be conceited. **∼nción** *f* presumption. **∼nto** *a* presumed. **∼ntuoso** *a* presumptuous

presup|oner [34] *vt* presuppose. **∼uesto** *m* budget

presuroso *a* quick

preten|cioso *a* pretentious. **∼der** *vt* try to; (*afirmar*) claim; (*solicitar*) apply for; (*cortejar*) court. **∼dido** *a* so-called. **∼diente** *m* pretender; (*a una mujer*) suitor. **∼sión** *f* pretension; (*aspiración*) aspiration

pretérito *m* preterite, past

pretexto *m* pretext. **a ∼ de** on the pretext of

prevalec|er [11] *vi* prevail. **∼iente** *a* prevalent

prevalerse [42] *vpr* take advantage

preven|ción *f* prevention; (*prejuicio*) prejudice. **∼ido** *a* ready;

(*precavido*) cautious. ~**ir** [53] *vt*
prepare; (*proveer*) provide; (*precaver*) prevent; (*advertir*) warn.
~**tivo** *a* preventive

prever [43] *vt* foresee; (*prepararse*) plan

previo *a* previous

previs|ible *a* predictable. ~**ión**
f forecast; (*prudencia*) prudence.
~**ión de tiempo** weather forecast. ~**to** *a* foreseen

prima *f* (*pariente*) cousin; (*cantidad*) bonus

primario *a* primary

primate *m* primate; (*fig, persona*) important person

primavera *f* spring. ~**l** *a* spring

primer *a véase* **primero**

primer|a *f* (*auto*) first (gear); (*en tren etc*) first class. ~**o** *a* (*delante de nombre masculino en singular* **primer**) first; (*principal*) main; (*anterior*) former; (*mejor*) best. —*n* (the) first. —*adv* first.
~**a enseñanza** primary education. **a** ~**os de** at the beginning of. **de** ~**a** first-class

primitivo *a* primitive

primo *m* cousin; (*fam*) fool.
hacer el ~ be taken for a ride

primogénito *a* & *m* first-born, eldest

primor *m* delicacy; (*cosa*) beautiful thing

primordial *a* basic

princesa *f* princess

principado *m* principality

principal *a* principal. —*m* (*jefe*) head, boss (*fam*)

príncipe *m* prince

principi|ante *m* & *f* beginner.
~**ar** *vt/i* begin, start. ~**o** *m* beginning; (*moral, idea*) principle; (*origen*) origin. **al** ~**o** at first. **a** ~**o(s) de** at the beginning of. **dar** ~**o a** a start. **desde el** ~**o** from the outset. **en** ~ in principle. ~**os** *mpl* (*nociones*) rudiments

pring|oso *a* greasy. ~**ue** *m* dripping; (*mancha*) grease mark

prior *m* prior. ~**ato** *m* priory

prioridad *f* priority

prisa *f* hurry, haste. **a** ~ quickly.
a toda ~ (*fam*) as quickly as possible. **correr** ~ be urgent. **darse** ~ hurry (up). **de** ~ quickly.
tener ~ be in a hurry

prisi|ón *f* prison; (*encarcelamiento*) imprisonment. ~**onero** *m* prisoner

prism|a *m* prism. ~**áticos** *mpl* binoculars

priva|ción *f* deprivation. ~**do** *a* (*particular*) private. ~**r** *vt* deprive (**de** of); (*prohibir*) prevent (**de** from). —*vi* be popular.
~**tivo** *a* exclusive (**de** to)

privilegi|ado *a* privileged; (*muy bueno*) exceptional. ~**o** *m* privilege

pro *prep* for. —*m* advantage.
—*pref* pro-. **el** ~ **y el contra** the pros and cons. **en** ~ **de** on behalf of. **los** ~**s y los contras** the pros and cons

proa *f* bows

probab|ilidad *f* probability. ~**le** *a* probable, likely. ~**lemente** *adv* probably

proba|dor *m* fitting-room. ~**r** [2] *vt* try; try on (*ropa*); (*demostrar*) prove. —*vi* try. ~**rse** *vpr* try on

probeta *f* test-tube

problem|a *m* problem. ~**ático** *a* problematic

procaz *a* insolent

proced|encia *f* origin. ~**ente** *a* (*razonable*) reasonable. ~**ente de** (coming) from. —*m* **er** *m* conduct. —*vi* proceed. ~**er contra** start legal proceedings against. ~**er de** come from. ~**imiento** *m* procedure; (*sistema*) process; (*jurid*) proceedings

procesador *m*. ~ **de textos** word processor

procesal *a.* **costas ~es** legal costs

procesamiento *m* processing. **~ de textos** word-processing

procesar *vt* prosecute

procesión *f* procession

proceso *m* process; *(jurid)* trial; *(transcurso)* course

proclama *f* proclamation. **~ción** *f* proclamation. **~r** *vt* proclaim

procreación *f* procreation. **~r** *vt* procreate

procurador *m* attorney, solicitor. **~r** *vt* try; *(obtener)* get; *(dar)* give

prodigar [12] *vt* lavish. **~se** *vpr* do one's best

prodigio *m* prodigy; *(milagro)* miracle. **~ioso** *a* prodigious

pródigo *a* prodigal

producción *f* production. **~ir** [47] *vt* produce; *(causar)* cause. **~irse** *vpr (aparecer)* appear; *(suceder)* happen. **~tivo** *a* productive. **~to** *m* product. **~tor** *m* producer. **~to derivado** by-product. **~tos agrícolas** farm produce. **~tos de belleza** cosmetics. **~tos de consumo** consumer goods

proeza *f* exploit

profanación *f* desecration. **~ar** *vt* desecrate. **~o** *a* profane

profecía *f* prophecy

proferir [4] *vt* utter; hurl *‹insultos etc›*

profesar *vt* profess; practise *‹profesión›*. **~ión** *f* profession. **~ional** *a* professional. **~or** *m* teacher; *(en universidad etc)* lecturer. **~orado** *m* teaching profession; *(conjunto de profesores)* staff

profeta *m* prophet. **~ético** *a* prophetic. **~etizar** [10] *vt/i* prophesize

prófugo *a & m* fugitive

profundidad *f* depth. **~o** *a* deep; *(fig)* profound

profusión *f* profusion. **~o** *a* profuse. **con ~ión** profusely

progenie *f* progeny

programa *m* programme; *(de ordenador)* program; *(de estudios)* curriculum. **~ción** *f* programming; *(TV etc)* programmes; *(en periódico)* TV guide. **~r** *vt* programme; program *‹ordenador›*. **~dor** *m* computer programmer

progresar *vi* (make) progress. **~ión** *f* progression. **~ista** *a* progressive. **~ivo** *a* progressive. **~o** *m* progress. **hacer ~os** make progress

prohibición *f* prohibition. **~do** *a* forbidden. **~r** *vt* forbid. **~tivo** *a* prohibitive

prójimo *m* fellow man

prole *f* offspring

proletariado *m* proletariat. **~o** *a & m* proletarian

proliferación *f* proliferation. **~iferar** *vi* proliferate. **~ífico** *a* prolific

prolijo *a* long-winded, extensive

prólogo *m* prologue

prolongar [12] *vt* prolong; *(alargar)* lengthen. **~se** *vpr* go on

promedio *m* average

prometer *vt* promise. **~ter** *vt/i* promise. **~terse** *vpr ‹novios›* get engaged. **~térselas muy felices** have high hopes. **~tida** *f* fiancée. **~tido** *a* promised; *(novios)* engaged. —*m* fiancé

prominencia *f* prominence. **~te** *a* prominent

promiscuidad *f* promiscuity. **~o** *a* promiscuous

promoción *f* promotion

promontorio *m* promontory

promotor *m* promoter. **~ver** [2] *vt* promote; *(causar)* cause

promulgar [12] *vt* promulgate

pronombre *m* pronoun

pronos|ticar [7] *vt* predict. **∼ós-
tico** *m* prediction; (*del tiempo*)
forecast; (*med*) prognosis

pront|itud *f* quickness. **∼o** *a*
quick; (*preparado*) ready. —*adv*
quickly; (*dentro de poco*) soon;
(*temprano*) early. —*m* urge. **al
∼o** at first. **de ∼o** suddenly. **por
lo ∼o** for the time being; (*al
menos*) anyway. **tan ∼o como**
as soon as

pronuncia|ción *f* pronun-
ciation. **∼miento** *m* revolt. **∼r**
vt pronounce; deliver (*discurso*).
∼rse *vpr* be pronounced; (*decla-
rase*) declare o.s.; (*sublevarse*)
rise up

propagación *f* propagation

propaganda *f* propaganda;
(*anuncios*) advertising

propagar [12] *vt/i* propagate.
∼se *vpr* spread

propano *m* propane

propasarse *vpr* go too far

propens|ión *f* inclination. **∼o** *a*
inclined

propiamente *adv* exactly

propici|ar *vt* (*provocar*) cause,
bring about. **∼o** *a* favourable

propie|dad *f* property; (*posesión*)
possession. **∼tario** *m* owner

propina *f* tip

propio *a* own; (*característico*)
typical; (*natural*) natural; (*apropiado*) proper. **de ∼** on purpose.
el médico ∼ the doctor himself

proponer [34] *vt* propose. **∼se**
vpr propose

proporci|ón *f* proportion. **∼on-
ado** *a* proportioned. **∼onal** *a*
proportional. **∼onar** *vt* proportion; (*facilitar*) supply

proposición *f* proposition

propósito *m* intention. **a ∼**
(*adrede*) on purpose; (*de paso*)
incidentally. **a ∼ de ∼** with regard
to. **de ∼** on purpose

propuesta *f* proposal

propuls|ar *vt* propel; (*fig*) pro-
mote. **∼ión** *f* propulsion. **∼ión
a chorro** jet propulsion

prórroga *f* extension

prorrogar [12] *vt* extend

prorrumpir *vi* burst out

prosa *f* prose. **∼ico** *a* prosaic

proscri|bir (*pp* **proscrito**) *vt*
banish; (*prohibido*) ban. **∼to** *a*
banned. —*m* exile; (*persona*)
outlaw

prosecución *f* continuation

proseguir [5 & 13] *vt/i* continue

prospección *f* prospecting

prospecto *m* prospectus

prosper|ar *vi* prosper. **∼idad** *f*
prosperity; (*éxito*) success

próspero *a* prosperous. **¡P∼
Año Nuevo!** Happy New Year!

prostit|ución *f* prostitution.
∼uta *f* prostitute

protagonista *m* & *f* protagonist

prote|cción *f* protection. **∼ctor**
a protective. —*m* protector;
(*patrocinador*) patron. **∼ger** [14]
vt protect. **∼gida** *f* protegée.
∼gido *a* protected. —*m* protegé

proteína *f* protein

protesta *f* protest; (*declaración*)
protestation

protestante *a* & *m* & *f* (*relig*)
Protestant

protestar *vt/i* protest

protocolo *m* protocol

protuberan|cia *f* protuberance.
∼te *a* protuberant

provecho *m* benefit. **¡buen ∼!**
enjoy your meal! **de ∼** useful. **en
∼ de** to the benefit of. **sacar ∼
de** benefit from

proveer [18] (*pp* **proveído** *y* **provisto**) *vt* supply, provide

provenir [53] *vi* come (**de** from)

proverbi|al *a* proverbial. **∼o** *m*
proverb

providencia *f* providence. **∼l** *a*
providential

provincia *f* province. **∼l** *a*, **∼no**
a provincial

provisi ón f provision; (medida) measure. **~onal** a provisional

provisto a provided (**de** with)

provoca ción f provocation. **~r** [7] vt provoke; (causar) cause. **~tivo** a provocative

próximamente adv soon

proximidad f proximity

próximo a next; (cerca) near

proyec ción f projection. **~tar** vt hurl; cast (luz); show (película). **~til** m missile. **~to** m plan. **~to de ley** bill. **~tor** m projector. **en ~to** planned

pruden cia f prudence. **~nte** a prudent, sensible

prueba f proof; (examen) test; (de ropa) fitting. **a ~** on trial. **a ~ de** proof against. **a ~ de agua** waterproof. **en ~ de** in proof of. **poner a ~** test

pruebo vb véase **probar**

psicoan álisis f psychoanalysis. **~alista** m & f psychoanalyst. **~alizar** [10] vt psychoanalyse

psicodélico a psychedelic

psic ología f psychology. **~ológico** a psychological. **~ólogo** m psychologist

psicópata m & f psychopath

psicosis f psychosis

psique f psyche

psiqui atra m & f psychiatrist. **~atría** f psychiatry. **~átrico** a psychiatric

psíquico a psychic

ptas, pts abrev (pesetas) pesetas

púa f sharp point; (bot) thorn; (de erizo) quill; (de peine) tooth; (mus) plectrum

pubertad f puberty

publica ción f publication. **~r** [7] vt publish; (anunciar) announce

publici dad f publicity; (com) advertising. **~tario** a advertising

público a public. —m public; (de espectáculo etc) audience. **dar al ~** publish

puchero m cooking pot; (guisado) stew. **hacer ~s** (fig, fam) pout

pude vb véase **poder**

púdico a modest

pudiente a rich

pudín m pudding

pudor m modesty. **~oso** a modest

pudrir (pp podrido) vt rot; (fig, molestar) annoy. **~se** vpr rot

puebl ecito m small village. **~o** m town; (aldea) village; (nación) nation, people

puedo vb véase **poder**

puente m bridge; (fig, fam) long weekend. **~ colgante** suspension bridge. **~ levadizo** drawbridge. **hacer ~** (fam) have a long weekend

puerco a filthy; (grosero) coarse. —m pig. **~ espín** porcupine

pueril a childish

puerro m leek

puerta f door; (en deportes) goal; (de ciudad) gate. **~ principal** main entrance. **a ~ cerrada** behind closed doors

puerto m port; (fig, refugio) refuge; (entre montañas) pass. **~ franco** free port

Puerto Rico m Puerto Rico

puertorriqueño a & m Puerto Rican

pues adv (entonces) then; (bueno) well. —conj since

puest a f setting; (en juegos) bet. **~a de sol** sunset. **~a en escena** staging. **~a en marcha** starting. **~o** a put; (vestido) dressed. —m place; (empleo) position, job; (en mercado etc) stall. —conj. **~o que** since. **~o de socorro** first aid post

pugna f fight. **~r** vt fight

puja f effort; (en subasta) bid. **~r** vt struggle; (en subasta) bid

pulcro a neat

pulga f flea; (de juego) tiddly-wink. **tener malas ~s** be bad-tempered

pulga|da f inch. **~r** m thumb; (del pie) big toe

puli|do a neat. **~mentar** vt polish. **~mento** m polishing; (substancia) polish. **~r** vt polish; (suavizar) smooth

pulm|ón m lung. **~onar** a pulmonary. **~onía** f pneumonia

pulpa f pulp

pulpería f (LAm) grocer's shop (Brit), grocery store (Amer)

púlpito m pulpit

pulpo m octopus

pulque m (Mex) pulque, alcoholic Mexican drink

pulsa|ción f pulsation. **~dor** a pulsating. —m button. **~r** vt (mus) play

pulsera f bracelet; (de reloj) strap

pulso m pulse; (muñeca) wrist; (firmeza) steady hand; (fuerza) strength; (fig, tacto) tact. **tomar el ~ a** uno take s.o.'s pulse

pulular vi teem with

pulveriza|dor m (de perfume) atomizer. **~r** [10] vt pulverize; atomize (líquido)

pulla f cutting remark

pum int bang!

puma m puma

puna f puna, high plateau

punitivo a punitive

punta f point; (extremo) tip; (clavo) (small) nail. **estar de ~** be in a bad mood. **estar de ~ con uno** be at odds with s.o. **ponerse de ~ con uno** fall out with s.o. **sacar ~ a** sharpen; (fig) find fault with

puntada f stitch

puntal m prop, support

puntapié m kick

puntear vt mark; (mus) pluck

puntera f toe

puntería f aim; (destreza) markmanship

puntiagudo a sharp, pointed

puntilla f (encaje) lace. **de ~s** on tiptoe

punto m point; (señal) dot; (de examen) mark; (lugar) spot, place; (de taxis) stand; (momento) moment; (punto final) full stop (Brit), period (Amer); (puntada) stitch; (de tela) mesh. **~ de admiración** exclamation mark. **~ de arranque** starting point. **~ de exclamación** exclamation mark. **~ de interrogación** question mark. **~ de vista** point of view. **~ final** full stop. **~ muerto** (auto) neutral (gear). **~ y aparte** full stop, new paragraph (Brit), period, new paragraph (Amer). **~ y coma** semicolon. **a ~** on time; (listo) ready. **a ~ de** on the point of. **de ~** knitted. **dos ~s** colon. **en ~** exactly. **hacer ~** knit. **hasta cierto ~** to a certain extent

puntuación f punctuation; (en deportes, acción) scoring; (en deportes, número de puntos) score

puntual a punctual; (exacto) accurate. **~idad** f punctuality; (exactitud) accuracy

puntuar [21] vt punctuate. —vi score

punza|da f prick; (dolor) pain; (fig) pang. **~nte** a sharp. **~r** [10] vt prick

puñado m handful. **a ~s** by the handful

puñal m dagger. **~ada** f stab

puñetazo m punch. **~o** m fist; (de ropa) cuff; (mango) handle. **de su ~o (y letra)** in his own handwriting

pupa f spot; (en los labios) cold sore. **hacer ~** hurt. **hacerse ~** hurt o.s.

pupila f pupil

pupitre m desk

puquío *m* (Arg) spring

puré *m* purée; (sopa) thick soup. **~ de patatas** mashed potato

pureza *f* purity

purga *f* purge. **~r** [12] *vt* purge. **~torio** *m* purgatory

purificación *f* purification. **~r** [7] *vt* purify

purista *m & f* purist

puritano *a* puritanical. **—m.** puritan

puro *a* pure; ⟨cielo⟩ clear; (fig) simple. **—m** cigar. **de ~** so. **de pura casualidad** by sheer chance

púrpura *f* purple

purpúreo *a* purple

pus *m* pus

puse *vb véase* **poner**

pusilánime *a* cowardly

pústula *f* spot

puta *f* whore

putrefacción *f* putrefaction

pútrido *a* rotten, putrid

Q

que *pron rel* (personas, sujeto) who; (personas, complemento) whom; (cosas) which, that. **—** *conj* that. **¡~ tengan Vds buen viaje!** have a good journey! **¡que venga!** let him come! **~ venga o no venga** whether he comes or not. **a que I bet**. **creo que tiene razón** I think (that) he is right. **de ~** from which. **yo ~ tú** if I were you

qué *a* (con sustantivo) what (con a o adv) how. **—pron** what. **¡~ bonito!** how nice. **¿en ~ piensas?** what are you thinking about?

quebrada *f* gorge; (paso) pass. **~dizo** *a* fragile. **~do** *a* broken; (com) bankrupt. **—m** (math) fraction. **~dura** *f* fracture.

(hondonada) gorge. **~ntar** *vt* break; (debilitar) weaken. **~nto** *m* (pérdida) loss; (daño) damage. **~r** [1] *vt* break. **—vi** break; (com) go bankrupt. **~rse** *vpr* break

quechua *a & m & f* Quechuan

queda *f* curfew

quedar *vi* stay, remain; (estar) be; (faltar, sobrar) be left. **~ bien** come off well. **~se** *vpr* stay. **~ con** arrange to meet. **~ en** agree to. **~ en nada** come to nothing. **~ por** (+ infinitivo) remain to be (+ pp)

quehacer *m* job. **~es domésticos** household chores

queja *f* complaint; (de dolor) moan. **~arse** *vpr* complain (de about); (gemir) moan. **~ido** *m* moan. **~oso** *a* complaining

quemado *a* burnt; (fig, fam) bitter. **~dor** *m* burner. **~dura** *f* burn. **~r** *vt* burn; (prender fuego a) set fire to. **—vi** burn; (estar muy caliente) be very hot. **~rse** *vpr* burn o.s.; (consumirse) burn up; (con el sol) get sunburnt. **~rropa** *adv.* **a ~rropa** point-blank

quena *f* Indian flute

quepo *vb véase* **caber**

queque *m* (Mex) cake

querella *f* (riña) quarrel, dispute; (jurid) charge

querer [35] *vt* want; (amar) love; (necesitar) need. **~er decir** mean. **~ido** *a* dear; (amado) loved. **—m** darling; (amante) lover. **como quiera que** since; (de cualquier modo) however. **cuando quiera que** whenever. **donde quiera** wherever. **¿quieres darme ese libro?** would you pass me that book? **quiere llover** it's trying to rain. **¿quieres un helado?** would you like an ice-cream? **quisiera ir a la playa** I'd like to go to the beach. **sin ~er** without meaning to

queroseno *m* kerosene

querubín *m* cherub

quesadilla *f* cheesecake; *(Mex, empanadilla)* pie. ~**o** *m* cheese. ~**o de bola** Edam cheese

quiá *int* never!, surely not!

quicio *m* frame. **sacar de** ~ **a uno** infuriate s.o.

quiebra *f* break; *(fig)* collapse; *(com)* bankruptcy

quiebro *m* dodge

quien *pron rel (sujeto)* who; *(complemento)* whom

quién *pron interrogativo (sujeto)* who; *(tras preposición)* whom; ¿**de** ~? whose. ¿**de** ~ **son estos libros?** whose are these books?

quienquiera *pron* whoever

quiero *vb véase* **querer**

quieto *a* still; *(inmóvil)* motionless; *(carácter etc)* calm. ~**ud** *f* stillness

quijada *f* jaw

quilate *m* carat

quilla *f* keel

quimera *f (fig)* illusion

químic|a *f* chemistry. ~**o** *a* chemical. —*m* chemist

quincalla *f* hardware; *(de adorno)* trinket

quince *a & m* fifteen. ~ **días** a fortnight. ~**na** *f* fortnight. ~**nal** *a* fortnightly

quincuagésimo *a* fiftieth

quiniela *f* pools coupon. ~**s** *fpl* (football) pools

quinientos *a & m* five hundred

quinino *m* quinine

quinqué *m* oil-lamp; *(fig, fam)* shrewdness

quinquenio *m* (period of) five years

quinta *f (casa)* villa

quintaesencia *f* quintessence

quintal *m* a hundred kilograms

quinteto *m* quintet

quinto *a & m* fifth

quiosco *m* kiosk; *(en jardín)* summerhouse; *(en parque etc)* bandstand

quirúrgico *a* surgical

quise *vb véase* **querer**

quisque *pron.* **cada** ~ *(fam)* (absolutely) everybody

quisquilla *f* trifle; *(camarón)* shrimp. ~**oso** *a* irritable; *(chinchorrero)* fussy

quita|manchas *m invar* stain remover. ~**nieves** *m invar* snow plough. ~**r** *vt* remove, take away; take off *(ropa)*; *(robar)* steal. ~**ndo** *(a excepción de, fam)* apart from. ~**rse** *upr* be removed; take off *(ropa)*. ~**rse de** *(no hacerlo más)* stop. ~**rse de en medio** get out of the way. ~**sol** *m invar* sunshade

Quito *m* Quito

quizá(s) *adv* perhaps

quórum *m* quorum

R

rábano *m* radish. ~ **picante** horseradish. **me importa un** ~ I couldn't care less

rabi|a *f* rabies; *(fig)* rage. ~**ar** *vi (de dolor)* be in great pain; *(estar enfadado)* be furious; *(fig, tener ganas, fam)* long. ~**ar por algo** long for sth. ~**ar por hacer algo** long to do sth. ~**eta** *f* tantrum. **dar** ~**a** infuriate

rabino *m* Rabbi

rabioso *a* rabid; *(furioso)* furious; *(dolor etc)* violent

rabo *m* tail

racial *a* racial

racimo *m* bunch

raciocinio *m* reason; *(razonamiento)* reasoning

ración *f* share, ration; *(de comida)* portion

racional *a* rational. ~**izar** [10] *vt* rationalize

racionar *vt (limitar)* ration; *(repartir)* ration out

racis|mo *m* racism. **~ta** *a* racist

racha *f* gust of wind; (*fig*) spate

radar *m* radar

radiación *f* radiation

radiactiv|idad *f* radioactivity. **~o** *a* radioactive

radiador *m* radiator

radial *a* radial

radiante *a* radiant

radical *a* & *m* & *f* radical

radicar [7] *vi* (*estar*) be. **~ en** (*fig*) lie in

radio *m* radius; (*de rueda*) spoke; (*elemento metálico*) radium. **—f** radio

radioactiv|idad *f* radioactivity. **~o** *a* radioactive

radio|difusión *f* broadcasting. **~emisora** *f* radio station. **~escucha** *m* & *f* listener

radiografía *f* radiography

radi|ología *f* radiology. **~ólogo** *m* radiologist

radioterapia *f* radiotherapy

radioyente *m* & *f* listener

raer [36] *vt* scrape off

ráfaga *f* (*de viento*) gust; (*de luz*) flash; (*de ametralladora*) burst

rafia *f* raffia

raído *a* threadbare

raigambre *f* roots; (*fig*) tradition

raíz *f* root. **a ~ de** immediately after. **echar raíces** (*fig*) settle

raja *f* split; (*culin*) slice. **~r** *vt* split. **~rse** *vpr* split; (*fig*) back out

rajatabla. a ~ vigorously

ralea *f* sort

ralo *a* sparse

ralla|dor *m* grater. **~r** *vt* grate

rama *f* branch. **~je** *m* branches. **~l** *m* branch. **en ~** raw

rambla *f* gully; (*avenida*) avenue

ramera *f* prostitute

ramifica|ción *f* ramification. **~rse** [7] *vpr* branch out

ramilla *f* twig

ramillete *m* bunch

ramo *m* branch; (*de flores*) bouquet

rampa *f* ramp, slope

ramplón *a* vulgar

rana *f* frog. **ancas** *fpl* **de ~** frogs' legs. **no ser ~** not be stupid

rancio *a* rancid; (*vino*) old; (*fig*) ancient

ranch|ero *m* cook; (*LAm, jefe de rancho*) farmer. **~o** *m* (*LAm*) ranch, farm

rango *m* rank

ranúnculo *m* buttercup

ranura *f* groove; (*para moneda*) slot

rapar *vt* shave; crop (*pelo*)

rapaz *a* rapacious; (*ave*) of prey. **—m** bird of prey

rapidez *f* speed

rápido *a* fast, quick. **—adv** quickly. **—m** (*tren*) express. **~s** *mpl* rapids

rapiña *f* robbery. **ave** *f* **de ~** bird of prey

rapsodia *f* rhapsody

rapt|ar *vt* kidnap. **~o** *m* kidnapping; (*de ira etc*) fit; (*éxtasis*) ecstasy

raqueta *f* racquet

raramente *adv* seldom, rarely

rarefacción *f* rarefaction

rar|eza *f* rarity; (*cosa rara*) oddity. **~o** *a* rare; (*extraño*) odd. **es ~o que** it is strange that. **¡qué ~o!** how strange!

ras *m.* **a ~ de** level with

rasar *vt* level; (*rozar*) graze

rasca|cielos *m invar* skyscraper. **~dura** *f* scratch. **~r** [7] *vt* scratch; (*raspar*) scrape

rasgar [12] *vt* tear

rasgo *m* stroke. **~s** *mpl* (*facciones*) features

rasguear *vt* strum; (*fig, escribir*) write

rasguñ|ar *vt* scratch. **~o** *m* scratch

raso *a* (*llano*) flat; (*liso*) smooth; (*cielo*) clear; (*cucharada etc*)

raspa level; ⟨vuelo etc⟩ low. —m satin. **al ∼** in the open air. **soldado** m **∼** private

raspa f ⟨de pescado⟩ backbone

raspa|dura f scratch; ⟨acción⟩ scratching. **∼r** vt scratch; ⟨rozar⟩ scrape

rastr|a f rake. **a ∼as** dragging. **∼ear** vt track. **∼eo** m dragging. **∼ero** a creeping; ⟨vuelo⟩ low. **∼illar** vt rake. **∼illo** m rake. **∼o** m rake; ⟨huella⟩ track; ⟨señal⟩ sign. **el R∼o** the flea market in Madrid. **ni ∼o** not a trace

rata f rat

rate|ar vt steal. **∼ría** f pilfering. **∼ro** m petty thief

ratifica|ción f ratification. **∼r** [7] vt ratify

rato m moment, short time. **∼s libres** spare time. **a ∼s** at times. **hace un ∼** a moment ago. **¡hasta otro ∼!** ⟨fam⟩ see you soon! **pasar mal ∼** have a rough time

rat|ón m mouse. **∼onera** f mousetrap; ⟨madriguera⟩ mouse hole

raud|al m torrent; ⟨fig⟩ floods. **∼o** a swift

raya f line; ⟨lista⟩ stripe; ⟨de pelo⟩ parting. **∼r** vt rule. —vi border ⟨con on⟩. **a ∼s** striped. **pasar de la ∼** go too far

rayo m ray; ⟨descarga eléctrica⟩ lightning. **∼s X** X-rays

raza f race; ⟨de animal⟩ breed. **de ∼** ⟨caballo⟩ thoroughbred; ⟨perro⟩ pedigree

raz|ón f reason. **a ∼ón de** at the rate of. **perder la ∼ón** go out of one's mind. **tener ∼ón** be right. **∼onable** a reasonable. **∼onamiento** m reasoning. **∼onar** vt reason out. —vi reason

re m D; ⟨solfa⟩ re

reac|ción f reaction. **∼cionario** a & m reactionary. **∼ción en**

cadena chain reaction. **∼tor** m reactor; ⟨avión⟩ jet

real a real; ⟨de rey etc⟩ royal. —m real, old Spanish coin

realce m relief; ⟨fig⟩ splendour

realidad f reality; ⟨verdad⟩ truth. **en ∼** in fact

realis|mo m realism. **∼ta** a realistic. —m & f realist; ⟨monárquico⟩ royalist

realiza|ción f fulfilment. **∼r** [10] vt carry out; make ⟨viaje⟩; achieve ⟨meta⟩; ⟨vender⟩ sell. **∼rse** upr ⟨plan etc⟩ be carried out; ⟨sueño, predicción etc⟩ come true; ⟨persona⟩ fulfil o.s.

realzar [10] vt ⟨fig⟩ enhance

reanima|ción f revival. **∼r** vt revive. **∼rse** upr revive

reanudar vt resume; renew ⟨amistad⟩

reaparecer [11] vi reappear

rearm|ar vt rearm. **∼e** m rearmament

reavivar vt revive

rebaj|a f reduction. **∼do** a ⟨precio⟩ reduced. **∼r** vt lower. **en ∼s** in the sale

rebanada f slice

rebaño m herd; ⟨de ovejas⟩ flock

rebasar vt exceed; ⟨dejar atrás⟩ leave behind

rebatir vt refute

rebel|arse upr rebel. **∼de** a rebellious. —m rebel. **∼día** f rebelliousness. **∼ión** f rebellion

reblandecer [11] vt soften

rebosa|nte a overflowing. **∼r** vi overflow; ⟨abundar⟩ abound

rebot|ar vt bounce; ⟨rechazar⟩ repel. —vi bounce; ⟨bala⟩ ricochet. **∼e** m bounce, rebound. **de ∼e** on the rebound

rebozar [10] vt wrap up; ⟨culin⟩ coat in batter

rebullir [22] vi stir

rebusca|do a affected. **∼r** [7] vt search thoroughly

rebuznar vi bray

recabar vt claim

recado m errand; (mensaje) message. **dejar ~** leave a message

reca|er [29] vi fall back; (med) relapse; (fig) fall. **~ida** f relapse

recalcar [7] vt squeeze; (fig) stress

recalcitrante a recalcitrant

recalentar [1] vt (de nuevo) reheat; (demasiado) overheat

recamar vt embroider

recámara f small room; (de arma de fuego) chamber; (LAm, dormitorio) bedroom

recambio m change; (de pluma etc) refill. **~s** mpl spare parts. **de ~** spare

recapitula|ción f summing up. **~r** vt sum up

recargar [12] vt overload; (aumentar) increase; recharge (batería). **~o** m increase

recat|ado a modest. **~ar** vt hide. **~arse** upr hide o.s. away; (actuar discretamente) act discreetly. **~o** m prudence; (modestia) modesty. **sin ~arse**, **sin ~o** openly

recauda|ción f (cantidad) takings. **~dor** m tax collector. **~r** vt collect

recel|ar vt/i suspect. **~o** m distrust; (temor) fear. **~oso** a suspicious

recepción f reception. **~onista** m & f receptionist

receptáculo m receptacle

recept|ivo a receptive. **~or** m receiver

recesión f recession

receta f recipe; (med) prescription

recib|imiento m (acogida) welcome. **~ir** vt receive; (acoger) welcome. **~vi** entertain. **~irse** upr graduate. **~o** m receipt. **acusar ~o** acknowledge receipt

reci|én adv recently; (casado, nacido etc) newly. **~ente** a recent; (culin) fresh

recinto m enclosure

recio a strong; (voz) loud. **—adv** hard; (en voz alta) loudly

recipiente m (persona) recipient; (cosa) receptacle

recíproco a reciprocal. **a la recíproca** vice versa

recita|l m recital; (de poesías) reading. **~r** vt recite

reclama|ción f claim; (queja) complaint. **~r** vt claim. **—vi** appeal

reclinar vi lean. **~se** upr recline

reclu|ir [17] vt shut away. **~sión** f seclusion; (cárcel) prison. **~so** m prisoner

recluta m recruit. **—f** recruitment. **~miento** m recruitment; (conjunto de reclutas) recruits. **~r** vt recruit

recobrar vt recover. **~se** upr recover

recodo m bend

recog|er [14] vt collect; pick up (cosa caída); (cosechar) harvest; (dar asilo) shelter. **~erse** upr withdraw; (ir a casa) go home; (acostarse) go to bed. **~ida** f collection; (cosecha) harvest. **~ido** a withdrawn; (pequeño) small

recolección f harvest

recomenda|ción f recommendation. **~r** [1] vt recommend; (encomendar) entrust

recomenzar [1 & 10] vt/i start again

recompensa f reward. **~r** vt reward

recomponer [34] vt mend

reconcilia|ción f reconciliation. **~r** vt reconcile. **~rse** upr reconciled

recóndito a hidden

reconoc|er [11] vt recognize; (admitir) acknowledge; (examinar) examine. **~imiento** m recognition; (admisión) acknowledgement; (agradecimiento) gratitude; (*examen*) examination

reconozco *vb véase* **reconocer**

reconquista *f* reconquest. ~r *vt* reconquer; (*fig*) win back

reconsiderar *vt* reconsider

reconstitu|ir [17] *vt* reconstitute. ~yente *m* tonic

reconstru|cción *f* reconstruction. ~ir [17] *vt* reconstruct

récord /'rekor/ *m* record. **batir un** ~ break a record

recordar [2] *vt* remember; (*hacer acordar*) remind; (*Lam, despertar*) wake up. —*vi* remember. **que yo recuerde** as far as I remember. **si mal no recuerdo** if I remember rightly

recorr|er *vt* tour (*país*); (*pasar por*) travel through; cover (*distancia*); (*registrar*) look over. ~ido *m* journey; (*itinerario*) route

recort|ado *a* jagged. ~ar *vt* cut (out). ~e *m* cutting (out); (*de periódico etc*) cutting

recoser *vt* mend

recostar [2] *vt* lean. ~se *vpr* lie back

recoveco *m* bend; (*rincón*) nook

recre|ación *f* recreation. ~ar *vt* re-create; (*divertir*) entertain. ~arse *vpr* amuse o.s. ~ativo *a* recreational. ~o *m* recreation; (*escol*) break

recrimina|ción *f* recrimination. ~r *vt* reproach

recrudecer [11] *vi* increase, worsen, get worse

recta *f* straight line

rect|angular *a* rectangular; (*triángulo*) right-angled. ~ángulo *a* rectangular; (*triángulo*) right-angled. —*m* rectangle

rectifica|ción *f* rectification. ~r [7] *vt* rectify

rect|itud *f* straightness; (*fig*) honesty. ~o *a* straight; (*fig,*

justo) fair; (*fig, honrado*) honest. —*m* rectum. **todo** ~o straight on

rector *a* governing. —*m* rector

recuadro *m* (*en periódico*) box

recubrir [*pp* **recubierto**] *vt* cover

recuerdo *m* memory; (*regalo*) souvenir. —*vb véase* **recordar**. ~s *mpl* (*saludos*) regards

recupera|ción *f* recovery. ~r *vt* recover. ~rse *vpr* recover. ~r **el tiempo perdido** make up for lost time

recur|rir *vi*. ~rir a resort to (*cosa*); turn to (*persona*). ~so *m* resort; (*medio*) resource; (*jurid*) appeal. ~sos *mpl* resources

recusar *vt* refuse

rechaz|ar [10] *vt* repel; reflect (*luz*); (*no aceptar*) refuse; (*negar*) deny. ~o *m*. **de** ~o on the rebound; (*fig*) consequently

rechifla *f* booing; (*burla*) derision

rechinar *vi* squeak; (*madera etc*) creak; (*dientes*) grind

rechistar *vi* murmur. **sin** ~ without saying a word

rechoncho *a* stout

red *f* network; (*malla*) net; (*para equipaje*) luggage rack; (*fig, engaño*) trap

redac|ción *f* editing; (*conjunto de redactores*) editorial staff; (*oficina*) editorial office; (*escol, univ*) essay. ~tar *vt* write. ~tor *m* writer; (*de periódico*) editor

redada *f* casting; (*de policía*) raid

redecilla *f* small net; (*para el pelo*) hairnet

rededor *m*. **al** ~, **en** ~ around

reden|ción *f* redemption. ~tor *a* redeeming

redil *f* sheepfold

redimir *vt* redeem

rédito *m* interest

redoblar *vt* redouble; (*doblar*) bend back

redoma f flask
redomado a sly
redond|a f (de imprenta) roman (type); (mus) semibreve (Brit), whole note (Amer). **~amente** adv (categóricamente) flatly. **~ear** vt round off. **~el** m circle; (de plaza de toros) arena. **~o** a round; (completo) complete. — m circle. **a la ~a** around. **en ~o** round; (categóricamente) flatly
reduc|ción f reduction. **~ido** a reduced; (limitado) limited; (pequeño) small; (precio) low. **~ir** [47] vt reduce. **~irse** vpr be reduced; (fig) amount
reduje vb véase **reducir**
redundan|cia f redundancy. **~te** a redundant
reduplicar [7] vt (aumentar) redouble
reduzco vb véase **reducir**
reedificar [7] vt reconstruct
reembols|ar vt reimburse. **~o** m repayment. **contra ~o** cash on delivery
reemplaz|ar [10] vt replace. **~o** m replacement
reemprender vt start again
reenviar [20] vt, **reexpedir** [5] vt forward
referencia f reference; (información) report. **con ~** a with reference to. **hacer ~** a refer to
referéndum m (pl referéndums) referendum
referir [4] vt tell; (remitir) refer. **~se** vpr refer. **por lo que se refiere a** as regards
refiero vb véase **referir**
refilón. de ~ obliquely
refin|amiento m refinement. **~ar** vt refine. **~ería** f refinery
reflector m reflector; (proyector) searchlight
reflej|ar vt reflect. **~o** a reflected; (med) reflex. — m reflection; (med) reflex; (en el pelo) highlights

reflexi|ón f reflection. **~onar** vi reflect. **~vo** a (persona) thoughtful; (gram) reflexive. **con ~ón** on reflection. **sin ~ón** without thinking
reflujo m ebb
reforma f reform. **~s** fpl (reparaciones) repairs. **~r** vt reform. **~rse** vpr reform
reforzar [2 & 10] vt reinforce
refrac|ción f refraction. **~tar** vt refract. **~tario** a heat-resistant
refrán m saying
refregar [1 & 12] vt rub
refrenar vt rein in (caballo); (fig) restrain
refrendar vt endorse
refresc|ar [7] vt refresh; (enfriar) cool. — vi get cooler. **~arse** vpr refresh o.s.; (salir) go out for a walk. **~o** m cold drink. **~os** mpl refreshments
refrigera|ción f refrigeration; (aire acondicionado) air-conditioning. **~r** vt refrigerate. **~dor** m, **~dora** f refrigerator
refuerzo m reinforcement
refugi|ado m refugee. **~arse** vpr take refuge. **~o** m refuge, shelter
refulgir [14] vi shine
refundir vt (fig) revise, rehash
refunfuñar vi grumble
refutar vt refute
regadera f watering-can; (Mex, ducha) shower
regala|damente adv very well. **~do** a as a present, free; (cómodo) comfortable. **~r** vt give; (agasajar) treat very well. **~rse** vpr indulge o.s.
regaliz m liquorice
regalo m present, gift; (placer) joy; (comodidad) comfort
regañ|adientes. a ~adientes reluctantly. **~ar** vt scold. — vi moan; (dos personas) quarrel. **~o** m (reprensión) scolding
regar [1 & 12] vt water

regata *f* regatta

regate *m* dodge; (*en deportes*) dribbling. **~ar** *vt* haggle over; (*economizar*) economize on. **—vi** haggle; (*en deportes*) dribble. **~o** *m* haggling; (*en deportes*) dribbling

regazo *m* lap

regencia *f* regency

regenerar *vt* regenerate

regente *m* & *f* regent; (*director*) manager

régimen *m* (*pl* **regímenes**) rule; (*pol*) regime; (*med*) diet. **~ alimenticio** *m* diet

regimiento *m* regiment

regio *a* royal

regi|ón *f* region. **~onal** *a* regional

regir [5 & 14] *vt* rule; govern (*país*); run (*colegio, empresa*). **—vi** apply, be in force

registr|ado *a* registered. **~ador** *m* recorder; (*persona*) registrar. **~ar** *vt* register; (*grabar*) record; (*examinar*) search. **~arse** *vpr* register; (*darse*) be reported. **~o** *m* (*acción de registrar*) registration; (*libro*) register; (*cosa anotada*) entry; (*inspección*) search. **~o civil** (*oficina*) register office

regla *f* ruler; (*norma*) rule; (*menstruación*) period, menstruation. **~mentación** *f* regulation. **~mentar** *vt* regulate. **~mentario** *a* obligatory. **~mento** *m* regulations. **en ~** in order. **por ~ general** as a rule

regocij|ar *vt* delight. **~arse** *vpr* be delighted. **~o** *m* delight. **~os** *mpl* festivities

regode|arse *vpr* be delighted. **~o** *m* delight

regordete *a* chubby

regres|ar *vi* return. **~ión** *f* regression. **~ivo** *a* backward. **~o** *m* return

reguer|a *f* irrigation ditch. **~o** *m* irrigation ditch; (*señal*) trail

regula|dor *m* control. **~r** *a* regular; (*mediano*) average; (*no bueno*) so-so. **—vt** regulate; (*controlar*) control. **~ridad** *f* regularity. **con ~ridad** regularly. **por lo ~r** as a rule

rehabilita|ción *f* rehabilitation; (*en un empleo etc*) reinstatement. **~r** *vt* rehabilitate; (*al empleo etc*) reinstate

rehacer [31] *vt* redo; (*repetir*) repeat; (*reparar*) repair. **~se** *vpr* recover

rehén *m* hostage

rehogar [12] *vt* sauté

rehuir [17] *vt* avoid

rehusar *vt/i* refuse

reimpr|esión *f* reprinting. **~imir** (*pp* **reimpreso**) *vt* reprint

reina *f* queen. **~do** *m* reign. **~nte** *a* ruling; (*fig*) prevailing. **~r** *vi* reign; (*fig*) prevail

reincidir *vi* relapse, repeat an offence

reino *m* kingdom. **R~ Unido** United Kingdom

reinstaurar *vt* restore

reintegr|ar *vt* reinstate (*persona*); refund (*cantidad*). **~arse** *vpr* return. **~o** *m* refund

reír [51] *vi* laugh. **~se de** *vpr* laugh at. **echarse a ~** burst out laughing

reivindica|ción *f* claim. **~r** [7] *vt* claim; (*restaurar*) restore

rej|a *f* grille, grating. **~illa** *f* grille, grating; (*red*) luggage rack; (*de mimbre*) wickerwork. **entre ~as** behind bars

rejuvenecer [11] *vt/i* rejuvenate. **~se** *vpr* be rejuvenated

relaci|ón *f* relation(ship); (*relato*) tale; (*lista*) list. **~onado** *a* concerning. **~onar** *vt* relate (**con** to). **~onarse** *vpr* be connected. **bien ~onado** well-connected. **con ~ón a, en ~ón**

a in relation to. **hacer ∼ón a** refer to

relaja|ción f relaxation; (*aflojamiento*) slackening. **∼do** a loose. **∼r** vt relax; (*aflojar*) slacken. **∼rse** vpr relax

relamerse vpr lick one's lips

relamido a overdressed

rel|ámpago m (flash of) lightning. **∼ampaguear** vi thunder; (*fig*) sparkle

relatar vt tell, relate

relativ|idad f relativity. **∼o** a relative. **en lo ∼o a** in relation to

relato m tale; (*informe*) report

relegar [12] vt relegate. **∼ al olvido** forget about

relev|ante a outstanding. **∼ar** vt relieve; (*substituir*) replace. **∼o** m relief. **carrera f de ∼os** relay race

relieve m relief; (*fig*) importance. **de ∼** important. **poner de ∼** emphasize

religi|ón f religion. **∼osa** f nun. **∼oso** a religious. —m monk

relinch|ar vi neigh. **∼o** m neigh

reliquia f relic

reloj m clock; (*de bolsillo o pulsera*) watch. **∼ de caja** grandfather clock. **∼ de pulsera** wrist-watch. **∼ de sol** sundial. **∼ despertador** alarm clock. **∼ería** f watchmaker's (shop). **∼ero** m watchmaker

reluci|ente a shining. **∼r** [11] vi shine; (*destellar*) sparkle

relumbrar vi shine

rellano m landing

rellen|ar vt refill; (*culin*) stuff; fill in (*formulario*). **∼o** a full up; (*culin*) stuffed. —m filling; (*culin*) stuffing

remach|ar vt rivet; (*fig*) drive home. **∼e** m rivet

remangar [12] vt roll up

remanso m pool; (*fig*) haven

remar vi row

remat|ado a (*total*) complete; (*niño*) very naughty. **∼ar** vt finish off; (*agotar*) use up; (*com*) sell off cheap. **∼e** m end; (*fig*) finishing touch. **de ∼e** completely

remedar vt imitate

remedi|ar vt remedy; (*ayudar*) help; (*poner fin a*) put a stop to; (*fig, resolver*) solve. **∼o** m remedy; (*fig*) solution. **como último ∼o** as a last resort. **no hay más ∼o** there's no other way. **no tener más ∼o** have no choice

remedo m imitation

rem|endar [1] vt repair. **∼iendo** m patch; (*fig, mejora*) improvement

remilg|ado a fussy; (*afectado*) affected. **∼o** m fussiness; (*afectación*) affectation

reminiscencia f reminiscence

remirar vt look again at

remisión f sending; (*referencia*) reference; (*perdón*) forgiveness

remiso a remiss

remit|e m sender's name and address. **∼ente** m sender. **∼ir** vt send; (*referir*) refer. —vi diminish

remo m oar

remoj|ar vt soak; (*fig, fam*) celebrate. **∼o** m soaking. **poner a ∼o** soak

remolacha f beetroot. **∼ azucarera** sugar beet

remolcar [7] vt tow

remolino m swirl; (*de aire etc*) whirl; (*de gente*) throng

remolque m towing; (*cabo*) towrope; (*vehículo*) trailer. **a ∼ on** tow. **dar ∼ a** tow

remontar vt mend. **∼se** vpr soar; (*con tiempo*) go back to

rémora f (*fig*) hindrance

remord|er [2] (*fig*) worry. **∼imiento** m remorse. **tener ∼imientos** feel remorse

remoto a remote

remover [2] *vt* move; stir ‹*líquido*›; turn over ‹*tierra*›; ‹*quitar*› remove; ‹*fig, activar*› revive

remozar [10] *vt* rejuvenate ‹*persona*›; renovate ‹*edificio etc*›

remunera|ción *f* remuneration. ~**r** *vt* remunerate

renac|er [11] *vi* be reborn; ‹*fig*› revive. ~**imiento** *m* rebirth. **R~** Renaissance

renacuajo *m* tadpole; ‹*fig*› tiddler

rencilla *f* quarrel

rencor *m* bitterness. ~**oso** *a* (*estar*) resentful; (*ser*) spiteful. **guardar** ~ **a** have a grudge against

rendi|ción *f* surrender. ~**do** *a* submissive; (*agotado*) exhausted

rendija *f* crack

rendi|miento *m* efficiency; (*com*) yield. ~**r** [5] *vt* yield; (*vencer*) defeat; (*agotar*) exhaust; pay ‹*homenaje*›. —*vi* pay; (*producir*) produce. ~**rse** *vpr* surrender

renega|do *a* & *m* renegade. ~**r** [1 & 12] *vt* deny. —*vi* grumble. ~**r de** renounce ‹*fe etc*›; disown ‹*personas*›

RENFE *abrev* (*Red Nacional de los Ferrocarriles Españoles*) Spanish National Railways

renglón *m* line; (*com*) item. **a** ~ **seguido** straight away

reno *m* reindeer

renombr|ado *a* renowned. ~**e** *m* renown

renova|ción *f* renewal; (*de edificio*) renovation; (*de cuarto*) decorating. ~**r** *vt* renew; renovate ‹*edificio*›; decorate ‹*cuarto*›

rent|a *f* income; (*alquiler*) rent; (*deuda*) national debt. ~**able** *a* profitable. ~**ar** *vt* produce, yield; (*LAm, alquilar*) rent, hire. ~**a vitalicia** (life) annuity. ~**ista** *m* & *f* person of independent means

renuncia *f* renunciation. ~**r** *vi*. ~**r a** renounce, give up

reñi|do *a* hard-fought. ~**r** [5 & 22] *vt* tell off. —*vi* quarrel. **estar** ~**do con** be incompatible with ‹*cosas*›; be on bad terms with ‹*personas*›

reo *m* & *f* culprit; (*jurid*) accused. ~ **de Estado** person accused of treason. ~ **de muerte** prisoner sentenced to death

reojo. mirar de ~ look out of the corner of one's eye at; (*fig*) look askance at

reorganizar [10] *vt* reorganize

repanchigarse [12] *vpr*, **repantigarse** [12] *vpr* sprawl out

repar|ación *f* repair; (*acción*) repairing; (*fig, compensación*) reparation. ~**ar** *vt* repair; (*fig*) make amends for; (*notar*) notice. —*vi*. ~**ar en** notice; (*hacer caso de*) pay attention to. ~**o** *m* fault; (*objeción*) objection. **poner** ~**os** raise objections

repart|ición *f* division. ~**idor** *m* delivery man. ~**imiento** *m* distribution. ~**ir** *vt* distribute, share out; deliver ‹*cartas, leche etc*›; hand out ‹*folleto, premio*›. ~**o** *m* distribution; (*de cartas, leche etc*) delivery; (*actores*) cast

repas|ar *vt* go over; check ‹*cuenta*›; revise ‹*texto*›; (*leer a la ligera*) glance through; (*coser*) mend. —*vi* go back. ~**o** *m* revision; (*de ropa*) mending. **dar un** ~**o** look through

repatria|ción *f* repatriation. ~**r** *vt* repatriate

repecho *m* steep slope

repele|nte *a* repulsive. ~**r** *vt* repel

repensar [1] *vt* reconsider

repente. de ~ suddenly. ~**ino** *a* sudden

repercu|sión *f* repercussion. ~**tir** *vi* reverberate; (*fig*) have repercussions (**en** on)

repertorio m repertoire; (lista) index

repeti|ción f repetition; (mus) repeat. ~**damente** adv repeatedly. ~**r** [5] vt repeat; (imitar) copy; —vi. ~**r** de have a second helping of. **¡que se repita!** encore!

repi|car [7] vt ring (campanas). ~**que** m peal

repisa f shelf. ~ **de chimenea** mantlepiece

repito vb véase **repetir**

replegarse [1 & 12] vpr withdraw

repleto a full up

réplica a answer; (copia) replica

replicar [7] vi answer

repliegue m crease; (mil) withdrawal

repollo m cabbage

reponer [34] vt replace; revive (obra de teatro); (contestar) reply. ~**se** vpr recover

report|aje m report. ~**ero** m reporter

repos|ado a quiet; (sin prisa) unhurried. ~**ar** vi rest. ~**arse** vpr settle. ~**o** m rest

repost|ar vt replenish; refuel (avión); fill up (coche etc). ~**ería** f cake shop

repren|der vt reprimand. ~**sible** a reprehensible

represalia f reprisal. **tomar** ~**s** retaliate

representa|ción f representation; (en el teatro) performance. **en** ~**ción de** of representing. ~**nte** m representative; (actor) actor. ~**r** vt represent; perform (obra de teatro); play (papel); (aparentar) look. ~**rse** vpr imagine. ~**tivo** a representative

represi|ón f repression. ~**vo** a repressive

reprimenda f reprimand

reprimir vt suppress. ~**se** vpr stop o.s.

reprobar [2] vt condemn; reproach (persona)

réprobo a & m reprobate

reproch|ar vt reproach. ~**e** m reproach

reproduc|ción f reproduction. ~**ir** [47] vt reproduce. ~**tor** a reproductive

reptil m reptile

rep|ública f republic. ~**ublicano** a & m republican

repudiar vt repudiate

repuesto m store; (auto) spare (part). **de** ~ in reserve

repugna|ncia f disgust. ~**nte** a repugnant. ~**r** vt disgust

repujar vt emboss

repuls|a f rebuff. ~**ión** f repulsion. ~**ivo** a repulsive

reputa|ción f reputation. ~**do** a reputable. ~**r** vt consider

requebrar [1] vt flatter

requemar vt scorch; (culin) burn; tan (piel)

requeri|miento m request; (jurid) summons. ~**r** [4] vt need; (pedir) ask

requesón m cottage cheese

requete... pref extremely

requiebro m compliment

réquiem m (pl réquiems) m requiem

requis|a f inspection; (mil) requisition. ~**ar** vt requisition. ~**ito** m requirement

res f animal. ~ **lanar** sheep. ~ **vacuna** (vaca) cow; (toro) bull; (buey) ox. **carne de** ~ (Mex) beef

resabido a well-known; (persona) pedantic

resabio m (unpleasant) aftertaste; (vicio) bad habit

resaca f undercurrent; (después de beber alcohol) hangover

resaltar vi stand out. **hacer** ~ emphasize

resarcir [9] *vt* repay; (*compensar*) compensate. ~**se** *vpr* make up for

resbal|**adizo** *a* slippery. ~**ar** *vi* slip; (*auto*) skid; (*líquido*) trickle. ~**arse** *vpr* slip; (*auto*) skid; (*líquido*) trickle. ~**ón** *m* slip; (*de vehículo*) skid

rescat|**ar** *vt* ransom; (*recuperar*) recapture; (*fig*) recover. ~**e** *m* ransom; (*recuperación*) recapture; (*salvamento*) rescue

rescindir *vt* cancel

rescoldo *m* embers

resecar [7] *vt* dry up; (*med*) remove. ~**se** *vpr* dry up

resenti|**do** *a* resentful. ~**miento** *m* resentment. ~**rse** *vpr* feel the effects; (*debilitarse*) be weakened; (*ofenderse*) take offence (**de** at)

reseña *f* account; (*en periódico*) report, review. ~**r** *vt* describe; (*en periódico*) report on, review

resero *m* (*Arg*) herdsman

reserva *f* reservation; (*provisión*) reserve(s). ~**ción** *f* reservation. ~**do** *a* reserved. ~**r** *vt* reserve; (*guardar*) keep, save. ~**rse** *vpr* save o.s. **a** ~ **de** except for. **a** ~ **de que** unless. **de** ~ in reserve

resfria|**do** *m* cold; (*enfriamiento*) chill. ~**r** *vt.* ~**r a uno** give s.o. a cold. ~**rse** *vpr* catch a cold; (*fig*) cool off

resguard|**ar** *vt* protect. ~**arse** *vpr* protect o.s.; (*fig*) take care. ~**o** *m* protection; (*garantía*) guarantee; (*recibo*) receipt

resid|**encia** *f* residence; (*univ*) hall of residence, dormitory (*Amer*); (*de ancianos etc*) home. ~**encial** *a* residential. ~**ente** *a* & *m* & *f* resident. ~**ir** *vi* reside; (*fig*) lie

residu|**al** *a* residual. ~**o** *m* remainder. ~**os** *mpl* waste

resigna|**ción** *f* resignation. ~**damente** *adv* with resignation. ~**r** *vt* resign. ~**rse** *vpr* resign o.s. (**a**, **con** to)

resina *f* resin

resist|**encia** *f* resistence. ~**ente** *a* resistent. ~**ir** *vt* resist; (*soportar*) bear. —*vi* resist. **oponer** ~**encia a** resist

resma *f* ream

resobado *a* trite

resol|**ución** *f* resolution; (*solución*) solution; (*decisión*) decision. ~**ver** [2] (*pp* **resuelto**) resolve; solve (*problema etc*). ~**verse** *vpr* be solved; (*resultar bien*) work out; (*decidirse*) make up one's mind

resollar [2] *vi* breathe heavily. **sin** ~ without saying a word

resona|**ncia** *f* resonance. ~**nte** *a* resonant; (*fig*) resounding. ~**r** [2] *vi* resound. **tener** ~**ncia** cause a stir

resopl|**ar** *vi* puff; (*por enfado*) snort; (*por cansancio*) pant. ~**ido** *m* heavy breathing; (*de enfado*) snort; (*de cansancio*) panting

resorte *m* spring. **tocar** (**todos los**) ~**s** (*fig*) pull strings

respald|**ar** *vt* back; (*escribir*) endorse. ~**arse** *vpr* lean back. ~**o** *m* back

respect|**ar** *vi* concern. ~**ivo** *a* respective. ~**o** *m* respect. **al** ~**o** on the matter. (**con**) ~**o a** as regards. **en/por lo que** ~**a** as regards

respet|**able** *a* respectable. —*m* audience. ~**ar** *vt* respect. ~**o** *m* respect. ~**uoso** *a* respectful. **de** ~**o** best. **faltar al** ~**o a** be disrespectful to. **hacerse** ~**ar** command respect

respingo *m* start

respira|**ción** *f* breathing; (*med*) respiration; (*ventilación*) ventilation. ~**ador** *a* respiratory.

~**ar** *vi* breathe; (*fig*) breathe a sigh of relief. **no** ~**ar** (*no hablar*) not say a word. ~**o** *m* breathing; (*fig*) rest

resplandecer [11] *vi* shine. ~**eciente** *a* shining. ~**or** *m* brilliance; (*de llamas*) glow

responder *vi* answer; (*replicar*) answer back; (*fig*) reply, respond. ~ **de** answer for

responsabilidad *f* responsibility. ~**le** *a* responsible. **hacerse** ~**le de** assume responsibility for

respuesta *f* reply, answer

resquebradura *f* crack. ~**jar** *vt* crack. ~**jarse** *vpr* crack

resquemor *m* (*fig*) uneasiness

resquicio *m* crack; (*fig*) possibility

resta *f* subtraction

restablecer [11] *vt* restore. ~**se** *vpr* recover

restallar *vi* crack

restante *a* remaining. **lo** ~ the rest

restar *vt* take away; (*substraer*) subtract. —*vi* be left

restauración *f* restoration. ~**nte** *m* restaurant. ~**r** *vt* restore

restitución *f* restitution. ~**ir** [17] *vt* return; (*restaurar*) restore

resto *m* rest, remainder; (*en matemática*) remainder. ~**s** *mpl* remains; (*de comida*) leftovers

restorán *m* restaurant

restregar [1 & 12] *vt* rub

restricción *f* restriction. ~**ngir** [14] *vt* restrict, limit

resucitar *vt* resuscitate; (*fig*) revive. —*vi* return to life

resuelto *a* resolute

resuello *m* breath; (*respiración*) breathing

resultado *m* result. ~**r** *vi* result; (*salir*) turn out; (*ser*) be; (*ocurrir*) happen; (*costar*) come to

resumen *m* summary. ~**ir** *vt* summarize; (*recapitular*) sum up; (*abreviar*) abridge. **en** ~**en** in short

resurgir [14] *vi* reappear; (*fig*) revive. ~**gimiento** *m* resurgence. ~**rección** *f* resurrection

retaguardia *f* (*mil*) rearguard

retahíla *f* string

retal *m* remnant

retama *f*, **retamo** *m* (*LAm*) broom

retar *vt* challenge

retardar *vt* slow down; (*demorar*) delay

retazo *m* remnant; (*fig*) piece, bit

retemblar [1] *vi* shake

rete... *pref* extremely

retención *f* retention. ~**er** [40] *vt* keep; (*en la memoria*) retain; (*no dar*) withhold

reticencia *f* insinuation; (*reserva*) reticence, reluctance

retina *f* retina

retintín *m* ringing. **con** ~ (*fig*) sarcastically

retirada *f* withdrawal. ~**ado** *a* secluded; (*jubilado*) retired. ~**ar** *vt* move away; (*quitar*) remove; withdraw (*dinero*); (*jubilar*) pension off. ~**arse** *vpr* draw back; (*mil*) withdraw; (*jubilarse*) retire; (*acostarse*) go to bed. ~**o** *m* retirement; (*pensión*) pension; (*lugar apartado*) retreat

reto *m* challenge

retocar [7] *vt* retouch

retoño *m* shoot

retoque *m* (*acción*) retouching; (*efecto*) finishing touch

retorcer [2 & 9] *vt* twist; wring (*ropa*). ~**erse** *vpr* get twisted up; (*de dolor*) writhe. ~**imiento** *m* twisting; (*de ropa*) wringing

retórica *f* rhetoric; (*grandilocuencia*) grandiloquence. ~**o** *m* rhetorical

retorn|ar *vt/i* return. **~o** *m* return

retortijón *m* twist; *(de tripas)* stomach cramp

retoz|ar [10] *vi* romp, frolic. **~ón** *a* playful

retractar *vt* retract. **~se** *vpr* retract

retra|er [41] *vt* retract. **~erse** *vpr* withdraw. **~ido** *a* retiring

retransmitir *vt* relay

retras|ado *a* behind; *(reloj)* slow; *(poco desarrollado)* backward; *(anticuado)* old-fashioned; *(med)* mentally retarded. **~ar** *vt* delay; put back *(reloj)*; *(retardar)* slow down. —*vi* fall behind; *(reloj)* be slow. **~arse** *vpr* be behind; *(reloj)* be slow. **~o** *m* delay; *(poco desarrollo)* backwardness; *(de reloj)* slowness. **~os** *mpl* arrears. **con 5 minutos de ~** 5 minutes late. **traer ~o** be late

retrat|ar *vt* paint a portrait of; *(foto)* photograph; *(fig)* protray. **~ista** *m & f* portrait painter. **~o** *m* portrait; *(fig, descripción)* description. **ser el vivo ~o de** be the living image of

retreparse *vpr* lean back

retreta *f* retreat

retrete *m* toilet

retribu|ción *f* payment. **~ir** [17] *vt* pay

retroce|der *vi* move back; *(fig)* back down. **~so** *m* backward movement; *(de arma de fuego)* recoil; *(med)* relapse

retrógrado *a & m* *(pol)* reactionary

retropropulsión *f* jet propulsion

retrospectivo *a* retrospective

retrovisor *m* rear-view mirror

retumbar *vt* echo; *(trueno etc)* boom

reuma *m*, **reúma** *m* rheumatism

reum|ático *a* rheumatic. **~atismo** *m* rheumatism

reuni|ón *f* meeting; *(entre amigos)* reunion. **~r** [23] *vt* join together; *(recoger)* gather (together). **~rse** *vpr* join together; *(personas)* meet

rev|álida *f* final exam. **~alidar** *vt* confirm; *(escol)* take an exam in

revancha *f* revenge. **tomar la ~** get one's own back

revela|ción *f* revelation. **~do** *m* developing. **~dor** *a* revealing. **~r** *vt* reveal; *(foto)* develop

revent|ar [1] *vi* burst; *(tener ganas)* be dying to. **~arse** *vpr* burst. **~ón** *m* burst; *(auto)* puncture

reverbera|ción *f* *(de luz)* reflection; *(de sonido)* reverberation. **~r** *vi* *(luz)* be reflected; *(sonido)* reverberate

reveren|cia *f* reverence; *(muestra de respeto)* bow; *(muestra de respeto de mujer)* curtsy. **~ciar** *vt* revere. **~do** *a* respected; *(relig)* reverend. **~te** *a* reverent

revers|ible *a* reversible. **~o** *m* reverse

revertir [4] *vi* revert

revés *m* wrong side; *(desgracia)* misfortune; *(en deportes)* backhand. **al ~** the other way round; *(con lo de arriba abajo)* upside down; *(con lo de dentro fuera)* inside out

revesti|miento *m* coating. **~r** [5] *vt* cover; put on *(ropa)*; *(fig)* take on

revis|ar *vt* check; overhaul *(mecanismo)*; service *(coche etc)*. **~ión** *f* check(ing); *(inspección)* inspection; *(de coche etc)* service. **~or** *m* inspector

revist|a *f* magazine; *(inspección)* inspection; *(artículo)* review; *(espectáculo)* revue. **~ero** *m* critic; *(mueble)* magazine rack. **pasar ~a** inspect

revivir *vi* come to life again

revocar [7] *vt* revoke; whitewash ⟨*pared*⟩

revolcar [2 & 7] *vt* knock over. **∼se** *vpr* roll

revolotear *vi* flutter

revoltijo *m*, **revoltillo** *m* mess. **∼ de huevos** scrambled eggs

revoltoso *a* rebellious; ⟨*niño*⟩ naughty

revoluci|ón *f* revolution. **∼onar** *vt* revolutionize. **∼onario** *a & m* revolutionary

revolver [2, pp **revuelto**] *vt* mix; stir ⟨*líquido*⟩; ⟨*desordenar*⟩ mess up; ⟨*pol*⟩ stir up. **∼se** *vpr* turn round. **∼se contra** turn on

revólver *m* revolver

revoque *m* ⟨*con cal*⟩ whitewashing

revuelo *m* fluttering; ⟨*fig*⟩ stir

revuelt|a *f* turn; ⟨*de calle etc*⟩ bend; ⟨*motín*⟩ revolt; ⟨*conmoción*⟩ disturbance. **∼o** *a* mixed up; ⟨*líquido*⟩ cloudy; ⟨*mar*⟩ rough; ⟨*tiempo*⟩ unsettled; ⟨*huevos*⟩ scrambled

rey *m* king. **∼es** *mpl* king and queen

reyerta *f* quarrel

rezagarse [12] *vpr* fall behind

rez|ar [10] *vt* say. **∼vi** pray; ⟨*decir*⟩ say. **∼o** *m* praying; ⟨*oración*⟩ prayer

rezongar [12] *vi* grumble

rezumar *vt/i* ooze

ría *f* estuary

riachuelo *m* stream

riada *f* flood

ribera *f* bank

ribete *m* border; ⟨*fig*⟩ embellishment

ricino *m*. **aceite de ∼** castor oil

rico *a* rich; ⟨*culin, fam*⟩ delicious. **∼m** rich person

rid|ículo *a* ridiculous. **∼iculizar** [10] *vt* ridicule

riego *m* watering; ⟨*irrigación*⟩ irrigation

riel *m* rail

rienda *f* rein

riesgo *m* risk. **a ∼ de** at the risk of. **correr (el) ∼ de** run the risk of

rifa *f* raffle. **∼r** *vt* raffle. **∼rse** *vpr* ⟨*fam*⟩ quarrel over

rifle *m* rifle

rigidez *f* rigidity; ⟨*fig*⟩ inflexibility

rígido *a* rigid; ⟨*fig*⟩ inflexible

rig|or *m* strictness; ⟨*exactitud*⟩ exactness; ⟨*de clima*⟩ severity. **∼uroso** *a* rigorous. **de ∼or** compulsory. **en ∼or** strictly speaking

rima *f* rhyme. **∼r** *vt/i* rhyme

rimbombante *a* resounding; ⟨*lenguaje*⟩ pompous; ⟨*fig, ostentoso*⟩ showy

rimel *m* mascara

rincón *m* corner

rinoceronte *m* rhinoceros

riña *f* quarrel; ⟨*pelea*⟩ fight

riñ|ón *m* kidney. **∼onada** *f* loin; ⟨*guiso*⟩ kidney stew

río *m* river; ⟨*fig*⟩ stream. **—vb** *véase* **reír**. **∼ abajo** downstream. **∼ arriba** upstream

rioja *m* Rioja wine

riqueza *f* wealth; ⟨*fig*⟩ richness. **∼s** *fpl* riches

riquísimo *a* delicious

risa *f* laugh. **desternillarse de ∼** split one's sides laughing. **la ∼** laughter

risco *m* cliff

ris|ible *a* laughable. **∼otada** *f* guffaw

ristra *f* string

risueño *a* smiling; ⟨*fig*⟩ happy

rítmico *a* rhythmic(al)

ritmo *m* rhythm; ⟨*fig*⟩ rate

rit|o *m* rite; ⟨*fig*⟩ ritual. **∼ual** *a & m* ritual. **de ∼ual** customary

rival *a & m & f* rival. **∼idad** *f* rivalry. **∼izar** [10] *vi* rival

riz|ado *a* curly. **∼ar** [10] *vt* curl; ripple ⟨*agua*⟩. **∼o** *m* curl; ⟨*en agua*⟩ ripple. **∼oso** *a* curly

róbalo m bass

robar vt steal (cosa); rob (persona); (raptar) kidnap

roble m oak (tree)

roblón m rivet

robo (pl robots) m robot

robot (pl robots) m robot

robust|ez f strength. ~o a strong

roca f rock

roce m rubbing; (toque ligero) touch; (señal) mark; (fig, entre personas) contact

rociar [20] vt spray

rocín m nag

rocío m dew

rodaballo m turbot

rodado m (Arg, vehículo) vehicle

rodaja f disc; (culin) slice

rodaje m (de película) shooting; (de coche) running in. ~r [2] vt shoot (película); run in (coche); (recorrer) travel. —vi (coche) run; (hacer una película) shoot

rode|ar vt surround. ~arse vpr surround o.s. (de with). ~o m long way round; (de ganado) round-up. **andar con ~os** beat about the bush. **sin ~os** plainly

rodilla f knee. ~era f knee-pad. **de ~as** kneeling

rodillo m roller; (culin) rolling-pin

rododendro m rhododendron

rodrigón m stake

roe|dor m rodent. ~r [37] vt gnaw

rogar [2 & 12] vt/i ask; (relig) pray. **se ruega a los Sres pasajeros...** passengers are requested... **se ruega no fumar** please do not smoke

roj|ete m rouge. ~ez f redness. ~izo a reddish. ~o a & m red. **ponerse ~o** blush

roll|izo a round; (persona) plump. ~o m roll; (de cuerda) coil; (culin, rodillo) rolling-pin; (fig, pesadez, fam) bore

romance a Romance. —m Romance language; (poema) romance. **hablar en ~** speak plainly

rom|ánico a Romanesque; (lengua) Romance. ~ano a & m Roman. **a la ~ana** (culin) (deep-)fried in batter

rom|anticismo m romanticism. ~ántico a romantic

romería f pilgrimage

romero m rosemary

romo a blunt; (nariz) snub; (fig, torpe) dull

rompe|cabezas m invar puzzle; (con tacos de madera) jigsaw (puzzle). ~nueces m invar nutcrackers. ~olas m invar breakwater

romper (pp roto) vt break; break off (relaciones etc). —vi break; (sol) break through. ~erse vpr break. ~er a burst out. ~imiento m (de relaciones etc) breaking off

ron m rum

ronc|ar [7] vi snore. ~o a hoarse

roncha f lump; (culin) slice

ronda f round; (patrulla) patrol; (carretera) ring road. ~lla f group of serenaders; (invención) story. ~r vt/i patrol

rondón. de ~ unannounced

ronquedad f, **ronquera** f hoarseness

ronquido m snore

ronronear vi purr

ronzal m halter

roña f (suciedad) grime. ~oso a dirty; (oxidado) rusty; (tacaño) mean

ropa f clothes, clothing. ~a blanca linen; (ropa interior) underwear. ~a de cama bedclothes. ~a hecha ready-made clothes. ~a interior underwear. ~aje m robes; (excesivo) heavy clothing. ~ero m wardrobe

ros|a *a invar* pink. **~f** rose; *(color)* pink. **~áceo** *a* pink. **~ado** *a* rosy. **—m** *(vino)* rosé. **~al** *m* rose-bush

rosario *m* rosary; *(fig)* series

rosbif *m* roast beef

rosc|a *f* coil; *(de tornillo)* thread; *(de pan)* roll. **~o** *m* roll

rosetón *m* rosette

rosquilla *f* doughnut; *(oruga)* grub

rostro *m* face

rota|ción *f* rotation. **~tivo** *a* rotary

roto *a* broken

rótula *f* kneecap

rotulador *m* felt-tip pen

rótulo *m* sign; *(etiqueta)* label

rotundo *a* emphatic

rotura *f* break

roturar *vt* plough

roza *f* groove. **~dura** *f* scratch

rozagante *a* showy

rozar [10] *vt* rub against; *(ligeramente)* brush against; *(ensuciar)* dirty; *(fig)* touch on. **~se** *vpr* rub; *(con otras personas)* mix

Rte. *abrev* (Remite(nte)) sender

rúa *f* (small) street

rubéola *f* German measles

rubí *m* ruby

rubicundo *a* ruddy

rubio *a* *(pelo)* fair; *(persona)* fair-haired; *(tabaco)* Virginian

rubor *m* blush; *(fig)* shame. **~izado** *a* blushing; *(fig)* ashamed. **~izar** [10] *vt* make blush. **~izarse** *vpr* blush

rúbrica *f* red mark; *(de firma)* flourish; *(título)* heading

rudeza *f* roughness

rudiment|al *a* rudimentary. **~os** *mpl* rudiments

rudo *a* rough; *(sencillo)* simple

rueda *f* wheel; *(de mueble)* castor; *(de personas)* ring; *(culin)* slice. **~ de prensa** press conference

ruedo *m* edge; *(redondel)* arena

ruego *m* request; *(súplica)* entreaty. *—vb véase* **rogar**

rufi|án *m* pimp; *(granuja)* villain. **~anesco** *a* roguish

rugby *m* Rugby

rugi|do *m* roar. **~r** [14] *vi* roar

ruibarbo *m* rhubarb

ruido *m* noise; *(alboroto)* din; *(escándalo)* commotion. **~so** *a* noisy; *(fig)* sensational

ruin *a* despicable; *(tacaño)* mean

ruina *f* ruin; *(colapso)* collapse

ruindad *f* meanness

ruinoso *a* ruinous

ruiseñor *m* nightingale

ruleta *f* roulette

rulo *m* *(culin)* rolling-pin; *(del pelo)* curler

Rumania *f* Romania

rumano *a* & *m* Romanian

rumba *f* rumba

rumbo *m* direction; *(fig)* course; *(fig, generosidad)* lavishness. **~so** *a* lavish. **con ~ a** in the direction of. **hacer ~ a** head for

rumia|nte *a* & *m* ruminant. **~r** *vt* chew; *(fig)* chew over. *—ví* ruminate

rumor *m* rumour; *(ruido)* murmur. **~earse** *vpr* be rumoured. **~oso** *a* murmuring

runr|ún *m* rumour; *(ruido)* murmur. **~unearse** *vpr* be rumoured

ruptura *f* break; *(de relaciones etc)* breaking off

rural *a* rural

Rusia *f* Russia

ruso *a* & *m* Russian

rústico *a* rural; *(de carácter)* coarse. **en rústica** paperback

ruta *f* route; *(camino)* road; *(fig)* course

rutilante *a* shining

rutina *f* routine. **~rio** *a* routine

S

Ltd, Limited, plc, Public Limited Company

sábado *m* Saturday

sabana *f* (*esp LAm*) savannah

sábana *f* sheet

sabandija *f* bug

sabañón *m* chilblain

sabático *a* sabbatical

sab|elotodo *m* & *f invar* know-all (*fam*). **~er** [38] *vt* know; (*ser capaz de*) be able to, know how to; (*enterarse de*) learn. —*vi.* **~er** a taste of. **~er** *m* knowledge. **~ido** *a* well-known. **~iduría** *f* wisdom; (*conocimientos*) knowledge. a **~er** si I wonder if. **¡haberlo ~ido!** if only I'd known! **hacer ~er** let know. **no sé cuántos** what's-his-name. **para que lo sepas** let me tell you. **¡qué sé yo!** how should I know? **que yo sepa** as far as I know. **¿~es nadar?** can you swim? **un no sé qué** a certain sth. **¡yo qué sé!** how should I know?

sabiendas. a ~ knowingly; (*a propósito*) on purpose

sabio *a* learned; (*prudente*) wise

sabor *m* taste, flavour; (*fig*) flavour. **~ear** *vt* taste; (*fig*) savour

sabot|aje *m* sabotage. **~eador** *m* saboteur. **~ear** *vt* sabotage

sabroso *a* tasty; (*fig, substancioso*) meaty

sabueso *m* (*perro*) bloodhound; (*fig, detective*) detective

saca|corchos *m invar* corkscrew. **~puntas** *m invar* pencil-sharpener

sacar [7] *vt* take out; put out 〈*parte del cuerpo*〉; (*quitar*) remove; take 〈*foto*〉; win 〈*premio*〉; get 〈*billete, entrada etc*〉; withdraw 〈*dinero*〉; reach 〈*solución*〉; draw 〈*conclusión*〉; make 〈*copia*〉. **~ adelante** bring up 〈*niño*〉; carry on 〈*negocio*〉

sacarina *f* saccharin

sacerdo|cio *m* priesthood. **~tal** *a* priestly. **~te** *m* priest

saciar *vt* satisfy

saco *m* bag; (*anat*) sac; (*LAm, chaqueta*) jacket; (*de mentiras*) pack. **~ de dormir** sleeping-bag

sacramento *m* sacrament

sacrific|ar [7] *vt* sacrifice. **~arse** *vpr* sacrifice o.s. **~io** *m* sacrifice

sacr|ilegio *m* sacrilege. **~ílego** *a* sacrilegious

sacro *a* sacred, holy. **~santo** *a* sacrosanct

sacudi|da *f* shake; (*movimiento brusco*) jolt, jerk; (*fig*) shock. **~da eléctrica** electric shock. **~r** *vt* shake; (*golpear*) beat; (*ahuyentar*) chase away. **~rse** *vpr* shake off; (*fig*) get rid of

sádico *a* sadistic. —*m* sadist

sadismo *m* sadism

saeta *f* arrow; (*de reloj*) hand

safari *m* safari

sagaz *a* shrewd

Sagitario *m* Sagittarius

sagrado *a* sacred, holy. —*m* sanctuary

Sahara *m*, **Sáhara** /'saxara/ *m* Sahara

sainete *m* short comedy

sal *f* salt

sala *f* room; (*en teatro*) house. **~ de espectáculos** concert hall, auditorium. **~ de espera** waiting-room. **~ de estar** living-room. **~ de fiestas** nightclub

sala|do *a* salty; 〈*agua del mar*〉 salt; (*vivo*) lively; (*encantador*) cute; (*fig*) witty. **~r** *vt* salt

salario *m* wages

salazón *f* (*carne*) salted meat; (*pescado*) salted fish

salchich|a *f* (*pork*) sausage. **~ón** *m* salami

sald|ar *vt* pay 〈*cuenta*〉; (*vender*) sell off; (*fig*) settle. **~o** *m* balance; (*venta*) sale; (*lo que queda*) remnant

salero *m* salt-cellar

salgo *vb véase* **salir**

sali|da *f* departure; (*puerta*) exit, way out; (*de gas, de líquido*) leak; (*de astro*) rising; (*com, posibilidad de venta*) opening; (*chiste*) witty remark; (*fig*) way out. **~da de emergencia** emergency exit. **~ente** *a* projecting; (*fig*) outstanding. **~r** [52] *vi* leave; (*de casa etc*) go out; (*revista etc*) be published; (*resultar*) turn out; (*astro*) rise; (*aparecer*) appear. **~rse** *vpr* leave; (*recipiente, líquido etc*) leak. **~r adelante** get by. **~rse con la suya** get one's own way

saliva *f* saliva

salmo *m* psalm

salm|ón *m* salmon. **~onete** *m* red mullet

salmuera *f* brine

salón *m* lounge, sitting-room. **~ de actos** assembly hall. **~ de fiestas** dancehall

salpica|dero *m* (*auto*) dashboard. **~dura** *f* splash; (*acción*) splashing. **~r** [7] *vt* splash; (*rociar*) sprinkle

sals|a *f* sauce; (*para carne asada*) gravy; (*fig*) spice. **~ verde** parsley sauce. **~era** *f* sauce-boat

salt|amontes *m invar* grasshopper. **~ar** *vt* jump (over); (*fig*) miss out. **~** *vi* jump; (*romperse*) break; (*líquido*) spurt out; (*desprenderse*) come off; (*pelota*) bounce; (*estallar*) explode. **~eador** *m* highwayman. **~ear** *vt* rob; (*culin*) sauté. **~** *vi* skip through

saltimbanqui *m* acrobat

salt|o *m* jump; (*al agua*) dive. **~ de agua** waterfall. **~ón** *a* (*ojos*) bulging. **~** *m* grasshopper. **~os** by jumping; (*fig*) by leaps and bounds. **de un ~o** with one jump

salud *f* health; (*fig*) welfare. **—int** cheers! **~able** *a* healthy

salud|ar *vt* greet, say hello to; (*mil*) salute. **~o** *m* greeting; (*mil*) salute. **~os** *mpl* best wishes. **le ~a atentamente** (*en cartas*) yours faithfully

salva *f* salvo; (*de aplausos*) thunders

salvación *f* salvation

salvado *m* bran

Salvador *m*. **El ~** El Salvador

salvaguardia *f* safeguard

salvaje *a* (*planta, animal*) wild; (*primitivo*) savage. **—m & f** savage

salvamanteles *m invar* table-mat

salva|mento *m* rescue. **~r** *vt* save, rescue; (*atravesar*) cross; (*recorrer*) travel; (*fig*) overcome. **~rse** *vpr* save o.s. **~vidas** *m invar* lifebelt. **chaleco ~vidas** life-jacket

salvia *f* sage

salvo *a* safe. **—adv & prep** except (for). **~ que** unless. **~conducto** *m* safe-conduct. **a ~** out of danger. **poner a ~** put in a safe place

samba *f* samba

San *a* Saint, St. **~ Miguel** St Michael

sana|r *vt* cure. **—vi** recover. **~torio** *m* sanatorium

sanci|ón *f* sanction. **~onar** *vt* sanction

sancocho *m* (*LAm*) stew

sandalia *f* sandal

sándalo *m* sandalwood

sandía *f* water melon

sandwich /'sambitʃ/ *m* (*pl* **sandwichs**, **sandwiches**) sandwich

sanear *vt* drain

sangr|ante *a* bleeding; (*fig*) flagrant. **~ar** *vt/i* bleed. **~e** *f* blood. **a ~e fría** in cold blood

sangría *f* (*bebida*) sangria

sangriento *a* bloody

sangui|juela f leech. **~íneo** a blood

san|idad f health. **~itario** a sanitary. **~o** a healthy; (seguro) sound. **~o y salvo** safe and sound. **cortar por lo ~o** settle things once and for all

santiamén m. **en un ~** in an instant

sant|idad f sanctity. **~ificar** [7] vt sanctify. **~iguar** [15] vt make the sign of the cross over. **~iguarse** vpr cross o.s. **~o** a holy; (delante de nombre) Saint, St. —m saint; (día) saint's day, name day. **~uario** m sanctuary. **~urrón** a sanctimonious, hypocritical

saña f fury; (crueldad) cruelty. **~oso** a, **~udo** a furious

sapo m toad; (bicho, fam) small animal, creature

saque m (en tenis) service; (en fútbol) throw-in; (inicial en fútbol) kick-off

saque|ar vt loot. **~o** m looting

sarampión m measles

sarape m (Mex) blanket

sarc|asmo m sarcasm. **~ástico** a sarcastic

sardana f Catalonian dance

sardina f sardine

sardo a & m Sardinian

sardónico a sardonic

sargento m sergeant

sarmiento m vine shoot

sarpullido m rash

sarta f string

sartén f frying-pan (Brit), fry-pan (Amer)

sastre m tailor. **~ría** f tailoring; (tienda) tailor's (shop)

Satanás m Satan

satánico a satanic

satélite m satellite

satinado a shiny

sátira f satire

satírico a satirical. —m satirist

satisfac|ción f satisfaction. **~acer** [31] vt satisfy; (pagar) pay; (gustar) please; meet (gastos, requisitos). **~acerse** vpr satisfy o.s.; (vengarse) take revenge. **~actorio** a satisfactory. **~echo** a satisfied. **~echo de sí mismo** smug

satura|ción f saturation. **~r** vt saturate

Saturno m Saturn

sauce m willow. **~ llorón** weeping willow

saúco m elder

savia f sap

sauna f sauna

saxofón m, **saxófono** m saxophone

sazón f ripeness; (culin) seasoning. **~onado** a ripe; (culin) seasoned. **~onar** vt ripen; (culin) season. **en ~ón** in season

se pron (él) him; (ella) her; (Vd) you; (reflexivo, él) himself; (reflexivo, ella) herself; (reflexivo, ello) itself; (reflexivo, uno) oneself; (reflexivo, Vd) yourself; (reflexivo, ellos, ellas) themselves; (reflexivo, Vds) yourselves; (recíproco) (to) each other. **~ dice** people say, they say, it is said (que that). **~ habla español** Spanish spoken

sé vb véase **saber** y **ser**

sea vb véase **ser**

sebo m tallow; (culin) suet

seca|dor m drier; (de pelo) hairdrier. **~nte** a drying. —m blotting-paper. **~r** [7] vt dry. **~rse** vpr dry; (río etc) dry up; (persona) dry o.s.

sección f section

seco a dry; (frutos, flores) dried; (flaco) thin; (respuesta) curt; (escueto) plain. **a secas** just. **en ~** (bruscamente) suddenly. **lavar en ~** dry-clean

secre|ción f secretion. **~tar** vt secrete

secretaría f secretariat. ~**io** m secretary

secreto a & m secret

secta f sect. ~**rio** a sectarian

sector m sector

secuela f consequence

secuencia f sequence

secuestr|ar vt confiscate; kidnap (persona); hijack (avión). ~**o** m seizure; (de persona) kidnapping; (de avión) hijack(ing)

secular a secular

secundar vt second, help. ~**io** a secondary

sed f thirst. —vb véase **ser**. tener ~ be thirsty. tener ~ de (fig) be hungry for

seda f silk

sedante a & m, **sedativo** a & m sedative

sede f seat; (relig) see

sedentario a sedentary

sedici|ón f sedition. ~**oso** a seditious

sediento a thirsty

sediment|ar vi deposit. ~**arse** vpr settle. ~**o** m sediment

seduc|ción f seduction. ~**ir** [47] vt seduce; (atraer) attract. ~**tor** a seductive. —m seducer

sega|dor m harvester. ~**dora** f harvester, mower. ~**r** [1 & 12] vt reap

seglar a secular. —m layman

segmento m segment

segoviano m person from Segovia

segrega|ción f segregation. ~**r** [12] vt segregate

segui|da f. en ~**da** immediately. ~**do** a continuous; (en plural) consecutive. —adv straight; (después) after. **todo** ~**do** go straight ahead. ~**dor** a following. —m follower. ~**r** [5 & 13] vt follow (continuar) continue

según prep according to. —adv it depends; (a medida que) as

segundo a second. —m second; (culin) second course

segur|amente adv certainly; (muy probablemente) surely. ~**idad** f safety; (certeza) certainty; (aplomo) confidence. ~**idad en sí mismo** self-confidence. ~**idad social** social security. ~**o** a safe; (cierto) certain, sure; (firme) secure; (de fiar) reliable. —adv for certain. —m insurance; (dispositivo de seguridad) safety device. ~**o de sí mismo** self-confident. ~**o de terceros** third-party insurance

seis a & m six. ~**cientos** a & m six hundred

seísmo m earthquake

selec|ción f selection. ~**cionar** vt select, choose. ~**tivo** a selective. ~**to** a selected; (fig) choice

selva f forest; (jungla) jungle

sell|ar vt stamp; (cerrar) seal. ~**o** m stamp; (en documento oficial) seal; (fig, distintivo) hallmark

semáforo m semaphore; (auto) traffic lights; (rail) signal

semana f week. ~**l** a weekly. ~**rio** a & m weekly. **S~ Santa** Holy Week

semántic|a f semantics. ~**o** a semantic

semblante m face; (fig) look

sembrar [1] vt sow; (fig) scatter

semeja|nte a similar; (tal) such. —m fellow man; (cosa) equal. ~**nza** f similarity. ~**r** vi seem. ~**rse** vpr look alike. a ~**nza de** like. tener ~**nza con** resemble

semen m semen. ~**tal** a stud. —m stud animal

semestr|al a half-yearly. ~**e** m six months

semibreve m semibreve (Brit), whole note (Amer)

semic|ircular a semicircular. ~**írculo** m semicircle

semicorchea f semiquaver (*Brit*), sixteenth note (*Amer*)

semifinal f semifinal

semill a f seed. ~**ero** m nursery; (*fig*) hotbed

seminario m (*univ*) seminar; (*relig*) seminary

sem|ita a Semitic. —m Semite. ~**ítico** a Semitic

sémola f semolina

senado m senate; (*fig*) assembly. ~**r** m senator

sencill|ez f simplicity. ~**o** a simple; (*uno solo*) single

senda f, **sendero** m path

sendos apl each

seno m bosom. ~ **materno** womb

sensaci|ón f sensation. ~**onal** a sensational

sensat|ez f good sense. ~**o** a sensible

sensi|bilidad f sensibility. ~**ble** a sensitive; (*notable*) notable; (*lamentable*) lamentable. ~**tivo** a (*órgano*) sense

sensual a sensual. ~**idad** f sensuality

senta|do a sitting (down). **dar algo por** ~**do** take something for granted. ~**r** [1] vt place; (*establecer*) establish. —vi suit; (*de medidas*) fit; (*comida*) agree with. ~**rse** vpr sit (down); (*sedimento*) settle

sentencia f saying; (*jurid*) sentence. ~**r** vt sentence

sentido a deeply felt; (*sincero*) sincere; (*sensible*) sensitive. —m sense; (*dirección*) direction. ~ **común** common sense. ~ **del humor** sense of humour. ~ **único** one-way. **doble** ~ double meaning. **no tener** ~ not make sense. **perder el** ~ faint. **sin** ~ unconscious; (*cosa*) senseless

sentim|ental a sentimental. ~**iento** m feeling; (*sentido*) sense; (*pesar*) regret

sentir [4] vt feel; (*oír*) hear; (*lamentar*) be sorry for. —vi feel; (*lamentarse*) be sorry. —m (*opinión*) opinion. ~**se** vpr feel. **lo siento** I'm sorry

seña f sign. ~**s** fpl (*dirección*) address; (*descripción*) description

señal f sign; (*rail etc*) signal; (*telefónico*) tone; (*com*) deposit. ~**ado** a notable. ~**ar** vt signal; (*poner señales en*) mark; (*apuntar*) point out; (*manecilla, aguja*) point to; (*determinar*) fix. ~**arse** vpr stand out. **dar** ~**es de** show signs of. **en** ~ **de** as a token of

señero a alone; (*sin par*) unique

señor m man; (*caballero*) gentleman; (*delante de nombre propio*) Mr; (*tratamiento directo*) sir. ~**a** f lady, woman; (*delante de nombre propio*) Mrs; (*esposa*) wife; (*tratamiento directo*) madam. ~**ial** a (*casa*) stately. ~**ita** f young lady; (*delante de nombre propio*) Miss; (*tratamiento directo*) miss. ~**ito** m young gentleman. **el** ~ **alcalde** the mayor. **el** ~ **Mr. muy** ~ **mío** Dear Sir. **¡no** ~**!** certainly not! **ser** ~ **de** be master of, control

señuelo m lure

sepa vb véase **saber**

separa|ción f separation. ~**do** a separate. ~**r** vt separate; (*apartar*) move away; (*de empleo*) dismiss. ~**rse** vpr separate; (*amigos*) part. ~**tista** a & f separatist. **por** ~**do** separately

septentrional a north(ern)

séptico a septic

septiembre m September

séptimo a seventh

sepulcro m sepulchre

sepult|ar vt bury. ~**ura** f burial; (*tumba*) grave. ~**urero** m gravedigger

sequ|edad f dryness. **~ía** f
drought

séquito m entourage; (fig)
aftermath

ser [39] vi be. —m being. **~ de** be
made of; (provenir de) come
from; (pertenecer a) belong to.
a no ~ que unless. ¡así sea! so be it! **es
más** what is more. **lo que sea**
anything. **no sea que, no vaya
a ~ que** in case. **o sea** in other
words. **sea lo que** fuere be that
as it may. **sea... sea** either... or.
siendo así que since. **soy yo**
it's me

seren|ar vt calm down. **~arse**
vpr calm down; ⟨tiempo⟩ clear
up. **~ata** f serenade. **~idad** f
serenity. **~o** a ⟨cielo⟩ clear; ⟨ti-
empo⟩ fine; (fig) calm. —m night
watchman. **al ~o** in the open

seri|al m serial. **~e** f series.
fuera de ~e (fig, extraordinario) special. **producción
f en ~** mass production

seri|edad f seriousness. **~o** a ser-
ious; ⟨confiable⟩ reliable. **en ~o**
seriously. **poco ~o** frivolous

sermón m sermon

serp|enteante a winding. **~en-
tear** vi wind. **~iente** f snake.
~iente de cascabel rattlesnake

serrano a mountain; ⟨jamón⟩
cured

serr|ar [1] vt saw. **~ín** m
sawdust. **~ucho** m (hand)saw

servi|cial a helpful. **~cio** m ser-
vice; ⟨conjunto⟩ (aseo) toilet.
~cio a domicilio delivery service. **~dor** m servant. **~dum-
bre** f servitude; ⟨criados⟩
servants, staff. **~l** a servile. **su
(seguro) ~dor** (en cartas) yours
faithfully

servilleta f serviette, (table)
napkin

servir [5] vt serve; (ayudar) help;
(en restaurante) wait on. —vi
serve; (ser útil) be of use. **~se**
vpr help o.s. **~se de** use. **no ~
de nada** be useless. **para ~le** at
your service. **sírvase sentarse**
please sit down

sesear vi pronounce the Spanish
c as an s

sesent|a a & m sixty. **~ón** a & m
sixty-year-old

seseo m pronunciation of the
Spanish c as an s

sesg|ado a slanting. **~o** m slant;
(fig, rumbo) turn

sesión f session; (en el cine) showing; (en el teatro) performance

ses|o m brain; (fig) brains. **~udo**
a inteligent; ⟨sensato⟩ sensible

seta f mushroom

sete|cientos a & m seven
hundred. **~nta** a & m seventy.
~ntón a & m seventy-year-old

setiembre m September

seto m fence; (de plantas) hedge.
~ vivo hedge

seudo... pref pseudo...

seudónimo m pseudonym

sever|idad f severity. **~o** a
severe; ⟨disciplina, profesor etc⟩
strict

Sevilla f Seville

sevillan|as fpl popular dance
from Seville. **~o** m person from
Seville

sexo m sex

sext|eto m sextet. **~o** a sixth

sexual a sexual. **~idad** f
sexuality

si m (mus) B; (solfa) te. —conj if;
⟨dubitativo⟩ whether. **~ no** or
else. **por ~ (acaso)** in case

sí pron reflexivo (él) himself; (ella)
herself; (ello) itself; (uno) oneself; (Vd) yourself; (ellos, ellas)
themselves; (Vds) yourselves;
(recíproco) each other

sí adv yes. —m consent

Siamés a & m Siamese

Sicilia f Sicily

sida m Aids

siderurgia f iron and steel industry

sidra f cider

siega f harvesting; (*época*) harvest time

siembra f sowing; (*época*) sowing time

siempre *adv* always. ~ **que** if. **como** ~ as usual. **de** ~ (*acostumbrado*) usual. **lo de** ~ the same old story. **para** ~ for ever

sien f temple

siento *vb véase* **sentar** *y* **sentir**

sierra f saw; (*cordillera*) mountain range

siervo m slave

siesta f siesta

siete a & m seven

sífilis f syphilis

sifón m U-bend; (*de soda*) syphon

sigilo m secrecy

sigla f initials, abbreviation

siglo m century; (*época*) time, age; (*fig, mucho tiempo, fam*) ages; (*fig, mundo*) world

significa|**ción** f meaning; (*importancia*) significance. ~**do** a (*conocido*) well-known. —*m* meaning. ~**r** [7] *vt* mean; (*expresar*) express. ~**rse** *vpr* stand out. ~**tivo** a significant

signo m sign. ~ **de admiración** exclamation mark. ~ **de interrogación** question mark

sigo *vb véase* **seguir**

siguiente a following, next. **lo** ~ the following

sílaba f syllable

silb|**ar** *vt/i* whistle. ~**ato** m, ~**ido** m whistle

silenci|**ador** m silencer. ~**ar** *vt* hush up. ~**o** m silence. ~**oso** a silent

sílfide f sylph

silicio m silicon

silo m silo

silueta f silhouette; (*dibujo*) outline

silvestre a wild

silla f chair; (*de montar*) saddle; (*relig*) see. ~**a de ruedas** wheelchair. ~**in** m saddle. ~**ón** m armchair

simb|**ólico** a symbolic(al). ~**olismo** m symbolism. ~**olizar** [10] *vt* symbolize

símbolo m symbol

sim|**etría** f symmetry. ~**étrico** a symmetric(al)

simiente f seed

similar a similar

simp|**atía** f liking; (*cariño*) affection; (*fig, amigo*) friend. ~**ático** a nice, likeable; (*amable*) kind. ~**atizante** m & f sympathizer. ~**atizar** [10] *vi* get on (well together). **me es** ~**ático** I like

simple a simple; (*mero*) mere. ~**eza** f simplicity; (*tontería*) stupid thing; (*insignificancia*) trifle. ~**icidad** f simplicity. ~**ificar** [7] *vt* simplify. ~**ón** m simpleton

simposio m symposium

simula|**ción** f simulation. ~**r** *vt* feign

simultáneo a simultaneous

sin *prep* without. ~ **que** without

sinagoga f synagogue

sincer|**idad** f sincerity. ~**o** a sincere

síncopa f (*mus*) syncopation

sincopar *vt* syncopate

sincronizar [10] *vt* synchronize

sindica|**l** a (trade-)union. ~**lista** m & f trade-unionist. ~**to** m trade union

síndrome m syndrome

sinfín m endless number

sinf|**onía** f symphony. ~**ónico** a symphonic

singular a singular; (*excepcional*) exceptional. ~**izar** [10] *vt* single out. ~**izarse** *vpr* stand out

siniestro *a* sinister; *(desgraciado)* unlucky. —*m* disaster

sinnúmero *m* endless number

sino *m* fate. —*conj* but; *(salvo)* except

sínodo *m* synod

sinónimo *a* synoymous. —*m* synonym

sinrazón *f* wrong

sintaxis *f* syntax

síntesis *f* invar synthesis

sint|ético *a* synthetic. ~**etizar** [10] *vt* synthesize; *(resumir)* summarize

síntoma *f* sympton

sintomático *a* symptomatic

sinton|ía *f (en la radio)* signature tune. ~**izar** [10] *vt (con la radio)* tune (in)

sinuoso *a* winding

sinvergüenza *m & f* scoundrel

sionis|mo *m* Zionism. ~**ta** *m & f* Zionist

siquiera *conj* even if. —*adv* at least. **ni** ~ not even

sirena *f* siren

Siria *f* Syria

sirio *a & m* Syrian

siroco *m* sirocco

sirvienta *f*, **sirviente** *m* servant

sirvo *vb véase* **servir**

sise|ar *vt/i* hiss. ~**o** *m* hissing

sísmico *a* seismic

sismo *m* earthquake

sistem|a *m* system. ~**ático** *a* systematic. **por** ~**a** as a rule

sitiar *vt* besiege; *(fig)* surround

sitio *m* place; *(espacio)* space; *(mil)* siege. **en cualquier** ~ anywhere

situa|ción *f* position. ~**r** [21] *vt* situate; *(poner)* put; *(depositar)* deposit. ~**rse** *vpr* be successful, establish o.s.

slip /es'lip/ *m (pl* **slips** /es'lip/) underpants, briefs

slogan /es'logan/ *m (pl* **slogans** /es'logan/) slogan

smoking /es'mokin/ *m (pl* **smokings** /es'mokin/) dinner jacket *(Brit)*, tuxedo *(Amer)*

sobaco *m* armpit

sobar *vt* handle; knead *(masa)*

soberan|ía *f* sovereignty. ~**o** *a* sovereign; *(fig)* supreme. —*m* sovereign

soberbi|a *f* pride; *(altanería)* arrogance. ~**o** *a* proud; *(altivo)* arrogant

soborn|ar *vt* bribe. ~**o** *m* bribe

sobra *f* surplus. ~**s** *fpl* leftovers. ~**do** *a* more than enough. ~**nte** *a* surplus. ~**r** *vi* be left over; *(estorbar)* be in the way. **de** ~ more than enough

sobrasada *f* Majorcan sausage

sobre *prep* on; *(encima de)* on top of; *(más o menos)* about; *(encima de)* above; *(sin tocar)* over; *(además de)* on top of. —*m* envelope. ~**cargar** [12] *vt* overload. ~**coger** [14] *vt* startle. ~**cogerse** *vpr* be startled. ~**cubierta** *f* dust cover. ~**dicho** *a* aforementioned. ~**entender** [1] *vt* understand, infer. ~**entendido** *a* implicit. ~**humano** *a* superhuman. ~**llevar** *vt* bear. ~**mesa** *f.* **de** ~**mesa** after-dinner. ~**natural** *a* supernatural. ~**nombre** *m* nickname. ~**pasar** *vt* exceed. ~**poner** [34] *vt* superimpose; *(fig, anteponer)* put before. ~**ponerse** *vpr* overcome. ~**pujar** *vt* surpass. ~**saliente** *a (fig)* outstanding. —*m* excellent mark. ~**salir** [52] *vi* stick out; *(fig)* stand out. ~**saltar** *vt* startle. ~**salto** *m* fright. ~**sueldo** *m* bonus. ~**todo** *m* overall; *(abrigo)* overcoat. ~**todo** above all, especially. ~**venir** [53] *vi* happen. ~**viviente** *a* surviving. —*m & f* survivor. ~**vivir** *vi* survive. ~**volar** *vt* fly over

sobriedad *f* restraint

sobrin|a *f* niece. **~o** *m* nephew

sobrio *a* moderate, sober

socarr|ón *a* sarcastic; *(taimado)* sly. **~onería** *f* sarcasm

socavar *vt* undermine

soci|able *a* sociable. **~al** *a* social. **~aldemocracia** *f* social democracy. **~aldemócrata** *m* & *f* social democrat. **~alismo** *m* socialsim. **~alista** *a* *m* & *f* socialist. **~alizar** [10] *vt* nationalize. **~edad** *f* society; *(com)* company. **~edad anónima** limited company. **~o** *m* member; *(com)* partner. **~ología** *f* sociology. **~ólogo** *m* sociologist

socorr|er *vt* help. **~o** *m* help

soda *f (bebida)* soda (water)

sodio *m* sodium

sofá *m* sofa, settee

sofistica|ción *f* sophistication. **~do** *a* sophisticated. **~r** [7] *vt* adulterate

sofoca|ción *f* suffocation. **~nte** *a* *(fig)* stifling. **~r** [7] *vt* suffocate; *(fig)* stifle. **~rse** *vpr* suffocate; *(ruborizarse)* blush

soga *f* rope

soja *f* soya (bean)

sojuzgar [12] *vt* subdue

sol *m* sun; *(luz solar)* sunlight; *(mus)* G; *(solfa)* soh. **al ~** in the sun. **día** *m* **de ~** sunny day. **hace ~, hay ~** it is sunny. **tomar el ~** sunbathe

solamente *adv* only

solapa *f* lapel; *(de bolsillo etc)* flap. **~do** *a* sly. **~r** *vt/i* overlap

solar *a* solar. **—** *m* plot

solariego *a (casa)* ancestral

solaz *m* relaxation

solda|do *m* soldier. **~ raso** private

solda|dor *m* welder; *(utensilio)* soldering iron. **~r** [2] *vt* weld, solder

solea|do *a* sunny. **~r** *vt* put in the sun

soledad *f* solitude; *(aislamiento)* loneliness

solemn|e *a* solemn. **~idad** *f* solemnity; *(ceremonia)* ceremony

soler [2] *vi* be in the habit of. **suele despertarse a las 6** he usually wakes up at 6 o'clock

sol|icitar *vt* request; apply for *(empleo)*; attract *(atención)*. **~ícito** *a* solicitous. **~icitud** *f (atención)* concern; *(petición)* request; *(para un puesto)* application

solidaridad *f* solidarity

solid|ez *f* solidity; *(de color)* fastness. **~ificar** [7] *vt* solidify. **~ificarse** *vpr* solidify

sólido *a* solid; *(color)* fast; *(robusto)* strong. **—** *m* solid

soliloquio *m* soliloquy

solista *m* & *f* soloist

solitario *a* solitary; *(aislado)* lonely. **—** *m* recluse; *(juego, diamante)* solitaire

solo *a (sin compañía)* alone; *(aislado)* lonely; *(único)* only; *(mus)* solo; *(café)* black. **—** *m* solo; *(juego)* solitaire. **a solas** alone

sólo *adv* only. **~ que** only. **aunque ~** even if it is only. **con ~ que** if; *(con tal que)* as long as. **no ~... sino también** not only... but also... **tan ~** only

solomillo *m* sirloin

solsticio *m* solstice

soltar [2] *vt* let go of; *(dejar caer)* drop; *(dejar salir, decir)* let out; give *(golpe etc)*. **~se** *vpr* come undone; *(librarse)* break loose

solter|a *f* single woman. **~o** *a* single. **—** *m* bachelor. **apellido** *m* **de ~a** maiden name

soltura *f* looseness; *(agilidad)* agility; *(en hablar)* ease, fluency

solu|ble *a* soluble. **~ción** *f* solution. **~cionar** *vt* solve; settle *(huelga, asunto)*

solvent|ar *vt* resolve; settle *(deuda)*. ~e a & m solvent

sollo *m* sturgeon

solloz|ar [10] *vi* sob. ~o *m* sob

sombr|a *f* shade; *(imagen oscura)* shadow. ~**eado** *a* shady. **a la** ~**a** in the shade

sombrero *m* hat. ~ **hongo** bowler hat

sombrío *a* sombre

somero *a* shallow

someter *vt* subdue; subject *(persona)*; *(presentar)* submit. ~**se** *vpr* give in

somn|oliento *a* sleepy. ~**ífero** *m* sleeping-pill

somos *vb véase* **ser**

son *m* sound. —*vb véase* **ser**

sonámbulo *m* sleepwalker

sonar [2] *vt* blow; ring *(timbre)*. —*vi* sound; *(timbre, teléfono etc)* ring; *(reloj)* strike; *(pronunciarse)* be pronounced; *(mus)* play; *(fig, ser conocido)* be familiar. ~**se** *vpr* blow one's nose. ~ **a** sound like

sonata *f* sonata

sond|ear *vt* sound; *(fig)* sound out. ~**o** *m* sounding; *(fig)* poll

soneto *m* sonnet

sónico *a* sonic

sonido *m* sound

sonoro *a* sonorous; *(ruidoso)* loud

sonr|eír [51] *vi* smile. ~**eírse** *vpr* smile. ~**iente** *a* smiling. ~**isa** *f* smile

sonroj|ar *vt* make blush. ~**arse** *vpr* blush. ~**o** *m* blush

sonrosado *a* rosy, pink

sonsacar [7] *vt* wheedle out

soñ|ado *a* dream. ~**ador** *m* dreamer. ~**ar** [2] *vi* dream (**con** of). ¡**ni** ~**arlo!** not likely! (**que**) **ni** ~**ado** marvellous

sopa *f* soup

sopesar *vt* (*fig*) weigh up

sopl|ar *vt* blow; blow out *(vela)*; blow off *(polvo)*; *(inflar)* blow

up. —*vi* blow. ~**ete** *m* blowlamp. ~**o** *m* puff; *(fig, momento)* moment

soporífero *a* soporific. —*m* sleeping-pill

soport|al *m* porch. ~**ales** *mpl* arcade. ~**ar** *vt* support; *(fig)* bear. ~**e** *m* support

soprano *f* soprano

sor *f* sister

sorb|er *vt* suck; sip *(bebida)*; *(absorber)* absorb. ~**ete** *m* sorbet, water-ice. ~**o** *m* swallow; *(pequeña cantidad)* sip

sord|amente *adv* silently, dully. ~**era** *f* deafness

sórdido *a* squalid; *(tacaño)* mean

sordo *a* deaf; *(silencioso)* quiet. —*m* deaf person. ~**mudo** *a* deaf and dumb. **a la sorda, a sordas** on the quiet. **hacerse el** ~ turn a deaf ear

sorna *f* sarcasm. **con** ~ sarcastically

soroche *m* (*LAm*) mountain sickness

sorpren|dente *a* surprising. ~**nder** *vt* surprise; *(coger desprevenido)* catch. ~**sa** *f* surprise

sorte|ar *vt* draw lots for; *(rifar)* raffle; *(fig)* avoid. —*vi* draw lots; *(con moneda)* toss up. ~**o** *m* draw; *(rifa)* raffle; *(fig)* avoidance

sortija *f* ring; *(de pelo)* ringlet

sortilegio *m* witchcraft; *(fig)* spell

sos|egado *a* calm. ~**egar** [1 & 12] *vt* calm. —*vi* rest. ~**iego** *m* calmness. **con** ~**iego** calmly

soslayo. al ~**, de** ~ sideways

soso *a* tasteless; *(fig)* dull

sospech|a *f* suspicion. ~**ar** *vt/i* suspect. ~**oso** *a* suspicious. —*m* suspect

sost|én *m* support; *(prenda femenina)* bra *(fam)*, brassière. ~**ener** [40] *vt* support; *(sujetar)* hold; (*mantener*) maintain; (*alimentar*) sustain. **~enerse** *vpr* support o.s.; (*continuar*) remain. **~enido** *a* sustained; (*mus*) sharp. **—***m* (*mus*) sharp

sota *f* (*de naipes*) jack

sótano *m* basement

sotavento *m* lee

soto *m* grove; (*matorral*) thicket

soviético *a* (*historia*) Soviet

soy *vb* véase **ser**

Sr *abrev* (*Señor*) Mr. **~a** *abrev* (*Señora*) Mrs. **~ta** *abrev* (*Señorita*) Miss

su *a* (*de él*) his; (*de ella*) her; (*de ello*) its; (*de uno*) one's; (*de Vd*) your; (*de ellos, de ellas*) their; (*de Vds*) your

suav|e *a* smooth; (*fig*) gentle; ⟨*color, sonido*⟩ soft. **~idad** *f* smoothness, softness. **~izar** [10] *vt* smooth, soften

subalimentado *a* underfed

subalterno *a* secondary; (*persona*) auxiliary

subarrendar [1] *vt* sublet

subasta *f* auction; (*oferta*) tender. **~r** *vt* auction

sub|campeón *m* runner-up. **~consciencia** *f* subconscious. **~consciente** *a & m* subconscious. **~continente** *m* subcontinent. **~desarrollado** *a* under-developed. **~director** *m* assistant manager

súbdito *m* subject

sub|dividir *vt* subdivide. **~estimar** *vt* underestimate. **~gerente** *m & f* assistant manager

subi|da *f* ascent; (*aumento*) rise; (*pendiente*) slope. **~do** *a* ⟨*precio*⟩ high; ⟨*color*⟩ bright; ⟨*olor*⟩ strong. **~r** *vt* go up; (*poner*) put; (*llevar*) take up; (*aumentar*) increase. **—***vi* go up. **~r a** get into (*coche*); get on (*autobús, avión, barco, tren*); (*aumentar*) increase. **~rse** *vpr* climb up. **~rse a** get on (*tren etc*)

súbito *a* sudden. **—***adv* suddenly. **de ~** suddenly

subjetivo *a* subjective

subjuntivo *a & m* subjunctive

subleva|ción *f* uprising. **~r** *vt* incite to rebellion. **~rse** *vpr* rebel

sublim|ar *vt* sublimate. **~e** *a* sublime

submarino *a* underwater. **—***m* submarine

subordinado *a & m* subordinate

subrayar *vt* underline

subrepticio *a* surreptitious

subsanar *vt* remedy; overcome (*dificultad*)

subscri|bir *vt* (*pp* **subscrito**) sign. **~birse** *vpr* subscribe. **~pción** *f* subscription

subsidi|ario *a* subsidiary. **~o** *m* subsidy. **~o de paro** unemployment benefit

subsiguiente *a* subsequent

subsist|encia *f* subsistence. **~ir** *vi* subsist; (*perdurar*) survive

substanci|a *f* substance. **~al** *a* important. **~oso** *a* substantial

substantivo *m* noun

substitu|ción *f* substitution. **~ir** [17] *vt/i* substitute. **~to** *a & m* substitute

substraer [41] *vt* take away

subterfugio *m* subterfuge

subterráneo *a* underground. **—***m* (*bodega*) cellar; (*conducto*) underground passage

subtítulo *m* subtitle

suburb|ano *a* suburban. **—***m* suburban train. **~io** *m* suburb; (*en barrio pobre*) slum

subvenci|ón *f* grant. **~onar** *vt* subsidize

subver|sión *f* subversion. **~sivo** *a* subversive. **~tir** [4] *vt* subvert

subyugar [12] *vt* subjugate; (*fig*) subdue

succión *f* suction

suce|der *vi* happen; (*seguir*) follow; (*substituar*) succeed. **~dido**

m event. **lo** ∼**dido** what happened. ∼**sión** *f* succession. ∼**sivo** *a* successive; *(consecutivo)* consecutive. ∼**so** *m* event; *(incidente)* incident. ∼**sor** *m* successor. **en lo** ∼**sivo** in future. **lo que** ∼**de es que** the trouble is that. **¿qué** ∼**de?** what's the matter?

suciedad *f* dirt; *(estado)* dirtiness

sucinto *a* concise; *(prenda)* scanty

sucio *a* dirty; *(vil)* mean; *(conciencia)* guilty. **en** ∼ in rough

sucre *m* (unidad monetaria del Ecuador) sucre

suculento *a* succulent

sucumbir *vi* succumb

sucursal *f* branch (office)

Sudáfrica *m* & *f* South Africa

sudafricano *a* & *m* South African

Sudamérica *f* South America

sudamericano *a* & *m* South American

sudar *vt* work hard for. —*vi* sweat

sud|este *m* south-east; *(viento)* south-east wind. ∼**oeste** *m* south-west; *(viento)* south-west wind

sudor *m* sweat

Suecia *f* Sweden

sueco *a* Swedish. —*m* *(persona)* Swede; *(lengua)* Swedish. **hacerse el** ∼ pretend not to hear

suegr|a *f* mother-in-law. ∼**o** *m* father-in-law. **mis** ∼**os** my in-laws

suela *f* sole

sueldo *m* salary

suelo *m* ground; *(dentro de edificio)* floor; *(tierra)* land. —*m* *véase* **soler**

suelto *a* loose; *(libre)* free; *(sin pareja)* odd; *(lenguaje)* fluent. —*m* *(en periódico)* item; *(dinero)* change

sueño *m* sleep; *(ilusión)* dream. **tener** ∼ be sleepy

suero *m* serum; *(de leche)* whey

suerte *f* luck; *(destino)* fate; *(azar)* chance. **de otra** ∼ otherwise. **de** ∼ **que** so. **echar** ∼**s** draw lots. **por** ∼ fortunately. **tener** ∼ be lucky

suéter *m* jersey

suficien|cia *f* sufficiency; *(presunción)* smugness; *(aptitud)* suitability. ∼**te** *a* sufficient; *(presumido)* smug. ∼**temente** *adv* enough

sufijo *m* suffix

sufragio *m* *(voto)* vote

sufri|do *a* *(persona)* long-suffering; *(tela)* hard-wearing. ∼**miento** *m* suffering. ∼**r** *vt* suffer; *(experimentar)* undergo; *(soportar)* bear. —*vi* suffer

suge|rencia *f* suggestion. ∼**rir** [4] *vt* suggest. ∼**stión** *f* suggestion. ∼**stionable** *a* impressionable. ∼**stionar** *vt* influence. ∼**stivo** *a* *(estimulante)* stimulating; *(atractivo)* attractive

suicid|a *a* suicidal. —*m* & *f* suicide; *(fig)* maniac. ∼**arse** *vpr* commit suicide. ∼**io** *m* suicide

Suiza *f* Switzerland

suizo *a* Swiss. —*m* Swiss; *(bollo)* bun

suje|ción *f* subjection. ∼**tador** *m* fastener; *(de pelo, papeles etc)* clip; *(prenda femenina)* bra *(fam)*, brassière. ∼**tapapeles** *m invar* paper-clip. ∼**tar** *vt* fasten; *(agarrar)* hold; *(fig)* restrain. ∼**tarse** *vr* subject o.s.; *(ajustarse)* conform. ∼**to** *a* fastened; *(susceptible)* subject. —*m* individual

sulfamida *f* sulpha (drug)

sulfúrico *a* sulphuric

sult|án *m* sultan. ∼**ana** *f* sultana

suma *f* sum; *(total)* total. **en** ∼ in short. ∼**mente** *adv* extremely.

~r *vt* add (up); *(fig)* gather. —*vi* add up. ~**rse** *vpr*. ~**rse a** join in

sumario *a* brief. —*m* summary; *(jurid)* indictment

sumergi|ble *m* submarine. —*a* submersible. ~**r** [14] *vt* submerge

sumidero *m* drain

suministr|ar *vt* supply. ~**o** *m* supply; *(acción)* supplying

sumir *vt* sink; *(fig)* plunge

sumis|ión *f* submission. ~**o** *a* submissive

sumo *a* greatest; *(supremo)* supreme. **a lo** ~ at the most

suntuoso *a* sumptuous

supe *vb véase* **saber**

superar *vt* surpass; *(vencer)* overcome; *(dejar atrás)* get past. ~**se** *vpr* excel o.s.

superchería *f* swindle

superestructura *f* superstructure

superfici|al *a* superficial. ~**e** *f* surface; *(extensión)* area. **de** ~**e** surface

superfluo *a* superfluous

superhombre *m* superman

superintendente *m* superintendent

superior *a* superior; *(más alto)* higher; *(mejor)* better; *(piso)* upper. —*m* superior. ~**idad** *f* superiority

superlativo *a* & *m* superlative

supermercado *m* supermarket

supersónico *a* supersonic

superstici|ón *f* superstition. ~**oso** *a* superstitious

supervis|ión *f* supervision. ~**or** *m* supervisor

superviviente *a* surviving. —*m* & *f* survivor

suplantar *vt* supplant

suplement|ario *a* supplementary. ~**o** *m* supplement

suplente *a* & *m* & *f* substitute

súplica *f* entreaty; *(petición)* request

suplicar [7] *vt* beg

suplicio *m* torture

suplir *vt* make up for; *(reemplazar)* replace

suponer [34] *vt* suppose; *(significar)* mean; *(costar)* cost. ~**sición** *f* supposition

supositorio *m* suppository

suprem|acía *f* supremacy. ~**o** *a* supreme; *(momento etc)* critical

supres|ión *f* suppression. ~**imir** *vt* suppress; *(omitir)* omit

supuesto *a* supposed. —*m* assumption. ~**que** if. **¡por** ~**!** of course!

sur *m* south; *(viento)* south wind

surc|ar [7] *vt* plough. ~**o** *m* furrow; *(de rueda)* rut; *(en la piel)* wrinkle

surgir [14] *vi* spring up; *(elevarse)* loom up; *(aparecer)* appear; *(dificultad, oportunidad)* arise, crop up

surreali|smo *m* surrealism. ~**ta** *a* & *m* & *f* surrealist

surti|do *a* well-stocked; *(variado)* assorted. —*m* assortment, selection. ~**dor** *m (de gasolina)* petrol pump *(Brit)*, gas pump *(Amer)*. ~**r** *vt* supply; have *(efecto)*. ~**rse** *vpr* provide o.s. (**de** with)

suscep|tibilidad *f* susceptibility; *(sensibilidad)* sensitivity. ~**le** *a* susceptible; *(sensible)* sensitive

suscitar *vt* provoke; arouse *(curiosidad, interés, sospechas)*

suscr... *véase* **subscr...**

susodicho *a* aforementioned

suspen|der *vt* hang (up); *(interrumpir)* suspend; *(univ etc)* fail. ~**derse** *vpr* stop. ~**sión** *f* suspension. ~**so** *a* hanging; *(pasmado)* amazed; *(univ etc)* failed. —*m* fail. **en** ~**so** pending

suspicaz *a* suspicious

suspir|ar *vi* sigh. ~**o** *m* sigh

sust... *véase* **subst...**

sustent|ación f support. **~ar** vt support; (*alimentar*) sustain; (*mantener*) maintain. **~o** m support; (*alimento*) sustenance

susto m fright. **caerse del ~** be frightened to death

susurr|ar vi (*persona*) whisper; (*agua*) murmur; (*hojas*) rustle. **~o** m (*de persona*) whisper; (*de agua*) murmur; (*de hojas*) rustle

sutil a fine; (*fig*) subtle. **~eza** f fineness; (*fig*) subtlety

suyo a & pron (*de él*) his; (*de ella*) hers; (*de ello*) its; (*de uno*) one's; (*de Vd*) yours; (*de ellos, de ellas*) theirs; (*de Vds*) yours. **un amigo ~** a friend of his, a friend of theirs, etc

T

taba f (*anat*) ankle-bone; (*juego*) jacks

tabac|alera f (state) tobacconist. **~alero** a tobacco. **~o** m tobacco; (*cigarrillos*) cigarettes; (*rapé*) snuff

tabalear vi drum (with one's fingers)

Tabasco m Tabasco (P)

tabern|a f bar. **~ero** m barman; (*dueño*) landlord

tabernáculo m tabernacle

tabique m (thin) wall

tabl|a f plank; (*de piedra etc*) slab; (*estante*) shelf; (*de vestido*) pleat; (*lista*) list; (*índice*) index; (*en matemática etc*) table. **~ado** m platform; (*en el teatro*) stage. **~ao** m place where flamenco shows are held. **~as reales** backgammon. **~ero** m board. **~ero de mandos** dashboard. **hacer ~a rasa de** disregard

tableta f tablet; (*de chocolate*) bar

tabl|illa f small board. **~ón** m plank. **~ón de anuncios** notice

board (*esp Brit*), bulletin board (*Amer*)

tabú m taboo

tabular vt tabulate

taburete m stool

tacaño a mean

tacita f small cup

tácito a tacit

taciturno a taciturn; (*triste*) miserable

taco m plug; (*LAm, tacón*) heel; (*de billar*) cue; (*de billetes*) book; (*fig, lío, fam*) mess; (*Mex, culin*) filled tortilla

tacógrafo m tachograph

tacón m heel

táctic|a f tactics. **~o** a tactical

táctil a tactile

tacto m touch; (*fig*) tact

tacuara f (*Arg*) bamboo

tacurú m (small) ant

tacha f fault; (*clavo*) tack. **poner ~s a** find fault with. **sin ~** flawless

tachar vt (*borrar*) rub out; (*con raya*) cross out. **~ de** accuse of

tafia f (*LAm*) rum

tafilete m morocco

tahúr m card-sharp

Tailandia f Thailand

tailandés a & m Thai

taimado a sly

taj|ada f slice. **~ante** a sharp. **~o** m slash; (*fig, trabajo, fam*) job; (*culin*) chopping block. **sacar ~ada** profit

Tajo m Tagus

tal a such; (*ante sustantivo en singular*) such a. **—pron** (*persona*) someone; (*cosa*) such a thing. **—adv** so; (*de tal manera*) in such a way. **~ como** the way. **~ cual** (*tal como*) the way; (*regular*) fair. **~ para cual** (*fam*) two of a kind. **con ~ que** as long as. **¿qué ~?** how are you? **un ~** a certain

taladr|ar vt drill. **~o** m drill; (*agujero*) drill hole

talante *m* mood. **de buen ~** willingly

talar *vt* fell; (*fig*) destroy

talco *m* talcum powder

talcualillo *a* (*fam*) so so

talega *f*, **talego** *m* sack

talento *m* talent

TALGO *m* high-speed train

talismán *m* talisman

tal|ón *m* heel; (*recibo*) counterfoil; (*cheque*) cheque. **~onario** *m* receipt book; (*de cheques*) cheque book

talla *f* carving; (*grabado*) engraving; (*de piedra preciosa*) cutting; (*estatura*) height; (*medida*) size; (*palo*) measuring stick; (*Arg*, *charla*) gossip. **~do** *a* carved. —*m* carving. **~dor** *m* engraver

tallarín *m* noodle

talle *m* waist; (*figura*) figure; (*medida*) size

taller *m* workshop; (*de pintor etc*) studio

tallo *m* stem, stalk

tamal *m* (*LAm*) tamale

tamaño *a* (*tan grande*) so big a; (*tan pequeño*) so small a. —*m* size. **de ~ natural** life-size

tambalearse *vpr* (*persona*) stagger; (*cosa*) wobble

también *adv* also, too

tambor *m* drum. **~ del freno** brake drum. **~ilear** *vi* drum

Támesis *m* Thames

tamiz *m* sieve. **~ar** [10] *vt* sieve

tampoco *adv* nor, neither, not either

tampón *m* tampon; (*para entintar*) ink-pad

tan *adv* so. **tan... ~ as... as**

tanda *f* group; (*capa*) layer; (*de obreros*) shift

tangente *a & f* tangent

Tánger *m* Tangier

tangible *a* tangible

tango *m* tango

tanque *m* tank; (*camión*, *barco*) tanker

tante|ar *vt* estimate; (*ensayar*) test; (*fig*) weigh up. —*vi* score. **~o** *m* estimate; (*prueba*) test; (*en deportes*) score

tanto *a* (*en singular*) so much; (*en plural*) so many; (*comparación en singular*) as much; (*comparación en plural*) as many. —*pron* so much; (*en plural*) so many. —*adv* so much; (*tiempo*) so long. —*m* certain amount; (*punto*) point; (*gol*) goal. **~ como** as well as; (*cantidad*) as much as. **~ más... cuanto que** all the more... because. **~ si... como si** whether... or. **a ~s de** sometime in. **en ~**, **entre ~** meanwhile. **en ~ que** while. **entre ~** meanwhile. **estar al ~ de** be up to date with. **hasta ~ que** until. **no es para ~** it's not as bad as all that. **otro ~** the same; (*el doble*) as much again. **por (lo) ~** so. **un ~** *adv* somewhat

tañer [22] *vt* play

tapa *f* lid; (*de botella*) top; (*de libro*) cover. **~s** *fpl* savoury snacks

tapacubos *m invar* hub-cap

tapa|dera *f* cover, lid; (*fig*) cover. **~r** *vt* cover; (*abrigar*) wrap up; (*obturar*) plug; put the top on (*botella*)

taparrabo(s) *m invar* loincloth; (*bañador*) swimming-trunks

tapete *m* (*de mesa*) table cover; (*alfombra*) rug

tapia *f* wall. **~r** *vt* enclose

tapicería *f* tapestry; (*de muebles*) upholstery

tapioca *f* tapioca

tapiz *m* tapestry. **~ar** [10] *vt* hang with tapestries; upholster (*muebles*)

tap|ón *m* stopper; (*corcho*) cork; (*med*) tampon; (*tec*) plug. **~onazo** *m* pop

taqui|grafía f shorthand. **~í-grafo** m shorthand writer

taquill|a f ticket office; (*archivador*) filing cabinet; (*fig, dinero*) takings. **~ero** m clerk, ticket seller. **—a** box-office

tara f (*peso*) tare; (*defecto*) defect

taracea f marquetry

tarántula f tarantula

tararear vt/i hum

tarda|nza f delay. **~r** vi take; (*mucho tiempo*) take a long time. **a más ~r** at the latest. **sin ~r** without delay

tard|e adv late. **—f** (*antes del atardecer*) afternoon; (*después del atardecer*) evening. **~e o temprano** sooner or later. **~ío** a late. **de ~e en ~e** from time to time. **por la ~e** in the afternoon

tardo a (*torpe*) slow

tarea f task, job

tarifa f rate, tariff

tarima f platform

tarjeta f card. **~ de crédito** credit card. **~ postal** postcard

tarro m jar

tarta f cake; (*torta*) tart. **~ helada** ice-cream gateau

tartamud|ear vi stammer. **~o** a stammering. **—m** stammerer. **es ~o** he stammers

tártaro m tartar

tarugo m chunk

tasa f valuation; (*precio*) fixed price; (*índice*) rate. **~r** vt fix a price for; (*limitar*) ration; (*evaluar*) value

tasca f bar

tatarabuel|a f great-great-grandmother. **~o** m great-great-gandfather

tatua|je m (*acción*) tattooing; (*dibujo*) tattoo. **~r** [21] vt tattoo

taurino a bullfighting

tauromaquia f bullfighting

taxi m taxi. **~ímetro** m taxi meter. **~ista** m & f taxi-driver

tayuyá m (*Arg*) water melon

taz|a f cup. **~ón** m bowl

te pron (*acusativo*) you; (*dativo*) (to) you; (*reflexivo*) (to) yourself

té m tea. **dar el ~** bore

tea f torch

teatr|al a theatre; (*exagerado*) theatrical. **~alizar** [10] vt dramatize. **~o** m theatre; (*literatura*) drama. **obra** f **~al** play

tebeo m comic

teca f teak

tecla f key. **~do** m keyboard. **tocar la ~, tocar una ~** pull strings

técnica f technique

tecn|icismo m technicality

técnico a technical. **—m** technician

tecnolog|ía f technology. **~óg-ico** a technological

tecolote m (*Mex*) owl

tecomate m (*Mex*) earthenware cup

tech|ado m roof. **~ar** vt roof. **~o** m (*interior*) ceiling; (*exterior*) roof. **~umbre** f roofing. **bajo ~ado** indoors

teja f tile. **~do** m roof. **a toca ~** cash

teje|dor m weaver. **~r** vt weave; (*hacer punto*) knit

tejemaneje m (*fam*) fuss; (*intriga*) scheming

tejido m material; (*anat, fig*) tissue. **~s** mpl textiles

tejón m badger

tela f material; (*de araña*) web; (*en líquido*) skin

telar m loom. **~es** mpl textile mill

telaraña f spider's web, cobweb

tele f (*fam*) television

tele|comunicación f telecommunication. **~diario** m television news. **~dirigido** a remote-controlled. **~férico** m cable-car; (*tren*) cable-railway

telefonear *vt/i* telephone. **~efónico** *a* telephone. **~efonista** *m* & *f* telephonist. **~éfono** *m* telephone. **al ~éfono** on the phone

telegrafía *f* telegraphy. **~egrafiar** [20] *vt* telegraph. **~egráfico** *a* telegraphic. **~égrafo** *m* telegraph

telegrama *m* telegram

telenovela *f* television soap opera

teleobjetivo *m* telephoto lens

telepatía *f* telepathy. **~ático** *a* telepathic

telescópico *a* telescopic. **~opio** *m* telescope

telesilla *m* ski-lift, chair-lift

telespectador *m* viewer

telesquí *m* ski-lift

televidente *m* & *f* viewer. **~sar** *vt* televise. **~sión** *f* television. **~sor** *m* television (set)

télex *m* telex

telón *m* curtain. **~ de acero** (*historia*) Iron Curtain

tema *m* subject; (*mus*) theme

temblar [1] *vi* shake; (*de miedo*) tremble; (*de frío*) shiver; (*fig*) shudder. **~or** *m* shaking; (*de miedo*) trembling; (*de frío*) shivering. **~or de tierra** earthquake. **~oroso** *a* trembling

temer *vt* be afraid (of). —*vi* be afraid. **~se** *vpr* be afraid

temerario *a* reckless

temeroso *a* frightened. **~ible** *a* fearsome. **~or** *m* fear

témpano *m* floe

temperamento *m* temperament

temperatura *f* temperature

temperie *f* weather

tempestad *f* storm. **~uoso** *a* stormy. **levantar ~ades** (*fig*) cause a storm

templado *a* moderate; (*tibio*) warm; (*clima, tiempo*) mild; (*valiente*) courageous; (*listo*) bright. **~anza** *f* moderation; (*de clima o*

tiempo) mildness. **~ar** *vt* temper; (*calentar*) warm; (*mus*) tune. **~e** *m* tempering; (*temperatura*) temperature; (*humor*) mood

templete *m* niche; (*pabellón*) pavillion. **~o** *m* temple

temporada *f* time; (*época*) season. **~l** *a* temporary. —*m* (*tempestad*) storm; (*periodo de lluvia*) rainy spell

temprano *a* ⟨*frutos*⟩ early. **~o** *a* & *adv* early. **ser ~ero** be an early riser

tenacidad *f* tenacity

tenacillas *fpl* tongs

tenaz *a* tenacious

tenaza *f*, **tenazas** *fpl* pliers; (*para arrancar clavos*) pincers; (*para el fuego, culin*) tongs

tendencia *f* tendency. **~nte** *a*. **~nte** *a* aimed at. **~r** [1] *vt* spread (out); hang out ⟨*ropa a secar*⟩; (*colocar*) lay. —*vi* have a tendency (**a** to). **~rse** *vpr* stretch out

tenderete *m* stall. **~o** *m* shopkeeper

tendido *a* spread out; ⟨*ropa*⟩ hung out; ⟨*persona*⟩ stretched out. —*m* (*en plaza de toros*) front rows. **~s** *mpl* ⟨*ropa lavada*⟩ washing

tendón *m* tendon

tenebroso *a* gloomy; (*turbio*) shady

tenedor *m* fork; (*poseedor*) holder

tener [40] *vt* have (got); (*agarrar*) hold; be ⟨*años, calor, celos, cuidado, frío, ganas, hambre, miedo, razón, sed etc*⟩. **¡ten cuidado!** be careful! **tengo calor** I'm hot. **tiene 3 años** he's 3 (years old). **~se** *vpr* stand up; (*considerarse*) consider o.s., think o.s. **~ al corriente**, **~ al día** keep up to date. **~ 2 cm de largo** be 2 cms long. **~ a uno**

por consider s.o. ~ **que** have (got) to. **tenemos que comprar pan** we've got to buy some bread. **¡ahí tienes!** there you are! **no ~ nada que ver con** have nothing to do with. **¿qué tienes?** what's the matter (with you)? **¡tenga!** here you are!

tengo vb véase **tener**

teniente m lieutenant. ~ **de alcalde** deputy mayor

tenis m tennis. ~**ta** m & f tennis player

tenor m sense; (mus) tenor. **a este ~** in this fashion

tensi|ión f tension; (presión) pressure; (arterial) blood pressure; (elec) voltage; (de persona) tenseness. ~**o** a tense

tentación f temptation

tentáculo m tentacle

tenta|dor a tempting. ~**r** [1] vt feel; (seducir) tempt

tentativa f attempt

tenue a thin; (luz, voz) faint

teñi|do m dye. ~**r** [5 & 22] vt dye; (fig) tinge (**de** with). ~**rse** vpr dye one's hair

teo|logía f theology. ~**lógico** a theological. ~**ólogo** m theologian

teorema m theorem

teo|ría f theory. ~**órico** a theoretical

tepache m (Mex) (alcoholic) drink

tequila f tequila

TER m high-speed train

terap|éutico a therapeutic. ~**ia** f therapy

tercer a véase **tercero**. ~**a** f (auto) third (gear). ~**o** a (delante de nombre masculino en singular **tercer**) third. —m third party

terceto m trio

terciar vi mediate. ~ **en** join in. ~**se** vpr occur

tercio m third

terciopelo m velvet

terco a obstinate

tergiversar vt distort

termal a thermal. ~**s** fpl thermal baths

termes m invar termite

térmico a thermal

termina|ción f ending; (conclusión) conclusion. ~**l** a & m terminal. ~**nte** a categorical. ~**r** vt finish, end. ~**rse** vpr come to an end. ~**r por** end up

término m end; (palabra) term; (plazo) period. ~ **medio** average. ~ **municipal** municipal district. **dar** ~ **a** finish off. **en último** ~ as a last resort. **estar en buenos** ~**s con** be on good terms with. **llevar a** ~ carry out. **poner** ~ **a** put an end to. **primer** ~ foreground

terminología f terminology

termita f termite

termo m Thermos flask (P), flask

termómetro m thermometer

termo|nuclear a thermonuclear. ~**sifón** m boiler. ~**stato** m thermostat

terner|a f (carne) veal. ~**o** m calf

ternura f tenderness

terquedad f stubbornness

terracota f terracotta

terrado m flat roof

terraplén m embankment

terrateniente m & f landowner

terraza f terrace; (terrado) flat roof

terremoto m earthquake

terre|no a earthly. —m land; (solar) plot; (fig) field. ~**stre** a earthly; (mil) ground

terr|ible a terrible. ~**iblemente** adv awfully. ~**ífico** a terrifying

territori|al a territorial. ~**o** m territory

terrón m (de tierra) clod; (culin) lump

terror m terror. ~**ífico** a terrifying. ~**ismo** m terrorism. ~**ista** m & f terrorist

terr|oso a earthy; (*color*) brown. **~uño** m land; (*patria*) native land

terso a polished; (*piel*) smooth

tertulia f social gathering, get-together (*fam*). **~r** vi (*LAm*) get together. **estar de ~** chat. **hacer ~** get together

tesi|na f dissertation. **~s** f inv thesis; (*opinión*) theory

tesón m perseverance

tesor|ería f treasury. **~ero** m treasurer. **~o** m treasure; (*tesorería*) treasury; (*libro*) thesaurus

testa f (*fam*) head. **~ferro** m figurehead

testa|mento m will. **T~mento** (*relig*) Testament. **~r** vi make a will

testarudo a stubborn

testículo m testicle

testi|ficar [7] vt/i testify. **~go** m witness. **~go de vista, ~go ocular, ~go presencial** eye-witness. **~monio** m testimony

teta f nipple; (*de biberón*) teat

tétanos m tetanus

tetera f (*para el té*) teapot; (*Mex, biberón*) feeding-bottle

tetilla f nipple; (*de biberón*) teat

tétrico a gloomy

textil a & m textile

text|o m text. **~ual** a textual

textura f texture

teyú m (*Arg*) iguana

tez f complexion

ti pron you

tía f aunt; (*fam*) woman

tiara f tiara

tibio a lukewarm. **ponerle ~ a uno** insult s.o.

tiburón m shark

tic m tic

tiempo m time; (*atmosférico*) weather; (*mus*) tempo; (*gram*) tense; (*en deportes*) half. **a su ~** in due course. **a ~** in time. **¿cuánto ~?** how long? **hace**

buen ~ the weather is fine. **hace ~** some time ago. **mucho ~** a long time. **perder el ~** waste time. **¿qué ~ hace?** what is the weather like?

tienda f shop; (*de campaña*) tent. **~ de comestibles, ~ de ultramarinos** grocer's (shop) (*Brit*), grocery store (*Amer*)

tiene vb *véase* **tener**

tienta. **a ~s** gropingly. **andar a ~s** grope one's way

tiento m touch; (*de ciego*) blind person's stick; (*fig*) tact

tierno a tender; (*joven*) young

tierra f land; (*planeta, elec*) earth; (*suelo*) ground; (*geol*) soil, earth. **caer por ~** (*fig*) crumble. **por ~** overland, by land

tieso a stiff; (*firme*) firm; (*engreído*) conceited; (*orgulloso*) proud

tiesto m flowerpot

tifoideo a typhoid

tifón m typhoon

tifus m typhus; (*fiebre tifoidea*) typhoid (fever); (*en el teatro*) people with complimentary tickets

tigre m tiger

tijera f, **tijeras** fpl scissors; (*de jardín*) shears

tijeret|a f (*insecto*) earwig; (*bot*) tendril. **~ear** vt snip

tila f lime(-tree); (*infusión*) lime tea

tild|ar vt. **~ar de** (*fig*) call. **~e** m tilde

tilín m tinkle. **hacer ~** appeal

tilingo a (*Arg, Mex*) silly

tilma f (*Mex*) poncho

tilo m lime(-tree)

timar vt swindle

timbal m drum; (*culin*) timbale, meat pie

timbiriche m (*Mex*) (alcoholic) drink

timbr|ar vt stamp. **~e** m (*sello*) stamp; (*elec*) bell; (*sonido*) timbre. **tocar el ~e** ring the bell

timidez f shyness

tímido a shy

timo m swindle

timón m rudder; (fig) helm

tímpano m kettledrum; (anat) eardrum. ~s mpl (mus) timpani

tina f tub. ~ja f large earthenware jar

tinglado m (fig) intrigue

tinieblas fpl darkness; (fig) confusion

tino f (habilidad) skill; (moderación) moderation; (tacto) tact

tint|a f ink. ~e m dyeing; (color) dye; (fig) tinge. ~ero m ink-well. **de buena** ~a on good authority

tint|ín m tinkle; (de vasos) chink, clink. ~inear vi tinkle; (vasos) chink, clink

tinto a (vino) red

tintorería f dyeing; (tienda) dry cleaner's

tintura f dyeing; (color) dye; (noción superficial) smattering

tío m uncle; (fam) man. ~s mpl uncle and aunt

tiovivo m merry-go-round

típico a typical

tipo m type; (persona, fam) person; (figura de mujer) figure; (figura de hombre) build; (com) rate

tip|ografía f typography. ~ográfico a typographic(al). ~ógrafo m printer

típula f crane-fly, daddy-long-legs

tique m, **tíquet** m ticket

tiquete m (LAm) ticket

tira f strip. **la** ~ **de** lots of

tirabuzón m corkscrew; (de pelo) ringlet

tirad|a f distance; (serie) series; (de libros etc) edition. ~o a (barato) very cheap; (fácil, fam) very easy. ~or m (asa) handle; (juguete) catapult (Brit), slingshot (Amer). **de una** ~a at one go

tiran|ía f tyranny. ~izar [10] vt tyrannize. ~o a tyrannical. —m tyrant

tirante a tight; (fig) tense; (relaciones) strained. —m shoulder strap. ~s mpl braces (esp Brit), suspenders (Amer)

tirar vt throw; (desechar) throw away; (derribar) knock over; give (golpe, coz etc); (imprimir) print. —vi (disparar) shoot. ~se upr throw o.s.; (tumbarse) lie down. ~ a tend to (be); (parecerse a) resemble. ~ **de** pull; (atraer) attract. **a todo** ~ at the most. **ir tirando** get by

tirita f sticking-plaster, plaster (Brit)

tirit|ar vi shiver. ~ón m shiver

tiro m throw; (disparo) shot; (alcance) range. ~ **a gol** shot at goal. **a** ~ within range. **errar el** ~ miss. **pegarse un** ~ shoot o.s.

tiroides m thyroid (gland)

tirón m tug. **de un** ~ in one go

tirote|ar vt shoot at. ~o m shooting

tisana f herb tea

tisis f tuberculosis

tisú m (pl tisus) tissue

títere m puppet. ~ **de guante** glove puppet. ~s mpl puppet show

titilar vi quiver; (estrella) twinkle

titiritero m puppeteer; (acróbata) acrobat; (malabarista) juggler

titube|ante a shaky; (fig) hesitant. ~ar vi stagger; (cosa) be unstable; (fig) hesitate. ~o m hesitation

titula|do a (libro) entitled; (persona) qualified. ~r m headline; (persona) holder. —vt call. ~rse upr be called

título m title; (persona) titled person; (académico) qualification; (univ) degree; (de periódico etc) headline; (*derecho*) right. **a ~ de** as, by way of

tiza *f* chalk

tiznar *vt* dirty. **~ne** *m* soot. **~ón** *m* half-burnt stick; (*fig*) stain

toalla *f* towel. **~ero** *m* towel-rail

tobillo *m* ankle

tobogán *m* slide; (*para la nieve*) toboggan

tocadiscos *m invar* record-player

tocado *a* (*con sombrero*) wearing. —*m* hat. **~dor** *m* dressing-table. **~dor de señoras** ladies' room. **~nte** *a* touching. **~r** [7] *vt* touch; (*mus*) play; ring (*timbre*); (*mencionar*) touch on; (*barco*) stop at. —*vi* knock; (*corresponder a uno*) be one's turn. **~rse** *vpr* touch each other; (*cubrir la cabeza*) cover one's head. **en lo que ~ a, en lo ~nte a** as for. **estar ~do (de la cabeza)** be mad. **te ~ a ti** it's your turn

tocateja. a ~ cash

tocayo *m* namesake

tocino *m* bacon

tocólogo *m* obstetrician

todavía *adv* still, yet. **~ no** not yet

todo *a* all; (*entero*) the whole; (*cada*) every. —*adv* completely, all. —*m* whole. —*pron* everything, all; (*en plural*) everyone. **~ el día** all day. **~ el mundo** everyone. **~ lo que** anyone who. **~ incluido** all in. **~ lo contrario** quite the opposite. **~ lo que** anything which. **~s los días** every day. **~s los dos** both (of them). **~s los tres** all three. **ante ~** above all. **a ~ ~** esto meanwhile. **con ~** still, however. **del ~** completely. **en ~ el mundo** anywhere. **estar en ~** be on the ball. **es ~ uno** it's all the same. **nosotros ~s** all of us. **sobre ~** above all

toldo *m* sunshade

tolerancia *f* tolerance. **~nte** *a* tolerant. **~r** *vt* tolerate

tolondro *m* (*chichón*) lump

toma *f* taking; (*med*) dose; (*de agua*) outlet; (*elec*) socket; (*elec, clavija*) plug. —*int* well!, fancy that! **~ de corriente** power point. **~dura** *f*. **~dura de pelo** hoax. **~r** *vt* take; catch (*autobús, tren etc*); (*beber*) drink, have; (*comer*) eat, have. —*vi* take; (*dirigirse*) go. **~rse** *vpr* take; (*beber*) drink, have; (*comer*) eat, have. **~r a bien** take well. **~r a mal** take badly. **~r en serio** take seriously. **~rla con uno** pick on s.o. **~r nota** take note. **~r por** take for. **~ y daca** give and take. **¿qué va a ~r?** what would you like?

tomate *m* tomato

tomavistas *m invar* cine-camera

tómbola *f* tombola

tomillo *m* thyme

tomo *m* volume

ton. sin ~ ni son without rhyme or reason

tonada *f*, **tonadilla** *f* tune

tonel *m* barrel. **~ada** *f* ton. **~aje** *m* tonnage

tónica *f* tonic water; (*mus*) tonic. **~o** *a* tonic; (*sílaba*) stressed. —*m* tonic

tonificar [7] *vt* invigorate

tono *m* tone; (*mus, modo*) key; (*color*) shade

tontería *f* silliness; (*cosa*) silly thing; (*dicho*) silly remark. **~o** *a* silly. —*m* fool, idiot; (*payaso*) clown. **dejarse de ~erías** stop wasting time. **hacer el ~o** act the fool. **hacerse el ~o** feign ignorance

topacio *m* topaz

topar *vt* (*animal*) butt; (*persona*) bump into; (*fig*) run into. —*vi*. **~ con** run into

tope a maximum. —m end; (de tren) buffer. **hasta los ~s** crammed full. **ir a ~** go flat out

tópico a topical. —m cliché

topo m mole

topografía f topography. **~áfico** a topographical

toque m touch; (sonido) sound; (de campana) peal; (de reloj) stroke; (fig) crux. **~ de queda** curfew. **~tear** vt keep fingering, fiddle with. **dar el último ~** put the finishing touches

toquilla f shawl

tórax m thorax

torbellino m whirlwind; (de polvo) cloud of dust; (fig) whirl

torcer [2 & 9] vt twist; (doblar) bend; wring out (ropa). —vi turn. **~se** vpr twist; (fig, desviarse) go astray; (fig, frustrarse) go wrong

tordo a dapple grey. —m thrush

torear vt fight; (evitar) dodge; (entretener) put off. —vi fight (bulls). **~o** m bullfighting. **~ro** m bullfighter

torment|a f storm. **~o** m torture. **~oso** a stormy

tornado m tornado

tornar vt return

tornasolado a irridescent

torneo m tournament

tornillo m screw

torniquete m (entrada) turnstile

torno m lathe; (de alfarero) wheel. **en ~ a** around

toro m bull. **~s** mpl bullfighting. **ir a los ~s** go to a bullfight

toronja f grapefruit

torpe a clumsy; (estúpido) stupid

torped|ero m torpedo-boat. **~o** m torpedo

torpeza f clumsiness; (de inteligencia) slowness

torpor m torpor

torrado m toasted chick-pea

torre f tower; (en ajedrez) castle, rook

torrefac|ción f roasting. **~to** a roasted

torren|cial a torrential. **~te** m torrent; (circulatorio) bloodstream; (fig) flood

tórrido a torrid

torrija f French toast

torsión f twisting

torso m torso

torta f tart; (bollo, fam) cake; (golpe) slap, punch; (Mex, bocadillo) sandwich. **~zo** m slap, punch. **no entender ni ~** not understand a word of it. **pegarse un ~zo** have a bad accident

tortícolis f stiff neck

tortilla f omelette; (Mex, de maíz) tortilla, maize cake. **~ francesa** plain omelette

tórtola f turtle-dove

tortuga f tortoise; (de mar) turtle

tortuoso a winding; (fig) devious

tortura f torture. **~r** vt torture

torvo a grim

tos f cough. **~ ferina** whooping cough

tosco a crude; (persona) coarse

toser vi cough

tósigo m poison

tosquedad f crudeness; (de persona) coarseness

tost|ada f toast. **~ado** a (pan) toasted; (café) roasted; (persona) tanned; (marrón) brown. **~ar** vt toast (pan); roast (café); tan (piel). **~ón** m (pan) crouton; (lata) bore

total a total. —adv after all. —m total; (totalidad) whole. **~idad** f whole. **~itario** a totalitarian. **~izar** [10] vt total. **~ que** so, to cut a long story short

tóxico a toxic

toxicómano m drug addict

toxina f toxin

tozudo a stubborn

traba f bond; (fig, obstáculo) obstacle. **poner ~s a** hinder

trabaj|ador a hard-working. —m worker. **~ar** vt work (de as); knead ⟨masa⟩; ⟨estudiar⟩ work at; ⟨actor⟩ act. —vi work. **~o** m work. **~os** mpl hardships. **~os forzados** hard labour. **~oso** a hard. **costar ~o** be difficult. **¿en qué ~as?** what work do you do?

trabalenguas m invar tongue-twister

traba|r vt ⟨sujetar⟩ fasten; ⟨unir⟩ join; ⟨empezar⟩ start; ⟨culin⟩ thicken. **~rse** vpr get tangled up. **trabársele la lengua** get tongue-tied. **~zón** f joining; ⟨fig⟩ connection

trabucar [7] vt mix up

trácala f ⟨Mex⟩ trick

tracción f traction

tractor m tractor

tradición f tradition. **~onal** a traditional. **~onalista** m & f traditionalist

traduc|ción f translation. **~ir** [47] vt translate (al into). **~tor** m translator

traer [41] vt bring; ⟨llevar⟩ carry; ⟨atraer⟩ attract. **traérselas** be difficult

trafica|nte m & f dealer. **~r** [7] vi deal

tráfico m traffic; ⟨com⟩ trade

traga|deras fpl ⟨fam⟩ throat. **tener buenas ~deras** ⟨ser crédulo⟩ swallow anything; ⟨ser tolerante⟩ be easygoing. **~luz** m skylight. **~perras** f invar slot-machine. **~r** [12] vt swallow; ⟨comer mucho⟩ devour; ⟨absorber⟩ absorb; ⟨fig⟩ swallow up. **no (poder) ~r** not be able to stand. **~rse** vpr swallow; swallow up

tragedia f tragedy

trágico a tragic. —m tragedian

trag|o m swallow, gulp; ⟨pequeña porción⟩ sip; ⟨fig, disgusto⟩ blow. **~ón** a greedy. —m glutton. **echar(se) un ~o** have a drink

trai|ción f treachery; ⟨pol⟩ treason. **~cionar** vt betray. **~cionero** a treacherous. **~dor** a treacherous. —m traitor

traigo vb véase **traer**

traje m dress; ⟨de hombre⟩ suit. —vb véase **traer**. **~ de baño** swimming-costume. **~ de ceremonia**, **~ de etiqueta**, **~ de noche** evening dress

traj|ín m ⟨transporte⟩ haulage; ⟨jaleo, fam⟩ bustle. **~inar** vt transport. —vi bustle about

trama f weft; ⟨fig⟩ link; ⟨fig, argumento⟩ plot. **~r** vt weave; ⟨fig⟩ plot

tramitar vt negotiate

trámite m step. **~s** mpl procedure. **en ~** in hand

tramo m ⟨parte⟩ section; ⟨de escalera⟩ flight

trampa f trap; ⟨puerta⟩ trapdoor; ⟨fig⟩ trick. **~illa** f trapdoor. **hacer ~a** cheat

trampolín m trampoline; ⟨fig, de piscina⟩ springboard

tramposo a cheating. —m cheat

tranca f stick; ⟨de puerta⟩ bar

trance m moment; ⟨hipnótico etc⟩ trance. **a todo ~** at all costs

tranco m stride

tranquil|idad f ⟨peace and⟩ quiet; ⟨de espíritu⟩ peace of mind. **~izar** [10] vt reassure. **~o** a quiet; ⟨conciencia⟩ clear; ⟨mar⟩ calm; ⟨despreocupado⟩ thoughtless. **estáte ~o** don't worry

trans... pref ⟨véase también **tras...**⟩ trans...

transacción f transaction; ⟨acuerdo⟩ compromise

transatlántico a transatlantic. —m ⟨ocean⟩ liner

transbord|ador m ferry. **~ar** vt transfer. **~arse** vpr change. **~o** m transfer. **hacer ~o** change (en at)

transcri|bir ⟨pp **transcrito**⟩ vt transcribe. **~pción** f transcription

transcur|rir *vi* pass. **~so** *m* course

transeúnte *a* temporary. **—***m* & *f* passer-by

transfer|encia *f* transfer. **~ir** [4] *vt* transfer

transfigurar *vt* transfigure

transforma|ción *f* transformation. **~dor** *m* transformer. **~r** *vt* transform

transfusión *f* transfusion. **hacer una ~** give a blood transfusion

transgre|dir *vt* transgress. **~sión** *f* transgression

transición *f* transition

transido *a* overcome

transigir [14] *vi* give in, compromise

transistor *m* transistor; (*radio*) radio

transita|ble *a* passable. **~r** *vi* go

transitivo *a* transitive

tránsito *m* transit; (*tráfico*) traffic

transitorio *a* transitory

translúcido *a* translucent

transmi|sión *f* transmission; (*radio, TV*) broadcast. **~sor** *m* transmitter. **~sora** *f* broadcasting station. **~tir** *vt* transmit; (*radio, TV*) broadcast; (*fig*) pass on

transparen|cia *f* transparency. **~tar** *vt* show. **~te** *a* transparent

transpira|ción *f* perspiration. **~r** *vi* transpire; (*sudar*) sweat

transponer [34] *vt* move. **—***vi* disappear round (*esquina etc*); disappear behind (*montaña etc*). **~se** *vpr* disappear

transport|ar *vt* transport. **~e** *m* transport. **empresa** *f* **de ~es** removals company

transversal *a* transverse; (*calle*) side

tranvía *m* tram

trapacería *f* swindle

trapear *vt* (*LAm*) mop

trapecio *m* trapeze; (*math*) trapezium

trapiche *m* (*para azúcar*) mill; (*para aceitunas*) press

trapicheo *m* fiddle

trapisonda *f* (*jaleo, fam*) row; (*enredo, fam*) plot

trapo *m* rag; (*para limpiar*) cloth. **~s** *mpl* (*fam*) clothes. **a todo ~** out of control

tráquea *f* windpipe, trachea

traquete|ar *vt* bang, rattle. **~o** *m* banging, rattle

tras *prep* after; (*detrás*) behind; (*encima de*) as well as

tras... *pref* (*véase también* **trans...**) trans...

trascende|ncia *f* importance. **~ntal** *a* transcendental; (*importante*) important. **~r** [1] *vi* (*oler*) smell (**a** of); (*saberse*) become known; (*extenderse*) spread

trasegar [1 & 12] *vt* move around

trasero *a* back, rear. **—***m* (*anat*) bottom

trasgo *m* goblin

traslad|ar *vt* move; (*aplazar*) postpone; (*traducir*) translate; (*copiar*) copy. **~o** *m* transfer; (*copia*) copy; (*mudanza*) removal. **dar ~o** send a copy

translúcido *a* translucent. **~ucirse** [11] *vpr* be translucent; (*dejarse ver*) show through; (*fig, revelarse*) be revealed. **~uz** *m*. **al ~uz** against the light

trasmano *m*. **a ~** out of reach; (*fig*) out of the way

trasnochar *vt* (*acostarse tarde*) go to bed late; (*no acostarse*) stay up all night; (*no dormir*) be unable to sleep; (*pernoctar*) spend the night

traspas|ar *vt* pierce; (*transferir*) transfer; (*pasar el límite*) go beyond. **~o** *m* transfer. **se ~a** for sale

traspié *m* trip; (*fig*) slip. **dar un ~** stumble; (*fig*) slip up

trasplantar vt transplant. **~e** m transplanting; (med) transplant

trastada f stupid thing; (jugada) dirty trick, practical joke

traste m fret. **dar al ~ con** ruin. **ir al ~** fall through

trastero m storeroom

trastienda f back room; (fig) shrewdness

trasto m piece of furniture; (cosa inútil) piece of junk; (persona) useless person, dead loss (fam)

trastornar vt drive a mad. **~ar** vt upset; (volver loco) drive mad; (fig, gustar mucho, fam) delight. **~arse** vpr get upset; (volverse loco) go mad. **~o** m (incl med) upset; (pol) disturbance; (fig) confusion

trastrocar [2 & 7] vt change round

tratable a friendly. **~ado** m treatise; (acuerdo) treaty. **~amiento** m treatment; (título) title. **~ante** m & f dealer. **~ar** vt (incl med) treat; deal with (asunto etc); (com) deal; (manejar) handle; (de tú, de Vd) address (de as); (llamar) call. —vi deal (with). **~ar con** have to do with; know (persona); (com) deal in. **~ar de** be about; (intentar) try. **~o** m treatment; (acuerdo) agreement; (título) title; (relación) relationship. **¡~o hecho!** agreed! **~os** mpl dealings. **¿de qué se ~a?** what's it about?

trauma m trauma. **~ático** a traumatic

través m (inclinación) slant. **a ~ de** through; (de un lado a otro) across. **de ~** across; (de lado) sideways. **mirar de ~** look askance at

travesaño m crosspiece

travesía f crossing; (calle) side-street

travesura f prank. **~ieso** a (niño) mischievous, naughty

trayecto m road; (tramo) stretch; (ruta) route; (viaje) journey. **~ria** f trajectory; (fig) course

traza f plan; (aspecto) look, appearance; (habilidad) skill. **~ado** a. **bien ~ado** good-looking. **mal ~ado** unattractive. —m plan. **~ar** [10] vt draw; (bosquejar) sketch. **~o** m line

trébol m clover. **~es** mpl (en naipes) clubs

trece a & m thirteen

trecho m stretch; (distancia) distance; (tiempo) while. **a ~s** in places. **de ~ en ~** at intervals

tregua f truce; (fig) respite

treinta a & m thirty

tremendo a terrible; (extraordinario) terrific

trementina f turpentine

tren m train; (equipaje) luggage. **~ de aterrizaje** landing gear. **~ de vida** lifestyle

trencilla f braid. **~za** f braid; (de pelo) plait. **~zar** [10] vt plait

trepador a climbing. **~r** vt/i climb

tres a & m three. **~cientos** a & m three hundred. **~illo** m three-piece suite; (mus) triplet

treta f trick

triangular a triangular. **~ángulo** m triangle

tribal a tribal. **~u** f tribe

tribulación f tribulation

tribuna f platform; (de espectadores) stand

tribunal m court; (de examen etc) board; (fig) tribunal

tributar vt pay. **~o** m tribute; (impuesto) tax

triciclo m tricycle

tricolor a three-coloured

tricornio m three-cornered. —m three-cornered hat

tricotar vt/i knit

tridimensional a three-dimensional

tridente m trident

trigésimo *a* thirtieth

trigal *m* wheat field. **∼o** *m* wheat

trigonometría *f* trigonometry

trigueño *a* olive-skinned; ⟨pelo⟩ dark blonde

trilogía *f* trilogy

trilla|do *a* ⟨fig, manoseado⟩ trite; ⟨fig, conocido⟩ well-known. **∼r** *vt* thresh

trimestr|al *a* quarterly. **∼e** *m* quarter; ⟨escol, univ⟩ term

trin|ar *vi* warble. **estar que trina** be furious

trinchar *vt* carve

trinche|ra *f* ditch; ⟨mil⟩ trench; ⟨rail⟩ cutting; ⟨abrigo⟩ trench coat

trineo *m* sledge

trinidad *f* trinity

Trinidad *f* Trinidad

trino *m* warble

trío *m* trio

tripa *f* intestine; ⟨culin⟩ tripe; ⟨fig, vientre⟩ tummy, belly. **∼s** *fpl* ⟨de máquina etc⟩ parts, workings. **me duele la ∼** I've got tummy-ache. **revolver las ∼s** turn one's stomach

tripicallos *mpl* tripe

triple *a* triple. **∼m. el ∼e (de)** three times as much (as). **∼icado a. por ∼icado** in triplicate. **∼icar** [7] *vt* treble

trípode *m* tripod

tríptico *m* triptych

tripula|ción *f* crew. **∼nte** *m & f* member of the crew. **∼r** *vt* man

triquitraque *m* ⟨ruido⟩ clatter

tris *m* crack; ⟨de papel etc⟩ ripping noise. **estar en un ∼** be on the point of

triste *a* sad; ⟨paisaje, tiempo etc⟩ gloomy; ⟨fig, insignificante⟩ miserable. **∼za** *f* sadness

tritón *m* newt

triturar *vt* crush

triunf|al *a* triumphal. **∼ante** *a* triumphant. **∼ar** *vi* triumph (de, sobre over). **∼o** *m* triumph

triunvirato *m* triumvirate

trivial *a* trivial

triza *f* piece. **hacer algo ∼s** smash sth to pieces

trocar [2 & 7] *vt* (ex)change

trocear *vt* cut up, chop

trocito *m* small piece

trocha *f* narrow path; ⟨atajo⟩ short cut

trofeo *m* trophy

tromba *f* waterspout. **∼ de agua** heavy downpour

trombón *m* trombone; ⟨músico⟩ trombonist

trombosis *f invar* thrombosis

trompa *f* horn; ⟨de orquesta⟩ French horn; ⟨de elefante⟩ trunk; ⟨hocico⟩ snout; ⟨juguete⟩ (spinning) top; ⟨anat⟩ tube. **—m** horn player. **coger una ∼** ⟨fam⟩ get drunk

trompada *f*, **trompazo** *m* bump

trompet|a *f* trumpet; ⟨músico⟩ trumpeter, trumpet player; ⟨clarín⟩ bugle. **∼illa** *f* ear-trumpet

trompicar [7] *vi* trip

trompo *m* ⟨juguete⟩ (spinning) top

trona|da *f* thunder storm. **∼r** *vt* ⟨Mex⟩ shoot. **—vi** thunder

tronco *m* trunk. **dormir como un ∼** sleep like a log

tronchar *vt* bring down; ⟨fig⟩ cut short. **∼se de risa** laugh a lot

trono *m* throne

trop|a *f* troops. **∼el** *m* mob. **ser de ∼a** be in the army

tropero *m* ⟨Arg, vaquero⟩ cowboy

tropez|ar [1 & 10] *vi* trip; ⟨fig⟩ slip up. **∼ar con** run into. **∼ón** *m* stumble; ⟨fig⟩ slip

tropical *a* tropical

trópico *a* tropical. **—m** tropic

tropiezo *m* slip; ⟨desgracia⟩ mishap

trotar *vi* trot. **∼e** *m* trot; ⟨fig⟩ toing and froing. **al ∼e** trotting;

(de prisa) in a rush. **de mucho**
~e hard-wearing

trozo *m* piece, bit. **a ~s** in bits

truco *m* knack; *(ardid)* trick.
coger el ~ get the knack

trucha *f* trout

trueno *m* thunder; *(estampido)*
bang

trueque *m* exchange. **aun a ~ de**
even at the expense of

trufa *f* truffle. **~r** *vt* stuff with
truffles

truhán *m* rogue; *(gracioso)* jester

truncar [7] *vt* truncate; *(fig)* cut
short

tu *a* your

tú *pron* you

tuba *f* tuba

tubérculo *m* tuber

tuberculosis *f* tuberculosis

tub|ería *f* pipes; *(oleoducto etc)*
pipeline. **~o** *m* tube. **~o de**
ensayo test tube. **~o de escape**
(auto) exhaust (pipe). **~ular** *a*
tubular

tuerca *f* nut

tuerto *a* one-eyed, blind in one
eye. *—m* one-eyed person

tuétano *m* marrow; *(fig)* heart.
hasta los ~s completely

tufo *m* fumes; *(olor)* bad smell

tugurio *m* hovel, slum

tul *m* tulle

tulipán *m* tulip

tulli|do *a* paralysed. **~r** [22] *vt*
cripple

tumba *f* grave, tomb

tumb|ar *vt* knock down, knock
over; *(fig, en examen, fam)* fail;
(pasmar, fam) overwhelm.
~arse *vpr* lie down. **~o** *m* jolt.
dar un ~o tumble. **~ona** *f* settee; *(sillón)* armchair; *(de lona)*
deckchair

tumefacción *f* swelling

tumido *a* swollen

tumor *m* tumour

tumulto *m* turmoil; *(pol)* riot

tuna *f* prickly pear; *(de estu-*
diantes) student band

tunante *m & f* rogue

túnel *m* tunnel

Túnez *m (ciudad)* Tunis; *(país)*
Tunisia

túnica *f* tunic

Tunicia *f* Tunisia

tupé *m* toupee; *(fig)* nerve

tupido *a* thick

turba *f* peat; *(muchedumbre)*
mob

turba|ción *f* disturbance, upset;
(confusión) confusion. **~do** *a*
upset

turbante *m* turban

turbar *vt* upset; *(molestar)*
disturb. **~se** *vpr* be upset

turbina *f* turbine

turbi|o *a* cloudy; *(vista)* blurred;
(asunto etc) unclear. **~ón** *m*
squall

turbulen|cia *f* turbulence; *(dis-*
turbio) disturbance. **~te** *a* tur-
bulent; *(persona)* restless

turco *a* Turkish. *—m* Turk; *(len-*
gua) Turkish

tur|ismo *m* tourism; *(coche)* car.
~ista *m & f* tourist. **~ístico** *a*
tourist. **oficina** *f* **de ~ismo**
tourist office

turn|arse *vpr* take turns **(para**
to). **~o** *m* turn; *(de trabajo)* shift.
por ~o in turn

turquesa *f* turquoise

Turquía *f* Turkey

turrón *m* nougat

turulato *a (fam)* stunned

tutear *vt* address as **tú**. **~se** *vpr*
be on familiar terms

tutela *f* *(jurid)* guardianship;
(fig) protection

tuteo *m* use of the familiar **tú**

tutor *m* guardian; *(escol)* form
master

tuve *vb véase* **tener**

tuyo *a & pron* yours. **un amigo**
~ a friend of yours

U

u *conj* or
ubicuidad *f* ubiquity
ubre *f* udder
ucraniano *a & m* Ukranian
Ud *abrev* (Usted) you
uf *int* phew!; (de repugnancia) ugh!
ufan|arse *upr* be proud (con, de of); (jactarse) boast (con, de about). ∼o *a* proud
ujier *m* usher
úlcera *f* ulcer
ulterior *a* later; (lugar) further. ∼mente *adv* later, subsequently
últimamente *adv* (recientemente) recently; (al final) finally; (en último caso) as a last resort
ultim|ar *vt* complete. ∼átum *m* ultimatum
último *a* last; (más reciente) latest; (más lejano) furthest; (más alto) top; (más bajo) bottom; (fig, extremo) extreme. **estar en las últimas** be on one's last legs; (sin dinero) be down to one's last penny. **por** ∼ finally. **ser lo** ∼ (muy bueno) be marvellous; (muy malo) be awful. **vestido a la última** dressed in the latest fashion
ultra *a* ultra, extreme
ultraj|ante *a* outrageous. ∼e *m* outrage
ultramar *m* overseas countries. **de** ∼, **en** ∼ overseas
ultramarino *a* overseas. ∼s *mpl* groceries. **tienda de** ∼s grocer's (shop) (Brit), grocery store (Amer)
ultranza a ∼ (con decisión) decisively; (extremo) extreme
ultra|sónico *a* ultrasonic. ∼violeta *a invar* ultraviolet
ulular *vi* howl; (búho) hoot

umbilical *a* umbilical
umbral *m* threshold
umbrío *a*, **umbroso** *a* shady
un *art indef m* (pl unos) a. —*a* one. —**os** *a pl* some
una *art indef* a. **la** ∼ one o'clock
un|ánime *a* unanimous. ∼**animidad** *f* unanimity
undécimo *a* eleventh
ung|ir [14] *vt* anoint. ∼**üento** *m* ointment
únic|amente *adv* only. ∼o *a* only; (fig, incomparable) unique
unicornio *m* unicorn
unidad *f* unit; (cualidad) unity. ∼o *a* united
unifica|ción *f* unification. ∼r [7] *vt* unite, unify
uniform|ar *vt* standardize; (poner uniforme a) put into uniform. ∼e *a & m* uniform. ∼**idad** *f* uniformity
uni|génito *a* only. ∼**lateral** *a* unilateral
uni|ón *f* union; (cualidad) unity; (tec) joint. ∼r *vt* join; mix (liquidos). ∼**rse** *upr* join together
unísono *m* unison. **al** ∼ in unison
unitario *a* unitary
universal *a* universal
universi|dad *f* university. **U-**∼**dad a Distancia** Open University. ∼**tario** *a* university
universo *m* universe
uno *a* one; (en plural) some. —*pron* one; (alguien) someone, somebody. —*m* one. ∼ **a otro** each other. ∼ **y otro** both. (los) ∼**s...** (los) otros some... others
untar *vt* grease; (med) rub; (fig, sobornar, fam) bribe
uña *f* nail; (de animal) claw; (casco) hoof
upa *int* up!
uranio *m* uranium
Urano *m* Uranus
urban|idad *f* politeness. ∼**ismo** *m* town planning. ∼**ístico** *a*

V

urban. ~**ización** f development. ~**izar** [10] vt civilize; develop ⟨terreno⟩. ~**o** a urban

urbe f big city

urdimbre f warp

urdir vt (fig) plot

urg|encia f urgency; (emergencia) emergency; (necesidad) urgent need. ~**ente** a urgent. ~**ir** [14] vi be urgent. **carta** f ~**ente** express letter

urinario m urinal

urna f urn; (pol) ballot box

urraca f magpie

URSS abrev (historia) (Unión de Repúblicas Socialistas Soviéticas) USSR, Union of Soviet Socialist Republics

Uruguay m. el ~ Uruguay

uruguayo a & m Uruguayan

us|ado a used; ⟨ropa etc⟩ worn. ~**anza** f usage, custom. ~**ar** vt use; (llevar) wear. ~**o** m use; (costumbre) usage, custom. **al** ~**o** (de moda) in fashion; (a la manera de) in the style of. **de** ~**o externo** for external use

usted pron you

usual a usual

usuario a user

usur|a f usury. ~**ero** m usurer

usurpar vt usurp

usuta f (Arg) sandal

utensilio m tool; (de cocina) utensil. ~**s** mpl equipment

útero m womb

útil a useful. ~**es** mpl implements

utili|dad f usefulness. ~**tario** a utilitarian; ⟨coche⟩ utility. ~**zación** f use, utilization. ~**zar** [10] vt use, utilize

uva f grape. ~ **pasa** raisin. **mala** ~ bad mood

vaca f cow; (carne) beef

vacaciones fpl holiday(s). **estar de** ~ be on holiday. **ir de** ~ go on holiday

vaca|nte a vacant. —f vacancy. ~**r** [7] vi fall vacant

vaci|ar [20] vt empty; (ahuecar) hollow out; (en molde) cast; (afilar) sharpen. ~**edad** f emptiness; (tontería) silly thing, frivolity

vacila|ción f hesitation. ~**nte** a unsteady; (fig) hesitant. ~**r** vi sway; (dudar) hesitate; (fam) tease

vacío a empty; (vanidoso) vain. —m empty space; (estado) emptiness; (en física) vacuum; (fig) void

vacuidad f emptiness; (tontería) silly thing, frivolity

vacuna f vaccine. ~**ción** f vaccination. ~**r** vt vaccinate

vacuno a bovine

vacuo a empty

vade m folder

vad|ear vt ford. ~**o** m ford

vaga|bundear vi wander. ~**bundo** a vagrant; ⟨perro⟩ stray. —m tramp. ~**r** [12] vi wander (about)

vagina f vagina

vago a vague; (holgazán) idle; (foto) blurred. —m idler

vag|ón m carriage; (de mercancías) truck, wagon. ~**ón restaurante** dining-car. ~**oneta** f truck

vahído m dizzy spell

vaho m breath; (vapor) steam. ~**s** mpl inhalation

vaina f sheath; (bot) pod

vainilla f vanilla

vaivén m swaying; (de tráfico) coming and going; (fig, de suerte)

change. **vaivenes** *mpl* (*fig*) ups
and downs

vajilla *f* dishes, crockery. **lavar
la** ~ wash up

vale *m* voucher; (*pagaré*) IOU.
~**dero** *a* valid

valenciano *a* from Valencia

valentía *f* courage; (*acción*)
brave deed. ~**ón** *m* braggart

valer [42] *vt* be worth; (*costar*)
cost; (*fig, significar*) mean. —*vi*
be worth; (*costar*) cost; (*servir*)
be of use; (*ser valedero*) be valid;
(*estar permitido*) be allowed.
—*m* worth. ~**la pena** be worthwhile, be worth it. **¿cuánto
vale?** how much is it?. **no** ~
para nada be useless. **¡vale!** all
right!, OK! (*fam*). **¿vale?** all
right?, OK? (*fam*)

valeroso *a* courageous

valgo *vb véase* **valer**

valía *f* worth

validez *f* validity. **dar** ~ **a**
validate

válido *a* valid

valiente *a* brave; (*valentón*)
boastful; (*en sentido irónico*)
fine. —*m* brave person; (*valentón*) braggart

valija *f* case; (*de correos*)
mailbag. ~ **diplomática** diplomatic bag

val|ioso *a* valuable. ~**or** *m*
value, worth; (*descaro, fam*)
nerve. ~**ores** *mpl* securities.
~**oración** *f* valuation. ~**orar** *vt*
value. **conceder** ~**or a** attach
importance to. **objetos** *mpl* **de**
~**or** valuables. **sin** ~**or**
worthless

vals *m invar* waltz

válvula *f* valve

valla *f* fence; (*fig*) barrier

valle *m* valley

vampiro *m* vampire

vanagloriarse [20 *o regular*] *vpr*
boast

vanamente *adv* uselessly, in
vain

vandalismo *m* vandalism

vándalo *m* vandal

vanguardia *f* vanguard. **de** ~
(*en arte, música etc*) avant-garde

vanidad *f* vanity. ~**oso** *a* vain

vano *a* vain; (*inútil*) useless. **en**
~ in vain

vapor *m* steam; (*gas*) vapour;
(*naut*) steamer. ~**izador** *m*
spray. ~**izar** [10] vaporize. **al** ~
(*culin*) steamed

vaquer|ía *f* dairy. ~**o** *m* cow-
herd, cowboy. ~**os** *mpl* jeans

vara *f* stick; (*de autoridad*) staff;
(*medida*) yard

varar *vi* run aground

varia|ble *a* & *f* variable. ~**ción** *f*
variation. ~**nte** *f* version.
~**ntes** *fpl* hors d'oeuvres. ~**r**
[20] *vt* change; (*dar variedad a*)
vary. —*vi* vary; (*cambiar*)
change

varice *f* varicose vein

varicela *f* chickenpox

varicoso *a* having varicose veins

variedad *f* variety

varilla *f* stick; (*de metal*) rod

vario *a* varied; (*en plural*)
several

varita *f* wand

variz *f* varicose vein

var|ón *a* male. —*m* man; (*niño*)
boy. ~**onil** *a* manly

vasc|o *a* & *m* Basque. ~**ongado** *a*
Basque. ~**uence** *a* & *m* Basque.
las V~**ongadas** the Basque
provinces

vasectomía *f* vasectomy

vaselina *f* Vaseline (P), petroleum jelly

vasija *f* pot, container

vaso *m* glass; (*anat*) vessel

vástago *m* shoot; (*descendiente*)
descendant; (*varilla*) rod

vasto *a* vast

Vaticano *m* Vatican

vaticinar *vt* prophesy. ∿io *m* prophesy

vatio *m* watt

vaya *vb véase* ir

Vd *abrev* (Usted) you

vecin|dad *f* neighbourhood, vicinity; (vecinos) neighbours. ∿dario *m* inhabitants, neighbourhood. ∿o *a* neighbouring; (de al lado) next-door. —*m* neighbour

veda|do *m* preserve. ∿do de caza game preserve. ∿r *vt* prohibit

vega *f* fertile plain

vegeta|ción *f* vegetation. ∿l *a* vegetable. —*m* plant, vegetable. ∿r *vi* grow; (persona) vegetate. ∿riano *a & m* vegetarian

vehemente *a* vehement

vehículo *m* vehicle

veinte *a & m* twenty. ∿na *f* score

veinti|cinco *a & m* twenty-five. ∿cuatro *a & m* twenty-four. ∿dós *a & m* twenty-two. ∿nueve *a & m* twenty-nine. ∿ocho *a & m* twenty-eight. ∿séis *a & m* twenty-six. ∿siete *a & m* twenty-seven. ∿trés *a & m* twenty-three. ∿ún *a* twenty-one. ∿uno *a & m* (delante de nombre masculino **veintún**) twenty-one

vejar *vt* humiliate; (molestar) vex

vejez *f* old age

vejiga *f* bladder; (med) blister

vela *f* (naut) sail; (de cera) candle; (falta de sueño) sleeplessness; (vigilia) vigil. **pasar la noche en** ∿ have a sleepless night

velada *f* evening party

vela|do *a* veiled; (foto) blurred. ∿r *vt* watch over; (encubrir) veil; (foto) blur. —*vi* stay awake, not sleep. ∿r **por** look after. ∿rse *vpr* (foto) blur

velero *m* sailing-ship

veleta *f* weather vane

velo *m* veil

veloc|idad *f* speed; (auto etc) gear. ∿ímetro *m* speedometer. ∿ista *m & f* sprinter. **a toda** ∿idad at full speed

velódromo *m* cycle-track

veloz *a* fast, quick

vell|o *m* down. ∿ón *m* fleece. ∿udo *a* hairy

vena *f* vein; (en madera) grain. **estar de/en** ∿ be in the mood

venado *m* deer; (culin) venison

vencedor *a* winning. —*m* winner

vencejo *m* (pájaro) swift

venc|er [9] *vt* beat; (superar) overcome. —*vi* win; (plazo) expire. ∿erse *vpr* collapse; (persona) control o.s. ∿ido *a* beaten; (com, atrasado) in arrears. **darse por** ∿ido give up. **los** ∿idos *mpl* (en deportes etc) the losers

venda *f* bandage. ∿je *m* dressing. ∿r *vt* bandage

vendaval *m* gale

vende|dor *a* selling. —*m* seller, salesman. ∿dor **ambulante** pedlar. ∿r *vt* sell. ∿r por sell. ∿rse **caro** play hard to get. **se** ∿ for sale

vendimia *f* grape harvest; (de vino) vintage, year

Venecia *f* Venice

veneciano *a* Venetian

veneno *m* poison; (fig, malevolencia) spite. ∿so *a* poisonous

venera *f* scallop shell

venera|ble *a* venerable. ∿ción *f* reverence. ∿r *vt* revere

venéreo *a* venereal

venero *m* (yacimiento) seam; (de agua) spring; (fig) source

venezolano *a & m* Venezuelan

Venezuela *f* Venezuela

venga|nza *f* revenge. ∿r [12] *vt* avenge. ∿rse *vpr* take revenge (de, por for) (de, en on). ∿tivo *a* vindictive

vengo *vb véase* venir

venia f (*permiso*) permission

venial a venial

veni|da f arrival; (*vuelta*) return. **~dero** a coming. **~r** [53] *vi* come; (*estar, ser*) be. **~r a para** come to. **~r bien** suit. **la semana que viene** next week. **¡venga!** come on!

venta f sale; (*posada*) inn. **en ~** for sale

ventaja f advantage. **~oso** a advantageous

ventana f window; (*de la nariz*) nostril. **~illa** f window

ventarrón m (*fam*) strong wind

ventear vt (*olfatear*) sniff

ventero m innkeeper

ventila|ción f ventilation. **~dor** m fan. **~r** vt air

vent|isca f blizzard. **~olera** f gust of wind. **~osa** f sucker. **~osidad** f wind, flatulence. **~oso** a windy

ventrílocuo m ventriloquist

ventrudo a pot-bellied

ventura f happiness; (*suerte*) luck. **~oso** a happy, lucky. **a la ~a** at random. **echar la buena ~a a uno** tell s.o.'s fortune. **por ~a** by chance; (*afortunadamente*) fortunately

Venus f Venus

ver [43] *vt* see; watch (*televisión*). **—vi** see. **~se** *vpr* see o.s.; (*encontrarse*) find o.s.; (*dos personas*) meet. **a mi (modo de) ~** in my view. **a ~** let's see. **de buen ~** good-looking. **dejarse ~** show. **¡habráse visto!** did you ever! **no poder ~** not be able to stand. **no tener nada que ~ con** have nothing to do with. **¡para que veas!** so there! **vamos a ~** let's see. **ya lo veo** that's obvious. **ya ~ás** you'll see. **ya ~emos** we'll see

vera f edge; (*de río*) bank

veracruzano a from Veracruz

veran|eante m & f tourist, holiday-maker. **~ear** vi spend one's holiday. **~eo** m (*summer*) holiday. **~iego** a summer. **~o** m summer. **casa** f **de ~eo** summer-holiday home. **ir de ~eo** go on holiday. **lugar** m **de ~eo** holiday resort

veras fpl. **de ~** really

veraz a truthful

verbal a verbal

verbena f (*bot*) verbena; (*fiesta*) fair; (*baile*) dance

verbo m verb. **~so** a verbose

verdad f truth. **¿~?** isn't it?, aren't they?, won't it? etc. **~eramente** *adv* really. **~ero** a true; (*fig*) real. **a decir ~** to tell the truth. **de ~** really. **la pura ~** the plain truth. **si bien es ~ que** although

verd|e a green; (*fruta etc*) unripe; (*chiste etc*) dirty, blue. **—m** green; (*hierba*) grass. **~or** m greenness

verdugo m executioner; (*fig*) tyrant

verdu|lería f greengrocer's (shop). **~lero** m greengrocer. **~ra** f (*green*) vegetable(s)

vereda f path; (*LAm, acera*) pavement (*Brit*), sidewalk (*Amer*)

veredicto m verdict

vergel m large garden; (*huerto*) orchard

verg|onzoso a shameful; (*tímido*) shy. **~üenza** f shame; (*timidez*) shyness. **¡es una ~üenza!** it's a disgrace! **me da ~üenza** I'm ashamed; (*tímido*) I'm shy about. **tener ~üenza** be ashamed; (*tímido*) be shy

verídico a true

verifica|ción f verification. **~r** [7] *vt* check. **~rse** *vpr* take place; (*resultar verdad*) come true

verja f grating; (*cerca*) railings; (*puerta*) iron gate

vermú m, **vermut** m vermouth

vernáculo *a* vernacular

verosímil *a* likely; ⟨*relato etc*⟩ credible

verraco *m* boar

verruga *f* wart

versado *a* versed

versar *vi* turn. ~ **sobre** be about

versátil *a* versatile; (*fig*) fickle

versión *f* version; (*traducción*) translation

verso *m* verse; (*línea*) line

vértebra *f* vertebra

vertedero *m* rubbish tip; (*desaguadero*) drain. ~**dor** *m* drain. ~**r** [1] *vt* pour; (*derramar*) spill. ─*vi* flow

vertical *a & f* vertical

vértice *f* vertex

vertiente *f* slope

vertiginoso *a* dizzy

vértigo *m* dizziness; (*med*) vertigo. **de** ~ (*fam*) amazing

vesania *f* rage; (*med*) insanity

vesícula *f* blister. ~ **biliar** gall-bladder

vespertino *a* evening

vestíbulo *m* hall; (*de hotel, teatro etc*) foyer

vestido *m* (*de mujer*) dress; (*ropa*) clothes

vestigio *m* trace. ~**s** *mpl* remains

vestimenta *f* clothing. ~**ir** [5] *vt* (*ponerse*) put on; (*llevar*) wear; dress ⟨*niño etc*⟩. ~ (*llevar*) wear. ~**irse** *upr* get dressed; (*llevar*) wear. ~**uario** *m* wardrobe; (*cuarto*) dressing-room

Vesuvio *m* Vesuvius

vetar *vt* veto

veterano *a* veteran

veterinaria *f* veterinary science. ~**o** *a* veterinary. ─*m* vet (*fam*), veterinary surgeon (*Brit*), veterinarian (*Amer*)

veto *m* veto. **poner el** ~ **a** veto

vetusto *a* ancient

vez *f* time; (*turno*) turn. **a la** ~ at the same time; (*de una vez*) in one go. **alguna que otra** ~ from time to time. **alguna** ~ sometimes; (*en preguntas*) ever. **algunas veces** sometimes. **a su** ~ in (his) turn. **a veces** sometimes. **cada** ~ **más** more and more. **de una** ~ in one go. **de una** ~ **para siempre** once and for all. **de** ~ **en cuando** from time to time. **dos veces** twice. **2 veces 4** 2 times 4. **en** ~ **de** instead of. **érase una** ~, **había una** ~ once upon a time. **muchas veces** often. **otra** ~ again. **pocas veces**, **rara** ~ rarely. **repetidas veces** again and again. **tal** ~ perhaps. **una** ~ (**que**) once

vía *f* road; (*rail*) line; (*anat*) tract; (*fig*) way. ─*prep* via. ~ **aérea** by air. ~ **de comunicación** *f* means of communication. ~ **férrea** railway (*Brit*), railroad (*Amer*). ~ **rápida** fast lane. **estar en** ~**s de** be in the process of

viabilidad *f* viability. ~**le** *a* viable

viaducto *m* viaduct

viajante *m & f* commercial traveller. ~**ar** *vi* travel. ~**e** *m* journey; (*corto*) trip. ~**e de novios** honeymoon. ~**ero** *m* traveller; (*pasajero*) passenger. ¡**buen** ~**e**! have a good journey!

víbora *f* viper

vibración *f* vibration. ~**nte** *a* vibrant. ~**r** *vt/i* vibrate

vicario *m* vicar

vice... *pref* vice-...

viceversa *adv* vice versa

viciado *a* corrupt; (*aire*) stale. ~**ar** *vt* corrupt; (*estropear*) spoil. ~**o** *m* vice; (*mala costumbre*) bad habit. ~**oso** *a* dissolute; ⟨*círculo*⟩ vicious

vicisitud *f* vicissitude

víctima f victim; (de un accidente) casualty

victoria f victory. **~oso** a victorious

vid f vine

vida f life; (duración) lifetime. ¡**~ mía!** my darling! **de por ~** for life. **en mi ~** never (in my life). **en ~ de** during the lifetime of. **estar en ~** be alive

vídeo m video recorder

video|cinta f videotape. **~juego** m video game

vidriar vt glaze

vidri|era f stained glass window; (puerta) glass door; (LAm, escaparate) shop window. **~ería** f glass works. **~ero** m glazier. **~o** m glass. **~oso** a glassy

vieira f scallop

viejo a old. —m old person

Viena f Vienna

viene vb véase **venir**

viento m wind. **hacer ~** be windy

vientre m belly; (matriz) womb; (intestino) bowels. **llevar un niño en el ~** be pregnant

viernes m Friday. **V~ Santo** Good Friday

viga f beam; (de metal) girder

vigen|cia f validity. **~te** a valid; (ley) in force. **entrar en ~cia** come into force

vigésimo a twentieth

vigía f (torre) watch-tower; (persona) lookout

vigil|ancia f vigilance. **~ante** a vigilant. —m watchman, supervisor. **~ar** vt keep an eye on. —vi be vigilant; (vigía etc) keep watch. **~ia** f vigil; (relig) fasting

vigor m vigour; (vigencia) force. **~oso** a vigorous. **entrar en ~** come into force

vil a vile. **~eza** f vileness; (acción) vile deed

vilipendiar vt abuse

vilo. en ~ in the air

villa f town; (casa) villa. **la V~** Madrid

villancico m (Christmas) carol

villano a rustic; (grosero) coarse

vinagre m vinegar. **~ra** f vinegar bottle. **~ras** fpl cruet. **~ta** f vinaigrette (sauce)

vincular vt bind

vínculo m bond

vindicar [7] vt avenge; (justificar) vindicate

vine vb véase **venir**

vinicultor m wine-grower. **~ura** f wine growing

vino m wine. **~ de Jerez** sherry. **~ de la casa** house wine. **~ de mesa** table wine

viña f, **viñedo** m vineyard

viola f viola; (músico) viola player

violación f violation; (de una mujer) rape

violado a & m violet

violar vt violate; break (ley); rape (mujer)

violen|cia f violence; (fuerza) force; (embarazo) embarrassment. **~tar** vt force; break into (casa etc). **~tarse** vpr force o.s. **~to** a violent; (fig) awkward. **hacer ~cia** a force

violeta a invar & f violet

viol|ín m violin; (músico) violinist. **~inista** m & f violinist. **~ón** m double bass; (músico) double-bass player. **~onc(h)elista** m & f cellist. **~onc(h)elo** m cello

vira|je m turn. **~r** vt turn. —vi turn; (fig) change direction

virg|en a & f virgin. **~inal** a virginal. **~inidad** f virginity

Virgo m Virgo

viril a virile. **~idad** f virility

virtual a virtual

virtud f virtue; (capacidad) ability. **en ~ de** by virtue of

virtuoso a virtuous. —m virtuoso

viruela f smallpox. **picado de ~s** pock-marked

virulé. a la ~ (fam) crooked; (estropeado) damaged

virulento a virulent

virus m invar virus

visa|do m visa. **~r** vt endorse

vísceras fpl entrails

viscos|a f viscose. **~o** a viscous

visera f visor; (de gorra) peak

visib|ilidad f visibility. **~le** a visible

visig|odo a Visigothic. **—m** Visigoth. **~ótico** a Visigothic

visillo m (cortina) net curtain

visi|ón f vision; (vista) sight. **~onario** a & m visionary

visita f visit; (persona) visitor. **~ de cumplido** courtesy call. **~nte** m & f visitor. **~r** vt visit. **tener ~** have visitors

vislumbr|ar vt glimpse. **~e** f glimpse; (resplandor, fig) glimmer

viso m sheen; (aspecto) appearance

visón m mink

visor m viewfinder

víspera f day before, eve

vista f sight, vision; (aspecto, mirada) look; (panorama) view. **apartar la ~** turn away; (fig) turn a blind eye. **a primera ~, a simple ~** at first sight. **clavar la ~ en** stare at. **con ~s a** with a view to. **en ~ de** in view of, considering. **estar a la ~** be obvious. **hacer la ~ gorda** turn a blind eye. **perder de ~** lose sight of. **tener a la ~** have in front of one. **volver la ~ atrás** look back

vistazo m glance. **dar/echar un ~** a glance at

visto a seen; (corriente) common; (considerado) considered. **—vb** véase **vestir. ~ bueno** passed. **~ que** since. **bien ~** acceptable. **está ~ que** it's obvious that. **lo**

nunca ~ an unheard-of thing. **mal ~** unacceptable. **por lo ~** apparently

vistoso a colourful, bright

visual a visual. **—f** glance. **echar una ~ a** have a look at

vital a vital. **~icio** a life. **—m** (life) annuity. **~idad** f vitality

vitamina f vitamin

viticult|or m wine-grower. **~ura** f wine growing

vitorear vt cheer

vítreo a vitreous

vitrina f showcase

vituper|ar vt censure. **~io** m censure. **~ios** mpl abuse

viud|a f widow. **~ez** f widowhood. **~o** a widowed. **—m** widower

viva m cheer

vivacidad f liveliness

vivamente adv vividly; (sinceramente) sincerely

vivaz a (bot) perennial; (vivo) lively

víveres mpl supplies

vivero m nursery; (fig) hotbed

viveza f vividness; (de inteligencia) sharpness; (de carácter) liveliness

vivido a true

vívido a vivid

vivienda f housing; (casa) house; (piso) flat

viviente a living

vivificar [7] vt (animar) enliven

vivir vt live through. **—vi** live. **—m** life. **~ de** live on. **de mal ~** dissolute. **¡viva!** hurray! **¡viva el rey!** long live the king!

vivisección f vivisection

vivo a alive; (viviente) living; (color) bright; (listo) clever; (fig) lively. **a lo ~, al ~** vividly

Vizcaya f Biscay

vizconde m viscount. **~sa** f viscountess

vocablo m word. **~ulario** m vocabulary

vocación f vocation

vocal a vocal. —f vowel. —m & f member. ~ista m & f vocalist

voce ar vt call (*mercancías*); (*fig*) proclaim. —vi shout. ~río m shouting

vociferar vi shout

vodka m & f vodka

vola da f flight. ~dor a flying. —m rocket. ~ndas. en ~ndas in the air; (*fig, rápidamente*) very quickly. ~nte a flying. —m (*auto*) steering-wheel; (*nota*) note; (*rehilete*) shuttlecock; (*tec*) flywheel. ~r [2] vt blow up. —vi fly; (*desaparecer, fam*) disappear

volátil a volatile

volcán m volcano. ~ico a volcanic

vol car [2 & 7] vt knock over; (*adrede*) empty out. —vi overturn. ~carse vpr fall over; (*vehículo*) overturn; (*fig*) do one's utmost. ~carse en throw o.s. into

vol(e)ibol m volleyball

volquete m tipper, dump truck

voltaje m voltage

volte ar vt turn over; (*en el aire*) toss; ring (*campanas*). ~reta f somersault

voltio m volt

voluble a (*fig*) fickle

volum en m volume; (*importancia*) importance. ~inoso a voluminous

voluntad f will; (*fuerza de voluntad*) will-power; (*deseo*) wish; (*intención*) intention. **buena** ~ goodwill. **mala** ~ ill will

voluntario a voluntary. —m volunteer. ~so a willing; (*obstinado*) wilful

voluptuoso a voluptuous

volver [2, *pp* **vuelto**] vt turn; (*de arriba a abajo*) turn over; (*devolver*) restore. —vi return; (*fig*) revert. ~se vpr turn round; (*regresar*) return; (*hacerse*)

become. ~ **a hacer algo** do sth again. ~ **en sí** come round

vomit ar vt bring up. ~ví be sick, vomit. ~ivo m emetic. —a disgusting

vómito m vomit; (*acción*) vomiting

vorágine f maelstrom

voraz a voracious

vos pron (*LAm*) you

vosotros pron you; (*reflexivo*) yourselves. **el libro de** ~ your book

vot ación f voting; (*voto*) vote. ~ante m & f voter. ~ar vt vote for. —vi vote. ~o m vote; (*relig*) vow; (*maldición*) curse. **hacer** ~os por hope for

voy vb véase **ir**

voz f voice; (*grito*) shout; (*rumor*) rumour; (*palabra*) word. ~ **pública** public opinion. **aclarar la** ~ clear one's throat. **a media** ~ softly. **a una** ~ unanimously. **dar voces** shout. **en** ~ **alta** loudly

vuelco m upset. **el corazón me dio un** ~ my heart missed a beat

vuelo m flight; (*acción*) flying; (*de ropa*) flare. **al** ~ in flight; (*fig*) in passing

vuelta f turn; (*curva*) bend; (*paseo*) walk; (*revolución*) revolution; (*regreso*) return; (*dinero*) change. **a la** ~ on one's return; (*de página*) over the page. **a la** ~ **de la esquina** round the corner. **dar la** ~ **al mundo** go round the world. **dar una** ~ go for a walk. **estar de** ~ be back. **¡hasta la** ~! see you soon!

vuelvo vb véase **volver**

vuestro a your. —pron yours. **un amigo** ~ a friend of yours

vulg ar a vulgar; (*persona*) common. ~aridad f ordinariness; (*trivialidad*) triviality; (*grosería*) vulgarity. ~arizar [10] vt popularize. ∼o *m* common people

vulnerab|ilidad *f* vulnerability. ∼**le** *a* vulnerable

W

wáter *m* toilet
whisky /'wiski/ *m* whisky

X

xenofobia *f* xenophobia
xilófono *m* xylophone

Y

y *conj* and
ya *adv* already; (*ahora*) now; (*luego*) later; (*en seguida*) immediately; (*pronto*) soon. —*int* of course! ∼ **no** no longer. ∼ **que** since. ¡∼, ∼! oh yes!, all right!
yacaré *m* (*LAm*) alligator
yac|er [44] *vi* lie. ∼**imiento** *m* deposit; (*de petróleo*) oilfield
yanqui *m* & *f* American, Yank(ee)
yate *m* yacht
yegua *f* mare
yeísmo *m* pronunciation of the Spanish *ll* like the Spanish *y*
yelmo *m* helmet
yema *f* (*bot*) bud; (*de huevo*) yolk; (*golosina*) sweet. ∼ **del dedo** fingertip
yergo *vb véase* **erguir**
yermo *a* uninhabited; (*no cultivable*) barren. —*m* wasteland
yerno *m* son-in-law
yerro *m* mistake. —*vb véase* **errar**
yerto *a* stiff

yeso *m* gypsum; (*arquit*) plaster. ∼ **mate** plaster of Paris
yo *pron* I. —*m* ego. ∼ **mismo** I myself. **soy** ∼ it's me
yodo *m* iodine
yoga *m* yoga
yogur *m* yog(h)urt
York. de ∼ ⟨*jamón*⟩ cooked
yuca *f* yucca
Yucatán *m* Yucatán
yugo *m* yoke
Yugoslavia *f* Yugoslavia
yugoslavo *a* & *m* Yugoslav
yunque *m* anvil
yunta *f* yoke
yuxtaponer [34] *vt* juxtapose
yuyo *m* (*Arg*) weed

Z

zafarse *vpr* escape; get out of ⟨*obligación etc*⟩
zafarrancho *m* (*confusión*) mess; (*riña*) quarrel
zafio *a* coarse
zafiro *m* sapphire
zaga *f* rear. **no ir en** ∼ not be inferior
zaguán *m* hall
zaherir [4] *vt* hurt one's feelings
zahorí *m* clairvoyant; (*de agua*) water diviner
zaino *a* ⟨*caballo*⟩ chestnut; (*vaca*) black
zalamer|ía *f* flattery. ∼o *a* flattering. —*m* flatterer
zamarra *f* (*piel*) sheepskin; (*prenda*) sheepskin jacket
zamarrear *vt* shake
zamba *f* (*esp LAm*) South American dance; (*samba*) samba
zambulli|da *f* dive. ∼**r** [22] *vt* plunge. ∼**rse** *vpr* dive
zamparse *vpr* fall; (*comer*) gobble up
zanahoria *f* carrot

zancad|a f stride. ∼**illa** f trip.
echar la ∼**illa** a uno, poner la
∼**illa** a uno trip s.o. up

zanc|o m stilt. ∼**udo** a long-
legged. —m (*LAm*) mosquito

zanganear vi idle

zángano m drone; (*persona*)
idler

zangolotear vt fiddle with. —vi
rattle; (*persona*) fidget

zanja f ditch. ∼**r** vt (*fig*) settle

zapapico m pickaxe

zapat|ear vt/i tap with one's feet.
∼**ería** f shoe shop; (*arte*) shoe-
making. ∼**ero** m shoemaker; (*el
que remienda zapatos*) cobbler.
∼**illa** f slipper. ∼**illas deport-
ivas** trainers. ∼**o** m shoe

zaragata f turmoil

Zaragoza f Saragossa

zarand|a f sieve. ∼**ear** vt sieve;
(*sacudir*) shake

zarcillo m earring

zarpa f claw, paw

zarpar vi weigh anchor

zarza f bramble. ∼**mora** f
blackberry

zarzuela f musical, operetta

zascandil m scatterbrain

zenit m zenith

zigzag m zigzag. ∼**uear** vi zigzag

zinc m zinc

zipizape m (*fam*) row

zócalo m skirting-board; (*pedestal*) plinth

zodiaco m, **zodíaco** m zodiac

zona f zone; (*área*) area

zoo m zoo. ∼**logía** f zoology. ∼**lógico** a zoological

zoólogo m zoologist

zopenco a stupid. —m idiot

zoquete m (*de madera*) block;
(*persona*) blockhead

zorr|a f fox; (*hembra*) vixen. ∼**o**
m fox

zozobra f (*fig*) anxiety. ∼**r** vi be
shipwrecked; (*fig*) be ruined

zueco m clog

zulú a & m Zulu

zumb|ar vt (*fam*) give (*golpe
etc*). —vi buzz. ∼**ido** m buzzing

zumo m juice

zurci|do m darning. ∼**r** [9] vt
darn

zurdo a left-handed; (*mano*) left

zurrar vt (*fig, dar golpes, fam*)
beat up

zurriago m whip

zutano m so-and-so

ENGLISH-SPANISH
INGLÉS-ESPAÑOL

A

a /ə, eɪ/ *indef art* (*before vowel* **an**) un *m*; una *f*

aback /ə'bæk/ *adv.* **be taken ~** quedar desconcertado

abacus /'æbəkəs/ *n* ábaco *m*

abandon /ə'bændən/ *vt* abandonar. —*n* abandono *m*, desenfado *m*. **~ed** *a* abandonado; ⟨*behaviour*⟩ perdido. **~ment** *n* abandono *m*

abase /ə'beɪs/ *vt* degradar. **~ment** *n* degradación *f*

abashed /ə'bæʃt/ *a* confuso

abate /ə'beɪt/ *vt* disminuir. —*vi* disminuir; ⟨*storm etc*⟩ calmarse. **~ment** *n* disminución *f*

abattoir /'æbətwɑ:(r)/ *n* matadero *m*

abbess /'æbɪs/ *n* abadesa *f*

abbey /'æbɪ/ *n* abadía *f*

abbot /'æbət/ *n* abad *m*

abbreviat|e /ə'bri:vɪeɪt/ *vt* abreviar. **~ion** /-'eɪʃn/ *n* abreviatura *f*; (*act*) abreviación *f*

ABC /'eɪbi:'si:/ *n* abecé *m*, abecedario *m*

abdicat|e /'æbdɪkeɪt/ *vt/i* abdicar. **~ion** /-'eɪʃn/ *n* abdicación *f*

abdom|en /'æbdəmən/ *n* abdomen *m*. **~inal** /-'dɒmɪnl/ *a* abdominal

abduct /æb'dʌkt/ *vt* secuestrar. **~ion** /-ʃn/ *n* secuestro *m*. **~or** *n* secuestrador *m*

aberration /æbə'reɪʃn/ *n* aberración *f*

abet /ə'bet/ *vt* (*pt* **abetted**) (*jurid*) ser cómplice de

abeyance /ə'beɪəns/ *n*. **in ~** en suspenso

abhor /əb'hɔ:(r)/ *vt* (*pt* **abhorred**) aborrecer. **~rence** /-'hɒrəns/ *n* aborrecimiento *m*; (*thing*) abominación *f*. **~rent** /-'hɒrənt/ *a* aborrecible

abide /ə'baɪd/ *vt* (*pt* **abided**) soportar. —*vi* (*old use, pt* **abode**) morar. **~ by** atenerse a; cumplir ⟨*promise*⟩

abiding /ə'baɪdɪŋ/ *a* duradero, permanente

ability /ə'bɪlətɪ/ *n* capacidad *f*; (*cleverness*) habilidad *f*

abject /'æbdʒekt/ *a* (*wretched*) miserable; (*vile*) abyecto

ablaze /ə'bleɪz/ *a* en llamas

able /'eɪbl/ *a* (-**er**, -**est**) capaz. **be ~** poder; (*know how to*) saber

ablutions /ə'blu:ʃnz/ *npl* ablución *f*

ably /'eɪblɪ/ *adv* hábilmente

abnormal /æb'nɔ:ml/ *a* anormal. **~ity** /-'mælɪtɪ/ *n* anormalidad *f*

aboard /ə'bɔ:d/ *adv* a bordo. —*prep* a bordo de

abode /ə'bəʊd/ *see* **abide**. —*n* (*old use*) domicilio *m*

abolish /ə'bɒlɪʃ/ *vt* suprimir, abolir

abolition /æbə'lɪʃn/ n supresión f, abolición f

abominable /ə'bɒmɪnəbl/ a abominable

abominat|e /ə'bɒmɪneɪt/ vt abominar. ~**ion** /-'neɪʃn/ n abominación f

aboriginal /æbə'rɪdʒənl/ a & n aborigen (m & f), indígena (m & f). ~**es** /-iːz/ npl aborígenes mpl

abort /ə'bɔːt/ vt hacer abortar. — vi abortar. ~**ion** /-ʃn/ n aborto m provocado; (fig) aborto m. ~**ionist** n abortista m & f. ~**ive** a abortivo; (fig) fracasado

abound /ə'baʊnd/ vi abundar (**in** de, en)

about /ə'baʊt/ adv (approximately) alrededor de; (here and there) por todas partes; (in existence) por aquí. ~ **here** por aquí. **be** ~ **to** estar a punto de. **be up and** ~ estar levantado. —prep sobre; (around) alrededor de; (somewhere in) en. **talk** ~ hablar de. ~**face** n (fig) cambio m rotundo. ~**turn** n (fig) cambio m rotundo

above /ə'bʌv/ adv arriba. —prep encima de; (more than) más de. ~ **all** sobre todo. ~**board** a honrado. —adv abiertamente. ~**mentioned** a susodicho

abrasi|on /ə'breɪʒn/ n abrasión f. ~**ve** /ə'breɪsɪv/ a & n abrasivo (m); (fig) agresivo, brusco

abreast /ə'brest/ adv de frente. **keep** ~ **of** mantenerse al corriente de

abridge /ə'brɪdʒ/ vt abreviar. ~**ment** n abreviación f; (abstract) resumen m

abroad /ə'brɔːd/ adv (be) en el extranjero; (go) al extranjero; (far and wide) por todas partes

abrupt /ə'brʌpt/ a brusco. ~**ly** adv (suddenly) repentinamente; (curtly) bruscamente. ~**ness** n brusquedad f

abscess /'æbsɪs/ n absceso m

abscond /əb'skɒnd/ vi fugarse

absen|ce /'æbsəns/ n ausencia f; (lack) falta f. ~**t** /'æbsənt/ a ausente. /æb'sent/ vr. ~ **o.s.** ausentarse. ~**tly** adv distraídamente. ~**t-minded** a distraído. ~**t-mindedness** n distracción f, despiste m

absentee /æbsən'tiː/ n ausente m & f. ~**ism** n absentismo m

absinthe /'æbsɪnθ/ n ajenjo m

absolute /'æbsəluːt/ a absoluto. ~**ly** adv absolutamente

absolution /æbsə'luːʃn/ n absolución f

absolve /əb'zɒlv/ vt (from sin) absolver; (from obligation) liberar

absor|b /əb'zɔːb/ vt absorber. ~**bent** a absorbente. ~**ption** n absorción f

abstain /əb'steɪn/ vi abstenerse (**from** de)

abstemious /əb'stiːmɪəs/ a abstemio

abstention /əb'stenʃn/ n abstención f

abstinen|ce /'æbstɪnəns/ n abstinencia f. ~**t** a abstinente

abstract /'æbstrækt/ a abstracto. —n (quality) abstracto m; (summary) resumen m. /əb'strækt/ vt extraer; (summarize) resumir. ~**ion** /-ʃn/ n abstracción f

abstruse /əb'struːs/ a abstruso

absurd /əb'sɜːd/ a absurdo. ~**ity** n absurdo m, disparate m

abundan|ce /ə'bʌndəns/ n abundancia f. ~**t** a abundante

abuse /ə'bjuːz/ vt (misuse) abusar de; (ill-treat) maltratar; (insult) insultar. /ə'bjuːs/ n abuso m; (insults) insultos mpl

abusive /ə'bjuːsɪv/ a injurioso

abut /ə'bʌt/ vi (pt abutted) confinar (**on** con)

abysmal /ə'bɪzməl/ *a* abismal; (*bad, fam*) pésimo; (*fig*) profundo

abyss /ə'bɪs/ *n* abismo *m*

acacia /ə'keɪʃə/ *n* acacia *f*

academic /æke'demɪk/ *a* académico; (*pej*) teórico. —*n* universitario *m*, catedrático *m*. ~**ian** /-də'mɪʃn/ *n* académico *m*

academy /ə'kædəmɪ/ *n* academia *f*. ~ **of music** conservatorio *m*

accede /ək'siːd/ *vi*. ~ **to** acceder a (*request*); tomar posesión de ‹*office*›. ~ **to the throne** subir al trono

accelerate /ək'seləreɪt/ *vt* acelerar. ~**ion** /-'reɪʃn/ *n* aceleración *f*. ~**or** *n* acelerador *m*

accent /'æksənt/ *n* acento *m*. /æk'sent/ *vt* acentuar

accentuate /æk'sentʃʊeɪt/ *vt* acentuar

accept /ək'sept/ *vt* aceptar. ~**able** *a* aceptable. ~**ance** *n* aceptación *f*; (*approval*) aprobación *f*

access /'ækses/ *n* acceso *m*. ~**ibility** /-ɪ'bɪlɪtɪ/ *n* accesibilidad *f*. ~**ible** /-səbl/ *a* accesible; ‹*person*› tratable

accession /ək'seʃn/ *n* (*to power, throne etc*) ascenso *m*; (*thing added*) adquisición *f*

accessory /ək'sesərɪ/ *a* accesorio. —*n* accesorio *m*, complemento *m*; (*jurid*) cómplice *m & f*

accident /'æksɪdənt/ *n* accidente *m*; (*chance*) casualidad *f*. **by ~** por accidente, por descuido, sin querer; (*by chance*) por casualidad. ~**al** /-'dentl/ *a* accidental, fortuito. ~**ally** /-'dentlɪ/ *adv* por accidente, por descuido, sin querer; (*by chance*) por casualidad

acclaim /ə'kleɪm/ *vt* aclamar. —*n* aclamación *f*

acclimatiz|ation /əklaɪmətaɪ'zeɪʃn/ *n* aclimatación *f*. ~**e** /ə'klaɪmətaɪz/ *vt* aclimatar. —*vi* aclimatarse

accolade /'ækəleɪd/ *n* (*of knight*) acolada *f*; (*praise*) encomio *m*

accommodat|e /ə'kɒmədeɪt/ *vt* (*give hospitality to*) alojar; (*adapt*) acomodar; (*supply*) proveer; (*oblige*) complacer. ~**ing** *a* complaciente. ~**ion** /-'deɪʃn/ *n* alojamiento *m*; (*rooms*) habitaciones *fpl*

accompan|iment /ə'kʌmpənɪmənt/ *n* acompañamiento *m*. ~**ist** *n* acompañante *m & f*. ~**y** /ə'kʌmpənɪ/ *vt* acompañar

accomplice /ə'kʌmplɪs/ *n* cómplice *m & f*

accomplish /ə'kʌmplɪʃ/ *vt* (*complete*) acabar; (*achieve*) realizar; (*carry out*) llevar a cabo. ~**ed** *a* consumado. ~**ment** *n* realización *f*; (*ability*) talento *m*; (*thing achieved*) triunfo *m*, logro *m*

accord /ə'kɔːd/ *vi* concordar. —*vt* conceder. —*n* acuerdo *m*; (*harmony*) armonía *f*. **of one's own** ~ espontáneamente. ~**ance** *n*. **in** ~**ance with** de acuerdo con

according /ə'kɔːdɪŋ/ *adv*. ~ **to** según. ~**ly** *adv* en conformidad; (*therefore*) por consiguiente

accordion /ə'kɔːdɪən/ *n* acordeón *m*

accost /ə'kɒst/ *vt* abordar

account /ə'kaʊnt/ *n* cuenta *f*; (*description*) relato *m*; (*importance*) importancia *f*. **on** ~ **of** a causa de. **on no** ~ de ninguna manera. **on this** ~ por eso. **take into** ~ tener en cuenta. —*vt* considerar. ~ **for** dar cuenta de, explicar

accountab|ility /əkaʊntə'bɪlɪtɪ/ *n* responsabilidad *f*. ~**le** *a* responsable (**for de**)

accountan|cy /ə'kaʊntənsı/ *n* contabilidad *f*. ∼**t** *n* contable *m* & *f*

accoutrements /ə'ku:trəmənts/ *npl* equipo *m*

accredited /ə'kredɪtɪd/ *a* acreditado; (*authorized*) autorizado

accrue /ə'kru:/ *vi* acumularse

accumulat|e /ə'kju:mjʊleɪt/ *vt* acumular. —*vi* acumularse. ∼**ion** /-'leɪʃn/ *n* acumulación *f*. ∼**or** *n* (*elec*) acumulador *m*

accura|cy /'ækjərəsı/ *n* exactitud *f*, precisión *f*. ∼**te** *a* exacto, preciso

accus|ation /ækju:'zeɪʃn/ *n* acusación *f*. ∼**e** *vt* acusar

accustom /ə'kʌstəm/ *vt* acostumbrar. ∼**ed** *a* acostumbrado. **get** ∼**ed (to)** acostumbrarse (a)

ace /eɪs/ *n* as *m*

acetate /'æsɪteɪt/ *n* acetato *m*

ache /eɪk/ *n* dolor *m*. —*vi* doler. **my leg** ∼**s** me duele la pierna

achieve /ə'tʃi:v/ *vt* realizar; lograr (*success*). ∼**ment** *n* realización *f*; (*feat*) éxito *m*; (*thing achieved*) proeza *f*, logro *m*

acid /'æsɪd/ *a & n* ácido (*m*). ∼**ity** /ə'sɪdətı/ *n* acidez *f*

acknowledge /ək'nɒlɪdʒ/ *vt* reconocer. ∼ **receipt of** acusar recibo de. ∼**ment** *n* reconocimiento *m*; (*com*) acuse *m* de recibo

acme /'ækmı/ *n* cima *f*

acne /'æknı/ *n* acné *m*

acorn /'eɪkɔ:n/ *n* bellota *f*

acoustic /ə'ku:stɪk/ *a* acústico. ∼**s** *npl* acústica *f*

acquaint /ə'kweɪnt/ *vt*. ∼ **s.o. with** poner a uno al corriente de. **be** ∼**ed with** conocer (*person*); saber (*fact*). ∼**ance** *n* conocimiento *m*; (*person*) conocido *m*

acquiesce /ækwı'es/ *vi* consentir (**in** en). ∼**nce** *n* aquiescencia *f*, consentimiento *m*

acqui|re /ə'kwaɪə(r)/ *vt* adquirir; aprender (*language*). ∼**re a taste for** tomar gusto a. ∼**sition** /ækwı'zıʃn/ *n* adquisición *f*. ∼**sitive** /-'kwɪzɪtɪv/ *a* codicioso

acquit /ə'kwɪt/ *vt* (*pt* **acquitted**) absolver; ∼ **o.s. well** defenderse bien, tener éxito. ∼**tal** *n* absolución *f*

acre /'eɪkə(r)/ *n* acre *m*. ∼**age** *n* superficie *f* (en acres)

acrid /'ækrɪd/ *a* acre

acrimon|ious /ækrɪ'məʊnɪəs/ *a* cáustico, mordaz. ∼**y** /'ækrɪmənı/ *n* acrimonia *f*, acritud *f*

acrobat /'ækrəbæt/ *n* acróbata *m & f*. ∼**ic** /-'bætɪk/ *a* acrobático. ∼**ics** /-'bætɪks/ *npl* acrobacia *f*

acronym /'ækrənɪm/ *n* acrónimo *m*, siglas *fpl*

across /ə'krɒs/ *adv & prep* (*side to side*) de un lado a otro; (*on other side*) del otro lado de; (*crosswise*) a través de. **go** *or* **walk** ∼ atravesar

act /ækt/ *n* acto *m*; (*action*) acción *f*; (*in variety show*) número *m*; (*decree*) decreto *m*. —*vt* hacer (*part, role*). —*vi* actuar; (*pretend*) fingir; (*function*) funcionar. ∼ **as** actuar de. ∼ **for** representar. ∼**ing** *a* interino. —*n* (*of play*) representación *f*; (*by actor*) interpretación *f*; (*profession*) profesión *f* de actor

action /'ækʃn/ *n* acción *f*; (*jurid*) demanda *f*; (*plot*) argumento *m*. **out of** ∼ (*on sign*) no funciona. **put out of** ∼ inutilizar. **take** ∼ tomar medidas

activate /'æktɪveɪt/ *vt* activar

activ|e /'æktɪv/ *a* activo; (*energetic*) enérgico; (*volcano*) en actividad. ∼**ity** /-'tɪvətı/ *n* actividad *f*

act|or /'æktə(r)/ *n* actor *m*. ∼**ress** *n* actriz *f*

actual /ˈæktjʊəl/ a verdadero.
~ity /-ˈælətɪ/ n realidad f. **~ly**
adv en realidad, efectivamente;
(even) incluso

actuary /ˈæktjʊərɪ/ n actuario m

actuate /ˈæktjʊeɪt/ vt accionar,
impulsar

acumen /ˈækjʊmen/ n perspicacia f

acupuncture /ˈækjʊpʌŋktʃə(r)/
n acupuntura f. **~ist** n acupunturista m & f

acute /əˈkjuːt/ a agudo. **~ly** adv
agudamente. **~ness** n agudeza f

ad /æd/ n (fam) anuncio m

AD /eɪˈdiː/ abbr (Anno Domini)
d.J.C.

adamant /ˈædəmənt/ a inflexible

Adam's apple /ˈædəmzˈæpl/ —
nuez f (de Adán)

adapt /əˈdæpt/ vt adaptar. —vi
adaptarse

adaptab **ility** /ədæptəˈbɪlətɪ/ n
adaptabilidad f. **~le** /əˈdæptəbl/
a adaptable

adaptation /ædæpˈteɪʃn/ n adaptación f; (of book etc) versión f

adaptor /əˈdæptə(r)/ n (elec)
adaptador m

add /æd/ vt añadir. —vi sumar. **~
up** sumar; (fig) tener sentido. **~
up to** equivaler a

adder /ˈædə(r)/ n víbora f

addict /ˈædɪkt/ n adicto m; (fig)
entusiasta m & f. **~ed** /əˈdɪktɪd/
a. **~ed to** adicto a; (fig) fanático
de. **~ion** /-ʃn/ n (med) dependencia f; (fig) afición f. **~ive** a
que crea dependencia

adding machine /ˈædɪŋmæʃiːn/ n
máquina f de sumar, sumadora f

addition /əˈdɪʃn/ n suma f. **in ~**
además. **~al** /-ʃənl/ a suplementario

additive /ˈædɪtɪv/ a & n aditivo
(m)

address /əˈdres/ n señas fpl,
dirección f; (speech) discurso
m. —vt poner la dirección;

(speak to) dirigirse a. **~ee**
/ædreˈsiː/ n destinatario m

adenoids /ˈædɪnɔɪdz/ npl vegetaciones fpl adenoideas

adept /ˈædept/ a & n experto (m)

adequa **cy** /ˈædɪkwəsɪ/ n suficiencia f. **~te** a suficiente, adecuado. **~tely** adv suficientemente, adecuadamente

adhere /ədˈhɪə(r)/ vi adherirse
(to a); observar (rule). **~nce**
/-rəns/ n adhesión f; (to rules)
observancia f

adhesion /ədˈhiːʒn/ n adherencia
f

adhesive /ədˈhiːsɪv/ a & n adhesivo m f

ad infinitum /ædɪnfɪˈnaɪtəm/ adv
hasta el infinito

adjacent /əˈdʒeɪsnt/ a contiguo

adjective /ˈædʒɪktɪv/ n adjetivo
m

adjoin /əˈdʒɔɪn/ vt lindar con.
~ing a contiguo

adjourn /əˈdʒɜːn/ vt aplazar; suspender (meeting etc). —vi suspenderse. **~ to** trasladarse a

adjudicate /əˈdʒuːdɪkeɪt/ vt
juzgar. —vi actuar como juez

adjust /əˈdʒʌst/ vt ajustar (machine); (arrange) arreglar. —vi.
~ (to) adaptarse (a). **~able** a
ajustable. **~ment** n adaptación
f; (tec) ajuste m

ad lib /ædˈlɪb/ a improvisado. —
vi (pt -libbed) (fam) improvisar

administer /ədˈmɪnɪstə(r)/ vt
administrar, dar, proporcionar

administrat **ion** /ədmɪnɪˈstreɪʃn/ n administración f. **~or** n administrador m

admirable /ˈædmərəbl/ a admirable

admiral /ˈædmərəl/ n almirante
m

admiration /ædməˈreɪʃn/ n
admiración f

admire /əd'maɪə(r)/ vt admirar. **~r** /-'maɪərə(r)/ n admirador m; (suitor) enamorado m

admissible /əd'mɪsəbl/ a admisible

admission /əd'mɪʃn/ n admisión f; (entry) entrada f

admit /əd'mɪt/ vt (pt **admitted**) dejar entrar; (acknowledge) admitir, reconocer. **~ to** confesar. **be ~ted** (to hospital etc) ingresar. **~tance** n entrada f. **~tedly** adv es verdad que

admonish /əd'mɒnɪʃ/ vt reprender; (advise) aconsejar. **~tion** /-'nɪʃn/ n reprensión f

ado /ə'duː/ n alboroto m; (trouble) dificultad f. **without more ~** en seguida, sin más

adolescen|ce /ædə'lesns/ n adolescencia f. **~t** a & n adolescente (m & f)

adopt /ə'dɒpt/ vt adoptar. **~ed** a (child) adoptivo. **~ion** /-ʃn/ n adopción f. **~ive** a adoptivo

ador|able /ə'dɔːrəbl/ a adorable. **~ation** /ædə'reɪʃn/ n adoración f. **~e** /ə'dɔː(r)/ vt adorar

adorn /ə'dɔːn/ vt adornar. **~ment** n adorno m

adrenalin /ə'drenəlɪn/ n adrenalina f

adrift /ə'drɪft/ a & adv a la deriva

adroit /ə'drɔɪt/ a diestro

adulation /ædjʊ'leɪʃn/ n adulación f

adult /'ædʌlt/ a & n adulto (m)

adulterat|ion /ədʌltə'reɪʃn/ n adulteración f. **~e** /ə'dʌltəreɪt/ vt adulterar

adulter|er /ə'dʌltərə(r)/ n adúltero m. **~ess** n adúltera f. **~ous** a adúltero. **~y** n adulterio m

advance /əd'vɑːns/ vt adelantar. **~vi** adelantarse. **~n** adelanto m. **in ~** con anticipación, por adelantado. **~d** a avanzado; (studies) superior. **~ment** n adelanto m; (in job) promoción f

advantage /əd'vɑːntɪdʒ/ n ventaja f. **take ~ of** aprovecharse de; abusar de (person). **~ous** /ædvən'teɪdʒəs/ a ventajoso

advent /'ædvənt/ n venida f. **A~** n adviento m

adventur|e /əd'ventʃə(r)/ n aventura f. **~er** n aventurero m. **~ous** a (persona) aventurero; (cosa) arriesgado; (fig, bold) llamativo

adverb /'ædvɜːb/ n adverbio m

adversary /'ædvəsəri/ n adversario m

advers|e /'ædvɜːs/ a adverso, contrario, desfavorable. **~ity** /əd'vɜːsəti/ n infortunio m

advert /'ædvɜːt/ n (fam) anuncio m. **~ise** /'ædvətaɪz/ vt anunciar. **~vi** hacer publicidad; (seek, sell) poner un anuncio. **~isement** /əd'vɜːtɪsmənt/ n anuncio m. **~iser** /-ə(r)/ n anunciante m & f

advice /əd'vaɪs/ n consejo m; (report) informe m

advis|able /əd'vaɪzəbl/ a aconsejable. **~e** vt aconsejar; (inform) avisar. **~e against** aconsejar en contra de. **~er** n consejero m; (consultant) asesor m. **~ory** a consultivo

advocate /'ædvəkət/ n defensor m; (jurid) abogado m. /'ædvəkeɪt/ vt recomendar

aegis /'iːdʒɪs/ n égida f. **under the ~ of** bajo la tutela de, patrocinado por

aeon /'iːən/ n eternidad f

aerial /'eərɪəl/ a aéreo. **~n** antena f

aerobatics /eərə'bætɪks/ npl acrobacia f aérea

aerobics /eə'rəʊbɪks/ npl aeróbica f

aerodrome /'eərədrəʊm/ n aeródromo m

aerodynamic /eərəʊdaɪ'næmɪk/ a aerodinámico

aeroplane /'eərəpleɪn/ n avión m

aerosol /'eərəsɒl/ n aerosol m

aesthetic /i:s'θetɪk/ a estético

afar /ə'fɑ:(r)/ adv lejos

affable /'æfəbl/ a afable

affair /ə'feə(r)/ n asunto m. (love) ~ aventura f, amorío m. ~s npl (business) negocios mpl

affect /ə'fekt/ vt afectar; (pretend) fingir

affect|ation /æfek'teɪʃn/ n afectación f. ~ed a afectado, amanerado

affection /ə'fekʃn/ n cariño m; (disease) afección f. ~ate /-ʃənət/ a cariñoso

affiliat|e /ə'fɪlieɪt/ vt afiliar. ~ion /-'eɪʃn/ n afiliación f

affinity /ə'fɪnətɪ/ n afinidad f

affirm /ə'fɜ:m/ vt afirmar. ~ation /æfə'meɪʃn/ n afirmación f

affirmative /ə'fɜ:mətɪv/ a afirmativo. —n respuesta f afirmativa

affix /ə'fɪks/ vt sujetar; añadir (signature); pegar (stamp)

afflict /ə'flɪkt/ vt afligir. ~ion /-ʃn/ n aflicción f, pena f

affluen|ce /'æfluəns/ n riqueza f. ~t a rico. —n (geog) afluente m

afford /ə'fɔ:d/ vt permitirse; (provide) dar

affray /ə'freɪ/ n reyerta f

affront /ə'frʌnt/ n afrenta f, ofensa f. —vt afrentar, ofender

afield /ə'fi:ld/ adv. far ~ muy lejos

aflame /ə'fleɪm/ adv & a en llamas

afloat /ə'fləʊt/ adv a flote

afoot /ə'fʊt/ adv. sth is ~ se está tramando algo

aforesaid /ə'fɔ:sed/ a susodicho

afraid /ə'freɪd/ a. be ~ tener miedo (of a); (be sorry) sentir, lamentar

afresh /ə'freʃ/ adv de nuevo

Africa /'æfrɪkə/ n África f. ~n a & n africano (m)

after /'ɑ:ftə(r)/ adv después; (behind) detrás. —prep después de; (behind) detrás de. be ~ (seek) buscar, andar en busca de. —conj después de que. ~ posterior

afterbirth /'ɑ:ftəbɜ:θ/ n placenta f

after-effect /'ɑ:ftərɪfekt/ n consecuencia f, efecto m secundario

aftermath /'ɑ:ftəmæθ/ n secuelas fpl

afternoon /ɑ:ftə'nu:n/ n tarde f

aftershave /'ɑ:ftəʃeɪv/ n loción f para después del afeitado

afterthought /'ɑ:ftəθɔ:t/ n ocurrencia f tardía

afterwards /'ɑ:ftəwədz/ adv después

again /ə'gen/ adv otra vez; (besides) además. ~ and ~ una y otra vez

against /ə'genst/ prep contra, en contra de

age /eɪdʒ/ n edad f. ~ mayor de edad. under ~ menor de edad. —vt/i (pres p ageing) envejecer. ~d /'eɪdʒd/ a de ... años. ~d 10 de 10 años, que tiene 10 años. ~d /'eɪdʒɪd/ a viejo, anciano. ~less a siempre joven; (eternal) eterno, inmemorial. ~s (fam) siglos mpl

agency /'eɪdʒənsɪ/ n agencia f, organismo m, oficina f; (means) mediación f

agenda /ə'dʒendə/ npl orden m del día

agent /'eɪdʒənt/ n agente m & f; (representative) representante m & f

agglomeration /əglɒmə'reɪʃn/ n aglomeración f

aggravat|e /'ægrəveɪt/ vt agravar; (irritate, fam) irritar. ~ion /-'veɪʃn/ n agravación f, (irritation, fam) irritación f

aggregate /ˈægrɪgət/ a total. —n conjunto m. /ˈægrɪgeɪt/ vt agregar. —vi ascender a

aggression /əˈgreʃn/ n agresión f. ∼ive a agresivo. ∼iveness n agresividad f. ∼or n agresor m

aggrieved /əˈgriːvd/ a apenado, ofendido

aghast /əˈgɑːst/ a horrorizado

agile /ˈædʒaɪl/ a ágil. ∼ity /əˈdʒɪlətɪ/ n agilidad f

agitat|e /ˈædʒɪteɪt/ vt agitar. ∼ion /-ˈteɪʃn/ n agitación f, excitación f. ∼or n agitador m

agnostic /ægˈnɒstɪk/ a & n agnóstico (m). ∼ism /-sɪzəm/ n agnosticismo m

ago /əˈgəʊ/ adv hace. a long time ∼ hace mucho tiempo. 3 days ∼ hace 3 días

agog /əˈgɒg/ a ansioso

agon|ize /ˈægənaɪz/ vi atormentarse. ∼izing a atroz, angustioso, doloroso. ∼y n dolor m (agudo); (mental) angustia f

agree /əˈgriː/ vt acordar. —vi estar de acuerdo; (of figures) concordar; (get on) entenderse. ∼ with (of food etc) sentar bien a. ∼able /əˈgriːəbl/ a agradable. be ∼able (willing) estar de acuerdo. ∼d a (time, place) convenido. ∼ment /əˈgriːmənt/ n acuerdo m. in ∼ment de acuerdo

agricultur|al /ægrɪˈkʌltʃərəl/ a agrícola. ∼e /ˈægrɪkʌltʃə(r)/ n agricultura f

aground /əˈgraʊnd/ adv. run ∼ (of ship) varar, encallar

ahead /əˈhed/ adv delante; (of time) antes de. be ∼ ir delante

aid /eɪd/ vt ayudar. —n ayuda f. in ∼ of a beneficio de

aide /eɪd/ n (Amer) ayudante m & f

AIDS /eɪdz/ n (med) SIDA m

ail /eɪl/ vt afligir. ∼ing a enfermo. ∼ment n enfermedad f

aim /eɪm/ vt apuntar; (fig) dirigir. —vi apuntar; (fig) pretender. —n puntería f; (fig) propósito m. ∼less a, ∼lessly adv sin objeto, sin rumbo

air /eə(r)/ n aire m. be on the ∼ estar en el aire. put on ∼s darse aires. —vt airear. —a (base etc) aéreo. ∼borne a en el aire; (mil) aerotransportado. ∼conditioned a climatizado, con aire acondicionado. ∼craft /ˈeəkrɑːft/ n (pl invar) avión m. ∼field /ˈeəfiːld/ n aeródromo m. A∼ Force fuerzas fpl aéreas. ∼gun /ˈeəgʌn/ n escopeta f de aire comprimido. ∼lift /ˈeəlɪft/ n puente m aéreo. ∼line /ˈeəlaɪn/ n línea f aérea. ∼lock /ˈeəlɒk/ n (in pipe) burbuja f de aire; (chamber) esclusa f de aire. ∼ mail n correo m aéreo. ∼man /ˈeəmən/ (pl -men) n aviador m. ∼port /ˈeəpɔːt/ n aeropuerto m. ∼tight /ˈeətaɪt/ a hermético. ∼worthy /ˈeəwɜːðɪ/ a en condiciones de vuelo. ∼y /ˈeərɪ/ a (-ier, -iest) aireado; (manner) ligero

aisle /aɪl/ n nave f lateral; (gangway) pasillo m

ajar /əˈdʒɑː(r)/ adv & a entreabierto

akin /əˈkɪn/ a semejante (a to)

alabaster /ˈæləbɑːstə(r)/ n alabastro m

alacrity /əˈlækrətɪ/ n prontitud f

alarm /əˈlɑːm/ n alarma f; (clock) despertador m. —vt asustar. ∼ist n alarmista m & f

alas /əˈlæs/ int ¡ay!, ¡ay de mí!

albatross /ˈælbətrɒs/ n albatros m

albino /ælˈbiːnəʊ/ a & n albino (m)

album /ˈælbəm/ n álbum m

alchem|ist /ˈælkəmɪst/ n alquimista m & f. ~y n alquimia f

alcohol /ˈælkəhɒl/ n alcohol m. ~ic /-ˈhɒlɪk/ a & n alcohólico (m). ~ism n alcoholismo m

alcove /ˈælkəʊv/ n nicho m

ale /eɪl/ n cerveza f

alert /əˈlɜːt/ a vivo; (watchful) vigilante. —n alerta f. **on the** ~ alerta. —vt avisar. ~ness n vigilancia f

algebra /ˈældʒɪbrə/ n álgebra f

Algeria /ælˈdʒɪərɪə/ n Argelia f. ~n a & n argelino (m)

alias /ˈeɪlɪəs/ n (pl -ases) alias m invar. —adv alias

alibi /ˈælɪbaɪ/ n (pl -is) coartada f

alien /ˈeɪlɪən/ n extranjero m. — a ajeno

alienat|e /ˈeɪlɪəneɪt/ vt enajenar. ~ion /-ˈneɪʃn/ n enajenación f

alight[1] /əˈlaɪt/ vi bajar; (bird) posarse

alight[2] /əˈlaɪt/ a ardiendo; (light) encendido

align /əˈlaɪn/ vt alinear. ~ment n alineación f

alike /əˈlaɪk/ a parecido, semejante. **look or be** ~ parecerse. —adv de la misma manera

alimony /ˈælɪmənɪ/ n pensión f alimenticia

alive /əˈlaɪv/ a vivo. ~ **to** sensible a. ~ **with** lleno de

alkali /ˈælkəlaɪ/ n (pl -is) álcali m. ~**ne** a alcalino

all /ɔːl/ a & pron todo. ~ **but one** todos excepto uno. ~ **of it** todo. —adv completamente. ~ **but** casi. **in** (fam) rendido. ~ **of a sudden** de pronto. ~ **over** (finished) acabado; (everywhere) por todas partes. ~ **right!** ¡vale! **be** ~ **for** estar a favor de. **not at** ~ de ninguna manera; (after thanks) ¡no hay de qué!

allay /əˈleɪ/ vt aliviar (pain); aquietar (fears etc)

all-clear /ɔːlˈklɪə(r)/ n fin m de (la) alarma

allegation /ælɪˈgeɪʃn/ n alegato m

allege /əˈledʒ/ vt alegar. ~**dly** /-ɪdlɪ/ adv según se dice, supuestamente

allegiance /əˈliːdʒəns/ n lealtad f

allegor|ical /ælɪˈgɒrɪkl/ a alegórico. ~**y** /ˈælɪgərɪ/ n alegoría f

allerg|ic /əˈlɜːdʒɪk/ a alérgico. ~**y** /ˈælədʒɪ/ n alergia f

alleviat|e /əˈliːvɪeɪt/ vt aliviar. ~**ion** /-ˈeɪʃn/ n alivio m

alley /ˈælɪ/ n (pl -eys) n callejuela f; (for bowling) bolera f

alliance /əˈlaɪəns/ n alianza f

allied /ˈælaɪd/ a aliado

alligator /ˈælɪgeɪtə(r)/ n caimán m

allocat|e /ˈæləkeɪt/ vt asignar; (share out) repartir. ~**ion** /-ˈkeɪʃn/ n asignación f; (share) ración f; (distribution) reparto m

allot /əˈlɒt/ vt (pt allotted) asignar. ~**ment** n asignación f; (share) ración f; (land) parcela f

all-out /ɔːlˈaʊt/ a máximo

allow /əˈlaʊ/ vt permitir; (grant) conceder; (reckon on) prever; (agree) admitir. ~ **for** tener en cuenta. ~**ance** /əˈlaʊəns/ n concesión f; (pension) pensión f; (com) rebaja f. **make** ~**ances for** ser indulgente con; (take into account) tener en cuenta

alloy /ˈælɔɪ/ n aleación f. /əˈlɔɪ/ vt alear

all-round /ɔːlˈraʊnd/ a completo

allude /əˈluːd/ vi aludir

allure /əˈlʊə(r)/ vt atraer. —n atractivo m

allusion /əˈluːʒn/ n alusión f

ally /ˈælaɪ/ n aliado m. /əˈlaɪ/ vt aliarse

almanac /ˈɔːlmənæk/ n almanaque m

almighty /ɔːlˈmaɪtɪ/ a todopoderoso; (big, fam) enorme. —n. **the A~** el Todopoderoso m

almond /'ɑːmənd/ n almendra f; (tree) almendro (m)

almost /'ɔːlməʊst/ adv casi

alms /ɑːmz/ n limosna f

alone /ə'ləʊn/ a solo. —adv sólo, solamente

along /ə'lɒŋ/ prep por, a lo largo de. —adv. ~ with junto con. all ~ todo el tiempo. come ~ venga

alongside /əlɒŋ'saɪd/ adv (naut) al costado. —prep al lado de

aloof /ə'luːf/ adv apartado. —a reservado. ~ness n reserva f

aloud /ə'laʊd/ adv en voz alta

alphabet /'ælfəbet/ n alfabeto m. ~ical /-'betɪk/ a alfabético

alpine /'ælpaɪn/ a alpino

Alps /ælps/ npl. the ~ los Alpes mpl

already /ɔːl'redɪ/ adv ya

Alsatian /æl'seɪʃn/ n (geog) alsaciano m; (dog) pastor m alemán

also /'ɔːlsəʊ/ adv también; (moreover) además

altar /'ɔːltə(r)/ n altar m

alter /'ɔːltə(r)/ vt cambiar. —vi cambiarse. ~ation /-'reɪʃn/ n modificación f; (to garment) arreglo m

alternate /ɔːl'tɜːnət/ a alterno. /'ɔːltəneɪt/ vt/i alternar. ~ly adv alternativamente

alternative /ɔːl'tɜːnətɪv/ a alternativo. —n alternativa f. ~ly adv en cambio, por otra parte

although /ɔːl'ðəʊ/ conj aunque

altitude /'æltɪtjuːd/ n altitud f

altogether /ɔːltə'geðə(r)/ adv completamente; (on the whole) en total

altruis|m /'æltruːɪzəm/ n altruismo m. ~t /'æltruːɪst/ n altruista m & f. ~tic /-'ɪstɪk/ a altruista

aluminium /æljʊ'mɪnɪəm/ n aluminio m

always /'ɔːlweɪz/ adv siempre

am /æm/ see **be**

a.m. /'eɪem/ abbr (ante meridiem) de la mañana

amalgamate /ə'mælgəmeɪt/ vt amalgamar. —vi amalgamarse

amass /ə'mæs/ vt amontonar

amateur /'æmətə(r)/ n aficionado m. —a no profesional; (in sports) amateur. ~ish a (pej) torpe, chapucero

amaz|e /ə'meɪz/ vt asombrar. ~ed a asombrado, estupefacto. be ~ed at quedarse asombrado de, asombrarse de. ~ement n asombro m. ~ingly adv extraordinariamente

ambassador /æm'bæsədə(r)/ n embajador m

amber /'æmbə(r)/ n ámbar m; (auto) luz f amarilla

ambidextrous /æmbɪ'dekstrəs/ a ambidextro

ambience /'æmbɪəns/ n ambiente m

ambigu|ity /æmbɪ'gjuːətɪ/ n ambigüedad f. ~ous /æm'bɪgjʊəs/ a ambiguo

ambit /'æmbɪt/ n ámbito m

ambiti|on /æm'bɪʃn/ n ambición f. ~ous a ambicioso

ambivalen|ce /æm'bɪvələns/ n ambivalencia f. ~t a ambivalente

amble /'æmbl/ vi andar despacio, andar sin prisa

ambulance /'æmbjʊləns/ n ambulancia f

ambush /'æmbʊʃ/ n emboscada f. —vt tender una emboscada a

amen /ɑː'men/ int amén

amenable /ə'miːnəbl/ a. ~ to (responsive) sensible a, flexible a

amend /ə'mend/ vt enmendar. ~ment n enmienda f. ~s npl. make ~s reparar

amenities /ə'miːnətɪz/ npl atractivos mpl, comodidades fpl, instalaciones fpl

America /ə'merɪkə/ n América; (North America) Estados mpl

Unidos. ~n a & n americano (m); (North American) estadounidense (m & f). ~nism n americanismo m. ~nize vt americanizar

amethyst /'æmıθıst/ n amatista f

amiable /'eımıəbl/ a simpático

amicable /'æmıkəbl/ a amistoso. ~y adv amistosamente

amid(st) /ə'mıd(st)/ prep entre, en medio de

amiss /ə'mıs/ a malo. —adv mal. sth ~ algo que no va bien. take sth ~ llevar algo a mal

ammonia /ə'məʊnıə/ n amoníaco m, amoniaco m

ammunition /æmjʊ'nıʃn/ n municiones fpl

amnesia /æm'ni:zıə/ n amnesia f

amnesty /'æmnəstı/ n amnistía f

amok /ə'mɒk/ adv. run ~ volverse loco

among(st) /ə'mʌŋ(st)/ prep entre

amoral /eı'mɒrəl/ a amoral

amorous /'æmərəs/ a amoroso

amorphous /ə'mɔ:fəs/ a amorfo

amount /ə'maʊnt/ n cantidad f, (total) total m, suma f. —vi. ~ to sumar; (fig) equivaler a, significar

amp(ere) /'amp(eə(r))/ n amperio m

amphibi|an /æm'fıbıən/ n anfibio m. ~ous a anfibio

amphitheatre /'æmfıθıətə(r)/ n anfiteatro m

ample /'æmpl/ a (-er, -est) amplio; (enough) suficiente; (plentiful) abundante. ~y adv ampliamente, bastante

amplif|ier /'æmplıfaıə(r)/ n amplificador m. ~y vt amplificar

amputat|e /'æmpjʊteıt/ vt amputar. ~ion /-'teıʃn/ n amputación f

amuse /ə'mju:z/ vt divertir. ~ement n diversión f. ~ing a divertido

an /ən, æn/ see a

anachronism /ə'nækrənızəm/ n anacronismo m

anaemi|a /ə'ni:mıə/ n anemia f. ~c a anémico

anaesthe|sia /ænıs'θi:zıə/ n anestesia f. ~tic /ænıs'θetık/ n anestésico m. ~tist /ə'ni:sθıtıst/ n anestesista m & f

anagram /'ænəgræm/ n anagrama m

analogy /ə'nælədʒı/ n analogía f

analy|se /'ænəlaız/ vt analizar. ~is /ə'næləsıs/ n (pl -yses /-si:z/) n análisis m. ~t /'ænəlıst/ n analista m & f

analytic(al) /ænə'lıtık(əl)/ a analítico

anarch|ist /'ænəkıst/ n anarquista m & f. ~y n anarquía f

anathema /ə'næθəmə/ n anatema m

anatom|ical /ænə'tɒmıkl/ a anatómico. ~y /ə'nætəmı/ n anatomía f

ancest|or /'ænsestə(r)/ n antepasado m. ~ral /-'sestrəl/ a ancestral. ~ry /'ænsestrı/ n ascendencia f

anchor /'æŋkə(r)/ n ancla f. —vt anclar; (fig) sujetar. —vi anclar

anchovy /'æntʃəvı/ n (fresh) boquerón m; (tinned) anchoa f

ancient /'eınʃənt/ a antiguo, viejo

ancillary /æn'sılərı/ a auxiliar

and /ənd, ænd/ conj y; (before i- and hi-) e. go ~ see him vete a verle. more ~ more siempre más, cada vez más. try ~ come ven si puedes, trata de venir

Andalusia /ændə'lu:zjə/ f Andalucía f

anecdote /'ænıkdəʊt/ n anécdota f

anew /ə'nju:/ adv de nuevo

angel /'eındʒl/ n ángel m. ~ic /æn'dʒelık/ a angélico

anger /'æŋgə(r)/ *n* ira *f*. —*vt* enojar

angle[1] /'æŋgl/ *n* ángulo *m*; (*fig*) punto *m* de vista

angle[2] /'æŋgl/ *vi* pescar con caña. ~ **for** (*fig*) buscar. ~**r** /-ə(r)/ *n* pescador *m*

Anglican /'æŋglɪkən/ *a* & *n* anglicano (*m*)

Anglo-... /'æŋgləʊ/ *pref* anglo...

Anglo-Saxon /'æŋgləʊ'sæksn/ *a* & *n* anglosajón (*m*)

angr|ily /'æŋgrɪlɪ/ *adv* con enojo. ~**y** /'æŋgrɪ/ *a* (-**ier**, -**iest**) enojado. **get** ~**y** enfadarse

anguish /'æŋgwɪʃ/ *n* angustia *f*

angular /'æŋgjʊlə(r)/ *a* angular; (*face*) anguloso

animal /'ænɪml/ *a* & *n* animal (*m*)

animat|e /'ænɪmət/ *a* vivo. /'ænɪmeɪt/ *vt* animar. ~**ion** /-'meɪʃn/ *n* animación *f*

animosity /ænɪ'mɒsətɪ/ *n* animosidad *f*

aniseed /'ænɪsi:d/ *n* anís *m*

ankle /'æŋkl/ *n* tobillo *m*. ~ **sock** escarpín *m*, calcetín *m*

annals /'ænlz/ *npl* anales *mpl*

annex /ə'neks/ *vt* anexionar. ~**ation** /ænek'seɪʃn/ *n* anexión *f*

annexe /'æneks/ *n* anexo *m*, dependencia *f*

annihilat|e /ə'naɪəleɪt/ *vt* aniquilar. ~**ion** /-'leɪʃn/ *n* aniquilación *f*

anniversary /ænɪ'vɜːsərɪ/ *n* aniversario *m*

annotat|e /'ænəteɪt/ *vt* anotar. ~**ion** /-'teɪʃn/ *n* anotación *f*

announce /ə'naʊns/ *vt* anunciar, comunicar. ~**ment** *n* anuncio *m*, aviso *m*, declaración *f*. ~**r** /-ə(r)/ *n* (*radio*, *TV*) locutor *m*

annoy /ə'nɔɪ/ *vt* molestar. ~**ance** *n* disgusto *m*. ~**ed** *a* enfadado. ~**ing** *a* molesto

annual /'ænjʊəl/ *a* anual. —*n* anuario *m*. ~**ly** *adv* cada año

annuity /ə'nju:ətɪ/ *n* anualidad *f*. **life** ~ renta *f* vitalicia

annul /ə'nʌl/ *vt* (*pt* **annulled**) anular. ~**ment** *n* anulación *f*

anoint /ə'nɔɪnt/ *vt* ungir

anomal|ous /ə'nɒmələs/ *a* anómalo. ~**y** *n* anomalía *f*

anon /ə'nɒn/ *adv* (*old use*) dentro de poco

anonymous /ə'nɒnɪməs/ *a* anónimo

anorak /'ænəræk/ *n* anorac *m*

another /ə'nʌðə(r)/ *a* & *pron* otro (*m*). ~ **10 minutes** 10 minutos más. **in** ~ **way** de otra manera. **one** ~ unos a otros

answer /'ɑːnsə(r)/ *n* respuesta *f*; (*solution*) solución *f*. —*vt* contestar a; escuchar, oír (*prayer*). ~ **the door** abrir la puerta. —*vi* contestar. ~ **back** replicar. ~ **for** ser responsable de. ~**able** *a* responsable. ~**ing-machine** *n* contestador *m* automático

ant /ænt/ *n* hormiga *f*

antagon|ism /æn'tægənɪzəm/ *n* antagonismo *m*. ~**stic** /-'nɪstɪk/ *a* antagónico, opuesto. ~**ze** /æn'tægənaɪz/ *vt* provocar la enemistad de

Antarctic /æn'tɑːktɪk/ *a* antártico. —*n* Antártico *m*

ante-... /'ænti/ *pref* ante...

antecedent /æntɪ'siːdnt/ *n* antecedente *m*

antelope /'æntɪləʊp/ *n* antílope *m*

antenatal /'æntɪneɪtl/ *a* prenatal

antenna /æn'tenə/ *n* antena *f*

anthem /'ænθəm/ *n* himno *m*

anthill /'ænthɪl/ *n* hormiguero *m*

anthology /æn'θɒlədʒɪ/ *n* antología *f*

anthropolog|ist /ænθrə'pɒlədʒɪst/ *n* antropólogo *m*. ~**y** *n* antropología *f*

anti-... /'ænti/ *pref* anti... ~**aircraft** *a* antiaéreo

antibiotic /æntɪbaɪ'ɒtɪk/ *a* & *n* antibiótico (*m*)

antibody /'æntɪbɒdɪ/ n anticuerpo m

antic /'æntɪk/ n payasada f, travesura f

anticipat|e /æn'tɪsɪpeɪt/ vt anticiparse a; (foresee) prever; (forestall) prevenir. ~ion /-'peɪʃn/ n anticipación f; (expectation) esperanza f

anticlimax /æntɪ'klaɪmæks/ n decepción f

anticlockwise /æntɪ'klɒkwaɪz/ adv & a en sentido contrario al de las agujas del reloj, hacia la izquierda

anticyclone /æntɪ'saɪkləʊn/ n anticiclón m

antidote /'æntɪdəʊt/ m antídoto m

antifreeze /'æntɪfriːz/ n anticongelante m

antipathy /æn'tɪpəθɪ/ n antipatía f

antiquarian /æntɪ'kweərɪən/ a & n anticuario (m)

antiquated /'æntɪkweɪtɪd/ a anticuado

antique /æn'tiːk/ a antiguo. —n antigüedad f. ~ **dealer** anticuario m. ~ **shop** tienda f de antigüedades

antiquity /æn'tɪkwətɪ/ n antigüedad f

anti-Semitic /æntɪsɪ'mɪtɪk/ a antisemítico

antiseptic /æntɪ'septɪk/ a & n antiséptico (m)

antisocial /æntɪ'səʊʃl/ a antisocial

antithesis /æn'tɪθəsɪs/ n (pl -eses /-siːz/) antítesis f

antler /'æntlər/ n cornamenta f

anus /'eɪnəs/ n ano m

anvil /'ænvɪl/ n yunque m

anxiety /æŋ'zaɪətɪ/ n ansiedad f; (worry) inquietud f; (eagerness) anhelo m

anxious /'æŋkʃəs/ a inquieto; (eager) deseoso. ~ly adv con

inquietud; (eagerly) con impaciencia

any /'enɪ/ a algún m; (negative) ningún m; (whatever) cualquier; (every) todo. at ~ moment en cualquier momento. have you ~ wine? ¿tienes vino? —pron alguno; (negative) ninguno. have we ~? ¿tenemos algunos? not ~ ninguno. —adv (a little) un poco, algo. is it ~ better? ¿está algo mejor? it isn't ~ good no sirve para nada

anybody /'enɪbɒdɪ/ pron alguien; (after negative) nadie. ~ can do it cualquiera sabe hacerlo, cualquiera puede hacerlo

anyhow /'enɪhaʊ/ adv de todas formas; (in spite of all) a pesar de todo; (badly) de cualquier modo

anyone /'enɪwʌn/ pron alguien; (after negative) nadie

anything /'enɪθɪŋ/ pron algo; (whatever) cualquier cosa; (after negative) nada. ~ **but** todo menos

anyway /'enɪweɪ/ adv de todas formas

anywhere /'enɪweə(r)/ adv en cualquier parte; (after negative) en ningún sitio; (everywhere) en todas partes. ~ **else** en cualquier otro lugar. ~ **you go** dondequiera que vayas

apace /ə'peɪs/ adv rápidamente

apart /ə'pɑːt/ adv aparte; (separated) apartado, separado. ~ **from** aparte de. **come** ~ romperse. **take** ~ desmontar

apartheid /ə'pɑːtheɪt/ n segregación f racial, apartheid m

apartment /ə'pɑːtmənt/ n (Amer) apartamento m

apath|etic /æpə'θetɪk/ a apático, indiferente. ~y /'æpəθɪ/ n apatía f

ape /eɪp/ n mono m. —vt imitar

aperient /ə'pɪərɪənt/ a & n laxante (m)

aperitif /ə'perətif/ n aperitivo m

aperture /'æpətʃʊə(r)/ n abertura f

apex /'eɪpeks/ n ápice m

aphorism /'æfərɪzəm/ n aforismo m

aphrodisiac /æfrə'dɪzɪæk/ a & n afrodisíaco (m), afrodisiaco (m)

apiece /ə'piːs/ adv cada uno

aplomb /ə'plɒm/ n aplomo m

apologetic /əpɒlə'dʒetɪk/ a lleno de disculpas. be ~etic disculparse. ~ize /ə'pɒlədʒaɪz/ vi disculparse (for a). ~y /ə'pɒlədʒɪ/ n disculpa f; (poor specimen) birria f

apople|ctic /æpə'plektɪk/ a apoplético. ~xy /'æpəpleksɪ/ n apoplejía f

apostle /ə'pɒsl/ n apóstol m

apostrophe /ə'pɒstrəfɪ/ n (punctuation mark) apóstrofo m

appal /ə'pɔːl/ vt (pt appalled) horrorizar. ~ling a espantoso

apparatus /æpə'reɪtəs/ n aparato m

apparel /ə'pærəl/ n ropa f, indumentaria f

apparent /ə'pærənt/ a aparente; (clear) evidente. ~ly adv por lo visto

apparition /æpə'rɪʃn/ n aparición f

appeal /ə'piːl/ vi apelar; (attract) atraer. —n llamamiento m; (attraction) atractivo m; (jurid) apelación f. ~ing a atrayente

appear /ə'pɪə(r)/ vi aparecer; (arrive) llegar; (seem) parecer; (on stage) actuar. ~ance n aparición f; (aspect) aspecto m

appease /ə'piːz/ vt aplacar; (pacify) apaciguar

append /ə'pend/ vt adjuntar. ~age /ə'pendɪdʒ/ n añadidura f

appendicitis /əpendɪ'saɪtɪs/ n apendicitis f

appendix /ə'pendɪks/ n (pl -ices /-siːz/) (of book) apéndice m. (pl -ixes) (anat) apéndice m

appertain /æpə'teɪn/ vi relacionarse (to con)

appetite /'æpɪtaɪt/ n apetito m

appetizer /'æpɪtaɪzə(r)/ n aperitivo m. ~ing a apetitoso

applaud /ə'plɔːd/ vt/i aplaudir. ~se n aplausos mpl

apple /'æpl/ n manzana f. ~-tree n manzano m

appliance /ə'plaɪəns/ n aparato m. electrical ~ electrodoméstico m

applicable /'æplɪkəbl/ a aplicable; (relevant) pertinente

applicant /'æplɪkənt/ n candidato m, solicitante m & f

application /æplɪ'keɪʃn/ n aplicación f; (request) solicitud f. ~ form formulario m (de solicitud)

applied /ə'plaɪd/ a aplicado. ~y /ə'plaɪ/ vt aplicar. —vi aplicarse; (ask) dirigirse. ~y for solicitar (job etc)

appoint /ə'pɔɪnt/ vt nombrar; (fix) señalar. ~ment n cita f; (job) empleo m

apportion /ə'pɔːʃn/ vt repartir

apposite /'æpəzɪt/ a apropiado

apprais|al /ə'preɪzl/ n evaluación f. ~e vt evaluar

appreciable /ə'priːʃəbl/ a sensible; (considerable) considerable

appreciat|e /ə'priːʃɪeɪt/ vt apreciar; (understand) comprender; (be grateful for) agradecer. —vi (increase value) aumentar en valor. ~ion /-'eɪʃn/ n aprecio m; (gratitude) agradecimiento m. ~ive /ə'priːʃɪətɪv/ a (grateful) agradecido

apprehen|d /æprɪ'hend/ vt detener; (understand) comprender. ~sion /-ʃn/ n detención f; (fear) recelo m

apprehensive /æprɪ'hensɪv/ a aprensivo

apprentice /ə'prentɪs/ n aprendiz m. —vt poner de aprendiz. ~ship n aprendizaje m

approach /ə'prəʊtʃ/ *vt* acercarse a. —*vi* acercarse. —*n* acercamiento *m*; (*to problem*) enfoque *m*; (*access*) acceso *m*. **make ~es to** dirigirse a. **~able** *a* accesible

approbation /æprə'beɪʃn/ *n* aprobación *f*

appropriate /ə'prəʊprɪət/ *a* apropiado. /ə'prəʊprɪeɪt/ *vt* apropiarse de. **~ly** *adv* apropiadamente

approval /ə'pruːvl/ *n* aprobación *f*. **on ~** a prueba

approv|**e** /ə'pruːv/ *vt/i* aprobar. **~ingly** *adv* con aprobación

approximat|**e** /ə'prɒksɪmət/ *a* aproximado. /ə'prɒksɪmeɪt/ *vt* aproximarse a. **~ely** *adv* aproximadamente. **~ion** /-'meɪʃn/ *n* aproximación *f*

apricot /'eɪprɪkɒt/ *n* albaricoque *m*, chabacano *m* (*Mex*). **~-tree** *n* albaricoquero *m*, chabacano *m* (*Mex*)

April /'eɪprəl/ *n* abril *m*. **~ fool!** ¡inocentón!

apron /'eɪprən/ *n* delantal *m*

apropos /'æprəpəʊ/ *adv* a propósito

apse /æps/ *n* ábside *m*

apt /æpt/ *a* apropiado; (*pupil*) listo. **be ~ to** tener tendencia a

aptitude /'æptɪtjuːd/ *n* aptitud *f*

aptly /'æptli/ *adv* acertadamente

aqualung /'ækwʌlʌŋ/ *n* pulmón *m* acuático

aquarium /ə'kweərɪəm/ *n* (*pl* -ums) acuario *m*

Aquarius /ə'kweərɪəs/ *n* Acuario *m*

aquatic /ə'kwætɪk/ *a* acuático

aqueduct /'ækwɪdʌkt/ *n* acueducto *m*

aquiline /'ækwɪlaɪn/ *a* aquilino

Arab /'ærəb/ *a & n* árabe *m*. **~ian** /ə'reɪbɪən/ *a* árabe. **~ic** /'ærəbɪk/ *a & n* árabe (*m*). **~ic numerals** números *mpl* arábigos

arable /'ærəbl/ *a* cultivable

arbiter /'ɑːbɪtə(r)/ *n* árbitro *m*

arbitrary /'ɑːbɪtrərɪ/ *a* arbitrario

arbitrat|**e** /'ɑːbɪtreɪt/ *vi* arbitrar. **~ion** /-'treɪʃn/ *n* arbitraje *m*. **~or** *n* árbitro *m*

arc /ɑːk/ *n* arco *m*

arcade /ɑː'keɪd/ *n* arcada *f*; (*around square*) soportales *mpl*; (*shops*) galería *f*. **amusement ~** galería *f* de atracciones

arcane /ɑː'keɪn/ *a* misterioso

arch[1] /ɑːtʃ/ *n* arco *m*. —*vt* arquear. —*vi* arquearse

arch[2] /ɑːtʃ/ *a* malicioso

archaeolog|**ical** /ɑːkɪə'lɒdʒɪkl/ *a* arqueológico. **~ist** /ɑːkɪ'ɒlədʒɪst/ *n* arqueólogo *m*. **~y** /ɑːkɪ'ɒlədʒɪ/ *n* arqueología *f*

archaic /ɑː'keɪɪk/ *a* arcaico

archbishop /ɑːtʃ'bɪʃəp/ *n* arzobispo *m*

arch-enemy /ɑːtʃ'enəmɪ/ *n* enemigo *m* jurado

archer /ɑːtʃə(r)/ *n* arquero *m*. **~y** *n* tiro *m* al arco

archetype /'ɑːkɪtaɪp/ *n* arquetipo *m*

archipelago /ɑːkɪ'peləgəʊ/ *n* (*pl* -os) archipiélago *m*

architect /'ɑːkɪtekt/ *n* arquitecto *m*. **~ure** /'ɑːkɪtektʃə(r)/ *n* arquitectura *f*. **~ural** /-'tektʃərəl/ *a* arquitectónico

archives /'ɑːkaɪvz/ *npl* archivo *m*. **~ist** /-ɪvɪst/ *n* archivero *m*

archway /'ɑːtʃweɪ/ *n* arco *m*

Arctic /'ɑːktɪk/ *a* ártico. —*n* Ártico *m*

arctic /'ɑːktɪk/ *a* glacial

ardent /'ɑːdənt/ *a* ardiente, fervoroso, apasionado. **~ly** *adv* ardientemente

ardour /'ɑːdə(r)/ *n* ardor *m*, fervor *m*, pasión *f*

arduous /'ɑːdjʊəs/ *a* arduo

are /ɑː(r)/ *see* **be**

area /'eərɪə/ *n* (*surface*) superficie *f*; (*region*) zona *f*; (*fig*) campo *m*

arena /ə'ri:nə/ n arena f; (in circus) pista f; (in bullring) ruedo m

aren't /ɑ:nt/ = **are not**

Argentin|a /ɑ:dʒən'ti:nə/ n Argentina f. **~ian** /-'tɪnɪən/ a & n argentino (m)

arguable /'ɑ:ɡjʊəbl/ a discutible

argue /'ɑ:ɡju:/ vi discutir; (reason) razonar

argument /'ɑ:ɡjʊmənt/ n disputa f; (reasoning) argumento m. **~ative** /-'mentətɪv/ a discutidor

arid /'ærɪd/ a árido

Aries /'eəri:z/ n Aries m

arise /ə'raɪz/ vi (pt **arose**, pp **arisen**) levantarse; (fig) surgir. **~ from** resultar de

aristocra|cy /ærɪ'stɒkrəsɪ/ n aristocracia f. **~t** /'ærɪstəkræt/ n aristócrata m & f. **~tic** /-'krætɪk/ a aristocrático

arithmetic /ə'rɪθmətɪk/ n aritmética f

ark /ɑ:k/ n (relig) arca f

arm[1] /ɑ:m/ n brazo m. **~ in ~** cogidos del brazo

arm[2] /ɑ:m/ n. **~s** npl armas fpl. —vt armar

armada /ɑ:'mɑ:də/ n armada f

armament /'ɑ:məmənt/ n armamento m

armchair /'ɑ:mtʃeə(r)/ n sillón m

armed robbery /ɑ:md'rɒbərɪ/ n robo m a mano armada

armful /'ɑ:mfʊl/ n brazada f

armistice /'ɑ:mɪstɪs/ n armisticio m

armlet /'ɑ:mlɪt/ n brazalete m

armour /'ɑ:mə(r)/ n armadura f. **~ed** a blindado

armoury /'ɑ:mərɪ/ n arsenal m

armpit /'ɑ:mpɪt/ n sobaco m, axila f

army /'ɑ:mɪ/ n ejército m

aroma /ə'rəʊmə/ n aroma m. **~tic** /ærə'mætɪk/ a aromático

arose /ə'rəʊz/ see **arise**

around /ə'raʊnd/ adv alrededor; (near) cerca. **all ~** por todas

partes. —prep alrededor de; (with time) a eso de

arouse /ə'raʊz/ vt despertar

arpeggio /ɑ:'pedʒɪəʊ/ n arpegio m

arrange /ə'reɪndʒ/ vt arreglar; (fix) fijar. **~ment** n arreglo m; (agreement) acuerdo m; (pl, plans) preparativos mpl

array /ə'reɪ/ vt (dress) ataviar; (mil) formar. —n atavio m; (mil) orden m; (fig) colección f, conjunto m

arrears /ə'rɪəz/ npl atrasos mpl. **in ~** atrasado en pagos

arrest /ə'rest/ vt detener; llamar (attention). —n detención f. **under ~** detenido

arrival /ə'raɪvl/ n llegada f. **new ~al** recien llegado m. **~e** /ə'raɪv/ vi llegar

arrogan|ce /'ærəɡəns/ n arrogancia f. **~t** a arrogante. **~tly** adv con arrogancia

arrow /'ærəʊ/ n flecha f

arsenal /'ɑ:sənl/ n arsenal m

arsenic /'ɑ:snɪk/ n arsénico m

arson /'ɑ:sn/ n incendio m provocado. **~ist** n incendiario m

art[1] /ɑ:t/ n arte m. **A~s** npl (Univ) Filosofía y Letras fpl. **fine ~s** bellas artes fpl

art[2] /ɑ:t/ (old use, with thou) = **are**

artefact /'ɑ:tɪfækt/ n artefacto m

arterial /ɑ:'tɪərɪəl/ a arterial. **~ road** n carretera f nacional

artery /'ɑ:tərɪ/ n arteria f

artesian /ɑ:'ti:zjən/ a. **~ well** pozo m artesiano

artful /'ɑ:tfʊl/ a astuto. **~ness** n astucia f

art gallery /ɑ:t'ɡælərɪ/ n museo m de pinturas, pinacoteca f, galería f de arte

arthritic /ɑ:'θrɪtɪk/ a artrítico. **~s** /ɑ:'θraɪtɪs/ n artritis f

artichoke /'ɑ:tɪtʃəʊk/ n alcachofa f. **Jerusalem ~** pataca f

article /ˈɑːtɪkl/ n artículo m. ~ **of clothing** prenda f de vestir. **leading** ~ artículo de fondo

articulat|e /ɑːˈtɪkjʊlət/ a articulado; ⟨person⟩ elocuente. /ɑːˈtɪkjʊleɪt/ vt/i articular. ~**ed lorry** n camión m con remolque. ~**ion** /-ˈleɪʃn/ n articulación f

artifice /ˈɑːtɪfɪs/ n artificio m

artificial /ɑːtɪˈfɪʃl/ a artificial; ⟨hair etc⟩ postizo

artillery /ɑːˈtɪlərɪ/ n artillería f

artisan /ɑːtɪˈzæn/ n artesano m

artist /ˈɑːtɪst/ n artista m & f

artiste /ɑːˈtiːst/ n (in theatre) artista m & f

artist|ic /ɑːˈtɪstɪk/ a artístico. ~**ry** n arte m, habilidad f

artless /ˈɑːtlɪs/ a ingenuo

arty /ˈɑːtɪ/ a (fam) que se las da de artista

as /æz, əz/ adv & conj como; (since) ya que; (while) mientras. ~ **big** ~ tan grande como. ~ **far** ~ (distance) hasta; (qualitative) en cuanto a. ~ **far** ~ **I know** que yo sepa. ~ **if** como si. ~ **long** ~ mientras. ~ **much** ~ tanto como. ~ **soon** ~ tan pronto como. ~ **well** también

asbestos /æzˈbestɒs/ n amianto m, asbesto m

ascend /əˈsend/ vt/i subir. ~**t** /əˈsent/ n subida f

ascertain /æsəˈteɪn/ vt averiguar

ascetic /əˈsetɪk/ a ascético. —n asceta m & f

ascribe /əˈskraɪb/ vt atribuir

ash[1] /æʃ/ n ceniza f

ash[2] /æʃ/ n. ~**(-tree)** fresno m

ashamed /əˈʃeɪmd/ a avergonzado. **be** ~ avergonzarse

ashen /ˈæʃn/ a ceniciento

ashore /əˈʃɔː(r)/ adv a tierra. **go** ~ desembarcar

ash: ~**tray** /ˈæʃtreɪ/ n cenicero m. **A~ Wednesday** n Miércoles m de Ceniza

Asia /ˈeɪʃə/ n Asia f. ~**n** a & n asiático (m). ~**tic** /-ɪˈætɪk/ a asiático

aside /əˈsaɪd/ adv a un lado. —n (in theatre) aparte m

asinine /ˈæsɪnaɪn/ a estúpido

ask /ɑːsk/ vt pedir; preguntar (question); (invite) invitar. ~ **about** enterarse de. ~ **after** pedir noticias de. ~ **for help** pedir ayuda. ~ **for trouble** buscarse problemas. ~ **s.o. in** invitar a uno a pasar

askance /əˈskæns/ adv. **look** ~ at mirar de soslayo

askew /əˈskjuː/ adv & a ladeado

asleep /əˈsliːp/ adv & a dormido. **fall** ~ dormirse, quedar dormido

asparagus /əˈspærəgəs/ n espárrago m

aspect /ˈæspekt/ n aspecto m; (of house etc) orientación f

aspersions /əˈspɜːʃnz/ npl. **cast** ~ **on** difamar

asphalt /ˈæsfælt/ n asfalto m. —vt asfaltar

asphyxia /æsˈfɪksɪə/ n asfixia f. ~**te** /əsˈfɪksɪeɪt/ vt asfixiar. ~**tion** /-ˈeɪʃn/ n asfixia f

aspic /ˈæspɪk/ n gelatina f

aspiration /æspəˈreɪʃn/ n aspiración f. ~**e** /əˈspaɪə(r)/ vi aspirar

aspirin /ˈæsprɪn/ n aspirina f

ass /æs/ n asno m; (fig, fam) imbécil m

assail /əˈseɪl/ vt asaltar. ~**ant** n asaltador m

assassin /əˈsæsɪn/ n asesino m. ~**ate** /əˈsæsɪneɪt/ vt asesinar. ~**ation** /-ˈeɪʃn/ n asesinato m

assault /əˈsɔːlt/ n (mil) ataque m; (jurid) atentado m. —vt asaltar

assemblage /əˈsemblɪdʒ/ n (of things) colección f; (of people) reunión f; (mec) montaje m

assemble /əˈsembl/ vt reunir; (mec) montar. —vi reunirse

assembly /ə'semblɪ/ n reunión f; (pol etc) asamblea f. ~ **line** n línea f de montaje

assent /ə'sent/ n asentimiento m. —vi asentir

assert /ə'sɜːt/ vt afirmar; hacer valer ⟨one's rights⟩. ~**ion** /-ʃn/ n afirmación f. ~**ive** a positivo, firme

assess /ə'ses/ vt valorar; (determine) determinar; fijar ⟨tax etc⟩. ~**ment** n valoración f

asset /'æset/ n (advantage) ventaja f; (pl, com) bienes mpl

assiduous /ə'sɪdjʊəs/ a asiduo

assign /ə'saɪn/ vt asignar; (appoint) nombrar

assignation /æsɪg'neɪʃn/ n asignación f; (meeting) cita f

assignment /ə'saɪnmənt/ n asignación f, misión f; (task) tarea f

assimilat|**e** /ə'sɪmɪleɪt/ vt asimilar. —vi asimilarse. ~**ion** /-'eɪʃn/ n asimilación f

assist /ə'sɪst/ vt/i ayudar. ~**ance** n ayuda f. ~**ant** /ə'sɪstənt/ n ayudante m & f; (shop) dependienta f, dependiente m. —a auxiliar, adjunto

associat|**e** /ə'səʊʃɪeɪt/ vt asociar. —vi asociarse. /ə'səʊ-ʃɪət/ a asociado. —n colega m & f; (com) socio m. ~**ion** /-'eɪʃn/ n asociación f. **A~ion** football n fútbol m

assorted /ə'sɔːtɪd/ a surtido. ~**ment** n surtido m

assume /ə'sjuːm/ vt suponer; tomar ⟨power, attitude⟩; asumir ⟨role, burden⟩

assumption /ə'sʌmpʃn/ n suposición f. **the A~** la Asunción f

assur|**ance** /ə'ʃʊərəns/ n seguridad f; (insurance) seguro m. ~**e** /ə'ʃʊə(r)/ vt asegurar. ~**ed** a seguro. ~**edly** /-rɪdlɪ/ adv seguramente

asterisk /'æstərɪsk/ n asterisco m

astern /ə'stɜːn/ adv a popa

asthma /'æsmə/ n asma f. ~**tic** /-'mætɪk/ a & n asmático (m)

astonish /ə'stɒnɪʃ/ vt asombrar. ~**ing** a asombroso. ~**ment** n asombro m

astound /ə'staʊnd/ vt asombrar

astray /ə'streɪ/ adv & a. **go ~** extraviarse. **lead ~** llevar por mal camino

astride /ə'straɪd/ adv a horcajadas. —prep a horcajadas sobre

astringent /ə'strɪndʒənt/ a astringente; (fig) austero. —n astringente m

astrolog|**er** /ə'strɒlədʒə(r)/ n astrólogo m. ~**y** n astrología f

astronaut /'æstrənɔːt/ n astronauta m & f

astronom|**er** /ə'strɒnəmə(r)/ n astrónomo m. ~**ical** /æstrə-'nɒmɪkl/ a astronómico. ~**y** /ə'strɒnəmɪ/ n astronomía f

astute /ə'stjuːt/ a astuto. ~**ness** n astucia f

asunder /ə'sʌndə(r)/ adv en pedazos; (in two) en dos

asylum /ə'saɪləm/ n asilo m. **lunatic ~** manicomio m

at /ət, æt/ prep a. ~ **home** en casa. ~ **night** por la noche. ~ **Robert's** en casa de Roberto. ~ **once** en seguida; (simultaneously) a la vez. ~ **sea** en el mar. ~ **the station** en la estación. ~ **times** a veces. **not ~ all** nada; (after thanks) ¡de nada!

ate /et/ see **eat**

atheism /'eɪθɪɪzəm/ n ateísmo m. ~**t** /'eɪθɪɪst/ n ateo m

athlet|**e** /'æθliːt/ n atleta m & f. ~**ic** /-'letɪk/ a atlético. ~**ics** /-'letɪks/ npl atletismo m

Atlantic /ət'læntɪk/ a & n atlántico (m). —n. ~ **(Ocean)** (Océano m) Atlántico m

atlas /'ætləs/ n atlas m

atmospher|**e** /'ætməsfɪə(r)/ n atmósfera f; (fig) ambiente m.

~ic /-'ferɪk/ a atmosférico. ~ics /-'ferɪks/ npl parásitos mpl

atom /'ætəm/ n átomo m. ~ic /ə'tɒmɪk/ a atómico

atomize /'ætəmaɪz/ vt atomizar. ~r /'ætəmaɪzə(r)/ n atomizador m

atone /ə'təʊn/ vi. ~ for expiar. ~ment n expiación f

atrocious /ə'trəʊʃəs/ a atroz. ~ty /-'trɒsətɪ/ n atrocidad f

atrophy /'ætrəfɪ/ n atrofia f

attach /ə'tætʃ/ vt sujetar; adjuntar (document etc). be ~ed to (be fond of) tener cariño a

attaché /ə'tæʃeɪ/ n agregado m. ~ case maletín m

attachment /ə'tætʃmənt/ n (affection) cariño m; (tool) accesorio m

attack /ə'tæk/ n ataque m. —vt/i atacar. ~er n agresor m

attain /ə'teɪn/ vt conseguir. ~able a alcanzable. ~ment n logro m. ~ments npl conocimientos mpl, talento m

attempt /ə'tempt/ vt intentar. — n tentativa f; (attack) atentado m

attend /ə'tend/ vt asistir a; (escort) acompañar. —vi prestar atención. ~ to (look after) ocuparse de. ~ance n asistencia f; (people present) concurrencia f. ~ant a concomitante. —n encargado m; (servant) sirviente m

attention /ə'tenʃn/ n atención f. ~! (mil) ¡firmes! **pay** ~ prestar atención

attentive /ə'tentɪv/ a atento. ~ness n atención f

attenuate /ə'tenjʊeɪt/ vt atenuar

attest /ə'test/ vt atestiguar. —vi dar testimonio. ~ation /æte'steɪʃn/ n testimonio m

attic /'ætɪk/ n desván m.

attire /ə'taɪə(r)/ n atavío m. —vt vestir

attitude /'ætɪtjuːd/ n postura f

attorney /ə'tɜːnɪ/ n (pl -eys) apoderado m; (Amer) abogado m

attract /ə'trækt/ vt atraer. ~ion /-ʃn/ n atracción f; (charm) atractivo m

attractive /ə'træktɪv/ a atractivo; (interesting) atrayente. ~ness n atractivo m

attribute /ə'trɪbjuːt/ vt atribuir. /'ætrɪbjuːt/ n atributo m

attrition /ə'trɪʃn/ n desgaste m

aubergine /'əʊbəʒiːn/ n berenjena f

auburn /'ɔːbən/ a castaño

auction /'ɔːkʃn/ n subasta f. —vt subastar. ~eer /-ə'nɪə(r)/ n subastador m

audacious /ɔː'deɪʃəs/ a audaz. ~ty /-æsətɪ/ n audacia f

audible /'ɔːdəbl/ a audible

audience /'ɔːdɪəns/ n (interview) audiencia f; (teatro, radio) público m

audio-visual /ɔːdɪəʊ'vɪʒʊəl/ a audiovisual

audit /'ɔːdɪt/ n revisión f de cuentas. —vt revisar

audition /ɔː'dɪʃn/ n audición f. — vt dar audición a

auditor /'ɔːdɪtə(r)/ n interventor m de cuentas

auditorium /ɔːdɪ'tɔːrɪəm/ n sala f, auditorio m

augment /ɔːg'ment/ vt aumentar

augur /'ɔːgə(r)/ vt augurar. it ~s well es de buen agüero

august /ɔː'gʌst/ a augusto

August /'ɔːgəst/ n agosto m

aunt /ɑːnt/ n tía f

au pair /əʊ'peə(r)/ n chica f au pair

aura /'ɔːrə/ n atmósfera f, halo m

auspices /'ɔːspɪsɪz/ npl auspicios mpl

auspicious /ɔː'spɪʃəs/ a propicio

austere /ɔː'stɪə(r)/ a austero. ~ity /-erətɪ/ n austeridad f

Australia /ɒ'streɪlɪə/ n Australia f. ~n a & n australiano (m)

Austria /'ɒstrɪə/ n Austria f. ~**n** a & n austríaco (m)

authentic /ɔː'θentɪk/ a auténtico. ~**ate** /ɔː'θentɪkeɪt/ vt autenticar. ~**ity** /-ən'tɪsətɪ/ n autenticidad f

author /'ɔːθə(r)/ n autor m. ~**ess** n autora f

authoritarian /ɔː'θɒrɪ'teərɪən/ a autoritario

authoritative /ɔː'θɒrɪtətɪv/ a autorizado; (manner) autoritario

authority /ɔː'θɒrətɪ/ n autoridad f; (permission) autorización f

authoriz|ation /ɔːθəraɪ'zeɪʃn/ n autorización f. ~**e** /'ɔːθəraɪz/ vt autorizar

authorship /'ɔːθəʃɪp/ n profesión f de autor; (origin) paternidad f literaria

autistic /ɔː'tɪstɪk/ a autista

autobiography /ɔːtəubaɪ'ɒgrəfɪ/ n autobiografía f

autocra|cy /ɔː'tɒkrəsɪ/ n autocracia f. ~**t** /'ɔːtəkræt/ n autócrata m & f. ~**tic** /-'krætɪk/ a autocrático

autograph /'ɔːtəgrɑːf/ n autógrafo m. ~ vt firmar

automat|e /'ɔːtəmeɪt/ vt automatizar. ~**ic** /ɔːtə'mætɪk/ a automático. ~**ion** /-'meɪʃn/ n automatización f. ~**on** /ɔː'tɒmətən/ n autómata m

automobile /'ɔːtəməbiːl/ n (Amer) coche m, automóvil m

autonom|ous /ɔː'tɒnəməs/ a autónomo. ~**y** n autonomía f

autopsy /'ɔːtɒpsɪ/ n autopsia f

autumn /'ɔːtəm/ n otoño m. ~**al** /-'tʌmnəl/ a de otoño, otoñal

auxiliary /ɔːg'zɪlɪərɪ/ a auxiliar. —n asistente m; (verb) verbo m auxiliar; (pl, troops) tropas fpl auxiliares

avail /ə'veɪl/ vt/i servir. ~ **o.s. of** aprovecharse de. —n ventaja f. **to no** ~ inútil

availab|ility /əveɪlə'bɪlətɪ/ n disponibilidad f. ~**le** /ə'veɪləbl/ a disponible

avalanche /'ævəlɑːnʃ/ n avalancha f

avaric|e /'ævərɪs/ n avaricia f. ~**ious** /-'rɪʃəs/ a avaro

avenge /ə'vendʒ/ vt vengar

avenue /'ævənjuː/ n avenida f; (fig) vía f

average /'ævərɪdʒ/ n promedio m. **on** ~ por término medio. —a medio. —vt calcular el promedio de. —vi alcanzar un promedio de

avers|e /ə'vɜːs/ a enemigo (**to** de). **be** ~**e** to sentir repugnancia por, no gustarle. ~**ion** /-ʃn/ n repugnancia f

avert /ə'vɜːt/ vt (turn away) apartar; (ward off) desviar

aviary /'eɪvɪərɪ/ n pajarera f

aviat|ion /eɪvɪ'eɪʃn/ n aviación f. ~**or** /'eɪvɪeɪtə(r)/ n (old use) aviador m

avid /'ævɪd/ a ávido. ~**ity** /-'vɪdətɪ/ n avidez f

avocado /ævə'kɑːdəʊ/ n (pl -os) aguacate m

avoid /ə'vɔɪd/ vt evitar. ~**able** a evitable. ~**ance** n el evitar m

avuncular /ə'vʌŋkjʊlə(r)/ a de tío

await /ə'weɪt/ vt esperar

awake /ə'weɪk/ vt/i (pt awoke, pp awoken) despertar. —a despierto. **wide** ~ completamente despierto; (fig) despabilado. ~**n** /ə'weɪkən/ vt/i despertar. ~**ning** n el despertar m

award /ə'wɔːd/ vt otorgar; (jurid) adjudicar. —n premio m; (jurid) adjudicación f; (scholarship) beca f

aware /ə'weə(r)/ a consciente. **are you** ~ **that?** ¿te das cuenta de que? ~**ness** n conciencia f

awash /ə'wɒʃ/ a inundado

away /ə'weɪ/ adv (absent) fuera; (far) lejos; (persistently) sin parar. —a & n. ~ (match) partido m fuera de casa

awe /ɔː/ n temor m. ~some a imponente. ~struck a atemorizado

awful /'ɔːfʊl/ a terrible, malísimo. ~ly adv terriblemente

awhile /ə'waɪl/ adv un rato

awkward /'ɔːkwəd/ a difícil; (inconvenient) inoportuno; (clumsy) desmañado; (embarrassed) incómodo. ~ly adv con dificultad; (clumsily) de manera torpe. ~ness n dificultad f; (discomfort) molestia f; (clumsiness) torpeza f

awning /'ɔːnɪŋ/ n toldo m

awoke, awoken /ə'wəʊk, ə'wəʊkən/ see awake

awry /ə'raɪ/ adv & a ladeado. go ~ salir mal

axe /æks/ n hacha f. —vt (pres p axing) cortar con hacha; (fig) recortar

axiom /'æksɪəm/ n axioma m

axis /'æksɪs/ n (pl axes /-iːz/) eje m

axle /'æksl/ n eje m

ay(e) /aɪ/ adv & n sí (m)

B

BA abbr see bachelor

babble /'bæbl/ vi balbucir; (chatter) parlotear; (of stream) murmullar. —n balbuceo m; (chatter) parloteo m; (of stream) murmullo m

baboon /bə'buːn/ n mandril m

baby /'beɪbɪ/ n niño m, bebé m; (Amer, sl) chica f. ~ish /'beɪbɪʃ/ a infantil. ~-sit vi cuidar a los niños, hacer de canguro. ~-sitter n persona f que cuida a los niños, canguro m

bachelor /'bætʃələ(r)/ n soltero m. B~ of Arts (BA) licenciado

m en filosofía y letras. B~ of Science (BSc) licenciado m en ciencias

back /bæk/ n espalda f; (of car) parte f trasera; (of chair) respaldo m; (of cloth) revés m; (of house) parte f de atrás; (of animal, book) lomo m; (of hand, document) dorso m; (football) defensa m & f. ~ of beyond en el quinto pino. —a trasero; (taxes) atrasado. —adv atrás; (returned) de vuelta. —vt apoyar; (betting) apostar a; dar marcha atrás a (car). —vi retroceder; (car) dar marcha atrás. ~ down vi volverse atrás. ~ out vi retirarse. ~ up vi (auto) retroceder. ~ache /'bækeɪk/ n dolor m de espalda. ~-bencher n (pol) diputado m sin poder ministerial. ~biting /'bækbaɪtɪŋ/ n maledicencia f. ~bone /'bækbəʊn/ n columna f vertebral; (fig) pilar m. ~chat /'bæktʃæt/ n impertinencias fpl. ~date /bæk'deɪt/ vt antedatar. ~er /'bækə(r)/ n partidario m; (com) financiador m. ~fire /bæk'faɪə(r)/ vi (auto) petardear; (fig) fallar, salir el tiro por la culata. ~gammon /bæk'gæmən/ n backgamon m. ~ground /'bækgraʊnd/ n fondo m; (environment) antecedentes mpl. ~hand /'bækhænd/ n (sport) revés m. ~handed a dado con el dorso de la mano; (fig) equívoco, ambiguo. ~hander n (sport) revés m; (fig) ataque m indirecto; (bribe, sl) soborno m. ~ing /'bækɪŋ/ n apoyo m. ~lash /'bæklæʃ/ n reacción f. ~log /'bæklɒg/ n atrasos mpl. ~side /bæk'saɪd/ n (fam) trasero m. ~stage /bæk'steɪdʒ/ a de bastidores. —adv entre bastidores. ~stroke /'bækstrəʊk/ n (tennis etc) revés m; (swimming) braza *f* de espaldas. **~up** *n* apoyo *m*. **~ward** /'bækwəd/ *a* (step *etc*) hacia atrás; (retarded) atrasado. **~wards** /'bækwədz/ *adv* hacia atrás; (fall) de espaldas; (back to front) al revés. **go ~wards and forwards** ir de acá para allá. **~water** /'bækwɔ:tə(r)/ *n* agua *f* estancada; (fig) lugar *m* apartado

bacon /'beɪkən/ *n* tocino *m*

bacteria /bæk'tɪərɪə/ *npl* bacterias *fpl*. **~l** *a* bacteriano

bad /bæd/ *a* (worse, worst) malo; (serious) grave; (harmful) nocivo; (language) indecente. **feel ~** sentirse mal

bade /beɪd/ *see* bid

badge /bædʒ/ *n* distintivo *m*, chapa *f*

badger /'bædʒə(r)/ *n* tejón *m*. —*vt* acosar

bad: **~ly** *adv* mal. **want ~ly** desear muchísimo. **~ly off** mal de dinero. **~mannered** *a* mal educado

badminton /'bædmɪntən/ *n* bádminton *m*

bad-tempered /bæd'tempəd/ *a* (always) de mal genio; (temporarily) de mal humor

baffle /'bæfl/ *vt* desconcertar

bag /bæg/ *n* bolsa *f*; (handbag) bolso *m*. —*vt* (pt bagged) ensacar; (take) coger (not LAm), agarrar (LAm). **~s** *npl* (luggage) equipaje *m*. **~s of** (fam) montones de

baggage /'bægɪdʒ/ *n* equipaje *m*

baggy /'bægɪ/ *a* (clothes) holgado

bagpipes /'bægpaɪps/ *npl* gaita *f*

Bahamas /bə'hɑ:məz/ *npl*. **the ~** las Bahamas *fpl*

bail[1] /beɪl/ *n* caución *f*, fianza *f*. —*vt* poner en libertad bajo fianza. **~ s.o. out** obtener la libertad de uno bajo fianza

bail[2] /beɪl/ *n* (cricket) travesaño *m*

bail[3] /beɪl/ *vt* (naut) achicar

bailiff /'beɪlɪf/ *n* alguacil *m*; (estate) administrador *m*

bait /beɪt/ *n* cebo *m*. —*vt* cebar; (torment) atormentar

bak|e /beɪk/ *vt* cocer al horno. —*vi* cocerse. **~er** *n* panadero *m*. **~ery** /'beɪkərɪ/ *n* panadería *f*. **~ing** *n* cocción *f*; (batch) hornada *f*. **~ing-powder** *n* levadura *f* en polvo

balance /'bæləns/ *n* equilibrio *m*; (com) balance *m*; (sum) saldo *m*; (scales) balanza *f*; (remainder) resto *m*. —*vt* equilibrar; (com) saldar; nivelar (budget). —*vi* equilibrarse; (com) saldarse. **~d** *a* equilibrado

balcony /'bælkənɪ/ *n* balcón *m*

bald /bɔ:ld/ *a* (-er, -est) calvo; (tyre) desgastado

balderdash /'bɔ:ldədæʃ/ *n* tonterías *fpl*

bald: **~ly** *adv* escuetamente. **~ness** *n* calvicie *f*

bale /beɪl/ *n* bala *f*, fardo *m*. —*vi*. **~ out** lanzarse en paracaídas

Balearic /bælɪ'ærɪk/ *a*. **~ Islands** Islas *fpl* Baleares

baleful /'beɪlfʊl/ *a* funesto

balk /bɔ:k/ *n* frustrar. —*vi*. **~ (at)** resistirse (a)

ball[1] /bɔ:l/ *n* bola *f*; (tennis *etc*) pelota *f*; (football *etc*) balón *m*; (of yarn) ovillo *m*

ball[2] /bɔ:l/ *n* (dance) baile *m*

ballad /'bæləd/ *n* balada *f*

ballast /'bæləst/ *n* lastre *m*

ball: **~-bearing** *n* cojinete *m* de bolas. **~-cock** *n* llave *f* de bola

ballerina /bælə'ri:nə/ *f* bailarina *f*

ballet /'bæleɪ/ *n* ballet *m*

ballistic /bə'lɪstɪk/ *a* balístico. **~s** *n* balística *f*

balloon /bə'lu:n/ *n* globo *m*

balloonist /bə'lu:nɪst/ *n* aeronauta *m* & *f*

ballot /'bælət/ n votación f. ~ (-paper) n papeleta f. ~-box n urna f

ball-point /'bɔːlpɔɪnt/ n. ~ (pen) bolígrafo m

ballroom /'bɔːlruːm/ n salón m de baile

ballyhoo /bælɪ'huː/ n (publicity) publicidad f sensacionalista; (uproar) jaleo m

balm /bɑːm/ n bálsamo m. ~y a (mild) suave; (sl) chiflado

baloney /bə'ləʊnɪ/ n (sl) tonterías fpl

balsam /'bɔːlsəm/ n bálsamo m

balustrade /bælə'streɪd/ n barandilla f

bamboo /bæm'buː/ n bambú m

bamboozle /bæm'buːzl/ vt engatusar

ban /bæn/ vt (pt banned) prohibir. ~ from excluir de. —n prohibición f

banal /bə'nɑːl/ a banal. ~ity /-ælətɪ/ n banalidad f

banana /bə'nɑːnə/ n plátano m, banana f (LAm). ~-tree plátano m, banano m

band[1] /bænd/ n banda f

band[2] /bænd/ n (mus) orquesta f; (military, brass) banda f. —vi. ~ together juntarse

bandage /'bændɪdʒ/ n venda f. —vt vendar

b & b abbr (bed and breakfast) cama f y desayuno

bandit /'bændɪt/ n bandido m

bandstand /'bændstænd/ n quiosco m de música

bandwagon /'bændwægən/ n. jump on the ~ (fig) subirse al carro

bandy[1] /'bændɪ/ a (-ier, -iest) patizambo

bandy[2] /'bændɪ/ vt. ~ about repetir. **be bandied about** estar en boca de todos

bandy-legged /'bændɪlegd/ a patizambo

bane /beɪn/ n (fig) perdición f. ~ful a funesto

bang /bæŋ/ n (noise) ruido m; (blow) golpe m; (of gun) estampido m; (of door) golpe m. —vt/i golpear. —adv exactamente. —int ¡pum!

banger /'bæŋə(r)/ n petardo m; (culin, sl) salchicha f

bangle /'bæŋgl/ n brazalete m

banish /'bænɪʃ/ vt desterrar

banisters /'bænɪstəz/ npl barandilla f

banjo /'bændʒəʊ/ n (pl -os) banjo m

bank[1] /bæŋk/ n (of river) orilla f. —vt cubrir (fire). —vi (aviat) ladearse

bank[2] /bæŋk/ n banco m. —vt depositar. ~ on vt contar con. ~ with tener una cuenta con. ~er n banquero m. ~ holiday n día m festivo, fiesta f. ~ing n (com) banca f. ~note f billete m de banco

bankrupt /'bæŋkrʌpt/ a & n quebrado (m). —vt hacer quebrar. ~cy n bancarrota f, quiebra f

banner /'bænə(r)/ n bandera f; (in demonstration) pancarta f

banns /bænz/ npl amonestaciones fpl

banquet /'bæŋkwɪt/ n banquete m

bantamweight /'bæntəmweɪt/ n peso m gallo

banter /'bæntə(r)/ n chanza f. —vi chancearse

bap /bæp/ n panecillo m blando

baptism /'bæptɪzəm/ n bautismo m; (act) bautizo m

Baptist /'bæptɪst/ n bautista m & f

baptize /bæp'taɪz/ vt bautizar

bar /bɑː(r)/ n barra f; (on window) reja f; (of chocolate) tableta f; (of soap) pastilla f; (pub) bar m; (mus) compás m; (jurid) abogacía f; (fig) obstáculo m. —vt (pt barred) atrancar ‹door›; (exclude) excluir; (prohibit) prohibir. —prep excepto

barbar|ian /baːˈbeərɪən/ a & n bárbaro (m). ~**ic** /baːˈbærɪk/ a bárbaro. ~**ity** /-əti/ n barbaridad f. ~**ous** a /ˈbaːbərəs/ a bárbaro

barbecue /ˈbaːbɪkjuː/ n barbacoa f. —vt asar a la parilla

barbed /baːbd/ a. ~ **wire** alambre m de espinas

barber /ˈbaːbə(r)/ n peluquero m, barbero m

barbiturate /baːˈbɪtjʊrət/ n barbitúrico m

bare /beə(r)/ a (-er, est) desnudo; ‹room› con pocos muebles; (mere) simple; (empty) vacío. —vt desnudar; (uncover) descubrir. ~ **one's teeth** mostrar los dientes. ~**back** /ˈbeəbæk/ adv a pelo. ~**faced** /ˈbeəfeɪst/ a descarado. ~**foot** a descalzo. ~**headed** /ˈbeəhedɪd/ a descubierto. ~**ly** adv apenas. ~**ness** n desnudez f

bargain /ˈbaːgɪn/ n (agreement) pacto m; (good buy) ganga f. —vi negociar; (haggle) regatear. ~ **for** esperar, contar con

barge /baːdʒ/ n barcaza f. —vi. ~ **in** irrumpir

baritone /ˈbærɪtəʊn/ n barítono m

barium /ˈbeərɪəm/ n bario m

bark[1] /baːk/ n (of dog) ladrido m. —vi ladrar

bark[2] /baːk/ (of tree) corteza f

barley /ˈbaːlɪ/ n cebada f. ~**water** n hordiate m

bar: ~**maid** /ˈbaːmeɪd/ n camarera f. ~**man** /ˈbaːmən/ n (pl -men) camarero m

barmy /ˈbaːmɪ/ a (sl) chiflado

barn /baːn/ n granero m

barometer /bəˈrɒmɪtə(r)/ n barómetro m

baron /ˈbærən/ n barón m. ~**ess** n baronesa f

baroque /bəˈrɒk/ a & n barroco (m)

barracks /ˈbærəks/ npl cuartel m

barrage /ˈbæraːʒ/ n (mil) barrera f; (dam) presa f; (of questions) bombardeo m

barrel /ˈbærəl/ n tonel m; (of gun) cañón m. ~**organ** n organillo m

barren /ˈbærən/ a estéril. ~**ness** n esterilidad f, aridez f

barricade /ˌbærɪˈkeɪd/ n barricada f. —vt cerrar con barricadas

barrier /ˈbærɪə(r)/ n barrera f

barring /ˈbaːrɪŋ/ prep salvo

barrister /ˈbærɪstə(r)/ n abogado m

barrow /ˈbærəʊ/ n carro m; (wheelbarrow) carretilla f

barter /ˈbaːtə(r)/ n trueque m. —vt trocar

base /beɪs/ n base f. —vt basar. —a vil

baseball /ˈbeɪsbɔːl/ n béisbol m

baseless /ˈbeɪslɪs/ a infundado

basement /ˈbeɪsmənt/ n sótano m

bash /bæʃ/ vt golpear. —n golpe m. **have a** ~ (sl) probar

bashful /ˈbæʃfl/ a tímido

basic /ˈbeɪsɪk/ a básico, fundamental. ~**ally** adv fundamentalmente

basil /ˈbæzl/ n albahaca f

basilica /bəˈzɪlɪkə/ n basílica f

basin /ˈbeɪsn/ n (for washing) palangana f; (for food) cuenco m; (geog) cuenca f

basis /ˈbeɪsɪs/ n (pl **bases** /-siːz/) base f

bask /baːsk/ vi asolearse; (fig) gozar (**in** de)

basket /ˈbaːskɪt/ n cesta f; (big) cesto m. ~**ball** /ˈbaːskɪtbɔːl/ n baloncesto m

Basque /baːsk/ a & n vasco (m). ~ **Country** n País m Vasco. ~ **Provinces** npl Vascongadas f

bass¹ /beɪs/ a bajo. —n (mus) bajo m

bass² /bæs/ n (marine fish) róbalo m; (freshwater fish) perca f

bassoon /bə'su:n/ n fagot m

bastard /'bɑːstəd/ a & n bastardo (m). **you ~!** (fam) ¡cabrón!

baste /beɪst/ vt (sew) hilvanar; (culin) lard(e)ar

bastion /'bæstɪən/ n baluarte m

bat¹ /bæt/ n bate m; (for table tennis) raqueta f. **off one's own ~** por sí solo. —vi (pt batted) golpear. —vi batear

bat² /bæt/ n (mammal) murciélago m

bat³ /bæt/ vt. **without ~ting an eyelid** sin pestañear

batch /bætʃ/ n (of people) grupo m; (of papers) lío m; (of goods) remesa f; (of bread) hornada f

bated /'beɪtɪd/ a. **with ~ breath** con aliento entrecortado

bath /bɑːθ/ n (pl -s /bɑːðz/) baño m; (tub) bañera f; (pl, swimming pool) piscina f. —vt bañar. —vi bañarse

bathe /beɪð/ vt bañar. —vi bañarse. —n baño m. **~r** /-ə(r)/ n bañista m & f

bathing /'beɪðɪŋ/ n baños mpl. **~-costume** n traje m de baño

bathroom /'bɑːθrʊm/ n cuarto m de baño

batman /'bætmən/ n (pl -men) (mil) ordenanza f

baton /'bætən/ n (mil) bastón m; (mus) batuta f

batsman /'bætsmən/ n (pl -men) bateador m

battalion /bə'tælɪən/ n batallón m

batter¹ /'bætə(r)/ vt apalear

batter² /'bætə(r)/ n batido m para rebozar, albardilla f

batter: **~ed** a (car etc) estropeado; (wife etc) golpeado. **~ing** n (fam) bombardeo m

battery /'bætərɪ/ n (mil, auto) batería f; (of torch, radio) pila f

battle /'bætl/ n batalla f; (fig) lucha f. —vi luchar. **~-axe** /'bætlæks/ n (woman, fam) arpía f. **~field** /'bætlfiːld/ n campo m de batalla. **~ments** /'bætlmənts/ npl almenas fpl. **~ship** /'bætlʃɪp/ n acorazado m

batty /'bætɪ/ a (sl) chiflado

baulk /bɔːlk/ vt frustrar. —vi. **~ (at)** resistirse (a)

bawdiness /'bɔːdɪnəs/ n obscenidad f. **~y** /'bɔːdɪ/ a (-ier, -iest) obsceno, verde

bawl /bɔːl/ vt/i gritar

bay¹ /beɪ/ n (geog) bahía f

bay² /beɪ/ n (bot) laurel m

bay³ /beɪ/ n (of dog) ladrido m. **keep a ~** mantener a raya. —vi ladrar

bayonet /'beɪənet/ n bayoneta f

bay window /beɪ'wɪndəʊ/ n ventana f salediza

bazaar /bə'zɑː(r)/ n bazar m

BC /biː'siː/ abbr (before Christ) a. de C., antes de Cristo

be /biː/ vi (pres **am**, **are**, **is**; pt **was**, **were**; pp **been**) (position or temporary) estar; (permanent) ser. **~ cold/hot**, etc tener frío/calor, etc. **~ reading/singing**, etc (aux) leer/cantar, etc. **~ that as it may** sea como fuere. **he is 30** (age) tiene 30 años. **he is to come** (must) tiene que venir. **how are you?** ¿cómo estás? **how much is it?** ¿cuánto vale?, ¿cuánto es? **have been to** haber estado en. **it is cold/hot**, etc (weather) hace frío/calor, etc

beach /biːtʃ/ n playa f

beachcomber /'biːtʃkəʊmə(r)/ n raquero m

beacon /'biːkən/ n faro m

bead /biːd/ n cuenta f; (of glass) abalorio m

beak /biːk/ n pico m

beaker /'biːkə(r)/ n jarra f, vaso m

beam /biːm/ n viga f; (of light) rayo m; (naut) bao m. —vi emitir. —vi irradiar; (smile) sonreír. ~ends npl. be on one's ~ends no tener más dinero. ~ing a radiante

bean /biːn/ n judía; (broad bean) haba f; (of coffee) grano m

beano /'biːnəʊ/ n (pl -os) (fam) juerga f

bear¹ /beə(r)/ vt (pt bore, pp borne) llevar; parir (niño); (endure) soportar. ~ right torcer a la derecha. ~ in mind tener en cuenta. ~ with tener paciencia con

bear² /beə(r)/ n oso m

bearable /'beərəbl/ a soportable

beard /bɪəd/ n barba f. ~ed a barbudo

bearer /'beərə(r)/ n portador m; (of passport) poseedor m

bearing /'beərɪŋ/ n comportamiento m; (relevance) relación f; (mec) cojinete m. get one's ~s orientarse

beast /biːst/ n bestia f; (person) bruto m. ~ly /'biːstlɪ/ a (-ier, -iest) bestial; (fam) horrible

beat /biːt/ vt (pt beat, pp beaten) golpear; (culin) batir; (defeat) derrotar; (better) sobrepasar; (baffle) dejar perplejo. ~ a retreat (mil) batirse en retirada. ~ it (sl) largarse. —vi (heart) latir. —n latido m; (mus) ritmo m; (of policeman) ronda f. ~ up dar una paliza a; (culin) batir. ~er n batidor m. ~ing n paliza f

beautician /bjuː'tɪʃn/ n esteticista m & f

beautiful /'bjuːtɪfl/ a hermoso. ~ly adv maravillosamente

beautify /'bjuːtɪfaɪ/ vt embellecer

beauty /'bjuːtɪ/ n belleza f. ~ parlour n salón m de belleza. ~ spot (on face) lunar m; (site) lugar m pintoresco

beaver /'biːvə(r)/ n castor m

became /bɪ'keɪm/ see become

because /bɪ'kɒz/ conj porque. —adv. ~ of a causa de

beck /bek/ n. be at the ~ and call of estar a disposición de

beckon /'bekən/ vt/i. ~ (to) hacer señas a

become /bɪ'kʌm/ vt (pt became, pp become) (clothes) sentar bien. —vi hacerse, llegar a ser, volverse, convertirse en. what has ~ of her? ¿qué es de ella?

becoming /bɪ'kʌmɪŋ/ a (clothes) favorecedor

bed /bed/ n cama f; (layer) estrato m; (of sea, river) fondo m; (of flowers) macizo m. —vi (pt bedded). ~ down acostarse. ~ and breakfast (b & b) cama y desayuno. ~bug /'bedbʌg/ n chinche f. ~clothes /'bedkləʊðz/ npl, ~ding n ropa f de cama

bedevil /bɪ'devl/ vt (pt bedevilled) (torment) atormentar

bedlam /'bedləm/ n confusión f, manicomio m

bed: ~pan /'bedpæn/ n orinal m de cama. ~post /'bedpəʊst/ n columna f de la cama

bedraggled /bɪ'drægld/ a sucio

bed: ~ridden /'bedrɪdn/ a encamado. ~room /'bedrʊm/ n dormitorio m, habitación f. ~side /'bedsaɪd/ n cabecera f. ~-sitting-room /bed'sɪtɪŋrʊːm/ n salón m con cama, estudio m. ~spread /'bedspred/ n colcha f. ~time /'bedtaɪm/ n hora f de acostarse

bee /biː/ n abeja f. make a ~-line for ir en línea recta hacia

beech /biːtʃ/ n haya f

beef /biːf/ n carne f de vaca, carne f de res (LAm). —vi (sl) quejarse. ∼burger /'biːfbɜːgə(r)/ n hamburguesa f

beefeater /'biːfiːtə(r)/ n alabardero m de la torre de Londres

beefsteak /biːfsteik/ n filete m, bistec m, bife m (Arg)

beefy /biːfɪ/ a (-ier, -iest) musculoso

beehive /'biːhaɪv/ n colmena f

been /biːn/ see be

beer /bɪə(r)/ n cerveza f

beet /biːt/ n remolacha f

beetle /'biːtl/ n escarabajo m

beetroot /'biːtruːt/ n invar remolacha f

befall /bɪˈfɔːl/ vt (pt befell, pp befallen) acontecer a. —vi acontecer

befit /bɪˈfɪt/ vt (pt befitted) convenir a

before /bɪˈfɔː(r)/ prep (time) antes de; (place) delante de. ∼ leaving antes de marcharse. —adv (place) delante; (time) antes. a week ∼ una semana antes. the week ∼ la semana anterior. —conj (time) antes de que. ∼ he leaves antes de que se vaya. ∼hand /bɪˈfɔːhænd/ adv de antemano

befriend /bɪˈfrend/ vt ofrecer amistad a

beg /beg/ vt/i (pt begged) mendigar; (entreat) suplicar; (ask) pedir. ∼ s.o.'s pardon pedir perdón a uno. I ∼ your pardon! ¡perdone Vd! I ∼ your pardon? ¿cómo? it's going ∼ging no lo quiere nadie

began /bɪˈgæn/ see begin

beget /bɪˈget/ vt (pt begot, pp begotten, pres p begetting) engendrar

beggar /'begə(r)/ n mendigo m; (sl) individuo m, tío m (fam)

begin /bɪˈgɪn/ vt/i (pt began, pp begun, pres p beginning) comenzar, empezar. ∼ner n principiante m & f. ∼ning n principio m

begot, begotten /bɪˈgɒt, bɪˈgɒtn/ see beget

begrudge /bɪˈgrʌdʒ/ vt envidiar; (give) dar de mala gana

beguile /bɪˈgaɪl/ vt engañar, seducir; (entertain) entretener

begun /bɪˈgʌn/ see begin

behalf /bɪˈhɑːf/ n. on ∼ of de parte de, en nombre de

behave /bɪˈheɪv/ vi comportarse, portarse. ∼ (o.s.) portarse bien. ∼iour /bɪˈheɪvjə(r)/ n comportamiento m

behead /bɪˈhed/ vt decapitar

beheld /bɪˈheld/ see behold

behind /bɪˈhaɪnd/ prep detrás de. —adv detrás; (late) atrasado. —n (fam) trasero m

behold /bɪˈhəʊld/ vt (pt beheld) (old use) mirar, contemplar

beholden /bɪˈhəʊldən/ a agradecido

being /'biːɪŋ/ n ser m. come into ∼ nacer

belated /bɪˈleɪtɪd/ a tardío

belch /beltʃ/ vi eructar. —vt. ∼ out arrojar (smoke)

belfry /'belfrɪ/ n campanario m

Belgian /'beldʒən/ a & n belga (m & f). ∼um /'beldʒəm/ n Bélgica f

belie /bɪˈlaɪ/ vt desmentir

belief /bɪˈliːf/ n (trust) fe f; (opinion) creencia f. ∼ve /bɪˈliːv/ vt/i creer. make ∼ve fingir. ∼ver /-ə(r)/ n creyente m & f; (supporter) partidario m

belittle /bɪˈlɪtl/ vt empequeñecer; (fig) despreciar

bell /bel/ n campana f; (on door) timbre m

belligerent /bɪˈlɪdʒərənt/ a & n beligerante (m & f)

bellow /'beləʊ/ vt gritar. —vi bramar

bellows /'beləʊz/ npl fuelle m

belly /'belɪ/ n vientre m. ~ful /'belɪfʊl/ n panzada f. have a ~ful of (sl) estar harto de

belong /bɪ'lɒŋ/ vi pertenecer; (club) ser socio (to de)

belongings /bɪ'lɒŋɪŋz/ npl pertenencias fpl. personal ~ efectos mpl personales

beloved /bɪ'lʌvɪd/ a & n querido (m)

below /bɪ'ləʊ/ prep debajo de; (fig) inferior a. —adv abajo

belt /belt/ n cinturón m; (area) zona f. —vt (fig) rodear; (sl) pegar

bemused /bɪ'mjuːzd/ a perplejo

bench /bentʃ/ n banco m. the B~ (jurid) la magistratura f

bend /bend/ vt (pt & pp bent) doblar; torcer (arm, leg). —vi doblarse; (road) torcerse. —n curva f. ~ down/over inclinarse

beneath /bɪ'niːθ/ prep debajo de; (fig) inferior a. —adv abajo

benediction /benɪ'dɪkʃn/ n bendición f

benefactor /'benɪfæktə(r)/ n bienhechor m, benefactor m

beneficial /benɪ'fɪʃl/ a provechoso

beneficiary /benɪ'fɪʃərɪ/ a & n beneficiario (m)

benefit /'benɪfɪt/ n provecho m, ventaja f; (allowance) subsidio m; (financial gain) beneficio m. —vt (pt benefited, pres p benefiting) aprovechar. —vi aprovecharse

benevolence /bɪ'nevələns/ n benevolencia f. ~t a benévolo

benign /bɪ'naɪn/ a benigno

bent /bent/ see bend. —n inclinación f. —a encorvado; (sl) corrompido

bequeath /bɪ'kwiːð/ vt legar

bequest /bɪ'kwest/ n legado m

bereave|d /bɪ'riːvd/ n. the ~d la familia f del difunto. ~ment n pérdida f; (mourning) luto m

bereft /bɪ'reft/ a. ~ of privado de.

beret /'bereɪ/ n boina f

Bermuda /bə'mjuːdə/ n Islas fpl Bermudas

berry /'berɪ/ n baya f

berserk /bə'sɜːk/ a. go ~ volverse loco, perder los estribos

berth /bɜːθ/ n litera f; (anchorage) amarradero m. give a wide ~ to evitar. —vi atracar

beseech /bɪ'siːtʃ/ vt (pt besought) suplicar

beset /bɪ'set/ vt (pt beset, pres p besetting) acosar

beside /bɪ'saɪd/ prep al lado de. be ~ o.s. estar fuera de sí

besides /bɪ'saɪdz/ prep además de; (except) excepto. —adv además

besiege /bɪ'siːdʒ/ vt asediar; (fig) acosar

besought /bɪ'sɔːt/ see beseech

bespoke /bɪ'spəʊk/ a (tailor) que confecciona a la medida

best /best/ a (el) mejor. the ~ thing is to... lo mejor es... —adv (lo) mejor. like ~ preferir. —n lo mejor. at ~ a lo más. do one's ~ hacer todo lo posible. make the ~ of contentarse con. ~ man n padrino m (de boda)

bestow /bɪ'stəʊ/ vt conceder

bestseller /best'selə(r)/ n éxito m de librería, bestseller m

bet /bet/ n apuesta f. —vt/i (pt bet or betted) apostar

betray /bɪ'treɪ/ vt traicionar. ~al n traición f

betroth|al /bɪ'trəʊðəl/ n esponsales mpl. ~ed a prometido

better /'betə(r)/ a & adv mejor. ~ off en mejores condiciones; (richer) más rico. get ~ mejorar. all the ~ tanto mejor. I'd ~ más vale que. the ~ part of la mayor

parte de. **the sooner the** ~
cuanto antes mejor. —*vt*
mejorar; (*beat*) sobrepasar. —*n*
superior *m*. **get the** ~ **of** vencer
a. **one's** ~**s** sus superiores *mpl*

between /bɪ'twiːn/ *prep* entre. —
adv en medio

beverage /'bevərɪdʒ/ *n* bebida *f*

bevy /'bevɪ/ *n* grupo *m*

beware /bɪ'weə(r)/ *vi* tener cuidado. —*int* ¡cuidado!

bewilder /bɪ'wɪldə(r)/ *vt* desconcertar. ~**ment** *n* aturdimiento *m*

bewitch /bɪ'wɪtʃ/ *vt* hechizar

beyond /bɪ'jɒnd/ *prep* más allá
de; (*fig*) fuera de. ~ **doubt** sin
lugar a duda. ~ **reason** irrazonable. —*adv* más allá

bias /'baɪəs/ *n* predisposición *f*;
(*prejudice*) prejuicio *m*; (*sewing*)
sesgo *m*. —*vt* (*pt* biased) influir
en. ~**ed** *a* parcial

bib /bɪb/ *n* babero *m*

Bible /'baɪbl/ *n* Biblia *f*

biblical /'bɪblɪkl/ *a* bíblico

bibliography /bɪblɪ'ɒgrəfɪ/ *n*
bibliografía *f*

biceps /'baɪseps/ *n* bíceps *m*

bicker /'bɪkə(r)/ *vi* altercar

bicycle /'baɪsɪkl/ *n* bicicleta *f*. —
vi ir en bicicleta

bid /bɪd/ *n* (*offer*) oferta *f*;
(*attempt*) tentativa *f*. —*vi* hacer
una oferta. —*vt* (*pt* bid, *pp*
bidding) ofrecer; (*pt* bid, *pp*
bidden, *pres p* bidding) mandar; dar (*welcome, good-day etc*).
~**der** *n* postor *m*. ~**ding** *n* (*at
auction*) ofertas *fpl*; (*order*) mandato *m*

bide /baɪd/ *vt*. ~ **one's time**
esperar el momento oportuno

biennial /baɪ'enɪəl/ *a* bienal. —
n (*event*) bienal *f*; (*bot*) planta *f*
bienal

bifocals /baɪ'fəʊklz/ *npl* gafas *fpl*
bifocales, anteojos *mpl* bifocales
(*LAm*)

big /bɪg/ *a* (**bigger, biggest**)
grande; (*generous, sl*) generoso. —*adv.* **talk** ~ fanfarronear

bigamist /'bɪgəmɪst/ *n* bígamo
m. ~**ous** *a* bígamo. ~**y** *n* biga-
mia *f*

big-headed /bɪg'hedɪd/ *a* engreído

bigot /'bɪgət/ *n* fanático *m*. ~**ed** *a*
fanático. ~**ry** *n* fanatismo *m*

bigwig /'bɪgwɪg/ *n* (*fam*) pez *m*
gordo

bike /baɪk/ *n* (*fam*) bicicleta *f*,
bici *f* (*fam*)

bikini /bɪ'kiːnɪ/ *n* (*pl* -is) biquini
m, bikini *m*

bilberry /'bɪlbərɪ/ *n* arándano *m*

bile /baɪl/ *n* bilis *f*

bilingual /baɪ'lɪŋgwəl/ *a* bilingüe

bilious /'bɪlɪəs/ *a* (*med*) bilioso

bill[1] /bɪl/ *n* cuenta *f*; (*invoice*) factura *f*; (*notice*) cartel *m*; (*Amer,
banknote*) billete *m*; (*pol*) proyecto *m* de ley. —*vt* pasar la factura; (*in theatre*) anunciar

bill[2] /bɪl/ *n* (*of bird*) pico *m*

billet /'bɪlɪt/ *n* (*mil*) alojamiento
m. —*vt* alojar

billiards /'bɪlɪədz/ *n* billar *m*

billion /'bɪlɪən/ *n* billón *m*;
(*Amer*) mil millones *mpl*

billy-goat /'bɪlɪgəʊt/ *n* macho *m*
cabrío

bin /bɪn/ *n* recipiente *m*; (*for rubbish*) cubo *m*; (*for waste paper*)
papelera *f*

bind /baɪnd/ *vt* (*pt* bound) atar;
encuadernar (*book*); (*jurid*)
obligar. —*n* (*sl*) lata *f*. ~**ing**
/'baɪndɪŋ/ *n* (*of books*) en-
cuadernación *f*; (*braid*) ribete *m*

binge /bɪndʒ/ *n* (*sl*) (*of food*) comilona *f*; (*of drink*) borrachera *f*.
go on a ~ ir de juerga

bingo /'bɪŋgəʊ/ *n* bingo *m*

binoculars /bɪ'nɒkjʊləz/ *npl*
prismáticos *mpl*

biochemistry /baɪəʊˈkemɪstrɪ/ n bioquímica f

biographer /baɪˈɒɡrəfə(r)/ n biógrafo m. ~y n biografía f

biological /baɪəˈlɒdʒɪkl/ a biológico. ~ist n biólogo m. ~y /baɪˈɒlədʒɪ/ n biología f

biped /ˈbaɪped/ n bípedo m

birch /bɜːtʃ/ n (tree) abedul m; (whip) férula f

bird /bɜːd/ n ave f; (small) pájaro m; (fam) tipo m; (girl, sl) chica f

Biro /ˈbaɪərəʊ/ n (pl -os) (P) bolígrafo m, biromen m (Arg)

birth /bɜːθ/ n nacimiento m. ~ certificate n partida f de nacimiento. ~control n control m de la natalidad f. ~day /ˈbɜːθdeɪ/ n cumpleaños m invar. ~mark /ˈbɜːθmɑːk/ n marca f de nacimiento. ~rate n natalidad f. ~right /ˈbɜːθraɪt/ n derechos mpl de nacimiento

biscuit /ˈbɪskɪt/ n galleta f

bisect /baɪˈsekt/ vt bisecar

bishop /ˈbɪʃəp/ n obispo m

bit[1] /bɪt/ n trozo m; (quantity) poco m

bit[2] /bɪt/ see bite

bit[3] /bɪt/ n (of horse) bocado m; (mec) broca f

bitch /bɪtʃ/ n perra f; (woman, fam) mujer f maligna, bruja f (fam). —vi (fam) quejarse (about de). ~y a malintencionado

bit|**e** /baɪt/ vt/i (pt bit, pp bitten) morder. ~e one's nails morderse las uñas. —n mordisco m; (mouthful) bocado m; (of insect etc) picadura f. ~ing /ˈbaɪtɪŋ/ a mordaz

bitter /ˈbɪtə(r)/ a amargo; (of weather) glacial. to the ~ end hasta el final. —n cerveza f amarga. ~ly adv amargamente. it's ~ly cold hace un frío glacial. ~ness n amargor m; (resentment) amargura f

bizarre /bɪˈzɑː(r)/ a extraño

blab /blæb/ vi (pt blabbed) chismear

black /blæk/ a (-er, -est) negro. ~ and blue amoratado. —n negro m. —vt ennegrecer; limpiar (shoes). ~out desmayarse; (make dark) apagar las luces de

blackball /ˈblækbɔːl/ vt votar en contra de

blackberry /ˈblækbərɪ/ n zarzamora f

blackbird /ˈblækbɜːd/ n mirlo m

blackboard /ˈblækbɔːd/ n pizarra f

blackcurrant /blækˈkʌrənt/ n casis f

blacken /ˈblækən/ vt ennegrecer. —vi ennegrecerse

blackguard /ˈblægɑːd/ n canalla m

blackleg /ˈblækleg/ n esquirol m

blacklist /ˈblæklɪst/ vt poner en la lista negra

blackmail /ˈblækmeɪl/ n chantaje m. —vt chantajear. ~er n chantajista m & f

black-out /ˈblækaʊt/ n apagón m; (med) desmayo m; (of news) censura f

blacksmith /ˈblæksmɪθ/ n herrero m

bladder /ˈblædə(r)/ n vejiga f

blade /bleɪd/ n hoja f; (razor-blade) cuchilla f. ~ of grass brizna f de hierba

blame /bleɪm/ vt echar la culpa a. be to ~ tener la culpa. —n culpa f. ~less a inocente

bland /blænd/ a (-er, -est) suave

blandishments /ˈblændɪʃmənts/ npl halagos mpl

blank /blæŋk/ a en blanco; (cartridge) sin bala; (fig) vacío. ~ verse n verso m suelto. ~ n blanco m

blanket /ˈblæŋkɪt/ n manta f; (fig) capa f. —vt (pt blanketed) (fig) cubrir (in, with de)

blare /bleə(r)/ *vi* sonar muy fuerte. —*n* estrépito *m*

blarney /'blɑːnɪ/ *n* coba *f*. —*vt* dar coba

blasé /'blɑːzeɪ/ *a* hastiado

blasphem|e /blæs'fiːm/ *vt/i* blasfemar. ~**er** *n* blasfemador *m*. ~**ous** /'blæsfəməs/ *a* blasfemo. ~**y** /'blæsfəmɪ/ *n* blasfemia *f*

blast /blɑːst/ *n* explosión *f*; (*gust*) ráfaga *f*; (*sound*) toque *m*. —*vt* volar. ~**ed** *a* maldito. ~**furnace** *n* alto horno *m*. ~**-off** *n* (*of missile*) despegue *m*

blatant /'bleɪtnt/ *a* patente; (*shameless*) descarado

blaze /bleɪz/ *n* llamarada *f*; (*of light*) resplandor *m*; (*fig*) arranque *m*. —*vi* arder en llamas; (*fig*) brillar. ~**a trail** abrir un camino

blazer /'bleɪzə(r)/ *n* chaqueta *f*

bleach /bliːtʃ/ *n* lejía *f*; (*for hair*) decolorante *m*. —*vt* blanquear; decolorar ⟨*hair*⟩. —*vi* blanquearse

bleak /bliːk/ *a* (-**er**, -**est**) desolado; (*fig*) sombrío

bleary /'blɪərɪ/ *a* ⟨*eyes*⟩ nublado; (*indistinct*) indistinto

bleat /bliːt/ *n* balido *m*. —*vi* balar

bleed /bliːd/ *vt/i* (*pt* **bled**) sangrar

bleep /bliːp/ *n* pitido *m*. ~**er** *n* busca *m*, buscapersonas *m*

blemish /'blemɪʃ/ *n* tacha *f*

blend /blend/ *n* mezcla *f*. —*vt* mezclar. —*vi* combinarse

bless /bles/ *vt* bendecir. ~ **you!** (*on sneezing*) ¡Jesús! ~**ed** *a* bendito. **be** ~**ed with** estar dotado de. ~**ing** *n* bendición *f*; (*advantage*) ventaja *f*

blew /bluː/ *see* **blow¹**

blight /blaɪt/ *n* añublo *m*, tizón *m*; (*fig*) plaga *f*. —*vt* añublar, atizonar; (*fig*) destrozar

blighter /'blaɪtə(r)/ *n* (*sl*) tío *m* (*fam*), sinvergüenza *m*

blind /blaɪnd/ *a* ciego. ~ **alley** *n* callejón *m* sin salida. —*n* persiana *f*; (*fig*) pretexto *m*. —*vt* cegar. ~**fold** /'blaɪndfəʊld/ *a* & *adv* con los ojos vendados. —*n* venda *f*. —*vt* vendar los ojos. ~**ly** *adv* a ciegas. ~**ness** *n* ceguera *f*

blink /blɪŋk/ *n* parpadear; (*of light*) centellear

blinkers /'blɪŋkəz/ *npl* anteojeras *fpl*; (*auto*) intermitente *m*

bliss /blɪs/ *n* felicidad *f*. ~**ful** *a* feliz. ~**fully** *adv* felizmente; (*completely*) completamente

blister /'blɪstə(r)/ *n* ampolla *f*. —*vi* formarse ampollas

blithe /blaɪð/ *a* alegre

blitz /blɪts/ *n* bombardeo *m* aéreo. —*vt* bombardear

blizzard /'blɪzəd/ *n* ventisca *f*

bloated /'bləʊtɪd/ *a* hinchado (**with** de)

bloater /'bləʊtə(r)/ *n* arenque *m* ahumado

blob /blɒb/ *n* gota *f*; (*stain*) mancha *f*

bloc /blɒk/ *n* (*pol*) bloque *m*

block /blɒk/ *n* bloque *m*; (*of wood*) zoquete *m*; (*of buildings*) manzana *f*, cuadra *f* (*LAm*); (*in pipe*) obstrucción *f*. **in** ~ **letters** en letra de imprenta. **traffic** ~ embotellamiento *m*. —*vt* obstruir. ~**ade** /blɒ'keɪd/ *n* bloqueo *m*. —*vt* bloquear. ~**age** *n* obstrucción *f*

blockhead /'blɒkhed/ *n* (*fam*) zopenco *m*

bloke /bləʊk/ *n* (*fam*) tío *m* (*fam*), tipo *m*

blond /blɒnd/ *a* & *n* rubio (*m*). ~**e** *a* & *n* rubia (*f*)

blood /blʌd/ *n* sangre *f*. ~ **count** *n* recuento *m* sanguíneo. ~**curdling** *a* horripilante

bloodhound /'blʌdhaʊnd/ *n* sabueso *m*

blood: ~ **pressure** n tensión f arterial. **high** ~ **pressure** hipertensión f. ~**shed** /ˈblʌdʃed/ n efusión f de sangre, derramamiento m de sangre, matanza f. ~**shot** /ˈblʌdʃɒt/ a sanguinolento; ⟨eye⟩ inyectado de sangre. ~**stream** /ˈblʌdstriːm/ n sangre f

bloodthirsty /ˈblʌdθɜːstɪ/ a sanguinario

bloody /ˈblʌdɪ/ a (-ier, -iest) sangriento; ⟨stained⟩ ensangrentado; ⟨sl⟩ maldito. ~**-minded** a (fam) terco

bloom /bluːm/ n flor f. —vi florecer

bloomer /ˈbluːmə(r)/ n (sl) metedura f de pata

blooming a floreciente; (fam) maldito

blossom /ˈblɒsəm/ n flor f. —vi florecer. ~ **out (into)** (fig) llegar a ser

blot /blɒt/ n borrón m. —vt (pt blotted) manchar; (dry) secar. ~ **out** oscurecer

blotch /blɒtʃ/ n mancha f. ~**y** a lleno de manchas

blotter /ˈblɒtə(r)/ n, **blotting-paper** /ˈblɒtɪŋpeɪpə(r)/ n papel m secante

blouse /blaʊz/ n blusa f

blow¹ /bləʊ/ vt (pt blew, pp blown) soplar; fundir ⟨fuse⟩; tocar ⟨trumpet⟩. —vi soplar; ⟨fuse⟩ fundirse; ⟨sound⟩ sonar. —n (puff) soplo m. ~ **down** vt derribar. ~ **out** apagar ⟨candle⟩. ~ **over** pasar. ~ **up** vt inflar; ⟨explode⟩ volar; (photo) ampliar. —vi ⟨explode⟩ estallar; ⟨burst⟩ reventar

blow² /bləʊ/ n (incl fig) golpe m

blow-dry /ˈbləʊdraɪ/ vt secar con secador

blowlamp /ˈbləʊlæmp/ n soplete m

blow: ~**out** n (of tyre) reventón m. ~**up** n (photo) ampliación f

blowzy /ˈblaʊzɪ/ a desaliñado

blubber /ˈblʌbə(r)/ n grasa f de ballena

bludgeon /ˈblʌdʒən/ n cachiporra f. —vt aporrear

blue /bluː/ a (-er, -est) azul; ⟨joke⟩ verde. —n azul m. **out of the** ~ totalmente inesperado. ~**s** npl. **have the** ~**s** tener tristeza

bluebell /ˈbluːbel/ n campanilla f

bluebottle /ˈbluːbɒtl/ n moscarda f

blueprint /ˈbluːprɪnt/ n ferroprusiato m; (fig, plan) anteproyecto m

bluff /blʌf/ a (person) brusco. —n (poker) farol m. —vt engañar. —vi (poker) tirarse un farol

blunder /ˈblʌndə(r)/ vi cometer un error. —n metedura f de pata

blunt /blʌnt/ a desafilado; ⟨person⟩ directo, abrupto. —vt desafilar. ~**ly** adv francamente. ~**ness** n embotadura f; (fig) franqueza f, brusquedad f

blur /blɜː(r)/ n impresión f indistinta. —vt (pt blurred) hacer borroso

blurb /blɜːb/ n resumen m publicitario

blurt /blɜːt/ vt. ~ **out** dejar escapar

blush /blʌʃ/ vi ruborizarse. —n sonrojo m

bluster /ˈblʌstə(r)/ vi (weather) bramar; ⟨person⟩ fanfarronear. ~**y** a tempestuoso

boar /bɔː(r)/ n verraco m

board /bɔːd/ n tabla f, tablero m; (for notices) tablón m; (food) pensión f; (admin) junta f. ~ **and lodging** casa y comida. **above** ~ correcto. **full** ~ pensión f completa. **go by the** ~ ser abandonado. —vt alojar; (naut) embarcar en. —*vi* alojarse (**with** en casa de); (*at school*) ser interno. ∼**er** *n* huésped *m*; (*schl*) interno *m*. ∼**ing-house** *n* casa *f* de huéspedes, pensión *f*. ∼**ing-school** *n* internado *m*

boast /bəʊst/ *vt* enorgullecerse de. —*vi* jactarse. —*n* jactancia *f*. ∼**er** *n* jactancioso *m*. ∼**ful** *a* jactancioso

boat /bəʊt/ *n* barco *m*; (*large*) navío *m*; (*small*) barca *f*

boater /ˈbəʊtə(r)/ *n* (*hat*) canotié *m*

boatswain /ˈbəʊsn/ *n* contramaestre *m*

bob[1] /bɒb/ *vi* (*pt* bobbed) menearse, subir y bajar. ∼ **up** presentarse súbitamente

bob[2] /bɒb/ *n invar* (*sl*) chelín *m*

bobbin /ˈbɒbɪn/ *n* carrete *m*; (*in sewing machine*) canilla *f*

bobby /ˈbɒbɪ/ *n* (*fam*) policía *m*, poli *m* (*fam*)

bobsleigh /ˈbɒbsleɪ/ *n* bob(sleigh) *m*

bode /bəʊd/ *vi* presagiar. ∼ **well/ill** ser de buen/mal agüero

bodice /ˈbɒdɪs/ *n* corpiño *m*

bodily /ˈbɒdɪlɪ/ *a* físico, corporal. —*adv* físicamente; (*in person*) en persona

body /ˈbɒdɪ/ *n* cuerpo *m*. ∼**guard** /ˈbɒdɪgɑːd/ *n* guardaespaldas *m invar*. ∼**work** *n* carrocería *f*

boffin /ˈbɒfɪn/ *n* (*sl*) científico *m*

bog /bɒg/ *n* ciénaga *f*. —*vt* (*pt* bogged). **get** ∼**ged down** empantanarse

bogey /ˈbəʊgɪ/ *n* duende *m*; (*nuisance*) pesadilla *f*

boggle /ˈbɒgl/ *vi* sobresaltarse. **the mind** ∼**s** ¡no es posible!

bogus /ˈbəʊgəs/ *a* falso

bogy /ˈbəʊgɪ/ *n* duende *m*; (*nuisance*) pesadilla *f*

boil[1] /bɔɪl/ *vt/i* hervir. **be** ∼**ing hot** estar ardiendo; (*weather*)

hacer mucho calor. ∼ **away** evaporarse. ∼ **down to** reducirse a. ∼ **over** rebosar

boil[2] /bɔɪl/ *n* furúnculo *m*

boiled /bɔɪld/ *a* hervido; (*egg*) pasado por agua

boiler /ˈbɔɪlə(r)/ *n* caldera *f*. ∼ **suit** *n* mono *m*

boisterous /ˈbɔɪstərəs/ *a* ruidoso, bullicioso

bold /bəʊld/ *a* (-**er**, -**est**) audaz. ∼**ness** *n* audacia *f*

Bolivia /bəˈlɪvɪə/ *n* Bolivia *f*. ∼**n** *a* & *n* boliviano (*m*)

bollard /ˈbɒləd/ *n* (*naut*) noray *m*; (*Brit, auto*) poste *m*

bolster /ˈbəʊlstə(r)/ *n* cabezal *m*. —*vt*. ∼ **up** sostener

bolt /bəʊlt/ *n* cerrojo *m*; (*for nut*) perno *m*; (*lightning*) rayo *m*; (*leap*) fuga *f*. —*vt* echar el cerrojo a (*door*); engullir (*food*). —*vi* fugarse. —*adv*. ∼ **upright** rígido

bomb /bɒm/ *n* bomba *f*. —*vt* bombardear. ∼**ard** /bɒmˈbɑːd/ *vt* bombardear

bombastic /bɒmˈbæstɪk/ *a* ampuloso

bomb: ∼**er** /ˈbɒmə(r)/ *n* bombardero *m*. ∼**ing** *n* bombardeo *m*. ∼**shell** *n* bomba *f*

bonanza /bəˈnænzə/ *n* bonanza *f*

bond /bɒnd/ *n* (*agreement*) obligación *f*; (*link*) lazo *m*; (*com*) bono *m*

bondage /ˈbɒndɪdʒ/ *n* esclavitud *f*

bone /bəʊn/ *n* hueso *m*; (*of fish*) espina *f*. —*vt* deshuesar. ∼**-dry** *a* completamente seco. ∼ **idle** *a* holgazán

bonfire /ˈbɒnfaɪə(r)/ *n* hoguera *f*

bonnet /ˈbɒnɪt/ *n* gorra *f*; (*auto*) capó *m*, tapa *f* del motor (*Mex*)

bonny /ˈbɒnɪ/ *a* (-**ier**, -**iest**) bonito

bonus /ˈbəʊnəs/ *n* prima *f*; (*fig*) plus *m*

bony /'bəʊnɪ/ a (-ier, -iest) huesudo; (fish) lleno de espinas

boo /buː/ int ¡bu! —vt/i abuchear

boob /buːb/ n (mistake, sl) metedura f de pata. —vi (sl) meter la pata

booby /'buːbɪ/ n bobo m. ~ **trap** trampa f; (mil) trampa f explosiva

book /bʊk/ n libro m; (of cheques etc) talonario m; (notebook) libreta f; (exercise book) cuaderno m; (pl, com) cuentas fpl. —vt (enter) registrar; (reserve) reservar. —vi reservar. ~**able** a que se puede reservar. ~**case** /'bʊkkeɪs/ n estantería f, librería f. ~**ing-office** (in theatre) taquilla f; (rail) despacho m de billetes. ~**let** /'bʊklɪt/ n folleto m

bookkeeping /'bʊkkiːpɪŋ/ n contabilidad f

bookmaker /'bʊkmeɪkə(r)/ n corredor m de apuestas

book: ~**mark** /'bʊkmɑː(r)k/ n señal f. ~**seller** /'bʊkselə(r)/ n librero m. ~**shop** /'bʊkʃɒp/ n librería f. ~**stall** /'bʊkstɔːl/ n quiosco m de libros. ~**worm** /'bʊkwɜːm/ n (fig) ratón m de biblioteca

boom /buːm/ vi retumbar; (fig) prosperar. —n estampido m; (com) auge m

boon /buːn/ n beneficio m

boor /bʊə(r)/ n patán m. ~**ish** a grosero

boost /buːst/ vt estimular; reforzar ⟨morale⟩; aumentar ⟨price⟩; (publicize) hacer publicidad por. —n empuje m. ~**er** n (med) revacunación f

boot /buːt/ n bota f; (auto) maletero m, baúl m (LAm). **get the** ~ (sl) ser despedido

booth /buːð/ n cabina f; (at fair) puesto m

booty /'buːtɪ/ n botín m

booze /buːz/ vi (fam) beber mucho. —n (fam) alcohol m; (spree) borrachera f

border /'bɔːdə(r)/ n borde m; (frontier) frontera f; (in garden) arriate m. —vi. ~ **on** lindar con

borderline /'bɔːdəlaɪn/ n línea f divisoria. ~ **case** n caso m dudoso

bore[1] /bɔː(r)/ vt (tec) taladrar. —vi taladrar

bore[2] /bɔː(r)/ vt (annoy) aburrir. —n (person) pelmazo m; (thing) lata f

bore[3] /bɔː(r)/ see **bear**[1]

boredom /'bɔːdəm/ n aburrimiento m

boring /'bɔːrɪŋ/ a aburrido, pesado

born /bɔːn/ a nato. **be** ~ nacer

borne /bɔːn/ see **bear**[1]

borough /'bʌrə/ n municipio m

borrow /'bɒrəʊ/ vt pedir prestado

Borstal /'bɔːstl/ n reformatorio m

bosh /bɒʃ/ int & n (sl) tonterías (fpl)

bosom /'bʊzəm/ n seno m. ~ **friend** n amigo m íntimo

boss /bɒs/ n (fam) jefe m. —vt. ~ (about) (fam) dar órdenes a. ~**y** /'bɒsɪ/ a mandón

botan|ical /bə'tænɪkl/ a botánico. ~**ist** /'bɒtənɪst/ n botánico m. ~**y** /'bɒtənɪ/ n botánica f

botch /bɒtʃ/ vt chapucear. —n chapuza f

both /bəʊθ/ a & pron ambos (mpl), los dos (mpl). —adv al mismo tiempo, a la vez

bother /'bɒðə(r)/ vt molestar; (worry) preocupar. ~ **it!** int ¡caramba! —vi molestarse. ~ **about** preocuparse de. ~ **doing** tenerse la molestia de hacer. —n molestia f

bottle /'bɒtl/ n botella f; (for baby) biberón m. —vt embotellar. ~

up (fig) reprimir. ~neck
/ˈbɒtlnek/ n (traffic jam)
embotellamiento m. ~opener
n destapador m, abrebotellas m
invar; (corkscrew) sacacorchos
m invar

bottom /ˈbɒtəm/ n fondo m; (of
hill) pie m; (buttocks) trasero
m. —a último, inferior. ~less a
sin fondo

bough /baʊ/ n rama f

bought /bɔːt/ see buy

boulder /ˈbəʊldə(r)/ n canto m

boulevard /ˈbuːləvɑːd/ n bulevar
m

bounce /baʊns/ vt hacer
rebotar. —vi rebotar; (person)
saltar; (cheque, sl) ser rechaz-
ado. —n rebote m. ~ing
/ˈbaʊnsɪŋ/ a robusto

bound¹ /baʊnd/ vi saltar. —n
salto m

bound² /baʊnd/ n. out of ~s
zona f prohibida

bound³ /baʊnd/ a. be ~ for dirigirse a

bound⁴ /baʊnd/ see bind. ~ to
obligado a; (certain) seguro de

boundary /ˈbaʊndərɪ/ n límite m

boundless /ˈbaʊndləs/ a ilimitado

bountiful /ˈbaʊntɪfl/ a abundante

bouquet /buˈkeɪ/ n ramo m; (perfume) aroma m; (of wine) buqué
m, nariz f

bout /baʊt/ n período m; (med)
ataque m; (sport) encuentro m

bow¹ /bəʊ/ n (weapon, mus) arco
m; (knot) lazo m

bow² /baʊ/ n reverencia f. —vi
inclinarse. —vt inclinar

bow³ /baʊ/ n (naut) proa f

bowels /ˈbaʊəlz/ npl intestino
mpl; (fig) entrañas fpl

bowl¹ /bəʊl/ n cuenco m; (for
washing) palangana f; (of pipe)
cazoleta f

bowl² /bəʊl/ n (ball) bola f. —vt
(cricket) arrojar. —vi (cricket)
arrojar la pelota. ~ over
derribar

bow-legged /ˈbəʊˈlegɪd/ a
estevado

bowler¹ /ˈbəʊlə(r)/ n (cricket) lan-
zador m

bowler² /ˈbəʊlə(r)/ n. ~ (hat)
hongo m, bombín m

bowling /ˈbəʊlɪŋ/ n bolos mpl

bow-tie /bəʊˈtaɪ/ n corbata f de
lazo, pajarita f

box¹ /bɒks/ n caja f; (for jewels
etc) estuche m; (in theatre) palco
m

box² /bɒks/ vt boxear contra. ~
s.o.'s ears dar una manotada a
uno. —vi boxear. ~er n boxeador m. ~ing n boxeo m

box: B~ing Day n el 26 de diciembre. ~-office n taquilla f.
~-room n trastero m

boy /bɔɪ/ n chico m, muchacho m;
(young) niño m

boycott /ˈbɔɪkɒt/ vt boicotear. —
n boicoteo m

boy: ~-friend n novio m. ~hood
n niñez f. ~ish a de muchacho;
(childish) infantil

bra /brɑː/ n sostén m, sujetador m

brace /breɪs/ n abrazadera f;
(dental) aparato m. —vt asegurar. ~ o.s. prepararse. ~s npl
tirantes mpl

bracelet /ˈbreɪslɪt/ n pulsera f

bracing /ˈbreɪsɪŋ/ a vigorizante

bracken /ˈbrækən/ n helecho m

bracket /ˈbrækɪt/ n soporte m;
(group) categoría f; (typ) paréntesis m invar. square ~s
corchetes mpl. —vt poner entre
paréntesis; (join together)
agrupar

brag /bræg/ vi (pt bragged) jactarse (about de)

braid /breɪd/ n galón m; (of hair)
trenza f

brain /breɪn/ n cerebro m. —vt romper la cabeza
brain-child /'breɪntʃaɪld/ n invento m
brain: ～ **drain** (fam) fuga f de cerebros. ～**less** a estúpido. ～**s** npl (fig) inteligencia f
brainstorm /'breɪnstɔːm/ n ataque m de locura; (Amer, brainwave) idea f genial
brainwash /'breɪnwɒʃ/ vt lavar el cerebro
brainwave /'breɪnweɪv/ n idea f genial
brainy /breɪnɪ/ a (-ier, -iest) inteligente
braise /breɪz/ vt cocer a fuego lento
brake /breɪk/ n freno m. **disc** ～ freno de disco. **hand** ～ freno de mano. —vt/i frenar. ～ **fluid** n líquido m de freno. ～ **lining** n forro m del freno. ～ **shoe** n zapata f del freno
bramble /bræmbl/ n zarza f
bran /bræn/ n salvado m
branch /brɑːntʃ/ n rama f; (of road) bifurcación f; (com) sucursal m; (fig) ramo m. —vi. ～ **off** bifurcarse. ～ **out** ramificarse
brand /brænd/ n marca f; (iron) hierro m. —vt marcar; (reputation) tildar de
brandish /'brændɪʃ/ vt blandir
brand-new /brænd'njuː/ a flamante
brandy /'brændɪ/ n coñac m
brash /bræʃ/ a descarado
brass /brɑːs/ n latón m. **get down to** ～ **tacks** (fig) ir al grano. **top** ～ (sl) peces mpl gordos. ～**y** a (-ier, -iest) descarado
brassière /'bræsjeə(r)/ n sostén m, sujetador m
brat /bræt/ n (pej) mocoso m
bravado /brə'vɑːdəʊ/ n bravata f
brave /breɪv/ a (-er, -est) valiente. —n (Red Indian) guerrero

m indio. —vt afrontar. ～**ry** /-ərɪ/ n valentía f, valor m
brawl /brɔːl/ n alboroto m. —vi pelearse
brawn /brɔːn/ n músculo m; (strength) fuerza f muscular. ～**y** a musculoso
bray /breɪ/ n rebuzno m. —vi rebuznar
brazen /'breɪzn/ a descarado
brazier /'breɪzɪə(r)/ n brasero m
Brazil /brə'zɪl/ n el Brasil m. ～**ian** a & n brasileño (m)
breach /briːtʃ/ n violación f; (of contract) incumplimiento m; (gap) brecha f. —vt abrir una brecha en
bread /bred/ n pan m. **loaf of** ～ pan. ～**crumbs** /'bredkrʌmz/ npl migajas fpl; (culin) pan rallado. ～**line** n. **on the** ～**line** en la miseria
breadth /bredθ/ n anchura f
bread-winner /'bredwɪnə(r)/ n sostén m de la familia, cabeza f de familia
break /breɪk/ vt (pt broke, pp broken) romper; quebrantar (law); batir (record); comunicar (news); interrumpir (journey). —vi romperse; (news) divulgarse. —n ruptura f; (interval) intervalo m; (chance, fam) oportunidad f; (in weather) cambio m. ～ **away** escapar. ～ **down** vt derribar; analizar (figures). —vi estropearse; (auto) averiarse; (med) sufrir un colapso; (cry) deshacerse en lágrimas. ～ **into** forzar (house etc); (start doing) ponerse a. ～ **off** interrumpirse. ～ **out** (war, disease) estallar; (run away) escaparse. ～ **up** romperse; (schools) terminar. ～**able** a frágil. ～**age** n rotura f
breakdown /'breɪkdaʊn/ n (tec) falla f; (med) colapso m, crisis f nerviosa; (of figures) análisis f

breaker /'breɪkə(r)/ n (wave) cachón m

breakfast /'brekfəst/ n desayuno m

breakthrough /'breɪkθru:/ n adelanto m

breakwater /'breɪkwɔ:tə(r)/ n rompeolas m invar

breast /brest/ n pecho m; (of chicken etc) pechuga f. ~-**stroke** n braza f de pecho

breath /breθ/ n aliento m, respiración f. out of ~ sin aliento. under one's ~ a media voz. ~**alyser** /'breθəlaɪzə(r)/ n alcoholímetro m

breath|e /bri:ð/ vt/i respirar. ~**er** /bri:ðə(r)/ n descanso m, pausa f. ~**ing** n respiración f

breathtaking /'breθteɪkɪŋ/ a impresionante

bred /bred/ see **breed**

breeches /'brɪtʃɪz/ npl calzones mpl

breed /bri:d/ vt/i (pt bred) reproducirse; (fig) engendrar. —n raza f. ~**er** n criador m. ~**ing** n cría f; (manners) educación f

breez|e /bri:z/ n brisa f. ~**y** a de mucho viento; (person) despreocupado. it is ~**y** hace viento

Breton /'bretən/ a & n bretón (m)

brew /bru:/ vt hacer. —vi fermentar; (tea) reposar; (fig) prepararse. —n infusión f. ~**er** n cervecero m. ~**ery** n fábrica f de cerveza, cervecería f

bribe /braɪb/ n soborno m. —vt sobornar. ~**ry** /-ərɪ/ n soborno m

brick /brɪk/ n ladrillo m. —vt. ~ up tapar con ladrillos. ~**layer** /'brɪkleɪə(r)/ n albañil m

bridal /braɪdl/ a nupcial

bride /braɪd/ n novia f. ~**groom** /'braɪdgrʊm/ n novio m. ~**smaid** /'braɪdzmeɪd/ n dama f de honor

bridge[1] /brɪdʒ/ n puente m; (of nose) caballete m. —vt tender un puente sobre. ~ **a gap** llenar un vacío

bridge[2] /brɪdʒ/ n (cards) bridge m

bridle /braɪdl/ n brida f. —vt embridar. ~-**path** n camino m de herradura

brief /bri:f/ a (-er, -est) breve. —n (jurid) escrito m. —vt dar instrucciones a. ~**case** /'bri:fkeɪs/ n maletín m. ~**ly** adv brevemente. ~**s** npl (man's) calzoncillos mpl; (woman's) bragas fpl

brigad|e /brɪ'geɪd/ n brigada f. ~**ier** /-ə'dɪə(r)/ n general m de brigada

bright /braɪt/ a (-er, -est) brillante, claro; (clever) listo; (cheerful) alegre. ~**en** /'braɪtn/ vt aclarar; hacer más alegre (house etc). —vi (weather) aclararse; (face) animarse. ~**ly** adv brillantemente. ~**ness** n claridad f

brillian|ce /'brɪljəns/ n brillantez f, brillo m. ~**t** a brillante

brim /brɪm/ n borde m; (of hat) ala f. —vi (pt brimmed). ~ **over** desbordarse

brine /braɪn/ n salmuera f

bring /brɪŋ/ vt (pt brought) traer (thing); conducir (person, vehicle). ~ **about** causar. ~ **back** devolver. ~ **down** derribar; rebajar (price). ~ **off** lograr. ~ **on** causar. ~ **out** sacar; lanzar (product); publicar (book). ~ **round/to** hacer volver en sí (unconscious person). ~ **up** (med) vomitar; educar (children); plantear (question)

brink /brɪŋk/ n borde m

brisk /brɪsk/ a (-er, -est) enérgico, vivo. ~**ness** n energía f

bristl|e /'brɪsl/ n cerda f. —vi erizarse. ~**ing with** erizado de

Brit|ain /ˈbrɪtən/ n Gran Bretaña f. **~ish** /ˈbrɪtɪʃ/ a británico. the **~ish** los británicos. **~on** /ˈbrɪtən/ n británico m

Brittany /ˈbrɪtəni/ n Bretaña f

brittle /ˈbrɪtl/ a frágil, quebradizo

broach /brəʊtʃ/ vt abordar (subject); espitar (cask)

broad /brɔːd/ a (-er, -est) ancho. **in ~ daylight** en pleno día. **~ bean** n haba f

broadcast /ˈbrɔːdkɑːst/ n emisión f. —vt (pt **broadcast**) emitir. —vi hablar por la radio. **~ing** a de radiodifusión. —n radiodifusión f

broad: ~en /ˈbrɔːdn/ vt ensanchar. —vi ensancharse. **~ly** adv en general. **~-minded** a de miras amplias, tolerante, liberal

brocade /brəˈkeɪd/ n brocado m

broccoli /ˈbrɒkəli/ n invar brécol m

brochure /ˈbrəʊʃə(r)/ n folleto m

brogue /brəʊg/ n abarca f; (accent) acento m regional

broke /brəʊk/ see **break**. —a (sl) sin blanca

broken /ˈbrəʊkən/ see **break**. —a. **~ English** inglés m chapurreado. **~-hearted** a con el corazón destrozado

broker /ˈbrəʊkə(r)/ n corredor m

brolly /ˈbrɒli/ n (fam) paraguas m invar

bronchitis /brɒŋˈkaɪtɪs/ n bronquitis f

bronze /brɒnz/ n bronce m. —vt broncear. —vi broncearse

brooch /brəʊtʃ/ n broche m

brood /bruːd/ n cría f; (joc) prole m. —vi empollar; (fig) meditar. **~y** a contemplativo

brook[1] /brʊk/ n arroyo m

brook[2] /brʊk/ vt soportar

broom /bruːm/ n hiniesta f; (brush) escoba f. **~stick** /ˈbruːmstɪk/ n palo m de escoba

broth /brɒθ/ n caldo m

brothel /ˈbrɒθl/ n burdel m

brother /ˈbrʌðə(r)/ n hermano m. **~hood** n fraternidad f, (relig) hermandad f. **~-in-law** n cuñado m. **~ly** a fraternal

brought /brɔːt/ see **bring**

brow /braʊ/ n frente f; (of hill) cima f

browbeat /ˈbraʊbiːt/ vt (pt **-beat**, pp **-beaten**) intimidar

brown /braʊn/ a (-er, -est) marrón; (skin) moreno; (hair) castaño. —n marrón m. —vt poner moreno; (culin) dorar. —vi ponerse moreno; (culin) dorarse. **be ~ed off** (sl) estar hasta la coronilla

Brownie /ˈbraʊni/ n niña f exploradora

browse /braʊz/ vi (in a shop) curiosear; (animal) pacer

bruise /bruːz/ n magulladura f. —vt magullar; machucar (fruit). —vi magullarse; (fruit) machacarse

brunch /brʌntʃ/ n (fam) desayuno m tardío

brunette /bruːˈnet/ n morena f

brunt /brʌnt/ n. the **~ of** lo más fuerte de

brush /brʌʃ/ n cepillo m; (large) escoba; (for decorating) brocha f; (artist's) pincel; (skirmish) escaramuza f. —vt cepillar. **~ against** rozar. **~ aside** rechazar. **~ off** (rebuff) desairar. **~ up (on)** refrescar

brusque /bruːsk/ a brusco. **~ly** adv bruscamente

Brussels /ˈbrʌslz/ n Bruselas f. **~ sprout** col m de Bruselas

brutal /ˈbruːtl/ a brutal. **~ity** /-ˈtælətɪ/ n brutalidad f

brute /bruːt/ n bestia f. **~ force** fuerza f bruta

BSc abbr see **bachelor**

bubble /ˈbʌbl/ n burbuja f. —vi burbujear. **~ over** desbordarse

bubbly 315 bum

bubbly /ˈbʌblɪ/ a burbujeante. — n (fam) champaña m, champán m (fam)

buck¹ /bʌk/ a macho. —n (deer) ciervo m. —vi (of horse) corcovear. ~ **up** (hurry, sl) darse prisa; (cheer up, sl) animarse

buck² /bʌk/ (Amer, sl) dólar m

buck³ /bʌk/ n. **pass the** ~ **to s.o.** echarle a uno el muerto

bucket /ˈbʌkɪt/ n cubo m

buckle /ˈbʌkl/ n hebilla f. —vt abrochar. —vi torcerse. ~ **down to** dedicarse con empeño a

bud /bʌd/ n brote m. —vi (pt budded) brotar.

Buddhis|m /ˈbʊdɪzəm/ n budismo m. ~t /ˈbʊdɪst/ a & n budista (m & f)

budding /ˈbʌdɪŋ/ a (fig) en ciernes

buddy /ˈbʌdɪ/ n (fam) compañero m, amigote m (fam)

budge /bʌdʒ/ vt mover. —vi moverse

budgerigar /ˈbʌdʒərɪgɑː(r)/ n periquito m

budget /ˈbʌdʒɪt/ n presupuesto m. —vi (pt budgeted) presupuestar

buff /bʌf/ n (colour) color m de ante; (fam) aficionado m. —vt pulir

buffalo /ˈbʌfələʊ/ n (pl -oes or -o) búfalo m

buffer /ˈbʌfə(r)/ n parachoques m invar. ~ **state** n estado m tapón

buffet /ˈbʊfeɪ/ n (meal, counter) bufé m. /ˈbʌfɪt/ n golpe m; (slap) bofetada f. —vt (pt buffeted) golpear

buffoon /bəˈfuːn/ n payaso m, bufón m

bug /bʌg/ n bicho m; (germ, sl) microbio m; (device, sl) micrófono m oculto. —vt (pt bugged) ocultar un micrófono en; intervenir (telephone); (Amer, sl) molestar

bugbear /ˈbʌgbeə(r)/ n pesadilla f

buggy /ˈbʌgɪ/ n. **baby** ~ (esp Amer) cochecito m de niño

bugle /ˈbjuːgl/ n corneta f

build /bɪld/ vt/i (pt built) construir. ~ **up** vt urbanizar; (increase) aumentar. —n (of person) figura f, tipo m. ~**er** n constructor m. ~**up** n aumento m; (of gas etc) acumulación f; (fig) propaganda f

built /bɪlt/ see **build**. ~**-in** a empotrado. ~**-up area** n zona f urbanizada

bulb /bʌlb/ n bulbo m; (elec) bombilla f. ~**ous** a bulboso

Bulgaria /bʌlˈgeərɪə/ n Bulgaria f. ~**n** a & n búlgaro (m)

bulge /bʌldʒ/ n protuberancia f. —vi pandearse; (jut out) sobresalir. ~**ing** a abultado; (eyes) saltón

bulk /bʌlk/ n bulto m, volumen m. **in** ~ a granel; (loose) suelto. **the** ~ **of** la mayor parte de. ~**y** a voluminoso

bull /bʊl/ n toro m

bulldog /ˈbʊldɒg/ n buldog m

bulldozer /ˈbʊldəʊzə(r)/ n oruga f aplanadora, buldózer m

bullet /ˈbʊlɪt/ n bala f

bulletin /ˈbʊlɪtɪn/ n anuncio m; (journal) boletín m

bullet-proof /ˈbʊlɪtpruːf/ a a prueba de balas

bullfight /ˈbʊlfaɪt/ n corrida f (de toros). ~**er** n torero m

bullion /ˈbʊljən/ n (gold) oro m en barras; (silver) plata f en barras

bull: ~**ring** /ˈbʊlrɪŋ/ n plaza f de toros. ~**'s-eye** n centro m del blanco, diana f

bully /ˈbʊlɪ/ n matón m. —vt intimidar. ~**ing** n intimidación f

bum¹ /bʌm/ n (bottom, sl) trasero m

bum[2] /bʌm/ n (*Amer*, *sl*) holgazán *m*

bumble-bee /'bʌmblbi:/ n abejorro *m*

bump /bʌmp/ vt chocar contra. —vi dar sacudidas. —n choque *m*; (*swelling*) chichón *m*. ~ **into** chocar contra; (*meet*) encontrar

bumper /'bʌmpə(r)/ n parachoques *m invar*. —a abundante. ~ **edition** n edición *f* especial

bumpkin /'bʌmpkɪn/ n patán *m*, paleto *m* (*fam*)

bumptious /'bʌmpʃəs/ a presuntuoso

bun /bʌn/ n bollo *m*; (*hair*) moño *m*

bunch /bʌntʃ/ n manojo *m*; (*of people*) grupo *m*; (*of bananas, grapes*) racimo *m*, (*of flowers*) ramo *m*

bundle /'bʌndl/ n bulto *m*; (*of papers*) legajo *m*; (*of nerves*) manojo *m*. —vt. ~ **up** atar

bung /bʌŋ/ n tapón *m*. —vt tapar; (*sl*) tirar

bungalow /'bʌŋgələʊ/ n casa *f* de un solo piso, chalé *m*, bungalow *m*

bungle /'bʌŋgl/ vt chapucear

bunion /'bʌnjən/ n juanete *m*

bunk /bʌŋk/ n litera *f*

bunker /'bʌŋkə(r)/ n carbonera *f*; (*golf*) obstáculo *m*; (*mil*) refugio *m*, búnker *m*

bunkum /'bʌŋkəm/ n tonterías *fpl*

bunny /'bʌnɪ/ n conejito *m*

buoy /bɔɪ/ n boya *f*. —vt. ~ **up** hacer flotar; (*fig*) animar

buoyan|cy /'bɔɪənsɪ/ n flotabilidad *f*; (*fig*) optimismo *m*. ~**t** /'bɔɪənt/ a boyante; (*fig*) alegre

burden /'bɜ:dn/ n carga *f*. —vt cargar (**with** de). ~**some** a pesado

bureau /'bjʊərəʊ/ n (*pl* -**eaux** /-əʊz/) escritorio *m*; (*office*) oficina *f*

bureaucra|cy /bjʊə'rɒkrəsɪ/ n burocracia *f*. ~**t** /'bjʊərəkræt/ n burócrata *m & f*. ~**tic** /-'krætɪk/ a burocrático

burgeon /'bɜ:dʒən/ vi brotar; (*fig*) crecer

burgl|ar /'bɜ:glə(r)/ n ladrón *m*. ~**ary** n robo *m* con allanamiento de morada. ~**e** /'bɜ:gl/ vt robar con allanamiento

Burgundy /'bɜ:gəndɪ/ n Borgoña *f*; (*wine*) vino *m* de Borgoña

burial /'berɪəl/ n entierro *m*

burlesque /bɜ:'lesk/ n burlesco *m*

burly /'bɜ:lɪ/ a (-**ier**, -**iest**) corpulento

Burm|a /'bɜ:mə/ Birmania *f*. ~**ese** /-'mi:z/ a & n birmano (*m*)

burn /bɜ:n/ vt (*pt* **burned** o **burnt**) quemar. —vi quemarse. ~ **down** vt destruir con fuego. —n quemadura *f*. ~**er** n quemador *m*. ~**ing** a ardiente; (*food*) que quema; (*question*) candente

burnish /'bɜ:nɪʃ/ vt lustrar, pulir

burnt /bɜ:nt/ *see* **burn**

burp /bɜ:p/ n (*fam*) eructo *m*. —vi (*fam*) eructar

burr /bɜ:(r)/ n (*bot*) erizo *m*

burrow /'bʌrəʊ/ n madriguera *f*. —vt excavar

bursar /'bɜ:sə(r)/ n tesorero *m*. ~**y** /'bɜ:sərɪ/ n beca *f*

burst /bɜ:st/ vt (*pt* **burst**) reventar. —vi reventarse; (*tyre*) pincharse. —n reventón *m*; (*mil*) ráfaga *f*; (*fig*) explosión *f*. ~ **of laughter** carcajada *f*

bury /'berɪ/ vt enterrar; (*hide*) ocultar

bus /bʌs/ n (*pl* **buses**) autobús *m*, camión *m* (*Mex*). —vi (*pt* **bussed**) ir en autobús

bush /bʊʃ/ n arbusto m; (land) monte m. **~y** a espeso

busily /ˈbɪzɪlɪ/ adv afanosamente

business /ˈbɪznɪs/ n negocio m; (com) negocios mpl; (profession) ocupación f; (fig) asunto m. **mind one's own ~** ocuparse de sus propios asuntos. **~-like** a práctico, serio. **~man** n hombre m de negocios

busker /ˈbʌskə(r)/ n músico m ambulante

bus-stop /ˈbʌsstɒp/ n parada f de autobús

bust[1] /bʌst/ n busto m; (chest) pecho m

bust[2] /bʌst/ vt (pt busted or bust) (sl) romper. —vi romperse. —a roto. **go ~** (sl) quebrar

bustle /ˈbʌsl/ vi apresurarse. —n bullicio m

bust-up /ˈbʌstʌp/ n (sl) riña f

busy /ˈbɪzɪ/ a (-ier, -iest) ocupado; (street) concurrido. —vt. **~ o.s. with** ocuparse de

busybody /ˈbɪzɪbɒdɪ/ n entrometido m

but /bʌt/ conj pero; (after negative) sino. —prep menos. **~ for** si no fuera por. **last ~ one** penúltimo. —adv solamente

butane /ˈbjuːteɪn/ n butano m

butcher /ˈbʊtʃə(r)/ n carnicero m. —vt matar; (fig) hacer una carnicería con. **~y** n carnicería f, matanza f

butler /ˈbʌtlə(r)/ n mayordomo m

butt /bʌt/ n (of gun) culata f; (of cigarette) colilla f; (target) blanco m. —vi topar. **~ in** interrumpir

butter /ˈbʌtə(r)/ n mantequilla f. —vt untar con mantequilla. **~ up** vt (fam) lisonjear, dar jabón a. **~-bean** n judía f

buttercup /ˈbʌtəkʌp/ n ranúnculo m

butter-fingers /ˈbʌtəfɪŋgəz/ n manazas m invar, torpe m

butterfly /ˈbʌtəflaɪ/ n mariposa f

buttock /ˈbʌtək/ n nalga f

button /ˈbʌtn/ n botón m. —vt abotonar. —vi abotonarse. **~hole** /ˈbʌtnhəʊl/ n ojal m. —vt (fig) detener

buttress /ˈbʌtrɪs/ n contrafuerte m. —vt apoyar

buxom /ˈbʌksəm/ a ⟨woman⟩ rollizo

buy /baɪ/ vt (pt bought) comprar. —n compra f. **~er** n comprador m

buzz /bʌz/ n zumbido m; (phone call, fam) llamada f. —vi zumbar. **~ off** (sl) largarse. **~er** n timbre m

by /baɪ/ prep por; (near) cerca de; (before) antes de; (according to) según. **~ and large** en conjunto, en general. **~ car** en coche. **~ oneself** por sí solo

bye-bye /ˈbaɪbaɪ/ int (fam) ¡adiós!

by-election /ˈbaɪɪlekʃn/ n elección f parcial

bygone /ˈbaɪgɒn/ a pasado

by-law /ˈbaɪlɔː/ n reglamento m (local)

bypass /ˈbaɪpɑːs/ n carretera f de circunvalación. —vt evitar

by-product /ˈbaɪprɒdʌkt/ n subproducto m

bystander /ˈbaɪstændə(r)/ n espectador m

byword /ˈbaɪwɜːd/ n sinónimo m. **be a ~** for ser conocido por

C

cab /kæb/ n taxi m; (of lorry, train) cabina f

cabaret /ˈkæbəreɪ/ n espectáculo m

cabbage /'kæbɪdʒ/ n col m, repollo m

cabin /'kæbɪn/ n cabaña f; (in ship) camarote m; (in plane) cabina f

cabinet /'kæbɪnɪt/ n (cupboard) armario m; (for display) vitrina f. **C~** (pol) gabinete m. **~-maker** n ebanista m & f

cable /'keɪbl/ n cable m. —vt cablegrafiar. **~ railway** n funicular m

cache /kæʃ/ n (place) escondrijo m; (things) reservas fpl escondidas. —vt ocultar

cackle /'kækl/ n (of hen) cacareo m; (laugh) risotada f. —vi cacarear; (laugh) reírse a carcajadas

cacophon|ous /kə'kɒfənəs/ a cacofónico. **~y** n cacofonía f

cactus /'kæktəs/ n (pl -ti -taɪ) cacto m

cad /kæd/ n sinvergüenza m. **~dish** a desvergonzado

caddie /'kædɪ/ n (golf) portador m de palos

caddy /'kædɪ/ n cajita f

cadence /'keɪdəns/ n cadencia f

cadet /kə'det/ n cadete m

cadge /kædʒ/ vt/i gorronear. **~r** /-ə(r)/ n gorrón m

Caesarean /sɪ'zeərɪən/ a cesáreo. **~ section** n cesárea f

café /'kæfeɪ/ n cafetería f

cafeteria /kæfɪ'tɪərɪə/ n autoservicio m

caffeine /'kæfiːn/ n cafeína f

cage /keɪdʒ/ n jaula f. —vt enjaular

cagey /'keɪdʒɪ/ a (fam) evasivo

Cairo /'kaɪərəʊ/ n el Cairo m

cajole /kə'dʒəʊl/ vt engatusar. **~ry** n engatusamiento m

cake /keɪk/ n pastel m, tarta f; (sponge) bizcocho m. **~ of soap** pastilla f de jabón. **~d** a incrustado

calamit|ous /kə'læmɪtəs/ a desastroso. **~y** /kə'læmətɪ/ n calamidad f

calcium /'kælsɪəm/ n calcio m

calculat|e /'kælkjʊleɪt/ vt/i calcular; (Amer) suponer. **~ing** a calculador. **~ion** /-'leɪʃn/ n cálculo m. **~or** n calculadora f

calculus /'kælkjʊləs/ n (pl -li) cálculo m

calendar /'kælɪndə(r)/ n calendario m

calf[1] /kɑːf/ n (pl calves) ternero m

calf[2] /kɑːf/ n (pl calves) (of leg) pantorrilla f

calibre /'kælɪbə(r)/ n calibre m

calico /'kælɪkəʊ/ n calicó m

call /kɔːl/ vt/i llamar. —n llamada f; (shout) grito m; (visit) visita f. **be on ~** estar de guardia. **long distance ~** conferencia f. **~ back** vt hacer volver; (on phone) volver a llamar. —vi volver; (on phone) volver a llamar. **~ for** pedir; (fetch) ir a buscar. **~ off** cancelar. **~ on** visitar. **~ out** dar voces. **~ together** convocar. **~ up** (mil) llamar al servicio militar; (phone) llamar. **~-box** n cabina f telefónica. **~er** n visita f; (phone) el que llama m. **~ing** n vocación f

callous /'kæləs/ a insensible, cruel. **~ness** n crueldad f

callow /'kæləʊ/ a (-er, -est) inexperto

calm /kɑːm/ a (-er, -est) tranquilo; (weather) calmoso. —n tranquilidad f, calma f. —vt calmar. —vi calmarse. **~ness** n tranquilidad f, calma f

came /keɪm/ see **come**

camel /'kæml/ n camello m

camellia /kə'miːlɪə/ n camelia f

cameo /'kæmɪəʊ/ n (pl -os) camafeo m

camera /'kæmərə/ n máquina f (fotográfica); (TV) cámara f.

~man n (pl **-men**) operador m, cámara m

camouflage /ˈkæməflɑːʒ/ n camuflaje m. —vt encubrir; (mil) camuflar

camp[1] /kæmp/ n campamento m. —vi acamparse

camp[2] /kæmp/ a (affected) amanerado

campaign /kæmˈpeɪn/ n campaña f. —vi hacer campaña

camp: **~bed** n catre m de tijera. **~er** n campista m & f; (vehicle) caravana f. **~ing** n camping m. **go ~ing** hacer camping. **~site** /ˈkæmpsaɪt/ n camping m

campus /ˈkæmpəs/ n (pl **-puses**) ciudad f universitaria

can[1] /kæn/ v aux (pt **could**) (be able to) poder; (know how to) saber. **~not** (neg), **~'t** (neg, fam). **I ~not/~'t go** no puedo ir

can[2] /kæn/ n lata f. —vt (pt **canned**) enlatar. **~ned music** música f grabada

Canad|a /ˈkænədə/ n el Canadá m. **~ian** /kəˈneɪdɪən/ a & n canadiense (m & f)

canal /kəˈnæl/ n canal m

canary /kəˈneərɪ/ n canario m

cancel /ˈkænsl/ vt/i (pt **cancelled**) anular; cancelar (contract etc); suspender (appointment etc); (delete) tachar. **~lation** /-ˈleɪʃn/ n cancelación f

cancer /ˈkænsə(r)/ n cáncer m. **C~** n (Astr) Cáncer m. **~ous** a canceroso

candid /ˈkændɪd/ a franco

candida|cy /ˈkændɪdəsɪ/ n candidatura f. **~te** /ˈkændɪdeɪt/ n candidato m

candle /ˈkændl/ n vela f. **~stick** /ˈkændlstɪk/ n candelero m

candour /ˈkændə(r)/ n franqueza f

candy /ˈkændɪ/ n (Amer) caramelo m. **~-floss** n algodón m de azúcar

cane /keɪn/ n caña f; (for baskets) mimbre m; (stick) bastón m. —vt (strike) castigar con palmeta

canine /ˈkeɪnaɪn/ a canino

canister /ˈkænɪstə(r)/ n bote m

cannabis /ˈkænəbɪs/ n cáñamo m índico, hachís m, mariguana f

cannibal /ˈkænɪbl/ n caníbal m. **~ism** n canibalismo m

cannon /ˈkænən/ n invar cañón m. **~ shot** cañonazo m

cannot /ˈkænɒt/ see **can**[1]

canny /ˈkænɪ/ a astuto

canoe /kəˈnuː/ n canoa f, piragua f. —vi ir en canoa. **~ist** n piragüista m & f

canon /ˈkænən/ n canon m; (person) canónigo m. **~ize** /ˈkænənaɪz/ vt canonizar

can-opener /ˈkænəʊpnə(r)/ n abrelatas m invar

canopy /ˈkænəpɪ/ n dosel m; (of parachute) casquete m

cant /kænt/ n jerga f

can't /kɑːnt/ see **can**[1]

cantankerous /kænˈtæŋkərəs/ a malhumorado

canteen /kænˈtiːn/ n cantina f; (of cutlery) juego m; (flask) cantimplora f

canter /ˈkæntə(r)/ n medio galope m. —vi ir a medio galope

canvas /ˈkænvəs/ n lona f; (artist's) lienzo m

canvass /ˈkænvəs/ vi hacer campaña, solicitar votos. **~ing** n solicitación f (de votos)

canyon /ˈkænjən/ n cañón m

cap /kæp/ n gorra f; (lid) tapa f; (of cartridge) cápsula f; (academic) birrete m; (of pen) capuchón m; (mec) casquete m. —vt (pt **capped**) tapar, poner cápsula a; (outdo) superar

capab|ility /keɪpəˈbɪlətɪ/ n capacidad f. **~le** /ˈkeɪpəbl/ a capaz. **~ly** adv competentemente

capacity /kəˈpæsɪtɪ/ n capacidad f; (function) calidad f

cape[1] /keɪp/ n (cloak) capa f

cape[2] /keɪp/ n (geog) cabo m

caper[1] /'keɪpə(r)/ vi brincar. —n salto m; (fig) travesura f

caper[2] /'keɪpə(r)/ n (culin) alcaparra f

capital /'kæpɪtl/ a capital. ~ letter n mayúscula f. —n (town) capital f; (money) capital m

capitalism /'kæpɪtəlɪzəm/ n capitalismo m. ~t a & n capitalista (m & f)

capitalize /'kæpɪtəlaɪz/ vt capitalizar; (typ) escribir con mayúsculas. ~ on aprovechar

capitulate /kə'pɪtʃʊleɪt/ vi capitular. ~ion /-'leɪʃn/ n capitulación f

capon /'keɪpən/ n capón m

capricious /kə'prɪʃəs/ a caprichoso

Capricorn /'kæprɪkɔːn/ n Capricornio m

capsicum /'kæpsɪkəm/ n pimiento m

capsize /kæp'saɪz/ vt hacer zozobrar. —vi zozobrar

capsule /'kæpsjuːl/ n cápsula f

captain /'kæptɪn/ n capitán m. —vt capitanear

caption /'kæpʃn/ n (heading) título m; (of cartoon etc) leyenda f

captivate /'kæptɪveɪt/ vt encantar

captive /'kæptɪv/ a & n cautivo (m). ~ity /-'tɪvɪtɪ/ n cautiverio m, cautividad f

capture /'kæptʃə(r)/ vt prender; llamar (attention); (mil) tomar. —n apresamiento m; (mil) toma f

car /kɑː(r)/ n coche m, carro m (LAm)

carafe /kə'ræf/ n jarro m, garrafa f

caramel /'kærəmel/ n azúcar m quemado; (sweet) caramelo m

carat /'kærət/ n quilate m

caravan /'kærəvæn/ n caravana f

carbohydrate /kɑːbəʊ'haɪdreɪt/ n hidrato m de carbono

carbon /'kɑːbən/ n carbono m; (paper) carbón m. ~ copy copia f al carbón

carburettor /kɑːbjʊ'retə(r)/ n carburador m

carcass /'kɑːkəs/ n cadáver m, esqueleto m

card /kɑːd/ n tarjeta f; (for games) carta f; (membership) carnet m; (records) ficha f

cardboard /'kɑːdbɔːd/ n cartón m

cardiac /'kɑːdɪæk/ a cardíaco

cardigan /'kɑːdɪgən/ n chaqueta f de punto, rebeca f

cardinal /'kɑːdɪnl/ a cardinal. — n cardenal m

card-index /'kɑːdɪndeks/ n fichero m

care /keə(r)/ n cuidado m; (worry) preocupación f; (protection) cargo m. ~ of a cuidado de, en casa de. take ~ of cuidar de (person); ocuparse de (matter). —vi interesarse. I don't ~ me es igual. ~ about interesarse por. ~ for cuidar de; (like) querer

career /kə'rɪə(r)/ n carrera f. —vi correr a toda velocidad

carefree /'keəfriː/ a despreocupado

careful /'keəfʊl/ a cuidadoso; (cautious) prudente. ~ly adv con cuidado

careless /'keəlɪs/ a negligente; (not worried) indiferente. ~ly adv descuidadamente. ~ness n descuido m

caress /kə'res/ n caricia f. —vt acariciar

caretaker /'keəteɪkə(r)/ n vigilante m; (of flats etc) portero m

car-ferry /'kɑːferɪ/ n transbordador m de coches

cargo /'kɑːgəʊ/ n (pl -oes) carga f

Caribbean /kærɪ'biːən/ a caribe. ~ Sea n mar m Caribe

caricature /ˈkærɪkətʃʊə(r)/ n caricatura f. —vt caricaturizar

carnage /ˈkɑːnɪdʒ/ n carnicería f, matanza f

carnal /ˈkɑːnl/ a carnal

carnation /kɑːˈneɪʃn/ n clavel m

carnival /ˈkɑːnɪvl/ n carnaval m

carol /ˈkærəl/ n villancico m

carouse /kəˈraʊz/ vi correrse una juerga

carousel /ˈkærəˈsel/ n tiovivo m

carp[1] /kɑːp/ n invar carpa f

carp[2] /kɑːp/ vi ~ at quejarse de

car park /ˈkɑːpɑːk/ n aparcamiento m

carpent|er /ˈkɑːpɪntə(r)/ n carpintero m. ~ry n carpintería f

carpet /ˈkɑːpɪt/ n alfombra f. **be on the** ~ (fam) recibir un rapapolvo; (under consideration) estar sobre el tapete. —vt alfombrar. ~-sweeper n escoba f mecánica

carriage /ˈkærɪdʒ/ n coche m; (mec) carro m; (transport) transporte m; (cost, bearing) porte m

carriageway /ˈkærɪdʒweɪ/ n calzada f, carretera f

carrier /ˈkærɪə(r)/ n transportista m & f; (company) empresa f de transportes; (med) portador m. ~-bag bolsa f

carrot /ˈkærət/ n zanahoria f

carry /ˈkærɪ/ vt llevar; transportar (goods); (involve) llevar consigo, implicar; —vi (sounds) llegar, oírse. ~ off llevarse. ~ on continuar; (complain, fam) quejarse. ~ out realizar; cumplir (promise, threat). ~-cot n capazo m

cart /kɑːt/ n carro m. —vt acarrear; (carry, fam) llevar

cartilage /ˈkɑːtɪlɪdʒ/ n cartílago m

carton /ˈkɑːtən/ n caja f (de cartón)

cartoon /kɑːˈtuːn/ n caricatura f, chiste m; (strip) historieta f; (film) dibujos mpl animados. ~ist n caricaturista m & f

cartridge /ˈkɑːtrɪdʒ/ n cartucho m

carve /kɑːv/ vt tallar; trinchar (meat)

cascade /kæsˈkeɪd/ n cascada f. —vi caer en cascadas

case /keɪs/ n caso m; (jurid) proceso m; (crate) cajón m; (box) caja f; (suitcase) maleta f. **in any** ~ en todo caso. **in** ~ **he comes** por si viene. **in** ~ **of** en caso de. **lower** ~ caja f baja, minúscula f. **upper** ~ caja f alta, mayúscula f

cash /kæʃ/ n dinero m efectivo. **pay (in)** ~ pagar al contado. —vt cobrar. ~ **in** (on) aprovecharse de. ~ **desk** n caja f

cashew /ˈkæʃuː/ n anacardo m

cashier /kæˈʃɪə(r)/ n cajero m

cashmere /kæʃˈmɪə(r)/ n casimir m, cachemir m

casino /kəˈsiːnəʊ/ n (pl -os) casino m

cask /kɑːsk/ n barril m

casket /ˈkɑːskɪt/ n cajita f

casserole /ˈkæsərəʊl/ n cacerola f; (stew) cazuela f

cassette /kəˈset/ n casete m

cast /kɑːst/ vt (pt cast) arrojar; fundir (metal); dar (vote); (in theatre) repartir. —n lanzamiento m; (in play) reparto m; (mould) molde m

castanets /kæstəˈnets/ npl castañuelas fpl

castaway /ˈkɑːstəweɪ/ n náufrago m

caste /kɑːst/ n casta f

cast: ~ **iron** n hierro m fundido. ~**-iron** a de hierro fundido; (fig) sólido

castle /ˈkɑːsl/ n castillo m; (chess) torre f

cast-offs /ˈkɑːstɒfs/ npl desechos mpl

castor /ˈkɑːstə(r)/ n ruedecilla f

castor oil /ˈkɑːstərˈɔɪl/ n aceite m de ricino

castor sugar /ˈkɑːstəˈʃʊgə(r)/ n azúcar m extrafino

castrate /kæ'streɪt/ vt castrar. ~ion /-ʃn/ n castración f

casual /'kæʒʊəl/ a casual; ⟨meeting⟩ fortuito; ⟨work⟩ ocasional; ⟨attitude⟩ despreocupado; ⟨clothes⟩ informal, de sport. ~ly adv de paso

casualty /'kæʒʊəltɪ/ n accidente m; ⟨injured⟩ víctima f, herido m; ⟨dead⟩ víctima f, muerto m. ~ies npl (mil) bajas fpl

cat /kæt/ n gato m

cataclysm /'kætəklɪzəm/ n cataclismo m

catacomb /'kætəku:m/ n catacumba f

catalogue /'kætəlɒg/ n catálogo m. —vt catalogar

catalyst /'kætəlɪst/ n catalizador m

catamaran /'kætəmə'ræn/ n catamarán m

catapult /'kætəpʌlt/ n catapulta f; ⟨child's⟩ tirador m, tirachinos m invar

cataract /'kætərækt/ n catarata f

catarrh /kə'tɑ:(r)/ n catarro m

catastrophe /kə'tæstrəfɪ/ n catástrofe m. ~ic /kætə'strɒfɪk/ a catastrófico

catch /kætʃ/ vt (pt caught) coger (not LAm), agarrar; ⟨grab⟩ asir; tomar ⟨train, bus⟩; ⟨unawares⟩ sorprender; ⟨understand⟩ comprender; contraer ⟨disease⟩. ~ a cold resfriarse. ~ sight of avistar. —vi ⟨get stuck⟩ engancharse; ⟨fire⟩ prenderse. —n cogida f; ⟨of fish⟩ pesca f; ⟨on door⟩ pestillo m; ⟨on window⟩ cerradura f. ~ on (fam) hacerse popular. ~ up poner al día. ~ up with alcanzar; ponerse al corriente de ⟨news etc⟩

catching /'kætʃɪŋ/ a contagioso

catchment /'kætʃmənt/ n. ~ area n zona f de captación

catch-phrase /'kætʃfreɪz/ n eslogan m

catchword /'kætʃwɜ:d/ n eslogan m, consigna f

catchy /'kætʃɪ/ a pegadizo

catechism /'kætɪkɪzəm/ n catecismo m

categorical /kætɪ'gɒrɪkl/ a categórico

category /'kætɪgɔrɪ/ n categoría f

cater /'keɪtə(r)/ vi proveer comida a. ~ for proveer a ⟨needs⟩. ~er n proveedor m

caterpillar /'kætəpɪlə(r)/ n oruga f

cathedral /kə'θi:drəl/ n catedral f

catholic /'kæθəlɪk/ a universal. C~ a & n católico (m). C~ism /kə'θɒlɪsɪzəm/ n catolicismo m

catnap /'kætnæp/ n sueñecito m

cat's eyes /'kætsaɪz/ npl catafotos mpl

cattle /'kætl/ npl ganado m (vacuno)

catty /'kætɪ/ a malicioso. ~walk /'kætwɔ:k/ n pasarela f

caucus /'kɔ:kəs/ n comité m electoral

caught /kɔ:t/ see **catch**

cauldron /'kɔ:ldrən/ n caldera f

cauliflower /'kɒlɪflaʊə(r)/ n coliflor f

cause /kɔ:z/ n causa f, motivo m. —vt causar

causeway /'kɔ:zweɪ/ n calzada f elevada, carretera f elevada

caustic /'kɔ:stɪk/ a & n cáustico (m)

cauterize /'kɔ:təraɪz/ vt cauterizar

caution /'kɔ:ʃn/ n cautela f; ⟨warning⟩ advertencia f. —vt advertir; ⟨jurid⟩ amonestar

cautious /'kɔ:ʃəs/ a cauteloso, prudente. ~ly adv con precaución, cautelosamente

cavalcade /kævəl'keɪd/ n cabalgata f

cavalier /kævə'lɪə(r)/ a arrogante

cavalry /'kævəlrɪ/ n caballería f
cave /keɪv/ n cueva f. —vi. ~ in hundirse. ~-man n (pl -men) troglodita m
cavern /'kævən/ n caverna f, cueva f
caviare /'kævɪɑ:(r)/ n caviar m
caving /'keɪvɪŋ/ n espeleología f
cavity /'kævətɪ/ n cavidad f; (in tooth) caries f
cavort /kə'vɔːt/ vi brincar
cease /siːs/ vt/i cesar. —n. without ~ sin cesar. ~-fire n tregua f, alto m el fuego. ~less a incesante
cedar /'siːdə/r/ n cedro m
cede /siːd/ vt ceder
cedilla /sɪ'dɪlə/ n cedilla f
ceiling /'siːlɪŋ/ n techo m
celebrat|e /'selɪbreɪt/ vt celebrar. —vi divertirse. ~ed /'selɪbreɪtɪd/ a célebre. ~ion /-'breɪʃn/ n celebración f; (party) fiesta f
celebrity /sɪ'lebrətɪ/ n celebridad f
celery /'selərɪ/ n apio m
celestial /sɪ'lestjəl/ a celestial
celiba|cy /'selɪbəsɪ/ n celibato m. ~te /'selɪbət/ a & n célibe (m & f)
cell /sel/ n celda f; (biol) célula f; (elec) pila f
cellar /'selə(r)/ n sótano m; (for wine) bodega f
cell|ist /'tʃelɪst/ n violonc(h)elo m & f, violonc(h)elista m & f. ~o /'tʃeləʊ/ n (pl -os) violonc(h)elo m
Cellophane /'seləfeɪn/ n (P) celofán m (P)
cellular /'seljʊlə(r)/ a celular
celluloid /'seljʊlɔɪd/ n celuloide m
cellulose /'seljʊləʊs/ n celulosa f
Celt /kelt/ n celta m & f. ~ic a céltico
cement /sɪ'ment/ n cemento m. —vt cementar; (fig) consolidar

cemetery /'semətrɪ/ n cementerio m
cenotaph /'senətɑːf/ n cenotafio m
censor /'sensə(r)/ n censor m. —vt censurar. ~ship n censura f
censure /'senʃə(r)/ n censura f. —vt censurar
census /'sensəs/ n censo m
cent /sent/ n centavo m
centenary /sen'tiːnərɪ/ n centenario m
centigrade /'sentɪɡreɪd/ a centígrado
centilitre /'sentɪliːtə(r)/ n centilitro m
centimetre /'sentɪmiːtə(r)/ n centímetro m
centipede /'sentɪpiːd/ n ciempiés m invar
central /'sentrəl/ a central; (of town) céntrico. ~ heating n calefacción f central. ~ize vt centralizar. ~ly adv (situated) en el centro
centre /'sentə(r)/ n centro m. —vt (pt centred) concentrarse
centrifugal /sen'trɪfjʊɡəl/ a centrífugo
century /'sentʃərɪ/ n siglo m
ceramic /sɪ'ræmɪk/ a cerámico. ~s npl cerámica f
cereal /'sɪərɪəl/ n cereal m
cerebral /'serɪbrəl/ a cerebral
ceremon|ial /serɪ'məʊnɪəl/ a & n ceremonial (m). ~ious /-'məʊnɪəs/ a ceremonioso. ~y /'serɪmənɪ/ n ceremonia f
certain /'sɜːtn/ a cierto. for ~ seguro. make ~ of asegurarse de. ~ly adv desde luego. ~ty n certeza f
certificate /sə'tɪfɪkət/ n certificado m; (of birth, death etc) partida f
certify /'sɜːtɪfaɪ/ vt certificar
cessation /se'seɪʃən/ n cesación f
cesspit /'sespɪt/ n, cesspool /'sespuːl/ n pozo m negro; (fam) sentina f

chafe /tʃeɪf/ vt rozar. —vi rozarse; (fig) irritarse

chaff /tʃæf/ vt zumbarse de

chaffinch /'tʃæfɪntʃ/ n pinzón m

chagrin /'ʃægrɪn/ n disgusto m

chain /tʃeɪn/ n cadena f. —vt encadenar. ~ **reaction** n reacción f en cadena. ~**smoker** n fumador m que siempre tiene un cigarrillo encendido. ~ **store** n sucursal m

chair /tʃeə(r)/ n silla f; (univ) cátedra f. —vt presidir. ~**lift** n telesilla m

chairman /'tʃeəmən/ n (pl -men) presidente m

chalet /'ʃæleɪ/ n chalé m

chalice /'tʃælɪs/ n cáliz m

chalk /tʃɔːk/ n creta f; (stick) tiza f. ~**y** a cretáceo

challenge /'tʃælɪndʒ/ n desafío m; (fig) reto m. —vt desafiar; (question) poner en duda. ~**ing** a estimulante

chamber /'tʃeɪmbə(r)/ n (old use) cámara f. ~**maid** /'tʃeɪmbəmeɪd/ n camarera f. ~**pot** n orinal m. ~**s** npl despacho m, bufete m

chameleon /kə'miːljən/ n camaleón m

chamois /'ʃæmɪ/ n gamuza f

champagne /ʃæm'peɪn/ n champaña m, champán m (fam)

champion /'tʃæmpjən/ n campeón m. —vt defender. ~**ship** n campeonato m

chance /tʃɑːns/ n casualidad f; (likelihood) probabilidad f; (opportunity) oportunidad f; (risk) riesgo m. **by** ~ por casualidad. —a fortuito. —vi arriesgar. —vi suceder. ~ **upon** tropezar con

chancellor /'tʃɑːnsələ(r)/ n canciller m; (univ) rector m. **C~ of the Exchequer** Ministro m de Hacienda

chancy /'tʃɑːnsɪ/ a arriesgado; (uncertain) incierto

chandelier /ʃændə'lɪə(r)/ n araña f (de luces)

change /tʃeɪndʒ/ vt cambiar; (substitute) reemplazar. ~ **one's mind** cambiar de idea. —vi cambiarse. —n cambio m; (small coins) suelto m. ~ **of life** menopausia f. ~**able** a cambiable; (weather) variable. ~**over** n cambio m

channel /'tʃænl/ n canal m; (fig) medio m. **the C~ Islands** npl las islas fpl Anglonormandas. **the (English) C~** el canal de la Mancha. —vt (pt **channelled**) acanalar; (fig) encauzar

chant /tʃɑːnt/ n canto m. —vt/i cantar; (fig) salmodiar

chaos /'keɪɒs/ n caos m, desorden m. ~**tic** /-'ɒtɪk/ a caótico, desordenado

chap¹ /tʃæp/ n (crack) grieta f. —vt (pt **chapped**) agrietar. —vi agrietarse

chap² /tʃæp/ n (fam) hombre m, tío m (fam)

chapel /'tʃæpl/ n capilla f

chaperon /'ʃæpərəʊn/ n acompañanta f. —vt acompañar

chaplain /'tʃæplɪn/ n capellán m

chapter /'tʃæptə(r)/ n capítulo m

char¹ /tʃɑː(r)/ vt (pt **charred**) carbonizar

char² /tʃɑː(r)/ n asistenta f

character /'kærəktə(r)/ n carácter m; (in play) personaje m. **in** ~ característico

characteristic /kærəktə'rɪstɪk/ a característico. ~**ally** adv típicamente

characterize /'kærəktəraɪz/ vt caracterizar

charade /ʃə'rɑːd/ n charada f, farsa f

charcoal /'tʃɑːkəʊl/ n carbón m vegetal; (for drawing) carboncillo m

charge /tʃɑːdʒ/ n precio m; (elec, mil) carga f; (jurid) acusación f; (task, custody) encargo m; (responsibility) responsabilidad f. **in ~ of** responsable de, encargado de. **take ~ of** encargarse de. —vt pedir; (elec, mil) cargar; (jurid) acusar; (entrust) encargar. —vi cargar; (money) cobrar. **~able** a a cargo (de)

chariot /'tʃæriət/ n carro m

charisma /kə'rɪzmə/ n carisma m. **~tic** /-'mætɪk/ a carismático

charitable /'tʃærɪtəbl/ a caritativo

charity /'tʃærɪtɪ/ n caridad f; (society) institución f benéfica

charlatan /'ʃɑːlətən/ n charlatán m

charm /tʃɑːm/ n encanto m; (spell) hechizo m; (on bracelet) dije m, amuleto m. —vt encantar. **~ing** a encantador

chart /tʃɑːt/ n (naut) carta f de marear; (table) tabla f. —vt poner una carta de marear

charter /'tʃɑːtə(r)/ n carta f. —vt conceder carta a, estatuir; alquilar (bus, train); fletar (plane, ship). **~ed accountant** n contador m titulado. **~ flight** n vuelo m charter

charwoman /'tʃɑːwʊmən/ n (pl -women) asistenta f

chary /'tʃeərɪ/ a cauteloso

chase /tʃeɪs/ vt perseguir. —vi correr. —n persecución f. **~ away, ~ off** ahuyentar

chasm /'kæzəm/ n abismo m

chassis /'ʃæsɪ/ n chasis m

chaste /tʃeɪst/ a casto

chastise /tʃæs'taɪz/ vt castigar

chastity /'tʃæstətɪ/ n castidad f

chat /tʃæt/ n charla f. **have a ~** charlar. —vi (pt chatted) charlar

chattels /'tʃætlz/ n bienes mpl muebles

chatter /'tʃætə(r)/ n charla f. —vi charlar. **his teeth are ~ing** le castañetean los dientes. **~box** /'tʃætəbɒks/ n parlanchín m

chatty /'tʃætɪ/ a hablador; (style) familiar

chauffeur /'ʃəʊfə(r)/ n chófer m

chauvinis|**m** /'ʃəʊvɪnɪzəm/ n patriotería f; (male) machismo m. **~t** /'ʃəʊvɪnɪst/ n patriotero m; (male) machista m & f

cheap /tʃiːp/ a (-er, -est) barato; (poor quality) de baja calidad; (rate) económico. **~en** /'tʃiːpən/ vt abaratar. **~(ly)** adv barato, a bajo precio. **~ness** n baratura f

cheat /tʃiːt/ vt defraudar; (deceive) engañar. —vi (at cards) hacer trampas. —n trampa f; (person) tramposo m

check[1] /tʃek/ vt comprobar; (examine) inspeccionar; (curb) detener; (chess) dar jaque a. —vi comprobar. —n comprobación f; (of tickets) control m; (curb) freno m; (chess) jaque m; (bill, Amer) cuenta f. **~ in** registrarse; (at airport) facturar el equipaje. **~ out** pagar la cuenta y marcharse. **~ up** comprobar. **~ up on** investigar

check[2] /tʃek/ n (pattern) cuadro m. **~ed** a a cuadros

checkmate /'tʃekmeɪt/ n jaque m mate. —vt dar mate a

check-up /'tʃekʌp/ n examen m

cheek /tʃiːk/ n mejilla f; (fig) descaro m. **~bone** n pómulo m. **~y** a descarado

cheep /tʃiːp/ vi piar

cheer /tʃɪə(r)/ n alegría f; (applause) viva m. —vt alegrar; (applaud) aplaudir. —vi alegrarse; (applaud) aplaudir. **~ up!** ¡anímate! ¡anímese! **~ful** a alegre. **~fulness** n alegría f

cheerio /tʃɪərɪ'əʊ/ int (fam) ¡adiós!, ¡hasta luego!

cheer: ~less /'tʃɪəlɪs/ a triste. ~s! ¡salud!

cheese /tʃiːz/ n queso m

cheetah /'tʃiːtə/ n guepardo m

chef /ʃef/ n cocinero m

chemical /'kemɪkl/ a químico. —n producto m químico

chemist /'kemɪst/ n farmacéutico m; (scientist) químico m. ~ry n química f. ~'s (shop) n farmacia f

cheque /tʃek/ n cheque m, talón m. ~-book n talonario m

chequered /'tʃekəd/ a a cuadros; (fig) con altibajos

cherish /'tʃerɪʃ/ vt cuidar; (love) querer; abrigar (hope)

cherry /'tʃerɪ/ n cereza f. ~-tree n cerezo m

cherub /'tʃerəb/ n (pl -im) (angel) querubín m

chess /tʃes/ n ajedrez m. ~-board n tablero m de ajedrez

chest /tʃest/ n pecho m; (box) cofre m, cajón m. ~ of drawers n cómoda f

chestnut /'tʃesnʌt/ n castaña f. ~-tree n castaño m

chew /tʃuː/ vt masticar; (fig) rumiar. ~ing-gum n chicle m

chic /ʃiːk/ a elegante. —n elegancia f

chick /tʃɪk/ n polluelo m. ~en /'tʃɪkɪn/ n pollo m. —a (sl) cobarde. —vi. ~en out (sl) retirarse. ~en-pox n varicela f

chicory /'tʃɪkərɪ/ n (in coffee) achicoria f; (in salad) escarola f

chide /tʃaɪd/ vt (pt chided) reprender

chief /tʃiːf/ n jefe m. —a principal. ~ly adv principalmente

chilblain /'tʃɪlbleɪn/ n sabañón m

child /tʃaɪld/ n (pl children /'tʃɪldrən/) niño m; (offspring) hijo m. ~birth /'tʃaɪldbɜːθ/ n parto m. ~hood n niñez f. ~ish

a infantil. ~less a sin hijos. ~like a inocente, infantil

Chile /'tʃɪlɪ/ n Chile m. ~an a & n chileno (m)

chill /tʃɪl/ n frío m; (illness) resfriado m. —a frío. —vt enfriar; refrigerar (food)

chilli /'tʃɪlɪ/ n (pl -ies) chile m

chilly /'tʃɪlɪ/ a frío

chime /tʃaɪm/ n carillón m. —vt tocar (bells); dar (hours). —vi repicar

chimney /'tʃɪmnɪ/ n (pl -eys) chimenea f. ~-pot n cañón m de chimenea. ~-sweep n deshollinador m

chimpanzee /tʃɪmpæn'ziː/ n chimpancé m

chin /tʃɪn/ n barbilla f

china /'tʃaɪnə/ n porcelana f

China /'tʃaɪnə/ n China f. ~ese /-'niːz/ a & n chino (m)

chink[1] /tʃɪŋk/ n (crack) grieta f

chink[2] /tʃɪŋk/ n (sound) tintín m. —vt hacer tintinear. —vi tintinear

chip /tʃɪp/ n pedacito m; (splinter) astilla f; (culin) patata f frita; (gambling) ficha f. have a ~ on one's shoulder guardar rencor. —vt (pt chipped) desportillar. —vi desportillarse. ~ in (fam) interrumpir; (with money) contribuir

chiropodist /kɪ'rɒpədɪst/ n callista m & f

chirp /tʃɜːp/ n pío m. —vi piar

chirpy /'tʃɜːpɪ/ a alegre

chisel /'tʃɪzl/ n formón m. —vt (pt chiselled) cincelar

chit /tʃɪt/ n vale m, nota f

chit-chat /'tʃɪttʃæt/ n cháchara f

chivalrous /'ʃɪvəlrəs/ a caballeroso. ~y /'ʃɪvəlrɪ/ n caballerosidad f

chive /tʃaɪv/ n cebollino m

chlorine /'klɔːriːn/ n cloro m

chock /tʃɒk/ n calzo m. ~-a-block a, ~-full a atestado

chocolate /'tʃɒklɪt/ n chocolate m; (individual sweet) bombón m
choice /tʃɔɪs/ n elección f; (preference) preferencia f. —a escogido
choir /'kwaɪə(r)/ n coro m. ~boy /'kwaɪəbɔɪ/ n niño m de coro
choke /tʃəʊk/ vt sofocar. —vi sofocarse. —n (auto) estrangulador m, estárter m
cholera /'kɒlərə/ n cólera m
cholesterol /kə'lestərɒl/ n colesterol m
choose /tʃuːz/ vt/i (pt chose, pp chosen) elegir. ~y /'tʃuːzɪ/ a (fam) exigente
chop /tʃɒp/ vt (pt chopped) cortar. —n (culin) chuleta f. ~ down talar. ~ off cortar. ~per n hacha f; (butcher's) cuchilla f; (sl) helicóptero m
choppy /'tʃɒpɪ/ a picado
chopstick /'tʃɒpstɪk/ n palillo m (chino)
choral /'kɔːrəl/ a coral
chord /kɔːd/ n cuerda f; (mus) acorde m
chore /tʃɔː(r)/ n tarea f, faena f. **household** ~s npl faenas fpl domésticas
choreographer /kɒrɪ'ɒɡrəfə(r)/ n coreógrafa m
chorister /'kɒrɪstə(r)/ n (singer) corista m & f
chortle /'tʃɔːtl/ n risita f alegre. —vi reírse alegremente
chorus /'kɔːrəs/ n coro m; (of song) estribillo m
chose, chosen /tʃəʊz, 'tʃəʊzn/ see **choose**
Christ /kraɪst/ n Cristo m
christen /'krɪsn/ vt bautizar. ~ing n bautizo m
Christian /'krɪstʃən/ a & n cristiano (m). ~ **name** n nombre m de pila
Christmas /'krɪsməs/ n Navidad f; (period) Navidades fpl. —a de Navidad, navideño. ~-**box** n

aguinaldo m. ~ **day** n día m de Navidad. ~ **Eve** n Nochebuena f. **Father** ~ n Papá m Noel. **Happy** ~! ¡Felices Pascuas!
chrome /krəʊm/ n cromo m. ~**ium** /'krəʊmɪəm/ n cromo m. ~**ium plating** n cromado m
chromosome /'krəʊməssʊm/ n cromosoma m
chronic /'krɒnɪk/ a crónico; (bad, fam) terrible
chronicle /'krɒnɪkl/ n crónica f. —vt historiar
chronological /krɒnə'lɒdʒɪkl/ a cronológico. ~y /krə'nɒlədʒɪ/ n cronología f
chrysanthemum /krɪ'sæn θəməm/ n crisantemo m
chubby /'tʃʌbɪ/ a (-ier, -iest) regordete; (face) mofletudo
chuck /tʃʌk/ vt (fam) arrojar. ~ **out** tirar
chuckle /'tʃʌkl/ n risa f ahogada. —vi reírse entre dientes
chuffed /tʃʌft/ a (sl) contento
chug /tʃʌg/ vi (pt chugged) (of motor) traquetear
chum /tʃʌm/ n amigo m, compinche m. ~**my** a. **be** ~**my** (2 people) ser muy amigos. **be** ~**my with** ser muy amigo de
chump /tʃʌmp/ n (sl) tonto m. ~ **chop** n chuleta f
chunk /tʃʌŋk/ n trozo m grueso. ~y /tʃʌŋkɪ/ a macizo
church /tʃɜːtʃ/ n iglesia f. ~**yard** /'tʃɜːtʃjɑːd/ n cementerio m
churlish /'tʃɜːlɪʃ/ a grosero
churn /tʃɜːn/ n (for milk) lechera f, cántara f; (for butter) mantequera f. —vt agitar. ~ **out** producir en profusión
chute /ʃuːt/ n tobogán m
chutney /'tʃʌtnɪ/ n (pl -eys) condimento m agridulce
cider /'saɪdə(r)/ n sidra f
cigar /sɪ'ɡɑː(r)/ n puro m

cigarette /sɪgəˈret/ n cigarillo m.
~**-holder** n boquilla f

cine-camera /ˈsɪnɪkæmərə/ n
cámara f, tomavistas m invar

cinema /ˈsɪnəmə/ n cine m

cinnamon /ˈsɪnəmən/ n canela f

cipher /ˈsaɪfə(r)/ n (math, fig)
cero m; (secret system) cifra f

circle /ˈsɜːkl/ n círculo m; (in
theatre) anfiteatro m. —vt girar
alrededor de. —vi dar vueltas

circuit /ˈsɜːkɪt/ n circuito m;
(chain) cadena f

circuitous /sɜːˈkjuːɪtəs/ a
indirecto

circular /ˈsɜːkjʊlə(r)/ a & n circular (f)

circularize /ˈsɜːkjʊləraɪz/ vt
enviar circulares a

circulate /ˈsɜːkjʊleɪt/ vt hacer
circular. —vi circular. ~**ion**
/-ˈleɪʃn/ n circulación f; (of
journals) tirada f

circumcis|**e** /ˈsɜːkəmsaɪz/ vt cir-
cuncidar. ~**ion** /-ˈsɪʒn/ n cir-
cuncisión f

circumference /səˈkʌmfərəns/ n
circunferencia f

circumflex /ˈsɜːkəmfleks/ a & n
circunflejo (m)

circumspect /ˈsɜːkəmspekt/ a
circunspecto

circumstance /ˈsɜːkəmstəns/ n
circunstancia f. ~**s** (means) npl
situación f económica

circus /ˈsɜːkəs/ n circo m

cistern /ˈsɪstən/ n depósito m; (of
WC) cisterna f

citadel /ˈsɪtədl/ n ciudadela f

citation /saɪˈteɪʃn/ n citación f

cite /saɪt/ vt citar

citizen /ˈsɪtɪzn/ n ciudadano m;
(inhabitant) habitante m & f.
~**ship** n ciudadanía f

citrus /ˈsɪtrəs/ n. ~ **fruits** cít-
ricos mpl

city /ˈsɪtɪ/ n ciudad f; **the C**~ el
centro m financiero de Londres

civic /ˈsɪvɪk/ a cívico. ~**s** npl
cívica f

civil /ˈsɪvl/ a civil, cortés

civilian /sɪˈvɪlɪən/ a & n civil (m
& f). ~ **clothes** npl traje m de
paisano

civility /sɪˈvɪlətɪ/ n cortesía f

civiliz|**ation** /sɪvɪlaɪˈzeɪʃn/ n
civilización f. ~**e** /ˈsɪvəlaɪz/ vt
civilizar

civil: ~ **servant** n funcionario
m. ~ **service** n administración f
pública

civvies /ˈsɪvɪz/ npl. **in** ~ (sl) en
traje m de paisano

clad /klæd/ see **clothe**

claim /kleɪm/ vt reclamar;
(assert) pretender. —n reclamación f; (right) derecho m;
(jurid) demanda f. ~**ant**
n demandante m & f; (to throne)
pretendiente m

clairvoyant /kleəˈvɔɪənt/ n clarividente m & f

clam /klæm/ n almeja f

clamber /ˈklæmbə(r)/ vi trepar a
gatas

clammy /ˈklæmɪ/ a (-ier, -iest)
húmedo

clamour /ˈklæmə(r)/ n clamor
m. —vi. ~ **for** pedir a voces

clamp /klæmp/ n abrazadera f;
(auto) cepo m. —vt sujetar con
abrazadera. ~ **down on**
reprimir

clan /klæn/ n clan m

clandestine /klænˈdestɪn/ a
clandestino

clang /klæŋ/ n sonido m metálico

clanger /ˈklæŋə(r)/ n (sl) metedura f de pata

clap /klæp/ vt (pt clapped) aplaudir; batir (hands). —vi
aplaudir. —n palmada f; (of
thunder) trueno m

claptrap /ˈklæptræp/ n charlatanería f, tonterías fpl

claret /ˈklærət/ n clarete m

clarif|ication /klærɪfɪˈkeɪʃn/ n aclaración f. ~**y** /ˈklærɪfaɪ/ vt aclarar. —vi aclararse

clarinet /klærɪˈnet/ n clarinete m

clarity /ˈklærətɪ/ n claridad f

clash /klæʃ/ n choque m; (noise) estruendo m; (contrast) contraste m; (fig) conflicto m. —vt golpear. —vi encontrarse; (dates) coincidir; (opinions) estar en desacuerdo; (colours) desentonar

clasp /klɑːsp/ n cierre m. —vt agarrar; apretar ⟨hand⟩; (fasten) abrochar

class /klɑːs/ n clase f. **evening** ~ n clase nocturna. —vt clasificar

classic /ˈklæsɪk/ a & n clásico (m). ~**al** a clásico. ~**s** npl estudios mpl clásicos

classif|ication /klæsɪfɪˈkeɪʃn/ n clasificación f. ~**y** /ˈklæsɪfaɪ/ vt clasificar

classroom /ˈklɑːsruːm/ n aula f

classy /ˈklɑːsɪ/ a (sl) elegante

clatter /ˈklætə(r)/ n estrépito m. —vi hacer ruido

clause /klɔːz/ n cláusula f; (gram) oración f

claustrophobia /klɔːstrəˈfəʊbɪə/ n claustrofobia f

claw /klɔː/ n garra f; (of cat) uña f; (of crab) pinza f; (device) garfio m. —vt arañar

clay /kleɪ/ n arcilla f

clean /kliːn/ a (-er, -est) limpio; (stroke) neto. —adv completamente. —vt limpiar. —vi hacer la limpieza. ~ **up** hacer la limpieza. ~-**cut** a bien definido. ~**er** n mujer f de la limpieza. ~**liness** /ˈklenlɪnɪs/ n limpieza f

cleans|e /klenz/ vt limpiar; (fig) purificar. ~**ing cream** n crema f desmaquilladora

clear /klɪə(r)/ a (-er, -est) claro; (transparent) transparente; (without obstacles) libre; (profit) neto; (sky) despejado. **keep** ~ **of**

evitar. —adv claramente. —vt despejar; liquidar (goods); (jurid) absolver; (jump over) saltar por encima de; quitar (table). —vi (weather) despejarse; (fog) disolverse. ~ **off** vi (sl), ~ **out** vi (sl) largarse. ~ **up** vt (tidy) poner en orden; aclarar (mystery); —vi (weather) despejarse

clearance /ˈklɪərəns/ n espacio m libre; (removal of obstructions) despeje m; (authorization) permiso m; (by customs) despacho m; (by security) acreditación f. ~ **sale** n liquidación f

clearing /ˈklɪərɪŋ/ n claro m

clearly /ˈklɪəlɪ/ adv evidentemente

clearway /ˈklɪəweɪ/ n carretera f en la que no se permite parar

cleavage /ˈkliːvɪdʒ/ n escote m; (fig) división f

cleave /kliːv/ vt (pt **cleaved**, **clove** or **cleft**; pp **cloven** or **cleft**) hender. —vi henderse

clef /klef/ n (mus) clave f

cleft /kleft/ see **cleave**

clemen|cy /ˈklemənsɪ/ n clemencia f. ~**t** a clemente

clench /klentʃ/ vt apretar

clergy /ˈklɜːdʒɪ/ n clero m. ~**man** n (pl -**men**) clérigo m

cleric /ˈklerɪk/ n clérigo m. ~**al** a clerical; (of clerks) de oficina

clerk /klɑːk/ n empleado m; (jurid) escribano m

clever /ˈklevə(r)/ a (-er, -est) listo; (skilful) hábil. ~**ly** adv inteligentemente; (with skill) hábilmente. ~**ness** n inteligencia f

cliché /ˈkliːʃeɪ/ n tópico m, frase f hecha

click /klɪk/ n golpecito m. —vi chascar; (sl) llevarse bien

client /ˈklaɪənt/ n cliente m & f

clientele /kliːɒnˈtel/ n clientela f

cliff /klɪf/ n acantilado m

climate /'klaɪmɪt/ n clima m. **∼ic** /-'mætɪk/ a climático

climax /'klaɪmæks/ n punto m culminante

climb /klaɪm/ vt subir (stairs); trepar (tree); escalar (mountain). —vi subir. —n subida f. **∼ down** bajar; (fig) volverse atrás, rajarse. **∼er** n (sport) alpinista m & f; (plant) trepadora f

clinch /klɪntʃ/ vt cerrar (deal)

cling /klɪŋ/ vi (pt clung) agarrarse; (stick) pegarse

clinic /'klɪnɪk/ n clínica f. **∼al** /'klɪnɪkl/ a clínico

clink /klɪŋk/ n sonido m metálico. —vt hacer tintinear. —vi tintinear

clinker /'klɪŋkə(r)/ n escoria f

clip¹ /klɪp/ n (for paper) sujetapapeles m invar; (for hair) horquilla f. —vt (pt clipped) (join) sujetar

clip² /klɪp/ n (with scissors) tijeretada f; (blow, fam) golpe m. —vt (pt clipped) (cut) cortar; (fam) golpear. **∼pers** /'klɪpəz/ npl (for hair) maquinilla f para cortar el pelo; (for nails) cortaúñas m invar. **∼ping** n recorte m

clique /kliːk/ n pandilla f

cloak /kləʊk/ n capa f. **∼room** /'kləʊkruːm/ n guardarropa m; (toilet) servicios mpl

clobber /'klɒbə(r)/ n (sl) trastos mpl. —vt (sl) dar una paliza a

clock /klɒk/ n reloj m. **grandfather ∼** reloj de caja. —vi. **∼ in** fichar, registrar la llegada. **∼wise** /'klɒkwaɪz/ a & adv en el sentido de las agujas del reloj, a la derecha. **∼work** /'klɒkwɜːk/ n mecanismo m de relojería. **like ∼work** con precisión

clod /klɒd/ n terrón m

clog /klɒg/ n zueco m. —vt (pt clogged) atascar. —vi atascarse

cloister /'klɔɪstə(r)/ n claustro m

close¹ /kləʊs/ a (-er, -est) cercano; (together) apretado; (friend) íntimo; (weather) bochornoso; (link etc) estrecho; (game, battle) reñido. **have a ∼ shave** (fig) escaparse de milagro. —adv cerca. —n recinto m

close² /kləʊz/ vt cerrar. —vi cerrarse; (end) terminar. —n fin m. **∼d shop** n empresa f que emplea solamente a miembros del sindicato

close: **∼ly** adv de cerca; (with attention) atentamente; (exactly) exactamente. **∼ness** n proximidad f; (togetherness) intimidad f

closet /'klɒzɪt/ n (Amer) armario m

close-up /'kləʊsʌp/ n (cinema etc) primer plano m

closure /'kləʊʒə(r)/ n cierre m

clot /klɒt/ n (culin) grumo m; (med) coágulo m; (sl) tonto m. —vi (pt clotted) cuajarse

cloth /klɒθ/ n tela f; (duster) trapo m; (table-cloth) mantel m

clothe /kləʊð/ vt (pt clothed or clad) vestir. **∼es** /kləʊðz/ npl, **∼ing** n ropa f

cloud /klaʊd/ n nube f. —vi nublarse. **∼burst** /'klaʊdbɜːst/ n chaparrón m. **∼y** a (-ier, -iest) nublado; (liquid) turbio

clout /klaʊt/ n bofetada f. —vt abofetear

clove¹ /kləʊv/ n clavo m

clove² /kləʊv/ n. **∼ of garlic** n diente m de ajo

clove³ /kləʊv/ see **cleave**

clover /'kləʊvə(r)/ n trébol m

clown /klaʊn/ n payaso m. —vi hacer el payaso

cloy /klɔɪ/ vt empalagar

club /klʌb/ n club m; (weapon) porra f; (at cards) trébol m. —vt (pt clubbed) aporrear. —vi. **∼**

together reunirse, pagar a escote

cluck /klʌk/ *vi* cloquear

clue /kluː/ *n* pista *f*; (*in cross-words*) indicación *f*. **not to have a** ~ no tener la menor idea

clump /klʌmp/ *n* grupo *m*. —*vi* agrupar. —*vi* pisar fuertemente

clums|iness /ˈklʌmzɪnɪs/ *n* torpeza *f*. ~**y** /ˈklʌmzɪ/ *a* (**-ier, -iest**) torpe

clung /klʌŋ/ *see* **cling**

cluster /ˈklʌstə(r)/ *n* grupo *m*. —*vi* agruparse

clutch /klʌtʃ/ *vt* agarrar. —*n* (*auto*) embrague *m*

clutter /ˈklʌtə(r)/ *n* desorden *m*. —*vt* llenar desordenadamente

coach /kəʊtʃ/ *n* autocar *m*; (*of train*) vagón *m*; (*horse-drawn*) coche *m*; (*sport*) entrenador *m*. —*vt* dar clases particulares; (*sport*) entrenar

coagulate /kəʊˈægjʊleɪt/ *vt* coagular. —*vi* coagularse

coal /kəʊl/ *n* carbón *m*. ~**field** /ˈkəʊlfiːld/ *n* yacimiento *m* de carbón

coalition /kəʊəˈlɪʃn/ *n* coalición *f*

coarse /kɔːs/ *a* (**-er, -est**) grosero; (*material*) basto. ~**ness** *n* grosería *f*; (*texture*) basteza *f*

coast /kəʊst/ *n* costa *f*. —*vi* (*with cycle*) deslizarse cuesta abajo; (*with car*) ir en punto muerto. ~**al** *a* costero. ~**er** /ˈkəʊstə(r)/ *n* (*ship*) barco *m* de cabotaje; (*for glass*) posavasos *m* invar. ~**guard** /ˈkəʊstɡɑːd/ *n* guardacostas *m* invar. ~**line** /ˈkəʊstlaɪn/ *n* litoral *m*

coat /kəʊt/ *n* abrigo *m*; (*jacket*) chaqueta *f*; (*of animal*) pelo *m*; (*of paint*) mano *f*. —*vt* cubrir, revestir. ~**ing** *n* capa *f*. ~ **of arms** *n* escudo *m* de armas

coax /kəʊks/ *vt* engatusar

cob /kɒb/ *n* (*of corn*) mazorca *f*

cobble[1] /ˈkɒbl/ *n* guijarro *m*, adoquín *m*. —*vt* empedrar con guijarros, adoquinar

cobble[2] /ˈkɒbl/ *vt* (*mend*) remendar. ~**r** /ˈkɒblə(r)/ *n* (*old use*) remendón *m*

cobweb /ˈkɒbweb/ *n* telaraña *f*

cocaine /kəˈkeɪn/ *n* cocaína *f*

cock /kɒk/ *n* gallo *m*; (*mec*) grifo *m*; (*of gun*) martillo *m*. —*vt* amartillar (*gun*); aguzar (*ears*). ~**-and-bull story** *n* patraña *f*. ~**erel** /ˈkɒkərəl/ *n* gallo *m*. ~**-eyed** *a* (*sl*) torcido

cockle /ˈkɒkl/ *n* berberecho *m*

cockney /ˈkɒknɪ/ *a* & *n* (*pl* **-eys**) londinense (*m* & *f*) (del este de Londres)

cockpit /ˈkɒkpɪt/ *n* (*in aircraft*) cabina *f* del piloto

cockroach /ˈkɒkrəʊtʃ/ *n* cucaracha *f*

cocksure /kɒkˈʃʊə(r)/ *a* presuntuoso

cocktail /ˈkɒkteɪl/ *n* cóctel *m*. **fruit** ~ macedonia *f* de frutas

cock-up /ˈkɒkʌp/ *n* (*sl*) lío *m*

cocky /ˈkɒkɪ/ *a* (**-ier, -iest**) engreído

cocoa /ˈkəʊkəʊ/ *n* cacao *m*; (*drink*) chocolate *m*

coconut /ˈkəʊkənʌt/ *n* coco *m*

cocoon /kəˈkuːn/ *n* capullo *m*

cod /kɒd/ *n* (*pl* **cod**) bacalao *m*, abadejo *m*

coddle /ˈkɒdl/ *vt* mimar; (*culin*) cocer a fuego lento

code /kəʊd/ *n* código *m*; (*secret*) cifra *f*

codify /ˈkəʊdɪfaɪ/ *vt* codificar

cod-liver oil /ˈkɒdlɪvə(r)ɔɪl/ *n* aceite *m* de hígado de bacalao

coeducational /kəʊedʒʊˈkeɪʃənl/ *a* mixto

coerc|e /kəʊˈɜːs/ *vt* obligar. ~**ion** /-ʃn/ *n* coacción *f*

coexist /kəʊɪɡˈzɪst/ *vi* coexistir. ~**ence** *n* coexistencia *f*

coffee /'kɒfɪ/ n café m. ~-**mill** n molinillo m de café. ~-**pot** n cafetera f

coffer /'kɒfə(r)/ n cofre m

coffin /'kɒfɪn/ n ataúd m

cog /kɒg/ n diente m; (fig) pieza f

cogent /'kəʊdʒənt/ a convincente

cohabit /kəʊ'hæbɪt/ vi cohabitar

coherent /kəʊ'hɪərənt/ a coherente

coil /kɔɪl/ vt enrollar. —n rollo m; (one ring) vuelta f

coin /kɔɪn/ n moneda f. —vt acuñar. ~**age** n sistema m monetario

coincide /kəʊɪn'saɪd/ vi coincidir

coinciden|ce /kəʊ'ɪnsɪdəns/ n casualidad f. ~**tal** /-'dentl/ a casual; (coinciding) coincidente

coke /kəʊk/ n (coal) coque m

colander /'kʌləndə(r)/ n colador m

cold /kəʊld/ a (-er, -est) frío. be ~ tener frío. it is ~ hace frío. —n frío m; (med) resfriado m. **have a** ~ estar constipado. ~**-blooded** a insensible. ~**cream** n crema f. ~ **feet** (fig) miedītis f. ~**ness** n frialdad f. ~**-shoulder** vt tratar con frialdad. ~ **sore** n herpes m labial. ~ **storage** n conservación f en frigorífico

coleslaw /'kəʊlslɔː/ n ensalada f de col

colic /'kɒlɪk/ n cólico m

collaborat|e /kə'læbəreɪt/ vi colaborar. ~**ion** /-'reɪʃn/ n colaboración f. ~**or** n colaborador m

collage /kɒlɑːʒ/ n collage m

collaps|e /kə'læps/ vi derrumbarse; (med) sufrir un colapso. —n derrumbamiento m; (med) colapso m. ~**ible** /kə'læpsəbl/ a plegable

collar /'kɒlə(r)/ n cuello m; (for animals) collar m. —vt (fam) hurtar. ~**-bone** n clavícula f

colleague /'kɒliːg/ n colega m & f

collect /kə'lekt/ vt reunir; (hobby) coleccionar; (pick up) recoger; recaudar (rent). —vi (people) reunirse; (things) acumularse. ~**ed** /kə'lektɪd/ a reunido; (person) tranquilo. ~**ion** /-ʃn/ n colección f; (in church) colecta f; (of post) recogida f. ~**ive** /kə'lektɪv/ a colectivo. ~**or** n coleccionista m & f; (of taxes) recaudador m

college /'kɒlɪdʒ/ n colegio m; (of art, music etc) escuela f; (univ) colegio m mayor

collide /kə'laɪd/ vi chocar

colliery /'kɒlɪərɪ/ n mina f de carbón

collision /kə'lɪʒn/ n choque m

colloquial /kə'ləʊkwɪəl/ a familiar. ~**ism** n expresión f familiar

collusion /kə'luːʒn/ n connivencia f

colon /'kəʊlən/ n (gram) dos puntos mpl; (med) colon m

colonel /'kɜːnl/ n coronel m

colon|ial /kə'ləʊnɪəl/ a colonial. ~**ize** /'kɒlənaɪz/ vt colonizar. ~**y** /'kɒlənɪ/ n colonia f

colossal /kə'lɒsl/ a colosal

colour /'kʌlə(r)/ n color m. off ~ (fig) indispuesto. —a de color(es), en color(es). —vt colorar; (dye) teñir. —vi (blush) sonrojarse. ~ **bar** n barrera f racial. ~**-blind** a daltoniano. ~**ed** /'kʌləd/ a de color. ~**ful** a lleno de color; (fig) pintoresco. ~**less** a incoloro. ~**s** npl (flag) bandera f

colt /kəʊlt/ n potro m

column /'kɒləm/ n columna f. ~**ist** /'kɒləmnɪst/ n columnista m & f

coma /'kəʊmə/ n coma m

comb /kəʊm/ n peine m —vt peinar; (search) registrar

combat /'kɒmbæt/ n combate m. —vt (pt **combated**) combatir.

~ant /-ətənt/ n combatiente m & f

combination /kɒmbɪˈneɪʃn/ n combinación f

combine /kəmˈbaɪn/ vt combinar. —vi combinarse. /ˈkɒmbaɪn/ n asociación f. ~ **harvester** n cosechadora f

combustion /kəmˈbʌstʃən/ n combustión f

come /kʌm/ vi (pt **came**, pp **come**) venir; (occur) pasar. ~ **about** ocurrir. ~ **across** encontrarse con (person); encontrar (object). ~ **apart** deshacerse. ~ **away** marcharse. ~ **back** volver. ~ **by** obtener; (pass) pasar. ~ **down** bajar. ~ **in** entrar. ~ **in for** recibir. ~ **into** heredar (money). ~ **off** desprenderse; (succeed) tener éxito. ~ **off it!** (fam) ¡no me vengas con eso! ~ **out** salir; (result) resultar. ~ **round** (after fainting) volver en sí; (be converted) cambiar de idea. ~ **to** llegar a (decision etc). ~ **up** subir; (fig) salir. ~ **up with** proponer (idea)

comeback /ˈkʌmbæk/ n retorno m; (retort) réplica f

comedian /kəˈmiːdɪən/ n cómico m

comedown /ˈkʌmdaʊn/ n revés m

comedy /ˈkɒmədɪ/ n comedia f

comely /ˈkʌmlɪ/ a (-ier, -iest) (old use) bonito

comet /ˈkɒmɪt/ n cometa m

comeuppance /kʌmˈʌpəns/ n (Amer) merecido m

comfort /ˈkʌmfət/ n bienestar m; (consolation) consuelo m. —vt consolar. **~ortable** a cómodo; (wealthy) holgado. **~y** /ˈkʌmfɪ/ a (fam) cómodo

comic /ˈkɒmɪk/ a cómico. —n cómico m; (periodical) tebeo m. **~al** a cómico. ~ **strip** n historieta f

coming /ˈkʌmɪŋ/ n llegada f. —a próximo; (week, month etc) que viene. ~ **and going** ir y venir

comma /ˈkɒmə/ n coma f

command /kəˈmɑːnd/ n orden f; (mastery) dominio m. —vt mandar; (deserve) merecer

commandeer /kɒmənˈdɪə(r)/ vt requisar

commander /kəˈmɑːndə(r)/ n comandante m

commanding /kəˈmɑːndɪŋ/ a imponente

commandment /kəˈmɑːndmənt/ n mandamiento m

commando /kəˈmɑːndəʊ/ n (pl -os) comando m

commemorat|e /kəˈmeməreɪt/ vt conmemorar. **~ion** /-ˈreɪʃn/ n conmemoración f. **~ive** /-ətɪv/ a conmemorativo

commence /kəˈmens/ vt/i empezar. **~ment** n principio m

commend /kəˈmend/ vt alabar; (entrust) encomendar. **~able** a loable. **~ation** /kɒmenˈdeɪʃn/ n elogio m

commensurate /kəˈmenʃərət/ a proporcionado

comment /ˈkɒment/ n observación f. —vi hacer observaciones

commentary /ˈkɒməntrɪ/ n comentario m; (radio, TV) reportaje m

commentat|e /ˈkɒmənteɪt/ vi narrar. **~or** n (radio, TV) locutor m

commerc|e /ˈkɒmɜːs/ n comercio m. **~ial** /kəˈmɜːʃl/ a comercial. —n anuncio m. **~ialize** vt comercializar

commiserat|e /kəˈmɪzəreɪt/ vt compadecer. —vi compadecerse (with de). **~ion** /-ˈreɪʃn/ n conmiseración f

commission /kəˈmɪʃn/ n comisión f. out of ~ fuera de servicio. —vt encargar; (mil) nombrar

commissionaire /kəmɪʃəˈneə(r)/ n portero m

commissioner /kəˈmɪʃənə(r)/ n comisario m; (of police) jefe m

commit /kəˈmɪt/ vt (pt committed) cometer; (entrust) confiar. ~ o.s. comprometerse. ~ to memory aprender de memoria. ~ment n compromiso m

committee /kəˈmɪtɪ/ n comité m

commodity /kəˈmɒdətɪ/ n producto m, artículo m

common /ˈkɒmən/ a (-er, -est) común; (usual) corriente; (vulgar) ordinario. —n ejido m

commoner /ˈkɒmənə(r)/ n plebeyo m

common. ~ **law** n derecho m consuetudinario. ~**ly** adv comúnmente. **C~ Market** n Mercado m Común

commonplace /ˈkɒmənpleɪs/ a banal. —n banalidad f

common. ~**-room** n sala f común, salón m común. ~ **sense** n sentido m común

Commonwealth /ˈkɒmənwelθ/ n. **the** ~ la Mancomunidad f Británica

commotion /kəˈməʊʃn/ n confusión f

communal /ˈkɒmjʊnl/ a comunal

commune[1] /ˈkɒmjuːn/ n comuna f

commune[2] /kəˈmjuːn/ vi comunicarse

communicat|e /kəˈmjuːnɪkeɪt/ vt comunicar. —vi comunicarse. ~**ion** /-ˈkeɪʃn/ n comunicación f. ~**ive** /-ətɪv/ a comunicativo

communion /kəˈmjuːnɪən/ n comunión f

communiqué /kəˈmjuːnɪkeɪ/ n comunicado m

communis|m /ˈkɒmjʊnɪsəm/ n comunismo m. ~**t** /ˈkɒmjʊnɪst/ n comunista m & f

community /kəˈmjuːnətɪ/ n comunidad f. ~ **centre** n centro m social

commute /kəˈmjuːt/ vi viajar diariamente. —vt (jurid) conmutar. ~**r** /-ə(r)/ n viajero m diario

compact /kəmˈpækt/ a compacto. /ˈkɒmpækt/ n (for powder) polvera f. ~ **disc** /ˈkɒm-/ n disco m compacto

companion /kəmˈpænɪən/ n compañero m. ~**ship** n compañerismo m

company /ˈkʌmpənɪ/ n compañía f; (guests, fam) visita f; (com) sociedad f

compar|able /ˈkɒmpərəbl/ a comparable. ~**ative** /kəmˈpærətɪv/ a comparativo; (fig) relativo. —n (gram) comparativo m. ~**e** /kəmˈpeə(r)/ vt comparar. —vi poderse comparar. ~**ison** /kəmˈpærɪsn/ n comparación f

compartment /kəmˈpɑːtmənt/ n compartimiento m; (on train) departamento m

compass /ˈkʌmpəs/ n brújula f. ~**es** npl compás m

compassion /kəmˈpæʃn/ n compasión f. ~**ate** a compasivo

compatib|ility /kəmpætəˈbɪlətɪ/ n compatibilidad f. ~**le** /kəmˈpætəbl/ a compatible

compatriot /kəmˈpætrɪət/ n compatriota m & f

compel /kəmˈpel/ vt (pt compelled) obligar. ~**ling** a irresistible

compendium /kəmˈpendɪəm/ n compendio m

compensat|e /ˈkɒmpənseɪt/ vt compensar; (for loss) indemnizar. —vi compensar. ~**ion** /-ˈseɪʃn/ n compensación f; (financial) indemnización f

compère /ˈkɒmpeə(r)/ n presentador m. —vt presentar

compete /kəm'piːt/ *vi* competir

competen|ce /'kɒmpətəns/ *n* competencia *f*, aptitud *f*. ~t /'kɒmpɪtənt/ *a* competente, capaz

competition /kɒmpə'tɪʃn/ *n* (*contest*) concurso *m*; (*com*) competencia *f*. ~ive /kəm'petɪtɪv/ *a* competidor; (*price*) competitivo. ~or /kəm'petɪtə(r)/ *n* competidor *m*; (*in contest*) concursante *m & f*

compile /kəm'paɪl/ *vt* compilar. ~r /-ə(r)/ *n* recopilador *m*, compilador *m*

complacen|cy /kəm'pleɪsnsɪ/ *n* satisfacción *f* de sí mismo. ~t /kəm'pleɪsnt/ *a* satisfecho de sí mismo

complain /kəm'pleɪn/ *vi*. ~ (**about**) quejarse (de). ~ **of** (*med*) sufrir de. ~t /kəm'pleɪnt/ *n* queja *f*; (*med*) enfermedad *f*

complement /'kɒmplɪmənt/ *n* complemento *m*. —*vt* complementar. ~ary /-'mentrɪ/ *a* complementario

complet|e /kəm'pliːt/ *a* completo; (*finished*) acabado; (*downright*) total. —*vt* acabar; llenar ⟨*a form*⟩. ~ely *adv* completamente. ~ion /-ʃn/ *n* conclusión *f*

complex /'kɒmpleks/ *a* complejo. —*n* complejo *m*

complexion /kəm'plekʃn/ *n* tez *f*; (*fig*) aspecto *m*

complexity /kəm'pleksətɪ/ *n* complejidad *f*

complian|ce /kəm'plaɪəns/ *n* sumisión *f*. **in** ~**ce with** de acuerdo con. ~t *a* sumiso

complicat|e /'kɒmplɪkeɪt/ *vt* complicar. ~ed *a* complicado. ~ion /-'keɪʃn/ *n* complicación *f*

complicity /kəm'plɪsətɪ/ *n* complicidad *f*

compliment /'kɒmplɪmənt/ *n* cumplido *m*; (*amorous*) piropo *m*. —*vt* felicitar. ~ary /-'mentrɪ/ *a* halagador; (*given free*) de favor. ~s *npl* saludos *mpl*

comply /kəm'plaɪ/ *vi*. ~ **with** conformarse con

component /kəm'pəʊnənt/ *a & n* componente (*m*)

compose /kəm'pəʊz/ *vt* componer. ~ **o.s.** tranquilizarse. ~**d** *a* sereno

compos|er /kəm'pəʊzə(r)/ *n* compositor *m*. ~**ition** /kɒmpə'zɪʃn/ *n* composición *f*

compost /'kɒmpɒst/ *n* abono *m*

composure /kəm'pəʊʒə(r)/ *n* serenidad *f*

compound[1] /'kɒmpaʊnd/ *n* compuesto *m*. —*a* compuesto; (*fracture*) complicado. /kəm'paʊnd/ *vt* componer; agravar ⟨*problem etc*⟩. —*vi* (*settle*) arreglarse

compound[2] /'kɒmpaʊnd/ *n* (*enclosure*) recinto *m*

comprehen|d /kɒmprɪ'hend/ *vt* comprender. ~**sion** /kɒmprɪ'henʃn/ *n* comprensión *f*

comprehensive /kɒmprɪ'hensɪv/ *a* extenso; (*insurance*) a todo riesgo. ~ **school** *n* instituto *m*

compress /'kɒmpres/ *n* (*med*) compresa *f*. /kəm'pres/ *vt* comprimir; (*fig*) condensar. ~**ion** /-ʃn/ *n* compresión *f*

comprise /kəm'praɪz/ *vt* comprender

compromise /'kɒmprəmaɪz/ *n* acuerdo *m*, acomodo *m*, arreglo *m*. —*vt* comprometer. —*vi* llegar a un acuerdo

compuls|ion /kəm'pʌlʃn/ *n* obligación *f*, impulso *m*. ~**ive** /kəm'pʌlsɪv/ *a* compulsivo. ~**ory** /kəm'pʌlsərɪ/ *a* obligatorio

compunction /kəm'pʌŋkʃn/ *n* remordimiento *m*

computer /kəm'pju:tə(r)/ n ordenador m. **~ize** vt instalar ordenadores en. **be ~ized** tener ordenador

comrade /'kɒmreɪd/ n camarada m & f. **~ship** n camaradería f

con[1] /kɒn/ vt (pt **conned**) (fam) estafar. —n (fam) estafa f

con[2] /kɒn/ see **pro and con**

concave /'kɒŋkeɪv/ a cóncavo

conceal /kən'si:l/ vt ocultar. **~ment** n encubrimiento m

concede /kən'si:d/ vt conceder

conceit /kən'si:t/ n vanidad f. **~ed** a engreído

conceiv|able /kən'si:vəbl/ a concebible. **~ably** adv. **may ~ably** es concebible que. **~e** /kən'si:v/ vt/i concebir

concentrat|e /'kɒnsəntreɪt/ vt concentrar. —vi concentrarse. **~ion** /-'treɪʃn/ n concentración f. **~ion camp** n campo m de concentración

concept /'kɒnsept/ n concepto m

conception /kən'sepʃn/ n concepción f

conceptual /kən'septʃʊəl/ a conceptual

concern /kən'sɜ:n/ n asunto m; (worry) preocupación f; (com) empresa f. —vt tener que ver con; (deal with) tratar de. **as far as I'm ~ed** en cuanto a mí. **be ~ed about** preocuparse por. **~ing** prep acerca de

concert /'kɒnsət/ n concierto m. **in ~** de común acuerdo. **~ed** /kən'sɜ:tɪd/ a concertado

concertina /kɒnsə'ti:nə/ n concertina f

concerto /kən'tʃɜ:təʊ/ n (pl -os) concierto m

concession /kən'seʃn/ n concesión f

conciliat|e /kən'sɪlɪeɪt/ vt conciliar. **~ion** /-'eɪʃn/ n conciliación f

concise /kən'saɪs/ a conciso. **~ly** adv concisamente. **~ness** n concisión f

conclu|de /kən'klu:d/ vt concluir. —vi concluirse. **~ding** a final. **~sion** n conclusión f

conclusive /kən'klu:sɪv/ a decisivo. **~ly** adv concluyentemente

concoct /kən'kɒkt/ vt confeccionar; (fig) inventar. **~ion** /-ʃn/ n mezcla f; (drink) brebaje m

concourse /'kɒŋkɔ:s/ n (rail) vestíbulo m

concrete /'kɒŋkri:t/ n hormigón m. —a concreto. —vt cubrir con hormigón

concur /kən'kɜ:(r)/ vi (pt concurred) estar de acuerdo

concussion /kən'kʌʃn/ n conmoción f cerebral

condemn /kən'dem/ vt condenar. **~ation** /kɒndem'neɪʃn/ n condenación f, condena f; (censure) censura f

condens|ation /kɒnden'seɪʃn/ n condensación f. **~e** /kən'dens/ vt condensar. —vi condensarse

condescend /kɒndɪ'send/ vi dignarse (**to** a). **~ing** a superior

condiment /'kɒndɪmənt/ n condimento m

condition /kən'dɪʃn/ n condición f. **on ~ that** a condición de que. —vt condicionar. **~al** a condicional. **~er** n acondicionador m; (for hair) suavizante m

condolences /kən'dəʊlənsɪz/ npl pésame m

condom /'kɒndəm/ n condón m

condone /kən'dəʊn/ vt condonar

conducive /kən'dju:sɪv/ a. **be ~** to ser favorable a

conduct /kən'dʌkt/ vt conducir; dirigir ⟨orchestra⟩. /'kɒndʌkt/ n conducta f. **~or** /kən'dʌktə(r)/ n director m; (of bus) cobrador m. **~ress** n cobradora f

cone /kəʊn/ n cono m; (*for ice-cream*) cucurucho m

confectioner /kənˈfekʃənə(r)/ n pastelero m. **~y** n dulces mpl, golosinas fpl

confederation /kənfedəˈreɪʃn/ n confederación f

confer /kənˈfɜː(r)/ vt (pt **conferred**) conferir. —vi consultar

conference /ˈkɒnfərəns/ n congreso m

confess /kənˈfes/ vt confesar. — vi confesarse. **~ion** /-ʃn/ n confesión f. **~ional** n confes(i)onario m. **~or** n confesor m

confetti /kənˈfetɪ/ n confeti m, confetis mpl

confide /kənˈfaɪd/ vt/i confiar

confiden|ce /ˈkɒnfɪdəns/ n confianza f; (*secret*) confidencia f. **~ce trick** n estafa f, timo m. **~t** /ˈkɒnfɪdənt/ a seguro

confidential /kɒnfɪˈdenʃl/ a confidencial

confine /kənˈfaɪn/ vt confinar; (*limit*) limitar. **~ment** n (*imprisonment*) prisión f; (*med*) parto m

confines /ˈkɒnfaɪnz/ npl confines mpl

confirm /kənˈfɜːm/ vt confirmar. **~ation** /kɒnfəˈmeɪʃn/ n confirmación f. **~ed** a inveterado

confiscat|e /ˈkɒnfɪskeɪt/ vt confiscar. **~ion** /-ˈkeɪʃn/ n confiscación f

conflagration /kɒnfləˈgreɪʃn/ n conflagración f

conflict /ˈkɒnflɪkt/ n conflicto m. /kənˈflɪkt/ vi chocar. **~ing** /kən-/ a contradictorio

conform /kənˈfɔːm/ vt conformar. —vi conformarse. **~ist** n conformista m & f

confound /kənˈfaʊnd/ vt confundir. **~ed** a (*fam*) maldito

confront /kənˈfrʌnt/ vt hacer frente a; (*face*) enfrentarse con.

~ation /kɒnfrʌnˈteɪʃn/ n confrontación f

confus|e /kənˈfjuːz/ vt confundir. **~ing** a desconcertante. **~ion** /-ʒn/ n confusión f

congeal /kənˈdʒiːl/ vt coagular. —vi coagularse

congenial /kənˈdʒiːnɪəl/ a simpático

congenital /kənˈdʒenɪtl/ a congénito

congest|ed /kənˈdʒestɪd/ a congestionado. **~ion** /-tʃən/ n congestión f

congratulat|e /kənˈgrætjʊleɪt/ vt felicitar. **~ions** /-ˈleɪʃnz/ npl felicitaciones fpl

congregat|e /ˈkɒngrɪgeɪt/ vi congregarse. **~ion** /-ˈgeɪʃn/ n asamblea f; (*relig*) fieles mpl, feligreses mpl

congress /ˈkɒngres/ n congreso m. **C~** (*Amer*) el Congreso

conic(al) /ˈkɒnɪk(l)/ a cónico

conifer /ˈkɒnɪfə(r)/ n conífera f

conjecture /kənˈdʒektʃə(r)/ n conjetura f. —vt conjeturar. —vi hacer conjeturas

conjugal /ˈkɒndʒʊgl/ a conyugal

conjugat|e /ˈkɒndʒʊgeɪt/ vt conjugar. **~ion** /-ˈgeɪʃn/ n conjugación f

conjunction /kənˈdʒʌŋkʃn/ n conjunción f

conjur|e /ˈkʌndʒə(r)/ vi hacer juegos de manos. —vt. **~ up** evocar. **~or** n prestidigitador m

conk /kɒŋk/ vi. **~ out** (*sl*) fallar; (*person*) desmayarse

conker /ˈkɒŋkə(r)/ n (*fam*) castaña f de Indias

conman /ˈkɒnmæn/ n (*fam*) estafador m, timador m

connect /kəˈnekt/ vt juntar; (*elec*) conectar. —vi unirse; (*elec*) conectarse. **~ with** (*train*) enlazar con. **~ed** a unido; (*related*) relacionado. **be ~ed with** tener que ver con, estar emparentado con

connection /kə'nekʃn/ n unión f; (rail) enlace m; (elec, mec) conexión f; (fig) relación f. **in ~ with** a propósito de, con respecto a. **~s** npl relaciones fpl

conniv|ance /kə'naɪvəns/ n connivencia f. **~e** /kə'naɪv/ vi. **~e at** hacer la vista gorda a

connoisseur /kɒnə'sɜː(r)/ n experto m

connot|ation /kɒnə'teɪʃn/ n connotación f. **~e** /kə'nəʊt/ vt connotar; (imply) implicar

conquer /'kɒŋkə(r)/ vt conquistar; (fig) vencer. **~or** n conquistador m

conquest /'kɒŋkwest/ n conquista f

conscience /'kɒnʃəns/ n conciencia f

conscientious /kɒnʃɪ'enʃəs/ a concienzudo

conscious /'kɒnʃəs/ a consciente; (deliberate) intencional. **~ly** adv a sabiendas. **~ness** n consciencia f; (med) conocimiento m

conscript /'kɒnskrɪpt/ n recluta m. /kən'skrɪpt/ vt reclutar. **~ion** /kən'skrɪpʃn/ n reclutamiento m

consecrat|e /'kɒnsɪkreɪt/ vt consagrar. **~ion** /-'kreɪʃn/ n consagración f

consecutive /kən'sekjʊtɪv/ a sucesivo

consensus /kən'sensəs/ n consenso m

consent /kən'sent/ vi consentir. **~n** consentimiento m

consequen|ce /'kɒnsɪkwəns/ n consecuencia f. **~t** /'kɒnsɪkwənt/ a consiguiente. **~tly** adv por consiguiente

conservation /kɒnsə'veɪʃn/ n conservación f, preservación f. **~ist** /kɒnsə'veɪʃənɪst/ n conservacionista m & f

conservative /kən'sɜːvətɪv/ a conservador; (modest) prudente,

moderado. **C~** /kən's3ːvətɪv/ a & n conservador (m)

conservatory /kən'sɜːvətrɪ/ n (greenhouse) invernadero m

conserve /kən'sɜːv/ vt conservar

consider /kən'sɪdə(r)/ vt considerar; (take into account) tomar en cuenta. **~able** /kən'sɪdərəbl/ a considerable. **~ably** adv considerablemente

considerate /kən'sɪdərət/ a considerado. **~ion** /-'reɪʃn/ n consideración f

considering /kən'sɪdərɪŋ/ prep en vista de

consign /kən'saɪn/ vt consignar; (send) enviar. **~ment** n envío m

consist /kən'sɪst/ vi. **~ of** consistir en

consistency /kən'sɪstənsɪ/ n consistencia f; (fig) coherencia f

consistent /kən'sɪstənt/ a coherente; (unchanging) constante. **~ with** compatible con. **~ly** adv constantemente

consolation /kɒnsə'leɪʃn/ n consuelo m

console /kən'səʊl/ vt consolar

consolidat|e /kən'sɒlɪdeɪt/ vt consolidar. *—vi* consolidarse. **~ion** /-'deɪʃn/ n consolidación f

consonant /'kɒnsənənt/ n consonante f

consort /'kɒnsɔːt/ n consorte m & f. /kən'sɔːt/ vi. **~ with** asociarse con

consortium /kən'sɔːtɪəm/ n (pl **-tia**) consorcio m

conspicuous /kən'spɪkjʊəs/ a (easily seen) visible; (showy) llamativo; (noteworthy) notable

conspir|acy /kən'spɪrəsɪ/ n complot m, conspiración f. **~e** /kən'spaɪə(r)/ vi conspirar

constable /'kʌnstəbl/ n policía m, guardia m. **~ulary** /kən'stæbjʊlərɪ/ n policía f

constant /'kɒnstənt/ a constante. **~ly** adv constantemente

constellation /kɒnstəˈleɪʃn/ n
constelación f

consternation /kɒnstəˈneɪʃn/ n
consternación f

constipat|ed /ˈkɒnstɪpeɪtɪd/ a
estreñido. **~ion** /-ˈpeɪʃn/ n
estreñimiento m

constituen|cy /kənˈstɪtjʊənsɪ/ n
distrito m electoral. **~t**
/kənˈstɪtjʊənt/ n componente m;
(pol) elector m

constitut|e /ˈkɒnstɪtjuːt/ vt con-
stituir. **~ion** /-ˈtjuːʃn/ n constitución f. **~ional** /-ˈtjuːʃənl/ a
constitucional. —n paseo m

constrain /kənˈstreɪn/ vt forzar,
obligar, constreñir. **~t**
/kənˈstreɪnt/ n fuerza f

constrict /kənˈstrɪkt/ vt apretar.
~ion /-ʃn/ n constricción f

construct /kənˈstrʌkt/ vt construir. **~ion** /-ʃn/ n construcción f. **~ive** /kənˈstrʌktɪv/
a constructivo

construe /kənˈstruː/ vt interpretar; (gram) construir

consul /ˈkɒnsl/ n cónsul m. **~ar**
/-jʊlə(r)/ a consular. **~ate** /-ət/ n
consulado m

consult /kənˈsʌlt/ vt/i consultar.
~ant /kənˈsʌltənt/ n asesor m;
(med) especialista m & f; (tec)
consejero m técnico. **~ation**
/kɒnsəlˈteɪʃn/ n consulta f

consume /kənˈsjuːm/ vt consumir; (eat) comer; (drink)
beber. **~r** /-ə(r)/ n consumidor
m. —a de consumo. **~rism**
/kənˈsjuːmərɪzəm/ n protección f
del consumidor, consumismo m

consummat|e /ˈkɒnsəmeɪt/ vt
consumar. **~ion** /-ˈmeɪʃn/ n con-
sumación f

consumption /kənˈsʌmpʃn/ n
consumo m; (med) tisis f

contact /ˈkɒntækt/ n contacto
m. —vt ponerse en contacto con

contagious /kənˈteɪdʒəs/ a
contagioso

contain /kənˈteɪn/ vt contener. **~**
o.s. contenerse. **~er** n recipiente m; (com) contenedor m

contaminat|e /kənˈtæmɪneɪt/ vt
contaminar. **~ion** /-ˈneɪʃn/ n
contaminación f

contemplat|e /ˈkɒntəmpleɪt/ vt
contemplar; (consider) considerar. **~ion** /-ˈpleɪʃn/ n contem-
plación f

contemporary /kənˈtempərərɪ/
a & n contemporáneo (m)

contempt /kənˈtempt/ n desprecio m. **~ible** a despreciable.
~uous /-tjʊəs/ a desdeñoso

contend /kənˈtend/ vt sostener. —vi contender. **~er** n
contendiente m & f

content[1] /kənˈtent/ a satisfecho. —vt contentar

content[2] /ˈkɒntent/ n contenido
m

contented /kənˈtentɪd/ a satisfecho

contention /kənˈtenʃn/ n contienda f; (opinion) opinión f,
argumento m

contentment /kənˈtentmənt/ n
contento m

contest /ˈkɒntest/ n (competition)
concurso m; (fight) contienda f.
/kənˈtest/ vt disputar. **~ant** n
contendiente m & f, concursante
m & f

context /ˈkɒntekst/ n contexto m

continent /ˈkɒntɪnənt/ n continente m. **the C~** Europa f. **~al**
/-ˈnentl/ a continental

contingency /kənˈtɪndʒənsɪ/ n
contingencia f

contingent /kənˈtɪndʒənt/ a & n
contingente (m)

continu|al /kənˈtɪnjʊəl/ a
continuo. **~ance** /kənˈtɪnjʊəns/
n continuación f. **~ation**
/-ʊˈeɪʃn/ n continuación f. **~e**
/kənˈtɪnjuː/ vt/i continuar;
(resume) seguir. **~ed** a
continuo. **~ity** /kɒntɪˈnjuːətɪ/ n

continuidad f. **~ity girl** (*cinema*, *TV*) secretaria f de rodaje. **~ous** /kən'tɪnjʊəs/ a continuo. **~ously** adv continuamente

contort /kən'tɔːt/ vt retorcer. **~ion** /-ʃn/ n contorsión f. **~ionist** /-ʃənɪst/ n contorsionista m & f

contour /'kɒntʊə(r)/ n contorno m. **~ line** n curva f de nivel

contraband /'kɒntrəbænd/ n contrabando m

contraception /kɒntrə'sepʃn/ n contracepción f. **~ve** /kɒntrə'septɪv/ a & n anticonceptivo m

contract /'kɒntrækt/ n contrato m. /kən'trækt/ vt contraer. —vi contraerse. **~ion** /kən'trækʃn/ n contracción f. **~or** /kən'træktə(r)/ n contratista m & f

contradict /kɒntrə'dɪkt/ vt contradecir. **~ion** /-ʃn/ n contradicción f. **~ory** a contradictorio

contraption /kən'træpʃn/ n (*fam*) artilugio m

contrary /'kɒntrərɪ/ a & n contrario (m). **on the ~** al contrario. —adv. **~ to** contrariamente a. /kən'treərɪ/ a terco

contrast /'kɒntrɑːst/ n contraste m. /kən'trɑːst/ vt poner en contraste. —vi contrastar. **~ing** a contrastante

contraven|e /kɒntrə'viːn/ vt contravenir. **~tion** /-'venʃn/ n contravención f

contribut|e /kən'trɪbjuːt/ vt/i contribuir. **~e to** escribir para 〈*newspaper*〉. **~ion** /kɒntrɪ'bjuːʃn/ n contribución f; (*from salary*) cotización f. **~or** n contribuyente m & f; (*to newspaper*) colaborador m

contrite /'kɒntraɪt/ a arrepentido, pesaroso

contriv|ance /kən'traɪvəns/ n invención f. **~e** /kən'traɪv/ vt idear. **~e to** conseguir

control /kən'trəʊl/ vt (*pt* controlled) controlar. —n control m. **~s** npl (*mec*) mandos mpl

controvers|ial /kɒntrə'vɜːʃl/ a polémico, discutible. **~y** /'kɒntrəvɜːsɪ/ n controversia f

conundrum /kə'nʌndrəm/ n adivinanza f; (*problem*) enigma m

conurbation /kɒnɜː'beɪʃn/ n conurbación f

convalesce /kɒnvə'les/ vi convalecer. **~nce** n convalecencia f. **~nt** a & n convaleciente (m & f). **~nt home** n casa f de convalecencia

convector /kən'vektə(r)/ n estufa f de convección

convene /kən'viːn/ vt convocar. —vi reunirse

convenien|ce /kən'viːnɪəns/ n conveniencia f, comodidad f. **all modern ~ces** todas las comodidades. **at your ~ce** según le convenga. **~ces** npl servicios mpl. **~t** /kən'viːnɪənt/ a cómodo; 〈*place*〉 bien situado; 〈*time*〉 oportuno. **be ~t** convenir. **~tly** adv convenientemente

convent /'kɒnvənt/ n convento m

convention /kən'venʃn/ n convención f; (*meeting*) congreso m. **~al** a convencional

converge /kən'vɜːdʒ/ vi convergir

conversant /kən'vɜːsənt/ a. **~ with** versado en

conversation /kɒnvə'seɪʃn/ n conversación f. **~al** a de la conversación. **~alist** n hábil conversador m

converse[1] /kən'vɜːs/ vi conversar

converse[2] /'kɒnvɜːs/ a inverso. —n lo contrario. **~ly** adv a la inversa

conver|sion /kən'vɜːʃn/ n conversión f. **~t** /kən'vɜːt/ vt convertir. /'kɒnvɜːt/ n converso m.

~tible /kən'vɜːtɪbl/ a convertible. —n (auto) descapotable m

convex /'kɒnveks/ a convexo

convey /kən'veɪ/ vt llevar; transportar ⟨goods⟩; comunicar ⟨idea, feeling⟩. ~ance n transporte m. ~or belt n cinta f transportadora

convict /kən'vɪkt/ vt condenar. /'kɒnvɪkt/ n presidiario m. ~ion /kən'vɪkʃn/ n condena f; ⟨belief⟩ creencia f

convinc|e /kən'vɪns/ vt convencer. ~ing a convincente

convivial /kən'vɪvɪəl/ a alegre

convoke /kən'vəʊk/ vt convocar

convoluted /'kɒnvəluːtɪd/ a enrollado; ⟨argument⟩ complicado

convoy /'kɒnvɔɪ/ n convoy m

convuls|e /kən'vʌls/ vt convulsionar. be ~ed with laughter desternillarse de risa. ~ion /-ʃn/ n convulsión f

coo /kuː/ vi arrullar

cook /kʊk/ vt cocinar; ⟨alter, fam⟩ falsificar. ~ up ⟨fam⟩ inventar. —n cocinero m

cooker /'kʊkə(r)/ n cocina f

cookery /'kʊkərɪ/ n cocina f

cookie /'kʊkɪ/ n ⟨Amer⟩ galleta f

cool /kuːl/ a (-er, -est) fresco; ⟨calm⟩ tranquilo; ⟨unfriendly⟩ frío. —n fresco m; ⟨sl⟩ calma f. —vt enfriar. —vi enfriarse. ~ down ⟨person⟩ calmarse. ~ly adv tranquilamente. ~ness n frescura f

coop /kuːp/ n gallinero m. —vt. ~ up encerrar

co-operat|e /kəʊ'ɒpəreɪt/ vi cooperar. ~ion /-'reɪʃn/ n cooperación f

cooperative /kəʊ'ɒpərətɪv/ a cooperativo. —n cooperativa f

co-opt /kəʊ'ɒpt/ vt cooptar

co-ordinat|e /kəʊ'ɔːdɪneɪt/ vt coordinar. ~ion /-'neɪʃn/ n coordinación f

cop /kɒp/ vt (pt copped) ⟨sl⟩ prender. —n ⟨sl⟩ policía m

cope /kəʊp/ vi ⟨fam⟩ arreglárselas. ~ with enfrentarse con

copious /'kəʊpɪəs/ a abundante

copper¹ /'kɒpə(r)/ n cobre m; ⟨coin⟩ perra f. —a de cobre

copper² /'kɒpə(r)/ n ⟨sl⟩ policía m

coppice /'kɒpɪs/ n, copse /kɒps/ n bosquecillo m

Coptic /'kɒptɪk/ a copto

copulat|e /'kɒpjʊleɪt/ vi copular. ~ion /-'leɪʃn/ n cópula f

copy /'kɒpɪ/ n copia f; ⟨typ⟩ material m. —vt copiar

copyright /'kɒpɪraɪt/ n derechos mpl de autor

copy-writer /'kɒpɪraɪtə(r)/ n redactor m de textos publicitarios

coral /'kɒrəl/ n coral m

cord /kɔːd/ n cuerda f; ⟨fabric⟩ pana f. ~s npl pantalones mpl de pana

cordial /'kɔːdɪəl/ a & n cordial ⟨m⟩

cordon /'kɔːdn/ n cordón m. —vt. ~ off acordonar

corduroy /'kɔːdərɔɪ/ n pana f

core /kɔː(r)/ n ⟨of apple⟩ corazón m; ⟨fig⟩ meollo m

cork /kɔːk/ n corcho m. —vt taponar. ~screw /'kɔːkskruː/ n sacacorchos m invar

corn¹ /kɔːn/ n ⟨wheat⟩ trigo m; ⟨Amer⟩ maíz m; ⟨seed⟩ grano m

corn² /kɔːn/ n ⟨hard skin⟩ callo m

corned /kɔːnd/ a. ~ beef n carne f de vaca en lata

corner /'kɔːnə(r)/ n ángulo m; ⟨inside⟩ rincón m; ⟨outside⟩ esquina f; ⟨football⟩ saque m de esquina. —vt arrinconar; ⟨com⟩ acaparar. ~stone n piedra f angular

cornet /'kɔːnɪt/ n ⟨mus⟩ corneta f; ⟨for ice-cream⟩ cucurucho m

cornflakes /'kɔːnfleɪks/ npl copos mpl de maíz

cornflour /'kɔːnflaʊə(r)/ n harina f de maíz

cornice /'kɔːnɪs/ n cornisa f

cornucopia /kɔːnjʊ'kəʊpɪə/ n cuerno m de la abundancia

Corn|ish /'kɔːnɪʃ/ a de Cornualles. ~**wall** /'kɔːnwəl/ n Cornualles m

corny /'kɔːnɪ/ a (trite, fam) gastado; (mawkish) sentimental, sensiblero

corollary /kə'rɒlərɪ/ n corolario m

coronary /'kɒrənərɪ/ n trombosis f coronaria

coronation /kɒrə'neɪʃn/ n coronación f

coroner /'kɒrənə(r)/ n juez m de primera instancia

corporal[1] /'kɔːpərəl/ n cabo m

corporal[2] /'kɔːpərəl/ a corporal

corporate /'kɔːpərət/ a corporativo

corporation /kɔːpə'reɪʃn/ n corporación f; (of town) ayuntamiento m

corps /kɔː(r)/ n (pl **corps** /kɔːz/) cuerpo m

corpse /kɔːps/ n cadáver m

corpulent /'kɔːpjʊlənt/ a gordo, corpulento

corpuscle /'kɔːpʌsl/ n glóbulo m

corral /kə'rɑːl/ n (Amer) corral m

correct /kə'rekt/ a correcto; (time) exacto. —vt corregir. ~**ion** /-ʃn/ n corrección f

correlat|e /'kɒrəleɪt/ vt poner en correlación. ~**ion** /-'leɪʃn/ n correlación f

correspond /kɒrɪ'spɒnd/ vi corresponder; (write) escribirse. ~**ence** n correspondencia f. ~**ent** n corresponsal m & f

corridor /'kɒrɪdɔː(r)/ n pasillo m

corroborate /kə'rɒbəreɪt/ vt corroborar

corro|de /kə'rəʊd/ vt corroer. —vi corroerse. ~**sion** n corrosión f

corrugated /'kɒrəgeɪtɪd/ a ondulado. ~ **iron** n hierro m ondulado

corrupt /kə'rʌpt/ a corrompido. —vt corromper. ~**ion** /-ʃn/ n corrupción f

corset /'kɔːsɪt/ n corsé m

Corsica /'kɔːsɪkə/ n Córcega f. ~**n** a & n corso (m)

cortège /kɔː'teɪʒ/ n cortejo m

cos /kɒs/ n lechuga f romana

cosh /kɒʃ/ n cachiporra f. —vt aporrear

cosiness /'kəʊzɪnɪs/ n comodidad f

cosmetic /kɒz'metɪk/ a & n cosmético (m)

cosmic /'kɒzmɪk/ a cósmico

cosmonaut /'kɒzmənɔːt/ n cosmonauta m & f

cosmopolitan /kɒzmə'pɒlɪtən/ a & n cosmopolita (m & f)

cosmos /'kɒzmɒs/ n cosmos m

Cossack /'kɒsæk/ a & n cosaco (m)

cosset /'kɒsɪt/ vt mimar

cost /kɒst/ vi (pt cost) costar, valer. —vt (pt costed) calcular el coste de. —n precio m. **at all** ~**s** cueste lo que cueste. **to one's** ~ a sus expensas. ~**s** npl (jurid) costas fpl

Costa Rica /kɒstə'riːkə/ n Costa f Rica. ~**n** a & n costarricense (m & f), costarriqueño (m)

costly /'kɒstlɪ/ a (-ier, -iest) caro, costoso

costume /'kɒstjuːm/ n traje m

cosy /'kəʊzɪ/ a (-ier, -iest) cómodo; (place) acogedor. —n cubierta f (de tetera)

cot /kɒt/ n cuna f

cottage /'kɒtɪdʒ/ n casita f de campo. ~ **cheese** n requesón m. ~ **industry** n industria f casera.

cotton /'kɒtn/ n algodón m. —vi. ~ **on** (sl) comprender. ~ **wool** n algodón hidrófilo

couch /kaʊtʃ/ n sofá m. —vt expresar

couchette /ku:'ʃet/ n litera f

cough /kɒf/ vi toser. —n tos f. ~ **up** (sl) pagar. ~ **mixture** n jarabe m para la tos

could /kʊd, kəd/ pt of **can**

couldn't /'kʊdnt/ = **could not**

council /'kaʊnsl/ n consejo m; (of town) ayuntamiento m. ~**house** n vivienda f protegida. ~**lor** /'kaʊnsələ(r)/ n concejal m

counsel /'kaʊnsl/ n consejo m; (pl invar) (jurid) abogado m. ~**lor** n consejero m

count[1] /kaʊnt/ n recuento m. —vt/i contar

count[2] /kaʊnt/ n (nobleman) conde m

countdown /'kaʊntdaʊn/ n cuenta f atrás

countenance /'kaʊntɪnəns/ n semblante m. —vt aprobar

counter /'kaʊntə(r)/ n (in shop etc) mostrador m; (token) ficha f. —adv. ~ **to** en contra de. —vt oponerse a; parar (blow). —vi contraatacar

counter... /'kaʊntə(r)/ pref contra-

counteract /kaʊntər'ækt/ vt contrarrestar

counter-attack /'kaʊntərətæk/ n contraataque m. —vt/i contraatacar

counterbalance /'kaʊntəbæləns/ n contrapeso m. —vt/i contrapesar

counterfeit /'kaʊntəfɪt/ a falsificado. —n falsificación f. —vt falsificar

counterfoil /'kaʊntəfɔɪl/ n talón m

counterpart /'kaʊntəpɑ:t/ n equivalente m; (person) homólogo m

counter-productive /'kaʊntəprə'dʌktɪv/ a contraproducente

countersign /'kaʊntəsaɪn/ vt refrendar

countess /'kaʊntɪs/ n condesa f

countless /'kaʊntlɪs/ a innumerable

countrified /'kʌntrɪfaɪd/ a rústico

country /'kʌntrɪ/ n (native land) país m; (countryside) campo m. ~ **folk** n gente f del campo. **go to the** ~ ir al campo; (pol) convocar elecciones generales

countryman /'kʌntrɪmən/ n (pl -men) campesino m; (of one's own country) compatriota m

countryside /'kʌntrɪsaɪd/ n campo m

county /'kaʊntɪ/ n condado m, provincia f

coup /ku:/ n golpe m

coupé /'ku:peɪ/ n cupé m

couple /'kʌpl/ n (of things) par m; (of people) pareja f; (married) matrimonio m. **a** ~ **of** un par de. —vt unir; (tec) acoplar. —vi copularse

coupon /'ku:pɒn/ n cupón m

courage /'kʌrɪdʒ/ n valor m. ~**ous** /kə'reɪdʒəs/ a valiente. ~**ously** adv valientemente

courgette /kʊə'ʒet/ n calabacín m

courier /'kʊrɪə(r)/ n mensajero m; (for tourists) guía m & f

course /kɔ:s/ n curso m; (behaviour) conducta f; (aviat, naut) rumbo m; (culin) plato m; (for golf) campo m. **in due** ~ a su debido tiempo. **in the** ~ **of** en el transcurso de, durante. **of** ~ desde luego, por supuesto

court /kɔ:t/ n corte f; (tennis) pista f; (jurid) tribunal m. —vt cortejar; buscar (danger)

courteous /'kɜ:tɪəs/ a cortés

courtesan /ˌkɔːtɪˈzæn/ n (old use) cortesana f

courtesy /ˈkɜːtəsɪ/ n cortesía f

court: ~**ier** /ˈkɔːtɪə(r)/ n (old use) cortesano m. ~ **martial** n (pl **courts martial**) consejo m de guerra. ~**martial** vt (pt ~**martialled**) juzgar en consejo de guerra. ~**ship** /ˈkɔːtʃɪp/ n cortejo m

courtyard /ˈkɔːtjɑːd/ n patio m

cousin /ˈkʌzn/ n primo m. **first** ~ primo carnal. **second** ~ primo segundo

cove /kəʊv/ n cala f

covenant /ˈkʌvənənt/ n acuerdo m

Coventry /ˈkɒvntrɪ/ n. **send to** ~ hacer el vacío

cover /ˈkʌvə(r)/ vt cubrir; (journalism) hacer un reportaje sobre. ~ **up** cubrir; (fig) ocultar. —n cubierta f; (shelter) abrigo m; (lid) tapa f; (for furniture) funda f; (pretext) pretexto m; (of magazine) portada f. ~**age** /ˈkʌvərɪdʒ/ n reportaje m. ~ **charge** f precio m del cubierto. ~**ing** n cubierta f. ~**ing letter** n carta f explicatoria, carta f adjunta

covet /ˈkʌvɪt/ vt codiciar

cow /kaʊ/ n vaca f

coward /ˈkaʊəd/ n cobarde m. ~**ly** a cobarde. ~**ice** /ˈkaʊədɪs/ n cobardía f

cowboy /ˈkaʊbɔɪ/ n vaquero m

cower /ˈkaʊə(r)/ vi encogerse, acobardarse

cowl /kaʊl/ n capucha f; (of chimney) sombrerete m

cowshed /ˈkaʊʃed/ n establo m

coxswain /ˈkɒksn/ n timonel m

coy /kɔɪ/ a (-er, -est) (falsamente) tímido, remilgado

crab[1] /kræb/ n cangrejo m

crab[2] /kræb/ vi (pt **crabbed**) quejarse

crab-apple /ˈkræbæpl/ n manzana f silvestre

crack /kræk/ n grieta f; (noise) crujido m; (of whip) chasquido m; (joke, sl) chiste m. —a (fam) de primera. —vt agrietar; chasquear ⟨whip, fingers⟩; cascar ⟨nut⟩; gastar ⟨joke⟩; resolver ⟨problem⟩. —vi agrietarse. **get** ~**ing** (fam) darse prisa. ~ **down on** (fam) tomar medidas enérgicas contra. ~ **up** vi fallar; ⟨person⟩ volverse loco. ~**ed** /krækt/ a (sl) chiflado

cracker /ˈkrækə(r)/ n petardo m; (culin) galleta f (soso); (culin, Amer) galleta f

crackers /ˈkrækəz/ a (sl) chiflado

crackl|e /ˈkrækl/ vi crepitar. —n crepitación f, crujido m. ~**ing** /ˈkræklɪŋ/ n crepitación f, crujido m; (of pork) chicharrón m

crackpot /ˈkrækpɒt/ n (sl) chiflado m

cradle /ˈkreɪdl/ n cuna f. —vt acunar

craft /krɑːft/ n destreza f; (technique) arte f; (cunning) astucia f. —n invar (boat) barco m

craftsman /ˈkrɑːftsmən/ n (pl -**men**) artesano m. ~**ship** n artesanía f

crafty /ˈkrɑːftɪ/ a (-**ier**, -**iest**) astuto

crag /kræg/ n despeñadero m. ~**gy** a peñascoso

cram /kræm/ vt (pt **crammed**) rellenar. ~ **with** llenar de. —vi (for exams) empollar. ~**full** a atestado

cramp /kræmp/ n calambre m

cramped /kræmpt/ a apretado

cranberry /ˈkrænbərɪ/ n arándano m

crane /kreɪn/ n grúa f; (bird) grulla f. —vt estirar ⟨neck⟩

crank[1] /kræŋk/ n manivela f

crank[2] /kræŋk/ n (person) excéntrico m. ~**y** a excéntrico

cranny /ˈkrænɪ/ n grieta f

crash

crew

crash /kræʃ/ *n* accidente *m*;
(*noise*) estruendo *m*; (*collision*)
choque *m*; (*com*) quiebra *f*. —*vt*
estrellar. —*vi* quebrar con estrépito; (*have accident*) tener un
accidente; (*car etc*) chocar; (*fail*)
fracasar. **∼ course** *n* curso *m*
intensivo. **∼-helmet** *n* casco *m*
protector. **∼-land** *vi* hacer un
aterrizaje de emergencia, hacer
un aterrizaje forzoso

crass /kræs/ *a* craso, burdo

crate /kreɪt/ *n* cajón *m*. —*vt*
embalar

crater /'kreɪtə(r)/ *n* cráter *m*

cravat /krə'væt/ *n* corbata *f*, fular
m

crav|e /kreɪv/ *vi*. **∼e for** anhelar.
∼ing *n* ansia *f*

crawl /krɔːl/ *vi* andar a gatas;
(*move slowly*) avanzar lentamente; (*drag o.s.*) arrastrarse. —*n* (*swimming*) crol *m*.
at a ∼ a paso lento. **∼ to** humillarse ante. **∼ with** hervir de

crayon /'kreɪən/ *n* lápiz *m* de
color

craze /kreɪz/ *n* manía *f*

craz|iness /'kreɪzɪnɪs/ *n* locura *f*.
∼y /'kreɪzɪ/ *a* (**-ier, -iest**) loco.
be ∼y about andar loco por. **∼y
paving** *n* enlosado *m* irregular

creak /kriːk/ *n* crujido *m*; (*of
hinge*) chirrido *m*. —*vi* crujir;
(*hinge*) chirriar

cream /kriːm/ *n* crema *f*; (*fresh*)
nata *f*. —*a* (*colour*) color de
crema. —*vt* (*remove*) desnatar;
(*beat*) batir. **∼ cheese** *n* queso *m*
de nata. **∼y** *a* cremoso

crease /kriːs/ *n* pliegue *m*;
(*crumple*) arruga *f*. —*vt* plegar;
(*wrinkle*) arrugar. —*vi* arrugarse

creat|e /kriː'eɪt/ *vt* crear. **∼ion**
/-ʃn/ *n* creación *f*. **∼ive** *a* crea-
tivo. **∼or** *n* creador *m*

creature /'kriːtʃə(r)/ *n* criatura *f*,
bicho *m*, animal *m*

crèche /kreɪʃ/ *n* guardería *f*
infantil

credence /'kriːdns/ *n* creencia *f*,
fe *f*

credentials /krɪ'denʃlz/ *npl*
credenciales *mpl*

credib|ility /kredə'bɪlɪtɪ/ *n* cre-
dibilidad *f*. **∼le** /'kredəbl/ *a*
creíble

credit /'kredɪt/ *n* crédito *m*; (*honour*) honor *m*. **take the ∼ for**
atribuirse el mérito de. —*vt* (*pt*
credited) acreditar; (*believe*)
creer. **∼ s.o. with** atribuir a
uno. **∼able** *a* loable. **∼ card** *n*
tarjeta *f* de crédito. **∼or** *n*
acreedor *m*

credulous /'kredjʊləs/ *a* crédulo

creed /kriːd/ *n* credo *m*

creek /kriːk/ *n* ensenada *f*. **up
the ∼** (*sl*) en apuros

creep /kriːp/ *vi* (*pt* **crept**) arrastrarse; (*plant*) trepar. —*n* (*sl*)
persona *f* desagradable. **∼er** *n*
enredadera *f*. **∼s** /kriːps/ *npl*.
give s.o. the ∼s dar repugnancia a uno

cremat|e /krɪ'meɪt/ *vt* incinerar.
∼ion /-ʃn/ *n* cremación *f*. **∼or-
ium** /kremə'tɔːrɪəm/ *n* (*pl* **-ia**)
crematorio *m*

Creole /'kriːəʊl/ *a* & *n* criollo (*m*)

crêpe /kreɪp/ *n* crespón *m*

crept /krept/ *see* **creep**

crescendo /krɪ'ʃendəʊ/ *n* (*pl* **-os**)
crescendo *m*

crescent /'kresnt/ *n* media luna *f*;
(*street*) calle *f* en forma de media
luna

cress /kres/ *n* berro *m*

crest /krest/ *n* cresta *f*; (*coat of
arms*) blasón *m*

Crete /kriːt/ *n* Creta *f*

cretin /'kretɪn/ *n* cretino *m*

crevasse /krɪ'væs/ *n* grieta *f*

crevice /'krevɪs/ *n* grieta *f*

crew¹ /kruː/ *n* tripulación *f*;
(*gang*) pandilla *f*

crew² /kruː/ *see* **crow²**

crew: ∼ **cut** *n* corte *m* al rape. ∼ **neck** *n* cuello *m* redondo

crib /krɪb/ *n* cuna *f*; (*relig*) belén *m*; (*plagiarism*) plagio *m*. —*vt/i* (*pt* **cribbed**) plagiar

crick /krɪk/ *n* calambre *m*; (*in neck*) tortícolis *f*

cricket[1] /ˈkrɪkɪt/ *n* criquet *m*

cricket[2] /ˈkrɪkɪt/ *n* (*insect*) grillo *m*

cricketer /ˈkrɪkɪtə(r)/ *n* jugador *m* de criquet

crim|e /kraɪm/ *n* crimen *m*; (*acts*) criminalidad *f*. ∼**inal** /ˈkrɪmɪnl/ *a* & *n* criminal (*m*)

crimp /krɪmp/ *vt* rizar

crimson /ˈkrɪmzn/ *a* & *n* carmesí (*m*)

cringe /krɪndʒ/ *vi* encogerse; (*fig*) humillarse

crinkle /ˈkrɪŋkl/ *vt* arrugar. —*vi* arrugarse. —*n* arruga *f*

crinoline /ˈkrɪnəlɪn/ *n* miriñaque *m*

cripple /ˈkrɪpl/ *n* lisiado *m*, mutilado *m*. —*vt* lisiar; (*fig*) paralizar

crisis /ˈkraɪsɪs/ *n* (*pl* **crises** /ˈkraɪsiːz/) crisis *f*

crisp /krɪsp/ *a* (-**er**, -**est**) (*culin*) crujiente; (*air*) vigorizador. ∼**s** *npl* patatas *fpl* fritas a la inglesa

criss-cross /ˈkrɪskrɒs/ *a* entrecruzado. —*vt* entrecruzar. —*vi* entrecruzarse

criterion /kraɪˈtɪərɪən/ *n* (*pl* -**ia**) criterio *m*

critic /ˈkrɪtɪk/ *n* crítico *m*

critical /ˈkrɪtɪkl/ *a* crítico. ∼**ly** *adv* críticamente; (*ill*) gravemente

critic|ism /ˈkrɪtɪsɪzəm/ *n* crítica *f*. ∼**ze** /ˈkrɪtɪsaɪz/ *vt/i* criticar

croak /krəʊk/ *n* (*of person*) gruñido *m*; (*of frog*) canto *m*. —*vi* gruñir; (*frog*) croar

crochet /ˈkrəʊʃeɪ/ *n* croché *m*, ganchillo *m*. —*vt* hacer ganchillo

crock[1] /krɒk/ *n* (*person*, *fam*) vejancón *m*; (*old car*) cacharro *m*

crock[2] /krɒk/ *n* vasija *f* de loza

crockery /ˈkrɒkərɪ/ *n* loza *f*

crocodile /ˈkrɒkədaɪl/ *n* cocodrilo *m*. ∼ **tears** *npl* lágrimas *fpl* de cocodrilo

crocus /ˈkrəʊkəs/ *n* (*pl* -**es**) azafrán *m*

crony /ˈkrəʊnɪ/ *n* amigote *m*

crook /krʊk/ *n* (*fam*) maleante *m* & *f*, estafador *m*, criminal *m*; (*stick*) cayado *m*; (*of arm*) pliegue *m*

crooked /ˈkrʊkɪd/ *a* torcido; (*winding*) tortuoso; (*dishonest*) poco honrado

croon /kruːn/ *vt/i* canturrear

crop /krɒp/ *n* cosecha *f*; (*fig*) montón *m*. —*vt* (*pt* **cropped**) *vi* cortar. ∼ **up** surgir

cropper /ˈkrɒpə/ *n*. **come a** ∼ (*fall*, *fam*) caer; (*fail*, *fam*) fracasar

croquet /ˈkrəʊkeɪ/ *n* croquet *m*

croquette /krəˈket/ *n* croqueta *f*

cross /krɒs/ *n* cruz *f*; (*of animals*) cruce *m*. —*vt/i* cruzar; (*oppose*) contrariar. ∼ **off** tachar. ∼ **o.s.** santiguarse. ∼ **out** tachar. ∼ **s.o.'s mind** ocurrírsele a uno. — *a* enfadado. **talk at** ∼ **purposes** hablar sin entenderse

crossbar /ˈkrɒsbɑː(r)/ *n* travesaño *m*

cross-examine /krɒsɪgˈzæmɪn/ *vt* interrogar

cross-eyed /ˈkrɒsaɪd/ *a* bizco

crossfire /ˈkrɒsfaɪə(r)/ *n* fuego *m* cruzado

crossing /ˈkrɒsɪŋ/ *n* (*by boat*) travesía *f*; (*on road*) paso *m* para peatones

crossly /ˈkrɒslɪ/ *adv* con enfado

cross-reference /krɒsˈrefrəns/ *n* referencia *f*

crossroads /ˈkrɒsrəʊdz/ *n* cruce *m* (de carreteras)

cross-section /krɒs'sekʃn/ n sección f transversal; (fig) muestra f representativa

crosswise /'krɒswaɪz/ adv al través

crossword /'krɒswɜːd/ n crucigrama m

crotch /krɒtʃ/ n entrepiernas fpl

crotchety /'krɒtʃɪti/ a de mal genio

crouch /kraʊtʃ/ vi agacharse

crow[1] /krəʊ/ n cuervo m. **as the ~ flies** en línea recta

crow[2] /krəʊ/ vi (pt **crew**) cacarear

crowbar /'krəʊbɑː(r)/ n palanca f

crowd /kraʊd/ n muchedumbre f. —vt amontonar; (fill) llenar. —vi amontonarse; (gather) reunirse. **~ed** a atestado

crown /kraʊn/ n corona f; (of hill) cumbre f; (of head) coronilla f. —vt coronar; poner una corona a (tooth). **C~ Court** n tribunal m regional. **C~ prince** n príncipe m heredero

crucial /'kruːʃl/ a crucial

crucifix /'kruːsɪfɪks/ n crucifijo m. **~ion** /-'fɪkʃn/ n crucifixión f

crucify /'kruːsɪfaɪ/ vt crucificar

crude /kruːd/ a (**-er, -est**) (raw) crudo; (rough) tosco; (vulgar) ordinario

cruel /kruːəl/ a (**crueller, cruellest**) cruel. **~ty** n crueldad f

cruet /'kruːɪt/ n vinagreras fpl

cruise /kruːz/ n crucero m. —vi hacer un crucero; (of car) circular lentamente. **~r** n crucero m

crumb /krʌm/ n migaja f

crumble /'krʌmbl/ vt desmenuzar. —vi desmenuzarse; (collapse) derrumbarse

crummy /'krʌmi/ a (**-ier, -iest**) (sl) miserable

crumpet /'krʌmpɪt/ n bollo m blando

crumple /'krʌmpl/ vt arrugar; estrujar (paper). —vi arrugarse

crunch /krʌntʃ/ vt hacer crujir; (bite) ronzar, morder, masticar. —n crujido m; (fig) momento m decisivo

crusade /kruː'seɪd/ n cruzada f. **~r** /-ə(r)/ n cruzado m

crush /krʌʃ/ vt aplastar; arrugar (clothes); estrujar (paper). —n (crowd) aglomeración f. **have a ~ on** (sl) estar perdido por. **orange ~** n naranjada f

crust /krʌst/ n corteza f. **~y** a (bread) de corteza dura; (person) malhumorado

crutch /krʌtʃ/ n muleta f; (anat) entrepiernas fpl

crux /krʌks/ n (pl **cruxes**) punto m más importante, quid m, busilis m

cry /kraɪ/ n grito m. **be a far ~ from** (fig) distar mucho de. —vi llorar; (call out) gritar. **~ off** rajarse. **~-baby** n llorón m

crypt /krɪpt/ n cripta f

cryptic /'krɪptɪk/ a enigmático

crystal /'krɪstl/ n cristal m. **~lize** vt cristalizar. —vi cristalizarse

cub /kʌb/ n cachorro m. **C~ (Scout)** n niño m explorador

Cuba /'kjuːbə/ n Cuba f. **~n** a & n cubano (m)

cubby-hole /'kʌbɪhəʊl/ n casilla f; (room) chiribitil m, cuchitril m

cube /kjuːb/ n cubo m. **~ic** a cúbico

cubicle /'kjuːbɪkl/ n cubículo m; (changing room) caseta f

cubism /'kjuːbɪzm/ n cubismo m. **~t** a & n cubista (m & f)

cuckold /'kʌkəʊld/ n cornudo m

cuckoo /'kʊkuː/ n cuco m, cuclillo m

cucumber /'kjuːkʌmbə(r)/ n pepino m

cuddle /'kʌdl/ vt abrazar. —vi abrazarse. —n abrazo m. **~y** a mimoso

cudgel /'kʌdʒl/ n porra f. —vt (pt **cudgelled**) aporrear

cue[1] /kju:/ n indicación f; (in theatre) pie m

cue[2] /kju:/ n (in billiards) taco m

cuff /kʌf/ n puño m; (blow) bofetada f. **speak off the ~** hablar de improviso. —vt abofetear.
~link n gemelo m

cul-de-sac /'kʌldəsæk/ n callejón m sin salida

culinary /'kʌlɪnərɪ/ a culinario

cull /kʌl/ vt coger (flowers); entresacar (animals)

culminat|e /'kʌlmɪneɪt/ vi culminar. **~ion** /-'neɪʃn/ n culminación f

culottes /ku:'lɒts/ npl falda f pantalón

culprit /'kʌlprɪt/ n culpable m

cult /kʌlt/ n culto m

cultivat|e /'kʌltɪveɪt/ vt cultivar.
~ion /-'veɪʃn/ n cultivo m; (fig) cultura f

cultur|al /'kʌltʃərəl/ a cultural.
~e /'kʌltʃə(r)/ n cultura f; (bot etc) cultivo m. **~ed** a cultivado; (person) culto

cumbersome /'kʌmbəsəm/ a incómodo; (heavy) pesado

cumulative /'kju:mjʊlətɪv/ a cumulativo

cunning /'kʌnɪŋ/ a astuto. —n astucia f

cup /kʌp/ n taza f; (prize) copa f

cupboard /'kʌbəd/ n armario m

Cup Final /kʌp'faɪnl/ n final f del campeonato

cupful /'kʌpfʊl/ n taza f

cupidity /kju:'pɪdɪtɪ/ n codicia f

curable /'kjʊərəbl/ a curable

curate /'kjʊərət/ n coadjutor m

curator /kjʊə'reɪtə(r)/ n (of museum) conservador m

curb /kɜ:b/ n freno m. —vt refrenar

curdle /'kɜ:dl/ vt cuajar. —vi cuajarse; (milk) cortarse

curds /kɜ:dz/ npl cuajada f, requesón m

cure /kjʊə(r)/ vt curar. —n cura f

curfew /'kɜ:fju:/ n queda f; (signal) toque m de queda

curio /'kjʊərɪəʊ/ n (pl -os) curiosidad f

curio|us /'kjʊərɪəs/ a curioso.
~sity /-'ɒsɪtɪ/ n curiosidad f

curl /kɜ:l/ vt rizar (hair). **~ o.s. up** acurrucarse. —vi (hair) rizarse; (paper) arrollarse. —n rizo m. **~er** /'kɜ:lə(r)/ n bigudí m, rulo m. **~y** /'kɜ:lɪ/ a (-ier, -iest) rizado

currant /'kʌrənt/ n pasa f de Corinto

currency /'kʌrənsɪ/ n moneda f; (acceptance) uso m (corriente)

current /'kʌrənt/ a & n corriente (f). **~ events** asuntos mpl de actualidad. **~ly** adv actualmente

curriculum /kə'rɪkjʊləm/ n (pl -la) programa m de estudios. **~ vitae** n curriculum m vitae

curry[1] /'kʌrɪ/ n curry m

curry[2] /'kʌrɪ/ vt. **~ favour with** congraciarse con

curse /kɜ:s/ n maldición f; (oath) palabrota f. —vt maldecir. —vi decir palabrotas

cursory /'kɜ:sərɪ/ a superficial

curt /kɜ:t/ a brusco

curtail /kɜ:'teɪl/ vt abreviar; reducir (expenses)

curtain /'kɜ:tn/ n cortina f; (in theatre) telón m

curtsy /'kɜ:tsɪ/ n reverencia f. —vi hacer una reverencia

curve /kɜ:v/ n curva f. —vt encurvar. —vi encorvarse; (road) torcerse

cushion /'kʊʃn/ n cojín m. —vt amortiguar (a blow); (fig) proteger

cushy /'kʊʃɪ/ a (-ier, -iest) (fam) fácil

custard /'kʌstəd/ n natillas fpl

custodian /kʌˈstəʊdɪən/ n custodio m

custody /ˈkʌstədɪ/ n custodia f. be in ~ (jurid) estar detenido

custom /ˈkʌstəm/ n costumbre f; (com) clientela f

customary /ˈkʌstəmərɪ/ a acostumbrado

customer /ˈkʌstəmə(r)/ n cliente m

customs /ˈkʌstəmz/ npl aduana f. ~ officer n aduanero m

cut /kʌt/ vt/i (pt cut, pres p cutting) cortar; reducir ‹prices›. ~ n corte m; (reduction) reducción f. ~ across atravesar. ~ back, ~ down reducir. ~ in interrumpir. ~ off cortar; (phone) desconectar; (fig) aislar. ~ out recortar; (omit) suprimir. ~ through atravesar. ~ up cortar en pedazos. be ~ up about (fig) afligirse por

cute /kjuːt/ a (-er, -est) (fam) listo; (Amer) mono

cuticle /ˈkjuːtɪkl/ n cutícula f

cutlery /ˈkʌtlərɪ/ n cubiertos mpl

cutlet /ˈkʌtlɪt/ n chuleta f

cut-price /ˈkʌtpraɪs/ a a precio reducido

cut-throat /ˈkʌtθrəʊt/ a despiadado

cutting /ˈkʌtɪŋ/ a cortante; ‹remark› mordaz. —n (from newspaper) recorte m; (of plant) esqueje m

cyanide /ˈsaɪənaɪd/ n cianuro m

cybernetics /saɪbəˈnetɪks/ n cibernética f

cyclamen /ˈsɪkləmən/ n ciclamen m

cycle /ˈsaɪkl/ n ciclo m; (bicycle) bicicleta f. —vi ir en bicicleta

cyclic(al) /ˈsaɪklɪk(l)/ a cíclico

cycling /ˈsaɪklɪŋ/ n ciclismo m. ~st n ciclista m & f

cyclone /ˈsaɪkləʊn/ n ciclón m

cylinder /ˈsɪlɪndə(r)/ n cilindro m. ~er head (auto) n culata f. ~rical /-ˈlɪndrɪkl/ a cilíndrico

cymbal /ˈsɪmbl/ n címbalo m

cynic /ˈsɪnɪk/ n cínico m. ~al a cínico. ~ism /-sɪzəm/ n cinismo m

cypress /ˈsaɪprəs/ n ciprés m

Cypriot /ˈsɪprɪət/ a & n chipriota (m & f). ~us /ˈsaɪprəs/ n Chipre f

cyst /sɪst/ n quiste m

czar /zɑː(r)/ n zar m

Czech /tʃek/ a & n checo (m). the ~ Republic n la república f Checa

Czechoslovak /tʃekəʊˈsləʊvæk/ a & n (history) checoslovaco (m). ~ia /-əˈvækɪə/ n (history) Checoslovaquia f

D

dab /dæb/ vt (pt dabbed) tocar ligeramente. —n toque m suave. a ~ of un poquito de

dabble /ˈdæbl/ vi. ~ in meterse (superficialmente) en. ~r /ə(r)/ n aficionado m

dad /dæd/ n (fam) papá m. ~dy n (children's use) papá m. ~dy-long-legs n típula f

daffodil /ˈdæfədɪl/ n narciso m

daft /dɑːft/ a (-er, -est) tonto

dagger /ˈdægə(r)/ n puñal m

dahlia /ˈdeɪlɪə/ n dalia f

daily /ˈdeɪlɪ/ a diario. —adv diariamente, cada día. —n diario m; (cleaner, fam) asistenta f

dainty /ˈdeɪntɪ/ a (-ier, -iest) delicado

dairy /ˈdeərɪ/ n vaquería f; (shop) lechería f. —a lechero

dais /deɪːs/ n estrado m

daisy /ˈdeɪzɪ/ n margarita f

dale /deɪl/ n valle m

dally /ˈdælɪ/ vi tardar; (waste time) perder el tiempo

dam /dæm/ n presa f. —vt (pt dammed) embalsar

damag|e /'dæmɪdʒ/ n daño m; (pl, jurid) daños mpl y perjuicios mpl. —vt (fig) dañar, estropear. ~ing a perjudicial

damask /'dæməsk/ n damasco m.

dame /deɪm/ n (old use) dama f; (Amer, sl) chica f

damn /dæm/ vt condenar; (curse) maldecir. —int ¡córcholis! —a maldito. **I don't care a ~** (no) me importa un comino. ~ation /-'neɪʃn/ n condenación f, perdición f

damp /dæmp/ n humedad f. —a (-er, -est) húmedo. —vt mojar; (fig) ahogar. ~er /'dæmpə(r)/ n apagador m, sordina f; (fig) aguafiestas m invar. ~ness f humedad f

damsel /'dæmzl/ n (old use) doncella f

dance /dɑːns/ vt/i bailar. —n baile m. ~hall n salón m de baile. ~r /-ə(r)/ n bailador m; (professional) bailarín m

dandelion /'dændɪlaɪən/ n diente m de león

dandruff /'dændrʌf/ n caspa f

dandy /'dændɪ/ n petimetre m

Dane /deɪn/ n danés m

danger /'deɪndʒə(r)/ n peligro m; (risk) riesgo m. ~ous a peligroso

dangle /'dæŋgl/ vt balancear. — vi suspender, colgar

Danish /'deɪnɪʃ/ a danés. —n (lang) danés m

dank /dæŋk/ a (-er, -est) húmedo, malsano

dare /deə(r)/ vt desafiar. —vi atreverse a. **I ~ say** probablemente. —n desafío m

daredevil /'deədevl/ n atrevido m

daring /'deərɪŋ/ a atrevido

dark /dɑːk/ a (-er, -est) oscuro; (gloomy) sombrío; (skin, hair) moreno. —n oscuridad f; (nightfall) atardecer. **in the ~** a oscuras. ~en /'dɑːkən/ vt oscurecer. —

vi oscurecerse. **~ horse** n persona f de talentos desconocidos. **~ness** n oscuridad f. **~room** n cámara f oscura

darling /'dɑːlɪŋ/ a querido. —n querido m

darn /dɑːn/ vt zurcir

dart /dɑːt/ n dardo m. —vi lanzarse; (run) precipitarse. **~board** /'dɑːtbɔːd/ n blanco m. **~s** npl los dardos mpl

dash /dæʃ/ vi precipitarse. **~ off** marcharse apresuradamente. **~ out** salir corriendo. —vt lanzar; (break) romper; defraudar (hopes). —n carrera f; (small amount) poquito m; (stroke) raya f. **cut a ~** causar sensación

dashboard /'dæʃbɔːd/ n tablero m de mandos

dashing /'dæʃɪŋ/ a vivo; (showy) vistoso

data /'deɪtə/ npl datos mpl. **~ processing** n proceso m de datos

date¹ /deɪt/ n fecha f; (fam) cita f. **to ~** hasta la fecha. —vt fechar; (go out with, fam) salir con. —vi datar; (be old-fashioned) quedar anticuado

date² /deɪt/ n (fruit) dátil m

dated /'deɪtɪd/ a pasado de moda

daub /dɔːb/ vt embadurnar

daughter /'dɔːtə(r)/ n hija f. **~-in-law** n nuera f

daunt /dɔːnt/ vt intimidar

dauntless /'dɔːntlɪs/ a intrépido

dawdle /'dɔːdl/ vi andar despacio; (waste time) perder el tiempo. ~r /-ə(r)/ n rezagado m

dawn /dɔːn/ n amanecer m. —vi amanecer; (fig) nacer. **it ~ed on me that** caí en la cuenta de que, comprendí que

day /deɪ/ n día m; (whole day) jornada f; (period) época f. **~-break** n amanecer m. **~-dream** n ensueño m. —vi soñar despierto.

~**light** /'deɪlaɪt/ n luz f del día.
~**time** /'deɪtaɪm/ n día m

daze /deɪz/ vt aturdir. —n aturdimiento m. **in a** ~ aturdido

dazzle /'dæzl/ vt deslumbrar

deacon /'diːkən/ n diácono m

dead /ded/ a muerto; (numb) entumecido. ~ **centre** justo en medio. —adv completamente. ~ **beat** rendido. ~ **on time** justo a tiempo. ~ **slow** muy lento. **stop** ~ parar en seco. —n muertos mpl. **in the** ~ **of night** en plena noche. **the** ~ los muertos mpl. ~**en** /'dedn/ vt amortiguar (sound, blow); calmar (pain). ~**end** n callejón m sin salida. ~ **heat** n empate m

deadline /'dedlaɪn/ n fecha f tope, fin m de plazo

deadlock /'dedlɒk/ n punto m muerto

deadly /'dedlɪ/ a (-ier, -iest) mortal; (harmful) nocivo; (dreary) aburrido

deadpan /'dedpæn/ a impasible

deaf /def/ a (-er, -est) sordo. ~-**aid** n audífono m. ~**en** /'defn/ vt ensordecer. ~**ening** a ensordecedor. ~ **mute** n sordomudo m. ~**ness** n sordera f

deal /diːl/ n (transaction) negocio m; (agreement) pacto m; (of cards) reparto m; (treatment) trato m; (amount) cantidad f. **a great** ~ muchísimo. —vt (pt **dealt**) distribuir; dar (a blow, cards). —vi. ~ **in** comerciar en. ~ **with** tratar con (person); tratar de (subject etc); ocuparse de (problem etc). ~**er** n comerciante m. ~**ings** /'diːlɪŋz/ npl trato m

dean /diːn/ n deán m; (univ) decano m

dear /dɪə(r)/ a (-er, -est) querido; (expensive) caro. —n querido m; (child) pequeño m. —adv caro. —int ¡Dios mío! ~ **me!** ¡Dios mío!

~**ly** adv tiernamente; (pay) caro; (very much) muchísimo

dearth /dɜːθ/ n escasez f

death /deθ/ n muerte f. ~ **duty** n derechos mpl reales. ~**ly** a mortal; (silence) profundo. —adv como la muerte. ~'**s head** n calavera f. ~-**trap** n lugar m peligroso

débâcle /deɪ'bɑːkl/ n fracaso m, desastre m

debar /dɪ'bɑː(r)/ vt (pt **debarred**) excluir

debase /dɪ'beɪs/ vt degradar

debat|**able** /dɪ'beɪtəbl/ a discutible. ~**e** /dɪ'beɪt/ n debate m. —vt debatir, discutir. —vi discutir; (consider) considerar

debauch /dɪ'bɔːtʃ/ vt corromper. ~**ery** n libertinaje m

debilit|**ate** /dɪ'bɪlɪteɪt/ vt debilitar. ~**y** /dɪ'bɪlɪtɪ/ n debilidad f

debit /'debɪt/ n debe m. —vt. ~ **s.o.'s account** cargar en cuenta a uno

debonair /debə'neə(r)/ a alegre

debris /'debriː/ n escombros mpl

debt /det/ n deuda f. **be in** ~ tener deudas. ~**or** n deudor m

debutante /'debjuːtɑːnt/ n (old use) debutante f

decade /'dekeɪd/ n década f

decaden|**ce** /'dekədəns/ n decadencia f. ~**t** /'dekədənt/ a decadente

decant /dɪ'kænt/ vt decantar. ~**er** /ə(r)/ n garrafa f

decapitate /dɪ'kæpɪteɪt/ vt decapitar

decay /dɪ'keɪ/ vi decaer; (tooth) cariarse. —n decadencia f; (of tooth) caries f

deceased /dɪ'siːst/ a difunto

deceit /dɪ'siːt/ n engaño m. ~**ful** a falso. ~**fully** adv falsamente

deceive /dɪ'siːv/ vt engañar

December /dɪ'sembə(r)/ n diciembre m

decen|cy /'diːsənsɪ/ n decencia f.
~**t** /'diːsnt/ a decente; (good,
fam) bueno; (kind, fam) amable.
~**tly** adv decentemente

decentralize /diː'sentrəlaɪz/ vt
descentralizar

decep|tion /dɪ'sepʃn/ n engaño
m. ~**ve** /dɪ'septɪv/ a engañoso

decibel /'desɪbel/ n decibel(io) m

decide /dɪ'saɪd/ vt/i decidir. ~**d**
/-ɪd/ a resuelto; (unquestionable) indudable. ~**dly** /-ɪdlɪ/
adv decididamente; (unques-
tionably) indudablemente

decimal /'desɪml/ a & n decimal
(f). ~ **point** n coma f (decimal)

decimate /'desɪmeɪt/ vt diezmar

decipher /dɪ'saɪfə(r)/ vt descifrar

decision /dɪ'sɪʒn/ n decisión f

decisive /dɪ'saɪsɪv/ a decisivo;
(manner) decidido. ~**ly** adv de
manera decisiva

deck /dek/ n cubierta f; (of cards,
Amer) baraja f. **top** ~ (of bus)
imperial m. —vt adornar. ~
chair n tumbona f

declaim /dɪ'kleɪm/ vt declamar

declar|ation /deklə'reɪʃn/ n
declaración f. ~**e** /dɪ'kleə(r)/ vt
declarar

decline /dɪ'klaɪn/ vt rehusar;
(gram) declinar. —vi disminuir;
(deteriorate) deteriorarse; (fall)
bajar. —n decadencia f;
(decrease) disminución f; (fall)
baja f

decode /diː'kəʊd/ vt descifrar

decompos|e /diːkəm'pəʊz/ vt
descomponer. —vi descom-
ponerse. ~**ition** /-ɒmpə'zɪʃn/ n
descomposición f

décor /'deɪkɔː(r)/ n decoración f

decorat|e /'dekəreɪt/ vt decorar;
empapelar y pintar (room).
~**ion** /-'reɪʃn/ n (act) decoración
f; (ornament) adorno m. ~**ive**
/-ətɪv/ a decorativo. ~**or**
/'dekəreɪtə(r)/ n pintor m decorador. **interior** ~**or** n decorador
m de interiores

decorum /dɪ'kɔːrəm/ n decoro m

decoy /'diːkɔɪ/ n señuelo m.
/dɪ'kɔɪ/ vt atraer con señuelo

decrease /dɪ'kriːs/ vt disminuir. —vi disminuirse. /'diːkriːs/
n disminución f

decree /dɪ'kriː/ n decreto m;
(jurid) sentencia f. —vt (pt
decreed) decretar

decrepit /dɪ'krepɪt/ a decrépito

decry /dɪ'kraɪ/ vt denigrar

dedicat|e /'dedɪkeɪt/ vt dedicar.
~**ion** /-'keɪʃn/ n dedicación f; (in
book) dedicatoria f

deduce /dɪ'djuːs/ vt deducir

deduct /dɪ'dʌkt/ vt deducir.
~**ion** /-ʃn/ n deducción f

deed /diːd/ n hecho m; (jurid)
escritura f

deem /diːm/ vt juzgar, considerar

deep /diːp/ a (-er, est) adv profundo. **get into** ~ **waters** meterse en honduras. **go off the** ~
end enfadarse. —adv profundamente. **be** ~ **in thought**
estar absorto en sus pen-
samientos. ~**en** /'diːpən/ a pro-
fundizar. —vi hacerse más
profundo. ~**freeze** n congelador m. ~**ly** adv pro-
fundamente

deer /dɪə(r)/ n invar ciervo m

deface /dɪ'feɪs/ vt desfigurar

defamation /defə'meɪʃn/ n difamación f

default /dɪ'fɔːlt/ vi faltar. —n. **by**
~ en rebeldía. **in** ~ **of** en ausencia de

defeat /dɪ'fiːt/ vt vencer; (frustrate) frustrar. —n derrota f; (of
plan etc) fracaso m. ~**ism** /dɪ'fiː-
tɪzm/ n derrotismo m. ~**ist** /dɪ'fiː-
tɪst/ n derrotista m & f

defect /dɪ'fekt/ n defecto m.
/dɪ'fekt/ vi desertar. ~ **to** pasar
a. ~**ion** /dɪ'fekʃn/ n deserción f.
~**ive** /dɪ'fektɪv/ a defectuoso

defence /dɪˈfens/ n defensa f.
∼**less** a indefenso

defend /dɪˈfend/ vt defender.
∼**ant** n ⟨jurid⟩ acusado m

defensive /dɪˈfensɪv/ a defensivo. —n defensiva f

defer /dɪˈfɜː(r)/ vt (pt **deferred**) aplazar

deferen|ce /ˈdefərəns/ n deferencia f. ∼**tial** /-ˈrenʃl/ a deferente

defian|ce /dɪˈfaɪəns/ n desafío m.
in ∼**ce** of a despecho de. ∼**t** a desafiante. ∼**tly** adv con tono retador

deficien|cy /dɪˈfɪʃənsɪ/ n falta f.
∼**t** /dɪˈfɪʃnt/ a deficiente. be ∼**t** in carecer de

deficit /ˈdefɪsɪt/ n déficit m

defile /dɪˈfaɪl/ vt ensuciar; ⟨fig⟩ deshonrar

define /dɪˈfaɪn/ vt definir

definite /ˈdefɪnɪt/ a determinado;
⟨clear⟩ claro; ⟨firm⟩ categórico.
∼**ly** adv claramente; ⟨certainly⟩ seguramente

definition /defɪˈnɪʃn/ n definición f

definitive /dɪˈfɪnɪtɪv/ a definitivo

deflate /dɪˈfleɪt/ vt desinflar. —vi desinflarse. ∼**ion** /-ʃn/ n ⟨com⟩ deflación f

deflect /dɪˈflekt/ vt desviar. —vi desviarse

deform /dɪˈfɔːm/ vt deformar.
∼**ed** a deforme. ∼**ity** n deformidad f

defraud /dɪˈfrɔːd/ vt defraudar

defray /dɪˈfreɪ/ vt pagar

defrost /diːˈfrɒst/ vt descongelar

deft /deft/ a (-**er**, -**est**) hábil.
∼**ness** n destreza f

defunct /dɪˈfʌŋkt/ a difunto

defuse /diːˈfjuːz/ vt desactivar
⟨bomb⟩; ⟨fig⟩ calmar

defy /dɪˈfaɪ/ vt desafiar; ⟨resist⟩ resistir

degenerate /dɪˈdʒenəreɪt/ vi degenerar. /dɪˈdʒenərət/ a & n degenerado ⟨m⟩

degrad|ation /degrəˈdeɪʃn/ n degradación f. ∼**e** /dɪˈgreɪd/ vt degradar

degree /dɪˈgriː/ n grado m; ⟨univ⟩ licenciatura f; ⟨rank⟩ rango m.
to a certain ∼ hasta cierto punto. to a ∼ ⟨fam⟩ sumamente

dehydrate /diːˈhaɪdreɪt/ vt deshidratar

de-ice /diːˈaɪs/ vt descongelar

deign /deɪn/ vi. ∼ to dignarse

deity /ˈdiːɪtɪ/ n deidad f

deject|ed /dɪˈdʒektɪd/ a desanimado. ∼**ion** /-ʃn/ n abatimiento m

delay /dɪˈleɪ/ vt retardar; ⟨postpone⟩ aplazar. —vi demorarse. —n demora f

delectable /dɪˈlektəbl/ a deleitable

delegat|e /ˈdelɪgeɪt/ vt delegar.
/ˈdelɪgət/ n delegado m. ∼**ion** /-ˈgeɪʃn/ n delegación f

delete /dɪˈliːt/ vt tachar. ∼**ion** /-ʃn/ n tachadura f

deliberat|e /dɪˈlɪbəreɪt/ vt/i deliberar. /dɪˈlɪbərət/ a intencionado; ⟨steps etc⟩ pausado.
∼**ely** adv a propósito. ∼**ion** /-ˈreɪʃn/ n deliberación f

delica|cy /ˈdelɪkəsɪ/ n delicadeza f; ⟨food⟩ manjar m; ⟨sweet food⟩ golosina f. ∼**te** /ˈdelɪkət/ a delicado

delicatessen /delɪkəˈtesn/ n charcutería f fina

delicious /dɪˈlɪʃəs/ a delicioso

delight /dɪˈlaɪt/ n placer m. —vt encantar. —vi deleitarse. ∼**ed** a encantado. ∼**ful** a delicioso

delineate /dɪˈlɪnɪeɪt/ vt delinear.
∼**ion** /-ˈeɪʃn/ n delineación f

delinquen|cy /dɪˈlɪŋkwənsɪ/ n delincuencia f. ∼**t** /dɪˈlɪŋkwənt/ a & n delincuente ⟨m & f⟩

deliri|ous /dɪˈlɪrɪəs/ *a* delirante.
~um *n* delirio *m*

deliver /dɪˈlɪvə(r)/ *vt* entregar;
(*utter*) pronunciar; (*aim*) lanzar;
(*set free*) librar; (*med*) asistir al
parto de. **~ance** *n* liberación *f*.
~y *n* entrega *f*; (*of post*) reparto
m; (*med*) parto *m*

delta /ˈdeltə/ *n* (*geog*) delta *m*

delude /dɪˈluːd/ *vt* engañar. **~
o.s.** engañarse

deluge /ˈdeljuːdʒ/ *n* diluvio *m*

delusion /dɪˈluːʒn/ *n* ilusión *f*

de luxe /dɪˈlʌks/ *a* de lujo

delve /delv/ *vi* cavar. **~ into**
(*investigate*) investigar

demagogue /ˈdeməgɒg/ *n* demagogo *m*

demand /dɪˈmɑːnd/ *vt* exigir. **—***n*
petición *f*; (*claim*) reclamación *f*;
(*com*) demanda *f*. **in ~** muy popular, muy solicitado. **on ~** a solicitud. **~ing** *a* exigente. **~s** *npl*
exigencias *fpl*

demarcation /diːmɑːˈkeɪʃn/ *n*
demarcación *f*

demean /dɪˈmiːn/ *vt*. **~ o.s.**
degradarse. **~our** /dɪˈmiːnə(r)/
n conducta *f*

demented /dɪˈmentɪd/ *a* demente

demerara /deməˈreərə/ *n*. **~
(sugar)** *n* azúcar *m* moreno

demise /dɪˈmaɪz/ *n* fallecimiento
m

demo /ˈdeməʊ/ *n* (*pl* **-os**) (*fam*)
manifestación *f*

demobilize /diːˈməʊbəlaɪz/ *vt*
desmovilizar

democra|cy /dɪˈmɒkrəsɪ/ *n* demo-
cracia *f*. **~t** /ˈdeməkræt/ *n* demó-
crata *m* & *f*. **~tic** /-ˈkrætɪk/ *a*
democrático

demoli|sh /dɪˈmɒlɪʃ/ *vt* derribar.
~tion /deməˈlɪʃn/ *n* demolición
f

demon /ˈdiːmən/ *n* demonio *m*

demonstrat|e /ˈdemənstreɪt/ *vt*
demostrar. **—***vi* manifestarse,
hacer una manifestación. **~ion**

/-ˈstreɪʃn/ *n* demostración *f*; (*pol
etc*) manifestación *f*

demonstrative /dɪˈmɒnstrətɪv/
a demostrativo

demonstrator /ˈdemənstreɪtə(r)/
n demostrador *m*; (*pol etc*) manifestante *m* & *f*

demoralize /dɪˈmɒrəlaɪz/ *vt*
desmoralizar

demote /dɪˈməʊt/ *vt* degradar

demure /dɪˈmjʊə(r)/ *a* recatado

den /den/ *n* (*of animal*) guarida *f*,
madriguera *f*

denial /dɪˈnaɪəl/ *n* denegación *f*;
(*statement*) desmentimiento *m*

denigrate /ˈdenɪgreɪt/ *vt* denigrar

denim /ˈdenɪm/ *n* dril *m* (de algodón azul grueso). **~s** *npl* pantalón *m* vaquero

Denmark /ˈdenmɑːk/ *n* Dinamarca *f*

denomination /dɪnɒmɪˈneɪʃn/ *n*
denominación *f*; (*relig*) secta *f*

denote /dɪˈnəʊt/ *vt* denotar

denounce /dɪˈnaʊns/ *vt* denunciar

dens|e /dens/ *a* (**-er, -est**) espeso;
(*person*) torpe. **~ely** *adv* densamente. **~ity** *n* densidad *f*

dent /dent/ *n* abolladura *f*. **—***vt*
abollar

dental /ˈdentl/ *a* dental. **~ surgeon** *n* dentista *m* & *f*

dentist /ˈdentɪst/ *n* dentista *m* &
f. **~ry** *n* odontología *f*

denture /ˈdentʃə(r)/ *n* dentadura
f postiza

denude /dɪˈnjuːd/ *vt* desnudar;
(*fig*) despojar

denunciation /dɪnʌnsɪˈeɪʃn/ *n*
denuncia *f*

deny /dɪˈnaɪ/ *vt* negar; desmentir
(*rumour*); (*disown*) renegar

deodorant /diːˈəʊdərənt/ *a* & *n*
desodorante (*m*)

depart /dɪˈpɑːt/ *vi* marcharse;
(*train etc*) salir. **~ from** apartarse de

department /dɪˈpɑːtmənt/ n departamento m; (com) sección f. ~ **store** n grandes almacenes mpl

departure /dɪˈpɑːtʃə(r)/ n partida f, (of train etc) salida f. ~ **from** (fig) desviación f

depend /dɪˈpend/ vi depender. ~ **on** depender de; (rely) contar con. ~**able** a seguro. ~**ant** /dɪˈpendənt/ n familiar m & f dependiente. ~**ence** n dependencia f. ~**ent** a dependiente. be ~**ent on** depender de

depict /dɪˈpɪkt/ vt pintar; (in words) describir

deplete /dɪˈpliːt/ vt agotar

deplor|able /dɪˈplɔːrəbl/ a lamentable. ~**e** /dɪˈplɔː(r)/ vt lamentar

deploy /dɪˈplɔɪ/ vt desplegar. —vi desplegarse

depopulate /diːˈpɒpjʊleɪt/ vt despoblar

deport /dɪˈpɔːt/ vt deportar. ~**ation** /diːpɔːˈteɪʃn/ n deportación f

depose /dɪˈpəʊz/ vt deponer

deposit /dɪˈpɒzɪt/ vt (pt deposited) depositar. —n depósito m. ~**or** n depositante m & f

depot /ˈdepəʊ/ n depósito m; (Amer) estación f

deprav|e /dɪˈpreɪv/ vt depravar. ~**ity** /-ˈprævətɪ/ n depravación f

deprecate /ˈdeprɪkeɪt/ vt desaprobar

depreciat|e /dɪˈpriːʃɪeɪt/ vt depreciar. —vi depreciarse. ~**ion** /-ˈeɪʃn/ n depreciación f

depress /dɪˈpres/ vt deprimir; (press down) apretar. ~**ion** /-ʃn/ n depresión f

depriv|ation /deprɪˈveɪʃn/ n privación f. ~**e** /dɪˈpraɪv/ vt. ~ **of** privar de

depth /depθ/ n profundidad f. be out of one's ~ perder pie; (fig)

meterse en honduras. in the ~**s** of en lo más hondo de

deputation /depjʊˈteɪʃn/ n diputación f

deputize /ˈdepjʊtaɪz/ vi. ~ **for** sustituir a

deputy /ˈdepjʊtɪ/ n sustituto m. ~ **chairman** n vicepresidente m

derail /dɪˈreɪl/ vt hacer descarrilar. ~**ment** n descarrilamiento m

deranged /dɪˈreɪndʒd/ a (mind) trastornado

derelict /ˈderəlɪkt/ a abandonado

deri|de /dɪˈraɪd/ vt mofarse de. ~**sion** /-ˈrɪʒn/ n mofa f. ~**sive** a burlón. ~**sory** /dɪˈraɪsərɪ/ a mofador; (offer etc) irrisorio

deriv|ation /derɪˈveɪʃn/ n derivación f. ~**ative** /dɪˈrɪvətɪv/ a & n derivado (m). ~**e** /dɪˈraɪv/ vt/i derivar

derogatory /dɪˈrɒgətrɪ/ a despectivo

derv /dɜːv/ n gasóleo m

descen|d /dɪˈsend/ vt/i descender, bajar. ~**dant** n descendiente m & f. ~**t** /dɪˈsent/ n descenso m; (lineage) descendencia f

descri|be /dɪsˈkraɪb/ vt describir. ~**ption** /-ˈkrɪpʃn/ n descripción f. ~**ptive** /-ˈkrɪptɪv/ a descriptivo

desecrat|e /ˈdesɪkreɪt/ vt profanar. ~**ion** /-ˈkreɪʃn/ n profanación f

desert[1] /dɪˈzɜːt/ vt abandonar. —vi (mil) desertar

desert[2] /ˈdezət/ a & n desierto (m)

deserter /dɪˈzɜːtə(r)/ n desertor m

deserts /dɪˈzɜːts/ npl lo merecido. get one's ~ llevarse su merecido

deserv|e /dɪˈzɜːv/ vt merecer. ~**edly** adv merecidamente.

~ing a ⟨person⟩ digno de; ⟨action⟩ meritorio

design /dɪˈzaɪn/ n diseño m; (plan) proyecto m; (pattern) modelo m; (aim) propósito m. have ~s on poner la mira en. — vt diseñar; (plan) proyectar

designat|e /ˈdezɪgneɪt/ vt designar; (appoint) nombrar. ~ion /-ˈneɪʃn/ n denominación f; (appointment) nombramiento m

designer /dɪˈzaɪnə(r)/ n diseñador m; (of clothing) modisto m; (in theatre) escenógrafo m

desirab|ility /dɪzaɪərəˈbɪlətɪ/ n conveniencia f. ~le /dɪˈzaɪrəbl/ a deseable

desire /dɪˈzaɪə(r)/ n deseo m. —vt desear

desist /dɪˈzɪst/ vi desistir

desk /desk/ n escritorio m; (at school) pupitre m; (in hotel) recepción f; (com) caja f

desolat|e /ˈdesələt/ a desolado; (uninhabited) deshabitado. ~ion /-ˈleɪʃn/ n desolación f

despair /dɪˈspeə(r)/ n desesperación f. —vi. ~ of desesperarse de

desperat|e /ˈdespərət/ a desesperado; (dangerous) peligroso. ~ely adv desesperadamente. ~ion /-ˈreɪʃn/ n desesperación f

despicable /dɪˈspɪkəbl/ a despreciable

despise /dɪˈspaɪz/ vt despreciar

despite /dɪˈspaɪt/ prep a pesar de

desponden|cy /dɪˈspɒndənsɪ/ n abatimiento m. ~t /dɪˈspɒndənt/ a desanimado

despot /ˈdespɒt/ n déspota m

dessert /dɪˈzɜːt/ n postre m. ~spoon n cuchara f de postre

destination /destɪˈneɪʃn/ n destino m

destine /ˈdestɪn/ vt destinar

destiny /ˈdestɪnɪ/ n destino m

destitute /ˈdestɪtjuːt/ a indigente. ~ of desprovisto de

destroy /dɪˈstrɔɪ/ vt destruir

destroyer /dɪˈstrɔɪə(r)/ n (naut) destructor m

destruct|ion /dɪˈstrʌkʃn/ n destrucción f. ~ve a destructivo

desultory /ˈdesəltrɪ/ a irregular

detach /dɪˈtætʃ/ vt separar. ~able a separable. ~ed a separado. ~ed house n chalet m. ~ment /dɪˈtætʃmənt/ n separación f; (mil) destacamento m; (fig) indiferencia f

detail /ˈdiːteɪl/ n detalle m. —vt detallar; (mil) destacar. ~ed a detallado

detain /dɪˈteɪn/ vt detener; (delay) retener. ~ee /diːteɪˈniː/ n detenido m

detect /dɪˈtekt/ vt percibir; (discover) descubrir. ~ion /-ʃn/ n descubrimiento m, detección f. ~or n detector m

detective /dɪˈtektɪv/ n detective m. ~ story n novela f policíaca

detention /dɪˈtenʃn/ n detención f

deter /dɪˈtɜː(r)/ vt (pt deterred) disuadir; (prevent) impedir

detergent /dɪˈtɜːdʒənt/ a & n detergente (m)

deteriorat|e /dɪˈtɪərɪəreɪt/ vi deteriorarse. ~ion /-ˈreɪʃn/ n deterioro m

determination /dɪtɜːmɪˈneɪʃn/ n determinación f

determine /dɪˈtɜːmɪn/ vt determinar; (decide) decidir. ~d a determinado; (resolute) resuelto

deterrent /dɪˈterənt/ n fuerza f de disuasión

detest /dɪˈtest/ vt aborrecer. ~able a odioso

detonat|e /ˈdetəneɪt/ vt hacer detonar. —vi detonar. ~ion /-ˈneɪʃn/ n detonación f. ~or n detonador m

detour /ˈdiːtʊə(r)/ n desviación f

detract /dɪˈtrækt/ vi. ~ from (lessen) disminuir

detriment /'detrɪmənt/ n perjuicio m. **~al** /-'mentl/ a perjudicial

devalu|ation /diːvæljuˈeɪʃn/ n desvalorización f. **~e** /diːˈvæljuː/ vt desvalorizar

devastat|e /'devəsteɪt/ vt devastar. **~ing** a devastador; (fig) arrollador

develop /dɪ'veləp/ vt desarrollar; contraer (illness); urbanizar (land). **~i** desarrollarse; (show) aparecerse. **~er** n (foto) revelador m. **~ing country** n país m en vías de desarrollo. **~ment** n desarrollo m. (new) **~ment** novedad f

deviant /'diːvɪənt/ a desviado

deviat|e /'diːvɪeɪt/ vi desviarse. **~ion** /-'eɪʃn/ n desviación f

device /dɪ'vaɪs/ n dispositivo m; (scheme) estratagema f

devil /'devl/ n diablo m. **~ish** a diabólico

devious /'diːvɪəs/ a tortuoso

devise /dɪ'vaɪz/ vt idear

devoid /dɪ'vɔɪd/ a. **~ of** desprovisto de

devolution /diːvəˈluːʃn/ n descentralización f, (of power) delegación f

devot|e /dɪ'vəʊt/ vt dedicar. **~ed** a leal. **~edly** adv con devoción f. **~ee** /devəˈtiː/ n partidario m. **~ion** /-ʃn/ n dedicación f. **~ions** npl (relig) oraciones fpl

devour /dɪ'vaʊə(r)/ vt devorar

devout /dɪ'vaʊt/ a devoto

dew /djuː/ n rocío m

dexter|ity /dek'sterətɪ/ n destreza f. **~(e)rous** /'dekstrəs/ a diestro

diabet|es /daɪəˈbiːtiːz/ n diabetes f. **~ic** /-'betɪk/ a & n diabético (m)

diabolical /daɪəˈbɒlɪkl/ a diabólico

diadem /'daɪədem/ n diadema f

diagnos|e /'daɪəgnəʊz/ vt diagnosticar. **~is** /daɪəgˈnəʊsɪs/ n (pl -oses /-siːz/) diagnóstico m

diagonal /daɪˈægənl/ a & n diagonal (f)

diagram /'daɪəgræm/ n diagrama m

dial /'daɪəl/ n cuadrante m; (on phone) disco m. **—vt** (pt dialled) marcar

dialect /'daɪəlekt/ n dialecto m

dial: **~ling code** n prefijo m. **~ling tone** n señal f para marcar

dialogue /'daɪəlɒg/ n diálogo m

diameter /daɪˈæmɪtə(r)/ n diámetro m

diamond /'daɪəmənd/ n diamante m; (shape) rombo m. **~s** npl (cards) diamantes mpl

diaper /'daɪəpə(r)/ n (Amer) pañal m

diaphanous /daɪˈæfənəs/ a diáfano

diaphragm /'daɪəfræm/ n diafragma m

diarrhoea /daɪəˈrɪə/ n diarrea f

diary /'daɪərɪ/ n diario m; (book) agenda f

diatribe /'daɪətraɪb/ n diatriba f

dice /daɪs/ n invar dado m. **—vt** (culin) cortar en cubitos

dicey /'daɪsɪ/ a (sl) arriesgado

dictat|e /dɪk'teɪt/ vt/i dictar. **~es** /'dɪkteɪts/ npl dictados mpl. **~ion** /dɪk'teɪʃn/ n dictado m

dictator /dɪk'teɪtə(r)/ n dictador m. **~ship** n dictadura f

diction /'dɪkʃn/ n dicción f

dictionary /'dɪkʃənərɪ/ n diccionario m

did /dɪd/ see **do**

didactic /daɪˈdæktɪk/ a didáctico

diddle /'dɪdl/ vt (sl) estafar

didn't /'dɪdnt/ = **did not**

die[1] /daɪ/ vi (pres p dying) morir. **be dying to** morirse por. **~ down** disminuir. **~ out** extinguirse

die² /daɪ/ n (tec) cuño m

die-hard /'daɪhɑːd/ n intransigente m & f

diesel /'diːzl/ n (fuel) gasóleo m. ~ **engine** n motor m diesel

diet /'daɪət/ n alimentación f; (restricted) régimen m. —vi estar a régimen. ~**etic** /daɪə'tetɪk/ a dietético. ~**itian** n dietético m

differ /'dɪfə(r)/ vi ser distinto; (disagree) no estar de acuerdo. ~**ence** /'dɪfrəns/ n diferencia f; (disagreement) desacuerdo m. ~**ent** /'dɪfrənt/ a distinto, diferente

differentia|l /dɪfə'renʃl/ a & n diferencial (f). ~**te** /dɪfə'renʃɪeɪt/ vt diferenciar. —vi diferenciarse

differently /'dɪfrəntlɪ/ adv de otra manera

difficult /'dɪfɪkəlt/ a difícil. ~**y** n dificultad f

diffiden|ce /'dɪfɪdəns/ n falta f de confianza. ~**t** /'dɪfɪdənt/ a que falta confianza

diffus|e /dɪ'fjuːs/ a difuso. /dɪ'fjuːz/ vt difundir. —vi difundirse. ~**ion** /-ʒn/ n difusión f

dig /dɪg/ n (poke) empujón m; (poke with elbow) codazo m; (remark) indirecta f; (archaeol) excavación f. —vt (pt dug, pres p digging) cavar; (thrust) empujar. —vi cavar. ~ **out** extraer. ~ **up** desenterrar. ~**s** npl (fam) alojamiento m

digest /'daɪdʒest/ n resumen m. —vt digerir. ~**ible** a digerible. ~**ion** /-ʃn/ n digestión f. ~**ive** a digestivo

digger /'dɪgə(r)/ n (mec) excavadora f

digit /'dɪdʒɪt/ n cifra f; (finger) dedo m. ~**al** /'dɪdʒɪtl/ a digital

dignif|ied /'dɪgnɪfaɪd/ a solemne. ~**y** /'dɪgnɪfaɪ/ vt dignificar

dignitary /'dɪgnɪtərɪ/ n dignatario m

dignity /'dɪgnətɪ/ n dignidad f

digress /daɪ'gres/ vi divagar. ~ **from** apartarse de. ~**ion** /-ʃn/ n digresión f

dike /daɪk/ n dique m

dilapidated /dɪ'læpɪdeɪtɪd/ a ruinoso

dilat|e /daɪ'leɪt/ vt dilatar. —vi dilatarse. ~**ion** /-ʃn/ n dilatación f

dilatory /'dɪlətərɪ/ a dilatorio, lento

dilemma /daɪ'lemə/ n dilema m

diligen|ce /'dɪlɪdʒəns/ n diligencia f. ~**t** /'dɪlɪdʒənt/ a diligente

dilly-dally /'dɪlɪdælɪ/ vi (fam) perder el tiempo

dilute /daɪ'ljuːt/ vt diluir

dim /dɪm/ a (dimmer, dimmest) (weak) débil; (dark) oscuro; (stupid, fam) torpe. —vt (pt dimmed) amortiguar. —vi apagarse. ~ **the headlights** bajar los faros

dime /daɪm/ n (Amer) moneda f de diez centavos

dimension /daɪ'menʃn/ n dimensión f

diminish /dɪ'mɪnɪʃ/ vt/i disminuir

diminutive /dɪ'mɪnjʊtɪv/ a diminuto. —n diminutivo m

dimness /'dɪmnɪs/ n debilidad f; (of room etc) oscuridad f

dimple /'dɪmpl/ n hoyuelo m

din /dɪn/ n jaleo m

dine /daɪn/ vi cenar. ~**r** /-ə(r)/ n comensal m & f; (rail) coche m restaurante

dinghy /'dɪŋgɪ/ n (inflatable) bote m neumático

ding|iness /'dɪndʒɪnɪs/ n suciedad f. ~**y** /'dɪndʒɪ/ a (-ier, -iest) miserable, sucio

dining-room /'daɪnɪŋruːm/ n comedor m

dinner /'dɪnə(r)/ n cena f. ~**-jacket** n esmoquin m. ~ **party** n cena f

dinosaur /'daɪnəsɔː(r)/ n dinosaurio m

dint /dɪnt/ n. **by ~ of** a fuerza de

diocese /'daɪəsɪs/ n diócesis f

dip /dɪp/ vt (pt **dipped**) sumergir. —vi bajar. **~ into** hojear ⟨book⟩. —n ⟨slope⟩ inclinación f; (in sea) baño m

diphtheria /dɪf'θɪərɪə/ n difteria f

diphthong /'dɪfθɒŋ/ n diptongo m

diploma /dɪ'pləʊmə/ n diploma m

diplomacy /dɪ'pləʊməsɪ/ n diplomacia f

diplomat /'dɪpləmæt/ n diplomático m. **~ic** /-'mætɪk/ a diplomático

dipstick /'dɪpstɪk/ n (auto) varilla f del nivel de aceite

dire /daɪə(r)/ a (-er, -est) terrible; ⟨need, poverty⟩ extremo

direct /dɪ'rekt/ a directo. —adv directamente. —vt dirigir; ⟨show the way⟩ indicar

direction /dɪ'rekʃn/ n dirección f. **~s** npl instrucciones fpl

directly /dɪ'rektlɪ/ adv directamente; (at once) en seguida. —conj (fam) en cuanto

director /dɪ'rektə(r)/ n director m

directory /dɪ'rektərɪ/ n guía f

dirge /dɜːdʒ/ n canto m fúnebre

dirt /dɜːt/ n suciedad f. **~-track** n (sport) pista f de ceniza. **~y** /'dɜːtɪ/ a (-ier, -iest) sucio. **~y trick** n mala jugada f. **~y word** n palabrota f. —vt ensuciar

disability /dɪsə'bɪlɪtɪ/ n invalidez f

disable /dɪs'eɪbl/ vt incapacitar. **~d** a minusválido

disabuse /dɪsə'bjuːz/ vt desengañar

disadvantage /dɪsəd'vɑːntɪdʒ/ n desventaja f. **~d** a desventajado

disagree /dɪsə'griː/ vi no estar de acuerdo; ⟨food, climate⟩ sentar mal a. **~able** /dɪsə'griːəbl/ a desagradable. **~ment** n desacuerdo m; ⟨quarrel⟩ riña f

disappear /dɪsə'pɪə(r)/ vi desaparecer. **~ance** n desaparición f

disappoint /dɪsə'pɔɪnt/ vt desilusionar, decepcionar. **~ment** n desilusión f, decepción f

disapproval /dɪsə'pruːvl/ n desaprobación f. **~e** /dɪsə'pruːv/ vi. **~ of** desaprobar

disarm /dɪs'ɑːm/ vt/i desarmar. **~ament** n desarme m

disarray /dɪsə'reɪ/ n desorden m

disaster /dɪ'zɑːstə(r)/ n desastre m. **~rous** a catastrófico

disband /dɪs'bænd/ vt disolver. —vi disolverse

disbelief /dɪsbɪ'liːf/ n incredulidad f

disc /dɪsk/ n disco m

discard /dɪs'kɑːd/ vt descartar; abandonar ⟨beliefs etc⟩

discern /dɪ'sɜːn/ vt percibir. **~ible** a perceptible. **~ing** a perspicaz

discharge /dɪs'tʃɑːdʒ/ vt descargar; cumplir ⟨duty⟩; ⟨dismiss⟩ despedir; poner en libertad ⟨prisoner⟩; ⟨mil⟩ licenciar. /'dɪstʃɑːdʒ/ n descarga f; ⟨med⟩ secreción f; ⟨mil⟩ licenciamiento m; ⟨dismissal⟩ despedida f

disciple /dɪ'saɪpl/ n discípulo m

disciplinarian /dɪsəplɪ'neərɪən/ n ordenancista m & f. **~ary** a disciplinario. **~e** /'dɪsɪplɪn/ n disciplina f. —vt disciplinar; (punish) castigar

disc jockey /'dɪskdʒɒkɪ/ n (on radio) pinchadiscos m & f invar

disclaim /dɪs'kleɪm/ vt desconocer. **~er** n renuncia f

disclose /dɪs'kləʊz/ vt revelar. **~ure** /-ʒə(r)/ n revelación f

disco /'dɪskəʊ/ n (pl -os) (fam) discoteca f

discolour /dɪsˈkʌlə(r)/ vt decolorar. —vi decolorarse. ~ration /-ˈreɪʃn/ n decoloración f

discomfort /dɪsˈkʌmfət/ n malestar m; (lack of comfort) incomodidad f

disconcert /dɪskənˈsɜːt/ vt desconcertar

disconnect /dɪskəˈnekt/ vt separar; (elec) desconectar

disconsolate /dɪsˈkɒnsələt/ a desconsolado

discontent /dɪskənˈtent/ n descontento m. ~ed a descontento

discontinue /dɪskənˈtɪnjuː/ vt interrumpir

discord /ˈdɪskɔːd/ n discordia f; (mus) disonancia f. ~ant /-ˈskɔːdənt/ a discorde; (mus) disonante

discothèque /ˈdɪskətek/ n discoteca f

discount /ˈdɪskaʊnt/ n descuento m. /dɪsˈkaʊnt/ vt hacer caso omiso de; (com) descontar

discourage /dɪsˈkʌrɪdʒ/ vt desanimar; (dissuade) disuadir

discourse /ˈdɪskɔːs/ n discurso m

discourteous /dɪsˈkɜːtɪəs/ a descortés

discover /dɪsˈkʌvə(r)/ vt descubrir. ~y n descubrimiento m

discredit /dɪsˈkredɪt/ vt (pt discredited) desacreditar. —n descrédito m

discreet /dɪsˈkriːt/ a discreto. ~ly adv discretamente

discrepancy /dɪˈskrepənsɪ/ n discrepancia f

discretion /dɪˈskreʃn/ n discreción f

discriminat|e /dɪˈskrɪmɪneɪt/ vt/i discriminar. ~e between distinguir entre. ~ing a perspicaz. ~ion /-ˈneɪʃn/ n discernimiento m; (bias) discriminación f

discus /ˈdɪskəs/ n disco m

discuss /dɪˈskʌs/ vt discutir. ~ion /-ʃn/ n discusión f

disdain /dɪsˈdeɪn/ n desdén m. —vt desdeñar. ~ful a desdeñoso

disease /dɪˈziːz/ n enfermedad f. ~d a enfermo

disembark /dɪsɪmˈbɑːk/ vt/i desembarcar

disembodied /dɪsɪmˈbɒdɪd/ a incorpóreo

disenchant /dɪsɪnˈtʃɑːnt/ vt desencantar. ~ment n desencanto m

disengage /dɪsɪnˈɡeɪdʒ/ vt soltar. ~ the clutch desembragar. ~ment n soltura f

disentangle /dɪsɪnˈtæŋɡl/ vt desenredar

disfavour /dɪsˈfeɪvə(r)/ n desaprobación f. fall into ~ (person) caer en desgracia; (custom, word) caer en desuso

disfigure /dɪsˈfɪɡə(r)/ vt desfigurar

disgorge /dɪsˈɡɔːdʒ/ vt arrojar; (river) descargar; (fig) restituir

disgrace /dɪsˈɡreɪs/ n deshonra f; (disfavour) desgracia f. —vt deshonrar. ~ful a vergonzoso

disgruntled /dɪsˈɡrʌntld/ a descontento

disguise /dɪsˈɡaɪz/ vt disfrazar. —n disfraz m. in ~ disfrazado

disgust /dɪsˈɡʌst/ n repugnancia f, asco m. —vt repugnar, dar asco. ~ing a repugnante, asqueroso

dish /dɪʃ/ n plato m. —vt. ~ out (fam) distribuir. ~ up servir. ~cloth /ˈdɪʃklɒθ/ n bayeta f

dishearten /dɪsˈhɑːtn/ vt desanimar

dishevelled /dɪˈʃevld/ a desaliñado; (hair) despeinado

dishonest /dɪsˈɒnɪst/ a (person) poco honrado; (means) fraudulento. ~y n falta f de honradez

dishonour /dɪsˈɒnə(r)/ n deshonra f. —vt deshonrar. ~able a deshonroso. ~ably adv deshonrosamente

dishwasher /ˈdɪʃwɒʃə(r)/ n lavaplatos m & f

disillusion /dɪsɪˈluːʒn/ vt desilusionar. ~ment n desilusión

disincentive /dɪsɪnˈsentɪv/ n freno m

disinclined /dɪsɪnˈklaɪnd/ a poco dispuesto

disinfect /dɪsɪnˈfekt/ vt desinfectar. ~ant n desinfectante m

disinherit /dɪsɪnˈherɪt/ vt desheredar

disintegrate /dɪsˈɪntɪɡreɪt/ vt desintegrar. —vi desintegrarse

disinterested /dɪsˈɪntrəstɪd/ a desinteresado

disjointed /dɪsˈdʒɔɪntɪd/ a inconexo

disk /dɪsk/ n disco m

dislike /dɪsˈlaɪk/ n aversión f. — vt tener aversión a

dislocat|e /ˈdɪsləkeɪt/ vt dislocar(se) ⟨limb⟩. ~ion /-ˈkeɪʃn/ n dislocación f

dislodge /dɪsˈlɒdʒ/ vt sacar; ⟨oust⟩ desalojar

disloyal /dɪsˈlɔɪəl/ a desleal. ~ty n deslealtad f

dismal /ˈdɪzməl/ a triste; ⟨bad⟩ fatal

dismantle /dɪsˈmæntl/ vt desarmar

dismay /dɪsˈmeɪ/ n consternación f. —vt consternar

dismiss /dɪsˈmɪs/ vt despedir; ⟨reject⟩ rechazar. ~al n despedida f; ⟨of idea⟩ abandono m

dismount /dɪsˈmaʊnt/ vi apearse

disobedien|ce /dɪsəˈbiːdɪəns/ n desobediencia f. ~t /dɪsəˈbiːdɪənt/ a desobediente

disobey /dɪsəˈbeɪ/ vt/i desobedecer

disorder /dɪsˈɔːdə(r)/ n desorden m; ⟨ailment⟩ trastorno m. ~ly a desordenado

disorganize /dɪsˈɔːɡənaɪz/ vt desorganizar

disorientate /dɪsˈɔːrɪənteɪt/ vt desorientar

disown /dɪsˈəʊn/ vt repudiar

disparaging /dɪsˈpærɪdʒɪŋ/ a despreciativo. ~ly adv con desprecio

disparity /dɪsˈpærətɪ/ n disparidad f

dispassionate /dɪsˈpæʃənət/ a desapasionado

dispatch /dɪsˈpætʃ/ vt enviar. — n envío m; ⟨report⟩ despacho m. ~-rider n correo m

dispel /dɪsˈpel/ vt (pt dispelled) disipar

dispensable /dɪsˈpensəbl/ a prescindible

dispensary /dɪsˈpensərɪ/ n farmacia f

dispensation /dɪspenˈseɪʃn/ n distribución f; ⟨relig⟩ dispensa f

dispense /dɪsˈpens/ vt distribuir; ⟨med⟩ preparar; ⟨relig⟩ dispensar; administrar ⟨justice⟩. ~ with prescindir de. ~r /-ə(r)/ n ⟨mec⟩ distribuidor m automático; ⟨med⟩ farmacéutico m

dispers|al /dɪsˈpɜːsl/ n dispersión f. ~e /dɪsˈpɜːs/ vt dispersar. —vi dispersarse

dispirited /dɪsˈpɪrɪtɪd/ a desanimado

displace /dɪsˈpleɪs/ vt desplazar

display /dɪsˈpleɪ/ vt mostrar; exhibir ⟨goods⟩; manifestar ⟨feelings⟩. —n exposición f; ⟨of feelings⟩ manifestación f; ⟨pej⟩ ostentación f

displeas|e /dɪsˈpliːz/ vt desagradar. be ~ed with estar disgustado con. ~ure /-ˈpleʒə(r)/ n desagrado m

dispos|able /dɪsˈpəʊzəbl/ a desechable. ~al n ⟨of waste⟩ eliminación f. at s.o.'s ~al a la disposición de uno. ~e /dɪsˈpəʊz/ vt disponer. be well

~ed towards estar bien dispuesto hacia. —vi. ~e of deshacerse de

disposition /dɪspəˈzɪʃn/ n disposición f

disproportionate /dɪsprəˈpɔːʃənət/ a desproporcionado

disprove /dɪsˈpruːv/ vt refutar

dispute /dɪsˈpjuːt/ vt disputar. — n disputa f. in ~ disputado

disqualification /dɪskwɒlɪfɪˈkeɪʃn/ n descalificación f. ~y /dɪsˈkwɒlɪfaɪ/ vt incapacitar; (sport) descalificar

disquiet /dɪsˈkwaɪət/ n inquietud f

disregard /dɪsrɪˈgɑːd/ vt no hacer caso de. —n indiferencia f (for a)

disrepair /dɪsrɪˈpeə(r)/ n mal estado m

disreputable /dɪsˈrepjʊtəbl/ a de mala fama

disrepute /dɪsrɪˈpjuːt/ n descrédito m

disrespect /dɪsrɪsˈpekt/ n falta f de respeto

disrobe /dɪsˈrəʊb/ vt desvestir. — vi desvestirse

disrupt /dɪsˈrʌpt/ vt interrumpir; trastornar (plans). ~ion /-ʃn/ n interrupción f; (disorder) desorganización f. ~ive a desbaratador

dissatisfaction /dɪsætɪsˈfækʃn/ n descontento m

dissatisfied /dɪsˈsætɪsfaɪd/ a descontento

dissect /dɪˈsekt/ vt disecar. ~ion /-ʃn/ n disección f

disseminate /dɪˈsemɪneɪt/ vt diseminar. ~ion /-ˈneɪʃn/ n diseminación f

dissent /dɪˈsent/ vi disentir. —n disentimiento m

dissertation /dɪsəˈteɪʃn/ n disertación f; (univ) tesis f

disservice /dɪsˈsɜːvɪs/ n mal servicio m

dissident /ˈdɪsɪdənt/ a & n disidente (m & f)

dissimilar /dɪˈsɪmɪlə(r)/ a distinto

dissipate /ˈdɪsɪpeɪt/ vt disipar; (fig) desvanecer. ~d a disoluto

dissociate /dɪˈsəʊʃɪeɪt/ vt disociar

dissolute /ˈdɪsəluːt/ a disoluto. ~ion /dɪsəˈluːʃn/ n disolución f

dissolve /dɪˈzɒlv/ vt disolver. —vi disolverse

dissuade /dɪˈsweɪd/ vt disuadir

distance /ˈdɪstəns/ n distancia f. from a ~ce desde lejos. in the ~ce a lo lejos. ~t /ˈdɪstənt/ a lejano; (aloof) frío

distaste /dɪsˈteɪst/ n aversión f. ~ful a desagradable

distemper[1] /dɪˈstempə(r)/ n (paint) temple m. —vt pintar al temple

distemper[2] /dɪˈstempə(r)/ n (of dogs) moquillo m

distend /dɪsˈtend/ vt dilatar. —vi dilatarse

distil /dɪsˈtɪl/ vt (pt distilled) destilar. ~lation /-ˈleɪʃn/ n destilación f. ~lery /dɪsˈtɪləri/ n destilería f

distinct /dɪsˈtɪŋkt/ a distinto; (clear) claro; (marked) marcado. ~ion /-ʃn/ n distinción f; (in exam) sobresaliente m. ~ive a distintivo. ~ly adv claramente

distinguish /dɪsˈtɪŋgwɪʃ/ vt/i distinguir. ~ed a distinguido

distort /dɪsˈtɔːt/ vt torcer. ~ion /-ʃn/ n deformación f

distract /dɪsˈtrækt/ vt distraer. ~ed a aturdido. ~ing a molesto. ~ion /-ʃn/ n distracción f; (confusion) aturdimiento m

distraught /dɪsˈtrɔːt/ a aturdido

distress /dɪsˈtres/ n angustia f; (poverty) miseria f; (danger) peligro m. —vt afligir. ~ing a penoso

distribut|e /dɪsˈtrɪbjuːt/ vt distribuir. ~**ion** /-ˈbjuːʃn/ n distribución f. ~**or** n distribuidor m; (auto) distribuidor m de encendido

district /ˈdɪstrɪkt/ n distrito m; (of town) barrio m

distrust /dɪsˈtrʌst/ n desconfianza f. —vt desconfiar de

disturb /dɪsˈtɜːb/ vt molestar; (perturb) inquietar; (move) desordenar; (interrupt) interrumpir. ~**ance** n disturbio m; (tumult) alboroto m. ~**ed** a trastornado. ~**ing** a inquietante

disused /dɪsˈjuːzd/ a fuera de uso

ditch /dɪtʃ/ n zanja f; (for irrigation) acequia f. —vt (sl) abandonar

dither /ˈdɪðə(r)/ vi vacilar

ditto /ˈdɪtəʊ/ adv ídem

divan /dɪˈvæn/ n diván m

dive /daɪv/ vi tirarse de cabeza; (rush) meterse (precipitadamente); (underwater) bucear. —n salto m; (of plane) picado m; (place, fam) taberna f. ~**r** n saltador m; (underwater) buzo m

diverge /daɪˈvɜːdʒ/ vi divergir. ~**nt** /daɪˈvɜːdʒənt/ a divergente

divers|e /daɪˈvɜːs/ a diverso. ~**ify** /daɪˈvɜːsɪfaɪ/ vt diversificar. ~**ity** /daɪˈvɜːsətɪ/ n diversidad f

diver|sion /daɪˈvɜːʃn/ n desvío m; (distraction) diversión f. ~**t** /daɪˈvɜːt/ vt desviar; (entertain) divertir

divest /daɪˈvest/ vt. ~ **of** despojar de

divide /dɪˈvaɪd/ vt dividir. —vi dividirse

dividend /ˈdɪvɪdend/ n dividendo m

divine /dɪˈvaɪn/ a divino

diving-board /ˈdaɪvɪŋbɔːd/ n trampolín m

diving-suit /ˈdaɪvɪŋsuːt/ n escafandra f

divinity /dɪˈvɪnɪtɪ/ n divinidad f

division /dɪˈvɪʒn/ n división f

divorce /dɪˈvɔːs/ n divorcio m. —vt divorciarse de; (judge) divorciar. —vi divorciarse. ~**e** /dɪvɔːˈsiː/ n divorciado m

divulge /daɪˈvʌldʒ/ vt divulgar

DIY abbr see **do-it-yourself**

dizz|iness /ˈdɪzɪnɪs/ n vértigo m. ~**y** /ˈdɪzɪ/ a (-ier, -iest) mareado; (speed) vertiginoso. **be** or **feel** ~**y** marearse

do /duː/ vt (3 sing pres **does**, pt **did**, pp **done**) hacer; (swindle, sl) engañar. —vi hacer; (fare) ir; (be suitable) convenir; (be enough) bastar. —n (pl **dos** or **do's**) (fam) fiesta f. —v aux. ~ **you speak Spanish? Yes I** ~ ¿habla Vd español? Sí. **doesn't he?, don't you?** ¿verdad? ~ **come in!** (emphatic) ¡pase Vd! ~ **away with** abolir. ~ **in** (exhaust, fam) agotar; (kill, sl) matar. ~ **out** (clean) limpiar. ~ **up** abotonar (coat etc); renovar (house). ~ **with** tener que ver con; (need) necesitar. ~ **without** prescindir de. ~**ne for** (fam) arruinado. ~**ne in** (fam) agotado. **well** ~**ne** (culin) bien hecho. **well** ~**ne!** ¡muy bien!

docile /ˈdəʊsaɪl/ a dócil

dock[1] /dɒk/ n dique m. —vt poner en dique. —vi atracar al muelle

dock[2] /dɒk/ n (jurid) banquillo m de los acusados

dock: ~**er** n estibador m. ~**yard** /ˈdɒkjɑːd/ n astillero m

doctor /ˈdɒktə(r)/ n médico m, doctor m; (univ) doctor m. —vt castrar (cat); (fig) adulterar

doctorate /ˈdɒktərət/ n doctorado m

doctrine /ˈdɒktrɪn/ n doctrina f

document /ˈdɒkjʊmənt/ n documento m. ~**ary** /-ˈmentrɪ/ a & n documental (m)

doddering /ˈdɒdərɪŋ/ a chocho

dodge /dɒdʒ/ *vt* esquivar. —*vi* esquivarse. —*n* regate *m*; (*fam*) truco *m*

dodgems /'dɒdʒəmz/ *npl* autos *mpl* de choque

dodgy /'dɒdʒɪ/ *a* (-ier, -iest) (*awkward*) difícil

does /dʌz/ *see* do

doesn't /'dʌznt/ = does not

dog /dɒg/ *n* perro *m*. —*vt* (*pt* dogged) perseguir. ~collar *n* (*relig, fam*) alzacuello *m*. ~-eared *a* ⟨*book*⟩ sobado

dogged /'dɒgɪd/ *a* obstinado

doghouse /'dɒghaʊs/ *n* (*Amer*) perrera *f*. in the ~ (*sl*) en desgracia

dogma /'dɒgmə/ *n* dogma *m*. ~tic /-'mætɪk/ *a* dogmático

dogsbody /'dɒgzbɒdɪ/ *n* (*fam*) burro *m* de carga

doh /dəʊ/ *n* (*mus, first note of any musical scale*) do *m*

doily /'dɔɪlɪ/ *n* tapete *m*

doings /'duːɪŋz/ *npl* (*fam*) actividades *fpl*

do-it-yourself /duːɪtjɔː'self/ (*abbr* DIY) *n* bricolaje *m*. ~ enthusiast *n* manitas *m*

doldrums /'dɒldrəmz/ *npl*. be in the ~ estar abatido

dole /dəʊl/ *vt*. ~ out distribuir. —*n* (*fam*) subsidio *m* de paro. on the ~ (*fam*) parado

doleful /'dəʊlfl/ *a* triste

doll /dɒl/ *n* muñeca *f*. —*vt*. ~ up (*fam*) emperejilar

dollar /'dɒlə(r)/ *n* dólar *m*

dollop /'dɒləp/ *n* (*fam*) masa *f*

dolphin /'dɒlfɪn/ *n* delfín *m*

domain /dəˈmeɪn/ *n* dominio *m*; (*fig*) campo *m*

dome /dəʊm/ *n* cúpula *f*. ~d *a* abovedado

domestic /dəˈmestɪk/ *a* doméstico; ⟨*trade, flights, etc*⟩ nacional

domesticated *a* ⟨*animal*⟩ domesticado

domesticity /dɒmeˈstɪsətɪ/ *n* domesticidad *f*

domestic: ~ science *n* economía *f* doméstica. ~ servant *n* doméstico *m*

dominant /'dɒmɪnənt/ *a* dominante

dominat|e /'dɒmɪneɪt/ *vt/i* dominar. ~ion /-'neɪʃn/ *n* dominación *f*

domineer /dɒmɪ'nɪə(r)/ *vi* tiranizar

Dominican Republic /dəmɪnkən rɪ'pʌblɪk/ *n* República *f* Dominicana

dominion /dəˈmɪnjən/ *n* dominio *m*

domino /'dɒmɪnəʊ/ *n* (*pl* ~es) ficha *f* de dominó. ~es *npl* (*game*) dominó *m*

don¹ /dɒn/ *n* profesor *m*

don² /dɒn/ *vt* (*pt* donned) ponerse

donat|e /dəʊ'neɪt/ *vt* donar. ~ion /-ʃn/ *n* donativo *m*

done /dʌn/ *see* do

donkey /'dɒŋkɪ/ *n* burro *m*. ~-work *n* trabajo *m* penoso

donor /'dəʊnə(r)/ *n* donante *m* & *f*

don't /dəʊnt/ = do not

doodle /'duːdl/ *vi* garrapatear

doom /duːm/ *n* destino *m*; (*death*) muerte *f*. —*vt*. be ~ed to ser condenado a

doomsday /'duːmzdeɪ/ *n* día *m* del juicio final

door /dɔː(r)/ *n* puerta *f*. ~man /'dɔːmən/ *n* (*pl* -men) portero *m*. ~mat /'dɔːmæt/ *n* felpudo *m*. ~step /'dɔːstep/ *n* peldaño *m*. ~way /'dɔːweɪ/ *n* entrada *f*

dope /dəʊp/ *n* (*fam*) droga *f*; (*idiot, sl*) imbécil *m*. —*vt* (*fam*) drogar. ~y *a* (*sl*) torpe

dormant /'dɔːmənt/ *a* inactivo

dormer /'dɔːmə(r)/ *n*. ~ (window) buhardilla *f*

dormitory /ˈdɔːmɪtrɪ/ n dormitorio m

dormouse /ˈdɔːmaʊs/ n (pl -mice) lirón m

dos|age /ˈdəʊsɪdʒ/ n dosis f. **~e** /dəʊs/ n dosis f

doss /dɒs/ vi (sl) dormir. **~-house** n refugio m

dot /dɒt/ n punto m. **on the ~** en punto. —vt (pt dotted) salpicar. **be ~ted with** estar salpicado de

dote /dəʊt/ vi. **~ on** adorar

dotted line /dɒtɪdˈlaɪn/ n línea f de puntos

dotty /ˈdɒtɪ/ a (-ier, -iest) (fam) chiflado

double /ˈdʌbl/ a doble. —adv doble, dos veces. —n doble m; (person) doble m & f. **at the ~** corriendo. —vt doblar; redoblar (efforts etc). —vi doblarse. **~bass** n contrabajo m. **~ bed** n cama f de matrimonio. **~breasted** a cruzado. **~ chin** n papada f. **~cross** vt traicionar. **~dealing** n doblez m & f. **~decker** n autobús m de dos pisos. **~ Dutch** n galimatías m. **~jointed** a con articulaciones dobles. **~s** npl (tennis) doble m

doubt /daʊt/ n duda f. —vt dudar; (distrust) dudar de, desconfiar de. **~ful** a dudoso. **~less** adv sin duda

doubly /ˈdʌblɪ/ adv doblemente

dough /dəʊ/ n masa f; (money, sl) dinero m, pasta f (sl)

doughnut /ˈdəʊnʌt/ n buñuelo m

douse /daʊs/ vt mojar; apagar (fire)

dove /dʌv/ n paloma f

dowager /ˈdaʊədʒə(r)/ n viuda f (con bienes o título del marido)

dowdy /ˈdaʊdɪ/ a (-ier, -iest) poco atractivo

down¹ /daʊn/ adv abajo. —n abajo. **come ~** bajar. **go ~** bajar; (sun) ponerse. —prep

abajo. —a (sad) triste. —vt derribar; (drink, fam) beber

down² /daʊn/ n (feathers) plumón m

down-and-out /ˈdaʊnəndaʊt/ n vagabundo m

downcast /ˈdaʊnkɑːst/ a abatido

downfall /ˈdaʊnfɔːl/ n caída f, (fig) perdición f

downgrade /daʊnˈgreɪd/ vt degradar

down-hearted /daʊnˈhɑːtɪd/ a abatido

downhill /daʊnˈhɪl/ adv cuesta abajo

down payment /ˈdaʊnpeɪmənt/ n pago/pago m a cuenta

downpour /ˈdaʊnpɔː(r)/ n aguacero m

downright /ˈdaʊnraɪt/ a completo; (honest) franco. —adv completamente

downs /daʊnz/ npl colinas fpl

downstairs /daʊnˈsteəz/ adv abajo. /ˈdaʊnsteəz/ a de abajo

downstream /ˈdaʊnstriːm/ adv río abajo

down-to-earth /daʊntəˈɜːθ/ a práctico

downtrodden /ˈdaʊntrɒdn/ a oprimido

down: **~ under** en las antípodas; (in Australia) en Australia. **~ward** /ˈdaʊnwəd/ a & adv, **~wards** adv hacia abajo

dowry /ˈdaʊərɪ/ n dote f

doze /dəʊz/ vi dormitar. **~ off** dormirse, dar una cabezada. —n sueño m ligero

dozen /ˈdʌzn/ n docena f. **~s** of (fam) miles de, muchos

Dr abbr (Doctor) Dr, Doctor m. **~ Broadley** (el) Doctor Broadley

drab /dræb/ a monótono

draft /drɑːft/ n borrador m; (outline) bosquejo m; (com) letra f de cambio; (Amer, mil) reclutamiento m; (Amer, of air) corriente f de aire. —vt bosquejar;

(*mil*) destacar; (*Amer*, *conscript*) reclutar

drag /dræg/ *vt* (*pt* **dragged**) arrastrar; rastrear (*river*). —*vi* arrastrarse por el suelo. —*n* (*fam*) lata *f*. **in ~** (*man*, *sl*) vestido de mujer

dragon /'drægən/ *n* dragón *m*

dragon-fly /'drægənflaɪ/ *n* libélula *f*

drain /dreɪn/ *vt* desaguar; apurar (*tank*, *glass*); (*fig*) agotar. —*vi* escurrirse. —*n* desaguadero *m*. **be a ~ on** agotar. **~ing-board** *n* escurridero *m*

drama /'drɑːmə/ *n* drama *m*; (*art*) arte *m* teatral. **~tic** /drə'mætɪk/ *a* dramático. **~tist** /'dræmətɪst/ *n* dramaturgo *m*. **~tize** /'dræmətaɪz/ *vt* adaptar al teatro; (*fig*) dramatizar

drank /dræŋk/ *see* **drink**

drape /dreɪp/ *vt* cubrir; (*hang*) colgar. **~s** *npl* (*Amer*) cortinas *fpl*

drastic /'dræstɪk/ *a* drástico

draught /drɑːft/ *n* corriente *f* de aire. **~ beer** *n* cerveza *f* de barril. **~s** *n* *pl* (*game*) juego *m* de damas

draughtsman /'drɑːftsmən/ *n* (*pl* -**men**) diseñador *m*

draughty /'drɑːftɪ/ *a* lleno de corrientes de aire

draw /drɔː/ *vt* (*pt* **drew**, *pp* **drawn**) tirar; (*attract*) atraer; dibujar (*picture*); trazar (*line*); retirar (*money*). **~ the line at** trazar el límite. —*vi* (*sport*) empatar; dibujar (*pictures*); (*in lottery*) sortear. —*n* (*sport*) empate *m*; (*in lottery*) sorteo *m*. **~ in** (*days*) acortarse. **~ out** sacar (*money*). **~ up** pararse; redactar (*document*); acercar (*chair*)

drawback /'drɔːbæk/ *n* desventaja *f*

drawbridge /'drɔːbrɪdʒ/ *n* puente *m* levadizo

drawer /drɔː(r)/ *n* cajón *m*. **~s** /drɔːz/ *npl* calzoncillos *mpl*; (*women's*) bragas *fpl*

drawing /'drɔːɪŋ/ *n* dibujo *m*. **~-pin** *n* chinche *m*, chincheta *f*

drawing-room /'drɔːɪŋruːm/ *n* salón *m*

drawl /drɔːl/ *n* habla *f* lenta

drawn /drɔːn/ *see* **draw**. —*a* (*face*) ojeroso

dread /dred/ *n* terror *m*. —*vt* temer. **~ful** /'dredfl/ *a* terrible. **~fully** *adv* terriblemente

dream /driːm/ *n* sueño *m*. —*vt/i* (*pt* **dreamed** *or* **dreamt**) soñar. —*a* ideal. **~ up** idear. **~er** *n* soñador *m*. **~y** *a* soñador

dreariness /'drɪərɪnɪs/ *n* tristeza *f*; (*monotony*) monotonía *f*. **~y** /'drɪərɪ/ *a* (-**ier**, -**iest**) triste; (*boring*) monótono

dredge[1] /dredʒ/ *n* draga *f*. —*vt* dragar

dredge[2] /dredʒ/ *n* (*culin*) espolvorear

dredger[1] /'dredʒə(r)/ *n* draga *f*

dredger[2] /'dredʒə(r)/ *n* (*for sugar*) espolvoreador *m*

dregs /dregz/ *npl* heces *fpl*; (*fig*) hez *f*

drench /drentʃ/ *vt* empapar

dress /dres/ *n* vestido *m*; (*clothing*) ropa *f*. —*vt* vestir; (*decorate*) adornar; (*med*) vendar; (*culin*) aderezar, aliñar. —*vi* vestirse. **~ circle** *n* primer palco *m*

dresser[1] /'dresə(r)/ *n* (*furniture*) aparador *m*

dresser[2] /'dresə(r)/ *n* (*in theatre*) camarero *m*

dressing /'dresɪŋ/ *n* (*sauce*) aliño *m*; (*bandage*) vendaje *m*. **~-case** *n* neceser *m*. **~-down** *n* rapapolvo *m*, reprensión *f*. **~-gown** *n* bata *f*. **~-room** *n* tocador *m*; (*in theatre*) camarín *m*. **~-table** *n* tocador *m*

dressmaker /'dresmeɪkə(r)/ n modista m & f. ~ing n costura f

dress rehearsal /'dresrɪhɜːsl/ n ensayo m general

dressy /'dresɪ/ a (-ier, -iest) elegante

drew /druː/ see **draw**

dribble /'drɪbl/ vi gotear; ⟨baby⟩ babear; (in football) regatear

dribs and drabs /drɪbzn'dræbz/ npl. **in** ~ poco a poco, en cantidades pequeñas

dried /draɪd/ a ⟨food⟩ seco; ⟨fruit⟩ paso. ~r /'draɪə(r)/ n secador m

drift /drɪft/ vi ir a la deriva; ⟨snow⟩ amontonarse. —n (movement) dirección f; (of snow) montón m; (meaning) significado m. ~er n persona f sin rumbo. ~wood /'drɪftwʊd/ n madera f flotante

drill /drɪl/ n (tool) taladro m; (training) ejercicio m; (fig) lo normal. —vt taladrar, perforar; (train) entrenar. —vi entrenarse

drily /'draɪlɪ/ adv secamente

drink /drɪŋk/ vt/i (pt drank, pp drunk) beber. —n bebida f. ~able a bebible; ⟨water⟩ potable. ~er n bebedor m. ~ing-water n agua f potable

drip /drɪp/ vi (pt dripped) gotear. —n gota f; (med) goteo m intravenoso; (person, sl) mentecato m. ~-dry a que no necesita plancharse

dripping /'drɪpɪŋ/ n (culin) pringue m

drive /draɪv/ vt (pt drove, pp driven) empujar; conducir, manejar (LAm) ⟨car etc⟩. —n clavar ⟨nail⟩. ~ s.o. mad volver loco a uno. —vi conducir. ~ in (in car) entrar en coche. —n paseo m; (road) calle f; (private road) camino m de entrada; (fig) energía f; (pol) campaña f. ~ at

querer decir. ~r /'draɪvə(r)/ n conductor m, chófer m (LAm)

drivel /'drɪvl/ n tonterías fpl

driving /'draɪvɪŋ/ n conducción f. ~-licence n carné m de conducir. ~ school n autoescuela f

drizzle /'drɪzl/ n llovizna f. —vi lloviznar. ~y a lloviznoso

dromedary /'drɒmədərɪ/ n dromedario m

drone /drəʊn/ n (noise) zumbido m; (bee) zángano m. —vi zumbar; (fig) hablar en voz monótona; (idle, fam) holgazanear

drool /druːl/ vi babear

droop /druːp/ vt inclinar. —vi inclinarse; ⟨flowers⟩ marchitarse

drop /drɒp/ n gota f; ⟨fall⟩ caída f; ⟨decrease⟩ baja f; (of cliff) precipicio m. —vt (pt dropped) dejar caer; (lower) bajar. —vi caer. ~ in on pasar por casa de. ~ off (sleep) dormirse. ~ out retirarse; ⟨student⟩ abandonar los estudios. ~-out n marginado m

droppings /'drɒpɪŋz/ npl excremento m

dross /drɒs/ n escoria f

drought /draʊt/ n sequía f

drove[1] /drəʊv/ see **drive**

drove[2] /drəʊv/ n manada f

drown /draʊn/ vt ahogar. —vi ahogarse

drowsy /'draʊzɪ/ a soñoliento

drudge /drʌdʒ/ n esclavo m del trabajo. ~ry /-ərɪ/ n trabajo m pesado

drug /drʌg/ n droga f; (med) medicamento m. —vt (pt drugged) drogar. ~ addict n toxicómano m

drugstore /'drʌgstɔː(r)/ n (Amer) farmacia f (que vende otros artículos también)

drum /drʌm/ n tambor m; (for oil) bidón m. —vi (pt drummed) tocar el tambor. —vt. ~ into s.o.

inculcar en la mente de uno.
~**mer** n tambor m; (in group)
batería f. ~**s** npl batería f.
~**stick** /ˈdrʌmstɪk/ n baqueta f;
(culin) pierna f (de pollo)

drunk /drʌŋk/ see **drink**. —a
borracho. **get** ~ embo-
rracharse. ~**ard** n borracho m.
~**en** a borracho. ~**enness** n
embriaguez f

dry /draɪ/ a (**drier, driest**)
seco. —vt secar. —vi secarse. ~
up (fam) secar los platos.
~**clean** vt limpiar en seco.
~**cleaner** n tintorero m. ~
cleaner's (shop) tintorería f.
~**ness** n sequedad f

dual /ˈdjuːəl/ a doble. ~ **carriageway** n autovía f, carretera
f de doble calzada. ~**purpose** a
de doble uso

dub /dʌb/ vt (pt **dubbed**) doblar
(film); (nickname) apodar

dubious /ˈdjuːbɪəs/ a dudoso;
(person) sospechoso

duchess /ˈdʌtʃɪs/ n duquesa f

duck[1] /dʌk/ n pato m

duck[2] /dʌk/ vt sumergir; bajar
(head etc). —vi agacharse

duckling /ˈdʌklɪŋ/ n patito m

duct /dʌkt/ n conducto m

dud /dʌd/ a inútil; (cheque) sin
fondos; (coin) falso

due /djuː/ a debido; (expected)
esperado. ~ **to** debido a. —adv.
~ **north** n derecho hacia el
norte. ~**s** npl derechos mpl

duel /ˈdjuːəl/ n duelo m

duet /djuːˈet/ n dúo m

duffle /ˈdʌfl/ a. ~ **bag** n bolsa f de
lona. ~**coat** n trenca f

dug /dʌg/ see **dig**

duke /djuːk/ n duque m

dull /dʌl/ a (**-er, -est**) (weather)
gris; (colour) apagado; (person,
play, etc) pesado; (sound) sordo;
(stupid) torpe. —vt aliviar
(pain); entorpecer (mind)

duly /ˈdjuːlɪ/ adv debidamente

dumb /dʌm/ a (**-er, -est**) mudo;
(fam) estúpido

dumbfound /dʌmˈfaʊnd/ vt
pasmar

dummy /ˈdʌmɪ/ n muñeco m; (of
tailor) maniquí m; (of baby) chu-
pete m. —a falso. ~ **run** n
prueba f

dump /dʌmp/ vt descargar; (fam)
deshacerse de. —n vertedero m;
(mil) depósito m; (fam) lugar m
desagradable. **be down in the
~s** estar deprimido

dumpling /ˈdʌmplɪŋ/ n bola f de
masa hervida

dumpy /ˈdʌmpɪ/ a (**-ier, -iest**)
regordete

dunce /dʌns/ n burro m

dung /dʌŋ/ n excremento m;
(manure) estiércol m

dungarees /dʌŋgəˈriːz/ npl mono
m, peto m

dungeon /ˈdʌndʒən/ n calabozo
m

dunk /dʌŋk/ vt remojar

duo /ˈdjuːəʊ/ n dúo m

dupe /djuːp/ vt engañar. —n
inocentón m

duplicat|e /ˈdjuːplɪkət/ a & n
duplicado (m). /ˈdjuːplɪkeɪt/ vt
duplicar; (on machine) repro-
ducir. ~**or** n multicopista f

duplicity /djuːˈplɪsətɪ/ n doblez f

durable /ˈdjʊərəbl/ a resistente;
(enduring) duradero

duration /djʊˈreɪʃn/ n duración f

duress /djʊˈres/ n coacción f

during /ˈdjʊərɪŋ/ prep durante

dusk /dʌsk/ n crepúsculo m

dusky /ˈdʌskɪ/ a (**-ier, -iest**)
oscuro

dust /dʌst/ n polvo m. —vt quitar
el polvo a; (sprinkle) espolvorear

dustbin /ˈdʌstbɪn/ n cubo m de la
basura

dust-cover /ˈdʌstkʌvə(r)/ n
sobrecubierta f

duster /ˈdʌstə(r)/ n trapo m

dust-jacket /'dʌstdʒækɪt/ n sobre-cubierta f

dustman /'dʌstmən/ n (pl -men) basurero m

dustpan /'dʌstpæn/ n recogedor m

dusty /'dʌstɪ/ a (-ier, -iest) polvoriento

Dutch /dʌtʃ/ a & n holandés (m). go ~ pagar a escote. ~man m holandés m. ~woman n holandesa f

dutiful /'dju:tɪfl/ a obediente

duty /'dju:tɪ/ n deber m; (tax) derechos mpl de aduana. on ~ de servicio. ~-free a libre de impuestos

duvet /'dju:veɪ/ n edredón m

dwarf /dwɔ:f/ n (pl -s) enano m. —vt empequeñecer

dwell /dwel/ vi (pt dwelt) morar. ~ on dilatarse. ~er n habitante m & f. ~ing n morada f

dwindle /'dwɪndl/ vi disminuir

dye /daɪ/ vt (pres p **dyeing**) teñir. —n tinte m

dying /'daɪɪŋ/ see **die**

dynamic /daɪ'næmɪk/ a diná-mico. ~s npl dinámica f

dynamite /'daɪnəmaɪt/ n dina-mita f. —vt dinamitar

dynamo /'daɪnəməʊ/ n dinamo f, dínamo f

dynasty /'dɪnəstɪ/ n dinastía f

dysentery /'dɪsəntrɪ/ n dis-entería f

dyslexia /dɪs'leksɪə/ n dislexia f

E

each /i:tʃ/ a cada. —pron cada uno. ~ one cada uno. ~ other uno a otro, el uno al otro. they love ~ other se aman

eager /'i:gə(r)/ a impaciente; (enthusiastic) ávido. ~ly adv

con impaciencia. ~ness n impa-ciencia f, ansia f

eagle /'i:gl/ n águila f

ear[1] /ɪə(r)/ n oído m; (outer) oreja f

ear[2] /ɪə(r)/ n (of corn) espiga f

ear: ~ache /'ɪəreɪk/ n dolor m de oído. ~drum n tímpano m

earl /ɜ:l/ n conde m

early /'ɜ:lɪ/ a (-ier, -iest) tem-prano; (before expected time) pre-maturo. in the ~ spring a principios de la primavera. — adv temprano; (ahead of time) con anticipación

earmark /'ɪəmɑ:k/ vt. ~ for desti-nar a

earn /ɜ:n/ vt ganar; (deserve) merecer

earnest /'ɜ:nɪst/ a serio. in ~ en serio

earnings /'ɜ:nɪŋz/ npl ingresos mpl; (com) ganacias fpl

ear: ~phones /'ɪəfəʊnz/ npl auri-cular m. ~ring n pendiente m

earshot /'ɪəʃɒt/ n. within ~ al alcance del oído

earth /ɜ:θ/ n tierra f. —vt (elec) conectar a tierra. ~ly a terrenal

earthenware /'ɜ:θnweə(r)/ n loza f de barro

earthquake /'ɜ:θkweɪk/ n terre-moto m

earthy /'ɜ:θɪ/ a terroso; (coarse) grosero

earwig /'ɪəwɪg/ n tijereta f

ease /i:z/ n facilidad f; (comfort) tranquilidad f. at ~ a gusto; (mil) en posición de descanso. ill at ~ molesto. with ~ fácil-mente. —vt calmar; aliviar (pain); tranquilizar (mind); (loosen) aflojar. —vi calmarse; (lessen) disminuir

easel /'i:zl/ n caballete m

east /i:st/ n este m, oriente m. —a del este, oriental. —adv hacia el este.

Easter /'i:stə(r)/ n Semana f
Santa; (relig) Pascua f de Resu-
rrección. — **egg** n huevo m de
Pascua

east: ~**erly** a este; (wind) del
este. ~**ern** a del este, oriental.
~**ward** adv, ~**wards** adv hacia
el este

easy /'i:zɪ/ a (-ier, -iest) fácil;
(relaxed) tranquilo. **go** ~ **on**
(fam) tener cuidado con. **take it**
~ no preocuparse. —int ¡despacio! ~ **chair** n sillón m. ~**going** a acomodadizo

eat /i:t/ vt/i (pt **ate**, pp **eaten**)
comer. ~ **into** corroer. ~**able** a
comestible. ~**er** n comedor m

eau-de-Cologne /ˌəʊdəkə'ləʊn/ n
agua f de colonia

eaves /i:vz/ npl alero m

eavesdrop /'i:vzdrɒp/ vi (pt
-**dropped**) escuchar a escondidas

ebb /eb/ n reflujo m. —vi bajar;
(fig) decaer

ebony /'ebənɪ/ n ébano m

ebullient /ɪ'bʌlɪənt/ a exuberante

EC /i:'si:/ abbr (European Community) CE (Comunidad f
Europea)

eccentric /ɪk'sentrɪk/ a & n
excéntrico (m). ~**ity**
/eksen'trɪsətɪ/ n excentricidad f

ecclesiastical /ɪklɪ:zɪ'æstɪkl/ a
eclesiástico

echelon /'eʃəlɒn/ n escalón m

echo /'ekəʊ/ n (pl -**oes**) eco m. —
vt (pt **echoed**, pres p **echoing**)
repetir; (imitate) imitar. —vi
hacer eco

eclectic /ɪk'lektɪk/ a & n ecléc-
tico (m)

eclipse /ɪ'klɪps/ n eclipse m. —vt
eclipsar

ecology /ɪ'kɒlədʒɪ/ n ecología f

economic /i:kə'nɒmɪk/ a económico. ~**ical** a económico.
~**ics** n economía f. ~**ist**

/ɪ'kɒnəmɪst/ n economista m & f.
~**ize** /ɪ'kɒnəmaɪz/ vi economizar. ~**y** /ɪ'kɒnəmɪ/ n economía f

ecstasy /'ekstəsɪ/ n éxtasis f.
~**tic** /ɪk'stætɪk/ a extático.
~**tically** adv con éxtasis

Ecuador /'ekwədɔ:(r)/ n el Ecuador m

ecumenical /i:kju:'menɪkl/ a
ecuménico

eddy /'edɪ/ n remolino m

edge /edʒ/ n borde m, margen m;
(of knife) filo m; (of town) afueras
fpl. **have the** ~ **on** (fam) llevar
la ventaja a. **on** ~ nervioso. —
vt ribetear; (move) mover poco a
poco. —vi avanzar cau-
telosamente. ~**ways** adv de
lado

edging /'edʒɪŋ/ n borde m; (sewing) ribete m

edgy /'edʒɪ/ a nervioso

edible /'edɪbl/ a comestible

edict /'i:dɪkt/ n edicto m

edifice /'edɪfɪs/ n edificio m

edify /'edɪfaɪ/ vt edificar

edit /'edɪt/ vt dirigir (newspaper);
preparar una edición de (text);
(write) redactar; montar (film).
~**ed by** a cargo de. ~**ion** /ɪ'dɪʃn/
n edición f. ~**or** /'edɪtə(r)/ n (of
newspaper) director m; (of text)
redactor m. ~**orial** /edɪ'tɔ:rɪəl/ a
editorial. — n artículo m de
fondo. ~**or in chief** n jefe m de
redacción

educate /'edʒʊkeɪt/ vt instruir,
educar. ~**ed** a culto. ~**ion**
/-'keɪʃn/ n enseñanza f; (culture)
cultura f; (upbringing) educación f. ~**ional** /-'keɪʃənl/ a
instructivo

EEC /i:i:'si:/ abbr (European Economic Community) CEE (Comunidad f Económica Europea)

eel /i:l/ n anguila f

eerie /'ɪərɪ/ a (-ier, -iest)
misterioso

efface /ɪˈfeɪs/ vt borrar

effect /ɪˈfekt/ n efecto m. **in ~** efectivamente. **take ~** entrar en vigor. —vt efectuar

effective /ɪˈfektɪv/ a eficaz; (striking) impresionante; (mil) efectivo. **~ly** adv eficazmente. **~ness** n eficacia f

effeminate /ɪˈfemɪnət/ a afeminado

effervescent /efəˈvesnt/ a efervescente

effete /eˈfiːt/ a agotado

efficien|cy /ɪˈfɪʃənsɪ/ n eficiencia f; (mec) rendimiento m. **~t** /ɪˈfɪʃnt/ a eficiente. **~tly** adv eficientemente

effigy /ˈefɪdʒɪ/ n efigie f

effort /ˈefət/ n esfuerzo m. **~less** a fácil

effrontery /ɪˈfrʌntərɪ/ n descaro m

effusive /ɪˈfjuːsɪv/ a efusivo

e.g. /iːˈdʒiː/ abbr (exempli gratia) p.ej., por ejemplo

egalitarian /ɪgælɪˈteərɪən/ a & n igualitario (m)

egg[1] /eg/ n huevo m

egg[2] /eg/ vt. **~ on** (fam) incitar

egg-cup /ˈegkʌp/ n huevera f

egg-plant /ˈegplɑːnt/ n berenjena f

eggshell /ˈegʃel/ n cáscara f de huevo

ego /ˈiːgəʊ/ n (pl -os) yo m. **~ism** n egoísmo m. **~ist** n egoísta m & f. **~centric** /ˌiːgəʊˈsentrɪk/ a egocéntrico. **~tism** n egotismo m. **~tist** n egotista m & f

Egypt /ˈiːdʒɪpt/ n Egipto m. **~ian** /ɪˈdʒɪpʃn/ a & n egipcio (m)

eh /eɪ/ int (fam) ¡eh!

eiderdown /ˈaɪdədaʊn/ n edredón m

eight /eɪt/ a & n ocho (m)

eighteen /eɪˈtiːn/ a & n dieciocho (m). **~th** a & n decimoctavo (m)

eighth /eɪtθ/ a & n octavo (m)

eight|ieth /ˈeɪtɪəθ/ a & n ochenta (m), octogésimo (m). **~y** /ˈeɪtɪ/ a & n ochenta (m)

either /ˈaɪðə(r)/ a cualquiera de los dos; (negative) ninguno de los dos; (each) cada. —pron uno u otro; (with negative) ni uno ni otro. —adv (negative) tampoco. —conj o. **~ he** or o él o; (with negative) ni él ni

ejaculate /ɪˈdʒækjʊleɪt/ vt/i (exclaim) exclamar

eject /ɪˈdʒekt/ vt expulsar, echar

eke /iːk/ vt. **~ out** hacer bastar; (increase) complementar

elaborate /ɪˈlæbərət/ a complicado. /ɪˈlæbəreɪt/ vt elaborar. —vi explicarse

elapse /ɪˈlæps/ vi (of time) transcurrir

elastic /ɪˈlæstɪk/ a & n elástico (m). **~ band** n goma f (elástica)

elasticity /ɪlæˈstɪsətɪ/ n elasticidad f

elat|ed /ɪˈleɪtɪd/ a regocijado. **~ion** /-ʃn/ n regocijo m

elbow /ˈelbəʊ/ n codo m

elder[1] /ˈeldə(r)/ a mayor (m)

elder[2] /ˈeldə(r)/ n (tree) saúco m

elderly /ˈeldəlɪ/ a mayor, anciano

eldest /ˈeldɪst/ a & n el mayor (m)

elect /ɪˈlekt/ vt elegir. **~ to** decidir hacer. —a electo. **~ion** /-ʃn/ n elección f

elector /ɪˈlektə(r)/ n elector m. **~al** a electoral. **~ate** n electorado m

electric /ɪˈlektrɪk/ a eléctrico. **~al** a eléctrico. **~ blanket** n manta f eléctrica. **~ian** /ɪlekˈtrɪʃn/ n electricista m & f. **~ity** /ɪlekˈtrɪsətɪ/ n electricidad f

electrify /ɪˈlektrɪfaɪ/ vt electrificar; (fig) electrizar

electrocute /ɪˈlektrəkjuːt/ vt electrocutar

electrolysis /ɪlekˈtrɒlɪsɪs/ n electrólisis f

electron /ɪˈlektrɒn/ n electrón m

electronic /ɪlek'trɒnɪk/ a electrónico. ~s n electrónica f

elegan|ce /'elɪɡəns/ n elegancia f. ~t /'elɪɡənt/ a elegante. ~tly adv elegantemente

element /'elɪmənt/ n elemento m. ~ary /-'mentrɪ/ a elemental

elephant /'elɪfənt/ n elefante m

elevat|e /'elɪveɪt/ vt elevar. ~ion /-'veɪʃn/ n elevación f. ~or /'elɪveɪtə(r)/ n (Amer) ascensor m

eleven /ɪ'levn/ a & n once (m). ~th a & n undécimo (m)

elf /elf/ n (pl elves) duende m

elicit /ɪ'lɪsɪt/ vt sacar

eligible /'elɪdʒəbl/ a elegible. be ~ for tener derecho a

eliminat|e /ɪ'lɪmɪneɪt/ vt eliminar. ~ion /-'neɪʃn/ n eliminación f

élite /eɪ'liːt/ n elite f, élite m

elixir /ɪ'lɪksɪə(r)/ n elixir m

ellip|se /ɪ'lɪps/ n elipse f. ~tical a elíptico

elm /elm/ n olmo m

elocution /elə'kjuːʃn/ n elocución f

elongate /'iːlɒŋɡeɪt/ vt alargar

elope /ɪ'ləʊp/ vi fugarse con el amante. ~ment n fuga f

eloquen|ce /'eləkwəns/ n elocuencia f. ~t /'eləkwənt/ a elocuente. ~tly adv con elocuencia

El Salvador /el'sælvədɔː(r)/ n El Salvador m

else /els/ adv más. everybody ~ todos los demás. nobody ~ ningún otro, nadie más. nothing ~ nada más. or ~ o bien. somewhere ~ en otra parte

elsewhere /els'weə(r)/ adv en otra parte

elucidate /ɪ'luːsɪdeɪt/ vt aclarar

elude /ɪ'luːd/ vt eludir

elusive /ɪ'luːsɪv/ a esquivo

emaciated /ɪ'meɪʃɪeɪtɪd/ a esquelético

emanate /'eməneɪt/ vi emanar

emancipat|e /ɪ'mænsɪpeɪt/ vt emancipar. ~ion /-'peɪʃn/ n emancipación f

embalm /ɪm'bɑːm/ vt embalsamar

embankment /ɪm'bæŋkmənt/ n terraplén m; (of river) dique m

embargo /ɪm'bɑːɡəʊ/ n (pl -oes) prohibición f

embark /ɪm'bɑːk/ vt embarcar. —vi embarcarse. ~ on (fig) emprender. ~ation /emba'keɪʃn/ n (of people) embarco m; (of goods) embarque m

embarrass /ɪm'bærəs/ vt desconcertar; (shame) dar vergüenza. ~ment n desconcierto m; (shame) vergüenza f

embassy /'embəsɪ/ n embajada f

embed /ɪm'bed/ vt (pt embedded) embutir; (fig) fijar

embellish /ɪm'belɪʃ/ vt embellecer. ~ment n embellecimiento m

embers /'embəz/ npl ascua f

embezzle /ɪm'bezl/ vt desfalcar. ~ment n desfalco m

embitter /ɪm'bɪtə(r)/ vt amargar

emblem /'embləm/ n emblema m

embod|iment /ɪm'bɒdɪmənt/ n encarnación f. ~y /ɪm'bɒdɪ/ vt encarnar; (include) incluir

emboss /ɪm'bɒs/ vt grabar en relieve, repujar. ~ed a en relieve, repujado

embrace /ɪm'breɪs/ vt abrazar; (fig) abarcar. —vi abrazarse. —n abrazo m

embroider /ɪm'brɔɪdə(r)/ vt bordar. ~y n bordado m

embroil /ɪm'brɔɪl/ vt enredar

embryo /'embrɪəʊ/ n (pl -os) embrión m. ~nic /-'ɒnɪk/ a embrionario

emend /ɪ'mend/ vt enmendar

emerald /'emərəld/ n esmeralda f

emerge /ɪ'mɜːdʒ/ vi salir. ~nce /-əns/ n aparición f

emergency /ɪˈmɜːdʒənsɪ/ n emergencia f. **in an ~** en caso de emergencia. **~ exit** n salida f de emergencia

emery /ˈemərɪ/ n esmeril m. **~-board** n lima f de uñas

emigrant /ˈemɪɡrənt/ n emigrante m & f

emigrat|e /ˈemɪɡreɪt/ vi emigrar. **~ion** /-ˈɡreɪʃn/ n emigración f

eminen|ce /ˈemɪnəns/ n eminencia f. **~t** /ˈemɪnənt/ a eminente. **~tly** adv eminentemente

emissary /ˈemɪsərɪ/ n emisario m

emission /ɪˈmɪʃn/ n emisión f

emit /ɪˈmɪt/ vt (pt emitted) emitir

emollient /ɪˈmɒlɪənt/ a & n emoliente (m)

emotion /ɪˈməʊʃn/ n emoción f. **~onal** a emocional; ⟨person⟩ emotivo; ⟨moving⟩ conmovedor. **~ve** /ɪˈməʊtɪv/ a emotivo

empathy /ˈempəθɪ/ n empatía f

emperor /ˈempərə(r)/ n emperador m

emphas|is /ˈemfəsɪs/ n (pl **~ses** /-siːz/) énfasis m. **~ze** /ˈemfəsaɪz/ vt subrayar; ⟨single out⟩ destacar

emphatic /ɪmˈfætɪk/ a categórico; ⟨resolute⟩ decidido

empire /ˈempaɪə(r)/ n imperio m

empirical /ɪmˈpɪrɪkl/ a empírico

employ /ɪmˈplɔɪ/ vt emplear. **~ee** /emplɔɪˈiː/ n empleado m. **~er** n patrón m. **~ment** n empleo m. **~ment agency** n agencia f de colocaciones

empower /ɪmˈpaʊə(r)/ vt autorizar (**to do** a hacer)

empress /ˈemprɪs/ n emperatriz f

empt|y /ˈemptɪ/ a vacío. npl envases mpl. **~iness** n vacío m. **~y** /ˈemptɪ/ a vacío; ⟨promise⟩ vano. **on an ~y stomach** con el estómago vacío. *vt* vaciar. *vi* vaciarse

emulate /ˈemjʊleɪt/ vt emular

emulsion /ɪˈmʌlʃn/ n emulsión f

enable /ɪˈneɪbl/ vt. **~ s.o. to** permitir a uno

enact /ɪˈnækt/ vt ⟨jurid⟩ decretar; ⟨in theatre⟩ representar

enamel /ɪˈnæml/ n esmalte m. — vt (pt **enamelled**) esmaltar

enamoured /ɪˈnæməd/ a. **be ~ of** estar enamorado de

encampment /ɪnˈkæmpmənt/ n campamento m

encase /ɪnˈkeɪs/ vt encerrar

enchant /ɪnˈtʃɑːnt/ vt encantar. **~ing** a encantador. **~ment** n encanto m

encircle /ɪnˈsɜːkl/ vt rodear

enclave /ˈenkleɪv/ n enclave m

enclos|e /ɪnˈkləʊz/ vt cercar ⟨land⟩; ⟨with letter⟩ adjuntar; ⟨in receptacle⟩ encerrar. **~ed** a ⟨space⟩ encerrado; ⟨com⟩ adjunto. **~ure** /ɪnˈkləʊʒə(r)/ n cercamiento m; ⟨area⟩ recinto m; ⟨com⟩ documento m adjunto

encompass /ɪnˈkʌmpəs/ vt cercar; ⟨include⟩ incluir, abarcar

encore /ˈɒŋkɔː(r)/ int ¡bis! — n bis m, repetición f

encounter /ɪnˈkaʊntə(r)/ vt encontrar. — n encuentro m

encourage /ɪnˈkʌrɪdʒ/ vt animar; ⟨stimulate⟩ estimular. **~ment** n estímulo m

encroach /ɪnˈkrəʊtʃ/ vi. **~ on** invadir ⟨land⟩; quitar ⟨time⟩. **~ment** n usurpación f

encumb|er /ɪnˈkʌmbə(r)/ vt ⟨hamper⟩ estorbar; ⟨burden⟩ cargar. **be ~ered with** estar cargado de. **~rance** n estorbo m; ⟨burden⟩ carga f

encyclical /ɪnˈsɪklɪkl/ n encíclica f

encyclopaedi|a /ɪnsaɪkləˈpiːdɪə/ n enciclopedia f. **~c** a enciclopédico

end /end/ n fin m; ⟨furthest point⟩ extremo m. **in the ~** por fin.

make ~**s meet** poder llegar a fin de mes. **no** ~ (fam) muy. **no** ~ **of** muchísimos. **on** ~ de pie; (consecutive) seguido. —vt/i terminar, acabar

endanger /ɪn'deɪndʒə(r)/ vt arriesgar

endear|ing /ɪn'dɪərɪŋ/ a simpático. ~**ment** n palabra f cariñosa

endeavour /ɪn'devə(r)/ n tentativa f. —vi. ~ **to** esforzarse por

ending /'endɪŋ/ n fin m

endive /'endɪv/ n escarola f, endibia f

endless /'endlɪs/ a interminable; (patience) infinito

endorse /ɪn'dɔ:s/ vt endosar; (fig) aprobar. ~**ment** n endoso m; (fig) aprobación f; (auto) nota f de inhabilitación

endow /ɪn'daʊ/ vt dotar

endur|able /ɪn'djʊərəbl/ a aguantable. ~**ance** n resistencia f. ~**e** /ɪn'djʊə(r)/ vt aguantar. —vi durar. ~**ing** a perdurable

enemy /'enəmɪ/ n & a enemigo (m)

energ|etic /enə'dʒetɪk/ a enérgico. ~**y** /'enədʒɪ/ n energía f

enervate /'enəveɪt/ vt debilitar. ~**ing** a debilitante

enfold /ɪn'fəʊld/ vt envolver; (in arms) abrazar

enforce /ɪn'fɔ:s/ vt aplicar; (impose) imponer; hacer cumplir (law). ~**d** a forzado

engage /ɪn'geɪdʒ/ vt emplear (staff); (reserve) reservar; ocupar (attention); (mec) hacer engranar. —vi (mec) engranar. ~**d** a prometido; (busy) ocupado. **get** ~**d** prometerse. ~**ment** n compromiso m; (undertaking) obligación f

engaging /ɪn'geɪdʒɪŋ/ a atractivo

engender /ɪn'dʒendə(r)/ vt engendrar

engine /'endʒɪn/ n motor m; (of train) locomotora f. ~**driver** n maquinista m

engineer /endʒɪ'nɪə(r)/ n ingeniero m; (mechanic) mecánico m. —vt (contrive, fam) lograr. ~**ing** n ingeniería f

England /'ɪŋglənd/ n Inglaterra f

English /'ɪŋglɪʃ/ a inglés. —n (lang) inglés m; (people) ingleses mpl. ~**man** n inglés m. ~**woman** n inglesa f. **the** ~ **Channel** el canal m de la Mancha

engrave /ɪn'greɪv/ vt grabar. ~**ing** n grabado m

engrossed /ɪn'grəʊst/ a absorto

engulf /ɪn'gʌlf/ vt tragar(se)

enhance /ɪn'hɑ:ns/ vt aumentar

enigma /ɪ'nɪgmə/ n enigma m. ~**tic** /enɪg'mætɪk/ a enigmático

enjoy /ɪn'dʒɔɪ/ vt gozar de. ~ **o.s.** divertirse. **I** ~ **reading** me gusta la lectura. ~**able** a agradable. ~**ment** n placer m

enlarge /ɪn'lɑ:dʒ/ vt agrandar; (foto) ampliar. —vi agrandarse. ~ **upon** extenderse sobre. ~**ment** n (foto) ampliación f

enlighten /ɪn'laɪtn/ vt aclarar; (inform) informar. ~**ment** n aclaración f. **the E**~**ment** el siglo m de las luces

enlist /ɪn'lɪst/ vt alistar; (fig) conseguir. —vi alistarse

enliven /ɪn'laɪvn/ vt animar

enmity /'enmətɪ/ n enemistad f

ennoble /ɪ'nəʊbl/ vt ennoblecer

enormity /ɪ'nɔːmətɪ/ n enormidad f. ~**ous** /ɪ'nɔːməs/ a enorme

enough /ɪ'nʌf/ a & adv bastante. —n bastante m, suficiente m. —int ¡basta!

enquir|e /ɪn'kwaɪə(r)/ vt/i preguntar. ~**e** about informarse de. ~**y** n pregunta f; (investigation) investigación f

enrage /ɪn'reɪdʒ/ vt enfurecer

enrapture /ɪnˈræptʃə(r)/ vt extasiar

enrich /ɪnˈrɪtʃ/ vt enriquecer

enrol /ɪnˈrəʊl/ vt (pt **enrolled**) inscribir; matricular ⟨student⟩. —vi inscribirse; ⟨student⟩ matricularse. ~**ment** n inscripción f; ⟨of student⟩ matrícula f

ensconce /ɪnˈskɒns/ vt. ~ **o.s.** arrellanarse

ensemble /ɒnˈsɒmbl/ n conjunto m

enshrine /ɪnˈʃraɪn/ vt encerrar

ensign /ˈensaɪn/ n enseña f

enslave /ɪnˈsleɪv/ vt esclavizar

ensue /ɪnˈsjuː/ vi resultar, seguirse

ensure /ɪnˈʃʊə(r)/ vt asegurar

entail /ɪnˈteɪl/ vt suponer; acarrear ⟨trouble etc⟩

entangle /ɪnˈtæŋgl/ vt enredar. ~**ment** n enredo m; ⟨mil⟩ alambrada f

enter /ˈentə(r)/ vt entrar en; ⟨write⟩ escribir; matricular ⟨school etc⟩; hacerse socio de ⟨club⟩. —vi entrar

enterprise /ˈentəpraɪz/ n empresa f; ⟨fig⟩ iniciativa f

enterprising /ˈentəpraɪzɪŋ/ a emprendedor

entertain /entəˈteɪn/ vt divertir; recibir ⟨guests⟩; abrigar ⟨ideas, hopes⟩; ⟨consider⟩ considerar. ~**ment** n diversión f; ⟨performance⟩ espectáculo m; ⟨reception⟩ recepción f

enthral /ɪnˈθrɔːl/ vt (pt **enthralled**) cautivar

enthuse /ɪnˈθjuːz/ vi. ~ **over** entusiasmarse por

enthusiasm /ɪnˈθjuːzɪæzəm/ n entusiasmo m. ~**tic** /-ˈæstɪk/ a entusiasta; ⟨thing⟩ entusiástico. ~**tically** /-ˈæstɪklɪ/ adv con entusiasmo. ~**t** /ɪnˈθjuːzɪæst/ n entusiasta m & f

entice /ɪnˈtaɪs/ vt atraer. ~**ment** n atracción f

entire /ɪnˈtaɪə(r)/ a entero. ~**ly** adv completamente. ~**ty** /ɪnˈtaɪərətɪ/ n. in its ~**ty** en su totalidad

entitle /ɪnˈtaɪtl/ vt titular; ⟨give a right⟩ dar derecho a. be ~**d to** tener derecho a. ~**ment** n derecho m

entity /ˈentɪtɪ/ n entidad f

entomb /ɪnˈtuːm/ vt sepultar

entrails /ˈentreɪlz/ npl entrañas fpl

entrance[1] /ˈentrəns/ n entrada f; ⟨right to enter⟩ admisión f

entrance[2] /ɪnˈtrɑːns/ vt encantar

entrant /ˈentrənt/ n participante m & f; ⟨in exam⟩ candidato m

entreat /ɪnˈtriːt/ vt suplicar. ~**y** n súplica f

entrench /ɪnˈtrentʃ/ vt atrincherar

entrust /ɪnˈtrʌst/ vt confiar

entry /ˈentrɪ/ n entrada f; ⟨of street⟩ bocacalle f; ⟨note⟩ apunte m

entwine /ɪnˈtwaɪn/ vt entrelazar

enumerate /ɪˈnjuːməreɪt/ vt enumerar

enunciate /ɪˈnʌnsɪeɪt/ vt pronunciar; ⟨state⟩ enunciar

envelop /ɪnˈveləp/ vt (pt **enveloped**) envolver

envelope /ˈenvələʊp/ n sobre m

enviable /ˈenvɪəbl/ a envidiable

envious /ˈenvɪəs/ a envidioso. ~**ly** adv con envidia

environment /ɪnˈvaɪərənmənt/ n medio m ambiente. ~**al** /-ˈmentl/ a ambiental

envisage /ɪnˈvɪzɪdʒ/ vt prever; ⟨imagine⟩ imaginar

envoy /ˈenvɔɪ/ n enviado m

envy /ˈenvɪ/ n envidia f. —vt envidiar

enzyme /ˈenzaɪm/ n enzima f

epaulette /ˈepəʊlet/ n charretera f

ephemeral /ɪ'femərəl/ a efímero

epic /'epik/ n épica f. —a épico

epicentre /'episentə(r)/ n epicentro m

epicure /'epɪkjʊə(r)/ n sibarita m & f; (gourmet) gastrónomo m

epidemic /epɪ'demɪk/ n epidemia f. —a epidémico

epileps|sy /'epɪlepsɪ/ n epilepsia f. ~tic /-'leptɪk/ a & n epiléptico (m)

epilogue /'epɪlog/ n epílogo m

episode /'epɪsəʊd/ n episodio m

epistle /ɪ'pɪsl/ n epístola f

epitaph /'epɪtɑːf/ n epitafio m

epithet /'epɪθet/ n epíteto m

epitom|e /ɪ'pɪtəmɪ/ n epítome m, personificación f. ~ize vt epitomar, personificar, ser la personificación de

epoch /'iːpok/ n época f. ~-making a que hace época

equal /'iːkwəl/ a & n igual (m & f). ~ to (a task) a la altura de. — vt (pt equalled) ser igual a; (math) ser. ~ity /ɪ'kwolətɪ/ n igualdad f. ~ize /'iːkwəlaɪz/ vt/i igualar. ~izer /-ə(r)/ n (sport) tanto m de empate. ~ly adv igualmente

equanimity /ekwə'nɪmətɪ/ n ecuanimidad f

equate /ɪ'kweɪt/ vt igualar

equation /ɪ'kweɪʒn/ n ecuación f

equator /ɪ'kweɪtə(r)/ n ecuador m. ~ial /ekwə'tɔːrɪəl/ a ecuatorial

equestrian /ɪ'kwestrɪən/ a ecuestre

equilateral /iːkwɪ'lætərl/ a equilátero

equilibrium /iːkwɪ'lɪbrɪəm/ n equilibrio m

equinox /'iːkwɪnoks/ n equinoccio m

equip /ɪ'kwɪp/ vt (pt equipped) equipar. ~ment n equipo m

equitable /'ekwɪtəbl/ a equitativo

equity /'ekwətɪ/ n equidad f; (pl, com) acciones fpl ordinarias

equivalen|ce /ɪ'kwɪvələns/ n equivalencia f. ~t /ɪ'kwɪvələnt/ a & n equivalente (m)

equivocal /ɪ'kwɪvəkl/ a equívoco

era /'ɪərə/ n era f

eradicate /ɪ'rædɪkeɪt/ vt extirpar

erase /ɪ'reɪz/ vt borrar. ~r /-ə(r)/ n borrador m

erect /ɪ'rekt/ a erguido. —vt levantar. ~ion /-ʃn/ n erección f, montaje m

ermine /'ɜːmɪn/ n armiño m

erode /ɪ'rəʊd/ vt desgastar. ~sion /-ʒn/ n desgaste m

erotic /ɪ'rotɪk/ a erótico. ~ism /-sɪzəm/ n erotismo m

err /ɜː(r)/ vi errar; (sin) pecar

errand /'erənd/ n recado m

erratic /ɪ'rætɪk/ a irregular; (person) voluble

erroneous /ɪ'rəʊnɪəs/ a erróneo

error /'erə(r)/ n error m

erudit|e /'eruːdaɪt/ a erudito. ~ion /-'dɪʃn/ n erudición f

erupt /ɪ'rʌpt/ vi estar en erupción; (fig) estallar. ~ion /-ʃn/ n erupción f

escalat|e /'eskəleɪt/ vt intensificar. —vi intensificarse. ~ion /-'leɪʃn/ n intensificación f

escalator /'eskəleɪtə(r)/ n escalera f mecánica

escapade /eskə'peɪd/ n aventura f

escap|e /ɪ'skeɪp/ vi escaparse. — vt evitar. —n fuga f; (avoidance) evasión f. have a narrow ~e escapar por un pelo. ~ism /ɪ'skeɪpɪzəm/ n escapismo m

escarpment /esˈkɑːpmənt/ n escarpa f

escort /'eskɔːt/ n acompañante m; (mil) escolta f. /ɪ'skɔːt/ vt acompañar; (mil) escoltar

Eskimo /'eskɪməʊ/ n (pl -os, -o) esquimal (m & f)

especial /ɪˈspeʃl/ a especial. **~ly** adv especialmente

espionage /ˈespɪɒnɑːʒ/ n espionaje m

esplanade /espləˈneɪd/ n paseo m marítimo

Esq. /ɪˈskweɪə(r)/ abbr (*Esquire*) (*in address*). E. Ashton, **~** Sr. D. E. Ashton

essay /ˈeseɪ/ n ensayo m; (*at school*) composición f

essence /ˈesns/ n esencia f. **in ~** esencialmente

essential /ɪˈsenʃl/ a esencial. **—n** lo esencial. **~ly** adv esencialmente

establish /ɪˈstæblɪʃ/ vt establecer; (*prove*) probar. **~ment** n establecimiento m. **the E~ment** los que mandan, el sistema m

estate /ɪˈsteɪt/ n finca f; (*possessions*) bienes mpl. **~ agent** n agente m inmobiliario. **~ car** n furgoneta f

esteem /ɪˈstiːm/ vt estimar. **—n** estimación f, estima f

estimate /ˈestɪmət/ n cálculo m; (*com*) presupuesto m. /ˈestɪmeɪt/ vt calcular. **~ion** /-ˈmeɪʃn/ n estima f, estimación f; (*opinion*) opinión f

estranged /ɪsˈtreɪndʒd/ a alejado

estuary /ˈestjʊərɪ/ n estuario m

etc. /etˈsetrə/ abbr (*et cetera*) etc., etcétera

etching /ˈetʃɪŋ/ n aguafuerte m

eternal /ɪˈtɜːnl/ a eterno

eternity /ɪˈtɜːnətɪ/ n eternidad f

ether /ˈiːθə(r)/ n éter m

ethereal /ɪˈθɪərɪəl/ a etéreo

ethic /ˈeθɪk/ n ética f. **~s** npl ética f. **~al** a ético

ethnic /ˈeθnɪk/ a étnico

ethos /ˈiːθɒs/ n carácter m distintivo

etiquette /ˈetɪket/ n etiqueta f

etymology /etɪˈmɒlədʒɪ/ n etimología f

eucalyptus /juːkəˈlɪptəs/ n (*pl -tuses*) eucalipto m

eulogy /ˈjuːlədʒɪ/ n encomio m

euphemism /ˈjuːfəmɪzəm/ n eufemismo m

euphoria /juːˈfɔːrɪə/ n euforia f

Europe /ˈjʊərəp/ n Europa f. **~an** /-ˈpɪən/ a & n europeo (m)

euthanasia /juːθəˈneɪzɪə/ n eutanasia f

evacuate /ɪˈvækjʊeɪt/ vt evacuar; desocupar (*building*). **~ion** /-ˈeɪʃn/ n evacuación f

evade /ɪˈveɪd/ vt evadir

evaluate /ɪˈvæljʊeɪt/ vt evaluar

evangelical /iːvænˈdʒelɪkl/ a evangélico. **~st** /ɪˈvændʒəlɪst/ n evangelista m & f

evaporate /ɪˈvæpəreɪt/ vi evaporarse. **~ion** /-ˈreɪʃn/ n evaporación f

evasion /ɪˈveɪʒn/ n evasión f

evasive /ɪˈveɪsɪv/ a evasivo

eve /iːv/ n víspera f

even /ˈiːvn/ a regular; (*flat*) llano; (*surface*) liso; (*amount*) igual; (*number*) par. **get ~ with** desquitarse con. **—vt** nivelar. **~ up** igualar. **—adv** aun, hasta, incluso. **~ if** aunque. **so even** así. **not ~** ni siquiera

evening /ˈiːvnɪŋ/ n tarde f; (*after dark*) noche f. **~ class** n clase f nocturna. **~ dress** n (*man's*) traje m de etiqueta; (*woman's*) traje m de noche

evensong /ˈiːvənsɒŋ/ n vísperas fpl

event /ɪˈvent/ n acontecimiento m; (*sport*) prueba f. **in the ~ of** en caso de. **~ful** a lleno de acontecimientos

eventual /ɪˈventʃʊəl/ a final, definitivo. **~ity** /-ˈælətɪ/ n eventualidad f. **~ly** adv finalmente

ever /ˈevə(r)/ adv jamás, nunca; (*at all times*) siempre. **~ after** desde entonces. **~ since** desde entonces. **—conj** después de que.

~ **so** (*fam*) muy. **for** ~ para
siempre. **hardly** ~ casi nunca
evergreen /'evəgriːn/ *a* de hoja
perenne. —*n* árbol *m* de hoja
perenne
everlasting /'evəlɑːstɪŋ/ *a* eterno
every /'evrɪ/ *a* cada, todo. ~
child todos los niños. ~ **one**
cada uno. ~ **other day** cada dos
días
everybody /'evrɪbɒdɪ/ *pron* todo
el mundo
everyday /'evrɪdeɪ/ *a* todos los
días
everyone /'evrɪwʌn/ *pron* todo el
mundo. ~ **else** todos los demás
everything /'evrɪθɪŋ/ *pron* todo
everywhere /'evrɪweə(r)/ *adv* en
todas partes
evict /ɪ'vɪkt/ *vt* desahuciar. ~**ion**
/-ʃn/ *n* desahucio *m*
eviden|ce /'evɪdəns/ *n* evidencia
f; (*proof*) pruebas *fpl*; (*jurid*) testimonio *m*. ~**ce of** señales de. **in**
~**ce** visible. ~**t** /'evɪdənt/ *a* evidente. ~**tly** *adv* evidentemente
evil /'iːvl/ *a* malo. —*n* mal *m*, maldad *f*
evocative /ɪ'vɒkətɪv/ *a* evocador
evoke /ɪ'vəʊk/ *vt* evocar
evolution /iːvə'luːʃn/ *n* evolución *f*
evolve /ɪ'vɒlv/ *vt* desarrollar. —
vi desarrollarse, evolucionar
ewe /juː/ *n* oveja *f*
ex... /eks/ *pref* ex...
exacerbate /ɪg'zæsəbeɪt/ *vt* exacerbar
exact /ɪg'zækt/ *a* exacto. —*vt*
exigir (**from** a). ~**ing** *a* exigente. ~**itude** /n* exactitud *f*. ~**ly**
adv exactamente
exaggerat|e /ɪg'zædʒəreɪt/ *vt*
exagerar. ~**ion** /n* exageración *f*
exalt /ɪg'zɔːlt/ *vt* exaltar
exam /ɪg'zæm/ *n* (*fam*) examen
m. ~**ination** /ɪgzæmɪ'neɪʃn/ *n*
examen *m*. ~**ine** /ɪg'zæmɪn/ *vt*

examinar; interrogar ⟨*witness*⟩.
~**iner** /-ə(r)/ *n* examinador *m*
example /ɪg'zɑːmpl/ *n* ejemplo *m*.
make an ~ **of** infligir castigo
ejemplar a
exasperat|e /ɪg'zæspəreɪt/ *vt*
exasperar. ~**ion** /-'reɪʃn/ *n*
exasperación *f*
excavat|e /'ekskəveɪt/ *vt* excavar. ~**ion** /-'veɪʃn/ *n* excavación *f*
exceed /ɪk'siːd/ *vt* exceder.
~**ingly** *adv* extremadamente
excel /ɪk'sel/ *vi* (*pt* **excelled**)
sobresalir. —*vt* superar
excellen|ce /'eksələns/ *n* excelencia *f*. ~**t** /'eksələnt/ *a* excelente. ~**tly** *adv* excelentemente
except /ɪk'sept/ *prep* excepto,
con excepción de. ~ **for** con
excepción de. —*vt* exceptuar.
~**ing** *prep* con excepción de
exception /ɪk'sepʃn/ *n* excepción *f*. **take** ~ **to** ofenderse por.
~**al** /ɪk'sepʃənl/ *a* excepcional.
~**ally** *adv* excepcionalmente
excerpt /'eksɜːpt/ *n* extracto *m*
excess /ɪk'ses/ *n* exceso *m*.
/'ekses/ *a* excedente. ~ **fare** *n*
suplemento *m*. ~ **luggage** *n*
exceso *m* de equipaje
excessive /ɪk'sesɪv/ *a* excesivo.
~**ly** *adv* excesivamente
exchange /ɪks'tʃeɪndʒ/ *vt* cambiar. —*n* cambio *m*. (**telephone**)
~ **central** *f* telefónica
exchequer /ɪks'tʃekə(r)/ *n* (*pol*)
erario *m*, hacienda *f*
excise¹ /'eksaɪz/ *n* impuestos *mpl*
indirectos
excise² /ek'saɪz/ *vt* quitar
excit|able /ɪk'saɪtəbl/ *a* excitable. ~**e** /ɪk'saɪt/ *vt* emocionar;
(*stimulate*) excitar. ~**ed** *a* entusiasmado. ~**ement** *n* emoción *f*;
(*enthusiasm*) entusiasmo *m*.
~**ing** *a* emocionante
exclaim /ɪk'skleɪm/ *vi* exclamar. ~**mation** /ekskləˈmeɪʃn/ *n*

exclamación f. ∼**mation mark** n signo m de admiración f, punto m de exclamación

exclu|de /ɪk'sklu:d/ vt excluir. ∼**sion** /-ʒən/ n exclusión f

exclusive /ɪk'sklu:sɪv/ a exclusivo; ⟨club⟩ selecto. ∼ **of** excluyendo. ∼**ly** adv exclusivamente

excommunicate /ekskə'mju:nɪkeɪt/ vt excomulgar

excrement /'ekskrɪmənt/ n excremento m

excruciating /ɪk'skru:ʃɪeɪtɪŋ/ a atroz, insoportable

excursion /ɪk'ska:ʃn/ n excursión f

excus|able a /ɪk'skju:zəbl/ a perdonable. ∼**e** /ɪk'skju:z/ vt perdonar. ∼**e from** dispensar de. ∼**e me!** ¡perdón! /ɪk'skju:s/ n excusa f

ex-directory /eksdɪ'rektərɪ/ a que no está en la guía telefónica

execrable /'eksɪkrəbl/ a execrable

execut|e /'eksɪkju:t/ vt ejecutar. ∼**ion** /eksɪ'kju:ʃn/ n ejecución f. ∼**ioner** n verdugo m

executive /ɪg'zekjʊtɪv/ a & n ejecutivo (m)

executor /ɪg'zekjʊtə(r)/ n (jurid) testamentario m

exemplary /ɪg'zemplərɪ/ a ejemplar

exemplify /ɪg'zemplɪfaɪ/ vt ilustrar

exempt /ɪg'zempt/ a exento. —vt dispensar. ∼**ion** /-ʃn/ n exención f

exercise /'eksəsaɪz/ n ejercicio m. —vt ejercer. —vi hacer ejercicios. ∼ **book** n cuaderno m

exert /ɪg'zɜ:t/ vt ejercer. ∼**o.s.** esforzarse. ∼**ion** /-ʃn/ n esfuerzo m

exhal|ation /ekshə'leɪʃn/ n exhalación f. ∼**e** /eks'heɪl/ vt/i exhalar

exhaust /ɪg'zɔ:st/ vt agotar. —n (auto) tubo m de escape. ∼**ed** a agotado. ∼**ion** /-stʃən/ n agotamiento m. ∼**ive** /ɪg'zɔ:stɪv/ a exhaustivo

exhibit /ɪg'zɪbɪt/ vt exponer; (jurid) exhibir; (fig) mostrar. —n objeto m expuesto; (jurid) documento m

exhibition /eksɪ'bɪʃn/ n exposición f; (act of showing) demostración f; (univ) beca f. ∼**ist** n exhibicionista m & f

exhibitor /ɪg'zɪbɪtə(r)/ n expositor m

exhilarat|e /ɪg'zɪləreɪt/ vt alegrar. ∼**ion** /-'reɪʃn/ n regocijo m

exhort /ɪg'zɔ:t/ vt exhortar

exile /'eksaɪl/ n exilio m; (person) exiliado m. —vt desterrar

exist /ɪg'zɪst/ vi existir. ∼**ence** n existencia f. **in** ∼**ence** existente

existentialism /egzɪs'tenʃəlɪzəm/ n existencialismo m

exit /'eksɪt/ n salida f

exodus /'eksədəs/ n éxodo m

exonerate /ɪg'zɒnəreɪt/ vt disculpar

exorbitant /ɪg'zɔ:bɪtənt/ a exorbitante

exorcis|e /'eksɔ:saɪz/ vt exorcizar. ∼**m** /-sɪzəm/ n exorcismo m

exotic /ɪg'zɒtɪk/ a exótico

expand /ɪk'spænd/ vt extender; dilatar ⟨metal⟩; (develop) desarrollar. —vi extenderse; (develop) desarrollarse; ⟨metal⟩ dilatarse

expanse /ɪk'spæns/ n extensión f

expansion /ɪk'spænʃn/ n extensión f; (of metal) dilatación f

expansive /ɪk'spænsɪv/ a expansivo

expatriate /eks'pætrɪət/ a & n expatriado (m)

expect /ɪk'spekt/ vt esperar; (suppose) suponer; (demand)

contar con. **I ~ so** supongo que
sí

expectan|cy /ɪk'spektənsɪ/ *n*
esperanza *f*. **life ~cy** esperanza
f de vida. **~t** /ɪk'spektənt/ *a*
expectante. **~t mother** *n* futura
madre *f*

expectation /ekspek'teɪʃn/ *n*
esperanza *f*

expedien|cy /ɪk'spiːdɪənsɪ/ *n*
conveniencia *f*. **~t** /ɪk'spiːdɪənt/
a conveniente

expedite /'ekspɪdaɪt/ *vt* acelerar

expedition /ekspɪ'dɪʃn/ *n* expedición *f*. **~ary** *a* expedicionario

expel /ɪk'spel/ *vt* (*pt* **expelled**)
expulsar

expend /ɪk'spend/ *vt* gastar.
~able *a* prescindible

expenditure /ɪk'spendɪtʃə(r)/ *n*
gastos *mpl*

expens|e /ɪk'spens/ *n* gasto *m*,
(*fig*) costa *f*. **at s.o.'s ~e** a costa
de uno. **~ive** /ɪk'spensɪv/ *a* caro.
~ively *adv* costosamente

experience /ɪk'spɪərɪəns/ *n*
experiencia. **~d** *a* experto

experiment /ɪk'sperɪmənt/ *n*
experimento *m*. **~i** /ɪk'sper-
ɪment/ *vi* experimentar. **~al** /-'mentl/ *a*
experimental

expert /'ekspɜːt/ *a & n* experto
(*m*). **~ise** /eksp3ː'tiːz/ *n* pericia *f*.
~ly *adv* hábilmente

expir|e /ɪk'spaɪə(r)/ *vi* expirar.
~y *n* expiración *f*

expla|in /ɪk'spleɪn/ *vt* explicar.
~nation /eksplə'neɪʃn/ *n* expli-
cación *f*. **~natory** /ɪks'plæn-
ətərɪ/ *a* explicatorio

expletive /ɪk'spliːtɪv/ *n* palabrota *f*

explicit /ɪk'splɪsɪt/ *a* explícito

explode /ɪk'spləʊd/ *vt* hacer
explotar; (*tec*) explosionar. —*vi*
estallar

exploit /'eksplɔɪt/ *n* hazaña *f*.
/ɪk'splɔɪt/ *vt* explotar. **~ation**
/eksplɔɪ'teɪʃn/ *n* explotación *f*

explor|ation /eksplə'reɪʃn/ *n*
exploración *f*. **~atory** /ɪk-
'splɒrətrɪ/ *a* exploratorio. **~e** /ɪk-
'splɔː(r)/ *vt* explorar. **~er** *n* explorador *m*

explos|ion /ɪk'spləʊʒn/ *n* explo-
sión *f*. **~ve** *a* & *n* explosivo (*m*)

exponent /ɪk'spəʊnənt/ *n* exponente *m*

export /ɪk'spɔːt/ *vt* exportar.
/'ekspɔːt/ *n* exportación *f*. **~er**
/ɪks'pɔːtə(r)/ exportador *m*

expos|e /ɪk'spəʊz/ *vt* exponer;
(*reveal*) descubrir. **~ure** /-ʒə(r)/
n exposición *f*. **die of ~ure**
morir de frío

expound /ɪk'spaʊnd/ *vt* exponer

express[1] /ɪk'spres/ *vt* expresar

express[2] /ɪk'spres/ *a* expreso; (*letter*) urgente. —*adv* (*by express
post*) por correo urgente. **—n**
(*train*) rápido *m*, expreso *m*

expression /ɪk'spreʃn/ *n* expresión *f*

expressive /ɪk'spresɪv/ *a* ex-
presivo

expressly /ɪk'spreslɪ/ *adv* expresamente

expulsion /ɪk'spʌlʃn/ *n* expul-
sión *f*

expurgate /'ekspəgeɪt/ *vt* expurgar

exquisite /'ekskwɪzɪt/ *a* exqui-
sito. **~ly** *adv* primorosamente

ex-serviceman /eks'sɜːvɪsmən/
n (*pl* -**men**) excombatiente *m*

extant /ek'stænt/ *a* existente

extempore /ek'stempərɪ/ *a* improvisado. —*adv* de improviso

extend /ɪk'stend/ *vt* extender;
(*prolong*) prolongar; ensanchar
(*house*). —*vi* extenderse. **~sion**
n extensión *f*; (*of road, time*) pro-
longación *f*; (*building*) anejo *m*;
(*com*) prórroga *f*

extensive /ɪk'stensɪv/ *a* extenso.
~ly *adv* extensamente

extent /ɪk'stent/ n extensión f; (fig) alcance f. **to a certain ~** hasta cierto punto

extenuate /ɪk'stenjʊeɪt/ vt atenuar

exterior /ɪk'stɪərɪə(r)/ a & n exterior (m)

exterminate /ɪk'stɜːmɪneɪt/ vt exterminar. **~ion** /-'neɪʃn/ n exterminio m

external /ɪk'stɜːnl/ a externo. **~ly** adv externamente

extinct /ɪk'stɪŋkt/ a extinto. **~ion** /-ʃn/ n extinción f

extinguish /ɪk'stɪŋgwɪʃ/ vt extinguir. **~er** n extintor m

extol /ɪk'stəʊl/ vt (pt extolled) alabar

extort /ɪk'stɔːt/ vt sacar por la fuerza. **~ion** /-ʃn/ n exacción f. **~ionate** /ɪk'stɔːʃənət/ a exorbitante

extra /'ekstrə/ a suplementario. —adv extraordinariamente. —n suplemento m; (cinema) extra m & f

extract /'ekstrækt/ n extracto m. /ɪk'strækt/ vt extraer; (fig) arrancar. **~ion** /-ʃn/ n extracción f; (lineage) origen m

extradite /'ekstrədaɪt/ vt extraditar. **~ion** /-'dɪʃn/ n extradición f

extramarital /ekstrə'mærɪtl/ a fuera del matrimonio

extramural /ekstrə'mjʊərəl/ a fuera del recinto universitario; (for external students) para estudiantes externos

extraordinary /ɪk'strɔːdnrɪ/ a extraordinario

extra-sensory /ekstrə'sensərɪ/ a extrasensorial

extravagan|ce /ɪk'strævəgəns/ n prodigalidad f, extravagancia f. **~t** /ɪk'strævəgənt/ a pródigo, extravagante

extreme /ɪk'striːm/ a & n extremo (m). **~ely** adv extremadamente. **~ist** n extremista

m & f. **~ity** /ɪk'stremətɪ/ n extremidad f

extricate /'ekstrɪkeɪt/ vt desenredar, librar

extrovert /'ekstrəvɜːt/ n extrovertido m

exuberan|ce /ɪg'zjuːbərəns/ n exuberancia f. **~t** /ɪg'zjuːbərənt/ a exuberante

exude /ɪg'zjuːd/ vt rezumar

exult /ɪg'zʌlt/ vi exultar

eye /aɪ/ n ojo m. **keep an ~ on** no perder de vista. **see ~ to ~** estar de acuerdo con. —vt (pt eyed, pres p eyeing) mirar. **~ball** /'aɪbɔːl/ n globo m del ojo. **~brow** /'aɪbraʊ/ n ceja f. **~ful** /'aɪfʊl/ n (fam) espectáculo m sorprendente. **~lash** /'aɪlæʃ/ n pestaña f. **~let** /'aɪlɪt/ n ojete m. **~lid** /'aɪlɪd/ n párpado m. **~opener** n (fam) revelación f. **~shadow** n sombra f de ojos, sombreador m. **~sight** /'aɪsaɪt/ n vista f. **~sore** /'aɪsɔː(r)/ n (fig, fam) monstruosidad f, horror m. **~witness** /'aɪwɪtnɪs/ n testigo m ocular

F

fable /'feɪbl/ n fábula f

fabric /'fæbrɪk/ n tejido m, tela f

fabrication /fæbrɪ'keɪʃn/ n invención f

fabulous /'fæbjʊləs/ a fabuloso

façade /fə'sɑːd/ n fachada f

face /feɪs/ n cara f, rostro m; (of watch) esfera f; (aspect) aspecto m. **~ down(wards)** boca abajo. **~ up(wards)** boca arriba. **in the ~** of frente a. **lose ~** quedar mal. **pull ~s** hacer muecas. —vt mirar hacia; (house) dar a; (confront) enfrentarse con. —vi volverse. **~ up to** enfrentarse con.

~ **flannel** n paño m (para lavarse la cara). ~**less** a anónimo.
~-**lift** n cirugía f estética en la cara

facet /'fæsɪt/ n faceta f

facetious /fə'si:ʃəs/ a chistoso, gracioso

facial /'feɪʃl/ a facial. —n masaje m facial

facile /'fæsaɪl/ a fácil

facilitate /fə'sɪlɪteɪt/ vt facilitar

facility /fə'sɪlɪtɪ/ n facilidad f

facing /'feɪsɪŋ/ n revestimiento m. ~s npl (on clothes) vueltas fpl

facsimile /fæk'sɪmɪlɪ/ n facsímile m

fact /fækt/ n hecho m. **as a matter of** ~, **in** ~ en realidad, a decir verdad

faction /'fækʃn/ n facción f

factor /'fæktə(r)/ n factor m

factory /'fæktərɪ/ n fábrica f

factual /'fæktʃʊəl/ a basado en hechos, factual

faculty /'fækəltɪ/ n facultad f

fad /fæd/ n manía f, capricho m

fade /feɪd/ vi ⟨colour⟩ descolorarse; ⟨flowers⟩ marchitarse; ⟨light⟩ apagarse; ⟨memory, sound⟩ desvanecerse

faeces /'fi:si:z/ npl excrementos mpl

fag[1] /fæg/ n ⟨chore, fam⟩ faena f; ⟨cigarette, sl⟩ cigarillo m, pitillo m

fag[2] /fæg/ n ⟨homosexual, Amer, sl⟩ marica m

fagged /fægd/ a. ~ (**out**) rendido

fah /fɑ/ n ⟨mus, fourth note of any musical scale⟩ fa m

fail /feɪl/ vi fallar; ⟨run short⟩ acabarse. **he** ~**ed to arrive** no llegó. —vt no aprobar ⟨exam⟩; suspender ⟨candidate⟩; ⟨disappoint⟩ fallar. ~ **s.o.** ⟨words etc⟩ faltarle a uno. —n. **without** ~ sin falta

failing /'feɪlɪŋ/ n defecto m. —prep a falta de

failure /'feɪljə(r)/ n fracaso m; ⟨person⟩ fracasado m; ⟨med⟩ ataque m; ⟨mec⟩ fallo m. ~ **to do** dejar m de hacer

faint /feɪnt/ a (-er, -est) ⟨weak⟩ débil; ⟨indistinct⟩ indistinto. **feel** ~ estar mareado. **the** ~**est idea** la más remota idea. —vi desmayarse. —n desmayo m. ~-**hearted** a pusilánime, cobarde. ~**ly** adv ⟨weakly⟩ débilmente; ⟨indistinctly⟩ indistintamente. ~**ness** n debilidad f

fair[1] /feə(r)/ a (-er, -est) ⟨just⟩ justo; ⟨weather⟩ bueno; ⟨amount⟩ razonable; ⟨hair⟩ rubio; ⟨skin⟩ blanco. ~ **play** n juego m limpio. —adv limpio

fair[2] /feə(r)/ n feria f

fair: ~**ly** adv ⟨justly⟩ justamente; ⟨rather⟩ bastante. ~**ness** n justicia f

fairy /'feərɪ/ n hada f. ~**land** n país m de las hadas. ~ **story**, ~-**tale** cuento m de hadas

fait accompli /feɪtə'komplɪ/ n hecho m consumado

faith /feɪθ/ n ⟨trust⟩ confianza f; ⟨relig⟩ fe f. ~**ful** a fiel. ~**fully** adv fielmente. ~**fulness** n fidelidad f. ~-**healing** n curación f por la fe

fake /feɪk/ n falsificación f; ⟨person⟩ impostor m. —a falso. —vt falsificar; ⟨pretend⟩ fingir

fakir /'feɪkɪə(r)/ n faquir m

falcon /'fɔ:lkən/ n halcón m

Falkland /'fɔ:lklənd/ n. **the** ~ **Islands** npl las islas fpl Malvinas

fall /fɔ:l/ vi (pt **fell**, pp **fallen**) caer. —n caída f; ⟨autumn, Amer⟩ otoño m; ⟨in price⟩ baja f. ~ **back on** recurrir a. ~ **down** ⟨fall⟩ caer; ⟨be unsuccessful⟩ fracasar. ~ **for** ⟨person⟩ enamorarse de ⟨person⟩; ⟨fam⟩ dejarse engañar por ⟨trick⟩. ~ **in** ⟨mil⟩ formar filas. ~ **off** ⟨diminish⟩ disminuir. ~ **out**

fallacy /'fæləsɪ/ n error m

fallible /'fæləbl/ a falible

fallout /'fɔːlaʊt/ n lluvia f radiactiva

fallow /'fæləʊ/ a en barbecho

false /fɔːls/ a falso. **~hood** /-hʊd/ n mentira f. **~ly** adv falsamente. **~ness** n falsedad f

falsetto /fɔːl'setəʊ/ n (pl -os) falsete m

falsify /'fɔːlsɪfaɪ/ vt falsificar

falter /'fɔːltə(r)/ vi vacilar

fame /feɪm/ n fama f. **~d** a famoso

familiar /fə'mɪlɪə(r)/ a familiar. be **~** with conocer. **~ity** /-'ærɪtɪ/ n familiaridad f. **~ize** vt familiarizar

family /'fæməlɪ/ n familia f. **—a** de (la) familia, familiar

famine /'fæmɪn/ n hambre f, hambruna f (Amer)

famished /'fæmɪʃt/ a hambriento

famous /'feɪməs/ a famoso. **~ly** adv (fam) a las mil maravillas

fan[1] /fæn/ n abanico m; (mec) ventilador m. —vt (pt fanned) abanicar; soplar (fire). —vi. **~ out** desparramarse en forma de abanico

fan[2] /fæn/ n (of person) admirador m; (enthusiast) aficionado m, entusiasta m & f

fanatic /fə'nætɪk/ n fanático m. **~al** a fanático. **~ism** /-sɪzəm/ n fanatismo m

fan belt /'fænbelt/ n correa f de ventilador

fancier /'fænsɪə(r)/ n aficionado m

fanciful /'fænsɪfl/ a (imaginative) imaginativo; (unreal) imaginario

fancy /'fænsɪ/ n fantasía f; (liking) gusto m. take a **~** to tomar cariño a (person); aficionarse a (thing). —a de lujo; (extravagant) excesivo. —vt (imagine) imaginar; (believe) creer; (want, fam) apetecer a. **~ dress** n disfraz m

fanfare /'fænfeə(r)/ n fanfarria f

fang /fæŋ/ n (of animal) colmillo m; (of snake) diente m

fanlight /'fænlaɪt/ n montante m

fantasize /'fæntəsaɪz/ vi fantasear

fantastic /fæn'tæstɪk/ a fantástico

fantasy /'fæntəsɪ/ n fantasía f

far /fɑː(r)/ adv lejos; (much) mucho. as **~** as hasta. as **~** as I know que yo sepa. by **~** con mucho. —a (further, furthest or farther, farthest) lejano

far-away /'fɑːrəweɪ/ a lejano

farce /fɑːs/ n farsa f. **~ical** a ridículo

fare /feə(r)/ n (for transport) tarifa f; (food) comida f. —vi irle. **how did you ~?** ¿qué tal te fue?

Far East /fɑː(r)'iːst/ n Extremo, Lejano Oriente m

farewell /feə'wel/ int & n adiós (m)

far-fetched /fɑː'fetʃt/ a improbable

farm /fɑːm/ n granja f. —vt cultivar. **~ out** arrendar. —vi ser agricultor. **~er** n agricultor m. **~house** n granja f. **~ing** n agricultura f. **~yard** n corral m

far: **~-off** a lejano. **~-reaching** a trascendental. **~-seeing** a clarividente. **~-sighted** a hipermétrope; (fig) clarividente

farther, farthest /'fɑːðə(r), 'fɑːðəst/ see **far**

fascinat|e /'fæsɪneɪt/ vt fascinar. **~ion** /-'eɪ∫n/ n fascinación f

fascis|m /'fæʃɪzəm/ n fascismo m. **~t** /'fæʃɪst/ a & n fascista (m & f)

fashion /'fæʃn/ n (*manner*) manera f; (*vogue*) moda f. ~**able** a de moda

fast[1] /fɑːst/ a (**-er, -est**) rápido; (*clock*) adelantado; (*secure*) fijo; (*colours*) sólido. —adv rápidamente; (*securely*) firmemente. ~ **asleep** profundamente dormido

fast[2] /fɑːst/ vi ayunar. —n ayuno m

fasten /'fɑːsn/ vt/i sujetar; cerrar (*windows, doors*); abrochar (*belt etc*). ~**er** n, ~**ing** n (*on box, window*) cierre m; (*on door*) cerrojo m

fastidious /fə'stɪdɪəs/ a exigente, minucioso

fat /fæt/ n grasa f. —a (**fatter, fattest**) gordo; (*meat*) que tiene mucha grasa; (*thick*) grueso. **a ~ lot of** (*sl*) muy poco

fatal /'feɪtl/ a mortal; (*fateful*) fatídico

fatalism /'feɪtəlɪzəm/ n fatalismo m. ~**t** n fatalista m & f

fatality /fə'tælətɪ/ n calamidad f; (*death*) muerte f

fatally /'feɪtəlɪ/ adv mortalmente; (*by fate*) fatalmente

fate /feɪt/ n destino m; (*one's lot*) suerte f. ~**d** a predestinado. ~**ful** a fatídico

fat-head /'fæthed/ n imbécil m

father /'fɑːðə(r)/ n padre m. ~**hood** n paternidad f. ~**in-law** m (pl **fathers-in-law**) m suegro m. ~**ly** a paternal

fathom /'fæðəm/ n braza f. —vt. ~ (**out**) comprender

fatigue /fə'tiːg/ n fatiga f. —vt fatigar

fat: ~**ness** n gordura f. ~**ten** vt/i engordar. ~**tening** a que engorda. ~**ty** a graso. —n (*fam*) gordinflón m

fatuous /'fætjʊəs/ a fatuo

faucet /'fɔːsɪt/ n (*Amer*) grifo m

fault /fɔːlt/ n defecto m; (*blame*) culpa f; (*tennis*) falta f; (*geol*)

falla f. **at ~** culpable. —vt criticar. ~**less** a impecable. ~**y** a defectuoso

fauna /'fɔːnə/ n fauna f

faux pas /fəʊ'pɑː/ (pl **faux pas** /fəʊ'pɑː/) n metedura f de pata, paso m en falso

favour /'feɪvə(r)/ n favor m. —vt favorecer; (*support*) estar a favor de; (*prefer*) preferir. ~**able** a favorable. ~**ably** adv favorablemente

favourite /'feɪvərɪt/ a & n preferido (m). ~**ism** n favoritismo m

fawn[1] /fɔːn/ n cervato m. —a color de cervato, beige, bern

fawn[2] /fɔːn/ vi. ~ **on** adular

fax /fæks/ n telefacsímil m, fax m

fear /fɪə(r)/ n miedo m. —vt temer. ~**ful** a (*frightening*) espantoso; (*frightened*) temeroso. ~**less** a intrépido. ~**lessness** n intrepidez f. ~**some** a espantoso

feasibility /fiːzə'bɪlətɪ/ n viabilidad f. ~**le** /'fiːzəbl/ a factible; (*likely*) posible

feast /fiːst/ n (*relig*) fiesta f; (*meal*) banquete m, comilona f. —vt banquetear, festejar. ~ **on** regalarse con

feat /fiːt/ n hazaña f

feather /'feðə(r)/ n pluma f. —vt. ~ **one's nest** hacer su agosto. ~**brained** a tonto. ~**weight** n peso m pluma

feature /'fiːtʃə(r)/ n (*on face*) facción f; (*characteristic*) característica f; (*in newspaper*) artículo m; ~ (**film**) película f principal, largometraje m. —vt presentar; (*give prominence to*) destacar. —vi figurar

February /'februərɪ/ n febrero m

feckless /'feklɪs/ a inepto; (*irresponsible*) irreflexivo

fed /fed/ see **feed**. —a. ~ **up** (*sl*) harto (**with** de)

federal /ˈfedərəl/ a federal

federation /fedəˈreɪʃn/ n federación f

fee /fiː/ n (professional) honorarios mpl; (enrolment) derechos mpl; (club) cuota f

feeble /ˈfiːbl/ a (-er, -est) débil. ~-minded a imbécil

feed /fiːd/ vt (pt fed) dar de comer a; (supply) alimentar. —vi comer. —n (for animals) pienso m; (for babies) comida f. ~back n reacciones fpl, comentarios mpl

feel /fiːl/ vt (pt felt) sentir; (touch) tocar; (think) parecerle. do you ~ it's a good idea? te parece buena idea? I ~ it is necessary me parece necesario. ~ as if tener la impresión de que. ~ hot/hungry tener calor/hambre. ~ like (want, fam) tener ganas de. ~ up to sentirse capaz de

feeler /ˈfiːlə(r)/ n (of insects) antena f. put out a ~ (fig) hacer un sondeo

feeling /ˈfiːlɪŋ/ n sentimiento m; (physical) sensación f

feet /fiːt/ see foot

feign /feɪn/ vt fingir

feint /feɪnt/ n finta f

felicitous /fəˈlɪsɪtəs/ a feliz, oportuno

feline /ˈfiːlaɪn/ a felino

fell[1] /fel/ see fall

fell[2] /fel/ vt derribar

fellow /ˈfeləʊ/ n (fam) tipo m; (comrade) compañero m; (society) socio m. ~ countryman n compatriota m & f. ~-passenger/traveller n compañero m de viaje. ~ship n compañerismo m; (group) asociación f

felony /ˈfeləni/ n crimen m

felt[1] /felt/ n fieltro m

felt[2] /felt/ see feel

female /ˈfiːmeɪl/ a hembra; (voice, sex etc) femenino. —n mujer f; (animal) hembra f

feminine /ˈfemənɪn/ a & n femenino (m). ~nity /-ˈnɪnəti/ n feminidad f. ~st n feminista m & f

fence /fens/ n cerca f; (person, sl) perista m & f (fam). —vt. ~e(in) encerrar, cercar. —vi (sport) practicar la esgrima. ~er n esgrimidor m. ~ing n (sport) esgrima f

fend /fend/ vi. ~ for o.s. valerse por sí mismo. —vt. ~ off defenderse de

fender /ˈfendə(r)/ n guardafuego m; (mudguard, Amer) guardabarros m invar; (naut) defensa f

fennel /ˈfenl/ n hinojo m

ferment /ˈfɜːment/ n fermento m; (fig) agitación f. /fəˈment/ vt/i fermentar. ~ation /-ˈteɪʃn/ n fermentación f

fern /fɜːn/ n helecho m

feroci|ous /fəˈrəʊʃəs/ a feroz. ~ty /fəˈrɒsəti/ n ferocidad f

ferret /ˈferɪt/ n hurón m. —vi (pt ferreted) huronear. —vt. ~ out descubrir

ferry /ˈferi/ n ferry m. —vt transportar

fertile /ˈfɜːtaɪl/ a fértil; (biol) fecundo. ~ity /-ˈtɪləti/ n fertilidad f; (biol) fecundidad f

fertilize /ˈfɜːtəlaɪz/ vt abonar; (biol) fecundar. ~r n abono m

fervent /ˈfɜːvənt/ a ferviente

fervour /ˈfɜːvə(r)/ n fervor m

fester /ˈfestə(r)/ vi enconarse

festival /ˈfestəvl/ n fiesta f; (arts) festival m

festive /ˈfestɪv/ a festivo. ~ season n temporada f de fiestas

festivity /feˈstɪvəti/ n festividad f

festoon /feˈstuːn/ vi. ~ with adornar de

fetch /fetʃ/ vt (go for) ir a buscar; (bring) traer; (be sold for) venderse por

fetching /ˈfetʃɪŋ/ a atractivo

fête /feɪt/ n fiesta f. —vt festejar

fetid /ˈfetɪd/ a fétido

fetish /ˈfetɪʃ/ n fetiche m; (psych) obsesión f

fetter /ˈfetə(r)/ vt encadenar. —s npl grilletes mpl

fettle /ˈfetl/ n condición f

feud /fjuːd/ n enemistad f (inveterada)

feudal /ˈfjuːdl/ a feudal. —ism n feudalismo m

fever /ˈfiːvə(r)/ n fiebre f. —ish a febril

few /fjuː/ a pocos. —n pocos mpl. **a** ~ unos (pocos). **a good** ~, **quite a** ~ (fam) muchos. —**er** a & n menos. —**est** a & n el menor número de

fiancé /frˈɒnseɪ/ n novio m. ~e /frˈɒnseɪ/ n novia f

fiasco /frˈæskəʊ/ n (pl -os) fiasco m

fib /fɪb/ n mentirijilla f. ~**ber** n mentiroso m

fibre /ˈfaɪbə(r)/ n fibra f. ~**glass** n fibra f de vidrio

fickle /ˈfɪkl/ a inconstante

fiction /ˈfɪkʃn/ n ficción f. (**works of** ~) novelas fpl. ~**al** a novelesco

fictitious /fɪkˈtɪʃəs/ a ficticio

fiddle /ˈfɪdl/ n (fam) violín m; (swindle, sl) trampa f. —vt (sl) falsificar. ~ **with** juguetear con, toquetear, manosear. ~**r** n (fam) violinista m & f; (cheat, sl) tramposo m

fidelity /frˈdelətɪ/ n fidelidad f

fidget /ˈfɪdʒɪt/ vi (pt **fidgeted**) moverse, ponerse nervioso. ~ **with** juguetear con. ~ n azogado m. ~**y** a azogado

field /fiːld/ n campo m. ~ **day** n gran ocasión f. ~ **glasses** npl gemelos mpl. **F**~ **Marshal** n mariscal m de campo, capitán m general. ~**work** n investigaciones fpl en el terreno

fiend /fiːnd/ n demonio m. ~**ish** a diabólico

fierce /fɪəs/ a (-er, -est) feroz; (attack) violento. ~**ness** n ferocidad f, violencia f

fiery /ˈfaɪərɪ/ a (-ier, -iest) ardiente

fifteen /fɪfˈtiːn/ a & n quince (m). ~**th** a & n quince (m), decimoquinto (m). —n (fraction) quinzavo m

fifth /fɪfθ/ a & n quinto (m). ~ **column** n quinta columna f

fiftieth /ˈfɪftɪəθ/ a & n cincuenta (m). ~**y** a & n cincuenta (m). ~**y-~y** mitad y mitad, a medias. **a** ~**y-~y chance** una posibilidad f de cada dos

fig /fɪg/ n higo m

fight /faɪt/ vt/i (pt **fought**) luchar; (quarrel) disputar. ~ **shy of** evitar. —n lucha f; (quarrel) disputa f; (mil) combate m. ~ **back** defenderse. ~ **off** rechazar (attack); luchar contra (illness). ~**er** n luchador m; (mil) combatiente m & f; (aircraft) avión m de caza. ~**ing** n luchas fpl

figment /ˈfɪgmənt/ n invención f

figurative /ˈfɪgjʊrətɪv/ a figurado

figure /ˈfɪgə(r)/ n (number) cifra f; (diagram) figura f; (shape) forma f; (of woman) tipo m. —vt imaginar. —vi figurar. **that** ~**s** (Amer, fam) es lógico. ~ **out** explicarse. ~**head** n testaferro m, mascarón m de proa. ~ **of speech** n tropo m, figura f. ~**s** npl (arithmetic) aritmética f

filament /ˈfɪləmənt/ n filamento m

filch /fɪltʃ/ vt hurtar

file[1] /faɪl/ n carpeta f; (set of papers) expediente m. —vt archivar (papers)

file[2] /faɪl/ n (row) fila f. —vi. ~ **in** entrar en fila. ~ **past** desfilar ante

file[3] /faɪl/ n (*tool*) lima f. —vt limar

filings /ˈfaɪlɪŋz/ npl limaduras fpl

fill /fɪl/ vt llenar. —vi llenarse. ~ **in** rellenar ⟨*form*⟩. ~ **out** (*get fatter*) engordar. ~ **up** (*auto*) llenar, repostar. —n. **eat one's** ~ hartarse de comer. **have had one's** ~ **of** estar harto de

fillet /ˈfɪlɪt/ n filete m. —vt (pt **filleted**) cortar en filetes

filling /ˈfɪlɪŋ/ n (*in tooth*) empaste m. ~ **station** n estación f de servicio

film /fɪlm/ n película f. —vt filmar. ~ **star** n estrella f de cine. ~**strip** n tira f de película

filter /ˈfɪltə(r)/ n filtro m. —vt filtrar. —vi filtrarse. ~**tipped** a con filtro

filth /fɪlθ/ n inmundicia f. ~**iness** n inmundicia f. ~**y** a inmundo

fin /fɪn/ n aleta f

final /ˈfaɪnl/ a último; (*conclusive*) decisivo. —n (*sport*) final f. ~**s** npl (*schol*) exámenes mpl de fin de curso

finale /fɪˈnɑːlɪ/ n final m

finalist n finalista m & f. ~**ize** vt concluir. ~**ly** adv (*lastly*) finalmente, por fin; (*once and for all*) definitivamente

financ|e /ˈfaɪnæns/ n finanzas fpl. —vt financiar. ~**ial** /faɪˈnænʃl/ a financiero. ~**ially** adv económicamente. ~**ier** /faɪˈnænsɪə(r)/ n financiero m

finch /fɪntʃ/ n pinzón m

find /faɪnd/ vt (pt **found**) encontrar. ~ **out** enterarse de. ~**er** n el m que encuentra, descubridor m. ~**ings** npl resultados mpl

fine[1] /faɪn/ a (-**er**, -**est**) fino; (*excellent*) excelente. —adv muy bien; (*small*) en trozos pequeños

fine[2] /faɪn/ n multa f. —vt multar

fine: ~ **arts** npl bellas artes fpl. ~**ly** adv (*admirably*) espléndidamente; (*cut*) en trozos pequeños. ~**ry** /ˈfaɪnərɪ/ n galas fpl

finesse /fɪˈnes/ n tino m

finger /ˈfɪŋgə(r)/ n dedo m. —vt tocar. ~**nail** n uña f. ~**print** n huella f dactilar. ~**stall** n dedil m. ~**tip** n punta f del dedo

finicky /ˈfɪnɪkɪ/ a, **finicky** /ˈfɪnɪkɪ/ a melindroso

finish /ˈfɪnɪʃ/ vt/i terminar. ~ **doing** terminar de hacer. ~ **up doing** terminar por hacer. —n fin m; (*of race*) llegada f, meta f; (*appearance*) acabado m

finite /ˈfaɪnaɪt/ a finito

Fin|land /ˈfɪnlənd/ n Finlandia f. ~**n** n finlandés m. ~**nish** a & n finlandés (m)

fiord /fjɔːd/ n fiordo m

fir /fɜː(r)/ n abeto m

fire /ˈfaɪə(r)/ n fuego m; (*conflagration*) incendio m. —vt disparar ⟨*bullet etc*⟩; (*dismiss*) despedir; (*fig*) excitar, enardecer, inflamar. —vi tirar. ~**arm** n arma f de fuego. ~ **brigade** n cuerpo m de bomberos. ~**cracker** n (*Amer*) petardo m. ~ **department** n (*Amer*) cuerpo m de bomberos. ~**engine** n coche m de bomberos. ~**escape** n escalera f de incendios. ~**light** n lumbre f. ~**man** n bombero m. ~**place** n chimenea f. ~**side** n hogar m. ~ **station** n parque m de bomberos. ~**wood** n leña f. ~**work** n fuego m artificial

firing-squad /ˈfaɪərɪŋskwɒd/ n pelotón m de ejecución

firm[1] /fɜːm/ n empresa f

firm[2] /fɜːm/ a (-**er**, -**est**) firme. ~**ly** adv firmemente. ~**ness** n firmeza f

first /fɜːst/ a primero. **at** ~ **hand** directamente. **at** ~ **sight** a primera vista. —n primero m. —adv primero; (*first time*) por

primera vez. ~ of all ante todo.
~ aid n primeros auxilios mpl.
~-born a primogénito. ~-class
a de primera clase. ~ floor n
primer piso m; (Amer) planta f
baja. F~ Lady n (Amer) Primera Dama f. ~ly adv en primer
lugar. ~ name n nombre m de
pila. ~-rate a excelente

fiscal /'fɪskl/ a fiscal

fish /fɪʃ/ n (usually invar) (alive
in water) pez m; (food) pescado
m. —vi pescar. ~ for pescar. ~
out (take out, fam) sacar. go
~ing ir de pesca. ~erman
/'fɪʃəmən/ n pescador m. ~ing n
pesca f. ~ing-rod n caña f de
pesca. ~monger n pescadero m.
~shop n pescadería f. ~y a
⟨smell⟩ a pescado; (questionable,
fam) sospechoso

fission /'fɪʃn/ n fisión f

fist /fɪst/ n puño m

fit¹ /fɪt/ a (fitter, fittest) conveniente; (healthy) sano; (good
enough) adecuado; (able)
capaz. —n (of clothes) corte m. —
vt (pt fitted) (adapt) adaptar; (be
the right size for) sentar bien a;
(install) colocar. —vi encajar; (in
certain space) caber; (clothes)
sentar. ~ out equipar. ~ up
equipar

fit² /fɪt/ n ataque m

fitful /'fɪtfl/ a irregular

fitment /'fɪtmənt/ n mueble m

fitness /'fɪtnɪs/ n (buena) salud f;
(of remark) conveniencia f

fitting /'fɪtɪŋ/ a apropiado. —n
(of clothes) prueba f. ~s /'fɪtɪŋz/
npl (in house) accesorios mpl

five /faɪv/ a & n cinco (m). ~r
/'faɪvə(r)/ n (fam) billete m de
cinco libras

fix /fɪks/ vt (make firm, attach,
decide) fijar; (mend, deal with)
arreglar. —n. in a ~ en un aprieto. ~ation /-eɪʃn/ n fijación f.
~ed a fijo

fixture /'fɪkstʃə(r)/ n (sport) partido m. ~s (in house) accesorios
mpl

fizz /fɪz/ vi burbujear. —n efer-
vescencia f. ~le /fɪzl/ vi burbujear. ~le out fracasar. ~y a
efervescente; (water) con gas

flab /flæb/ n (fam) flaccidez f

flabbergast /'flæbəgɑːst/ vt pasmar

flabby /'flæbi/ a flojo

flag /flæg/ n bandera f. —vt (pt
flagged). ~ down bajar señales
de parada a. —vi (pt flagged)
(weaken) flaquear; (interest)
decaer; (conversation) languidecer

flagon /'flægən/ n botella f
grande, jarro m

flag-pole /'flægpəʊl/ n asta f de
bandera

flagrant /'fleɪgrənt/ a (glaring)
flagrante; (scandalous) escandaloso

flagstone /'flægstəʊn/ n losa f

flair /fleə(r)/ n don m (for de)

flak|e /fleɪk/ n copo m; (of paint,
metal) escama f. —vi descon-
charse. ~e out (fam) caer rendido. ~y a escamoso

flamboyant /flæm'bɔɪənt/ a (clothes) vistoso; (manner) extravagante

flame /fleɪm/ n llama f. —vi
llamear

flamingo /flə'mɪŋgəʊ/ n (pl
-o(e)s) flamenco m

flammable /'flæməbl/ a inflamable

flan /flæn/ n tartaleta f, tarteleta
f

flank /flæŋk/ n (of animal) ijada
f, flanco m; (of person) costado m;
(of mountain) falda f; (mil) flanco
m

flannel /'flænl/ n franela f (de
lana); (for face) paño m (para lavarse la cara). ~ette n franela f
(de algodón), muletón m

flap /flæp/ *vi* (*pt* flapped) ondear; ⟨*wings*⟩ aletear; ⟨*become agitated, fam*⟩ ponerse nervioso. —*vt* sacudir; batir ⟨*wings*⟩. —*n* ⟨*of pocket*⟩ cartera *f*, ⟨*of table*⟩ ala *f*. **get into a** ∼ ponerse nervioso

flare /fleə(r)/ *n* llamarada *f*, ⟨*mil*⟩ bengala *f*; ⟨*in skirt*⟩ vuelo *m*. —*vi*. ∼ **up** llamear; ⟨*fighting*⟩ estallar; ⟨*person*⟩ encolerizarse. ∼**d** *a* ⟨*skirt*⟩ acampanado

flash /flæʃ/ —*vi* brillar; ⟨*on and off*⟩ destellar. —*vt* despedir; ⟨*aim torch*⟩ dirigir; ⟨*flaunt*⟩ hacer ostentación de. ∼ **past** pasar como un rayo. —*n* relámpago *m*; ⟨*of news, camera*⟩ flash *m*. ∼**back** *n* escena *f* retrospectiva. ∼**light** *n* ⟨*torch*⟩ linterna *f*

flashy /flæʃɪ/ *a* ostentoso

flask /flɑːsk/ *n* frasco *m*; ⟨*vacuum flask*⟩ termo *m*

flat[1] /flæt/ *a* (**flatter, flattest**) llano; ⟨*tyre*⟩ desinflado; ⟨*refusal*⟩ categórico; ⟨*fare, rate*⟩ fijo; ⟨*mus*⟩ desafinado. —*adv.* ∼ **out** ⟨*at top speed*⟩ a toda velocidad

flat[2] /flæt/ *n* ⟨*rooms*⟩ piso *m*, apartamento *m*; ⟨*tyre*⟩ ⟨*fam*⟩ pinchazo *m*; ⟨*mus*⟩ bemol *m*

flat: ∼**ly** *adv* categóricamente. ∼**ness** *n* llanura *f*. ∼**ten** /flætn/ *vt* allanar, aplanar. —*vi* allanarse, aplanarse

flatter /flætə(r)/ *vt* adular. ∼**er** *n* adulador *m*. ∼**ing** *a* ⟨*person*⟩ lisonjero; ⟨*clothes*⟩ favorecedor. ∼**y** *n* adulación *f*

flatulence /flætjʊlʌns/ *n* flatulencia *f*

flaunt /flɔːnt/ *vt* hacer ostentación de

flautist /flɔːtɪst/ *n* flautista *m* & *f*

flavour /fleɪvə(r)/ *n* sabor *m*. —*vt* condimentar. ∼**ing** *n* condimento *m*

flaw /flɔː/ *n* defecto *m*. ∼**less** *a* perfecto

flax /flæks/ *n* lino *m*. ∼**en** *a* de lino; ⟨*hair*⟩ rubio

flea /fliː/ *n* pulga *f*

fleck /flek/ *n* mancha *f*, pinta *f*

fled /fled/ *see* **flee**

fledged /fledʒd/ *a*. **fully** ∼ ⟨*doctor etc*⟩ hecho y derecho; ⟨*member*⟩ de pleno derecho

fledg(e)ling /fledʒlɪŋ/ *n* pájaro *m* volantón

flee /fliː/ *vi* (*pt* fled) huir. —*vt* huir de

fleece /fliːs/ *n* vellón *m*. —*vt* ⟨*rob*⟩ desplumar

fleet /fliːt/ *n* ⟨*naut, aviat*⟩ flota *f*; ⟨*of cars*⟩ parque *m*

fleeting /fliːtɪŋ/ *a* fugaz

Flemish /flemɪʃ/ *a* & *n* flamenco (*m*)

flesh /fleʃ/ *n* carne *f*. **in the** ∼ en persona. **one's own** ∼ **and blood** los de su sangre. ∼**y** *a* ⟨*fruit*⟩ carnoso

flew /fluː/ *see* **fly**[1]

flex /fleks/ *vt* doblar; flexionar ⟨*muscle*⟩. —*n* ⟨*elec*⟩ cable *m*, flexible *m*

flexibility /fleksəbɪlətɪ/ *n* flexibilidad *f*. ∼**le** /fleksəbl/ *a* flexible

flexitime /fleksɪtaɪm/ *n* horario *m* flexible

flick /flɪk/ *n* golpecito *m*. —*vt* dar un golpecito a. ∼ **through** hojear

flicker /flɪkə(r)/ *vi* temblar; ⟨*light*⟩ parpadear. —*n* temblor *m*; ⟨*of hope*⟩ resquicio *m*; ⟨*of light*⟩ parpadeo *m*

flick: ∼**knife** *n* navaja *f* de muelle. ∼**s** *npl* cine *m*

flier /flaɪə(r)/ *n* aviador *m*; ⟨*circular, Amer*⟩ prospecto *m*, folleto *m*

flies /flaɪz/ *npl* ⟨*on trousers, fam*⟩ bragueta *f*

flight /flaɪt/ *n* vuelo *m*; ⟨*fleeing*⟩ huida *f*, fuga *f*. ∼ **of stairs** tramo *m* de escalera *f*. **put to** ∼ poner en fuga. **take (to)** ~ darse a la fuga. ~**deck** n cubierta f de vuelo

flighty /'flaɪtɪ/ a (-**ier, -iest**) frívolo

flimsy /'flɪmzɪ/ a (-**ier, -iest**) flojo, débil, poco substancioso

flinch /flɪntʃ/ vi (*draw back*) retroceder (**from** ante). **without** ~**ing** (*without wincing*) sin pestañear

fling /flɪŋ/ vt (pt **flung**) arrojar. —n. **have a** ~ echar una cana al aire

flint /flɪnt/ n pedernal m; (*for lighter*) piedra f

flip /flɪp/ vt (pt **flipped**) dar un golpecito a. ~ **through** hojear. —n golpecito m. ~ **side** n otra cara f

flippant /'flɪpənt/ a poco serio; (*disrespectful*) irrespetuoso

flipper /'flɪpə(r)/ n aleta f

flirt /flɜ:t/ vi coquetear. —n (*woman*) coqueta f; (*man*) mariposón m, coqueta f. ~**ation** /-'teɪʃn/ n coqueteo m

flit /flɪt/ vi (pt **flitted**) revolotear

float /fləʊt/ vi flotar. —vt hacer flotar. —n flotador m; (*on fishing line*) corcho m; (*cart*) carroza f

flock /flɒk/ n (*of birds*) bandada f; (*of sheep*) rebaño m; (*of people*) muchedumbre f, multitud f. —vi congregarse

flog /flɒg/ vt (pt **flogged**) (*beat*) azotar; (*sell, sl*) vender

flood /flʌd/ n inundación f; (*fig*) torrente m. —vt inundar. —vi (*building etc*) inundarse; (*river*) desbordar

floodlight /'flʌdlaɪt/ n foco m. — vt (pt **floodlit**) iluminar (con focos)

floor /flɔ:(r)/ n suelo m; (*storey*) piso m; (*for dancing*) pista f. — vt (*knock down*) derribar; (*baffle*) confundir

flop /flɒp/ vi (pt **flopped**) dejarse caer pesadamente; (*fail, sl*) fracasar. —n (*sl*) fracaso m. ~**py** a flojo

flora /'flɔːrə/ n flora f

floral /'flɔːrəl/ a floral

florid /'flɒrɪd/ a florido

florist /'flɒrɪst/ n florista m & f

flounce /flaʊns/ n volante m

flounder[1] /'flaʊndə(r)/ vi avanzar con dificultad, no saber qué hacer

flounder[2] /'flaʊndə(r)/ n (*fish*) platija f

flour /flaʊə(r)/ n harina f

flourish /'flʌrɪʃ/ vi prosperar. — vt blandir. —n ademán m elegante; (*in handwriting*) rasgo m. ~**ing** a próspero

floury /'flaʊərɪ/ a harinoso

flout /flaʊt/ vt burlarse de

flow /fləʊ/ vi correr; (*hang loosely*) caer. ~ **into** (*river*) desembocar en. —n flujo m; (*jet*) chorro m; (*stream*) corriente f; (*of words, tears*) torrente m. ~ **chart** n organigrama f

flower /'flaʊə(r)/ n flor f. ~**-bed** n macizo m de flores. ~**ed** a floreado, de flores. ~**y** a florido

flown /fləʊn/ see **fly**[1]

flu /fluː/ n (*fam*) gripe f

fluctuate /'flʌktjʊeɪt/ vi fluctuar. ~**ion** /-eɪʃn/ n fluctuación f

flue /fluː/ n humero m

fluen|cy /'fluːənsɪ/ n facilidad f. ~**t** a (*style*) fluido; (*speaker*) elocuente. **be** ~**t (in a language)** hablar (un idioma) con soltura. ~**tly** adv con fluidez; (*lang*) con soltura

fluff /flʌf/ n pelusa f. ~**y** a (-**ier, -iest**) velloso

fluid /'fluːɪd/ a & n fluido (m)

fluke /fluːk/ n (*stroke of luck*) chiripa f

flung /flʌŋ/ see **fling**

flunk /flʌŋk/ vt (Amer, fam) ser suspendido en (exam); suspender (person). —vi (fam) ser suspendido

fluorescent /fluə'resnt/ a fluorescente

fluoride /'fluəraɪd/ n fluoruro m

flurry /'flʌrɪ/ n (squall) ráfaga f; (fig) agitación f

flush¹ /flʌʃ/ vi ruborizarse. —vt limpiar con agua. ~ **the toilet** tirar de la cadena. —n (blush) rubor m; (fig) emoción f

flush² /flʌʃ/ a. ~ **(with)** a nivel (con)

flush³ /flʌʃ/ vt/i. ~ **out** (drive out) echar fuera

fluster /'flʌstə(r)/ vt poner nervioso

flute /flu:t/ n flauta f

flutter /'flʌtə(r)/ vi ondear; (bird) revolotear. —n (of wings) revoloteo m; (fig) agitación f

flux /flʌks/ n flujo m. **be in a state of** ~ estar siempre cambiando

fly¹ /flaɪ/ vi (pt **flew**, pp **flown**) volar; (passenger) ir en avión; (flag) flotar; (rush) correr. —vt pilotar (aircraft); transportar en avión (passengers, goods); izar (flag). —n (of trousers) bragueta f

fly² /flaɪ/ n mosca f

flyer /'flaɪə(r)/ n aviador m; (circular, Amer) prospecto m, folleto m

flying /'flaɪɪŋ/ a volante; (hasty) relámpago invar. —n (activity) aviación f. ~ **visit** n visita f relámpago

fly: ~**leaf** n guarda f. ~**over** n paso m elevado. ~**weight** n peso m mosca

foal /fəʊl/ n potro m

foam /fəʊm/ n espuma f. ~ **(rubber)** n goma f espuma. —vi espumar

fob /fɒb/ vt (pt **fobbed**). ~ **off on** s.o. (palm off) encajar a uno

focal /'fəʊkl/ a focal

focus /'fəʊkəs/ n (pl -**cuses** or -**ci** /-saɪ/) foco m; (fig) centro m. **in** ~ enfocado. **out of** ~ desenfocado. —vt/i (pt **focused**) enfocar(se); (fig) concentrar

fodder /'fɒdə(r)/ n forraje m

foe /fəʊ/ n enemigo m

foetus /'fi:təs/ n (pl -**tuses**) feto m

fog /fɒg/ n niebla f. —vt (pt **fogged**) envolver en niebla; (photo) velar. —vi. ~ **(up)** empañarse; (photo) velarse

fog(e)y /'fəʊgɪ/ n. **be an old** ~ estar chapado a la antigua

foggy /'fɒgɪ/ a (-**ier**, -**iest**) nebuloso. **it is** ~ hay niebla

foghorn /'fɒghɔ:n/ n sirena f de niebla

foible /'fɔɪbl/ n punto m débil

foil¹ /fɔɪl/ vt (thwart) frustrar

foil² /fɔɪl/ n papel m de plata; (fig) contraste m

foist /fɔɪst/ vt encajar (on a)

fold¹ /fəʊld/ vt doblar; cruzar (arms). —vi doblarse; (fail) fracasar. —n pliegue m

fold² /fəʊld/ n (for sheep) redil m

folder /'fəʊldə(r)/ n (file) carpeta f; (leaflet) folleto m

folding /'fəʊldɪŋ/ a plegable

foliage /'fəʊlɪɪdʒ/ n follaje m

folk /fəʊk/ n gente f. —a popular. ~**lore** n folklore m. ~**s** npl (one's relatives) familia f

follow /'fɒləʊ/ vt/i seguir. ~ **up** seguir; (investigate further) investigar. ~**er** n seguidor m. ~**ing** n partidarios mpl. —a siguiente. —prep después de

folly /'fɒlɪ/ n locura f

foment /fə'ment/ vt fomentar

fond /fɒnd/ a (-**er**, -**est**) (loving) cariñoso; (hope) vivo. **be** ~ **of** s.o. tener(le) cariño a uno. **be** ~ **of sth** ser aficionado a algo

fondle /'fɒndl/ vt acariciar

fondness /'fɒndnɪs/ n cariño m; (for things) afición f

font /fɒnt/ n pila f bautismal

food /fu:d/ n alimento m, comida f. ~ **processor** n robot m de cocina, batidora f

fool /fu:l/ n tonto m. —vt engañar. —vi hacer el tonto

foolhardy /'fu:lhɑːdɪ/ a temerario

foolish /'fu:lɪʃ/ a tonto. ~**ly** adv tontamente. ~**ness** n tontería f

foolproof /'fu:lpru:f/ a infalible, a toda prueba, a prueba de tontos

foot /fʊt/ n (pl feet) pie m; (measure) pie m (= 30,48 cm); (of animal, furniture) pata f. **get under s.o.'s feet** estorbar a uno. **on ~ a pie. on/to one's feet** de pie. **put one's ~ in it** meter la pata. —vt pagar ⟨bill⟩. ~ **it** ir andando

footage /'fʊtɪdʒ/ n (of film) secuencia f

football /'fʊtbɔːl/ n (ball) balón m; (game) fútbol m. ~**er** n futbolista m & f

footbridge /'fʊtbrɪdʒ/ n puente m para peatones

foothills /'fʊthɪlz/ npl estribaciones fpl

foothold /'fʊthəʊld/ n punto m de apoyo m

footing /'fʊtɪŋ/ n pie m

footlights /'fʊtlaɪts/ npl candilejas fpl

footloose /'fʊtlu:s/ a libre

footman /'fʊtmən/ n lacayo m

footnote /'fʊtnəʊt/ n nota f (al pie de la página)

foot: ~**path** n (in country) senda f; (in town) acera f, vereda f (Arg), banqueta f (Mex). ~**print** n huella f. ~**sore** a. **be** ~**sore** tener los pies doloridos. ~**step** n paso m. ~**stool** n escabel m. ~**wear** n calzado m

for /fɔː(r)/, unstressed /fə(r)/ prep (expressing purpose) para; (on behalf of) por; (in spite of) a pesar de; (during) durante; (in favour of) a favor de. **he has been in Madrid ~ two months** hace dos meses que está en Madrid. —conj ya que

forage /'fɒrɪdʒ/ vi forrajear. —n forraje m

foray /'fɒreɪ/ n incursión f

forbade /fə'bæd/ see **forbid**

forbear /fɔː'beə(r)/ vt/i (pt forbore, pp forborne) contenerse. ~**ance** n paciencia f

forbid /fə'bɪd/ vt (pt forbade, pp forbidden) prohibir (s.o. to do a uno hacer). ~ **s.o. sth** prohibir algo a uno

forbidding /fə'bɪdɪŋ/ a imponente

force /fɔːs/ n fuerza f. **come into ~** entrar en vigor. **the ~s** las fuerzas fpl armadas. —vt forzar. ~ **on** imponer a. ~**d** a forzado. ~**feed** vt alimentar a la fuerza. ~**ful** /'fɔːsfʊl/ a enérgico

forceps /'fɔːseps/ n invar tenazas fpl; (for obstetric use) fórceps m invar; (for dental use) gatillo m

forcible /'fɔːsəbl/ a a la fuerza. ~**y** adv a la fuerza

ford /fɔːd/ n vado m, botadero m (Mex). —vt vadear

fore /fɔː(r)/ a anterior. —n. **come to the ~** hacerse evidente

forearm /'fɔːrɑːm/ n antebrazo m

foreboding /fɔː'bəʊdɪŋ/ n presentimiento m

forecast /'fɔːkɑːst/ vt (pt forecast) pronosticar. —n pronóstico m

forecourt /'fɔːkɔːt/ n patio m

forefathers /'fɔːfɑːðəz/ npl antepasados mpl

forefinger /'fɔːfɪŋgə(r)/ n (dedo m) índice m

forefront /'fɔːfrʌnt/ n vanguardia f. **in the ~** a/en vanguardia, en primer plano

foregone /'fɔːgɒn/ a. ~ **conclusion** resultado m previsto

foreground /ˈfɔːɡraʊnd/ n primer plano m

forehead /ˈfɒrɪd/ n frente f

foreign /ˈfɒrən/ a extranjero; ⟨trade⟩ exterior; ⟨travel⟩ al extranjero, en el extranjero. ~er n extranjero m. F~ Secretary n ministro m de Asuntos Exteriores

foreman /ˈfɔːmən/ n capataz m, caporal m

foremost /ˈfɔːməʊst/ a primero. —adv. first and ~ ante todo

forensic /fəˈrensɪk/ a forense

forerunner /ˈfɔːrʌnə(r)/ n precursor m

foresee /fɔːˈsiː/ vt (pt -saw, pp -seen) prever. ~able a previsible

foreshadow /fɔːˈʃædəʊ/ vt presagiar

foresight /ˈfɔːsaɪt/ n previsión f

forest /ˈfɒrɪst/ n bosque m

forestall /fɔːˈstɔːl/ vt anticiparse a

forestry /ˈfɒrɪstrɪ/ n silvicultura f

foretaste /ˈfɔːteɪst/ n anticipación f

foretell /fɔːˈtel/ vt (pt foretold) predecir

forever /fəˈrevə(r)/ adv para siempre

forewarn /fɔːˈwɔːn/ vt prevenir

foreword /ˈfɔːwɜːd/ n prefacio m

forfeit /ˈfɔːfɪt/ n (penalty) pena f; (in game) prenda f; (fine) multa f. —vt perder

forgave /fəˈɡeɪv/ see **forgive**

forge¹ /fɔːdʒ/ n fragua f. —vt fraguar; (copy) falsificar

forge² /fɔːdʒ/ vi avanzar. ~ ahead adelantarse rápidamente

forge: ~r /ˈfɔːdʒə(r)/ n falsificador m. ~ry n falsificación f

forget /fəˈɡet/ vt (pt forgot, pp forgotten) olvidar. ~ o.s. propasarse, extralimitarse. —vi

olvidar(se). I forgot se me olvidó. ~ful a olvidadizo. ~ful of olvidando. ~-me-not n nomeolvides f invar

forgive /fəˈɡɪv/ vt (pt forgave, pp forgiven) perdonar. ~ness n perdón m

forgo /fɔːˈɡəʊ/ vt (pt forwent, pp forgone) renunciar a

fork /fɔːk/ n tenedor m; (for digging) horca f; (in road) bifurcación f. —vi ⟨road⟩ bifurcarse. ~ out (sl) aflojar la bolsa (fam), pagar. ~ed a ahorquillado; ⟨road⟩ bifurcado. ~-lift truck n carretilla f elevadora

forlorn /fəˈlɔːn/ a (hopeless) desesperado; (abandoned) abandonado. ~ hope n empresa f desesperada

form /fɔːm/ n forma f; (document) impreso m, formulario m; (sch) clase f. —vt formar. —vi formarse

formal /ˈfɔːml/ a formal; (person) formalista; ⟨dress⟩ de etiqueta. ~ity /-ˈmælɪtɪ/ n formalidad f. ~ly adv oficialmente

format /ˈfɔːmæt/ n formato m

formation /fɔːˈmeɪʃn/ n formación f

formative /ˈfɔːmətɪv/ a formativo

former /ˈfɔːmə(r)/ a anterior; (first of two) primero. ~ly adv antes

formidable /ˈfɔːmɪdəbl/ a formidable

formless /ˈfɔːmlɪs/ a informe

formula /ˈfɔːmjʊlə/ n (pl -ae /-iː/ or -as) fórmula f

formulate /ˈfɔːmjʊleɪt/ vt formular

fornicate /ˈfɔːnɪkeɪt/ vi fornicar. ~ion /-ˈkeɪʃn/ n fornicación f

forsake /fəˈseɪk/ vt (pt forsook, pp forsaken) abandonar

fort /fɔːt/ n (mil) fuerte m

forte /ˈfɔːteɪ/ n (talent) fuerte m

forth /fɔ:θ/ *adv* en adelante. **and so ~** y así sucesivamente. **go back and ~** ir y venir

forthcoming /fɔ:θ'kʌmɪŋ/ *a* próximo, venidero; (*sociable, fam*) comunicativo

forthright /fɔ:θraɪt/ *a* franco

forthwith /fɔ:θ'wɪθ/ *adv* inmediatamente

fortieth /'fɔ:tɪɪθ/ *a* cuarenta, cuadragésimo. **—n** cuadragésima parte *f*

fortification /fɔ:tɪfɪ'keɪʃn/ *n* fortificación *f*. **~y** /'fɔ:tɪfaɪ/ *vt* fortificar

fortitude /'fɔ:tɪtju:d/ *n* valor *m*

fortnight /'fɔ:tnaɪt/ *n* quince días *mpl*, quincena *f*. **~ly** *a* bimensual. **—adv** cada quince días

fortress /'fɔ:trɪs/ *n* fortaleza *f*

fortuitous /fɔ:'tju:ɪtəs/ *a* fortuito

fortunate /'fɔ:tʃənət/ *a* afortunado. **be ~** tener suerte. **~ly** *adv* afortunadamente

fortune /'fɔ:tʃu:n/ *n* fortuna *f*. **have the good ~ to** tener la suerte de. **~-teller** *n* adivino *m*

forty /'fɔ:tɪ/ *a & n* cuarenta (*m*). **~ winks** un sueñecito *m*

forum /'fɔ:rəm/ *n* foro *m*

forward /'fɔ:wəd/ *a* delantero; (*advanced*) precoz; (*pert*) impertinente. **—n** (*sport*) delantero *m*. **—adv** adelante. **come ~** presentarse. **go ~** avanzar. **—vt** hacer seguir ‹*letter*›; enviar ‹*goods*›; (*fig*) favorecer. **~ness** *n* precocidad *f*

forwards /'fɔ:wədz/ *adv* adelante

fossil /'fɒsl/ *a & n* fósil (*m*)

foster /'fɒstə(r)/ *vt* (*promote*) fomentar; criar ‹*child*›. **~-child** *n* hijo *m* adoptivo. **~-mother** *n* madre *f* adoptiva

fought /fɔ:t/ *see* **fight**

foul /faʊl/ *a* (-er, -est) (*smell, weather*) asqueroso; (*dirty*) sucio; (*language*) obsceno; (*air*) viciado. **~ play** jugada *f* sucia;

(*crime*) delito *m*. **—n** (*sport*) falta *f*. **—vt** ensuciar; manchar (*reputation*). **~-mouthed** *a* obsceno

found[1] /faʊnd/ *see* **find**

found[2] /faʊnd/ *vt* fundar

found[3] /faʊnd/ *vt* (*tec*) fundir

foundation /faʊn'deɪʃn/ *n* fundación *f*; (*basis*) fundamento. **~s** *npl* (*archit*) cimientos *mpl*

founder[1] /'faʊndə(r)/ *n* fundador *m*

founder[2] /'faʊndə(r)/ *vi* (*ship*) hundirse

foundry /'faʊndrɪ/ *n* fundición *f*

fountain /'faʊntɪn/ *n* fuente *f*. **~-pen** *n* estilográfica *f*

four /fɔ:(r)/ *a & n* cuatro (*m*). **~fold** *a* cuádruple. **—adv** cuatro veces. **~-poster** *n* cama *f* con cuatro columnas

foursome /'fɔ:səm/ *n* grupo *m* de cuatro personas

fourteen /fɔ:'ti:n/ *a & n* catorce (*m*). **~th** *a & n* catorce (*m*), decimocuarto (*m*). **—n** (*fraction*) catorceavo *m*

fourth /fɔ:θ/ *a & n* cuarto (*m*)

fowl /faʊl/ *n* ave *f*

fox /fɒks/ *n* zorro *m*, zorra *f*. **—vt** (*baffle*) dejar perplejo; (*deceive*) engañar

foyer /'fɔɪeɪ/ *n* (*hall*) vestíbulo *m*

fraction /'frækʃn/ *n* fracción *f*

fractious /'frækʃəs/ *a* díscolo

fracture /'fræktʃə(r)/ *n* fractura *f*. **—vt** fracturar. **—vi** fracturarse

fragile /'frædʒaɪl/ *a* frágil

fragment /'frægmənt/ *n* fragmento *m*. **~ary** *a* fragmentario

fragrance /'freɪgrəns/ *n* fragancia *f*. **~t** *a* fragante

frail /freɪl/ *a* (-er, -est) frágil

frame /freɪm/ *n* (*of picture, door, window*) marco *m*; (*of spectacles*) montura *f*; (*fig, structure*) estructura *f*; (*temporary state*) estado *m*. **~ of mind** estado *m* de ánimo. **—vt** enmarcar; (*fig*) formular; *(jurid, sl)* incriminar falsamente. ~**up** *n (sl)* complot *m*

framework /ˈfreɪmwɜːk/ *n* estructura *f*; *(context)* marco *m*

France /frɑːns/ *n* Francia *f*

franchise /ˈfræntʃaɪz/ *n (pol)* derecho *m* a votar; *(com)* concesión *f*

Franco... /ˈfræŋkəʊ/ *pref* franco...

frank /fræŋk/ *a* sincero. —*vt* franquear. ~**ly** *adv* sinceramente. ~**ness** *n* sinceridad *f*

frantic /ˈfræntɪk/ *a* frenético. ~ **with** loco de

fraternal /frəˈtɜːnl/ *a* fraternal

fraternity /frəˈtɜːnɪtɪ/ *n* fraternidad *f*; *(club)* asociación *f*

fraternize /ˈfrætənaɪz/ *vi* fraternizar

fraud /frɔːd/ *n (deception)* fraude *m*; *(person)* impostor *m*. ~**ulent** *a* fraudulento

fraught /frɔːt/ *a (tense)* tenso. ~ **with** cargado de

fray[1] /freɪ/ *vt* desgastar. —*vi* deshilacharse

fray[2] /freɪ/ *n* riña *f*

freak /friːk/ *n, (caprice)* capricho *m*; *(monster)* monstruo *m*; *(person)* chalado *m*. —*a* anormal. ~**ish** *a* anormal

freckle /ˈfrekl/ *n* peca *f*. ~**d** *a* pecoso

free /friː/ *a (freer* /ˈfriːə(r)/, *freest* /ˈfriːɪst/) libre; *(gratis)* gratis; *(lavish)* generoso. ~ **kick** *n* golpe *m* franco. ~ **of charge** gratis. ~ **speech** *n* libertad *f* de expresión. **give a** ~ **hand** dar carta blanca. —*vt (pt* **freed)** *(set at liberty)* poner en libertad; *(relieve from)* liberar *(from/of* de); *(untangle)* desenredar; *(loosen)* soltar

freedom /ˈfriːdəm/ *n* libertad *f*

freehold /ˈfriːhəʊld/ *n* propiedad *f* absoluta

freelance /ˈfriːlɑːns/ *a* independiente

freely /ˈfriːlɪ/ *adv* libremente

Freemason /ˈfriːmeɪsn/ *n* masón *m*. ~**ry** *n* masonería *f*

free-range /ˈfriːreɪndʒ/ *a (eggs)* de granja

freesia /ˈfriːzjə/ *n* fresia *f*

freeway /ˈfriːweɪ/ *n (Amer)* autopista *f*

freeze /friːz/ *vt (pt* **froze,** *pp* **frozen)** helar; congelar *(food, wages).* —*vi* helarse, congelarse; *(become motionless)* quedarse inmóvil. —*n* helada *f*; *(of wages, prices)* congelación *f*. ~**er** *n* congelador *m*. ~**ing** *a* glacial. —*n* congelación *f*. **below** ~**ing** bajo cero

freight /freɪt/ *n (goods)* mercancías *fpl*; *(hire of ship etc)* flete *m*. ~**er** *n (ship)* buque *m* de carga

French /frentʃ/ *a* francés. —*n (lang)* francés *m*. ~**man** *n* francés *m*. ~**-speaking** *a* francófono. ~ **window** *n* puertaventana *f*. ~**woman** *f* francesa *f*

frenzied /ˈfrenzɪd/ *a* frenético. ~**y** *n* frenesí *m*

frequency /ˈfriːkwənsɪ/ *n* frecuencia *f*

frequent /frɪˈkwent/ *vt* frecuentar. /ˈfriːkwənt/ *a* frecuente. ~**ly** *adv* frecuentemente

fresco /ˈfreskəʊ/ *n (pl* **-o(e)s)** fresco *m*

fresh /freʃ/ *a* (-**er,** -**est)** fresco; *(different, additional)* nuevo; *(cheeky)* fresco, descarado; *(water)* dulce. ~**en** *vi* refrescar. ~**en up** *(person)* refrescarse. ~**ly** *adv* recientemente. ~**man** *n* estudiante *m* de primer año. ~**ness** *n* frescura *f*

fret /fret/ *vi (pt* **fretted)** inquietarse. ~**ful** *a (discontented)* quejoso; *(irritable)* irritable

Freudian /'frɔɪdjən/ a freudiano

friar /'fraɪə(r)/ n fraile m

friction /'frɪkʃn/ n fricción f

Friday /'fraɪdeɪ/ n viernes m. **Good** ~ Viernes Santo

fridge /frɪdʒ/ n (fam) nevera f, refrigerador m, refrigeradora f

fried /fraɪd/ see **fry**. —a frito

friend /frend/ n amigo m. ~**liness** /'frendlɪnɪs/ n simpatía f. ~**ly** a (**-ier, -iest**) simpático. **F~ly Society** n mutualidad f. ~**ship** /'frendʃɪp/ n amistad f

frieze /friːz/ n friso m

frigate /'frɪgət/ n fragata f

fright /fraɪt/ n susto m; (person) espantajo m; (thing) horror m

frighten /'fraɪtn/ vt asustar. ~ **off** ahuyentar. ~**ed** a asustado. **be** ~**ed** tener miedo (**of** de)

frightful /'fraɪtfl/ a espantoso, horrible. ~**ly** adv terriblemente

frigid /'frɪdʒɪd/ a frío; (psych) frígido. ~**ity** /-'dʒɪdətɪ/ n frigidez f

frill /frɪl/ n volante m. ~**s** npl (fig) adornos mpl. **with no** ~**s** sencillo

fringe /frɪndʒ/ n (sewing) fleco m; (ornamental border) franja f; (of hair) flequillo m; (of area) periferia f; (of society) margen m. ~ **benefits** npl beneficios mpl suplementarios. ~ **theatre** n teatro m de vanguardia

frisk /frɪsk/ vt (search) cachear

frisky /'frɪskɪ/ a (**-ier, -iest**) retozón; (horse) fogoso

fritter[1] /'frɪtə(r)/ n buñuelo m

fritter[2] /'frɪtə(r)/ vt. ~ **away** desperdiciar

frivol|ity /frɪ'vɒlətɪ/ n frivolidad f. ~**ous** /'frɪvələs/ a frívolo

frizzy /'frɪzɪ/ a crespo

fro /frəʊ/ see **to and fro**

frock /frɒk/ n vestido m; (of monk) hábito m

frog /frɒg/ n rana f. **have a** ~ **in one's throat** tener carraspera

frogman /'frɒgmən/ n hombre m rana

frolic /'frɒlɪk/ vi (pt **frolicked**) retozar. —n broma f

from /frɒm/, unstressed /frəm/ prep de; (with time, prices, etc) a partir de; (habit, conviction) por; (according to) según. **take** ~ (away from) quitar a

front /frʌnt/ n parte f delantera; (of building) fachada f; (of clothes) delantera f; (mil, pol) frente f; (of book) principio m; (fig, appearance) apariencia f; (sea front) paseo m marítimo. **in** ~ **of** delante de. **put a bold** ~ **on** hacer de tripas corazón, mostrar firmeza. —a delantero; (first) primero. ~**age** n fachada f. ~**al** a frontal; (attack) de frente. ~ **door** n puerta f principal. ~ **page** n (of newspaper) primera plana f

frontier /'frʌntɪə(r)/ n frontera f

frost /frɒst/ n (freezing) helada f; (frozen dew) escarcha f. ~**-bite** n congelación f. ~**-bitten** a congelado. ~**ed** a (glass) esmerilado

frosting /'frɒstɪŋ/ n (icing, Amer) azúcar m glaseado

frosty a (weather) de helada; (window) escarchado; (fig) glacial

froth /frɒθ/ n espuma f. —vi espumar. ~**y** a espumoso

frown /fraʊn/ vi fruncir el entrecejo. ~ **on** desaprobar. —n ceño m

froze /frəʊz/, **frozen** /'frəʊzn/ see **freeze**

frugal /'fruːgl/ a frugal. ~**ly** adv frugalmente

fruit /fruːt/ n (bot, on tree, fig) fruto m; (as food) fruta f. ~**erer** n frutero m. ~**ful** /'fruːtfl/ a fértil; (fig) fructífero. ~**less** a infructuoso. ~ **machine** n (máquina f) tragaperras m. ~ **salad** n macedonia f de frutas.

~y /'fru:tɪ/ *a* ⟨*taste*⟩ que sabe a fruta

fruition /fru:'ɪʃn/ *n*. **come to** ~ realizarse

frump /frʌmp/ *n* espantajo *m*

frustrat|e /frʌ'streɪt/ *vt* frustrar. ~**ion** /-ʃn/ *n* frustración *f*; ⟨*disappointment*⟩ decepción *f*

fry[1] /fraɪ/ *vt* (*pt* **fried**) freír. —*vi* freírse

fry[2] /fraɪ/ *n* (*pl* **fry**). **small** ~ gente *f* de poca monta

frying-pan /'fraɪɪŋpæn/ *n* sartén *f*

fuchsia /'fju:ʃə/ *n* fucsia *f*

fuddy-duddy /'fʌdɪdʌdɪ/ *n*. **be a** ~ (*sl*) estar chapado a la antigua

fudge /fʌdʒ/ *n* dulce *m* de azúcar

fuel /'fju:əl/ *n* combustible *m*; ⟨*for car engine*⟩ carburante *m*; ⟨*fig*⟩ pábulo *m*. —*vt* (*pt* **fuelled**) alimentar de combustible

fugitive /'fju:dʒɪtɪv/ *a* & *n* fugitivo (*m*)

fugue /fju:g/ *n* (*mus*) fuga *f*

fulfil /fʊl'fɪl/ *vt* (*pt* **fulfilled**) cumplir (con) ⟨*promise, obligation*⟩; satisfacer ⟨*condition*⟩; realizar ⟨*hopes, plans*⟩; llevar a cabo ⟨*task*⟩. ~**ment** *n* ⟨*of promise, obligation*⟩ cumplimiento *m*; ⟨*of conditions*⟩ satisfacción *f*; ⟨*of hopes, plans*⟩ realización *f*; ⟨*of task*⟩ ejecución *f*

full /fʊl/ *a* (-**er, -est**) lleno; ⟨*bus, hotel*⟩ completo; ⟨*skirt*⟩ amplio; ⟨*account*⟩ detallado. **at** ~ **speed** a máxima velocidad. **be** ~ (**up**) ⟨*with food*⟩ no poder más. **in** ~ **swing** en plena marcha. —*n*. **in** ~ sin quitar nada. **to the** ~ completamente. **write in** ~ escribir con todas las letras. ~ **back** *n* ⟨*sport*⟩ defensa *m* & *f*. ~-**blooded** *a* vigoroso. ~ **moon** *n* plenilunio *m*. ~-**scale** *a* ⟨*drawing*⟩ de tamaño natural; ⟨*fig*⟩ amplio. ~ **stop** *n* punto *m*; ⟨*at*

end of paragraph, fig⟩ punto *m* final. ~ **time** *a* de jornada completa. ~**y** *adv* completamente

fulsome /'fʊlsəm/ *a* excesivo (torpemente)

fumble /'fʌmbl/ *vi* buscar (torpemente)

fume /fju:m/ *vi* humear; ⟨*fig, be furious*⟩ estar furioso. ~**s** *npl* humo *m*

fumigate /'fju:mɪgeɪt/ *vt* fumigar

fun /fʌn/ *n* ⟨*amusement*⟩ diversión *f*; ⟨*merriment*⟩ alegría *f*. **for** ~ en broma. **have** ~ divertirse. **make** ~ **of** burlarse de

function /'fʌŋkʃn/ *n* ⟨*purpose, duty*⟩ función *f*; ⟨*reception*⟩ recepción *f*. —*vi* funcionar. ~**al** *a* funcional

fund /fʌnd/ *n* fondo *m*. —*vt* proveer fondos para

fundamental /fʌndə'mentl/ *a* fundamental

funeral /'fju:nərəl/ *n* funeral *m*, funerales *mpl*. —*a* fúnebre

fun-fair /'fʌnfeə(r)/ *n* parque *m* de atracciones

fungus /'fʌŋgəs/ *n* (*pl* **-gi** /-gaɪ/) hongo *m*

funicular /fju:'nɪkjʊlə(r)/ *n* funicular *m*

funk /fʌŋk/ *m* ⟨*fear, sl*⟩ miedo *m*; ⟨*state of depression, Amer, sl*⟩ depresión *f*. **be in a (blue)** ~ tener (mucho) miedo; ⟨*Amer*⟩ estar (muy) deprimido. —*vi* rajarse

funnel /'fʌnl/ *n* ⟨*for pouring*⟩ embudo *m*; ⟨*of ship*⟩ chimenea *f*

funn|ily /'fʌnɪlɪ/ *adv* graciosamente; ⟨*oddly*⟩ curiosamente. ~**y** *a* (-**ier, -iest**) divertido, gracioso; ⟨*odd*⟩ curioso, raro. ~**y-bone** *n* cóndilo *m* del húmero. ~**y business** *n* engaño *m*

fur /fɜ:(r)/ *n* pelo *m*; ⟨*pelt*⟩ piel *f*; ⟨*in kettle*⟩ sarro *m*

furbish /'fɜ:bɪʃ/ *vt* pulir; ⟨*renovate*⟩ renovar

furious /'fjʊərɪəs/ a furioso. ∼ly adv furiosamente

furnace /'fɜːnɪs/ n horno m

furnish /'fɜːnɪʃ/ vt (with furniture) amueblar; (supply) proveer. ∼ings npl muebles mpl, mobiliario m

furniture /'fɜːnɪtʃə(r)/ n muebles mpl, mobiliario m

furrier /'fʌrɪə(r)/ n peletero m

furrow /'fʌrəʊ/ n surco m

furry /'fɜːrɪ/ a peludo

furthe|r /'fɜːðə(r)/ a más lejano; (additional) nuevo. —adv más lejos; (more) además. —vt fomentar. ∼rmore adv además. ∼rmost a más lejano. ∼st a más lejano. —adv más lejos

furtive /'fɜːtɪv/ a furtivo

fury /'fjʊərɪ/ n furia f

fuse[1] /fjuːz/ vt (melt) fundir; (fig, unite) fusionar. ∼ the lights fundir los plomos. —vi fundirse; (fig) fusionarse. —n fusible m, plomo m

fuse[2] /fjuːz/ n (of bomb) mecha f

fuse-box /'fjuːzbɒks/ n caja f de fusibles

fuselage /'fjuːzəlɑːʒ/ n fuselaje m

fusion /'fjuːʒn/ n fusión f

fuss /fʌs/ n (commotion) jaleo m. **kick up a** ∼ armar un lío, armar una bronca, protestar. **make a** ∼ **of** tratar con mucha atención. ∼y a (-ier, -iest) (finicky) remilgado; (demanding) exigente; (ornate) recargado

fusty /'fʌstɪ/ a (-ier, -iest) que huele a cerrado

futile /'fjuːtaɪl/ a inútil, vano

future /'fjuːtʃə(r)/ a futuro. —n futuro m, porvenir m; (gram) futuro m. **in** ∼ en lo sucesivo, de ahora en adelante

futuristic /fjuːtʃə'rɪstɪk/ a futurista

fuzz /fʌz/ n (fluff) pelusa f; (police, sl) policía f, poli f (fam)

fuzzy /'fʌzɪ/ a (hair) crespo; (photograph) borroso

G

gab /gæb/ n charla f. **have the gift of the** ∼ tener un pico de oro

gabardine /gæbə'diːn/ n gabardina f

gabble /'gæbl/ vt decir atropelladamente. —vi hablar atropelladamente. —n torrente m de palabras

gable /'geɪbl/ n aguilón m

gad /gæd/ vi (pt **gadded**). ∼ **about** callejear

gadget /'gædʒɪt/ n chisme m

Gaelic /'geɪlɪk/ a & n gaélico (m)

gaffe /gæf/ n plancha f, metedura f de pata

gag /gæg/ n mordaza f; (joke) chiste m. —vt (pt **gagged**) amordazar

gaga /'gɑːgɑː/ a (sl) chocho

gaiety /'geɪətɪ/ n alegría f

gaily /'geɪlɪ/ adv alegremente

gain /geɪn/ vt ganar; (acquire) adquirir; (obtain) conseguir. —vi (clock) adelantar. —n ganancia f; (increase) aumento m. ∼**ful** a lucrativo

gainsay /geɪn'seɪ/ vt (pt **gainsaid**) (formal) negar

gait /geɪt/ n modo m de andar

gala /'gɑːlə/ n fiesta f; (sport) competición f

galaxy /'gæləksɪ/ n galaxia f

gale /geɪl/ n vendaval m; (storm) tempestad f

gall /gɔːl/ n bilis f; (fig) hiel f; (impudence) descaro m

gallant /'gælənt/ a (brave) valiente; (chivalrous) galante. ∼**ry** n valor m

gall-bladder /'gɔːlblædə(r)/ n vesícula f biliar

galleon /ˈgælɪən/ n galeón m

gallery /ˈgælərɪ/ n galería f

galley /ˈgælɪ/ n (ship) galera f; (ship's kitchen) cocina f. ~ (proof) n (typ) galerada f

Gallic /ˈgælɪk/ a gálico. ~ism /n galicismo m

gallivant /ˈgælɪvænt/ vi (fam) callejear

gallon /ˈgælən/ n galón m (imperial = 4,546l; Amer = 3,785l)

gallop /ˈgæləp/ n galope m. —vi (pt galloped) galopar

gallows /ˈgæləʊz/ n horca f

galore /gəˈlɔː(r)/ adv en abundancia

galosh /gəˈlɒʃ/ n chanclo m

galvanize /ˈgælvənaɪz/ vt galvanizar

gambit /ˈgæmbɪt/ n (in chess) gambito m; (fig) táctica f

gamble /ˈgæmbl/ vt/i jugar. ~e on contar con. —n (venture) empresa f arriesgada; (bet) jugada f; (risk) riesgo m. ~er n jugador m. ~ing n juego m

game[1] /geɪm/ n juego m; (match) partido m; (animals, birds) caza f. —a valiente. ~ for listo para

game[2] /geɪm/ a (lame) cojo

gamekeeper /ˈgeɪmkiːpə(r)/ n guardabosque m

gammon /ˈgæmən/ n jamón m ahumado

gamut /ˈgæmət/ n gama f

gamy /ˈgeɪmɪ/ a manido

gander /ˈgændə(r)/ n ganso m

gang /gæŋ/ n pandilla f; (of workmen) equipo m. —vi. ~ up unirse (on contra)

gangling /ˈgæŋglɪŋ/ a larguirucho

gangrene /ˈgæŋgriːn/ n gangrena f

gangster /ˈgæŋstə(r)/ n bandido m, gángster m

gangway /ˈgæŋweɪ/ n pasillo m; (of ship) pasarela f

gaol /dʒeɪl/ n cárcel f. ~bird n criminal m empedernido. ~er n carcelero m

gap /gæp/ n vacío m; (breach) brecha f; (in time) intervalo m; (deficiency) laguna f; (difference) diferencia f

gape /geɪp/ vi quedarse boquiabierto; (be wide open) estar muy abierto. ~ing a abierto; (person) boquiabierto

garage /ˈgærɑːʒ/ n garaje m; (petrol station) gasolinera f; (for repairs) taller m. —vt dejar en (el) garaje

garb /gɑːb/ n vestido m

garbage /ˈgɑːbɪdʒ/ n basura f

garble /ˈgɑːbl/ vt mutilar

garden /ˈgɑːdn/ n (of flowers) jardín m; (of vegetables/fruit) huerto m. —vi trabajar en el jardín/huerto. ~er n jardinero/hortelano m. ~ing n jardinería/horticultura f

gargantuan /gɑːˈgæntjʊən/ a gigantesco

gargle /ˈgɑːgl/ vi hacer gárgaras. n gargarismo m

gargoyle /ˈgɑːgɔɪl/ n gárgola f

garish /ˈgeərɪʃ/ a chillón

garland /ˈgɑːlənd/ n guirnalda f

garlic /ˈgɑːlɪk/ n ajo m

garment /ˈgɑːmənt/ n prenda f (de vestir)

garnet /ˈgɑːnɪt/ n granate m

garnish /ˈgɑːnɪʃ/ vt aderezar. —n aderezo m

garret /ˈgærət/ n guardilla f, buhardilla f

garrison /ˈgærɪsn/ n guarnición f

garrulous /ˈgærələs/ a hablador

garter /ˈgɑːtə(r)/ n liga f

gas /gæs/ n (pl gases) gas m; (med) anestésico m; (petrol, Amer, fam) gasolina f. —vt (pt gassed) asfixiar con gas. —vi (fam) charlar. ~ fire n estufa f de gas

gash /gæʃ/ *n* cuchillada *f*. —*vt* acuchillar

gasket /'gæskɪt/ *n* junta *f*

gas: ~ **mask** *n* careta *f* antigás *a invar.* ~ **meter** *n* contador *m* de gas

gasoline /'gæsəliːn/ *n* (*petrol*, *Amer*) gasolina *f*

gasometer /gæ'sɒmɪtə(r)/ *n* gasómetro *m*

gasp /gɑːsp/ *vi* jadear; (*with surprise*) quedarse boquiabierto. — *n* jadeo *m*

gas: ~ **ring** *n* hornillo *m* de gas. ~ **station** *n* (*Amer*) gasolinera *f*

gastric /'gæstrɪk/ *a* gástrico

gastronomy /gæ'strɒnəmɪ/ *n* gastronomía *f*

gate /geɪt/ *n* puerta *f*; (*of metal*) verja *f*; (*barrier*) barrera *f*

gateau /'gætəʊ/ *n* (*pl* **gateaux**) tarta *f*

gate: ~**crasher** *n* intruso *m* (que ha entrado sin ser invitado o sin pagar). ~**way** *n* puerta *f*

gather /'gæðə(r)/ *vt* reunir (*people*, *things*); (*accumulate*) acumular; (*pick up*) recoger; recoger (*flowers*); (*fig*, *infer*) deducir; (*sewing*) fruncir. ~ **speed** acelerar. —*vi* (*people*) reunirse; (*things*) acumularse. ~**ing** *n* reunión *f*

gauche /gəʊʃ/ *a* torpe

gaudy /'gɔːdɪ/ *a* (**-ier**, **-iest**) chillón

gauge /geɪdʒ/ *n* (*measurement*) medida *f*; (*rail*) entrevía *f*; (*instrument*) indicador *m*. —*vt* medir; (*fig*) estimar

gaunt /gɔːnt/ *a* macilento; (*grim*) lúgubre

gauntlet /'gɔːntlɪt/ *n*. **run the** ~ **of** estar sometido a

gauze /gɔːz/ *n* gasa *f*

gave /geɪv/ *see* **give**

gawk /gɔːk/ *vi.* ~ **at** mirar como un tonto

gawky /'gɔːkɪ/ *a* (**-ier**, **-iest**) torpe

gawp /gɔːp/ *vi.* ~ **at** mirar como un tonto

gay /geɪ/ *a* (**-er**, **-est**) (*joyful*) alegre; (*homosexual*, *fam*) homosexual, gay (*fam*)

gaze /geɪz/ *vi.* ~ (**at**) mirar (fijamente). —*n* mirada *f* (fija)

gazelle /gə'zel/ *n* gacela *f*

gazette /gə'zet/ *n* boletín *m* oficial, gaceta *f*

gazump /gə'zʌmp/ *vt* aceptar un precio más elevado de otro comprador

GB *abbr see* **Great Britain**

gear /gɪə(r)/ *n* equipo *m*; (*tec*) engranaje *m*; (*auto*) marcha *f*. **in** ~ engranado. **out of** ~ desengranado. —*vt* adaptar. ~**box** *n* (*auto*) caja *f* de cambios

geese /giːs/ *see* **goose**

geezer /'giːzə(r)/ *n* (*sl*) tipo *m*

gelatine /'dʒelətiːn/ *n* gelatina *f*

gelignite /'dʒelɪgnaɪt/ *n* gelignita *f*

gem /dʒem/ *n* piedra *f* preciosa

Gemini /'dʒeminaɪ/ *n* (*astr*) Gemelos *mpl*, Géminis *mpl*

gen /dʒen/ *n* (*sl*) información *f*

gender /'dʒendə(r)/ *n* género *m*

gene /dʒiːn/ *n* gene *m*

genealogy /dʒiːnɪ'ælədʒɪ/ *n* genealogía *f*

general /'dʒenərəl/ *a* general. —*n* general *m*. **in** ~ generalmente. ~ **election** *n* elecciones *fpl* generales

generaliz|ation /dʒenərəlaɪ'zeɪʃn/ *n* generalización *f*. ~**e** *vt/i* generalizar

generally /'dʒenərəlɪ/ *adv* generalmente

general practitioner /'dʒenərəl prækˈtɪʃənə(r)/ *n* médico *m* de cabecera

generate /'dʒenəreɪt/ *vt* producir; (*elec*) generar

generation /dʒenəˈreɪʃn/ n generación f

generator /ˈdʒenəreɪtə(r)/ n (elec) generador m

genero|sity /dʒenəˈrɒsəti/ n generosidad f. ~us /ˈdʒenərəs/ a generoso; (plentiful) abundante

genetic /dʒɪˈnetɪk/ a genético. ~s n genética f

Geneva /dʒɪˈniːvə/ n Ginebra f

genial /ˈdʒiːnɪəl/ a simpático, afable; (climate) suave, templado

genital /ˈdʒenɪtl/ a genital. ~s npl genitales mpl

genitive /ˈdʒenɪtɪv/ a & n genitivo (m)

genius /ˈdʒiːnɪəs/ n (pl -uses) genio m

genocide /ˈdʒenəsaɪd/ n genocidio m

genre /ʒɑːnr/ n género m

gent /dʒent/ n (sl) señor m. ~s n aseo m de caballeros

genteel /dʒenˈtiːl/ a distinguido; (excessively refined) cursi

gentle /ˈdʒentl/ a (-er, -est) (mild, kind) amable, dulce; (slight) ligero; (hint) discreto

gentlefolk /ˈdʒentlfəʊk/ npl gente f de buena familia

gentleman /ˈdʒentlmən/ n señor m; (well-bred) caballero m

gentleness /ˈdʒentlnɪs/ n amabilidad f

gentlewoman /ˈdʒentlwʊmən/ n señora f (de buena familia)

gently /ˈdʒentlɪ/ adv amablemente; (slowly) despacio

gentry /ˈdʒentrɪ/ npl pequeña aristocracia f

genuflect /ˈdʒenjuːflekt/ vi doblar la rodilla

genuine /ˈdʒenjʊɪn/ a verdadero; (person) sincero

geograph|er /dʒɪˈɒɡrəfə(r)/ n geógrafo m. ~ical /dʒɪəˈɡræfɪkl/ a geográfico. ~y /dʒɪˈɒɡrəfɪ/ n geografía f

geolog|ical /dʒɪəˈlɒdʒɪkl/ a geológico. ~ist n geólogo m. ~y /dʒɪˈɒlədʒɪ/ n geología f

geometr|ic(al) /dʒɪəˈmetrɪk(l)/ a geométrico. ~y /dʒɪˈɒmətrɪ/ n geometría f

geranium /dʒəˈreɪnɪəm/ n geranio m

geriatrics /dʒerɪˈætrɪks/ n geriatría f

germ /dʒɜːm/ n (rudiment, seed) germen m; (med) microbio m

German /ˈdʒɜːmən/ a & n alemán (m). ~ic /dʒɜːˈmænɪk/ a germánico. ~ measles n rubéola f. ~ shepherd (dog) n (perro m) pastor m alemán. ~y n Alemania f

germicide /ˈdʒɜːmɪsaɪd/ n germicida m

germinate /ˈdʒɜːmɪneɪt/ vi germinar. —vt hacer germinar

gerrymander /ˈdʒerɪmændə(r)/ n falsificación f electoral

gestation /dʒeˈsteɪʃn/ n gestación f

gesticulate /dʒeˈstɪkjʊleɪt/ vi hacer ademanes, gesticular

gesture /ˈdʒestʃə(r)/ n ademán m; (fig) gesto m

get /get/ vt (pt & pp got, pp Amer gotten, pres p getting) obtener, tener; (catch) coger (not LAm), agarrar (esp LAm); (buy) comprar; (find) encontrar; (fetch) buscar, traer; (understand, sl) comprender, caer (fam). ~ s.o. to do sth conseguir que uno haga algo. —vi (go) ir; (become) hacerse; (start to) empezar a; (manage) conseguir. ~ married casarse. ~ ready prepararse. ~ about (person) salir mucho; (after illness) levantarse. ~ along (manage) ir tirando; (progress) hacer progresos. ~ along with llevarse bien con. ~ at (reach) llegar a; (imply) querer decir. ~ away salir; (escape) escaparse. ~ **back** *vi* volver. — *vt* (*manage*) ir tirando; (*pass*) pasar. ~ **down** bajar; (*depress*) deprimir. ~ **in** entrar; subir (*vehicle*); (*arrive*) llegar. ~ **off** bajar de (*train, car etc*); (*leave*) irse; (*jurid*) salir absuelto. ~ **on** (*progress*) hacer progresos; (*succeed*) tener éxito. ~ **on with** (*be on good terms with*) llevarse bien con; (*continue*) seguir. ~ **out** (*person*) salir; (*take out*) sacar. ~ **out of** (*fig*) librarse de. ~ **over** reponerse de (*illness*). ~ **round** soslayar (*difficulty etc*); engatusar (*person*). ~ **through** (*pass*) pasar; (*finish*) terminar; (*on phone*) comunicar con. ~ **up** levantarse; (*climb*) subir; (*organize*) preparar. ~**away** *n* huida *f*. ~**up** *n* traje *m*

geyser /'giːzə(r)/ *n* calentador *m* de agua; (*geog*) géiser *m*

Ghana /'gɑːnə/ *n* Ghana *f*

ghastly /'gɑːstlɪ/ *a* (-**ier**, -**iest**) horrible; (*pale*) pálido

gherkin /'gɜːkɪn/ *n* pepinillo *m*

ghetto /'getəʊ/ *n* (*pl* -**os**) (*Jewish quarter*) judería *f*; (*ethnic settlement*) barrio *m* pobre habitado por un grupo étnico

ghost /gəʊst/ *n* fantasma *m*. ~**ly** *a* espectral

ghoulish /'guːlɪʃ/ *a* macabro

giant /'dʒaɪənt/ *n* gigante *m*. —*a* gigantesco

gibberish /'dʒɪbərɪʃ/ *n* jerigonza *f*

gibe /dʒaɪb/ *n* mofa *f*

giblets /'dʒɪblɪts/ *npl* menudillos *mpl*

Gibraltar /dʒɪ'brɔːltə(r)/ *n* Gibraltar *m*

gidd|**iness** /'gɪdɪnɪs/ *n* vértigo *m*. ~**y** *a* (-**ier**, -**iest**) mareado; by (*speed*) vertiginoso. **be/feel** ~**y** estar/sentirse mareado

gift /gɪft/ *n* regalo *m*; (*ability*) don *m*. ~**ed** *a* dotado de talento. ~**wrap** *vt* envolver para regalo

gig /gɪg/ *n* (*fam*) concierto *m*

gigantic /dʒaɪ'gæntɪk/ *a* gigantesco

giggle /'gɪgl/ *vi* reírse tontamente. —*n* risita *f*. **the** ~**s** la risa *f* tonta

gild /gɪld/ *vt* dorar

gills /gɪlz/ *npl* agallas *fpl*

gilt /gɪlt/ *a* dorado. ~**edged** *a* (*com*) de máxima garantía

gimmick /'gɪmɪk/ *n* truco *m*

gin /dʒɪn/ *n* ginebra *f*

ginger /'dʒɪndʒə(r)/ *n* jengibre *m*. —*a* rojizo. —*vt*. ~ **up** animar. ~ **ale** *n*, ~ **beer** *n* cerveza *f* de jengibre. ~**bread** *n* pan *m* de jengibre

gingerly /'dʒɪndʒəlɪ/ *adv* cautelosamente

gingham /'gɪŋəm/ *n* guinga *f*

gipsy /'dʒɪpsɪ/ *n* gitano *m*

giraffe /dʒɪ'rɑːf/ *n* jirafa *f*

girder /'gɜːdə(r)/ *n* viga *f*

girdle /'gɜːdl/ *n* (*belt*) cinturón *m*; (*corset*) corsé *m*

girl /gɜːl/ *n* chica *f*, muchacha *f*; (*child*) niña *f*. ~**friend** *n* amiga *f*; (*of boy*) novia *f*. ~**hood** *n* (*up to adolescence*) niñez *f*; (*adolescence*) juventud *f*. ~**ish** *a* de niña; (*boy*) afeminado

giro /'dʒaɪrəʊ/ *n* (*pl* -**os**) giro *m* (*bancario*)

girth /gɜːθ/ *n* circunferencia *f*

gist /dʒɪst/ *n* lo esencial *invar*

give /gɪv/ *vt* (*pt* **gave**, *pp* **given**) dar; (*deliver*) entregar; regalar (*present*); prestar (*aid, attention*); (*grant*) conceder; (*yield*) ceder; (*devote*) dedicar. ~ **o.s. to** darse a. —*vi* dar; (*yield*) ceder; (*stretch*) estirarse. —*n* elasticidad *f*. ~ **away** regalar; descubrir (*secret*). ~ **back** devolver. ~ **in** (*yield*) rendirse. ~ **off** emitir. ~ **o.s. up** entregarse (a). ~ **out**

distribuir; *(announce)* anunciar; *(become used up)* agotarse. ~ **over** *(devote)* dedicar; *(stop, fam)* dejar (de). ~ **up** *(renounce)* renunciar a; *(yield)* ceder

given /'gɪvn/ *see* **give**. —*a* dado. ~ **name** *n* nombre *m* de pila

glacier /'glæsɪə(r)/ *n* glaciar *m*

glad /glæd/ *a* contento. ~**den** *vt* alegrar

glade /gleɪd/ *n* claro *m*

gladiator /'glædɪeɪtə(r)/ *n* gladiador *m*

gladiolus /glædɪ'əʊləs/ *n* (*pl* -li /-laɪ/) estoque *m*, gladiolo *m*, gladíolo *m*

gladly /'glædlɪ/ *adv* alegremente; *(willingly)* con mucho gusto

glamorize /'glæməraɪz/ *vt* embellecer. ~**rous** *a* atractivo. ~**ur** *n* encanto *m*

glance /glɑːns/ *n* ojeada *f*. —*vi.* ~ **at** dar un vistazo a

gland /glænd/ *n* glándula *f*

glare /gleə(r)/ *vi* deslumbrar; *(stare angrily)* mirar airadamente. —*n* deslumbramiento *m*; *(stare, fig)* mirada *f* airada. ~**ing** *a* deslumbrador; *(obvious)* manifiesto

glass /glɑːs/ *n* *(material)* vidrio *m*; *(without stem or for wine)* vaso *m*; *(with stem)* copa *f*; *(for beer)* caña *f*; *(mirror)* espejo *m*. ~**es** *npl* *(spectacles)* gafas *fpl*, anteojos *(LAm)* *mpl*. ~**y** *a* vítreo

glaze /gleɪz/ *vt* poner cristales a *(windows, doors)*; vidriar *(pottery)*. —*n* barniz *m*; *(for pottery)* esmalte *m*. ~**d** *a* *(object)* vidriado; *(eye)* vidrioso

gleam /gliːm/ *n* destello *m*. —*vi* destellar

glean /gliːn/ *vt* espigar

glee /gliː/ *n* regocijo *m*. ~ **club** *n* orfeón *m*. ~**ful** *a* regocijado

glen /glen/ *n* cañada *f*

glib /glɪb/ *a* de mucha labia; *(reply)* fácil. ~**ly** *adv* con poca sinceridad

glide /glaɪd/ *vi* deslizarse; *(plane)* planear. ~**er** / *n* planeador *m*. ~**ing** *n* planeo *m*

glimmer /'glɪmə(r)/ *n* destello *m*. —*vi* destellar

glimpse /glɪmps/ *n* vislumbre *f*. **catch a** ~ *of* vislumbrar. —*vt* vislumbrar

glint /glɪnt/ *n* destello *m*. —*vi* destellar

glisten /'glɪsn/ *vi* brillar

glitter /'glɪtə(r)/ *vi* brillar. —*n* brillo *m*

gloat /gləʊt/ *vi.* ~ **on/over** regodearse

global /'gləʊbl/ *a* *(world-wide)* mundial; *(all-embracing)* global

globe /gləʊb/ *n* globo *m*

globule /'glɒbjuːl/ *n* glóbulo *m*

gloom /gluːm/ *n* oscuridad *f*; *(sadness, fig)* tristeza *f*. ~**y** *a* (-**ier**, -**iest**) triste; *(pessimistic)* pesimista

glorify /'glɔːrɪfaɪ/ *vt* glorificar

glorious /'glɔːrɪəs/ *a* espléndido; *(deed, hero etc)* glorioso

glory /'glɔːrɪ/ *n* gloria *f*; *(beauty)* esplendor *m*. —*vi.* ~ **in** enorgullecerse de. ~**hole** *n* *(untidy room)* leonera *f*

gloss /glɒs/ *n* lustre *m*. —*a* brillante. —*vi.* ~ **over** *(make light of)* minimizar; *(cover up)* encubrir

glossary /'glɒsərɪ/ *n* glosario *m*

glossy /'glɒsɪ/ *a* brillante

glove /glʌv/ *n* guante *m*. ~ **compartment** *n* *(auto)* guantera *f*, gaveta *f*. ~**d** *a* enguantado

glow /gləʊ/ *vi* brillar; *(with health)* rebosar de; *(with passion)* enardecerse. —*n* incandescencia *f*; *(of cheeks)* rubor *m*

glower /'glaʊə(r)/ *vi.* ~ **(at)** mirar airadamente

glowing /'gləʊɪŋ/ *a* incandescente; *(account)* entusiasta; *(complexion)* rojo; *(with health)* rebosante de

glucose /'gluːkəʊs/ *n* glucosa *f*

glue /glu:/ n cola f. —vt (pres p gluing) pegar

glum /glʌm/ a (**glummer, glummest**) triste

glut /glʌt/ n superabundancia f

glutton /'glʌtn/ n glotón m. **~ous** a glotón. **~y** n glotonería f

glycerine /'glɪsəriːn/ n glicerina f

gnarled /nɑːld/ a nudoso

gnash /næʃ/ vt. **~ one's teeth** rechinar los dientes

gnat /næt/ n mosquito m

gnaw /nɔː/ vt/i roer

gnome /nəʊm/ n gnomo m

go /ɡəʊ/ vi (pt **went**, pp **gone**) ir; (leave) irse; (work) funcionar; (become) hacerse; (be sold) venderse; (vanish) desaparecer. **~ ahead!** ¡adelante! **~ bad** pasarse. **~ riding** montar a caballo. **~ shopping** ir de compras. **be ~ing to do** ir a hacer. —n (pl **goes**) (energy) energía f. **be on the ~** trabajar sin cesar. **have a ~** intentar. **it's your ~** te toca a ti. **make a ~ of** tener éxito en. **~ across** cruzar. **~ away** irse. **~ back** volver. **~ back on** faltar a (promise etc). **~ by** pasar. **~ down** bajar; (sun) ponerse. **~ for** buscar, traer; (like) gustar; (attack, sl) atacar. **~ in** entrar. **~ in for** presentarse para (exam). **~ off** (leave) irse; (go bad) pasarse; (explode) estallar. **~ on** seguir; (happen) pasar. **~ out** salir; (light, fire) apagarse. **~ over** (check) examinar. **~ round** (be enough) ser bastante. **~ through** (suffer) sufrir; (check) examinar. **~ under** hundirse. **~ up** subir. **~ without** pasarse sin

goad /ɡəʊd/ vt aguijonear

go-ahead /'ɡəʊəhed/ n luz f verde. —a dinámico

goal /ɡəʊl/ n fin m, objeto m; (sport) gol m. **~ie** n (fam) portero m. **~keeper** n portero m.

~post n poste m (de la portería)

goat /ɡəʊt/ n cabra f

goatee /ɡəʊ'tiː/ n perilla f, barbas fpl de chivo

gobble /'ɡɒbl/ vt engullir

go-between /'ɡəʊbɪtwiːn/ n intermediario m

goblet /'ɡɒblɪt/ n copa f

goblin /'ɡɒblɪn/ n duende m

God /ɡɒd/ n Dios m. **~-forsaken** a olvidado de Dios

god /ɡɒd/ n dios m. **~child** n ahijado m. **~daughter** n ahijada f. **~dess** /'ɡɒdɪs/ n diosa f. **~father** n padrino m. **~ly** a devoto. **~mother** n madrina f. **~send** n beneficio m inesperado. **~son** n ahijado m

go-getter /ɡəʊ'ɡetə(r)/ n persona f ambiciosa

goggle /'ɡɒɡl/ vi. **~ (at)** mirar con los ojos desmesuradamente abiertos

goggles /'ɡɒɡlz/ npl gafas fpl protectoras

going /'ɡəʊɪŋ/ n camino m; (racing) (estado m del) terreno m. **it is slow/hard ~** es lento/difícil. —a (price) actual; (concern) en funcionamiento. **~s-on** npl actividades fpl anormales, tejemaneje m

gold /ɡəʊld/ n oro m. —a de oro. **~en** /'ɡəʊldən/ a de oro; (in colour) dorado; (opportunity) único. **~en wedding** n bodas fpl de oro. **~fish** n invar pez m de colores, carpa f dorada. **~mine** n mina f de oro; (fig) fuente f de gran riqueza. **~plated** a chapado en oro. **~smith** n orfebre m

golf /ɡɒlf/ n golf m. **~course** n campo m de golf. **~er** n jugador m de golf

golly /'ɡɒli/ int ¡caramba!

golosh /ɡə'lɒʃ/ n chanclo m

gondola /'ɡɒndələ/ n góndola f. **~ier** /ɡɒndə'lɪə(r)/ n gondolero m

gone /gɒn/ *see* go. —*a* pasado. ~ **six o'clock** después de las seis

gong /gɒŋ/ *n* gong(o) *m*

good /gʊd/ *a* (**better, best**) bueno, (*before masculine singular noun*) buen. ~ **afternoon!** ¡buenas tardes! ~ **evening!** (*before dark*) ¡buenas tardes!; (*after dark*) ¡buenas noches! **G~ Friday** *n* Viernes *m* Santo. ~ **morning!** ¡buenos días! ~ **name** *n* (buena) reputación *f*. ~ **night!** ¡buenas noches! **a ~ deal** bastante. **as ~ as** (*almost*) casi. **be ~ with** entender. **do ~** hacer bien. **feel ~** sentirse bien. **have a ~ time** divertirse. **it is ~ for you** le sentará bien. —*n* bien *m*. **for ~** para siempre. **it is no ~ shouting/etc** es inútil gritar/etc.

goodbye /gʊdˈbaɪ/ *int* ¡adiós! —*n* adiós *m*. **say ~ to** despedirse de

good-for-nothing *a* & *n* inútil (*m*). ~**looking** *a* guapo

goodness /ˈgʊdnɪs/ *n* bondad *f*. ~!, ~ **gracious!,** ~ **me!, my ~!** ¡Dios mío!

goods /gʊdz/ *npl* (*merchandise*) mercancías *fpl*

goodwill /gʊdˈwɪl/ *n* buena voluntad *f*

goody /ˈgʊdɪ/ *n* (*culin, fam*) golosina *f*; (*in film*) bueno *m*. ~**goody** *n* mojigato *m*

gooey /ˈguːɪ/ *a* (**gooier, gooiest**) (*sl*) pegajoso; (*fig*) sentimental

goof /guːf/ *vi* (*Amer, blunder*) cometer una pifia. ~**y** *a* (*sl*) necio

goose /guːs/ *n* (*pl* **geese**) oca *f*

gooseberry /ˈgʊzbərɪ/ *n* uva *f* espina, grosella *f*

goose-flesh /ˈguːsfleʃ/ *n*, **goose-pimples** /ˈguːspɪmplz/ *n* carne *f* de gallina

gore /gɔː(r)/ *n* sangre *f*. —*vt* cornear

gorge /gɔːdʒ/ *n* (*geog*) garganta *f*. —*vt*. **o.s.** hartarse (**on** de)

gorgeous /ˈgɔːdʒəs/ *a* magnífico

gorilla /gəˈrɪlə/ *n* gorila *m*

gormless /ˈgɔːmlɪs/ *a* (*sl*) idiota

gorse /gɔːs/ *n* aulaga *f*

gory /ˈgɔːrɪ/ *a* (**-ier, -iest**) (*covered in blood*) ensangrentado; (*horrific, fig*) horrible

gosh /gɒʃ/ *int* ¡caramba!

go-slow /gəʊˈsləʊ/ *n* huelga *f* de celo

gospel /ˈgɒspl/ *n* evangelio *m*

gossip /ˈgɒsɪp/ *n* (*idle chatter*) charla *f*; (*tittle-tattle*) comadreo *m*; (*person*) chismoso *m*. —*vi* (*pt* **gossiped**) (*chatter*) charlar; (*repeat scandal*) comadrear. ~**y** *a* chismoso

got /gɒt/ *see* get. **have ~** tener. **have ~ to do** tener que hacer

Gothic /ˈgɒθɪk/ *a* (*archit*) gótico; (*people*) godo

gouge /gaʊdʒ/ *vt*. ~ **out** arrancar

gourmet /ˈɡʊəmeɪ/ *n* gastrónomo *m*

gout /gaʊt/ *n* (*med*) gota *f*

govern /ˈɡʌvn/ *vt/i* gobernar

governess /ˈɡʌvənɪs/ *n* institutriz *f*

government /ˈɡʌvənmənt/ *n* gobierno *m*. ~**al** /ɡʌvənˈmentl/ *a* gubernamental

governor /ˈɡʌvənə(r)/ *n* gobernador *m*

gown /gaʊn/ *n* vestido *m*; (*of judge, teacher*) toga *f*

GP *abbr* *see* **general practitioner**

grab /ɡræb/ *vt* (*pt* **grabbed**) agarrar

grace /ɡreɪs/ *n* gracia *f*. ~**ful** *a* elegante

gracious /ˈɡreɪʃəs/ *a* (*kind*) amable; (*elegant*) elegante

gradation /ɡrəˈdeɪʃn/ *n* gradación *f*

grade /ɡreɪd/ *n* clase *f*, categoría *f*; (*of goods*) clase *f*, calidad *f*; (*on*

scale) grado *m*; (*school mark*) nota *f*; (*class, Amer*) curso *m*.
school /n (*Amer*) escuela *f* primaria. —*vt* clasificar; (*schol*) calificar
gradient /'greɪdɪənt/ *n* (*slope*) pendiente *f*
gradual /'grædʒʊəl/ *a* gradual. ∼**ly** *adv* gradualmente
graduat|e /'grædʒʊət/ *n* (*univ*) licenciado. —*vi* /'grædʒʊeɪt/ licenciarse. —*vt* graduar. ∼**ion** /-'eɪʃn/ *n* entrega *f* de títulos
graffiti /grə'fiːtɪ/ *npl* pintada *f*
graft[1] /grɑːft/ *n* (*med, bot*) injerto *m*. —*vt* injertar
graft[2] /grɑːft/ *n* (*bribery, fam*) corrupción *f*
grain /greɪn/ *n* grano *m*
gram /græm/ *n* gramo *m*
gramma|r /'græmə(r)/ *n* gramática *f*. ∼**tical** /grə'mætɪkl/ *a* gramatical
gramophone /'græməfəʊn/ *n* tocadiscos *m invar*
grand /grænd/ *a* (-**er**, -**est**) magnífico; (*excellent, fam*) estupendo. ∼**child** *n* nieto *m*. ∼**daughter** *n* nieta *f*
grandeur /'grændʒə(r)/ *n* grandiosidad *f*
grandfather /'grændfɑːðə(r)/ *n* abuelo *m*
grandiose /'grændɪəʊs/ *a* grandioso
grand: ∼**mother** *n* abuela *f*. ∼**parents** *npl* abuelos *mpl*. ∼**piano** *n* piano *m* de cola. ∼**son** *n* nieto *m*
grandstand /'grænstænd/ *n* tribuna *f*
granite /'grænɪt/ *n* granito *m*
granny /'grænɪ/ *n* (*fam*) abuela *f*, nana *f* (*fam*)
grant /grɑːnt/ *vt* conceder; (*give*) donar; (*admit*) admitir (*that* que). **take for** ∼**ed** dar por sentado. —*n* concesión *f*; (*univ*) beca *f*

granulated /'grænjʊleɪtɪd/ *a*. ∼ **sugar** *n* azúcar *m* granulado
granule /'grænuːl/ *n* gránulo *m*
grape /greɪp/ *n* uva *f*
grapefruit /'greɪpfruːt/ *n invar* toronja *f*, pomelo *m*
graph /grɑːf/ *n* gráfica *f*
graphic /'græfɪk/ *a* gráfico
grapple /'græpl/ *vi*. ∼ **with** intentar vencer
grasp /grɑːsp/ *vt* agarrar. —*n* (*hold*) agarro *m*; (*strength of hand*) apretón *m*; (*reach*) alcance *m*; (*fig*) comprensión *f*
grasping /'grɑːspɪŋ/ *a* avaro
grass /grɑːs/ *n* hierba *f*. ∼**hopper** *n* saltamontes *m invar*. ∼**land** *n* pradera *f*. ∼ **roots** *npl* base *f* popular. —*a* popular. ∼**y** *a* cubierto de hierba
grate /greɪt/ *n* (*fireplace*) parrilla *f*. —*vt* rallar. ∼ **one's teeth** hacer rechinar los dientes. —*vi* rechinar
grateful /'greɪtfl/ *a* agradecido. ∼**ly** *adv* con gratitud
grater /'greɪtə(r)/ *n* rallador *m*
gratif|ied /'grætɪfaɪd/ *a* contento. ∼**y** *vt* satisfacer; (*please*) agradar a. ∼**ying** *a* agradable
grating /'greɪtɪŋ/ *n* reja *f*
gratis /'grɑːtɪs/ *a & adv* gratis (*a invar*)
gratitude /'grætɪtjuːd/ *n* gratitud *f*
gratuitous /grə'tjuːɪtəs/ *a* gratuito
gratuity /grə'tjuːətɪ/ *n* (*tip*) propina *f*; (*gift of money*) gratificación *f*
grave[1] /greɪv/ *n* sepultura *f*
grave[2] /greɪv/ *a* (-**er**, -**est**) (*serious*) serio. /grɑːv/ *a*. ∼ **accent** *n* acento *m* grave
grave-digger /'greɪvdɪgə(r)/ *n* sepulturero *m*
gravel /'grævl/ *n* grava *f*
gravely /'greɪvlɪ/ *a* (*seriously*) seriamente

grave: ~**stone** n lápida f. ~**yard** n cementerio m

gravitate /'græviteit/ vi gravitar. ~**ion** /-'teiʃn/ n gravitación f

gravity /'grævəti/ n gravedad f

gravy /'greivi/ n salsa f

graze[1] /greiz/ vt/i (eat) pacer

graze[2] /greiz/ vt (touch) rozar; (scrape) raspar. —n rozadura f

grease /gri:s/ n grasa f. —vt engrasar. ~**e-paint** n maquillaje m. ~**e-proof paper** n papel m a prueba de grasa, apergaminado m. ~**y** a grasiento

great /greit/ a (-er, -est) grande, (before singular noun) gran; (very good, fam) estupendo. G~ **Britain** n Gran Bretaña f. ~**grandfather** n bisabuelo m. ~**grandmother** n bisabuela f. ~**ly** /'greitli/ adv (very) muy; (much) mucho. ~**ness** n grandeza f

Greece /gri:s/ n Grecia f

greed /gri:d/ n avaricia f; (for food) glotonería f. ~**y** a avaro; (for food) glotón

Greek /gri:k/ a & n griego (m)

green /gri:n/ a (-er, -est) verde; (fig) crédulo. —n verde m; (grass) césped m. ~ **belt** n zona f verde. ~**ery** n verdor m. ~ **fingers** npl habilidad f con las plantas

greengage /'gri:ngeidʒ/ n (plum) claudia f

greengrocer /'gri:ngrəʊsə(r)/ n verdulero m

greenhouse /'gri:nhaʊs/ n invernadero m

green: ~ **light** n luz f verde. ~**s** npl verduras fpl

Greenwich Mean Time /grenitʃ 'mi:ntaim/ n hora f media de Greenwich

greet /gri:t/ vt saludar; (receive) recibir. ~**ing** n saludo m. ~**ings** npl (in letter) recuerdos mpl

gregarious /gri'geəriəs/ a gregario

grenade /gri'neid/ n granada f

grew /gru:/ see **grow**

grey /grei/ a & n (-er, -est) gris (m). —vi (hair) encanecer

greyhound /'greihaʊnd/ n galgo m

grid /grid/ n reja f; (network, elec) red f; (culin) parrilla f; (on map) cuadrícula f

grief /gri:f/ n dolor m. **come to** ~ (person) sufrir un accidente; (fail) fracasar

grievance /'gri:vns/ n queja f

grieve /gri:v/ vt afligir. —vi afligirse. ~ **for** llorar

grievous /'gri:vəs/ a doloroso; (serious) grave

grill /gril/ n (cooking device) parrilla f; (food) parrillada f, asado m, asada f. —vt asar a la parrilla; (interrogate) interrogar

grille /gril/ n rejilla f

grim /grim/ a (grimmer, grimmest) severo

grimace /'griməs/ n mueca f. —vi hacer muecas

grime /graim/ n mugre f. ~**y** a mugriento

grin /grin/ vt (pt grinned) sonreír. —n sonrisa f (abierta)

grind /graind/ vt (pt ground) moler (coffee, corn etc); (pulverize) pulverizar; (sharpen) afilar. ~ **one's teeth** hacer rechinar los dientes. —n faena f

grip /grip/ vt (pt gripped) agarrar; (interest) captar la atención de. —n (hold) agarro m; (strength of hand) apretón m. **come to** ~**s** encararse (**with** a/con)

gripe /graip/ n. ~**s** npl (med) cólico m

grisly /'grizli/ a (-ier, -iest) horrible

gristle /'grisl/ n cartílago m

grit /grɪt/ n arena f; (fig) valor m, aguante m. —vt (pt **gritted**) echar arena en ⟨road⟩. ∼ one's teeth (fig) acorazarse

grizzle /'grɪzl/ vi lloriquear

groan /grəʊn/ vi gemir. —n gemido m

grocer /'grəʊsə(r)/ n tendero m. ∼ies npl comestibles mpl. ∼y n tienda f de comestibles

grog /grɒg/ n grog m

groggy /'grɒgɪ/ a (weak) débil; (unsteady) inseguro; (ill) malucho

groin /grɔɪn/ n ingle f

groom /gruːm/ n mozo m de caballos; (bridegroom) novio m. —vt almohazar ⟨horses⟩; (fig) preparar. **well-∼ed** a bien arreglado

groove /gruːv/ n ranura f; (in record) surco m

grope /grəʊp/ vi (find one's way) moverse a tientas. ∼ for buscar a tientas

gross /grəʊs/ a (-er, -est) (coarse) grosero; (com) bruto; (fat) grueso; (flagrant) grave. —n invar gruesa f. ∼ly adv groseramente; (very) enormemente

grotesque /grəʊ'tesk/ a grotesco

grotto /'grɒtəʊ/ n (pl -oes) gruta f

grotty /'grɒtɪ/ a (sl) desagradable; (dirty) sucio

grouch /graʊtʃ/ vi (grumble, fam) rezongar

ground[1] /graʊnd/ n suelo m; (area) terreno m; (reason) razón f; (elec, Amer) toma f de tierra. —vt varar ⟨ship⟩; prohibir despegar ⟨aircraft⟩. ∼s npl jardines mpl; (sediment) poso m

ground[2] /graʊnd/ see **grind**

ground: ∼ **floor** n planta f baja. ∼ **rent** n alquiler m del terreno

grounding /'graʊndɪŋ/ n base f, conocimientos mpl (in de)

groundless /'graʊndlɪs/ a infundado

ground: ∼**sheet** n tela f impermeable. ∼**swell** n mar m de fondo. ∼**work** n trabajo m preparatorio

group /gruːp/ n grupo m. —vt agrupar. —vi agruparse

grouse[1] /graʊs/ n invar (bird) urogallo m. **red** ∼ lagópodo m escocés

grouse[2] /graʊs/ vi (grumble, fam) rezongar

grove /grəʊv/ n arboleda f. **lemon** ∼ n limonar m. **olive** ∼ n olivar m. **orange** ∼ n naranjal m. **pine** ∼ n pinar m

grovel /'grɒvl/ vi (pt **grovelled**) arrastrarse, humillarse. ∼**ling** a servil

grow /grəʊ/ vi (pt **grew**, pp **grown**) crecer; (cultivated plant) cultivarse; (become) volverse, ponerse. —vt cultivar. ∼ **up** hacerse mayor. ∼**er** n cultivador m

growl /graʊl/ vi gruñir. —n gruñido m

grown /grəʊn/ see **grow**. —a adulto. ∼**-up** a & n adulto (m)

growth /grəʊθ/ n crecimiento m; (increase) aumento m; (development) desarrollo m; (med) tumor m

grub /grʌb/ n (larva) larva f; (food, sl) comida f

grubby /'grʌbɪ/ a (-ier, -iest) mugriento

grudg|e /grʌdʒ/ vt dar de mala gana; (envy) envidiar. ∼**e doing** molestarle hacer. **he** ∼**ed pay**ing le molestó pagar. —n rencor m. **bear/have a** ∼**e against s.o.** guardar rencor a alguien. ∼**ingly** adv de mala gana

gruelling /'gruːəlɪŋ/ a agotador

gruesome /'gruːsəm/ a horrible

gruff /grʌf/ a (-er, -est) (manners) brusco; (voice) ronco

grumble /'grʌmbl/ vi rezongar

grumpy /'grʌmpɪ/ a (-ier, -iest) malhumorado

grunt /grʌnt/ vi gruñir. —n gruñido m

guarantee /gærən'tiː/ n garantía f. —vt garantizar. **~or** n garante m & f

guard /gɑːd/ vt proteger; (watch) vigilar. —vi. **~ against** guardar de. —n (vigilance, mil group) guardia f; (person) guardia m; (on train) jefe m de tren

guarded /'gɑːdɪd/ a cauteloso

guardian /'gɑːdɪən/ n guardián m; (of orphan) tutor m

guer(r)illa /gə'rɪlə/ n guerrillero m. **~ warfare** n guerra f de guerrillas

guess /ges/ vt/i adivinar; (suppose, Amer) creer. —n conjetura f. **~work** n conjetura(s) f(pl)

guest /gest/ n invitado m; (in hotel) huésped m. **~house** n casa f de huéspedes

guffaw /gʌ'fɔː/ n carcajada f. —vi reírse a carcajadas

guidance /'gaɪdəns/ n (advice) consejos mpl; (information) información f

guide /gaɪd/ n (person) guía m & f; (book) guía f. **Girl G~** exploradora f, guía f (fam). —vt guiar. **~book** n guía f. **~d missile** n proyectil m teledirigido. **~lines** npl pauta f

guild /gɪld/ n gremio m

guile /gaɪl/ n astucia f

guillotine /'gɪlətiːn/ n guillotina f

guilt /gɪlt/ n culpabilidad f. **~y** a culpable

guinea-pig /'gɪnɪpɪg/ n (including fig) cobaya f

guise /gaɪz/ n (external appearance) apariencia f; (style) manera f

guitar /gɪ'tɑː(r)/ n guitarra f. **~ist** n guitarrista m & f

gulf /gʌlf/ n (part of sea) golfo m; (hollow) abismo m

gull /gʌl/ n gaviota f

gullet /'gʌlɪt/ n esófago m

gullible /'gʌləbl/ a crédulo

gully /'gʌlɪ/ n (ravine) barranco m

gulp /gʌlp/ vt. **~ down** tragarse de prisa. —vi tragar; (from fear etc) sentir dificultad para tragar. —n trago m

gum[1] /gʌm/ n goma f; (for chewing) chicle m. —vt (pt **gummed**) engomar

gum[2] /gʌm/ n (anat) encía f. **~boil** /'gʌmbɔɪl/ n flemón m

gumboot /'gʌmbuːt/ n bota f de agua

gumption /'gʌmpʃn/ n (fam) iniciativa f; (common sense) sentido m común

gun /gʌn/ n (pistol) pistola f; (rifle) fusil m; (large) cañón m. —vt (pt **gunned**). **~ down** abatir a tiros. **~fire** n tiros mpl

gunge /gʌndʒ/ n (sl) materia f sucia (y pegajosa)

gun: **~man** /'gʌnmən/ n pistolero m. **~ner** /'gʌnə(r)/ n artillero m. **~powder** n pólvora f. **~shot** n disparo m

gurgle /'ɡɜːgl/ n (of liquid) gorgoteo m; (of baby) gorjeo m. —vi (liquid) gorgotear; (baby) gorjear

guru /'ɡuruː/ n (pl -us) mentor m

gush /gʌʃ/ vi. **~ (out)** salir a borbotones. —n (of liquid) chorro m; (fig) torrente m. **~ing** a efusivo

gusset /'gʌsɪt/ n escudete m

gust /gʌst/ n ráfaga f; (of smoke) bocanada f

gusto /'gʌstəʊ/ n entusiasmo m

gusty /'gʌstɪ/ a borrascoso

gut /gʌt/ n tripa f, intestino m. —vt (pt **gutted**) destripar; (fire) destruir. **~s** npl tripas fpl; (courage, fam) valor m

gutter /'gʌtə(r)/ n (on roof) canalón m; (in street) cuneta f; (slum, fig) arroyo m. ~**snipe** n golfillo m

guttural /'gʌtərəl/ a gutural

guy /gaɪ/ n (man, fam) hombre m, tío m (fam)

guzzle /'gʌzl/ vt/i soplarse, tragarse

gym /dʒɪm/ n (gymnasium, fam) gimnasio m; (gymnastics, fam) gimnasia f

gymkhana /dʒɪmkɑ:nə/ n gincana f, gymkhana f

gymnasium /dʒɪm'neɪzɪəm/ n gimnasio m

gymnast /'dʒɪmnæst/ n gimnasta m & f. ~**ics** npl gimnasia f

gym-slip /'dʒɪmslɪp/ n túnica f (de gimnasia)

gynaecolog|**ist** /gaɪnɪ'kɒlədʒɪst/ n ginecólogo m. ~**y** n ginecología f

gypsy /'dʒɪpsɪ/ n gitano m

gyrate /dʒaɪə'reɪt/ vi girar

gyroscope /'dʒaɪərəskəʊp/ n giroscopio m

H

haberdashery /hæbə'dæʃərɪ/ n mercería f

habit /'hæbɪt/ n costumbre f; (costume, relig) hábito m. **be in the** ~ **of** (+ gerund) tener la costumbre de (+ infinitive), soler (+ infinitive). **get into the** ~ **of** (+ gerund) acostumbrarse a (+ infinitive)

habitable /'hæbɪtəbl/ a habitable

habitat /'hæbɪtæt/ n hábitat m

habitation /hæbɪ'teɪʃn/ n habitación f

habitual /hə'bɪtjʊəl/ a habitual; ⟨smoker, liar⟩ inveterado. ~**ly** adv de costumbre

hack /hæk/ n (old horse) jamelgo m; (writer) escritorzuelo m. —vt cortar. ~ **to pieces** cortar en pedazos

hackney /'hæknɪ/ a. ~ **carriage** n coche m de alquiler, taxi m

hackneyed /'hæknɪd/ a manido

had /hæd/ see **have**

haddock /'hædək/ n invar eglefino m. **smoked** ~ n eglefino m ahumado

haemorrhage /'hemərɪdʒ/ n hemorragia f

haemorrhoids /'hemərɔɪdz/ npl hemorroides fpl, almorranas fpl

hag /hæg/ n bruja f

haggard /'hægəd/ a ojeroso

haggle /'hægl/ vi regatear

Hague /heɪg/ n. **The** ~ La Haya f

hail¹ /heɪl/ n granizo m. —vi granizar

hail² /heɪl/ vt (greet) saludar; llamar ⟨taxi⟩. —vi. ~ **from** venir de

hailstone /'heɪlstəʊn/ n grano m de granizo

hair /heə(r)/ n pelo m. ~**brush** n cepillo m para el pelo. ~**cut** n corte m de pelo. **have a** ~**cut** cortarse el pelo. ~**do** n (fam) peinado m. ~**dresser** n peluquero m. ~**dresser's (shop)** n peluquería f. ~**dryer** n secador m. ~**pin** n horquilla f. ~**pin bend** n curva f cerrada. ~**raising** a espeluznante. ~**style** n peinado m

hairy /'heərɪ/ a (-ier, -iest) peludo; (terrifying, sl) espeluznante

hake /heɪk/ n invar merluza f

halcyon /'hælsɪən/ a sereno. ~ **days** npl época f feliz

hale /heɪl/ a robusto

half /hɑ:f/ n (pl **halves**) mitad f. —a medio. ~ **a dozen** media docena f. ~ **an hour** media hora f. —adv medio, a medias. ~**back** n (sport) medio m. ~**caste** n mestizo (m). ~**hearted** a poco entusiasta.

~**-term** *n* vacaciones *fpl* de medio trimestre. ~**-time** *n* (*sport*) descanso *m*. ~**-way** *a* medio. ~**-wit** *n* imbécil *m* & *f*. at ~**-mast** a media asta

halibut /'hælɪbət/ *n invar* hipogloso *m*, halibut *m*

hall /hɔːl/ *n* (*room*) sala *f*; (*mansion*) casa *f* solariega; (*entrance*) vestíbulo *m*. ~ **of residence** *n* colegio *m* mayor

hallelujah /hælɪ'luːjə/ *int* & *n* aleluya (*f*)

hallmark /'hɔːlmɑːk/ *n* (*on gold etc*) contraste *m*; (*fig*) sello *m* (distintivo)

hallo /hə'ləʊ/ *int* = **hello**

hallow /'hæləʊ/ *vt* santificar. **H~e'en** *n* víspera *f* de Todos los Santos

hallucination /həluːsɪ'neɪʃn/ *n* alucinación *f*

halo /'heɪləʊ/ *n* (*pl* -oes) aureola *f*

halt /hɔːlt/ *n* alto *m*. —*vt* parar. —*vi* pararse

halve /hɑːv/ *vt* dividir por mitad

ham /hæm/ *n* jamón *m*; (*theatre, sl*) racionista *m* & *f*

hamburger /'hæmbɜːgə(r)/ *n* hamburguesa *f*

hamlet /'hæmlɪt/ *n* aldea *f*, caserío *m*

hammer /'hæmə(r)/ *n* martillo *m*. —*vt* martill(e)ar; (*defeat, fam*) machacar

hammock /'hæmək/ *n* hamaca *f*

hamper[1] /'hæmpə(r)/ *n* cesta *f*

hamper[2] /'hæmpə(r)/ *vt* estorbar, poner trabas

hamster /'hæmstə(r)/ *n* hámster *m*

hand /hænd/ *n* (*including cards*) mano *f*; (*of clock*) manecilla *f*; (*writing*) escritura *f*, letra *f*; (*worker*) obrero *m*. at ~ a mano. **by** ~ a mano. **lend a** ~ echar una mano. **on** ~ a mano. **on**

one's ~**s** (*fig*) en (las) manos de uno. **on the one** ~... **on the other** ~ por un lado... por otro. **out of** ~ fuera de control. **to** ~ a mano. —*vt* dar. ~ **down** pasar. ~ **in** entregar. ~ **over** entregar. ~ **out** distribuir. ~**bag** *n* bolso *m*, cartera *f* (*LAm*). ~**book** *n* (*manual*) manual *m*; (*guidebook*) guía *f*. ~**cuffs** *npl* esposas *fpl*. ~**ful** /hændfʊl/ *n* puñado *m*; (*person, fam*) persona *f* difícil. ~**luggage** *n* equipaje *m* de mano. ~**out** *n* folleto *m*; (*money*) limosna *f*

handicap /'hændɪkæp/ *n* desventaja *f*; (*sport*) handicap *m*. —*vt* (*pt* **handicapped**) imponer impedimentos a

handicraft /'hændɪkrɑːft/ *n* artesanía *f*

handiwork /'hændɪwɜːk/ *n* obra *f*, trabajo *m* manual

handkerchief /'hæŋkətʃɪf/ *n* (*pl* -fs) pañuelo *m*

handle /'hændl/ *n* (*of door etc*) tirador *m*; (*of implement*) mango *m*; (*of cup, bag, basket etc*) asa *f*. —*vt* manejar; (*touch*) tocar; (*control*) controlar

handlebar /'hændlbɑː(r)/ *n* (*on bicycle*) manillar *m*

handshake /'hændʃeɪk/ *n* apretón *m* de manos

handsome /'hænsəm/ *a* (*good-looking*) guapo; (*generous*) generoso; (*large*) considerable

handwriting /'hændraɪtɪŋ/ *n* escritura *f*, letra *f*

handy /'hændɪ/ *a* (-ier, -iest) (*useful*) cómodo; (*person*) diestro; (*near*) a mano. ~**man** *n* hombre *m* habilidoso

hang /hæŋ/ *vt* (*pt* **hung**) colgar; (*pt* **hanged**) (*capital punishment*) ahorcar. —*vi* colgar; (*hair*) caer. —*n*. **get the** ~ **of sth** coger el truco de algo. ~ **about** holgazanear. ~ **on** (*hold out*) resistir; (*wait*, *sl*) esperar. ~ **out** *vi* tender; (*live*, *sl*) vivir. ~ **up** (*telephone*) colgar

hangar /'hæŋə(r)/ *n* hangar *m*

hanger /'hæŋə(r)/ *n* (*for clothes*) percha *f*. ~**on** *n* parásito *m*, pegote *m*

hang-gliding /'hæŋglaɪdɪŋ/ *n* vuelo *m* libre

hangman /'hæŋmən/ *n* verdugo *m*

hangover /'hæŋəʊvə(r)/ *n* (*after drinking*) resaca *f*

hang-up /'hæŋʌp/ *n* (*sl*) complejo *m*

hanker /'hæŋkə(r)/ *vi*. ~ **after** anhelar. ~**ing** *n* anhelo *m*

hanky-panky /'hæŋkɪpæŋkɪ/ *n* (*trickery*, *sl*) trucos *mpl*

haphazard /hæp'hæzəd/ *a* fortuito. ~**ly** *adv* al azar

hapless /'hæplɪs/ *a* desafortunado

happen /'hæpən/ *vi* pasar, suceder, ocurrir. **if he ~s to come** si acaso viene. ~**ing** *n* acontecimiento *m*

happ|ily /'hæpɪlɪ/ *adv* felizmente; (*fortunately*) afortunadamente. ~**iness** *n* felicidad *f*. ~**y** *a* (-*ier*, -*iest*) feliz. ~**y-go-lucky** *a* despreocupado. ~**y medium** *n* término *m* medio

harangue /hə'ræŋ/ *n* arenga *f*. — *vt* arengar

harass /'hærəs/ *vt* acosar. ~**ment** *n* tormento *m*

harbour /'hɑːbə(r)/ *n* puerto *m*. — *vt* encubrir ⟨*criminal*⟩; abrigar ⟨*feelings*⟩

hard /hɑːd/ *a* (-*er*, -*est*) duro; (*difficult*) difícil. ~ **of hearing** duro de oído. —*adv* mucho; (*pull*) fuerte. ~ **by** (muy) cerca. ~ **done by** tratado injustamente. ~ **up** (*fam*) sin un cuarto. ~**board** *n* chapa *f* de madera, tabla *f*. ~**boiled egg** *n* huevo *m* duro. ~**en** /'hɑːdn/ *vt*

endurecer. —*vi* endurecerse. ~**headed** *a* realista

hardly /'hɑːdlɪ/ *adv* apenas. ~ **ever** casi nunca

hardness /'hɑːdnɪs/ *n* dureza *f*

hardship /'hɑːdʃɪp/ *n* apuro *m*

hard: ~ **shoulder** *n* arcén *m*. ~**ware** *n* ferretería *f*; ⟨*computer*⟩ hardware *m*. ~**working** *a* trabajador

hardy /'hɑːdɪ/ *a* (-*ier*, -*iest*) (*bold*) audaz; (*robust*) robusto; (*bot*) resistente

hare /heə(r)/ *n* liebre *f*. ~**brained** *a* aturdido

harem /'hɑːriːm/ *n* harén *m*

haricot /'hærɪkəʊ/ *n*. ~ **bean** alubia *f*, judía *f*

hark /hɑːk/ *vi* escuchar. ~ **back to** volver a

harlot /'hɑːlət/ *n* prostituta *f*

harm /hɑːm/ *n* daño *m*. **there is no ~ in** (+ *gerund*) no hay ningún mal en (+ *infinitive*). —*vt* hacer daño a ⟨*person*⟩; dañar ⟨*thing*⟩; perjudicar ⟨*interests*⟩. ~**ful** *a* perjudicial. ~**less** *a* inofensivo

harmonica /hɑː'mɒnɪkə/ *n* armónica *f*

harmon|ious /hɑː'məʊnɪəs/ *a* armonioso. ~**ize** *vt*/*i* armonizar. ~**y** *n* armonía *f*

harness /'hɑːnɪs/ *n* (*for horses*) guarniciones *fpl*; (*for children*) andadores *mpl*. —*vt* poner guarniciones a ⟨*horse*⟩; (*fig*) aprovechar

harp /hɑːp/ *n* arpa *f*. —*vi*. ~ **on** (**about**) machacar. ~**ist** /'hɑː pɪst/ *n* arpista *m* & *f*

harpoon /hɑː'puːn/ *n* arpón *m*

harpsichord /'hɑːpsɪkɔːd/ *n* clavicémbalo *m*, clave *m*

harrowing /'hærəʊɪŋ/ *a* desgarrador

harsh /hɑːʃ/ *a* (-*er*, -*est*) duro, severo; ⟨*taste*, *sound*⟩ áspero.

~ly *adv* severamente. **~ness** *n* severidad *f*

harvest /'hɑːvɪst/ *n* cosecha *f*. —*vt* cosechar. **~er** *n* (*person*) segador; (*machine*) cosechadora *f*

has /hæz/ *see* **have**

hash /hæʃ/ *n* picadillo *m*. **make a ~ of** sth hacer algo con los pies, estropear algo

hashish /'hæʃiːʃ/ *n* hachís *m*

hassle /'hæsl/ *n* (*quarrel*) pelea *f*; (*difficulty*) problema *m*, dificultad *f*; (*bother, fam*) pena *f*, follón *m*, lío *m*. —*vt* (*harass*) acosar, dar la lata

haste /heɪst/ *n* prisa *f*. **in ~ de** prisa. **make ~** darse prisa

hasten /'heɪsn/ *vt* apresurar. —*vi* apresurarse, darse prisa

hast|**ily** /'heɪstɪlɪ/ *adv* de prisa. **~y** *a* (*-ier, -iest*) precipitado; (*rash*) irreflexivo

hat /hæt/ *n* sombrero *m*. **a ~ trick** *n* tres victorias *fpl* consecutivas

hatch[1] /hætʃ/ *n* (*for food*) ventanilla *f*; (*naut*) escotilla *f*

hatch[2] /hætʃ/ *vt* empollar (*eggs*); tramar (*plot*). —*vi* salir del cascarón

hatchback /'hætʃbæk/ *n* (*coche m*) cincopuertas *m* *invar*, coche *m* con puerta trasera

hatchet /'hætʃɪt/ *n* hacha *f*

hate /heɪt/ *n* odio *m*. —*vt* odiar. **~ful** *a* odioso

hatred /'heɪtrɪd/ *n* odio *m*

haughty /'hɔːtɪ/ *a* (*-ier, -iest*) altivo

haul /hɔːl/ *vt* arrastrar; transportar (*goods*). —*n* (*catch*) redada *f*; (*stolen goods*) botín *m*; (*journey*) recorrido *m*. **~age** *n* transporte *m*. **~ier** *n* transportista *m* & *f*

haunch /hɔːntʃ/ *n* anca *f*

haunt /hɔːnt/ *vt* frecuentar. —*n* sitio *m* preferido. **~ed house** *n*

casa *f* frecuentada por fantasmas

Havana /həˈvænə/ *n* La Habana *f*

have /hæv/ *vt* (*3 sing pres tense* **has,** *pt* **had**) tener; (*eat, drink*) tomar. **~ it out with** resolver el asunto. **~ sth done** hacer hacer algo. **~ to do** tener que hacer. —*v aux* haber. **~ just done** acabar de hacer. —*n*. **the ~s and ~nots** los ricos *mpl* y los pobres *mpl*

haven /'heɪvn/ *n* puerto *m*; (*refuge*) refugio *m*

haversack /'hævəsæk/ *n* mochila *f*

havoc /'hævək/ *n* estragos *mpl*

haw /hɔː/ *see* **hum**

hawk[1] /hɔːk/ *n* halcón *m*

hawk[2] /hɔːk/ *vt* vender por las calles. **~er** *n* vendedor *m* ambulante

hawthorn /'hɔːθɔːn/ *n* espino *m* (blanco)

hay /heɪ/ *n* heno *m*. **~ fever** *n* fiebre *f* del heno. **~stack** *n* almiar *m*

haywire /'heɪwaɪə(r)/ *a*. **go ~** (*plans*) desorganizarse; (*machine*) estropearse

hazard /'hæzəd/ *n* riesgo *m*. —*vt* arriesgar; aventurar (*guess*). **~ous** *a* arriesgado

haze /heɪz/ *n* neblina *f*

hazel /'heɪzl/ *n* avellano *m*. **~nut** *n* avellana *f*

hazy /'heɪzɪ/ *a* (*-ier, -iest*) nebuloso

he /hiː/ *pron* él. —*n* (*animal*) macho *m*; (*man*) varón *m*

head /hed/ *n* cabeza *f*; (*leader*) jefe *m*; (*of beer*) espuma *f*. **~s or tails** cara o cruz. —*a* principal. **~ waiter** *n* jefe *m* de comedor. —*vt* encabezar. **~ the ball** dar un cabezazo a. **~ for** dirigirse a. **~ache** *n* dolor *m* de cabeza. **~dress** *n* tocado *m*. **~er** *n* (*football*) cabezazo *m*. **~ first**

adv de cabeza. **∼gear** *n* tocado *m*

heading /'hedɪŋ/ *n* título *m*, encabezamiento *m*

headlamp /'hedlæmp/ *n* faro *m*

headland /'hedlənd/ *n* promontorio *m*

headlight /'hedlaɪt/ *n* faro *m*

headline /'hedlaɪn/ *n* titular *m*

headlong /'hedlɒŋ/ *adv* de cabeza; (*precipitately*) precipitadamente

head: **∼master** *n* director *m*. **∼mistress** *n* directora *f*. **∼on** *a* & *adv* de frente. **∼phone** *n* auricular *m*, audífono *m* (*LAm*)

headquarters /hed'kwɔːtəz/ *n* (*of organization*) sede *f*; (*of business*) oficina *f* central; (*mil*) cuartel *m* general

headstrong /'hedstrɒŋ/ *a* testarudo

headway /'hedweɪ/ *n* progreso *m*. **make ∼** hacer progresos

heady /'hedɪ/ *a* (**-ier, -iest**) (*impetuous*) impetuoso; (*intoxicating*) embriagador

heal /hiːl/ *vt* curar. **—***vi* cicatrizarse; (*fig*) curarse

health /helθ/ *n* salud *f*. **∼y** *a* sano

heap /hiːp/ *n* montón *m*. **—***vt* amontonar. **∼s of** (*fam*) montones de, muchísimos

hear /hɪə(r)/ *vt*/*i* (*pt* **heard** /hɜːd/) oír. **∼, ∼!** ¡bravo! **not ∼ of** (*refuse to allow*) no querer oír. **∼ about** oír hablar de. **∼ from** recibir noticias de. **∼ of** oír hablar de

hearing /'hɪərɪŋ/ *n* oído *m*; (*of witness*) audición *f*. **∼-aid** *n* audífono *m*

hearsay /'hɪəseɪ/ *n* rumores *mpl*. **from ∼** según los rumores

hearse /hɜːs/ *n* coche *m* fúnebre

heart /hɑːt/ *n* corazón *m*. **at ∼** en el fondo. **by ∼** de memoria. **lose ∼** descorazonarse. **∼ache** *n* pena *f*. **∼ attack** *n* ataque *m* al

corazón. **∼break** *n* pena *f*. **∼breaking** *a* desgarrador. **∼-broken** *a*. **be ∼-broken** partírsele el corazón

heartburn /'hɑːtbɜːn/ *n* acedía *f*

hearten /'hɑːtn/ *vt* animar

heartfelt /'hɑːtfelt/ *a* sincero

hearth /hɑːθ/ *n* hogar *m*

heartily /'hɑːtɪlɪ/ *adv* de buena gana; (*sincerely*) sinceramente

heart: **∼less** *a* cruel. **∼-searching** *n* examen *m* de conciencia. **∼-to-∼** *a* abierto

hearty /'hɑːtɪ/ *a* (*sincere*) sincero; (*meal*) abundante

heat /hiːt/ *n* calor *m*; (*contest*) eliminatoria *f*. **—***vt* calentar. **—***vi* calentarse. **∼ed** *a* (*fig*) acalorado. **∼er** /'hiːtə(r)/ *n* calentador *m*

heath /hiːθ/ *n* brezal *m*, descampado *m*, terreno *m* baldío

heathen /'hiːðn/ *n* & *a* pagano (*m*)

heather /'heðə(r)/ *n* brezo *m*

heat: **∼ing** *n* calefacción *f*. **∼-stroke** *n* insolación *f*. **∼wave** *n* ola *f* de calor

heave /hiːv/ *vt* (*lift*) levantar; exhalar (*sigh*); (*throw, fam*) lanzar. **—***vi* (*retch*) sentir náuseas

heaven /'hevn/ *n* cielo *m*. **∼ly** *a* celestial; (*astronomy*) celeste; (*excellent, fam*) divino

heavily /'hevɪlɪ/ *adv* pesadamente; (*smoke, drink*) mucho. **∼y** *a* (**-ier, -iest**) pesado; (*sea*) grueso; (*traffic*) denso; (*work*) duro. **∼yweight** *n* peso *m* pesado

Hebrew /'hiːbruː/ *a* & *n* hebreo (*m*)

heckle /'hekl/ *vt* interrumpir (*speaker*)

hectic /'hektɪk/ *a* febril

hedge /hedʒ/ *n* seto *m* vivo. **—***vt* rodear con seto vivo. **—***vi* escaparse por la tangente

hedgehog /'hedʒhɒg/ *n* erizo *m*

heed /hiːd/ vt hacer caso de. —n atención f. **pay ~ to** hacer caso de. **~less** a desatento

heel /hiːl/ n talón m; (of shoe) tacón m. **down at ~, down at the ~s** (Amer) desharrapado

hefty /ˈheftɪ/ a (-ier, -iest) (sturdy) fuerte; (heavy) pesado

heifer /ˈhefə(r)/ n novilla f

height /haɪt/ n altura f; (of person) estatura f; (of fame, glory) cumbre f; (of joy, folly, pain) colmo m

heighten /ˈhaɪtn/ vt (raise) elevar; (fig) aumentar

heinous /ˈheɪnəs/ a atroz

heir /eə(r)/ n heredero m. **~ess** n heredera f. **~loom** /ˈeəluːm/ n reliquia f heredada

held /held/ see **hold**[1]

helicopter /ˈhelɪkɒptə(r)/ n helicóptero m

heliport /ˈhelɪpɔːt/ n helipuerto m

hell /hel/ n infierno m. **~-bent** a resuelto. **~ish** a infernal

hello /həˈləʊ/ int ¡hola!; (telephone, caller) ¡oiga!, ¡bueno! (Mex), ¡hola! (Arg); (telephone, person answering) ¡diga!, ¡bueno! (Mex), ¡hola! (Arg); (surprise) ¡vaya! **say ~ to** saludar

helm /helm/ n (of ship) timón m

helmet /ˈhelmɪt/ n casco m

help /help/ vt/i ayudar. **he cannot ~ laughing** no puede menos de reír. **~ o.s. to** servirse. **it cannot be ~ed** no hay más remedio. —n ayuda f; (charwoman) asistenta f. **~er** n ayudante m. **~ful** a útil; (person) amable

helping /ˈhelpɪŋ/ n porción f

helpless /ˈhelplɪs/ a (unable to manage) incapaz; (powerless) impotente

helter-skelter /heltəˈskeltə(r)/ n tobogán m. —adv atropelladamente

hem /hem/ n dobladillo m. —vt (pt **hemmed**) hacer un dobladillo. **~ in** encerrar

hemisphere /ˈhemɪsfɪə(r)/ n hemisferio m

hemp /hemp/ n (plant) cáñamo m; (hashish) hachís m

hen /hen/ n gallina f

hence /hens/ adv de aquí. **~forth** adv de ahora en adelante

henchman /ˈhentʃmən/ n secuaz m

henna /ˈhenə/ n alheña f

hen-party /ˈhenpɑːtɪ/ n (fam) reunión f de mujeres

henpecked /ˈhenpekt/ a dominado por su mujer

her /hɜː(r)/ pron (accusative) la; (dative) le; (after prep) ella. **I know ~** la conozco. —a su, sus pl

herald /ˈherəld/ vt anunciar

heraldry /ˈherəldrɪ/ n heráldica f

herb /hɜːb/ n hierba f. **~s** npl hierbas fpl finas

herbaceous /hɜːˈbeɪʃəs/ a herbáceo

herbalist /ˈhɜːbəlɪst/ n herbolario m

herculean /hɜːkjuˈliːən/ a hercúleo

herd /hɜːd/ n rebaño m. —vt. **~ together** reunir

here /hɪə(r)/ adv aquí. **~!** (take this) ¡tenga! **~abouts** adv por aquí. **~after** adv en el futuro. **~by** adv por este medio; (in letter) por la presente

hereditary /hɪˈredɪtərɪ/ a hereditario. **~y** /hɪˈredɪtɪ/ n herencia f

heresy /ˈherəsɪ/ n herejía f. **~tic** n hereje m & f

herewith /hɪəˈwɪð/ adv adjunto

heritage /ˈherɪtɪdʒ/ n herencia f; (fig) patrimonio m

hermetic /hɜːˈmetɪk/ a hermético

hermit /ˈhɜːmɪt/ n ermitaño m

hernia /ˈhɜːnɪə/ n hernia f

hero /ˈhɪərəʊ/ n (pl -oes) héroe m. ~ic a heroico

heroin /ˈherəʊɪn/ n heroína f

hero: ~ine /ˈherəʊɪn/ n heroína f. ~ism /ˈherəʊɪzm/ n heroísmo m

heron /ˈherən/ n garza f real

herring /ˈherɪŋ/ n arenque m

hers /hɜːz/ poss pron suyo m, suya f, suyos mpl, suyas fpl, de ella

herself /hɜːˈself/ pron ella misma; (reflexive) se; (after prep) sí

hesitant /ˈhezɪtənt/ a vacilante

hesitat|e /ˈhezɪteɪt/ vi vacilar. ~ion /-ˈteɪʃn/ n vacilación f

hessian /ˈhesɪən/ n arpillera f

het /het/ a. ~ up (sl) nervioso

heterogeneous /hetərəʊˈdʒiːnɪəs/ a heterogéneo

heterosexual /hetərəʊˈseksjʊəl/ a heterosexual

hew /hjuː/ vt (pt pp hewn) cortar; (cut into shape) tallar

hexagon /ˈheksəgən/ n hexágono m. ~al /-ˈægənl/ a hexagonal

hey /heɪ/ int ¡eh!

heyday /ˈheɪdeɪ/ n apogeo m

hi /haɪ/ int (fam) ¡hola!

hiatus /haɪˈeɪtəs/ n (pl -tuses) hiato m

hibernat|e /ˈhaɪbəneɪt/ vi hibernar. ~ion n hibernación f

hibiscus /hɪˈbɪskəs/ n hibisco m

hiccup /ˈhɪkʌp/ n hipo m. have (the) ~s tener hipo. —vi tener hipo

hide[1] /haɪd/ vt (pt hid, pp hidden) esconder. —vi esconderse

hide[2] /haɪd/ n piel f, cuero m

hideous /ˈhɪdɪəs/ a (dreadful) horrible; (ugly) feo

hide-out /ˈhaɪdaʊt/ n escondrijo m

hiding[1] /ˈhaɪdɪŋ/ n (thrashing) paliza f

hiding[2] /ˈhaɪdɪŋ/ n. go into ~ esconderse

hierarchy /ˈhaɪərɑːkɪ/ n jerarquía f

hieroglyph /ˈhaɪərəglɪf/ n jeroglífico m

hi-fi /ˈhaɪfaɪ/ a de alta fidelidad. —n (equipo m de) alta fidelidad (f)

higgledy-piggledy /hɪgldɪˈpɪgldɪ/ adv en desorden

high /haɪ/ a (-er, -est) alto; (price) elevado; (number, speed) grande; (wind) fuerte; (intoxicated, fam) ebrio; (voice) agudo; (meat) manido. in the ~ season en plena temporada. —n alto nivel m. a (new) ~ un récord m. —adv alto

highbrow /ˈhaɪbraʊ/ a & n intelectual (m & f)

higher education /haɪər edʒʊˈkeɪʃn/ n enseñanza f superior

high-falutin /haɪfəˈluːtɪn/ a pomposo

high-handed /haɪˈhændɪd/ a despótico

high jump /ˈhaɪdʒʌmp/ n salto m de altura

highlight /ˈhaɪlaɪt/ n punto m culminante. —vt destacar

highly /ˈhaɪlɪ/ adv muy; (paid) muy bien. ~ strung a nervioso

highness /ˈhaɪnɪs/ n (title) alteza f

high: ~-rise building n rascacielos m. ~ school n instituto m. ~-speed a de gran velocidad. ~ spot n (fam) punto m culminante. ~ street n calle f mayor. ~-strung a (Amer) nervioso. ~ tea n merienda f substanciosa

highway /ˈhaɪweɪ/ n carretera f. ~man n salteador m de caminos

hijack /'haɪdʒæk/ vt secuestrar. —n secuestro m. **~er** n secuestrador

hike /haɪk/ n caminata f. —vi darse la caminata. **~r** n excursionista m & f

hilarious /hɪ'leərɪəs/ a (funny) muy divertido

hill /hɪl/ n colina f; (slope) cuesta f. **~billy** n rústico m. **~side** n ladera f. **~y** a montuoso

hilt /hɪlt/ n (of sword) puño m. **to the ~** totalmente

him /hɪm/ pron le, lo; (after prep) él. **I know ~** le/lo conozco

himself /hɪm'self/ pron él mismo; (reflexive) se

hind /haɪnd/ a trasero

hinder /'hɪndə(r)/ vt estorbar; (prevent) impedir

hindrance /'hɪndrəns/ n obstáculo m

hindsight /'haɪnsaɪt/ n. **with ~** retrospectivamente

Hindu /hɪn'du:/ n & a hindú (m & f). **~ism** n hinduismo m

hinge /hɪndʒ/ n bisagra f. —vi. **~ on** (depend on) depender de

hint /hɪnt/ n indirecta f; (advice) consejo m. —vt dar a entender. —vi soltar una indirecta. **~ at** hacer alusión a

hinterland /'hɪntəlænd/ n interior m

hip /hɪp/ n cadera f

hippie /'hɪpɪ/ n hippie m & f

hippopotamus /hɪpə'pɒtəməs/ n (pl -muses or -mi) hipopótamo m

hire /haɪə(r)/ vt alquilar (thing); contratar (person). —n alquiler m. **~-purchase** n compra f a plazos

hirsute /'hɜ:sju:t/ a hirsuto

his /hɪz/ a su, sus pl. —poss pron el suyo m, la suya f, los suyos mpl, las suyas fpl

Hispanic /hɪ'spænɪk/ a hispánico. **~ist** n hispanista m & f. **~o...** pref hispano...

hiss /hɪs/ n silbido. —vt/i silbar

histor|ian /hɪ'stɔ:rɪən/ n historiador m. **~ic(al)** /hɪ'stɒrɪk/ a histórico. **~y** /'hɪstərɪ/ n historia f. **make ~y** pasar a la historia

histrionic /hɪstrɪ'ɒnɪk/ a histriónico

hit /hɪt/ vt (pt hit, pres p hitting) golpear; (collide with) chocar con; (find) dar con; (affect) afectar. **~ it off** hacer buenas migas con. —n (blow) golpe m; (fig) éxito m. **~ on** vi encontrar, dar con

hitch /hɪtʃ/ vt (fasten) atar. —n (snag) problema m. **~ a lift**, **~-hike** vi hacer autostop, hacer dedo (Arg), pedir aventón (Mex). **~-hiker** n autostopista m

hither /'hɪðə(r)/ adv acá. **~ and thither** acá y allá

hitherto /'hɪðətu:/ adv hasta ahora

hit-or-miss /'hɪtɔ:'mɪs/ a (fam) a la buena de Dios, a ojo

hive /haɪv/ n colmena f. —vt. **~ off** separar; (industry) desnacionalizar

hoard /hɔ:d/ vt acumular. —n provisión f; (of money) tesoro m

hoarding /'hɔ:dɪŋ/ n cartelera f, valla f publicitaria

hoar-frost /'hɔ:frɒst/ n escarcha f

hoarse /hɔ:s/ a (-er, -est) ronco. **~ness** n (of voice) ronquera f; (of sound) ronquedad f

hoax /həʊks/ n engaño m. —vt engañar

hob /hɒb/ n repisa f; (of cooker) fogón m

hobble /'hɒbl/ vi cojear

hobby /'hɒbɪ/ n pasatiempo m

hobby-horse /'hɒbɪhɔ:s/ n (toy) caballito m (de niño); (fixation) caballo m de batalla

hobnail /'hɒbneɪl/ n clavo m

hob-nob /'hɒbnɒb/ vi (pt **hob-nobbed**). ~ **with** codearse con

hock[1] /hɒk/ n vino m del Rin

hock[2] /hɒk/ vt (pawn, sl) empeñar

hockey /'hɒkɪ/ n hockey m

hodgepodge /'hɒdʒpɒdʒ/ n mezcolanza f

hoe /həʊ/ n azada f. −vt (pres p **hoeing**) azadonar

hog /hɒg/ n cerdo m. −vt (pt **hogged**) (fam) acaparar

hoist /hɔɪst/ vt levantar; izar (flag). −n montacargas m invar

hold[1] /həʊld/ vt (pt **held**) tener; (grasp) coger (not LAm), agarrar; (contain) contener; mantener (interest); (believe) creer; contener (breath). ~ **one's tongue** callarse. −vi mantenerse. −n asidero m; (influence) influencia f. **get** ~ **of** agarrar; (fig, acquire) adquirir. ~ **back** (contain) contener; (conceal) ocultar. ~ **on** (stand firm) resistir; (wait) esperar. ~ **on to** (keep) guardar; (cling to) agarrarse a. ~ **out** vt (offer) ofrecer. −vi (resist) resistir. ~ **over** aplazar. ~ **up** (support) sostener; (delay) retrasar; (rob) atracar. ~ **with** aprobar

hold[2] /həʊld/ n (of ship) bodega f

holdall /'həʊldɔːl/ n bolsa f (de viaje)

holder /'həʊldə(r)/ n tenedor m; (of post) titular m; (for object) soporte m

holding /'həʊldɪŋ/ n (land) propiedad f

hold-up /'həʊldʌp/ n atraco m

hole /həʊl/ n agujero m; (in ground) hoyo m; (in road) bache m. −vt agujerear

holiday /'hɒlɪdeɪ/ n vacaciones fpl; (public) fiesta f. −vi pasar las vacaciones. ~**maker** n veraneante m

holiness /'həʊlɪnɪs/ n santidad f

Holland /'hɒlənd/ n Holanda f

hollow /'hɒləʊ/ a & n hueco (m). −vt ahuecar

holly /'hɒlɪ/ n acebo m. ~**hock** n malva f real

holocaust /'hɒləkɔːst/ n holocausto m

holster /'həʊlstə(r)/ n pistolera f

holy /'həʊlɪ/ a (-ier, -iest) santo, sagrado. **H~ Ghost** n, **H~ Spirit** n Espíritu m Santo. ~ **water** n agua f bendita

homage /'hɒmɪdʒ/ n homenaje m

home /həʊm/ n casa f; (institution) asilo m; (for soldiers) hogar m; (native land) patria f. **feel at** ~ **with** sentirse como en su casa. −a casera, de casa; (of family) de familia; (pol) interior; (match) de casa. −adv. en casa. **H~ Counties** npl región f alrededor de Londres. ~**land** n patria f. ~**less** a sin hogar. ~**ly** /'həʊmlɪ/ a (-ier, -iest) casero; (ugly) feo. **H~ Office** n Ministerio m del Interior. ~**Secretary** n Ministro m del Interior. ~**sick** a. **be** ~**sick** tener morriña. ~**town** n ciudad f natal. ~ **truths** npl las verdades fpl del barquero, las cuatro verdades fpl. ~**ward** /'həʊmwəd/ a (journey) de vuelta. −adv hacia casa. ~**work** n deberes mpl

homicide /'hɒmɪsaɪd/ n homicidio m

homoeopath|ic /həʊmɪəʊ'pæθɪk/ a homeopático. ~**y** /-'ɒpəθɪ/ n homeopatía f

homogeneous /həʊməʊ'dʒiːnɪəs/ a homogéneo

homosexual /həʊməʊ'seksjʊəl/ a & n homosexual (m)

hone /həʊn/ vt afilar

honest /'ɒnɪst/ a honrado; (frank) sincero. ~**ly** adv honradamente, sinceramente. ~**y** n honradez f

honey /ˈhʌnɪ/ n miel f; (person, fam) cielo m, cariño m. **∼comb** /ˈhʌnɪkəʊm/ n panal m

honeymoon /ˈhʌnɪmuːn/ n luna f de miel

honeysuckle /ˈhʌnɪsʌkl/ n madreselva f

honk /hɒŋk/ vi tocar la bocina

honorary /ˈɒnərərɪ/ a honorario

honour /ˈɒnə(r)/ n honor m. —vt honrar. **∼able** a honorable

hood /hʊd/ n capucha f; (car roof) capota f; (car bonnet) capó m

hoodlum /ˈhuːdləm/ n gamberro m, matón m

hoodwink /ˈhʊdwɪŋk/ vt engañar

hoof /huːf/ n (pl hoofs or hooves) casco m

hook /hʊk/ n gancho m; (on garment) corchete m; (for fishing) anzuelo m. **by ∼ or by crook** por fas o por nefas, por las buenas o por las malas. **get s.o. off the ∼** sacar a uno de un apuro. **off the ∼** (telephone) descolgado. —vt enganchar. —vi engancharse

hooked /hʊkt/ a ganchudo. **∼ on** (sl) adicto a

hooker /ˈhʊkə(r)/ n (rugby) talonador m; (Amer, sl) prostituta f

hookey /ˈhʊkɪ/ n. **play ∼** (Amer, sl) hacer novillos

hooligan /ˈhuːlɪɡən/ n gamberro m

hoop /huːp/ n aro m

hooray /hʊˈreɪ/ int & n ¡viva! m

hoot /huːt/ n (of horn) bocinazo m; (of owl) ululato m. —vi tocar la bocina; (owl) ulular

hooter /ˈhuːtə(r)/ n (of car) bocina f; (of factory) sirena f

Hoover /ˈhuːvə(r)/ n (P) aspiradora f. —vt pasar la aspiradora

hop¹ /hɒp/ vi (pt hopped) saltar a la pata coja. **∼ in** (fam) subir. **∼ it** (sl) largarse. **∼ out** (fam) bajar. —n salto m; (flight) etapa f

hop² /hɒp/ n. **∼(s)** lúpulo m

hope /həʊp/ n esperanza f. —vt/i esperar. **∼ for** esperar. **∼ful** a esperanzador. **∼fully** adv con optimismo; (it is hoped) se espera. **∼less** a desesperado. **∼lessly** adv sin esperanza

hopscotch /ˈhɒpskɒtʃ/ n tejo m

horde /hɔːd/ n horda f

horizon /həˈraɪzn/ n horizonte m

horizontal /hɒrɪˈzɒntl/ a horizontal. **∼ly** adv horizontalmente

hormone /ˈhɔːməʊn/ n hormona f

horn /hɔːn/ n cuerno m; (of car) bocina f; (mus) trompa f. —vt. **∼ in** (sl) entrometerse. **∼ed** a con cuernos

hornet /ˈhɔːnɪt/ n avispón m

horny /ˈhɔːnɪ/ a (hands) calloso

horoscope /ˈhɒrəskəʊp/ n horóscopo m

horrible /ˈhɒrəbl/ a horrible. **∼d** /ˈhɒrɪd/ a horrible

horrific /həˈrɪfɪk/ a horroroso. **∼y** /ˈhɒrɪfaɪ/ vt horrorizar

horror /ˈhɒrə(r)/ n horror m. **∼ film** n película f de miedo

hors-d'oevre /ɔːˈdɜːvr/ n entremés m

horse /hɔːs/ n caballo m. **∼back** n. **on ∼back** a caballo

horse chestnut /hɔːsˈtʃesnʌt/ n castaña f de Indias

horse: ∼man n jinete m. **∼play** n payasadas fpl. **∼power** n (unit) caballo m (de fuerza). **∼racing** n carreras fpl de caballos

horseradish /ˈhɔːsrædɪʃ/ n rábano m picante

horse: ∼sense n (fam) sentido m común. **∼shoe** /ˈhɔːsʃuː/ n herradura f

horsy /ˈhɔːsɪ/ a ⟨face etc⟩ caballuno

horticultur|al /hɔːtɪˈkʌltʃərəl/ a hortícola. **~e** /ˈhɔːtɪkʌltʃə(r)/ n horticultura f

hose /həʊz/ n ⟨tube⟩ manga f. —vt ⟨water⟩ regar con una manga; ⟨clean⟩ limpiar con una manga.
~pipe n manga f

hosiery /ˈhəʊzɪərɪ/ n calcetería f

hospice /ˈhɒspɪs/ n hospicio m

hospitabl|e /hɒˈspɪtəbl/ a hospitalario. **~y** adv con hospitalidad

hospital /ˈhɒspɪtl/ n hospital m

hospitality /hɒspɪˈtælɪtɪ/ n hospitalidad f

host[1] /həʊst/ n. **a ~ of** un montón de

host[2] n ⟨master of house⟩ huésped m, anfitrión m

host[3] n ⟨relig⟩ hostia f

hostage /ˈhɒstɪdʒ/ n rehén m

hostel /ˈhɒstl/ n ⟨for students⟩ residencia f. **~ youth ~** albergue m juvenil

hostess /ˈhəʊstɪs/ n huéspeda f, anfitriona f

hostil|e /ˈhɒstaɪl/ a hostil. **~ity** n hostilidad f

hot /hɒt/ a (**hotter, hottest**) caliente; ⟨culin⟩ picante; ⟨news⟩ de última hora. **be/feel ~** tener calor. **in ~ water** ⟨fam⟩ en un apuro. **it is ~** hace calor. —vt/i. **~ up** ⟨fam⟩ calentarse

hotbed /ˈhɒtbed/ n ⟨fig⟩ semillero m

hotchpotch /ˈhɒtʃpɒtʃ/ n mezcolanza f

hot dog /hɒtˈdɒg/ n perrito m caliente

hotel /həʊˈtel/ n hotel m. **~ier** n hotelero m

hot: **~head** n impetuoso m. **~headed** a impetuoso. **~house** n invernadero m. **~line** n teléfono m rojo. **~plate**

calentador m. **~-water bottle** n bolsa f de agua caliente

hound /haʊnd/ n perro m de caza. —vt perseguir

hour /aʊə(r)/ n hora f. **~ly** a & adv cada hora. **~ly pay** n sueldo m por hora. **paid ~ly** pagado por hora

house /haʊs/ n (pl **-s** /ˈhaʊzɪz/) casa f; ⟨theatre building⟩ sala f; ⟨theatre audience⟩ público m; ⟨pol⟩ cámara f. /haʊz/ vt alojar; ⟨keep⟩ guardar. **~boat** n casa f flotante. **~breaking** n robo m de casa. **~hold** /ˈhaʊshəʊld/ n casa f, familia f. **~holder** n dueño m de una casa; ⟨head of household⟩ cabeza f de familia. **~keeper** n ama f de llaves. **~keeping** n gobierno m de la casa. **~maid** n criada f, mucama f (LAm). **H~ of Commons** n Cámara f de los Comunes. **~-proud** a meticuloso. **~-warming** n inauguración f de una casa. **~wife** /ˈhaʊswaɪf/ n ama f de casa. **~work** n quehaceres mpl domésticos

housing /ˈhaʊzɪŋ/ n alojamiento m. **~ estate** n urbanización f

hovel /ˈhɒvl/ n casucha f

hover /ˈhɒvə(r)/ vi ⟨bird, threat etc⟩ cernerse; ⟨loiter⟩ rondar. **~craft** n aerodeslizador m

how /haʊ/ adv cómo. **~ about a walk?** ¿qué le parece si damos un paseo? **~ are you?** ¿cómo está Vd? **~ do you do?** ⟨in introduction⟩ mucho gusto. **~ long?** ¿cuánto tiempo? **~ many?** ¿cuántos? **~ much?** ¿cuánto? **~ often?** ¿cuántas veces? **and ~!** ¡y cómo!

however /haʊˈevə(r)/ adv ⟨with verb⟩ de cualquier manera que (+ subjunctive); ⟨with adjective or adverb⟩ por... que (+ subjunctive); ⟨nevertheless⟩ no obstante, sin embargo. ~ **much it rains** por mucho que llueva

howl /haʊl/ *n* aullido. —*vi* aullar

howler /'haʊlə(r)/ *n* ⟨*fam*⟩ plancha *f*

HP *abbr see* **hire-purchase**

hp *abbr see* **horsepower**

hub /hʌb/ *n* ⟨*of wheel*⟩ cubo *m*; ⟨*fig*⟩ centro *m*

hubbub /'hʌbʌb/ *n* barahúnda *f*

hub-cap /'hʌbkæp/ *n* tapacubos *m invar*

huddle /'hʌdl/ *vi* apiñarse

hue[1] /hju:/ *n* ⟨*colour*⟩ color *m*

hue[2] /hju:/ *n.* ~ **and cry** clamor *m*

huff /hʌf/ *n.* **in a** ~ enojado

hug /hʌg/ *vt* ⟨*pt* **hugged**⟩ abrazar; ⟨*keep close to*⟩ no apartarse de. —*n* abrazo *m*

huge /hju:dʒ/ *a* enorme. ~**ly** *adv* enormemente

hulk /hʌlk/ *n* ⟨*of ship*⟩ barco *m* viejo; ⟨*person*⟩ armatoste *m*

hull /hʌl/ *n* ⟨*of ship*⟩ casco *m*

hullabaloo /hʌləbə'lu:/ *n* tumulto *m*

hullo /hə'ləʊ/ *int* = **hello**

hum /hʌm/ *vt/i* ⟨*pt* **hummed**⟩ ⟨*person*⟩ canturrear; ⟨*insect, engine*⟩ zumbar. —*n* zumbido *m.* ~ **(or hem) and haw (or ha)** vacilar

human /'hju:mən/ *a & n* humano (*m*). ~ **being** *n* ser *m* humano

humane /hju:'meɪn/ *a* humano

humanism /'hju:mənɪzəm/ *n* humanismo *m*

humanitarian /hju:mænɪ'teərɪən/ *a* humanitario

humanity /hju:'mænətɪ/ *n* humanidad *f*

humble /'hʌmbl/ *a* (-er, -est) humilde. —*vt* humillar. ~**y** *adv* humildemente

humbug /'hʌmbʌg/ *n* ⟨*false talk*⟩ charlatanería *f*; ⟨*person*⟩ charlatán *m*; ⟨*sweet*⟩ caramelo *m* de menta

humdrum /'hʌmdrʌm/ *a* monótono

humid /'hju:mɪd/ *a* húmedo. ~**ifier** *n* humedecedor *m*. ~**ity** /hju:'mɪdətɪ/ *n* humedad *f*

humiliat|**e** /hju:'mɪlɪeɪt/ *vt* humillar. ~**ion** /-'eɪʃn/ *n* humillación *f*

humility /hju:'mɪlətɪ/ *n* humildad *f*

humorist /'hju:mərɪst/ *n* humorista *m & f*

humo|**rous** /'hju:mərəs/ *a* divertido. ~**rously** *adv* con gracia. ~**ur** *n* humorismo *m*; ⟨*mood*⟩ humor *m*. **sense of** ~**ur** *n* sentido *m* del humor

hump /hʌmp/ *n* montecillo *m*; ⟨*of the spine*⟩ joroba *f*. **the** ~ ⟨*sl*⟩ malhumor *m*. —*vt* encorvarse; ⟨*hoist up*⟩ llevar al hombro

hunch /hʌntʃ/ *vt* encorvar. ~**ed up** encorvado. —*n* presentimiento *m*; ⟨*lump*⟩ joroba *f*. ~**back** /'hʌntʃbæk/ *n* jorobado *m*

hundred /'hʌndrəd/ *a* ciento, ⟨*before noun*⟩ cien. —*n* ciento *m*. ~**fold** *a* céntuplo. —*adv* cien veces. ~**s of** centenares de. ~**th** *a* centésimo. —*n* centésimo *m*, centésima parte *f*

hundredweight /'hʌndrədweɪt/ *n* 50,8kg; ⟨*Amer*⟩ 45,36kg

hung /hʌŋ/ *see* **hang**

Hungar|**ian** /hʌŋ'geərɪən/ *a & n* húngaro (*m*). ~**y** /'hʌŋgərɪ/ *n* Hungría *f*

hunger /'hʌŋgə(r)/ *n* hambre *f*. —*vi.* ~ **for** tener hambre de. ~**strike** *n* huelga *f* de hambre

hungr|**ily** /'hʌŋgrəlɪ/ *adv* ávidamente. ~**y** *a* (-ier, -iest) hambriento. **be** ~**y** tener hambre

hunk /hʌŋk/ *n* ⟨*buen*⟩ pedazo *m*

hunt /hʌnt/ *vt/i* cazar. ~ **for** buscar. —*n* caza *f*. ~**er** *n* cazador *m*. ~**ing** *n* caza *f*

hurdle /'hɜːdl/ n (sport) valla f; (fig) obstáculo m

hurdy-gurdy /'hɜːdɪgɜːdɪ/ n organillo m

hurl /hɜːl/ vt lanzar

hurly-burly /'hɜːlɪbɜːlɪ/ n tumulto m

hurrah /hʊ'rɑː/, **hurray** /hʊ'reɪ/ int & n ¡viva! (m)

hurricane /'hʌrɪkən/ n huracán m

hurried /'hʌrɪd/ a apresurado. **~ly** adv apresuradamente

hurry /'hʌrɪ/ vi apresurarse, darse prisa. —vt apresurar, dar prisa a. —n prisa f. **be in a ~** tener prisa

hurt /hɜːt/ vt/i (pt **hurt**) herir. —n (injury) herida f; (harm) daño m. **~ful** a hiriente; (harmful) dañoso

hurtle /'hɜːtl/ vt lanzar. —vi. **~ along** mover rápidamente

husband /'hʌzbənd/ n marido m

hush /hʌʃ/ vt acallar. —n silencio m. **~ up** ocultar ⟨affair⟩. **~-~** a (fam) muy secreto

husk /hʌsk/ n cáscara f

husky /'hʌskɪ/ a (-ier, -iest) (hoarse) ronco; (burly) fornido

hussy /'hʌsɪ/ n desvergonzada f

hustle /'hʌsl/ vt (jostle) empujar. —vi (hurry) darse prisa. —n empuje m. **~ and bustle** n bullicio m

hut /hʌt/ n cabaña f

hutch /hʌtʃ/ n conejera f

hyacinth /'haɪəsɪnθ/ n jacinto m

hybrid /'haɪbrɪd/ a & n híbrido (m)

hydrangea /haɪ'dreɪndʒə/ n hortensia f

hydrant /'haɪdrənt/ n. (fire) **~** n boca f de riego

hydraulic /haɪ'drɔːlɪk/ a hidráulico

hydroelectric /haɪdrəʊɪ'lektrɪk/ a hidroeléctrico

hydrofoil /'haɪdrəfɔɪl/ n aerodeslizador m

hydrogen /'haɪdrədʒən/ n hidrógeno m. **~ bomb** n bomba f de hidrógeno. **~ peroxide** n peróxido m de hidrógeno

hyena /haɪ'iːnə/ n hiena f

hygien|e /'haɪdʒiːn/ n higiene f. **~ic** a higiénico

hymn /hɪm/ n himno m

hyper... /'haɪpə(r)/ pref hiper...

hypermarket /'haɪpəmɑːkɪt/ n hipermercado m

hyphen /'haɪfn/ n guión m. **~ate** vt escribir con guión

hypno|sis /hɪp'nəʊsɪs/ n hipnosis f. **~tic** /-'nɒtɪk/ a hipnótico. **~tism** /hɪpnə'tɪzəm/ n hipnotismo m. **~tist** n hipnotista m & f. **~tize** vt hipnotizar

hypochondriac /haɪpə'kɒn drɪæk/ n hipocondríaco m

hypocrisy /hɪ'pɒkrəsɪ/ n hipocresía f

hypocrit|e /'hɪpəkrɪt/ n hipócrita m & f. **~ical** a hipócrita

hypodermic /haɪpə'dɜːmɪk/ a hipodérmico. —n jeringa f hipodérmica

hypothe|sis /haɪ'pɒθəsɪs/ n (pl -theses /-siːz/) hipótesis f. **~tical** /-ə'θetɪkl/ a hipotético

hysteri|a /hɪ'stɪərɪə/ n histerismo m. **~cal** /-'terɪkl/ a histérico. **~cs** /hɪ'sterɪks/ npl histerismo m. **have ~cs** ponerse histérico; (laugh) morir de risa

I

I /aɪ/ pron yo

ice /aɪs/ n hielo m. —vt helar; glasear ⟨cake⟩. —vi. **~ (up)** helarse. **~berg** n iceberg m, témpano m. **~-cream** n helado m. **~-cube** n cubito *m* de hielo. ~ **hockey** *n* hockey *m* sobre hielo

Iceland /'aɪslənd/ *n* Islandia *f*. ~**er** *n* islandés *m*. ~**ic** /-'lændɪk/ *a* islandés

ice lolly /aɪs'lɒlɪ/ polo *m*, paleta *f* (*LAm*)

icicle /'aɪsɪkl/ *n* carámbano *m*

icing /'aɪsɪŋ/ *n* (*sugar*) azúcar *m* glaseado

icon /'aɪkon/ *n* icono *m*

icy /'aɪsɪ/ *a* (-ier, -iest) glacial

idea /aɪ'dɪə/ *n* idea *f*

ideal /aɪ'dɪəl/ *a* ideal. —*n* ideal *m*. ~**ism** *n* idealismo *m*. ~**ist** *n* idealista *m* & *f*. ~**istic** /-'lɪstɪk/ *a* idealista. ~**ize** *vt* idealizar. ~**ly** *adv* idealmente

identical /aɪ'dentɪkl/ *a* idéntico

identif|ication /aɪdentɪfɪ'keɪʃn/ *n* identificación *f*. ~**y** /aɪ'dentɪfaɪ/ *vt* identificar. —*vi*. ~**y with** identificarse con

identikit /aɪ'dentɪkɪt/ *n* retrato-robot *m*

identity /aɪ'dentɪtɪ/ *n* identidad *f*

ideolog|ical /aɪdɪə'lɒdʒɪkl/ *a* ideológico. ~**y** /aɪdɪ'ɒlədʒɪ/ *n* ideología *f*

idiocy /'ɪdɪəsɪ/ *n* idiotez *f*

idiom /'ɪdɪəm/ *n* locución *f*. ~**atic** /-'mætɪk/ *a* idiomático

idiosyncrasy /ɪdɪəʊ'sɪŋkrəsɪ/ *n* idiosincrasia *f*

idiot /'ɪdɪət/ *n* idiota *m* & *f*. ~**ic** /-'ɒtɪk/ *a* idiota

idle /'aɪdl/ *a* (-er, -est) ocioso; (*lazy*) holgazán; (*out of work*) desocupado; (*machine*) parado. —*vi* (*engine*) marchar en vacío. —*vt*. ~ **away** perder. ~**ness** *n* ociosidad *f*. ~**r** /-ə(r)/ *n* ocioso *m*

idol /'aɪdl/ *n* ídolo *m*. ~**ize** *vt* idolatrar

idyllic /ɪ'dɪlɪk/ *a* idílico

i.e. /aɪ'i/ *abbr* (*id est*) es decir

if /ɪf/ *conj* si

igloo /'ɪɡlu:/ *n* iglú *m*

ignite /ɪɡ'naɪt/ *vt* encender. —*vi* encenderse

ignition /ɪɡ'nɪʃn/ *n* ignición *f*; (*auto*) encendido *m*. ~ (**switch**) *n* contacto *m*

ignoramus /ɪɡnə'reɪməs/ *n* (*pl* -muses) ignorante

ignoran|ce /'ɪɡnərəns/ *n* ignorancia *f*. ~**t** *a* ignorante. ~**tly** *adv* por ignorancia

ignore /ɪɡ'nɔ:(r)/ *vt* no hacer caso de

ilk /ɪlk/ *n* ralea *f*

ill /ɪl/ *a* enfermo; (*bad*) malo. ~ **will** *n* mala voluntad *f*. —*adv* mal. ~ **at ease** inquieto. —*n* mal *m*. ~**advised** *a* imprudente. ~**bred** *a* mal educado

illegal /ɪ'li:ɡl/ *a* ilegal

illegible /ɪ'ledʒɪbl/ *a* ilegible

illegitima|cy /ɪlɪ'dʒɪtɪməsɪ/ *n* ilegitimidad *f*. ~**te** *a* ilegítimo

ill: ~**fated** *a* malogrado. ~**gotten** *a* mal adquirido

illitera|cy /ɪ'lɪtərəsɪ/ *n* analfabetismo *m*. ~**te** *a* & *n* analfabeto (*m*)

ill: ~**natured** *a* poco afable. ~**ness** *n* enfermedad *f*

illogical /ɪ'lɒdʒɪkl/ *a* ilógico

ill: ~**starred** *a* malogrado. ~**treat** *vt* maltratar

illuminat|e /ɪ'lu:mɪneɪt/ *vt* iluminar. ~**ion** /-'neɪʃn/ *n* iluminación *f*

illusion /ɪ'lu:ʒn/ *n* ilusión *f*. ~**sory** *a* ilusorio

illustrat|e /'ɪləstreɪt/ *vt* ilustrar. ~**ion** *n* (*example*) ejemplo *m*; (*picture in book*) grabado *m*, lámina *f*. ~**ive** *a* ilustrativo

illustrious /ɪ'lʌstrɪəs/ *a* ilustre

image /'ɪmɪdʒ/ *n* imagen *f*. ~**ry** *n* imágenes *fpl*

imagin|able /ɪ'mædʒɪnəbl/ *a* imaginable. ~**ary** *a* imaginario. ~**ation** /-'neɪʃn/ *n* imaginación *f*. ~**ative** *a* imaginativo. ~**e** *vt* imaginar(se)

imbalance /ɪm'bæləns/ n desequilibrio m

imbecil|**e** /'ɪmbəsiːl/ a & n imbécil (m & f). **∼ity** /-'sɪlətɪ/ n imbecilidad f

imbibe /ɪm'baɪb/ vt embeber; (drink) beber

imbue /ɪm'bjuː/ vt empapar (with de)

imitat|**e** /'ɪmɪteɪt/ vt imitar. **∼ion** /-'teɪʃn/ n imitación f. **∼or** n imitador m

immaculate /ɪ'mækjʊlət/ a inmaculado

immaterial /ɪmə'tɪərɪəl/ a inmaterial; (unimportant) insignificante

immature /ɪmə'tjʊə(r)/ a inmaduro

immediate /ɪ'miːdɪət/ a inmediato. **∼ly** adv inmediatamente. **∼ly you hear me** en cuanto me oigas. —conj en cuanto (+ subj)

immense /ɪ'mens/ a inmenso. **∼ely** adv inmensamente; (very much, fam) muchísimo. **∼ity** n inmensidad f

immers|**e** /ɪ'mɜːs/ vt sumergir. **∼ion** /-ʃn/ n inmersión f. **∼ion heater** n calentador m de inmersión

immigra|**nt** /'ɪmɪgrənt/ a & n inmigrante (m & f). **∼te** vi inmigrar. **∼tion** /-'greɪʃn/ n inmigración f

imminen|**ce** /'ɪmɪnəns/ n inminencia f. **∼t** a inminente

immobil|**e** /ɪ'məʊbaɪl/ a inmóvil. **∼ize** /-bɪlaɪz/ vt inmovilizar

immoderate /ɪ'mɒdərət/ a inmoderado

immodest /ɪ'mɒdɪst/ a inmodesto

immoral /ɪ'mɒrəl/ a inmoral. **∼ity** /ɪmə'rælətɪ/ n inmoralidad f

immortal /ɪ'mɔːtl/ a inmortal. **∼ity** /-'tælətɪ/ n inmortalidad f. **∼ize** vt inmortalizar

immun|**e** /ɪ'mjuːn/ a inmune (from, to a, contra). **∼ity** n inmunidad f. **∼ization** /ɪmjʊnaɪ'zeɪʃn/ n inmunización f. **∼ize** vt inmunizar

imp /ɪmp/ n diablillo m

impact /'ɪmpækt/ n impacto m

impair /ɪm'peə(r)/ vt perjudicar

impale /ɪm'peɪl/ vt empalar

impart /ɪm'pɑːt/ vt comunicar

impartial /ɪm'pɑːʃl/ a imparcial. **∼ity** /-ɪ'ælətɪ/ n imparcialidad f

impassable /ɪm'pɑːsəbl/ a (barrier etc) infranqueable; (road) impracticable

impasse /æm'pɑːs/ n callejón m sin salida

impassioned /ɪm'pæʃnd/ a apasionado

impassive /ɪm'pæsɪv/ a impasible

impatien|**ce** /ɪm'peɪʃəns/ n impaciencia f. **∼t** a impaciente. **∼tly** adv con impaciencia

impeach /ɪm'piːtʃ/ vt acusar

impeccable /ɪm'pekəbl/ a impecable

impede /ɪm'piːd/ vt estorbar

impediment /ɪm'pedɪmənt/ n obstáculo m. (speech) **∼** n defecto m del habla

impel /ɪm'pel/ vt (pt impelled) impeler

impending /ɪm'pendɪŋ/ a inminente

impenetrable /ɪm'penɪtrəbl/ a impenetrable

imperative /ɪm'perətɪv/ a imprescindible. —n (gram) imperativo m

imperceptible /ɪmpə'septəbl/ a imperceptible

imperfect /ɪm'pɜːfɪkt/ a imperfecto. **∼ion** /-'fekʃn/ n imperfección f

imperial /ɪm'pɪərɪəl/ a imperial. **∼ism** n imperialismo m

imperil /ɪm'perəl/ vt (pt imperilled) poner en peligro

imperious /ɪm'pɪərɪəs/ a imperioso

impersonal /ɪm'pɜːsənl/ a impersonal

impersonat|e /ɪm'pɜːsəneɪt/ vt hacerse pasar por; (mimic) imitar. ∼ion /-'neɪʃn/ n imitación f. ∼or n imitador m

impertinen|ce /ɪm'pɜːtɪnəns/ n impertinencia f. ∼t a impertinente. ∼tly adv impertinentemente

impervious /ɪm'pɜːvɪəs/ a. ∼ to impermeable a; (fig) insensible a

impetuous /ɪm'petjʊəs/ a impetuoso

impetus /'ɪmpɪtəs/ n ímpetu m

impinge /ɪm'pɪndʒ/ vi. ∼ on afectar a

impish /'ɪmpɪʃ/ a travieso

implacable /ɪm'plækəbl/ a implacable

implant /ɪm'plɑːnt/ vt implantar

implement /'ɪmplɪmənt/ n herramienta f. /'ɪmplɪment/ vt realizar

implicat|e /'ɪmplɪkeɪt/ vt implicar. ∼ion /-'keɪʃn/ n implicación f

implicit /ɪm'plɪsɪt/ a (implied) implícito; (unquestioning) absoluto

implied /ɪm'plaɪd/ a implícito

implore /ɪm'plɔː(r)/ vt implorar

imply /ɪm'plaɪ/ vt implicar; (mean) querer decir; (insinuate) dar a entender

impolite /ɪmpə'laɪt/ a mal educado

imponderable /ɪm'pɒndərəbl/ a & n imponderable (m)

import /ɪm'pɔːt/ vt importar. /'ɪmpɔːt/ n (article) importación f; (meaning) significación f

importan|ce /ɪm'pɔːtəns/ n importancia f. ∼t a importante

importation /ɪmpɔː'teɪʃn/ n importación f

importer /ɪm'pɔːtə(r)/ n importador m

impose /ɪm'pəʊz/ vt imponer. — vi. ∼ on abusar de la amabilidad de

imposing /ɪm'pəʊzɪŋ/ a imponente

imposition /ɪmpə'zɪʃn/ n imposición f; (fig) molestia f

impossib|ility /ɪmpɒsə'bɪlətɪ/ n imposibilidad f. ∼le a imposible

impostor /ɪm'pɒstə(r)/ n impostor m

impoten|ce /'ɪmpətəns/ n impotencia f. ∼t a impotente

impound /ɪm'paʊnd/ vt confiscar

impoverish /ɪm'pɒvərɪʃ/ vt empobrecer

impracticable /ɪm'præktɪkəbl/ a impracticable

impractical /ɪm'præktɪkl/ a poco práctico

imprecise /ɪmprɪ'saɪs/ a impreciso

impregnable /ɪm'pregnəbl/ a inexpugnable

impregnate /'ɪmpregneɪt/ vt impregnar (with de)

impresario /ɪmprɪ'sɑːrɪəʊ/ n (pl -os) empresario m

impress /ɪm'pres/ vt impresionar; (imprint) imprimir. ∼ on s.o. hacer entender a uno

impression /ɪm'preʃn/ n impresión f. ∼able a impresionable

impressive /ɪm'presɪv/ a impresionante

imprint /'ɪmprɪnt/ n impresión f. /ɪm'prɪnt/ vt imprimir

imprison /ɪm'prɪzn/ vt encarcelar. ∼ment n encarcelamiento m

improbab|ility /ɪmprɒbə'bɪlətɪ/ n improbabilidad f. ∼le a improbable

impromptu /ɪm'prɒmptjuː/ a improvisado. —adv de improviso

improper /ɪm'prɒpə(r)/ a impropio; (incorrect) incorrecto

impropriety /ɪmprə'praɪətɪ/ n inconveniencia f

improve /ɪm'pruːv/ vt mejorar. —vi mejorar(se). —**ment** n mejora f

improvis|ation /ɪmprəvaɪ'zeɪʃn/ n improvisación f. —**e** vt/i improvisar

imprudent /ɪm'pruːdənt/ a imprudente

impuden|ce /'ɪmpjʊdəns/ n insolencia f. —**t** a insolente

impulse /'ɪmpʌls/ n impulso m. **on** ~ sin reflexionar

impulsive /ɪm'pʌlsɪv/ a irreflexivo. —**ly** adv sin reflexionar

impunity /ɪm'pjuːnətɪ/ n impunidad f. **with** ~ impunemente

impur|e /ɪm'pjʊə(r)/ a impuro. —**ity** n impureza f

impute /ɪm'pjuːt/ vt imputar

in /ɪn/ prep en, dentro de. ~ **a firm manner** de una manera terminante. ~ **an hour('s time)** dentro de una hora. ~ **doing** al hacer. ~ **so far as** en cuanto que. ~ **the evening** por la tarde. ~ **the main** por la mayor parte. ~ **the rain** bajo la lluvia. **the sun** al sol. **one** ~ **ten** uno de cada diez. **the best** ~ el mejor de. —adv (inside) dentro; (at home) en casa; (in fashion) de moda. —n. **the** ~**s and outs of** los detalles mpl de

inability /ɪnə'bɪlətɪ/ n incapacidad f

inaccessible /ɪnæk'sesəbl/ a inaccesible

inaccura|cy /ɪn'ækjʊrəsɪ/ n inexactitud f. —**te** a inexacto

inaction /ɪn'ækʃn/ n inacción f

inactive /ɪn'æktɪv/ a inactivo. —**ity** n inactividad f

inadequa|cy /ɪn'ædɪkwəsɪ/ a insuficiencia f. —**te** a insuficiente

inadmissible /ɪnəd'mɪsəbl/ a inadmisible

inadvertently /ɪnəd'vɜːtəntlɪ/ adv por descuido

inadvisable /ɪnəd'vaɪzəbl/ a no aconsejable

inane /ɪ'neɪn/ a estúpido

inanimate /ɪn'ænɪmət/ a inanimado

inappropriate /ɪnə'prəʊprɪət/ a inoportuno

inarticulate /ɪnɑː'tɪkjʊlət/ a incapaz de expresarse claramente

inasmuch as /ɪnəz'mʌtʃəz/ adv ya que

inattentive /ɪnə'tentɪv/ a desatento

inaudible /ɪn'ɔːdəbl/ a inaudible

inaugural /ɪ'nɔːɡjʊrəl/ a inaugural

inaugurat|e /ɪ'nɔːɡjʊreɪt/ vt inaugurar. —**ion** /-'reɪʃn/ n inauguración f

inauspicious /ɪnɔː'spɪʃəs/ a poco propicio

inborn /'ɪnbɔːn/ a innato

inbred /ɪn'bred/ a (inborn) innato

incalculable /ɪn'kælkjʊləbl/ a incalculable

incapab|ility /ɪnkeɪpə'bɪlətɪ/ n incapacidad f. —**le** a incapaz

incapacit|ate /ɪnkə'pæsɪteɪt/ vt incapacitar. —**y** n incapacidad f

incarcerat|e /ɪn'kɑːsəreɪt/ vt encarcelar. —**ion** /-'reɪʃn/ n encarcelamiento m

incarnat|e /ɪn'kɑːnət/ a encarnado. —**ion** /-'neɪʃn/ n encarnación f

incautious /ɪn'kɔːʃəs/ a incauto. —**ly** adv incautamente

incendiary /ɪn'sendɪərɪ/ a incendiario. —n (person) incendiario m; (bomb) bomba f incendiaria

incense[1] /'ɪnsens/ n incienso m

incense[2] /ɪn'sens/ vt enfurecer

incentive /ɪn'sentɪv/ n incentivo m; (payment) prima f de incentivo

inception /ɪnˈsepʃn/ n principio m

incertitude /ɪnˈsɜːtɪtjuːd/ n incertidumbre f

incessant /ɪnˈsesnt/ a incesante. ~ly adv sin cesar

incest /ˈɪnsest/ n incesto m. ~uous /-ˈsestjʊəs/ a incestuoso

inch /ɪntʃ/ n pulgada f (= 2,54cm). —vi avanzar palmo a palmo

incidence /ˈɪnsɪdəns/ n frecuencia f

incident /ˈɪnsɪdənt/ n incidente m

incidental /ɪnsɪˈdentl/ a fortuito. ~ly adv incidentemente; (by the way) a propósito

incinerate /ɪnˈsɪnəreɪt/ vt incinerar. ~or n incinerador m

incipient /ɪnˈsɪpɪənt/ a incipiente

incision /ɪnˈsɪʒn/ n incisión f

incisive /ɪnˈsaɪsɪv/ a incisivo

incite /ɪnˈsaɪt/ vt incitar. ~ment n incitación f

inclement /ɪnˈklemənt/ a inclemente

inclination /ɪnklɪˈneɪʃn/ n inclinación f

incline[1] /ɪnˈklaɪn/ vt inclinar. —vi inclinarse. be ~d to tener tendencia a

incline[2] /ˈɪnklaɪn/ n cuesta f

include /ɪnˈkluːd/ vt incluir. ~ding prep incluso. ~sion /-ʒn/ n inclusión f

inclusive /ɪnˈkluːsɪv/ a inclusivo. be ~ of incluir. —adv inclusive

incognito /ɪnkɒgˈniːtəʊ/ adv de incógnito

incoherent /ɪnkəʊˈhɪərənt/ a incoherente

income /ˈɪnkʌm/ n ingresos mpl. ~ tax n impuesto m sobre la renta

incoming /ˈɪnkʌmɪŋ/ a ⟨tide⟩ ascendente; ⟨tenant etc⟩ nuevo

incomparable /ɪnˈkɒmpərəbl/ a incomparable

incompatible /ɪnkəmˈpætəbl/ a incompatible

incompeten|ce /ɪnˈkɒmpɪtəns/ n incompetencia f. ~t a incompetente

incomplete /ɪnkəmˈpliːt/ a incompleto

incomprehensible /ɪnkɒmprɪˈhensəbl/ a incomprensible

inconceivable /ɪnkənˈsiːvəbl/ a inconcebible

inconclusive /ɪnkənˈkluːsɪv/ a poco concluyente

incongruous /ɪnˈkɒŋgrʊəs/ a incongruente

inconsequential /ɪnkɒnsɪˈkwenʃl/ a sin importancia

inconsiderate /ɪnkənˈsɪdərət/ a desconsiderado

inconsisten|cy /ɪnkənˈsɪstənsɪ/ n inconsecuencia f. ~t a inconsecuente. be ~t with no concordar con

inconspicuous /ɪnkənˈspɪkjʊəs/ a que no llama la atención. ~ly adv sin llamar la atención

incontinen|ce /ɪnˈkɒntɪnəns/ a incontinencia f. ~t a incontinente

inconvenien|ce /ɪnkənˈviːnɪəns/ a incomodidad f; ⟨drawback⟩ inconveniente m. ~t a incómodo; ⟨time⟩ inoportuno

incorporat|e /ɪnˈkɔːpəreɪt/ vt incorporar; ⟨include⟩ incluir. ~ion /-ˈreɪʃn/ n incorporación f

incorrect /ɪnkəˈrekt/ a incorrecto

incorrigible /ɪnˈkɒrɪdʒəbl/ a incorregible

incorruptible /ɪnkəˈrʌptəbl/ a incorruptible

increase /ˈɪnkriːs/ n aumento m (in, of de). /ɪnˈkriːs/ vt/i aumentar

increasing /ɪnˈkriːsɪŋ/ a creciente. ~ly adv cada vez más

incredible /ɪnˈkredəbl/ a increíble

incredulous /ɪnˈkredjʊləs/ a incrédulo

increment /ˈɪnkrɪmənt/ n aumento m

incriminat|e /ɪnˈkrɪmɪneɪt/ vt acriminar. ~ing a acriminador

incubat|e /ˈɪŋkjʊbeɪt/ vt incubar. ~ion /-ˈbeɪʃn/ n incubación f. ~or n incubadora f

inculcate /ˈɪnkʌlkeɪt/ vt inculcar

incumbent /ɪnˈkʌmbənt/ n titular. —a. **be** ~ **on** incumbir a

incur /ɪnˈkɜː(r)/ vt (pt incurred) incurrir en; contraer ‹debts›

incurable /ɪnˈkjʊərəbl/ a incurable

incursion /ɪnˈkɜːʃn/ n incursión f

indebted /ɪnˈdetɪd/ a. ~ **to s.o.** estar en deuda con uno

indecen|cy /ɪnˈdiːsnsɪ/ n indecencia f. ~t a indecente

indecisi|on /ɪndɪˈsɪʒn/ n indecisión f. ~ve /ɪndɪˈsaɪsɪv/ a indeciso

indeed /ɪnˈdiːd/ adv en efecto; ⟨really?⟩ ¿de veras?

indefatigable /ɪndɪˈfætɪgəbl/ a incansable

indefinable /ɪndɪˈfaɪnəbl/ a indefinible

indefinite /ɪnˈdefɪnət/ a indefinido. ~**ly** adv indefinidamente

indelible /ɪnˈdelɪbl/ a indeleble

indemni|fy /ɪnˈdemnɪfaɪ/ vt indemnizar. ~**ty** /-ətɪ/ n indemnización f

indent /ɪnˈdent/ vt endentar ⟨text⟩. ~**ation** /-ˈteɪʃn/ n mella f

independen|ce /ɪndɪˈpendəns/ n independencia f. ~t a independiente. ~**tly** adv independientemente. ~**tly of** independientemente de

indescribable /ɪndɪˈskraɪbəbl/ a indescriptible

indestructible /ɪndɪˈstrʌktəbl/ a indestructible

indeterminate /ɪndɪˈtɜːmɪnət/ a indeterminado

index /ˈɪndeks/ n (pl indexes) índice m. —vt poner índice a; ⟨enter in the/an index⟩ poner en el/un índice. ~ **finger** n (dedo m) índice m. ~**-linked** a indexado

India /ˈɪndɪə/ n la India f. ~**n** a & n indio (m). ~**n summer** n veranillo m de San Martín

indicat|e /ˈɪndɪkeɪt/ vt indicar. ~**ion** /-ˈkeɪʃn/ n indicación f. ~**ive** /ɪnˈdɪkətɪv/ a & n indicativo (m). ~**or** /ˈɪndɪkeɪtə(r)/ n indicador m

indict /ɪnˈdaɪt/ vt acusar. ~**ment** n acusación f

indifferen|ce /ɪnˈdɪfrəns/ n indiferencia f. ~**t** a indiferente; ⟨not good⟩ mediocre

indigenous /ɪnˈdɪdʒɪnəs/ a indígena

indigesti|ble /ɪndɪˈdʒestəbl/ a indigesto. ~**on** /-tʃən/ n indigestión f

indigna|nt /ɪnˈdɪgnənt/ a indignado. ~**tion** /-ˈneɪʃn/ n indignación f

indignity /ɪnˈdɪgnətɪ/ n indignidad f

indigo /ˈɪndɪgəʊ/ n añil (m)

indirect /ɪndɪˈrekt/ a indirecto. ~**ly** adv indirectamente

indiscre|et /ɪndɪˈskriːt/ a indiscreto. ~**tion** /-ˈkreʃn/ n indiscreción f

indiscriminate /ɪndɪˈskrɪmɪnət/ a indistinto. ~**ly** adv indistintamente

indispensable /ɪndɪˈspensəbl/ a imprescindible

indispos|ed /ɪndɪˈspəʊzd/ a indispuesto. ~**ition** /-əˈzɪʃn/ n indisposición f

indisputable /ɪndɪˈspjuːtəbl/ a indiscutible

indissoluble /ˌɪndɪˈsɒljʊbl/ a indisoluble

indistinct /ˌɪndɪˈstɪŋkt/ a indistinto

indistinguishable /ˌɪndɪˈstɪŋgwɪʃəbl/ a indistinguible

individual /ˌɪndɪˈvɪdjʊəl/ a individual. —n individuo m. ∼ist n individualista m & f. ∼ity n individualidad f. ∼ly adv individualmente

indivisible /ˌɪndɪˈvɪzəbl/ a indivisible

Indo-China /ˌɪndəʊˈtʃaɪnə/ n Indochina f

indoctrinate /ɪnˈdɒktrɪneɪt/ vt adoctrinar. ∼ion /-ˈneɪʃn/ n adoctrinamiento m

indolen|ce /ˈɪndələns/ n indolencia f. ∼t a indolente

indomitable /ɪnˈdɒmɪtəbl/ a indomable

Indonesia /ˌɪndəʊˈniːzɪə/ n Indonesia f. ∼n a & n indonesio (m)

indoor /ˈɪndɔː(r)/ a interior; (clothes etc) de casa; (covered) cubierto. ∼s adv dentro; (at home) en casa

induce /ɪnˈdjuːs/ vt inducir; (cause) provocar. ∼ment n incentivo m

induct /ɪnˈdʌkt/ vt instalar; (mil, Amer) incorporar

indulge /ɪnˈdʌldʒ/ vt satisfacer (desires); complacer (person). —vi. ∼ in entregarse a. ∼nce /ɪnˈdʌldʒəns/ n (of desires) satisfacción f; (relig) indulgencia f. ∼nt a indulgente

industrial /ɪnˈdʌstrɪəl/ a industrial; (unrest) laboral. ∼ist n industrial m & f. ∼ized a industrializado

industrious /ɪnˈdʌstrɪəs/ a trabajador

industry /ˈɪndəstrɪ/ n industria f; (zeal) aplicación f

inebriated /ɪˈniːbrɪeɪtɪd/ a borracho

inedible /ɪnˈedɪbl/ a incomible

ineffable /ɪnˈefəbl/ a inefable

ineffective /ˌɪnɪˈfektɪv/ a ineficaz; (person) incapaz

ineffectual /ˌɪnɪˈfektjʊəl/ a ineficaz

inefficien|cy /ˌɪnɪˈfɪʃnsɪ/ n ineficacia f; (of person) incompetencia f. ∼t a ineficaz; (person) incompetente

ineligible /ɪnˈelɪdʒəbl/ a inelegible. be ∼ for no tener derecho a

inept /ɪˈnept/ a inepto

inequality /ˌɪnɪˈkwɒlɪtɪ/ n desigualdad f

inert /ɪˈnɜːt/ a inerte

inertia /ɪˈnɜːʃə/ n inercia f

inescapable /ˌɪnɪˈskeɪpəbl/ a ineludible

inestimable /ɪnˈestɪməbl/ a inestimable

inevitabl|e /ɪnˈevɪtəbl/ a inevitable. ∼ly adv inevitablemente

inexact /ˌɪnɪgˈzækt/ a inexacto

inexcusable /ˌɪnɪkˈskjuːsəbl/ a imperdonable

inexhaustible /ˌɪnɪgˈzɔːstəbl/ a inagotable

inexorable /ɪnˈeksərəbl/ a inexorable

inexpensive /ˌɪnɪkˈspensɪv/ a económico, barato

inexperience /ˌɪnɪkˈspɪərɪəns/ n falta f de experiencia. ∼d a inexperto

inexplicable /ˌɪnɪkˈsplɪkəbl/ a inexplicable

inextricable /ˌɪnɪkˈstrɪkəbl/ a inextricable

infallib|ility /ɪnˌfæləbɪlətɪ/ n infalibilidad f. ∼le a infalible

infam|ous /ˈɪnfəməs/ a infame. ∼y n infamia f

infan|cy /ˈɪnfənsɪ/ n infancia f. ∼t n niño m. ∼tile /ˈɪnfəntaɪl/ a infantil

infantry /ˈɪnfəntrɪ/ n infantería f

infatuat|ed /ɪnˈfætjʊeɪtɪd/ a. be ∼ed with encapricharse por.

~ion /-'eɪʃn/ n encaprichamiento m

infect /ɪn'fekt/ vt infectar; (fig) contagiar. ~ s.o. with contagiar a uno. ~ion /ɪn'fekʃn/ n infección f; (fig) contagio m. ~ious /ɪn'fekʃəs/ a contagioso

infer /ɪn'fɜ:(r)/ vt (pt inferred) deducir. ~ence /'ɪnfərəns/ n deducción f

inferior /ɪn'fɪərɪə(r)/ a inferior. —n inferior m & f. ~ity /-'ɒrətɪ/ n inferioridad f

infernal /ɪn'fɜ:nl/ a infernal. ~ly adv (fam) atrozmente

inferno /ɪn'fɜ:nəʊ/ n (pl -os) infierno m

infertil|e /ɪn'fɜ:taɪl/ a estéril. ~ity /-'tɪlətɪ/ n esterilidad f

infest /ɪn'fest/ vt infestar. ~ation /-'steɪʃn/ n infestación f

infidelity /ɪnfɪ'delətɪ/ n infidelidad f

infighting /'ɪnfaɪtɪŋ/ n lucha f cuerpo a cuerpo; (fig) riñas fpl (internas)

infiltrat|e /ɪnfɪl'treɪt/ vt infiltrar. —vi infiltrarse. ~ion /-'treɪʃn/ n infiltración f

infinite /'ɪnfɪnət/ a infinito. ~ly adv infinitamente

infinitesimal /ɪnfɪnɪ'tesɪml/ a infinitesimal

infinitive /ɪn'fɪnətɪv/ n infinitivo m

infinity /ɪn'fɪnətɪ/ n (infinite distance) infinito m; (infinite quantity) infinidad f

infirm /ɪn'fɜ:m/ a enfermizo

infirmary /ɪn'fɜ:mərɪ/ n hospital m; (sick bay) enfermería f

infirmity /ɪn'fɜ:mətɪ/ n enfermedad f; (weakness) debilidad f

inflame /ɪn'fleɪm/ vt inflamar. ~mable /ɪn'flæməbl/ a inflamable. ~mation /-ə'meɪʃn/ n inflamación f. ~matory /ɪn'flæmətərɪ/ a inflamatorio

inflate /ɪn'fleɪt/ vt inflar

inflation /ɪn'fleɪʃn/ n inflación f. ~ary a inflacionario

inflection /ɪn'flekʃn/ n inflexión f

inflexible /ɪn'fleksəbl/ a inflexible

inflict /ɪn'flɪkt/ vt infligir (on a)

inflow /'ɪnfləʊ/ n afluencia f

influence /'ɪnfluəns/ n influencia f. under the ~ (drunk, fam) borracho. —vt influir, influenciar (esp LAm)

influential /ɪnflu'enʃl/ a influyente

influenza /ɪnflu'enzə/ n gripe f

influx /'ɪnflʌks/ n afluencia f

inform /ɪn'fɔ:m/ vt informar. keep ~ed tener al corriente

informal /ɪn'fɔ:ml/ a (simple) sencillo, sin ceremonia; (unofficial) oficioso. ~ity /'mæləti/ n falta f de ceremonia. ~ly adv sin ceremonia

inform|ant /ɪn'fɔ:mənt/ n informador m. ~ation /ɪnfə'meɪʃn/ n información f. ~ative /ɪn'fɔ:mətɪv/ a informativo. ~er /ɪn'fɔ:mə(r)/ n denunciante m

infra-red /ɪnfrə'red/ a infrarrojo

infrequent /ɪn'fri:kwənt/ a poco frecuente. ~ly adv raramente

infringe /ɪn'frɪndʒ/ vt infringir. ~ on usurpar. ~ment n infracción f

infuriate /ɪn'fjʊərɪeɪt/ vt enfurecer

infuse /ɪn'fju:z/ vt infundir. ~ion /-ʒn/ n infusión f

ingen|ious /ɪn'dʒi:nɪəs/ a ingenioso. ~uity /ɪndʒɪ'nju:ətɪ/ n ingeniosidad f

ingenuous /ɪn'dʒenjʊəs/ a ingenuo

ingest /ɪn'dʒest/ vt ingerir

ingot /'ɪŋgət/ n lingote m

ingrained /ɪn'greɪnd/ a arraigado

ingratiate /ɪn'greɪʃɪeɪt/ vt. ~ o.s. with congraciarse con

ingratitude /ɪnˈɡrætɪtjuːd/ n ingratitud f

ingredient /ɪnˈɡriːdɪənt/ n ingrediente m

ingrowing /ˈɪnɡrəʊɪŋ/ a. ~ **nail** n uñero m, uña f encarnada

inhabit /ɪnˈhæbɪt/ vt habitar. ~**able** a habitable. ~**ant** n habitante m

inhale /ɪnˈheɪl/ vt aspirar. —vi ‹tobacco› aspirar el humo

inherent /ɪnˈhɪərənt/ a inherente. ~**ly** adv intrínsecamente

inherit /ɪnˈherɪt/ vt heredar. ~**ance** n herencia f

inhibit /ɪnˈhɪbɪt/ vt inhibir. be ~**ed** tener inhibiciones. ~**ion** /-ˈbɪʃn/ n inhibición f

inhospitable /ɪnhəˈspɪtəbl/ a ‹place› inhóspito; ‹person› inhospitalario

inhuman /ɪnˈhjuːmən/ a inhumano. ~**e** /ɪnhjuːˈmeɪn/ a inhumano. ~**ity** /ɪnhjuːˈmænətɪ/ n inhumanidad f

inimical /ɪˈnɪmɪkl/ a hostil

inimitable /ɪˈnɪmɪtəbl/ a inimitable

iniquit|ous /ɪˈnɪkwɪtəs/ a inicuo. ~**y** /-ətɪ/ n iniquidad f

initial /ɪˈnɪʃl/ n inicial f. —vt (pt **initialled**) firmar con iniciales. he ~**led the document** firmó el documento con sus iniciales. —a inicial. ~**ly** adv al principio

initiat|e /ɪˈnɪʃɪeɪt/ vt iniciar; promover ‹scheme etc›. ~**ion** /-ˈeɪʃn/ n iniciación f

initiative /ɪˈnɪʃɪtɪv/ n iniciativa f

inject /ɪnˈdʒekt/ vt inyectar; (fig) injertar ‹new element›. ~**ion** /-ʃn/ n inyección f

injunction /ɪnˈdʒʌŋkʃn/ n ‹court order› entredicho m

injur|e /ˈɪndʒə(r)/ vt ‹wound› herir; ‹fig, damage› perjudicar. ~**y** /ˈɪndʒərɪ/ n herida f; ‹damage› perjuicio m

injustice /ɪnˈdʒʌstɪs/ n injusticia f

ink /ɪŋk/ n tinta f

inkling /ˈɪŋklɪŋ/ n atisbo m

ink: ~**-well** n tintero m. ~**y** a manchado de tinta

inland /ˈɪnlənd/ a interior. —adv tierra adentro. **I~ Revenue** n Hacienda f

in-laws /ˈɪnlɔːz/ npl parientes mpl políticos

inlay /ɪnˈleɪ/ vt (pt **inlaid**) taracear, incrustar. /ˈɪnleɪ/ n taracea f, incrustación f

inlet /ˈɪnlet/ n ensenada f; ‹tec› entrada f

inmate /ˈɪnmeɪt/ n (of asylum) internado m; (of prison) preso m

inn /ɪn/ n posada f

innards /ˈɪnədz/ npl tripas fpl

innate /ɪˈneɪt/ a innato

inner /ˈɪnə(r)/ a interior; (fig) íntimo. ~**most** a más íntimo. ~**tube** n cámara f de aire, llanta f (LAm)

innings /ˈɪnɪŋz/ n invar turno m

innkeeper /ˈɪnkiːpə(r)/ n posadero m

innocen|ce /ˈɪnəsns/ n inocencia f. ~**t** a & n inocente (m & f)

innocuous /ɪˈnɒkjuəs/ a inocuo

innovat|e /ˈɪnəveɪt/ vi innovar. ~**ion** /-ˈveɪʃn/ n innovación f. ~**or** n innovador m

innuendo /ɪnjuːˈendəʊ/ n (pl -oes) insinuación f

innumerable /ɪˈnjuːmərəbl/ a innumerable

inoculat|e /ɪˈnɒkjʊleɪt/ vt inocular. ~**ion** /-ˈleɪʃn/ n inoculación f

inoffensive /ɪnəˈfensɪv/ a inofensivo

inoperative /ɪnˈɒpərətɪv/ a inoperante

inopportune /ɪnˈɒpətjuːn/ a inoportuno

inordinate /ɪˈnɔːdɪnət/ a excesivo. ~**ly** adv excesivamente

in-patient /'ɪnpeɪʃnt/ n paciente m interno

input /'ɪnput/ n (data) datos mpl; (comput process) entrada f, input m; (elec) energía f

inquest /'ɪnkwest/ n investigación f judicial

inquir|e /ɪn'kwaɪə(r)/ vi preguntar. ~y n (question) pregunta f; (investigation) investigación f

inquisition /ɪnkwɪ'zɪʃn/ n inquisición f

inquisitive /ɪn'kwɪzətɪv/ a inquisitivo

inroad /'ɪnrəʊd/ n incursión f

inrush /'ɪnrʌʃ/ n irrupción f

insan|e /ɪn'seɪn/ a loco. ~ity /-'sænətɪ/ n locura f

insanitary /ɪn'sænɪtərɪ/ a insalubre

insatiable /ɪn'seɪʃəbl/ a insaciable

inscri|be /ɪn'skraɪb/ vt inscribir; dedicar (book). ~ption /-ɪpʃn/ n inscripción f, (in book) dedicatoria f

inscrutable /ɪn'skruːtəbl/ a inescrutable

insect /'ɪnsekt/ n insecto m. ~icide /ɪn'sektɪsaɪd/ n insecticida f

insecur|e /ɪnsɪ'kjʊə(r)/ a inseguro. ~ity n inseguridad f

insemination /ɪnsemɪ'neɪʃn/ n inseminación f

insensible /ɪn'sensəbl/ a insensible; (unconscious) sin conocimiento

insensitive /ɪn'sensətɪv/ a insensible

inseparable /ɪn'sepərəbl/ a inseparable

insert /'ɪnsɜːt/ n materia f insertada. /ɪn'sɜːt/ vt insertar. ~ion /-ʃn/ n inserción f

inshore /ɪn'ʃɔː(r)/ a costero

inside /ɪn'saɪd/ n interior m. ~ out al revés; (thoroughly) a fondo. —a interior. —adv

dentro. —prep dentro de. ~s npl tripas fpl

insidious /ɪn'sɪdɪəs/ a insidioso

insight /'ɪnsaɪt/ n (perception) penetración f, revelación f

insignia /ɪn'sɪgnɪə/ npl insignias fpl

insignificant /ɪnsɪg'nɪfɪkənt/ a insignificante

insincer|e /ɪnsɪn'sɪə(r)/ a poco sincero. ~ity /-'serətɪ/ n falta f de sinceridad f

insinuat|e /ɪn'sɪnjʊeɪt/ vt insinuar. ~ion /-'eɪʃn/ n insinuación f

insipid /ɪn'sɪpɪd/ a insípido

insist /ɪn'sɪst/ vt/i insistir. ~ on insistir en; (demand) exigir

insisten|ce /ɪn'sɪstəns/ n insistencia f. ~t a insistente. ~tly adv con insistencia

insolen|ce /'ɪnsələns/ n insolencia f. ~t a insolente

insoluble /ɪn'sɒljʊbl/ a insoluble

insolvent /ɪn'sɒlvənt/ a insolvente

insomnia /ɪn'sɒmnɪə/ n insomnio m. ~c /-læk/ n insomne m & f

inspect /ɪn'spekt/ vt inspeccionar; revisar (ticket). ~ion /-ʃn/ n inspección f. ~or n inspector m; (on train, bus) revisor m

inspir|ation /ɪnspə'reɪʃn/ n inspiración f. ~e /ɪn'spaɪə(r)/ vt inspirar

instability /ɪnstə'bɪlətɪ/ n inestabilidad f

install /ɪn'stɔːl/ vt instalar. ~ation /-ə'leɪʃn/ n instalación f

instalment /ɪn'stɔːlmənt/ n (payment) plazo m; (of serial) entrega f

instance /'ɪnstəns/ n ejemplo m; (case) caso m. for ~ por ejemplo. in the first ~ en primer lugar

instant /'ɪnstənt/ a inmediato; (food) instantáneo. —n instante

m. **~aneous** /ɪnstənˈteɪnɪəs/ *a*
instantáneo. **~ly** /ˈɪnstəntli/ *adv*
inmediatamente

instead /ɪnˈsted/ *adv* en cambio.
~ of doing en vez de hacer. **~ of**
s.o. en lugar de uno

instep /ˈɪnstep/ *n* empeine *m*

instigat|**e** /ˈɪnstɪɡeɪt/ *vt* instigar.
~ion /-ˈɡeɪʃn/ *n* instigación *f*.
~or *n* instigador *m*

instil /ɪnˈstɪl/ *vt* (*pt* **instilled**)
infundir

instinct /ˈɪnstɪŋkt/ *n* instinto *m*.
~ive /ɪnˈstɪŋktɪv/ *a* instintivo

institut|**e** /ˈɪnstɪtjuːt/ *n* instituto
m. —*vt* instituir; iniciar (*enquiry*
etc). **~ion** /-ˈtjuːʃn/ *n* institución
f

instruct /ɪnˈstrʌkt/ *vt* instruir;
(*order*) mandar. **~ s.o. in sth**
enseñar algo a uno. **~ion** /-ʃn/
n instrucción *f*. **~ions** /-ʃnz/ *npl*
(*for use*) modo *m* de empleo.
~ive *a* instructivo

instrument /ˈɪnstrəmənt/ *n* instrumento *m*. **~al** /ɪnstrə-
ˈmentl/ *a* instrumental. **be ~al in**
contribuir a. **~alist** *n* instru-
mentalista *m* & *f*

insubordinat|**e** /ɪnsəˈbɔːdɪnət/ *a*
insubordinado. **~ion** /-ˈneɪʃn/ *n*
insubordinación *f*

insufferable /ɪnˈsʌfərəbl/ *a* insufrible, insoportable

insufficient /ɪnsəˈfɪʃnt/ *a* insuficiente. **~ly** *adv* insuficientemente

insular /ˈɪnsjʊlə(r)/ *a* insular;
(*narrow-minded*) de miras
estrechas

insulat|**e** /ˈɪnsjʊleɪt/ *vt* aislar.
~ing tape *n* cinta *f* aisladora/
aislante. **~ion** /-ˈleɪʃn/ *n* aislamiento *m*

insulin /ˈɪnsjʊlɪn/ *n* insulina *f*

insult /ɪnˈsʌlt/ *vt* insultar.
/ˈɪnsʌlt/ *n* insulto *m*

insuperable /ɪnˈsjuːpərəbl/ *a*
insuperable

insur|**ance** /ɪnˈʃʊərəns/ *n* seguro
m. **~e** *vt* asegurar. **~e that** asegurarse de que

insurgent /ɪnˈsɜːdʒənt/ *a* & *n*
insurrecto (*m*)

insurmountable /ɪnsəˈmaʊnt-
əbl/ *a* insuperable

insurrection /ɪnsəˈrekʃn/ *n* in-
surrección *f*

intact /ɪnˈtækt/ *a* intacto

intake /ˈɪnteɪk/ *n* (*quantity*)
número *m*; (*mec*) admisión *f*; (*of*
food) consumo *m*

intangible /ɪnˈtændʒəbl/ *a* intangible

integral /ˈɪntɪɡrəl/ *a* íntegro. **be**
an ~ part of ser parte inte-
grante de

integrat|**e** /ˈɪntɪɡreɪt/ *vt*
integrar. —*vi* integrarse. **~ion**
/-ˈɡreɪʃn/ *n* integración *f*

integrity /ɪnˈteɡrɪti/ *n* integridad *f*

intellect /ˈɪntəlekt/ *n* intelecto *m*.
~ual *a* & *n* intelectual (*m*)

intelligen|**ce** /ɪnˈtelɪdʒəns/ *n*
inteligencia *f*; (*information*)
información *f*. **~t** *a* inteligente.
~tly *adv* inteligentemente.
~tsia /ɪntelɪˈdʒentsɪə/ *n* inte-
lectualidad *f*

intelligible /ɪnˈtelɪdʒəbl/ *a* inteligible

intemperance /ɪnˈtempərəns/ *n*
inmoderación *f*

intend /ɪnˈtend/ *vt* destinar. **~ to**
do tener la intención de hacer.
~ed *a* intencionado. —*n* (*future*
spouse) novio *m*

intense /ɪnˈtens/ *a* intenso; (*per-*
son) apasionado. **~ly** *adv* intensamente; (*very*) sumamente

intensi|**fication** /ɪntensɪfɪˈkeɪʃn/
n intensificación *f*. **~y** /-faɪ/
vt intensificar

intensity /ɪnˈtensɪti/ *n* intensidad *f*

intensive /ɪnˈtensɪv/ *a* intensivo.
~ care *n* asistencia *f* intensiva,
cuidados *mpl* intensivos

intent /ɪn'tent/ n propósito m. — a atento. ~ on absorto en. ~ on doing resuelto a hacer

intention /ɪn'tenʃn/ n intención f. ~al a intencional

intently /ɪn'tentli/ adv atentamente

inter /ɪn'tɜ:(r)/ vt (pt interred) enterrar

inter... /'ɪntə(r)/ pref inter..., entre...

interact /ɪntər'ækt/ vi obrar recíprocamente. ~ion /-ʃn/ n interacción f

intercede /ɪntə'si:d/ vi interceder

intercept /ɪntə'sept/ vt interceptar. ~ion /-ʃn/ n interceptación f; (in geometry) intersección f

interchange /'ɪntətʃeɪndʒ/ n (road junction) cruce m. ~able /-'tʃeɪndʒəbl/ a intercambiable

intercom /'ɪntəkɒm/ n intercomunicador m

interconnected /ɪntəkə'nektɪd/ a relacionado

intercourse /'ɪntəkɔ:s/ n trato m; (sexual) trato m sexual

interest /'ɪntrest/ n interés m; (advantage) ventaja f. —vt interesar. ~ed a interesado. be ~ed in interesarse por. ~ing a interesante

interfere /ɪntə'fɪə(r)/ vi entrometerse. ~ in entrometerse en. ~ with entrometerse en, interferir en; interferir (radio). ~nce n interferencia f

interim a provisional. —n. in the ~ entre tanto

interior /ɪn'tɪərɪə(r)/ a & n interior (m)

interjection /ɪntə'dʒekʃn/ n interjección f

interlock /ɪntə'lɒk/ vt/i (tec) engranar

interloper /'ɪntələʊpə(r)/ n intruso m

interlude /'ɪntəlu:d/ n intervalo m; (theatre, music) interludio m

intermarr|**iage** /ɪntə'mærɪdʒ/ n matrimonio m entre personas de distintas razas. ~y vi casarse (con personas de distintas razas)

intermediary /ɪntə'mi:dɪərɪ/ a & n intermediario (m)

intermediate /ɪntə'mi:dɪət/ a intermedio

interminable /ɪn'tɜ:mɪnəbl/ a interminable

intermission /ɪntə'mɪʃn/ n pausa f; (theatre) descanso m

intermittent /ɪntə'mɪtnt/ a intermitente. ~ly adv con discontinuidad

intern /ɪn'tɜ:n/ vt internar. /'ɪntɜ:n/ n (doctor, Amer) interno m

internal /ɪn'tɜ:nl/ a interior. ~ly adv interiormente

international /ɪntə'næʃənl/ a & n internacional (m)

internee /ˌɪntɜ:'ni:/ n internado m

internment /ɪn'tɜ:nmənt/ n internamiento m

interplay /'ɪntəpleɪ/ n interacción f

interpolate /ɪn'tɜ:pəleɪt/ vt interpolar

interpret /ɪn'tɜ:prɪt/ vt/i interpretar. ~ation /-'teɪʃn/ n interpretación f. ~er n intérprete m & f

interrelated /ɪntərɪ'leɪtɪd/ a interrelacionado

interrogat|**e** /ɪn'terəgeɪt/ vt interrogar. ~ion /-'geɪʃn/ n interrogación f; (session of questions) interrogatorio m

interrogative /ɪntə'rɒgətɪv/ a & n interrogativo (m)

interrupt /ɪntə'rʌpt/ vt interrumpir. ~ion /-ʃn/ n interrupción f

intersect /ɪntə'sekt/ vt cruzar. —vi (roads) cruzarse; (geometry) intersecarse. ~ion /-ʃn/ n (*roads*) cruce *m*; (*geometry*) intersección *f*

interspersed /ɪntə'spɜ:st/ *a* disperso. ∼ **with** salpicado de

intertwine /ɪntə'twaɪn/ *vt* entrelazar. —*vi* entrelazarse

interval /'ɪntəvl/ *n* intervalo *m*; (*theatre*) descanso *m*. **at** ∼**s** a intervalos

interven|e /ɪntə'vi:n/ *vi* intervenir. ∼**tion** /-'venʃn/ *n* intervención *f*

interview /'ɪntəvju:/ *n* entrevista *f*. —*vt* entrevistarse con. ∼**er** *n* entrevistador *m*

intestin|al /ɪnte'staɪnl/ *a* intestinal. ∼**e** /ɪn'testɪn/ *n* intestino *m*

intimacy /'ɪntɪməsɪ/ *n* intimidad *f*

intimate[1] /'ɪntɪmət/ *a* íntimo

intimate[2] /'ɪntɪmeɪt/ *vt* (*state*) anunciar; (*imply*) dar a entender

intimately /'ɪntɪmətlɪ/ *adv* íntimamente

intimidat|e /ɪn'tɪmɪdeɪt/ *vt* intimidar. ∼**ion** /-'deɪʃn/ *n* intimidación *f*

into /'ɪntu:/, *unstressed* /'ɪntə/ *prep* en; (*translate*) a

intolerable /ɪn'tɒlərəbl/ *a* intolerable

intoleran|ce /ɪn'tɒlərəns/ *n* intolerancia *f*. ∼**t** *a* intolerante

intonation /ɪntə'neɪʃn/ *n* entonación *f*

intoxicat|e /ɪn'tɒksɪkeɪt/ *vt* embriagar; (*med*) intoxicar. ∼**ed** *a* ebrio. ∼**ion** /-'keɪʃn/ *n* embriaguez *f*; (*med*) intoxicación *f*

intra... /'ɪntrə/ *pref* intra...

intractable /ɪn'træktəbl/ *a* (*person*) intratable; (*thing*) muy difícil

intransigent /ɪn'trænsɪdʒənt/ *a* intransigente

intransitive /ɪn'trænsɪtɪv/ *a* intransitivo

intravenous /ɪntrə'vi:nəs/ *a* intravenoso

intrepid /ɪn'trepɪd/ *a* intrépido

intrica|cy /'ɪntrɪkəsɪ/ *n* complejidad *f*. ∼**te** *a* complejo

intrigu|e /ɪn'tri:g/ *vt/i* intrigar. —*n* intriga *f*. ∼**ing** *a* intrigante

intrinsic /ɪn'trɪnsɪk/ *a* intrínseco. ∼**ally** *adv* intrínsecamente

introduc|e /ɪntrə'dju:s/ *vt* introducir; presentar (*person*). ∼**tion** /ɪntrə'dʌkʃn/ *n* introducción *f*; (*to person*) presentación *f*. ∼**tory** /-təri/ *a* preliminar

introspective /ɪntrə'spektɪv/ *a* introspectivo

introvert /'ɪntrəvɜ:t/ *n* introvertido *m*

intru|de /ɪn'tru:d/ *vi* entrometerse; (*disturb*) molestar. ∼**der** *n* intruso *m*. ∼**sion** /-ʒn/ *n* intrusión *f*

intuiti|on /ɪntju:'ɪʃn/ *n* intuición *f*. ∼**ve** /ɪn'tju:ɪtɪv/ *a* intuitivo

inundat|e /'ɪnʌndeɪt/ *vt* inundar. ∼**ion** /-'deɪʃn/ *n* inundación *f*

invade /ɪn'veɪd/ *vt* invadir. ∼**r** /-ə(r)/ *n* invasor *m*

invalid[1] /'ɪnvəlɪd/ *n* enfermo *m*, inválido *m*

invalid[2] /ɪn'vælɪd/ *a* nulo. ∼**ate** *vt* invalidar

invaluable /ɪn'væljʊəbl/ *a* inestimable

invariable /ɪn'veərɪəbl/ *a* invariable. ∼**y** *adv* invariablemente

invasion /ɪn'veɪʒn/ *n* invasión *f*

invective /ɪn'vektɪv/ *n* invectiva *f*

inveigh /ɪn'veɪ/ *vi* dirigir invectivas (**against** contra)

inveigle /ɪn'veɪgl/ *vt* engatusar, persuadir

invent /ɪn'vent/ *vt* inventar. ∼**ion** /-'venʃn/ *n* invención *f*. ∼**ive** *a* inventivo. ∼**or** *n* inventor *m*

inventory /'ɪnvəntərɪ/ n inventario m

invers|e /ɪn'vɜ:s/ a & n inverso (m). **~ely** adv inversamente. **~ion** /ɪn'vɜ:ʃn/ n inversión f

invert /ɪn'vɜ:t/ vt invertir. **~ed commas** npl comillas fpl

invest /ɪn'vest/ vt invertir. —vi. **~ in** hacer una inversión f

investigat|e /ɪn'vestɪgeɪt/ vt investigar. **~ion** /-'geɪʃn/ n investigación f. **under ~ion** sometido a examen. **~or** n investigador m

inveterate /ɪn'vetərət/ a inveterado

invidious /ɪn'vɪdɪəs/ a (hateful) odioso; (unfair) injusto

invigilat|e /ɪn'vɪdʒɪleɪt/ vi vigilar. **~or** n celador m

invigorate /ɪn'vɪgəreɪt/ vt vigorizar; (stimulate) estimular

invincible /ɪn'vɪnsɪbl/ a invencible

invisible /ɪn'vɪzəbl/ a invisible

invit|ation /ɪnvɪ'teɪʃn/ n invitación f. **~e** /ɪn'vaɪt/ vt invitar; (ask for) pedir. **~ing** a atrayente

invoice /'ɪnvɔɪs/ n factura f. —vt facturar

invoke /ɪn'vəʊk/ vt invocar

involuntary /ɪn'vɒləntərɪ/ a involuntario

involve /ɪn'vɒlv/ vt enredar. **~d** a (complex) complicado. **~d in** embrollado en. **~ment** n enredo m

invulnerable /ɪn'vʌlnərəbl/ a invulnerable

inward /'ɪnwəd/ a interior. —adv interiormente. **~s** adv hacia/para dentro

iodine /'aɪədi:n/ n yodo m

iota /aɪ'əʊtə/ n (amount) pizca f

IOU /aɪəʊ'ju:/ abbr (I owe you) pagaré m

IQ /aɪ'kju:/ abbr (intelligence quotient) cociente m intelectual

Iran /ɪ'rɑ:n/ n Irán m. **~ian** /ɪ'reɪnɪən/ a & n iraní (m)

Iraq /ɪ'rɑ:k/ n Irak m. **~i** a & n iraquí (m)

irascible /ɪ'ræsəbl/ a irascible

irate /aɪ'reɪt/ a colérico

ire /aɪə(r)/ n ira f

Ireland /'aɪələnd/ n Irlanda f

iris /'aɪərɪs/ n (anat) iris m; (bot) lirio m

Irish /'aɪərɪʃ/ a irlandés. —n (lang) irlandés m. **~man** n irlandés m. **~woman** n irlandesa f

irk /ɜ:k/ vt fastidiar. **~some** a fastidioso

iron /'aɪən/ n hierro m; (appliance) plancha f. —a de hierro. —vt planchar. **~ out** allanar. **I~ Curtain** n telón m de acero

ironic(al) /aɪ'rɒnɪk(l)/ a irónico

ironing-board /'aɪənɪŋbɔ:d/ n tabla f de planchar

ironmonger /'aɪənmʌŋgə(r)/ n ferretero m. **~y** n ferretería f

ironwork /'aɪənwɜ:k/ n herraje m

irony /'aɪərənɪ/ n ironía f

irrational /ɪ'ræʃənl/ a irracional

irreconcilable /ɪrekən'saɪləbl/ a irreconciliable

irrefutable /ɪrɪ'fju:təbl/ a irrefutable

irregular /ɪ'regjʊlə(r)/ a irregular. **~ity** /-'lærətɪ/ n irregularidad f

irrelevan|ce /ɪ'reləvəns/ n inoportunidad f, impertinencia f. **~t** a no pertinente

irreparable /ɪ'repərəbl/ a irreparable

irreplaceable /ɪrɪ'pleɪsəbl/ a irremplazable

irrepressible /ɪrɪ'presəbl/ a irreprimible

irresistible /ɪrɪ'zɪstəbl/ a irresistible

irresolute /ɪˈrezəluːt/ a irresoluto, indeciso

irrespective /ɪrɪˈspektɪv/ a. ~ of sin tomar en cuenta

irresponsible /ɪrɪˈtrɒnsəbl/ a irresponsable

irretrievable /ɪrɪˈtriːvəbl/ a irrecuperable

irreverent /ɪˈrevərənt/ a irreverente

irreversible /ɪrɪˈvɜːsəbl/ a irreversible; ⟨decision⟩ irrevocable

irrevocable /ɪˈrevəkəbl/ a irrevocable

irrigate /ˈɪrɪgeɪt/ vt regar; (med) irrigar. ~ion /-ˈgeɪʃn/ n riego m; (med) irrigación f

irritable /ˈɪrɪtəbl/ a irritable

irritate /ˈɪrɪteɪt/ vt irritar. ~ion /-ˈteɪʃn/ n irritación f

is /ɪz/ see **be**

Islam /ˈɪzlɑːm/ n Islam m. ~ic /ɪzˈlæmɪk/ a islámico

island /ˈaɪlənd/ n isla f. traffic ~ n refugio m (en la calle). ~er n isleño m

isle /aɪl/ n isla f

isolate /ˈaɪsəleɪt/ vt aislar. ~ion /-ˈleɪʃn/ n aislamiento m

isotope /ˈaɪsətəʊp/ n isotopo m

Israel /ˈɪzreɪl/ n Israel m. ~i /ɪzˈreɪlɪ/ a & n israelí (m)

issue /ˈɪʃuː/ n asunto m; (outcome) resultado m; (of magazine etc) número m; (of stamps) emisión f; (offspring) descendencia f. at ~ en cuestión. take ~ with oponerse a. —vt distribuir; emitir ⟨stamps etc⟩; publicar ⟨book⟩. —vi. ~ from salir de

isthmus /ˈɪsməs/ n istmo m

it /ɪt/ pron (subject) el, ella, ello; (direct object) lo, la; (indirect object) le; (after preposition) él, ella, ello. ~ is hot hace calor. ~ is me soy yo. far from ~ ni mucho menos. that's ~ eso es. who is ~? ¿quién es?

italic /ɪˈtælɪk/ a bastardillo m. ~s npl (letra f) bastardilla f

italian /ɪˈtæljən/ a & n italiano (m). I~y /ˈɪtəlɪ/ n Italia f

itch /ɪtʃ/ n picazón f. —vi picar. I'm ~ing to rabio por. my arm ~es me pica el brazo. ~y a que pica

item /ˈaɪtəm/ n artículo m; (on agenda) asunto m. news ~ n noticia f. ~ize vt detallar

itinerant /aɪˈtɪnərənt/ a ambulante

itinerary /aɪˈtɪnərərɪ/ n itinerario m

its /ɪts/ a su, sus (pl). —pron (el) suyo m, (la) suya f, (los) suyos mpl, (las) suyas fpl

it's /ɪts/ = it is, it has

itself /ɪtˈself/ pron él mismo, ella misma, ello mismo; (reflexive) se; (after prep) sí mismo, sí misma

ivory /ˈaɪvərɪ/ n marfil m. ~ tower n torre f de marfil

ivy /ˈaɪvɪ/ n hiedra f

J

jab /dʒæb/ vt (pt jabbed) pinchar; (thrust) hurgonear. —n pinchazo m

jabber /ˈdʒæbə(r)/ vi barbullar. —n farfulla f

jack /dʒæk/ n (mec) gato m; (cards) sota f. —vt. ~ up alzar con gato

jackal /ˈdʒækl/ n chacal m

jackass /ˈdʒækæs/ n burro m

jackdaw /ˈdʒækdɔː/ n grajilla f

jacket /ˈdʒækɪt/ n chaqueta f, saco m (LAm); (of book) sobrecubierta f, camisa f

jack-knife /ˈdʒæknaɪf/ n navaja f

jackpot /ˈdʒækpɒt/ n premio m gordo. hit the ~ sacar el premio gordo

jade /dʒeɪd/ n (*stone*) jade m

jaded /'dʒeɪdɪd/ a cansado

jagged /'dʒægɪd/ a dentado

jaguar /'dʒægjʊə(r)/ n jaguar m

jail /dʒeɪl/ n cárcel m. ~**bird** n criminal m empedernido. ~**er** n carcelero m

jalopy /dʒə'lɒpɪ/ n cacharro m

jam[1] /dʒæm/ vt (pt **jammed**) interferir con (*radio*); (*traffic*) embotellar; (*people*) atestar en. —vi obstruirse; (*mechanism etc*) atascarse. —n (*of people*) aglomeración m; (*of traffic*) embotellamiento m; (*situation, fam*) apuro m

jam[2] /dʒæm/ n mermelada f

Jamaica /dʒə'meɪkə/ n Jamaica f

jamboree /dʒæmbə'ri:/ n reunión f

jam-packed /'dʒæm'pækt/ a atestado

jangle /'dʒæŋgl/ n sonido m metálico (y áspero). —vt/i sonar discordemente

janitor /'dʒænɪtə(r)/ n portero m

January /'dʒænjʊərɪ/ n enero m

Japan /dʒə'pæn/ n el Japón m. ~**ese** /dʒæpə'niːz/ a n japonés (m)

jar[1] /dʒɑː(r)/ n tarro m, frasco m

jar[2] /dʒɑː(r)/ vi (pt **jarred**) (*sound*) sonar mal; (*colours*) chillar. —vt sacudir

jar[3] /dʒɑː(r)/ n. on the ~ (*ajar*) entreabierto

jargon /'dʒɑːgən/ n jerga f

jarring /'dʒɑːrɪŋ/ a discorde

jasmine /'dʒæsmɪn/ n jazmín m

jaundice /'dʒɔːndɪs/ n ictericia f. ~**d** a (*envious*) envidioso; (*bitter*) amargado

jaunt /dʒɔːnt/ n excursión f

jaunty /'dʒɔːntɪ/ a (-**ier**, -**iest**) garboso

javelin /'dʒævəlɪn/ n jabalina f

jaw /dʒɔː/ n mandíbula f. —vi (*talk lengthily, sl*) hablar por los codos

jay /dʒeɪ/ n arrendajo m. ~**walk** vi cruzar la calle descuidadamente

jazz /dʒæz/ n jazz m. —vt. ~ **up** animar. ~**y** a chillón

jealous /'dʒeləs/ a celoso. ~**y** n celos mpl

jeans /dʒiːnz/ npl (*pantalones mpl*) vaqueros mpl

jeep /dʒiːp/ n jeep m

jeer /dʒɪə(r)/ vt/i. ~ **at** mofarse de, befar; (*boo*) abuchear. —n mofa f; (*boo*) abucheo m

jell /dʒel/ vi cuajar. ~**ied** a en gelatina

jelly /'dʒelɪ/ n jalea f. ~**fish** n medusa f

jeopard|**ize** /'dʒepədaɪz/ vt arriesgar. ~**y** n peligro m

jerk /dʒɜːk/ n sacudida f; (*fool, sl*) idiota m & f. —vt sacudir. ~**ily** adv a sacudidas. ~**y** a espasmódico

jersey /'dʒɜːzɪ/ n (pl -**eys**) jersey m

jest /dʒest/ n broma f. —vi bromear. ~**er** n bufón m

Jesus /'dʒiːzəs/ n Jesús m

jet[1] /dʒet/ n (*stream*) chorro m; (*plane*) yet m, avión m de propulsión por reacción

jet[2] /dʒet/ n (*mineral*) azabache m. ~**black** a de azabache, como el azabache

jet: ~ **lag** n cansancio m retardado después de un vuelo largo. **have** ~ **lag** estar desfasado. ~**propelled** a (de propulsión) a reacción

jettison /'dʒetɪsn/ vt echar al mar; (*fig, discard*) deshacerse de

jetty /'dʒetɪ/ n muelle m

Jew /dʒuː/ n judío m

jewel /'dʒuːəl/ n joya f. ~**led** a enjoyado. ~**ler** n joyero m. ~**lery** n joyas fpl

Jew: ~**ess** n judía f. ~**ish** a judío. ~**ry** /'dʒʊərɪ/ n los judíos mpl

jib[1] /dʒɪb/ n (*sail*) foque m

jib² /dʒɪb/ vi (pt jibbed) rehusar. ~ at oponerse a.

jiffy /'dʒɪfɪ/ n momentito m. do sth in a ~ hacer algo en un santiamén

jig /dʒɪg/ n (dance) giga f

jiggle /'dʒɪgl/ vt zangolotear

jigsaw /'dʒɪgsɔː/ n rompecabezas m invar

jilt /dʒɪlt/ vt plantar, dejar plantado

jingle /'dʒɪŋgl/ vt hacer sonar. — vi tintinear. —n tintineo m; (advert) anuncio m cantado

jinx /dʒɪŋks/ n (person) gafe m; (spell) maleficio m

jitters /'dʒɪtəz/ npl. have the ~s estar nervioso. ~y /-ərɪ/ a nervioso. be ~y estar nervioso

job /dʒɒb/ n trabajo m; (post) empleo m, puesto m. have a ~ doing costar trabajo hacer. it is a good ~ that menos mal que. ~centre n bolsa f de trabajo. ~less a sin trabajo.

jockey /'dʒɒkɪ/ n jockey m. —vi (manoeuvre) maniobrar (for para)

jocular /'dʒɒkjʊlə(r)/ a jocoso

jog /dʒɒg/ vt (pt jogged) empujar; refrescar (memory). —vi hacer footing. ~ging n jogging m

join /dʒɔɪn/ vt unir, juntar; hacerse socio de (club); hacerse miembro de (political group); alistarse en (army); reunirse con (another person). —vi (roads etc) empalmar; (rivers) confluir. ~ in participar (en). ~ up (mil) alistarse. —n juntura

joiner /'dʒɔɪnə(r)/ n carpintero m

joint /dʒɔɪnt/ a común. — author n coautor m. —n (join) juntura f; (anat) articulación f; (culin) asado m; (place, sl) garito m; (marijuana, sl) cigarillo m de marijuana. out of ~ descoyuntado. ~ly adv conjuntamente

joist /dʒɔɪst/ n viga f

joke /dʒəʊk/ n broma f; (funny story) chiste m. —vi bromear. ~er n bromista m & f; (cards) comodín m. ~ingly adv en broma

jollification /dʒɒlɪfɪ'keɪʃn/ n jolgorio m. ~ity n jolgorio m. ~y a (-ier, -iest) alegre. —adv (fam) muy

jolt /dʒɒlt/ vt sacudir. —vt (vehicle) traquetear. —n sacudida f

Jordan /dʒɔː'dən/ n Jordania f. ~ian a & n /-'deɪnɪən/ jordano (m)

jostle /'dʒɒsl/ vt/i empujar(se)

jot /dʒɒt/ n pizca f. —vt (pt jotted) apuntar. ~ter n bloc m

journal /'dʒɜːnl/ n (diary) diario m; (newspaper) periódico m; (magazine) revista f. ~ese /dʒɜː nəˈliːz/ n jerga f periodística. ~ism n periodismo m. ~ist n periodista m f

journey /'dʒɜːnɪ/ n viaje m. —vi viajar

jovial /'dʒəʊvɪəl/ a jovial

jowl /dʒaʊl/ n (jaw) quijada f; (cheek) mejilla f. cheek by ~ muy cerca

joy /dʒɔɪ/ n alegría f. ~ful a alegre. ~ride n paseo m en coche sin permiso del dueño. ~ous a alegre

jubilant /'dʒuːbɪlənt/ a jubiloso. ~tion /-'leɪʃn/ n júbilo m

jubilee /'dʒuːbɪliː/ n aniversario m especial

Judaism /'dʒuːdeɪɪzəm/ n judaísmo m

judder /'dʒʌdə(r)/ vi vibrar. —n vibración f

judge /dʒʌdʒ/ n juez m. —vt juzgar. ~ment n juicio m

judicial /dʒuː'dɪʃl/ a judicial. ~ry n magistratura f

judicious /dʒuː'dɪʃəs/ a juicioso

judo /'dʒuːdəʊ/ n judo m

jug /dʒʌg/ n jarra f

juggernaut /'dʒʌgənɔːt/ n (lorry) camión m grande

juggle /'dʒʌgl/ vt/i hacer juegos malabares (con). ~r n malabarista m & f

juic|e /dʒuːs/ n jugo m, zumo m. ~y a jugoso, zumoso; (story etc) (fam) picante

juke-box /'dʒuːkbɒks/ n tocadiscos m invar tragaperras

July /dʒuː'laɪ/ n julio m

jumble /'dʒʌmbl/ vt mezclar. —n (muddle) revoltijo m. ~ sale n venta f de objetos usados, mercadillo m

jumbo /'dʒʌmbəʊ/ a. ~ jet n jumbo m

jump /dʒʌmp/ vt/i saltar. ~ the gun obrar prematuramente. ~ the queue colarse. —vi saltar; (start) asustarse; (prices) alzarse. ~ at apresurarse a aprovechar. —n salto m; (start) susto m; (increase) aumento m

jumper /'dʒʌmpə(r)/ n jersey m; (dress, Amer) mandil m, falda f con peto

jumpy /'dʒʌmpɪ/ a nervioso

junction /'dʒʌŋkʃn/ n juntura f; (of roads) cruce m, entronque m (LAm); (rail) empalme m, entronque m (LAm)

juncture /'dʒʌŋktʃə(r)/ n momento m; (state of affairs) coyuntura f

June /dʒuːn/ n junio m

jungle /'dʒʌŋgl/ n selva f

junior /'dʒuːnɪə(r)/ a (in age) más joven (to que); (in rank) subalterno. —n menor m. ~ school n escuela f

junk /dʒʌŋk/ n trastos mpl viejos. —vt (fam) tirar

junkie /'dʒʌŋkɪ/ n (sl) drogadicto m

junk shop /'dʒʌŋkʃɒp/ n tienda f de trastos viejos

junta /'dʒʌntə/ n junta f

jurisdiction /dʒʊərɪs'dɪkʃn/ n jurisdicción f

jurisprudence /dʒʊərɪs'pruːdəns/ n jurisprudencia f

juror /'dʒʊərə(r)/ n jurado m

jury /'dʒʊərɪ/ n jurado m

just /dʒʌst/ a (fair) justo. —adv exactamente; (slightly) apenas; (only) sólo, solamente. ~ as tall tan alto (as como). ~ listen! ¡escucha! he has ~ left acaba de marcharse

justice /'dʒʌstɪs/ n justicia f. J~ of the Peace juez m de paz

justifiable /dʒʌstɪ'faɪəbl/ a justificable. ~iably adv con razón. ~ication /dʒʌstɪfɪ'keɪʃn/ n justificación f. ~y /'dʒʌstɪfaɪ/ vt justificar

justly /'dʒʌstlɪ/ adv con justicia

jut /dʒʌt/ vi (pt jutted). ~ out sobresalir

juvenile /'dʒuːvənaɪl/ a juvenil; (childish) infantil. —n joven m & f. ~ court n tribunal m de menores

juxtapose /dʒʌkstə'pəʊz/ vt yuxtaponer

K

kaleidoscope /kə'laɪdəskəʊp/ n calidoscopio m

kangaroo /kæŋgə'ruː/ n canguro m

kapok /'keɪpɒk/ n miraguano m

karate /kə'rɑːtɪ/ n karate m

kebab /kɪ'bæb/ n broqueta f

keel /kiːl/ n (of ship) quilla f. —vi. ~ over volcarse

keen /kiːn/ a (-er, -est) ⟨interest, feeling⟩ vivo; ⟨wind, mind, analysis⟩ penetrante; ⟨edge⟩ afilado; ⟨appetite⟩ bueno; ⟨eyesight⟩ agudo; ⟨eager⟩ entusiasta. be ~ on gustarle a uno. he's ~ on

Shostakovich le gusta Shostakovich. ~**ly** *adv* vivamente; (*enthusiastically*) con entusiasmo. ~**ness** *n* intensidad *f*; (*enthusiasm*) entusiasmo *m*.

keep /kiːp/ *vt* (*pt* **kept**) guardar; cumplir (*promise*); tener (*shop, animals*); mantener (*family*); observar (*rule*); (*celebrate*) celebrar; (*delay*) detener; (*prevent*) impedir. ~ (*food*) conservarse; (*remain*) quedarse. —*n* subsistencia *f*; (*of castle*) torreón *m*. **for** ~**s** (*fam*) para siempre. ~ **back** *vt* retener. —*vi* no acercarse. ~ **in** no dejar salir. ~ **in with** mantenerse en buenas relaciones con. ~ **out** no dejar entrar. ~ **up** mantener. ~ **up** (**with**) estar al día (en). ~**er** *n* guarda *m*

keeping /ˈkiːpɪŋ/ *n* cuidado *m*. **in** ~ **with** de acuerdo con

keepsake /ˈkiːpseɪk/ *n* recuerdo *m*

keg /keɡ/ *n* barrilete *m*

kennel /ˈkenl/ *n* perrera *f*

Kenya /ˈkenjə/ *n* Kenia *f*

kept /kept/ *see* **keep**

kerb /kɜːb/ *n* bordillo *m*

kerfuffle /kəˈfʌfl/ *n* (*fuss, fam*) lío *m*

kernel /ˈkɜːnl/ *n* almendra *f*; (*fig*) meollo *m*

kerosene /ˈkerəsiːn/ *n* queroseno *m*

ketchup /ˈketʃʌp/ *n* salsa *f* de tomate

kettle /ˈketl/ *n* hervidor *m*

key /kiː/ *n* llave *f*; (*of typewriter, piano etc*) tecla *f*. —*a* clave. —*vt*. ~ **up** excitar. ~**board** *n* teclado *m*. ~**hole** *n* ojo *m* de la cerradura. ~**note** *n* (*mus*) tónica *f*; (*speech*) idea *f* fundamental. ~**ring** *n* llavero *m*. ~**stone** *n* piedra *f* clave

khaki /ˈkɑːkiː/ *a* caqui

kibbutz /kɪˈbʊts/ *n* (*pl* -**im** /-iːm/ *or* -**es**) kibbutz *m*

kick /kɪk/ *vt* dar una patada a; (*animals*) tirar una coz a. —*vi* dar patadas; (*firearm*) dar culatazo. —*n* patada *f*; (*of animal*) coz *f*; (*of firearm*) culatazo *m*; (*thrill, fam*) placer *m*. ~ **out** (*fam*) echar a patadas. ~ **up** armar (*fuss etc*). ~**back** *n* culatazo *m*; (*payment*) soborno *m*. ~**off** *n* (*sport*) saque *m* inicial

kid /kɪd/ *n* (*young goat*) cabrito *m*; (*leather*) cabritilla *f*; (*child, sl*) chaval *m*. —*vt* (*pt* **kidded**) tomar el pelo a. —*vi* bromear

kidnap /ˈkɪdnæp/ *vt* (*pt* **kidnapped**) secuestrar. ~**ping** *n* secuestro *m*

kidney /ˈkɪdnɪ/ *n* riñón *m*. —*a* renal

kill /kɪl/ *vt* matar; (*fig*) acabar con. —*n* matanza *f*; (*in hunt*) pieza(s) *f*(*pl*). ~**er** *n* matador *m*; (*murderer*) asesino *m*. ~**ing** *n* matanza *f*; (*murder*) asesinato *m*. —*a* (*funny, fam*) para morirse de risa; (*tiring, fam*) agotador. ~**joy** *n* aguafiestas *m* & *f* invar

kiln /kɪln/ *n* horno *m*

kilo /ˈkiːləʊ/ *n* (*pl* -**os**) kilo *m*

kilogram(me) /ˈkɪləɡræm/ *n* kilogramo *m*

kilohertz /ˈkɪləhɜːts/ *n* kilohercio *m*

kilometre /ˈkɪləmiːtə(r)/ *n* kilómetro *m*

kilowatt /ˈkɪləwɒt/ *n* kilovatio *m*

kilt /kɪlt/ *n* falda *f* escocesa

kin /kɪn/ *n* parientes *mpl*. **next of** ~ pariente *m* más próximo, parientes *mpl* más próximos

kind[1] /kaɪnd/ *n* clase *f*. ~ **of** (*somewhat, fam*) un poco. **in** ~ en especie. **be two of a** ~ ser tal para cual

kind[2] /kaɪnd/ *a* amable

kindergarten /ˈkɪndəɡɑːtn/ *n* escuela *f* de párvulos

kind-hearted /kaɪnd'hɑ:tɪd/ a bondadoso

kindle /'kɪndl/ vt/i encender(se)

kind: ~**liness** n bondad f. ~**ly** a (-ier, -iest) bondadoso. —adv bondadosamente; (please) haga el favor de. ~**ness** n bondad f

kindred /'kɪndrɪd/ a emparentado. ~ **spirits** npl almas fpl afines

kinetic /kɪ'netɪk/ a cinético

king /kɪŋ/ n rey m

kingdom /'kɪŋdəm/ n reino m

kingpin /'kɪŋpɪn/ n (person) persona f clave; (thing) piedra f angular

king-size(d) /'kɪŋsaɪz(d)/ a extraordinariamente grande

kink /kɪŋk/ n (in rope) retorcimiento m; (fig) manía f. ~**y** a (fam) pervertido

kiosk /'ki:ɒsk/ n quiosco m. **telephone** ~ cabina f telefónica

kip /kɪp/ n (sl) sueño m. —vi (pt kipped) dormir

kipper /'kɪpə(r)/ n arenque m ahumado

kiss /kɪs/ n beso m. —vt/i besar(se)

kit /kɪt/ n avíos mpl; (tools) herramientos mpl. —vt (pt kitted). ~ **out** vt equipar de. ~**bag** n mochila f

kitchen /'kɪtʃɪn/ n cocina f. ~**ette** /kɪtʃɪ'net/ n cocina f pequeña. ~ **garden** n huerto m

kite /kaɪt/ n (toy) cometa f

kith /kɪθ/ n. ~ **and kin** n amigos mpl y parientes mpl

kitten /'kɪtn/ n gatito m

kitty /'kɪtɪ/ n (fund) fondo m común

kleptomaniac /kleptəʊ-'meɪnɪæk/ n cleptómano m

knack /næk/ n truco m

knapsack /'næpsæk/ n mochila f

knave /neɪv/ n (cards) sota f

knead /ni:d/ vt amasar

knee /ni:/ n rodilla f. ~**cap** n rótula f

kneel /ni:l/ vi (pt knelt). ~ (**down**) arrodillarse

knees-up /'ni:zʌp/ n (fam) baile m

knell /nel/ n toque m de difuntos

knelt /nelt/ see **kneel**

knew /nju:/ see **know**

knickerbockers /'nɪkəbɒkəz/ npl pantalón m bombacho

knickers /'nɪkəz/ npl bragas fpl

knick-knack /'nɪknæk/ n chuchería f

knife /naɪf/ n (pl knives) cuchillo m. —vt acuchillar

knight /naɪt/ n caballero m; (chess) caballo m. —vt conceder el título de Sir a. ~**hood** n título m de Sir

knit /nɪt/ vt (pt knitted or knit) tejer. —vi hacer punto. ~ **one's brow** fruncir el ceño. ~**ting** n labor f de punto. ~**wear** n artículos mpl de punto

knob /nɒb/ n botón m; (of door, drawer etc) tirador m. ~**bly** a nudoso

knock /nɒk/ vt golpear; (criticize) criticar. —vi golpear; (at door) llamar. —n golpe m. ~ **about** vt maltratar. —vi rodar. ~ **down** derribar; atropellar (person); rebajar (prices). ~ **off** vt hacer caer; (complete quickly, fam) despachar; (steal, sl) birlar. —vi (finish work, fam) terminar, salir del trabajo. ~ **out** (by blow) dejar sin conocimiento; (eliminate) eliminar; (tire) agotar. ~ **over** tirar; atropellar (person). ~ **up** preparar de prisa (meal etc). ~**down** a (price) de saldo. ~ n aldaba f. ~**kneed** a patizambo. ~**out** n (boxing) knock-out m

knot /nɒt/ n nudo m. —vt (pt knotted) anudar. ~**ty** a (nɒtɪ) a nudoso

know
443
lame

know /nɘʊ/ *vt* (*pt* **knew**) saber; (*be acquainted with*) conocer. — *vi* saber. —*n*. **be in the** ~ estar al tanto. ~ **about** entender de ⟨*cars etc*⟩. ~ **of** saber de. ~**all** *n*, ~**it-all** (*Amer*) *n* sabelotodo *m & f*. ~**how** *n* habilidad *f*. ~**ingly** *adv* deliberadamente

knowledge /'nɒlɪdʒ/ *n* conocimiento *m*; (*learning*) conocimientos *mpl*. ~**able** *a* informado

known /nɘʊn/ *see* **know**. —*a* conocido

knuckle /'nʌkl/ *n* nudillo *m*. — *vi*. ~ **under** someterse

Koran /kɘ'rɑːn/ *n* Corán *m*, Alcorán *m*

Korea /kɘ'rɪɘ/ *n* Corea *f*

kosher /'kɘʊʃɘ(r)/ *a* preparado según la ley judía

kowtow /kaʊ'taʊ/ *vi* humillarse (**to** ante)

kudos /'kjuːdɒs/ *n* prestigio *m*

L

lab /læb/ *n* (*fam*) laboratorio *m*

label /'leɪbl/ *n* etiqueta *f*. —*vt* (*pt* **labelled**) poner etiqueta a; (*fig, describe as*) describir como

laboratory /lɘ'bɒrɘtɘrɪ/ *n* laboratorio *m*

laborious /lɘ'bɔːrɪɘs/ *a* penoso

labour /'leɪbɘ(r)/ *n* trabajo *m*; (*workers*) mano *f* de obra. **in** ~ de parto. —*vi* trabajar. —*vt* insistir en

Labour /'leɪbɘ(r)/ *n* el partido *m* laborista. *a* laborista

laboured /'leɪbɘd/ *a* penoso

labourer /'leɪbɘrɘ(r)/ *n* obrero *m*; (*on farm*) labriego *m*

labyrinth /'læbɘrɪnθ/ *n* laberinto *m*

lace /leɪs/ *n* encaje *m*; (*of shoe*) cordón *m*, agujeta *f* (*Mex*). —*vt*

(*fasten*) atar. ~ **with** echar a ⟨*a drink*⟩

lacerate /'læsɘreɪt/ *vt* lacerar

lack /læk/ *n* falta *f*. **for** ~ **of** por falta de. —*vt* faltarle a uno. **be** ~**s money** carece de dinero. **be** ~**ing** faltar

lackadaisical /lækɘ'deɪzɪkl/ *a* indolente, apático

lackey /'lækɪ/ *n* lacayo *m*

laconic /lɘ'kɒnɪk/ *a* lacónico

lacquer /'lækɘ(r)/ *n* laca *f*

lad /læd/ *n* muchacho *m*

ladder /'lædɘ(r)/ *n* escalera *f* (de mano); (*in stocking*) carrera *f*. — *vt* hacer una carrera en. —*vi* hacerse una carrera

laden /'leɪdn/ *a* cargado (**with** de)

ladle /'leɪdl/ *n* cucharón *m*

lady /'leɪdɪ/ *n* señora *f*. **young** ~ señorita *f*. ~**bird** *n*, ~**bug** *n* (*Amer*) mariquita *f*. ~ **friend** *n* amiga *f*. ~**in-waiting** *n* dama *f* de honor. ~**like** *a* distinguido. ~**ship** *n* Señora *f*

lag[1] /læg/ *vi* (*pt* **lagged**). ~ (**behind**) retrasarse. —*n* (*interval*) intervalo *m*

lag[2] /læg/ *vt* (*pt* **lagged**) revestir ⟨*pipes*⟩

lager /'lɑːgɘ(r)/ *n* cerveza *f* dorada

laggard /'lægɘd/ *n* holgazán *m*

lagging /'lægɪŋ/ *n* revestimiento *m* calorífugo

lagoon /lɘ'guːn/ *n* laguna *f*

lah /lɑː/ *n* (*mus, sixth note of any musical scale*) la *m*

laid /leɪd/ *see* **lay**[1]

lain /leɪn/ *see* **lie**[1]

lair /leɘ(r)/ *n* guarida *f*

laity /'leɪɪtɪ/ *n* laicado *m*

lake /leɪk/ *n* lago *m*

lamb /læm/ *n* cordero *m*. ~**swool** *n* lana *f* de cordero

lame /leɪm/ *a* (**-er, -est**) cojo; (*excuse*) poco convincente. ~**ly** *adv* (*argue*) con poca convicción *f*

lament /lə'ment/ n lamento m. — vt/i lamentarse (de). ~able /'læməntəbl/ a lamentable

laminated /'læmɪneɪtɪd/ a laminado

lamp /læmp/ n lámpara f. ~post n farol m. ~shade n pantalla f

lance /lɑːns/ n lanza f. —vt (med) abrir con lanceta. ~corporal n cabo m interino

lancet /'lɑːnsɪt/ n lanceta f

land /lænd/ n tierra f; (country) país m; (plot) terreno m. —a terrestre; (breeze) de tierra; (policy, reform) agrario. —vt desembarcar; (obtain) conseguir; dar (blow); (put) meter. —vi (from ship) desembarcar; (aircraft) aterrizar; (fall) caer. ~ up ir a parar

landed /'lændɪd/ a hacendado

landing /'lændɪŋ/ n desembarque m; (aviat) aterrizaje m; (top of stairs) descanso m. ~stage n desembarcadero m

landlady /'lændleɪdɪ/ n propietaria f; (of inn) patrona f

land-locked /'lændlɒkt/ a rodeado de tierra

landlord /'lændlɔːd/ n propietario m; (of inn) patrón m

land: ~mark n punto m destacado. ~scape /'lændskeɪp/ n paisaje m. —vt ajardinar. ~slide n desprendimiento m de tierras; (pol) victoria f arrolladora

lane /leɪn/ n (path, road) camino m; (strip of road) carril m; (aviat) ruta f

language /'læŋgwɪdʒ/ n idioma m; (speech, style) lenguaje m

languid /'læŋgwɪd/ a lánguido. ~ish /'læŋgwɪʃ/ vi languidecer. ~or /'læŋgə(r)/ n languidez f

lank /læŋk/ a larguirucho; (hair) lacio. ~y /'læŋkɪ/ a (-ier, -iest) larguirucho

lantern /'læntən/ n linterna f

lap [1] /læp/ n regazo m

lap [2] /læp/ n (sport) vuelta f. —vt/i (pt lapped). ~ over traslapar(se)

lap [3] /læp/ vt (pt lapped). ~ up beber a lengüetazos; (fig) aceptar con entusiasmo. —vi (waves) chapotear

lapel /lə'pel/ n solapa f

lapse /læps/ vi (decline) degradarse; (expire) caducar; (time) transcurrir. ~ into recaer en. —n error m; (of time) intervalo m

larceny /'lɑːsənɪ/ n robo m

lard /lɑːd/ n manteca f de cerdo

larder /'lɑːdə(r)/ n despensa f

large /lɑːdʒ/ a (-er, -est) grande, (before singular noun) gran. —n. at ~ en libertad. ~ly adv en gran parte. ~ness f (gran) tamaño m

largesse /lɑː'ʒes/ n generosidad f

lark [1] /lɑːk/ n alondra f

lark [2] /lɑːk/ n broma f; (bit of fun) travesura f. —vi andar de juerga

larva /'lɑːvə/ n (pl -vae /-viː/) larva f

laryngitis /lærɪn'dʒaɪtɪs/ n laringitis f. ~x /'lærɪŋks/ n laringe f

lascivious /lə'sɪvɪəs/ a lascivo

laser /'leɪzə(r)/ n láser m

lash /læʃ/ vt azotar. ~ out (spend) gastar. ~ out against atacar. —n latigazo m; (eyelash) pestaña f

lashings /'læʃɪŋz/ npl. ~ of (cream etc, sl) montones de

lass /læs/ n muchacha f

lassitude /'læsɪtjuːd/ n lasitud f

lasso /læ'suː/ n (pl -os) lazo m

last [1] /lɑːst/ a último; (week etc) pasado. ~ **Monday** n el lunes pasado. **have the ~ word** decir la última palabra. **the ~ straw** n el colmo m. —adv por último; (most recently) la última vez. **he came ~** llegó el último. —n último m; (remainder) lo que queda. ~ **but one** penúltimo. **at (long) ~** en fin.

last[2] /lɑːst/ *vi* durar. ~ **out**
sobrevivir

last[3] /lɑːst/ *n* horma *f*

lasting /'lɑːstɪŋ/ *a* duradero

last: ~**ly** *adv* por último. ~ **night**
n anoche *m*

latch /lætʃ/ *n* picaporte *m*

late /leɪt/ *a* (-**er**, -**est**) (*not on
time*) tarde; (*recent*) reciente;
(*former*) antiguo, ex; ⟨*fruit*⟩ tardío; ⟨*hour*⟩ avanzado; (*deceased*)
difunto. **in** ~ **July** a fines de
julio. **the** ~ **Dr Phillips** el
difunto Dr. Phillips. —*adv* tarde.
of ~ últimamente. ~**ly** *adv*
últimamente. ~**ness** *n* (*delay*)
retraso *m*; (*of hour*) lo avanzado

latent /'leɪtnt/ *a* latente

lateral /'lætərəl/ *a* lateral

latest /'leɪtɪst/ *a* último. **at the** ~
a más tardar

lathe /leɪð/ *n* torno *m*

lather /'lɑːðə(r)/ *n* espuma *f*. —*vt*
enjabonar. —*vi* hacer espuma

Latin /'lætɪn/ *n* (*lang*) latín *m*. —
a latino

latitude /'lætɪtjuːd/ *n* latitud *m*

latrine /lə'triːn/ *n* letrina *f*

latter /'lætə(r)/ *a* último; (*of two*)
segundo. —*n*. **the** ~ éste *m*, ésta
f, éstos *mpl*, éstas *fpl*. ~-**day** *a*
moderno. ~**ly** *adv* últimamente

lattice /'lætɪs/ *n* enrejado *m*

laudable /'lɔːdəbl/ *a* laudable

laugh /lɑːf/ *vi* reír(se) (**at** de). —*n*
risa *f*. ~**able** *a* ridículo. ~**ing-
stock** *n* hazmerreír *m invar*.
~**ter** /'lɑːftə(r)/ *n* (*act*) risa *f*;
(*sound of laughs*) risas *fpl*

launch[1] /lɔːntʃ/ *vt* lanzar. —*n*
lanzamiento *m*. ~ (**out**) **into**
lanzarse a

launch[2] /lɔːntʃ/ *n* (*boat*) lancha *f*

launching pad /'lɔːntʃɪŋpæd/ *n*
plataforma *f* de lanzamiento

launder /'lɔːndə(r)/ *vt* lavar (*y
planchar*). ~**erette** *n* lavandería
f automática. ~**ress** *n* lavandera

f. ~**ry** /'lɔːndrɪ/ *n* (*place*) lavandería *f*; (*dirty clothes*) ropa *f*
sucia; (*clean clothes*) colada *f*

laurel /'lɒrəl/ *n* laurel *m*

lava /'lɑːvə/ *n* lava *f*

lavatory /'lævətərɪ/ *n* retrete *m*.
public ~ servicios *mpl*

lavender /'lævəndə(r)/ *n* lavanda
f

lavish /'lævɪʃ/ *a* ⟨*person*⟩ pro-
digo; (*plentiful*) abundante;
(*lush*) suntuoso. —*vt* prodigar.
~**ly** *adv* profusamente

law /lɔː/ *n* ley *f*; (*profession, subject of study*) derecho *m*. ~-
abiding *a* observante de la ley.
~ **and order** *n* orden *m* público.
~ **court** *n* tribunal *m*. ~**ful** *a*
(*permitted by law*) lícito; (*recognized by law*) legítimo. ~**fully**
adv legalmente. ~**less** *a* sin
leyes

lawn /lɔːn/ *n* césped *m*.
~-**mower** *n* cortacésped *f*. ~
tennis *n* tenis *m* (sobre hierba)

lawsuit /'lɔːsuːt/ *n* pleito *m*

lawyer /'lɔːjə(r)/ *n* abogado *m*

lax /læks/ *a* descuidado; ⟨*morals
etc*⟩ laxo

laxative /'læksətɪv/ *n* laxante *m*

laxity /'læksətɪ/ *n* descuido *m*

lay[1] /leɪ/ *vt* (*pt* **laid**) poner ⟨*incl
table, eggs*⟩; tender ⟨*trap*⟩;
formar ⟨*plan*⟩. ~ **hands on**
echar mano a. ~ **hold of**
agarrar. ~ **waste** asolar. ~
aside dejar a un lado. ~ **down**
dejar a un lado; imponer ⟨*condition*⟩. ~ **into** col dar una paliza a. ~ **off** *vt* despedir
⟨*worker*⟩. —*vi* (*fam*) terminar. ~
on (*provide*) proveer. ~ **out**
(*design*) disponer; (*display*)
exponer; desembolsar ⟨*money*⟩.
~ **up** (*store*) guardar; obligar a
guardar cama ⟨*person*⟩

lay[2] /leɪ/ *a* (*non-clerical*) laico;
⟨*opinion etc*⟩ profano

lay[3] /leɪ/ *see* **lie**

layabout /'leɪəbaʊt/ n holgazán m

lay-by /'leɪbaɪ/ n apartadero m

layer /'leɪə(r)/ n capa f

layette /leɪ'et/ n canastilla f

layman /'leɪmən/ n lego m

lay-off /'leɪɒf/ n paro m forzoso

layout /'leɪaʊt/ n disposición f

laze /leɪz/ vi holgazanear; ⟨relax⟩ descansar

laz|iness /'leɪzɪnɪs/ n pereza f. **∼y** a perezoso. **∼y-bones** n holgazán m

lb. abbr (pound) libra f

lead[1] /li:d/ vt (pt led) conducir; dirigir ⟨team⟩; llevar ⟨life⟩; ⟨induce⟩ inducir a. —vi (go first) ir delante; ⟨road⟩ ir, conducir; ⟨in cards⟩ salir. —n mando m; ⟨clue⟩ pista f; ⟨leash⟩ correa f; ⟨in theatre⟩ primer papel m; ⟨wire⟩ cable m; ⟨example⟩ ejemplo m. **in the ∼** en cabeza. **∼ away** llevar. **∼ up to** preparar el terreno para

lead[2] /led/ n plomo m; ⟨of pencil⟩ mina f. **∼en** /'ledn/ a de plomo

leader /'li:də(r)/ n jefe m; ⟨leading article⟩ editorial m. **∼ship** n dirección f

leading /'li:dɪŋ/ a principal; ⟨in front⟩ delantero. **∼ article** n editorial m

leaf /li:f/ n (pl leaves) hoja f. —vi. **∼ through** hojear

leaflet /'li:flɪt/ n folleto m

leafy /'li:fɪ/ a frondoso

league /li:g/ n liga f. **be in ∼ with** conchabarse con

leak /li:k/ n ⟨hole⟩ agujero m; ⟨of gas, liquid⟩ escape m; ⟨of information⟩ filtración f; ⟨in roof⟩ gotera f; ⟨in boat⟩ vía f de agua. —vi ⟨receptacle, gas, liquid⟩ salirse; ⟨information⟩ filtrarse; ⟨drip⟩ gotear; ⟨boat⟩ hacer agua. —vt dejar escapar; filtrar ⟨information⟩. **∼age** n = leak. **∼y** a ⟨receptacle⟩ agujereado;

⟨roof⟩ que tiene goteras; ⟨boat⟩ que hace agua

lean[1] /li:n/ vt (pt leaned or leant /lent/) apoyar. —vi inclinarse. **∼ against** apoyarse en. **∼ on** apoyarse en. **∼ out** asomarse (of a). **∼ over** inclinarse

lean[2] /li:n/ a (-er, -est) magro. —n carne f magra

leaning /'li:nɪŋ/ a inclinado. —n inclinación f

leanness /'li:nnɪs/ n ⟨of meat⟩ magrez f; ⟨of person⟩ flaqueza f

lean-to /'li:ntu:/ n colgadizo m

leap /li:p/ vi (pt leaped or leapt /lept/) saltar. —n salto m. **∼-frog** n salto m, saltacabrilla f. —vi (pt -frogged) jugar a saltacabrilla. **∼ year** n año m bisiesto

learn /lɜ:n/ vt/i (pt learned or learnt) aprender (to do a hacer). **∼ed** /'lɜ:nɪd/ a culto. **∼er** /'lɜ:nə(r)/ n principiante m; ⟨apprentice⟩ aprendiz m; ⟨student⟩ estudiante m & f. **∼ing** n saber m

lease /li:s/ n arriendo m. —vt arrendar

leash /li:ʃ/ n correa f

least /li:st/ a. **the ∼** ⟨smallest amount of⟩ mínimo; ⟨slightest⟩ menor; ⟨smallest⟩ más pequeño. —n lo menos. **at ∼** por lo menos. **not in the ∼** en absoluto. **—adv** menos

leather /'leðə(r)/ n piel f, cuero m

leave /li:v/ vt (pt left) dejar; ⟨depart from⟩ marcharse de. **∼ alone** dejar de tocar ⟨thing⟩; dejar en paz ⟨person⟩. **be left ⟨over⟩** quedar. —vi marcharse; ⟨train⟩ salir. —n permiso m. **∼ on** ⟨mil⟩ de permiso. **take one's ∼ of** despedirse de. **∼ out** omitir

leavings /'li:vɪŋz/ npl restos mpl

Lebanon /'lebənən/ n el Líbano m. **∼ese** /-'ni:z/ a & n libanés (m)

lecher /'letʃə(r)/ n libertino m. **~ous** a lascivo. **~y** n lascivia f

lectern /'lektɜːn/ n atril m; (in church) facistol m

lecture /'lektʃə(r)/ n conferencia f; (univ) clase f; (rebuke) sermón m. —vt/i dar una conferencia (a); (univ) dar clases (a); (rebuke) sermonear. **~r** n conferenciante m; (univ) profesor m

led /led/ see **lead**[1]

ledge /ledʒ/ n repisa f; (of window) antepecho m

ledger /'ledʒə(r)/ n libro m mayor

lee /liː/ n sotavento m, (fig) abrigo m

leech /liːtʃ/ n sanguijuela f

leek /liːk/ n puerro m

leer /'lɪə(r)/ vi. ~ (at) mirar impúdicamente. —n mirada f impúdica

leeway /'liːweɪ/ n deriva f; (fig, freedom of action) libertad f de acción. **make up ~** recuperar los atrasos

left[1] /left/ a izquierdo. —adv a la izquierda. —n izquierda f

left[2] /left/ see **leave**

left: **~-hand** a izquierdo. **~-handed** a zurdo. **~ist** n izquierdista m & f. **~ luggage** n consigna f. **~overs** npl restos mpl

left-wing /left'wɪŋ/ a izquierdista

leg /leg/ n pierna f; (of animal, furniture) pata f; (of pork) pernil m; (of lamb) pierna f; (of journey) etapa f. **on its last ~s** en las últimas

legacy /'legəsɪ/ n herencia f

legal /'liːgl/ a (permitted by law) lícito; (recognized by law) legítimo; (affairs etc) jurídico. **~ aid** n abogacía f de pobres. **~ity** /-'gælɪtɪ/ n legalidad f. **~ize** vt legalizar. **~ly** adv legalmente

legation /lɪ'geɪʃn/ n legación f

legend /'ledʒənd/ n leyenda f. **~ary** a legendario

leggings /'legɪŋz/ npl polainas fpl

legib|ility /ledʒəbɪlətɪ/ n legibilidad f. **~le** a legible. **~ly** a legiblemente

legion /'liːdʒən/ n legión f

legislat|e /'ledʒɪsleɪt/ vi legislar. **~ion** /-'leɪʃn/ n legislación f. **~ive** a legislativo. **~ure** /-eɪtʃə(r)/ n cuerpo m legislativo

legitima|cy /lɪ'dʒɪtɪməsɪ/ f legitimidad f. **~te** a legítimo

leisure /'leʒə(r)/ n ocio m. **at one's ~** cuando tenga tiempo. **~ly** adv sin prisa

lemon /'lemən/ n limón m. **~ade** /lemə'neɪd/ n (fizzy) gaseosa f (de limón); (still) limonada f

lend /lend/ vt (pt **lent**) prestar. **~ itself to** prestarse a. **~er** n prestador m; (moneylender) prestamista m & f. **~ing** n préstamo m. **~ing library** n biblioteca f de préstamo

length /leŋθ/ n largo m; (in time) duración f; (of cloth) largo m; (of road) tramo m. **at ~** (at last) por fin. **at (great) ~** detalladamente. **~en** /'leŋθən/ vt alargar. —vi alargarse. **~ways** adv a lo largo. **~y** a largo

lenien|cy /'liːnɪənsɪ/ n indulgencia f. **~t** a indulgente. **~tly** adv con indulgencia

lens /lenz/ n lente f. **~ contact ~es** npl lentillas fpl

lent /lent/ see **lend**

Lent /lent/ n cuaresma f

lentil /'lentl/ n (bean) lenteja f

Leo /'liːəʊ/ n (astr) Leo m

leopard /'lepəd/ n leopardo m

leotard /'liːətɑːd/ n leotardo m

lep|er /'lepə(r)/ n leproso m. **~rosy** /'leprəsɪ/ n lepra f

lesbian /'lezbɪən/ n lesbiana f. —a lesbiano

lesion /'liːʒn/ n lesión f

less /les/ a (in quantity) menos; (in size) menor. —adv & prep

menos. ~ than menos que;
(with numbers) menos de. —
menor m. ~ and ~ cada vez
menos. none the ~ sin
embargo. ~en /'lesn/ vt/i disminuir. ~er /'lesə(r)/ a menor

lesson /'lesn/ n clase f

lest /lest/ conj por miedo de que

let /let/ vt (pt let, pres p letting)
dejar; (lease) alquilar. ~ me do
it déjame hacerlo. —v aux. ~'s
go! ¡vamos!, ¡vámonos! ~'s see
(vamos) a ver. ~'s talk/drink
hablemos/bebamos. —n alquiler m. ~ down bajar; (deflate)
desinflar; (fig) defraudar. ~ go
soltar. ~ in dejar entrar. ~ off
disparar (gun); (cause to
explode) hacer explotar; hacer
estallar (firework); (excuse) perdonar. ~ off steam (fig)
desfogarse. ~ on (sl) revelar. ~
o.s. in for meterse en. ~ out
dejar salir. ~ through dejar
pasar. ~ up disminuir. ~down
n desilusión f

lethal /'li:θl/ a (dose, wound)
mortal; (weapon) mortífero

letharg|ic /lɪ'tɑ:dʒɪk/ a letárgico.
~y /'leθədʒɪ/ n letargo m

letter /'letə(r)/ n (of alphabet)
letra f; (written message) carta f.
~-bomb n carta f explosiva.
~-box n buzón m. ~-head n
membrete m. ~ing n letras fpl

lettuce /'letɪs/ n lechuga f

let-up /'letʌp/ n (fam) descanso m

leukaemia /lu:'ki:mɪə/ n leucemia f

level /'levl/ a (flat) llano; (on surface) horizontal; (in height) a
nivel; (in score) igual; (spoonful)
raso. —n nivel m. be on the ~
(fam) ser honrado. —vt (pt levelled) nivelar; (aim) apuntar. ~
crossing n paso m a nivel.
~-headed a juicioso

lever /'li:və(r)/ n palanca f. —vt
apalancar. ~age /'li:vərɪdʒ/ n
apalancamiento m

levity /'levətɪ/ n ligereza f

levy /'levɪ/ vt exigir (tax). —n
impuesto m

lewd /lu:d/ a (-er, -est) lascivo

lexicography /leksɪ'kɒgrəfɪ/ n
lexicografía f

lexicon /'leksɪkən/ n léxico m

liable /'laɪəbl/ a. be ~ to do
tener tendencia a hacer. ~ for
responsable de. ~ to susceptible
de; expuesto a (fine)

liability /laɪə'bɪlətɪ/ n responsabilidad f; (disadvantage, fam)
inconveniente m. **liabilities** npl
(debts) deudas fpl

liais|e /lɪ'eɪz/ vi hacer un enlace,
enlazar. ~on /lɪ'eɪzɒn/ n enlace
m; (love affair) lío m

liar /'laɪə(r)/ n mentiroso m

libel /'laɪbl/ n libelo m. —vt (pt
libelled) difamar (por escrito)

Liberal /'lɪbərəl/ a & n liberal (m
& f)

liberal /'lɪbərəl/ a liberal; (generous) generoso; (tolerant) tolerante. ~ly adv liberalmente;
(generously) generosamente;
(tolerantly) tolerantemente

liberat|e /'lɪbəreɪt/ vt liberar.
~ion /-'reɪʃn/ n liberación f

libertine /'lɪbəti:n/ n libertino m

liberty /'lɪbətɪ/ n libertad f. be at
~ to estar autorizado para. take
liberties tomarse libertades. take
the ~ of tomarse la libertad de

libido /lɪ'bi:dəʊ/ n (pl -os) libido
m

Libra /'li:brə/ n (astr) Libra f

librar|ian /laɪ'breərɪən/ n bibliotecario m. ~y /'laɪbrərɪ/ n biblioteca f

libretto /lɪ'bretəʊ/ n (pl -os)
libreto m

Libya /'lɪbɪə/ n Libia f. ~n a & n
libio (m)

lice /laɪs/ see louse

licence /'laɪsns/ n licencia f, permiso m; (fig, liberty) libertad f. ~

plate *n* (placa *f* de) matrícula *f*. **driving** ~ carné *m* de conducir

license /'laɪsns/ *vt* autorizar

licentious /laɪ'senʃəs/ *a* licencioso

lichen /'laɪkən/ *n* liquen *m*

lick /lɪk/ *vt* lamer; (*defeat, sl*) dar una paliza a. ~ **one's chops** relamerse. —*n* lametón *m*

licorice /'lɪkərɪs/ *n* (*Amer*) regaliz *m*

lid /lɪd/ *n* tapa *f*; (*of pan*) cobertera *f*

lido /'li:dəʊ/ *n* (*pl* -os) piscina *f*

lie¹ /laɪ/ *vi* (*pt* lay, *pp* lain, *pres p* lying) echarse; (*state*) estar echado; (*remain*) quedarse; (*be*) estar, encontrarse; (*in grave*) yacer. **be lying** estar echado. ~ **down** acostarse. ~ **low** quedarse escondido

lie² /laɪ/ *n* mentira *f*. —*vi* (*pt* lied, *pres p* lying) mentir. **give the** ~ **to** desmentir

lie-in /laɪ'ɪn/ *n*. **have a** ~**in** quedarse en la cama

lieu /lju:/ *n*. **in** ~ **of** en lugar de

lieutenant /leftenənt/ *n* (*mil*) teniente *m*

life /laɪf/ *n* (*pl* lives) vida *f*. ~**belt** *n* cinturón *m* salvavidas. ~**boat** *n* lancha *f* de salvamento; (*on ship*) bote *m* salvavidas. ~**buoy** *n* boya *f* salvavidas. ~ **cycle** *n* ciclo *m* vital. ~**guard** *n* bañero *m*. ~**jacket** *n* chaleco *m* salvavidas. ~**less** *a* sin vida. ~**like** *a* natural. ~**line** *n* cuerda *f* salvavidas; (*fig*) cordón *m* umbilical. ~**long** *a* de toda la vida. ~**size(d)** *a* de tamaño natural. ~**time** *n* vida *f*

lift /lɪft/ *vt* levantar; (*steal, fam*) robar. —*vi* (*fog*) disiparse. —*n* ascensor *m*, elevador *m* (*LAm*). **give a** ~ **to s.o.** llevar a uno en su coche, dar aventón a uno (*LAm*). ~**off** *n* (*aviat*) despegue *m*

ligament /'lɪgəmənt/ *n* ligamento *m*

light¹ /laɪt/ *n* luz *f*; (*lamp*) lámpara *f*, luz *f*; (*flame*) fuego *m*; (*headlight*) faro *m*. **bring to** ~ sacar a luz. **come to** ~ salir a luz. **have you got a** ~? ¿tienes fuego? **the** ~**s** *npl* (*auto, traffic signals*) el semáforo *m*. —*a* claro. —*vt* (*pt* lit *or* lighted) encender; (*illuminate*) alumbrar. ~ **up** *vt/i* iluminar(se)

light² /laɪt/ *a* (-er, -est) (*not heavy*) ligero

lighten¹ /'laɪtn/ *vt* (*make less heavy*) aligerar

lighten² /'laɪtn/ *vt* (*give light to*) iluminar; (*make brighter*) aclarar

lighter /'laɪtə(r)/ *n* (*for cigarettes*) mechero *m*

light-fingered /laɪt'fɪŋgəd/ *a* largo de uñas

light-headed /laɪt'hedɪd/ *a* (*dizzy*) mareado; (*frivolous*) casquivano

light-hearted /laɪt'hɑ:tɪd/ *a* alegre

lighthouse /'laɪthaʊs/ *n* faro *m*

lighting /'laɪtɪŋ/ *n* (*system*) alumbrado *m*; (*act*) iluminación *f*

light: ~**ly** *adv* ligeramente. ~**ness** *n* ligereza *f*

lightning /'laɪtnɪŋ/ *n* relámpago *m*. —*a* relámpago

lightweight /'laɪtweɪt/ *a* ligero. —*n* (*boxing*) peso *m* ligero

light-year /'laɪtjɪə(r)/ *n* año *m* luz

like¹ /laɪk/ *a* parecido. —*prep* como. —*conj* (*fam*) como. —*n* igual. **the** ~**s of you** la gente como tú

like² /laɪk/ *vt* gustarle (a uno). **I** ~ **chocolate** me gusta el chocolate. **I should** ~ quisiera. **they** ~ **swimming** (a ellos) les gusta

nadar. **would** you ~? ¿quieres?
~able a simpático. **~s** npl
gustos mpl

likelihood /ˈlaɪklɪhʊd/ n probabilidad f

likely a (-ier, -iest) probable. **he
is ~ to come** es probable que
venga. —adv probablemente.
not ~! ¡ni hablar!

like-minded /laɪkˈmaɪndɪd/ a.
be ~ tener las mismas opiniones

liken /ˈlaɪkən/ vt comparar

likeness /ˈlaɪknɪs/ n parecido m.
be a good ~ parecerse mucho

likewise /ˈlaɪkwaɪz/ adv (also)
también; (the same way) lo
mismo

liking /ˈlaɪkɪŋ/ n (for thing) afición f; (for person) simpatía f

lilac /ˈlaɪlək/ n lila f. —a color de
lila

lilt /lɪlt/ n ritmo m

lily /ˈlɪlɪ/ n lirio m. **~ of the valley** lirio m de los valles

limb /lɪm/ n miembro m. **out on
a ~** aislado

limber /ˈlɪmbə(r)/ vi. **~ up** hacer
ejercicios preliminares

limbo /ˈlɪmbəʊ/ n limbo m. **be in
~** (forgotten) estar olvidado

lime[1] /laɪm/ n (white substance)
cal f

lime[2] /laɪm/ n (fruit) lima f

lime[3] /laɪm/ n. **~-(tree)** (linden
tree) tilo m

limelight /ˈlaɪmlaɪt/ n. **be in the
~** estar muy a la vista

limerick /ˈlɪmərɪk/ n quintilla f
humorística

limestone /ˈlaɪmstəʊn/ n caliza f

limit /ˈlɪmɪt/ n límite m. —vt
limitar. **~ation** /-ˈteɪʃn/ n limitación f. **~ed** a limitado. **~ed
company** n sociedad f anónima

limousine /ˈlɪməziːn/ n limusina f

limp[1] /lɪmp/ vi cojear. —n cojera
f. **have a ~** cojear

limp[2] /lɪmp/ a (-er, -est) flojo

limpid /ˈlɪmpɪd/ a límpido

linctus /ˈlɪŋktəs/ n jarabe m
(para la tos)

line[1] /laɪn/ n línea f; (track) vía f;
(wrinkle) arruga f; (row) fila f; (of
poem) verso m; (rope) cuerda f;
(of goods) surtido m; (queue,
Amer) cola f. **in ~ with** de
acuerdo con. —vt (on paper etc)
rayar; bordear (streets etc). **~ up**
alinearse; (in queue) hacer cola

line[2] /laɪn/ vt forrar; (fill) llenar

lineage /ˈlɪnɪɪdʒ/ n linaje m

linear /ˈlɪnɪə(r)/ a lineal

linen /ˈlɪnɪn/ n (sheets etc) ropa f
blanca; (material) lino m

liner /ˈlaɪnə(r)/ n transatlántico
m

linesman /ˈlaɪnzmən/ n (football)
juez m de línea

linger /ˈlɪŋgə(r)/ vi tardar en
marcharse; (smells etc) persistir.
~ over dilatarse en

lingerie /ˈlænʒəri/ n ropa f interior, lencería f

lingo /ˈlɪŋgəʊ/ n (pl -os) idioma
m; (specialized vocabulary) jerga
f

linguist /ˈlɪŋgwɪst/ n (specialist
in languages) políglota m & f;
(specialist in linguistics) lingüista m & f. **~ic** /lɪŋˈgwɪstɪk/ a
lingüístico. **~ics** n lingüística f

lining /ˈlaɪnɪŋ/ n forro m; (auto,
of brakes) guarnición f

link /lɪŋk/ n (of chain) eslabón m;
(fig) lazo m. —vt eslabonar; (fig)
enlazar. **~ up with** reunirse
con. **~age** n enlace m

links /lɪŋks/ n invar campo m de
golf

lino /ˈlaɪnəʊ/ n (pl -os) linóleo m.
~leum /lɪˈnəʊliəm/ n linóleo m

lint /lɪnt/ n (med) hilas fpl; (fluff)
pelusa f

lion /ˈlaɪən/ n león m. **the ~'s
share** la parte f del león. **~ess** n
leona f

lionize /ˈlaɪənaɪz/ vt tratar como una celebridad

lip /lɪp/ n labio m; (edge) borde m. **pay ~ service** to aprobar de boquilla. **stiff upper ~** n imperturbabilidad f. **~read** vt/i leer en los labios. **~salve** n crema f para los labios. **~stick** n lápiz m de labios.

liquefy /ˈlɪkwɪfaɪ/ vt/i licuar(se)

liqueur /lɪˈkjʊə(r)/ n licor m

liquid /ˈlɪkwɪd/ a & n líquido (m)

liquidate /ˈlɪkwɪdeɪt/ vt liquidar. **~ion** /-ˈdeɪʃn/ n liquidación f

liquidize /ˈlɪkwɪdaɪz/ vt licuar. **~r** n licuadora f

liquor /ˈlɪkə(r)/ n bebida f alcohólica

liquorice /ˈlɪkərɪs/ n regaliz m

lira /ˈlɪərə/ n (pl **lire** /ˈlɪəreɪ/ or **liras**) lira f

lisle /laɪl/ n hilo m de Escocia

lisp /lɪsp/ n ceceo m. **speak with a ~** cecear. —vi cecear

lissom /ˈlɪsəm/ a flexible, ágil

list[1] /lɪst/ n lista f. —vt hacer una lista de; (enter in a list) inscribir

list[2] /lɪst/ vi (ship) escorar

listen /ˈlɪsn/ vi escuchar. **~ in (to)** escuchar. **~ to** escuchar. **~er** n oyente m & f

listless /ˈlɪstlɪs/ a apático

lit /lɪt/ see **light**[1]

litany /ˈlɪtənɪ/ n letanía f

literacy /ˈlɪtərəsɪ/ n capacidad f de leer y escribir

literal /ˈlɪtərəl/ a literal; (fig) prosaico. **~ly** adv al pie de la letra, literalmente

literary /ˈlɪtərərɪ/ a literario

literate /ˈlɪtərət/ a que sabe leer y escribir

literature /ˈlɪtərətʃə(r)/ n literatura f; (fig) impresos mpl

lithe /laɪð/ a ágil

lithograph /ˈlɪθəɡrɑːf/ n litografía f

litigation /lɪtɪˈɡeɪʃn/ n litigio m

litre /ˈliːtə(r)/ n litro m

litter /ˈlɪtə(r)/ n basura f; (of animals) camada f. —vt ensuciar; (scatter) esparcir. **~ed with** lleno de. **~bin** n papelera f

little /ˈlɪtl/ a pequeño; (not much) poco de. —n poco m. **a ~** un poco. **a ~ water** un poco de agua. —adv poco. **~ by ~** poco a poco. **~ finger** n meñique m

liturgy /ˈlɪtədʒɪ/ n liturgia f

live[1] /lɪv/ vt/i vivir. **~ down** lograr borrar. **~ it up** echar una cana al aire. **~ on** (feed o.s. on) vivir de; (continue) perdurar. **~ up to** vivir de acuerdo con; cumplir (a promise)

live[2] /laɪv/ a vivo; (wire) con corriente; (broadcast) en directo. **be a ~ wire** ser una persona enérgica

livelihood /ˈlaɪvlɪhʊd/ n sustento m

livel|iness /ˈlaɪvlɪnɪs/ n vivacidad f. **~y** a (-ier, -iest) vivo

liven /ˈlaɪvn/ vt/i. **~ up** animar(se); (cheer up) alegrar(se)

liver /ˈlɪvə(r)/ n hígado m

livery /ˈlɪvərɪ/ n librea f

livestock /ˈlaɪvstɒk/ n ganado m

livid /ˈlɪvɪd/ a lívido; (angry, fam) furioso

living /ˈlɪvɪŋ/ a vivo. —n vida f. **~room** n cuarto m de estar, cuarto m de estancia (LAm)

lizard /ˈlɪzəd/ n lagartija f; (big) lagarto m

llama /ˈlɑːmə/ n llama f

load /ləʊd/ n (incl elec) carga f; (quantity) cantidad f; (weight, strain) peso m. —vt cargar. **~ed** a (incl dice) cargado; (wealthy, sl) muy rico. **~s of** (fam) montones de

loaf[1] /ləʊf/ n (pl **loaves**) pan m; (stick of bread) barra f

loaf[2] /ləʊf/ vi. **~ (about)** holgazanear. **~er** n holgazán m

loam /ləʊm/ n marga f

loan /ləʊn/ n préstamo m. **on ~** prestado. —vt prestar

loath /ləʊθ/ a poco dispuesto (**to** a)

loath|e /ləʊð/ vt odiar. **~ing** n odio m (**of** a). **~some** a odioso

lobby /'lɒbɪ/ n vestíbulo m; (pol) grupo m de presión. —vt hacer presión sobre

lobe /ləʊb/ n lóbulo m

lobster /'lɒbstə(r)/ n langosta f

local /'ləʊkl/ a local. —n (pub, fam) bar m. **the ~s** los vecinos mpl

locale /ləʊ'kɑːl/ n escenario m

local government /ləʊkl 'gʌvənmənt/ n gobierno m municipal

locality /ləʊ'kælətɪ/ n localidad f

localized /'ləʊkəlaɪzd/ a localizado

locally /'ləʊkəlɪ/ adv localmente; (nearby) en la localidad

locate /ləʊ'keɪt/ vt (situate) situar; (find) encontrar

location /ləʊ'keɪʃn/ n colocación f; (place) situación f. **on ~** fuera del estudio. **to film on ~ in Andalusia** rodar en Andalucía

lock[1] /lɒk/ n (**of** door etc) cerradura f; (on canal) esclusa f. —vt/i cerrar(se) con llave. **~ in** encerrar. **~ out** cerrar la puerta a. **~ up** encerrar

lock[2] /lɒk/ n (of hair) mechón m. **~s** npl pelo m

locker /'lɒkə(r)/ n armario m

locket /'lɒkɪt/ n medallón m

lock-out /'lɒkaʊt/ n lock-out m

locksmith /'lɒksmɪθ/ n cerrajero m

locomotion /ləʊkə'məʊʃn/ n locomoción f

locomotive /ləʊkə'məʊtɪv/ n locomotora f

locum /'ləʊkəm/ n interino m

locust /'ləʊkəst/ n langosta f

lodge /lɒdʒ/ n (in park) casa f del guarda; (of porter) portería f. —vt alojar; presentar (complaint); depositar (money). —vi alojarse. **~r** /-ə(r)/ n huésped m

lodgings /'lɒdʒɪŋz/ n alojamiento m; (room) habitación f

loft /lɒft/ n desván m

lofty /'lɒftɪ/ a (-ier, -iest) elevado; (haughty) altanero

log /lɒg/ n (of wood) leño m; (naut) cuaderno m de bitácora. **sleep like a ~** dormir como un lirón. —vt (pt logged) apuntar; (travel) recorrer

logarithm /'lɒgərɪðm/ n logaritmo m

log-book /'lɒgbʊk/ n cuaderno m de bitácora; (aviat) diario m de vuelo

loggerheads /'lɒgəhedz/ npl. be **at ~** with estar a matar con

logic /'lɒdʒɪk/ a lógica f. **~al** a lógico. **~ally** adv lógicamente

logistics /lə'dʒɪstɪks/ n logística f

logo /'ləʊgəʊ/ n (pl -os) logotipo m

loin /lɔɪn/ n (culin) solomillo m. **~s** npl ijadas fpl

loiter /'lɔɪtə(r)/ vi holgazanear

loll /lɒl/ vi repantigarse

lollipop /'lɒlɪpɒp/ n (boiled sweet) pirulí m. **~y** n (iced) polo m; (money, sl) dinero m

London /'lʌndən/ n Londres m. —a londinense. **~er** n londinense m & f

lone /ləʊn/ a solitario. **~ly** /'ləʊnlɪ/ a (-ier, -iest) solitario. **feel ~ly** sentirse muy solo. **~r** /'ləʊnə(r)/ n solitario m. **~some** a solitario

long[1] /lɒŋ/ a (-er, -est) largo. **a ~ time** mucho tiempo. **how ~ is it?** ¿cuánto tiene de largo? **in the ~ run** a la larga. —adv largo/mucho tiempo. **as ~ as** (while) mientras; (provided that) con tal que (+ subjunctive).

before ~ dentro de poco. **so** ~!
¡hasta luego! **so** ~ **as** (*provided
that*) con tal que (+ *subjunctive*)
long² /lɒŋ/ *vi.* ~ **for** anhelar
long-distance /lɒŋ'dɪstns/ *a* de
larga distancia. ~ **(tele)phone
call** *n* conferencia *f*
longer /'lɒŋgə(r)/ *adv.* **no** ~**er** ya
no
longevity /lɒn'dʒevɪtɪ/ *n* longevidad *f*
long: ~ **face** *n* cara *f* triste.
~**hand** *n* escritura *f* a mano. ~
johns *npl* (*fam*) calzoncillos *mpl*
largos. ~ **jump** *n* salto *m* de
longitud
longing /'lɒŋɪŋ/ *n* anhelo *m*,
ansia *f*
longitude /'lɒŋgɪtjuːd/ *n* longitud *f*
long: ~**playing record** *n* elepé
m. ~**range** *a* de gran alcance.
~**sighted** *a* présbita. ~
standing *a* de mucho tiempo. ~
suffering *a* sufrido. ~**term**
a a largo plazo. ~ **wave** *n* onda *f*
larga. ~**winded** *a* (*speaker etc*)
prolijo
loo /luː/ *n* (*fam*) servicios *mpl*
look /lʊk/ *vt* mirar; (*seem*) parecer; representar ⟨*age*⟩. —*vi*
mirar; (*seem*) parecer; (*search*)
buscar. ~ *n* mirada *f*; (*appearance*) aspecto *m*. ~ **after** ocuparse de; cuidar ⟨*person*⟩. ~ **at**
mirar. ~ **down** on despreciar.
~ **for** buscar. ~ **forward** to
esperar con ansia. ~ **in on** pasar
por casa de. ~ **into** investigar.
~ **like** (*resemble*) parecerse a. ~
on to ⟨*room, window*⟩ dar a. ~
out tener cuidado. ~ **out for**
buscar; (*watch*) tener cuidado
con. ~ **round** volver la cabeza.
~ **through** hojear. ~ **up** buscar
⟨*word*⟩; (*visit*) ir a ver. ~ **up** to
respetar. ~**er-on** *n* espectador
m. ~**ing-glass** *n* espejo *m*.
~**out** *n* (*mil*) atalaya *f*; (*person*)

vigía *m.* ~**s** *npl* belleza *f.* **good**
~**s** *mpl* belleza *f*
loom¹ /luːm/ *n* telar *m*
loom² /luːm/ *vi* aparecerse
loony /'luːnɪ/ *a & n* (*sl*) chiflado
(*m*) (*fam*), loco (*m*). ~ **bin** *n* (*sl*)
manicomio *m*
loop /luːp/ *n* lazo *m.* —*vt* hacer
presilla con
loophole /'luːphəʊl/ *n* (*in rule*)
escapatoria *f*
loose /luːs/ *a* (-**er**, -**est**) (*untied*)
suelto; (*not tight*) flojo; (*inexact*)
vago; (*immoral*) inmoral; (*not
packed*) suelto. **be at a** ~ **end**,
be at ~ **ends** (*Amer*) no tener
nada que hacer. ~**ly** *adv* sueltamente; (*roughly*) aproximadamente. ~**n** /'luːsn/ *vt*
(*slacken*) aflojar; (*untie*) desatar
loot /luːt/ *n* botín *m.* —*vt* saquear.
~**er** *n* saqueador *m.* ~**ing** *n*
saqueo *m*
lop /lɒp/ *vt* (*pt* lopped) ~ **off**
cortar
lop-sided /lɒp'saɪdɪd/ *a* ladeado
loquacious /ləʊ'kweɪʃəs/ *a*
locuaz
lord /lɔːd/ *n* señor *m*; (*British
title*) lord *m.* (**good**) **L~**! ¡Dios
mío! **the L~** el Señor *m.* (**the
House of**) **L~s** la Cámara *f* de
los Lores. ~**ly** *a* señorial;
(*haughty*) altivo. ~**ship** *n*
señoría *f*
lore /lɔː(r)/ *n* tradiciones *fpl*
lorgnette /lɔː'njet/ *n* impertinentes *mpl*
lorry /'lɒrɪ/ *n* camión *m*
lose /luːz/ *vt/i* (*pt* lost) perder.
~**r** *n* perdedor *m*
loss /lɒs/ *n* pérdida *f.* **be at a** ~
estar perplejo. **be at a** ~ **for
words** no encontrar palabras.
be at a ~ to no saber cómo
lost /lɒst/ *see* lose. —*a* perdido.
~ **property** *n*, ~ **and found**
(*Amer*) *n* oficina *f* de objetos perdidos. **get** ~ perderse

lot /lɒt/ n (fate) suerte f; (at auction) lote m; (land) solar m. **a ~ (of)** muchos. **quite a ~ of** (fam) bastante. **~s (of)** (fam) muchos. **the ~** todos mpl

lotion /'ləʊʃn/ n loción f

lottery /'lɒtəri/ n lotería f

lotto /'lɒtəʊ/ n lotería f

lotus /'ləʊtəs/ n (pl -uses) loto m

loud /laʊd/ a (-er, -est) fuerte; (noisy) ruidoso; (gaudy) chillón. **out ~** en voz alta. **~ hailer** n megáfono m. **~ly** adv (speak etc) en voz alta; (noisily) ruidosamente. **~speaker** n altavoz m

lounge /laʊndʒ/ vi repantigarse. —n salón m. **~ suit** n traje m de calle

louse /laʊs/ n (pl lice) piojo m

lousy /'laʊzi/ a (-ier, -iest) piojoso; (bad, sl) malísimo

lout /laʊt/ n patán m

lovable /'lʌvəbl/ a adorable

love /lʌv/ n amor m; (tennis) cero m. **be in ~ with** estar enamorado de. **fall in ~ with** enamorarse de. —vt querer (person); gustarle mucho a uno, encantarle a uno (things). **I ~ milk** me encanta la leche. **~ affair** n amores mpl

lovely /'lʌvli/ a (-ier, -iest) hermoso; (delightful, fam) precioso. **have a ~ time** divertirse

lover /'lʌvə(r)/ n amante m & f

lovesick /'lʌvsik/ a atortolado

loving /'lʌviŋ/ a cariñoso

low[1] /ləʊ/ a & adv (-er, -est) bajo. —n (low pressure) área f de baja presión

low[2] /ləʊ/ vi mugir

lowbrow /'ləʊbraʊ/ a poco culto

low-cut /'ləʊkʌt/ a escotado

low-down /'ləʊdaʊn/ a bajo. —n (sl) informes mpl

lower /'ləʊə(r)/ a & adv see **low**[2]. —vt bajar. **o.s.** envilecerse

low-key /'ləʊ'ki:/ a moderado

lowlands /'ləʊləndz/ npl tierra f baja

lowly /'ləʊli/ a (-ier, -iest) humilde

loyal /'lɔɪəl/ a leal. **~ly** adv lealmente. **~ty** n lealtad f

lozenge /'lɒzɪndʒ/ n (shape) rombo m; (tablet) pastilla f

LP /el'pi:/ abbr (long-playing record) elepé m

Ltd /'lɪmɪtɪd/ abbr (Limited) S.A., Sociedad Anónima

lubricant /'lu:brɪkənt/ n lubricante m. **~te** /-'keɪt/ vt lubricar. **~tion** /-'keɪʃn/ n lubricación f

lucid /'lu:sɪd/ a lúcido. **~ity** /-'sɪdətɪ/ n lucidez f

luck /lʌk/ n suerte f. **bad ~** n mala suerte f. **~ily** /'lʌkɪlɪ/ adv afortunadamente. **~y** a (-ier, -iest) afortunado

lucrative /'lu:krətɪv/ a lucrativo

lucre /'lu:kə(r)/ n (pej) dinero m. **filthy ~** vil metal m

ludicrous /'lu:dɪkrəs/ a ridículo

lug /lʌg/ vt (pt lugged) arrastrar

luggage /'lʌgɪdʒ/ n equipaje m. **~-rack** n rejilla f. **~-van** n furgón m

lugubrious /lu:'gu:brɪəs/ a lúgubre

lukewarm /'lu:kwɔ:m/ a tibio

lull /lʌl/ vt (soothe, send to sleep) adormecer; (calm) calmar. —n periodo m de calma

lullaby /'lʌləbaɪ/ n canción f de cuna

lumbago /lʌm'beɪgəʊ/ n lumbago m

lumber /'lʌmbə(r)/ n trastos mpl viejos; (wood) maderos mpl. —vt. **~ s.o. with** hacer que uno cargue con. **~jack** n leñador m

luminous /'lu:mɪnəs/ a luminoso

lump[1] /lʌmp/ n protuberancia f; (in liquid) grumo m; (of sugar)

terrón m; (in throat) nudo m. —
vt. ∼ **together** agrupar
lump² /lʌmp/ vt. ∼ **it** (fam)
aguantarlo
lump: ∼ **sum** n suma f global. ∼**y**
a ⟨sauce⟩ grumoso; (bumpy) cubierto de protuberancias
lunacy /'luːnəsi/ n locura f
lunar /'luːnə(r)/ a lunar
lunatic /'luːnətik/ n loco m
lunch /lʌntʃ/ n comida f,
almuerzo m. —vi comer
luncheon /'lʌntʃən/ n comida f,
almuerzo m. ∼ **meat** n carne f
en lata. ∼ **voucher** n vale m de
comida
lung /lʌŋ/ n pulmón m
lunge /lʌndʒ/ n arremetida f
lurch¹ /lɜːtʃ/ vi tambalearse
lurch² /lɜːtʃ/ n. **leave in the** ∼
dejar en la estacada
lure /ljʊə(r)/ vt atraer. —n
(attraction) atractivo m
lurid /'ljʊərɪd/ a chillón; (shocking) espeluznante
lurk /lɜːk/ vi esconderse; (in
ambush) estar al acecho; (prowl)
rondar
luscious /'lʌʃəs/ a delicioso
lush /lʌʃ/ a exuberante. —n
(Amer, sl) borracho m
lust /lʌst/ n lujuria f; (fig) ansia
f. —vi. ∼ **after** codiciar. ∼**ful** a
lujurioso
lustre /'lʌstə(r)/ n lustre m
lusty /'lʌsti/ a (-ier, -iest) fuerte
lute /luːt/ n laúd m
Luxemburg /'lʌksəmbɜːg/ n Luxemburgo m
luxuriant /lʌg'zjʊərɪənt/ a exuberante
luxur|ious /lʌg'zjʊərɪəs/ a
lujoso. ∼**y** /'lʌkʃəri/ n lujo m. —
a de lujo
lye /laɪ/ n lejía f
lying /'laɪɪŋ/ see **lie¹**, **lie²**. —n
mentiras fpl
lynch /lɪntʃ/ vt linchar
lynx /lɪŋks/ n lince m

lyre /'laɪə(r)/ n lira f
lyric /'lɪrɪk/ a lírico. ∼**al** a lírico.
∼**ism** /-sɪzəm/ n lirismo m. ∼**s**
npl letra f

M

MA abbr (Master of Arts) Master
m, grado m universitario entre
el de licenciado y doctor
mac /mæk/ n (fam) impermeable
m
macabre /məˈkɑːbrə/ a macabro
macaroni /mækəˈrəʊni/ n maca-
rrones mpl
macaroon /mækəˈruːn/ n mostachón m
mace¹ /meɪs/ n (staff) maza f
mace² /meɪs/ n (spice) macis f
Mach /mɑːk/ n. ∼ **(number)** n
(número m de) Mach m
machiavellian /mækɪəˈveliən/ a
maquiavélico
machinations /mækɪˈneɪʃnz/ npl
maquinaciones fpl
machine /məˈʃiːn/ n máquina
f. —vt (sew) coser a máquina;
(tec) trabajar a máquina. ∼**gun**
n ametralladora f. ∼**ry** /məˈʃiː-
nəri/ n maquinaria f; (working
parts, fig) mecanismo m. ∼ **tool**
n máquina f herramienta
machinist /məˈʃiːnɪst/ n maquinista m & f
mach|ismo /mæˈtʃɪzməʊ/ n
machismo m. ∼**o** a macho
mackerel /'mækrəl/ n invar
(fish) caballa f
mackintosh /'mækɪntɒʃ/ n
impermeable m
macrobiotic /mækrəʊbaɪˈɒtɪk/ a
macrobiótico
mad /mæd/ a (madder, mad-
dest) loco; (foolish) insensato;
⟨dog⟩ rabioso; (angry, fam)
furioso. **be** ∼ **about** estar loco

por. **like** ~ como un loco; (*a lot*) muchísimo

Madagascar /mædə'gæskə(r)/ *n* Madagascar *m*

madam /'mædəm/ *n* señora *f*; (*unmarried*) señorita *f*

madcap /'mædkæp/ *a* atolondrado. —*n* locuelo *m*

madden /'mædn/ *vt* (*make mad*) enloquecer; (*make angry*) enfurecer

made /meɪd/ *see* **make**. ~ **to measure** hecho a la medida

Madeira /mə'dɪərə/ *n* (*wine*) vino *m* de Madera

mad: ~**house** *n* manicomio *m*. ~**ly** *adv* (*interested, in love etc*) locamente; (*frantically*) como un loco. ~**man** *n* loco *m*. ~**ness** *n* locura *f*

madonna /mə'dɒnə/ *n* Virgen *f* María

madrigal /'mædrɪgl/ *n* madrigal *m*

maelstrom /'meɪlstrəm/ *n* remolino *m*

maestro /'maɪstrəʊ/ *n* (*pl* **maestri** /-striː/ *or* **os**) maestro *m*

Mafia /'mæfɪə/ *n* mafia *f*

magazine /mægə'ziːn/ *n* revista *f*; (*of gun*) recámara *f*

magenta /mə'dʒentə/ *a* rojo purpúreo

maggot /'mægət/ *n* gusano *m*. ~**y** *a* agusanado

Magi /'meɪdʒaɪ/ *npl*. **the** ~ los Reyes *mpl* Magos

magic /'mædʒɪk/ *n* magia *f*. —*a* mágico. ~**al** *a* mágico. ~**ian** /mə'dʒɪʃn/ *n* mago *m*

magisterial /mædʒɪ'stɪərɪəl/ *a* magistral; (*imperious*) autoritario

magistrate /'mædʒɪstreɪt/ *n* magistrado *m*, juez *m*

magnanim|ity /mægnə'nɪmətɪ/ *n* magnanimidad *f*. ~**ous** /-'næn ɪməs/ *a* magnánimo

magnate /'mægneɪt/ *n* magnate *m*

magnesia /mæg'niːʒə/ *n* magnesia *f*

magnet /'mægnɪt/ *n* imán *m*. ~**ic** /-'netɪk/ *a* magnético. ~**ism** *n* magnetismo *m*. ~**ize** *vt* magnetizar

magnificen|ce /mæg'nɪfɪsns/ *a* magnificencia *f*. ~**t** *a* magnífico

magnif|ication /mægnɪfɪ'keɪʃn/ *n* aumento *m*. ~**ier** /-'faɪə(r)/ *n* lupa *f*, lente *f* de aumento. ~**y** /-'faɪ/ *vt* aumentar. ~**ying-glass** *n* lupa *f*, lente *f* de aumento

magnitude /'mægnɪtjuːd/ *n* magnitud *f*

magnolia /mæg'nəʊlɪə/ *n* magnolia *f*

magnum /'mægnəm/ *n* botella *f* de litro y medio

magpie /'mægpaɪ/ *n* urraca *f*

mahogany /mə'hɒgənɪ/ *n* caoba *f*

maid /meɪd/ *n* (*servant*) criada *f*; (*girl, old use*) doncella *f*. **old** ~ solterona *f*

maiden /'meɪdn/ *n* doncella *f*. — *a* (*aunt*) soltera; (*voyage*) inaugural. ~**hood** /n doncellez *f*, virginidad *f*, soltería *f*. ~**ly** *adv* virginal. ~ **name** *n* apellido de soltera

mail[1] /meɪl/ *n* correo *m*; (*letters*) cartas *fpl*. —*a* postal, de correos. —*vt* (*post*) echar al correo; (*send*) enviar por correo

mail[2] /meɪl/ *n* (*armour*) (cota *f* de) malla *f*

mail: ~**ing-list** *n* lista *f* de direcciones. ~**man** *n* (*Amer*) cartero *m*. ~**order** *n* venta *f* por correo

maim /meɪm/ *vt* mutilar

main /meɪn/ *n*. (**water/gas**) ~ cañería *f* principal. **in the** ~ en su mayor parte. **the** ~**s** *npl* (*elec*) la red *f* eléctrica. —*a* principal. **a** ~ **road** *n* una carretera *f*. ~**land**

n continente *m*. ~ly *adv* principalmente. ~spring *n* muelle *m* real; (*fig, motive*) móvil *m* principal. ~stay *n* sostén *m* principal. ~stream *n* corriente *f* principal. ~ **street** *n* calle *f* principal

maintain /meɪnˈteɪn/ *vt* mantener

maintenance /ˈmeɪntənəns/ *n* mantenimiento *m*; (*allowance*) pensión *f* alimenticia

maisonette /meɪzəˈnet/ *n* (*small house*) casita *f*; (*part of house*) dúplex *m*

maize /meɪz/ *n* maíz *m*

majestic /məˈdʒestɪk/ *a* majestuoso

majesty /ˈmædʒəstɪ/ *n* majestad *f*

major /ˈmeɪdʒə(r)/ *a* mayor. **a ~ road** una calle *f* prioritaria. ~ *n* comandante *m*. ~*vi.* **~ in** (*univ, Amer*) especializarse en

Majorca /məˈjɔːkə/ *n* Mallorca *f*

majority /məˈdʒɒrətɪ/ *n* mayoría *f*. **the ~ of people** la mayoría *f* de la gente. ~*a* mayoritario

make /meɪk/ *vt/i* (*pt* **made**) hacer; (*manufacture*) fabricar; ganar (*money*); tomar (*decision*); llegar a (*destination*). ~ **s.o. do sth** obligar a uno a hacer algo. **be made of** estar hecho de. **I cannot ~ anything of it** no me lo explico. **I ~ it two o'clock** yo tengo las dos. ~*n* fabricación *f*; (*brand*) marca *f*. ~ **as if to** estar a punto de. ~ **believe** fingir. ~ **do** (*manage*) arreglarse. ~ **do with** (*content o.s.*) contentarse con. ~ **for** dirigirse a. ~ **good** *vi* tener éxito. ~*vt* compensar; (*repair*) reparar. ~ **it** llegar; (*succeed*) tener éxito. ~ **it up** (*become reconciled*) hacer las paces. ~ **much of** dar mucha importancia a. ~ **off** escaparse (*with con*). ~ **out** *vt* distinguir; (*understand*) entender; (*draw*

up) extender; (*assert*) dar a entender. ~*vi* arreglárselas. ~ **over** ceder (**to a**). ~ **up** formar; (*prepare*) preparar; inventar (*story*); (*compensate*) compensar. ~*vi* hacer las paces. ~ **up (one's face)** maquillarse. ~ **up for** compensar; recuperar (*time*). ~ **up to** congraciarse con. ~**believe** *a* fingido, simulado. ~*n* ficción *f*

maker /ˈmeɪkə(r)/ *n* fabricante *m* & *f*. **the M~** el Hacedor *m*, el Creador *m*

makeshift /ˈmeɪkʃɪft/ *n* expediente *m*. ~*a* (*temporary*) provisional; (*improvised*) improvisado

make-up /ˈmeɪkʌp/ *n* maquillaje *m*

makeweight /ˈmeɪkweɪt/ *n* complemento *m*

making /ˈmeɪkɪŋ/ *n.* **be the ~ of** ser la causa del éxito de. **he has the ~s of** tiene madera de. **in the ~** en vías de formación

maladjusted /mæləˈdʒʌstɪd/ *a* inadaptado. ~**ment** *n* inadaptación *f*

maladministration /mælədmɪnɪˈstreɪʃn/ *n* mala administración *f*

malady /ˈmælədɪ/ *n* enfermedad *f*

malaise /mæˈleɪz/ *n* malestar *m*

malaria /məˈleərɪə/ *n* paludismo *m*

Malay /məˈleɪ/ *a* & *n* malayo (*m*). ~**sia** *n* Malasia *f*

male /meɪl/ *a* masculino; (*bot, tec*) macho. ~*n* macho *m*; (*man*) varón *m*

malefactor /ˈmælɪfæktə(r)/ *n* malhechor *m*

malevolen|ce /məˈlevələns/ *n* malevolencia *f*. ~**t** *a* malévolo

malform|ation /mælfɔːˈmeɪʃn/ *n* malformación *f*. ~**ed** *a* deforme

malfunction /mælˈfʌŋkʃn/ *n* funcionamiento *m* defectuoso. ~*vi* funcionar mal

malic|e /'mælɪs/ n rencor m.
bear s.o. ~e guardar rencor a
uno. ~ious /mə'lɪʃəs/ a malévolo. ~iously adv con
malevolencia

malign /mə'laɪn/ a maligno. —vt
calumniar

malignan|cy /mə'lɪgnənsɪ/ n
malignidad f. ~t a maligno

malinger /mə'lɪŋgə(r)/ vi fingirse
enfermo. ~er n enfermo m
fingido

malleable /'mælɪəbl/ a maleable

mallet /'mælɪt/ n mazo m

malnutrition /mælnju:'trɪʃn/ n
desnutrición f

malpractice /mæl'præktɪs/ n
falta f profesional

malt /mɔ:lt/ n malta f

Malt|a /'mɔ:ltə/ n Malta f. ~ese
/-'ti:z/ a & n maltés (m)

maltreat /mæl'tri:t/ vt maltratar.
~ment n maltrato m

malt whisky /mɔ:lt'wɪskɪ/ n
güisqui m de malta

mammal /'mæml/ n mamífero m

mammoth /'mæməθ/ n mamut
m. —a gigantesco

man /mæn/ n (pl men) hombre
m; (in sports team) jugador m;
(chess) pieza f. ~ in the street
hombre m de la calle. ~ to ~ de
hombre a hombre. —vt (pt
manned) guarnecer (de hombres); tripular (ship); servir
(guns)

manacle /'mænəkl/ n manilla
f. —vt poner esposas a

manage /'mænɪdʒ/ vt dirigir; llevar (shop, affairs); (handle)
manejar. —vi arreglárselas. ~
to do lograr hacer. ~able a
manejable. ~ment n dirección f

manager /'mænɪdʒə(r)/ n director m; (of actor) empresario m.
~ess /-'res/ n directora f. ~ial
/-'dʒɪərɪəl/ a directivo. ~ial
staff n personal m dirigente

managing director /mænɪdʒɪŋ
daɪ'rektə(r)/ n director m
gerente

mandarin /'mændərɪn/ n mandarín m; (orange) mandarina f

mandate /'mændeɪt/ n mandato
m

mandatory /'mændətərɪ/ a obligatorio

mane /meɪn/ n (of horse) crin f;
(of lion) melena f

manful /'mænfl/ a valiente

manganese /'mæŋgəni:z/ n man-
ganeso m

manger /'meɪndʒə(r)/ n pesebre
m

mangle¹ /'mæŋgl/ n (for wringing) exprimidor m; (for smooth-
ing) máquina f de planchar

mangle² /'mæŋgl/ vt destrozar

mango /'mæŋgəʊ/ n (pl -oes)
mango m

mangy /'meɪndʒɪ/ a sarnoso

man: ~handle vt maltratar.
~hole n registro m. ~hole
cover n tapa f de registro.
~hood n edad f viril; (quality)
virilidad f. ~hour n hora-
hombre f. ~hunt n persecución
f

mania /'meɪnɪə/ n manía f. ~c
/-ɪæk/ n maníaco m

manicur|e /'mænɪkjʊə(r)/ n
manicura f. —vt hacer la manicura a (person). ~ist n manicuro
m

manifest /'mænɪfest/ a manifiesto. —vt mostrar. ~ation
/-'steɪʃn/ n manifestación f

manifesto /mænɪ'festəʊ/ n (pl
-os) manifiesto m

manifold /'mænɪfəʊld/ a
múltiple

manipulat|e /mə'nɪpjʊleɪt/ vt
manipular. ~ion /-'leɪʃn/ n manipulación f

mankind /mæn'kaɪnd/ n la
humanidad f

man; ∼ly adv viril. ∼made a artificial

mannequin /'mænɪkɪn/ n maniquí m

manner /'mænə(r)/ n manera f; (behaviour) comportamiento m; (kind) clase f. ∼ed a amanerado. bad-∼ed a mal educado. ∼s npl (social behaviour) educación f. have no ∼s no tener educación

mannerism /'mænərɪzəm/ n peculiaridad f

mannish /'mænɪʃ/ a (woman) hombruna

manoevre /mə'nu:və(r)/ n maniobra f. ∼vt/i maniobrar

man-of-war /mænəv'wɔ:(r)/ n buque m de guerra

manor /'mænə(r)/ n casa f solariega

manpower /'mænpaʊə(r)/ n mano f de obra

manservant /'mænsə:vənt/ n criado m

mansion /'mænʃn/ n mansión f

man; ∼-size(d) a grande. ∼slaughter n homicidio m impremeditado

mantelpiece /'mæntlpi:s/ n repisa f de chimenea

mantilla /mæn'tɪlə/ n mantilla f

mantle /'mæntl/ n manto m

manual /'mænjʊəl/ a manual. – n (handbook) manual m

manufacture /mænju'fæktʃə(r)/ vt fabricar. –n fabricación f. ∼r /-ə(r)/ n fabricante m

manure /mə'njʊə(r)/ n estiércol m

manuscript /'mænjuskrɪpt/ n manuscrito m

many /'menɪ/ a & n muchos (mpl). ∼ people mucha gente f. ∼ a time muchas veces. a great/good ∼ muchísimos

map /mæp/ n mapa m; (of streets etc) plano m. –vt (pt mapped) levantar un mapa de. ∼ out organizar

maple /'meɪpl/ n arce m

mar /ma:/ vt (pt marred) estropear; aguar (enjoyment)

marathon /'mærəθən/ n maratón m

marauder /mə'rɔ:də(r)/ n merodeador m. ∼ing a merodeador

marble /'ma:bl/ n mármol m; (for game) canica f

March /ma:tʃ/ n marzo m

march /ma:tʃ/ vi (mil) marchar. ∼ off irse. –vt. ∼ off (lead away) llevarse. –n marcha f

marchioness /ma:ʃə'nes/ n marquesa f

march-past /'ma:tʃpa:st/ n desfile m

mare /meə(r)/ n yegua f

margarine /ma:dʒə'ri:n/ n margarina f

margin /'ma:dʒɪn/ n margen f. ∼al a marginal. ∼al seat n (pol) escaño m inseguro. ∼ally adv muy poco

marguerite /ma:gə'ri:t/ n margarita f

marigold /'mærɪgəʊld/ n caléndula f

marijuana /mærɪ'hwa:nə/ n marihuana f

marina /mə'ri:nə/ n puerto m deportivo

marinade /mærɪ'neɪd/ n escabeche m. ∼te /'mærɪneɪt/ vt escabechar

marine /mə'ri:n/ a marino. –n (sailor) soldado m de infantería de marina; (shipping) marina f

marionette /mærɪə'net/ n marioneta f

marital /'mærɪtl/ a marital, matrimonial. ∼ status n estado m civil

maritime /'mærɪtaɪm/ a marítimo

marjoram /'ma:dʒərəm/ n mejorana f

mark[1] /ma:k/ n marca f; (trace) huella f; (schol) nota f; (target) blanco *m*. —*vt* marcar; poner nota a ‹*exam*›. ~ **out** trazar; escoger ‹*person*›

mark² /mɑːk/ *n* (*currency*) marco *m*

marked /mɑːkt/ *a* marcado. ~**ly** /-kɪdlɪ/ *adv* marcadamente

marker /ˈmɑːkə(r)/ *n* marcador *m*; (*for book*) registro *m*

market /ˈmɑːkɪt/ *n* mercado *m*. **on the** ~ en venta. —*vt* (*sell*) vender; (*launch*) comercializar. ~ **garden** *n* huerto *m*. ~**ing** *n* marketing *m*

marking /ˈmɑːkɪŋ/ *n* (*marks*) marcas *fpl*

marksman /ˈmɑːksmən/ *n* tirador *m*. ~**ship** *n* puntería *f*

marmalade /ˈmɑːməleɪd/ *n* mermelada *f* de naranja

marmot /ˈmɑːmət/ *n* marmota *f*

maroon /məˈruːn/ *n* granate *m*. —*a* de color granate

marooned /məˈruːnd/ *a* abandonado; (*snow-bound etc*) aislado

marquee /mɑːˈkiː/ *n* tienda de campaña *f* grande; (*awning*, *Amer*) marquesina *f*

marquetry /ˈmɑːkɪtrɪ/ *n* marquetería *f*

marquis /ˈmɑːkwɪs/ *n* marqués *m*

marriage /ˈmærɪdʒ/ *n* matrimonio *m*; (*wedding*) boda *f*. ~**able** *a* casadero

married /ˈmærɪd/ *a* casado; ‹*life*› conjugal

marrow /ˈmærəʊ/ *n* (*of bone*) tuétano *m*; (*vegetable*) calabacín *m*

marry /ˈmærɪ/ *vt* casarse con; (*give or unite in marriage*) casar. —*vi* casarse. **get married** casarse

marsh /mɑːʃ/ *n* pantano *m*

marshal /ˈmɑːʃl/ *n* (*mil*) mariscal *m*; (*master of ceremonies*) maestro *m* de ceremonias; (*at sports*

events) oficial *m*. —*vt* (*pt* **marshalled**) ordenar; formar ‹*troops*›

marsh mallow /mɑːʃˈmæləʊ/ *n* (*plant*) malvavisco *m*

marshmallow /mɑːʃˈmæləʊ/ *n* (*sweet*) caramelo *m* blando

marshy /ˈmɑːʃɪ/ *a* pantanoso

martial /ˈmɑːʃl/ *a* marcial. ~ **law** *n* ley *f* marcial

Martian /ˈmɑːʃn/ *a* & *n* marciano (*m*)

martinet /mɑːtɪˈnet/ *n* ordenancista *m* & *f*

martyr /ˈmɑːtə(r)/ *n* mártir *m* & *f*. —*vt* martirizar. ~**dom** *n* martirio *m*

marvel /ˈmɑːvl/ *n* maravilla *f*. —*vi* (*pt* **marvelled**) maravillarse (**at** con, de). ~**lous** /ˈmɑːvələs/ *a* maravilloso

Marxis|m /ˈmɑːksɪzəm/ *n* marxismo *m*. ~**t** *a* & *n* marxista (*m* & *f*)

marzipan /ˈmɑːzɪpæn/ *n* mazapán *m*

mascara /mæˈskɑːrə/ *n* rímel *m*

mascot /ˈmæskɒt/ *n* mascota *f*

masculin|e /ˈmæskjʊlɪn/ *a* & *n* masculino (*m*). ~**ity** /-ˈlɪnɪtɪ/ *n* masculinidad *f*

mash /mæʃ/ *n* mezcla *f*; (*potatoes*, *fam*) puré *m* de patatas. —*vt* (*crush*) machacar; (*mix*) mezclar. ~**ed potatoes** *n* puré *m* de patatas

mask /mɑːsk/ *n* máscara *f*. —*vt* enmascarar

masochis|m /ˈmæsəkɪzəm/ *n* masoquismo *m*. ~**t** *n* masoquista *m* & *f*

mason /ˈmeɪsn/ *n* (*builder*) albañil *m*

Mason /ˈmeɪsn/ *n*. ~ **mason** *m*. ~**ic** /məˈsɒnɪk/ *a* masónico

masonry /ˈmeɪsnrɪ/ *n* albañilería *f*

masquerade /mɑːskəˈreɪd/ n mascarada f. —vi. ∼ **as** hacerse pasar por

mass[1] /mæs/ n masa f. (large quantity) montón m. **the ∼es** npl las masas fpl. —vt/i agrupar(se)

mass[2] /mæs/ n (relig) misa f. **high ∼** misa f mayor

massacre /ˈmæsəkə(r)/ n masacre f, matanza f. —vt masacrar

massage /ˈmæsɑːʒ/ n masaje m. —vt dar masaje a

masseur /mæˈsɜː(r)/ n masajista m. ∼**se** /mæˈsɜːz/ n masajista f

massive /ˈmæsɪv/ a masivo; (heavy) macizo; (huge) enorme

mass: ∼ **media** n medios mpl de comunicación. ∼**-produce** vt fabricar en serie

mast /mɑːst/ n mástil m; (for radio, TV) torre f

master /ˈmɑːstə(r)/ n maestro m; (in secondary school) profesor m; (of ship) capitán m. —vt dominar. ∼**-key** n llave f maestra. ∼**ly** a magistral. ∼**mind** n cerebro m. —vt dirigir. **M∼ of Arts** master m, grado m universitario entre el de licenciado y el de doctor

masterpiece /ˈmɑːstəpiːs/ n obra f maestra

master-stroke /ˈmɑːstəstrəʊk/ n golpe m maestro

mastery /ˈmɑːstərɪ/ n dominio m; (skill) maestría f

masturbate /ˈmæstəbeɪt/ vi masturbarse. ∼**ion** /-ˈbeɪʃn/ n masturbación f

mat /mæt/ n estera f; (at door) felpudo m

match[1] /mætʃ/ n (sport) partido m; (equal) igual m; (marriage) matrimonio m; (s.o. to marry) partido m. —vt emparejar; (equal) igualar; (clothes, colours) hacer juego con. —vi hacer juego

match[2] /mætʃ/ n (of wood) fósforo m; (of wax) cerilla f. ∼**box** /ˈmætʃbɒks/ n (for wooden matches) caja f de fósforos; (for wax matches) caja f de cerillas

matching /ˈmætʃɪŋ/ a que hace juego

mate[1] /meɪt/ n compañero m; (of animals) macho m, hembra f; (assistant) ayudante m. —vt/i acoplar(se)

mate[2] /meɪt/ n (chess) mate m

material /məˈtɪərɪəl/ n material m; (cloth) tela f. —a material; (fig) importante. ∼**istic** /-ˈlɪstɪk/ a materialista. ∼**s** npl materiales mpl. **raw ∼s** npl materias fpl primas

materialize /məˈtɪərɪəlaɪz/ vi materializarse

maternal /məˈtɜːnl/ a maternal; (relation) materno

maternity /məˈtɜːnɪtɪ/ n maternidad f. —a de maternidad. ∼ **clothes** npl vestido m premamá. ∼ **hospital** n maternidad f

matey /ˈmeɪtɪ/ a (fam) simpático

mathematic|**ian** /mæθəməˈtɪʃn/ n matemático m. ∼**al** /-ˈmætɪkl/ a matemático. ∼**s** /-ˈmætɪks/ n & npl matemáticas fpl

maths /mæθs/, **math** (Amer) n & npl matemáticas fpl

matinée /ˈmætɪneɪ/ n función f de tarde

matriculate /məˈtrɪkjʊleɪt/ vt/i matricular(se). ∼**ion** /-ˈleɪʃn/ n matriculación f

matrimon|**ial** /mætrɪˈməʊnɪəl/ a matrimonial. ∼**y** /ˈmætrɪmənɪ/ n matrimonio m

matrix /ˈmeɪtrɪks/ n (pl **matrices** /-sɪːz/) matriz f

matron /ˈmeɪtrən/ n (married, elderly) matrona f; (in school) ama f de llaves; (former use, in hospital) enfermera f jefe. ∼**ly** a matronil matt /mæt/ a mate

matted /'mætid/ a enmarañado

matter /'mætə(r)/ n (substance) materia f; (affair) asunto m; (pus) pus m. as a ~ of fact en realidad. no ~ no importa. what is the ~? ¿qué pasa? —vi importar. it does not ~ no importa. ~-of-fact a realista

matting /'mætiŋ/ n estera f

mattress /'mætris/ n colchón m

matur|e /mə'tjʊə(r)/ a maduro. —vt/i madurar. ~ity n madurez f

maul /mɔːl/ vt maltratar

Mauritius /mə'rɪʃəs/ n Mauricio m

mausoleum /mɔːsə'lɪəm/ n mausoleo m

mauve /məʊv/ a & n color (m) de malva

mawkish /'mɔːkɪʃ/ a empalagoso

maxim /'mæksɪm/ n máxima f

maxim|ize /'mæksɪmaɪz/ vt llevar al máximo. ~um a & n (pl -ima) máximo (m)

may /meɪ/ v aux (pt might) poder. ~ I smoke? ¿se permite fumar? ~ he be happy ¡que sea feliz! he ~/might come puede que venga. I ~/might as well stay más vale quedarme. it ~/might be true puede ser verdad

May /meɪ/ n mayo m. ~ Day n el primero m de mayo

maybe /'meɪbɪ/ adv quizá(s)

mayhem /'meɪhem/ n (havoc) alboroto m

mayonnaise /meɪə'neɪz/ n mayonesa f

mayor /meə(r)/ n alcalde m, alcaldesa f. ~ess n alcaldesa f

maze /meɪz/ n laberinto m

me¹ /miː/ pron me; (after prep) mí. he knows ~ me conoce. it's ~ soy yo

me² /miː/ n (mus, third note of any musical scale) mi m

meadow /'medəʊ/ n prado m

meagre /'miːgə(r)/ a escaso

meal¹ /miːl/ n comida f

meal² /miːl/ n (grain) harina f

mealy-mouthed /miːlɪ'maʊðd/ a hipócrita

mean¹ /miːn/ vt (pt meant) (intend) tener la intención de, querer; (signify) querer decir, significar. ~ to do tener la intención de hacer. ~ well tener buenas intenciones. be meant for estar destinado a

mean² /miːn/ a (-er, -est) (miserly) tacaño; (unkind) malo; (poor) pobre

mean³ /miːn/ a medio. —n medio m; (average) promedio m

meander /mɪ'ændə(r)/ vi (river) serpentear; (person) vagar

meaning /'miːnɪŋ/ n sentido m. ~ful a significativo. ~less a sin sentido

meanness /'miːnnɪs/ n (miserliness) tacañería f; (unkindness) maldad f

means /miːnz/ n medio m. by all ~ por supuesto. by no ~ de ninguna manera. —npl (wealth) recursos mpl. ~ test n investigación f financial

meant /ment/ see mean¹

meantime /'miːntaɪm/ adv entretanto. in the ~ entretanto

meanwhile /'miːnwaɪl/ adv entretanto

measles /'miːzlz/ n sarampión m

measly /'miːzlɪ/ a (sl) miserable

measurable /'meʒərəbl/ a mensurable

measure /'meʒə(r)/ n medida f; (ruler) regla f. —vt/i medir. ~ up to estar a la altura de. ~d a (rhythmical) acompasado; (carefully considered) prudente. ~ment n medida f

meat /miːt/ n carne f. ~y a carnoso; (fig) sustancioso

mechanic /mɪˈkænɪk/ n mecánico m. ∼al /mɪˈkænɪkl/ a mecánico. ∼s n mecánica f

mechanism /ˈmekənɪzəm/ n mecanismo m. ∼ze vt mecanizar

medal /ˈmedl/ n medalla f

medallion /mɪˈdælɪən/ n medallón m

medallist /ˈmedəlɪst/ n ganador m de una medalla. **be a gold** ∼ ganar una medalla de oro

meddle /ˈmedl/ vi entrometerse (**in** en); (tinker) tocar. ∼ **with** (tinker) tocar. ∼**some** a entrometido

media /ˈmiːdɪə/ see **medium**. —npl. **the** ∼ npl los medios mpl de comunicación

mediate /ˈmiːdɪeɪt/ vi mediar. ∼**ion** /-ˈeɪʃn/ n mediación f. ∼**or** n mediador m

medical /ˈmedɪkl/ a médico; (student) de medicina. —n (fam) reconocimiento m médico

medicat|ed /ˈmedɪkeɪtɪd/ a medicinal. ∼**ion** /-ˈkeɪʃn/ n medicación f

medicin|e /ˈmedsɪn/ n medicina f. ∼**al** /mɪˈdɪsɪnl/ a medicinal

medieval /medɪˈiːvl/ a medieval

mediocr|e /miːdɪˈəʊkə(r)/ a mediocre. ∼**ity** /-ˈɒkrətɪ/ n mediocridad f

meditat|e /ˈmedɪteɪt/ vt/i meditar. ∼**ion** /-ˈteɪʃn/ n meditación f

Mediterranean /medɪtəˈreɪnɪən/ a mediterráneo. —n. **the** ∼ el Mediterráneo m

medium /ˈmiːdɪəm/ n (pl **media**) medio m; (pl **mediums**) (person) médium m. —a mediano

medley /ˈmedlɪ/ n popurrí m

meek /miːk/ a (-er, -est) manso

meet /miːt/ vt (pt **met**) encontrar; (bump into s.o.) encontrarse con; (see again) ver; (fetch) ir a buscar; (get to know, be introduced to) conocer. ∼ **the** bill pagar la cuenta. —vi encontrarse; (get to know) conocerse; (in session) reunirse. ∼ **with** tropezar con (obstacles)

meeting /ˈmiːtɪŋ/ n reunión f; (accidental between two people) encuentro m; (arranged between two people) cita f

megalomania /megələʊˈmeɪnɪə/ n megalomanía f

megaphone /ˈmegəfəʊn/ n megáfono m

melanchol|ic /melənˈkɒlɪk/ a melancólico. ∼**y** /ˈmelənkɒlɪ/ n melancolía f. —a melancólico

mêlée /ˈmeleɪ/ n pelea f confusa

mellow /ˈmeləʊ/ a (-er, -est) (fruit, person) maduro; (sound, colour) dulce. —vt/i madurar(se)

melod|ic /mɪˈlɒdɪk/ a melódico. ∼**ous** /mɪˈləʊdɪəs/ a melodioso

melodrama /ˈmelədrɑːmə/ n melodrama m. ∼**tic** /-əˈmætɪk/ a melodramático

melody /ˈmelədɪ/ n melodía f

melon /ˈmelən/ n melón m

melt /melt/ vt (make liquid) derretir; fundir (metals). —vi (become liquid) derretirse; (metals) fundirse. ∼**ing-pot** n crisol m

member /ˈmembə(r)/ n miembro m. **M**∼ **of Parliament** n diputado m. ∼**ship** n calidad f de miembro; (members) miembros mpl

membrane /ˈmembreɪn/ n membrana f

memento /mɪˈmentəʊ/ n (pl -oes) recuerdo m

memo /ˈmeməʊ/ n (pl -os) (fam) nota f

memoir /ˈmemwɑː(r)/ n memoria f

memorable /ˈmemərəbl/ a memorable

memorandum /meməˈrændəm/ n (pl -ums) nota f

memorial /mɪˈmɔːrɪəl/ n monumento m. —a conmemorativo

memorize /ˈmeməraɪz/ vt aprender de memoria

memory /ˈmemərɪ/ n (faculty) memoria f; (thing remembered) recuerdo m. **from ~ de** memoria. **in ~ of** en memoria de

men /men/ see **man**

menac|e /ˈmenəs/ n amenaza f; (nuisance) pesado m. —vt amenazar. **~ingly** adv de manera amenazadora

menagerie /mɪˈnædʒərɪ/ n casa f de fieras

mend /mend/ vt reparar; (darn) zurcir. **~ one's ways** enmendarse. —n remiendo m. **be on the ~** ir mejorando

menfolk /ˈmenfəʊk/ n hombres mpl

menial /ˈmiːnɪəl/ a servil

meningitis /menɪnˈdʒaɪtɪs/ n meningitis f

menopause /ˈmenəpɔːz/ n menopausia f

menstruat|e /ˈmenstrʊeɪt/ vi menstruar. **~ion** /-eɪʃn/ n menstruación f

mental /ˈmentl/ a mental; (hospital) psiquiátrico

mentality /menˈtælətɪ/ n mentalidad f

menthol /ˈmenθɒl/ n mentol m. **~ated** a mentolado

mention /ˈmenʃn/ vt mencionar. **don't ~ it!** ¡no hay de qué! —n mención f

mentor /ˈmentɔː(r)/ n mentor m

menu /ˈmenjuː/ n (set meal) menú m; (a la carte) lista f (de platos)

mercantile /ˈmɜːkəntaɪl/ a mercantil

mercenary /ˈmɜːsɪnərɪ/ a & n mercenario (m)

merchandise /ˈmɜːtʃəndaɪz/ n mercancías fpl

merchant /ˈmɜːtʃənt/ n comerciante m. —a (ship, navy) mercante. **~ bank** n banco m mercantil

merci|ful /ˈmɜːsɪfl/ a misericordioso. **~fully** adv (fortunately, fam) gracias a Dios. **~less** /ˈmɜːsɪlɪs/ a despiadado

mercur|ial /mɜːˈkjʊərɪəl/ a mercurial; (fig, active) vivo. **~y** /ˈmɜːkjʊrɪ/ n mercurio m

mercy /ˈmɜːsɪ/ n compasión f. **at the ~ of** a merced de

mere /mɪə(r)/ a simple. **~ly** adv simplemente

merest /ˈmɪərɪst/ a mínimo

merge /mɜːdʒ/ vt unir; fusionar (companies). —vi unirse; (companies) fusionarse. **~r** /-ə(r)/ n fusión f

meridian /məˈrɪdɪən/ n meridiano m

meringue /məˈræŋ/ n merengue m

merit /ˈmerɪt/ n mérito m. —vt (pt merited) merecer. **~orious** /-ˈtɔːrɪəs/ a meritorio

mermaid /ˈmɜːmeɪd/ n sirena f

merr|ily /ˈmerɪlɪ/ adv alegremente. **~iment** /ˈmerɪmənt/ n alegría f. **~y** /ˈmerɪ/ a (-ier, -iest) alegre. **make ~** divertirse. **~y-go-round** n tiovivo m. **~y-making** n holgorio m

mesh /meʃ/ n malla f; (network) red f

mesmerize /ˈmezməraɪz/ vt hipnotizar

mess /mes/ n desorden m; (dirt) suciedad f; (mil) rancho m. **make a ~ of** chapucear, estropear. —vt. **~ up** desordenar; (dirty) ensuciar. —vi. **~ about** entretenerse. **~ with** (tinker with) manosear

message /ˈmesɪdʒ/ n recado m

messenger /ˈmesɪndʒə(r)/ n mensajero m

Messiah /mɪˈsaɪə/ n Mesías m

Messrs /'mesəz/ npl. ~ Smith los señores mpl or Sres. Smith

messy /'mesɪ/ a (-ier, -iest) en desorden; (dirty) sucio

met /met/ see meet

metabolism /mɪ'tæbəlɪzəm/ n metabolismo m

metal /'metl/ n metal. —a de metal. ~lic /mɪ'tælɪk/ a metálico

metallurgy /mɪ'tælədʒɪ/ n metalurgia f

metamorphosis /metə'mɔːfəsɪs/ n (pl -phoses /-sɪːz/) metamorfosis f

metaphor /'metəfə(r)/ n metáfora f. ~ical /-'fɒrɪkl/ a metafórico

mete /miːt/ vt. ~ out repartir; dar ⟨punishment⟩

meteor /'miːtɪə(r)/ n meteoro m

meteorite /'miːtɪəraɪt/ n meteorito m

meteorolog|ical /miːtɪərə'lɒdʒɪkl/ a meteorológico. ~y /-'rɒlədʒɪ/ n meteorología f

meter[1] /'miːtə(r)/ n contador m

meter[2] /'miːtə(r)/ n (Amer) = metre

method /'meθəd/ n método m

methodical /mɪ'θɒdɪkl/ a metódico

Methodist /'meθədɪst/ a & n metodista (m & f)

methylated /'meθɪleɪtɪd/ a. ~ spirit n alcohol m desnaturalizado

meticulous /mɪ'tɪkjʊləs/ a meticuloso

metre /'miːtə(r)/ n metro m

metric /'metrɪk/ a métrico. ~ation /-'keɪʃn/ n cambio m al sistema métrico

metropolis /mɪ'trɒpəlɪs/ n metrópoli f

metropolitan /metrə'pɒlɪtən/ a metropolitano

mettle /'metl/ n valor m

mew /mjuː/ n maullido m. —vi maullar

mews /mjuːz/ npl casas fpl pequeñas (que antes eran caballerizas)

Mexic|an /'meksɪkən/ a & n mejicano (m); (in Mexico) mexicano (m). ~o /-kəʊ/ n Méjico m; (in Mexico) México m

mezzanine /'metsəniːn/ n entresuelo m

mi /miː/ n (mus, third note of any musical scale) mi m

miaow /miː'aʊ/ n & vi = mew

mice /maɪs/ see mouse

mickey /'mɪkɪ/ n. take the ~ out of (sl) tomar el pelo a

micro... /'maɪkrəʊ/ pref micro...

microbe /'maɪkrəʊb/ n microbio m

microchip /'maɪkrəʊtʃɪp/ n pastilla f

microfilm /'maɪkrəʊfɪlm/ n microfilme m

microphone /'maɪkrəfəʊn/ n micrófono m

microprocessor /maɪkrəʊ'prəʊsesə(r)/ n microprocesador m

microscop|e /'maɪkrəskəʊp/ n microscopio m. ~ic /-'skɒpɪk/ a microscópico

microwave /'maɪkrəʊweɪv/ n microonda f. ~ oven n horno m de microondas

mid /mɪd/ a. in ~ air en pleno aire. in ~ March a mediados de marzo. in ~ ocean en medio del océano

midday /mɪd'deɪ/ n mediodía m

middle /'mɪdl/ a de en medio; ⟨quality⟩ mediano. —n medio m. in the ~ of en medio de. ~-aged a de mediana edad. M~ Ages npl Edad f Media. ~ class n clase f media. ~-class a de la clase media. M~ East n Oriente m Medio. ~man n intermediario m

middling /'mɪdlɪŋ/ a regular

midge /mɪdʒ/ n mosquito m

midget /'mɪdʒɪt/ n enano m. —a minúsculo

Midlands /'mɪdləndz/ npl región f central de Inglaterra

midnight /'mɪdnaɪt/ n medianoche f

midriff /'mɪdrɪf/ n diafragma m; (fam) vientre m

midst /mɪdst/ n. **in our ~** entre nosotros. **in the ~ of** en medio de

midsummer /mɪd'sʌmə(r)/ n pleno verano m; (solstice) solsticio m de verano

midway /mɪd'weɪ/ adv a medio camino

midwife /'mɪdwaɪf/ n comadrona f

midwinter /mɪd'wɪntə(r)/ n pleno invierno m

might[1] /maɪt/ see **may**

might[2] /maɪt/ n (strength) fuerza f; (power) poder m. **~y** a (strong) fuerte; (powerful) poderoso; (very great, fam) enorme. —adv (fam) muy

migraine /'mi:greɪn/ n jaqueca f

migrant /'maɪgrənt/ a migratorio. —n (person) emigrante m & f

migrat|e /maɪ'greɪt/ vi emigrar. **~ion** /-ʃn/ n migración f

mike /maɪk/ a (fam) micrófono m

mild /maɪld/ a (-er, -est) (person) apacible; (climate) templado; (slight) ligero; (taste) suave; (illness) benigno

mildew /'mɪldju:/ n moho m

mild: **~ly** adv (slightly) ligeramente. **~ness** n (of person) apacibilidad f; (of climate, illness) benignidad f; (of taste) suavidad f

mile /maɪl/ n milla f. **~s better** (fam) mucho mejor. **~s too big** (fam) demasiado grande. **~age** n (loosely) kilometraje m.

~stone n mojón m; (event, stage, fig) hito m

milieu /mɪ'ljɜ:/ n ambiente m

militant /'mɪlɪtənt/ a & n militante (m & f)

military /'mɪlɪtərɪ/ a militar

militate /'mɪlɪteɪt/ vi militar (**against** contra)

militia /mɪ'lɪʃə/ n milicia f

milk /mɪlk/ n leche f. —a (product) lácteo; (chocolate) con leche. —vt ordeñar (cow); (exploit) chupar. **~man** n repartidor m de leche. **~ shake** n batido m de leche. **~y** a lechoso. **M~y Way** n Vía f Láctea

mill /mɪl/ n molino m; (for coffee, pepper) molinillo m; (factory) fábrica f. —vt moler. —vi. **~ about/around** apiñarse, circular

millennium /mɪ'lenɪəm/ n (pl -ia or -iums) milenio m

miller /'mɪlə(r)/ n molinero m

millet /'mɪlɪt/ n mijo m

milli... /'mɪlɪ/ pref mili...

milligram(me) /'mɪlɪgræm/ n miligramo m

millimetre /'mɪlɪmiːtə(r)/ n milímetro m

milliner /'mɪlɪnə(r)/ n sombrerero m

million /'mɪlɪən/ n millón m. **a ~ pounds** un millón m de libras. **~aire** n millonario m

millstone /'mɪlstəʊn/ n muela f (de molino); (fig, burden) losa f

mime /maɪm/ n pantomima f. —vt hacer en pantomima. —vi actuar de mimo

mimic /'mɪmɪk/ vt (pt **mimicked**) imitar. —n imitador m. **~ry** n imitación f

mimosa /mɪ'məʊzə/ n mimosa f

minaret /mɪnə'ret/ n alminar m

mince /mɪns/ vt desmenuzar; picar (meat). **not to ~ matters/words** no tener pelos en la lengua. —n carne f picada.

~**meat** n conserva f de fruta picada. **make** ~**meat of** s.o. hacer trizas a uno. ~**pie** n pastel m con frutas picadas. ~**r** n máquina f de picar carne

mind /maɪnd/ n mente f; (sanity) juicio m; (opinion) parecer m; (intention) intención f. **be on one's** ~ preocuparle a uno. ~vt (look after) cuidar; (heed) hacer caso de. **I don't** ~ me da igual. **I don't** ~ **the noise** no me molesta el ruido. **never** ~ no te preocupes, no se preocupe. ~**er** n cuidador m. ~**ful** a atento (**of** a). ~**less** a estúpido

mine[1] /maɪn/ poss pron (el) mío m, (la) mía f, (los) míos mpl, (las) mías fpl. **it is** ~ es mío

mine[2] /maɪn/ n mina f. —vt extraer. ~**field** n campo m de minas. ~**r** n minero m

mineral /ˈmɪnərəl/ a & n mineral (m). ~ (**water**) n (fizzy soft drink) gaseosa f. ~ **water** n (natural) agua f mineral

minesweeper /ˈmaɪnswiːpə(r)/ n (ship) dragaminas m invar

mingle /ˈmɪŋgl/ vt/i mezclar(se)

mingy /ˈmɪndʒɪ/ a tacaño

mini... /ˈmɪnɪ/ pref mini...

miniature /ˈmɪnɪtʃə(r)/ a & n miniatura (f)

mini: ~**bus** n microbús m. ~**cab** n taxi m

minim /ˈmɪnɪm/ n (mus) blanca f

minim|al /ˈmɪnɪml/ a mínimo. ~**ize** vt minimizar. ~**um** a & n (pl -**ima**) mínimo (m)

mining /ˈmaɪnɪŋ/ n explotación f. —a minero

miniskirt /ˈmɪnɪskɜːt/ n minifalda f

minist|er /ˈmɪnɪstə(r)/ n ministro m; (relig) pastor m. ~**erial** /-ˈstɪərɪəl/ a ministerial. ~**ry** n ministerio m

mink /mɪŋk/ n visón m

minor /ˈmaɪnə(r)/ a (incl mus) sin importancia. —n menor m & f de edad

minority /maɪˈnɒrətɪ/ n minoría f. —a minoritario

minster /ˈmɪnstə(r)/ n catedral f

minstrel /ˈmɪnstrəl/ n juglar m

mint[1] /mɪnt/ n (plant) menta f; (sweet) caramelo m de menta

mint[2] /mɪnt/ n. **the M~** n casa f de la moneda. **a** ~ un dineral m. —vt acuñar. **in** ~ **condition** como nuevo

minuet /mɪnjʊˈet/ n minué m

minus /ˈmaɪnəs/ prep menos; (without, fam) sin. —n (sign) menos m. ~ **sign** n menos m

minuscule /ˈmɪnəskjuːl/ a minúsculo

minute[1] /ˈmɪnɪt/ n minuto m. ~**s** npl (of meeting) actas fpl

minute[2] /maɪˈnjuːt/ a minúsculo; (detailed) minucioso

minx /mɪŋks/ n chica f descarada

miracle /ˈmɪrəkl/ n milagro m. ~**ulous** /mɪˈrækjʊləs/ a milagroso

mirage /ˈmɪrɑːʒ/ n espejismo m

mire /ˈmaɪə(r)/ n fango m

mirror /ˈmɪrə(r)/ n espejo m. —vt reflejar

mirth /mɜːθ/ n (merriment) alegría f; (laughter) risas fpl

misadventure /mɪsədˈventʃə(r)/ n desgracia f

misanthropist /mɪˈzænθrəpɪst/ n misántropo m

misapprehension /mɪsæprɪˈhenʃn/ n malentendido m

misbehav|e /mɪsbɪˈheɪv/ vi portarse mal. ~**iour** n mala conducta f

miscalculat|e /mɪsˈkælkjʊleɪt/ vt/i calcular mal. ~**ion** /-ˈleɪʃn/ n desacierto m

miscarr|iage /ˈmɪskærɪdʒ/ n aborto m. ~**iage of justice** n error m judicial. ~**y** vi abortar

miscellaneous /ˌmɪsəˈleɪnɪəs/ a vario

mischief /ˈmɪstʃɪf/ n (foolish conduct) travesura f; (harm) daño m. **get into ~** cometer travesuras. **make ~** armar un lío

mischievous /ˈmɪstʃɪvəs/ a travieso; (malicious) perjudicial

misconception /ˌmɪskənˈsepʃn/ n equivocación f

misconduct /mɪsˈkɒndʌkt/ n mala conducta f

misconstrue /ˌmɪskənˈstruː/ vt interpretar mal

misdeed /mɪsˈdiːd/ n fechoría f

misdemeanour /ˌmɪsdɪˈmiːnə(r)/ n fechoría f

misdirect /ˌmɪsdɪˈrekt/ vt dirigir mal (person)

miser /ˈmaɪzə(r)/ n avaro m

miserable /ˈmɪzərəbl/ a (sad) triste; (wretched) miserable; (weather) malo

miserly /ˈmaɪzəlɪ/ a avariento

misery /ˈmɪzərɪ/ n (unhappiness) tristeza f; (pain) sufrimiento m; (poverty) pobreza f; (person, fam) aguafiestas m & f

misfire /mɪsˈfaɪə(r)/ vi fallar

misfit /ˈmɪsfɪt/ n (person) inadaptado m; (thing) cosa f mal ajustada

misfortune /mɪsˈfɔːtʃuːn/ n desgracia f

misgiving /mɪsˈɡɪvɪŋ/ n (doubt) duda f; (apprehension) presentimiento m

misguided /mɪsˈɡaɪdɪd/ a equivocado. **be ~** equivocarse

mishap /ˈmɪshæp/ n desgracia f

misinform /ˌmɪsɪnˈfɔːm/ vt informar mal

misinterpret /ˌmɪsɪnˈtɜːprɪt/ vt interpretar mal

misjudge /mɪsˈdʒʌdʒ/ vt juzgar mal

mislay /mɪsˈleɪ/ vt (pt mislaid) extraviar

mislead /mɪsˈliːd/ vt (pt misled) engañar. **~ing** a engañoso

mismanage /mɪsˈmænɪdʒ/ vt administrar mal. **~ment** n mala administración f

misnomer /mɪsˈnəʊmə(r)/ n nombre m equivocado

misplace /mɪsˈpleɪs/ vt colocar mal; (lose) extraviar

misprint /ˈmɪsprɪnt/ n errata f

misquote /mɪsˈkwəʊt/ vt citar mal

misrepresent /ˌmɪsreprɪˈzent/ vt describir engañosamente

miss[1] /mɪs/ vt (fail to hit) errar; (notice absence of) echar de menos; perder (train). **~ the point** no comprender. **—n** fallo m. **~ out** omitir

miss[2] /mɪs/ n (pl misses) señorita f

misshapen /mɪsˈʃeɪpən/ a deforme

missile /ˈmɪsaɪl/ n proyectil m

missing /ˈmɪsɪŋ/ a (person) (absent) ausente; (person) (after disaster) desaparecido; (lost) perdido. **be ~** faltar

mission /ˈmɪʃn/ n misión f. **~ary** /ˈmɪʃənərɪ/ n misionero m

missive /ˈmɪsɪv/ n misiva f

misspell /mɪsˈspel/ vt (pt misspelt or misspelled) escribir mal

mist /mɪst/ n neblina f; (at sea) bruma f. **—vt/i** empañar(se)

mistake /mɪsˈteɪk/ n error m. **—vt** (pt mistook, pp mistaken) equivocarse de; (misunderstand) entender mal. **~ for** tomar por. **~n** /-ən/ a equivocado. **be ~n** equivocarse. **~nly** adv equivocadamente

mistletoe /ˈmɪsltəʊ/ n muérdago m

mistreat /mɪsˈtriːt/ vt maltratar

mistress /ˈmɪstrɪs/ n (of house) señora f; (primary school teacher) maestra f; (secondary

school teacher) profesora *f*;
(*lover*) amante *f*

mistrust /mɪs'trʌst/ *vt* desconfiar de. —*n* desconfianza *f*

misty /'mɪstɪ/ *a* (-ier, -iest) nebuloso; (*day*) de niebla; (*glass*) empañado. **it is ~** hay neblina

misunderstand /mɪsʌndə-'stænd/ *vt* (*pt* -**stood**) entender mal. **~ing** *n* malentendido *m*

misuse /mɪs'juːz/ *vt* emplear mal; abusar de (*power etc*). /mɪs'juːs/ *n* mal uso *m*; (*unfair use*) abuso *m*

mite /maɪt/ *n* (*insect*) ácaro *m*, garrapata *f*; (*child*) niño *m* pequeño

mitigate /'mɪtɪgeɪt/ *vt* mitigar

mitre /'maɪtə(r)/ *n* (*head-dress*) mitra *f*

mitten /'mɪtn/ *n* manopla *f*; (*leaving fingers exposed*) mitón *m*

mix /mɪks/ *vt/i* mezclar(se). **~ up** mezclar; (*confuse*) confundir. **~ with** frecuentar (*people*). —*n* mezcla *f*

mixed /mɪkst/ *a* (*school etc*) mixto; (*assorted*) variado. **be ~ up** estar confuso

mixer /'mɪksə(r)/ *n* (*culin*) batidora *f*. **be a good ~** tener don de gentes

mixture /'mɪkstʃə(r)/ *n* mezcla *f*

mix-up /'mɪksʌp/ *n* lío *m*

moan /məʊn/ *n* gemido *m*. —*vi* gemir; (*complain*) quejarse (*about* de). **~er** *n* refunfuñador *m*

moat /məʊt/ *n* foso *m*

mob /mɒb/ *n* (*crowd*) muchedumbre *f*; (*gang*) pandilla *f*; (*masses*) populacho *m*. —*vt* (*pt* mobbed) acosar

mobile /'məʊbaɪl/ *a* móvil. **~ home** caravana *f*. —*n* móvil *m*. **~ity** /mə'bɪlɪtɪ/ *n* movilidad *f*

mobiliz|ation /məʊbɪlaɪ'zeɪʃn/ *n* movilización *f*. **~e** /'məʊbɪlaɪz/ *vt/i* movilizar

moccasin /'mɒkəsɪn/ *n* mocasín *m*

mocha /'mɒkə/ *n* moca *m*

mock /mɒk/ *vt* burlarse de. —*vi* burlarse. —*a* fingido

mockery /'mɒkərɪ/ *n* burla *f*. **a ~ of** una parodia *f* de

mock-up /'mɒkʌp/ *n* maqueta *f*

mode /məʊd/ *n* (*way, method*) modo *m*; (*fashion*) moda *f*

model /'mɒdl/ *n* modelo *m*; (*mock-up*) maqueta *f*; (*for fashion*) maniquí *m*. —*a* (*exemplary*) ejemplar; (*car etc*) en miniatura. —*vt* (*pt* modelled) modelar; presentar (*clothes*). —*vi* ser maniquí; (*pose*) posar. **~ling** *n* profesión *f* de maniquí

moderate /'mɒdərət/ *a & n* moderado (*m*). /'mɒdəreɪt/ *vt/i* moderar(se). **~ly** /'mɒdərətlɪ/ *adv* (*in moderation*) moderadamente; (*fairly*) medianamente

moderation /mɒdə'reɪʃn/ *n* moderación *f*. **in ~** con moderación

modern /'mɒdn/ *a* moderno. **~ize** *vt* modernizar

modest /'mɒdɪst/ *a* modesto. **~y** *n* modestia *f*

modicum /'mɒdɪkəm/ *n*. **a ~ of** un poquito *m* de

modification /mɒdɪfɪ'keɪʃn/ *n* modificación *f*. **~y** /-faɪ/ *vt/i* modificar(se)

modulat|e /'mɒdjʊleɪt/ *vt/i* modular. **~ion** /-'leɪʃn/ *n* modulación *f*

module /'mɒdjuːl/ *n* módulo *m*

mogul /'məʊgəl/ *n* (*fam*) magnate *m*

mohair /'məʊheə(r)/ *n* mohair *m*

moist /mɔɪst/ *a* (-er, -est) húmedo. **~en** /'mɔɪsn/ *vt* humedecer

moistur|e /'mɔɪstʃə(r)/ *n* humedad *f*. **~ize** /'mɔɪstʃəraɪz/ *vt* humedecer. **~izer** *n* crema *f* hidratante

molar 470 mood

molar /ˈməʊlə(r)/ n muela f

molasses /məˈlæsɪz/ n melaza f

mold /məʊld/ (Amer) = mould

mole[1] /məʊl/ n (animal) topo m

mole[2] /məʊl/ n (on skin) lunar m

mole[3] /məʊl/ n (breakwater) malecón m

molecule /ˈmɒlɪkjuːl/ n molécula f

molehill /ˈməʊlhɪl/ n topera f

molest /məˈlest/ vt importunar

mollify /ˈmɒlɪfaɪ/ vt apaciguar

mollusc /ˈmɒləsk/ n molusco m

mollycoddle /ˈmɒlɪkɒdl/ vt mimar

molten /ˈməʊltən/ a fundido

mom /mɒm/ n (Amer) mamá f

moment /ˈməʊmənt/ n momento m. **~arily** /ˈməʊməntərɪlɪ/ adv momentáneamente. **~ary** a momentáneo

momentous /məˈmentəs/ a importante

momentum /məˈmentəm/ n momento m; (speed) velocidad f; (fig) ímpetu m

Monaco /ˈmɒnəkəʊ/ n Mónaco m

monarch /ˈmɒnək/ n monarca m. **~ist** n monárquico m. **~y** n monarquía f

monastery /ˈmɒnəstərɪ/ n monasterio m. **~ic** /məˈnæstɪk/ a monástico

Monday /ˈmʌndeɪ/ n lunes m

monetarist /ˈmʌnɪtərɪst/ n monetarista m & f. **~y** a monetario

money /ˈmʌnɪ/ n dinero m. **~box** n hucha f. **~ed** a adinerado. **~lender** n prestamista m & f. **~ order** n giro m postal. **~s** npl cantidades fpl de dinero. **~spinner** n mina f de dinero

mongol /ˈmɒŋgl/ n & a (med) mongólico (m)

mongrel /ˈmʌŋgrəl/ n perro m mestizo

monitor /ˈmɒnɪtə(r)/ n (pupil) monitor m & f; (tec) monitor

m. —vt controlar; escuchar ‹a broadcast›

monk /mʌŋk/ n monje m

monkey /ˈmʌŋkɪ/ n mono m. **~nut** n cacahuete m, maní m (LAm). **~wrench** n llave f inglesa

mono /ˈmɒnəʊ/ a monofónico

monocle /ˈmɒnəkl/ n monóculo m

monogram /ˈmɒnəgræm/ n monograma m

monologue /ˈmɒnəlɒg/ n monólogo m

monopolize /məˈnɒpəlaɪz/ vt monopolizar. **~y** n monopolio m

monosyllabic /mɒnəsɪˈlæbɪk/ a monosilábico. **~le** /-ˈsɪləbl/ n monosílabo m

monotone /ˈmɒnətəʊn/ n monotonía f. **speak in a ~** hablar con una voz monótona

monotonous /məˈnɒtənəs/ a monótono. **~y** n monotonía f

monsoon /mɒnˈsuːn/ n monzón m

monster /ˈmɒnstə(r)/ n monstruo m

monstrosity /mɒnˈstrɒsətɪ/ n monstruosidad f

monstrous /ˈmɒnstrəs/ a monstruoso

montage /mɒnˈtɑːʒ/ n montaje m

month /mʌnθ/ n mes m. **~ly** /ˈmʌnθlɪ/ a mensual. —adv mensualmente. —n (periodical) revista f mensual

monument /ˈmɒnjʊmənt/ n monumento m. **~al** /-ˈmentl/ a monumental

moo /muː/ n mugido m. —vi mugir

mooch /muːtʃ/ vi (sl) haraganear. —vt (Amer, sl) birlar

mood /muːd/ n humor m. **be in the ~ for** tener ganas de. **in a good/bad ~** de buen/mal humor. **~y** a (-ier, -iest) de

humor cambiadizo; (*bad-tempered*) malhumorado
moon /muːn/ *n* luna *f*. ~**light** *n* luz *f* de la luna. ~**lighting** *n* (*fam*) pluriempleo *m*. ~**lit** *a* iluminado por la luna; (*night*) de luna
moor[1] /mʊə(r)/ *n* (*open land*) páramo *m*
moor[2] /mʊə(r)/ *vt* amarrar. ~**ings** *npl* (*ropes*) amarras *fpl*; (*place*) amarradero *m*
Moor /mʊə(r)/ *n* moro *m*
moose /muːs/ *n invar* alce *m*
moot /muːt/ *a* discutible. —*vt* proponer 〈*question*〉
mop /mɒp/ *n* fregona *f*. ~ **of hair** pelambrera *f*. —*vt* (*pt* **mopped**) fregar. ~ **(up)** limpiar
mope /məʊp/ *vi* estar abatido
moped /ˈməʊped/ *n* ciclomotor *m*
moral /ˈmɒrəl/ *a* moral. —*n* moraleja *f*. ~**s** *npl* moralidad *f*
morale /məˈrɑːl/ *n* moral *f*
moral|**ist** /ˈmɒrəlɪst/ *n* moralista *m* & *f*. ~**ity** /məˈrælɪtɪ/ *n* moralidad *f*. ~**ize** *vi* moralizar. ~**ly** *adv* moralmente
morass /məˈræs/ *n* (*marsh*) pantano *m*; (*fig, entanglement*) embrollo *m*
morbid /ˈmɔːbɪd/ *a* morboso
more /mɔː(r)/ *a* & *n* & *adv* más. ~ **and** ~ cada vez más. ~ **or less** más o menos. **once** ~ una vez más. **some** ~ más
moreover /mɔːˈrəʊvə(r)/ *adv* además
morgue /mɔːg/ *n* depósito *m* de cadáveres
moribund /ˈmɒrɪbʌnd/ *a* moribundo
morning /ˈmɔːnɪŋ/ *n* mañana *f*; (*early hours*) madrugada *f*. **at 11 o'clock in the** ~ a las once de la mañana. **in the** ~ por la mañana
Morocc|**an** /məˈrɒkən/ *a* & *n* marroquí (*m* & *f*). ~**o** /-kəʊ/ *n* Marruecos *mpl*

moron /ˈmɔːrɒn/ *n* imbécil *m* & *f*
morose /məˈrəʊs/ *a* malhumorado
morphine /ˈmɔːfiːn/ *n* morfina *f*
Morse /mɔːs/ *n* Morse *m*. ~ (**code**) *n* alfabeto *m* Morse
morsel /ˈmɔːsl/ *n* pedazo *m*; (*mouthful*) bocado *m*
mortal /ˈmɔːtl/ *a* & *n* mortal (*m*). ~**ity** /-ˈtælətɪ/ *n* mortalidad *f*
mortar /ˈmɔːtə(r)/ *n* (*all senses*) mortero *m*
mortgage /ˈmɔːgɪdʒ/ *n* hipoteca *f*. —*vt* hipotecar
mortify /ˈmɔːtɪfaɪ/ *vt* mortificar
mortuary /ˈmɔːtjʊərɪ/ *n* depósito *m* de cadáveres
mosaic /məʊˈzeɪk/ *n* mosaico *m*
Moscow /ˈmɒskəʊ/ *n* Moscú *m*
Moses /ˈməʊzɪz/ *a*. ~ **basket** *n* moisés *m*
mosque /mɒsk/ *n* mezquita *f*
mosquito /mɒsˈkiːtəʊ/ *n* (*pl* -oes) mosquito *m*
moss /mɒs/ *n* musgo *m*. ~**y** *a* musgoso
most /məʊst/ *a* más. **for the** ~ **part** en su mayor parte. —*n* la mayoría *f*. ~ **of** la mayor parte de. **at** ~ a lo más. **make the** ~ **of** aprovechar al máximo. ~ **ly** *adv* principalmente
MOT *abbr* (*Ministry of Transport*). ~ (**test**) *n* ITV, inspección *f* técnica de vehículos
motel /məʊˈtel/ *n* motel *m*
moth /mɒθ/ *n* mariposa *f* (nocturna); (*in clothes*) polilla *f*. ~**ball** *n* bola *f* de naftalina. ~**eaten** *a* apolillado
mother /ˈmʌðə(r)/ *n* madre *f*. —*vt* cuidar como a un hijo. ~**hood** *n* maternidad *f*. ~**in-law** *n* (*pl* ~**s-in-law**) suegra *f*. ~**land** *n* patria *f*. ~**ly** *adv* maternalmente. ~**of-pearl** *n* nácar *m*. **M~'s Day** *n* el día *m* de la

Madre. **∼-to-be** n futura madre f. **∼ tongue** n lengua f materna

motif /məʊˈtiːf/ n motivo m

motion /ˈməʊʃn/ n movimiento m; (proposal) moción f. —vt/i. **∼ (to) s.o. to** hacer señas a uno para que. **∼less** a inmóvil

motivat|e /ˈməʊtɪveɪt/ vt motivar. **∼ion** /-ˈveɪʃn/ n motivación f

motive /ˈməʊtɪv/ n motivo m

motley /ˈmɒtlɪ/ a abigarrado

motor /ˈməʊtə(r)/ n motor m; (car) coche m. —a motor; (fem) motora, motriz. —vi ir en coche. **∼ bike** n (fam) motocicleta f, moto f (fam). **∼ boat** n lancha f motora. **∼cade** /ˈməʊtəkeɪd/ n (Amer) desfile m de automóviles. **∼ car** n coche m, automóvil m. **∼ cycle** n motocicleta f. **∼cyclist** n motociclista m & f. **∼ing** n automovilismo m. **∼ist** n automovilista m & f. **∼ize** vt motorizar. **∼way** n autopista f

mottled /ˈmɒtld/ a abigarrado

motto /ˈmɒtəʊ/ n (pl **-oes**) lema m

mould[1] /məʊld/ n molde m. —vt moldear

mould[2] /məʊld/ n (fungus, rot) moho m

moulding /ˈməʊldɪŋ/ n (on wall etc) moldura f

mouldy /ˈməʊldɪ/ a mohoso

moult /məʊlt/ vi mudar

mound /maʊnd/ n montículo m; (pile, fig) montón m

mount[1] /maʊnt/ vt/i subir. —n montura f. **∼ up** aumentar

mount[2] /maʊnt/ n (hill) monte m

mountain /ˈmaʊntɪn/ n montaña f. **∼eer** /maʊntɪˈnɪə(r)/ n alpinista m & f. **∼eering** n alpinismo m. **∼ous** /ˈmaʊntɪnəs/ a montañoso

mourn /mɔːn/ vt llorar. —vi lamentarse. **∼ for** llorar la muerte de. **∼er** n persona f que

acompaña el cortejo fúnebre. **∼ful** a triste. **∼ing** n luto m

mouse /maʊs/ n (pl **mice**) ratón m. **∼trap** n ratonera f

mousse /muːs/ n (dish) crema f batida

moustache /məˈstɑːʃ/ n bigote m

mousy /ˈmaʊsɪ/ a (hair) pardusco; (fig) tímido

mouth /maʊθ/ vt formar con los labios. /maʊθ/ n boca f. **∼ful** n bocado m. **∼organ** n armónica f. **∼piece** n (mus) boquilla f; (fig, person) portavoz f, vocero m (LAm). **∼wash** n enjuague m

movable /ˈmuːvəbl/ a móvil, movible

move /muːv/ vt mover; mudarse de (house); (with emotion) conmover; (propose) proponer. —vi moverse; (be in motion) estar en movimiento; (progress) hacer progresos; (take action) tomar medidas; (depart) irse. **∼ (out)** irse. —n movimiento m; (in game) jugada f; (player's turn) turno m; (removal) mudanza f. **on the ∼** en movimiento. **∼ along** (hacer) circular. **∼ away** alejarse. **∼ back** (hacer) retroceder. **∼ forward** (hacer) avanzar. **∼ in** instalarse. **∼ on** (hacer) circular. **∼ over** apartarse. **∼ment** /ˈmuːvmənt/ n movimiento m

movie /ˈmuːvɪ/ n (Amer) película f. the **∼s** npl el cine m

moving /ˈmuːvɪŋ/ a en movimiento; (touching) conmovedor

mow /məʊ/ vt (pt **mowed** or **mown**) segar. **∼ down** derribar. **∼er** n (for lawn) cortacésped m inv

MP abbr see **Member of Parliament**

Mr /ˈmɪstə(r)/ abbr (pl **Messrs**) (Mister) señor m. **∼ Coldbeck** (el) Sr. Coldbeck

Mrs /'mɪsɪz/ *abbr* (*pl* **Mrs**) (*Missis*) señora *f*. ~ **Andrews** (la) Sra. Andrews. **the ~ Andrews** (las) Sras. Andrews

Ms /mɪz/ *abbr* (*title of married or unmarried woman*) señora *f*, señorita. **Ms** Lawton (la) Sra. Lawton

much /mʌtʃ/ *a & n* mucho (*m*). — *adv* mucho; (*before pp*) muy. ~ **as** por mucho que. ~ **the same** más o menos lo mismo. **so** ~ tanto. **too** ~ demasiado

muck /mʌk/ *n* estiércol *m*; (*dirt, fam*) suciedad *f*. —*vi*. ~ **about** (*sl*) perder el tiempo. ~ **about with** (*sl*) juguetear con. —*vt*. ~ **up** (*sl*) echar a perder. ~ **in** (*sl*) participar. ~**y** *a* sucio

mucus /'mjuːkəs/ *n* moco *m*

mud /mʌd/ *n* lodo *m*, barro *m*

muddle /'mʌdl/ *vt* embrollar. —*vi*. ~ **through** salir del paso. —*n* desorden *m*; (*mix-up*) lío *m*

muddy /'mʌdɪ/ *a* lodoso; (*hands etc*) cubierto de lodo

mudguard /'mʌdgɑːd/ *n* guardabarros *m invar*

muff /mʌf/ *n* manguito *m*

muffin /'mʌfɪn/ *n* mollete *m*

muffle /'mʌfl/ *vt* tapar; amortiguar (*a sound*). ~**r** *n* (*scarf*) bufanda *f*

mug /mʌg/ *n* tazón *m*; (*for beer*) jarra *f*; (*face, sl*) cara *f*, jeta *f* (*sl*); (*fool, sl*) primo *m*. —*vt* (*pt* **mugged**) asaltar. ~**ger** *n* asaltador *m*. ~**ging** *n* asalto *m*

muggy /'mʌgɪ/ *a* bochornoso

Muhammadan /mə'hæmɪdən/ *a & n* mahometano (*m*)

mule¹ /mjuːl/ *n* mula *f*, mulo *m*

mule² /mjuːl/ *n* (*slipper*) babucha *f*

mull¹ /mʌl/ *vt*. ~ **over** reflexionar sobre

mull² /mʌl/ *vt* calentar con especias (*wine*)

multi... /'mʌltɪ/ *pref* multi...

multicoloured /mʌltɪ'kʌləd/ *a* multicolor

multifarious /mʌltɪ'feərɪəs/ *a* múltiple

multinational /mʌltɪ'næʃənl/ *a & n* multinacional (*f*)

multiple /'mʌltɪpl/ *a & n* múltiplo (*m*). ~**ication** /mʌltɪplɪ'keɪʃn/ *n* multiplicación *f*. ~**y** /'mʌltɪplaɪ/ *vt/i* multiplicar(se)

multitude /'mʌltɪtjuːd/ *n* multitud *f*

mum¹ /mʌm/ *n* (*fam*) mamá *f* (*fam*)

mum² /mʌm/ *a*. **keep** ~ (*fam*) guardar silencio

mumble /'mʌmbl/ *vt* decir entre dientes. —*vi* hablar entre dientes

mummify /'mʌmɪfaɪ/ *vt/i* momificar(se)

mummy¹ /'mʌmɪ/ *n* (*mother, fam*) mamá *f* (*fam*)

mummy² /'mʌmɪ/ *n* momia *f*

mumps /mʌmps/ *n* paperas *fpl*

munch /mʌntʃ/ *vt/i* mascar

mundane /mʌn'deɪn/ *a* mundano

municipal /mjuː'nɪsɪpl/ *a* municipal. ~**ity** /-'pælətɪ/ *n* municipio *m*

munificent /mjuː'nɪfɪsənt/ *a* munífico

munitions /mjuː'nɪʃnz/ *npl* municiones *fpl*

mural /'mjʊərəl/ *a & n* mural (*f*)

murder /'mɜːdə(r)/ *n* asesinato *m*. —*vt* asesinar. ~**er** *n* asesino *m*. ~**ess** *n* asesina *f*. ~**ous** *a* homicida

murky /'mɜːkɪ/ *a* (**-ier, -iest**) oscuro

murmur /'mɜːmə(r)/ *n* murmullo *m*. —*vt/i* murmurar

muscle /'mʌsl/ *n* músculo *m*. —*vi*. ~ **in** (*Amer, sl*) meterse por fuerza en

muscular /'mʌskjʊlə(r)/ *a* muscular; *(having well-developed muscles)* musculoso

muse /mjuːz/ *vi* meditar

museum /mjuːˈzɪəm/ *n* museo *m*

mush /mʌʃ/ *n* pulpa *f*

mushrom /'mʌʃrʊm/ *n* champiñón *m*; *(bot)* seta *f.* —*vi (appear in large numbers)* crecer como hongos

mushy /'mʌʃɪ/ *a* pulposo

music /'mjuːzɪk/ *n* música *f.* ~al *a* musical; *(instrument)* de música; *(talented)* que tiene don de música. —*n* comedia *f* musical. ~ hall *n* teatro *m* de variedades. ~ian /mjuːˈzɪʃn/ *n* músico *m*

musk /mʌsk/ *n* almizcle *m*

Muslim /'mʊzlɪm/ *a* & *n* musulmán *(m)*

muslin /'mʌzlɪn/ *n* muselina *f*

musquash /'mʌskwɒʃ/ *n* ratón *m* almizclero

mussel /mʌsl/ *n* mejillón *m*

must /mʌst/ *v aux* deber, tener que. **he ~ be old** debe ser viejo. **I ~ have done it** debo haberlo hecho. **you ~ go** debes marcharte. —*n.* **be a ~** ser imprescindible

mustard /'mʌstəd/ *n* mostaza *f*

muster /'mʌstə(r)/ *vt/i* reunir(se)

musty /'mʌstɪ/ *a* (-**ier**, -**iest**) que huele a cerrado

mutation /mjuːˈteɪʃn/ *n* mutación *f*

mute /mjuːt/ *a* & *n* mudo *(m)*. ~**d** *a* *(sound)* sordo; *(criticism)* callado

mutilat|e /'mjuːtɪleɪt/ *vt* mutilar. ~**ion** /-ˈleɪʃn/ *n* mutilación *f*

mutin|ous /'mjuːtɪnəs/ *a* *(sailor etc)* amotinado; *(fig)* rebelde. ~**y** *n* motín *m.* —*vi* amotinarse

mutter /'mʌtə(r)/ *vt/i* murmurar

mutton /'mʌtn/ *n* cordero *m*

mutual /'mjuːtʃʊəl/ *a* mutuo; *(common, fam)* común. ~**ly** *adv* mutuamente

muzzle /mʌzl/ *n* (*snout*) hocico *m*; *(device)* bozal *m*; *(of gun)* boca *f.* —*vt* poner el bozal a

my /maɪ/ *a* mi, mis *pl*

myopic /maɪˈɒpɪk/ *a* miope

myriad /'mɪrɪəd/ *n* miríada *f*

myself /maɪˈself/ *pron* yo mismo *m*, yo misma *f*; *(reflexive)* me; *(after prep)* mí (mismo) *m*, mí (misma) *f*

myster|ious /mɪˈstɪərɪəs/ *a* misterioso. ~**y** /'mɪstərɪ/ *n* misterio *m*

mystic /'mɪstɪk/ *a* & *n* místico *(m).* ~**al** *a* místico. ~**ism** /-sɪzəm/ *n* misticismo *m*

mystification /mɪstɪfɪˈkeɪʃn/ *n* confusión *f.* ~**y** /-faɪ/ *vt* dejar perplejo

mystique /mɪˈstiːk/ *n* mística *f*

myth /mɪθ/ *n* mito *m.* ~**ical** *a* mítico. ~**ology** /mɪˈθɒlədʒɪ/ *n* mitología *f*

N

N *abbr (north)* norte *m*

nab /næb/ *vt* (*pt* **nabbed**) *(arrest, sl)* coger (*not LAm*), agarrar (*esp LAm*)

nag /næg/ *vt* (*pt* **nagged**) fastidiar; *(scold)* regañar. —*vi* criticar

nagging /'nægɪŋ/ *a* persistente, regañón

nail /neɪl/ *n* clavo *m*; *(of finger, toe)* uña *f.* **pay on the ~** pagar a tocateja. —*vt* clavar. ~ **polish** *n* esmalte *m* para las uñas

naïve /naɪˈiːv/ *a* ingenuo

naked /'neɪkɪd/ *a* desnudo. **to the ~ eye** a simple vista. ~**ly** *adv* desnudamente. ~**ness** *n* desnudez *f*

namby-pamby /næmbɪˈpæmbɪ/ *a* & *n* ñoño *(m)*

name /neɪm/ n nombre m; (fig) fama f. —vt nombrar; (fix) fijar. **be ~d after** llevar el nombre de. **~less** a anónimo. **~ly** /ˈneɪmlɪ/ adv a saber. **~sake** /ˈneɪmseɪk/ n (person) tocayo m

nanny /ˈnænɪ/ n niñera f. **~-goat** n cabra f

nap[1] /næp/ n (sleep) sueñecito m; (after lunch) siesta f. —vi (pt napped) echarse un sueño. **catch s.o. ~ping** coger a uno desprevenido

nap[2] /næp/ n (fibres) lanilla f

nape /neɪp/ n nuca f

napkin /ˈnæpkɪn/ n (at meals) servilleta f; (for baby) pañal m

nappy /ˈnæpɪ/ n pañal m

narcotic /nɑːˈkɒtɪk/ a & n narcótico (m)

narrate /nəˈreɪt/ vt contar. **~ion** /-ʃn/ n narración f. **~ive** /ˈnærətɪv/ n relato m. **~or** /nəˈreɪtə(r)/ n narrador m

narrow /ˈnærəʊ/ a (-er, -est) estrecho. **have a ~ escape** escaparse por los pelos. —vt estrechar; (limit) limitar. —vi estrecharse. **~ly** adv estrechamente; (just) por poco. **~-minded** a de miras estrechas. **~ness** n estrechez f

nasal /ˈneɪzl/ a nasal

nast|**ily** /ˈnɑːstɪlɪ/ adv desagradablemente; (maliciously) con malevolencia. **~iness** n (malice) malevolencia f. **~y** a /ˈnɑːstɪ/ (-ier, -iest) desagradable; (malicious) malévolo; (weather) malo; (taste, smell) asqueroso; (wound) grave; (person) antipático

natal /ˈneɪtl/ a natal

nation /ˈneɪʃn/ n nación f

national /ˈnæʃənl/ a nacional. — n súbdito m. **~ anthem** n himno m nacional. **~ism** n nacionalismo m. **~ity** /næʃəˈnælɪtɪ/ n

nacionalidad f. **~ize** vt nacionalizar. **~ly** adv a nivel nacional

nationwide /ˈneɪʃnwaɪd/ a nacional

native /ˈneɪtɪv/ n natural m & f. **be a ~ of** ser natural de. —a nativo; (country, town) natal; (inborn) innato. **~ speaker of Spanish** hispanohablante m & f. **~ language** n lengua f materna

Nativity /nəˈtɪvətɪ/ n. **the ~** la Natividad f

NATO /ˈneɪtəʊ/ abbr (North Atlantic Treaty Organization) OTAN f, Organización f del Tratado del Atlántico Norte

natter /ˈnætə(r)/ vi (fam) charlar. —n (fam) charla f

natural /ˈnætʃərəl/ a natural. **~ history** n historia f natural. **~ist** n naturalista m & f

naturaliz|**ation** /nætʃərəlaɪˈzeɪʃn/ n naturalización f. **~e** vt naturalizar

naturally /ˈnætʃərəlɪ/ adv (of course) naturalmente; (by nature) por naturaleza

nature /ˈneɪtʃə(r)/ n naturaleza f; (kind) género m; (of person) carácter m

naught /nɔːt/ n (old use) nada f; (maths) cero m

naught|**ily** /ˈnɔːtɪlɪ/ adv mal. **~y** a (-ier, -iest) malo; (child) travieso; (joke) verde

nause|**a** /ˈnɔːzɪə/ n náusea f. **~ate** vt dar náuseas a. **~ous** a nauseabundo

nautical /ˈnɔːtɪkl/ a náutico. **~ mile** n milla f marina

naval /ˈneɪvl/ a naval; (officer) de marina

Navarre /nəˈvɑː(r)/ n Navarra f. **~se** a navarro

nave /neɪv/ n (of church) nave f

navel /ˈneɪvl/ n ombligo m

navigable /ˈnævɪgəbl/ a navegable

navigate /'nævɪgeɪt/ *vt* navegar por ⟨*sea etc*⟩; gobernar ⟨*ship*⟩. — *vi* navegar. **~ion** *n* navegación *f*. **~or** *n* navegante *m*

navvy /'nævɪ/ *n* peón *m* caminero

navy /'neɪvɪ/ *n* marina *f*. **~ (blue)** azul *m* marino

NE *abbr* (*north-east*) noreste *m*

near /'nɪə(r)/ *adv* cerca. **~ at hand** muy cerca. **~ by** *adv* cerca. **draw ~** acercarse. — *prep.* **~ (to)** cerca de. — *a* cercano. — *vt* acercarse a. **~by** *a* cercano. **N~ East** *n* Oriente *m* Próximo. **~ly** /'nɪəlɪ/ *adv* casi. **not ~ly as pretty as** no es ni con mucho tan guapa como. **~ness** /'nɪənɪs/ *n* proximidad *f*

neat /niːt/ *a* (-er, -est) pulcro; ⟨*room etc*⟩ bien arreglado; ⟨*clever*⟩ diestro; ⟨*ingenious*⟩ hábil; ⟨*whisky, brandy etc*⟩ solo. **~ly** *adv* pulcramente. **~ness** *n* pulcritud *f*

nebulous /'nebjʊləs/ *a* nebuloso

necessar|ies /'nesəsərɪz/ *npl* lo indispensable. **~ily** /nesə'serɪlɪ/ *adv* necesariamente. **~y** *a* necesario, imprescindible

necessit|ate /nə'sesɪteɪt/ *vt* necesitar. **~y** /nɪ'sesɪtɪ/ *n* necesidad *f*; ⟨*thing*⟩ cosa *f* indispensable

neck /nek/ *n* ⟨*of person, bottle, dress*⟩ cuello *m*; ⟨*of animal*⟩ pescuezo *m*. **~ and ~** parejos. **~lace** /'nekləs/ *n* collar *m*. **~line** *n* escote *m*. **~tie** *n* corbata *f*

nectar /'nektə(r)/ *n* néctar *m*

nectarine /'nektəri:n/ *n* nectarina *f*

née /neɪ/ *a* de soltera

need /ni:d/ *n* necesidad *f*. — *vt* necesitar; ⟨*demand*⟩ exigir. **you ~ not speak** no tienes que hablar

needle /'ni:dl/ *n* aguja *f*. — *vt* ⟨*annoy, fam*⟩ pinchar

needless /'ni:dlɪs/ *a* innecesario. **~ly** *adv* innecesariamente

needlework /'ni:dlwɜ:k/ *n* costura *f*; ⟨*embroidery*⟩ bordado *m*

needy /'ni:dɪ/ *a* (-ier, -iest) necesitado

negation /nɪ'geɪʃn/ *n* negación *f*

negative /'negətɪv/ *a* negativo. — *n* ⟨*of photograph*⟩ negativo *m*; ⟨*word, gram*⟩ negativa *f*. **~ly** *adv* negativamente

neglect /nɪ'glekt/ *vt* descuidar; no cumplir con ⟨*duty*⟩. **~ to do** dejar de hacer. — *n* descuido *m*, negligencia *f*. **(state of) ~** abandono *m*. **~ful** *a* descuidado

négligé /'neglɪʒeɪ/ *n* bata *f*, salto *m* de cama

negligen|ce /'neglɪdʒəns/ *n* negligencia *f*, descuido *m*. **~t** *a* descuidado

negligible /'neglɪdʒəbl/ *a* insignificante

negotiable /nɪ'gəʊʃəbl/ *a* negociable

negotiat|e /nɪ'gəʊʃɪeɪt/ *vt/i* negociar. **~ion** /-'eɪʃn/ *n* negociación *f*. **~or** *n* negociador *m*

Negr|ess /'ni:grɪs/ *n* negra *f*. **~o** *n* (*pl* -oes) negro *m*. — *a* negro

neigh /neɪ/ *n* relincho *m*. — *vi* relinchar

neighbour /'neɪbə(r)/ *n* vecino *m*. **~hood** *n* vecindad *f*, barrio *m*. **in the ~hood of** alrededor de. **~ing** *a* vecino. **~ly** /'neɪbəlɪ/ *a* amable

neither /'naɪðə(r)/ *a & pron* ninguno *m* de los dos, ni el uno *m* ni el otro *m*. — *adv* ni. **~ big nor small** ni grande ni pequeño. **~ shall I come** no voy yo tampoco. — *conj* tampoco

neon /'ni:ɒn/ *n* neón *m*. — *a* ⟨*lamp etc*⟩ de neón

nephew /'nevju:/ *n* sobrino *m*

nepotism /'nepətɪzəm/ *m* nepotismo *m*

nerve /nɜːv/ n nervio m; (*courage*) valor m; (*calm*) sangre f fría; (*impudence*, fam) descaro m. **~-racking** a exasperante. **~s** npl (*before exams etc*) nervios mpl

nervous /ˈnɜːvəs/ a nervioso. **be/feel ~** (*afraid*) tener miedo (**of** a). **~ly** adv (*tensely*) nerviosamente; (*timidly*) tímidamente. **~ness** n nerviosidad f; (*fear*) miedo m

nervy /ˈnɜːvɪ/ a see **nervous**; (*Amer*, fam) descarado

nest /nest/ n nido m. — vi anidar. **~-egg** n (*money*) ahorros mpl

nestle /ˈnesl/ vi acomodarse. **~ up to** arrimarse a

net /net/ n red f. — vt (pt netted) coger (*not LAm*), agarrar (*esp LAm*). — a (*weight etc*) neto

netball /ˈnetbɔːl/ n baloncesto m

Netherlands /ˈneðələndz/ npl. **the ~** los Países mpl Bajos

netting /ˈnetɪŋ/ n (*nets*) redes fpl; (*wire*) malla f; (*fabric*) tul m

nettle /ˈnetl/ n ortiga f

network /ˈnetwɜːk/ n red f

neuralgia /njʊəˈrældʒɪə/ n neuralgia f

neuro|sis /njʊəˈrəʊsɪs/ n (pl -oses /-siːz/) neurosis f. **~tic** a & n neurótico m

neuter /ˈnjuːtə(r)/ a & n neutro (m). — vt castrar (*animals*)

neutral /ˈnjuːtrəl/ a neutral; (*colour*) neutro; (*elec*) neutro. **~** (**gear**) (*auto*) punto m muerto. **~ity** /-ˈtrælɪtɪ/ n neutralidad f

neutron /ˈnjuːtrɒn/ n neutrón m. **~ bomb** n bomba f de neutrones

never /ˈnevə(r)/ adv nunca, jamás; (*not*, fam) no. **~ again** nunca más. **~ mind** (*don't worry*) no te preocupes, no se preocupe; (*it doesn't matter*) no importa. **he ~ smiles** no sonríe nunca. **I ~ saw him** (*fam*) no le vi. **~-ending** a interminable

nevertheless /nevəðəˈles/ adv sin embargo, no obstante

new /njuː/ a (-er, -est) (*new to owner*) nuevo (*placed before noun*); (*brand new*) nuevo (*placed after noun*). **~-born** a recién nacido. **~comer** n recién llegado m. **~fangled** a (*pej*) moderno. **~-laid egg** n huevo m fresco. **~ly** adv nuevamente; (*recently*) recién. **~ly-weds** npl recién casados mpl. **~ moon** n luna f nueva. **~ness** n novedad f

news /njuːz/ n noticias fpl; (*broadcasting, press*) informaciones fpl; (*on TV*) telediario m; (*on radio*) diario m hablado. **~agent** n vendedor m de periódicos. **~caster** n locutor m. **~letter** n boletín m. **~paper** n periódico m. **~reader** n locutor m. **~reel** n noticiario m, nodo m (*in Spain*)

newt /njuːt/ n tritón m

new year /njuːˈjɪə(r)/ n año m nuevo. **N~'s Day** n día m de Año Nuevo. **N~'s Eve** n noche f vieja

New Zealand /njuːˈziːlənd/ n Nueva Zelanda f. **~er** n neozelandés m

next /nekst/ a próximo; (*week, month etc*) que viene, próximo; (*adjoining*) vecino; (*following*) siguiente. — adv la próxima vez; (*afterwards*) después. — n siguiente m. **~ to** junto a. **~ to nothing** casi nada. **~ door** al lado (**to** de). **~-door** al lado de. **~-best** mejor alternativa f. **~ of kin** n pariente m más próximo, parientes mpl más próximos

nib /nɪb/ n (*of pen*) plumilla f

nibble /ˈnɪbl/ vt/i mordisquear. — n mordisco m

nice /naɪs/ a (-er, -est) agradable; (*likeable*) simpático; (*kind*) amable; (*pretty*) bonito; (*weather*) bueno; (*subtle*) sutil. **~ly** adv agradablemente;

(*kindly*) amablemente; (*well*) bien

nicety /'naɪsətɪ/ n (*precision*) precisión f; (*detail*) detalle m. **to a ~** exactamente

niche /nɪtʃ, niːʃ/ n (*recess*) nicho m; (*fig*) buena posición f

nick /nɪk/ n corte m; (*prison, sl*) cárcel f. **in the ~ of time** justo a tiempo. —vt (*steal, arrest, sl*) birlar

nickel /'nɪkl/ n níquel m; (*Amer*) moneda f de cinco centavos

nickname /'nɪkneɪm/ n apodo m; (*short form*) diminutivo m. —vt apodar

nicotine /'nɪkətiːn/ n nicotina f

niece /niːs/ n sobrina f

nifty /'nɪftɪ/ a (*sl*) (*smart*) elegante

Nigeria /naɪ'dʒɪərɪə/ n Nigeria f. **~n** a & n nigeriano (m)

niggardly /'nɪgədlɪ/ a (*person*) tacaño; (*thing*) miserable

niggling /'nɪglɪŋ/ a molesto

night /naɪt/ n noche f; (*evening*) tarde f. —a nocturno, de noche. **~-cap** n (*hat*) gorro m de dormir; (*drink*) bebida f (tomada antes de acostarse). **~club** n sala f de fiestas, boîte f. **~-dress** n camisón m. **~fall** n anochecer m. **~-gown** n camisón m

nightingale /'naɪtɪŋgeɪl/ n ruiseñor m

night: **~-life** n vida f nocturna. **~ly** adv todas las noches. **~mare** n pesadilla f. **~-school** n escuela f nocturna. **~-time** n noche f. **~-watchman** n sereno m

nil /nɪl/ n nada f; (*sport*) cero m

nimble /'nɪmbl/ a (-er, -est) ágil

nine /naɪn/ a & n nueve (m)

nineteen /naɪn'tiːn/ a & n diecinueve (m). **~th** a & n diecinueve (m), decimonoveno (m)

ninetieth /'naɪntɪɪθ/ a noventa, nonagésimo. **~y** a & n noventa (m)

ninth /naɪnθ/ a & n noveno (m)

nip[1] /nɪp/ vt (pt **nipped**) (*pinch*) pellizcar; (*bite*) mordisquear. —vi (*rush, sl*) correr. —n (*pinch*) pellizco m; (*cold*) frío m

nip[2] /nɪp/ n (*of drink*) trago m

nipper /'nɪpə(r)/ n (*sl*) chaval m

nipple /'nɪpl/ n pezón m; (*of baby's bottle*) tetilla f

nippy /'nɪpɪ/ a (-ier, -iest) (*nimble, fam*) ágil; (*quick, fam*) rápido; (*chilly, fam*) fresquito

nitrogen /'naɪtrədʒən/ n nitrógeno m

nitwit /'nɪtwɪt/ n (*fam*) imbécil m & f

no /nəʊ/ a ninguno. **~ entry** prohibido el paso. **~ man's land** n tierra f de nadie. **~ smoking** se prohibe fumar. **~ way!** (*Amer, fam*) ¡ni hablar! —adv no. —n (pl **noes**) no m

nobility /nəʊ'bɪlətɪ/ n nobleza f

noble /'nəʊbl/ a (-er, -est) noble. **~man** n noble m

nobody /'nəʊbədɪ/ pron nadie m. —n nadie m. **~ is there** no hay nadie. **he knows ~** no conoce a nadie

nocturnal /nɒk'tɜːnl/ a nocturno

nod /nɒd/ vt (pt **nodded**). **~ one's head** asentir con la cabeza. —vi (*in agreement*) asentir con la cabeza; (*in greeting*) saludar; (*be drowsy*) dar cabezadas. —n inclinación f de cabeza

nodule /'nɒdjuːl/ n nódulo m

noise /nɔɪz/ n ruido m. **~eless** a silencioso. **~ily** /'nɔɪzɪlɪ/ adv ruidosamente. **~y** a (-ier, -iest) ruidoso

nomad /'nəʊmæd/ n nómada m & f. **~ic** /-'mædɪk/ a nómada

nominal /'nɒmɪnl/ a nominal

nominate /'nɒmɪneɪt/ vt nombrar; (*put forward*) proponer. **~ion** /-'neɪʃn/ n nombramiento m non-... /nɒn/ pref *no* ...

nonagenarian /nəʊnədʒɪ-'neərɪən/ *a* & *n* nonagenario (*m*), noventón (*m*)

nonchalant /'nɒnʃələnt/ *a* imperturbable

non-commissioned /nɒnkə-'mɪʃnd/ *a*. ~ officer *n* suboficial *m*

non-comittal /nɒnkə'mɪtl/ *a* evasivo

nondescript /'nɒndɪskrɪpt/ *a* inclasificable, anodino

none /nʌn/ *pron* (*person*) nadie, ninguno; (*thing*) ninguno, nada. ~ of nada de. ~ of us ninguno de nosotros. I have ~ no tengo nada. —*adv* no, de ninguna manera. he is ~ the happier no está más contento

nonentity /nɒ'nentətɪ/ *n* nulidad *f*

non-existent /nɒnɪg'zɪstənt/ *a* inexistente

nonplussed /nɒn'plʌst/ *a* perplejo

nonsens|e /'nɒnsns/ *n* tonterías *fpl*, disparates *mpl*. ~ical /-'sensɪkl/ *a* absurdo

non-smoker /nɒn'sməʊkə(r)/ *n* persona *f* que no fuma; (*rail*) departamento *m* de no fumadores

non-starter /nɒn'stɑːtə(r)/ *n* (*fam*) proyecto *m* imposible

non-stop /nɒn'stɒp/ *a* (*train*) directo; (*flight*) sin escalas. —*adv* sin parar; (*by train*) directamente; (*by air*) sin escalas

noodles /'nuːdlz/ *npl* fideos *mpl*

nook /nʊk/ *n* rincón *m*

noon /nuːn/ *n* mediodía *m*

no-one /'nəʊwʌn/ *pron* nadie. *see* nobody

noose /nuːs/ *n* nudo *m* corredizo

nor /nɔː(r)/ *conj* ni, tampoco. neither blue ~ red ni azul ni rojo.
he doesn't play the piano, ~

do I no sabe tocar el piano, ni yo tampoco

Nordic /'nɔːdɪk/ *a* nórdico

norm /nɔːm/ *n* norma *f*; (*normal*) lo normal

normal /'nɔːml/ *a* normal. ~cy *n* (*Amer*) normalidad *f*. ~ity /-'mælətɪ/ *n* normalidad *f*. ~ly *adv* normalmente

Norman /'nɔːmən/ *a* & *n* normando (*m*)

Normandy /'nɔːməndɪ/ *n* Normandía *f*

north /nɔːθ/ *n* norte *m*. —*a* del norte, norteño. —*adv* hacia el norte. N~ America *n* América *f* del Norte, Norteamérica *f*. N~ American *a* & *n* norteamericano (*m*). ~east *n* nordeste *m*. ~erly /'nɔːðəlɪ/ *a* del norte. ~ern /'nɔːðən/ *a* del norte. ~erner *n* norteño *m*. N~ Sea *n* mar *m* del Norte. ~ward *a* hacia el norte. ~wards *adv* hacia el norte. ~west *n* noroeste *m*

Norw|ay /'nɔːweɪ/ *n* Noruega *f*. ~egian *a* & *n* noruego (*m*)

nose /nəʊz/ *n* nariz *f*. —*vi*. ~ about *v* curiosear. ~bleed *n* hemorragia *f* nasal. ~dive *n* picado *m*

nostalgia /nɒ'stældʒə/ *n* nostalgia *f*. ~c *a* nostálgico

nostril /'nɒstrɪl/ *n* nariz *f*; (*of horse*) ollar *m*

nosy /'nəʊzɪ/ *a* (-ier, -iest) (*fam*) entrometido

not /nɒt/ *adv* no. ~ at all no... nada; (*after thank you*) de nada. ~ yet aún no. I do ~ know no sé. I suppose ~ supongo que no

notable /'nəʊtəbl/ *a* notable. —*n* (*person*) notabilidad *f*. ~y /'nəʊtəblɪ/ *adv* notablemente

notary /'nəʊtərɪ/ *n* notario *m*

notation /nəʊ'teɪʃn/ *n* notación *f*

notch /nɒtʃ/ *n* muesca *f*. —*vt*. ~ up apuntar ‹*score etc*›

note /nəʊt/ n nota f; (banknote)
billete m. **take ~s** tomar apuntes. —vt notar. **~book** n libreta
f. **~d** a célebre. **~paper** n papel
m de escribir. **~worthy** a
notable

nothing /ˈnʌθɪŋ/ pron nada. **he
eats ~** no come nada. **for ~**
(free) gratis; (in vain) inútilmente. —n nada f; (person) nulidad f; (thing of no importance)
fruslería f; (zero) cero m. —adv
de ninguna manera. **~ big** nada
grande. **~ else** nada más. **~
much** poca cosa

notice /ˈnəʊtɪs/ n (attention)
atención f; (advert) anuncio m;
(sign) letrero m; (poster) cartel
m; (termination of employment)
despido m; (warning) aviso m.
(advance) ~ previo aviso m.
(of dismissal) despido m. **take
~ of** prestar atención a, hacer
caso a (person); hacer caso de
(thing). —vt notar. **~able** a evidente. **~ably** adv visiblemente.
~board n tablón m de anuncios

notification /nəʊtɪfɪˈkeɪʃn/ n
aviso m, notificación f. **~y** vt
avisar

notion /ˈnəʊʃn/ n (concept) concepto m; (idea) idea f. **~s** npl
(sewing goods etc, Amer) artículos mpl de mercería

notoriety /nəʊtəˈraɪətɪ/ n notoriedad f; (pej) mala fama f. **~ous**
/nəʊˈtɔːrɪəs/ a notorio. **~ously**
adv notoriamente

notwithstanding /nɒtwɪθ
ˈstændɪŋ/ prep a pesar de. —adv
sin embargo

nougat /ˈnuːgɑː/ n turrón m

nought /nɔːt/ n cero m

noun /naʊn/ n sustantivo m,
nombre m

nourish /ˈnʌrɪʃ/ vt alimentar;
(incl fig) nutrir. **~ment** n alimento m

novel /ˈnɒvl/ n novela f. —a
nuevo. **~ist** n novelista m & f.
~ty n novedad f

November /nəʊˈvembə(r)/ n noviembre m

novice /ˈnɒvɪs/ n principiante m
& f

now /naʊ/ adv ahora. **~ and
again, ~ and then** de vez en
cuando. **just ~** ahora mismo; (a
moment ago) hace poco. —conj
ahora que

nowadays /ˈnaʊədeɪz/ adv hoy
(en) día

nowhere /ˈnəʊweə(r)/ adv
en/por ninguna parte; (after
motion towards) a ninguna parte

noxious /ˈnɒkʃəs/ a nocivo

nozzle /ˈnɒzl/ n boquilla f; (tec)
tobera f

nuance /ˈnjuːɑːns/ n matiz m

nuclear /ˈnjuːklɪə(r)/ a nuclear

nucleus /ˈnjuːklɪəs/ n (pl -lei
/-lɪaɪ/) núcleo m

nude /njuːd/ a & n desnudo (m).
in the ~ desnudo

nudge /nʌdʒ/ vt dar un codazo
a. —n codazo m

nudi|sm /ˈnjuːdɪzəm/ n desnudismo m. **~st** n nudista m & f.
~ty /ˈnjuːdətɪ/ n desnudez f

nuisance /ˈnjuːsns/ n (thing,
event) fastidio m; (person) pesado m. **be a ~** dar la lata

null /nʌl/ a nulo. **~ify** vt anular

numb /nʌm/ a entumecido. —vt
entumecer

number /ˈnʌmbə(r)/ n número
m. —vt numerar; (count, include)
contar. **~plate** n matrícula f

numeracy /ˈnjuːmərəsɪ/ n conocimientos mpl de matemáticas

numeral /ˈnjuːmərəl/ n número
m

numerate /ˈnjuːmərət/ a que
tiene buenos conocimientos de
matemáticas

numerical /njuːˈmerɪkl/ a numérico

numerous /'nju:mərəs/ a numeroso

nun /nʌn/ n monja f

nurse /nɜ:s/ n enfermera f, enfermero m; *(nanny)* niñera f. wet ~ n nodriza f. ~ vt cuidar; abrigar *(hope etc)*. ~maid n niñera f

nursery /'nɜ:səri/ n cuarto m de los niños; *(for plants)* vivero m. ~ (day) ~ n guardería f infantil. ~ rhyme n canción f infantil. ~ school n escuela f de párvulos

nursing home /'nɜ:sɪŋhəʊm/ n *(for old people)* asilo m de ancianos

nurture /'nɜ:tʃə(r)/ vt alimentar

nut /nʌt/ n *(walnut, Brazil nut etc)* nuez f; *(hazelnut)* avellana f; *(peanut)* cacahuete m; *(tec)* tuerca f; *(crazy person, sl)* chiflado m. ~crackers npl cascanueces m invar

nutmeg /'nʌtmeg/ n nuez f moscada

nutrient /'nju:trɪənt/ n alimento m

nutrition /nju:'trɪʃn/ n nutrición f. ~ious a nutritivo

nuts /nʌts/ a *(crazy, sl)* chiflado

nutshell /'nʌtʃel/ n cáscara f de nuez. in a ~ en pocas palabras

nuzzle /'nʌzl/ vt acariciar con el hocico

NW abbr *(north-west)* noroeste m

nylon /'naɪlɒn/ n nailon m. ~s npl medias fpl de nailon

nymph /nɪmf/ n ninfa f

O

oaf /əʊf/ n *(pl oafs)* zoquete m

oak /əʊk/ n roble m

OAP /əʊer'pi:/ abbr *(old-age pensioner)* n pensionista m & f

oar /ɔ:(r)/ n remo m. ~sman /'ɔ:zmən/ n *(pl -men)* remero m

oasis /əʊ'eɪsɪs/ n *(pl oases* /-si:z/) oasis m invar

oath /əʊθ/ n juramento m; *(swear-word)* palabrota f

oatmeal /'əʊtmi:l/ n harina f de avena. ~s /əʊts/ npl avena f

obedien|ce /ə'bi:dɪəns/ n obediencia f. ~t /ə'bi:dɪənt/ a obediente. ~tly adv obedientemente

obelisk /'ɒbəlɪsk/ n obelisco m

obes|e /əʊ'bi:s/ a obeso. ~ity n obesidad f

obey /ə'beɪ/ vt obedecer; cumplir *(instructions etc)*

obituary /ə'bɪtʃʊəri/ n necrología f

object /'ɒbdʒɪkt/ n objeto m. /əb'dʒekt/ vi oponerse

objection /əb'dʒekʃn/ n objeción f. ~able /əb'dʒekʃnəbl/ a censurable; *(unpleasant)* desagradable

objective /əb'dʒektɪv/ a & n objetivo *(m)*. ~ively adv objetivamente

objector /əb'dʒektə(r)/ n objetante m & f

obligation /ɒblɪ'geɪʃn/ n obligación f. be under an ~ation to tener obligación de. ~atory /ə'blɪgətrɪ/ a obligatorio. ~e /ə'blaɪdʒ/ vt obligar; *(do a small service)* hacer un favor a. ~ed a agradecido. much ~ed! ¡muchas gracias! ~ing a atento

oblique /ə'bli:k/ a oblicuo

obliterate /ə'blɪtəreɪt/ vt borrar. ~ion /-'reɪʃn/ n borradura f

oblivion /ə'blɪvɪən/ n olvido m. ~us /ə'blɪvɪəs/ a *(unaware)* inconsciente (to, of de)

oblong /'ɒblɒŋ/ a & n oblongo *(m)*

obnoxious /əb'nɒkʃəs/ a odioso

oboe /'əʊbəʊ/ n oboe m

obscene /əb'si:n/ a obsceno. ~ity /-enəti/ n obscenidad f

obscure /əb'skjʊə(r)/ a oscuro. ~vt oscurecer; *(conceal)*

esconder; (confuse) confundir. ~ity n oscuridad f

obsequious /əb'si:kwɪəs/ a obsequioso

observan|ce /əb'zɜ:vəns/ n observancia f. ~t /əb'zɜ:vənt/ a observador

observation /ɒbzə'veɪʃn/ n observación f

observatory /əb'zɜ:vətrɪ/ n observatorio m

observe /əb'zɜ:v/ vt observar. ~r n observador m

obsess /əb'ses/ vt obsesionar. ~ion /-ʃn/ n obsesión f. ~ive a obsesivo

obsolete /'ɒbsəli:t/ a desusado

obstacle /'ɒbstəkl/ n obstáculo m

obstetrics /əb'stetrɪks/ n obstetricia f

obstina|cy /'ɒbstɪnəsɪ/ n obstinación f. ~te /'ɒbstɪnət/ a obstinado. ~tely adv obstinadamente

obstreperous /əb'strepərəs/ a turbulento, ruidoso, protestón

obstruct /əb'strʌkt/ vt obstruir. ~ion /-ʃn/ n obstrucción f

obtain /əb'teɪn/ vt obtener. —vi prevalecer. ~able a asequible

obtrusive /əb'tru:sɪv/ a importuno

obtuse /əb'tju:s/ a obtuso

obviate /'ɒbvɪeɪt/ vt evitar

obvious /'ɒbvɪəs/ a obvio. ~ly obviamente

occasion /ə'keɪʒn/ n ocasión f, oportunidad f. on ~ de vez en cuando. —vt ocasionar. ~al /ə'keɪʒənl/ a poco frecuente. ~ally adv de vez en cuando

occult /ɒ'kʌlt/ a oculto

occup|ant /'ɒkjʊpənt/ n ocupante m & f. ~ation /ɒkjʊ'peɪʃn/ n ocupación f. (job) trabajo m, profesión f. ~ational a profesional. ~ier n ocupante m & f. ~y /'ɒkjʊpaɪ/ vt ocupar

occur /ə'kɜ:(r)/ vi (pt occurred) ocurrir, suceder; (exist) encontrarse. it ~red to me that se me ocurrió que. ~rence /ə'kʌrəns/ n suceso m, acontecimiento m

ocean /'əʊʃn/ n océano m

o'clock /ə'klɒk/ adv. it is 7 ~ son las siete

octagon /'ɒktəgən/ n octágono m

octane /'ɒkteɪn/ n octano m

octave /'ɒktɪv/ n octava f

October /ɒk'təʊbə(r)/ n octubre m

octopus /'ɒktəpəs/ n (pl -puses) pulpo m

oculist /'ɒkjʊlɪst/ n oculista m & f

odd /ɒd/ a (-er, -est) extraño, raro; (number) impar; (one of pair) sin pareja; (occasional) poco frecuente; (left over) sobrante. fifty-~ unos cincuenta, cincuenta y pico. the ~ one out la excepción f. ~ity n (thing) curiosidad f. (person) excéntrico m. ~ly adv extrañamente. ~ly enough por extraño que parezca. ~ment /'ɒdmənt/ n retazo m. ~s /ɒdz/ npl probabilidades fpl; (in betting) apuesta f. ~s and ends retazos mpl. at ~s de punta, de malas

ode /əʊd/ n oda f

odious /'əʊdɪəs/ a odioso

odour /'əʊdə(r)/ n olor m. ~less a inodoro

of /ɒv, əv/ prep de. a friend ~ mine un amigo mío. how kind ~ you es Vd muy amable

off /ɒf/ adv lejos; (light etc) apagado; (tap) cerrado; (food) pasado. —prep de, desde; (away from) fuera de; (distant from) lejos de. be better ~ estar mejor. be ~ marcharse. day ~ n día m de asueto, día m libre

offal /'ɒfl/ n menudos mpl, asaduras fpl

off: ~**beat** a insólito. ~ **chance** n posibilidad f remota. ~ **colour** a indispuesto

offen|ce /ɔ'fens/ n ofensa f; (illegal act) delito m. **take** ~**ce** ofenderse. ~**d** /ɔ'fend/ vt ofender. ~**der** n delincuente m & f. ~**sive** /ɔ'fensɪv/ a ofensivo; (disgusting) repugnante. —n ofensiva f

offer /'ɒfə(r)/ vt ofrecer. —n oferta f. **on** ~ en oferta

offhand /ɒf'hænd/ a (casual) desenvuelto; (brusque) descortés. —adv de improviso

office /'ɒfɪs/ n oficina f; (post) cargo m

officer /'ɒfɪsə(r)/ n oficial m; (policeman) policía f, guardia m; (of organization) director m

official /ɔ'fɪʃl/ a & n oficial (m). ~**ly** adv oficialmente

officiate /ɔ'fɪʃɪeɪt/ vi oficiar. ~ **as** desempeñar las funciones de

officious /ɔ'fɪʃəs/ a oficioso

offing /'ɒfɪŋ/ n. **in the** ~ en perspectiva

off: ~**licence** n tienda f de bebidas alcohólicas. ~**load** vt descargar. ~**putting** a (disconcerting, fam) desconcertante; (repellent, fam) repugnante. ~**set** /'ɒfset/ vt (pt ~**set**, pres p ~**setting**) contrapesar. ~**shoot** /'ɒfʃuːt/ n retoño m; (fig) ramificación f. ~**side** /ɒf'saɪd/ a (sport) fuera de juego. ~**spring** /'ɒfsprɪŋ/ n invar progenie f. ~**stage** a entre bastidores. ~**white** a blancuzco, color hueso

often /'ɒfn/ adv muchas veces, con frecuencia, a menudo. **how** ~? ¿cuántas veces?

ogle /'əʊgl/ vt comerse con los ojos

ogre /'əʊgə(r)/ n ogro m

oh /əʊ/ int ¡oh!, ¡ay!

oil /ɔɪl/ n aceite m; (petroleum) petróleo m. —vt lubricar. ~**field** /'ɔɪlfiːld/ n yacimiento m petrolífero. ~**painting** n pintura f al óleo. ~**rig** /'ɔɪlrɪg/ n plataforma f de perforación. ~**skins** /'ɔɪlskɪnz/ npl chubasquero m. ~**y** a aceitoso; (food) grasiento

ointment /'ɔɪntmənt/ n ungüento m

OK /əʊ'keɪ/ int ¡vale!, ¡de acuerdo! —a bien; (satisfactory) satisfactorio. —adv muy bien

old /əʊld/ a (-**er**, -**est**) viejo; (not modern) anticuado; (former) antiguo. **how** ~ **is she?** ¿cuántos años tiene? **she is ten years** ~ tiene diez años. **of** ~ de antaño. ~ **age** n vejez f. ~**fashioned** a anticuado. ~ **maid** n solterona f. ~**world** a antiguo

oleander /əʊlɪ'ændə(r)/ n adelfa f

olive /'ɒlɪv/ n (fruit) aceituna f; (tree) olivo m. —a de oliva; (colour) aceitunado

Olympic /ɔ'lɪmpɪk/ a olímpico. ~**s** npl, ~ **Games** npl Juegos mpl Olímpicos

omelette /'ɒmlɪt/ n tortilla f, tortilla f de huevos (Mex)

om|en /'əʊmen/ n agüero m. ~**inous** /'ɒmɪnəs/ a siniestro

omi|ssion /ɔ'mɪʃn/ n omisión f. ~**t** /ɔ'mɪt/ vt (pt **omitted**) omitir

omnipotent /ɒm'nɪpətənt/ a omnipotente

on /ɒn/ prep en, sobre. ~ **foot** a pie. ~ **Monday** el lunes. ~ **Mondays** los lunes. ~ **seeing** al ver. ~ **the way** de camino. —adv (light etc) encendido; (put on) puesto, poco natural; (machine) en marcha; (tap) abierto. ~ **and off** de vez en cuando. ~ **and** ~ sin cesar. **and so** ~ y así sucesivamente. **be** ~ **at** (fam) criticar. **go** ~ continuar. **later** ~ más tarde

once /wʌns/ *adv* una vez; (*formerly*) antes. —*conj* una vez que. **at ~** en seguida. **~-over** *n* (*fam*) ojeada *f*

oncoming /ˈɒnkʌmɪŋ/ *a* que se acerca; (*traffic*) que viene en sentido contrario, de frente

one /wʌn/ *a* & *n* uno (*m*). —*pron* uno. **~ another** el uno al otro. **~ by ~** uno a uno. **~ never knows** nunca se sabe. **the blue ~** el azul. **this ~** éste. **~-off** *a* (*fam*) único

onerous /ˈɒnərəs/ *a* oneroso

one: **~self** /wʌnˈself/ *pron* (*subject*) uno mismo; (*object*) se; (*after prep*) sí (mismo). **by ~self** solo. **~-sided** *a* unilateral. **~-way** *a* (*street*) de dirección única; (*ticket*) de ida

onion /ˈʌnɪən/ *n* cebolla *f*

onlooker /ˈɒnlʊkə(r)/ *n* espectador *m*

only /ˈəʊnlɪ/ *a* único. **~ son** *n* hijo *m* único. —*adv* sólo, solamente. **~ just** apenas. **~ too** de veras. —*conj* pero, sólo que

onset /ˈɒnset/ *n* principio *m*; (*attack*) ataque *m*

onslaught /ˈɒnslɔːt/ *n* ataque *m* violento

onus /ˈəʊnəs/ *n* responsabilidad *f*

onward(s) /ˈɒnwəd(z)/ *a* & *adv* hacia adelante

onyx /ˈɒnɪks/ *n* ónice *f*

ooze /uːz/ *vt/i* rezumar

opal /ˈəʊpl/ *n* ópalo *m*

opaque /əʊˈpeɪk/ *a* opaco

open /ˈəʊpən/ *a* abierto; (*free to all*) público; (*undisguised*) manifiesto; (*question*) discutible; (*view*) despejado. **~ sea** *n* alta mar *f*. **~ secret** *n* secreto *m* a voces. **O~ University** *n* Universidad *f* a Distancia. **half-~** *a* medio abierto. **in the ~** *n* al aire libre. —*vt/i* abrir. **~-ended** *a* abierto. **~er** /ˈəʊpənə(r)/ *n* (*for tins*) abrelatas *m invar*; (*for

bottles with caps) abrebotellas *m invar*; (*corkscrew*) sacacorchos *m invar*. **eye~er** *n* (*fam*) revelación *f*. **~ing** /ˈəʊpənɪŋ/ *n* abertura *f*; (*beginning*) principio *m*; (*job*) vacante *m*. **~ly** /ˈəʊpənlɪ/ *adv* abiertamente. **~-minded** *a* imparcial

opera /ˈɒprə/ *n* ópera *f*. **~glasses** *npl* gemelos *mpl* de teatro

operate /ˈɒpəreɪt/ *vt* hacer funcionar. —*vi* funcionar; (*medicine etc*) operar. **~ on** (*med*) operar *a*

operatic /ɒpəˈrætɪk/ *a* operístico

operation /ɒpəˈreɪʃn/ *n* operación *f*; (*mec*) funcionamiento *m*. **in ~** en vigor. **~al** /ɒpəˈreɪʃnl/ *a* operacional

operative /ˈɒpərətɪv/ *a* operativo; (*law etc*) en vigor

operator /ˈɒpəreɪtə(r)/ *n* operario *m*; (*telephonist*) telefonista *m* & *f*

operetta /ɒpəˈretə/ *n* opereta *f*

opinion /əˈpɪnɪən/ *n* opinión *f*. **in my ~** a mi parecer. **~ated** *a* dogmático

opium /ˈəʊpɪəm/ *n* opio *m*

opponent /əˈpəʊnənt/ *n* adversario *m*

opportune /ˈɒpətjuːn/ *a* oportuno. **~ist** /ɒpəˈtjuːnɪst/ *n* oportunista *m* & *f*. **~ity** /ɒpəˈtjuːnətɪ/ *n* oportunidad *f*

oppos|e /əˈpəʊz/ *vt* oponerse *a*. **~ed to** en contra de. **be ~ed to** oponerse *a*. **~ing** *a* opuesto

opposite /ˈɒpəzɪt/ *a* opuesto; (*facing*) de enfrente. —*n* contrario *m*. —*adv* enfrente. —*prep* enfrente de. **~ number** *n* homólogo *m*

opposition /ɒpəˈzɪʃn/ *n* oposición *f*; (*resistence*) resistencia *f*

oppress /əˈpres/ *vt* oprimir. **~ion** /-ʃn/ *n* opresión *f*. **~ive** *a* (*cruel*) opresivo; (*heat*) sofocante. **~or** *n* opresor *m*

opt /ɒpt/ vi. ~ **for** elegir. ~ **out** negarse a participar

optic|al /'ɒptɪkl/ a óptico. ~**ian** /ɒp'tɪʃn/ n óptico m

optimis|m /'ɒptɪmɪzəm/ n optimismo m. ~**t** /'ɒptɪmɪst/ n optimista m & f. ~**tic** /-'mɪstɪk/ a optimista

optimum /'ɒptɪməm/ n lo óptimo, lo mejor

option /'ɒpʃn/ n opción f. ~**al** /'ɒpʃənl/ a facultativo

opulen|ce /'ɒpjʊləns/ n opulencia f. ~**t** /'ɒpjʊlənt/ a opulento

or /ɔ:(r)/ conj o; (before Spanish o- and ho-) u; (after negative) ni. ~ **else** si no, o bien

oracle /'ɒrəkl/ n oráculo m

oral /'ɔ:rəl/ a oral. —n (fam) examen m oral

orange /'ɒrɪndʒ/ n naranja f; (tree) naranjo m; (colour) color m naranja. —a de color naranja. ~**ade** n naranjada f

orator /'ɒrətə(r)/ n orador m

oratorio /ɒrə'tɔ:rɪəʊ/ n (pl -os) oratorio m

oratory /'ɒrətrɪ/ n oratoria f

orb /ɔ:b/ n orbe m

orbit /'ɔ:bɪt/ n órbita f. —vt orbitar

orchard /'ɔ:tʃəd/ n huerto m

orchestra /'ɔ:kɪstrə/ n orquesta f. ~**l** /-'kestrəl/ a orquestal. ~**te** /'ɔ:kɪstreɪt/ vt orquestar

orchid /'ɔ:kɪd/ n orquídea f

ordain /ɔ:'deɪn/ vt ordenar

ordeal /ɔ:'di:l/ n prueba f dura

order /'ɔ:də(r)/ n orden m; (com) pedido m. **in** ~ **that** para que. **in** ~ **to** para. —vt (command) mandar; (com) pedir

orderly /'ɔ:dəlɪ/ a ordenado. —n asistente m & f

ordinary /'ɔ:dɪnrɪ/ a corriente; (average) medio; (mediocre) ordinario

ordination /ɔ:dɪ'neɪʃn/ n ordenación f

ore /ɔ:(r)/ n mineral m

organ /'ɔ:gən/ n órgano m

organic /ɔ:'gænɪk/ a orgánico

organism /'ɔ:gənɪzəm/ n organismo m

organist /'ɔ:gənɪst/ n organista m & f

organiz|ation /ɔ:gənaɪ'zeɪʃn/ n organización f. ~**e** /'ɔ:gənaɪz/ vt organizar. ~**er** n organizador m

orgasm /'ɔ:gæzəm/ n orgasmo m

orgy /'ɔ:dʒɪ/ n orgía f

Orient /'ɔ:rɪənt/ n Oriente m. ~**al** /-'entl/ a & n oriental (m & f)

orientat|e /'ɔ:rɪənteɪt/ vt orientar. ~**ion** /-'teɪʃn/ n orientación f

orifice /'ɒrɪfɪs/ n orificio m

origin /'ɒrɪdʒɪn/ n origen m. ~**al** /ə'rɪdʒənl/ a original. ~**ality** /-'nælətɪ/ n originalidad f. ~**ally** adv originalmente. ~**ate** /ə'rɪdʒɪneɪt/ vi. ~**ate from** provenir de. ~**ator** n autor m

ormolu /'ɔ:məlu:/ n similar m

ornament /'ɔ:nəmənt/ n adorno m. ~**al** /-'mentl/ a de adorno. ~**ation** /-en'teɪʃn/ n ornamentación f

ornate /ɔ:'neɪt/ a adornado; ⟨style⟩ florido

ornithology /ɔ:nɪ'θɒlədʒɪ/ n ornitología f

orphan /'ɔ:fn/ n huérfano m. —vt dejar huérfano. ~**age** n orfanato m

orthodox /'ɔ:θədɒks/ a ortodoxo. ~**y** n ortodoxia f

orthopaedic /ɔ:θə'pi:dɪk/ a ortopédico. ~**s** n ortopedia f

oscillate /'ɒsɪleɪt/ vi oscilar

ossify /'ɒsɪfaɪ/ vt osificar. —vi osificarse

ostensible /ɒs'tensɪbl/ a aparente. ~**y** adv aparentemente

ostentat|ion /ɒsten'teɪʃn/ n ostentación f. ~**ious** a ostentoso

osteopath /ˈɒstɪəpæθ/ n osteópata m & f. ~**y** /-ˈɒpəθɪ/ n osteopatía f

ostracize /ˈɒstrəsaɪz/ vt excluir

ostrich /ˈɒstrɪtʃ/ n avestruz m

other /ˈʌðə(r)/ a & n & pron otro (m). ~ **than** de otra manera que. **the** ~ **one** el otro. ~**wise** /ˈʌðəwaɪz/ adv de otra manera; (or) si no

otter /ˈɒtə(r)/ n nutria f

ouch /aʊtʃ/ int ¡ay!

ought /ɔːt/ v aux deber. **I** ~ **to see it** debería verlo. **he** ~ **to have done it** debería haberlo hecho

ounce /aʊns/ n onza f (= 28.35 gr.)

our /ˈaʊə(r)/ a nuestro. ~**s** /ˈaʊəz/ poss pron el nuestro, la nuestra, los nuestros, las nuestras. ~**selves** /aʊəˈselvz/ pron (subject) nosotros mismos, nosotras mismas; (reflexive) nos; (after prep) nosotros (mismos), nosotras (mismas)

oust /aʊst/ vt expulsar, desalojar

out /aʊt/ adv fuera; (light) apagado; (in blossom) en flor; (in error) equivocado. ~-**and**-~ a cien por cien. ~ **of date** anticuado; (not valid) caducado. ~ **of doors** fuera. ~ **of order** estropeado; (sign) no funciona. ~ **of pity** por compasión. ~ **of place** fuera de lugar; (fig) inoportuno. ~ **of print** agotado. ~ **of sorts** indispuesto. ~ **of stock** agotado. ~ **of tune** desafinado. ~ **of work** parado, desempleado. **be** ~ equivocarse. **be** ~ **of** quedarse sin. **be** ~ **to** estar resuelto a. **five** ~ **of six** cinco de cada seis. **made** ~ **of** hecho de

outbid /aʊtˈbɪd/ vt (pt **-bid**, pres p **-bidding**) ofrecer más que

outboard /ˈaʊtbɔːd/ a fuera borda

outbreak /ˈaʊtbreɪk/ n (of anger) arranque m; (of war) comienzo m; (of disease) epidemia f

outbuilding /ˈaʊtbɪldɪŋ/ n dependencia f

outburst /ˈaʊtbɜːst/ n explosión f

outcast /ˈaʊtkɑːst/ n paria m & f

outcome /ˈaʊtkʌm/ n resultado m

outcry /ˈaʊtkraɪ/ n protesta f

outdated /aʊtˈdeɪtɪd/ a anticuado

outdo /aʊtˈduː/ vt (pt **-did**, pp **-done**) superar

outdoor /ˈaʊtdɔː(r)/ a al aire libre. ~**s** /-ˈdɔːz/ adv al aire libre

outer /ˈaʊtə(r)/ a exterior

outfit /ˈaʊtfɪt/ n equipo m; (clothes) traje m. ~**ter** n camisero m

outgoing /ˈaʊtɡəʊɪŋ/ a (minister etc) saliente; (sociable) abierto. ~**s** npl gastos mpl

outgrow /aʊtˈɡrəʊ/ vt (pt **-grew**, pp **-grown**) crecer más que (person); hacerse demasiado grande para (clothes). **he's** ~**n his trousers** le quedan pequeños los pantalones

outhouse /ˈaʊthaʊs/ n dependencia f

outing /ˈaʊtɪŋ/ n excursión f

outlandish /aʊtˈlændɪʃ/ a extravagante

outlaw /ˈaʊtlɔː/ n proscrito m. — vt proscribir

outlay /ˈaʊtleɪ/ n gastos mpl

outlet /ˈaʊtlet/ n salida f

outline /ˈaʊtlaɪn/ n contorno m; (summary) resumen m. —vt trazar; (describe) dar un resumen de

outlive /aʊtˈlɪv/ vt sobrevivir a

outlook /ˈaʊtlʊk/ n perspectiva f

outlying /ˈaʊtlaɪɪŋ/ a remoto

outmoded /aʊtˈməʊdɪd/ a anticuado

outnumber /aʊtˈnʌmbə(r)/ vt sobrepasar en número

outpatient /'aʊt'peɪʃnt/ n paciente m externo

outpost /'aʊtpəʊst/ n avanzada f

output /'aʊtpʊt/ n producción f

outrage /'aʊtreɪdʒ/ n ultraje m. —vt ultrajar. **~ous** /aʊt'reɪdʒəs/ a escandaloso, atroz

outright /'aʊtraɪt/ adv completamente; (at once) inmediatamente; (frankly) francamente. —a completo; (refusal) rotundo

outset /'aʊtset/ n principio m

outside /'aʊtsaɪd/ a & n exterior (m). /'aʊtsaɪd/ adv fuera. /aʊt'saɪd/ prep fuera de. **~r** /aʊt'saɪdə(r)/ n forastero m; (in race) caballo m no favorito

outsize /'aʊtsaɪz/ a de tamaño extraordinario

outskirts /'aʊtskɜːts/ npl afueras fpl

outspoken /aʊt'spəʊkn/ a franco. **be ~** no tener pelos en la lengua

outstanding /aʊt'stændɪŋ/ a excepcional; (not settled) pendiente; (conspicuous) sobresaliente

outstretched /aʊt'stretʃt/ a extendido

outstrip /aʊt'strɪp/ vt (pt -stripped) aventajar

outward /'aʊtwəd/ a externo; (journey) de ida. **~ly** adv por fuera, exteriormente. **~(s)** adv hacia fuera

outweigh /aʊt'weɪ/ vt pesar más que; (fig) valer más que

outwit /aʊt'wɪt/ vt (pt -witted) ser más listo que

oval /'əʊvl/ a oval(ado). —n óvalo m

ovary /'əʊvərɪ/ n ovario m

ovation /əʊ'veɪʃn/ n ovación f

oven /'ʌvn/ n horno m

over /'əʊvə(r)/ prep por encima de; (across) al otro lado de; (during) durante; (more than) más

de. **~ and above** por encima de. —adv por encima; (ended) terminado; (more) más; (in excess) de sobra. **~ again** otra vez. **~ and ~** una y otra vez. **~ here** por aquí. **~ there** por allí. **all ~** por todas partes

over... /'əʊvə(r)/ pref sobre..., super...

overall /əʊvər'ɔːl/ a global; (length, cost) total. —adv en conjunto. /'əʊvərɔːl/ n, **~s** npl mono m

overawe /əʊvər'ɔː/ vt intimidar

overbalance /əʊvə'bæləns/ vt hacer perder el equilibrio. —vi perder el equilibrio

overbearing /əʊvə'beərɪŋ/ a dominante

overboard /'əʊvəbɔːd/ adv al agua

overbook /əʊvə'bʊk/ vt aceptar demasiadas reservaciones para

overcast /əʊvə'kɑːst/ a nublado

overcharge /əʊvə'tʃɑːdʒ/ vt (fill too much) sobrecargar; (charge too much) cobrar demasiado

overcoat /'əʊvəkəʊt/ n abrigo m

overcome /əʊvə'kʌm/ vt (pt -came, pp -come) superar, vencer. **be ~ by** estar abrumado de

overcrowded /əʊvə'kraʊdɪd/ a atestado (de gente)

overdo /əʊvə'duː/ vt (pt -did, pp -done) exagerar; (culin) cocer demasiado

overdose /'əʊvədəʊs/ n sobredosis f

overdraft /'əʊvədrɑːft/ n giro m en descubierto

overdraw /əʊvə'drɔː/ vt (pt -drew, pp -drawn) girar en descubierto. **be ~n** tener un saldo deudor

overdue /əʊvə'djuː/ a retrasado; (belated) tardío; (bill) vencido y no pagado

overestimate /əʊvə'restɪmeɪt/ vt sobrestimar

overflow /əʊvə'fləʊ/ vi desbordarse. /'əʊvəfləʊ/ n (excess) exceso m; (outlet) rebosadero m

overgrown /əʊvə'grəʊn/ a demasiado grande; (garden) cubierto de hierbas

overhang /əʊvə'hæŋ/ vt (pt -hung) sobresalir por encima de; (fig) amenazar. —vi sobresalir. /'əʊvəhæŋ/ n saliente f

overhaul /əʊvə'hɔːl/ vt revisar. /'əʊvəhɔːl/ n revisión f

overhead /əʊvə'hed/ adv por encima. /'əʊvəhed/ a de arriba. ~s npl gastos mpl generales

overhear /əʊvə'hɪə(r)/ vt (pt -heard) oír por casualidad

overjoyed /əʊvə'dʒɔɪd/ a muy contento. **he was ~** rebosaba de alegría

overland /'əʊvəlænd/ a terrestre. —adv por tierra

overlap /əʊvə'læp/ vt (pt -lapped) traslapar. —vi traslaparse

overleaf /əʊvə'liːf/ adv a la vuelta. **see ~** véase al dorso

overload /əʊvə'ləʊd/ vt sobrecargar

overlook /əʊvə'lʊk/ vt dominar; (building) dar a; (forget) olvidar; (oversee) inspeccionar; (forgive) perdonar

overnight /əʊvə'naɪt/ adv por la noche, durante la noche; (fig, instantly) de la noche a la mañana. **stay ~** pasar la noche. —a de noche

overpass /'əʊvəpɑːs/ n paso m a desnivel, paso m elevado

overpay /əʊvə'peɪ/ vt (pt -paid) pagar demasiado

overpower /əʊvə'paʊə(r)/ vt subyugar; dominar (opponent); (fig) abrumar. ~ing a abrumador

overpriced /əʊvə'praɪst/ a demasiado caro

overrate /əʊvə'reɪt/ vt supervalorar

overreach /əʊvə'riːtʃ/ ur. ~ o.s. extralimitarse

overreact /əʊvərɪ'ækt/ vi reaccionar excesivamente

override /əʊvə'raɪd/ vt (pt -rode, pp -ridden) pasar por encima de. ~ing a dominante

overripe /'əʊvəraɪp/ a pasado, demasiado maduro

overrule /əʊvə'ruːl/ vt anular; denegar (claim)

overrun /əʊvə'rʌn/ vt (pt -ran, pp -run, pres p -running) invadir; exceder (limit)

overseas /əʊvə'siːz/ a de ultramar. —adv al extranjero, en ultramar

oversee /əʊvə'siː/ vt (pt -saw, pp -seen) vigilar. ~r /'əʊvəsɪə(r)/ n supervisor m

overshadow /əʊvə'ʃædəʊ/ vt (darken) sombrear; (fig) eclipsar

overshoot /əʊvə'ʃuːt/ vt (pt -shot) excederse. ~ **the mark** pasarse de la raya

oversight /'əʊvəsaɪt/ n descuido m

oversleep /əʊvə'sliːp/ vi (pt -slept) despertarse tarde. **I overslept** se me pegaron las sábanas

overstep /əʊvə'step/ vt (pt -stepped) pasar de. ~ **the mark** pasarse de la raya

overt /'əʊvɜːt/ a manifiesto

overtake /əʊvə'teɪk/ vt/i (pt -took, pp -taken) sobrepasar; (auto) adelantar. ~ing n adelantamiento m

overtax /əʊvə'tæks/ vt exigir demasiado

overthrow /əʊvə'θrəʊ/ vt (pt -threw, pp -thrown) derrocar. /'əʊvəθrəʊ/ n derrocamiento m

overtime /'əʊvətaɪm/ n horas fpl extra

overtone /'ouvetoun/ n (fig) matiz m

overture /'ouvetjue(r)/ n obertura f. ~s npl (fig) propuestas fpl

overturn /ouve'tз:n/ vt/i volcar

overweight /ouve'weit/ a demasiado pesado. **be ~** ser demasiado, ser gordo

overwhelm /ouve'welm/ vt aplastar; (with emotion) abrumar. **~ing** a aplastante; (fig) abrumador

overwork /ouve'wз:k/ vt hacer trabajar demasiado. —vi trabajar demasiado. —n trabajo m excesivo

overwrought /ouve'rɔːt/ a agotado, muy nervioso

ovulation /ovju'leiʃn/ n ovulación f

ow|e /ou/ vt deber. **~ing** a debido. **~ing to** a causa de

owl /aul/ n lechuza f, búho m

own /oun/ a propio. **get one's ~ back** (fam) vengarse. **hold one's ~** mantenerse firme, saber defenderse. **on one's ~** por su cuenta. —vt poseer, tener. —vi. **~ up (to)** (fam) confesar. **~er** n propietario m, dueño m. **~ership** n posesión f; (right) propiedad f

ox /ɒks/ n (pl oxen) buey m

oxide /'ɒksaid/ n óxido m

oxygen /'ɒksidʒen/ n oxígeno m

oyster /'ɔistə(r)/ n ostra f

P

p /piː/ abbr (pence, penny) penique(s) (m(pl))

pace /peis/ n paso m. —vi. **~ up and down** pasearse de aquí para allá. **~-maker** n (runner) el que marca el paso; (med) marcapasos m invar. **keep ~ with** andar al mismo paso que

Pacific /pe'sifik/ a pacífico. —n. **~ (Ocean)** (Océano m) Pacífico (m)

pacif|ist /'pæsifist/ n pacifista m & f. **~y** /'pæsifai/ vt apaciguar

pack /pæk/ n fardo m; (of cards) baraja f; (of hounds) jauría f; (of wolves) manada f; (large amount) montón m. —vt empaquetar; hacer (suitcase); (press down) apretar. —vi hacer la maleta. **~age** /'pækidʒ/ n paquete m. —vt empaquetar. **~age deal** n acuerdo m global. **~age tour** n viaje m organizado. **~ed lunch** n almuerzo m frío. **~ed out** (fam) de bote en bote. **~et** /'pækit/ n paquete m. **send ~ing** echar a paseo

pact /pækt/ n pacto m, acuerdo m

pad /pæd/ n almohadilla f; (for writing) bloc m; (for ink) tampón m; (flat, fam) piso m. —vt (pt padded) rellenar. **~ding** n relleno m. —vi andar a pasos quedos. **launching ~** plataforma f de lanzamiento

paddle[1] /'pædl/ n canalete m

paddle[2] /'pædl/ vi mojarse los pies

paddle-steamer /'pædlstiːmə(r)/ n vapor m de ruedas

paddock /'pædək/ n recinto m; (field) prado m

paddy /'pædi/ n arroz m con cáscara. **~field** n arrozal m

padlock /'pædlɒk/ n candado m. —vt cerrar con candado

paediatrician /piːdiə'triʃn/ n pediatra m & f

pagan /'peigən/ a & n pagano (m)

page[1] /peidʒ/ n página f. —vt paginar

page[2] /peidʒ/ (in hotel) botones m invar. —vt llamar

pageant /'pædʒənt/ n espectáculo m (histórico). **~ry** n boato m

pagoda /pə'gəudə/ n pagoda f

paid /peɪd/ *see* pay. —*a.* put ~ to (*fam*) acabar con

pail /peɪl/ *n* cubo *m*

pain /peɪn/ *n* dolor *m*. ~ **in the neck** (*fam*) ⟨*persona*⟩ pesado *m*; ⟨*thing*⟩ lata *f*. **be in** ~ tener dolores. ~**s** *npl* (*effort*) esfuerzos *mpl*. **be at** ~**s** esmerarse. —*vt* doler. ~**ful** /peɪnfl/ *a* doloroso; (*laborious*) penoso. ~**killer** *n* calmante *m*. ~**less** *a* indoloro. ~**staking** /ˈpeɪnzteɪkɪŋ/ *a* esmerado

paint /peɪnt/ *n* pintura *f.* —*vt*/*i* pintar. ~**er** *n* pintor *m*. ~**ing** *n* pintura *f*

pair /peə(r)/ *n* par *m*; (*of people*) pareja *f*. ~ **of trousers** pantalón *m*, pantalones *mpl*. —*vi* emparejarse. ~ **off** emparejarse

pajamas /pəˈdʒɑːməz/ *npl* pijama *m*

Pakistan /pɑːkɪˈstɑːn/ *n* el Pakistán *m*. ~**i** *a* & *n* paquistaní (*m* & *f*)

pal /pæl/ *n* (*fam*) amigo *m*

palace /ˈpælɪs/ *n* palacio *m*

palat|able /ˈpælətəbl/ *a* sabroso; (*fig*) aceptable. ~**e** /ˈpælət/ *n* paladar *m*

palatial /pəˈleɪʃl/ *a* suntuoso

palaver /pəˈlɑːvə(r)/ *n* (*fam*) lío *m*

pale[1] /peɪl/ *a* (-er, -est) pálido; ⟨*colour*⟩ claro. —*vi* palidecer

pale[2] /peɪl/ *n* estaca *n*

paleness /ˈpeɪlnɪs/ *n* palidez *f*

Palestin|e /ˈpælɪstaɪn/ *n* Palestina *f*. ~**ian** /-ˈstɪnɪən/ *a* & *n* palestino *m*

palette /ˈpælɪt/ *n* paleta *f*. ~**knife** *n* espátula *f*

pall[1] /pɔːl/ *n* paño *m* mortuorio; (*fig*) capa *f*

pall[2] /pɔːl/ *vi.* ~ **(on)** perder su sabor (para)

pallid /ˈpælɪd/ *a* pálido

palm /pɑːm/ *n* palma *f*. —*vt.* ~ **off** encajar (on a). ~**ist** /ˈpɑːmɪst/ *n* quiromántico *m*. **P**~ **Sunday** *n* Domingo *m* de Ramos

palpable /ˈpælpəbl/ *a* palpable

palpitat|e /ˈpælpɪteɪt/ *vi* palpitar. ~**ion** /-ˈteɪʃn/ *n* palpitación *f*

paltry /ˈpɔːltrɪ/ *a* (-ier, -iest) insignificante

pamper /ˈpæmpə(r)/ *vt* mimar

pamphlet /ˈpæmflɪt/ *n* folleto *m*

pan /pæn/ *n* cacerola *f*; (*for frying*) sartén *f*; (*of scales*) platillo *m*; (*of lavatory*) taza *f*

panacea /pænəˈsɪə/ *n* panacea *f*

panache /pæˈnæʃ/ *n* brío *m*

pancake /ˈpænkeɪk/ *n* hojuela *f*, crêpe *f*

panda /ˈpændə/ *n* panda *m*. ~ **car** *n* coche *m* de la policía

pandemonium /pændɪˈməʊnɪəm/ *n* pandemonio *m*

pander /ˈpændə(r)/ *vi.* ~ **to** complacer

pane /peɪn/ *n* (*of glass*) vidrio *m*

panel /ˈpænl/ *n* panel *m*; (*group of people*) jurado *m*. ~**ling** *n* paneles *mpl*

pang /pæŋ/ *n* punzada *f*

panic /ˈpænɪk/ *n* pánico *m*. —*vi* (*pt* **panicked**) ser preso de pánico. ~**-stricken** *a* preso de pánico

panoram|a /pænəˈrɑːmə/ *n* panorama *m*. ~**ic** /-ˈræmɪk/ *a* panorámico

pansy /ˈpænzɪ/ *n* pensamiento *m*; (*effeminate man, fam*) maricón *m*

pant /pænt/ *vi* jadear

pantechnicon /pænˈteknɪkən/ *n* camión *m* de mudanzas

panther /ˈpænθə(r)/ *n* pantera *f*

panties /ˈpæntɪz/ *npl* bragas *fpl*

pantomime /ˈpæntəmaɪm/ *n* pantomima *f*

pantry /ˈpæntrɪ/ *n* despensa *f*

pants /pænts/ *npl* (*man's underwear, fam*) calzoncillos *mpl*; (*woman's underwear, fam*) bragas *fpl*; (*trousers, fam*) pantalones *mpl*

papacy /'peɪpəsɪ/ n papado m. ∼l a papal

paper /'peɪpə(r)/ n papel m; (newspaper) periódico m; (exam) examen m; (document) documento m. **on** ∼ en teoría. −vt empapelar, tapizar (LAm). ∼**back** /'peɪpəbæk/ a en rústica. −n libro m en rústica. ∼**clip** n sujetapapeles m invar, clip m. ∼**weight** /'peɪpəweɪt/ n pisapapeles m invar. ∼**work** n papeleo m, trabajo m de oficina

papier mâché /pæpɪeɪ'mæʃeɪ/ n cartón m piedra

par /pɑː(r)/ n par f; (golf) par m. **feel below** ∼ no estar en forma. **on a** ∼ **with** a la par con

parable /'pærəbl/ n parábola f

parachut|**e** /'pærəʃuːt/ n paracaídas m invar. −vi lanzarse en paracaídas. ∼**ist** n paracaidista m & f

parade /pə'reɪd/ n desfile m; (street) paseo m; (display) alarde m. −vi desfilar. −vt hacer alarde de

paradise /'pærədaɪs/ n paraíso m

paradox /'pærədɒks/ n paradoja f. ∼**ical** /-'dɒksɪkl/ a paradójico

paraffin /'pærəfɪn/ n queroseno m

paragon /'pærəgən/ n dechado m

paragraph /'pærəgrɑːf/ n párrafo m

parallel /'pærəlel/ a paralelo. −n paralelo m; (line) paralela f. −vt ser paralelo a

paraly|**se** /'pærəlaɪz/ vt paralizar. ∼**sis** /pə'ræləsɪs/ n (pl -ses /-siːz/) parálisis f. ∼**tic** /pærə'lɪtɪk/ a & n paralítico (m)

parameter /pə'ræmɪtə(r)/ n parámetro m

paramount /'pærəmaʊnt/ a supremo

paranoia /pærə'nɔɪə/ n paranoia f

parapet /'pærəpɪt/ n parapeto m

paraphernalia /pærəfə'neɪlɪə/ n trastos mpl

paraphrase /'pærəfreɪz/ n paráfrasis f. −vt parafrasear

paraplegic /pærə'pliːdʒɪk/ n parapléjico m

parasite /'pærəsaɪt/ n parásito m

parasol /'pærəsɒl/ n sombrilla f

paratrooper /'pærətruːpə(r)/ n paracaidista m

parcel /'pɑːsl/ n paquete m

parch /pɑːtʃ/ vt resecar. **be** ∼**ed** tener mucha sed

parchment /'pɑːtʃmənt/ n pergamino m

pardon /'pɑːdn/ n perdón m; (jurid) indulto m. **I beg your** ∼! ¡perdón Vd! **I beg your** ∼? ¿cómo?, ¿mande? (Mex). −vt perdonar

pare /peə(r)/ vt cortar ⟨nails⟩; (peel) pelar, mondar

parent /'peərənt/ n (father) padre m; (mother) madre f; (source) origen m. ∼**s** npl padres mpl. ∼**al** /pə'rentl/ a de los padres

parenthesis /pə'renθəsɪs/ n (pl -theses /-siːz/) paréntesis m invar

parenthood /'peərənthʊd/ n paternidad f, maternidad f

Paris /'pærɪs/ n París m

parish /'pærɪʃ/ n parroquia f; (municipal) municipio m. ∼**ioner** /pə'rɪʃənə(r)/ n feligrés m

Parisian /pə'rɪzɪən/ a & n parisino (m)

parity /'pærətɪ/ n igualdad f

park /pɑːk/ n parque m. −vt/i aparcar. ∼ **oneself** vr (fam) instalarse

parka /'pɑːkə/ n anorak m

parking-meter /'pɑːkɪŋmiːtə(r)/ n parquímetro m

parliament /'pɑːləmənt/ n parlamento m. ∼**ary** /-'mentrɪ/ a parlamentario

parlour /'pɑːlə(r)/ n salón m

parochial /pə'rəʊkɪəl/ a parroquial; (fig) pueblerino

parody /'pærədɪ/ n parodia f. —vt parodiar

parole /pə'rəʊl/ n libertad f bajo palabra, libertad f provisional. **on ~** libre bajo palabra. —vt liberar bajo palabra

paroxysm /'pærəksɪzəm/ n paroxismo m

parquet /'pɑːkeɪ/ n. **~ floor** n parqué m

parrot /'pærət/ n papagayo m

parry /'pærɪ/ vt parar; (avoid) esquivar. —n parada f

parsimonious /pɑːsɪ'məʊnɪəs/ a parsimonioso

parsley /'pɑːslɪ/ n perejil m

parsnip /'pɑːsnɪp/ n pastinaca f

parson /'pɑːsn/ n cura m, párroco m

part /pɑːt/ n parte f; (of machine) pieza f; (of serial) entrega f; (in play) papel m; (side in dispute) partido m. **on the ~ of** por parte de. —adv en parte. —vt separar. **~ with** vt separarse de. —vi separarse

partake /pɑː'teɪk/ vt (pt -took, pp -taken) participar. **~ of** compartir

partial /'pɑːʃl/ a parcial. **be ~ to** ser aficionado a. **~ity** /-ɪ'ælɪtɪ/ n parcialidad f. **~ly** adv parcialmente

participa|nt /pɑː'tɪsɪpənt/ n participante m & f. **~te** /pɑː'tɪsɪpeɪt/ vi participar. **~tion** /-'peɪʃn/ n participación f

participle /'pɑːtɪsɪpl/ n participio m

particle /'pɑːtɪkl/ n partícula f

particular /pə'tɪkjʊlə(r)/ a particular; (precise) meticuloso; (fastidious) quisquilloso. —n. **in ~** especialmente. **~ly** adv especialmente. **~s** npl detalles mpl

parting /'pɑːtɪŋ/ n separación f; (in hair) raya f. —a de despedida

partisan /pɑːtɪ'zæn/ n partidario m

partition /pɑː'tɪʃn/ n partición f; (wall) tabique m. —vt dividir

partly /'pɑːtlɪ/ adv en parte

partner /'pɑːtnə(r)/ n socio m; (sport) pareja f. **~ship** n asociación f; (com) sociedad f

partridge /'pɑːtrɪdʒ/ n perdiz f

part-time /pɑːt'taɪm/ a & adv a tiempo parcial

party /'pɑːtɪ/ n reunión f, fiesta f; (group) grupo m; (pol) partido m; (jurid) parte f. **~ line** n (telephone) línea f colectiva

pass /pɑːs/ vt pasar; (in front of) pasar por delante de; (overtake) adelantar; (approve) aprobar ⟨exam, bill, law⟩; hacer ⟨remark⟩; pronunciar ⟨judgement⟩. **~ down** transmitir. **~ over** pasar por alto de. **~ round** distribuir. **~ through** pasar por; (cross) atravesar. **~ up** (fam) dejar pasar. —vi pasar; (in exam) aprobar. **~ away** morir. **~ out** (fam) desmayarse. —n (permit) permiso m; (in mountains) puerto m, desfiladero m; (sport) pase m; (in exam) aprobado m. **make a ~ at** (fam) hacer proposiciones amorosas a. **~able** /'pɑːsəbl/ a pasable; ⟨road⟩ transitable

passage /'pæsɪdʒ/ n paso m; (voyage) travesía f; (corridor) pasillo m; (in book) pasaje m

passenger /'pæsɪndʒə(r)/ n pasajero m

passer-by /pɑːsə'baɪ/ n (pl passers-by) transeúnte m & f

passion /'pæʃn/ n pasión f. **~ate** a apasionado. **~ately** adv apasionadamente

passive /'pæsɪv/ a pasivo. **~ness** n pasividad f

passmark /'pɑːsmɑːk/ n aprobado m

Passover /ˈpɑːsəʊvə(r)/ n Pascua f de los hebreos

passport /ˈpɑːspɔːt/ n pasaporte m

password /ˈpɑːswɜːd/ n contraseña f

past /pɑːst/ a & n pasado (m). in times ~ en tiempos pasados. the ~ week n la semana f pasada. —prep por delante de; (beyond) más allá de. —adv por delante. drive ~ pasar en coche. go ~ pasar

paste /peɪst/ n pasta f; (adhesive) engrudo m. —vt (fasten) pegar; (cover) engrudar. ~board /ˈpeɪstbɔːd/ n cartón m. ~jewellery n joyas fpl de imitación

pastel /ˈpæstl/ a & n pastel (m)

pasteurize /ˈpæstʃəraɪz/ vt pasteurizar

pastiche /pæˈstiːʃ/ n pastiche m

pastille /ˈpæstɪl/ n pastilla f

pastime /ˈpɑːstaɪm/ n pasatiempo m

pastoral /ˈpɑːstərəl/ a pastoral

pastries npl pasteles mpl, pastas fpl. ~y /ˈpeɪstrɪ/ n pasta f

pasture /ˈpɑːstʃə(r)/ n pasto m

pasty[1] /ˈpæstɪ/ n empanada f

pasty[2] /ˈpeɪstɪ/ a pastoso; (pale) pálido

pat[1] /pæt/ vt (pt patted) dar palmaditas en; acariciar (dog etc). —n palmadita f; (of butter) porción f

pat[2] /pæt/ adv en el momento oportuno

patch /pætʃ/ n pedazo m; (period) período m; (repair) remiendo m; (piece of ground) terreno m. not a ~ on (fam) muy inferior a. —vt remendar. ~ up arreglar. ~work n labor m de retazos; (fig) mosaico m. ~y a desigual

pâté /ˈpæteɪ/ n pasta f, paté m

patent /ˈpeɪtnt/ a patente. —n patente f. —vt patentar. ~ leather n charol m. ~ly adv evidentemente

paternal /pəˈtɜːnl/ a paterno. ~ity /pəˈtɜːnətɪ/ n paternidad f

path /pɑːθ/ n (pl -s /pɑːðz/) sendero m; (sport) pista f; (of rocket) trayectoria f; (fig) camino m

pathetic /pəˈθetɪk/ a patético, lastimoso

pathology /pəˈθɒlədʒɪ/ n patología f

pathos /ˈpeɪθɒs/ n patetismo m

patience /ˈpeɪʃns/ n paciencia f. ~t /ˈpeɪʃnt/ a & n paciente (m & f). ~tly adv con paciencia

patio /ˈpætɪəʊ/ n (pl -os) patio m

patriarch /ˈpeɪtrɪɑːk/ n patriarca m

patrician /pəˈtrɪʃn/ a & n patricio (m)

patriot /ˈpætrɪət/ n patriota m & f. ~ic /-ˈɒtɪk/ a patriótico. ~ism n patriotismo m

patrol /pəˈtrəʊl/ n patrulla f. —vt/i patrullar

patron /ˈpeɪtrən/ n (of the arts etc) mecenas m & f; (customer) cliente m & f; (of charity) patrocinador m. ~age /ˈpætrənɪdʒ/ n patrocinio m; (of shop etc) clientela f. ~ize vt ser cliente de; (fig) tratar con condescendencia

patter[1] /ˈpætə(r)/ n (of steps) golpeteo m; (of rain) tamborileo m. —vi correr con pasos ligeros; (rain) tamborilear

patter[2] /ˈpætə(r)/ n (speech) jerga f; (chatter) parloteo m

pattern /ˈpætn/ n diseño m; (model) modelo m; (sample) muestra f; (manner) modo m; (in dressmaking) patrón m

paunch /pɔːntʃ/ n panza f

pauper /ˈpɔːpə(r)/ n indigente m & f, pobre m & f

pause /pɔːz/ n pausa f. —vi hacer una pausa

pave /peɪv/ vt pavimentar. ~ the way for preparar el terreno para pavement /'peɪvmənt/ n pavimento m; (at side of road) acera f

pavilion /pə'vɪlɪən/ n pabellón m

paving-stone /'peɪvɪŋstəʊn/ n losa f

paw /pɔː/ n pata f; (of cat) garra f. —vi tocar con la pata; (person) manosear

pawn¹ /pɔːn/ n (chess) peón m; (fig) instrumento m

pawn² /pɔːn/ vt empeñar. —n. in ~ en prenda. ~broker /'pɔːnbrəʊkə(r)/ n prestamista m & f. ~shop n monte m de piedad

pawpaw /'pɔːpɔː/ n papaya f

pay /peɪ/ vt (pt paid) pagar; prestar (attention); hacer (compliment, visit). ~ back devolver. ~ cash pagar al contado. ~ in ingresar. ~ off pagar. ~ out pagar. —vi pagar; (be profitable) rendir. —n paga f. in the ~ of al servicio de. ~able /'peɪəbl/ a pagadero. ~ment /'peɪmənt/ n pago m. ~-off n (sl) liquidación f; (fig) ajuste m de cuentas. ~roll /'peɪrəʊl/ n nómina f. ~ up pagar

pea /piː/ n guisante m

peace /piːs/ n paz f. ~ of mind tranquilidad f. ~able a pacífico. ~ful /'piːsfl/ a tranquilo. ~maker /'piːsmeɪkə(r)/ n pacificador m

peach /piːtʃ/ n melocotón m, durazno m (LAm); (tree) melocotonero m, duraznero m (LAm)

peacock /'piːkɒk/ n pavo m real

peak /piːk/ n cumbre f; (maximum) máximo m. ~ hours npl horas fpl punta. ~ed cap n gorra f de visera

peaky /'piːkɪ/ a pálido

peal /piːl/ n repique m. ~s of laughter risotadas fpl

peanut /'piːnʌt/ n cacahuete m, maní m (Mex). ~s (sl) una bagatela f

pear /peə(r)/ n pera f; (tree) peral m

pearl /pɜːl/ n perla f. ~y a nacarado

peasant /'peznt/ n campesino m

peat /piːt/ n turba f

pebble /'pebl/ n guijarro m

peck /pek/ vt picotear; (kiss, fam) dar un besito a. —n picotazo m; (kiss) besito m. ~ish /'pekɪʃ/ a. be ~ish (fam) tener hambre, tener gazuza (fam)

peculiar /pɪ'kjuːlɪə(r)/ a raro; (special) especial. ~ity /·'ærəti/ n rareza f; (feature) particularidad f

pedal /'pedl/ n pedal m. —vi pedalear

pedantic /pɪ'dæntɪk/ a pedante

peddle /'pedl/ vt vender por las calles

pedestal /'pedɪstl/ n pedestal m

pedestrian /pɪ'destrɪən/ n peatón m. —a de peatones; (dull) prosaico. ~ crossing n paso m de peatones

pedigree /'pedɪgriː/ n linaje m; (of animal) pedigrí m. —a (animal) de raza

pedlar /'pedlə(r)/ n buhonero m, vendedor m ambulante

peek /piːk/ vi mirar a hurtadillas

peel /piːl/ n cáscara f. —vt pelar (fruit, vegetables). —vi pelarse. ~ings npl peladuras fpl, monda f

peep¹ /piːp/ vi mirar a hurtadillas. —n mirada f furtiva

peep-hole /'piːphəʊl/ n mirilla f

peep² /piːp/ (bird) piar. —n pío m

peer¹ /pɪə(r)/ vi mirar. ~ at escudriñar

peer² /pɪə(r)/ n par m, compañero m. ~age n pares mpl

peeved /piːvd/ a (sl) irritado. ~ish /'piːvɪʃ/ a picajoso

peg /peg/ n clavija f; (for washing) pinza f; (hook) gancho m; (for tent) estaca f. off the ~ de percha. —vt (pt **pegged**) fijar (precios). ~ **away at** afanarse por

pejorative /pɪ'dʒɒrətɪv/ a peyorativo, despectivo

pelican /'pelɪkən/ n pelícano m. ~ **crossing** n paso m de peatones (con semáforo)

pellet /'pelɪt/ n pelotilla f; (for gun) perdigón m

pelt[1] /pelt/ n pellejo m

pelt[2] /pelt/ vt tirar. —vi llover a cántaros

pelvis /'pelvɪs/ n pelvis f

pen[1] /pen/ n (enclosure) recinto m

pen[2] /pen/ (for writing) pluma f, estilográfica f; (ball-point) bolígrafo m

penal /'piːnl/ a penal. ~**ize** vt castigar. ~**ty** /'penltɪ/ n castigo m; (fine) multa f. ~**ty kick** n (football) penalty m

penance /'penəns/ n penitencia f

pence /pens/ see **penny**

pencil /'pensl/ n lápiz m. —vt (pt **pencilled**) escribir con lápiz. ~**sharpener** n sacapuntas m invar

pendant /'pendənt/ n dije m, medallón m

pending /'pendɪŋ/ a pendiente. —prep hasta

pendulum /'pendjʊləm/ n péndulo m

penetrat|**e** /'penɪtreɪt/ vt/i penetrar. ~**ing** a penetrante. ~**ion** /-'treɪʃn/ n penetración f

penguin /'pengwɪn/ n pingüino m

penicillin /penɪ'sɪlɪn/ n penicilina f

peninsula /pə'nɪnsjʊlə/ n península f

penis /'piːnɪs/ n pene m

peniten|**ce** /'penɪtəns/ n penitencia f. ~**t** /'penɪtənt/ a & n penitente (m & f). ~**tiary** /penɪ'tenʃərɪ/ n (Amer) cárcel m

pen: ~**knife** /'pennaɪf/ n (pl **pen-knives**) navaja f; (small) cortaplumas m invar. ~**name** n seudónimo m

pennant /'penənt/ n banderín m

penn|**iless** /'penɪlɪs/ a sin un céntimo. ~**y** /'penɪ/ n (pl **pennies** or **pence**) penique m

pension /'penʃn/ n pensión f; (for retirement) jubilación f. —vt pensionar. ~**able** a con derecho a pensión; (age) de la jubilación. ~**er** n jubilado m. ~ **off** jubilar

pensive /'pensɪv/ a pensativo

pent-up /pent'ʌp/ a reprimido; (confined) encerrado

pentagon /'pentəgən/ n pentágono m

Pentecost /'pentɪkɒst/ n Pentecostés m

penthouse /'penthaʊs/ n ático m

penultimate /pen'ʌltɪmət/ a penúltimo

penury /'penjʊərɪ/ n penuria f

peony /'piːənɪ/ n peonía f

people /'piːpl/ npl gente f; (citizens) pueblo m. ~ **say** se dice. **English** ~ los ingleses mpl. **my** ~ (fam) mi familia f. —vt poblar

pep /pep/ n vigor m. —vt. ~ **up** animar

pepper /'pepə(r)/ n pimienta f; (vegetable) pimiento m. —vt sazonar con pimienta. ~**y** a picante. ~**corn** /'pepəkɔːn/ n grano m de pimienta. ~**corn rent** n alquiler m nominal

peppermint /'pepəmɪnt/ n menta f; (sweet) pastilla f de menta

pep talk /'peptɔːk/ n palabras fpl animadoras

per /pɜː(r)/ prep por. ~ **annum** al año. ~ **cent** por ciento. ~ **head** por cabeza, por persona. **ten miles** ~ **hour** diez millas por hora

perceive /pə'siːv/ vt percibir; (notice) darse cuenta de

percentage /pə'sentɪdʒ/ n porcentaje m

percepti|ble /pə'septəbl/ a perceptible. ~**on** /pə'sepʃn/ n percepción f. ~**ve** a perspicaz

perch[1] /pɜːtʃ/ n (of bird) percha f. —vi posarse

perch[2] /pɜːtʃ/ (fish) perca f

percolat|e /'pɜːkəleɪt/ vt filtrar. —vi filtrarse. ~**or** n cafetera f

percussion /pə'kʌʃn/ n percusión f

peremptory /pə'remptərɪ/ a perentorio

perennial /pə'renɪəl/ a & n perenne (m)

perfect /'pɜːfɪkt/ a perfecto. /pə'fekt/ vt perfeccionar. ~**ion** /pə'fekʃn/ n perfección f. to ~**ion** a la perfección. ~**ionist** n perfeccionista m & f. ~**ly** /'pɜːfɪktlɪ/ adv perfectamente

perforat|e /'pɜːfəreɪt/ vt perforar. ~**ion** /-'reɪʃn/ n perforación f

perform /pə'fɔːm/ vt hacer, realizar; representar ⟨play⟩; desempeñar ⟨role⟩; (mus) interpretar. ~ **an operation** (med) operar. ~**ance** n ejecución f; (of play) representación f; (of car) rendimiento m; (fuss, fam) jaleo m. ~**er** n artista m & f

perfume /'pɜːfjuːm/ n perfume m

perfunctory /pə'fʌŋktərɪ/ a superficial

perhaps /pə'hæps/ adv quizá(s), tal vez

peril /'perəl/ n peligro m. ~**ous** a arriesgado, peligroso

perimeter /pə'rɪmɪtə(r)/ n perímetro m

period /'pɪərɪəd/ n período m; (lesson) clase f; (gram) punto m. —a de (la) época m. ~**ic** /-'ɒdɪk/ a periódico. ~**ical** /pɪərɪ'ɒdɪkl/ n revista f. ~**ically** /-'ɒdɪklɪ/ adv periódico

peripher|al /pə'rɪfərəl/ a periférico. ~**y** /pə'rɪfərɪ/ n periferia f

periscope /'perɪskəʊp/ n periscopio m

perish /'perɪʃ/ vi perecer; (rot) estropearse. ~**able** a perecedero. ~**ing** a (fam) glacial

perjur|e /'pɜːdʒə(r)/ vr. ~**e o.s.** perjurarse. ~**y** n perjurio m

perk[1] /pɜːk/ n gaje m

perk[2] /pɜːk/ vt/i. ~ **up** vt reanimar. —vi reanimarse. ~**y** a alegre

perm /pɜːm/ n permanente f. —vt hacer una permanente

permanen|ce /'pɜːmənəns/ n permanencia f. ~**t** /'pɜːmənənt/ a permanente. ~**tly** adv permanentemente

permea|ble /'pɜːmɪəbl/ a permeable. ~**te** /'pɜːmɪeɪt/ vt penetrar; (soak) empapar

permissible /pə'mɪsəbl/ a permisible

permission /pə'mɪʃn/ n permiso m

permissive /pə'mɪsɪv/ a indulgente. ~**ness** n tolerancia f. ~ **society** n sociedad f permisiva

permit /pə'mɪt/ vt (pt permitted) permitir. /'pɜːmɪt/ n permiso m

permutation /pɜːmjuː'teɪʃn/ n permutación f

pernicious /pə'nɪʃəs/ a pernicioso

peroxide /pə'rɒksaɪd/ n peróxido m

perpendicular /pɜːpən'dɪkjʊlə(r)/ a & n perpendicular (f)

perpetrat|e /'pɜːpɪtreɪt/ vt cometer. ~**or** n autor m

perpetual /pə'petʃʊəl/ a perpetuo. ~**te** /pə'petʃʊeɪt/ vt perpetuar. ~**tion** /-'eɪʃn/ n perpetuación f

perplex /pə'pleks/ vt dejar perplejo. ~**ed** a perplejo. ~**ing** a desconcertante. **~ity** n perplejidad f

persecut|e /'pɜːsɪkjuːt/ vt perseguir. **~ion** /-'kjuːʃn/ n persecución f

persever|ance /pɜːsɪ'vɪərəns/ n perseverancia f. **~e** /pɜːsɪ'vɪə(r)/ vi perseverar, persistir

Persian /'pɜːʃn/ a persa. **the ~ Gulf** n el golfo m Pérsico. **~** persa (m & f); (lang) persa m

persist /pə'sɪst/ vi persistir. **~ence** n persistencia f. **~ent** a persistente; (continual) continuo. **~ently** adv persistentemente

person /'pɜːsn/ n persona f

personal /'pɜːsənl/ a personal

personality /pɜːsə'nælətɪ/ n personalidad f; (on TV) personaje m

personally /'pɜːsənlɪ/ adv personalmente; (in person) en persona

personify /pə'sɒnɪfaɪ/ vt personificar

personnel /pɜːsə'nel/ n personal m

perspective /pə'spektɪv/ n perspectiva f

perspicacious /pɜːspɪ'keɪʃəs/ a perspicaz

perspir|ation /pɜːspə'reɪʃn/ n sudor m. **~e** /pəs'paɪə(r)/ vi sudar

persua|de /pə'sweɪd/ vt persuadir. **~sion** n persuasión f. **~sive** /pə'sweɪsɪv/ a persuasivo. **~sively** adv de manera persuasiva

pert /pɜːt/ a (saucy) impertinente; (lively) animado

pertain /pə'teɪn/ vi. **~ to** relacionarse con

pertinent /'pɜːtɪnənt/ a pertinente. **~ly** adv pertinentemente

pertly /'pɜːtlɪ/ adv impertinentemente

perturb /pə'tɜːb/ vt perturbar

Peru /pə'ruː/ n el Perú m

perus|al /pə'ruːzl/ n lectura f cuidadosa. **~e** /pə'ruːz/ vt leer cuidadosamente

Peruvian /pə'ruːvɪən/ a & n peruano (m)

pervade /pə'veɪd/ vt difundirse por. **~sive** a penetrante

perver|se /pə'vɜːs/ a (stubborn) terco; (wicked) perverso. **~sity** n terquedad f; (wickedness) perversidad f. **~sion** n perversión f. **~t** /pə'vɜːt/ vt pervertir. /'pɜːvɜːt/ n pervertido m

pessimis|m /'pesɪmɪzəm/ n pesimismo m. **~t** /'pesɪmɪst/ n pesimista m & f. **~tic** /-'mɪstɪk/ a pesimista

pest /pest/ n insecto m nocivo, plaga f; (person) pelma m; (thing) lata f

pester /'pestə(r)/ vt importunar

pesticide /'pestɪsaɪd/ n pesticida f

pet /pet/ n animal m doméstico; (favourite) favorito m. —a preferido. —vt (pt petted) acariciar

petal /'petl/ n pétalo m

peter /'piːtə(r)/ vi. **~ out** (supplies) agotarse; (disappear) desparecer

petite /pə'tiːt/ a (of woman) chiquita

petition /pɪ'tɪʃn/ n petición f. —vt dirigir una petición a

pet name /'petneɪm/ n apodo m cariñoso

petrify /'petrɪfaɪ/ vt petrificar. —vi petrificarse

petrol /'petrəl/ n gasolina f. **~eum** /pɪ'trəʊlɪəm/ n petróleo m. **~ gauge** n indicador m de nivel de gasolina. **~ pump** n (in car) bomba f de gasolina; (at garage) surtidor m de gasolina. **~ station** n gasolinera f. **~ tank** n depósito m de gasolina

petticoat /'petɪkəʊt/ n enaguas fpl

pett|iness /'petɪnɪs/ n mezquindad f. **~y** /'petɪ/ a (-ier,

-iest) insignificante; (mean) mezquino. ~y cash n dinero m para gastos menores. ~y officer n suboficial m de marina

petulan|ce /'petjʊləns/ n irritabilidad f. ~t /'petjʊlənt/ a irritable

pew /pju:/ n banco m (de iglesia)

pewter /'pju:tə(r)/ n peltre m

phallic /'fælɪk/ a fálico

phantom /'fæntəm/ n fantasma m

pharmaceutical /fɑ:mə'sju:tɪkl/ a farmacéutico

pharmac|ist /'fɑ:məsɪst/ n farmacéutico m. ~y /'fɑ:məsɪ/ n farmacia f

pharyngitis /færɪn'dʒaɪtɪs/ n faringitis f

phase /feɪz/ n etapa f. —vt. ~ in introducir progresivamente. ~ out retirar progresivamente. ~

PhD abbr (Doctor of Philosophy) n Doctor m en Filosofía

pheasant /'feznt/ n faisán m

phenomenal /fɪ'nɒmɪnl/ a fenomenal

phenomenon /fɪ'nɒmɪnən/ n (pl -ena) fenómeno m

phew /fju:/ int ¡uy!

phial /'faɪəl/ n frasco m

philanderer /fɪ'lændərə(r)/ n mariposón m

philanthrop|ic /fɪlən'θrɒpɪk/ a filantrópico. ~ist /fɪ'lænθrəpɪst/ n filántropo m

philatel|ist /fɪ'lætəlɪst/ n filatelista m & f. ~y /fɪ'lætəlɪ/ n filatelia f

philharmonic /fɪlhɑ:'mɒnɪk/ a filarmónico

Philippines /'fɪlɪpi:nz/ npl Filipinas fpl

philistine /'fɪlɪstaɪn/ a & n filisteo (m)

philosoph|er /fɪ'lɒsəfə(r)/ n filósofo m. ~ical /-ə'sɒfɪkl/ a filosófico. ~y /fɪ'lɒsəfɪ/ n filosofía f

phlegm /flem/ n flema f. ~atic /fleg'mætɪk/ a flemático

phobia /'fəʊbɪə/ n fobia f

phone /fəʊn/ n (fam) teléfono m. —vt/i llamar por teléfono. ~ back ⟨caller⟩ volver a llamar; ⟨person called⟩ llamar. ~ box n cabina f telefónica

phonetic /fə'netɪk/ a fonético. ~s n fonética f

phoney /'fəʊnɪ/ a (-ier, -iest) (sl) falso. —n (sl) farsante m & f

phosphate /'fosfeɪt/ n fosfato m

phosphorus /'fosfərəs/ n fósforo m

photo /'fəʊtəʊ/ n (pl -os) (fam) fotografía f, foto f (fam)

photocopy /'fəʊtəʊkɒpɪ/ n fotocopia f. —vt fotocopiar

photogenic /fəʊtəʊ'dʒenɪk/ a fotogénico

photograph /'fəʊtəgrɑ:f/ n fotografía f. —vt hacer una fotografía de, sacar fotos de. ~er /fə'tɒgrəfə(r)/ n fotógrafo m. ~ic /-'græfɪk/ a fotográfico. ~y /fə'tɒgrəfɪ/ n fotografía f

phrase /freɪz/ n frase f, locución f, expresión f. —vt expresar. ~book n libro m de frases

physical /'fɪzɪkl/ a físico

physician /fɪ'zɪʃn/ n médico m

physic|ist /'fɪzɪsɪst/ n físico m. ~s /'fɪzɪks/ n física f

physiology /fɪzɪ'ɒlədʒɪ/ n fisiología f

physiotherap|ist /fɪzɪəʊ'θerəpɪst/ n fisioterapeuta m & f. ~y /fɪzɪəʊ'θerəpɪ/ n fisioterapia f

physique /fɪ'zi:k/ n constitución f; (appearance) físico m

pian|ist /'pɪənɪst/ n pianista m & f. ~o /pɪ'ænəʊ/ n (pl -os) piano m

piccolo /'pɪkələʊ/ n flautín m, píccolo m

pick¹ /pɪk/ (tool) pico m

pick² /pɪk/ vt escoger; recoger ⟨flowers etc⟩; forzar ⟨a lock⟩; ⟨dig⟩

picar. ~ **a quarrel** buscar camorra. ~ **holes in** criticar. —n *(choice)* selección *f*; *(the best)* lo mejor. ~ **on** *vt (nag)* meterse con. ~ **out** *vt* escoger; *(identify)* identificar; destacar *(colour)*. ~ **up** *vt* recoger; *(lift)* levantar; *(learn)* aprender; adquirir *(habit, etc)*; obtener *(information)*; contagiarse de *(illness)*. —*vi* mejorar; *(med)* reponerse

pickaxe /'pɪkæks/ *n* pico *m*

picket /'pɪkɪt/ *n (striker)* huelguista *m* & *f*; *(group of strikers)* piquete *m*; *(stake)* estaca *f*. ~ **line** *n* piquete *m*. —*vi* estar de guardia

pickle /'pɪkl/ *n (in vinegar)* encurtido *m*; *(in brine)* salmuera *f*. **in a** ~ *(fam)* en un apuro. —*vt* encurtir. ~**s** *npl* encurtido *m*

pick ~**pocket** /'pɪkpɒkɪt/ *n* ratero *m*. ~**up** *n (sl)* ligue *m*; *(truck)* camioneta *f*; *(stylus-holder)* fonocaptor *m*, brazo *m*

picnic /'pɪknɪk/ *n* comida *f* campestre. —*vi (pt* **picnicked***)* merendar en el campo

pictorial /pɪk'tɔːrɪəl/ *a* ilustrado

picture /'pɪktʃə(r)/ *n (painting)* cuadro *m*; *(photo)* fotografía *f*; *(drawing)* dibujo *m*; *(beautiful thing)* preciosidad *f*; *(film)* película *f*; *(fig)* descripción *f*. **the** ~**s** *npl* el cine *m*. —*vt* imaginarse; *(describe)* describir

picturesque /pɪktʃə'resk/ *a* pintoresco

piddling /'pɪdlɪŋ/ *a (fam)* insignificante

pidgin /'pɪdʒɪn/ *a*. ~ **English** *n* inglés *m* corrompido

pie /paɪ/ *n* empanada *f*; *(sweet)* pastel *m*, tarta *f*

piebald /'paɪbɔːld/ *a* pío

piece /piːs/ *n* pedazo *m*; *(coin)* moneda *f*; *(in game)* pieza *f*. **a** ~ **of advice** un consejo *m*. **a** ~ **of news** una noticia *f*. **take to** ~**s**

desmontar. —*vt*. ~ **together** juntar. ~**meal** /'piːsmiːl/ *a* gradual; *(unsystematic)* poco sistemático. —*adv* poco a poco. ~**work** *n* trabajo *m* a destajo

pier /pɪə(r)/ *n* muelle *m*

pierc|**e** /pɪəs/ *vt* perforar. ~**ing** *a* penetrante

piety /'paɪətɪ/ *n* piedad *f*

piffl|**e** /'pɪfl/ *n (sl)* tonterías *fpl*. ~**ing** *a (sl)* insignificante

pig /pɪg/ *n* cerdo *m*

pigeon /'pɪdʒɪn/ *n* paloma *f*; *(culin)* pichón *m*. ~**hole** *n* casilla *f*

pig: ~**gy** /'pɪgɪ/ *a (greedy, fam)* glotón. ~**gy-back** *adv* a cuestas. ~**gy bank** *n* hucha *f*. ~**headed** *a* terco

pigment /'pɪgmənt/ *n* pigmento *m*. ~**ation** /-'teɪʃn/ *n* pigmentación *f*

pig: ~**skin** /'pɪgskɪn/ *n* piel *m* de cerdo. ~**sty** /'pɪgstaɪ/ *n* pocilga *f*

pigtail /'pɪgteɪl/ *n (plait)* trenza *f*

pike /paɪk/ *n (fish)* lucio *m*

pilchard /'pɪltʃəd/ *n* sardina *f*

pile[1] /paɪl/ *n (heap)* montón *m*. —*vt* amontonar. ~ **it on** exagerar. —*vi* amontonarse. ~ **up** *vt* amontonar. —*vi* amontonarse. ~**s** /paɪlz/ *npl (med)* almorranas *fpl*

pile[2] /paɪl/ *n (of fabric)* pelo *m*

pile-up /'paɪlʌp/ *n* accidente *m* múltiple

pilfer /'pɪlfə(r)/ *vt/i* hurtar. ~**age** /-ɪdʒ/, ~**ing** *n* hurto *m*

pilgrim /'pɪlgrɪm/ *n* peregrino. ~**age** *n* peregrinación *f*

pill /pɪl/ *n* píldora *f*

pillage /'pɪlɪdʒ/ *n* saqueo *m*. —*vt* saquear

pillar /'pɪlə(r)/ *n* columna *f*. ~**box** *n* buzón *m*

pillion /'pɪlɪən/ *n* asiento *m* trasero. **ride** ~ ir en el asiento trasero

pillory /'pɪlərɪ/ *n* picota *f*

pillow /'pɪləʊ/ n almohada f.
~case /'pɪləʊkeɪs/ n funda f de almohada

pilot /'paɪlət/ n piloto m. —vt pilotar. ~light n fuego m piloto

pimp /pɪmp/ n alcahuete m

pimple /'pɪmpl/ n grano m

pin /pɪn/ n alfiler m; (mec) perno m. ~s and needles hormigueo m. —vt (pt pinned) prender con alfileres; (hold down) enclavijar; (fix) sujetar. ~ s.o. down obligar a uno a que se decida. ~ up fijar

pinafore /'pɪnəfɔːr/ n delantal m. ~dress n mandil m

pincers /'pɪnsəz/ npl tenazas fpl

pinch /pɪntʃ/ vt pellizcar; (steal, sl) hurtar. —vi (shoe) apretar. — n pellizco m; (small amount) pizca f. at a ~ en caso de necesidad

pincushion /'pɪnkʊʃn/ n acerico m

pine¹ /paɪn/ n pino m

pine² /paɪn/ vi. ~ away consumirse. ~ for suspirar por

pineapple /'paɪnæpl/ n piña f, ananás m

ping /pɪŋ/ n sonido m agudo. ~pong /'pɪŋpɒŋ/ n pimpón m, ping-pong m

pinion /'pɪnjən/ vt maniatar

pink /pɪŋk/ a & n color (m) de rosa

pinnacle /'pɪnəkl/ n pináculo m

pin: ~point vt determinar con precisión. ~stripe /'pɪnstraɪp/ n raya f fina

pint /paɪnt/ n pinta f (= 0.57 litre)

pin-up /'pɪnʌp/ n (fam) fotografía f de mujer

pioneer /paɪə'nɪər/ n pionero m. —vt ser el primer promotor de, promover

pious /'paɪəs/ a piadoso

pip¹ /pɪp/ n (seed) pepita f

pip² /pɪp/ n (time signal) señal f

pip³ /pɪp/ n (on uniform) estrella f

pipe /paɪp/ n tubo m; (mus) caramillo m; (for smoking) pipa f. —vt conducir por tuberías. ~ down (fam) bajar la voz, callarse. ~cleaner n limpiapipas m invar. ~dream n ilusión f. ~line /'paɪplaɪn/ n tubería f; (for oil) oleoducto m. in the ~line en preparación f. ~r n flautista m & f

piping /'paɪpɪŋ/ n tubería f. ~ hot muy caliente, hirviendo

piquant /'piːkənt/ a picante

pique /piːk/ n resentimiento m

piracy /'paɪərəsɪ/ n piratería f. ~te /'paɪərət/ n pirata m

pirouette /pɪrʊ'et/ n pirueta f. —vi piruetear

Pisces /'paɪsiːz/ n (astr) Piscis m

pistol /'pɪstl/ n pistola f

piston /'pɪstən/ n pistón m

pit /pɪt/ n foso m; (mine) mina f; (of stomach) boca f. —vt (pt pitted) marcar con hoyos; (fig) oponer. ~ o.s. against medirse con

pitch¹ /pɪtʃ/ n brea f

pitch² /pɪtʃ/ (degree) grado m; (mus) tono m; (sport) campo m. —vt lanzar; armar ‹tent›. ~ into (fam) atacar. —vi caerse; ‹ship› cabecear. ~ in (fam) contribuir. ~ed battle n batalla f campal

pitch-black /pɪtʃ'blæk/ a oscuro como boca de lobo

pitcher /'pɪtʃə(r)/ n jarro m

pitchfork /'pɪtʃfɔːk/ n horca f

piteous /'pɪtɪəs/ a lastimoso

pitfall /'pɪtfɔːl/ n trampa f

pith /pɪθ/ n (of orange, lemon) médula f; (fig) meollo m

pithy /'pɪθɪ/ a (-ier, -iest) conciso

pitiful /'pɪtɪfl/ a lastimoso. ~less a despiadado

pittance /'pɪtns/ n sueldo m irrisorio

pity /'pɪtɪ/ n piedad f; (regret) lástima f. —vt compadecerse de

pivot /'pɪvət/ n pivote m. —vt montonar sobre un pivote. —vi girar sobre un pivote; (fig) depender (**on** de)

pixie /'pɪksɪ/ n duende m

placard /'plækɑːd/ n pancarta f; (poster) cartel m

placate /plə'keɪt/ vt apaciguar

place /pleɪs/ n lugar m; (seat) asiento m; (post) puesto m; (house, fam) casa f. **take** ~ tener lugar. —vt poner, colocar; (remember) recordar; (identify) identificar. **be** ~**d** (in race) colocarse. ~**mat** n salvamanteles m invar. ~**ment** /'pleɪsmənt/ n colocación f

placid /'plæsɪd/ a plácido

plagiarism /'pleɪdʒərɪzm/ n plagio m. ~**ze** /'pleɪdʒəraɪz/ vt plagiar

plague /pleɪg/ n peste f; (fig) plaga f. —vt atormentar

plaice /pleɪs/ n invar platija f

plaid /plæd/ n tartán m

plain /pleɪn/ a (-er, -est) claro; (simple) sencillo; (candid) franco; (ugly) feo. **in** ~ **clothes** en traje de paisano. —adv claramente. —n llanura f. ~**ly** adv claramente; (frankly) francamente; (simply) sencillamente. ~**ness** n claridad f; (simplicity) sencillez f

plaintiff /'pleɪntɪf/ n demandante m & f

plait /plæt/ vt trenzar. —n trenza f

plan /plæn/ n proyecto m; (map) plano m. —vt (pt **planned**) planear, proyectar; (intend) proponerse

plane[1] /pleɪn/ n (tree) plátano m

plane[2] /pleɪn/ (level) nivel m; (aviat) avión m. —a plano

plane[3] /pleɪn/ (tool) cepillo m. —vt cepillar

planet /'plænɪt/ n planeta m. ~**ary** a planetario

plank /plæŋk/ n tabla f

planning /'plænɪŋ/ n planificación f. **family** ~ n planificación familiar. **town** ~ n urbanismo m

plant /plɑːnt/ n planta f; (mec) maquinaria f; (factory) fábrica f. —vt plantar; (place in position) colocar. ~**ation** /plæn'teɪʃn/ n plantación f

plaque /plæk/ n placa f

plasma /'plæzmə/ n plasma m

plaster /'plɑːstə(r)/ n yeso m; (adhesive) esparadrapo m; (for setting bones) escayola f. ~ **of Paris** n yeso m mate. —vt enyesar; (med) escayolar (broken bone); (cover) cubrir (**with** de). ~**ed** a (fam) borracho

plastic /'plæstɪk/ a & n plástico (m)

Plasticine /'plæstɪsiːn/ n (P) pasta f de modelar, plastilina f (P)

plastic surgery /plæstɪk'sɜː-dʒərɪ/ n cirugía f estética

plate /pleɪt/ n plato m; (of metal) chapa f; (silverware) vajilla f de plata; (in book) lámina f. —vt (cover with metal) chapear

plateau /'plætəʊ/ n (pl **plateaux**) n meseta f

plateful /'pleɪtfl/ n (pl **-fuls**) plato m

platform /'plætfɔːm/ n plataforma f; (rail) andén m

platinum /'plætɪnəm/ n platino m

platitude /'plætɪtjuːd/ n tópico m, perogrullada f, lugar m común

platonic /plə'tonɪk/ a platónico

platoon /plə'tuːn/ n pelotón m

platter /'plætə(r)/ n fuente f, plato m grande

plausible /'plɔːzəbl/ a plausible; (person) convincente

play /pleɪ/ *vt* jugar; (*act role*) desempeñar el papel de; tocar ‹*instrument*›. ~ **safe** no arriesgarse. ~ **up to** halagar. —*vi* jugar. ~**ed out** agotado. —*n* juego *m*; (*drama*) obra *f* de teatro. ~ **on words** *n* juego *m* de palabras. ~**down** *vt* minimizar. ~ **on** *vt* aprovecharse de. ~ **up** *vi* (*fam*) causar problemas. ~**act** *vi* hacer la comedia. ~**boy** /pleɪbɔɪ/ *n* calavera *m*. ~**er** *n* jugador *m*; (*mus*) músico *m*. ~**ful** /pleɪfl/ *a* juguetón. ~**fully** *adv* jugando; (*jokingly*) en broma. ~**ground** /pleɪ graʊnd/ *n* parque *m* de juegos infantiles; (*in school*) campo *m* de recreo. ~**group** *n* jardín *m* de la infancia. ~**ing** /pleɪɪŋ/ *n* juego *m*. ~**ing-card** *n* naipe *m*. ~**ing-field** *n* campo *m* de deportes. ~**mate** /pleɪmeɪt/ *n* compañero *m* (de juego). ~**pen** *n* corralito *m*. ~**thing** *n* juguete *m*. ~**wright** /pleɪraɪt/ *n* dramaturgo *m*

plc /piːelˈsiː/ *abbr* (*public limited company*) S.A., sociedad *f* anónima

plea /pliː/ *n* súplica *f*; (*excuse*) excusa *f*; (*jurid*) defensa *f*

plead /pliːd/ *vt* (*jurid*) alegar; (*as excuse*) pretextar. —*vi* suplicar; (*jurid*) abogar. ~ **with** suplicar

pleasant /ˈpleznt/ *a* agradable

pleas|e /pliːz/ *int* por favor. —*vt* agradar, dar gusto a. —*vi* agradar; (*wish*) querer. ~ **e o.s.** hacer lo que quiera. **do as you** ~ haz lo que quieras. ~**ed** a contento. ~**ed with** satisfecho de. ~**ing** *a* agradable

pleasur|e /ˈpleʒə(r)/ *n* placer *m*. ~**able** *a* agradable

pleat /pliːt/ *n* pliegue *m*. —*vt* hacer pliegues en

plebiscite /ˈplebɪsɪt/ *n* plebiscito *m*

plectrum /ˈplektrəm/ *n* plectro *m*

pledge /pledʒ/ *n* prenda *f*; (*promise*) promesa *f*. —*vt* empeñar; (*promise*) prometer

plent|iful /ˈplentɪfl/ *a* abundante. ~**y** /ˈplentɪ/ *n* abundancia *f*. ~**y (of)** muchos (de)

pleurisy /ˈplʊərəsɪ/ *n* pleuresía *f*

pliable /ˈplaɪəbl/ *a* flexible

pliers /ˈplaɪəz/ *npl* alicates *mpl*

plight /plaɪt/ *n* situación *f* (difícil)

plimsolls /ˈplɪmsəlz/ *npl* zapatillas *fpl* de lona

plinth /plɪnθ/ *n* plinto *m*

plod /plɒd/ *vi* (*pt* **plodded**) caminar con paso pesado; (*work hard*) trabajar laboriosamente. ~**der** *n* empollón *m*

plonk /plɒŋk/ *n* (*sl*) vino *m* peleón

plop /plɒp/ *n* paf *m*. —*vi* (*pt* **plopped**) caerse con un paf

plot /plɒt/ *n* complot *m*; (*of novel etc*) argumento *m*; (*piece of land*) parcela *f*. —*vt* (*pt* **plotted**) tramar; (*mark out*) trazar. —*vi* conspirar

plough /plaʊ/ *n* arado *m*. —*vt/i* arar. ~ **through** avanzar laboriosamente por

ploy /plɔɪ/ *n* (*fam*) estratagema *f*, truco *m*

pluck /plʌk/ *vt* arrancar; depilarse (*eyebrows*); desplumar (*bird*); recoger (*flowers*). ~ **up courage** hacer de tripas corazón. —*n* valor *m*. ~**y** *a* (-**ier**, -**iest**) valiente

plug /plʌg/ *n* tapón *m*; (*elec*) enchufe *m*; (*auto*) bujía *f*. —*vt* (*pt* **plugged**) tapar; (*advertise*, *fam*) dar publicidad a. ~ **in** (*elec*) enchufar

plum /plʌm/ *n* ciruela *f*; (*tree*) ciruelo *m*

plumage /ˈpluːmɪdʒ/ *n* plumaje *m*

plumb /plʌm/ a vertical. —n plomada f. —adv verticalmente; (exactly) exactamente. —vt sondar

plumber /'plʌmə(r)/ n fontanero m. ~ing n instalación f sanitaria, instalación f de cañerías

plume /plu:m/ n pluma f

plum job /plʌm'dʒɒb/ n (fam) puesto m estupendo

plummet /'plʌmɪt/ n plomada f. —vi caer a plomo, caer en picado

plump /plʌmp/ a (-er, -est) rechoncho. —vt. ~ for elegir. ~ness n gordura f

plum pudding /plʌm'pʊdɪŋ/ n budín m de pasas

plunder /'plʌndə(r)/ n (act) saqueo m; (goods) botín m. —vt saquear

plunge /plʌndʒ/ vt hundir; (in water) sumergir. —vi zambullirse; (fall) caer. —n salto m. ~er n (for sink) desatascador m; (mec) émbolo m. ~ing a (neck-line) bajo, escotado

plural /'plʊərəl/ a & n plural (m)

plus /plʌs/ prep más. —a positivo. —n signo m más; (fig) ventaja f. five ~ más de cinco

plush /plʌʃ/ n felpa f. —a de felpa, afelpado; (fig) lujoso. ~y a lujoso

plutocrat /'plu:təkræt/ n plutócrata m & f

plutonium /plu:'təʊnjəm/ n plutonio m

ply /plaɪ/ vt manejar (tools); ejercer (trade). ~ s.o. with drink dar continuamente de beber a uno. ~wood n contrachapado m

p.m. /pi:'em/ abbr (post meridiem) de la tarde

pneumatic /nju:'mætɪk/ a neumático

pneumonia /nju:'məʊnjə/ n pulmonía f

PO /pi:'əʊ/ abbr (Post Office) oficina f de correos

poach /pəʊtʃ/ vt escalfar (egg); cocer (fish etc); (steal) cazar en vedado. ~er n cazador m furtivo

pocket /'pɒkɪt/ n bolsillo m; (of air, resistance) bolsa f. be in ~ salir ganado. be out of ~ salir perdiendo. —vt poner en el bolsillo. ~-book n (notebook) libro m de bolsillo; (purse, Amer) cartera f; (handbag, Amer) bolso m. ~-money n dinero m para los gastos personales

pock-marked /'pɒkmɑːkt/ a (face) picado de viruelas

pod /pɒd/ n vaina f

podgy /'pɒdʒɪ/ a (-ier, -iest) rechoncho

poem /'pəʊɪm/ n poesía f

poet /'pəʊɪt/ n poeta m. ~ess n poetisa f. ~ic /-'etɪk/ a, ~ical /-'etɪkl/ a poético. P~ Laureate n poeta laureado. ~ry /'pəʊɪtrɪ/ n poesía f

poignant /'pɔɪnjənt/ a conmovedor

point /pɔɪnt/ n punto m; (sharp end) punta f; (significance) lo importante; (elec) toma f de corriente. good ~s cualidades fpl. to the ~ pertinente. up to a ~ hasta cierto punto. what is the ~? ¿para qué?, ¿a qué fin? —vt (aim) apuntar; (show) indicar. ~ out señalar. —vi señalar. ~-blank a & adv a boca de jarro, a quemarropa. ~ed /'pɔɪntɪd/ a puntiagudo; (fig) mordaz. ~er n (indicador m; (dog) perro m de muestra; (clue, fam) indicación f. ~less /'pɔɪntlɪs/ a inútil

poise /pɔɪz/ n equilibrio m; (elegance) elegancia f; (fig) aplomo m. ~d a en equilibrio. ~d for listo para

poison /'pɔɪzn/ n veneno m. —vt envenenar. ~ous a venenoso; (chemical etc) tóxico

poke /pəʊk/ vt empujar; atizar ⟨fire⟩. ~ **fun at** burlarse de. ~ **out** asomar ⟨head⟩. —vi hurgar; (pry) meterse. ~ **about** de fisgonear. —n empuje m

poker[1] /ˈpəʊkə(r)/ n atizador m

poker[2] /ˈpəʊkə(r)/ n (cards) póquer m. ~**-face** n cara f inmutable

poky /ˈpəʊkɪ/ a (-ier, -iest) estrecho

Poland /ˈpəʊlənd/ n Polonia f

polar /ˈpəʊlə(r)/ a polar. ~ **bear** n oso m blanco

polarize /ˈpəʊləraɪz/ vt polarizar

Pole /pəʊl/ n polaco m

pole[1] /pəʊl/ n palo m; (for flag) asta f

pole[2] /pəʊl/ (geog) polo m. ~**-star** n estrella f polar

polemic /pəˈlemɪk/ a polémico. —n polémica f

police /pəˈliːs/ n policía f. —vt vigilar. ~**man** /-ˈliːsmən/ n (pl -men) policía m, guardia m. ~ **record** n antecedentes mpl penales. ~ **state** n estado m policíaco. ~ **station** n comisaría f. ~**woman** /-wʊmən/ n (pl -women) mujer m policía

policy[1] /ˈpɒlɪsɪ/ n política f

policy[2] /ˈpɒlɪsɪ/ (insurance) póliza f (de seguros)

polio(myelitis) /ˈpəʊlɪəʊ(maɪəˈlaɪtɪs)/ n polio(mielitis) f

polish /ˈpɒlɪʃ/ n (for shoes) betún m; (for floor) cera f; (for nails) esmalte m de uñas; (shine) brillo m; (fig) finura f. **nail** ~ esmalte m de uñas. —vt pulir; limpiar (shoes); encerar (floor). ~ **off** despachar. ~**ed** a pulido; (manner) refinado. ~**er** n pulidor m; (machine) pulidora f

Polish /ˈpəʊlɪʃ/ a & n polaco (m)

polite /pəˈlaɪt/ a cortés. ~**ly** adv cortésmente. ~**ness** n cortesía f

politic|**al** /pəˈlɪtɪkl/ a político. ~**ian** /pɒlɪˈtɪʃn/ n político m. ~**s** /ˈpɒlətɪks/ n política f

polka /ˈpɒlkə/ n polca f. ~ **dots** npl diseño m de puntos

poll /pəʊl/ n elección f; (survey) encuesta f. —vt obtener ⟨votes⟩

pollen /ˈpɒlən/ n polen m

polling-booth /ˈpəʊlɪŋbuːð/ n cabina f de votar

pollute /pəˈluːt/ vt contaminar. ~**ion** /-ʃn/ n contaminación f

polo /ˈpəʊləʊ/ n polo m. ~**-neck** n cuello m vuelto

poltergeist /ˈpɒltəgaɪst/ n duende m

polyester /pɒlɪˈestə(r)/ n poliéster m

polygam|**ist** /pəˈlɪɡəmɪst/ n polígamo m. ~**ous** a polígamo. ~**y** /pəˈlɪɡəmɪ/ n poligamia f

polyglot /ˈpɒlɪɡlɒt/ a & n políglota (m & f)

polygon /ˈpɒlɪɡən/ n polígono m

polyp /ˈpɒlɪp/ n pólipo m

polystyrene /pɒlɪˈstaɪriːn/ n poliestireno m

polytechnic /pɒlɪˈteknɪk/ n escuela f politécnica

polythene /ˈpɒlɪθiːn/ n polietileno m. ~ **bag** n bolsa f de plástico

pomegranate /ˈpɒmɪɡrænɪt/ n (fruit) granada f

pommel /ˈpʌml/ n pomo m

pomp /pɒmp/ n pompa f

pompon /ˈpɒmpɒn/ n pompón m

pompo|**sity** /pɒmˈpɒsətɪ/ n pomposidad f. ~**us** /ˈpɒmpəs/ a pomposo

poncho /ˈpɒntʃəʊ/ n (pl -os) poncho m

pond /pɒnd/ n charca f; (artificial) estanque m

ponder /ˈpɒndə(r)/ vt considerar. —vi reflexionar. ~**ous** a pesado

pong /pɒŋ/ n (sl) hedor m. —vi (sl) apestar

pontiff /ˈpɒntɪf/ n pontífice m. ~**ical** /-ˈtɪfɪkl/ a pontifical; (fig)

dogmático. **~icate** /pɒnˈtɪfɪkeɪt/
vi pontificar

pontoon /pɒnˈtuːn/ *n* pontón *m*.
~ bridge *n* puente *m* de
pontones

pony /ˈpəʊnɪ/ *n* poni *m*. **~tail** *n*
cola *f* de caballo. **~trekking** *n*
excursionismo *m* en poni

poodle /ˈpuːdl/ *n* perro *m* de
lanas, caniche *m*

pool[1] /puːl/ *n* charca *f*; (*artificial*)
estanque *m*. (**swimming-**)**~** *n*
piscina *f*

pool[2] /puːl/ *n* (*common fund*)
fondos *mpl* comunes; (*snooker*)
billar *m* americano. —*vt* aunar.
~s *npl* quinielas *fpl*

poor /pʊə(r)/ *a* (-**er**, -**est**) pobre;
(*not good*) malo. **be in ~ health**
estar mal de salud. **~ly** *a* (*fam*)
indispuesto. —*adv* pobremente;
(*badly*) mal

pop[1] /pɒp/ *n* ruido *m* seco; (*of
bottle*) taponazo *m.* —*vt* (*pt
popped*) hacer reventar; (*put*)
poner. **~ in** *vi* entrar; (*visit*)
pasar por. **~ out** *vi* saltar; (*person*) salir un rato. **~ up** *vi*
surgir, aparecer

pop[2] /pɒp/ *a* (*popular*) pop
invar. —*n* (*fam*) música *f* pop. **~-
art** *n* arte *m* pop

popcorn /ˈpɒpkɔːn/ *n* palomitas
fpl

pope /pəʊp/ *n* papa *m*

popgun /ˈpɒpɡʌn/ *n* pistola *f* de
aire comprimido

poplar /ˈpɒplə(r)/ *n* chopo *m*

poplin /ˈpɒplɪn/ *n* popelina *f*

poppy /ˈpɒpɪ/ *n* amapola *f*

popular /ˈpɒpjʊlə(r)/ *a* popular.
~ity /-ˈlærɪt/ *n* popularidad *f*.
~ize *vt* popularizar

populat|**e** /ˈpɒpjʊleɪt/ *vt* poblar.
~ion /-ˈleɪʃn/ *n* población *f*.
(*number of inhabitants*) habitantes *mpl*

porcelain /ˈpɔːsəlɪn/ *n* porcelana
f

porch /pɔːtʃ/ *n* porche *m*

porcupine /ˈpɔːkjʊpaɪn/ *n*
puerco *m* espín

pore[1] /pɔː(r)/ *n* poro *m*

pore[2] /pɔː(r)/ *vi.* **~ over** estudiar
detenidamente

pork /pɔːk/ *n* cerdo *m*

porn /pɔːn/ *n* (*fam*) pornografía *f*.
~ographic /-əˈɡræfɪk/ *a* porno-
gráfico. **~ography** /pɔːˈnɒɡrəfɪ/
n pornografía *f*

porous /ˈpɔːrəs/ *a* poroso

porpoise /ˈpɔːpəs/ *n* marsopa *f*

porridge /ˈpɒrɪdʒ/ *n* gachas *fpl*
de avena

port[1] /pɔːt/ *n* puerto *m*; (*porthole*)
portilla *f*. **~ of call** puerto de
escala

port[2] /pɔːt/ *n* (*naut, left*) babor
m. —*a* de babor

port[3] /pɔːt/ *n* (*wine*) oporto *m*

portable /ˈpɔːtəbl/ *a* portátil

portal /ˈpɔːtl/ *n* portal *m*

portent /ˈpɔːtent/ *n* presagio *m*

porter /ˈpɔːtə(r)/ *n* portero *m*; (*for
luggage*) mozo *m.* **~age** *n* porte
m

portfolio /pɔːtˈfəʊljəʊ/ *n* (*pl* -**os**)
cartera *f*

porthole /ˈpɔːthəʊl/ *n* portilla *f*

portico /ˈpɔːtɪkəʊ/ *n* (*pl* -**oes**) pórtico *m*

portion /ˈpɔːʃn/ *n* porción *f*. —*vt*
repartir

portly /ˈpɔːtlɪ/ *a* (-**ier**, -**iest**)
corpulento

portrait /ˈpɔːtrɪt/ *n* retrato *m*

portray /pɔːˈtreɪ/ *vt* retratar;
(*represent*) representar. **~al** *n*
retrato *m*

Portug|**al** /ˈpɔːtjʊɡl/ *n* Portugal
m. **~uese** /-ˈɡiːz/ *a* & *n* portugués (*m*)

pose /pəʊz/ *n* postura *f.* —*vt* colocar; hacer ⟨*question*⟩; plantear
⟨*problem*⟩. —*vi* posar. **~ as**
hacerse pasar por. **~r** /ˈpəʊzə(r)/
n pregunta *f* difícil

posh /pɒʃ/ *a* (*sl*) elegante

position /pə'zɪʃn/ n posición f;
(job) puesto m; (status) rango
m. —vt colocar

positive /'pɒzɪtɪv/ a positivo;
(real) verdadero; (certain)
seguro. —n (foto) positiva f. ~ly
adv positivamente

possess /pə'zes/ vt poseer. ~ion
/pə'zeʃn/ n posesión f. take
~ion of tomar posesión de.
~ions npl posesiones fpl; (jurid)
bienes mpl. ~ive /pə'zesɪv/ a
posesivo. ~or n poseedor m

possib|ility /pɒsə'bɪlətɪ/ n posi-
bilidad f. ~le /'pɒsəbl/ a
posible. ~ly adv posiblemente

post¹ /pəust/ n (pole) poste m. —
vt fijar (notice)

post² /pəust/ (place) puesto m

post³ /pəust/ (mail) correo m. —
vt echar (letter). keep s.o. ~ed
tener a uno al corriente

post... /pəust/ pref post

post: ~age /'pəustɪdʒ/ n fran-
queo m. ~al /'pəustl/ a postal.
~al order n giro m postal.
~-box n buzón m. ~card
/'pəustkɑːd/ n (tarjeta f) postal f.
~-code n código m postal

post-date /pəust'deɪt/ vt poner
fecha posterior a

poster /'pəustə(r)/ n cartel m

poste restante /pəust'restɑːnt/ n
lista f de correos

posteri|or /pɒ'stɪərɪə(r)/ a pos-
terior. —n trasero m. ~ty
/pɒs'terətɪ/ n posteridad f

posthumous /'pɒstjʊməs/ a
póstumo. ~ly adv después de la
muerte

post: ~man /'pəustmən/ n (pl
-men) cartero m. ~mark
/'pəustmɑːk/ n matasellos m
invar. ~master /'pəustmɑːstə(r)/ n
administrador m de correos. ~mis-
tress /'pəustmɪstrɪs/ n admin-
istradora f de correos

post-mortem /pəust'mɔːtəm/ n
autopsia f

Post Office /'pəustɒfɪs/ n oficina
f de correos, correos mpl

postpone /pəust'pəun/ vt
aplazar. ~ment n aplazamiento
m

postscript /'pəustskrɪpt/ n posdata f

postulant /'pɒstjʊlənt/ n post-
ulante m & f

postulate /'pɒstjʊleɪt/ vt
postular

posture /'pɒstʃə(r)/ n postura
f. —vi adoptar una postura

posy /'pəuzɪ/ n ramillete m

pot /pɒt/ n (for cooking) olla f; (for
flowers) tiesto m; (marijuana, sl)
mariguana f. go to ~ (sl) echarse a perder. —vt (pt potted)
poner en tiesto

potassium /pə'tæsjəm/ n potasio
m

potato /pə'teɪtəu/ n (pl -oes) patata f, papa f (LAm)

pot: ~-belly n barriga f.
~-boiler n obra f literaria
escrita sólo para ganar dinero

poten|cy /'pəutənsɪ/ n potencia f.
~t /'pəutnt/ a potente; (drink)
fuerte

potentate /'pəutənteɪt/ n potent-
ado m

potential /pəu'tenʃl/ a & n pot-
encial (m). ~ity /-ʃɪ'ælətɪ/ n pot-
encialidad f. ~ly adv
potencialmente

pot-hole /'pɒthəul/ n caverna f;
(in road) bache m. ~r n espeleólogo m

potion /'pəuʃn/ n poción f

pot: ~ luck n lo que haya.
~-shot n tiro m al azar. ~ted
/'pɒtɪd/ see pot. ~a (food) en
conserva

potter¹ /'pɒtə(r)/ n alfarero m

potter² /'pɒtə(r)/ vi hacer pequeños trabajos agradables, no
hacer nada de particular

pottery /'pɒtərɪ/ n cerámica f

potty /ˈpɒtɪ/ a (-ier, -iest) (sl) chiflado. —n orinal m

pouch /pautʃ/ n bolsa f pequeña

pouffe /puːf/ n (stool) taburete m

poulterer /ˈpəultərə(r)/ n pollero m

poultice /ˈpəultɪs/ n cataplasma f

poultry /ˈpəultrɪ/ n aves fpl de corral

pounce /pauns/ vi saltar, atacar de repente. —n salto m, ataque m repentino

pound[1] /paund/ n (weight) libra f (= 454g); (money) libra f (esterlina)

pound[2] /paund/ n (for cars) depósito m

pound[3] /paund/ vt (crush) machacar; (bombard) bombardear. — vi golpear; (heart) palpitar; (walk) ir con pasos pesados

pour /pɔː(r)/ vt verter. ~ out servir (drink). —vi fluir; (rain) llover a cántaros. ~ in (people) entrar en tropel. ~ing rain n lluvia f torrencial. ~ out (people) salir en tropel

pout /paut/ vi hacer pucheros. — n puchero m, mala cara f

poverty /ˈpɒvətɪ/ n pobreza f

powder /ˈpaudə(r)/ n polvo m; (cosmetic) polvos mpl. —vt polvorear; (pulverize) pulverizar. ~ one's face ponerse polvos en la cara. ~ed a en polvo. ~y a polvoriento

power /ˈpauə(r)/ n poder m; (elec) corriente f; (energy) energía f; (nation) potencia f. ~ cut n apagón m. ~ed a con motor. ~ed by impulsado por. ~ful a poderoso. ~less a impotente. ~station n central f eléctrica

practicable /ˈpræktɪkəbl/ a practicable

practical /ˈpræktɪkl/ a práctico. ~ joke n broma f pesada. ~ly adv prácticamente

practice /ˈpræktɪs/ n práctica f; (custom) costumbre f; (exercise) ejercicio m; (sport) entrenamiento m; (clients) clientela f. be in ~ce (doctor, lawyer) ejercer. be out of ~ce no estar en forma. in ~ce (in fact) en la práctica; (on form) en forma. ~se /ˈpræktɪs/ vt hacer ejercicios en; (put into practice) poner en práctica; (sport) entrenarse en; ejercer (profession). — vi ejercitarse; (professional) ejercer. —~sed a experto

practitioner /prækˈtɪʃənə(r)/ n profesional m & f. general ~ médico m de cabecera. medical ~ médico m

pragmatic /prægˈmætɪk/ a pragmático

prairie /ˈpreərɪ/ n pradera f

praise /preɪz/ vt alabar. —n alabanza f. ~worthy a loable

pram /præm/ n cochecito m de niño

prance /prɑːns/ vi (horse) hacer cabriolas; (person) pavonearse

prank /præŋk/ n travesura f

prattle /ˈprætl/ vi parlotear. —n parloteo m

prawn /prɔːn/ n gamba f

pray /preɪ/ vi rezar. ~er /preə(r)/ n oración f. ~ for rogar

pre... /priː/ pref pre...

preach /priːtʃ/ vt/i predicar. ~er n predicador m

preamble /priːˈæmbl/ n preámbulo m

pre-arrange /priːəˈreɪndʒ/ vt arreglar de antemano. ~ment n arreglo m previo

precarious /prɪˈkeərɪəs/ a precario. ~ly adv precariamente

precaution /prɪˈkɔːʃn/ n precaución f. ~ary a de precaución; (preventive) preventivo

precede /prɪˈsiːd/ vt preceder

precedence /ˈpresɪdəns/ n precedencia f. ~t /ˈpresɪdənt/ n precedente m

preceding /prɪ'siːdɪŋ/ *a* precedente

precept /'priːsept/ *n* precepto *m*

precinct /'priːsɪŋkt/ *n* recinto *m*. **pedestrian ~ zona** *f* peatonal. **~s** *npl* contornos *mpl*

precious /'preʃəs/ *a* precioso. —*adv* (*fam*) muy

precipice /'presɪpɪs/ *n* precipicio *m*

precipitat|e /prɪ'sɪpɪteɪt/ *vt* precipitar. /prɪ'sɪpɪtət/ *n* precipitado *m*. —*a* precipitado. **~ion** /-'teɪʃn/ *n* precipitación *f*

precipitous /prɪ'sɪpɪtəs/ *a* escarpado

précis /'preɪsiː/ *n* (*pl* **précis** /-siːz/) resumen *m*

precis|e /prɪ'saɪs/ *a* preciso; (*careful*) meticuloso. **~ely** *adv* precisamente. **~ion** /-'sɪʒn/ *n* precisión *f*

preclude /prɪ'kluːd/ *vt* (*prevent*) impedir; (*exclude*) excluir

precocious /prɪ'kəʊʃəs/ *a* precoz. **~ly** *adv* precozmente

preconce|ived /priːkən'siːvd/ *a* preconcebido. **~ption** /-'sepʃn/ *n* preconcepción *f*

precursor /priː'kɜːsə(r)/ *n* precursor *m*

predator /'predətə(r)/ *n* animal *m* de rapiña. **~y** *a* de rapiña

predecessor /'priːdɪsesə(r)/ *n* predecesor *m*, antecesor *m*

predestin|ation /priːdestɪ'neɪʃn/ *n* predestinación *f*. **~e** /priː'destɪn/ *vt* predestinar

predicament /prɪ'dɪkəmənt/ *n* apuro *m*

predicat|e /'predɪkət/ *n* predicado *m*. **~ive** /prɪ'dɪkətɪv/ *a* predicativo

predict /prɪ'dɪkt/ *vt* predecir. **~ion** /-ʃn/ *n* predicción *f*

predilection /priːdɪ'lekʃn/ *n* predilección *f*

predispose /priːdɪs'pəʊz/ *vt* predisponer

predominan|t /prɪ'dɒmɪnənt/ *a* predominante. **~te** /prɪ'dɒmɪneɪt/ *vi* predominar

pre-eminent /priː'emɪnənt/ *a* preeminente

pre-empt /priː'empt/ *vt* adquirir por adelantado, adelantarse a

preen /priːn/ *vt* limpiar, arreglar. **~ o.s.** atildarse

prefab /'priːfæb/ *n* (*fam*) casa *f* prefabricada. **~ricated** /-'fæb rɪkeɪtɪd/ *a* prefabricado

preface /'prefəs/ *n* prólogo *m*

prefect /'priːfekt/ *n* monitor *m*; (*official*) prefecto *m*

prefer /prɪ'fɜː(r)/ *vt* (*pt* **preferred**) preferir. **~able** /'prefrəbl/ *a* preferible. **~ence** /'prefrəns/ *n* preferencia *f*. **~ential** /-ə'renʃl/ *a* preferente

prefix /'priːfɪks/ *n* (*pl* **-ixes**) prefijo *m*

pregnan|cy /'pregnənsɪ/ *n* embarazo *m*. **~t** /'pregnənt/ *a* embarazada

prehistoric /priːhɪ'stɒrɪk/ *a* prehistórico

prejudge /priː'dʒʌdʒ/ *vt* prejuzgar

prejudice /'predʒʊdɪs/ *n* prejuicio *m*; (*harm*) perjuicio *m*. —*vt* predisponer; (*harm*) perjudicar. **~d** *a* parcial

prelate /'prelət/ *n* prelado *m*

preliminar|ies /prɪ'lɪmɪnərɪz/ *npl* preliminares *mpl*. **~y** /prɪ'lɪmɪnərɪ/ *a* preliminar

prelude /'preljuːd/ *n* preludio *m*

pre-marital /priː'mærɪtl/ *a* prematrimonial

premature /'premətjʊə(r)/ *a* prematuro

premeditated /priː'medɪteɪtɪd/ *a* premeditado

premier /'premɪə(r)/ *a* primero. —*n* (*pol*) primer ministro

première /'premɪə(r)/ *n* estreno *m*

premises /'premɪsɪz/ *npl* local *m*.
on the ~ en el local

premiss /'premɪs/ *n* premisa *f*

premium /'priːmɪəm/ *n* premio
m. **at a ~** muy solicitado

premonition /priːmə'nɪʃn/ *n*
presentimiento *m*

preoccup|ation /priːɒkjʊ'peɪʃn/
n preocupación *f*. **~ied**
/-'ɒkjʊpaɪd/ *a* preocupado

prep /prep/ *n* deberes *mpl*

preparation /prepə'reɪʃn/ *n* preparación *f*. **~s** *npl* preparativos
mpl

preparatory /prɪ'pærətrɪ/ *a* preparatorio. **~ school** *n* escuela *f*
primaria privada

prepare /prɪ'peə(r)/ *vt* preparar. **–vi** prepararse. **~d to** *a*
dispuesto a

prepay /priː'peɪ/ *vt* (*pt* **-paid**)
pagar por adelantado

preponderance /prɪ'pɒndərəns/
n preponderancia *f*

preposition /prepə'zɪʃn/ *n* preposición *f*

prepossessing /priːpə'zesɪŋ/ *a*
atractivo

preposterous /prɪ'pɒstərəs/ *a*
absurdo

prep school /'prepskuːl/ *n*
escuela *f* primaria privada

prerequisite /priː'rekwɪzɪt/ *n*
requisito *m* previo

prerogative /prɪ'rɒgətɪv/ *n* prerrogativa *f*

Presbyterian /prezbɪ'tɪərɪən/ *a*
& *n* presbiteriano (*m*)

prescri|be /prɪ'skraɪb/ *vt* pres-
cribir; (*med*) recetar. **~ption**
/-'ɪpʃn/ *n* prescripción *f*; (*med*)
receta *f*

presence /'prezns/ *n* presencia *f*;
(*attendance*) asistencia *f*. **~ of
mind** presencia *f* de ánimo

present[1] /'preznt/ *a* & *n* presente
(*m* & *f*). **at ~** actualmente. **for
the ~** por ahora

present[2] /'preznt/ *n* (*gift*) regalo
m

present[3] /prɪ'zent/ *vt* presentar;
(*give*) obsequiar. **~ s.o. with**
obsequiar a uno con. **~able** *a*
presentable. **~ation** /prezn
'teɪʃn/ *n* presentación *f*; (*ceremony*) ceremonia *f* de entrega

presently /'prezntlɪ/ *adv* dentro
de poco

preserv|ation /prezə'veɪʃn/ *n*
conservación *f*. **~ative** /prɪ'zɜː
vətɪv/ *n* preservativo *m*. **~e**
/prɪ'zɜːv/ *vt* conservar; (*maintain*) mantener; (*culin*) poner en
conserva. **–n** coto *m*; (*jam*) con-
fitura *f*

preside /prɪ'zaɪd/ *vi* presidir. **~
over** presidir

presiden|cy /'prezɪdənsɪ/ *n*
presidencia *f*. **~t** /'prezɪdənt/
n presidente *m*. **~tial**
/-'denʃl/ *a* presidencial

press /pres/ *vt* apretar; exprimir
(*fruit etc*); (*insist on*) insistir en;
(*iron*) planchar. **be ~ed for**
tener poco. **–vi** apretar; (*time*)
apremiar; (*fig*) urgir. **~ on** seguir adelante. **–n** presión *f*;
(*mec*, *newspapers*) prensa *f*.
(*printing*) imprenta *f*. **~ conference** *n* rueda *f* de prensa. **~
cutting** *n* recorte *m* de periódico. **~ing** /'presɪŋ/ *a* urgente.
~stud *n* automático *m*. **~up** *n*
plancha *f*

pressure /'preʃə(r)/ *n* presión
f. **–vt** hacer presión sobre.
~cooker *n* olla *f* a presión. **~
group** *n* grupo *m* de presión

pressurize /'preʃəraɪz/ *vt* hacer
presión sobre

prestig|e /pre'stiːʒ/ *n* prestigio *m*.
~ious /pre'stɪdʒəs/ *a* prestigioso

presum|ably /prɪ'zjuːməblɪ/ *adv*
presumiblemente, prob-
ablemente. **~e** /prɪ'zjuːm/ *vt* presumir. **~e (up)on** *vi* abusar de.

~ption /-'zʌmpʃn/ n presunción f. ~ptuous /prɪ'zʌmptʃʊəs/ a presuntuoso

presuppose /pri:sə'pəʊz/ vt presuponer

preten|ce /prɪ'tens/ n fingimiento m; (claim) pretensión f; (pretext) pretexto m. ~d /prɪ'tend/ vt/i fingir. ~d to (lay claim) pretender

pretentious /prɪ'tenʃəs/ a pretencioso

pretext /'pri:tekst/ n pretexto m

pretty /'prɪtɪ/ a (-ier, -iest) adv bonito, lindo (esp LAm); (person) guapo

prevail /prɪ'veɪl/ vi predominar; (win) prevalecer. ~ on persuadir

prevalen|ce /'prevələns/ n costumbre f. ~t /'prevələnt/ a extendido

prevaricate /prɪ'værɪkeɪt/ vi despistar

prevent /prɪ'vent/ vt impedir. ~able a evitable. ~ion /-ʃn/ n prevención f. ~ive a preventivo

preview /'pri:vju:/ n preestreno m, avance m

previous /'pri:vɪəs/ a anterior. ~ to antes de. ~ly adv anteriormente, antes

pre-war /pri:'wɔ:(r)/ a de antes de la guerra

prey /preɪ/ n presa f; (fig) víctima f. bird of ~ n ave f de rapiña. — vi. ~ on alimentarse de; (worry) atormentar

price /praɪs/ n precio m. —vt fijar el precio de. ~less a inapreciable; (amusing, fam) muy divertido. ~y a (fam) caro

prick /prɪk/ vt/i pinchar. ~ up one's ears aguzar las orejas. — n pinchazo m

prickl|e /'prɪkl/ n (bot) espina f; (of animal) púa f; (sensation) picor m. ~y a espinoso; (animal) lleno de púas; (person) quisquilloso

pride /praɪd/ n orgullo m. ~ of place n puesto m de honor. —vr. ~ o.s. on enorgullecerse de

priest /pri:st/ n sacerdote m. ~hood n sacerdocio m. ~ly a sacerdotal

prig /prɪg/ n mojigato m. ~gish a mojigato

prim /prɪm/ a (primmer, primmest) estirado; (prudish) gazmoño

primarily /'praɪmərɪlɪ/ adv en primer lugar

primary /'praɪmərɪ/ a primario; (chief) principal. ~ school n escuela f primaria

prime¹ /praɪm/ vt cebar ⟨gun⟩; (prepare) preparar; aprestar ⟨surface⟩

prime² /praɪm/ a principal; (first rate) excelente. ~ minister n primer ministro m. —n. be in one's ~ estar en la flor de la vida

primer¹ /'praɪmə(r)/ n (of paint) primera mano f

primer² /'praɪmə(r)/ (book) silabario m

primeval /praɪ'mi:vl/ a primitivo

primitive /'prɪmɪtɪv/ a primitivo

primrose /'prɪmrəʊz/ n primavera f

prince /prɪns/ n príncipe m. ~ly a principesco. ~ss /prɪn'ses/ n princesa f

principal /'prɪnsəpl/ a principal. —n (of school etc) director m

principality /prɪnsɪ'pælətɪ/ n principado m

principally /'prɪnsɪplɪ/ adv principalmente

principle /'prɪnsəpl/ n principio m. in ~ en principio. on ~ por principio

print /prɪnt/ vt imprimir; (write in capitals) escribir con letras de molde. —n (of finger, foot) huella f; (letters) caracteres mpl; (of *design*) estampado *m*; (*picture*) grabado *m*; (*photo*) copia *f*. **in ~** ‹*book*› disponible. **out of ~** agotado. **~ed matter** *n* impresos *mpl*. **~er** /ˈprɪntə(r)/ *n* impresor *m*; (*machine*) impresora *f*. **~ing** *n* tipografía *f*. **~out** *n* listado *m*

prior /ˈpraɪə(r)/ *n* prior *m*. **~** anterior. **~ to** antes de

priority /praɪˈɒrətɪ/ *n* prioridad *f*

priory /ˈpraɪərɪ/ *n* priorato *m*

prise /praɪz/ *vt* apalancar. **~ open** abrir por fuerza

prism /ˈprɪzəm/ *n* prisma *m*

prison /ˈprɪzn/ *n* cárcel *m*. **~er** *n* prisionero *m*; (*in prison*) preso *m*; (*under arrest*) detenido *m*. **~ officer** *n* carcelero *m*

pristine /ˈprɪstiːn/ *a* prístino

privacy /ˈprɪvəsɪ/ *n* intimidad *f*; (*private life*) vida *f* privada. **in ~** en la intimidad

private /ˈpraɪvət/ *a* privado; (*confidential*) personal; ‹*lessons, house*› particular; ‹*ceremony*› en la intimidad. **—** *n* soldado *m* raso. **in ~** en privado; (*secretly*) en secreto. **~ eye** *n* (*fam*) detective *m* privado. **~ly** *adv* en privado; (*inwardly*) interiormente

privation /praɪˈveɪʃn/ *n* privación *f*

privet /ˈprɪvɪt/ *n* alheña *f*

privilege /ˈprɪvɪlɪdʒ/ *n* privilegio *m*. **~d** *a* privilegiado

privy /ˈprɪvɪ/ *a*. **~ to** al corriente de

prize /praɪz/ *n* premio *m*. **~** ‹*idiot etc*› de remate. **—** *vt* estimar. **~fighter** *n* boxeador *m* profesional. **~giving** *n* reparto *m* de premios. **~winner** *n* premiado *m*

pro /prəʊ/ *n*. **~s and cons** el pro *m* y el contra *m*

probability /prɒbəˈbɪlətɪ/ *n* probabilidad *f*. **~le** /ˈprɒbəbl/ *a* probable. **~ly** *adv* probablemente

probation /prəˈbeɪʃn/ *n* prueba *f*; (*jurid*) libertad *f* condicional. **~ary** *a* de prueba

probe /prəʊb/ *n* sonda *f*; (*fig*) encuesta *f*. **—** *vt* sondar. **—** *vi*. **~ into** investigar

problem /ˈprɒbləm/ *n* problema *m*. **—** *a* difícil. **~atic** /-ˈmætɪk/ *a* problemático

procedure /prəˈsiːdʒə(r)/ *n* procedimiento *m*

proceed /prəˈsiːd/ *vi* proceder. **~ing** *n* procedimiento *m*. **~ings** /prəˈsiːdɪŋz/ *npl* (*report*) actas *fpl*; (*jurid*) proceso *m*

proceeds /ˈprəʊsiːdz/ *npl* ganancias *fpl*

process /ˈprəʊses/ *n* proceso *m*. **in ~** en vías de. **in the ~ of time** con el tiempo. **—** *vt* tratar; revelar ‹*photo*›. **~ion** /prəˈseʃn/ *n* desfile *m*

proclaim /prəˈkleɪm/ *vt* proclamar. **~mation** /prɒkləˈmeɪʃn/ *n* proclamación *f*

procrastinate /prəˈkræstɪneɪt/ *vi* aplazar, demorar, diferir

procreation /prəʊkrɪˈeɪʃn/ *n* procreación *f*

procure /prəˈkjʊə(r)/ *vt* obtener

prod /prɒd/ *vt* (*pt* **prodded**) empujar; (*with elbow*) dar un codazo a. **—** *vi* dar con el dedo. **—** *n* empuje *m*; (*with elbow*) codazo *m*

prodigal /ˈprɒdɪgl/ *a* pródigo

prodigious /prəˈdɪdʒəs/ *a* prodigioso

prodigy /ˈprɒdɪdʒɪ/ *n* prodigio *m*

produce /prəˈdjuːs/ *vt* (*show*) presentar; (*bring out*) sacar; poner en escena ‹*play*›; (*cause*) causar; (*manufacture*) producir. /ˈprɒdjuːs/ *n* productos *mpl*. **~er** /prəˈdjuːsə(r)/ *n* productor *m*; (*in theatre*) director *m*

product /ˈprɒdʌkt/ *n* producto *m*. **~ion** /prəˈdʌkʃn/ *n* producción *f*; (*of play*) representación *f*

productive /prə'dʌktɪv/ a productivo. **~ity** /ˌprɒdʌk'tɪvətɪ/ n productividad f

profane /prə'feɪn/ a profano; (*blasphemous*) blasfemo. **~ity** /-'fænətɪ/ n profanidad f

profess /prə'fes/ vt profesar; (*pretend*) pretender

profession /prə'feʃn/ n profesión f. **~al** a & n profesional (m & f)

professor /prə'fesə(r)/ n catedrático m; (*Amer*) profesor m

proffer /'prɒfə(r)/ vt ofrecer

proficien|cy /prə'fɪʃənsɪ/ n competencia f. **~t** /prə'fɪʃnt/ a competente

profile /'prəʊfaɪl/ n perfil m

profit /'prɒfɪt/ n (*com*) ganancia f; (*fig*) provecho m. —vi. **~ from** sacar provecho de. **~able** a provechoso

profound /prə'faʊnd/ a profundo. **~ly** adv profundamente

profuse /prə'fjuːs/ a profuso. **~ely** adv profusamente. **~ion** /-ʒn/ n profusión f

progeny /'prɒdʒənɪ/ n progenie f

prognosis /prɒg'nəʊsɪs/ n (*pl* -oses) pronóstico m

program(me) /'prəʊgræm/ n programa m. —vt (*pt* programmed) programar. **~mer** n programador m

progress /'prəʊgres/ n progreso m, progresos mpl; (*development*) desarrollo m. **in ~** en curso. /prə'gres/ vi hacer progresos; (*develop*) desarrollarse. **~ion** /prə'greʃn/ n progresión f

progressive /prə'gresɪv/ a progresivo; (*reforming*) progresista. **~ly** adv progresivamente

prohibit /prə'hɪbɪt/ vt prohibir. **~ive** /-bətɪv/ a prohibitivo

project /prə'dʒekt/ vt proyectar. —vi (*stick out*) sobresalir. /'prɒdʒekt/ n proyecto m

projectile /prə'dʒektaɪl/ n proyectil m

projector /prə'dʒektə(r)/ n proyector m

proletari|an /prəʊlɪ'teərɪən/ a & n proletario (m). **~at** /prəʊlɪ'teərɪət/ n proletariado m

prolifer|ate /prə'lɪfəreɪt/ vi proliferar. **~ation** /-'reɪʃn/ n proliferación f. **~ic** /prə'lɪfɪk/ a prolífico

prologue /'prəʊlɒg/ n prólogo m

prolong /prə'lɒŋ/ vt prolongar

promenade /ˌprɒmə'nɑːd/ n paseo m; (*along beach*) paseo m marítimo. —vt pasear. —vi pasearse. **~ concert** n concierto m (que forma parte de un festival de música clásica en Londres, en que no todo el público tiene asientos)

prominen|ce /'prɒmɪnəns/ n prominencia f; (*fig*) importancia f. **~t** /'prɒmɪnənt/ a prominente; (*important*) importante; (*conspicuous*) conspicuo

promiscu|ity /ˌprɒmɪ'skjuːətɪ/ n libertinaje m. **~ous** /prə'mɪskjʊəs/ a libertino

promise /'prɒmɪs/ n promesa f. —vt/i prometer. **~ing** a prometedor; (*person*) que promete

promontory /'prɒməntrɪ/ n promontorio m

promot|e /prə'məʊt/ vt promover. **~ion** /-'məʊʃn/ n promoción f

prompt /prɒmpt/ a pronto; (*punctual*) puntual. —adv en punto. —vt incitar; apuntar (*actor*). **~er** n apuntador m. **~ly** adv puntualmente. **~ness** n prontitud f

promulgate /'prɒməlgeɪt/ vt promulgar

prone /prəʊn/ a echado boca abajo. **~ to** propenso a

prong /prɒŋ/ n (*of fork*) diente m

pronoun /'prəʊnaʊn/ n pronombre m

pronounce /prə'naʊns/ vt pronunciar; (declare) declarar. **~ement** n declaración f. **~ed** /prə'naʊnst/ a pronunciado; (noticeable) marcado

pronunciation /prənʌnsɪ'eɪʃn/ n pronunciación f

proof /pruːf/ n prueba f; (of alcohol) graduación f normal. —a. **~ against** a prueba de. **~-reading** n corrección f de pruebas

prop¹ /prɒp/ n puntal m; (fig) apoyo m. —vt (pt **propped**) apoyar. **~ against** (lean) apoyar en

prop² /prɒp/ (in theatre, fam) accesorio m

propaganda /prɒpə'gændə/ n propaganda f

propagate /'prɒpəgeɪt/ vt propagar. —vi propagarse. **~ion** /-'geɪʃn/ n propagación f

propel /prə'pel/ vt (pt **propelled**) propulsar. **~ler** /prə'pelə(r)/ n hélice f

propensity /prə'pensətɪ/ n propensión f

proper /'prɒpə(r)/ a correcto; (suitable) apropiado; (gram) propio; (real, fam) verdadero. **~ly** adv correctamente

property /'prɒpətɪ/ n propiedad f; (things owned) bienes mpl. —a inmobiliario

prophecy /'prɒfəsɪ/ n profecía f. **~sy** /'prɒfəsaɪ/ vt/i profetizar. **~t** /'prɒfɪt/ n profeta m. **~tic** /prə'fetɪk/ a profético

propitious /prə'pɪʃəs/ a propicio

proportion /prə'pɔːʃn/ n proporción f. **~al** a, **~ate** a proporcional

proposal /prə'pəʊzl/ n propuesta f. **~al of marriage** oferta f de matrimonio. **~e** /prə'pəʊz/ vt proponer. —vi hacer una oferta de matrimonio

proposition /prɒpə'zɪʃn/ n proposición f; (project, fam) asunto m

propound /prə'paʊnd/ vt proponer

proprietor /prə'praɪətə(r)/ n propietario m

propriety /prə'praɪətɪ/ n decoro m

propulsion /prə'pʌlʃn/ n propulsión f

prosaic /prə'zeɪk/ a prosaico

proscribe /prə'skraɪb/ vt proscribir

prose /prəʊz/ n prosa f

prosecute /'prɒsɪkjuːt/ vt procesar; (carry on) proseguir. **~ion** /-'kjuːʃn/ n proceso m. **~or** n acusador m. Public P**~or** fiscal m

prospect /'prɒspekt/ n vista f; (expectation) perspectiva f. /prə'spekt/ vi prospectar

prospective /prə'spektɪv/ a probable; (future) futuro

prospector /prə'spektə(r)/ n prospector m, explorador m

prospectus /prə'spektəs/ n prospecto m

prosper /'prɒspə(r)/ vi prosperar. **~ity** /-'sperətɪ/ n prosperidad f. **~ous** /'prɒspərəs/ a próspero

prostitute /'prɒstɪtjuːt/ n prostituta f. **~ion** /-'tjuːʃn/ n prostitución f

prostrate /'prɒstreɪt/ a echado boca abajo; (fig) postrado

protagonist /prə'tægənɪst/ n protagonista m & f

protect /prə'tekt/ vt proteger. **~ion** /-ʃn/ n protección f. **~ive** /prə'tektɪv/ a protector. **~or** n protector m

protégé /'prɒtɪʒeɪ/ n protegido m. **~e** n protegida f

protein /'prəʊtiːn/ n proteína f

protest /'prəʊtest/ n protesta f. **under ~** bajo protesta.

/prə'test/ vt/i protestar. ~er n
(demonstrator) manifestante m
& f

Protestant /'prɒtɪstənt/ a & n
protestante (m & f)

protocol /'prəʊtəkɒl/ n protocolo
m

prototype /'prəʊtətaɪp/ n prototipo m

protract /prə'trækt/ vt prolongar

protractor /prə'træktə(r)/ n
transportador m

protrude /prə'truːd/ vi
sobresalir

protuberance /prə'tjuːbərəns/ n
protuberancia f

proud /praʊd/ a orgulloso. ~ly
adv orgullosamente

prove /pruːv/ vt probar. —vi resultar. ~n a probado

provenance /'prɒvənəns/ n procedencia f

proverb /'prɒvɜːb/ n proverbio
m. ~ial /prə'vɜːbɪəl/ a
proverbial

provide /prə'vaɪd/ vt proveer. —
vi. ~ against precaverse de. ~
for (allow for) prever; mantener
(person). ~d /prə'vaɪdɪd/ conj. ~
(that) con tal que

providen|ce /'prɒvɪdəns/ n pro-
videncia f. ~t a providente.
~tial /prɒvɪ'denʃl/ a
providencial

providing /prə'vaɪdɪŋ/ conj. ~
that con tal que

provinc|e /'prɒvɪns/ n provincia
f; (fig) competencia f. ~ial
/prə'vɪnʃl/ a provincial

provision /prə'vɪʒn/ n provisión
f; (supply) suministro m; (stipu-
lation) condición f. ~s npl comestibles mpl

provisional /prə'vɪʒənl/ a provisional. ~ly adv provi-
sionalmente

proviso /prə'vaɪzəʊ/ n (pl -os)
condición f

provo|cation /prɒvə'keɪʃn/ n
provocación f. ~cative /-'vɒk
ətɪv/ a provocador. ~ke
/prə'vəʊk/ vt provocar

prow /praʊ/ n proa f

prowess /'praʊɪs/ n habilidad f;
(valour) valor m

prowl /praʊl/ vi merodear. —n
ronda f. be on the ~ merodear.
~er n merodeador m

proximity /prɒk'sɪmətɪ/ n proximidad f

proxy /'prɒksɪ/ n poder m. by ~
por poder

prude /pruːd/ n mojigato m

pruden|ce /'pruːdəns/ n pruden-
cia f. ~t /'pruːdənt/ a prudente.
~tly adv prudentemente

prudish /'pruːdɪʃ/ a mojigato

prune[1] /pruːn/ n ciruela f pasa

prune[2] /pruːn/ vt podar

pry /praɪ/ vi entrometerse

psalm /sɑːm/ n salmo m

pseudo... /'sjuːdəʊ/ pref seudo...

pseudonym /'sjuːdənɪm/ n seudónimo m

psychiatr|ic /saɪkɪ'ætrɪk/ a psi-
quiátrico. ~ist /saɪ'kaɪətrɪst/ n
psiquiatra m & f. ~y
/saɪ'kaɪətrɪ/ n psiquiatría f

physic /'saɪkɪk/ a psíquico

psycho-analys|e /saɪkəʊ
'ænəlaɪz/ vt psicoanalizar.
~is /saɪkəʊ'næləsɪs/ n psicoan-
álisis m. ~t /-ɪst/ n psico-
analista m & f

psycholog|ical /saɪkə'lɒdʒɪkl/ a
psicológico. ~ist /saɪ'kɒlədʒɪst/
n psicólogo m. ~y /saɪ'kɒlədʒɪ/ n
psicología f

psychopath /'saɪkəpæθ/ n psicópata m & f

pub /pʌb/ n bar m

puberty /'pjuːbətɪ/ n pubertad f

pubic /'pjuːbɪk/ a pubiano,
púbico

public /'pʌblɪk/ a público

publican /'pʌblɪkən/ n tabernero
m

publication /pʌblɪ'keɪʃn/ n publicación f

public house /pʌblɪk'haʊs/ n bar m

publicity /pʌb'lɪsətɪ/ n publicidad f

publicize /'pʌblɪsaɪz/ vt publicar, anunciar

publicly /'pʌblɪklɪ/ adv públicamente

public school /pʌblɪk'skuːl/ n colegio m privado; (Amer) instituto m

public-spirited /pʌblɪk'spɪrɪtɪd/ a cívico

publish /'pʌblɪʃ/ vt publicar. ~er n editor m. ~ing n publicación f

puck /pʌk/ n (ice hockey) disco m

pucker /'pʌkə(r)/ vt arrugar. —vi arrugarse

pudding /'pʊdɪŋ/ n postre m; (steamed) budín m

puddle /'pʌdl/ n charco m

pudgy /'pʌdʒɪ/ a (-ier, -iest) rechoncho

puerile /'pjʊəraɪl/ a pueril

puff /pʌf/ n soplo m; (for powder) borla f. —vt/i soplar. ~ at chupar ‹pipe›. ~ out apagar ‹candle›; (swell up) hinchar. ~ed a (out of breath) sin aliento. ~ pastry n hojaldre m. ~y /'pʌfɪ/ a hinchado

pugnacious /pʌg'neɪʃəs/ a belicoso

pug-nosed /'pʌgnəʊzd/ a chato

pull /pʊl/ vt tirar de; sacar ‹tooth›; torcer ‹muscle›. ~ a face hacer una mueca. ~ a fast one hacer una mala jugada. ~ down derribar ‹building›. ~ off quitarse; (fig) lograr. ~ one's weight poner de su parte. ~ out sacar. ~ s.o.'s leg tomarle el pelo a uno. ~ up (uproot) desarraigar; (reprimand) reprender. —vi tirar (at de). ~ away

(auto) alejarse. ~ back retirarse. ~ in (enter) entrar; (auto) parar. ~ o.s. together tranquilizarse. ~ out (auto) salirse. ~ through recobrar la salud. ~ up (auto) parar. —n tirón m; (fig) atracción f; (influence) influencia f. give a ~ tirar

pulley /'pʊlɪ/ n polea f

pullover /'pʊləʊvə(r)/ n jersey m

pulp /pʌlp/ n pulpa f; (for paper) pasta f

pulpit /'pʊlpɪt/ n púlpito m

pulsate /'pʌlseɪt/ vi pulsar

pulse /pʌls/ n (med) pulso m

pulverize /'pʌlvəraɪz/ vt pulverizar

pumice /'pʌmɪs/ n piedra f pómez

pummel /'pʌml/ vt (pt pummelled) aporrear

pump¹ /pʌmp/ n bomba f; —vt sacar con una bomba; (fig) sonsacar. ~ up inflar

pump² /pʌmp/ (plimsoll) zapatilla f de lona; (dancing shoe) escarpín m

pumpkin /'pʌmpkɪn/ n calabaza f

pun /pʌn/ n juego m de palabras

punch¹ /pʌntʃ/ vt dar un puñetazo a; (perforate) perforar; hacer ‹hole›. —n puñetazo m; (vigour, sl) empuje m; (device) punzón m

punch² /pʌntʃ/ (drink) ponche m. ~-drunk a aturdido a golpes. ~ line n gracia f. ~-up n riña f

punctilious /pʌŋk'tɪlɪəs/ a meticuloso

punctual /'pʌŋktjʊəl/ a puntual. ~ity /-'ælɪtɪ/ n puntualidad f. ~ly adv puntualmente

punctuate /'pʌŋktʃʊeɪt/ vt puntuar. ~ion n puntuación f

puncture /'pʌŋktʃə(r)/ n (in tyre) pinchazo m. —vt pinchar. —vi pincharse

pundit /'pʌndɪt/ n experto m

pungen|cy /'pʌndʒənsɪ/ n acritud f; (fig) mordacidad f. ~t /'pʌndʒənt/ a acre; (remark) mordaz

punish /'pʌnɪʃ/ vt castigar. ~able a castigable. ~ment n castigo m

punitive /'pju:nɪtɪv/ a punitivo

punk /pʌŋk/ a (music, person) punk

punnet /'pʌnɪt/ n canastilla f

punt[1] /pʌnt/ n (boat) batea f

punt[2] /pʌnt/ vi apostar. ~er n apostante m & f

puny /'pju:nɪ/ a (-ier, -iest) diminuto; (weak) débil; (petty) insignificante

pup /pʌp/ n cachorro m

pupil[1] /'pju:pl/ n alumno m

pupil[2] /'pju:pl/ (of eye) pupila f

puppet /'pʌpɪt/ n títere m

puppy /'pʌpɪ/ n cachorro m

purchase /'pɜ:tʃəs/ vt comprar. —n compra f. ~r n comprador m

pur|e /'pjʊə(r)/ a (-ier, -est) puro. ~ely adv puramente. ~ity n pureza f

purée /'pjʊəreɪ/ n puré m

purgatory /'pɜ:gətrɪ/ n purgatorio m

purge /pɜ:dʒ/ vt purgar. —n purga f

purif|ication /pjʊərɪfɪ'keɪʃn/ n purificación f. ~y /'pjʊərɪfaɪ/ vt purificar

purist /'pjʊərɪst/ n purista m & f

puritan /'pjʊərɪtən/ n puritano m. ~ical /-'tænɪkl/ a puritano

purl /pɜ:l/ n (knitting) punto m del revés

purple /'pɜ:pl/ a purpúreo, morado. —n púrpura f

purport /pə'pɔ:t/ vt. ~ to be pretender ser

purpose /'pɜ:pəs/ n propósito m; (determination) resolución f. on ~ a propósito. to no ~ en vano. ~

~-built a construido especialmente. ~ful a (resolute) resuelto. ~ly adv a propósito

purr /pɜ:(r)/ vi ronronear

purse /pɜ:s/ n monedero m; (Amer) bolso m, cartera f (LAm). —vt fruncir

pursu|e /pə'sju:/ vt perseguir, seguir. ~er n perseguidor m. ~it /pə'sju:t/ n persecución f; (fig) ocupación f

purveyor /pə'veɪə(r)/ n proveedor m

pus /pʌs/ n pus m

push /pʊʃ/ vt empujar; apretar (button). —vi empujar. —n empuje m; (effort) esfuerzo m; (drive) dinamismo m. at a ~ en caso de necesidad. get the ~ (sl) ser despedido. ~ aside vt apartar. ~ back vt hacer retroceder. ~ off vi (sl) marcharse. ~ on vi seguir adelante. ~ up vt levantar. ~-button telephone n teléfono m de teclas. ~-chair n sillita f con ruedas. ~ing /'pʊʃɪŋ/ a ambicioso. ~-over n (fam) cosa f muy fácil, pan comido. ~y a (pej) ambicioso

puss /pʊs/ n minino m

put /pʊt/ vt (pt put, pres p putting) poner; (express) expresar; (say) decir; (estimate) estimar; hacer ‹question›. ~ across comunicar; (deceive) engañar. ~ aside poner aparte. ~ away guardar. ~ back devolver; retrasar ‹clock›. ~ by guardar; ahorrar ‹money›. ~ down depositar; (suppress) suprimir; (write) apuntar; (kill) sacrificar. ~ forward avanzar. ~ in introducir; (submit) presentar. ~ in for pedir. ~ off aplazar; (disconcert) desconcertar. ~ on (wear) ponerse; cobrar ‹speed›; encender ‹light›. ~ one's foot down mantenerse firme. ~ out (*extinguish*) apagar; (*inconvenience*) incomodar; extender ⟨*hand*⟩ desconcertar. ~ **to sea** hacerse a la mar. ~ **through** (*phone*) poner. ~ **up** levantar; subir ⟨*price*⟩; alojar ⟨*guest*⟩. ~ **up with** soportar. **stay** ~ (*fam*) no moverse

putrefy /ˈpjuːtrɪfaɪ/ *vi* pudrirse

putt /pʌt/ *n* (*golf*) golpe *m* suave

putty /ˈpʌtɪ/ *n* masilla *f*

put-up /ˈpʊtʌp/ *a*. ~ **job** *n* confabulación *f*

puzzl|e /ˈpʌzl/ *n* enigma *m*; (*game*) rompecabezas *m* *invar*. —*vt* dejar perplejo. —*vi* calentarse los sesos. ~**ing** *a* incomprensible; (*odd*) curioso

pygmy /ˈpɪgmɪ/ *n* pigmeo *m*

pyjamas /pəˈdʒɑːməz/ *npl* pijama *f*

pylon /ˈpaɪlon/ *n* pilón *m*

pyramid /ˈpɪrəmɪd/ *n* pirámide *f*

python /ˈpaɪθn/ *n* pitón *m*

Q

quack[1] /kwæk/ *n* (*of duck*) graznido *m*

quack[2] /kwæk/ (*person*) charlatán *m*. ~ **doctor** *n* curandero *m*

quadrangle /ˈkwɒdræŋgl/ *n* cuadrilátero *m*; (*court*) patio *m*

quadruped /ˈkwɒdrʊped/ *n* cuadrúpedo *m*

quadruple /ˈkwɒdrʊpl/ *a* & *n* cuádruplo (*m*). —*vt* cuadruplicar. ~**t** /-plət/ *n* cuatrillizo *m*

quagmire /ˈkwæɡmaɪə(r)/ *n* ciénaga *f*; (*fig*) atolladero *m*

quail /kweɪl/ *n* codorniz *f*

quaint /kweɪnt/ *a* (-er, -est) pintoresco; (*odd*) curioso

quake /kweɪk/ *vi* temblar. —*n* ⟨*fam*⟩ terremoto *m*

Quaker /ˈkweɪkə(r)/ *n* cuáquero (*m*)

qualification /kwɒlɪfɪˈkeɪʃn/ *n* título *m*; (*requirement*) requisito *m*; (*ability*) capacidad *f*; (*fig*) reserva *f*

qualified /ˈkwɒlɪfaɪd/ *a* cualificado; (*limited*) limitado; (*with degree, diploma*) titulado. ~**y** /ˈkwɒlɪfaɪ/ *vt* calificar; (*limit*) limitar. —*vi* sacar el título; (*sport*) clasificarse; (*fig*) llenar los requisitos

qualitative /ˈkwɒlɪtətɪv/ *a* cualitativo

quality /ˈkwɒlɪtɪ/ *n* calidad *f*; (*attribute*) cualidad *f*

qualm /kwɑːm/ *n* escrúpulo *m*

quandary /ˈkwɒndrɪ/ *n*. **in a** ~ en un dilema

quantitative /ˈkwɒntɪtətɪv/ *a* cuantitativo

quantity /ˈkwɒntɪtɪ/ *n* cantidad *f*

quarantine /ˈkwɒrəntiːn/ *n* cuarentena *f*

quarrel /ˈkwɒrəl/ *n* riña *f*. —*vi* (*pt* **quarrelled**) reñir. ~**some** *a* pendenciero

quarry[1] /ˈkwɒrɪ/ *n* (*excavation*) cantera *f*

quarry[2] /ˈkwɒrɪ/ *n* (*animal*) presa *f*

quart /kwɔːt/ *n* (poco más de un) litro *m*

quarter /ˈkwɔːtə(r)/ *n* cuarto *m*; (*of year*) trimestre *m*; (*district*) barrio *m*. **from all** ~**s** de todas partes. —*vt* dividir en cuartos; (*mil*) acuartelar. ~**s** *npl* alojamiento *m*

quartermaster /ˈkwɔːtəmɑːstə(r)/ *n* intendente *m*

quarter: ~**final** *n* cuarto *m* de final. ~**ly** *a* trimestral. —*adv* cada tres meses

quartet /kwɔːˈtet/ *n* cuarteto *m*

quartz /kwɔːts/ *n* cuarzo *m*. —*a* ⟨*watch etc*⟩ de cuarzo

quash /kwɒʃ/ *vt* anular

quasi.. /'kweɪsaɪ/ *pref* cuasi...

quaver /'kweɪvə(r)/ *vi* temblar. —*n* (*mus*) corchea *f*

quay /kiː/ *n* muelle *m*

queasy /'kwiːzɪ/ *a* (*stomach*) delicado

queen /kwiːn/ *n* reina *f*. ~ **mother** *n* reina *f* madre

queer /kwɪə(r)/ *a* (-**er**, -**est**) extraño; (*dubious*) sospechoso; (*ill*) indispuesto. —*n* (*sl*) homosexual *m*

quell /kwel/ *vt* reprimir

quench /kwentʃ/ *vt* apagar; sofocar (*desire*)

querulous /'kwerʊləs/ *a* quejumbroso

query /'kwɪərɪ/ *n* pregunta *f*. —*vt* preguntar; (*doubt*) poner en duda

quest /kwest/ *n* busca *f*

question /'kwestʃən/ *n* pregunta *f*; (*for discussion*) cuestión *f*. in ~ en cuestión. out of the ~ imposible. without ~ sin duda. —*vt* preguntar; (*police etc*) interrogar; (*doubt*) poner en duda. ~**able** /'kwestʃənəbl/ *a* discutible. ~ **mark** *n* signo *m* de interrogación. ~**naire** /kwes tʃə'neə(r)/ *n* cuestionario *m*

queue /kjuː/ *n* cola *f*. —*vi* (*pres p* **queuing**) hacer cola

quibble /'kwɪbl/ *vi* discutir; (*split hairs*) sutilizar

quick /kwɪk/ *a* (-**er**, -**est**) rápido. **be** ~! ¡date prisa! —*adv* rápidamente. —*n*. **to the** ~ en lo vivo. ~**en** /'kwɪkən/ *vt* acelerar. —*vi* acelerarse. ~**ly** *adv* rápidamente. ~**sand** /'kwɪksænd/ *n* arena *f* movediza. ~**-tempered** *a* irascible

quid /kwɪd/ *n invar* (*sl*) libra *f* (esterlina)

quiet /'kwaɪət/ *a* (-**er**, -**est**) tranquilo; (*silent*) callado; (*discreet*) discreto. —*n* tranquilidad *f*. **on the** ~ a escondidas. ~**en**

/'kwaɪətn/ *vt* calmar. —*vi* calmarse. ~**ly** *adv* tranquilamente; (*silently*) silenciosamente; (*discreetly*) discretamente. ~**ness** *n* tranquilidad *f*

quill /kwɪl/ *n* pluma *f*

quilt /kwɪlt/ *n* edredón *m*. —*vt* acolchar

quince /kwɪns/ *n* membrillo *m*

quinine /kwɪ'niːn/ *n* quinina *f*

quintessence /kwɪn'tesns/ *n* quintaesencia *f*

quintet /kwɪn'tet/ *n* quinteto *m*

quintuplet /'kwɪntjʊ:plət/ *n* quintillizo *m*

quip /kwɪp/ *n* ocurrencia *f*

quirk /kwɜːk/ *n* peculiaridad *f*

quit /kwɪt/ *vt* (*pt* **quitted**) dejar. —*vi* abandonar; (*leave*) marcharse; (*resign*) dimitir. ~ **doing** (*cease*, *Amer*) dejar de hacer

quite /kwaɪt/ *adv* bastante; (*completely*) totalmente; (*really*) verdaderamente. ~ (**so**)! ¡claro! ~ **a few** bastante

quits /kwɪts/ *a* a la par. **call it** ~ darlo por terminado

quiver /'kwɪvə(r)/ *vi* temblar

quixotic /kwɪk'sɒtɪk/ *a* quijotesco

quiz /kwɪz/ *n* (*pl* **quizzes**) serie *f* de preguntas; (*game*) concurso *m*. —*vt* (*pt* **quizzed**) interrogar. ~**zical** /'kwɪzɪkl/ *a* burlón

quorum /'kwɔːrəm/ *n* quórum *m*

quota /'kwəʊtə/ *n* cuota *f*

quot|**ation** /kwəʊ'teɪʃn/ *n* cita *f*; (*price*) presupuesto *m*. ~**ation marks** *npl* comillas *fpl*. ~**e** /kwəʊt/ *vt* citar; (*com*) cotizar. —*n* (*fam*) cita *f*; (*price*) presupuesto *m*. **in** ~**s** *npl* entre comillas

quotient /'kwəʊʃnt/ *n* cociente *m*

R

rabbi /'ræbaɪ/ n rabino m

rabbit /'ræbɪt/ n conejo m

rabble /'ræbl/ n gentío m. **the ∼** (pej) el populacho m

rabid /'ræbɪd/ a feroz; ⟨dog⟩ rabioso. **∼es** /'reɪbiːz/ n rabia f

race[1] /reɪs/ n carrera f. —vt hacer correr ⟨horse⟩; acelerar ⟨engine⟩. —vi ⟨run⟩ correr, ir corriendo; ⟨rush⟩ ir de prisa

race[2] /reɪs/ ⟨group⟩ raza f

race: **∼course** /'reɪskɔːs/ n hipódromo m. **∼horse** /'reɪshɔːs/ n caballo m de carreras. **∼riots** /'reɪsraɪəts/ npl disturbios mpl raciales. **∼track** /'reɪstræk/ n hipódromo m

racial /'reɪʃl/ a racial. **∼ism** /-ɪzəm/ n racismo m

racing /'reɪsɪŋ/ n carreras fpl. **∼ car** n coche m de carreras

racis|m /'reɪsɪzəm/ n racismo m. **∼t** /'reɪsɪst/ a & n racista (m & f)

rack[1] /ræk/ n ⟨shelf⟩ estante m; ⟨for luggage⟩ rejilla f; ⟨for plates⟩ escurreplatos m invar. —vt. **∼ one's brains** devanarse los sesos

rack[2] /ræk/ n. **go to ∼ and ruin** quedarse en la ruina

racket[1] /'rækɪt/ n ⟨for sports⟩ raqueta f

racket[2] /'rækɪt/ ⟨din⟩ alboroto m; ⟨swindle⟩ estafa f. **∼eer** /-ə'tɪə(r)/ n estafador m

raconteur /rækɒn'tɜː/ n anecdotista m & f

racy /'reɪsɪ/ a (-ier, -iest) vivo

radar /'reɪdɑː(r)/ n radar m

radian|ce /'reɪdɪəns/ n resplandor m. **∼t** /'reɪdɪənt/ a radiante. **∼tly** adv con resplandor

radiat|e /'reɪdɪeɪt/ vt irradiar. —vi divergir. **∼ion** /-'eɪʃn/ n radiación f. **∼or** /'reɪdɪeɪtə(r)/ n radiador m

radical /'rædɪkl/ a & n radical (m)

radio /'reɪdɪəʊ/ n (pl -os) radio f. —vt transmitir por radio

radioactiv|e /reɪdɪəʊ'æktɪv/ a radiactivo. **∼ity** /-'tɪvətɪ/ n radiactividad f

radiograph|er /reɪdɪ'ɒgrəfə(r)/ n radiógrafo m. **∼y** n radiografía f

radish /'rædɪʃ/ n rábano m

radius /'reɪdɪəs/ n (pl -dii /-dɪaɪ/) radio m

raffish /'ræfɪʃ/ a disoluto

raffle /'ræfl/ n rifa f

raft /rɑːft/ n balsa f

rafter /'rɑːftə(r)/ n cabrio m

rag[1] /ræg/ n andrajo m; ⟨for wiping⟩ trapo m; ⟨newspaper⟩ periodicucho m. **in ∼s** ⟨person⟩ andrajoso; ⟨clothes⟩ hecho jirones

rag[2] /ræg/ n ⟨univ⟩ festival m estudiantil; ⟨prank, fam⟩ broma f pesada. —vt (pt ragged) ⟨sl⟩ tomar el pelo a

ragamuffin /'rægəmʌfɪn/ n granuja m, golfo m

rage /reɪdʒ/ n rabia f; ⟨fashion⟩ moda f. —vi estar furioso; ⟨storm⟩ bramar

ragged /'rægɪd/ a ⟨person⟩ andrajoso; ⟨clothes⟩ hecho jirones; ⟨edge⟩ mellado

raid /reɪd/ n ⟨mil⟩ incursión f; ⟨by police, etc⟩ redada f; ⟨by thieves⟩ asalto m. —vt ⟨mil⟩ atacar; ⟨police⟩ hacer una redada en; ⟨thieves⟩ asaltar. **∼er** n invasor m; ⟨thief⟩ ladrón m

rail[1] /reɪl/ n barandilla f; ⟨for train⟩ riel m; ⟨rod⟩ barra f. **by ∼** por ferrocarril

rail[2] /reɪl/ vi. **∼ against, ∼ at** insultar

railing /'reɪlɪŋ/ n barandilla f; ⟨fence⟩ verja f

rail|road /'reɪlrəʊd/ n (Amer), **∼way** /'reɪlweɪ/ n ferrocarril m

~**wayman** *n* (*pl* **-men**) ferroviario *m*. ~**way station** *n* estación *f* de ferrocarril

rain /reɪn/ *n* lluvia *f*. —*vi* llover. ~**bow** /'reɪnbəʊ/ *n* arco *m* iris. ~**coat** /'reɪnkəʊt/ *n* impermeable *m*. ~**fall** /'reɪnfɔːl/ *n* precipitación *f*. ~**water** *n* agua *f* de lluvia. ~**y** /'reɪnɪ/ *a* (**-ier, -iest**) lluvioso

raise /reɪz/ *vt* levantar; (*breed*) criar; obtener (*money etc*); hacer (*question*); plantear (*problem*); subir (*price*). ~ **one's glass** to brindar por. ~ **one's hat** descubrirse. —*n* (*Amer*) aumento *m*

raisin /'reɪzn/ *n* (uva *f*) pasa *f*

rake¹ /reɪk/ *n* rastrillo *m*. —*vt* rastrillar; (*search*) buscar en. ~ **up** remover

rake² /reɪk/ *n* (*man*) calavera *m*

rake-off /'reɪkɒf/ *n* (*fam*) comisión *f*

rally /'rælɪ/ *vt* reunir; (*revive*) reanimar. —*vi* reunirse; (*in sickness*) recuperarse. —*n* reunión *f*; (*recovery*) recuperación *f*; (*auto*) rallye *m*

ram /ræm/ *n* carnero *m*. —*vt* (*pt* **rammed**) (*thrust*) meter por la fuerza; (*crash into*) chocar con

ramble /'ræmbl/ *n* excursión *f* a pie. —*vi* ir de paseo; (*in speech*) divagar. ~**e** on divagar. ~**er** *n* excursionista *m* & *f*. ~**ing** *a* (*speech*) divagador

ramification /ræmɪfɪ'keɪʃn/ *n* ramificación *f*

ramp /ræmp/ *n* rampa *f*

rampage /ræm'peɪdʒ/ *vi* alborotarse. /'ræmpeɪdʒ/ *n*. **go on the** ~ alborotarse

rampant /'ræmpənt/ *a*. **be** ~ (*disease etc*) estar extendido

rampart /'ræmpɑːt/ *n* muralla *f*

ramshackle /'ræmʃækl/ *a* desvencijado

ran /ræn/ *see* **run**

ranch /rɑːntʃ/ *n* hacienda *f*

rancid /'rænsɪd/ *a* rancio

rancour /'ræŋkə(r)/ *n* rencor *m*

random /'rændəm/ *a* hecho al azar; (*chance*) fortuito. —*n*. **at** ~ al azar

randy /'rændɪ/ *a* (**-ier, -iest**) lujurioso, cachondo (*fam*)

rang /ræŋ/ *see* **ring**

range /reɪndʒ/ *n* alcance *m*; (*distance*) distancia *f*; (*series*) serie *f*; (*of mountains*) cordillera *f*; (*extent*) extensión *f*; (*com*) surtido *m*; (*open area*) dehesa *f*; (*stove*) cocina *f* económica. —*vi* extenderse; (*vary*) variar

ranger /'reɪndʒə(r)/ *n* guardabosque *m*

rank¹ /ræŋk/ *n* posición *f*, categoría *f*; (*row*) fila *f*; (*for taxis*) parada *f*. **the** ~ **and file** la masa *f*. —*vt* clasificar. —*vi* clasificarse. ~**s** *npl* soldados *mpl* rasos

rank² /ræŋk/ *a* (**-er, -est**) exuberante; (*smell*) fétido; (*fig*) completo

rankle /'ræŋkl/ *vi* (*fig*) causar rencor

ransack /'rænsæk/ *vt* registrar; (*pillage*) saquear

ransom /'rænsəm/ *n* rescate *m*. **hold s.o. to** ~ exigir rescate por uno; (*fig*) hacer chantaje a uno. —*vt* rescatar; (*redeem*) redimir

rant /rænt/ *vi* vociferar

rap /ræp/ *n* golpe *m* seco. —*vt*/*i* (*pt* **rapped**) golpear

rapacious /rə'peɪʃs/ *a* rapaz

rape /reɪp/ *vt* violar. —*n* violación *f*

rapid /'ræpɪd/ *a* rápido. ~**ity** /rə'pɪdətɪ/ *n* rapidez *f*. ~**s** /'ræpɪdz/ *npl* rápido *m*

rapist /'reɪpɪst/ *n* violador *m*

rapport /ræ'pɔː(r)/ *n* armonía *f*, relación *f*

rapt /ræpt/ *a* (*attention*) profundo. ~ **in** absorto en

rapture /'ræptʃə(r)/ n éxtasis m. **~ous** a extático

rare[1] /reə(r)/ a (-er, -est) raro

rare[2] /reə(r)/ a (culin) poco hecho

rarefied /'reərifaid/ a enrarecido

rarely /'reəli/ adv raramente

rarity /'reərəti/ n rareza f

raring /'reəriŋ/ a (fam). **~ to** impaciente por

rascal /'rɑːskl/ n tunante m & f

rash[1] /ræʃ/ a (-er, -est) imprudente, precipitado

rash[2] /ræʃ/ n erupción f

rasher /'ræʃə(r)/ n loncha f

rash|**ly** /'ræʃli/ adv imprudentemente, a la ligera. **~ness** n imprudencia f

rasp /rɑːsp/ n (file) escofina f

raspberry /'rɑːzbri/ n frambuesa f

rasping /'rɑːspiŋ/ a áspero

rat /ræt/ n rata f. **—vi** (pt ratted). **~ on** (desert) desertar; (inform on) denunciar, chivarse

rate /reit/ n (ratio) proporción f; (speed) velocidad f; (price) precio m; (of interest) tipo m. **at any ~** de todas formas. **at the ~ of** (on the basis of) a razón de. **at this ~** así. **—vt** valorar; (consider) considerar; (deserve, Amer) merecer. **—vi** ser considerado. **~able value** n valor m imponible. **~payer** /'reitpeiə(r)/ n contribuyente m & f. **~s** npl (taxes) impuestos mpl municipales

rather /'rɑːðə(r)/ adv mejor dicho; (fairly) bastante; (a little) un poco. **—int** claro. **I would ~ not** prefiero no

ratification /rætifi'keiʃn/ n ratificación f. **~y** /'rætifai/ vt ratificar

rating /'reitiŋ/ n clasificación f; (sailor) marinero m; (number, TV) índice m

ratio /'reiʃiəʊ/ n (pl -os) proporción f

ration /'ræʃn/ n ración f. **—vt** racionar

rational /'ræʃənl/ a racional. **~ize** /'ræʃənəlaiz/ vt racionalizar

rat race /'rætreis/ n lucha f incesante para triunfar

rattle /'rætl/ vi traquetear. **—vt** (shake) agitar; (sl) desconcertar. **—n** traqueteo m; (toy) sonajero m. **~ off** (fig) decir de corrida

rattlesnake /'rætlsneik/ n serpiente f de cascabel

ratty /'ræti/ a (-ier, -iest) (sl) irritable

raucous /'rɔːkəs/ a estridente

ravage /'rævidʒ/ vt estragar. **~s** /'rævidʒiz/ npl estragos mpl

rave /reiv/ vi delirar; (in anger) enfurecerse. **~ about** entusiasmarse por

raven /'reivn/ n cuervo m. **—a** ⟨hair⟩ negro

ravenous /'rævənəs/ a voraz; ⟨person⟩ hambriento. **be ~** morirse de hambre

ravine /rə'viːn/ n barranco m

raving /'reiviŋ/ a. **~ mad** loco de atar. **~s** npl divagaciones fpl

ravish /'ræviʃ/ vt (rape) violar. **~ing** a (enchanting) encantador

raw /rɔː/ a (-er, -est) crudo; (not processed) bruto; (wound) en carne viva; (inexperienced) inexperto; (weather) crudo. **~ deal** n tratamiento m injusto, injusticia f. **~ materials** npl materias fpl primas

ray /rei/ n rayo m

raze /reiz/ vt arrasar

razor /'reizə(r)/ n navaja f de afeitar; (electric) maquinilla f de afeitar

Rd abbr (Road) C/, Calle f

re[1] /riː/ prep con referencia a. **—pref** re...

re[2] /rei/ n (mus, second note of any musical scale) re m reach /riːtʃ/ vt alcanzar; (extend) extender; (arrive at) llegar a; (achieve) lograr; (hand over) pasar, dar. —vi extenderse. —n alcance m; (of river) tramo m recto. within ~ of al alcance de; (close to) a corta distancia de

react /rɪˈækt/ vi reaccionar. ~ion /rɪˈækʃn/ n reacción f. ~ionary a & n reaccionario (m)
reactor /rɪˈæktə(r)/ n reactor m
read /riːd/ vt (pt read /red/) leer; (study) estudiar; (interpret) interpretar. —vi leer; (instrument) indicar. —n (fam) lectura f. ~ out vi leer en voz alta. ~able a interesante, agradable; (clear) legible. ~er /ˈriːdə(r)/ n lector m. ~ership n lectores m

readily /ˈredɪlɪ/ adv (willingly) de buena gana; (easily) fácilmente. ~ness /ˈredmɪs/ n prontitud f. in ~ness preparado, listo

reading /ˈriːdɪŋ/ n lectura f

readjust /riːəˈdʒʌst/ vt reajustar. —vi readaptarse (to a)

ready /ˈredɪ/ a (-ier, -iest) listo, preparado; (quick) pronto. ~-made a confeccionado. ~ money n dinero m contante. ~ reckoner n baremo m. get ~ prepararse

real /rɪəl/ a verdadero. —adv (Amer, fam) verdaderamente. ~ estate n bienes mpl raíces

realism /ˈrɪəlɪzəm/ n realismo m. ~t /ˈrɪəlɪst/ n realista m & f. ~tic /-ˈlɪstɪk/ a realista. ~tically /-ˈlɪstɪklɪ/ adv de manera realista

reality /rɪˈælɪtɪ/ n realidad f

realization /rɪəlaɪˈzeɪʃn/ n comprensión f; (com) realización f. ~e /ˈrɪəlaɪz/ vt darse cuenta de; (fulfil, com) realizar

really /ˈrɪəlɪ/ adv verdaderamente

realm /relm/ n reino m

ream /riːm/ n resma f

reap /riːp/ vt segar; (fig) cosechar

re: ~appear /riːəˈpɪə(r)/ vi reaparecer. ~appraisal /riːəˈpreɪzl/ n revaluación f

rear¹ /rɪə(r)/ n parte f de atrás. —a posterior, trasero

rear² /rɪə(r)/ vt (bring up, breed) criar. ~ one's head levantar la cabeza. —vi (horse) encabritarse. ~ up (horse) encabritarse

rear: ~admiral n contraalmirante m. ~guard /ˈrɪəgɑːd/ n retaguardia f

re: ~arm /riːˈɑːm/ vi rearmar. —vi rearmarse. ~arrange /riːəˈreɪndʒ/ vt arreglar de otra manera

reason /ˈriːzn/ n razón f, motivo m. within ~ dentro de lo razonable. —vi razonar

reasonable /ˈriːzənəbl/ a razonable

reasoning /ˈriːznɪŋ/ n razonamiento m

reassur|ance /riːəˈʃʊərəns/ n promesa f tranquilizadora; (guarantee) garantía f. ~e /riːəˈʃʊə(r)/ vt tranquilizar

rebate /ˈriːbeɪt/ n reembolso m; (discount) rebaja f

rebel /ˈrebl/ n rebelde m & f. /rɪˈbel/ vi (pt rebelled) rebelarse. ~lion n rebelión f. ~lious a rebelde

rebound /rɪˈbaʊnd/ vi rebotar; (fig) recaer. /ˈriːbaʊnd/ n rebote m. on the ~ (fig) por reacción

rebuff /rɪˈbʌf/ vt rechazar. —n desaire m

rebuild /riːˈbɪld/ vt (pt rebuilt) reconstruir

rebuke /rɪˈbjuːk/ vt reprender. —n reprensión f

rebuttal /rɪˈbʌtl/ n refutación f

recall /rɪˈkɔːl/ vt (call s.o. back) llamar; (remember) recordar. —n llamada f

recant /rɪˈkænt/ vi retractarse

recap /ˈriːkæp/ vt/i (pt **recapped**) (fam) resumir. —n (fam) resumen m

recapitulat|e /riːkəˈpɪtʃʊleɪt/ vt/i resumir. **∼ion** /-ˈleɪʃn/ n resumen m

recapture /riːˈkæptʃə(r)/ vt recobrar; (recall) hacer revivir

reced|e /rɪˈsiːd/ vi retroceder. **∼ing** a (forehead) huidizo

receipt /rɪˈsiːt/ n recibo m. **∼s** npl (com) ingresos mpl

receive /rɪˈsiːv/ vt recibir. **∼r** /-ə(r)/ n (of stolen goods) perista m & f; (of phone) auricular m

recent /ˈriːsnt/ a reciente. **∼ly** adv recientemente

receptacle /rɪˈseptəkl/ n recipiente m

reception /rɪˈsepʃn/ n recepción f; (welcome) acogida f. **∼ist** n recepcionista m & f

receptive /rɪˈseptɪv/ a receptivo

recess /rɪˈses/ n hueco m; (holiday) vacaciones fpl; (fig) parte f recóndita

recession /rɪˈseʃn/ n recesión f

recharge /riːˈtʃɑːdʒ/ vt cargar de nuevo, recargar

recipe /ˈresɪpɪ/ n receta f

recipient /rɪˈsɪpɪənt/ n recipiente m & f; (of letter) destinatario m

reciprocal /rɪˈsɪprəkl/ a recíproco

reciprocate /rɪˈsɪprəkeɪt/ vt corresponder a

recital /rɪˈsaɪtl/ n (mus) recital m

recite /rɪˈsaɪt/ vt recitar; (list) enumerar

reckless /ˈreklɪs/ a imprudente. **∼ly** adv imprudentemente. **∼ness** n imprudencia f

reckon /ˈrekən/ vt/i calcular; (consider) considerar; (think) pensar. **∼ on** (rely) contar con. **∼ing** n cálculo m

reclaim /rɪˈkleɪm/ vt reclamar; recuperar (land)

reclin|e /rɪˈklaɪn/ vi recostarse. **∼ing** a acostado; (seat) reclinable

recluse /rɪˈkluːs/ n solitario m

recogni|tion /rekəɡˈnɪʃn/ n reconocimiento m. **beyond ∼tion** irreconocible. **∼ze** /ˈrekəɡnaɪz/ vt reconocer

recoil /rɪˈkɔɪl/ vi retroceder. —n (of gun) culatazo m

recollect /rekəˈlekt/ vt recordar. **∼ion** /-ʃn/ n recuerdo m

recommend /rekəˈmend/ vt recomendar. **∼ation** /-ˈdeɪʃn/ n recomendación f

recompense /ˈrekəmpens/ vt recompensar. —n recompensa f

reconcil|e /ˈrekənsaɪl/ vt conciliar (people); conciliar (facts). **∼e o.s.** resignarse (to a). **∼iation** /-sɪlɪˈeɪʃn/ n reconciliación f

recondition /riːkənˈdɪʃn/ vt reacondicionar, arreglar

reconnaissance /rɪˈkɒnɪsns/ n reconocimiento m

reconnoitre /rekəˈnɔɪtə(r)/ vt (pres p **-tring**) (mil) reconocer. —vi hacer un reconocimiento

re∼consider /riːkənˈsɪdə(r)/ vt volver a considerar. **∼construct** /riːkənˈstrʌkt/ vt reconstruir. **∼construction** /-ʃn/ n reconstrucción f

record /rɪˈkɔːd/ vt (in register) registrar; (in diary) apuntar; (mus) grabar. /ˈrekɔːd/ n (file) documentación f, expediente m; (mus) disco m; (sport) récord m. **off the ∼** en confianza. **∼er** /rɪˈkɔːdə(r)/ n registrador m; (mus) flauta f dulce. **∼ing** n grabación f. **∼-player** n tocadiscos m invar

recount /rɪˈkaʊnt/ vt contar, relatar, referir

re-count /riːˈkaʊnt/ vt recontar. /ˈriːkaʊnt/ n (pol) recuento m

recoup /rɪˈkuːp/ vt recuperar

recourse /rɪˈkɔːs/ n recurso m. **have ~ to** recurrir a

recover /rɪˈkʌvə(r)/ vt recuperar. —vi reponerse. **~y** n recuperación f

recreation /rekrɪˈeɪʃn/ n recreo m. **~al** a de recreo

recrimination /rɪkrɪmɪˈneɪʃn/ n recriminación f

recruit /rɪˈkruːt/ n recluta m. —vt reclutar. **~ment** n reclutamiento m

rectangle /ˈrektæŋgl/ n rectángulo m. **~ular** /-ˈtæŋgjʊlə(r)/ a rectangular

rectification /rektɪfɪˈkeɪʃn/ n rectificación f. **~y** /ˈrektɪfaɪ/ vt rectificar

rector /ˈrektə(r)/ n párroco m; (of college) rector m. **~y** n rectoría f

recumbent /rɪˈkʌmbənt/ a recostado

recuperat|e /rɪˈkuːpəreɪt/ vt recuperar. —vi reponerse. **~ion** /-ˈreɪʃn/ n recuperación f

recur /rɪˈkɜː(r)/ vi (pt recurred) repetirse. **~rence** /rɪˈkʌrns/ n repetición f. **~rent** /rɪˈkʌrənt/ a repetido

recycle /riːˈsaɪkl/ vt reciclar

red /red/ a (redder, reddest) rojo. —n rojo. **in the ~** (account) en descubierto. **~breast** /ˈredbrest/ n petirrojo m. **~brick** /ˈredbrɪk/ a (univ) de reciente fundación. **~den** /ˈredn/ vt enrojecer. —vi enrojecerse. **~dish** a rojizo

redecorate /riːˈdekəreɪt/ vt pintar de nuevo

rede|em /rɪˈdiːm/ vt redimir. **~eming quality** n cualidad f compensadora. **~mption** /-ˈdempʃn/ n redención f

redeploy /riːdɪˈplɔɪ/ vt disponer de otra manera; (mil) cambiar de frente

red: **~-handed** a en flagrante. **~ herring** n (fig) pista f falsa. **~-hot** a al rojo; (news) de última hora

Red Indian /red'ɪndjən/ n piel m & f roja

redirect /riːdɑɪˈrekt/ vt reexpedir

red: **~-letter day** n día m señalado, día m memorable. **~ light** n luz f roja. **~ness** n rojez f

redo /riːˈduː/ vt (pt redid, pp redone) rehacer

redouble /rɪˈdʌbl/ vt redoblar

redress /rɪˈdres/ vt reparar. —n reparación f

red tape /red'teɪp/ n (fig) papeleo m

reduc|e /rɪˈdjuːs/ vt reducir. —vi reducirse; (slim) adelgazar. **~tion** /ˈdʌkʃn/ n reducción f

redundan|cy /rɪˈdʌndənsɪ/ n superfluidad f; (unemployment) desempleo m. **~t** /rɪˈdʌndənt/ superfluo. **be made ~t** perder su empleo

reed /riːd/ n caña f; (mus) lengüeta f

reef /riːf/ n arrecife m

reek /riːk/ n mal olor m. —vi. **~ (of)** apestar a

reel /riːl/ n carrete m. —vi dar vueltas; (stagger) tambalearse. —vt. **~ off** (fig) enumerar

refectory /rɪˈfektərɪ/ n refectorio m

refer /rɪˈfɜː(r)/ vt (pt referred) remitir. —vi referirse. **~ to** referirse a; (consult) consultar

referee /refəˈriː/ n árbitro m; (for job) referencia f. —vi (pt refereed) arbitrar

reference /ˈrefrəns/ n referencia f. **~ book** n libro m de consulta. **in ~ to, with ~ to** en cuanto a; (com) respecto a

referendum /refə'rendəm/ n (pl -ums) referéndum m

refill /ri:'fil/ vt rellenar. /'ri:fil/ n recambio m

refine /ri'faɪn/ vt refinar. **~d** a refinado. **~ment** n refinamiento m; (tec) refinación f. **~ry** /-əri/ n refinería f

reflect /ri'flekt/ vt reflejar. —vi reflejar; (think) reflexionar. **~ upon** perjudicar. **~ion** /-ʃn/ n reflexión f; (image) reflejo m. **~ive** /ri'flektɪv/ a reflector; (thoughtful) pensativo. **~or** n reflector m

reflex /'ri:fleks/ a & n reflejo (m)

reflexive /ri'fleksɪv/ a (gram) reflexivo

reform /ri'fɔ:m/ vt reformar. —vi reformarse. —n reforma f. **~er** n reformador m

refract /ri'frækt/ vt refractar

refrain[1] /ri'freɪn/ n estribillo m

refrain[2] /ri'freɪn/ vi abstenerse (from de)

refresh /ri'freʃ/ vt refrescar. **~er** /ri'freʃə(r)/ a (course) de repaso. **~ing** a refrescante. **~ments** npl (food and drink) refrigerio m

refrigerate /ri'frɪdʒəreɪt/ vt refrigerar. **~or** n nevera f, refrigeradora f (LAm)

refuel /ri:'fju:əl/ vt/i (pt refuelled) repostar

refuge /'refju:dʒ/ n refugio m. **take ~** refugiarse. **~e** /refjʊ'dʒi:/ n refugiado m

refund /ri'fʌnd/ vt reembolsar. /'ri:fʌnd/ n reembolso m

refurbish /ri:'fɜ:bɪʃ/ vt renovar

refusal /ri'fju:zl/ n negativa f

refuse[1] /ri'fju:z/ vt rehusar. —vi negarse

refuse[2] /'refju:s/ n basura f

refute /ri'fju:t/ vt refutar

regain /ri'geɪn/ vt recobrar

regal /'ri:gl/ a real

regale /ri'geɪl/ vt festejar

regalia /ri'geɪlɪə/ npl insignias fpl

regard /ri'gɑ:d/ vt mirar; (consider) considerar. **as ~s** en cuanto a. —n mirada f; (care) atención f; (esteem) respeto m. **~ing** prep en cuanto a. **~less** /ri'gɑ:dlɪs/ adv a pesar de todo. **~less of** sin tener en cuenta. **~s** npl saludos mpl. **kind ~s** npl recuerdos mpl

regatta /ri'gætə/ n regata f

regency /'ri:dʒənsi/ n regencia f

regenerate /ri'dʒenəreɪt/ vt regenerar

regent /'ri:dʒənt/ n regente m & f

regime /reɪ'ʒi:m/ n régimen m

regiment /'redʒɪmənt/ n regimiento m. **~al** /-'mentl/ a del regimiento. **~ation** /-en'teɪʃn/ n reglamentación f rígida

region /'ri:dʒən/ n región f. **in the ~ of** alrededor de. **~al** a regional

register /'redʒɪstə(r)/ n registro m. —vt registrar; matricular (vehicle); declarar (birth); certificar (letter); facturar (luggage); (indicate) indicar; (express) expresar. —vi (enrol) inscribirse; (fig) producir impresión. **~ office** n registro m civil

registrar /redʒi'strɑ:(r)/ n secretario m del registro civil; (univ) secretario m general

registration /redʒi'streɪʃn/ n registración f; (in register) inscripción f; (of vehicle) matrícula f

registry /'redʒɪstri/ n. **~ office** n registro m civil

regression /ri'greʃn/ n regresión f

regret /ri'gret/ n pesar m. —vt (pt regretted) lamentar. **I ~ that** siento (que). **~fully** adv con pesar. **~table** a lamentable. **~tably** adv lamentablemente

regular /'regjʊlə(r)/ a regular; (*usual*) habitual. —n (*fam*) cliente m habitual. ~**ity** /-'lærətɪ/ n regularidad f. ~**ly** adv regularmente

regulat|e /'regjʊleɪt/ vt regular. ~**ion** /-'leɪʃn/ n arreglo m; (*rule*) regla f

rehabilitat|e /ri:hə'bɪlɪteɪt/ vt rehabilitar. ~**ion** /-'teɪʃn/ n rehabilitación f

rehash /ri:'hæʃ/ vt volver a presentar. /'ri:hæʃ/ n refrito m

rehears|al /rɪ'hɜ:sl/ n ensayo m. ~**e** /rɪ'hɜ:s/ vt ensayar

reign /reɪn/ n reinado m. —vi reinar

reimburse /ri:ɪm'bɜ:s/ vt reembolsar

reins /reɪnz/ npl riendas fpl

reindeer /'reɪndɪə(r)/ n invar reno m

reinforce /ri:ɪn'fɔ:s/ vt reforzar. ~**ment** n refuerzo m

reinstate /ri:ɪn'steɪt/ vt reintegrar

reiterate /ri:'ɪtəreɪt/ vt reiterar

reject /rɪ'dʒekt/ vt rechazar. /'rɪ-dʒekt/ n producto m defectuoso. ~**ion** /'dʒekʃn/ n rechazamiento m, rechazo m

rejoic|e /rɪ'dʒɔɪs/ vi regocijarse. ~**ing** n regocijo m

rejoin /rɪ'dʒɔɪn/ vt reunirse con; (*answer*) replicar. ~**der** /'dʒɔɪndə(r)/ n réplica f

rejuvenate /rɪ'dʒu:vəneɪt/ vt rejuvenecer

rekindle /ri:'kɪndl/ vt reavivar

relapse /rɪ'læps/ n recaída f. —vi recaer; (*into crime*) reincidir

relate /rɪ'leɪt/ vt contar; (*connect*) relacionar. —vi relacionarse (to con). ~**d** a emparentado; (*ideas etc*) relacionado

relation /rɪ'leɪʃn/ n relación f; (*person*) pariente m & f. ~**ship** n relación f; (*blood tie*) parentesco m; (*affair*) relaciones fpl

relative /'relətɪv/ n pariente m & f. —a relativo. ~**ly** adv relativamente

relax /rɪ'læks/ vt relajar. —vi relajarse. ~**ation** /ri:læk'seɪʃn/ n relajación f; (*rest*) descanso m; (*recreation*) recreo m. ~**ing** a relajante

relay /'ri:leɪ/ n relevo m. ~ (*race*) n carrera f de relevos. /rɪ'leɪ/ vt retransmitir

release /rɪ'li:s/ vt soltar; poner en libertad (*prisoner*); lanzar (*bomb*); estrenar (*film*); (*mec*) desenganchar; publicar (*news*); emitir (*smoke*). —n liberación f; (*of film*) estreno f; (*record*) disco m nuevo

relegate /'relɪgeɪt/ vt relegar

relent /rɪ'lent/ vi ceder. ~**less** a implacable; (*continuous*) incesante

relevan|ce /'reləvəns/ n pertinencia f. ~**t** /'reləvənt/ a pertinente

reliab|ility /rɪlaɪə'bɪlətɪ/ n fiabilidad f. ~**le** /rɪ'laɪəbl/ a seguro; (*person*) de fiar; (*com*) serio

relian|ce /rɪ'laɪəns/ n dependencia f; (*trust*) confianza f. ~**t** a confiado

relic /'relɪk/ n reliquia f. ~**s** npl restos mpl

relief /rɪ'li:f/ n alivio m; (*assistance*) socorro m; (*outline*) relieve m. ~**ve** /rɪ'li:v/ vt aliviar; (*take over from*) relevar

religio|n /rɪ'lɪdʒən/ n religión f. ~**us** /rɪ'lɪdʒəs/ a religioso

relinquish /rɪ'lɪŋkwɪʃ/ vt abandonar, renunciar

relish /'relɪʃ/ n gusto m; (*culin*) salsa f. —vt saborear. **I don't ~ the idea** no me gusta la idea

relocate /ri:ləʊ'keɪt/ vt colocar de nuevo

reluctan|ce /rɪ'lʌktəns/ n desgana f. ~**t** /rɪ'lʌktənt/ a mal dispuesto. **be ~t to** no tener ganas de. ~**tly** adv de mala gana

rely /rɪˈlaɪ/ vi. ~ **on** contar con; (trust) fiarse de; (depend) depender

remain /rɪˈmeɪn/ vi quedar. ~**der** /rɪˈmeɪndə(r)/ n resto m. ~**s** npl restos mpl. (left-overs) sobras fpl

remand /rɪˈmɑːnd/ vt. ~ **in custody** mantener bajo custodia. — n. **on** ~ bajo custodia

remark /rɪˈmɑːk/ n observación f. —vt observar. ~**able** a notable

remarry /riːˈmærɪ/ vi volver a casarse

remedial /rɪˈmiːdɪəl/ a remediador

remedy /ˈremədɪ/ n remedio m. —vt remediar

remember /rɪˈmembə(r)/ vt acordarse de. —vi acordarse. ~**rance** n recuerdo m

remind /rɪˈmaɪnd/ vt recordar. ~**er** n recordatorio m; (letter) notificación f

reminisce /remɪˈnɪs/ vi recordar el pasado. ~**nces** npl recuerdos mpl. ~**nt** /remɪˈnɪsnt/ a. **be** ~**nt of** recordar

remiss /rɪˈmɪs/ a negligente

remission /rɪˈmɪʃn/ n remisión f; (of sentence) reducción f de condena

remit /rɪˈmɪt/ vt (pt remitted) perdonar; enviar (money). —vi moderarse. ~**tance** n remesa f

remnant /ˈremnənt/ n resto m; (of cloth) retazo m; (trace) vestigio m

remonstrate /ˈremənstreɪt/ vi protestar

remorse /rɪˈmɔːs/ n remordimiento m. ~**ful** a lleno de remordimiento. ~**less** a implacable

remote /rɪˈməʊt/ a remoto; (slight) leve; (person) distante. ~ **control** n mando m a distancia. ~**ly** adv remotamente.

~**ness** n lejanía f; (isolation) aislamiento m, alejamiento m; (fig) improbabilidad f

remov|able /rɪˈmuːvəbl/ a movible; (detachable) de quita y pon, separable. ~**al** n eliminación f; (from house) mudanza f. ~**e** /rɪˈmuːv/ vt quitar; (dismiss) despedir; (get rid of) eliminar; (do away with) suprimir

remunerat|e /rɪˈmjuːnəreɪt/ vt remunerar. ~**ion** /-ˈreɪʃn/ n remuneración f. ~**ive** a remunerador

Renaissance /rəˈneɪsəns/ n Renacimiento m

rend /rend/ vt (pt rent) rasgar

render /ˈrendə(r)/ vt rendir; (com) presentar; (mus) interpretar; prestar (help etc). ~**ing** n (mus) interpretación f

rendezvous /ˈrɒndeɪvuː/ n (pl -vous /-vuːz/) cita f

renegade /ˈrenɪɡeɪd/ n renegado m

renew /rɪˈnjuː/ vt renovar; (resume) reanudar. ~**able** a renovable. ~**al** n renovación f

renounce /rɪˈnaʊns/ vt renunciar a; (disown) repudiar

renovat|e /ˈrenəveɪt/ vt renovar. ~**ion** /-ˈveɪʃn/ n renovación f

renown /rɪˈnaʊn/ n fama f. ~**ed** a célebre

rent[1] /rent/ n alquiler m. —vt alquilar

rent[2] /rent/ see **rend**

rental /ˈrentl/ n alquiler m

renunciation /rɪnʌnsɪˈeɪʃn/ n renuncia f

reopen /riːˈəʊpən/ vt reabrir. —vi reabrirse. ~**ing** n reapertura f

reorganize /riːˈɔːɡənaɪz/ vt reorganizar

rep[1] /rep/ n (com, fam) representante m & f

rep[2] /rep/ (theatre, fam) teatro m de repertorio

repair /rɪˈpeə(r)/ vt reparar; remendar *(clothes, shoes)*. —n reparación f; *(patch)* remiendo m. **in good** ~ en buen estado

repartee /repaˈtiː/ n ocurrencias fpl

repatriat|e /riːˈpætrɪeɪt/ vt repatriar. ~**ion** /-ˈeɪʃn/ n repatriación f

repay /riːˈpeɪ/ vt *(pt* **repaid)** reembolsar; pagar *(debt)*; *(reward)* recompensar. ~**ment** n reembolso m, pago m

repeal /rɪˈpiːl/ vt abrogar. —n abrogación f

repeat /rɪˈpiːt/ vt repetir. —vi repetir(se). —n repetición f. ~**edly** /rɪˈpiːtɪdlɪ/ adv repetidas veces

repel /rɪˈpel/ vt *(pt* **repelled)** repeler. ~**lent** a repelente

repent /rɪˈpent/ vt arrepentirse. ~**ance** n arrepentimiento m. ~**ant** a arrepentido

repercussion /riːpəˈkʌʃn/ n repercusión f

repertoire /ˈrepətwɑː(r)/ n repertorio m. ~**ry** /ˈrepətrɪ/ n repertorio m. ~**ry** **(theatre)** n teatro m de repertorio

repetit|ion /repɪˈtɪʃn/ n repetición f. ~**ious** /-ˈtɪʃəs/ a, ~**ive** /rɪˈpetɪtɪv/ a que se repite; *(dull)* monótono

replace /rɪˈpleɪs/ vt reponer; *(take the place of)* sustituir. ~**ment** n sustitución f; *(person)* sustituto m. ~**ment part** n recambio m

replay /ˈriːpleɪ/ n *(sport)* repetición f del partido; *(recording)* repetición f inmediata

replenish /rɪˈplenɪʃ/ vt reponer; *(refill)* rellenar

replete /rɪˈpliːt/ a repleto

replica /ˈreplɪkə/ n copia f

reply /rɪˈplaɪ/ vt/i contestar. —n respuesta f

report /rɪˈpɔːt/ vt anunciar; *(denounce)* denunciar. —vi presentar un informe; *(present o.s.)* presentarse. —n informe m; *(schol)* boletín m; *(rumour)* rumor m; *(newspaper)* reportaje m; *(sound)* estallido m. ~**age** /repɔːˈtɑːʒ/ n reportaje m. ~**edly** adv según se dice. ~**er** /rɪˈpɔːtə(r)/ n reportero m, informador m

repose /rɪˈpəʊz/ n reposo m

repository /rɪˈpɒzɪtrɪ/ n depósito m

repossess /riːpəˈzes/ vt recuperar

reprehen|d /reprɪˈhend/ vt reprender. ~**sible** /-səbl/ a reprensible

represent /reprɪˈzent/ vt representar. ~**ation** /-ˈteɪʃn/ n representación f. ~**ative** /reprɪˈzentətɪv/ a representativo. —n representante m & f

repress /rɪˈpres/ vt reprimir. ~**ion** /-ʃn/ n represión f. ~**ive** a represivo

reprieve /rɪˈpriːv/ n indulto m; *(fig)* respiro m. —vt indultar; *(fig)* aliviar

reprimand /ˈreprɪmɑːnd/ vt reprender. —n represión f

reprint /ˈriːprɪnt/ n reimpresión f; *(offprint)* tirada f aparte. /riːˈprɪnt/ vt reimprimir

reprisal /rɪˈpraɪzl/ n represalia f

reproach /rɪˈprəʊtʃ/ vt reprochar. —n reproche m. ~**ful** a de reproche, reprobador. ~**fully** adv con reproche

reprobate /ˈreprəbeɪt/ n malvado m; *(relig)* réprobo m

reproduc|e /riːprəˈdjuːs/ vt reproducir. —vi reproducirse. ~**tion** /-ˈdʌkʃn/ n reproducción f. ~**tive** /-ˈdʌktɪv/ a reproductor

reprove /rɪˈpruːv/ vt reprender

reptile /ˈreptaɪl/ n reptil m

republic /rɪˈpʌblɪk/ n república f. ~**an** a & n republicano (m)

repudiate /rɪˈpjuːdɪeɪt/ vt repudiar; (refuse to recognize) negarse a reconocer

repugnan|ce /rɪˈpʌgnəns/ n repugnancia f. ~**t** /rɪˈpʌgnənt/ a repugnante

repuls|e /rɪˈpʌls/ vt rechazar, repulsar. ~**ion** /-ʃn/ n repulsión f. ~**ive** a repulsivo

reputable /ˈrepjʊtəbl/ a acreditado, de confianza, honroso

reputation /repjʊˈteɪʃn/ n reputación f

repute /rɪˈpjuːt/ n reputación f. ~**d** /-ɪd/ a supuesto. ~**dly** adv según se dice

request /rɪˈkwest/ n petición f. — vt pedir. ~ **stop** n parada f discrecional

require /rɪˈkwaɪə(r)/ vt requerir; (need) necesitar; (demand) exigir. ~**d** a necesario. ~**ment** n requisito m

requisite /ˈrekwɪzɪt/ a necesario. —n requisito m

requisition /rekwɪˈzɪʃn/ n requisición f. —vt requisar

resale /ˈriːseɪl/ n reventa f

rescind /rɪˈsɪnd/ vt rescindir

rescue /ˈreskjuː/ vt salvar. —n salvamento m. ~**r** /-ə(r)/ n salvador m

research /rɪˈsɜːtʃ/ n investigación f. ~vt investigar. ~**er** n investigador m

resembl|ance /rɪˈzembləns/ n parecido m. ~**e** /rɪˈzembl/ vt parecerse a

resent /rɪˈzent/ vt resentirse por. ~**ful** a resentido. ~**ment** n resentimiento m

reservation /rezəˈveɪʃn/ n reserva f; (booking) reservación f

reserve /rɪˈzɜːv/ vt reservar. —n reserva f; (in sports) suplente m & f. ~**d** a reservado

reservist /rɪˈzɜːvɪst/ n reservista m & f

reservoir /ˈrezəvwɑː(r)/ n embalse m; (tank) depósito m

reshape /riːˈʃeɪp/ vt formar de nuevo, reorganizar

reshuffle /riːˈʃʌfl/ vt (pol) reorganizar. —n (pol) reorganización f

reside /rɪˈzaɪd/ vi residir

residen|ce /ˈrezɪdəns/ n residencia f. ~**ce permit** n permiso m de residencia. **be in** ~**ce** (doctor etc) interno. ~**t** /ˈrezɪdənt/ a & n residente (m & f). ~**tial** /-ˈʃl/ a residencial

residue /ˈrezɪdjuː/ n residuo m

resign /rɪˈzaɪn/ vt/i dimitir. ~ **o.s.** to resignarse a. ~**ation** /rezɪgˈneɪʃn/ n resignación f; (from job) dimisión f. ~**ed** a resignado

resilien|ce /rɪˈzɪlɪəns/ n elasticidad f; (of person) resistencia f. ~**t** /rɪˈzɪlɪənt/ a elástico; (person) resistente

resin /ˈrezɪn/ n resina f

resist /rɪˈzɪst/ vt resistir. —vi resistirse. ~**ance** n resistencia f. ~**ant** a resistente

resolute /ˈrezəluːt/ a resuelto. ~**ion** /-ˈluːʃn/ n resolución f

resolve /rɪˈzɒlv/ vt resolver. ~ **to** do resolverse a hacer. —n resolución f. ~**d** a resuelto

resonan|ce /ˈrezənəns/ n resonancia f. ~**t** /ˈrezənənt/ a resonante

resort /rɪˈzɔːt/ vi. ~ **to** recurrir a. —n recurso m; (place) lugar m turístico. **in the last** ~ como último recurso

resound /rɪˈzaʊnd/ vi resonar. ~**ing** a resonante

resource /rɪˈsɔːs/ n recurso m. ~**ful** a ingenioso. ~**fulness** n ingeniosidad f

respect /rɪˈspekt/ n (esteem) respeto m; (aspect) respecto m with ~ to con respecto a. —*vt* respetar

respectab|ility /rɪspektə'bɪlətɪ/ *n* respetabilidad *f*. ~**le** /rɪ'spektəbl/ *a* respetable. ~**ly** *adv* respetablemente

respectful /rɪ'spektfl/ *a* respetuoso

respective /rɪ'spektɪv/ *a* respectivo. ~**ly** *adv* respectivamente

respiration /respə'reɪʃn/ *n* respiración *f*

respite /'respaɪt/ *n* respiro *m*, tregua *f*

resplendent /rɪ'splendənt/ *a* resplandeciente

respon|d /rɪ'spond/ *vi* responder. ~**se** /rɪ'spons/ *n* respuesta *f*; (*reaction*) reacción *f*

responsib|ility /rɪsponsə'bɪlətɪ/ *n* responsabilidad *f*. ~**le** /rɪ'sponsəbl/ *a* responsable; ⟨*job*⟩ de responsabilidad. ~**ly** *adv* con formalidad

responsive /rɪ'sponsɪv/ *a* que reacciona bien. ~ **to** sensible a

rest[1] /rest/ *vt* descansar; (*lean*) apoyar; (*place*) poner, colocar. — *vi* descansar; (*lean*) apoyarse. —*n* descanso *m*; (*mus*) pausa *f*

rest[2] /rest/ *n* (*remainder*) resto *m*, lo demás; (*people*) los demás, los otros *mpl.* —*vi* (*remain*) quedar

restaurant /'restərɒnt/ *n* restaurante *m*

restful /'restfl/ *a* sosegado

restitution /restɪ'tjuːʃn/ *n* restitución *f*

restive /'restɪv/ *a* inquieto

restless /'restlɪs/ *a* inquieto. ~**ly** *adv* inquietamente. ~**ness** *n* inquietud *f*

restor|ation /restə'reɪʃn/ *n* restauración *f*. ~**e** /rɪ'stɔː(r)/ *vt* restablecer; restaurar (*building*); (*put back in position*) reponer; (*return*) devolver

restrain /rɪ'streɪn/ *vt* contener. ~ **o.s.** contenerse. ~**ed** *a* (*moderate*) moderado; (*in control of self*) comedido. ~**t** *n* restricción *f*; (*moderation*) moderación *f*

restrict /rɪ'strɪkt/ *vt* restringir. ~**ion** /-ʃn/ *n* restricción *f*. ~**ive** /rɪ'strɪktɪv/ *a* restrictivo

result /rɪ'zʌlt/ *n* resultado *m*. — *vi.* ~ **from** resultar de. ~ **in** dar como resultado

resume /rɪ'zjuːm/ *vt* reanudar. — *vi* continuar

résumé /'rezjʊmeɪ/ *n* resumen *m*

resumption /rɪ'zʌmpʃn/ *n* continuación *f*

resurgence /rɪ'sɜːdʒəns/ *n* resurgimiento *m*

resurrect /rezə'rekt/ *vt* resucitar. ~**ion** /-ʃn/ *n* resurrección *f*

resuscitate /rɪ'sʌsɪteɪt/ *vt* resucitar. ~**ion** /-'teɪʃn/ *n* resucitación *f*

retail /'riːteɪl/ *n* venta *f* al por menor. —*a* & *adv* al por menor. —*vt* vender al por menor. —*vi* venderse al por menor. ~**er** *n* minorista *m* & *f*

retain /rɪ'teɪn/ *vt* retener; (*keep*) conservar

retainer /rɪ'teɪnə(r)/ *n* (*fee*) anticipo *m*

retaliat|e /rɪ'tælɪeɪt/ *vi* desquitarse. ~**ion** /-ʃn/ *n* represalias *fpl*

retarded /rɪ'tɑːdɪd/ *a* retrasado

retentive /rɪ'tentɪv/ *a* ⟨*memory*⟩ bueno

rethink /riː'θɪŋk/ *vt* (*pt* **rethought**) considerar de nuevo

reticen|ce /'retɪsns/ *n* reserva *f*. ~**t** /'retɪsnt/ *a* reservado, callado

retina /'retɪnə/ *n* retina *f*

retinue /'retɪnjuː/ *n* séquito *m*

retire /rɪ'taɪə(r)/ *vi* (*from work*) jubilarse; (*withdraw*) retirarse; (*go to bed*) acostarse. —*vt* jubilar. ～**ed** *a* jubilado. ～**ement** *n* jubilación *f.* ～**ing** /rɪ'taɪərɪŋ/ *a* reservado

retort /rɪ'tɔːt/ *vt/i* replicar. —*n* réplica *f*

retrace /riː'treɪs/ *vt* repasar. ～ **one's steps** volver sobre sus pasos

retract /rɪ'trækt/ *vt* retirar. —*vi* retractarse

retrain /riː'treɪn/ *vt* reciclar, reeducar

retreat /rɪ'triːt/ *vi* retirarse. —*n* retirada *f*; (*place*) refugio *m*

retrial /riː'traɪəl/ *n* nuevo proceso *m*

retribution /retrɪ'bjuːʃn/ *n* justo *m* castigo

retriev|**al** /rɪ'triːvl/ *n* recuperación *f.* ～**e** /rɪ'triːv/ *vt* (*recover*) recuperar; (*save*) salvar; (*put right*) reparar. ～**er** *n* (*dog*) perro *m* cobrador

retrograde /'retrəgreɪd/ *a* retrógrado

retrospect /'retrəspekt/ *n* retrospección *f.* **in** ～ retrospectivamente. ～**ive** /-'spek tɪv/ *a* retrospectivo

return /rɪ'tɜːn/ *vi* volver; (*reappear*) reaparecer. —*vt* devolver; (*com*) declarar; (*pol*) elegir. —*n* vuelta *f*; (*com*) ganancia *f*; (*restitution*) devolución *f.* ～ **of income** *n* declaración *f* de ingresos. **in** ～ **for** a cambio de. **many happy** ～**s!** ¡feliz cumpleaños! ～**ing** /rɪ'tɜːnɪŋ/ *a.* ～**ing officer** *n* escrutador *m.* ～ **match** *n* partido *m* de desquite. ～ **ticket** *n* billete *m* de ida y vuelta. ～**s** *npl* (*com*) ingresos *mpl*

reunion /riː'juːnɪən/ *n* reunión *f*

reunite /riːjuː'naɪt/ *vt* reunir

rev /rev/ *n* (*auto, fam*) revolución *f.* —*vt/i.* ～ (**up**) (*pt* **revved**) (*auto, fam*) acelerar(se)

revamp /riː'væmp/ *vt* renovar

reveal /rɪ'viːl/ *vt* revelar. ～**ing** *a* revelador

revel /'revl/ *vi* (*pt* **revelled**) jaranear. ～ **in** deleitarse en. ～**ry** *n* juerga *f*

revelation /revə'leɪʃn/ *n* revelación *f*

revenge /rɪ'vendʒ/ *n* venganza *f*; (*sport*) desquite *m.* **take** ～ vengarse. —*vt* vengar. ～**ful** *a* vindicativo, vengativo

revenue /'revənjuː/ *n* ingresos *mpl*

reverberate /rɪ'vɜːbəreɪt/ *vi* (*light*) reverberar; (*sound*) resonar

revere /rɪ'vɪə(r)/ *vt* venerar

reverence /'revərəns/ *n* reverencia *f*

reverend /'revərənd/ *a* reverendo

reverent /'revərənt/ *a* reverente

reverie /'revərɪ/ *n* ensueño *m*

revers /rɪ'vɪə/ *n* (*pl* **revers** /rɪ'vɪəz/) *n* solapa *f*

revers|**al** /rɪ'vɜːsl/ *n* inversión *f.* ～**e** /rɪ'vɜːs/ *a* inverso. —*n* contrario *m*; (*back*) revés *m*; (*auto*) marcha *f* atrás. —*vt* invertir; anular (*decision*); (*auto*) dar marcha atrás a. —*vi* (*auto*) dar marcha atrás

revert /rɪ'vɜːt/ *vi.* ～ **to** volver a

review /rɪ'vjuː/ *n* repaso *m*; (*mil*) revista *f*; (*of book, play, etc*) crítica *f.* —*vt* analizar (*situation*); reseñar (*book, play, etc*). ～**er** *n* crítico *m*

revile /rɪ'vaɪl/ *vt* injuriar

revis|**e** /rɪ'vaɪz/ *vt* revisar; (*schol*) repasar. ～**ion** /-ʒn/ *n* revisión *f*; (*schol*) repaso *m*

revival /rɪ'vaɪvl/ *n* restablecimiento *m*; (*of faith*) despertar *m*; (*of play*) reestreno *m.* ～**e** /rɪ'vaɪv/ *vt* restablecer; resucitar (*person*). —*vi* restablecerse; (*person*) volver en sí

revoke /rɪ'vəʊk/ *vt* revocar

revolt /rɪˈvəʊlt/ *vi* sublevarse. — *vt* dar asco a. —*n* sublevación *f*

revolting /rɪˈvəʊltɪŋ/ *a* asqueroso

revolution /revəˈluːʃn/ *n* revolución *f*. ~**ary** *a* & *n* revolucionario (*m*). ~**ize** *vt* revolucionar

revolve /rɪˈvɒlv/ *vi* girar

revolver /rɪˈvɒlvə(r)/ *n* revólver *m*

revolving /rɪˈvɒlvɪŋ/ *a* giratorio

revue /rɪˈvjuː/ *n* revista *f*

revulsion /rɪˈvʌlʃn/ *n* asco *m*

reward /rɪˈwɔːd/ *n* recompensa *f*. —*vt* recompensar. ~**ing** *a* remunerador; (*worthwhile*) que vale la pena

rewrite /riːˈraɪt/ *vt* (*pt* **rewrote**, *pp* **rewritten**) escribir de nuevo; (*change*) redactar de nuevo

rhapsody /ˈræpsədɪ/ *n* rapsodia *f*

rhetoric /ˈretərɪk/ *n* retórica *f*. ~**al** /rɪˈtorɪkl/ *a* retórico

rheumatic /ruːˈmætɪk/ *a* reumático. ~**sm** /ˈruːmətɪzəm/ *n* reumatismo *m*

rhinoceros /raɪˈnɒsərəs/ *n* (*pl* **-oses**) rinoceronte *m*

rhubarb /ˈruːbɑːb/ *n* ruibarbo *m*

rhyme /raɪm/ *n* rima *f*; (*poem*) poesía *f*. —*vt/i* rimar

rhythm /ˈrɪðəm/ *n* ritmo *m*. ~**ic(al)** /ˈrɪðmɪk(l)/ *a* rítmico

rib /rɪb/ *n* costilla *f*. —*vt* (*pt* **ribbed**) (*fam*) tomar el pelo *a*

ribald /ˈrɪbld/ *a* obsceno, verde

ribbon /ˈrɪbən/ *n* cinta *f*

rice /raɪs/ *n* arroz *m*. ~ **pudding** *n* arroz con leche

rich /rɪtʃ/ *a* (*-er, -est*) rico. —*n* ricos *mpl*. ~**es** *npl* riquezas *fpl*. ~**ly** *adv* ricamente. ~**ness** *n* riqueza *f*

rickety /ˈrɪkətɪ/ *a* (*shaky*) cojo, desvencijado

ricochet /ˈrɪkəʃeɪ/ *n* rebote *m*. —*vi* rebotar

rid /rɪd/ *vt* (*pt* **rid**, *pres p* **ridding**) librar (**of** de). **get ~ of** deshacerse de. ~**dance** /ˈrɪdns/ *n*. **good ~dance!** ¡qué alivio!

ridden /ˈrɪdn/ *see* **ride**. —*a* (*infested*) infestado. ~ **by** (*oppressed*) agobiado de

riddle¹ /ˈrɪdl/ *n* acertijo *m*

riddle² /ˈrɪdl/ *vt* acribillar. **be ~d with** estar lleno de

ride /raɪd/ *vi* (*pt* **rode**, *pp* **ridden**) (*on horseback*) montar; (*go*) ir en bicicleta, a caballo etc). **take s.o. for a ~** (*fam*) engañarle a uno. —*vt* montar a (*horse*); ir en (*bicycle*); recorrer (*distance*). —*n* (*on horse*) cabalgata *f*; (*in car*) paseo *m* en coche. ~**r** /-ə(r)/ *n* (*on horse*) jinete *m*; (*cyclist*) ciclista *m* & *f*; (*in document*) cláusula *f* adicional

ridge /rɪdʒ/ *n* línea *f*, arruga *f*; (*of mountain*) cresta *f*; (*of roof*) caballete *m*

ridicule /ˈrɪdɪkjuːl/ *n* irrisión *f*. —*vt* ridiculizar. ~**ous** /rɪˈdɪkjʊləs/ *a* ridículo

riding /ˈraɪdɪŋ/ *n* equitación *f*

rife /raɪf/ *a* difundido. ~ **with** lleno de

riff-raff /ˈrɪfræf/ *n* gentuza *f*

rifle¹ /ˈraɪfl/ *n* fusil *m*

rifle² /ˈraɪfl/ *vt* saquear

rifle-range /ˈraɪflreɪndʒ/ *n* campo *m* de tiro

rift /rɪft/ *n* grieta *f*; (*fig*) ruptura *f*

rig¹ /rɪg/ *vt* (*pt* **rigged**) aparejar. —*n* (*at sea*) plataforma *f* de perforación. ~ **up** *vt* improvisar

rig² /rɪg/ *vt* (*pej*) amañar

right /raɪt/ *a* (*correct, fair*) exacto, justo; (*morally*) bueno; (*not left*) derecho; (*suitable*) adecuado. —*n* (*entitlement*) derecho *m*; (*not left*) derecha *f*; (*not evil*) bien *m*. ~ **of way** *n* (*auto*) prioridad *f*. **be in the ~**

tener razón. **on the ~** a la derecha. **put ~** rectificar. —vt enderezar; (fig) corregir. —adv a la derecha; (directly) derecho; (completely) completamente; (well) bien. **~ away** adv inmediatamente. **~ angle** n ángulo m recto

righteous /ˈraɪtʃəs/ a recto; (cause) justo

right: **~ful** /ˈraɪtfl/ a legítimo. **~fully** adv legítimamente. **~-hand** man n brazo m derecho. **~ly** adv justamente. **~wing** a (pol) n derechista

rigid /ˈrɪdʒɪd/ a rígido. **~ity** /-ˈdʒɪdɪtɪ/ n rigidez f

rigmarole /ˈrɪgmərəʊl/ n galimatías m invar

rig|**orous** /ˈrɪgərəs/ a riguroso. **~our** /ˈrɪgə(r)/ n rigor m

rig-out /ˈrɪgaʊt/ n (fam) atavío m

rile /raɪl/ vt (fam) irritar

rim /rɪm/ n borde m; (of wheel) llanta f; (of glasses) montura f. **~med** a bordeado

rind /raɪnd/ n corteza f; (of fruit) cáscara f

ring[1] /rɪŋ/ n (circle) círculo m; (circle of metal etc) aro m; (on finger) anillo m; (on finger with stone) sortija f; (boxing) cuadrilátero m; (bullring) ruedo m, redondel m, plaza f; (for circus) pista f; —vt rodear

ring[2] /rɪŋ/ n (of bell) toque m; (tinkle) tintineo m; (telephone call) llamada f. —vt (pt rang, pp rung) hacer sonar; (telephone) llamar por teléfono. **~ the bell** tocar el timbre. —vi sonar. **~ back** vt/i volver a llamar. **~ off** vi colgar. **~ up** vt llamar por teléfono

ring: **~leader** /ˈrɪŋliːdə(r)/ n cabecilla f. **~ road** n carretera f de circunvalación

rink /rɪŋk/ n pista f

rinse /rɪns/ vt enjuagar. —n aclarado m; (of dishes) enjuague m; (for hair) reflejo m

riot /ˈraɪət/ n disturbio m; (of colours) profusión f. **run ~** desenfrenarse. —vi amotinarse. **~er** n amotinador m. **~ous** a tumultuoso

rip /rɪp/ vt (pt ripped) rasgar. —vi rasgarse. **let ~** (fig) soltar. —n rasgadura f. **~ off** vt (sl) robar. **~cord** n (of parachute) cuerda f de abertura

ripe /raɪp/ a (-er, -est) maduro. **~n** /ˈraɪpən/ vt/i madurar. **~ness** n madurez f

rip-off /ˈrɪpɒf/ n (sl) timo m

ripple /ˈrɪpl/ n rizo m; (sound) murmullo m. —vt rizar. —vi rizarse

rise /raɪz/ vi (pt rose, pp risen) levantarse; (rebel) sublevarse; (river) crecer; (prices) subir. —n subida f; (land) altura f; (increase) aumento m; (to power) ascenso m. **give ~ to** ocasionar. **~r** /-ə(r)/ n. **early ~r** n madrugador m

rising /ˈraɪzɪŋ/ n (revolt) sublevación f. —a (sun) naciente. **~ generation** n nueva generación f

risk /rɪsk/ n riesgo m. —vt arriesgar. **~y** a (-ier, -iest) arriesgado

risqué /ˈriːskeɪ/ a subido de color

rissole /ˈrɪsəʊl/ n croqueta f

rite /raɪt/ n rito m

ritual /ˈrɪtʃʊəl/ a & n ritual (m)

rival /ˈraɪvl/ a & n rival (m). —vt (pt rivalled) rivalizar con. **~ry** n rivalidad f

river /ˈrɪvə(r)/ n río m

rivet /ˈrɪvɪt/ n remache m. —vt remachar. **~ing** a fascinante

Riviera /rɪvɪˈeərə/ n. **the (French) ~** la Costa f Azul. **the (Italian) ~** la Riviera f (Italiana)

rivulet /ˈrɪvjʊlɪt/ n riachuelo m

road /rəʊd/ n (in town) calle f; (between towns) carretera f; (way) camino m. **on the ~ en** camino. **~hog** n conductor m descortés. **~house** n albergue m. **~map** n mapa m de carreteras. **~side** /ˈrəʊdsaɪd/ n borde m de la carretera. **~sign** n señal f de tráfico. **~way** /ˈrəʊdweɪ/ n calzada f. **~works** npl obras fpl. **~worthy** /ˈrəʊdwɜːðɪ/ a (vehicle) seguro

roam /rəʊm/ vi vagar

roar /rɔː(r)/ n rugido m; (laughter) carcajada f. —vt/i rugir. **~ past** (vehicles) pasar con estruendo. **~ with laughter** reírse a carcajadas. **~ing** /ˈrɔːrɪŋ/ a (trade etc) activo

roast /rəʊst/ vt asar; tostar (coffee). —vi asarse; (person, coffee) tostarse. —a & n asado (m). **~ beef** n rosbif m

rob /rɒb/ vt (pt robbed) robar; asaltar (bank). **~ of** privar de. **~ber** n ladrón m; (of bank) atracador m. **~bery** n robo m

robe /rəʊb/ n manto m; (univ etc) toga f. **bath~** n albornoz m

robin /ˈrɒbɪn/ n petirrojo m

robot /ˈrəʊbɒt/ n robot m, autómata m

robust /rəʊˈbʌst/ a robusto

rock¹ /rɒk/ n roca f; (boulder) peñasco m; (sweet) caramelo m en forma de barra; (of Gibraltar) peñón m. **on the ~s** (drink) con hielo; (fig) arruinado. **be on the ~s** (marriage etc) andar mal

rock² /rɒk/ vt mecer; (shake) sacudir. —vi mecerse; (shake) sacudirse. —n (mus) música f rock

rock: **~bottom** a (fam) bajísimo. **~ery** /ˈrɒkərɪ/ n cuadro m alpino, rocalla f

rocket /ˈrɒkɪt/ n cohete m

rock: **~ing-chair** n mecedora f. **~ing-horse** n caballo m de balancín. **~y** /ˈrɒkɪ/ a (-ier, -iest)

rocoso; (fig, shaky) bamboleante

rod /rɒd/ n vara f; (for fishing) caña f; (metal) barra f

rode /rəʊd/ see **ride**

rodent /ˈrəʊdnt/ n roedor m

rodeo /rəˈdeɪəʊ/ n (pl -os) rodeo m

roe¹ /rəʊ/ n (fish eggs) hueva f

roe² /rəʊ/ (pl **roe**, or **roes**) (deer) corzo m

rogue /rəʊg/ n pícaro m. **~ish** a picaresco

role /rəʊl/ n papel m

roll /rəʊl/ vt hacer rodar; (roll up) enrollar; (flatten lawn) allanar; aplanar (pastry). —vi rodar; (ship) balancearse; (on floor) revolcarse. **be ~ing** (in money) (fam) nadar (en dinero). —n rollo m; (of ship) balanceo m; (of drum) redoble m; (of thunder) retumbo m; (bread) panecillo m; (list) lista f. **~ over** vi (turn over) dar una vuelta. **~ up** vt enrollar; arremangar (sleeve). —vi (fam) llegar. **~call** n lista f

roller /ˈrəʊlə(r)/ n rodillo m; (wheel) rueda f; (for hair) rulo m, bigudí m. **~coaster** n montaña f rusa. **~skate** n patín m de ruedas

rollicking /ˈrɒlɪkɪŋ/ a alegre

rolling /ˈrəʊlɪŋ/ a ondulado. **~pin** n rodillo m

Roman /ˈrəʊmən/ a & n romano (m). **~ Catholic** a & n católico (m) (romano)

romance /rəʊˈmæns/ n novela f romántica; (love) amor m; (affair) aventura f

Romania /rəʊˈmeɪnɪə/ n Rumania f. **~n** a & n rumano (m)

romantic /rəʊˈmæntɪk/ a romántico. **~ism** n romanticismo m

Rome /rəʊm/ n Roma f

romp /rɒmp/ vi retozar. —n retozo m

rompers /'rɒmpəz/ *npl* pelele *m*

roof /ruːf/ *n* techo *m*, tejado *m*; (*of mouth*) paladar *m*. —*vt* techar. ~**-garden** *n* jardín *m* en la azotea. ~**-rack** *n* baca *f*. ~**-top** *n* tejado *m*

rook[1] /rʊk/ *n* grajo *m*

rook[2] /rʊk/ (*in chess*) torre *f*

room /ruːm/ *n* cuarto *m*, habitación *f*; (*bedroom*) dormitorio *m*; (*space*) sitio *m*; (*large hall*) sala *f*. ~**y** *a* espacioso; (*clothes*) holgado

roost /ruːst/ *n* percha *f*. —*vi* descansar. ~**er** *n* gallo *m*

root[1] /ruːt/ *n* raíz *f*. **take** ~ echar raíces. —*vt* hacer arraigar. —*vi* echar raíces, arraigarse

root[2] /ruːt/ *vt*/*i*. ~ **about** *vi* hurgar. ~ **for** *vi* (*Amer, sl*) alentar. ~ **out** *vt* extirpar

rootless /'ruːtlɪs/ *a* desarraigado

rope /rəʊp/ *n* cuerda *f*. **know the** ~**s** estar al corriente. —*vt* atar. ~ **in** *vt* agarrar

rosary /'rəʊzərɪ/ *n* (*relig*) rosario *m*

rose[1] /rəʊz/ *n* rosa *f*; (*nozzle*) roseta *f*

rose[2] /rəʊz/ *see* **rise**

rosé /'rəʊzeɪ/ *n* (vino *m*) rosado *m*

rosette /rəʊ'zet/ *n* escarapela *f*

roster /'rɒstə(r)/ *n* lista *f*

rostrum /'rɒstrəm/ *n* tribuna *f*

rosy /'rəʊzɪ/ *a* (-**ier**, -**iest**) rosado; (*skin*) sonrosado

rot /rɒt/ *vi* (*pt* **rotted**) pudrir. —*vi* pudrirse. —*n* putrefacción *f*; (*sl*) tonterías *fpl*

rota /'rəʊtə/ *n* lista *f*

rotary /'rəʊtərɪ/ *a* giratorio, rotativo

rotat|e /rəʊ'teɪt/ *vt* girar; (*change round*) alternar. —*vi* girar; (*change round*) alternarse. ~**ion** /-ʃn/ *n* rotación *f*

rote /rəʊt/ *n*. **by** ~ maquinalmente, de memoria

rotten /'rɒtn/ *a* podrido; (*fam*) desagradable

rotund /rəʊ'tʌnd/ *a* redondo; (*person*) regordete

rouge /ruːʒ/ *n* colorete *m*

rough /rʌf/ *a* (-**er**, -**est**) áspero; (*person*) tosco; (*bad*) malo; (*ground*) accidentado; (*violent*) brutal; (*approximate*) aproximado; (*diamond*) bruto. —*adv* duro. ~ **copy** *n*, ~ **draft** *n* borrador *m*. —*n* (*ruffian*) matón *m*. —*vt*. ~ **it** vivir sin comodidades. ~ **out** *vt* esbozar

roughage /'rʌfɪdʒ/ *n* alimento *m* indigesto, afrecho *m*; (*for animals*) forraje *m*

rough: ~**-and-ready** *a* improvisado. ~**-and-tumble** *n* riña *f*. ~**ly** *adv* toscamente; (*more or less*) más o menos. ~**ness** *n* aspereza *f*; (*lack of manners*) incultura *f*; (*crudeness*) tosquedad *f*

roulette /ruː'let/ *n* ruleta *f*

round /raʊnd/ *a* (-**er**, -**est**) redondo. —*n* círculo *m*; (*slice*) tajada *f*; (*of visits, drinks*) ronda *f*; (*of competition*) vuelta *f*; (*boxing*) asalto *m*. —*prep* alrededor de. —*adv* alrededor. ~ **about** (*approximately*) aproximadamente. **come** ~ **to**, **go** ~ **to** (*a friend etc*) pasar por casa de. —*vt* redondear; doblar (*corner*). ~ **off** *vt* terminar. ~ **up** *vt* reunir; redondear (*price*)

roundabout /'raʊndəbaʊt/ *n* tiovivo *m*; (*for traffic*) glorieta *f*. —*a* indirecto

rounders /'raʊndəz/ *n* juego *m* parecido al béisbol

round: ~**ly** *adv* (*bluntly*) francamente. ~ **trip** *n* viaje *m* de ida y vuelta. ~**up** *n* reunión *f*; (*of suspects*) redada *f*

rous|e /raʊz/ *vt* despertar. ~**ing** *a* excitante

rout /raʊt/ n derrota f. —vt derrotar

route /ruːt/ n ruta f; (naut, aviat) rumbo m; (of bus) línea f

routine /ruːˈtiːn/ n rutina f. —a rutinario

rov|e /rəʊv/ vt/i vagar (por). ~ing a errante

row[1] /rəʊ/ n fila f

row[2] /rəʊ/ n (in boat) paseo m en bote (de remos). —vi remar

row[3] /raʊ/ n (noise, fam) ruido m; (quarrel) pelea f. —vi (fam) pelearse

rowdy /ˈraʊdɪ/ a (-ier, -iest) n ruidoso

rowing /ˈrəʊɪŋ/ n remo m. ~-boat n bote m de remos

royal /ˈrɔɪəl/ a real. ~ist a & n monárquico (m). ~ly adv magníficamente. ~ty n familia f real; (payment) derechos mpl de autor

rub /rʌb/ vt (pt rubbed) frotar. ~ it in insistir en algo. —n frotamiento m. ~ off on s.o. vi pegársele a uno. ~ out vt borrar

rubber /ˈrʌbə(r)/ n goma f. ~ band n goma f (elástica). ~ stamp n sello m de goma. ~-stamp vt (fig) aprobar maquinalmente. ~y a parecido al caucho

rubbish /ˈrʌbɪʃ/ n basura f; (junk) trastos mpl; (fig) tonterías fpl. ~y a sin valor

rubble /ˈrʌbl/ n escombros; (small) cascajo m

ruby /ˈruːbɪ/ n rubí m

rucksack /ˈrʌksæk/ n mochila f

rudder /ˈrʌdə(r)/ n timón m

ruddy /ˈrʌdɪ/ a (-ier, -iest) rubicundo; (sl) maldito

rude /ruːd/ a (-er, -est) descortés, mal educado; (improper) indecente; (brusque) brusco. ~ly adv con descortesía. ~ness n descortesía f

rudiment /ˈruːdɪmənt/ n rudimento m. ~ary /-ˈmentrɪ/ a rudimentario

rueful /ˈruːfl/ a triste

ruffian /ˈrʌfɪən/ n rufián m

ruffle /ˈrʌfl/ vt despeinar (hair); arrugar (clothes). —n (frill) volante m, fruncido m

rug /rʌg/ n tapete m; (blanket) manta f

Rugby /ˈrʌgbɪ/ n. ~ (football) n rugby m

rugged /ˈrʌgɪd/ a desigual; (landscape) accidentado; (fig) duro

ruin /ˈruːɪn/ n ruina f. —vt arruinar. ~ous a ruinoso

rule /ruːl/ n regla f; (custom) costumbre f; (pol) dominio m. as a ~ por regla general. —vt gobernar; (master) dominar; (jurid) decretar; (decide) decidir. ~ out vt descartar. ~d paper n papel m rayado

ruler /ˈruːlə(r)/ n (sovereign) soberano m; (leader) gobernante m & f; (measure) regla f

ruling /ˈruːlɪŋ/ a class dirigente. —n decisión f

rum /rʌm/ n ron m

rumble /ˈrʌmbl/ vi retumbar; (stomach) hacer ruidos. —n retumbo m; (of stomach) ruido m

ruminant /ˈruːmɪnənt/ a & n rumiante (m)

rummage /ˈrʌmɪdʒ/ vi hurgar

rumour /ˈruːmə(r)/ n rumor m. —vt. it is ~ed that se dice que

rump /rʌmp/ n (of horse) grupa f; (of fowl) rabadilla f. ~ steak n filete m

rumpus /ˈrʌmpəs/ n (fam) jaleo m

run /rʌn/ vi (pt ran, pp run, pres p running) correr; (flow) fluir; (pass) pasar; (function) funcionar; (melt) derretirse; (bus etc) circular; (play) representarse (continuamente);

⟨colours⟩ correrse; ⟨in election⟩ presentarse. —vt tener ⟨house⟩. ⟨control⟩ dirigir; correr ⟨risk⟩. ⟨drive⟩ conducir; ⟨pass⟩ pasar; ⟨present⟩ presentar; forzar ⟨blockade⟩. **~ a temperature** tener fiebre. —n corrida f, carrera f; ⟨journey⟩ viaje m; ⟨outing⟩ paseo m, excursión f; ⟨distance travelled⟩ recorrido m; ⟨ladder⟩ carrera f; ⟨ski⟩ pista f; ⟨series⟩ serie f. **at a ~** corriendo. **have the ~ of** tener a su disposición. **in the long ~** a la larga. **on the ~** de fuga. **~ across** vi toparse con ⟨friend⟩. **~ away** vi escaparse. **~ down** vi bajar corriendo; ⟨clock⟩ quedarse sin cuerda. —vt ⟨auto⟩ atropellar; ⟨belittle⟩ denigrar. **~ in** vt rodar ⟨vehicle⟩. —vi entrar corriendo. **~ into** vt toparse con ⟨friend⟩; ⟨hit⟩ chocar con. **~ off** vt tirar ⟨copies etc⟩. **~ out** vi salir corriendo; ⟨liquid⟩ salirse; ⟨fig⟩ agotarse. **~ out of** quedar sin. **~ over** vt ⟨auto⟩ atropellar. **~ through** vt traspasar; ⟨revise⟩ repasar. **~ up** vt hacerse ⟨bill⟩. —vi subir corriendo. **~ up against** vt toparse con ⟨difficulties⟩. **~away** /ˈrʌnəweɪ/ a fugitivo; ⟨success⟩ decisivo; ⟨inflation⟩ galopante. —n fugitivo m. **~ down** a ⟨person⟩ agotado. **~down** n informe m detallado

rung[1] /rʌŋ/ n ⟨of ladder⟩ peldaño m

rung[2] /rʌŋ/ see **ring**

run: **~ner** /ˈrʌnə(r)/ n corredor m; ⟨on sledge⟩ patín m. **~ner bean** n judía f escarlata. **~ner up** n sub-campeón m, segundo m. **~ning** /ˈrʌnɪŋ/ n ⟨race⟩ carrera f. **be in the ~ning** tener posibilidades de ganar. —a en marcha; ⟨water⟩ corriente; ⟨commentary⟩ en directo. **four times ~ning** cuatro veces seguidas.

~ny /ˈrʌnɪ/ a líquido; ⟨nose⟩ que moquea. **~-of-the-mill** a ordinario. **~up** n período m que precede. **~way** /ˈrʌnweɪ/ n pista f

rupture /ˈrʌptʃə(r)/ n ruptura f; ⟨med⟩ hernia f. —vt/i quebrarse

rural /ˈrʊərəl/ a rural

ruse /ru:z/ n ardid m

rush[1] /rʌʃ/ n ⟨haste⟩ prisa f; ⟨crush⟩ bullicio m. —vi precipitarse. —vt apresurar; ⟨mil⟩ asaltar

rush[2] /rʌʃ/ n ⟨plant⟩ junco m

rush-hour /ˈrʌʃaʊə(r)/ n hora f punta

rusk /rʌsk/ n galleta f, tostada f

russet /ˈrʌsɪt/ a rojizo. —n ⟨apple⟩ manzana f rojiza

Russia /ˈrʌʃə/ n Rusia f. **~n** a & n ruso (m)

rust /rʌst/ n orín m. —vt oxidar. —vi oxidarse

rustic /ˈrʌstɪk/ a rústico

rustle /ˈrʌsl/ vt hacer susurrar; ⟨Amer⟩ robar. **~ up** ⟨fam⟩ preparar. —vi susurrar

rust: **~proof** a inoxidable. **~y** a (-ier, -iest) oxidado

rut /rʌt/ n surco m. **in a ~** en la rutina de siempre

ruthless /ˈru:θlɪs/ a despiadado. **~ness** n crueldad f

rye /raɪ/ n centeno m

S

S abbr ⟨south⟩ sur m

sabbath /ˈsæbəθ/ n día m de descanso; ⟨Christian⟩ domingo m; ⟨Jewish⟩ sábado m

sabbatical /səˈbætɪkl/ a sabático

sabot|age /ˈsæbətɑ:ʒ/ n sabotaje m. —vt sabotear. **~eur** /-ˈtɜ:(r)/ n saboteador m

saccharin /ˈsækərɪn/ n sacarina f

sachet /ˈsæʃeɪ/ n bolsita f

sack[1] /sæk/ n saco m. **get the ~** (fam) ser despedido. —vt (fam) despedir. **~ing** n arpillera f; (fam) despido m

sack[2] /sæk/ vt (plunder) saquear

sacrament /'sækrəmənt/ n sacramento m

sacred /'seikrid/ a sagrado

sacrifice /'sækrifais/ n sacrificio m. —vt sacrificar

sacrileg|e /'sækrilidʒ/ n sacrilegio m. **~ious** /-'lidʒəs/ a sacrílego

sacrosanct /'sækrəʊsæŋkt/ a sacrosanto

sad /sæd/ a (**sadder, saddest**) triste. **~den** /'sædn/ vt entristecer

saddle /'sædl/ n silla f. **be in the ~** (fig) tener las riendas. —vt ensillar (horse). **~ s.o. with** (fig) cargar a uno con. **~bag** n alforja f

sad: **~ly** adv tristemente; (fig) desgraciadamente. **~ness** n tristeza f

sadis|**m** /'seidizəm/ n sadismo m. **~t** /'seidist/ n sádico m. **~tic** /sə'distik/ a sádico

safari /sə'fɑːrɪ/ n safari m

safe /seif/ a (**-er, -est**) seguro; (out of danger) salvo; (cautious) prudente. **~ and sound** sano y salvo. —n caja f fuerte. **~ deposit** n caja f de seguridad. **~guard** /'seifgɑːd/ n salvaguardia f. —vt salvaguardar. **~ly** adv sin peligro; (in safe place) en lugar seguro. **~ty** /'seifti/ n seguridad f. **~ty belt** n cinturón m de seguridad. **~ty-pin** n imperdible m. **~ty-valve** n válvula f de seguridad

saffron /'sæfrən/ n azafrán m

sag /sæg/ vi (pt **sagged**) hundirse; (give) aflojarse

saga /'sɑːgə/ n saga f

sage[1] /seidʒ/ n (wise person) sabio m. —a sabio

sage[2] /seidʒ/ n (herb) salvia f

sagging /'sægiŋ/ a hundido; (fig) decaído

Sagittarius /sædʒi'teəriəs/ n (astr) Sagitario m

sago /'seigəʊ/ n sagú m

said /sed/ see **say**

sail /seil/ n vela f; (trip) paseo m (en barco). —vi navegar; (leave) partir; (sport) practicar la vela; (fig) deslizarse. —vt manejar (boat). **~ing** n (sport) vela f. **~ing-boat** n, **~ing-ship** n barco m de vela. **~or** /'seilə(r)/ n marinero m

saint /seint, before name sənt/ n santo m. **~ly** a santo

sake /seik/ n. **for the ~ of** por, por el amor de

salacious /sə'leiʃəs/ a salaz

salad /'sæləd/ n ensalada f. **~ bowl** n ensaladera f. **~ cream** n mayonesa f. **~-dressing** n aliño m

salar|**ied** /'sælərid/ a asalariado. **~y** /'sæləri/ n sueldo m

sale /seil/ n venta f; (at reduced prices) liquidación f. **for ~** (sign) se vende. **on ~** en venta. **~able** /'seiləbl/ a vendible. **~sman** /'seilzmən/ n (pl **-men**) vendedor m; (in shop) dependiente m; (traveller) viajante m. **~swoman** /(pl **-women**) vendedora f; (in shop) dependienta f

salient /'seiliənt/ a saliente, destacado

saliva /sə'laivə/ n saliva f

sallow /'sæləʊ/ a (**-er, -est**) amarillento

salmon /'sæmən/ n invar salmón m. **~ trout** n trucha f salmonada

salon /'sælɒn/ n salón m

saloon /sə'luːn/ n (on ship) salón m; (Amer, bar) bar m; (auto) turismo m

salt /sɔːlt/ n sal f. —a salado. —vt salar. **~-cellar** n salero m. **~y** a salado

salutary /'sæljʊtrɪ/ a saludable

salute /sə'luːt/ n saludo m. —vt saludar. —vi hacer un saludo

salvage /'sælvɪdʒ/ n salvamento m; (goods) objetos mpl salvados. —vt salvar

salvation /sæl'veɪʃn/ n salvación f

salve /sælv/ n ungüento m

salver /'sælvə(r)/ n bandeja f

salvo /'sælvəʊ/ n (pl -os) salva f

same /seɪm/ a igual (as que); (before noun) mismo (as que). at the ~ time al mismo tiempo. —pron. the ~ el mismo, la misma, los mismos, las mismas. do the ~ as hacer como. —adv. de la misma manera. all the ~ de todas formas

sample /'saːmpl/ n muestra f. —vt probar (food)

sanatorium /sænə'tɔːrɪəm/ n (pl -ums) sanatorio m

sanctify /'sæŋktɪfaɪ/ vt santificar

sanctimonious /sæŋktɪ'məʊnɪəs/ a beato

sanction /'sæŋkʃn/ n sanción f. —vt sancionar

sanctity /'sæŋktɪtɪ/ n santidad f

sanctuary /'sæŋktʃʊərɪ/ n (relig) santuario m; (for wildlife) reserva f; (refuge) asilo m

sand /sænd/ n arena f. —vt enarenar. ~s npl (beach) playa f

sandal /'sændl/ n sandalia f

sand: ~castle n castillo m de arena. ~paper /'sændpeɪpə(r)/ n papel m de lija. —vt lijar. ~storm /'sændstɔːm/ n tempestad f de arena

sandwich /'sænwɪdʒ/ n bocadillo m, sandwich m. —vt. ~ed between intercalado

sandy /'sændɪ/ a arenoso

sane /seɪn/ a (-er, -est) (person) cuerdo; (judgement, policy) razonable. ~ly adv sensatamente

sang /sæŋ/ see sing

sanitary /'sænɪtrɪ/ a higiénico; (system etc) sanitario. ~ towel n, ~ napkin n (Amer) compresa f (higiénica)

sanitation /sænɪ'teɪʃn/ n higiene f; (drainage) sistema m sanitario

sanity /'sænɪtɪ/ n cordura f; (fig) sensatez f

sank /sæŋk/ see sink

Santa Claus /'sæntəklɔːz/ n Papá m Noel

sap /sæp/ n (in plants) savia f. —vt (pt sapped) agotar

sapling /'sæplɪŋ/ n árbol m joven

sapphire /'sæfaɪə(r)/ n zafiro m

sarcasm /'saːkæzəm/ n sarcasmo m. ~tic /-'kæstɪk/ a sarcástico

sardine /saː'diːn/ n sardina f

Sardinia /saː'dɪnɪə/ n Cerdeña f. ~n a & n sardo (m)

sardonic /saː'dɒnɪk/ a sardónico

sash /sæʃ/ n (over shoulder) banda f; (round waist) fajín m. ~window n ventana f de guillotina

sat /sæt/ see sit

satanic /sə'tænɪk/ a satánico

satchel /'sætʃl/ n cartera f

satellite /'sætəlaɪt/ n & a satélite (m)

satiate /'seɪʃɪeɪt/ vt saciar

satin /'sætɪn/ n raso m. —a de raso; (like satin) satinado

satire /'sætaɪə(r)/ n sátira f. ~ical /sə'tɪrɪkl/ a satírico. ~ist /'sætərɪst/ n satírico m. ~ize /'sætəraɪz/ vt satirizar

satisfaction /sætɪs'fækʃn/ n satisfacción f

satisfactor|ily /sætɪs'fæktərɪlɪ/ adv satisfactoriamente. ~y /sætɪs'fæktərɪ/ a satisfactorio

satisfy /'sætɪsfaɪ/ vt satisfacer; (convince) convencer. ~ing a satisfactorio

satsuma /sæt'suːmə/ n mandarina f

saturat|e /'sætʃəreɪt/ vt saturar, empapar. ~ed a saturado, empapado. **~ion** /-'reɪʃn/ n saturación f

Saturday /'sætədeɪ/ n sábado m

sauce /sɔːs/ n salsa f; (cheek) descaro m. **~pan** /'sɔːspən/ n cazo m

saucer /'sɔːsə(r)/ n platillo m

saucy /'sɔːsɪ/ a (-ier, -iest) descarado

Saudi Arabia /saʊdɪə'reɪbɪə/ n Arabia f Saudí

sauna /'sɔːnə/ n sauna f

saunter /'sɔːntə(r)/ vi deambular, pasearse

sausage /'sɒsɪdʒ/ n salchicha f

savage /'sævɪdʒ/ a salvaje; (fierce) feroz; (furious, fam) rabioso. —n salvaje m & f. —vt atacar. **~ry** n ferocidad f

sav|e /seɪv/ vt salvar; ahorrar (money, time); (prevent) evitar. —n (football) parada f. —prep salvo, con excepción de. **~er** n ahorrador m. **~ing** n ahorro m. **~ings** npl ahorros mpl

saviour /'seɪvɪə(r)/ n salvador m

savour /'seɪvə(r)/ n sabor m. —vt saborear. **~y** a (appetizing) sabroso; (not sweet) no dulce. —n aperitivo m (no dulce)

saw[1] /sɔː/ see **see**[1]

saw[2] /sɔː/ n sierra f. —vt (pt sawed, pp sawn) serrar. **~dust** /'sɔːdʌst/ n serrín m. **~n** /sɔːn/ see **saw**

saxophone /'sæksəfəʊn/ n saxófono m

say /seɪ/ vt/i (pt said /sed/) decir; rezar (prayer). **I ~!** no me digas! —n. have a **~** expresar una opinión; (in decision) tener voz en capítulo. have no **~** no tener ni voz ni voto. **~ing** /'seɪɪŋ/ n refrán m

scab /skæb/ n costra f; (blackleg, fam) esquirol m

scaffold /'skæfəʊld/ n (gallows) cadalso m, patíbulo m. **~ing** /'skæfəʊldɪŋ/ n (for workmen) andamio m

scald /skɔːld/ vt escaldar; calentar (milk etc). —n escaldadura f

scale[1] /skeɪl/ n escala f

scale[2] /skeɪl/ n (of fish) escama f

scale[3] /skeɪl/ vt (climb) escalar. **~ down** vt reducir (proporcionalmente)

scales /skeɪlz/ npl (for weighing) balanza f, peso m

scallop /'skɒləp/ n venera f; (on dress) festón m

scalp /skælp/ n cuero m cabelludo. —vt quitar el cuero cabelludo a

scalpel /'skælpəl/ n escalpelo m

scamp /skæmp/ n bribón m

scamper /'skæmpə(r)/ vi. **~ away** marcharse corriendo

scampi /'skæmpɪ/ npl gambas fpl grandes

scan /skæn/ vt (pt scanned) escudriñar; (quickly) echar un vistazo a; (radar) explorar. —vi (poetry) estar bien medido

scandal /'skændl/ n escándalo m; (gossip) chismorreo m. **~ize** /'skændəlaɪz/ vt escandalizar. **~ous** a escandaloso

Scandinavia /skændɪ'neɪvɪə/ n Escandinavia f. **~n** a & n escandinavo (m)

scant /skænt/ a escaso. **~ily** adv insuficientemente. **~y** /'skæntɪ/ a (-ier, -iest) escaso

scapegoat /'skeɪpɡəʊt/ n cabeza f de turco

scar /skɑː(r)/ n cicatriz f. —vt (pt scarred) dejar una cicatriz en. —vi cicatrizarse

scarc|e /skeəs/ a (-er, -est) escaso. make o.s. **~e** (fam) mantenerse lejos. **~ely** /'skeəslɪ/ adv apenas. **~ity** n escasez f

scare /skeə(r)/ vt asustar. be **~d** tener miedo. —n susto m.

~**crow** /'skeəkrəʊ/ n espantapájaros m invar. ~**monger** /'skeəmʌŋgə(r)/ n alarmista m & f

scarf /skɑːf/ n (pl **scarves**) bufanda f; (over head) pañuelo m

scarlet /'skɑːlət/ a escarlata f. ~ **fever** n escarlatina f

scary /'skeərɪ/ a (-ier, -iest) que da miedo

scathing /'skeɪðɪŋ/ a mordaz

scatter /'skætə(r)/ vt (throw) esparcir; (disperse) dispersar. — vi dispersarse. ~**brained** a atolondrado. ~**ed** a disperso; (occasional) esporádico

scatty /'skætɪ/ a (-ier, -iest) (sl) atolondrado

scavenge /'skævɪndʒ/ vi buscar (en la basura). ~**r** /-ə(r)/ n (vagrant) persona f que busca objetos en la basura

scenario /sɪ'nɑːrɪəʊ/ n (pl -os) argumento; (of film) guión m

scene /siːn/ n escena f; (sight) vista f; (fuss) lío m. **behind the** ~**es** entre bastidores. ~**ery** /'siːnərɪ/ n paisaje m; (in theatre) decorado m. ~**ic** /'siːnɪk/ a pintoresco

scent /sent/ n olor m; (perfume) perfume m; (trail) pista f. — vt presentir; (make fragrant) perfumar

sceptic /'skeptɪk/ n escéptico m. ~**al** a escéptico. ~**ism** /-sɪzm/ n escepticismo m

sceptre /'septə(r)/ n cetro m

schedule /'ʃedjuːl, 'skedjuːl/ n programa f; (timetable) horario m. **behind** ~ con retraso. **on** ~ sin retraso. — vt proyectar. ~**d flight** n vuelo m regular

scheme /skiːm/ n proyecto m; (plot) intriga f. — vi hacer proyectos; (pej) intrigar. ~**r** n intrigante m & f

schism /'sɪzm/ n cisma m

schizophrenic /skɪtsə'frenɪk/ a & n esquizofrénico (m)

scholar /'skɒlə(r)/ n erudito m. ~**ly** a erudito. ~**ship** n erudición f; (grant) beca f

scholastic /skə'læstɪk/ a escolar

school /skuːl/ n escuela f; (of univ) facultad f. —a (age, holidays, year) escolar. — vt enseñar; (discipline) disciplinar. ~**boy** /'skuːlbɔɪ/ n colegial m. ~**girl** /-gɜːl/ n colegiala f. ~**ing** n instrucción f. ~**master** /'skuːlmɑːstə(r)/ n (primary) maestro m; (secondary) profesor m. ~**mistress** n (primary) maestra f; (secondary) profesora f. ~**teacher** n (primary) maestro m; (secondary) profesor m

schooner /'skuːnə(r)/ n goleta f; (glass) vaso m grande

sciatica /saɪ'ætɪkə/ n ciática f

scien|ce /'saɪəns/ n ciencia f. ~**ce fiction** n ciencia f ficción. ~**tific** /-'tɪfɪk/ a científico. ~**tist** /'saɪəntɪst/ n científico m

scintillate /'sɪntɪleɪt/ vi centellear

scissors /'sɪsəz/ npl tijeras fpl

sclerosis /sklə'rəʊsɪs/ n esclerosis f

scoff /skɒf/ vt (sl) zamparse. — vi. ~ **at** mofarse de

scold /skəʊld/ vt regañar. ~**ing** n regaño m

scone /skɒn/ n (tipo m de) bollo m

scoop /skuːp/ n paleta f; (news) noticia f exclusiva. — vt. ~ **out** excavar. ~ **up** recoger

scoot /skuːt/ vi (fam) largarse corriendo. ~**er** /'skuːtə(r)/ n escúter m; (for child) patinete m

scope /skəʊp/ n alcance m; (opportunity) oportunidad f

scorch /skɔːtʃ/ vt chamuscar. ~**er** n (fam) día m de mucho calor. ~**ing** a (fam) de mucho calor

score /skɔ:(r)/ n tanteo m; (mus) partitura f; (twenty) veintena f; (reason) motivo m. **on that** ~ en cuanto a eso. —vt marcar; (slash) rayar; (mus) instrumentar; conseguir (success). —vi marcar un tanto; (keep score) tantear. ~ **over s.o.** aventajar a. ~**r** /-ə(r)/ n tanteador m

scorn /skɔ:n/ n desdén m. —vt desdeñar. ~**ful** a desdeñoso. ~**fully** adv desdeñosamente

Scorpio /'skɔ:pɪəʊ/ n (astr) Escorpión m

scorpion /'skɔ:pɪən/ n escorpión m

Scot /skɒt/ n escocés m. ~**ch** /skɒtʃ/ a escocés. —n güisqui m

scotch /skɒtʃ/ vt frustrar; (suppress) suprimir

scot-free /skɒt'fri:/ a impune; (gratis) sin pagar

Scot: ~**land** /'skɒtlənd/ n Escocia f. ~**s** a escocés. ~**sman** n escocés m. ~**swoman** n escocesa f. ~**tish** a escocés

scoundrel /'skaʊndrəl/ n canalla f

scour /'skaʊə(r)/ vt estregar; (search) registrar. ~**er** n estropajo m

scourge /skɜ:dʒ/ n azote m

scout /skaʊt/ n explorador m. **Boy S~** explorador m. —vi. ~ **(for)** buscar

scowl /skaʊl/ n ceño m. —vi fruncir el entrecejo

scraggy /'skrægɪ/ a (-ier, -iest) descarnado

scram /skræm/ vi (sl) largarse

scramble /'skræmbl/ vi (clamber) gatear. ~ **for** pelearse para obtener. —vt revolver (eggs). —n (difficult climb) subida f difícil; (struggle) lucha f

scrap /skræp/ n pedacito m; (fight, fam) pelea f. —vt (pt scrapped) desechar. ~**book** n

álbum m de recortes. ~**s** npl sobras fpl

scrape /skreɪp/ n raspadura f; (fig) apuro m. —vt raspar; (graze) arañar; (rub) frotar. —vi. ~ **through** lograr pasar; aprobar por los pelos (exam). ~ **together** reunir. ~**r** /-ə(r)/ n raspador m

scrap: ~**heap** n montón m de deshechos. ~**iron** n chatarra f

scrappy /'skræpɪ/ a fragmentario, pobre, de mala calidad

scratch /skrætʃ/ vt rayar; (with nail etc) arañar; rascar (itch). —vi arañar. —n raya f; (from nail etc) arañazo m. **start from** ~ empezar sin nada, empezar desde el principio. **up to** ~ al nivel requerido

scrawl /skrɔ:l/ n garrapato m. —vt/i garrapatear

scrawny /'skrɔ:nɪ/ a (-ier, -iest) descarnado

scream /skri:m/ vt/i gritar. —n grito m

screech /skri:tʃ/ vi gritar; (brakes etc) chirriar. —n grito m; (of brakes etc) chirrido m

screen /skri:n/ n pantalla f; (folding) biombo m. —vt (hide) ocultar; (protect) proteger; proyectar (film); seleccionar (candidates)

screw /skru:/ n tornillo m. —vt atornillar. ~**driver** /'skru:draɪvə(r)/ n destornillador m. ~ **up** atornillar; entornar (eyes); torcer (face); (ruin, sl) arruinar. ~**y** /'skru:ɪ/ a (-ier, -iest) (sl) chiflado

scribble /'skrɪbl/ vt/i garrapatear. —n garrapato m

scribe /skraɪb/ n copista m & f

script /skrɪpt/ n escritura f; (of film etc) guión m

Scriptures /'skrɪptʃəz/ npl Sagradas Escrituras fpl

script-writer /'skrɪptraɪtə(r)/ n guionista m & f

scroll /skrəʊl/ n rollo m (de pergamino)

scrounge /skraʊndʒ/ vt/i obtener de gorra; (steal) birlar. **~r** /-ə(r)/ n gorrón m

scrub /skrʌb/ n (land) maleza f; (clean) fregado m. —vt/i (pt scrubbed) fregar

scruff /skrʌf/ n. the **~** of the neck el cogote m

scruffy /'skrʌfɪ/ a (-ier, -iest) desaliñado

scrum /skrʌm/ n, **scrummage** /'skrʌmɪdʒ/ n (Rugby) melée f

scrup|le /'skru:pl/ n escrúpulo m. **~ulous** /'skru:pjʊləs/ a escrupuloso. **~ulously** adv escrupulosamente

scrutin|ize /'skru:tɪnaɪz/ vt escudriñar. **~y** /'skru:tɪnɪ/ n examen m minucioso

scuff /skʌf/ vt arañar ‹shoes›

scuffle /'skʌfl/ n pelea f

scullery /'skʌlərɪ/ n trascocina f

sculpt /skʌlpt/ vt/i esculpir. **~or** n escultor m. **~ure** /-tʃə(r)/ n escultura f. —vt/i esculpir

scum /skʌm/ n espuma f; (people, pej) escoria f

scurf /skɜ:f/ n caspa f

scurrilous /'skʌrɪləs/ a grosero

scurry /'skʌrɪ/ vi correr

scurvy /'skɜ:vɪ/ n escorbuto m

scuttle[1] /'skʌtl/ n cubo m del carbón

scuttle[2] /'skʌtl/ vt barrenar ‹ship›

scuttle[3] /'skʌtl/ vi. **~** away correr, irse de prisa

scythe /saɪð/ n guadaña f

SE abbr (south-east) sudeste m

sea /si:/ n mar m. **at ~** en el mar; (fig) confuso. **by ~** por mar. **~board** /'si:bɔ:d/ n litoral m. **~farer** /'si:feərə(r)/ n marinero m. **~food** /'si:fu:d/ n mariscos mpl. **~gull** /'si:gʌl/ n gaviota f. **~horse** n caballito m de mar, hipocampo m

seal[1] /si:l/ n sello m. —vt sellar. **~ off** acordonar ‹area›

seal[2] /si:l/ n (animal) foca f

sea level /'si:levl/ n nivel m del mar

sealing-wax /'si:lɪŋwæks/ n lacre m

sea lion /'si:laɪən/ n león m marino

seam /si:m/ n costura f; (of coal) veta f

seaman /'si:mən/ n (pl -men) marinero m

seamy /'si:mɪ/ a. the **~ side** n el lado m sórdido, el revés m

seance /'seɪɑ:ns/ n sesión f de espiritismo

sea: **~plane** /'si:pleɪn/ n hidroavión f. **~port** /'si:pɔ:t/ n puerto m de mar

search /sɜ:tʃ/ vt registrar; (examine) examinar. —vi buscar. —n (for sth) búsqueda f; (of sth) registro m. **in ~ of** en busca de. **~ for** buscar. **~ing** a penetrante. **~party** n equipo m de salvamento. **~light** /'sɜ:tʃlaɪt/ n reflector m

sea: **~scape** /'si:skeɪp/ n marina f. **~shore** n orilla f del mar. **~sick** /'si:sɪk/ a mareado. **be ~sick** marearse. **~side** /'si:saɪd/ n playa f

season /'si:zn/ n estación f; (period) temporada f. —vt (culin) sazonar; secar ‹wood›. **~able** a propio de la estación. **~al** a estacional. **~ed** /'si:znd/ a (fig) experto. **~ing** n condimento m. **~ticket** n billete m de abono

seat /si:t/ n asiento m; (place) lugar m; (of trousers) fondillos mpl; (bottom) trasero m. **take a ~** sentarse. —vt sentar; (have seats for) tener asientos para. **~belt** n cinturón m de seguridad

sea: ~**urchin** n erizo m de mar. ~**weed** /'si:wi:d/ n alga f. ~**worthy** /'si:wɜ:ðɪ/ a en estado de navegar

secateurs /'sekətз:/ npl tijeras fpl de podar

secede /sɪ'si:d/ vi separarse. ~**ssion** /-eʃn/ n secesión f

seclude /sɪ'klu:d/ vt aislar. ~**ded** a aislado. ~**sion** /-ʒn/ n aislamiento m

second¹ /'sekənd/ a & n segundo (m). on ~ **thoughts** pensándolo bien. —adv (in race etc) en segundo lugar. —vt apoyar. ~**s** npl (goods) artículos mpl de segunda calidad; (more food, fam) otra porción f

second² /sɪ'kɒnd/ vt (transfer) trasladar temporalmente

secondary /'sekəndrɪ/ a secundario. ~ **school** n instituto m

second: ~**best** a segundo. ~**class** a de segunda clase. ~**hand** a de segunda mano. ~**ly** adv en segundo lugar. ~**rate** a mediocre

secrecy /'si:krəsɪ/ n secreto m. ~**t** /'si:krɪt/ a & n secreto (m). in ~**t** en secreto

secretarial /sekrə'teərɪəl/ a de secretario. ~**iat** /sekrə'teərɪət/ n secretaría f. ~**y** /'sekrətrɪ/ n secretario m. **S~y of State** ministro m; (Amer) Ministro m de Asuntos Exteriores

secrete /sɪ'kri:t/ vt (med) secretar. ~**ion** /-ʃn/ n secreción f

secretive /'si:krɪtɪv/ a reservado

secretly /'si:krɪtlɪ/ adv en secreto

sect /sekt/ n secta f. ~**arian** /-'teərɪən/ a sectario

section /'sekʃn/ n sección f; (part) parte f

sector /'sektə(r)/ n sector m

secular /'sekjʊlə(r)/ a seglar

secure /sɪ'kjʊə(r)/ a seguro; (fixed) fijo. —vt asegurar; (obtain) obtener. ~**ely** adv seguramente. ~**ity** /sɪ'kjʊərətɪ/ n seguridad f; (for loan) garantía f, fianza f

sedate /sɪ'deɪt/ a sosegado

sedation /sɪ'deɪʃn/ n sedación f. ~**ive** /'sedətɪv/ a & n sedante (m)

sedentary /'sedəntrɪ/ a sedentario

sediment /'sedɪmənt/ n sedimento m

seduce /sɪ'dju:s/ vt seducir. ~**er** /-ə(r)/ n seductor m. ~**tion** /sɪ'dʌkʃn/ n seducción f. ~**tive** /-tɪv/ a seductor

see¹ /si:/ —vt (pt saw, pp seen) ver; (understand) comprender; (notice) notar; (escort) acompañar. ~**ing** that visto que. ~ **you later!** ¡hasta luego! —vi ver; (understand) comprender. ~ **about** ocuparse de. ~ **off** despedirse de. ~ **through** llevar a cabo; descubrir el juego de (person). ~ **to** ocuparse de

see² /si:/ n diócesis f

seed /si:d/ n semilla f; (fig) germen m; (tennis) preseleccionado m. ~**ling** n plantón m. **go to** ~ granar; (fig) echarse a perder. ~**y** /si:dɪ/ a (-ier, -iest) sórdido

seek /si:k/ vt (pt sought) buscar. ~ **out** buscar

seem /si:m/ vi parecer. ~**ingly** adv aparentemente

seemly /'si:mlɪ/ a (-ier, -iest) correcto

seen /si:n/ see **see¹**

seep /si:p/ vi filtrarse. ~**age** n filtración f

see-saw /si:sɔ:/ n balancín m

seethe /si:ð/ vi (fig) hervir. **be seething with anger** estar furioso

see-through /'si:θru:/ a transparente

segment /'segmənt/ n segmento m; (of orange) gajo m

segregat|e /'segrigeit/ vt segregar. **~ion** /-'geiʃn/ n segregación f

seiz|e /siːz/ vt agarrar; (jurid) incautarse de. **~e on** vi valerse de. **~e up** vi (tec) agarrotarse. **~ure** /'siːʒə(r)/ n incautación f; (med) ataque m

seldom /'seldəm/ adv raramente

select /si'lekt/ vt escoger; (sport) seleccionar. —a selecto; (exclusive) exclusivo. **~ion** /-ʃn/ n selección f. **~ive** a selectivo

self /self/ n (pl **selves**) sí mismo. **~-addressed** a con su propia dirección. **~-assurance** n confianza f en sí mismo. **~-assured** a seguro de sí mismo. **~-catering** a con facilidades para cocinar. **~-centred** a egocéntrico. **~-confidence** n confianza f en sí mismo. **~-confident** a seguro de sí mismo. **~-conscious** a cohibido. **~-contained** a independiente. **~-control** n dominio m de sí mismo. **~-defence** n defensa f propia. **~-denial** n abnegación f. **~-employed** a que trabaja por cuenta propia. **~-esteem** n amor m propio. **~-evident** a evidente. **~-government** n autonomía f. **~-important** a presumido. **~-indulgent** a inmoderado. **~-interest** n interés m propio. **~-ish** /selfiʃ/ a egoísta. **~-ishness** n egoísmo m. **~-less** /'selfis/ a desinteresado. **~-made** a rico por su propio esfuerzo. **~-opinionated** a intransigente; (arrogant) engreído. **~-pity** n compasión f de sí mismo. **~-portrait** n autorretrato m. **~-possessed** a dueño de sí mismo. **~-reliant** a independiente. **~-respect** n amor m propio. **~-righteous** a

santurrón. **~-sacrifice** n abnegación f. **~-satisfied** a satisfecho de sí mismo. **~-seeking** a egoísta. **~-service** a & n autoservicio (m). **~-styled** a sedicente, llamado. **~-sufficient** a independiente. **~-willed** a terco

sell /sel/ vt (pt **sold**) vender. **be sold on** (fam) entusiasmarse por. **be sold out** estar agotado. —vi venderse. **~-by date** n fecha f de caducidad. **~ off** vt liquidar. **~ up** vt vender todo. **~er** n vendedor m

Sellotape /'seləteip/ n (P) (papel m) celo m, cinta f adhesiva

sell-out n (betrayal, fam) traición f

semantic /si'mæntik/ a semántico. **~s** n semántica f

semaphore /'seməfɔː(r)/ n semáforo m

semblance /'sembləns/ n apariencia f

semen /'siːmən/ n semen m

semester /si'mestə(r)/ n (Amer) semestre m

semi... /'semi/ pref semi...

semibreve /'semibriːv/ n semibreve f, redonda f. **~circle** /'semisɜːkl/ n semicírculo m. **~circular** /-'sɜːkjʊlə(r)/ a semicircular. **~colon** /semi'kəʊlən/ n punto m y coma. **~detached** /semidi'tætʃt/ a (house) adosado. **~final** /semi'fainl/ n semifinal f

seminar /'seminɑː(r)/ n seminario m

seminary /'seminəri/ n (college) seminario m

semiquaver /'semikweivə(r)/ n (mus) semicorchea f

Semit|e /'siːmait/ n semita m & f. **~ic** /si'mitik/ a semítico

semolina /semə'liːnə/ n sémola f

senat|e /'senit/ n senado m. **~or** /-ətə(r)/ n senador m

send /send/ vt/i (pt **sent**) enviar. **~ away** despedir. **~ away for**

pedir (por correo). ∼ **for** enviar a buscar. ∼ **off for** pedir (por correo). ∼ **up** (*fam*) parodiar. ∼**er** *n* remitente *m*. ∼**off** *n* despedida *f*

senile /'si:naɪl/ *a* senil. ∼**ity** /sɪ'nɪlətɪ/ *n* senilidad *f*

senior /'si:nɪə(r)/ *a* mayor; (*in rank*) superior; (*partner etc*) principal. —*n* mayor *m* & *f*. ∼ **citizen** *n* jubilado *m*. ∼**ity** /-'ɒrətɪ/ *n* antigüedad *f*

sensation /sen'seɪʃn/ *n* sensación *f*. ∼**al** *a* sensacional

sense /sens/ *n* sentido *m*; (*common sense*) juicio *m*; (*feeling*) sensación *f*. **make** ∼ *vt* tener sentido. **make** ∼ **of** comprender. ∼**less** *a* insensato; (*med*) sin sentido

sensibilities /sensɪ'bɪlətɪz/ *npl* susceptibilidad *f*. ∼**ibility** /sensɪ'bɪlətɪ/ *n* sensibilidad *f*

sensible /'sensəbl/ *a* sensato; (*clothing*) práctico

sensitive /'sensɪtɪv/ *a* sensible; (*touchy*) susceptible. ∼**ity** /-'tɪvətɪ/ *n* sensibilidad *f*

sensory /'sensərɪ/ *a* sensorio

sensual /'senʃʊəl/ *a* sensual. ∼**ity** /-'æələtɪ/ *n* sensualidad *f*

sensuous /'sensʊəs/ *a* sensual

sent /sent/ *see* **send**

sentence /'sentəns/ *n* frase *f*; (*jurid*) sentencia *f*; (*punishment*) condena *f*. —*vt*. ∼ **to** condenar a

sentiment /'sentɪmənt/ *n* sentimiento *m*; (*opinion*) opinión *f*. ∼**al** /senti'mentl/ *a* sentimental. ∼**ality** /-'tælətɪ/ *n* sentimentalismo *m*

sentry /'sentrɪ/ *n* centinela *m*

separable /'sepərəbl/ *a* separable

separate¹ /'sepərət/ *a* separado; (*independent*) independiente. ∼**ly** *adv* por separado. ∼**s** *npl* coordinados *mpl*

separate² /'sepəreɪt/ *vt* separar. —*vi* separarse. ∼**ion** /-'reɪʃn/ *n* separación *f*. ∼**ist** /'sepərətɪst/ *n* separatista *m* & *f*

September /sep'tembə(r)/ *n* se(p)tiembre *m*

septic /'septɪk/ *a* séptico. ∼ **tank** *n* fosa *f* séptica

sequel /'si:kwəl/ *n* continuación *f*; (*consequence*) consecuencia *f*

sequence /'si:kwəns/ *n* sucesión *f*; (*of film*) secuencia *f*

sequin /'si:kwɪn/ *n* lentejuela *f*

serenade /serə'neɪd/ *n* serenata *f*. —*vt* dar serenata a

serene /sɪ'ri:n/ *a* sereno. ∼**ity** /-'enətɪ/ *n* serenidad *f*

sergeant /'sɑ:dʒənt/ *n* sargento *m*

serial /'sɪərɪəl/ *n* serial *m*. —*a* de serie. ∼**ize** *vt* publicar por entregas

series /'sɪəri:z/ *n* serie *f*

serious /'sɪərɪəs/ *a* serio. ∼**ly** *adv* seriamente; (*ill*) gravemente. **take** ∼**ly** tomar en serio. ∼**ness** *n* seriedad *f*

sermon /'sɜ:mən/ *n* sermón *m*

serpent /'sɜ:pənt/ *n* serpiente *f*

serrated /sɪ'reɪtɪd/ *a* serrado

serum /'sɪərəm/ *n* (*pl* **-a**) suero *m*

servant /'sɜ:vənt/ *n* criado *m*; (*fig*) servidor *m*

serve /sɜ:v/ *vt* servir; (*in the army etc*) prestar servicio; cumplir (*sentence*). ∼ **as** servir de. **its purpose** servir para el caso. **it** ∼**s you right** ¡bien te lo mereces! ¡te está bien merecido! —*vi* servir. —*n* (*in tennis*) saque *m*

service /'sɜ:vɪs/ *n* servicio *m*; (*maintenance*) revisión *f*. ∼ **of** ∼ **to** útil *a*. —*vt* revisar (*car etc*). ∼**able** /'sɜ:vɪsəbl/ *a* práctico; (*durable*) duradero. ∼ **charge** *n* servicio *m*. ∼**man** /'sɜ:vɪsmən/ *n* (*pl* **-men**) militar *m*. ∼**s** *npl* (*mil*) fuerzas *fpl* armadas. ∼ **station** *n* estación *f* de servicio

serviette /sɜ:vɪ'et/ *n* servilleta *f*

servile /'sɜːvaɪl/ a servil
session /'seʃn/ n sesión f; (univ) curso m
set /set/ vt (pt set, pres p setting) poner; poner en hora (clock etc); fijar (limit etc); (typ) componer. ~ **fire to** pegar fuego a. ~ **free** vt poner en libertad. —vi ponerse; (jelly) cuajarse. —n serie f; (of cutlery etc) juego m; (tennis) set m; (TV, radio) aparato m; (of hair) marcado m; (in theatre) decorado m; (of people) círculo m. —a fijo. **be** ~ **on** estar resuelto a. ~ **about** vi empezar a. ~ **back** vt (delay) retardar; (cost, sl) costar. ~ **off** vi salir. — vt (make start) poner en marcha; hacer estallar (bomb). ~ **out** vt (expound) (argument) exponer —vi (leave) salir. ~ **sail** salir. ~ **the table** poner la mesa. ~ **up** vt establecer. ~**back** n revés m. ~ **square** n escuadra f de dibujar
settee /se'tiː/ n sofá m
setting /'setɪŋ/ n (of sun) puesta f; (of jewel) engaste m; (in theatre) escenario m; (typ) composición f. ~**lotion** n fijador m
settle /'setl/ vt (arrange) arreglar; (pay) pagar; fijar (date); calmar (nerves). —vi (come to rest) posarse; (live) instalarse. ~ **down** calmarse; (become orderly) sentar la cabeza. ~ **for** aceptar. ~ **up** ajustar cuentas. ~**ment** /'setlmənt/ n establecimiento m; (agreement) acuerdo m; (com) liquidación f; (place) colonia f. ~**r** /-ə(r)/ n colonizador m
set-: ~**to** n pelea f. ~**up** n (fam) sistema m
seven /sevn/ a & n siete (m). ~**teen** /sevn'tiːn/ a & n diecisiete (m). ~**teenth** a & n decimoséptimo (m). ~**th** a & n séptimo (m). ~**tieth** a & n setenta (m), septuagésimo (m). ~**ty** /sevnti/ a & n setenta (m).

sever /'sevə(r)/ vt cortar; (fig) romper
several /'sevrəl/ a & pron varios
severance /'sevərəns/ n (breaking off) ruptura f
severe /sɪ'vɪə(r)/ a (-er, -est) severo; (violent) violento; (serious) grave; (weather) riguroso. ~**ely** adv severamente; (seriously) gravemente. ~**ity** /-'verətɪ/ n severidad f; (violence) violencia f; (seriousness) gravedad f
sew /səʊ/ vt/i (pt sewed, pp sewn, or sewed) coser
sew|age /'suːɪdʒ/ n aguas fpl residuales. ~**er** /'suːə(r)/ n cloaca f
sewing /'səʊɪŋ/ n costura f. ~ **machine** n máquina f de coser
sewn /səʊn/ see **sew**
sex /seks/ n sexo m. **have** ~ tener relaciones sexuales. —a sexual. ~**ist** /'seksɪst/ a & n sexista (m & f)
sextet /seks'tet/ n sexteto m
sexual /'seksjʊəl/ a sexual. ~ **intercourse** n relaciones fpl sexuales. ~**ity** /-'ælətɪ/ n sexualidad f
sexy /'seksɪ/ a (-ier, -iest) excitante, sexy, provocativo
shabb|ily /'ʃæbɪlɪ/ adv pobremente; (act) mezquinamente. ~**iness** n pobreza f; (meanness) mezquindad f. ~**y** /'ʃæbɪ/ a (-ier, -iest) (clothes) gastado; (person) pobremente vestido; (mean) mezquino
shack /ʃæk/ n choza f
shackles /'ʃæklz/ npl grillos mpl, grilletes mpl
shade /ʃeɪd/ n sombra f; (of colour) matiz m; (for lamp) pantalla f. **a** ~ **better** un poquito mejor. —vt dar sombra a
shadow /'ʃædəʊ/ n sombra f. **S~ Cabinet** n gobierno m en la

sombra. —vt (follow) seguir. **~y**
a (fig) vago

shady /ˈʃeɪdɪ/ a (-ier, -iest)
sombreado; (fig) dudoso

shaft /ʃɑːft/ n (of arrow) astil m;
(mec) eje m; (of light) rayo m; (of
lift, mine) pozo m

shaggy /ˈʃægɪ/ a (-ier, -iest)
peludo

shak|e /ʃeɪk/ vt (pt **shook**, pp
shaken) sacudir; agitar (bottle);
(shock) desconcertar. **~e hands
with** estrechar la mano a. —vi
temblar. **~e off** vt deshacerse
de. —n sacudida f. **~e-up** n
reorganización f. **~y** /ˈʃeɪkɪ/ a
(-ier, -iest) tembloroso; (table
etc) inestable; (unreliable) incierto

shall /ʃæl/ v, aux (first person in
future tense). **I ~ go** iré. **we ~
see** veremos

shallot /ʃəˈlɒt/ n chalote m

shallow /ˈʃæləʊ/ a (-er, -est) poco
profundo; (fig) superficial

sham /ʃæm/ n farsa f; (person)
impostor m. —a falso; (affected)
fingido. —vt (pt **shammed**)
fingir

shambles /ˈʃæmblz/ npl (mess,
fam) desorden m total

shame /ʃeɪm/ n vergüenza f.
what a ~! ¡qué lástima! —vt
avergonzar. **~faced** /ˈʃeɪmfeɪst/
a avergonzado. **~ful** a vergonzoso. **~fully** adv ver-
gonzosamente. **~less** a desvergonzado

shampoo /ʃæmˈpuː/ n champú
m. —vt lavar

shamrock /ˈʃæmrɒk/ n trébol m

shandy /ˈʃændɪ/ n cerveza f con
gaseosa, clara f

shan't /ʃɑːnt/ = **shall not**

shanty /ˈʃæntɪ/ n chabola f. **~
town** n chabolas fpl

shape /ʃeɪp/ n forma f. —vt
formar; determinar (future). —
vi formarse. **~ up** prometer.

~less a informe. **~ly** /ˈʃeɪplɪ/ a
(-ier, -iest) bien proporcionado

share /ʃeə(r)/ n porción f; (com)
acción f. **go ~s** compartir. —vt
compartir; (divide) dividir. —vi
participar. **~ in** participar en.
~holder /ˈʃeəhəʊldə(r)/ n
accionista m & f. **~-out** n
reparto m

shark /ʃɑːk/ n tiburón m; (fig)
estafador m

sharp /ʃɑːp/ a (-er, -est) (knife etc)
afilado; (pin etc) puntiagudo;
(pain, sound) agudo; (taste)
acre; (sudden, harsh) brusco;
(well defined) marcado; (dishonest) poco escrupuloso;
(clever) listo. —adv en punto. **at
seven o'clock ~** a las siete en
punto. —n (mus) sostenido m.
~en /ˈʃɑːpn/ vt afilar; sacar punta
a (pencil). **~ener** n (mec) afi-
lador m; (for pencils) sacapuntas
m invar. **~ly** adv bruscamente

shatter /ˈʃætə(r)/ vt hacer añicos;
(upset) perturbar. —vi hacerse
añicos. **~ed** a (exhausted)
agotado

shav|e /ʃeɪv/ vt afeitar. —vi afei-
tarse. —n afeitado m. **have a ~e**
afeitarse. **~en** a (face) afeitado;
(head) rapado. **~er** n maquinilla f (de afeitar). **~ing-brush**
n brocha f de afeitar. **~ing-
cream** n crema f de afeitar

shawl /ʃɔːl/ n chal m

she /ʃiː/ pron ella. —n hembra f

sheaf /ʃiːf/ n (pl **sheaves**) gavilla
f

shear /ʃɪə(r)/ vt (pp **shorn**, or
sheared) esquilar. **~s** /ʃɪəz/ npl
tijeras fpl grandes

sheath /ʃiːθ/ n (pl **-s** /ʃiːðz/) vaina
f; (contraceptive) condón m. **~e**
/ʃiːð/ vt envainar

shed[1] /ʃed/ n cobertizo m

shed[2] /ʃed/ vt (pt **shed**, pres p
shedding) perder; derramar (tears); despojarse de (clothes). **~
light on** aclarar

sheen /ʃiːn/ n lustre m

sheep /ʃiːp/ n invar oveja f. **∼-dog** n perro m pastor. **∼ish** /ʃiːpiʃ/ a vergonzoso. **∼ishly** adv tímidamente. **∼skin** /ʃiːpskɪn/ n piel f de carnero, zamarra f

sheer /ʃɪə(r)/ a puro; (steep) perpendicular; (fabric) muy fino. — adv a pico

sheet /ʃiːt/ n sábana f; (of paper) hoja f; (of glass) lámina f; (of ice) capa f

sheikh /ʃeɪk/ n jeque m

shelf /ʃelf/ n (pl **shelves**) estante m. **be on the ∼** quedarse para vestir santos

shell /ʃel/ n concha f; (of egg) cáscara f; (of building) casco m; (explosive) proyectil m. —vt desgranar (peas etc); (mil) bombardear. **∼fish** /ʃelfɪʃ/ n invar (crustacean) crustáceo m; (mollusc) marisco m

shelter /ʃeltə(r)/ n refugio m, abrigo m. —vt abrigar; (protect) proteger; (give lodging to) dar asilo a. —vi abrigarse. **∼ed** a (spot) abrigado; (life etc) protegido

shelve /ʃelv/ vt (fig) dar carpetazo a. **∼ing** /ʃelvɪŋ/ n estantería f

shepherd /ʃepəd/ n pastor m. —vt guiar. **∼ess** /-ˈdes/ n pastora f. **∼'s pie** n carne f picada con puré de patatas

sherbet /ʃɜːbət/ n (Amer, water-ice) sorbete m

sheriff /ʃerɪf/ n alguacil m, sheriff m

sherry /ʃerɪ/ n (vino m de) jerez m

shield /ʃiːld/ n escudo m. —vt proteger

shift /ʃɪft/ vt cambiar; cambiar de sitio (furniture etc); echar (blame etc). —n cambio m; (work) turno m; (workers) tanda

f. **make ∼** arreglárselas. **∼less** /ʃɪftlɪs/ a holgazán

shifty /ʃɪftɪ/ a (-ier, -iest) taimado

shilling /ʃɪlɪŋ/ n chelín m

shilly-shally /ʃɪlɪʃælɪ/ vi titubear

shimmer /ʃɪmə(r)/ vi rielar, relucir. —n luz f trémula

shin /ʃɪn/ n espinilla f

shine /ʃaɪn/ vi (pt **shone**) brillar. —vt sacar brillo a. **∼ on** dirigir (torch). —n brillo m

shingle /ʃɪŋgl/ n (pebbles) guijarros mpl

shingles /ʃɪŋglz/ npl (med) herpes mpl & fpl

shiny /ʃaɪnɪ/ a (-ier, -iest) brillante

ship /ʃɪp/ n buque m, barco m. — vt (pt **shipped**) transportar; (send) enviar; (load) embarcar. **∼building** /ʃɪpbɪldɪŋ/ n construcción f naval. **∼ment** n envío m. **∼per** n expedidor m. **∼ping** n envío m; (ships) barcos mpl. **∼shape** /ʃɪpʃeɪp/ adv & a en buen orden, en regla. **∼wreck** /ʃɪprek/ n naufragio m. **∼wrecked** a naufragado. **∼wrecked** naufragar. **∼yard** /ʃɪpjɑːd/ n astillero m

shirk /ʃɜːk/ vt esquivar. **∼er** n gandul m

shirt /ʃɜːt/ n camisa f. **in ∼ sleeves** en mangas de camisa. **∼y** /ʃɜːtɪ/ a (sl) enfadado

shiver /ʃɪvə(r)/ vi temblar. —n escalofrío m

shoal /ʃəʊl/ n banco m

shock /ʃɒk/ n sacudida f; (fig) susto m; (elec) descarga f; (med) choque m. —vt escandalizar. **∼ing** a escandaloso; (fam) espantoso. **∼ingly** adv terriblemente

shod /ʃɒd/ see **shoe**

shoddily /ʃɒdɪlɪ/ adv mal. **∼y** /ʃɒdɪ/ a (-ier, -iest) mal hecho, de pacotilla

shoe /ʃuː/ n zapato m; (of horse) herradura f. —vt (pt **shod**, pres p **shoeing**) herrar ⟨horse⟩. **be well shod** estar bien calzado. **~horn** /ˈʃuːhɔːn/ n calzador m. **~lace** n cordón m de zapato. **~maker** /ˈʃuːmeɪkə(r)/ n zapatero m. **~ polish** n betún m. **~string** n. **on a ~string** con poco dinero. **~tree** n horma f.

shone /ʃɒn/ see **shine**

shoo /ʃuː/ vt ahuyentar

shook /ʃʊk/ see **shake**

shoot /ʃuːt/ vt (pt **shot**) disparar; rodar ⟨film⟩. —vi (hunt) cazar. —n (bot) retoño m; (hunt) cacería f. **~ down** vt derribar. **~ out** vi (rush) salir disparado. **~ up** ⟨prices⟩ subir de repente; ⟨grow⟩ crecer. **~ing-range** n campo m de tiro

shop /ʃɒp/ n tienda f; (work-shop) taller m. **talk ~** hablar de su trabajo. —vi (pt **shopping**) hacer compras. **~ around** buscar el mejor precio. **go ~ping** ir de compras. **~ assistant** n dependiente m. **~keeper** /ˈʃɒpkiːpə(r)/ n tendero m. **~lifter** n ratero m (de tiendas). **~lifting** n ratería f (de tiendas). **~per** n comprador m. **~ping** /ˈʃɒpɪŋ/ n compras fpl. **~ping bag** n bolsa f de la compra. **~ping centre** n centro m comercial. **~ steward** n enlace m sindical. **~window** n escaparate m

shore /ʃɔː(r)/ n orilla f

shorn /ʃɔːn/ see **shear**

short /ʃɔːt/ a (-er, -est) corto; (not lasting) breve; ⟨person⟩ bajo; (curt) brusco. **a ~ time ago** hace poco. **be ~ of** necesitar. **Mick is ~ for Michael** Mick es el diminutivo de Michael. —adv (stop) en seco. **~ of doing** a menos que no hagamos. **in ~** en resumen.

~age /ˈʃɔːtɪdʒ/ n escasez f. **~bread** /ˈʃɔːtbred/ n galleta f de mantequilla. **~change** vt estafar, engañar. **~ circuit** n cortocircuito m. **~coming** /ˈʃɔːtkʌmɪŋ/ n deficiencia f. **~ cut** n atajo m. **~en** /ˈʃɔːtn/ vt acortar. **~hand** n taquigrafía f. **~hand typist** n taquimecanógrafo m, taquimeca f (fam). **~lived** a efímero. **~ly** /ˈʃɔːtlɪ/ adv dentro de poco. **~s** npl pantalón m corto. **~sighted** a miope. **~tempered** a de mal genio

shot /ʃɒt/ see **shoot**. —n tiro m; (person) tirador m; (photo) foto f; (injection) inyección f. **like a ~** como una bala; (willingly) de buena gana. **~gun** n escopeta f

should /ʃʊd, ʃəd/ v, aux. **I ~ go** debería ir. **I ~ have seen him** debiera haberlo visto. **I ~ like** me gustaría. **if he ~ come** si viniese

shoulder /ˈʃəʊldə(r)/ n hombro m. —vt cargar con ⟨responsibility⟩; llevar a hombros ⟨burden⟩. **~blade** n omóplato m. **~-strap** n correa f del hombro; (of bra etc) tirante m

shout /ʃaʊt/ n grito m. —vt/i gritar. **~ at s.o.** gritarle a uno. **~ down** hacer callar a gritos

shove /ʃʌv/ n empujón m. —vt empujar; (put, fam) poner. —vi empujar. **~ off** vi (fam) largarse

shovel /ˈʃʌvl/ n pala f. —vt (pt **shovelled**) mover con la pala

show /ʃəʊ/ vt (pt **showed**, pp **shown**) mostrar; (on display) exponer; poner ⟨film⟩. —vi (be visible) verse. —n demostración f; (exhibition) exposición f; (ostentation) pompa f; (in theatre) espectáculo m; (in cinema) sesión f. **~ on** expuesto. **~ off** vt lucir; (pej) ostentar. —vi presumir. **~ up** vi destacar; (be

present) presentarse. —*vt*
(*unmask*) desenmascarar. ~
case *n* vitrina *f*. ~down *n* confrontación *f*

shower /ˈʃaʊə(r)/ *n* chaparrón *m*;
(*of blows etc*) lluvia *f*; (*for washing*) ducha *f*. have a ~
ducharse. —*vi* ducharse. —*vt*. ~
with colmar de. ~proof
/ˈʃaʊəpruːf/ *a* impermeable. ~y
a lluvioso

show: ~jumping *n* concurso *m*
hípico. ~manship /ˈʃəʊmənʃɪp/
n teatralidad *f*, arte *f* de presentar espectáculos

shown /ʃəʊn/ *see* show

show: ~off *n* fanfarrón *m*.
~place *n* lugar *m* de interés
turístico. ~room /ˈʃəʊruːm/ *n*
sala *f* de exposición *f*

showy /ˈʃəʊɪ/ *a* (-ier, -iest)
llamativo; (*person*) ostentoso

shrank /ʃræŋk/ *see* shrink

shrapnel /ˈʃræpnəl/ *n* metralla *f*

shred /ʃred/ *n* pedazo *m*; (*fig*)
pizca *f*. —*vt* (*pt* shredded) hacer
tiras; (*culin*) cortar en tiras.
~der *n* desfibradora *f*, trituradora *f*

shrew /ʃruː/ *n* musaraña *f*;
(*woman*) arpía *f*

shrewd /ʃruːd/ *a* (-er, -est)
astuto. ~ness *n* astucia *f*

shriek /ʃriːk/ *n* chillido *m*. —*vt/i*
chillar

shrift /ʃrɪft/ *n*. give s.o. short ~
despachar a uno con
brusquedad

shrill /ʃrɪl/ *a* agudo

shrimp /ʃrɪmp/ *n* camarón *m*

shrine /ʃraɪn/ *n* (*place*) lugar *m*
santo; (*tomb*) sepulcro *m*

shrink /ʃrɪŋk/ *vt* (*pt* shrank, *pp*
shrunk) encoger. —*vi* encogerse; (*draw back*) retirarse;
(*lessen*) disminuir. ~age *n* encogimiento *m*

shrivel /ˈʃrɪvl/ *vi* (*pt* shrivelled)
(*dry up*) secarse; (*become
wrinkled*) arrugarse

shroud /ʃraʊd/ *n* sudario *m*; (*fig*)
velo *m*. —*vt* (*veil*) velar

Shrove /ʃrəʊv/ *n*. ~ Tuesday *n*
martes *m* de carnaval

shrub /ʃrʌb/ *n* arbusto *m*

shrug /ʃrʌg/ *vt* (*pt* shrugged)
encogerse de hombros. —*n* encogimiento *m* de hombros

shrunk /ʃrʌŋk/ *see* shrink

shrunken /ˈʃrʌŋkən/ *a* encogido

shudder /ˈʃʌdə(r)/ *vi* estremecerse. —*n* estremecimiento *m*

shuffle /ˈʃʌfl/ *vi* arrastrar los
pies. —*vt* barajar (*cards*). —*n*
arrastramiento *m* de los pies; (*of
cards*) barajadura *f*

shun /ʃʌn/ *vt* (*pt* shunned)
evitar

shunt /ʃʌnt/ *vt* apartar, desviar

shush /ʃʊʃ/ *int* ¡chitón!

shut /ʃʌt/ *vt* (*pt* shut, *pres p*
shutting) cerrar. —*vi* cerrarse.
~ down cerrar. ~ up *vt* cerrar;
(*fam*) hacer callar. —*vi* callarse.
~down *n* cierre *m*. ~ter
/ˈʃʌtə(r)/ *n* contraventana *f*;
(*photo*) obturador *m*

shuttle /ˈʃʌtl/ *n* lanzadera *f*;
(*train*) tren *m* de enlace. —*vt*
transportar. —*vi* ir y venir.
~cock /ˈʃʌtlkɒk/ *n* volante *m*. ~
service *n* servicio *m* de enlace

shy /ʃaɪ/ *a* (-er, -est) tímido. —
vi (*pt* shied) asustarse. ~ away
from huir. ~ness *n* timidez *f*

Siamese /saɪəˈmiːz/ *a* siamés

sibling /ˈsɪblɪŋ/ *n* hermano *m*,
hermana *f*

Sicilian /sɪˈsɪljən/ *a* & *n* siciliano (*m*). ~y /ˈsɪsɪlɪ/ *n* Sicilia *f*

sick /sɪk/ *a* enfermo; (*humour*)
negro; (*fed up, fam*) harto. be ~
(*vomit*) vomitar. be ~ of (*fig*)
estar harto de. feel ~ sentir
náuseas. ~en *vt* dar asco. —*vi* caer enfermo. be
~ening for incubar

sickle /ˈsɪkl/ *n* hoz *f*

sick: ~**ly** /'sɪklɪ/ a (-ier, -iest) enfermizo; (*taste, smell etc*) nauseabundo. ~**ness** /'sɪknɪs/ n enfermedad f. ~**room** n cuarto m del enfermo

side /saɪd/ n lado m; (*of river*) orilla f; (*of hill*) ladera f; (*team*) equipo m; (*fig*) parte f. ~ **by** ~ uno al lado del otro. **on the** ~ (*sideline*) como actividad secundaria; (*secretly*) a escondidas. —a lateral. —vi. ~ **with** tomar el partido de. ~**board** /'saɪdbɔːd/ n aparador m. ~**boards** npl, ~**burns** npl (sl) patillas fpl. ~**car** n sidecar m. ~**effect** n efecto m secundario. ~**light** /'saɪdlaɪt/ n luz f de posición. ~**line** /'saɪdlaɪn/ n actividad f secundaria. ~**long** /-lɒŋ/ a & adv de soslayo. ~**road** n calle f secundaria. ~**saddle** n silla f de mujer. **ride** ~**saddle** adv a mujeriegas. ~**show** n atracción f secundaria. ~**step** vt evitar. ~**track** vt desviar del asunto. ~**walk** /'saɪdwɔːk/ n (*Amer*) acera f, vereda f (LAm). ~**ways** /'saɪdweɪz/ a & adv de lado. ~**whiskers** npl patillas fpl

siding /'saɪdɪŋ/ n apartadero m

sidle /'saɪdl/ vi avanzar furtivamente. ~ **up to** acercarse furtivamente

siege /siːdʒ/ n sitio m, cerco m

siesta /sɪ'estə/ n siesta f

sieve /sɪv/ n cernedor m. —vt cerner

sift /sɪft/ vt cerner. —vi. ~ **through** examinar

sigh /saɪ/ n suspiro. —vi suspirar

sight /saɪt/ n vista f; (*spectacle*) espectáculo m; (*on gun*) mira f. **at** (**first**) ~ a primera vista. **catch** ~ **of** vislumbrar. **lose** ~ **of** perder de vista. **on** ~ a primera vista. **within** ~ **of** (*near*)

cerca de. —vt ver, divisar. ~**seeing** /'saɪtsiːɪŋ/ n visita f turística. ~**seer** /-ə(r)/ n turista m & f

sign /saɪn/ n señal f. —vt firmar. ~ **on**, ~ **up** vt inscribir. —vi inscribirse

signal /'sɪgnəl/ n señal f. —vt (pt **signalled**) comunicar; hacer señas a (*person*). ~**box** n casilla f del guardavía. ~**man** /'sɪgnəlmən/ n (pl -**men**) guardavía f

signatory /'sɪgnətrɪ/ n firmante m & f

signature /'sɪgnətʃə(r)/ n firma f. ~ **tune** n sintonía f

signet-ring /'sɪgnɪtrɪŋ/ n anillo m de sello

significan|ce /sɪg'nɪfɪkəns/ n significado m. ~**t** /sɪg'nɪfɪkənt/ a significativo; (*important*) importante. ~**tly** adv significativamente

signify /'sɪgnɪfaɪ/ vt significar. —vi (*matter*) importar, tener importancia

signpost /'saɪnpəʊst/ n poste m indicador

silen|ce /'saɪləns/ n silencio m. —vt hacer callar. ~**cer** /-ə(r)/ n silenciador m. ~**t** /saɪlənt/ a silencioso; (*film*) mudo. ~**tly** adv silenciosamente

silhouette /sɪlu:'et/ n silueta f. —vt. **be** ~**d** perfilarse, destacarse (**against** contra)

silicon /'sɪlɪkən/ n silicio m. ~ **chip** n pastilla f de silicio

silk /sɪlk/ n seda f. ~**en** a, ~**y** a (*of silk*) de seda; (*like silk*) sedoso. ~**worm** n gusano m de seda

sill /sɪl/ n antepecho m; (*of window*) alféizar m; (*of door*) umbral m

silly /'sɪlɪ/ a (-ier, -iest) tonto. —n. ~**billy** (*fam*) tonto m

silo /'saɪləʊ/ n (pl -os) silo m

silt /sɪlt/ n sedimento m

silver /'sɪlvə(r)/ n plata f. ~a de plata. ~ **plated** a bañado en plata, plateado. ~**side** /'sɪlvəsaɪd/ n (culin) contra f. ~**smith** /'sɪlvəsmɪθ/ n platero m. ~**ware** /'sɪlvəweə(r)/ n plata f. ~ **wedding** n bodas fpl de plata. ~**y** a plateado; (sound) argentino

similar /'sɪmɪlə(r)/ a parecido. ~**arity** /-ɪ'lærətɪ/ n parecido m. ~**arly** adv de igual manera

simile /'sɪmɪlɪ/ n símil m

simmer /'sɪmə(r)/ vt/i hervir a fuego lento; (fig) hervir. ~ **down** calmarse

simpl|e /'sɪmpl/ a (-er, -est) sencillo; (person) ingenuo. ~**e-minded** a ingenuo. ~**eton** /'sɪmpltən/ n simplón m. ~**icity** /-'plɪsɪtɪ/ n sencillez f. ~**ification** /-ɪ'keɪʃn/ n simplificación f. ~**ify** /'sɪmplɪfaɪ/ vt simplificar. ~**y** adv sencillamente; (absolutely) absolutamente

simulat|e /'sɪmjoleɪt/ vt simular. ~**ion** /-'leɪʃn/ n simulación f

simultaneous /sɪml'teɪnɪəs/ a simultáneo. ~**ly** adv simultáneamente

sin /sɪn/ n pecado m. —vi (pt sinned) pecar

since /sɪns/ prep desde. —adv desde entonces. —conj desde que; (because) ya que

sincer|e /sɪn'sɪə(r)/ a sincero. ~**ely** adv sinceramente. ~**ity** /-'serətɪ/ n sinceridad f

sinew /'sɪnju:/ n tendón m. ~**s** npl músculos mpl

sinful /'sɪnfl/ a pecaminoso; (shocking) escandaloso

sing /sɪŋ/ vt/i a (pt sang, pp sung) cantar

singe /sɪndʒ/ vt (pres p singeing) chamuscar

singer /'sɪŋə(r)/ n cantante m & f

single /'sɪŋgl/ a único; (not double) sencillo; (unmarried)

soltero; (bed, room) individual. —n (tennis) juego m individual; (ticket) billete m sencillo. —vt. ~ **e out** escoger; (distinguish) distinguir. ~**e-handed** a & adv sin ayuda. ~**e-minded** a resuelto

singlet /'sɪŋglɪt/ n camiseta f

singly /'sɪŋglɪ/ adv uno a uno

singsong /'sɪŋsɒŋ/ a monótono. —n. **have a** ~ cantar juntos

singular /'sɪŋgjolə(r)/ n singular f. —a singular; (uncommon) raro; (noun) en singular. ~**ly** adv singularmente

sinister /'sɪnɪstə(r)/ a siniestro

sink /sɪŋk/ vt (pt **sank**, pp **sunk**) hundir; perforar (well); invertir (money). —vi hundirse; (patient) debilitarse. —n fregadero m. ~ **in** vi penetrar

sinner /'sɪnə(r)/ n pecador m

sinuous /'sɪnjʊəs/ a sinuoso

sinus /'saɪnəs/ n (pl -**uses**) seno m

sip /sɪp/ n sorbo m. —vt (pt **sipped**) sorber

siphon /'saɪfən/ n sifón m. vt. ~ **out** sacar con sifón

sir /sɜ:(r)/ n señor m. **S~** n (title) sir m

siren /'saɪərən/ n sirena f

sirloin /'sɜ:lɔɪn/ n solomillo m, lomo m bajo

sirocco /sɪ'rɒkəʊ/ n siroco m

sissy /'sɪsɪ/ n hombre m afeminado, marica m, mariquita m; (coward) gallina m & f

sister /'sɪstə(r)/ n hermana f; (nurse) enfermera f jefe. **S~ Mary** Sor María. ~**in-law** (pl ~**s-in-law**) cuñada f. ~**ly** a de hermana; (like sister) como hermana

sit /sɪt/ vt (pt **sat**, pres p **sitting**) sentar. —vi sentarse; (committee etc) reunirse. **be** ~**ting** estar sentado. ~ **back** vi (fig) relajarse. ～ **down** vi sentarse. ～ **for** vi presentarse a ⟨exam⟩; posar para ⟨portrait⟩. ～ **up** vi enderezarse; ⟨stay awake⟩ velar. ～-**in** n ocupación f

site /saɪt/ n sitio m. **building** ～ n solar m. —vt situar

sit: ～**ting** n sesión f; ⟨in restaurant⟩ turno m. ～**ting-room** n cuarto m de estar

situate /'sɪtjʊeɪt/ vt situar. ～**ed** a situado. ～**ion** /-'eɪʃn/ n situación f; ⟨job⟩ puesto m

six /sɪks/ a & n seis (m). ～**teen** /sɪk'sti:n/ a & n dieciséis (m). ～**teenth** a & n decimosexto (m). ～**th** a & n sexto (m). ～**tieth** a & n sesenta (m), sexagésimo (m). ～**ty** /'sɪkstɪ/ a & n sesenta (m)

size /saɪz/ n tamaño m; ⟨of clothes⟩ talla f; ⟨of shoes⟩ número m; ⟨extent⟩ magnitud f. —vt. ～ **up** ⟨fam⟩ juzgar. ～**able** a bastante grande

sizzle /'sɪzl/ vi crepitar

skate¹ /skeɪt/ n patín m. —vi patinar. ～**board** /'skeɪtbɔːd/ n monopatín m. ～**r** n patinador m

skate² /skeɪt/ n invar ⟨fish⟩ raya f

skating /'skeɪtɪŋ/ n patinaje m. ～-**rink** n pista f de patinaje

skein /skeɪn/ n madeja f

skelet|al /'skelɪtl/ a esquelético. ～**on** /'skelɪtn/ n esqueleto m. ～**on staff** n personal m reducido

sketch /sketʃ/ n esbozo m; ⟨drawing⟩ dibujo m; ⟨in theatre⟩ pieza f corta y divertida. —vt esbozar. —vi dibujar. ～**y** /'sketʃɪ/ a (-**ier**, -**iest**) incompleto

skew /skju:/ n. **on the** ～ sesgado

skewer /'skjuːə(r)/ n broqueta f

ski /ski:/ n (pl **skis**) esquí m. —vi (pt **skied**, pres p **skiing**) esquiar. **go** ～**ing** ir a esquiar

ski: ～**er** n esquiador m. ～**ing** n esquí m

skilful /'skɪlfl/ a diestro

ski-lift /'ski:lɪft/ n telesquí m

skill /skɪl/ n destreza f, habilidad f. ～**ed** a hábil; ⟨worker⟩ cualificado

skim /skɪm/ vt (pt **skimmed**) espumar; desnatar ⟨milk⟩; ⟨glide over⟩ rozar. ～ **over** vt rasar. ～ **through** vi hojear

skimp /skɪmp/ vt escatimar. ～**y** /'skɪmpɪ/ a (-**ier**, -**iest**) insuficiente; ⟨skirt, dress⟩ corto

skin /skɪn/ n piel f. —vt (pt **skinned**) despellejar; pelar ⟨fruit⟩. ～**deep** a superficial. ～**diving** n natación f submarina. ～**flint** /'skɪnflɪnt/ n tacaño m. ～**ny** /'skɪnɪ/ a (-**ier**, -**iest**) flaco

skint /skɪnt/ a ⟨sl⟩ sin una perra

skip¹ /skɪp/ vi (pt **skipped**) vi saltar; ⟨with rope⟩ saltar a la comba. —vt saltarse. —n salto m

skip² /skɪp/ n ⟨container⟩ cuba f

skipper /'skɪpə(r)/ n capitán m

skipping-rope /'skɪpɪŋrəʊp/ n comba f

skirmish /'skɜːmɪʃ/ n escaramuza f

skirt /skɜːt/ n falda f. —vt rodear; ⟨go round⟩ ladear

skirting-board /'skɜːtɪŋbɔːd/ n rodapié m, zócalo m

skit /skɪt/ n pieza f satírica

skittish /'skɪtɪʃ/ a juguetón; ⟨horse⟩ nervioso

skittle /'skɪtl/ n bolo m

skive /skaɪv/ vi ⟨sl⟩ gandulear

skivvy /'skɪvɪ/ n ⟨fam⟩ criada f

skulk /skʌlk/ vi avanzar furtivamente; ⟨hide⟩ esconderse

skull /skʌl/ n cráneo m; ⟨remains⟩ calavera f. ～**cap** n casquete m

skunk /skʌŋk/ n mofeta f; ⟨person⟩ canalla f

sky /skaɪ/ n cielo m. ~-blue a &
n azul (m) celeste. ~jack
/'skaɪdʒæk/ vt secuestrar.
~jacker n secuestrador m.
~light /'skaɪlaɪt/ n tragaluz m.
~scraper /'skaɪskreɪpə(r)/ n
rascacielos m invar

slab /slæb/ n bloque m; (of stone)
losa f; (of chocolate) tableta f

slack /slæk/ a (-er, -est) flojo;
⟨person⟩ negligente; ⟨period⟩ de
poca actividad. —n (of rope)
parte f floja. —vt aflojar. —vi
aflojarse; (fig) descansar.
~en /'slækən/ vt aflojar. —vi
aflojarse; (fig) descansar.
~en (off) vt aflojar. ~ off (fam)
aflojar

slacks /slæks/ npl pantalones
mpl

slag /slæg/ n escoria f

slain /sleɪn/ see slay

slake /sleɪk/ vt apagar

slam /slæm/ vt (pt slammed) golpear; ⟨throw⟩ arrojar; ⟨criticize,
sl⟩ criticar. ~ the door dar un
portazo. —vi cerrarse de
golpe. —n golpe m; (of door) portazo m

slander /'slɑːndə(r)/ n calumnia
f. —vt difamar. ~ous a
calumnioso

slang /slæŋ/ n jerga f, argot m.
~y a vulgar

slant /slɑːnt/ vt inclinar; presentar con parcialidad ⟨news⟩. —
n inclinación f; (point of view)
punto m de vista

slap /slæp/ vt (pt slapped)
abofetear; (on the back) dar una
palmada; (put) arrojar. —n
bofetada f; (on back) palmada
f. —adv de lleno. ~dash
/'slæpdæʃ/ a descuidado.
~happy a (fam) despre-
ocupado; (dazed, fam) aturdido.
~stick /'slæpstɪk/ n payasada f.
~-up a (sl) de primera categoría

slash /slæʃ/ vt acuchillar; (fig)
reducir radicalmente. —n cuchillada f

slat /slæt/ n tablilla f

slate /sleɪt/ n pizarra f. —vt (fam)
criticar

slaughter /'slɔːtə(r)/ vt masacrar; matar ⟨animal⟩. —n carnicería f; (of animals) matanza f.
~house /'slɔːtəhaʊs/ n matadero m

Slav /slɑːv/ a & n eslavo (m)

slav|e /sleɪv/ n esclavo m. —vi
trabajar como un negro. ~e-
driver n negrero m. ~ery /-əri/
n esclavitud f. ~ish /'sleɪvɪʃ/ a
servil

Slavonic /sləˈvɒnɪk/ a eslavo

slay /sleɪ/ vt (pt slew, pp slain)
matar

sleazy /'sliːzɪ/ a (-ier, -iest) (fam)
sórdido

sledge /sledʒ/ n trineo m. ~-
hammer n almádena f

sleek /sliːk/ a (-er, -est) liso,
brillante; (elegant) elegante

sleep /sliːp/ n sueño m. go to ~
dormirse. —vi (pt slept)
dormir. —vt poder alojar. ~er n
durmiente m & f; (on track) tra-
viesa f; (berth) coche-cama m.
~ily adv soñolientamente.
~ing-bag n saco m de dormir.
~ing-pill n somnífero m. ~less
a insomne. ~lessness n insomnio m. ~walker n sonámbulo
m. ~y /'sliːpɪ/ a (-ier, -iest) soñoliento. be ~y tener sueño

sleet /sliːt/ n aguanieve f. —vi
caer aguanieve

sleeve /sliːv/ n manga f; (for
record) funda f. up one's ~ en
reserva. ~less a sin mangas

sleigh /sleɪ/ n trineo m

sleight /slaɪt/ n. ~ of hand pre-
stidigitación f

slender /'slendə(r)/ a delgado;
(fig) escaso

slept /slept/ see sleep

sleuth /sluːθ/ n investigador m
slew¹ /sluː/ see slay
slew² /sluː/ vi (turn) girar
slice /slaɪs/ n lonja f; (of bread) rebanada f; (of sth round) rodaja f; (implement) paleta f. —vt cortar; rebanar ⟨bread⟩
slick /slɪk/ a liso; (cunning) astuto. —n. (oil)-∼ capa f de aceite
slid|e /slaɪd/ vt (pt slid) deslizar. —vi resbalar. ∼e over pasar por alto de. —n resbalón m; (in playground) tobogán m; (for hair) pasador m; (photo) diapositiva f; (fig, fall) baja f. ∼e-rule n regla f de cálculo. ∼ing a corredizo. ∼ing scale n escala f móvil
slight /slaɪt/ a (-er, -est) ligero; (slender) delgado. —vt ofender. —n desaire m. ∼est a mínimo. not in the ∼est en absoluto. ∼ly adv un poco
slim /slɪm/ a (slimmer, slimmest) delgado. —vi (pt slimmed) adelgazar
slime /slaɪm/ n légamo m, lodo m, fango m
slimness /ˈslɪmnɪs/ n delgadez f
slimy /ˈslaɪmɪ/ a legamoso, fangoso, viscoso; (fig) rastrero
sling /slɪŋ/ n honda f; (toy) tirador; (med) cabestrillo m. —vt (pt slung) lanzar
slip /slɪp/ vt (pt slipped) deslizar. ∼ s.o.'s mind olvidársele a uno. —vi deslizarse. —n resbalón m; (mistake) error m; (petticoat) combinación f; (paper) trozo m. ∼ of the tongue n lapsus m linguae. give the ∼ to zafarse de, dar esquinazo a. ∼ away vi escabullirse. ∼ into vi ponerse ⟨clothes⟩. ∼ up vi (fam) equivocarse
slipper /ˈslɪpə(r)/ n zapatilla f
slippery /ˈslɪpərɪ/ a resbaladizo

slip: ∼-road n rampa f de acceso. ∼shod /ˈslɪpʃɒd/ a descuidado. ∼-up n (fam) error m
slit /slɪt/ n raja f; (cut) corte m. —vt (pt slit, pres p slitting) rajar; (cut) cortar
slither /ˈslɪðə(r)/ vi deslizarse
sliver /ˈslɪvə(r)/ n trocito m; (splinter) astilla f
slobber /ˈslɒbə(r)/ vi babear
slog /slɒg/ vt (pt slogged) golpear. —vi trabajar como un negro. —n golpetazo m; (hard work) trabajo m penoso
slogan /ˈsləʊgən/ n eslogan m
slop /slɒp/ vt (pt slopped) derramar. —vi derramarse. ∼s npl (fam) agua f sucia
slop|e /sləʊp/ vi inclinarse. —vt inclinar. —n declive m, pendiente m. ∼ing a inclinado
sloppy /ˈslɒpɪ/ a (-ier, -iest) (wet) mojado; (food) líquido; (work) descuidado; (person) desaliñado; (fig) sentimental
slosh /slɒʃ/ vi (fam) chapotear. —vt (hit, sl) pegar
slot /slɒt/ n ranura f. —vt (pt slotted) encajar
sloth /sləʊθ/ n pereza f
slot-machine /ˈslɒtməʃiːn/ n distribuidor m automático; (for gambling) máquina f tragaperras
slouch /slaʊtʃ/ vi andar cargado de espaldas; (in chair) repanchigarse
Slovak /ˈsləʊvæk/ a & n eslovaco (m). ∼ia /sləʊˈvækɪə/ n Eslovaquia f
sloven|liness /ˈslʌvnlɪnɪs/ n despreocupación f. ∼y /ˈslʌvnlɪ/ a descuidado
slow /sləʊ/ a (-er, -est) lento. be ∼ (clock) estar atrasado. in ∼ motion a cámara lenta. —adv despacio. —vt retardar. —vi ir más despacio. ∼ down, ∼ up vt retardar. —vi ir más despacio.

~**coach** /ˈsləʊkəʊtʃ/ n tardón m.
~**ly** adv despacio. ~**ness** n lentitud f

sludge /slʌdʒ/ n fango m; (sediment) sedimento m.

slug /slʌg/ n babosa f; (bullet) posta f. ~**gish** /ˈslʌgɪʃ/ a lento

sluice /sluːs/ n (gate) compuerta f; (channel) canal m

slum /slʌm/ n tugurio m

slumber /ˈslʌmbə(r)/ n sueño m. —vi dormir

slump /slʌmp/ n baja f repentina; (in business) depresión f. —vi bajar repentinamente; (collapse) desplomarse

slung /slʌŋ/ see **sling**

slur /slɜː(r)/ vt/i (pt **slurred**) articular mal. —n dicción f defectuosa; (discredit) calumnia f

slush /slʌʃ/ n nieve f medio derretida; (fig) sentimentalismo m. ~ **fund** n fondos mpl secretos para fines deshonestos. ~**y** a ⟨road⟩ cubierto de nieve medio derretida

slut /slʌt/ n mujer f desaseada

sly /slaɪ/ a (slyer, slyest) (crafty) astuto; (secretive) furtivo. —n. **on the** ~ a escondidas. ~**ly** adv astutamente

smack[1] /smæk/ n golpe m; (on face) bofetada f. —adv (fam) de lleno. —vt pegar

smack[2] /smæk/ vi. ~ **of** saber a; (fig) oler a

small /smɔːl/ a (-er, -est) pequeño. —n. the ~ **of the back** la región f lumbar. ~ **ads** npl anuncios mpl por palabras. ~**change** n cambio m. ~**holding** /ˈsmɔːlhəʊldɪŋ/ n parcela f. ~**pox** /ˈsmɔːlpɒks/ n viruela f. ~**talk** n charla f. ~**time** a (fam) de poca monta

smarmy /ˈsmɑːmɪ/ a (-ier, -iest) (fam) zalamero

smart /smɑːt/ a (-er, -est) elegante; (clever) inteligente; (brisk) rápido. —vi escocer. ~**en** /ˈsmɑːtn/ vt arreglar. —vi arreglarse. ~**en up** vi arreglarse. ~**ly** adv elegantemente; (quickly) rápidamente. ~**ness** n elegancia f

smash /smæʃ/ vt romper; (into little pieces) hacer pedazos; batir ⟨record⟩. —vi romperse; (collide) chocar (into con). —n (noise) estruendo m; (collision) choque m; (com) quiebra f. ~**ing** /ˈsmæʃɪŋ/ a (fam) estupendo

smattering /ˈsmætərɪŋ/ n conocimientos mpl superficiales

smear /smɪə(r)/ vt untar (with de); (stain) manchar (with de); (fig) difamar. —n mancha f; (med) frotis m

smell /smel/ n olor m; (sense) olfato m. —vt/i (pt **smelt**) oler. ~**y** a maloliente

smelt[1] /smelt/ see **smell**

smelt[2] /smelt/ vt fundir

smile /smaɪl/ n sonrisa f. —vi sonreír(se)

smirk /smɜːk/ n sonrisa f afectada

smite /smaɪt/ vt (pt **smote**, pp **smitten**) golpear

smith /smɪθ/ n herrero m

smithereens /smɪðəˈriːnz/ npl añicos mpl. **smash to** ~ hacer añicos

smitten /ˈsmɪtn/ see **smite**. —a encaprichado (with por)

smock /smɒk/ n blusa f, bata f

smog /smɒg/ n niebla f con humo

smoke /sməʊk/ n humo m. —vt/i fumar. ~**less** a sin humo. ~**r** /-ə(r)/ n fumador m. ~**e-screen** n cortina f de humo. ~**y** a ⟨room⟩ lleno de humo

smooth /smuːð/ a (-er, -est) liso; ⟨sound, movement⟩ suave; (sea) tranquilo; ⟨manners⟩ zalamero. —vt alisar; (fig) allanar. ~**ly** adv suavemente

smote /sməʊt/ *see* **smite**

smother /'smʌðə(r)/ *vt* sofocar; (*cover*) cubrir

smoulder /'sməʊldə(r)/ *vi* arder sin llama; (*fig*) arder

smudge /smʌdʒ/ *n* borrón *m*, mancha *f*. —*vt* tiznar. —*vi* tiznarse

smug /smʌg/ *a* (**smugger, smuggest**) satisfecho de sí mismo

smuggle /'smʌgl/ *vt* pasar de contrabando. ~**er** *n* contrabandista *m* & *f*. ~**ing** *n* contrabando *m*

smug: ~**ly** *adv* con suficiencia. ~**ness** *n* suficiencia *f*

smut /smʌt/ *n* tizne *m*; (*mark*) tiznajo *m*. ~**ty** *a* (-**ier, -iest**) tiznado; (*fig*) obsceno

snack /snæk/ *n* tentempié *m*. ~-**bar** *n* cafetería *f*

snag /snæg/ *n* problema *m*; (*in cloth*) rasgón *m*

snail /sneɪl/ *n* caracol *m*. ~'s **pace** *n* paso *m* de tortuga

snake /sneɪk/ *n* serpiente *f*

snap /snæp/ *vt* (*pt* **snapped**) (*break*) romper; castañetear (*fingers*). —*vi* romperse; (*dog*) intentar morder; (*say*) contestar bruscamente; (*whip*) chasquear. ~ **at** (*dog*) intentar morder; (*say*) contestar bruscamente. —*n* chasquido *m*; (*photo*) foto *f*. —*a* instantáneo. ~ **up** agarrar. ~**py** /'snæpɪ/ *a* (-**ier, -iest**) (*fam*) rápido. **make it** ~**py!** (*fam*) ¡date prisa! ~**shot** /'snæpʃɒt/ *n* foto *f*

snare /sneə(r)/ *n* trampa *f*

snarl /snɑːl/ *vi* gruñir. —*n* gruñido *m*

snatch /snætʃ/ *vt* agarrar; (*steal*) robar. —*n* arrebatamiento *m*; (*short part*) trocito *m*; (*theft*) robo *m*

sneak /sniːk/ *n* soplón *m*. —*vi*. ~ **in** entrar furtivamente. ~ **out** salir furtivamente

sneakers /'sniːkəz/ *npl* zapatillas *fpl* de lona

sneak: ~**ing** /'sniːkɪŋ/ *a* furtivo. ~**y** *a* furtivo

sneer /snɪə(r)/ *n* sonrisa *f* de desprecio. —*vi* sonreír con desprecio. ~ **at** hablar con desprecio a

sneeze /sniːz/ *n* estornudo *m*. —*vi* estornudar

snide /snaɪd/ *a* (*fam*) despreciativo

sniff /snɪf/ *vt* oler. —*vi* aspirar por la nariz. —*n* aspiración *f*

snigger /'snɪgə(r)/ *n* risa *f* disimulada. —*vi* reír disimuladamente

snip /snɪp/ *vt* (*pt* **snipped**) tijeretear. —*n* tijeretada *f*; (*bargain, sl*) ganga *f*

snipe /snaɪp/ *vi* disparar desde un escondite. ~**r** /ə(r)/ *n* tirador *m* emboscado, francotirador *m*

snippet /'snɪpɪt/ *n* retazo *m*

snivel /'snɪvl/ *vi* (*pt* **snivelled**) lloriquear. ~**ling** *a* llorón

snob /snɒb/ *n* esnob *m*. ~**bery** *n* esnobismo *m*. ~**bish** *a* esnob

snooker /'snuːkə(r)/ *n* billar *m*

snoop /snuːp/ *vi* (*fam*) curiosear

snooty /'snuːtɪ/ *a* (*fam*) desdeñoso

snooze /snuːz/ *n* sueñecito *m*. —*vi* echarse un sueñecito

snore /snɔː(r)/ *n* ronquido *m*. —*vi* roncar

snorkel /'snɔːkl/ *n* tubo *m* respiratorio

snort /snɔːt/ *n* bufido *m*. —*vi* bufar

snout /snaʊt/ *n* hocico *m*

snow /snəʊ/ *n* nieve *f*. —*vi* nevar. **be** ~**ed under with** estar inundado por. ~**ball** /'snəʊbɔːl/ *n* bola *f* de nieve. ~**drift** *n* nieve amontonada. ~**drop** /'snəʊdrɒp/ *n* campanilla *f* de invierno. ~**fall** /'snəʊfɔːl/ *n* nevada *f*. ~**flake** /'snəʊfleɪk/ *n* copo *m* de nieve. **~man** /'snəʊmæn/ *n* (*pl* **-men**) muñeco *m* de nieve. **~-plough** *n* quitanieves *m invar*. **~storm** /'snəʊstɔːm/ *n* nevasca *f*. **~y** *a* ⟨*place*⟩ de nieves abundantes; ⟨*weather*⟩ con nevadas seguidas

snub /snʌb/ *vt* (*pt* **snubbed**) desairar. **—n** desaire *m*. **~-nosed** /'snʌbnəʊzd/ *a* chato

snuff /snʌf/ *n* rapé *m*. **—vt** despabilar ⟨*candle*⟩. **~ out** apagar ⟨*candle*⟩

snuffle /'snʌfl/ *vi* respirar ruidosamente

snug /snʌg/ *a* (**snugger, snuggest**) cómodo; ⟨*tight*⟩ ajustado

snuggle /'snʌgl/ *vi* acomodarse

so /səʊ/ *adv* (*before a or adv*) tan; ⟨*thus*⟩ así. **—conj** así que. **~ am I** yo también. **~ as to** para. **~ far** *adv* ⟨*time*⟩ hasta ahora; ⟨*place*⟩ hasta aquí. **~ far as I know** que yo sepa. **~ long!** *(fam)* ¡hasta luego! **~ much** tanto. **~ that** *conj* para que. **and ~ forth, and ~ on** y así sucesivamente. **if ~** si es así. **I think ~** creo que sí. **or ~** más o menos

soak /səʊk/ *vt* remojar. **—vi** remojarse. **n** penetrar. **~ up** absorber. **~ing** *a* empapado. **—** *n* remojón *m*

so-and-so /'səʊənsəʊ/ *n* fulano *m*

soap /səʊp/ *n* jabón *m*. **—vt** enjabonar. **~ powder** *n* jabón en polvo. **~y** *a* jabonoso

soar /sɔː(r)/ *vi* elevarse; ⟨*price etc*⟩ ponerse por las nubes

sob /sɒb/ *n* sollozo *m*. **—vi** (*pt* **sobbed**) sollozar

sober /'səʊbə(r)/ *a* sobrio; ⟨*colour*⟩ discreto

so-called /'səʊkɔːld/ *a* llamado, supuesto

soccer /'sɒkə(r)/ *n* *(fam)* fútbol *m*

sociable /'səʊʃəbl/ *a* sociable

social /'səʊʃl/ *a* social; ⟨*sociable*⟩ sociable. **—n** reunión *f*. **~ism**

/-zəm/ *n* socialismo *m*. **~ist** /'səʊʃəlɪst/ *a & n* socialista *m & f*. **~ize** /'səʊʃəlaɪz/ *vt* socializar. **~ly** *adv* socialmente. **~ security** *n* seguridad *f* social. **~ worker** *n* asistente *m* social

society /sə'saɪətɪ/ *n* sociedad *f*

sociolog|ical /səʊsɪə'lɒdʒɪkl/ *a* sociológico. **~ist** *n* sociólogo *m*. **~y** /səʊsɪ'ɒlədʒɪ/ *n* sociología *f*

sock[1] /sɒk/ *n* calcetín *m*

sock[2] /sɒk/ *vt* *(sl)* pegar

socket /'sɒkɪt/ *n* hueco *m*; ⟨*of eye*⟩ cuenca *f*; ⟨*wall plug*⟩ enchufe *m*; ⟨*for bulb*⟩ portalámparas *m invar*, casquillo *m*

soda /'səʊdə/ *n* sosa *f*; ⟨*water*⟩ soda *f*. **~-water** *n* soda *f*

sodden /'sɒdn/ *a* empapado

sodium /'səʊdɪəm/ *n* sodio *m*

sofa /'səʊfə/ *n* sofá *m*

soft /sɒft/ *a* (**-er, -est**) blando; ⟨*sound, colour*⟩ suave; ⟨*gentle*⟩ dulce, tierno; ⟨*silly*⟩ estúpido. **~ drink** *n* bebida *f* no alcohólica. **~en** /'sɒfn/ *vt* ablandar; *(fig)* suavizar. **—vi** ablandarse; *(fig)* suavizarse. **~ly** *adv* dulcemente. **~ness** *n* blandura *f*; *(fig)* dulzura *f*. **~ware** /'sɒftweə(r)/ *n* programación *f*, software *m*

soggy /'sɒgɪ/ *a* (**-ier, -iest**) empapado

soh /səʊ/ *n* ⟨*mus, fifth note of any musical scale*⟩ sol *m*

soil[1] /sɔɪl/ *n* suelo *m*

soil[2] /sɔɪl/ *vt* ensuciar. **—vi** ensuciarse

solace /'sɒləs/ *n* consuelo *m*

solar /'səʊlə(r)/ *a* solar. **~ium** /sə'leərɪəm/ *n* (*pl* **-a**) solario *m*

sold /səʊld/ *see* **sell**

solder /'sɒldə(r)/ *n* soldadura *f*. **—vt** soldar

soldier /'səʊldʒə(r)/ *n* soldado *m*. **—vi. ~ on** *(fam)* perseverar

sole[1] /səʊl/ *n* ⟨*of foot*⟩ planta *f*; ⟨*of shoe*⟩ suela *f* sole² /səʊl/ (*fish*) lenguado *m*

sole³ /səʊl/ *a* único, solo. ~ly *adv* únicamente

solemn /'sɒləm/ *a* solemne. ~ity /sə'lemnəti/ *n* solemnidad *f*. ~ly *adv* solemnemente

solicit /sə'lɪsɪt/ *vt* solicitar. —*vi* importunar

solicitor /sə'lɪsɪtə(r)/ *n* abogado *m*; (*notary*) notario *m*

solicitous /sə'lɪsɪtəs/ *a* solícito

solid /'sɒlɪd/ *a* sólido; (*gold etc*) macizo; (*unanimous*) unánime; (*meal*) sustancioso. —*n* sólido *m*. ~arity /sɒlɪ'dærətɪ/ *n* solidaridad *f*. ~ify /sə'lɪdɪfaɪ/ *vt* solidificar. —*vi* solidificarse. ~ity /sə'lɪdətɪ/ *n* solidez *f*. ~ly *adv* sólidamente. ~s *npl* alimentos *mpl* sólidos

soliloquy /sə'lɪləkwɪ/ *n* soliloquio *m*

solitaire /sɒlɪ'teə(r)/ *n* solitario *m*

solitary /'sɒlɪtrɪ/ *a* solitario

solitude /'sɒlɪtjuːd/ *n* soledad *f*

solo /'səʊləʊ/ *n* (*pl* -os) (*mus*) solo *m*. ~ist *n* solista *m & f*

solstice /'sɒlstɪs/ *n* solsticio *m*

soluble /'sɒljʊbl/ *a* soluble

solution /sə'luːʃn/ *n* solución *f*

solvable /sə'səʊ/ *a* soluble

solve /sɒlv/ *vt* resolver

solvent /'sɒlvənt/ *a & n* solvente (*m*)

sombre /'sɒmbə(r)/ *a* sombrío

some /sʌm/ *a* alguno; (*a little*) un poco de. ~ day algún día. ~ two hours unas dos horas. will you have ~ wine? ¿quieres vino? —*pron* algunos; (*a little*) un poco. ~ of us algunos de nosotros. I want ~ quiero un poco. —*adv* (*approximately*) unos. ~body /'sʌmbədɪ/ *pron* alguien. —*n* personaje *m*. ~how /'sʌmhaʊ/ *adv* de algún modo. ~how or other de una manera u otra. ~one

/'sʌmwʌn/ *pron* alguien. —*n* personaje *m*

somersault /'sʌməsɔːlt/ *n* salto *m* mortal. —*vi* dar un salto mortal

some: ~thing /'sʌmθɪŋ/ *pron* algo *m*. ~thing like algo como; (*approximately*) cerca de. ~time /'sʌmtaɪm/ *a* ex. —*adv* algún día; (*in past*) durante. ~time last summer *a* (*durante*) el verano pasado. ~times /'sʌmtaɪmz/ *adv* de vez en cuando, a veces. ~what /'sʌmwɒt/ *adv* algo, un poco. ~where /'sʌmweə(r)/ *adv* en alguna parte

son /sʌn/ *n* hijo *m*

sonata /sə'nɑːtə/ *n* sonata *f*

song /sɒŋ/ *n* canción *f*. sell for a ~ vender muy barato. ~book /n* cancionero *m*

sonic /'sɒnɪk/ *a* sónico

son-in-law /'sʌnɪnlɔː/ *n* (*pl* sons-in-law) yerno *m*

sonnet /'sɒnɪt/ *n* soneto *m*

sonny /'sʌnɪ/ *n* (*fam*) hijo *m*

soon /suːn/ *adv* (-er, -est) pronto; (*in a short time*) dentro de poco; (*early*) temprano. ~ after poco después. ~er or later tarde o temprano. as ~ as en cuanto; as ~ as possible lo antes posible. I would ~er not go prefiero no ir

soot /sʊt/ *n* hollín *m*

soothe /suːð/ *vt* calmar. ~ing *a* calmante

sooty /'sʊtɪ/ *a* cubierto de hollín

sophisticated /sə'fɪstɪkeɪtɪd/ *a* sofisticado; (*complex*) complejo

soporific /sɒpə'rɪfɪk/ *a* soporífero

sopping /'sɒpɪŋ/ *a*. ~ (wet) empapado

soppy /'sɒpɪ/ *a* (-ier, -iest) (*fam*) sentimental; (*silly, fam*) tonto

soprano /sə'prɑːnəʊ/ *n* (*pl* -os) (*voice*) soprano *m*; (*singer*) soprano *f*

sorcerer /'sɔːsərə(r)/ n hechicero m

sordid /'sɔːdɪd/ a sórdido

sore /'sɔː(r)/ a (-er, -est) que duele, dolorido; (distressed) penoso; (vexed) enojado. —n llaga f. ~ly /'sɔːlɪ/ adv gravemente. ~ throat n dolor m de garganta. **I've got a ~ throat** me duele la garganta

sorrow /'sɔrəʊ/ n pena f, tristeza f. ~ful a triste

sorry /'sɒrɪ/ a (-ier, -ier) arrepentido; (wretched) lamentable; (sad) triste. **be ~** sentirlo; (repent) arrepentirse. **be ~ for s.o.** (pity) compadecerse de uno. **~!** ¡perdón!, ¡perdone!

sort /sɔːt/ n clase f; (person, fam) tipo m. **be out of ~s** estar indispuesto; (irritable) estar de mal humor. —vt clasificar. **~ out** (choose) escoger; (separate) separar; resolver (problem)

so-so /'səʊsəʊ/ a & adv regular

soufflé /'suːfleɪ/ n suflé m

sought /sɔːt/ see **seek**

soul /səʊl/ n alma f. ~ful /'səʊlfl/ a sentimental

sound[1] /saʊnd/ n sonido m; ruido m. —vt sonar; (test) sondar. —vi sonar; (seem) parecer (**as if** que)

sound[2] /saʊnd/ a (-er, -est) sano; (argument etc) lógico; (secure) seguro. **~ asleep** profundamente dormido

sound[3] /saʊnd/ n (strait) estrecho m

sound barrier /'saʊndbæriə(r)/ n barrera f del sonido

soundly /'saʊndlɪ/ adv sólidamente; (asleep) profundamente

sound: ~proof a insonorizado. **~track** n banda f sonora

soup /suːp/ n sopa f. **in the ~** (sl) en apuros

sour /'saʊə(r)/ a (-er, -est) agrio; (cream, milk) cortado. —vt agriar. —vi agriarse

source /sɔːs/ n fuente f

south /saʊθ/ n sur m. —a del sur. —adv hacia el sur. **S~ Africa** n Africa f del Sur. **S~ America** n América f (del Sur), Sudamérica f. **S~ American** a & n sudamericano (m). **~east** n sudeste m. **~erly** /'sʌðəlɪ/ a sur; (wind) del sur. **~ern** /'sʌðən/ a del sur, meridional. **~erner** n meridional m. **~ward** a sur; —adv hacia el sur. **~wards** adv hacia el sur. **~west** n sudoeste m

souvenir /suːvə'nɪə(r)/ n recuerdo m

sovereign /'sɒvrɪn/ n & a soberano (m). **~ty** n soberanía f

Soviet /'səʊvɪət/ a (history) soviético. **the ~ Union** n la Unión f Soviética

sow[1] /səʊ/ vt (pt **sowed**, pp **sowed** or **sown**) sembrar

sow[2] /saʊ/ n cerda f

soya /'sɔɪə/ n. **~ bean** n soja f

spa /spɑː/ n balneario m

space /speɪs/ n espacio m; (room) sitio m; (period) período m. —a (research etc) espacial. —vt espaciar. **~ out** espaciar. **~craft** /'speɪskrɑːft/ n, **~ship** n nave f espacial. **~suit** n traje m espacial

spacious /'speɪʃəs/ a espacioso

spade /speɪd/ n pala f. **~s** npl (cards) picos mpl, picas fpl; (in Spanish pack) espadas fpl. **~work** /'speɪdwɜːk/ n trabajo m preparatorio

spaghetti /spə'getɪ/ n espaguetis mpl

Spain /speɪn/ n España f

span[1] /spæn/ n (of arch) luz f; (of time) espacio m; (of wings) envergadura f. —vt (pt **spanned**) extenderse sobre

span[2] /spæn/ see **spick**

Spaniard /'spænjəd/ n español m

spaniel /'spænjəl/ *n* perro *m* de aguas

Spanish /'spænɪʃ/ *a* & *n* español (*m*)

spank /spæŋk/ *vt* dar un azote a. **~ing** *n* azote *m*

spanner /'spænə(r)/ *n* llave *f*

spar /spɑː(r)/ *vi* (*pt* **sparred**) entrenarse en el boxeo; (*argue*) disputar

spare /speə(r)/ *vt* salvar; (*do without*) prescindir de; (*afford to give*) dar; (*use with restraint*) escatimar. **—a** de reserva; (*surplus*) sobrante; (*person*) enjuto; (*meal etc*) frugal. **~ (part)** *n* repuesto *m*. **~ time** *n* tiempo *m* libre. **~ tyre** *n* neumático *m* de repuesto

sparing /'speərɪŋ/ *a* frugal. **~ly** *adv* frugalmente

spark /spɑːk/ *n* chispa *f*. **—vt.** **~ off** (*initiate*) provocar. **~ing-plug** *n* (*auto*) bujía *f*

sparkl|e /'spɑːkl/ *vi* centellear. **—** *n* centelleo *m*. **~ing** *a* centelleante; (*wine*) espumoso

sparrow /'spærəʊ/ *n* gorrión *m*

sparse /spɑːs/ *a* escaso; (*population*) poco denso. **~ly** *adv* escasamente

spartan /'spɑːtn/ *a* espartano

spasm /'spæzəm/ *n* espasmo *m*; (*of cough*) acceso *m*. **~odic** /spæz'mɒdɪk/ *a* espasmódico

spastic /'spæstɪk/ *n* víctima *f* de parálisis cerebral

spat /spæt/ *see* spit

spate /speɪt/ *n* avalancha *f*

spatial /'speɪʃl/ *a* espacial

spatter /'spætə(r)/ *vt* salpicar (**with** de)

spatula /'spætjʊlə/ *n* espátula *f*

spawn /spɔːn/ *n* hueva *f*. **—vt** engendrar. **—vi** desovar

speak /spiːk/ *vt/i* (*pt* **spoke**, *pp* **spoken**) hablar. **~ for** *vi* hablar en nombre de. **~ up** *vi* hablar más fuerte. **~er** /'spiːkə(r)/ *n* (*in*

public) orador *m*; (*loudspeaker*) altavoz *m*. **be a Spanish ~er** hablar español

spear /spɪə(r)/ *n* lanza *f*. **~head** /'spɪəhed/ *n* punta *f* de lanza. **—** *vt* (*lead*) encabezar. **~mint** /'spɪəmɪnt/ *n* menta *f* verde

spec /spek/ *n*. **on ~** (*fam*) por si acaso

special /'speʃl/ *a* especial. **~ist** /'speʃəlɪst/ *n* especialista *m* & *f*. **~ity** /-ɪ'ælɪtɪ/ *n* especialidad *f*. **~ization** /-'zeɪʃn/ *n* especialización *f*. **~ize** /'speʃəlaɪz/ *vi* especializarse. **~ized** *a* especializado. **~ty** *n* especialidad *f*. **~ly** *adv* especialmente

species /'spiːʃiːz/ *n* especie *f*

specific /spə'sɪfɪk/ *a* específico. **~ically** *adv* específicamente. **~ication** /-ɪ'keɪʃn/ *n* especificación *f*; (*details*) descripción *f*. **~y** /'spesɪfaɪ/ *vt* especificar

specimen /'spesɪmɪn/ *n* muestra *f*

speck /spek/ *n* manchita *f*; (*particle*) partícula *f*

speckled /'spekld/ *a* moteado

specs /speks/ *npl* (*fam*) gafas *fpl*, anteojos *mpl* (*LAm*)

spectac|le /'spektəkl/ *n* espectáculo *m*. **~les** *npl* gafas *fpl*, anteojos *mpl* (*LAm*). **~ular** /spek'tækjʊlə(r)/ *a* espectacular

spectator /spek'teɪtə(r)/ *n* espectador *m*

spectre /'spektə(r)/ *n* espectro *m*

spectrum /'spektrəm/ *n* (*pl* -**tra**) espectro *m*; (*of ideas*) gama *f*

speculat|e /'spekjʊleɪt/ *vi* especular. **~ion** /-'leɪʃn/ *n* especulación *f*. **~ive** /-lətɪv/ *a* especulativo. **~or** *n* especulador *m*

sped /sped/ *see* speed

speech /spiːtʃ/ *n* (*faculty*) habla *f*; (*address*) discurso *m*. **~less** *a* mudo

speed /spiːd/ n velocidad f; (rapidity) rapidez f; (haste) prisa f. ~vi (pt **speeded**) (drive too fast) ir a una velocidad excesiva. ~ **up** vt acelerar. —vi acelerarse. ~**boat** /'spiːdbəʊt/ n lancha f motora. ~**ily** adv rápidamente. ~**ing** n exceso m de velocidad. ~**ometer** /spiːˈdɒmɪtə(r)/ n velocímetro m. ~**way** /'spiːdweɪ/ n pista f; (Amer) autopista f. ~**y** /'spiːdɪ/ a (-ier, -iest) rápido

spell¹ /spel/ n (magic) hechizo m

spell² /spel/ vt/i (pt **spelled** or **spelt**) escribir; (mean) significar. ~ **out** vt deletrear; (fig) explicar. ~**ing** n ortografía f

spell³ /spel/ n (period) período m

spellbound /'spelbaʊnd/ a hechizado

spelt /spelt/ see **spell**²

spend /spend/ vt (pt **spent**) gastar; pasar (time etc); dedicar (care etc). —vi gastar dinero. ~**thrift** /'spendθrɪft/ n derrochador m

spent /spent/ see **spend**

sperm /spɜːm/ n (pl **sperms** or **sperm**) esperma f

spew /spjuː/ vt/i vomitar

sphere /sfɪə(r)/ n esfera f. ~**ical** /'sferɪkl/ a esférico

sphinx /sfɪŋks/ n esfinge f

spice /spaɪs/ n especia f; (fig) sabor m

spick /spɪk/ a. ~ **and span** impecable

spicy /'spaɪsɪ/ a picante

spider /'spaɪdə(r)/ n araña f

spik|e /spaɪk/ n (of metal etc) punta f. ~**y** a puntiagudo; (person) quisquilloso

spill /spɪl/ vt (pt **spilled** or **spilt**) derramar. —vi derramarse. ~ **over** desbordarse

spin /spɪn/ vt (pt **spun**, pres p **spinning**) hacer girar; hilar

(wool etc). —vi girar. —n vuelta f; (short drive) paseo m

spinach /'spɪnɪdʒ/ n espinacas fpl

spinal /'spaɪnl/ a espinal. ~ **cord** n médula f espinal

spindle /spɪndl/ n (for spinning) huso m. ~**y** a larguirucho

spin-drier /spɪn'draɪə(r)/ n secador m centrífugo

spine /spaɪn/ n columna f vertebral; (of book) lomo m. ~**less** a (fig) sin carácter

spinning /'spɪnɪŋ/ n hilado m. ~**top** n trompa f, peonza f. ~**wheel** n rueca f

spin-off /'spɪnɒf/ n beneficio m incidental; (by-product) subproducto m

spinster /'spɪnstə(r)/ n soltera f; (old maid, fam) solterona f

spiral /'spaɪərəl/ a espiral, helicoidal. —n hélice f. —vi (pt **spiralled**) moverse en espiral. ~ **staircase** n escalera f de caracol

spire /spaɪə(r)/ n (archit) aguja f

spirit /'spɪrɪt/ n espíritu m; (boldness) valor m. **in low ~s** abatido. —vt. ~ **away** hacer desaparecer. ~**ed** /'spɪrɪtɪd/ a animado, fogoso. ~**lamp** n lamparilla f de alcohol. ~**level** n nivel m de aire. ~**s** npl (drinks) bebidas fpl alcohólicas

spiritual /'spɪrɪtjʊəl/ a espiritual. —n canción f religiosa de los negros. ~**ualism** /-zəm/ n espiritismo m. ~**ualist** /'spɪrɪtjʊəlɪst/ n espiritista m & f

spit¹ /spɪt/ vt (pt **spat** or **spit**, pres p **spitting**) escupir. —vi escupir; (rain) lloviznar. —n esputo m; (spittle) saliva f

spit² /spɪt/ n (for roasting) asador m

spite /spaɪt/ n rencor m. **in ~ of** a pesar de. —vt fastidiar. ~**ful** a rencoroso. ~**fully** adv con rencor

spitting image /spɪtɪŋˈɪmɪdʒ/ n vivo retrato m

spittle /spɪtl/ n saliva f

splash /splæʃ/ vt salpicar. —vi esparcirse; ⟨person⟩ chapotear. —n salpicadura f; ⟨sound⟩ chapoteo m; ⟨of colour⟩ mancha f; ⟨drop, fam⟩ gota f. ~ **about** vi chapotear. ~ **down** vi ⟨spacecraft⟩ amerizar

spleen /spliːn/ n bazo m; (fig) esplín m

splendid /splendɪd/ a espléndido

splendour /splendə(r)/ n esplendor m

splint /splɪnt/ n tablilla f

splinter /splɪntə(r)/ n astilla f. —vi astillarse. ~ **group** n grupo m disidente

split /splɪt/ vt (pt **split**, pres p **splitting**) hender, rajar; ⟨tear⟩ rajar; ⟨divide⟩ dividir; ⟨share⟩ repartir. ~ **one's sides** caerse de risa. —vi partirse; ⟨divide⟩ dividirse. ~ **on s.o.** (sl) traicionar. —n hendidura f; ⟨tear⟩ desgarrón m; ⟨quarrel⟩ ruptura f; ⟨pol⟩ escisión f. ~ **up** vi separarse. ~ **second** n fracción f de segundo

splurge /splɜːdʒ/ vi (fam) derrochar

splutter /splʌtə(r)/ vi chisporrotear; ⟨person⟩ farfullar. —n chisporroteo m; ⟨speech⟩ farfulla f

spoil /spɔɪl/ vt (pt **spoilt** or **spoiled**) estropear, echar a perder; ⟨ruin⟩ arruinar; ⟨indulge⟩ mimar. —n botín m. ~s npl botín m. ~**sport** n aguafiestas m invar

spoke[1] /spəʊk/ see **speak**

spoke[2] /spəʊk/ n ⟨of wheel⟩ radio m

spoken /spəʊkən/ see **speak**

spokesman /spəʊksmən/ n (pl -**men**) portavoz m

spong|e /spʌndʒ/ n esponja f. —vt limpiar con una esponja. —vi. ~**e on** vivir a costa de. ~**e-cake** n bizcocho m. ~**er** /-ə(r)/ n gorrón m. ~**y** a esponjoso

sponsor /spɒnsə(r)/ n patrocinador m; ⟨surety⟩ garante m. —vt patrocinar. ~**ship** n patrocinio m

spontane|ity /spɒntəˈneɪtɪ/ n espontaneidad f. ~**ous** /spɒnˈteɪnjəs/ a espontáneo. ~**ously** adv espontáneamente

spoof /spuːf/ n (sl) parodia f

spooky /spuːkɪ/ a (-**ier**, -**iest**) (fam) escalofriante

spool /spuːl/ n carrete m; ⟨of sewing-machine⟩ canilla f

spoon /spuːn/ n cuchara f. ~**fed** a (fig) mimado. ~**feed** vt (pt -**fed**) dar de comer con cuchara. ~**ful** n (pl -**fuls**) cucharada f

sporadic /spəˈrædɪk/ a esporádico

sport /spɔːt/ n deporte m; ⟨amusement⟩ pasatiempo m; ⟨person, fam⟩ persona f alegre, buen chico m, buena chica f. **be a good** ~ ser buen perdedor. —vt lucir. ~**ing** a deportivo. ~**ing chance** n probabilidad f de éxito. ~**s car** n coche m deportivo. ~**s coat** n chaqueta f de sport. ~**sman** /spɔːtsmən/ n, (pl -**men**), ~**swoman** /spɔːts wʊmən/ n (pl -**women**) deportista m á f

spot /spɒt/ n mancha f; ⟨pimple⟩ grano m; ⟨place⟩ lugar m; ⟨in pattern⟩ punto m; ⟨drop⟩ gota f; ⟨a little, fam⟩ poquito m. **in a** ~ (fam) en un apuro. **on the** ~ n el lugar; ⟨without delay⟩ en el acto. —vt (pt **spotted**) manchar; ⟨notice, fam⟩ observar, ver. ~ **check** n control m hecho al azar. ~**less** a inmaculado. ~**light** /spɒtlaɪt/ n reflector m. ~**ted** a moteado; ⟨cloth⟩ a puntos. ~**ty**

a (-ier, -iest) manchado; ⟨skin⟩ con granos

spouse /spaʊz/ n cónyuge m & f

spout /spaʊt/ n pico m; ⟨jet⟩ chorro m. **up the** ~ ⟨ruined, sl⟩ perdido. —vi chorrear

sprain /spreɪn/ vt torcer. —n torcedura f

sprang /spræŋ/ see **spring**

sprat /spræt/ n espadín m

sprawl /sprɔːl/ vi ⟨person⟩ repanchigarse; ⟨city etc⟩ extenderse

spray /spreɪ/ n ⟨of flowers⟩ ramo m; ⟨water⟩ rociada f, ⟨from sea⟩ espuma f; ⟨device⟩ pulverizador m. —vt rociar. ~**gun** n pistola f pulverizadora

spread /spred/ vt ⟨pt **spread**⟩ ⟨stretch, extend⟩ extender; untar ⟨jam etc⟩; difundir ⟨idea, news⟩. —vi extenderse; ⟨disease⟩ propagarse; ⟨idea, news⟩ difundirse. —n extensión f; ⟨paste⟩ pasta f; ⟨of disease⟩ propagación f; ⟨feast, fam⟩ comilona f. ~**eagled** a con los brazos y piernas extendidos

spree /spriː/ n. **go on a** ~ ⟨have fun, fam⟩ ir de juerga

sprig /sprɪɡ/ n ramito m

sprightly /ˈspraɪtlɪ/ a (-ier, -iest) vivo

spring /sprɪŋ/ n ⟨season⟩ primavera f; ⟨device⟩ muelle m; ⟨elasticity⟩ elasticidad f; ⟨water⟩ manantial m. —a de primavera. —vt ⟨pt **sprang**, pp **sprung**⟩ hacer inesperadamente. —vi saltar; ⟨issue⟩ brotar. ~ **from** vi provenir de. ~ **up** vi surgir. ~**board** n trampolín m. ~**time** n primavera f. ~**y** a (-ier, -iest) elástico

sprinkle /ˈsprɪŋkl/ vt salpicar; ⟨with liquid⟩ rociar. —n salpicadura f; ⟨of liquid⟩ rociada f. ~**ed with** salpicado de. ~**er** /-ə(r)/ n regadera f. ~**ing**

/ˈsprɪŋklɪŋ/ n ⟨fig, amount⟩ poco m

sprint /sprɪnt/ n carrera f. —vi correr. ~**er** n corredor m

sprite /spraɪt/ n duende m, hada f

sprout /spraʊt/ vi brotar. —n brote m. **(Brussels)** ~**s** npl coles fpl de Bruselas

spruce /spruːs/ a elegante

sprung /sprʌŋ/ see **spring**. —a de muelles

spry /spraɪ/ a (**spryer**, **spryest**) vivo

spud /spʌd/ n ⟨sl⟩ patata f, papa f ⟨LAm⟩

spun /spʌn/ see **spin**

spur /spɜː(r)/ n espuela f; ⟨stimulus⟩ estímulo m. **on the** ~ **of the moment** impulsivamente. —vt ⟨pt **spurred**⟩. ~ **(on)** espolear; ⟨fig⟩ estimular

spurious /ˈspjʊərɪəs/ a falso. ~**ly** adv falsamente

spurn /spɜːn/ vt despreciar; ⟨reject⟩ rechazar

spurt /spɜːt/ vi chorrear; ⟨make sudden effort⟩ hacer un esfuerzo repentino. —n chorro m; ⟨effort⟩ esfuerzo m repentino

spy /spaɪ/ n espía m & f. —vt divisar. —vi espiar. ~ **out** vt reconocer. ~**ing** n espionaje m

squabble /ˈskwɒbl/ n riña f. —vi reñir

squad /skwɒd/ n ⟨mil⟩ pelotón m; ⟨of police⟩ brigada f; ⟨sport⟩ equipo m

squadron /ˈskwɒdrən/ n ⟨mil⟩ escuadrón m; ⟨naut, aviat⟩ escuadrilla f

squalid /ˈskwɒlɪd/ a asqueroso; ⟨wretched⟩ miserable

squall /skwɔːl/ n turbión m. —vi chillar. ~**y** a borrascoso

squalor /ˈskwɒlə(r)/ n miseria f

squander /ˈskwɒndə(r)/ vt derrochar

square /skweə(r)/ n cuadrado m; (open space in town) plaza f; (for drawing) escuadra f. —a cuadrado; (not owing) sin deudas, iguales; (honest) honrado; (meal) satisfactorio; (old-fashioned, sl) chapado a la antigua. **all ~ iguales.** —vt (settle) arreglar; (math) cuadrar. —vi (agree) cuadrar. **~ up to** enfrentarse con. **~ly** adv directamente

squash /skwɒʃ/ vt aplastar; (suppress) suprimir. —n apiñamiento m; (drink) zumo m; (sport) squash m. **~y** a blando

squat /skwɒt/ vi (pt squatted) ponerse en cuclillas; (occupy illegally) ocupar sin derecho. —n casa f ocupada sin derecho. —a (dumpy) achaparrado. **~ter** /-ə(r)/ n ocupante m & f ilegal

squawk /skwɔːk/ n graznido m. —vi graznar

squeak /skwiːk/ n chillido m; (of door etc) chirrido m. —vi chillar; (door etc) chirriar. **~y** a chirriador

squeal /skwiːl/ n chillido m. —vi chillar. **~ on** (inform on, sl) denunciar

squeamish /ˈskwiːmɪʃ/ a delicado; (scrupulous) escrupuloso. **be ~ about snakes** tener horror a las serpientes

squeeze /skwiːz/ vt apretar; exprimir (lemon etc); (extort) extorsionar (from de). —vi (force one's way) abrirse paso. —n estrujón m; (of hand) apretón m. **credit ~** n restricción f de crédito

squelch /skweltʃ/ vi chapotear. —n chapoteo m

squib /skwɪb/ n (firework) buscapiés m invar

squid /skwɪd/ n calamar m

squiggle /ˈskwɪgl/ n garabato m

squint /skwɪnt/ vi ser bizco; (look sideways) mirar de soslayo. —n estrabismo m

squire /ˈskwaɪə(r)/ n terrateniente m

squirm /skwɜːm/ vi retorcerse

squirrel /ˈskwɪrəl/ n ardilla f

squirt /skwɜːt/ vt arrojar a chorros. —vi salir a chorros. —n chorro m

St abbr (saint) /sənt/ S, San(to); (street) C/, Calle f

stab /stæb/ vt (pt stabbed) apuñalar. —n puñalada f; (pain) punzada f; (attempt, fam) tentativa f

stabili|ty /stəˈbɪlətɪ/ n estabilidad f. **~ze** /ˈsteɪbɪlaɪz/ vt estabilizar. **~zer** /-ə(r)/ n estabilizador m

stable[1] /ˈsteɪbl/ a (-er, -est) estable

stable[2] /ˈsteɪbl/ n cuadra f. —vt poner en una cuadra. **~-boy** n mozo m de cuadra

stack /stæk/ n montón m. —vt amontonar

stadium /ˈsteɪdjəm/ n estadio m

staff /stɑːf/ n (stick) palo m; (employees) personal m; (mil) estado m mayor; (in school) profesorado m. —vt proveer de personal

stag /stæg/ n ciervo m. **~party** n reunión f de hombres, fiesta f de despedida de soltero

stage /steɪdʒ/ n (in theatre) escena f; (phase) etapa f; (platform) plataforma f. **go on the ~** hacerse actor. —vt representar; (arrange) organizar. **~-coach** n (hist) diligencia f. **~ fright** n miedo m al público. **~-manager** n director m de escena. **~ whisper** n aparte m

stagger /ˈstægə(r)/ vi tambalearse. —vt asombrar; escalonar (holidays etc). —n tambaleo m. **~ing** a asombroso

stagna|nt /'stægnənt/ a estancado. **~te** /'stæg'neɪt/ vi estancarse. **~tion** /-ʃn/ n estancamiento m

staid /steɪd/ a serio, formal

stain /steɪn/ vt manchar; (*colour*) teñir. —n mancha f; (*liquid*) tinte m. **~ed glass window** n vidriera f de colores. **~less** /'steɪnlɪs/ a inmaculado. **~less steel** n acero m inoxidable. **~remover** n quitamanchas m invar

stair /steə(r)/ n escalón m. **~s** npl escalera f. **flight of ~s** tramo m de escalera. **~case** /'steəkeɪs/ n, **~way** n escalera f

stake /steɪk/ n estaca f; (*for execution*) hoguera f; (*wager*) apuesta f; (*com*) intereses mpl. **at ~** en juego. —vt estacar; (*wager*) apostar. **~ a claim** reclamar

stalactite /'stæləktaɪt/ n estalactita f

stalagmite /'stæləgmaɪt/ n estalagmita f

stale /steɪl/ a (-er, -est) no fresco; (*bread*) duro; (*smell*) viciado; (*news*) viejo; (*uninteresting*) gastado. **~mate** /'steɪlmeɪt/ n (*chess*) ahogado m; (*deadlock*) punto m muerto

stalk[1] /stɔːk/ n tallo m

stalk[2] /stɔːk/ vi andar majestuosamente. —vt seguir; (*animal*) acechar

stall[1] /stɔːl/ n (*stable*) cuadra f; (*in stable*) casilla f; (*in theatre*) butaca f; (*in market*) puesto m; (*kiosk*) quiosco m

stall[2] /stɔːl/ vi parar (*engine*). —vi (*engine*) pararse; (*fig*) andar con rodeos

stallion /'stælɪən/ n semental m

stalwart /'stɔːlwət/ n partidario m leal

stamina /'stæmɪnə/ n resistencia f

stammer /'stæmə(r)/ vi tartamudear. —n tartamudeo m

stamp /stæmp/ vt (*with feet*) patear; (*press*) estampar; poner un sello en (*envelope*); (*with rubber stamp*) sellar; (*fig*) señalar. —vi patear. —n sello m; (*with foot*) patada f; (*mark*) marca f, señal f. **~ out** (*fig*) acabar con

stampede /stæm'piːd/ n desbandada f; (*fam*) pánico m. —vi huir en desorden

stance /stɑːns/ n postura f

stand /stænd/ vi (*pt stood*) estar de pie; (*rise*) ponerse de pie; (*be*) encontrarse; (*stay firm*) mantenerse; (*pol*) presentarse como candidato (**for** en). **~ to reason** ser lógico. —vt (*endure*) soportar; (*place*) poner; (*offer*) ofrecer. **~ a chance** tener una posibilidad. **~ one's ground** mantenerse firme. **I'll ~ you a drink** te invito a una copa. —n posición f, postura f; (*mil*) resistencia f; (*for lamp etc*) pie m, sostén m; (*at market*) puesto m; (*booth*) quiosco m; (*sport*) tribuna f. **~ around** no hacer nada. **~ back** retroceder. **~ by** vi estar preparado. —vt (*support*) apoyar. **~ down** vi retirarse. **~ for** vt representar. **~ in for** suplir a. **~ out** destacarse. **~ up** vi ponerse de pie. **~ up for** defender. **~ up to** vt resistir a

standard /'stændəd/ n norma f; (*level*) nivel m; (*flag*) estandarte m. —a normal, corriente. **~ize** vt uniformar. **~ lamp** n lámpara f de pie. **~s** npl valores mpl

stand: **~by** n (*person*) reserva f; (*at airport*) lista f de espera. **~in** n suplente m & f. **~ing** /'stændɪŋ/ a de pie; (*upright*) derecho. —n posición f; (*duration*) duración f. **~offish** a (*fam*) frío. **~point** /'stændpɔɪnt/

n punto *m* de vista. ~**still**
/'stændstɪl/ *n.* **at a** ~**still**
parado. **come to a** ~**still**
pararse

stank /stæŋk/ *see* **stink**

staple[1] /'steɪpl/ *a* principal

staple[2] /'steɪpl/ *n* grapa *f.* —*vt*
sujetar con una grapa. ~**r** /-ə(r)/
n grapadora *f*

star /stɑː/ *n* (*incl cinema, theatre*)
estrella *f*; (*asterisk*) asterisco
m. —*vi* (*pt* **starred**) ser el
protagonista

starboard /'stɑːbəd/ *n* estribor *m*

starch /stɑːtʃ/ *n* almidón *m*; (*in
food*) fécula *f.* —*vt* almidonar.
~**y** *a* almidonado; (*food*) feculento; (*fig*) formal

stardom /'stɑːdəm/ *n* estrellato *m*

stare /steə(r)/ *n* mirada *f* fija. —
vi. ~ **at** mirar fijamente

starfish /'stɑːfɪʃ/ *n* estrella *f* de
mar

stark /stɑːk/ *a* (-**er, -est**) rígido;
(*utter*) completo. —*adv* completamente

starlight /'stɑːlaɪt/ *n* luz *f* de las
estrellas

starling /'stɑːlɪŋ/ *n* estornino *m*

starry /'stɑːrɪ/ *a* estrellado. ~-
eyed *a* (*fam*) ingenuo, idealista

start /stɑːt/ *vt* empezar; poner en
marcha ⟨*machine*⟩; (*cause*)
provocar. —*vi* empezar; (*jump*)
sobresaltarse; (*leave*) partir;
⟨*car etc*⟩ arrancar. —*n* principio
m; (*leaving*) salida *f*; (*sport*) ventaja *f*; (*jump*) susto *m.* ~**er** *n*
(*sport*) participante *m & f*; (*auto*)
motor *m* de arranque; (*culin*)
primer plato *m.* ~**ing-point** *n*
punto *m* de partida

startle /'stɑːtl/ *vt* asustar

starv|ation /stɑː'veɪʃn/ *n* hambre
f. ~**e** /stɑːv/ *vt* hacer morir de
hambre; (*deprive*) privar. —*vi*
morir de hambre

stash /stæʃ/ *vt* (*sl*) esconder

state /steɪt/ *n* estado *m*; (*grand
style*) pompa *f.* **S**~ *n* Estado *m*.
be in a ~ estar agitado. —*vt*
declarar; expresar ⟨*views*⟩; (*fix*)
fijar. —*a* del Estado; (*schol*) público; (*with ceremony*) de gala.
~**less** *a* sin patria

stately /'steɪtlɪ/ *a* (-**ier, -iest**)
majestuoso

statement /'steɪtmənt/ *n* declaración *f*; (*account*) informe *m*.
bank ~ *n* estado *m* de cuenta

stateroom /'steɪtrʊm/ *n* (*on ship*)
camarote *m*

statesman /'steɪtsmən/ *n* (*pl
-men*) estadista *m*

static /'stætɪk/ *a* inmóvil. ~**s** *n*
estática *f*; (*rad, TV*) parásitos
mpl atmosféricos, interferencias *fpl*

station /'steɪʃn/ *n* estación *f*; (*status*) posición *f* social. —*vt* colocar; (*mil*) estacionar

stationary /'steɪʃənrɪ/ *a* estacionario

stationer /'steɪʃənə(r)/ *n* papelero *m.* ~'**s (shop)** *n* papelería
f. ~**y** *n* artículos *mpl* de
escritorio

station-wagon /'steɪʃnwægən/ *n*
furgoneta *f*

statistic /stə'tɪstɪk/ *n* estadística
f. ~**al** /stə'tɪstɪkl/ *a* estadístico.
~**s** /stə'tɪstɪks/ *n* (*science*) estadística *f*

statue /'stætʃuː/ *n* estatua *f*.
~**sque** /-ʊ'esk/ *a* escultural.
~**tte** /-ʊ'et/ *n* figurilla *f*

stature /'stætʃə(r)/ *n* talla *f*, estatura *f*

status /'steɪtəs/ *n* posición *f*
social; (*prestige*) categoría *f*;
(*jurid*) estado *m*

statut|e /'stætʃuːt/ *n* estatuto *m*.
~**ory** /-ʊtrɪ/ *a* estatutario

staunch /stɔːnʃ/ *a* (-**er, -est**) leal.
~**ly** *adv* lealmente

stave /steɪv/ *n* (*mus*) pentagrama *m.* —*vt.* ~ **off** evitar

stay /steɪ/ n soporte m, sostén m; (of time) estancia f; (jurid) suspensión f. —vi quedar; (spend time) detenerse; (reside) alojarse. —vt matar ⟨hunger⟩. ~ **the course** terminar. ~ **in** quedar en casa. ~ **put** mantenerse firme. ~ **up** no acostarse. ~**ing-power** n resistencia f

stays /steɪz/ npl (old use) corsé m

stead /sted/ n. **in s.o.'s** ~ en lugar de uno. **stand s.o. in good** ~ ser útil a uno

steadfast /stedfɑːst/ a firme

steadily /stedɪlɪ/ adv firmemente; (regularly) regularmente. ~**y** /stedɪ/ a (-ier, -iest) firme; (regular) regular; (dependable) serio

steak /steɪk/ n filete m

steal /stiːl/ vt (pt stole, pp stolen) robar. ~ **the show** llevarse los aplausos. ~ **in** vi entrar a hurtadillas. ~ **out** vi salir a hurtadillas

stealth /stelθ/ n. **by** ~ sigilosamente. ~**y** a sigiloso

steam /stiːm/ n vapor m; (energy) energía f. —vt (cook) cocer al vapor; empañar ⟨window⟩. —vi echar vapor. ~ **ahead** (fam) hacer progresos. ~ **up** vi ⟨glass⟩ empañar. ~**engine** n máquina f de vapor. ~**er** /stiːmə(r)/ n (ship) barco m de vapor. ~**roller** /stiːmrəʊlə(r)/ n apisonadora f. ~**y** a húmedo

steel /stiːl/ n acero m. —vt. ~ **o.s.** fortalecerse. ~ **industry** n industria f siderúrgica. ~ **wool** n estropajo m de acero. ~**y** a acerado; (fig) duro, inflexible

steep /stiːp/ —a (-er, -est) escarpado; (price) (-est) exorbitante. —vt (soak) remojar. ~**ed in** (fig) empapado de

steeple /stiːpl/ n aguja f, campanario m. ~**chase** /stiːpltʃeɪs/ n carrera de obstáculos

steep: ~**ly** adv de modo empinado. ~**ness** n lo escarpado

steer /stɪə(r)/ vt guiar; gobernar ⟨ship⟩. —vi (in ship) gobernar. ~ **clear of** evitar. ~**ing** n (auto) dirección f. ~**ing-wheel** n volante m

stem /stem/ n tallo m; (of glass) pie m; (of word) raíz f; (of ship) roda f. —vt (pt **stemmed**) detener. —vi. ~ **from** provenir de

stench /stentʃ/ n hedor m

stencil /stensl/ n plantilla f; (for typing) cliché m. —vt (pt **stencilled**) estarcir

stenographer /stenɒgrəfə(r)/ n (Amer) estenógrafo m

step /step/ vi (pt **stepped**) ir. ~ **down** retirarse. ~ **in** entrar; (fig) intervenir. ~ **up** vt aumentar. ~ n paso m; (surface) escalón m; (fig) medida f. **in** ~ (fig) de acuerdo con. **out of** ~ (fig) en desacuerdo con. ~**brother** /stepbrʌðə(r)/ n hermanastro m. ~**daughter** n hijastra f. ~**father** n padrastro m. ~**ladder** n escalera f de tijeras. ~**mother** n madrastra f. ~**ping-stone** /stepɪŋstəʊn/ n pasadera f; (fig) escalón m. ~**sister** n hermanastra f. ~**son** n hijastro m

stereo /sterɪəʊ/ n (pl -os) cadena f estereofónica. —a estereofónico. ~**phonic** /sterɪəʊˈfɒnɪk/ a estereofónico. ~**type** /sterɪəʊtaɪp/ n estereotipo m. ~**typed** a estereotipado

sterile /steraɪl/ a estéril. ~**ity** /stəˈrɪlɪtɪ/ n esterilidad f. ~**ization** /-ˈzeɪʃn/ n esterilización f. ~**ize** /sterɪlaɪz/ vt esterilizar

sterling /stɜːlɪŋ/ n libras fpl esterlinas. —a (pound) esterlina; (fig) excelente. ~ **silver** n plata f de ley

stern[1] /stɜːn/ n (of boat) popa f

stern² /stɜ:n/ a (-er, -est) severo. ~ly adv severamente

stethoscope /'steθəskəʊp/ n estetoscopio m

stew /stju:/ vt/i guisar. —n guisado m. **in a ~** (fam) en un apuro

steward /stjʊəd/ n administrador m; (on ship, aircraft) camarero m. ~ess /-'des/ n camarera f; (on aircraft) azafata f

stick /stɪk/ n palo m; (for walking) bastón m; (of celery etc) tallo m. —vt (pt **stuck**) (glue) pegar; (put, fam) poner; (thrust) clavar; (endure, sl) soportar. —vi pegarse; (remain, fam) quedarse; (jam) bloquearse. ~ **at** (fam) perseverar en. ~ **out** sobresalir; (catch the eye, fam) resaltar. ~ **to** aferrarse a; cumplir (promise). ~ **up for** (fam) defender. ~er /'stɪkə(r)/ n pegatina f. ~ing-plaster n esparadrapo m. ~-in-the-mud n persona f chapada a la antigua

stickler /'stɪklə(r)/ n. **be a ~ for** insistir en

sticky /'stɪkɪ/ a (-ier, -iest) pegajoso; (label) engomado; (sl) difícil

stiff /stɪf/ a (-er, -est) rígido; (difficult) difícil; (manner) estirado; (drink) fuerte; (price) subido; (joint) tieso; (muscle) con agujetas. ~en /'stɪfn/ vt poner tieso. ~ly adv rígidamente. ~ **neck** n tortícolis f. ~ness n rigidez f

stifle /'staɪfl/ vt sofocar. ~ing a sofocante

stigma /'stɪgmə/ n (pl -as) estigma m. (pl **stigmata** /'stɪgmətə/) (relig) estigma m. ~**tize** vt estigmatizar

stile /staɪl/ n portillo m con escalones

stiletto /stɪ'letəʊ/ n (pl -os) estilete m. ~ **heels** npl tacones mpl aguja

still¹ /stɪl/ a inmóvil; (peaceful) tranquilo; (drink) sin gas. —n silencio m. —adv todavía; (nevertheless) sin embargo

still² /stɪl/ n (apparatus) alambique m

still: ~**born** a nacido muerto. ~ **life** n (pl -s) bodegón m. ~**ness** n tranquilidad f

stilted /'stɪltɪd/ a artificial

stilts /stɪlts/ npl zancos mpl

stimul|ant /'stɪmjʊlənt/ n estimulante m. ~**ate** /'stɪmjʊleɪt/ vt estimular. ~**ation** /-'leɪʃn/ n estímulo m. ~**us** /'stɪmjʊləs/ n (pl -li /-laɪ/) estímulo m

sting /stɪŋ/ n picadura f; (organ) aguijón m. —vt/i (pt **stung**) picar

stingi|ness /'stɪndʒɪnɪs/ n tacañería f. ~**y** /'stɪndʒɪ/ a (-ier, -iest) tacaño

stink /stɪŋk/ n hedor m. —vi (pt **stank** or **stunk**, pp **stunk**) oler mal. —vt. ~ **out** apestar (room). ~**er** /-ə(r)/ n (sl) problema m difícil; (person) mal bicho m

stint /stɪnt/ n (work) trabajo m. —vi. ~ **on** escatimar

stipple /'stɪpl/ vt puntear

stipulat|e /'stɪpjʊleɪt/ vt/i estipular. ~**ion** /-'leɪʃn/ n estipulación f

stir /stɜ:(r)/ vt (pt **stirred**) remover, agitar; (mix) mezclar; (stimulate) estimular. —vi moverse. —n agitación f; (commotion) conmoción f

stirrup /'stɪrəp/ n estribo m

stitch /stɪtʃ/ n (in sewing) puntada f; (in knitting) punto m; (pain) dolor m de costado; (med) punto m de sutura. **be in ~es** (fam) desternillarse de risa. —vt coser

stoat /stəʊt/ n armiño m

stock /stɒk/ n (com, supplies) existencias fpl; (com, variety) surtido *m*; (*livestock*) ganado *m*; (*lineage*) linaje *m*; (*finance*) acciones *fpl*; (*culin*) caldo *m*; (*plant*) alhelí *m*. **out of** ∼ agotado. **take** ∼ (*fig*) evaluar. —*a* corriente; (*fig*) trillado. —*vt* abastecer (**with** de). —*vi.* ∼ **up** abastecerse (**with** de). ∼**broker** /'stɒkbrəʊkə(r)/ *n* corredor *m* de bolsa. **S**∼ **Exchange** *n* bolsa *f*. **well**∼**ed** *a* bien provisto

stocking /'stɒkɪŋ/ *n* media *f*

stock: ∼**-in-trade** /stɒkɪntreɪd/ *n* existencias *fpl*. ∼**ist** /'stɒkɪst/ *n* distribuidor *m*. ∼**pile** /'stɒkpaɪl/ *n* reservas *fpl*. —*vt* acumular. ∼**still** *a* inmóvil. ∼**taking** *n* (*com*) inventario *m*

stocky /'stɒkɪ/ *a* (**-ier, -iest**) achaparrado

stodg|e /stɒdʒ/ *n* (*fam*) comida *f* pesada. ∼**y** *a* pesado

stoic /'stəʊɪk/ *n* estoico. ∼**al** *a* estoico. ∼**ally** *adv* estoicamente. ∼**ism** /-ɪsɪzəm/ *n* estoicismo *m*

stoke /stəʊk/ *vt* alimentar. ∼**r** /'stəʊkə(r)/ *n* fogonero *m*

stole[1] /stəʊl/ *see* **steal**

stole[2] /stəʊl/ *n* estola *f*

stolen /stəʊlən/ *see* **steal**

stolid /'stɒlɪd/ *a* impasible. ∼**ly** *adv* impasiblemente

stomach /'stʌmək/ *n* estómago *m*. —*vt* soportar. ∼**ache** *n* dolor *m* de estómago

ston|e /stəʊn/ *n* piedra *f*; (*med*) cálculo *m*; (*in fruit*) hueso *m*; (*weight, pl* **stone**) peso *m* de 14 libras (= *6,348 kg*). —*a* de piedra. —*vt* apedrear; deshuesar (*fruit*). ∼**e-deaf** *a* sordo como una tapia. ∼**emason** /'stəʊnmeɪsn/ *n* albañil *m*. ∼**ework** /'stəʊnwɜːk/ *n* cantería *f*. ∼**y** *a* pedregoso; (*like stone*) pétreo

stood /stʊd/ *see* **stand**

stooge /stuːdʒ/ *n* (*in theatre*) compañero *m*; (*underling*) lacayo *m*

stool /stuːl/ *n* taburete *m*

stoop /stuːp/ *vi* inclinarse; (*fig*) rebajarse. —*n.* **have a** ∼ ser cargado de espaldas

stop /stɒp/ *vt* (*pt* **stopped**) parar; (*cease*) terminar; tapar ⟨*a leak etc*⟩; (*prevent*) impedir; (*interrupt*) interrumpir. —*vi* pararse; (*stay, fam*) quedarse. —*n* (*bus etc*) parada *f*; (*gram*) punto *m*; (*mec*) tope *m*. ∼ **dead** *vi* pararse en seco. ∼**cock** /'stɒpkɒk/ *n* llave *f* de paso. ∼**gap** /'stɒpgæp/ *n* remedio *m* provisional. ∼**(-over)** *n* escala *f*. ∼**page** /'stɒpɪdʒ/ *n* parada *f*; (*of work*) paro *m*; (*interruption*) interrupción *f*; (*in pay*) interrupción *f*. ∼**per** /'stɒpə(r)/ *n* tapón *m*. ∼**-press** *n* noticias *fpl* de última hora. ∼ **light** *n* luz *f* de freno. ∼**-watch** *n* cronómetro *m*

storage /'stɔːrɪdʒ/ *n* almacenamiento *m*. ∼ **heater** *n* acumulador *m*. ∼ **in cold** ∼ almacenaje *m* frigorífico

store /stɔː(r)/ *n* provisión *f*; (*shop, depot*) almacén *m*; (*fig*) reserva *f*. **in** ∼ en reserva. **set** ∼ **by** dar importancia a. —*vt* (*for future*) poner en reserva; (*in warehouse*) almacenar. ∼ **up** acumular

storeroom /'stɔːruːm/ *n* despensa *f*

storey /'stɔːrɪ/ *n* (*pl* **-eys**) piso *m*

stork /stɔːk/ *n* cigüeña *f*

storm /stɔːm/ *n* tempestad *f*; (*mil*) asalto *m*. —*vi* rabiar. —*vt* (*mil*) asaltar. ∼**y** *a* tempestuoso

story /'stɔːrɪ/ *n* historia *f*; (*in newspaper*) artículo *m*; (*fam*) mentira *f*, cuento *m*. ∼**teller** *n* cuentista *m* & *f*

stout /staʊt/ *a* (**-er, -est**) (*fat*) gordo; (*brave*) valiente. —*n* cerveza *f* negra. ∼**ness** *n* corpulencia *f*

stove /stəʊv/ *n* estufa *f*

stow /stəʊ/ *vt* guardar; (*hide*) esconder. —*vi.* ∼ **away** viajar de polizón. ∼**away** /'stɔʊɔweɪ/ n polizón m

straddle /'strædl/ vt estar a horcajadas

straggle /'strægl/ vi rezagarse. ∼**y** a desordenado

straight /streɪt/ a (-er, -est) derecho, recto; (tidy) en orden; (frank) franco; (drink) solo, puro; (hair) lacio. —adv derecho; (direct) directamente; (without delay) inmediatamente. ∼ **on** todo recto. ∼ **out** sin vacilar. **go** ∼ enmendarse. —n recta f. ∼ **away** inmediatamente. ∼**en** /'streɪtn/ vt enderezar. —vi enderezarse. ∼**forward** /streɪt'fɔːwəd/ a franco; (easy) sencillo. ∼**forwardly** adv francamente. ∼**ness** n rectitud f

strain[1] /streɪn/ n (tension) tensión f; (injury) torcedura f. —vt estirar; (tire) cansar; (injure) torcer; (sieve) colar

strain[2] /streɪn/ n (lineage) linaje m; (streak) tendencia f

strained /streɪnd/ a forzado; (relations) tirante

strainer /'streɪnə(r)/ n colador m

strains /streɪnz/ npl (mus) acordes mpl

strait /streɪt/ n estrecho m. ∼**jacket** n camisa f de fuerza. ∼**laced** a remilgado, gazmoño. ∼**s** npl apuro m

strand /strænd/ n (thread) hebra f; (sand) playa f. —vi (ship) varar. **be** ∼**ed** quedarse sin recursos

strange /streɪndʒ/ a (-er, -est) extraño, raro; (not known) desconocido; (unaccustomed) nuevo. ∼**ly** adv extrañamente. ∼**ness** n extrañeza f. ∼**r** /'streɪndʒə(r)/ n desconocido m

strangle /'stræŋgl/ vt estrangular; (fig) ahogar. ∼**lehold** /'stræŋglhəʊld/ n (fig) dominio m

completo. ∼**ler** /-ə(r)/ n estrangulador m. ∼**ulation** /stræŋ gjʊ'leɪʃn/ n estrangulación f

strap /stræp/ n correa f. (of garment) tirante m. —vt (pt strapped) atar con correa; (flog) azotar

strapping /'stræpɪŋ/ a robusto

strata /'strɑːtə/ see **stratum**

stratagem /'strætədʒəm/ n estratagema f. ∼**egic** /strə'tiːdʒɪk/ a estratégico. ∼**egically** adv estratégicamente. ∼**egist** n estratega m & f. ∼**egy** /'strætədʒɪ/ n estrategia f

stratum /'strɑːtəm/ n (pl strata) estrato m

straw /strɔː/ n paja f. **the last** ∼ el colmo

strawberry /'strɔːbərɪ/ n fresa f

stray /streɪ/ vi vagar; (deviate) desviarse (from de). —a (animal) extraviado, callejero; (isolated) aislado. —n animal m extraviado, animal m callejero

streak /striːk/ n raya f; (of madness) vena f. —vt rayar. —vi moverse como un rayo. ∼**y** a (-ier, -iest) rayado; (bacon) entreverado

stream /striːm/ n arroyo m; (current) corriente f; (of people) desfile m; (schol) grupo m. —vi correr. ∼ **out** vi (people) salir en tropel

streamer /'striːmə(r)/ n (paper) serpentina f; (flag) gallardete m

streamline /'striːmlaɪn/ vt dar línea aerodinámica a; (simplify) simplificar. ∼**d** a aerodinámico

street /striːt/ n calle f. ∼**car** /'striːtkɑː/ n (Amer) tranvía m. ∼ **lamp** n farol m. ∼ **map** n, ∼ **plan** n plano m

strength /streŋθ/ n fuerza f; (of wall etc) solidez f. **on the** ∼ **of** a base de. ∼**en** /'streŋθn/ vt reforzar

strenuous /'strenjʊəs/ a enérgico; (*arduous*) arduo; (*tiring*) fatigoso. **~ly** *adv* enérgicamente

stress /stres/ n énfasis f; (*gram*) acento m; (*mec, med, tension*) tensión f. —vt insistir en

stretch /stretʃ/ vt estirar; (*extend*) extender; (*exaggerate*) forzar. **~ a point** hacer una excepción. —ví estirarse; (*extend*) extenderse. —n estirón m; (*period*) período m; (*of road*) tramo m. **at a ~** seguido; (*in one go*) de un tirón. **~er** /stretʃə(r)/ n camilla f

strew /struː/ vt (pt **strewed**, pp **strewn** or **strewed**) esparcir; (*cover*) cubrir

stricken /'strɪkən/ a. **~ with** afectado de

strict /strɪkt/ a (-er, -est) severo; (*precise*) estricto, preciso. **~ly** adv estrictamente. **~ly speaking** en rigor

stricture /'strɪktʃə(r)/ n crítica f; (*constriction*) constricción f

stride /straɪd/ vi (pt **strode**, pp **stridden**) andar a zancadas. —n zancada f. **take sth in one's ~** hacer algo con facilidad, tomarse las cosas con calma

strident /'straɪdnt/ a estridente

strife /straɪf/ n conflicto m

strike /straɪk/ vt (pt **struck**) golpear; encender (*match*); encontrar (*gold etc*); (*clock*) dar. —vi golpear; (*go on strike*) declararse en huelga; (*be on strike*) estar en huelga; (*attack*) atacar; (*clock*) dar la hora. —n (*of workers*) huelga f; (*attack*) ataque m; (*find*) descubrimiento m. **on ~** en huelga. **~ off, ~ out** tachar. **~ up a friendship** trabar amistad. **~r** /'straɪkə(r)/ n huelguista m & f

striking /'straɪkɪŋ/ a impresionante

string /strɪŋ/ n cuerda f; (*of lies, pearls*) sarta f. **pull ~s** tocar todos los resortes. —vt (pt **strung**) (*thread*) ensartar. **~ along** (*fam*) engañar. **~ out** extender(se). **~ed** a (*mus*) de cuerda

stringen|cy /'strɪndʒənsɪ/ n rigor m. **~t** /'strɪndʒənt/ a riguroso

stringy /'strɪŋɪ/ a fibroso

strip /strɪp/ vt (pt **stripped**) desnudar; (*tear away, deprive*) quitar; desmontar (*machine*). —vi desnudarse. —n tira f. **~ cartoon** n historieta f

stripe /straɪp/ n raya f; (*mil*) galón m. **~d** a a rayas, rayado

strip-: **~ light** n tubo m fluorescente. **~per** /-ə(r)/ n artista m & f de striptease. **~tease** n número m del desnudo, striptease m

strive /straɪv/ vi (pt **strove**, pp **striven**). **~ to** esforzarse por

strode /strəʊd/ see **stride**

stroke /strəʊk/ n golpe m; (*in swimming*) brazada f; (*med*) apoplejía f; (*of pen etc*) rasgo m; (*of clock*) campanada f; (*caress*) caricia f. —vt acariciar

stroll /strəʊl/ vi pasearse. —n paseo m

strong /strɒŋ/ a (-er, -est) fuerte. **~-box** n caja f fuerte. **~hold** /'strɒŋhəʊld/ n fortaleza f; (*fig*) baluarte m. **~ language** n palabras fpl fuertes, palabras fpl subidas de tono. **~ly** adv (*greatly*) fuertemente; (*with energy*) enérgicamente; (*deeply*) profundamente. **~ measures** npl medidas fpl enérgicas. **~-minded** a resuelto. **~-room** n cámara f acorazada

stroppy /'strɒpɪ/ a (sl) irascible

strove /strəʊv/ see **strive**

struck /strʌk/ see **strike**. **~ on** (sl) entusiasta de

structural /ˈstrʌktʃərəl/ a estructural. **~e** /ˈstrʌktʃə(r)/ n estructura f

struggle /ˈstrʌɡl/ vi luchar. **~ to one's feet** levantarse con dificultad. —n lucha f

strum /strʌm/ vt/i (pt **strummed**) rasguear

strung /strʌŋ/ see **string**. —a. **~ up** (tense) nervioso

strut /strʌt/ n puntal m; (walk) pavoneo m. —vi (pt **strutted**) pavonearse

stub /stʌb/ n cabo m; (counterfoil) talón m; (of cigarette) colilla f; (of tree) tocón m. —vt (pt **stubbed**). **~ out** apagar

stubble /ˈstʌbl/ n rastrojo m; (beard) barba f de varios días

stubborn /ˈstʌbən/ a terco. **~ly** adv tercamente. **~ness** n terquedad f

stubby /ˈstʌbɪ/ a (-ier, -iest) achaparrado

stucco /ˈstʌkəʊ/ n (pl -oes) estuco m

stuck /stʌk/ see **stick**. —a (jammed) bloqueado; (in difficulties) en un apuro. **~ on** (sl) encantado con. **~-up** a (sl) presumido

stud¹ /stʌd/ n tachón m; (for collar) botón m. —vt (pt **studded**) tachonar. **~ded with** sembrado de

stud² /stʌd/ n (of horses) caballeriza f

student /ˈstjuːdənt/ n estudiante m & f

studied /ˈstʌdɪd/ a deliberado

studio /ˈstjuːdɪəʊ/ n (pl -os) estudio m. **~ couch** n sofá m cama. **~ flat** n estudio m de artista

studious /ˈstjuːdɪəs/ a estudioso; (studied) deliberado. **~ly** adv estudiosamente; (carefully) cuidadosamente

study /ˈstʌdɪ/ n estudio m; (office) despacho m. —vt/i estudiar

stuff /stʌf/ n materia f, sustancia f; (sl) cosas fpl. —vt rellenar; disecar (animal); (cram) atiborrar; (block up) tapar; (put) meter de prisa. **~ing** n relleno m

stuffy /ˈstʌfɪ/ a (-ier, -iest) mal ventilado; (old-fashioned) chapado a la antigua

stumble /ˈstʌmbl/ vi tropezar. **~e across**, **~e on** tropezar con. —n tropezón m. **~ing-block** n tropiezo m, impedimento m

stump /stʌmp/ n cabo m; (of limb) muñón m; (of tree) tocón m. **~ed** /stʌmpt/ a (fam) perplejo. **~y** /ˈstʌmpɪ/ a (-ier, -iest) achaparrado

stun /stʌn/ vt (pt **stunned**) aturdir; (bewilder) pasmar. **~ning** a (fabulous, fam) estupendo

stung /stʌŋ/ see **sting**

stunk /stʌŋk/ see **stink**

stunt¹ /stʌnt/ n (fam) truco m publicitario

stunt² /stʌnt/ vt impedir el desarrollo de. **~ed** a enano

stupefy /ˈstjuːpɪfaɪ/ vt dejar estupefacto

stupendous /stjuːˈpendəs/ a estupendo. **~ly** adv estupendamente

stupid /ˈstjuːpɪd/ a estúpido. **~ity** /-ˈpɪdɪtɪ/ n estupidez f. **~ly** adv estúpidamente

stupor /ˈstjuːpə(r)/ n estupor m

sturd|iness /ˈstɜːdɪnɪs/ n robustez f. **~y** /ˈstɜːdɪ/ a (-ier, -iest) robusto

sturgeon /ˈstɜːdʒən/ n (pl **sturgeon**) esturión m

stutter /ˈstʌtə(r)/ vi tartamudear. —n tartamudeo m

sty¹ /staɪ/ n (pl **sties**) pocilga f

sty² /staɪ/ n, (pl **sties**) (med) orzuelo m

style /staɪl/ n estilo m; (fashion) moda f. **in ~** con todo lujo. —vt diseñar. **~ish** /ˈstaɪlɪʃ/ a elegante. ~ishly *adv* elegantemente. ~ist /'stailist/ *n* estilista *m & f*. hair ~ist *n* peluquero *m*. ~ized /'staɪlaɪzd/ *a* estilizado

stylus /'staɪləs/ *n* (*pl* -uses) aguja *f* (de tocadiscos)

suave /swɑ:v/ *a* (*pej*) zalamero

sub... /sʌb/ *pref* sub...

subaquatic /sʌbə'kwætɪk/ *a* subacuático

subconscious /sʌb'kɒnʃəs/ *a & n* subconsciente (*m*). ~**ly** *adv* de modo subconsciente

subcontinent /sʌb'kɒntɪnənt/ *n* subcontinente *m*

subcontract /sʌbkən'trækt/ *vt* subcontratar. ~**or** /-ə(r)/ *n* subcontratista *m & f*

subdivide /sʌbdɪ'vaɪd/ *vt* subdividir

subdue /səb'dju:/ *vt* dominar (*feelings*); sojuzgar (*country*). ~**d** *a* (*depressed*) abatido; (*light*) suave

subhuman /sʌb'hju:mən/ *a* infrahumano

subject /'sʌbdʒɪkt/ *a* sometido. ~ **to** sujeto a. —*n* súbdito *m*; (*theme*) asunto *m*; (*schol*) asignatura *f*; (*gram*) sujeto *m*; (*of painting, play, book etc*) tema *m*. /səb'dʒekt/ *vt* sojuzgar; (*submit*) someter. ~**ion** /-ʃn/ *n* sometimiento *m*

subjective /səb'dʒektɪv/ *a* subjetivo. ~**ly** *adv* subjetivamente

subjugate /'sʌbdʒugeɪt/ *vt* subyugar

subjunctive /səb'dʒʌŋktɪv/ *a & n* subjuntivo (*m*)

sublet /sʌb'let/ *vt* (*pt* sublet, *pres p* subletting) subarrendar

sublimate /'sʌblɪmeɪt/ *vt* sublimar. ~**ion** /-'meɪʃn/ *n* sublimación *f*

sublime /sə'blaɪm/ *a* sublime. ~**ly** *adv* sublimemente

submarine /sʌbmə'ri:n/ *n* submarino *m*

submerge /səb'mɜ:dʒ/ *vt* sumergir. —*vi* sumergirse

submi|**ssion** /səb'mɪʃn/ *n* sumisión *f*. ~**ssive** /-sɪv/ *a* sumiso. ~**t** /səb'mɪt/ *vt* (*pt* submitted) someter. —*vi* someterse

subordinat|**e** /sə'bɔ:dɪnət/ *a & n* subordinado (*m*). /sə'bɔ:dɪneɪt/ *vt* subordinar. ~**ion** /-'neɪʃn/ *n* subordinación *f*

subscri|**be** /səb'skraɪb/ *vi* suscribir. ~**be to** suscribir (*fund*); (*agree*) estar de acuerdo con; abonarse a (*newspaper*). ~**ber** /-ə(r)/ *n* abonado *m*. ~**ption** /-'rɪpʃn/ *n* suscripción *f*

subsequent /'sʌbsɪkwənt/ *a* subsiguiente. ~**ly** *adv* posteriormente

subservient /səb'sɜ:vjənt/ *a* servil

subside /səb'saɪd/ *vi* (*land*) hundirse; (*flood*) bajar; (*storm, wind*) amainar. ~**nce** *n* hundimiento *m*

subsidiary /səb'sɪdɪərɪ/ *a* subsidiario. —*n* (*com*) sucursal *m*

subsid|**ize** /'sʌbsɪdaɪz/ *vt* subvencionar. ~**y** /'sʌbsədɪ/ *n* subvención *f*

subsist /səb'sɪst/ *vi* subsistir. ~**ence** *n* subsistencia *f*

subsoil /'sʌbsɔɪl/ *n* subsuelo *m*

subsonic /sʌb'sɒnɪk/ *a* subsónico

substance /'sʌbstəns/ *n* substancia *f*

substandard /sʌb'stændəd/ *a* inferior

substantial /səb'stænʃl/ *a* sólido; (*meal*) substancial; (*considerable*) considerable. ~**ly** *adv* considerablemente

substantiate /səb'stænʃɪeɪt/ *vt* justificar

substitut|**e** /'sʌbstɪtju:t/ *n* substituto *m*. —*vt/i* substituir. ~**ion** /-'tju:ʃn/ *n* substitución *f*

subterfuge /ˈsʌbtəfjuːdʒ/ n subterfugio m

subterranean /sʌbtəˈreɪnjən/ a subterráneo

subtitle /ˈsʌbtaɪtl/ n subtítulo m

subtle /ˈsʌtl/ a (-er, -est) sutil. **~ty** n sutileza f

subtract /səbˈtrækt/ vt restar. **~ion** /-ʃn/ n resta f

suburb /ˈsʌbɜːb/ n barrio m. **the ~s** las afueras fpl. **~an** /səˈbɜːbən/ a suburbano. **~ia** /səˈbɜːbɪə/ n las afueras fpl

subvention /səbˈvenʃn/ n subvención f

subver|sion /səbˈvɜːʃn/ n subversión f. **~sive** /səbˈvɜːsɪv/ a subversivo. **~t** /səbˈvɜːt/ vt subvertir

subway /ˈsʌbweɪ/ n paso m subterráneo; (Amer) metro m

succeed /səkˈsiːd/ vi tener éxito. —vt suceder a. **~ in doing** lograr hacer. **~ing** a sucesivo

success /səkˈses/ n éxito m. **~ful** a que tiene éxito; (chosen) elegido

succession /səkˈseʃn/ n sucesión f. **in ~** sucesivamente, seguidos

successive /səkˈsesɪv/ a sucesivo. **~ly** adv sucesivamente

successor /səkˈsesə(r)/ n sucesor m

succinct /səkˈsɪŋkt/ a sucinto

succour /ˈsʌkə(r)/ vt socorrer. — n socorro m

succulent /ˈsʌkjʊlənt/ a suculento

succumb /səˈkʌm/ vi sucumbir

such /sʌtʃ/ a tal. —pron los que, las que; (so much) tanto. **and ~** y tal. —adv tan. **~ a big house** una casa tan grande. **~ and ~** tal o cual. **~ as it is** tal como es. **~like** a (fam) semejante, de ese tipo

suck /sʌk/ vt chupar; sorber (liquid). **~ up** absorber. **~ up to**

(sl) dar coba a. **~er** /ˈsʌkə(r)/ n (plant) chupón m; (person, fam) primo m

suckle /ˈsʌkl/ vt amamantar

suction /ˈsʌkʃn/ n succión f

sudden /ˈsʌdn/ a repentino. **all of a ~** de repente. **~ly** adv de repente. **~ness** n lo repentino

suds /sʌdz/ npl espuma f (de jabón)

sue /suː/ vt (pres p suing) demandar (for por)

suede /sweɪd/ n ante m

suet /ˈsuːɪt/ n sebo m

suffer /ˈsʌfə(r)/ vt sufrir; (tolerate) tolerar. —vi sufrir. **~ance** /ˈsʌfərəns/ n. **on ~ance** por tolerancia. **~ing** n sufrimiento m

suffice /səˈfaɪs/ vi bastar. **~iency** /səˈfɪʃənsɪ/ n suficiencia f. **~ient** /səˈfɪʃnt/ a suficiente; (enough) bastante. **~iently** adv suficientemente, bastante

suffix /ˈsʌfɪks/ n (pl -ixes) sufijo m

suffocat|e /ˈsʌfəkeɪt/ vt ahogar. —vi ahogarse. **~ion** /-ˈkeɪʃn/ n asfixia f

sugar /ˈʃʊɡə(r)/ n azúcar m & f. — vt azucarar. **~-bowl** n azucarero m. **~ lump** n terrón m de azúcar. **~y** a azucarado.

suggest /səˈdʒest/ vt sugerir. **~ible** /səˈdʒestɪbl/ a sugestionable. **~ion** /-tʃən/ n sugerencia f; (trace) traza f. **~ive** /səˈdʒestɪv/ a sugestivo. **be ~ive of** evocar, recordar. **~ively** adv sugestivamente

suicid|al /suːɪˈsaɪdl/ a suicida. **~e** /ˈsuːɪsaɪd/ n suicidio m; (person) suicida m & f. **commit ~e** suicidarse

suit /suːt/ n traje m; (woman's) traje m de chaqueta; (cards) palo m; (jurid) pleito m. —vt convenir; (clothes) sentar bien a; (adapt) adaptar. **be ~ed for** ser apto para. **~ability** *n* conveniencia *f*. **~able** *a* adecuado. **~ably** *adv* convenientemente. **~case** /'suːtkeɪs/ *n* maleta *f*, valija *f* (*LAm*)

suite /swiːt/ *n* (*of furniture*) juego *m*; (*of rooms*) apartamento *m*; (*retinue*) séquito *m*

suitor /'suːtə(r)/ *n* pretendiente *m*

sulk /sʌlk/ *vi* enfurruñarse. **~s** *npl* enfurruñamiento *m*. **~y** *a* enfurruñado

sullen /'sʌlən/ *a* resentido. **~ly** *adv* con resentimiento

sully /'sʌlɪ/ *vt* manchar

sulphur /'sʌlfə(r)/ *n* azufre *m*. **~ic** /-'fjʊərɪk/ *a* sulfúrico. **~ic acid** *n* ácido *m* sulfúrico

sultan /'sʌltən/ *n* sultán *m*

sultana /sʌl'tɑːnə/ *n* pasa *f* gorrona

sultry /'sʌltrɪ/ *a* (**-ier, -iest**) (*weather*) bochornoso; (*fig*) sensual

sum /sʌm/ *n* suma *f*. **~** *vt* (*pt* **summed**). **~ up** resumir (*situation*); (*assess*) evaluar

summar|ily /'sʌmərɪlɪ/ *adv* sumariamente. **~ize** *vt* resumir. **~y** /'sʌmərɪ/ *a* sumario. **~n** resumen *m*

summer /'sʌmə(r)/ *n* verano *m*. **~-house** *n* glorieta *f*, cenador *m*. **~time** *n* verano *m*. **~ time** *n* hora *f* de verano. **~y** *a* veraniego

summit /'sʌmɪt/ *n* cumbre *f*. **~ conference** *n* conferencia *f* cumbre

summon /'sʌmən/ *vt* llamar; convocar (*meeting, s.o. to meeting*); (*jurid*) citar. **~ up** armarse de. **~s** /'sʌmənz/ *n* llamada *f*; (*jurid*) citación *f*. **~** *vt* citar

sump /sʌmp/ *n* (*mec*) cárter *m*

sumptuous /'sʌmptjʊəs/ *a* suntuoso. **~ly** *adv* suntuosamente

sun /sʌn/ *n* sol *m*. **~** *vt* (*pt* **sunned**). **~ o.s.** tomar el sol.

~bathe /'sʌnbeɪð/ *vi* tomar el sol. **~beam** /'sʌnbiːm/ *n* rayo *m* de sol. **~burn** /'sʌnbɜːn/ *n* quemadura *f* de sol. **~burnt** *a* quemado por el sol

sundae /'sʌndeɪ/ *n* helado *m* con frutas y nueces

Sunday /'sʌndeɪ/ *n* domingo *m*. **~ school** *n* catequesis *f*

sun: **~dial** /'sʌndaɪl/ *n* reloj *m* de sol. **~down** /'sʌndaʊn/ *n* puesta *f* del sol

sundry /'sʌndrɪ/ *a* diversos. **all and ~** todo el mundo. **sundries** *npl* artículos *mpl* diversos

sunflower /'sʌnflaʊə(r)/ *n* girasol *m*

sung /sʌŋ/ *see* **sing**

sun-glasses /'sʌnglɑːsɪz/ *npl* gafas *fpl* de sol

sunk /sʌŋk/ *see* **sink**. **~en** /'sʌŋkən/ **—a** hundido

sunlight /'sʌnlaɪt/ *n* luz *f* del sol

sunny /'sʌnɪ/ *a* (**-ier, -iest**) (*day*) de sol; (*place*) soleado. **it is ~** hace sol

sun: **~rise** /'sʌnraɪz/ *n* amanecer *m*, salida *f* del sol. **~roof** *n* techo *m* corredizo. **~set** /'sʌnset/ *n* puesta *f* del sol. **~shade** /'sʌnʃeɪd/ *n* quitasol *m*, sombrilla *f*; (*awning*) toldo *m*. **~shine** /'sʌnʃaɪn/ *n* sol *m*. **~spot** /'sʌnspɒt/ *n* mancha *f* solar. **~stroke** /'sʌnstrəʊk/ *n* insolación *f*. **~tan** *n* bronceado *m*. **~tanned** *a* bronceado. **~tan lotion** *n* bronceador *m*

sup /sʌp/ *vt* (*pt* **supped**) sorber

super /'suːpə(r)/ *a* (*fam*) estupendo

superannuation /suːpərænjʊ'eɪʃn/ *n* jubilación *f*

superb /suː'pɜːb/ *a* espléndido. **~ly** *adv* espléndidamente

supercilious /suːpə'sɪlɪəs/ *a* desdeñoso

superficial /suːpəˈfɪʃl/ a superficial. **~ity** /-ˈælətɪ/ n superficialidad f. **~ly** adv superficialmente

superfluous /suːˈpɜːfluːəs/ a superfluo

superhuman /suːpəˈhjuːmən/ a sobrehumano

superimpose /suːpərɪmˈpəʊz/ vt sobreponer

superintend /suːpərɪnˈtend/ vt vigilar. **~ence** n dirección f. **~ent** n director m; (of police) comisario m

superior /suːˈpɪərɪə(r)/ a & n superior (m). **~ity** /-ˈɒrətɪ/ n superioridad f

superlative /suːˈpɜːlətɪv/ a & n superlativo (m)

superman /ˈsuːpəmæn/ n (pl -men) superhombre m

supermarket /ˈsuːpəmɑːkɪt/ n supermercado m

supernatural /suːpəˈnætʃrəl/ a sobrenatural

superpower /ˈsuːpəpaʊə(r)/ n superpotencia f

supersede /suːpəˈsiːd/ vt reemplazar, suplantar

supersonic /suːpəˈsɒnɪk/ a supersónico

superstition /suːpəˈstɪʃn/ n superstición f. **~us** a supersticioso

superstructure /ˈsuːpəstrʌktʃə(r)/ n superestructura f

supertanker /ˈsuːpətæŋkə(r)/ n petrolero m gigante

supervene /suːpəˈviːn/ vi sobrevenir

supervise /ˈsuːpəvaɪz/ vt supervisar. **~ion** /-ˈvɪʒn/ n supervisión f. **~or** /-ɪzə(r)/ n supervisor m. **~ory** a de supervisión

supper /ˈsʌpə(r)/ n cena f.

supplant /səˈplɑːnt/ vt suplantar

supple /ˈsʌpl/ a flexible. **~ness** n flexibilidad f

supplement /ˈsʌplɪmənt/ n suplemento m. **~vt** completar; (increase) aumentar. **~ary** /-ˈmentərɪ/ a suplementario

supplier /səˈplaɪə(r)/ n suministrador m; (com) proveedor m. **~y** /səˈplaɪ/ vt proveer; (feed) alimentar; satisfacer (a need). **~y** with abastece de. **—n** provisión f, suministro m. **~y and demand** oferta f y demanda

support /səˈpɔːt/ vt sostener; (endure) soportar, aguantar; (fig) apoyar. **—n** apoyo m, (tec) soporte m. **~er** /-ə(r)/ n soporte m, (sport) seguidor m, hincha m & f. **~ive** a alentador

suppose /səˈpəʊz/ vt suponer; (think) creer. **be ~ed to** deber. **not be ~ed to** (fam) no tener permiso para, no tener derecho a. **~edly** adv según cabe suponer; (before adjective) presuntamente. **~ition** /sʌpəˈzɪʃn/ n suposición f

suppository /səˈpɒzɪtərɪ/ n supositorio m

suppress /səˈpres/ vt suprimir. **~ion** n supresión f. **~or** /-ə(r)/ n supresor m

supremacy /suːˈpreməsɪ/ n supremacía f. **~e** /suːˈpriːm/ a supremo

surcharge /ˈsɜːtʃɑːdʒ/ n sobreprecio m; (tax) recargo m

sure /ʃʊə(r)/ a (-er, -est) seguro, cierto. **make ~** asegurarse. —adv (Amer, fam) ¡claro! **~ enough** efectivamente. **~footed** a de pie firme. **~ly** adv seguramente

surety /ˈʃʊərətɪ/ n garantía f

surf /sɜːf/ n oleaje m; (foam) espuma f

surface /ˈsɜːfɪs/ n superficie f. —a superficial, de la superficie. —vt (smoothe) alisar; (cover) recubrir (with de). —vi salir a la superficie; (emerge) emerger. ∼ mail n por via marítima

surfboard /'sɜːfbɔːd/ n tabla f de surf

surfeit /'sɜːfɪt/ n exceso m

surfing /'sɜːfɪŋ/ n, **surf-riding** /'sɜːfraɪdɪŋ/ n mar m

surge /sɜːdʒ/ vi (crowd) moverse en tropel; (waves) encresparse. —n oleada f; (elec) sobretensión f

surgeon /'sɜːdʒən/ n cirujano m

surgery /'sɜːdʒərɪ/ n cirugía f; (consulting room) consultorio m; (consulting hours) horas fpl de consulta

surgical /'sɜːrdʒɪkl/ a quirúrgico

surl|iness /'sɜːlɪnɪs/ n aspereza f. ∼y /'sɜːlɪ/ a (-ier, -iest) áspero

surmise /sə'maɪz/ vt conjeturar

surmount /sə'maʊnt/ vt superar

surname /'sɜːneɪm/ n apellido m

surpass /sə'pɑːs/ vt sobrepasar, exceder

surplus /'sɜːpləs/ a & n excedente (m)

surpris|e /sə'praɪz/ n sorpresa f. —vt sorprender. ∼ing a sorprendente. ∼ingly adv asombrosamente

surrealis|m /sə'rɪəlɪzəm/ n surrealismo m. ∼t n surrealista m & f

surrender /sə'rendə(r)/ vt entregar. —vi entregarse. —n entrega f; (mil) rendición f

surreptitious /sʌrəp'tɪʃəs/ a clandestino

surrogate /'sʌrəgət/ n substituto m

surround /sə'raʊnd/ vt rodear; (mil) cercar. —n borde m. ∼ing a circundante. ∼ings npl alrededores mpl

surveillance /sɜː'veɪləns/ n vigilancia f

survey /'sɜːveɪ/ n inspección f; (report) informe m; (general view) vista f de conjunto. /sə'veɪ/

vt examinar, inspeccionar; (inquire into) hacer una encuesta de. ∼or n topógrafo m, agrimensor m

surviv|al /sə'vaɪvl/ n supervivencia f. ∼e /sə'vaɪv/ vt/i sobrevivir. ∼or /-ə(r)/ n superviviente m & f

susceptib|ility /səseptə'bɪlətɪ/ n susceptibilidad f. ∼le /sə'septəbl/ a susceptible. ∼le to propenso a

suspect /sə'spekt/ vt sospechar. /'sʌspekt/ a & n sospechoso (m)

suspend /sə'spend/ vt suspender. ∼er /sə'spendə(r)/ n liga f. ∼er belt n liguero m. ∼ers npl (Amer) tirantes mpl

suspense /sə'spens/ n incertidumbre f; (in film etc) suspense m

suspension /sə'spenʃn/ n suspensión f. ∼ bridge n puente m colgante

suspicion /sə'spɪʃn/ n sospecha f; (trace) pizca f

suspicious /sə'spɪʃəs/ a desconfiado; (causing suspicion) sospechoso

sustain /sə'steɪn/ vt sostener; (suffer) sufrir

sustenance /'sʌstɪnəns/ n sustento m

svelte /svelt/ a esbelto

SW abbr (south-west) sudoeste m

swab /swɒb/ n (med) tapón m

swagger /'swægə(r)/ vi pavonearse

swallow[1] /'swɒləʊ/ vt/i tragar. —n trago m. ∼ **up** tragar; consumir (savings etc)

swallow[2] /'swɒləʊ/ n (bird) golondrina f

swam /swæm/ see swim

swamp /swɒmp/ n pantano m. —vt inundar; (with work) agobiar. ∼y a pantanoso

swan /swɒn/ n cisne m

swank /swæŋk/ n (fam) ostentación f. —vi (fam) fanfarronear

swap /swɒp/ vt/i (pt **swapped**) (fam) (inter)cambiar. —n (fam) (inter)cambio m

swarm /swɔːm/ n enjambre m. —vi ‹bees› enjambrar; (fig) hormiguear

swarthy /ˈswɔːðɪ/ a (-ier, -iest) moreno

swastika /ˈswɒstɪkə/ n cruz f gamada

swat /swɒt/ vt (pt **swatted**) aplastar

sway /sweɪ/ vi balancearse. —vt (influence) influir en. —n balanceo m; (rule) imperio m

swear /sweə(r)/ vt/i (pt **swore**, pp **sworn**) jurar. ~ **by** (fam) creer ciegamente en. ~**word** n palabrota f

sweat /swet/ n sudor m. —vi sudar

sweat|er /ˈswetə(r)/ n jersey m. ~**shirt** n sudadera f

swede /swiːd/ n naba f

Swede /swiːd/ n sueco m

Sweden /ˈswiːdn/ n Suecia f

Swedish /ˈswiːdɪʃ/ a & n sueco (m)

sweep /swiːp/ vt (pt **swept**) barrer; deshollinar ‹chimney›. ~ **the board** ganar todo. —vi barrer; ‹road› extenderse; (go majestically) moverse majestuosamente. —n barrido m; (curve) curva f; (movement) movimiento m; (person) deshollinador m. ~ **away** vt barrer. ~**ing** n (gesture) amplio; ‹changes etc› radical; ‹statement› demasiado general. ~**stake** /ˈswiːpsteɪk/ n lotería f

sweet /swiːt/ a (-er, -est) dulce; (fragrant) fragante; (pleasant) agradable. **have a ~ tooth** ser dulcero. —n caramelo m; (dish) postre m. ~**bread** /ˈswiːtbred/ n lechecillas fpl. ~**en** /ˈswiːtn/ vt

endulzar. ~**ener** /-ə(r)/ n dulcificante m. ~**heart** /ˈswiːthɑːt/ n amor m. ~**ly** adv dulcemente. ~**ness** n dulzura f. ~ **pea** n guisante m de olor

swell /swel/ vt (pt **swelled**, pp **swollen** or **swelled**) hinchar; (increase) aumentar. —vi hincharse; (increase) aumentarse; ‹river› crecer. —a (fam) estupendo. —n (of sea) oleaje m. ~**ing** n hinchazón m.

swelter /ˈsweltə(r)/ vi sofocarse de calor

swept /swept/ see **sweep**

swerve /swɜːv/ vi desviarse

swift /swɪft/ a (-er, -est) rápido. —n (bird) vencejo m. ~**ly** adv rápidamente. ~**ness** n rapidez f

swig /swɪg/ vt (pt **swigged**) (fam) beber a grandes tragos. —n (fam) trago m

swill /swɪl/ vt enjuagar; (drink) beber a grandes tragos. —n (food for pigs) bazofia f

swim /swɪm/ vi (pt **swam**, pp **swum**) nadar; ‹room, head› dar vueltas. —n baño m. ~**mer** n nadador m. ~**ming-bath** n piscina f. ~**mingly** /ˈswɪmɪŋlɪ/ adv a las mil maravillas. ~**ming-pool** n piscina f. ~**ming-trunks** npl bañador m. ~**suit** n traje m de baño

swindle /ˈswɪndl/ vt estafar. —n estafa f. ~**r** /-ə(r)/ n estafador m

swine /swaɪn/ npl cerdos mpl. —n (pl **swine**) (person, fam) canalla m

swing /swɪŋ/ vt (pt **swung**) balancear. —vi oscilar; (person) balancearse; (turn round) girar. —n balanceo m, vaivén m; (seat) columpio m; (mus) ritmo m. **in full ~** en plena actividad. ~ **bridge** n puente m giratorio

swingeing /ˈswɪndʒɪŋ/ a enorme

swipe   581   ~system

swipe /swaɪp/ vt golpear;   sympath|etic /sɪmpə'θetɪk/ a
(snatch, sl) birlar. —n (fam)   comprensivo; (showing pity)
golpe m   compasivo. ~ize /-aɪz/ vi com-
swirl /swɜ:l/ vi arremolinarse. —   prender; (pity) compadecerse
n remolino m   (with de). ~izer n (pol) sim-
swish /swɪʃ/ vt silbar. —a (fam)   patizante m & f. ~y /'sɪmpəθɪ/ n
elegante   comprensión f; (pity) compasión
Swiss /swɪs/ a & n suizo (m). ~   f; (condolences) pésame m. be in
roll n bizcocho m enrollado   ~y with estar de acuerdo con
switch /swɪtʃ/ n (elec) inte-   symphon|ic /sɪm'fɒnɪk/ a sin-
rruptor m; (change) cambio   fónico. ~y /'sɪmfənɪ/ n sinfonía f
m. —vt cambiar; (deviate)   symposium /sɪm'pəʊziəm/ n (pl
desviar. ~ off (elec) desconectar;   -ia) simposio m
apagar (light). ~ on (elec)   symptom /'sɪmptəm/ n síntoma
encender; arrancar (engine).   m. ~atic /-'mætɪk/ a sintomático
~back /'swɪtʃbæk/ n montaña f   synagogue /'sɪnəgɒg/ n sinagoga
rusa. ~board /'swɪtʃbɔ:d/ n   f
centralita f   synchroniz|ation /sɪnkrənaɪ-
Switzerland /'swɪtsələnd/ n   'zeɪʃn/ n sincronización f. ~e
Suiza f   /'sɪnkrənaɪz/ vt sincronizar
swivel /'swɪvl/ —vi (pt swiv-   syncopat|e /'sɪnkəpeɪt/ vt sin-
elled) girar   copar. ~ion /-'peɪʃn/ n síncopa f
swollen /'swəʊlən/ see swell. —a   syndicate /'sɪndɪkət/ n sindicato
hinchado   m
swoon /swu:n/ vi desmayarse   syndrome /'sɪndrəʊm/ n sín-
swoop /swu:p/ vi (bird) calarse;   drome m
(plane) bajar en picado. —n ca-   synod /'sɪnəd/ n sínodo m
lada f; (by police) redada f   synonym /'sɪnənɪm/ n sinónimo
sword /sɔ:d/ n espada f. ~fish   m. ~ous /-'nɒnɪməs/ a sinónimo
/'sɔ:dfɪʃ/ n pez m espada   synopsis /sɪ'nɒpsɪs/ n (pl -opses
swore /swɔ:(r)/ see swear   /-si:z/) sinopsis f, resumen m
sworn /swɔ:n/ see swear. —a   syntax /'sɪntæks/ n sintaxis f
(enemy) jurado; (friend) leal   invar
swot /swɒt/ vt/i (pt swotted)   synthesi|s /'sɪnθəsɪs/ n (pl
(schol, sl) empollar. —n (schol,   -theses /-si:z/) síntesis f. ~ze vt
sl) empollón m   sintetizar
swum /swʌm/ see swim   synthetic /sɪn'θetɪk/ a sintético
swung /swʌŋ/ see swing   syphilis /'sɪfɪlɪs/ n sífilis f
sycamore /'sɪkəmɔ:(r)/ n plátano   Syria /'sɪrɪə/ n Siria f. ~n a & n
m falso   sirio (m)
syllable /'sɪləbl/ n sílaba f   syringe /'sɪrɪndʒ/ n jeringa f. —
syllabus /'sɪləbəs/ n (pl -buses)   vt jeringar
programa m (de estudios)   syrup /'sɪrəp/ n jarabe m, almí-
symbol /'sɪmbl/ n símbolo m.   bar m; (treacle) melaza f. ~y a
~ic(al) /-'bɒlɪk(l)/ a simbólico.   almibarado
~ism n simbolismo m. ~ize vt   system /'sɪstəm/ n sistema m;
simbolizar   (body) organismo m; (order)
symmetr|ical /sɪ'metrɪkl/ a   método m. ~atic /-ə'mætɪk/
simétrico. ~y /'sɪmɪtrɪ/ n sime-   a sistemático. ~atically
tría f

tab 582 **take**

/-ə'mætɪklɪ/ adv sistemáticamente. **~s analyst** n analista m & f de sistemas

T

tab /tæb/ n (flap) lengüeta f; (label) etiqueta f. **keep ~s on** (fam) vigilar

tabby /'tæbɪ/ n gato m atigrado

tabernacle /'tæbənækl/ n tabernáculo m

table /'teɪbl/ n mesa f; (list) tabla f. **~ of contents** índice m. —vt presentar; (postpone) aplazar. **~cloth** n mantel m. **~mat** n salvamanteles m invar. **~spoon** /'teɪblspuːn/ n cucharón m, cuchara f sopera. **~spoonful** n (pl **-fuls**) cucharada f

tablet /'tæblɪt/ n (of stone) lápida f; (pill) tableta f; (of soap etc) pastilla f

table tennis /'teɪbltenɪs/ n tenis m de mesa, ping-pong m

tabloid /'tæbloɪd/ n tabloide m

taboo /tə'buː/ a & n tabú (m)

tabulator /'tæbjʊleɪtə(r)/ n tabulador m

tacit /'tæsɪt/ a tácito

taciturn /'tæsɪtɜːn/ a taciturno

tack /tæk/ n tachuela f; (stitch) hilván m; (naut) virada f; (fig) línea f de conducta. —vt sujetar con tachuelas; (sew) hilvanar. **~ on** añadir. —vi virar

tackle /'tækl/ n (equipment) equipo m; (football) placaje m. —vt abordar (problem etc); (in rugby) hacer un placaje a

tacky /'tækɪ/ a pegajoso; (in poor taste) vulgar, de pacotilla

tact /tækt/ n tacto m. **~ful** a discreto. **~fully** adv discretamente

tactic|al /'tæktɪkl/ a táctico. **~s** /'tæktɪks/ npl táctica f

tactile /'tæktaɪl/ a táctil

tact: **~less** a indiscreto. **~lessly** adv indiscretamente

tadpole /'tædpəʊl/ n renacuajo m

tag /tæg/ n (on shoe-lace) herrete m; (label) etiqueta f. —vt (pt **tagged**) poner etiqueta a; (trail) seguir. —vi. **~ along** (fam) seguir

tail /teɪl/ n cola f. **~s** npl (tailcoat) frac m; (of coin) cruz f. —vt (sl) seguir. —vi. **~ off** disminuir. **~-end** n extremo m final, cola f

tailor /'teɪlə(r)/ n sastre m. —vt confeccionar. **~-made** n hecho a la medida. **~-made for** (fig) hecho para

tailplane /'teɪlpleɪn/ n plano m de cola

taint /teɪnt/ n mancha f. —vt contaminar

take /teɪk/ vt (pt **took**, pp **taken**) tomar, coger (not LAm), agarrar (esp LAm); (contain) contener; (capture) capturar; (endure) aguantar; (require) requerir; tomar (bath); dar (walk); (carry) llevar; (accompany) acompañar; presentarse para (exam); sacar (photo); ganar (prize). **~ advantage of** aprovechar. **~ after** parecerse a. **~ away** quitar. **~ back** retirar (statement etc). **~ in** achicar (garment); (understand) comprender; (deceive) engañar. **~ off** quitarse (clothes); (mimic) imitar; (aviat) despegar. **~ o.s. off** marcharse. **~ on** (undertake) emprender; contratar (employee). **~ out** (remove) sacar. **~ over** tomar posesión de; (assume control) tomar el poder. **~ part** participar. **~ place** tener lugar. **~ sides** tomar partido. **~ to** dedicarse a; (like) tomar simpatía a (person); (like) aficionarse a (thing). **~ up** dedicarse a (hobby); (occupy) ocupar; (resume) reanudar. ~ up with trabar amistad con. be ~n ill ponerse enfermo. —n presa f; (photo, cinema, TV) toma f

takings /ˈteɪkɪnz/ npl ingresos mpl

take: ~-**off** n despegue m. ~-**over** n toma f de posesión.

talcum /ˈtælkəm/ n. ~ **powder** n (polvos mpl de) talco (m)

tale /teɪl/ n cuento m

talent /ˈtælənt/ n talento m. ~**ed** a talentoso

talisman /ˈtælɪzmən/ n talismán m

talk /tɔːk/ vt/i hablar. ~ **about** hablar de. ~ **over** discutir. —n conversación f; (lecture) conferencia f. **small** ~ charla f. ~**ative** a hablador. ~**er** n hablador m; (chatterbox) parlanchín m. ~**ing-to** n represión f

tall /tɔːl/ a (-er, -est) alto. ~ **story** n (fam) historia f inverosímil. **that's a ~ order** n (fam) eso es pedir mucho

tallboy /ˈtɔːlbɔɪ/ n cómoda f alta

tally /ˈtælɪ/ n tarja f; (total) total m. —vi corresponder (with a)

talon /ˈtælən/ n garra f

tambourine /tæmbəˈriːn/ n pandereta f

tame /teɪm/ a (-er, -est) (animal) doméstico; (person) dócil; (dull) insípido. —vt domesticar; domar (wild animal). ~**ly** adv dócilmente. ~**r** /-ə(r)/ n domador m

tamper /ˈtæmpə(r)/ vi. ~ **with** manosear; (alter) alterar, falsificar

tampon /ˈtæmpən/ n tampón m

tan /tæn/ vt (pt tanned) curtir (hide); (sun) broncear. —vi ponerse moreno. —n bronceado m. —a (colour) de color canela

tandem /ˈtændəm/ n tándem m

tang /tæŋ/ n sabor m fuerte; (smell) olor m fuerte

tangent /ˈtændʒənt/ n tangente f

tangerine /tændʒəˈriːn/ n mandarina f

tangibl|**e** /ˈtændʒəbl/ a tangible. ~**y** adv perceptiblemente

tangle /ˈtæŋgl/ vt enredar. —vi enredarse. —n enredo m

tango /ˈtæŋgəʊ/ n (pl -os) tango m

tank /tæŋk/ n depósito m; (mil) tanque m

tankard /ˈtæŋkəd/ n jarra f, bock m

tanker /ˈtæŋkə(r)/ n petrolero m; (truck) camión m cisterna

tantaliz|**e** /ˈtæntəlaɪz/ vt atormentar. ~**ing** a atormentador; (tempting) tentador

tantamount /ˈtæntəmaʊnt/ a. ~ **to** equivalente a

tantrum /ˈtæntrəm/ n rabieta f

tap[1] /tæp/ n grifo m. **on** ~ disponible. —vt explotar (resources); interceptar (phone)

tap[2] /tæp/ n (knock) golpe m ligero. —vt (pt tapped) golpear ligeramente. ~-**dance** n zapateado m

tape /teɪp/ n cinta f. —vt atar con cinta; (record) grabar. **have sth** ~**d** (sl) comprender perfectamente. ~-**measure** n cinta f métrica

taper /ˈteɪpə(r)/ n bujía f. —vt ahusar. —vi ahusarse. ~ **off** disminuir

tape: ~ **recorder** n magnetofón m, magnetófono m. ~ **recording** n grabación f

tapestry /ˈtæpɪstrɪ/ n tapicería f; (product) tapiz m

tapioca /tæpɪˈəʊkə/ n tapioca f

tar /tɑː(r)/ n alquitrán m. —vt (pt tarred) alquitranar

tardi|**ly** /ˈtɑːdɪlɪ/ adv lentamente; (late) tardíamente. ~**y** /ˈtɑːdɪ/ a (-ier, -iest) (slow) lento; (late) tardío

target /ˈtɑːgɪt/ n blanco m; (fig) objetivo m

tariff /ˈtærɪf/ n tarifa f

tarmac /'tɑːmæk/ *n* pista *f* de aterrizaje. **T~** *n* (*P*) macadán *m*

tarnish /'tɑːnɪʃ/ *vt* deslustrar. *—vi* deslustrarse

tarpaulin /tɑː'pɔːlɪn/ *n* alquitranado *m*

tarragon /'tærəgən/ *n* estragón *m*

tart[1] /tɑːt/ *n* pastel *m*; (*individual*) pastelillo *m*

tart[2] /tɑːt/ *n* (*sl, woman*) prostituta *f*, fulana *f* (*fam*). *—vt.* **~ o.s. up** (*fam*) engalanarse

tart[3] /tɑːt/ *a* (*-er, -est*) ácido; (*fig*) áspero

tartan /'tɑːtn/ *n* tartán *m*, tela *f* escocesa

tartar /'tɑːtə(r)/ *n* tártaro *m*. **~ sauce** *n* salsa *f* tártara

task /tɑːsk/ *n* tarea *f*. **take to ~** reprender. **~ force** *n* destacamiento *m* especial

tassel /'tæsl/ *n* borla *f*

taste /teɪst/ *n* sabor *m*, gusto *m*; (*small quantity*) poquito *m*. *—vt* probar. *—vi.* **~e of** saber a. **~eful** *a* de buen gusto. **~less** *a* soso; (*fig*) de mal gusto. **~y** *a* (*-ier, -iest*) sabroso

tat /tæt/ *see* **tit**[2]

tattered /'tætəd/ *a* hecho jirones. **~s** /'tætəz/ *npl* andrajos *mpl*

tattle /'tætl/ *vi* charlar. *—n* charla *f*

tattoo[1] /tə'tuː/ *n* (*mil*) espectáculo *m* militar

tattoo[2] /tə'tuː/ *vt* tatuar. *—n* tatuaje *m*

tatty /'tætɪ/ *a* (*-ier, -iest*) gastado, en mal estado

taught /tɔːt/ *see* **teach**

taunt /tɔːnt/ *vt* mofarse de. **~ s.o. with sth** echar algo en cara a uno. *—n* mofa *f*

Taurus /'tɔːrəs/ *n* (*astr*) Tauro *m*

taut /tɔːt/ *a* tenso

tavern /'tævən/ *n* taberna *f*

tawdry /'tɔːdrɪ/ *a* (*-ier, -iest*) charro

tawny /'tɔːnɪ/ *a* bronceado

tax /tæks/ *n* impuesto *m*. *—vt* imponer contribuciones a ⟨*person*⟩; gravar con un impuesto ⟨*thing*⟩; (*fig*) poner a prueba. **~able** *a* imponible. **~ation** /-'seɪʃn/ *n* impuestos *mpl.* **~ collector** *n* recaudador *m* de contribuciones. **~-free** *a* libre de impuestos

taxi /'tæksɪ/ *n* (*pl* **-is**) taxi *m*. *—vi* (*pt* **taxied**, *pres p* **taxiing**) ⟨*aircraft*⟩ rodar por la pista. **~ rank** *n* parada *f* de taxis

taxpayer /'tækspeɪə(r)/ *n* contribuyente *m* & *f*

te /tiː/ *n* (*mus, seventh note of any musical scale*) si *m*

tea /tiː/ *n* té *m*. **~-bag** *n* bolsita *f* de té. **~-break** *n* descanso *m* para el té

teach /tiːtʃ/ *vt/i* (*pt* **taught**) enseñar. **~er** *n* profesor *m*; (*primary*) maestro *m*. **~-in** *n* seminario *m*. **~ing** *n* enseñanza *f*. *—a* docente. **~ing staff** *n* profesorado *m*

teacup /'tiːkʌp/ *n* taza *f* de té

teak /tiːk/ *n* teca *f*

tea-leaf /'tiːliːf/ *n* hoja *f* de té

team /tiːm/ *n* equipo *m*; (*of horses*) tiro *m*. *—vi.* **~ up** unirse. **~-work** *n* trabajo *m* en equipo

teapot /'tiːpɒt/ *n* tetera *f*

tear[1] /teə(r)/ *vt* (*pt* **tore**, *pp* **torn**) rasgar. *—vi* rasgarse; (*run*) precipitarse. *—n* rasgón *m*. **~ apart** desgarrar. **~ o.s. away** separarse

tear[2] /tɪə(r)/ *n* lágrima *f*. **in ~s** llorando

tearaway /'teərəweɪ/ *n* gamberro *m*

tear /tɪə(r)/: **~ful** *a* lloroso. **~-gas** *n* gas *m* lacrimógeno

tease /tiːz/ *vt* tomar el pelo a; cardar ⟨*cloth etc*⟩. *—n* guasón *m*. **~r** /-ə(r)/ *n* (*fam*) problema *m* difícil

tea: **~-set** *n* juego *m* de té. **~spoon** /'tiːspuːn/ *n* cucharilla

f. ~spoonful n (pl -fuls) (amount) cucharadita f

teat /ti:t/ n (of animal) teta f; (for bottle) tetilla f

tea-towel /'ti:tauəl/ n paño m de cocina

technical /'teknɪkl/ a técnico. ~ity n /-'kælətɪ/ n detalle m técnico. ~ly adv técnicamente

technician /tek'nɪʃn/ n técnico m

technique /tek'ni:k/ n técnica f

technolog|ist /tek'nɒlədʒɪst/ n tecnólogo m. ~y /tek'nɒlədʒɪ/ n tecnología f

teddy bear /'tedɪbeə(r)/ n osito m de felpa, osito m de peluche

tedious /'ti:dɪəs/ a pesado. ~ly adv pesadamente

tedium /'ti:dɪəm/ n aburrimiento m

tee /ti:/ n (golf) tee m

teem /ti:m/ vi abundar; (rain) llover a cántaros

teen|age /'ti:neɪdʒ/ a adolescente; (for teenagers) para jóvenes. ~ager m & f, joven m & f. ~s /ti:nz/ npl. the ~s la adolescencia f

teeny /'ti:nɪ/ a (-ier, -iest) (fam) chiquito

teeter /'ti:tə(r)/ vi balancearse

teeth /ti:θ/ see **tooth**. ~e /ti:ð/ vi echar los dientes. ~ing troubles npl (fig) dificultades fpl iniciales

teetotaller /ti:'təʊtələ(r)/ n abstemio m

telecommunications /telɪkəmju:nɪ'keɪʃnz/ npl telecomunicaciones fpl

telegram /'telɪgræm/ n telegrama m

telegraph /'telɪgrɑ:f/ n telégrafo m. —vt telegrafiar. ~ic /-'græfɪk/ a telegráfico

telepath|ic /telɪ'pæθɪk/ a telepático. ~y /tɪ'lepəθɪ/ n telepatía f

telephon|e /'telɪfəʊn/ n teléfono m. —vt llamar por teléfono. ~e booth n cabina f telefónica. ~e directory n guía f telefónica. ~e exchange n central f telefónica. ~ic /-'fɒnɪk/ a telefónico. ~ist /tɪ'lefənɪst/ n telefonista m & f

telephoto /telɪ'fəʊtəʊ/ a. ~ lens n teleobjetivo m

teleprinter /'telɪprɪntə(r)/ n teleimpresor m

telescop|e /'telɪskəʊp/ n telescopio m. ~ic /-'kɒpɪk/ a telescópico

televis|e /'telɪvaɪz/ vt televisar. ~ion /'telɪvɪʒn/ n televisión f. ~ion set n televisor m

telex /'teleks/ n télex m. —vt enviar por télex

tell /tel/ vt (pt told) decir; contar (story); (distinguish) distinguir. —vi (produce an effect) tener efecto; (know) saber. ~ off vt reprender. ~er /'telə(r)/ n (in bank) cajero m

telling /'telɪŋ/ a eficaz

tell-tale /'telteɪl/ n soplón m. —a revelador

telly /'telɪ/ n (fam) televisión f, tele f (fam)

temerity /tɪ'merətɪ/ n temeridad f

temp /temp/ n (fam) empleado m temporal

temper /'tempə(r)/ n (disposition) disposición f; (mood) humor m; (fit of anger) cólera f; (of metal) temple m. **be in a ~** estar de mal humor. **keep one's ~** contenerse. **lose one's ~** enfadarse, perder la paciencia. —vt templar (metal)

temperament /'temprəmənt/ n temperamento m. ~al /-'mentl/ a caprichoso

temperance /'tempərəns/ n moderación f

temperate /'tempərət/ a moderado; (climate) templado

temperature /ˈtemprɪtʃə(r)/ *n* temperatura *f*. **have a ~** tener fiebre

tempest /ˈtempɪst/ *n* tempestad *f*. **~uous** /-ˈpestjʊəs/ *a* tempestuoso

temple[1] /ˈtempl/ *n* templo *m*

temple[2] /ˈtempl/ *n* (*anat*) sien *f*

tempo /ˈtempəʊ/ *n* (*pl* -os *or* tempi) ritmo *m*

temporar|ily /ˈtempərərəli/ *adv* temporalmente. **~y** /ˈtempərəri/ *a* temporal, provisional

tempt /tempt/ *vt* tentar. **~ s.o. to** inducir a uno a. **~ation** /-ˈteɪʃn/ *n* tentación *f*. **~ing** *a* tentador

ten /ten/ *a & n* diez (*m*)

tenable /ˈtenəbl/ *a* sostenible

tenaci|ous /tɪˈneɪʃəs/ *a* tenaz. **~ty** /-ˈæsəti/ *n* tenacidad *f*

tenan|cy /ˈtenənsi/ *n* alquiler *m*. **~t** /ˈtenənt/ *n* inquilino *m*

tend[1] /tend/ *vi*. **~ to** tener tendencia a

tend[2] /tend/ *vt* cuidar

tendency /ˈtendənsi/ *n* tendencia *f*

tender[1] /ˈtendə(r)/ *a* tierno; (*painful*) dolorido

tender[2] /ˈtendə(r)/ *n* (*com*) oferta *f*. **legal ~** *n* curso *m* legal. *—vt* ofrecer, presentar

tender: **~ly** *adv* tiernamente. **~ness** *n* ternura *f*

tendon /ˈtendən/ *n* tendón *m*

tenement /ˈtenəmənt/ *n* vivienda *f*

tenet /ˈtenɪt/ *n* principio *m*

tenfold /ˈtenfəʊld/ *a* diez veces mayor, décuplo. *—adv* diez veces

tenner /ˈtenə(r)/ *n* (*fam*) billete *m* de diez libras

tennis /ˈtenɪs/ *n* tenis *m*

tenor /ˈtenə(r)/ *n* tenor *m*

tens|e /tens/ *a* (-er, -est) tieso; (*fig*) tenso. *—n* (*gram*) tiempo *m*. *—vi*. **~ up** tensarse. **~eness** *n*, **~ion** /ˈtenʃn/ *n* tensión *f*

tent /tent/ *n* tienda *f*, carpa *f* (*LAm*)

tentacle /ˈtentəkl/ *n* tentáculo *m*

tentative /ˈtentətɪv/ *a* provisional; (*hesitant*) indeciso. **~ly** *adv* provisionalmente; (*timidly*) tímidamente

tenterhooks /ˈtentəhʊks/ *npl*. **on ~** en ascuas

tenth /tenθ/ *a & n* décimo (*m*)

tenuous /ˈtenjʊəs/ *a* tenue

tenure /ˈtenjʊə(r)/ *n* posesión *f*

tepid /ˈtepɪd/ *a* tibio

term /tɜːm/ *n* (*of time*) período *m*; (*schol*) trimestre *m*; (*word etc*) término *m*. *—vt* llamar. **~s** *npl* condiciones *fpl*; (*com*) precio *m*. **on bad ~s** en malas relaciones. **on good ~s** en buenas relaciones

terminal /ˈtɜːmɪnl/ *a* terminal, final. *—n* (*rail*) estación *f* terminal; (*elec*) borne *m*. (*air*) **~** *n* término *m*, terminal *m*

terminat|e /ˈtɜːmɪneɪt/ *vt* terminar. *—vi* terminarse. **~ion** /-ˈneɪʃn/ *n* terminación *f*

terminology /tɜːmɪˈnɒlədʒi/ *n* terminología *f*

terrace /ˈterəs/ *n* terraza *f*; (*houses*) hilera *f* de casas. **the ~s** *npl* (*sport*) las gradas *fpl*

terrain /təˈreɪn/ *n* terreno *m*

terrestrial /tɪˈrestrɪəl/ *a* terrestre

terrib|le /ˈterəbl/ *a* terrible. **~y** *adv* terriblemente

terrier /ˈterɪə(r)/ *n* terrier *m*

terrific /təˈrɪfɪk/ *a* (*excellent*, *fam*) estupendo; (*huge*, *fam*) enorme. **~ally** *adv* (*fam*) terriblemente; (*very well*) muy bien

terrify /ˈterɪfaɪ/ *vt* aterrorizar. **~ing** *a* espantoso

territor|ial /terɪˈtɔːrɪəl/ *a* territorial. **~y** /ˈterɪtri/ *n* territorio *m*

terror /'terə(r)/ n terror m. ∼**ism** /-zəm/ n terrorismo m. ∼**ist** /'terərist/ n terrorista m & f. ∼**ize** /'terəraiz/ vt aterrorizar

terse /tɜːs/ a conciso; (abrupt) brusco

test /test/ n prueba f; (exam) examen m. —vt probar; (examine) examinar

testament /'testəmənt/ n testamento m. **New T**∼ Nuevo Testamento. **Old T**∼ Antiguo Testamento

testicle /'testikl/ n testículo m

testify /'testifai/ vt atestiguar. —vi declarar

testimon|ial /testi'məʊniəl/ n certificado m; (of character) recomendación f. ∼**y** /'testiməni/ n testimonio m

test: ∼ match n partido m internacional. ∼**tube** n tubo m de ensayo, probeta f

testy /'testi/ a irritable

tetanus /'tetənəs/ n tétanos m invar

tetchy /'tetʃi/ a irritable

tether /'teðə(r)/ vt atar. —n. **be at the end of one's** ∼ no poder más

text /tekst/ n texto m. ∼**book** n libro m de texto

textile /'tekstail/ a & n textil (m)

texture /'tekstʃə(r)/ n textura f

Thai /tai/ a & n tailandés (m). ∼**land** n Tailandia f

Thames /temz/ n Támesis m

than /ðæn, ðən/ conj que; (with numbers) de

thank /θæŋk/ vt dar las gracias a, agradecer. ∼ **you** gracias. ∼**ful** /'θæŋkfl/ a agradecido. ∼**fully** adv con gratitud; (happily) afortunadamente. ∼**less** /'θæŋklis/ a ingrato. ∼**s** npl gracias fpl. ∼**s!** (fam) ¡gracias! ∼**s to** gracias a

that /ðæt, ðət/ a (pl those) ese, aquel, esa, aquella. —pron (pl those) ése, aquél, ésa, aquélla.

∼ **is** es decir. ∼'**s it!** ¡eso es! ∼ **is why** por eso. **is** ∼ **you?** ¿eres tú? **like** ∼ así. —adv tan. —rel pron que; (with prep) que, la que, el cual, la cual. —conj que

thatch /θætʃ/ n techo m de paja. ∼**ed** a con techo de paja

thaw /θɔː/ vt deshelar. —vi deshelarse; (snow) derretirse. —n deshielo m

the /ðə, ði, before vowel ðiː/ def art el, la, los, las. **at** ∼ al, a la, a los, a las. **from** ∼ del, de la, de los, de las. **to** ∼ al, a la, a los, a las. —adv. **all** ∼ **better** tanto mejor

theatr|e /'θiətə(r)/ n teatro m. ∼**ical** /θi'ætrikl/ a teatral

theft /θeft/ n hurto m

their /ðeə(r)/ a su, sus

theirs /ðeəz/ poss pron (el) suyo, (la) suya, (los) suyos, (las) suyas

them /ðem, ðəm/ pron (accusative) los, las; (dative) les; (after prep) ellos, ellas

theme /θiːm/ n tema m. ∼ **song** n motivo m principal

themselves /ðəm'selvz/ pron ellos mismos, ellas mismas; (reflexive) se; (after prep) sí mismos, sí mismas

then /ðen/ adv entonces; (next) luego, después. **by** ∼ para entonces. **now and** ∼ de vez en cuando. **since** ∼ desde entonces. —a de entonces

theolog|ian /θiə'ləʊdʒən/ n teólogo m. ∼**y** /θi'ɒlədʒi/ n teología f

theorem /'θiərəm/ n teorema m

theor|etical /θiə'retikl/ a teórico. ∼**y** /'θiəri/ n teoría f

therapeutic /θerə'pjuːtik/ a terapéutico. ∼**ist** n terapeuta m & f. ∼**y** /'θerəpi/ n terapia f

there /ðeə(r)/ adv ahí, allí. ∼ **are** hay. ∼ **he is** ahí está. ∼ **is** hay. ∼ **it is** ahí está. **down** ∼ ahí abajo. **up** ∼ ahí arriba. —int ¡vaya! ∼, ∼! ¡ya, ya! ∼**abouts**

adv por ahí. ~**after** *adv*
después. ~**by** *adv* por eso.
~**fore** /'ðeəfɔ:(r)/ *adv* por lo
tanto.

thermal /'θɜ:ml/ *a* termal

thermometer /θə'mɒmɪtə(r)/ *n*
termómetro *m*

thermonuclear /θɜ:məʊ'nju:-
klɪə(r)/ *a* termonuclear

Thermos /'θɜ:məs/ *n* (P) termo *m*

thermostat /'θɜ:məstæt/ *n* termostato *m*

thesaurus /θɪ'sɔ:rəs/ *n* (pl -ri
/-raɪ/) diccionario *m* de
sinónimos

these /ði:z/ *a* estos, estas. —*pron*
éstos, éstas

thesis /'θi:sɪs/ *n* (pl **theses** /-si:z/)
tesis *f*

they /ðeɪ/ *pron* ellos, ellas. ~ **say
that** se dice que

thick /θɪk/ *a* (-**er, -est**) espeso,
(*dense*) denso; (*stupid, fam*)
torpe; (*close, fam*) íntimo. —*adv*
espesamente, densamente. —*n*.
in the ~ en medio de. ~**en**
/'θɪkən/ *vt* espesar. —*vi* espesarse

thicket /'θɪkɪt/ *n* matorral *m*

thick: ~**ly** *adv* espesamente,
densamente. ~**ness** *n* espesor *m*

thickset /θɪk'set/ *a* fornido

thick-skinned /θɪk'skɪnd/ *a*
insensible

thief /θi:f/ *n* (pl **thieves**) ladrón
m

thieve /θi:v/ *vt/i* robar. ~**ing** *a*
ladrón

thigh /θaɪ/ *n* muslo *m*

thimble /'θɪmbl/ *n* dedal *m*

thin /θɪn/ *a* (**thinner, thinnest**)
delgado; (*person*) flaco; (*weak*)
débil; (*fine*) fino; (*sparse*)
escaso. —*adv* ligeramente. —*vt*
(*pt* **thinned**) adelgazar; (*dilute*)
diluir. ~ **out** hacer menos
denso. —*vi* adelgazarse (*diminish*) disminuir

thing /θɪŋ/ *n* cosa *f*. **for one** ~ en
primer lugar. **just the** ~ exactamente lo que se necesita. **poor**
~! ¡pobrecito! ~**s** *npl* (*belongings*) efectos *mpl*; (*clothing*) ropa
f

think /θɪŋk/ *vt* (*pt* **thought**) pensar, creer. —*vi* pensar (**about,
of** en); (*carefully*) reflexionar;
(*imagine*) imaginarse. ~ **better
of it** cambiar de idea. **I** ~ **so** creo
que sí. ~ **over** *vt* pensar bien. ~
up *vt* idear, inventar. ~**er** *n* pensador *m*. ~**tank** *n* grupo *m* de
expertos

thin: ~**ly** *adv* ligeramente.
~**ness** *n* delgadez *f*; (*of person*)
flaqueza *f*

third /θɜ:d/ *a* tercero. —*n* tercio
m, tercera parte *f*. ~**rate** *a* muy
inferior. **T**~ **World** *n* Tercer
Mundo *m*

thirst /θɜ:st/ *n* sed *f*. ~**y** *a* sediento. **be** ~**y** tener sed

thirteen /θɜ:'ti:n/ *a & n* trece (*m*).
~**th** *a & n* decimotercero (*m*)

thirtieth /'θɜ:tɪəθ/ *a & n* trigésimo (*m*). ~**y** /'θɜ:tɪ/ *a & n*
treinta (*m*)

this /ðɪs/ *a* (pl **these**) este, esta.
~ **one** éste, ésta. —*pron* (pl
these) éste, ésta, esto. **like** ~ así

thistle /'θɪsl/ *n* cardo *m*

thong /θɒŋ/ *n* correa *f*

thorn /θɔ:n/ *n* espina *f*. ~**y** *a*
espinoso

thorough /'θʌrə/ *a* completo;
(*deep*) profundo; (*cleaning etc*) a
fondo; (*person*) concienzudo

thoroughbred /'θʌrəbred/ *a* de
pura sangre

thoroughfare /'θʌrəfeə(r)/ *n*
calle *f*. **no** ~ prohibido el paso

thoroughly /'θʌrəlɪ/ *adv*
completamente

those /ðəʊz/ *a* esos, aquellos,
esas, aquellas. —*pron* ésos,
aquéllos, ésas, aquéllas

though /ðəʊ/ *conj* aunque. —*adv* sin embargo. **as ~** como si

thought /θɔːt/ *see* think. —*n* pensamiento *m*; (*idea*) idea *f*. **~ful** /ˈθɔːtfl/ *a* pensativo; (*considerate*) atento. **~fully** *adv* pensativamente; (*considerately*) atentamente. **~less** /ˈθɔːtlɪs/ *a* irreflexivo; (*inconsiderate*) desconsiderado

thousand /ˈθaʊznd/ *a & n* mil (*m*). **~th** *a & n* milésimo (*m*).

thrash /θræʃ/ *vt* azotar; (*defeat*) derrotar. **~ out** discutir a fondo

thread /θred/ *n* hilo *m*; (*of screw*) rosca *f*. —*vt* ensartar. **~ one's way** abrirse paso. **~bare** /ˈθredbeə(r)/ *a* raído

threat /θret/ *n* amenaza *f*. **~en** /ˈθretn/ *vt/i* amenazar. **~ening** *a* amenazador. **~eningly** *adv* de modo amenazador

three /θriː/ *a & n* tres (*m*). **~fold** *a* triple. —*adv* tres veces. **~some** /ˈθriːsəm/ *n* conjunto *m* de tres personas

thresh /θreʃ/ *vt* trillar

threshold /ˈθreʃhəʊld/ *n* umbral *m*

threw /θruː/ *see* throw

thrift /θrɪft/ *n* economía *f*, ahorro *m*. **~y** *a* frugal

thrill /θrɪl/ *n* emoción *f*. —*vt* emocionar. —*vi* emocionarse; (*quiver*) estremecerse. **be ~ed with** estar encantado de. **~er** /ˈθrɪlə(r)/ *n* (*book*) libro *m* de suspense; (*film*) película *f* de suspense. **~ing** *a* emocionante

thriv|e /θraɪv/ *vi* prosperar. **~ing** *a* próspero

throat /θrəʊt/ *n* garganta *f*. **have a sore ~** dolerle la garganta

throb /θrɒb/ *vi* (*pt* throbbed) palpitar; (*with pain*) dar punzadas; (*fig*) vibrar. —*n* palpitación *f*; (*pain*) punzada *f*; (*fig*) vibración *f*. **~bing** *a* (*pain*) punzante

throes /θrəʊz/ *npl*. **in the ~ of** en medio de

thrombosis /θrɒmˈbəʊsɪs/ *n* trombosis *f*

throne /θrəʊn/ *n* trono *m*

throng /θrɒŋ/ *n* multitud *f*

throttle /ˈθrɒtl/ *n* (*auto*) acelerador *m*. —*vt* ahogar

through /θruː/ *prep* por, a través de; (*during*) durante; (*by means of*) por medio de; (*thanks to*) gracias a. —*adv* de parte a parte, de un lado a otro; (*entirely*) completamente; (*to the end*) hasta el final. **be ~** (*finished*) haber terminado. —*a* (*train etc*) directo

throughout /θruːˈaʊt/ *prep* por todo; (*time*) en todo. —*adv* en todas partes; (*all the time*) todo el tiempo

throve /θrəʊv/ *see* thrive

throw /θrəʊ/ *vt* (*pt* threw, *pp* thrown) arrojar; (*baffle etc*) desconcertar. **~ a party** (*fam*) dar una fiesta. —*n* tiro *m*; (*of dice*) lance *m*. **~ away** *vt* tirar. **~ over** *vt* abandonar. **~ up** *vi* (*vomit*) vomitar. **~-away** *a* desechable

thrush /θrʌʃ/ *n* tordo *m*

thrust /θrʌst/ *vt* (*pt* thrust) empujar; (*push in*) meter. —*n* empuje *m*. **~ (up)on** imponer a

thud /θʌd/ *n* ruido *m* sordo

thug /θʌg/ *n* bruto *m*

thumb /θʌm/ *n* pulgar *m*. **under the ~ of** dominado por. —*vt* hojear (*book*). **~ a lift** hacer autostop. **~-index** *n* uñeros *mpl*

thump /θʌmp/ *vt* golpear. —*vi* (*heart*) latir fuertemente. —*n* porrazo *m*; (*noise*) ruido *m* sordo

thunder /ˈθʌndə(r)/ *n* trueno *m*. —*vi* tronar. **~ past** pasar con estruendo. **~bolt** /ˈθʌndəbəʊlt/ *n* rayo *m*. **~clap** /ˈθʌndəklæp/ *n* trueno *m*. **~storm** /ˈθʌndəstɔːm/ *n* tronada *f*. **~y** *a* con truenos

Thursday /ˈθɜːzdeɪ/ *n* jueves *m*

thus /ðʌs/ adv así

thwart /θwɔ:t/ vt frustrar

thyme /taɪm/ n tomillo m

thyroid /'θaɪrɔɪd/ n tiroides m
invar

tiara /tɪ'ɑ:rə/ n diadema f

tic /tɪk/ n tic m

tick[1] /tɪk/ n tictac m; (mark)
señal f, marca f; (instant, fam)
momentito m. —vi hacer
tictac. —vt. ~ (off) marcar. ~ off
vt (sl) reprender. ~ over vi (of
engine) marchar en vacío

tick[2] /tɪk/ n (insect) garrapata f

tick[3] /tɪk/ n. on ~ (fam) a crédito

ticket /'tɪkɪt/ n billete m, boleto
m (LAm); (label) etiqueta f; (fine)
multa f. ~-collector n revisor
m. ~-office n taquilla f

tickle /'tɪkl/ vt hacer cosquillas
a; (amuse) divertir. —n cosqui-
lleo m. ~ish /'tɪklɪʃ/ a
cosquilloso; (problem) delicado.
be ~ish tener cosquillas

tidal /'taɪdl/ a de marea. ~ wave
n maremoto m

tiddly-winks /'tɪdlɪwɪŋks/ n
juego m de pulgas

tide /taɪd/ n marea f; (of events)
curso m. —vt. ~ over ayudar a
salir de un apuro

tidings /'taɪdɪŋz/ npl noticias fpl

tidily /'taɪdɪlɪ/ adv en orden;
(well) bien. ~iness n orden m.
~y /'taɪdɪ/ a (-ier, -iest) orde-
nado; (amount, fam) considerable. —vt/i. ~y (up)
ordenar. ~y o.s. up arreglarse

tie /taɪ/ vt (pres p tying) atar;
hacer (a knot); (link)
vincular. —vi (sport) empatar.
—n atadura f; (necktie) corbata f;
(link) lazo m; (sport) empate m.
~ in with relacionar con. ~ up
atar; (com) inmovilizar. be ~d
up (busy) estar ocupado

tier /tɪə(r)/ n fila f; (in stadium
etc) grada f; (of cake) piso m

tie-up /'taɪʌp/ n enlace m

tiff /tɪf/ n riña f

tiger /'taɪgə(r)/ n tigre m

tight /taɪt/ a (-er, -est) (clothes)
ceñido; (taut) tieso; (control etc)
riguroso; (knot, nut) apretado;
(drunk, fam) borracho. —adv
bien; (shut) herméticamente. ~
corner n (fig) apuro m. ~en
/'taɪtn/ vt apretar. —vi apret-
arse. ~-fisted a tacaño. ~ly adv
bien; (shut) herméticamente.
~ness n estrechez f. ~rope
/'taɪtrəʊp/ n cuerda f floja. ~s
/taɪts/ npl leotardos mpl

tile /taɪl/ n (decorative) azulejo
m; (on roof) teja f; (on floor) baldosa f. —vt azulejar; tejar (roof);
embaldosar (floor)

till[1] /tɪl/ prep hasta. —conj hasta
que

till[2] /tɪl/ n caja f

till[3] /tɪl/ vt cultivar

tilt /tɪlt/ vt inclinar. —vi inclinarse. —n inclinación f. at full
~ a toda velocidad

timber /'tɪmbə(r)/ n madera f (de
construcción); (trees) árboles
mpl

time /taɪm/ n tiempo m;
(moment) momento m; (occasion) ocasión f; (by clock) hora f;
(epoch) época f; (rhythm) compás
m. ~ off tiempo libre. at ~s a
veces. behind the ~s anticuado. behind ~ atrasado. for
the ~ being por ahora. from ~
to ~ de vez en cuando. have a
good ~ divertirse, pasarlo bien.
in a year's ~ dentro de un año.
in no ~ en un abrir y cerrar de
ojos. in ~ a tiempo; (eventually)
con el tiempo. on ~ a la hora,
puntual. —vt elegir el momento;
cronometrar (race). ~ bomb n
bomba f de tiempo. ~-
honoured a consagrado. ~-lag
n intervalo m

timeless /'taɪmlɪs/ a eterno

timely /'taɪmlɪ/ a oportuno

timer /'taɪmə(r)/ *n* cronómetro *m*; (*culin*) avisador *m*; (*with sand*) reloj *m* de arena; (*elec*) interruptor *m* de reloj

timetable /'taɪmteɪbl/ *n* horario *m*

time zone /'taɪmzəʊn/ *n* huso *m* horario

timid /'tɪmɪd/ *a* tímido; (*fearful*) miedoso. **∼ly** *adv* tímidamente

timing /'taɪmɪŋ/ *n* medida *f* del tiempo; (*moment*) momento *m*; (*sport*) cronometraje *m*

timorous /'tɪmərəs/ *a* tímido; (*fearful*) miedoso. **∼ly** *adv* tímidamente

tin /tɪn/ *n* estaño *m*; (*container*) lata *f*. **∼ foil** *n* papel *m* de estaño. **∼ned** *a* (*pt* **tinned**) conservar en lata, enlatar

tinge /tɪndʒ/ *vt* teñir (**with** de); (*fig*) matizar (**with** de). **—** *n* matiz *m*

tingle /'tɪŋgl/ *vi* sentir hormigueo; (*with excitement*) estremecerse

tinker /'tɪŋkə(r)/ *n* hojalatero *m*. **—** *vi*. **∼** (**with**) jugar con; (*repair*) arreglar

tinkle /'tɪŋkl/ *n* retintín *m*; (*phone call*, *fam*) llamada *f*

tin: **∼ned** *a* en lata. **∼ny** *a* metálico. **∼opener** *n* abrelatas *m invar*. **∼ plate** *n* hojalata *f*

tinpot /'tɪnpɒt/ *a* (*pej*) inferior

tinsel /'tɪnsl/ *n* oropel *m*

tint /tɪnt/ *n* matiz *m*

tiny /'taɪnɪ/ *a* (**-ier, -iest**) diminuto

tip¹ /tɪp/ *n* punta *f*

tip² /tɪp/ *vt* (*pt* **tipped**) (*tilt*) inclinar; (*overturn*) volcar; (*pour*) verter. **—** *vi* inclinarse; (*overturn*) volcarse. **—** *n* (*for rubbish*) vertedero *m*. **∼** *out* verter

tip³ /tɪp/ *vt* (*reward*) dar una propina *a*. **∼ off** advertir. **—** *n* (*reward*) propina *f*; (*advice*) consejo *m*

tip-off /'tɪpɒf/ *n* advertencia *f*

tipped /'tɪpt/ *a* (*cigarette*) con filtro

tipple /'tɪpl/ *vi* beborrotear. **—** *n* bebida *f* alcohólica. **have a ∼** tomar una copa

tipsy /'tɪpsɪ/ *a* achispado

tiptoe /'tɪptəʊ/ *n*. **on ∼** de puntillas

tiptop /'tɪptɒp/ *a* (*fam*) de primera

tirade /taɪ'reɪd/ *n* diatriba *f*

tire /'taɪə(r)/ *vt* cansar. **—** *vi* cansarse. **∼d** /'taɪəd/ *a* cansado. **∼d of** harto de. **∼d out** agotado. **∼less** *a* incansable

tiresome /'taɪəsəm/ *a* (*annoying*) fastidioso; (*boring*) pesado

tiring /'taɪərɪŋ/ *a* cansado

tissue /'tɪʃuː/ *n* tisú *m*; (*handkerchief*) pañuelo *m* de papel. **∼-paper** *n* papel *m* de seda

tit¹ /tɪt/ *n* (*bird*) paro *m*

tit² /tɪt/ *n*. **∼ for tat** golpe por golpe

titbit /'tɪtbɪt/ *n* golosina *f*

titillate /'tɪtɪleɪt/ *vt* excitar

title /'taɪtl/ *n* título *m*. **∼d** *a* con título nobiliario. **∼deed** *n* título *m* de propiedad. **∼role** *n* papel *m* principal

tittle-tattle /'tɪtltætl/ *n* cháchara *f*

titular /'tɪtjʊlə(r)/ *a* nominal

tizzy /'tɪzɪ/ *n* (*sl*). **get in a ∼** ponerse nervioso

to /tu:, tə/ *prep* a; (*towards*) hacia; (*in order to*) para; (*according to*) según; (*as far as*) hasta; (*with times*) menos; (*of*). **give it to me** dámelo. **I don't want to** no quiero. **twenty ∼ seven** (*by clock*) las siete menos veinte. **∼ and fro** *adv* de aquí para allá

toad /təʊd/ *n* sapo *m*

toadstool /'təʊdstuːl/ *n* seta *f* venenosa

toast /təʊst/ n pan m tostado, tostada f; (drink) brindis m. drink a ~ to brindar por. —vt brindar por. ~er n tostador m de pan

tobacco /təˈbækəʊ/ n tabaco m. ~nist n estanquero m. ~nist's shop n estanco m

to-be /təˈbiː/ a futuro

toboggan /təˈbɒgən/ n tobogán m

today /təˈdeɪ/ n & adv hoy (m). ~ week dentro de una semana

toddler /ˈtɒdlə(r)/ n niño m que empieza a andar

toddy /ˈtɒdɪ/ n ponche m

to-do /təˈduː/ n lío m

toe /təʊ/ n dedo m del pie; (of shoe) punta f. **big** ~ dedo m gordo (del pie). **on one's ~s** (fig) alerta. —vt. ~ **the line** conformarse. ~**hold** n punto m de apoyo

toff /tɒf/ n (sl) petimetre m

toffee /ˈtɒfɪ/ n caramelo m

together /təˈgeðə(r)/ adv junto, juntos; (at same time) a la vez. ~ **with** junto con. ~**ness** n compañerismo m

toil /tɔɪl/ vi afanarse. —n trabajo m

toilet /ˈtɔɪlɪt/ n servicio m, retrete m; (grooming) arreglo m, tocado m. ~**paper** n papel m higiénico. ~**ries** /ˈtɔɪlɪtrɪz/ npl artículos mpl de tocador. ~ **water** n agua f de Colonia

token /ˈtəʊkən/ n señal f; (voucher) vale m; (coin) ficha f. —a simbólico

told /təʊld/ see **tell**. —a. **all** ~ con todo

tolerab|**le** /ˈtɒlərəbl/ a tolerable; (not bad) regular. ~**y** adv pasablemente

toleran|**ce** /ˈtɒlərəns/ n tolerancia f. ~**t** /ˈtɒlərənt/ a tolerante. ~**tly** adv con tolerancia

tolerate /ˈtɒləreɪt/ vt tolerar

toll[1] /təʊl/ n peaje m. **death** ~ número m de muertos. **take a**

heavy ~ dejar muchas víctimas

toll[2] /təʊl/ vi doblar, tocar a muerto

tom /tɒm/ n gato m (macho)

tomato /təˈmɑːtəʊ/ n (pl ~**oes**) tomate m

tomb /tuːm/ n tumba f, sepulcro m

tomboy /ˈtɒmbɔɪ/ n marimacho m

tombstone /ˈtuːmstəʊn/ n lápida f sepulcral

tom-cat /ˈtɒmkæt/ n gato m (macho)

tome /təʊm/ n librote m

tomfoolery /tɒmˈfuːlərɪ/ n payasadas fpl, tonterías fpl

tomorrow /təˈmɒrəʊ/ n & adv mañana (f). **see you** ~! ¡hasta mañana!

ton /tʌn/ n tonelada f (= 1,016 kg). ~**s of** (fam) montones de. **metric** ~ tonelada f (métrica) (= 1,000 kg)

tone /təʊn/ n tono m. —vt. ~ **down** atenuar. ~ **up** tonificar (muscles). —vi. ~ **in** armonizar. ~**deaf** a que no tiene buen oído

tongs /tɒŋz/ npl tenazas fpl; (for hair, sugar) tenacillas fpl

tongue /tʌŋ/ n lengua f. ~ **in cheek** adv irónicamente. ~**tied** a mudo. **get** ~**tied** trabársele la lengua. ~**twister** n trabalenguas m invar

tonic /ˈtɒnɪk/ a tónico. —n (tonic water) tónica f; (med, fig) tónico m. ~ **water** n tónica f.

tonight /təˈnaɪt/ adv & n esta noche (f); (evening) esta tarde (f)

tonne /tʌn/ n tonelada f (métrica)

tonsil /ˈtɒnsl/ n amígdala f. ~**litis** /-ˈlaɪtɪs/ n amigdalitis f

too /tuː/ adv demasiado; (also) también. ~ **many** a demasiados. ~ **much** a & adv demasiado

took /tʊk/ see **take**

tool /tu:l/ n herramienta f. ~**bag** n bolsa f de herramientas

toot /tu:t/ n bocinazo m. —vi tocar la bocina

tooth /tu:θ/ n (pl teeth) diente m; (molar) muela f. ~**ache** /'tu:θeɪk/ n dolor m de muelas. ~**brush** /'tu:θbrʌʃ/ n cepillo m de dientes. ~**comb** /tu:θkəʊm/ n peine m de púa fina. ~**less** a desdentado, sin dientes. ~**paste** /'tu:θpeɪst/ n pasta f dentífrica. ~**pick** /'tu:θpɪk/ n palillo m de dientes

top¹ /top/ n cima f; (upper part) parte f de arriba; (upper surface) superficie f; (lid, of bottle) tapa f; (of list) cabeza f. **from ~ to bottom** de arriba abajo. **on ~ (of)** encima de; (besides) además. ~ **floor** n último piso m. —vt (pt topped) cubrir; (exceed) exceder. ~ **up** vt llenar

top² /top/ n (toy) trompa f, peonza f

top: ~ **hat** n chistera f. ~**heavy** a más pesado arriba que abajo

topic /'topɪk/ n tema m. ~**al** /'topɪkl/ a de actualidad

top: ~**less** /'toplɪs/ a (bather) con los senos desnudos. ~**most** /'topməʊst/ a (el) más alto. ~**notch** a (fam) excelente

topography /tə'pogrəfi/ n topografía f

topple /'topl/ vi derribar; (overturn) volcar

top secret /top'si:krɪt/ a sumamente secreto

topsy-turvy /topsɪ'tɜ:vɪ/ adv & a patas arriba

torch /tɔ:tʃ/ n lámpara f de bolsillo; (flaming) antorcha f

tore /tɔ:(r)/ see **tear¹**

toreador /'toriədɔ:(r)/ n torero m

torment /'tɔ:ment/ n tormento m. /tɔ:'ment/ vt atormentar

torn /tɔ:n/ see **tear¹**

tornado /tɔ:'neɪdəʊ/ n (pl -oes) tornado m

torpedo /tɔ:'pi:dəʊ/ n (pl -oes) torpedo m. —vt torpedear

torpor /'tɔ:pə(r)/ n apatía f

torrent /'torənt/ n torrente m. ~**ial** /tə'renʃl/ a torrencial

torrid /'torɪd/ a tórrido

torso /'tɔ:səʊ/ n (pl -os) torso m

tortoise /'tɔ:təs/ n tortuga f. ~**shell** n carey m

tortuous /'tɔ:tjʊəs/ a tortuoso

torture /'tɔ:tʃə(r)/ n tortura f, tormento m. —vt atormentar. ~**r** /-ə(r)/ a atormentador m, verdugo m

Tory /'tɔ:rɪ/ a & n (fam) conservador (m)

toss /tos/ vt echar; (shake) sacudir. —vi agitarse. ~ **and turn** (in bed) revolverse. ~ **up** echar a cara o cruz

tot¹ /tot/ n nene m; (of liquor, fam) trago m

tot² /tot/ vt (pt totted). ~ **up** (fam) sumar

total /'təʊtl/ a & n total (m). —vt (pt totalled) sumar

totalitarian /təʊtælɪ'teərɪən/ a totalitario

total: ~**ity** /təʊ'tælɪtɪ/ n totalidad f. ~**ly** adv totalmente

totter /'totə(r)/ vi tambalearse. ~**y** a inseguro

touch /tʌtʃ/ vt tocar; (reach) alcanzar; (move) conmover. —vi tocarse. —n toque m; (sense) tacto m; (contact) contacto m; (trace) pizca f. **get in ~ with** ponerse en contacto con. ~ **down** (aircraft) aterrizar. ~ **off** disparar (gun); (fig) desencadenar. ~ **on** tratar levemente. ~ **up** retocar. ~**and-go** a incierto, dudoso

touching /'tʌtʃɪŋ/ a conmovedor

touchstone /'tʌtʃstəʊn/ n (fig) piedra f de toque

touchy /'tʌtʃɪ/ a quisquilloso

tough /tʌf/ a (-er, -est) duro; (*strong*) fuerte, resistente. ∼en /'tʌfn/ vt endurecer. ∼ness n dureza f, (*strength*) resistencia f

toupee /'tu:peɪ/ n postizo m, tupé m

tour /tʊə(r)/ n viaje m; (*visit*) visita f; (*excursion*) excursión f; (*by team etc*) gira f. —vt recorrer; (*visit*) visitar

tourism /'tʊərɪzəm/ n turismo m. ∼t /'tʊərɪst/ n turista m & f. —a turístico. ∼t office n oficina f de turismo

tournament /'tɔ:nəmənt/ n torneo m

tousle /'taʊzl/ vt despeinar

tout /taʊt/ vi. ∼ (**for**) solicitar. —n solicitador m

tow /təʊ/ vt remolcar. —n remolque m. on ∼ a remolque. with his family in ∼ (*fam*) acompañado por su familia

toward(s) /təˈwɔːd(z)/ prep hacia

towel /'taʊəl/ n toalla f. ∼ling n (*fabric*) toalla f

tower /'taʊə(r)/ n torre f. —vi. ∼ above dominar. ∼ block n edificio m alto. ∼ing a altísimo; (*rage*) violento

town /taʊn/ n ciudad f, pueblo m. go to ∼ (*fam*) no escatimar dinero. ∼ hall n ayuntamiento m. ∼ planning n urbanismo m

tow-path /'təʊpɑːθ/ n camino m de sirga

toxic /'tɒksɪk/ a tóxico. ∼n /'tɒksɪn/ n toxina f

toy /tɔɪ/ n juguete m. —vi. ∼ with jugar con ⟨*object*⟩; acariciar ⟨*idea*⟩. ∼shop n juguetería f

trace /treɪs/ n huella f, (*small amount*) pizca f. —vt seguir la pista de; (*draw*) dibujar; (*with tracing-paper*) calcar; (*track down*) encontrar. ∼ing /'treɪsɪŋ/ n calco m. ∼ing-paper n papel m de calcar

track /træk/ n huella f, (*path*) sendero m; (*sport*) pista f; (*of rocket etc*) trayectoria f; (*rail*) vía f. keep ∼ of vigilar. make ∼s (*sl*) marcharse. —vt seguir la pista de. ∼ down vt localizar. ∼ suit n traje m de deporte, chandal m

tract¹ /trækt/ n (*land*) extensión f; (*anat*) aparato m

tract² /trækt/ n (*pamphlet*) opúsculo m

traction /'trækʃn/ n tracción f

tractor /'træktə(r)/ n tractor m

trade /treɪd/ n comercio m; (*occupation*) oficio m; (*exchange*) cambio m; (*industry*) industria f. —vi cambiar. —vi comerciar. ∼ in (*give in part-exchange*) dar como parte del pago. ∼ on vi aprovecharse de. ∼ mark n marca f registrada. ∼r /-ə(r)/ n comerciante m & f. ∼sman /'treɪdzmən/ n (pl -men) (*shopkeeper*) tendero m. ∼ union n sindicato m. ∼ unionist n sindicalista m & f. ∼ wind n viento m alisio

trading /'treɪdɪŋ/ n comercio m. ∼ estate n zona f industrial

tradition /trə'dɪʃn/ n tradición f. ∼al a tradicional. ∼alist n tradicionalista m & f. ∼ally adv tradicionalmente

traffic /'træfɪk/ n tráfico m. —vi (*pt* trafficked) comerciar (in en). ∼-lights npl semáforo m. ∼ warden n guardia m, controlador m de tráfico

tragedy /'trædʒɪdɪ/ n tragedia f. ∼ic /'trædʒɪk/ a trágico. ∼ically adv trágicamente

trail /treɪl/ vi arrastrarse; (*lag*) rezagarse. —vt (*track*) seguir la pista de. —n estela f; (*track*) pista f. (*path*) sendero m. ∼er n remolque m; (*film*) avance m

train 595 **transplant**

train /treɪn/ n tren m; (of dress) cola f; (series) sucesión f; (retinue) séquito m. —vt adiestrar; (sport) entrenar; educar (child); guiar (plant); domar (animal). —vi adiestrarse; (sport) entrenarse. ~ed a (skilled) cualificado; (doctor) diplomado. ~ee n aprendiz m. ~er n (sport) entrenador m; (of animals) domador m. ~ers mpl zapatillas fpl de deporte. ~ing n instrucción f; (sport) entrenamiento m

traipse /treɪps/ vi (fam) vagar

trait /treɪ(t)/ n característica f, rasgo m

traitor /ˈtreɪtə(r)/ n traidor m

tram /træm/ n tranvía m

tramp /træmp/ vt recorrer a pie. —vi andar con pasos pesados. —n (vagrant) vagabundo m; (sound) ruido m de pasos; (hike) paseo m largo

trample /ˈtræmpl/ vt/i pisotear. ~ (on) pisotear

trampoline /ˈtræmpəlɪn/ n trampolín m

trance /trɑːns/ n trance m

tranquil /ˈtræŋkwɪl/ a tranquilo. ~lity /-ˈkwɪlɪtɪ/ n tranquilidad f

tranquillize /ˈtræŋkwɪlaɪz/ vt tranquilizar. ~r /-ə(r)/ n tranquilizante m

transact /trænˈzækt/ vt negociar. ~ion /-ʃn/ n transacción f

transatlantic /trænzətˈlæntɪk/ a transatlántico

transcend /trænˈsend/ vt exceder. ~ent a sobresaliente

transcendental /trænsenˈdentl/ a trascendental

transcribe /trænˈskraɪb/ vt transcribir; grabar (recorded sound)

transcript /ˈtrænskrɪpt/ n copia f. ~ion /-ɪpʃn/ n transcripción f

transfer /trænsˈfɜː(r)/ vt (pt transferred) trasladar; calcar (drawing). —vi trasladarse. ~ the charges (on telephone)

llamar a cobro revertido. /ˈtrænsfɜː/ n traslado m; (paper) calcomanía f. ~able a transferible

transfigur|ation /trænsfɪgjʊˈreɪʃn/ n transfiguración f. ~e /trænsˈfɪgə(r)/ vt transfigurar

transfix /trænsˈfɪks/ vt traspasar; (fig) paralizar

transform /trænsˈfɔːm/ vt transformar. ~ation /-əˈmeɪʃn/ n transformación f. ~er /-ə(r)/ n transformador m

transfusion /trænsˈfjuːʒn/ n transfusión f

transgress /trænsˈgres/ vt traspasar; infringir. ~ion /-ʃn/ n transgresión f; (sin) pecado m

transient /ˈtrænzɪənt/ a pasajero

transistor /trænˈzɪstə(r)/ n transistor m

transit /ˈtrænsɪt/ n tránsito m

transition /trænˈzɪʒn/ n transición f

transitive /ˈtrænsɪtɪv/ a transitivo

transitory /ˈtrænsɪtrɪ/ a transitorio

translat|e /trænzˈleɪt/ vt traducir. ~ion /-ʃn/ n traducción f. ~or /-ə(r)/ n traductor m

translucen|ce /trænzˈluːsns/ n traslucidez f. ~t /trænzˈluːsnt/ a traslúcido

transmission /trænsˈmɪʃn/ n transmisión f

transmit /trænzˈmɪt/ vt (pt transmitted) transmitir. ~ter /-ə(r)/ n transmisor m; (TV, radio) emisora f

transparen|cy /trænsˈpærənsɪ/ n transparencia f. (photo) diapositiva f. ~t /trænsˈpærənt/ a transparente

transpire /trænˈspaɪə(r)/ vi transpirar; (happen, fam) suceder, revelarse

transplant /trænsˈplɑːnt/ vt trasplantar. /ˈtrænsplɑːnt/ n trasplante m

transport /træn'spɔːt/ vt transportar. /'trænspɔːt/ n transporte m. ∼ation /-'teɪʃn/ n transporte m

transpos|e /træn'spəʊz/ vt transponer; (mus) transportar. ∼ition /-pə'zɪʃn/ n transposición f. (mus) transportación f

transverse /'trænzvɜːs/ a transverso

transvestite /trænz'vestaɪt/ n travestido m

trap /træp/ n trampa f. —vt (pt trapped) atrapar; (jam) atascar; (cut off) bloquear. ∼door /'træpdɔː(r)/ n trampa f; (in theatre) escotillón m

trapeze /trə'piːz/ n trapecio m

trappings /'træpɪŋz/ npl (fig) atavíos mpl

trash /træʃ/ n pacotilla f; (refuse) basura f; (nonsense) tonterías fpl. ∼ can n (Amer) cubo m de la basura. ∼y a de baja calidad

trauma /'trɔːmə/ n trauma m. ∼tic /-'mætɪk/ a traumático

travel /'trævl/ vi (pt travelled) viajar. —vt recorrer. —n viajar m. ∼ler /-ə(r)/ n viajero m. ∼ler's cheque n cheque m de viaje. ∼ling n viajar m

traverse /træ'vɜːs/ vt atravesar, recorrer

travesty /'trævɪstɪ/ n parodia f

trawler /'trɔːlə(r)/ n pesquero m de arrastre

tray /treɪ/ n bandeja f

treacher|ous a traidor; (deceptive) engañoso. ∼ously adv traidoramente. ∼y /'tretʃərɪ/ n traición f

treacle /'triːkl/ n melaza f

tread /tred/ vi (pt **trod**, pp **trodden**) andar. ∼ **on** pisar. —vt pisar. —n (step) paso m; (of tyre) banda f de rodadura. ∼le /'tredl/ n pedal m. ∼mill /'tredmɪl/ n rueda f de molino; (fig) rutina f

treason /'triːzn/ n traición f

treasure /'treʒə(r)/ n tesoro m. —vt apreciar mucho; (store) guardar

treasur|er /'treʒərə(r)/ n tesorero m. ∼y /'treʒərɪ/ n tesorería f. **the T**∼y n el Ministerio m de Hacienda

treat /triːt/ vt tratar; (consider) considerar. ∼ **s.o.** invitar a uno. —n placer m; (present) regalo m

treatise /'triːtɪz/ n tratado m

treatment /'triːtmənt/ n tratamiento m

treaty /'triːtɪ/ n tratado m

treble /'trebl/ a triple; (clef) de sol; (voice) de tiple. —vt triplicar. —vi triplicarse. —n tiple m & f

tree /triː/ n árbol m

trek /trek/ n viaje m arduo, caminata f. —vi (pt **trekked**) hacer un viaje arduo

trellis /'trelɪs/ n enrejado m

tremble /'trembl/ vi temblar

tremendous /trɪ'mendəs/ a tremendo; (huge, fam) enorme. ∼ly adv tremendamente

tremor /'tremə(r)/ n temblor m

tremulous /'tremjʊləs/ a tembloroso

trench /trentʃ/ n foso m, zanja f; (mil) trinchera f. ∼ **coat** n trinchera f

trend /trend/ n tendencia f; (fashion) moda f. ∼-**setter** n persona f que lanza la moda. ∼y a (-ier, -iest) (fam) a la última

trepidation /trepɪ'deɪʃn/ n inquietud f

trespass /'trespəs/ vi. ∼ **on** entrar sin derecho; (fig) abusar de. ∼er /-ə(r)/ n intruso m

tress /tres/ n trenza f

trestle /'tresl/ n caballete m. ∼-**table** n mesa f de caballete

trews /truːz/ npl pantalón m

trial /'traɪəl/ n prueba f; (jurid) proceso m; (ordeal) prueba f dura. ~ **and error** tanteo *m*. **be on** ~ estar a prueba; (*jurid*) ser procesado

triangl|e /'traɪæŋgl/ *n* triángulo *m*. **~ular** /-'æŋgjolə(r)/ *a* triangular

trib|al /'traɪbl/ *a* tribal. **~e** /traɪb/ *n* tribu *f*

tribulation /trɪbjʊ'leɪʃn/ *n* tribulación *f*

tribunal /traɪ'bju:nl/ *n* tribunal *m*

tributary /'trɪbjʊtrɪ/ *n* (*stream*) afluente *m*

tribute /'trɪbju:t/ *n* tributo *m*. **pay ~ to** rendir homenaje a

trice /traɪs/ *n*. **in a** ~ en un abrir y cerrar de ojos

trick /trɪk/ *n* trampa *f*; engaño *m*; (*joke*) broma *f*; (*at cards*) baza *f*; (*habit*) manía *f*. **do** ~ servir. **play a** ~ **on** gastar una broma a. —*vt* engañar. **~ery** /'trɪkərɪ/ *n* engaño *m*

trickle /'trɪkl/ *vi* gotear. ~ **in** (*fig*) entrar poco a poco. ~ **out** (*fig*) salir poco a poco

trickster /'trɪkstə(r)/ *n* estafador *m*

tricky /'trɪkɪ/ *a* delicado, difícil

tricolour /'trɪkələ(r)/ *n* bandera *f* tricolor

tricycle /'traɪsɪkl/ *n* triciclo *m*

trident /'traɪdənt/ *n* tridente *m*

tried /traɪd/ *see* **try**

trifl|e /'traɪfl/ *n* bagatela *f*; (*culin*) bizcocho *m* con natillas, jalea, frutas y nata. —*vi*. **~e with** jugar con. **~ing** *a* insignificante

trigger /'trɪgə(r)/ *n* (*of gun*) gatillo *m*. —*vt*. ~ (**off**) desencadenar

trigonometry /trɪgə'nɒmɪtrɪ/ *n* trigonometría *f*

trilby /'trɪlbɪ/ *n* sombrero *m* de fieltro

trilogy /'trɪlədʒɪ/ *n* trilogía *f*

trim /trɪm/ *a* (**trimmer, trimmest**) arreglado. —*vt* (*pt*

trimmed) cortar; recortar (*hair etc*); (*adorn*) adornar. —*n* (*cut*) recorte *m*; (*decoration*) adorno *m*; (*state*) estado *m*. **in** ~ en buen estado; (*fit*) en forma. **~ming** *n* adorno *m*. **~mings** *npl* recortes *mpl*; (*decorations*) adornos *mpl*; (*culin*) guarnición *f*

trinity /'trɪnɪtɪ/ *n* trinidad *f*. **the T~** la Trinidad

trinket /'trɪŋkɪt/ *n* chuchería *f*

trio /'tri:əʊ/ *n* (*pl* -**os**) trío *m*

trip /trɪp/ *vt* (*pt* **tripped**) hacer tropezar. —*vi* tropezar; (*go lightly*) andar con paso ligero. —*n* (*journey*) viaje *m*; (*outing*) excursión *f*; (*stumble*) traspié *m*. ~ **up** *vi* tropezar. —*vt* hacer tropezar

tripe /traɪp/ *n* callos *mpl*; (*nonsense, sl*) tonterías *fpl*

triple /'trɪpl/ *a* triple. —*vt* triplicar. —*vi* triplicarse. **~ts** /'trɪplɪts/ *npl* trillizos *mpl*

triplicate /'trɪplɪkət/ *a* triplicado. **in** ~ por triplicado

tripod /'traɪpɒd/ *n* trípode *m*

tripper /'trɪpə(r)/ *n* (*on day trip etc*) excursionista *m & f*

triptych /'trɪptɪk/ *n* tríptico *m*

trite /traɪt/ *a* trillado

triumph /'traɪʌmf/ *n* triunfo *m*. —*vi* triunfar (**over** sobre). **~al** /-'ʌmfl/ *a* triunfal. **~ant** /-'ʌmfnt/ *a* triunfante

trivial /'trɪvɪəl/ *a* insignificante. **~ity** /-'ælɪtɪ/ *n* insignificancia *f*

trod, trodden /trɒd, 'trɒdn/ *see* **tread**

trolley /'trɒlɪ/ *n* (*pl* -**eys**) carretón *m*. **tea** ~ *n* mesita *f* de ruedas. **~bus** *n* trolebús *m*

trombone /trɒm'bəʊn/ *n* trombón *m*

troop /tru:p/ *n* grupo *m*. —*vi*. ~ **in** entrar en tropel. ~ **out** salir en tropel. **~ing the colour** saludo *m* a la bandera. **~er** *n* soldado *m* de caballería. **~s** *npl* (*mil*) tropas *fpl*

trophy /'trəʊfɪ/ n trofeo m

tropic /'trɒpɪk/ n trópico m. ~**al** a tropical. ~s npl trópicos mpl

trot /trɒt/ n trote m. on the ~ (fam) seguidos. —vi (pt trotted) trotar. ~ out (produce, fam) producir

trotter /'trɒtə(r)/ n (culin) pie m de cerdo

trouble /'trʌbl/ n problema m; (awkward situation) apuro m; (inconvenience) molestia f; (conflict) conflicto m; (med) enfermedad f; (mec) avería f. be in ~ estar en un apuro. make ~ armar un lío. take ~ tomarse la molestia. —vt (bother) molestar; (worry) preocupar. —vi molestarse; (worry) preocuparse. be ~d about preocuparse por. ~-maker n alborotador m. ~some a molesto

trough /trɒf/ n (for drinking) abrevadero m; (for feeding) pesebre m; (of wave) seno m; (atmospheric) mínimo m de presión

trounce /traʊns/ vt (defeat) derrotar; (thrash) pegar

troupe /truːp/ n compañía f

trousers /'traʊzəz/ npl pantalón m; pantalones mpl

trousseau /'truːsəʊ/ n (pl -s /-əʊz/) ajuar m

trout /traʊt/ n (pl trout) trucha f

trowel /'traʊəl/ n (garden) desplantador m; (for mortar) paleta f

truant /'truːənt/ n. play ~ hacer novillos

truce /truːs/ n tregua f

truck[1] /trʌk/ n carro m; (rail) vagón m; (lorry) camión m

truck[2] /trʌk/ n (dealings) trato m

truculent /'trʌkjʊlənt/ a agresivo

trudge /trʌdʒ/ vi andar penosamente. —n caminata f penosa

true /truː/ a (-er, -est) verdadero; (loyal) leal; (genuine)

auténtico; (accurate) exacto. **come** ~ realizarse

truffle /'trʌfl/ n trufa f; (chocolate) trufa f de chocolate

truism /'truːɪzəm/ n perogrullada f

truly /'truːlɪ/ adv verdaderamente; (sincerely) sinceramente; (faithfully) fielmente. **yours** ~ (in letters) le saluda atentamente

trump /trʌmp/ n (cards) triunfo m. —vt fallar. ~ **up** inventar

trumpet /'trʌmpɪt/ n trompeta f. ~**er** /-ə(r)/ n trompetero m, trompeta m & f

truncated /trʌŋ'keɪtɪd/ a truncado

truncheon /'trʌntʃən/ n porra f

trundle /'trʌndl/ vt hacer rodar. —vi rodar

trunk /trʌŋk/ n tronco m; (box) baúl m; (of elephant) trompa f. ~**-call** n conferencia f. ~**-road** n carretera f (nacional). ~**s** npl bañador m

truss /trʌs/ n (med) braguero m. ~ **up** vt (culin) espetar

trust /trʌst/ n confianza f; (association) trust m. on ~ a ojos cerrados; (com) al fiado. —vi confiar. ~ **to** confiar en. —vt confiar en; (hope) esperar. ~**ed** a leal

trustee /trʌ'stiː/ n administrador m

trust: ~**ful** a confiado. ~**fully** adv confiadamente. ~**worthy** a, ~**y** a digno de confianza

truth /truːθ/ n (pl -s /truːðz/) verdad f. ~**ful** a veraz; (true) verídico. ~**fully** adv sinceramente

try /traɪ/ vt (pt tried) probar; (be a strain on) poner a prueba; (jurid) procesar. ~ **on** vt probarse (garment). ~ **out** vt probar. —vi probar. ~ **for** vt intentar conseguir. —n tentativa f, prueba f; (rugby) ensayo

m. ~ing *a* difícil; (*annoying*) molesto. ~out *n* prueba *f*
tryst /trɪst/ *n* cita *f*
T-shirt /ˈtiːʃɜːt/ *n* camiseta *f*
tub /tʌb/ *n* tina *f*; (*bath*, *fam*) baño *m*
tuba /ˈtjuːbə/ *n* tuba *f*
tubby /ˈtʌbɪ/ *a* (-ier, -iest) rechoncho
tube /tjuːb/ *n* tubo *m*; (*rail*, *fam*) metro *m*. **inner** ~ *n* cámara *f* de aire
tuber /ˈtjuːbə(r)/ *n* tubérculo *m*
tuberculosis /tjuːbɜːkjʊˈləʊsɪs/ *n* tuberculosis *f*
tub|ing /ˈtjuːbɪŋ/ *n* tubería *f*, tubos *mpl.* ~ular *a* tubular
tuck /tʌk/ *n* pliegue *m.* ~vt plegar; (*put*) meter; (*put away*) remeter; (*hide*) esconder. ~ **up** *vt* arropar (*child*). ~vi. ~ **in(to)** (*eat*, *sl*) comer con buen apetito. ~shop *n* confitería *f*
Tuesday /ˈtjuːzdeɪ/ *n* martes *m*
tuft /tʌft/ *n* (*of hair*) mechón *m*; (*of feathers*) penacho *m*; (*of grass*) manojo *m*
tug /tʌg/ *vt* (*pt* **tugged**) tirar de; (*tow*) remolcar. ~vi tirar fuerte. ~n tirón *m*; (*naut*) remolcador *m.* ~-of-war *n* lucha *f* de la cuerda; (*fig*) tira *m* y afloja
tuition /tjuːˈɪʃn/ *n* enseñanza *f*
tulip /ˈtjuːlɪp/ *n* tulipán *m*
tumble /ˈtʌmbl/ *vi* caerse. ~ **to** (*fam*) comprender. ~n caída *f*
tumbledown /ˈtʌmbldaʊn/ *a* ruinoso
tumble-drier /ˈtʌmbldraɪə(r)/ *n* secadora *f* (eléctrica con aire de salida)
tumbler /ˈtʌmblə(r)/ *n* (*glass*) vaso *m*
tummy /ˈtʌmɪ/ *n* (*fam*) estómago *m*
tumour /ˈtjuːmə(r)/ *n* tumor *m*
tumult /ˈtjuːmʌlt/ *n* tumulto *m*. ~uous /-ˈmʌltjʊəs/ *a* tumultuoso

tuna /ˈtjuːnə/ *n* (*pl* **tuna**) atún *m*
tune /tjuːn/ *n* aire *m.* **be in** ~ estar afinado. **be out of** ~ estar desafinado. ~vt afinar; (*radio*, *TV*); (*mec*) poner a punto. ~vi. ~ **in (to)** (*radio*, *TV*) sintonizarse. ~ **up** afinar. ~ful *a* melodioso. ~r /-ə(r)/ *n* afinador *m*; (*radio*, *TV*) sintonizador *m*
tunic /ˈtjuːnɪk/ *n* túnica *f*
tuning-fork /ˈtjuːnɪŋfɔːk/ *n* diapasón *m*
Tunisia /tjuːˈnɪzɪə/ *n* Túnez *m.* ~n *a* & *n* tunecino *m*
tunnel /ˈtʌnl/ *n* túnel *m.* ~vi (*pt* **tunnelled**) construir un túnel en
turban /ˈtɜːbən/ *n* turbante *m*
turbid /ˈtɜːbɪd/ *a* túrbido
turbine /ˈtɜːbaɪn/ *n* turbina *f*
turbo-jet /ˈtɜːbəʊdʒet/ *n* turborreactor *m*
turbot /ˈtɜːbət/ *n* rodaballo *m*
turbulen|ce /ˈtɜːbjʊləns/ *n* turbulencia *f.* ~t /ˈtɜːbjʊlənt/ *a* turbulento
tureen /tjʊˈriːn/ *n* sopera *f*
turf /tɜːf/ *n* (*pl* **turfs** or **turves**) césped *m*; (*segment*) tepe *m.* **the** ~ *n* las carreras *fpl* de caballos. ~vt. ~ **out** (*sl*) echar
turgid /ˈtɜːdʒɪd/ *a* (*language*) pomposo
Turk /tɜːk/ *n* turco *m*
turkey /ˈtɜːkɪ/ *n* (*pl* -eys) pavo *m*
Turk|ey /ˈtɜːkɪ/ *f* Turquía *f.* T~ish *a* & *n* turco *m*
turmoil /ˈtɜːmɔɪl/ *n* confusión *f*
turn /tɜːn/ *vt* hacer girar, dar vueltas a; volver (*direction*, *page*, *etc*); cumplir (*age*); dar (*hour*); doblar (*corner*); (*change*) cambiar; (*deflect*) desviar. ~ **the tables** volver las tornas. ~vi girar, dar vueltas; (*become*) hacerse; (*change*) cambiar. ~n vuelta *f*; (*in road*) curva *f*; (*change*) cambio *m*; (*sequence*)

turno *m*; (*of mind*) disposición *f*; (*in theatre*) número *m*; (*fright*) susto *m*; (*of illness, fam*) ataque *m*. **bad ~** mala jugada *f*. **good ~** favor *m*. **in ~** a su vez. **out of ~** fuera de lugar. **to a ~** (*culin*) en su punto. **~ against** *vt* volverse en contra de. **~ down** *vt* (*fold*) doblar; (*reduce*) bajar; (*reject*) rechazar. **~ in** *vt* entregar. —*vi* (*go to bed, fam*) acostarse. **~ off** *vt* cerrar ‹*tap*›; apagar ‹*light, TV, etc*›. —*vi* desviarse. **~ on** *vt* abrir ‹*tap*›; encender ‹*light etc*›; (*attack*) atacar; (*attract, fam*) excitar. **~ out** *vt* expulsar; apagar ‹*light etc*›; (*produce*) producir; (*empty*) vaciar. —*vi* (*result*) resultar. **~ round** *vi* dar la vuelta. **~ up** *vi* aparecer. —*vt* (*find*) encontrar; levantar ‹*collar*›; poner más fuerte ‹*gas*›. **~ed-up** *a* ‹*nose*› respingona. **~ing** /'tɜ:nɪŋ/ *n* vuelta *f*; (*road*) bocacalle *f*. **~ing-point** *n* punto *m* decisivo.

turnip /'tɜ:nɪp/ *n* nabo *m*

turn /tɜ:n/ **~out** *n* (*of people*) concurrencia *f*; (*of goods*) producción *f*. **~over** /'tɜ:nəʊvə(r)/ *n* (*culin*) empanada *f*; (*com*) volumen *m* de negocios; (*of staff*) rotación *f*. **~pike** /'tɜ:npaɪk/ *n* (*Amer*) autopista *f* de peaje. **~stile** /'tɜ:nstaɪl/ *n* torniquete *m*. **~table** /'tɜ:nteɪbl/ *n* plataforma *f* giratoria; (*on record-player*) plato *m* giratorio. **~up** *n* (*of trousers*) vuelta *f*

turpentine /'tɜ:pəntaɪn/ *n* trementina *f*

turquoise /'tɜ:kwɔɪz/ *a* & *n* turquesa (*f*)

turret /'tʌrɪt/ *n* torrecilla *f*; (*mil*) torreta *f*

turtle /'tɜ:tl/ *n* tortuga *f* de mar. **~neck** *n* cuello *m* alto

tusk /tʌsk/ *n* colmillo *m*

tussle /'tʌsl/ *vi* pelearse. —*n* pelea *f*

tussock /'tʌsək/ *n* montecillo *m* de hierbas

tutor /'tju:tə(r)/ *n* preceptor *m*; (*univ*) director *m* de estudios, profesor *m*. **~ial** /tju:'tɔ:rɪəl/ *n* clase *f* particular

tuxedo /tʌk'si:dəʊ/ *n* (*pl* **-os**) (*Amer*) esmoquin *m*

TV /ti:'vi:/ *n* televisión *f*

twaddle /'twɒdl/ *n* tonterías *fpl*

twang /twæŋ/ *n* tañido *m*; (*in voice*) gangueo *m*. —*vt* hacer vibrar. —*vi* vibrar

tweed /twi:d/ *n* tela *f* gruesa de lana

tweet /twi:t/ *n* piada *f*. —*vi* piar

tweezers /'twi:zəz/ *npl* pinzas *fpl*

twelfth /twelfθ/ *a* & *n* duodécimo (*m*). **~ve** /twelv/ *a* & *n* doce (*m*)

twentieth /'twentɪəθ/ *a* & *n* vigésimo (*m*). **~y** /'twentɪ/ *a* & *n* veinte (*m*)

twerp /twɜ:p/ *n* (*sl*) imbécil *m*

twice /twaɪs/ *adv* dos veces

twiddle /'twɪdl/ *vt* hacer girar. **~ one's thumbs** (*fig*) no tener nada que hacer. **~ with** jugar con

twig¹ /twɪg/ *n* ramita *f*

twig² /twɪg/ *vt/i* (*pt* **twigged**) (*fam*) comprender

twilight /'twaɪlaɪt/ *n* crepúsculo *m*

twin /twɪn/ *a* & *n* gemelo (*m*)

twine /twaɪn/ *n* bramante *m*. —*vt* torcer. —*vi* enroscarse

twinge /twɪndʒ/ *n* punzada *f*; (*fig*) remordimiento *m* (*de conciencia*)

twinkle /'twɪŋkl/ *vi* centellear. —*n* centelleo *m*

twirl /twɜ:l/ *vt* dar vueltas a. —*vi* dar vueltas. —*n* vuelta *f*

twist /twɪst/ *vt* torcer; (*roll*) enrollar; (*distort*) deformar. —*vi* torcerse; (*coil*) enroscarse;

U

⟨*road*⟩ serpentear. —*n* torsión *f*;
(*curve*) vuelta *f*; (*of character*)
peculiaridad *f*

twit[1] /twɪt/ *n* (*sl*) imbécil *m*

twit[2] /twɪt/ *vt* (*pt* **twitted**) tomar
el pelo a

twitch /twɪtʃ/ *vt* crispar. —*vi*
crisparse. —*n* tic *m*; (*jerk*) tirón
m

twitter /ˈtwɪtə(r)/ *vi* gorjear. —*n*
gorjeo *m*

two /tuː/ *a* & *n* dos (*m*). **in** ~
minds indeciso. ~**faced** *a*
falso, insincero. ~**piece** (suit)
n traje *m* (de dos piezas). ~**some**
/ˈtuːsəm/ *n* pareja *f*. ~**way** *a*
⟨*traffic*⟩ de doble sentido

tycoon /taɪˈkuːn/ *n* magnate *m*

tying /ˈtaɪɪŋ/ *see* **tie**

type /taɪp/ *n* tipo *m*. —*vt/i* escribir a máquina. ~**cast** *a* ⟨*actor*⟩
encasillado. ~**script** /ˈtaɪp
skrɪpt/ *n* texto *m* escrito a
máquina. ~**writer** /ˈtaɪpraɪtə(r)/
n máquina *f* de escribir.
~**written** /-ɪtn/ *a* escrito a
máquina, mecanografiado

typhoid /ˈtaɪfɔɪd/ *n*. ~ (**fever**)
fiebre *f* tifoidea

typhoon /taɪˈfuːn/ *n* tifón *m*

typical /ˈtɪpɪkl/ *a* típico. ~**ly** *adv*
típicamente

typify /ˈtɪpɪfaɪ/ *vt* tipificar

typi|ng /ˈtaɪpɪŋ/ *n* mecanografía
f. ~**st** *n* mecanógrafo *m*

typography /taɪˈpɒɡrəfɪ/ *n* tipografía *f*

tyran|nical /tɪˈrænɪkl/ *a* tirán-
ico. ~**nize** *vi* tiranizar. ~**ny**
/ˈtɪrənɪ/ *n* tiranía *f*. ~**t** /ˈtaɪərənt/
n tirano *m*

tyre /ˈtaɪə(r)/ *n* neumático *m*,
llanta *f* (*Amer*)

ubiquitous /juːˈbɪkwɪtəs/ *a*
omnipresente, ubicuo

udder /ˈʌdə(r)/ *n* ubre *f*

UFO /ˈjuːfəʊ/ *abbr* (*unidentified
flying object*) OVNI *m*, objeto *m*
volante no identificado

ugl|iness /ˈʌɡlɪnɪs/ *n* fealdad *f*.
~**y** /ˈʌɡlɪ/ *a* (-**ier**, -**iest**) feo

UK /juːˈkeɪ/ *abbr* (*United Kingdom*) Reino *m* Unido

ulcer /ˈʌlsə(r)/ *n* úlcera *f*. ~**ous** *a*
ulceroso

ulterior /ʌlˈtɪərɪə(r)/ *a* ulterior.
~ **motive** *n* segunda intención *f*

ultimate /ˈʌltɪmət/ *a* último;
(*definitive*) definitivo; (*fundamental*) fundamental. ~**ly**
adv al final; (*basically*) en el
fondo

ultimatum /ʌltɪˈmeɪtəm/ *n* (*pl*
-**ums**) ultimátum *m invar*

ultra... /ˈʌltrə/ *pref* ultra...

ultramarine /ʌltrəməˈriːn/ *n*
azul *m* marino

ultrasonic /ʌltrəˈsɒnɪk/ *a*
ultrasónico

ultraviolet /ʌltrəˈvaɪələt/ *a*
ultravioleta *a invar*

umbilical /ʌmˈbɪlɪkl/ *a* umbíl-
ical. ~ **cord** *n* cordón *m*
umbilical

umbrage /ˈʌmbrɪdʒ/ *n* resentimiento *m*. **take** ~ ofenderse (**at**
por)

umbrella /ʌmˈbrelə/ *n* paraguas
m invar

umpire /ˈʌmpaɪə(r)/ *n* árbitro
m. —*vt* arbitrar

umpteen /ˈʌmptiːn/ *a* (*sl*) muchísimos. ~**th** *a* (*sl*) enésimo

UN /juːˈen/ *abbr* (*United Nations*)
ONU *f*, Organización *f* de las
Naciones Unidas

un... /ʌn/ *pref* in..., des..., no,
poco, sin

unabated /ʌnə'beitid/ *a* no disminuido

unable /ʌn'eibl/ *a* incapaz (**to** de). **be ~ to** no poder

unabridged /ʌnə'bridʒd/ *a* íntegro

unacceptable /ʌnək'septəbl/ *a* inaceptable

unaccountabl|e /ʌnə'kauntəbl/ *a* inexplicable. **~y** *adv* inexplicablemente

unaccustomed /ʌnə'kʌstəmd/ *a* insólito. **be ~ to** a no estar acostumbrado a

unadopted /ʌnə'dɒptid/ *a (of road)* privado

unadulterated /ʌnə'dʌltəreitid/ *a* puro

unaffected /ʌnə'fektid/ *a* sin afectación, natural

unaided /ʌn'eidid/ *a* sin ayuda

unalloyed /ʌnə'lɔid/ *a* puro

unanimous /ju:'næniməs/ *a* unánime. **~ly** *adv* unánimemente

unannounced /ʌnə'naunst/ *a* sin previo aviso; *(unexpected)* inesperado

unarmed /ʌn'ɑ:md/ *a* desarmado

unassuming /ʌnə'sju:miŋ/ *a* modesto, sin pretensiones

unattached /ʌnə'tætʃt/ *a* suelto; *(unmarried)* soltero

unattended /ʌnə'tendid/ *a* sin vigilar

unattractive /ʌnə'træktiv/ *a* poco atractivo

unavoidabl|e /ʌnə'vɔidəbl/ *a* inevitable. **~y** *adv* inevitablemente

unaware /ʌnə'weə(r)/ *a* ignorante (**of** de). **be ~ of** ignorar. **~s** /-eəz/ *adv* desprevenido

unbalanced /ʌn'bælənst/ *a* desequilibrado

unbearabl|e /ʌn'beərəbl/ *a* inaguantable. **~y** *adv* inaguantablemente

unbeat|able /ʌn'bi:təbl/ *a* insuperable. **~en** *a* no vencido

unbeknown /ʌnbi'nəʊn/ *a* desconocido. **~ to me** *(fam)* sin saberlo yo

unbelievable /ʌnbi'li:vəbl/ *a* increíble

unbend /ʌn'bend/ *vt (pt unbent)* enderezar. —*vi (relax)* relajarse. **~ing** *a* inflexible

unbiased /ʌn'baiəst/ *a* imparcial

unbidden /ʌn'bidn/ *a* espontáneo; *(without invitation)* sin ser invitado

unblock /ʌn'blɒk/ *vt* desatascar

unbolt /ʌn'bəult/ *vt* desatrancar

unborn /ʌn'bɔ:n/ *a* no nacido todavía

unbounded /ʌn'baundid/ *a* ilimitado

unbreakable /ʌn'breikəbl/ *a* irrompible

unbridled /ʌn'braidld/ *a* desenfrenado

unbroken /ʌn'brəʊkən/ *a (intact)* intacto; *(continuous)* continuo

unburden /ʌn'bɜ:dn/ *vt.* **~ o.s.** desahogarse

unbutton /ʌn'bʌtn/ *vt* desabotonar, desabrochar

uncalled-for /ʌn'kɔ:ldfɔ:(r)/ *a* fuera de lugar; *(unjustified)* injustificado

uncanny /ʌn'kæni/ *a* (**-ier, -iest**) misterioso

unceasing /ʌn'si:siŋ/ *a* incesante

unceremonious /ʌnseri'məʊniəs/ *a* informal; *(abrupt)* brusco

uncertain /ʌn'sɜ:tn/ *a* incierto; *(changeable)* variable. **be ~ whether** no saber exactamente si. **~ty** *n* incertidumbre *f*

unchang|ed /ʌn'tʃeindʒd/ *a* igual. **~ing** *a* inmutable

uncharitable /ʌn'tʃæritəbl/ *a* severo

uncivilized /ʌn'sivilaizd/ *a* incivilizado

uncle /'ʌŋkl/ n tío m

unclean /ʌn'kliːn/ a sucio

unclear /ʌn'klɪə(r)/ a poco claro

uncomfortable /ʌn'kʌmfətəbl/ a incómodo; (unpleasant) desagradable. **feel** ~ no estar a gusto

uncommon /ʌn'kɒmən/ a raro. ~**ly** adv extraordinariamente

uncompromising /ʌn'kɒmprəmaɪzɪŋ/ a intransigente

unconcerned /ʌnkən'sɜːnd/ a indiferente

unconditional /ʌnkən'dɪʃənl/ a incondicional. ~**ly** adv incondicionalmente

unconscious /ʌn'kɒnʃəs/ a inconsciente; (med) sin sentido. ~**ly** adv inconscientemente

unconventional /ʌnkən'venʃənl/ a poco convencional

uncooperative /ʌnkəʊ'ɒpərətɪv/ a poco servicial

uncork /ʌn'kɔːk/ vt descorchar, destapar

uncouth /ʌn'kuːθ/ a grosero

uncover /ʌn'kʌvə(r)/ vt descubrir

unctuous /'ʌŋktjʊəs/ a untuoso; (fig) empalagoso

undecided /ʌndɪ'saɪdɪd/ a indeciso

undeniabl|e /ʌndɪ'naɪəbl/ a innegable. ~**y** adv indiscutiblemente

under /'ʌndə(r)/ prep debajo de; (less than) menos de; (in the course of) bajo, en. —adv debajo, abajo. ~ **age** a menor de edad. ~ **way** adv en curso; (on the way) en marcha

under... pref sub...

undercarriage /'ʌndəkærɪdʒ/ n (aviat) tren m de aterrizaje

underclothes /'ʌndəkləʊðz/ npl ropa f interior

undercoat /'ʌndəkəʊt/ n (of paint) primera mano f

undercover /ʌndə'kʌvə(r)/ a secreto

undercurrent /'ʌndəkʌrənt/ n corriente f submarina; (fig) tendencia f oculta

undercut /'ʌndəkʌt/ vt (pt **undercut**) (com) vender más barato que

underdeveloped /ʌndədɪ'veləpt/ a subdesarrollado

underdog /'ʌndədɒg/ n perdedor m. **the** ~**s** npl los de abajo

underdone /ʌndə'dʌn/ a (meat) poco hecho

underestimate /ʌndər'estɪmeɪt/ vt subestimar

underfed /ʌndə'fed/ a desnutrido

underfoot /ʌndə'fʊt/ adv bajo los pies

undergo /'ʌndəgəʊ/ vt (pt **-went**, pp **-gone**) sufrir

undergraduate /ʌndə'grædjʊət/ n estudiante m & f universitario (no licenciado)

underground /ʌndə'graʊnd/ adv bajo tierra; (in secret) clandestinamente. /'ʌndəgraʊnd/ a subterráneo; (secret) clandestino. —n metro m

undergrowth /'ʌndəgrəʊθ/ n maleza f

underhand /'ʌndəhænd/ a (secret) clandestino; (deceptive) fraudulento

underlie /ʌndə'laɪ/ vt (pt **-lay**, pp **-lain**, pres p **-lying**) estar debajo de; (fig) estar a la base de

underline /ʌndə'laɪn/ vt subrayar

underling /'ʌndəlɪŋ/ n subalterno m

underlying /ʌndə'laɪŋ/ a fundamental

undermine /ʌndə'maɪn/ vt socavar

underneath /ʌndə'niːθ/ prep debajo de. —adv por debajo

underpaid /ʌndə'peɪd/ *a* mal pagado

underpants /'ʌndəpænts/ *npl* calzoncillos *mpl*

underpass /'ʌndəpɑ:s/ *n* paso *m* subterráneo

underprivileged /ʌndə'prɪvɪlɪdʒd/ *a* desvalido

underrate /ʌndə'reɪt/ *vt* subestimar

undersell /ʌndə'sel/ *vt* (*pt* -**sold**) vender más barato que

undersigned /'ʌndəsaɪnd/ *a* abajo firmante

undersized /ʌndə'saɪzd/ *a* pequeño

understand /ʌndə'stænd/ *vt/i* (*pt* -**stood**) entender, comprender. ~**able** *a* comprensible. ~**ing** /ʌndə'stændɪŋ/ *a* comprensivo. —*n* comprensión *f*; (*agreement*) acuerdo *m*

understatement /ʌndə'steɪtmənt/ *n* subestimación *f*

understudy /'ʌndəstʌdɪ/ *n* sobresaliente *m* & *f* (en el teatro)

undertake /ʌndə'teɪk/ *vt* (*pt* -**took**, *pp* -**taken**) emprender; (*assume responsibility*) encargarse de

undertaker /'ʌndəteɪkə(r)/ *n* empresario *m* de pompas fúnebres

undertaking /'ʌndəteɪkɪŋ/ *n* empresa *f*; (*promise*) promesa *f*

undertone /'ʌndətəʊn/ *n*. **in an ~** en voz baja

undertow /'ʌndətəʊ/ *n* resaca *f*

undervalue /ʌndə'vælju:/ *vt* subvalorar

underwater /ʌndə'wɔ:tə(r)/ *a* submarino. —*adv* bajo el agua

underwear /'ʌndəweə(r)/ *n* ropa *f* interior

underweight /'ʌndəweɪt/ *a* de peso insuficiente. **be ~** estar flaco

underwent /ʌndə'went/ *see* **undergo**

underworld /'ʌndəwɜːld/ *n* (*criminals*) hampa *f*

underwrite /ʌndə'raɪt/ *vt* (*pt* -**wrote**, *pp* -**written**) (*com*) asegurar. ~**r** /-ə(r)/ *n* asegurador *m*

undeserved /ʌndɪ'zɜːvd/ *a* inmerecido

undesirable /ʌndɪ'zaɪərəbl/ *a* indeseable

undeveloped /ʌndɪ'veləpt/ *a* sin desarrollar

undies /'ʌndɪz/ *npl* (*fam*) ropa *f* interior

undignified /ʌn'dɪgnɪfaɪd/ *a* indecoroso

undisputed /ʌndɪs'pjuːtɪd/ *a* incontestable

undistinguished /ʌndɪs'tɪŋgwɪʃt/ *a* mediocre

undo /ʌn'duː/ *vt* (*pt* -**did**, *pp* -**done**) deshacer; (*ruin*) arruinar; reparar (*wrong*). **leave ~ne** dejar sin hacer

undoubted /ʌn'daʊtɪd/ *a* indudable. ~**ly** *adv* indudablemente

undress /ʌn'dres/ *vt* desnudar. —*vi* desnudarse

undue /ʌn'djuː/ *a* excesivo

undulat|e /'ʌndjʊleɪt/ *vi* ondular. ~**ion** /-'leɪʃn/ *n* ondulación *f*

unduly /ʌn'djuːlɪ/ *adv* excesivamente

undying /ʌn'daɪɪŋ/ *a* eterno

unearth /ʌn'ɜːθ/ *vt* desenterrar

unearthly /ʌn'ɜːθlɪ/ *a* sobrenatural; (*impossible*, *fam*) absurdo. **~ hour** *n* hora intempestiva

uneas|ily /ʌn'iːzɪlɪ/ *adv* inquietamente. ~**y** /ʌn'iːzɪ/ *a* incómodo; (*worrying*) inquieto

uneconomic /ʌniːkə'nɒmɪk/ *a* poco rentable

uneducated /ʌn'edjʊkeɪtɪd/ *a* inculto

unemploy|ed /ʌnɪmˈplɔɪd/ a parado, desempleado; (not in use) inutilizado. **~ment** n paro m, desempleo m

unending /ʌnˈendɪŋ/ a interminable, sin fin

unequal /ʌnˈiːkwəl/ a desigual

unequivocal /ʌnɪˈkwɪvəkl/ a inequívoco

unerring /ʌnˈɜːrɪŋ/ a infalible

unethical /ʌnˈeθɪkl/ a sin ética, inmoral

uneven /ʌnˈiːvn/ a desigual

unexceptional /ʌnɪkˈsepʃənl/ a corriente

unexpected /ʌnɪkˈspektɪd/ a inesperado

unfailing /ʌnˈfeɪlɪŋ/ a inagotable; (constant) constante; (loyal) leal

unfair /ʌnˈfeə(r)/ a injusto. **~ly** adv injustamente. **~ness** n injusticia f

unfaithful /ʌnˈfeɪθfl/ a infiel. **~ness** n infidelidad f

unfamiliar /ʌnfəˈmɪlɪə(r)/ a desconocido. **be ~ with** desconocer

unfasten /ʌnˈfɑːsn/ vt desabrochar (clothes); (untie) desatar

unfavourable /ʌnˈfeɪvərəbl/ a desfavorable

unfeeling /ʌnˈfiːlɪŋ/ a insensible

unfit /ʌnˈfɪt/ a inadecuado, no apto; (unwell) en mal estado físico; (incapable) incapaz

unflinching /ʌnˈflɪntʃɪŋ/ a resuelto

unfold /ʌnˈfəʊld/ vt desdoblar; (fig) revelar. —vi (view etc) extenderse

unforeseen /ʌnfəˈsiːn/ a imprevisto

unforgettable /ʌnfəˈgetəbl/ a inolvidable

unforgivable /ʌnfəˈgɪvəbl/ a imperdonable

unfortunate /ʌnˈfɔːtʃənət/ a desgraciado; (regrettable) lamentable. **~ly** adv desgraciadamente

unfounded /ʌnˈfaʊndɪd/ a infundado

unfriendly /ʌnˈfrendlɪ/ a poco amistoso, frío

unfurl /ʌnˈfɜːl/ vt desplegar

ungainly /ʌnˈgeɪnlɪ/ a desgarbado

ungodly /ʌnˈgɒdlɪ/ a impío. **~ hour** n (fam) hora f intempestiva

ungrateful /ʌnˈgreɪtfl/ a desagradecido

unguarded /ʌnˈgɑːdɪd/ a indefenso; (incautious) imprudente, incauto

unhapp|ily /ʌnˈhæpɪlɪ/ adv infelizmente; (unfortunately) desgraciadamente. **~iness** n tristeza f. **~y** /ʌnˈhæpɪ/ a (-ier, -iest) infeliz, triste; (unsuitable) inoportuno. **~y with** insatisfecho de (plans etc)

unharmed /ʌnˈhɑːmd/ a ileso, sano y salvo

unhealthy /ʌnˈhelθɪ/ a (-ier, -iest) enfermizo; (insanitary) malsano

unhinge /ʌnˈhɪndʒ/ vt desquiciar

unholy /ʌnˈhəʊlɪ/ a (-ier, -iest) impío; (terrible, fam) terrible

unhook /ʌnˈhʊk/ vt desenganchar

unhoped /ʌnˈhəʊpt/ a. **~ for** inesperado

unhurt /ʌnˈhɜːt/ a ileso

unicorn /ˈjuːnɪkɔːn/ n unicornio m

unification /juːnɪfɪˈkeɪʃn/ n unificación f

uniform /ˈjuːnɪfɔːm/ a & n uniforme (m). **~ity** /-ˈfɔːmətɪ/ n uniformidad f. **~ly** adv uniformemente

unify /ˈjuːnɪfaɪ/ vt unificar

unilateral /juːnɪˈlætərəl/ a unilateral

unimaginable /ʌnɪˈmædʒɪnəbl/ a inconcebible

unimpeachable /ʌnɪmˈpiːtʃəbl/ a irreprensible

unimportant /ʌnɪmˈpɔːtnt/ a insignificante

uninhabited /ʌnɪnˈhæbɪtɪd/ a inhabitado; (*abandoned*) despoblado

unintentional /ʌnɪnˈtenʃənl/ a involuntario

union /ˈjuːnjən/ n unión f; (*trade union*) sindicato m. ~ist n sindicalista m & f. U~ Jack n bandera f del Reino Unido

unique /juːˈniːk/ a único. ~ly adv extraordinariamente

unisex /ˈjuːnɪseks/ a unisex(o)

unison /ˈjuːnɪsn/ n. in ~ al unísono

unit /ˈjuːnɪt/ n unidad f; (*of furniture etc*) elemento m

unite /juːˈnaɪt/ vt unir. —vi unirse. U~d Kingdom (UK) n Reino m Unido. U~d Nations (UN) n Organización f de las Naciones Unidas (ONU). U~d States (of America) (USA) n Estados mpl Unidos de América) (EE.UU.)

unity /ˈjuːnɪtɪ/ n unidad f; (*fig*) acuerdo m

universal /juːnɪˈvɜːsl/ a universal. ~e /ˈjuːnɪvɜːs/ n universo m

university /juːnɪˈvɜːsətɪ/ n universidad f. —a universitario

unjust /ʌnˈdʒʌst/ a injusto

unkempt /ʌnˈkempt/ a desaseado

unkind /ʌnˈkaɪnd/ a poco amable; (*cruel*) cruel. ~ly adv poco amablemente. ~ness n falta f de amabilidad; (*cruelty*) crueldad f

unknown /ʌnˈnəʊn/ a desconocido

unlawful /ʌnˈlɔːfl/ a ilegal

unleash /ʌnˈliːʃ/ vt soltar; (*fig*) desencadenar

unless /ʌnˈles, ən'les/ conj a menos que, a no ser que

unlike /ʌnˈlaɪk/ a diferente; (*not typical*) impropio de. —prep a diferencia de. ~lihood n improbabilidad f. ~ly adv /ʌnˈlaɪklɪ/ a improbable

unlimited /ʌnˈlɪmɪtɪd/ a ilimitado

unload /ʌnˈləʊd/ vt descargar

unlock /ʌnˈlɒk/ vt abrir (con llave)

unluckily /ʌnˈlʌkɪlɪ/ adv desgraciadamente. ~y /ʌnˈlʌkɪ/ a (-ier, -iest) desgraciado; (*number*) de mala suerte

unmanly /ʌnˈmænlɪ/ a poco viril

unmanned /ʌnˈmænd/ a no tripulado

unmarried /ʌnˈmærɪd/ a soltero. ~ mother n madre f soltera

unmask /ʌnˈmɑːsk/ vt desenmascarar. —vi quitarse la máscara

unmentionable /ʌnˈmenʃənəbl/ a que no se debe aludir

unmistakable /ʌnmɪˈsteɪkəbl/ a inconfundible. ~y adv claramente

unmitigated /ʌnˈmɪtɪgeɪtɪd/ a (*absolute*) absoluto.

unmoved /ʌnˈmuːvd/ a (*fig*) indiferente (by a), insensible (by a)

unnatural /ʌnˈnætʃərəl/ a no natural; (*not normal*) anormal

unnecessarily /ʌnˈnesəsərɪlɪ/ adv innecesariamente. ~y /ʌnˈnesəsərɪ/ a innecesario

unnerve /ʌnˈnɜːv/ vt desconcertar

unnoticed /ʌnˈnəʊtɪst/ a inadvertido

unobtainable /ʌnəbˈteɪnəbl/ a inasequible; (*fig*) inalcanzable

unobtrusive /ʌnəbˈtruːsɪv/ a discreto

unofficial /ʌnəˈfɪʃl/ a no oficial. ~ly adv extraoficialmente

unpack /ʌnˈpæk/ vt desempaquetar (parcel); deshacer (suitcase). —vi deshacer la maleta

unpalatable /ʌnˈpælətəbl/ a desagradable

unparalleled /ʌnˈpærəleld/ a sin par

unpick /ʌnˈpɪk/ vt descoser

unpleasant /ʌnˈpleznt/ a desagradable. ~ness n lo desagradable

unplug /ʌnˈplʌg/ vt (elec) desenchufar

unpopular /ʌnˈpɒpjʊlə(r)/ a impopular

unprecedented /ʌnˈpresidentid/ a sin precedente

unpredictable /ʌnprɪˈdɪktəbl/ a imprevisible

unpremeditated /ʌnprɪˈmedɪteɪtɪd/ a impremeditado

unprepared /ʌnprɪˈpeəd/ a no preparado; (unready) desprevenido

unprepossessing /ʌnpriːpəˈzesɪŋ/ a poco atractivo

unpretentious /ʌnprɪˈtenʃəs/ a sin pretensiones, modesto

unprincipled /ʌnˈprɪnsɪpld/ a sin principios

unprofessional /ʌnprəˈfeʃənəl/ a contrario a la ética profesional

unpublished /ʌnˈpʌblɪʃt/ a inédito

unqualified /ʌnˈkwɒlɪfaɪd/ a sin título; (fig) absoluto

unquestionabl|e /ʌnˈkwestʃənəbl/ a indiscutible. ~y adv indiscutiblemente

unquote /ʌnˈkwəʊt/ vi cerrar comillas

unravel /ʌnˈrævl/ vt (pt unravelled) desenredar; deshacer (knitting etc). —vi desenredarse

unreal /ʌnˈrɪəl/ a irreal. ~istic a poco realista

unreasonable /ʌnˈriːzənəbl/ a irrazonable

unrecognizable /ʌnrekəgˈnaɪzəbl/ a irreconocible

unrelated /ʌnrɪˈleɪtɪd/ a (facts) inconexo, sin relación; (people) no emparentado

unreliable /ʌnrɪˈlaɪəbl/ a (person) poco formal; (machine) poco fiable

unrelieved /ʌnrɪˈliːvd/ a no aliviado

unremitting /ʌnrɪˈmɪtɪŋ/ a incesante

unrepentant /ʌnrɪˈpentənt/ a impenitente

unrequited /ʌnrɪˈkwaɪtɪd/ a no correspondido

unreservedly /ʌnrɪˈzɜːvɪdlɪ/ adv sin reserva

unrest /ʌnˈrest/ n inquietud f; (pol) agitación f

unrivalled /ʌnˈraɪvld/ a sin par

unroll /ʌnˈrəʊl/ vt desenrollar. —vi desenrollarse

unruffled /ʌnˈrʌfld/ (person) a imperturbable

unruly /ʌnˈruːlɪ/ a indisciplinado

unsafe /ʌnˈseɪf/ a peligroso; (person) en peligro

unsaid /ʌnˈsed/ a sin decir

unsatisfactory /ʌnsætɪsˈfæktərɪ/ a insatisfactorio

unsavoury /ʌnˈseɪvərɪ/ a desagradable

unscathed /ʌnˈskeɪðd/ a ileso

unscramble /ʌnˈskræmbl/ vt descifrar

unscrew /ʌnˈskruː/ vt destornillar

unscrupulous /ʌnˈskruːpjʊləs/ a sin escrúpulos

unseat /ʌnˈsiːt/ vt (pol) quitar el escaño a

unseemly /ʌnˈsiːmlɪ/ a indecoroso

unseen /ʌnˈsiːn/ a inadvertido. —n (translation) traducción f a primera vista

unselfish /ʌn'selfiʃ/ a desinteresado

unsettle /ʌn'setl/ vt perturbar. ~d a perturbado; ⟨weather⟩ variable; ⟨bill⟩ por pagar

unshakeable /ʌn'ʃeɪkəbl/ a firme

unshaven /ʌn'ʃeɪvn/ a sin afeitar

unsightly /ʌn'saɪtlɪ/ a feo

unskilled /ʌn'skɪld/ a inexperto. ~ **worker** n obrero m no cualificado

unsociable /ʌn'səʊʃəbl/ a insociable

unsolicited /ʌnsə'lɪsɪtɪd/ a no solicitado

unsophisticated /ʌnsə'fɪstɪkeɪtɪd/ a sencillo

unsound /ʌn'saʊnd/ a defectuoso, erróneo. **of** ~ **mind** demente

unsparing /ʌn'speərɪŋ/ a pródigo; ⟨cruel⟩ cruel

unspeakable /ʌn'spiːkəbl/ a indecible

unspecified /ʌn'spesɪfaɪd/ a no especificado

unstable /ʌn'steɪbl/ a inestable

unsteady /ʌn'stedɪ/ a inestable; ⟨hand⟩ poco firme; ⟨step⟩ inseguro

unstinted /ʌn'stɪntɪd/ a abundante

unstuck /ʌn'stʌk/ a suelto. **come** ~ **despegarse**; ⟨fail, fam⟩ fracasar

unstudied /ʌn'stʌdɪd/ a natural

unsuccessful /ʌnsək'sesfʊl/ a fracasado. **be** ~ no tener éxito, fracasar

unsuitable /ʌn'suːtəbl/ a inadecuado; ⟨inconvenient⟩ inconveniente

unsure /ʌn'ʃʊə(r)/ a inseguro

unsuspecting /ʌnsə'spektɪŋ/ a confiado

unthinkable /ʌn'θɪŋkəbl/ a inconcebible

untidy /ʌn'taɪdɪ/ adv desordenadamente. ~**iness** n desorden m. ~**y** /ʌn'taɪdɪ/ a (-ier, -iest) desordenado; ⟨person⟩ desaseado

untie /ʌn'taɪ/ vt desatar

until /ən'tɪl, ʌn'tɪl/ prep hasta. —conj hasta que

untimely /ʌn'taɪmlɪ/ a inoportuno; ⟨premature⟩ prematuro

untiring /ʌn'taɪərɪŋ/ a incansable

untold /ʌn'təʊld/ a incalculable

untoward /ʌntə'wɔːd/ a ⟨inconvenient⟩ inconveniente

untried /ʌn'traɪd/ a no probado

untrue /ʌn'truː/ a falso

unused /ʌn'juːzd/ a nuevo. /ʌn'juːst/ a. ~ **to** no acostumbrado a

unusual /ʌn'juːʒʊəl/ a insólito; ⟨exceptional⟩ excepcional. ~**ly** adv excepcionalmente

unutterable /ʌn'ʌtərəbl/ a indecible

unveil /ʌn'veɪl/ vt descubrir; ⟨disclose⟩ revelar

unwanted /ʌn'wɒntɪd/ a superfluo; ⟨child⟩ no deseado

unwarranted /ʌn'wɒrəntɪd/ a injustificado

unwelcome /ʌn'welkəm/ a desagradable; ⟨guest⟩ inoportuno

unwell /ʌn'wel/ a indispuesto

unwieldy /ʌn'wiːldɪ/ a difícil de manejar

unwilling /ʌn'wɪlɪŋ/ a no dispuesto. **be** ~ no querer. ~**ly** adv de mala gana

unwind /ʌn'waɪnd/ vt (pt **unwound**) desenvolver. —vi desenvolverse; ⟨relax, fam⟩ relajarse

unwise /ʌn'waɪz/ a imprudente

unwitting /ʌn'wɪtɪŋ/ a inconsciente; ⟨involuntary⟩ involuntario. ~**ly** adv involuntariamente

unworthy /ʌn'wɜːðɪ/ a indigno

unwrap /ʌnˈræp/ vt (pt unwrapped) desenvolver, deshacer

unwritten /ʌnˈrɪtn/ a no escrito; ⟨agreement⟩ tácito

up /ʌp/ adv arriba; (upwards) hacia arriba; (higher) más arriba; (out of bed) levantado; (finished) terminado. ~ here aquí arriba. ~ in (fam) versado en, fuerte en. ~ there allí arriba. ~ to hasta. be one ~ on llevar la ventaja a. be ~ against enfrentarse con. be ~ to tramar ⟨plot⟩; (one's turn) tocar a; a la altura de ⟨task⟩; (reach) llegar a. come ~ subir. feel ~ to it sentirse capaz. go ~ subir. it's ~ to you depende de ti. what is ~? ¿qué pasa? —prep arriba; (on top of) en lo alto de. —vt (pt upped) aumentar. —n. ~s and downs npl altibajos mpl

upbraid /ʌpˈbreɪd/ vt reprender

upbringing /ˈʌpbrɪŋɪŋ/ n educación f

update /ʌpˈdeɪt/ vt poner al día

upgrade /ʌpˈɡreɪd/ vt ascender ⟨person⟩; mejorar ⟨equipment⟩

upheaval /ʌpˈhiːvl/ n trastorno m

uphill /ˈʌphɪl/ a ascendente; (fig) arduo. —adv /ʌpˈhɪl/ cuesta arriba. go ~ subir

uphold /ʌpˈhəʊld/ vt (pt upheld) sostener

upholster /ʌpˈhəʊlstə(r)/ vt tapizar. ~er /-rə(r)/ n tapicero m. ~y n tapicería f

upkeep /ˈʌpkiːp/ n mantenimiento m

up-market /ʌpˈmɑːkɪt/ a superior

upon /əˈpɒn/ prep en; (on top of) encima de. once ~ a time érase una vez

upper /ˈʌpə(r)/ a superior. ~ class n clases fpl altas. ~hand n dominio m, ventaja f. ~most a (el) más alto. —n (of shoe) pala f

uppish /ˈʌpɪʃ/ a engreído

upright /ˈʌpraɪt/ a derecho; ⟨piano⟩ vertical. —n montante m

uprising /ˈʌpraɪzɪŋ/ n sublevación f

uproar /ˈʌprɔː(r)/ n tumulto m. ~ious /-ˈrɔːrɪəs/ a tumultuoso

uproot /ʌpˈruːt/ vt desarraigar

upset /ʌpˈset/ vt (pt upset, presp upsetting) trastornar; desbaratar ⟨plan etc⟩; (distress) alterar. /ˈʌpset/ n trastorno m

upshot /ˈʌpʃɒt/ n resultado m

upside-down /ˌʌpsaɪdˈdaʊn/ adv al revés; (in disorder) patas arriba. turn ~ volver

upstairs /ʌpˈsteəz/ adv arriba. /ˈʌpsteəz/ a de arriba

upstart /ˈʌpstɑːt/ n arribista m & f

upstream /ˈʌpstriːm/ adv río arriba; (against the current) contra la corriente

upsurge /ˈʌpsɜːdʒ/ n aumento m; (of anger etc) arrebato m

uptake /ˈʌpteɪk/ n. quick on the ~ muy listo

uptight /ˈʌptaɪt/ a (fam) nervioso

up-to-date /ʌptəˈdeɪt/ a al día; (news) de última hora; (modern) moderno

upturn /ˈʌptɜːn/ n aumento m; (improvement) mejora f

upward /ˈʌpwəd/ a ascendente. —adv hacia arriba. ~s adv hacia arriba

uranium /jʊˈreɪnɪəm/ n uranio m

urban /ˈɜːbən/ a urbano

urbane /ɜːˈbeɪn/ a cortés

urbanize /ˈɜːbənaɪz/ vt urbanizar

urchin /ˈɜːtʃɪn/ n pilluelo m

urge /ɜːdʒ/ vt incitar, animar. —n impulso m. ~ on animar

urgen|cy /ˈɜːdʒənsɪ/ n urgencia f. ~t /ˈɜːdʒənt/ a urgente. ~tly adv urgentemente

urin|ate /'juərɪneɪt/ *vi* orinar. **~e** /'juərɪn/ *n* orina *f*

urn /ɜːn/ *n* urna *f*

Uruguay /'juərəgwaɪ/ *n* el Uruguay *m*. **~an** *a* & *n* uruguayo (*m*)

us /ʌs, əs/ *pron* nos; (*after prep*) nosotros, nosotras

US(A) /ju:es'eɪ/ *abbr* (*United States (of America)*) EE.UU., Estados *mpl* Unidos

usage /'ju:zɪdʒ/ *n* uso *m*

use /ju:z/ *vt* emplear. /ju:s/ *n* uso *m*, empleo *m*. be of **~** servir. it is no **~** es inútil, no sirve para nada. make **~** of servirse de. **~** up agotar, consumir. **~d** /ju:zd/ *a* (*clothes*) gastado. /ju:st/ *pt*. he **~d** to say decía, solía decir. **—** *a*. **~d** to acostumbrado a. **~ful** /'ju:sfl/ *a* útil. **~fully** *adv* útilmente. **~less** *a* inútil; (*person*) incompetente. **~r** /-zə(r)/ *n* usuario *m*

usher /'ʌʃə(r)/ *n* ujier *m*; (*in theatre etc*) acomodador *m*. **—***vt*. **~ in** hacer entrar. **~ette** *n* acomodadora *f*

USSR *abbr* (*history*) (*Union of Soviet Socialist Republics*) URSS

usual /'ju:ʒʊəl/ *a* usual, corriente; (*habitual*) acostumbrado, habitual. as **~** como de costumbre, como siempre. **~ly** *adv* normalmente. he **~ly** wakes up early suele despertarse temprano

usurer /'ju:ʒərə(r)/ *n* usurero *m*

usurp /ju:'zɜːp/ *vt* usurpar. **~er** /-ɔ(r)/ *n* usurpador *m*

usury /'ju:ʒərɪ/ *n* usura *f*

utensil /ju:'tensl/ *n* utensilio *m*

uterus /'ju:tərəs/ *n* útero *m*

utilitarian /ju:tɪlɪ'teərɪən/ *a* utilitario

utility /ju:'tɪlətɪ/ *n* utilidad *f*. **public ~** *n* servicio *m* público. **—***a* utilitario

utilize /'ju:tɪlaɪz/ *vt* utilizar

utmost /'ʌtməʊst/ *a* extremo. **—** *n*. one's **~** todo lo posible

utter[1] /'ʌtə(r)/ *a* completo

utter[2] /'ʌtə(r)/ *vt* (*speak*) pronunciar; dar (*sigh*); emitir (*sound*). **~ance** *n* expresión *f*

utterly /'ʌtəlɪ/ *adv* totalmente

U-turn /'ju:tɜːn/ *n* vuelta *f*

V

vacan|cy /'veɪkənsɪ/ *n* (*job*) vacante *f*; (*room*) habitación *f* libre. **~t** *a* libre; (*empty*) vacío; (*look*) vago

vacate /və'keɪt/ *vt* dejar

vacation /və'keɪʃn/ *n* (*Amer*) vacaciones *fpl*

vaccin|ate /'væksɪneɪt/ *vt* vacunar. **~ation** /-'neɪʃn/ *n* vacunación *f*. **~e** /'væksi:n/ *n* vacuna *f*

vacuum /'vækjʊəm/ *n* (*pl* -cuums *or* -cua*) vacío *m*. **~ cleaner** *n* aspiradora *f*. **~ flask** *n* termo *m*

vagabond /'vægəbɒnd/ *n* vagabundo *m*

vagary /'veɪgərɪ/ *n* capricho *m*

vagina /və'dʒaɪnə/ *n* vagina *f*

vagrant /'veɪgrənt/ *n* vagabundo *m*

vague /veɪg/ *a* (-er, -est) vago; (*outline*) indistinto. be **~ about** no precisar. **~ly** *adv* vagamente

vain /veɪn/ *a* (-er, -est) vanidoso; (*useless*) vano, inútil. in **~** en vano. **~ly** *adv* vanamente

valance /'væləns/ *n* cenefa *f*

vale /veɪl/ *n* valle *m*

valentine /'væləntaɪn/ *n* (*card*) tarjeta *f* del día de San Valentín

valet /'vælɪt, 'væleɪ/ *n* ayuda *m* de cámara

valiant /'vælɪənt/ *a* valeroso

valid /'vælɪd/ *a* válido; (*ticket*) valedero. **~ate** *vt* dar validez a;

(*confirm*) convalidar. ∼ity
/ˈidəti/ n validez f

valley /ˈvælɪ/ n (pl -eys) valle m

valour /ˈvælə(r)/ n valor m

valuable /ˈvæljʊəbl/ a valioso.
∼s npl objetos mpl de valor

valuation /væljʊˈeɪʃn/ n valoración f

value /ˈvæljuː/ n valor m; (usefulness) utilidad f. **face** ∼ n valor
m nominal; (fig) significado m
literal. —vt valorar; (cherish)
apreciar. ∼ **added tax (VAT)** n
impuesto m sobre el valor añadido (IVA). ∼**d** a (appreciated)
apreciado, estimado. ∼**r** /-ə(r)/ n
tasador m

valve /vælv/ n válvula f

vampire /ˈvæmpaɪə(r)/ n vampiro m

van /væn/ n furgoneta f; (rail)
furgón m

vandal /ˈvændl/ n vándalo m.
∼**ism** /-əlɪzəm/ n vandalismo m.
∼**ize** vt destruir

vane /veɪn/ n (weathercock)
veleta f; (naut, aviat) paleta f

vanguard /ˈvænɡɑːd/ n vanguardia f

vanilla /vəˈnɪlə/ n vainilla f

vanish /ˈvænɪʃ/ vi desaparecer

vanity /ˈvænɪtɪ/ n vanidad f. ∼
case n neceser m

vantage /ˈvɑːntɪdʒ/ n ventaja f.
∼**point** n posición f ventajosa

vapour /ˈveɪpə(r)/ n vapor m

variable /ˈveərɪəbl/ a variable

varian|ce /ˈveərɪəns/ n. **at** ∼**ce**
en desacuerdo. ∼**t** /ˈveərɪənt/ a
diferente. —n variante m

variation /veərɪˈeɪʃn/ n variación f

varicoloured /ˈveərɪkʌləd/ a
multicolor

varied /ˈveərɪd/ a variado

varicose /ˈværɪkəʊs/ a varicoso.
∼ **veins** npl varices fpl

variety /vəˈraɪətɪ/ n variedad f.
∼ **show** n espectáculo m de
variedades

various /ˈveərɪəs/ a diverso. ∼**ly**
adv diversamente

varnish /ˈvɑːnɪʃ/ n barniz m; (for
nails) esmalte m. —vt barnizar

vary /ˈveərɪ/ vt/i variar. ∼**ing** a
diverso

vase /vɑːz, Amer veɪs/ n jarrón m

vasectomy /vəˈsektəmɪ/ n vasectomía f

vast /vɑːst/ a vasto, enorme. ∼**ly**
adv enormemente. ∼**ness** n
inmensidad f

vat /væt/ n tina f

VAT /viːeɪˈtiː/ abbr (value added
tax) IVA m, impuesto m sobre el
valor añadido

vault /vɔːlt/ n (roof) bóveda f; (in
bank) cámara f acorazada; (tomb)
cripta f; (cellar) sótano m; (jump)
salto m. —vt/i saltar

vaunt /vɔːnt/ vt jactarse de

veal /viːl/ n ternera f

veer /vɪə(r)/ vi cambiar de dirección; (naut) virar

vegetable /ˈvedʒɪtəbl/ a vegetal. —n legumbre m; (greens)
verduras fpl

vegetarian /vedʒɪˈteərɪən/ a & n
vegetariano (m)

vegetate /ˈvedʒɪteɪt/ vi vegetar

vegetation /vedʒɪˈteɪʃn/ n vegetación f

vehemen|ce /ˈviːəməns/ n
vehemencia f. ∼**t** /ˈviːəmənt/ a
vehemente. ∼**tly** adv con
vehemencia

vehicle /ˈviːɪkl/ n vehículo m

veil /veɪl/ n velo m. **take the** ∼
hacerse monja. —vt velar

vein /veɪn/ n vena f; (mood)
humor m. ∼**ed** a veteado

velocity /vɪˈlɒsɪtɪ/ n velocidad f

velvet /ˈvelvɪt/ n terciopelo m.
∼**y** a aterciopelado

venal /ˈviːnl/ a venal. ∼**ity**
/-ˈnælətɪ/ n venalidad f

vendetta /venˈdetə/ n enemistad
f prolongada

vending-machine /'vendɪŋ məʃi:n/ n distribuidor m automático

vendor /'vendə(r)/ n vendedor m

veneer /və'nɪə(r)/ n chapa f; (fig) barniz m, apariencia f

venerable /'venərəbl/ a venerable

venereal /və'nɪərɪəl/ a venéreo

Venetian /və'ni:ʃn/ a & n veneciano (m). v~ **blind** n persiana f veneciana

vengeance /'vendʒəns/ n venganza f. **with a ~** (fig) con creces

venison /'venɪzn/ n carne f de venado

venom /'venəm/ n veneno m. **~ous** a venenoso

vent /vent/ n abertura f; (for air) respiradero m. **give ~ to** dar salida a. —vt hacer un agujero en; (fig) desahogar

ventilat|e /'ventɪleɪt/ vt ventilar. **~ion** /-'leɪʃn/ n ventilación f. **~or** /-ɔ:(r)/ n ventilador m

ventriloquist /ven'trɪləkwɪst/ n ventrílocuo m

venture /'ventʃə(r)/ n empresa f (arriesgada). **at a ~** a la ventura. —vt arriesgar. —vi atreverse

venue /'venju:/ n lugar m (de reunión)

veranda /və'rændə/ n terraza f

verb /vɜ:b/ n verbo m

verbal /'vɜ:bl/ a verbal. **~ly** adv verbalmente

verbatim /vɜ:'beɪtɪm/ adv palabra por palabra, al pie de la letra

verbose /vɜ:'bəʊs/ a prolijo

verdant /'vɜ:dənt/ a verde

verdict /'vɜ:dɪkt/ n veredicto m; (opinion) opinión f

verge /vɜ:dʒ/ n borde m. —vt. **~ on** acercarse a

verger /'vɜ:dʒə(r)/ n sacristán m

verif|ication /verɪfɪ'keɪʃn/ n verificación f. **~y** /'verɪfaɪ/ vt verificar

veritable /'verɪtəbl/ a verdadero

vermicelli /vɜ:mɪ'tʃelɪ/ n fideos mpl

vermin /'vɜ:mɪn/ n sabandijas fpl

vermouth /'vɜ:məθ/ n vermut m

vernacular /və'nækjʊlə(r)/ n lengua f; (regional) dialecto m

versatil|e /'vɜ:sətaɪl/ a versátil. **~ity** /-'tɪlətɪ/ n versatilidad f

verse /vɜ:s/ n estrofa f; (poetry) poesías fpl; (of Bible) versículo m

versed /vɜ:st/ a. **~ in** versado en

version /'vɜ:ʃn/ n versión f

versus /'vɜ:səs/ prep contra

vertebra /'vɜ:tɪbrə/ n (pl -brae /-bri:/) vértebra f

vertical /'vɜ:tɪkl/ a & n vertical (f). **~ly** adv verticalmente

vertigo /'vɜ:tɪgəʊ/ n vértigo m

verve /vɜ:v/ n entusiasmo m, vigor m

very /'verɪ/ adv muy. **~ much** muchísimo. **~ well** muy bien. **the ~ first** el primero de todos. —a mismo. **the ~ thing** exactamente lo que hace falta

vespers /'vespəz/ npl vísperas fpl

vessel /'vesl/ n (receptacle) recipiente m; (ship) buque m; (anat) vaso m

vest /vest/ n camiseta f; (Amer) chaleco m. —vt conferir. **~ed interest** n interés m personal; (jurid) derecho m adquirido

vestige /'vestɪdʒ/ n vestigio m

vestment /'vestmənt/ n vestidura f

vestry /'vestrɪ/ n sacristía f

vet /vet/ n (fam) veterinario m. —vt (pt vetted) examinar

veteran /'vetərən/ n veterano m

veterinary /'vetərɪnərɪ/ a veterinario. **~ surgeon** n veterinario m

veto /'vi:təʊ/ n (pl -oes) veto m. —vt poner el veto a

vex /veks/ *vt* fastidiar. **~ation** /-ˈseɪʃn/ *n* fastidio *m*. **~ed question** *n* cuestión *f* controvertida. **~ing** *a* fastidioso

via /ˈvaɪə/ *prep* por, por vía de

viab|ility /vaɪəˈbɪlətɪ/ *n* viabilidad *f*. **~le** /ˈvaɪəbl/ *a* viable

viaduct /ˈvaɪədʌkt/ *n* viaducto *m*

vibrant /ˈvaɪbrənt/ *a* vibrante

vibrat|e /vaɪˈbreɪt/ *vt/i* vibrar. **~ion** /-ʃn/ *n* vibración *f*

vicar /ˈvɪkə(r)/ *n* párroco *m*. **~age** /-rɪdʒ/ *n* casa *f* del párroco

vicarious /vɪˈkeərɪəs/ *a* indirecto

vice[1] /vaɪs/ *n* vicio *m*

vice[2] /vaɪs/ *n* (*tec*) torno *m* de banco

vice... /vaɪs/ *pref* vice...

vice versa /vaɪsɪˈvɜːsə/ *adv* viceversa

vicinity /vɪˈsɪnətɪ/ *n* vecindad *f*. **in the ~ of** cerca de

vicious /ˈvɪʃəs/ *a* (*spiteful*) malicioso; (*violent*) atroz. **~ circle** *n* círculo *m* vicioso. **~ly** *adv* cruelmente

vicissitudes /vɪˈsɪsɪtjuːdz/ *npl* vicisitudes *fpl*

victim /ˈvɪktɪm/ *n* víctima *f*. **~ization** /-aɪˈzeɪʃn/ *n* persecución *f*. **~ize** *vt* victimizar

victor /ˈvɪktə(r)/ *n* vencedor *m*

Victorian /vɪkˈtɔːrɪən/ *a* victoriano

victor|ious /vɪkˈtɔːrɪəs/ *a* victorioso. **~y** /ˈvɪktərɪ/ *n* victoria *f*

video /ˈvɪdɪəʊ/ *a* video. **~n** (*fam*) magnetoscopio *m*. **~ recorder** *n* magnetoscopio *m*. **~tape** *n* videocassette *f*

vie /vaɪ/ *vi* (*pres p* **vying**) rivalizar

view /vjuː/ *n* vista *f*; (*mental survey*) visión *f* de conjunto; (*opinion*) opinión *f*. **in ~ of** en vista de. **on ~** expuesto. **with a ~ to** con miras

a. **~** *vt* ver; (*visit*) visitar; (*consider*) considerar. **~er** *n* espectador *m*; (*TV*) televidente *m & f*. **~finder** /ˈvjuːfaɪndə(r)/ *n* visor *m & f*. **~point** /ˈvjuːpɔɪnt/ *n* punto *m* de vista

vigil /ˈvɪdʒɪl/ *n* vigilia *f*. **~ance** *n* vigilancia *f*. **~ant** *a* vigilante. **keep ~** velar

vigor|ous /ˈvɪɡərəs/ *a* vigoroso. **~ur** /ˈvɪɡə(r)/ *n* vigor *m*.

vile /vaɪl/ *a* (*base*) vil; (*bad*) horrible; (*weather, temper*) de perros

vilification /vɪlɪfɪˈkeɪʃn/ *n* difamación *f*. **~y** /ˈvɪlɪfaɪ/ *vt* difamar

village /ˈvɪlɪdʒ/ *n* aldea *f*. **~r** /-ə(r)/ *n* aldeano *m*

villain /ˈvɪlən/ *n* malvado *m*; (*in story etc*) malo *m*. **~ous** *a* infame. **~y** *n* infamia *f*

vim /vɪm/ *n* (*fam*) energía *f*

vinaigrette /vɪnɪˈɡret/ *n*. **~ sauce** *n* vinagreta *f*

vindicat|e /ˈvɪndɪkeɪt/ *vt* vindicar. **~ion** /-ˈkeɪʃn/ *n* vindicación *f*

vindictive /vɪnˈdɪktɪv/ *a* vengativo. **~ness** *n* carácter *m* vengativo

vine /vaɪn/ *n* vid *f*

vinegar /ˈvɪnɪɡə(r)/ *n* vinagre *m*. **~y** *a* (*person*) avinagrado

vineyard /ˈvɪnjəd/ *n* viña *f*

vintage /ˈvɪntɪdʒ/ *n* (*year*) cosecha *f*. **—a** (*wine*) añejo; (*car*) de época

vinyl /ˈvaɪnɪl/ *n* vinilo *m*

viola /vɪˈəʊlə/ *n* viola *f*

violat|e /ˈvaɪəleɪt/ *vt* violar. **~ion** /-ˈleɪʃn/ *n* violación *f*

violen|ce /ˈvaɪələns/ *n* violencia *f*. **~t** *a* violento. **~tly** *adv* violentamente

violet /ˈvaɪələt/ *a & n* violeta (*f*)

violin /ˈvaɪəlɪn/ *n* violín *m*. **~ist** *n* violinista *m & f*

VIP /viːaɪˈpiː/ *abbr* (*very important person*) personaje *m* viper /ˈvaɪpə(r)/ n víbora f

virgin /ˈvɜːdʒɪn/ a & n virgen (f). ~al a virginal. ~ity /vəˈdʒɪnɪtɪ/ n virginidad f

Virgo /ˈvɜːgəʊ/ n (astr) Virgo f

virile /ˈvɪraɪl/ a viril. ~ity /-ˈrɪlɪtɪ/ n virilidad f

virtual /ˈvɜːtʃʊəl/ a verdadero. a ~ failure prácticamente un fracaso. ~ly adv prácticamente

virtue /ˈvɜːtʃuː/ n virtud f. by ~ of, in ~ of en virtud de

virtuoso /vɜːtjʊˈəʊzəʊ/ n (pl -si /-ziː/) virtuoso m

virtuous /ˈvɜːtʃʊəs/ a virtuoso

virulent /ˈvɪrʊlənt/ a virulento

virus /ˈvaɪərəs/ n (pl -uses) virus m

visa /ˈviːzə/ n visado m, visa f (LAm)

vis-a-vis /ˈviːzɑːˈviː/ adv frente a frente. —prep respecto a; (opposite) en frente de

viscount /ˈvaɪkaʊnt/ n vizconde m. ~ess n vizcondesa f

viscous /ˈvɪskəs/ a viscoso

visib|ility /vɪzɪˈbɪlɪtɪ/ n visibilidad f. ~le /ˈvɪzɪbl/ a visible. ~ly adv visiblemente

vision /ˈvɪʒn/ n visión f; (sight) vista f. ~ary /ˈvɪʒənərɪ/ a & n visionario (m)

visit /ˈvɪzɪt/ vt visitar; hacer una visita a (person). —vi hacer visitas. —n visita f. ~or n visitante m & f; (guest) visita f; (in hotel) cliente m & f

visor /ˈvaɪzə(r)/ n visera f

vista /ˈvɪstə/ n perspectiva f

visual /ˈvɪʒʊəl/ a visual. ~ize /ˈvɪʒʊəlaɪz/ vt imaginar(se); (foresee) prever. ~ly adv visualmente

vital /ˈvaɪtl/ a vital; (essential) esencial

vitality /vaɪˈtælɪtɪ/ n vitalidad f

vital|ly /ˈvaɪtəlɪ/ adv extremadamente. ~s npl órganos mpl

vitales. ~ statistics npl (fam) medidas fpl

vitamin /ˈvɪtəmɪn/ n vitamina f

vitiate /ˈvɪʃɪeɪt/ vt viciar

vitreous /ˈvɪtrɪəs/ a vítreo

vituperat|e /vɪˈtjuːpəreɪt/ vt vituperar. ~ion /-ˈreɪʃn/ n vituperación f

vivaci|ous /vɪˈveɪʃəs/ a animado, vivo. ~ously adv animadamente. ~ty /-ˈvæsətɪ/ n viveza f

vivid /ˈvɪvɪd/ a vivo. ~ly adv intensamente; (describe) gráficamente. ~ness n viveza f

vivisection /vɪvɪˈsekʃn/ n vivisección f

vixen /ˈvɪksn/ n zorra f

vocabulary /vəˈkæbjʊlərɪ/ n vocabulario m

vocal /ˈvəʊkl/ a vocal; (fig) franco. ~ist n cantante m & f

vocation /vəʊˈkeɪʃn/ n vocación f. ~al a profesional

vociferat|e /vəˈsɪfəreɪt/ vt/i vociferar. ~ous a vociferador

vogue /vəʊg/ n boga f. in ~ de moda

voice /vɔɪs/ n voz f. —vt expresar

void /vɔɪd/ a vacío; (not valid) nulo. ~ of desprovisto de. —n vacío m. —vt anular

volatile /ˈvɒlətaɪl/ a volátil; (person) voluble

volcan|ic /vɒlˈkænɪk/ a volcánico. ~o /vɒlˈkeɪnəʊ/ n (pl -oes) volcán m

volition /vəˈlɪʃn/ n. of one's own ~ de su propia voluntad

volley /ˈvɒlɪ/ n (pl -eys) (of blows) lluvia f; (of gunfire) descarga f cerrada

volt /vəʊlt/ n voltio m. ~age n voltaje m

voluble /ˈvɒljʊbl/ a locuaz

volume /ˈvɒljuːm/ n volumen m; (book) tomo m

voluminous /vəˈljuːmɪnəs/ a voluminoso

voluntar|ily /ˈvɒləntərəlɪ/ adv voluntariamente. ~**y** /ˈvɒləntərɪ/ a voluntario

volunteer /vɒlənˈtɪə(r)/ n voluntario m. −vt ofrecer. −vi ofrecerse voluntariamente; (mil) alistarse como voluntario

voluptuous /vəˈlʌptjʊəs/ a voluptuoso

vomit /ˈvɒmɪt/ vt/i vomitar. −n vómito m

voracious /vəˈreɪʃəs/ a voraz

vot|e /vəʊt/ n voto m; (right) derecho m de votar. −vi votar. ~**er** /-ə(r)/ n votante m & f. ~**ing** n votación f

vouch /vaʊtʃ/ vi. ~ **for** garantizar

voucher /ˈvaʊtʃə(r)/ n vale m

vow /vaʊ/ n voto m. −vi jurar

vowel /ˈvaʊəl/ n vocal f

voyage /ˈvɔɪɪdʒ/ n viaje m (en barco)

vulgar /ˈvʌlgə(r)/ a vulgar. ~**ity** /-ˈgærətɪ/ n vulgaridad f. ~**ize** vt vulgarizar

vulnerab|ility /vʌlnərəˈbɪlətɪ/ n vulnerabilidad f. ~**le** /ˈvʌlnərəbl/ a vulnerable

vulture /ˈvʌltʃə(r)/ n buitre m

vying /ˈvaɪɪŋ/ see **vie**

W

wad /wɒd/ n (pad) tapón m; (bundle) lío m; (of notes) fajo m; (of cotton wool etc) bolita f

wadding /ˈwɒdɪŋ/ n relleno m

waddle /ˈwɒdl/ vi contonearse

wade /weɪd/ vt vadear. −vi. ~ **through** abrirse paso entre; leer con dificultad (book)

wafer /ˈweɪfə(r)/ n barquillo m; (relig) hostia f

waffle[1] /ˈwɒfl/ n (fam) palabrería f. −vi (fam) divagar

waffle[2] /ˈwɒfl/ n (culin) gofre m

waft /wɒft/ vt llevar por el aire. −vi flotar

wag /wæg/ vt (pt **wagged**) menear. −vi menearse

wage /weɪdʒ/ n. ~**s** npl salario m. ~ **war** hacer la guerra. ~**r** /ˈweɪdʒə(r)/ n apuesta f. −vt apostar

waggle /ˈwægl/ vt menear. −vi menearse

wagon /ˈwægən/ n carro m; (rail) vagón m. **be on the** ~ (sl) no beber

waif /weɪf/ n niño m abandonado

wail /weɪl/ vi lamentarse. −n lamento m

wainscot /ˈweɪnskət/ n revestimiento m, zócalo m

waist /weɪst/ n cintura f. ~**band** n cinturón m

waistcoat /ˈweɪstkəʊt/ n chaleco m

waistline /ˈweɪstlaɪn/ n cintura f

wait /weɪt/ vt/i esperar; (at table) servir. ~ **for** esperar. ~ **on** servir. −n espera f. **lie in** ~ acechar

waiter /ˈweɪtə(r)/ n camarero m

wait: ~**ing-list** n lista f de espera. ~**ing-room** n sala f de espera

waitress /ˈweɪtrɪs/ n camarera f

waive /weɪv/ vt renunciar a

wake[1] /weɪk/ vt (pt **woke**, pp **woken**) despertar. −vi despertarse. −n velatorio m. ~ **up** vt despertar. −vi despertarse

wake[2] /weɪk/ n (naut) estela f. **in the** ~ **of** como resultado de, tras

waken /ˈweɪkən/ vt despertar. −vi despertarse

wakeful /ˈweɪkfl/ a insomne

Wales /weɪlz/ n País m de Gales

walk /wɔːk/ vi andar; (not ride) ir a pie; (stroll) pasearse. −vt salir; (workers) declararse en huelga. ~ **out** on abandonar. ~ **out on** abandonar. −vt andar por (streets); llevar de paseo (dog). −n paseo m; (gait)

modo *m* de andar; (*path*) sendero *m*. ~ **of life** clase *f* social.
~**about** /'wɔːkəbaʊt/ *n* (*of royalty*) encuentro *m* con el público.
~**er** /-ə(r)/ *n* paseante *m* & *f*

walkie-talkie /wɔːkɪ'tɔːkɪ/ *n*
transmisor-receptor *m* portátil

walking /'wɔːkɪŋ/ *n* paseo *m*.
~**stick** *n* bastón *m*

Walkman /'wɔːkmən/ *n* (P)
estereo *m* personal, Walkman *m*
(P), magnetófono *m* de bolsillo

walk: ~**out** *n* huelga *f*. ~**over**
n victoria *f* fácil

wall /wɔːl/ *n* (*interior*) pared *f*;
(*exterior*) muro *m*; (*in garden*)
tapia *f*; (*of city*) muralla *f*. **go to
the** ~ fracasar. **up the** ~ (*fam*)
loco. —*vt* amurallar ⟨*city*⟩

wallet /'wɒlɪt/ *n* cartera *f*, billetera *f* (*LAm*)

wallflower /'wɔːlflaʊə(r)/ *n*
alhelí *m*

wallop /'wɒləp/ *vt* (*pt* **walloped**)
(*sl*) golpear con fuerza. —*n* (*sl*)
golpe *m* fuerte

wallow /'wɒləʊ/ *vi* revolcarse

wallpaper /'wɔːlpeɪpə(r)/ *n* papel
m pintado

walnut /'wɔːlnʌt/ *n* nuez *f*; (*tree*)
nogal *m*

walrus /'wɔːlrəs/ *n* morsa *f*

waltz /wɔːls/ *n* vals *m*. —*vi* valsar

wan /wɒn/ *a* pálido

wand /wɒnd/ *n* varita *f*

wander /'wɒndə(r)/ *vi* vagar;
(*stroll*) pasearse; (*digress*) divagar; ⟨*road, river*⟩ serpentear. —
n paseo *m*. ~**er** /-ə(r)/ *n* vagabundo *m*. ~**lust** /'wɒndəlʌst/ *n*
pasión *f* por los viajes

wane /weɪn/ *vi* menguar. —*n*. **on
the** ~ disminuyendo

wangle /'wæŋgl/ *vt* (*sl*) agenciarse

want /wɒnt/ *vt* querer; (*need*)
necesitar; (*require*) exigir. —*vi*.
~ **for** carecer de. —*n* necesidad
f; (*lack*) falta *f*; (*desire*) deseo *m*.
~**ed** ⟨*criminal*⟩ buscado. ~**ing**

a (*lacking*) falto de. **be** ~**ing**
carecer de

wanton /'wɒntən/ *a* (*licentious*)
lascivo; (*motiveless*) sin motivo

war /wɔː(r)/ *n* guerra *f*. **at** ~ en
guerra

warble /'wɔːbl/ *vt* cantar trinando. —*vi* gorjear. —*n* gorjeo *m*.
~**r** /-ə(r)/ *n* curruca *f*

ward /wɔːd/ *n* (*in hospital*) sala *f*;
(*of town*) barrio *m*; (*child*) pupilo
m. —*vt*. ~ **off** parar

warden /'wɔːdn/ *n* guarda *m*

warder /'wɔːdə(r)/ *n* carcelero *m*

wardrobe /'wɔːdrəʊb/ *n* armario
m; (*clothes*) vestuario *m*

warehouse /'weəhaʊs/ *n* almacén *m*

wares /weəz/ *npl* mercancías *fpl*

war: ~**fare** /'wɔːfeə(r)/ *n* guerra
f. ~**head** /'wɔːhed/ *n* cabeza *f*
explosiva

warily /'weərɪlɪ/ *adv* cautelosamente

warlike /'wɔːlaɪk/ *a* belicoso

warm /wɔːm/ *a* (**-er, -est**) caliente; (*hearty*) caluroso. **be** ~
⟨*person*⟩ tener calor. **it is** ~ hace
calor. —*vt*. ~ (**up**) calentar;
recalentar ⟨*food*⟩; (*fig*) animar.
—*vi*. ~ (**up**) calentarse; (*fig*)
animarse. ~ **to** tomar simpatía a
⟨*person*⟩; ir entusiasmándose
por ⟨*idea etc*⟩. ~**-blooded** *a* de
sangre caliente. ~**-hearted** *a*
simpático. ~**ly** *adv* (*heartily*)
calurosamente

warmonger /'wɔːmʌŋgə(r)/ *n*
belicista *m* & *f*

warmth /wɔːmθ/ *n* calor *m*

warn /wɔːn/ *vt* avisar, advertir.
~**ing** *n* advertencia *f*; (*notice*)
aviso *m*. ~ **off** (*advise against*)
aconsejar en contra de; (*forbid*)
impedir

warp /wɔːp/ *vt* deformar; (*fig*)
pervertir. —*vi* deformarse

warpath /'wɔːpɑːθ/ *n*. **be on the** ~
buscar camorra

warrant /ˈwɒrənt/ n autorización f; (for arrest) orden f. — vt justificar. ~**officer** n suboficial m

warranty /ˈwɒrəntɪ/ n garantía f.

warring /ˈwɔːrɪŋ/ a en guerra

warrior /ˈwɒrɪə(r)/ n guerrero m

warship /ˈwɔːʃɪp/ n buque m de guerra

wart /wɔːt/ n verruga f

wartime /ˈwɔːtaɪm/ n tiempo m de guerra

wary /ˈweərɪ/ a (-ier, -iest) cauteloso

was /wɒz, wəz/ see **be**

wash /wɒʃ/ vt lavar; (flow over) bañar. —vi lavarse. —n lavado m; (dirty clothes) ropa f sucia; (wet clothes) colada f; (of ship) estela f. **have a** ~ lavarse. ~ **out** vt enjuagar; (fig) cancelar. ~ **up** vi fregar los platos. ~**able** a lavable. ~**basin** n lavabo m. ~**ed-out** a (pale) pálido; (tired) rendido. ~**er** /ˈwɒʃə(r)/ n arandela f; (washing-machine) lavadora f. ~**ing** /ˈwɒʃɪŋ/ n lavado m; (dirty clothes) ropa f sucia; (wet clothes) colada f. ~**ing-machine** n lavadora f. ~**ing-powder** n jabón m en polvo. ~**ing-up** n fregado m; (dirty plates etc) platos mpl para fregar. ~**out** n (sl) desastre m. ~**room** n (Amer) servicios mpl. ~**stand** n lavabo m. ~**tub** n tina f de lavar

wasp /wɒsp/ n avispa f

wastage /ˈweɪstɪdʒ/ n desperdicios mpl

waste /weɪst/ —a de desecho; (land) yermo. —n derroche m; (rubbish) desperdicio m; (of time) pérdida f. —vt derrochar; (not use) desperdiciar; perder (time). —vi. ~ **away** consumirse. ~**disposal unit** n trituradora f de basuras. ~**ful** a

dispendioso; (person) derrochador. ~**paper basket** n papelera f. ~**s** npl tierras fpl baldías

watch /wɒtʃ/ vt mirar; (keep an eye on) vigilar; (take heed) tener cuidado con; ver (TV). —vi mirar; (keep an eye on) vigilar. —n vigilancia f; (period of duty) guardia f; (timepiece) reloj m. **on the** ~ alerta. ~ **out** vi tener cuidado. ~**dog** n perro m guardián; (fig) guardián m. ~**ful** a vigilante. ~**maker** /ˈwɒtʃmeɪkə(r)/ n relojero m. ~**man** /ˈwɒtʃmən/ n (pl -men) vigilante m. ~**tower** n atalaya f. ~**word** /ˈwɒtʃwɜːd/ n santo m y seña

water /ˈwɔːtə(r)/ n agua f. **by** ~ (of travel) por mar. **in hot** ~ (fam) en un apuro. —vt regar (plants etc); (dilute) aguar, diluir. —vi (eyes) llorar. **make s.o.'s mouth** ~ hacérsele la boca agua. ~ **down** vt diluir; (fig) suavizar. ~**closet** n wáter m. ~**colour** n acuarela f. ~**course** /ˈwɔːtəkɔːs/ n arroyo m; (artificial) canal m. ~**cress** /ˈwɔːtəkres/ n berro m. ~**fall** /ˈwɔːtəfɔːl/ n cascada f. ~**ice** n sorbete m. ~**ing-can** /ˈwɔːtərɪŋkæn/ n regadera f. ~**lily** n nenúfar m. ~**line** n línea f de flotación. ~**logged** /ˈwɔːtəlɒgd/ a saturado de agua, empapado. ~ **main** n cañería f principal. ~ **melon** n sandía f. ~**mill** n molino m de agua. ~ **polo** n polo m acuático. ~**power** n energía f hidráulica. ~**proof** /ˈwɔːtəpruːf/ a & n impermeable (m); (watch) sumergible. ~**shed** /ˈwɔːtəʃed/ n punto m decisivo. ~**skiing** n esquí m acuático. ~**softener** n ablandador m de agua. ~**tight** /ˈwɔːtətaɪt/ a hermético, estanco; (fig) irrecusable. ~**way** n canal m navegable. ~**wheel** n rueda f hidráulica. ∼**wings** npl flotadores mpl. ∼**works** /'wɔ:ksɔ n sistema m de abastecimiento de agua. ∼**y** /'wɔ:tərɪ/ a acuoso; ⟨colour⟩ pálido; ⟨eyes⟩ lloroso

watt /wɒt/ n vatio m

wave /weɪv/ n onda f; ⟨of hand⟩ señal f; ⟨fig⟩ oleada f. —vt agitar; ondular ⟨hair⟩. —vi ⟨signal⟩ hacer señales con la mano; ⟨flag⟩. flotar. ∼**band** /'weɪvbænd/ n banda f de ondas. ∼**length** /'weɪvleŋθ/ n longitud f de onda

waver /'weɪvə(r)/ vi vacilar

wavy /'weɪvɪ/ a (-ier, -iest) ondulado

wax[1] /wæks/ n cera f. —vt encerar

wax[2] /wæks/ vi ⟨moon⟩ crecer

wax: ∼**en** a céreo. ∼**work** /'wækswɔ:k/ n figura f de cera. ∼**y** a céreo

way /weɪ/ n camino m; ⟨distance⟩ distancia f; ⟨manner⟩ manera f, modo m; ⟨direction⟩ dirección f; ⟨means⟩ medio m; ⟨habit⟩ costumbre f. **be in the** ∼ estorbar. **by the** ∼ a propósito. **by** ∼ **of** a título de, por. **either** ∼ de cualquier modo. **in a** ∼ en cierta manera. **in some** ∼**s** en ciertos modos. **lead the** ∼ mostrar el camino. **make** ∼ dejar paso a. **on the** ∼ en camino. **out of the** ∼ remoto; ⟨extraordinary⟩ fuera de lo común. **that** ∼ por allí. **this** ∼ por aquí. **under** ∼ en curso. ∼**bill** n hoja f de ruta. ∼**farer** /'weɪfeərə(r)/ n viajero m. ∼ **in** n entrada f

waylay /weɪ'leɪ/ vt (pt -laid) acechar; ⟨detain⟩ detener

way: ∼ **out** n salida f. ∼**out** a ultramoderno, original. ∼**s** npl costumbres fpl. ∼**side** /'weɪsaɪd/ n borde m del camino

wayward /'weɪwəd/ a caprichoso

we /wi:/ pron nosotros, nosotras

weak /wi:k/ a (-er, -est) débil; ⟨liquid⟩ aguado, acuoso; ⟨fig⟩ flojo. ∼**en** vt debilitar. ∼**kneed** a irresoluto. ∼**ling** /'wi:klɪŋ/ n persona f débil. ∼**ly** adv débilmente. —a enfermizo. ∼**ness** n debilidad f

weal /wi:l/ n verdugón m

wealth /welθ/ n riqueza f. ∼**y** a (-ier, -iest) rico

wean /wi:n/ vt destetar

weapon /'wepən/ n arma f

wear /weə(r)/ vt (pt **wore**, pp **worn**) llevar; ⟨put on⟩ ponerse; tener ⟨expression etc⟩; ⟨damage⟩ desgastar. —vi desgastarse; ⟨last⟩ durar. —n uso m; ⟨damage⟩ desgaste m; ⟨clothing⟩ ropa f. ∼ **down** vt desgastar; agotar ⟨opposition etc⟩. ∼ **off** vi desaparecer. ∼ **on** vi ⟨time⟩ pasar. ∼ **out** vt desgastar; ⟨tire⟩ agotar. ∼**able** a que se puede llevar. ∼ **and tear** desgaste m

wear: ∼**ily** /'wɪərɪlɪ/ adv cansadamente. ∼**iness** n cansancio m. ∼**isome** /'wɪərɪsəm/ a cansado. ∼**y** /'wɪərɪ/ a (-ier, -iest) cansado. —vt cansar. —vi cansarse. ∼**y** of cansarse de

weasel /'wi:zl/ n comadreja f

weather /'weðə(r)/ n tiempo m. **under the** ∼ ⟨fam⟩ indispuesto. —a meteorológico. —vt curar ⟨wood⟩; ⟨survive⟩ superar. ∼**beaten** a curtido. ∼**cock** /'weðəkɒk/ n, ∼**vane** n veleta f

weave /wi:v/ vt (pt **wove**, pp **woven**) tejer; entretejer ⟨story etc⟩; entrelazar ⟨flowers etc⟩. ∼ **one's way** abrirse paso. —n tejido m. ∼**r** /-ə(r)/ n tejedor m

web /web/ n tela f; ⟨of spider⟩ telaraña f; ⟨on foot⟩ membrana f. ∼**bing** n cincha f

wed /wed/ *vt* (*pt* **wedded**) casarse con; (*priest etc*) casar. —*vi* casarse. **~ded to** (*fig*) unido a

wedding /'wedɪŋ/ *n* boda *f*. **~cake** *n* pastel *m* de boda. **~ring** *n* anillo *m* de boda

wedge /wedʒ/ *n* cuña *f*; (*space filler*) calce *m*. —*vt* acuñar; (*push*) apretar

wedlock /'wedlɒk/ *n* matrimonio *m*

Wednesday /'wenzdeɪ/ *n* miércoles *m*

wee /wiː/ *a* (*fam*) pequeñito

weed /wiːd/ *n* mala hierba *f*. —*vt* desherbar. **~killer** *n* herbicida *m*. **~ out** eliminar. **~y** *a* (*person*) débil

week /wiːk/ *n* semana *f*. **~day** /'wiːkdeɪ/ *n* día *m* laborable. **~end** *n* fin *m* de semana. **~ly** /'wiːklɪ/ *a* semanal. —*n* semanario *m*. —*adv* semanalmente

weep /wiːp/ *vi* (*pt* **wept**) llorar. **~ing willow** *n* sauce *m* llorón

weevil /'wiːvɪl/ *n* gorgojo *m*

weigh /weɪ/ *vt/i* pesar. **~ anchor** levar anclas. **~ down** *vt* (*fig*) oprimir. **~ up** *vt* pesar; (*fig*) considerar

weight /weɪt/ *n* peso *m*. **~less** *a* ingrávido. **~lessness** *n* ingravidez *f*. **~lifting** *n* halterofilia *f*, levantamiento *m* de pesos. **~y** *a* (-**ier**, -**iest**) pesado; (*influential*) influyente

weir /wɪə(r)/ *n* presa *f*

weird /wɪəd/ *a* (-**er**, -**est**) misterioso; (*bizarre*) extraño

welcome /'welkəm/ *a* bienvenido. **~ to do** libre de hacer. **you're ~e!** (*after thank you*) ¡de nada! —*n* bienvenida *f*; (*reception*) acogida *f*. —*vt* dar la bienvenida a; (*appreciate*) alegrarse de

welcoming /'welkəmɪŋ/ *a* acogedor

weld /weld/ *vt* soldar. —*n* soldadura *f*. **~er** *n* soldador *m*

welfare /'welfeə(r)/ *n* bienestar *m*; (*aid*) asistencia *f* social. **W~ State** *n* estado *m* benefactor. **~ work** *n* asistencia *f* social

well¹ /wel/ *adv* (**better**, **best**) bien. **~ done!** ¡bravo! **as ~** también. **as ~ as** tanto... como. **be ~** estar bien. **do ~** (*succeed*) tener éxito. **very ~** muy bien. —*a* bien. —*int* bueno; (*surprise*) ¡vaya! **~ I never!** ¡no me digas!

well² /wel/ *n* pozo *m*; (*of staircase*) caja *f*

well: ~appointed *a* bien equipado. **~behaved** *a* bien educado. **~being** *n* bienestar *m*. **~bred** *a* bien educado. **~disposed** *a* benévolo. **~groomed** *a* bien aseado. **~heeled** *a* (*fam*) rico

wellington /'welɪŋtən/ *n* bota *f* de agua

well: ~knit *a* robusto. **~known** *a* conocido. **~meaning** *a*, **~ meant** *a* bienintencionado. **~ off** *a* acomodado. **~read** *a* culto. **~spoken** *a* bienhablado. **~to-do** *a* rico. **~wisher** *n* bienqueriente *m* & *f*

Welsh /welʃ/ *a* & *n* galés (*m*). **~ rabbit** *n* pan *m* tostado con queso

welsh /welʃ/ *vi*. **~ on** no cumplir con

wench /wentʃ/ *n* (*old use*) muchacha *f*

wend /wend/ *vt*. **~ one's way** encaminarse

went /went/ *see* **go**

wept /wept/ *see* **weep**

west /west/ *n* oeste *m*. **the ~** el Occidente *m*. —*a* del oeste. —*adv* hacia el oeste, al oeste. **go ~** (*sl*) morir. **W~ Germany** *n* Alemania *f* Occidental. **~erly** *a* del oeste. **~ern** *a* occidental. —*n* (*film*) película *f* del Oeste. **~erner** /-ʒnə(r)/ *n* occidental *m* & *f*. **W~ Indian** *a* & *n* antillano (*m*). **W~ Indies** *npl* Antillas *fpl*. **~ward** *a*, **~ward(s)** *adv* hacia el oeste

wet /wet/ *a* (**wetter, wettest**) mojado; (*rainy*) lluvioso, de lluvia; (*person, sl*) soso. **~ paint** recién pintado. **get ~** mojarse. —*vt* (*pt* **wetted**) mojar, humedecer. **~ blanket** *n* aguafiestas *m* & *f invar*. **~ suit** *n* traje *m* de buzo

whack /wæk/ *vt* (*fam*) golpear. —*n* (*fam*) golpe *m*. **~ed** /wækt/ *a* (*fam*) agotado. **~ing** *a* (*huge, sl*) enorme. —*n* paliza *f*

whale /weɪl/ *n* ballena *f*. **a ~ of a** (*fam*) maravilloso, enorme

wham /wæm/ *int* ¡zas!

wharf /wɔ:f/ *n* (*pl* **wharves** *or* **wharfs**) muelle *m*

what /wɒt/ *a* el que, la que, lo que, los que, las que; (*in questions & exclamations*) qué. — *pron* lo que; (*interrogative*) qué. **~ about going?** ¿si fuésemos? **~ about me?** ¿y yo? **~ for?** ¿para qué? **~ if?** ¿y si? **~ is it?** ¿qué es? **~ you need** lo que te haga falta. —*int* ¡cómo! **~ a fool!** ¡qué tonto!

whatever /wɒt'evə(r)/ *a* cualquiera. —*pron* (todo) lo que, cualquier cosa que

whatnot /'wɒtnɒt/ *n* chisme *m*

whatsoever /wɒtsəʊ'evə(r)/ *a* & *pron* **whatever**

wheat /wi:t/ *n* trigo *m*. **~en** *a* de trigo

wheedle /'wi:dl/ *vt* engatusar

wheel /wi:l/ *n* rueda *f*. **at the ~** al volante. **steering-~** *n* volante *m*. —*vt* empujar (*bicycle etc*). —*vi* girar. **~ round** girar. **~barrow** /'wi:lbærəʊ/ *n* carretilla *f*. **~ chair** /'wi:ltʃeə(r)/ *n* silla *f* de ruedas

wheeze /wi:z/ *vi* resollar. —*n* resuello *m*

when /wen/ *adv* cuándo. —*conj* cuando

whence /wens/ *adv* de dónde

whenever /wen'evə(r)/ *adv* en cualquier momento; (*every time that*) cada vez que

where /weə(r)/ *adv* & *conj* donde; (*interrogative adv*) dónde. **~ are you going?** ¿adónde vas? **~ are you from?** ¿de dónde eres?

whereabouts /'weərəbaʊts/ *adv* dónde. —*n* paradero *m*

whereas /weər'æz/ *conj* por cuanto; (*in contrast*) mientras (*que*)

whereby /weə'baɪ/ *adv* por lo cual

whereupon /weərə'pɒn/ *adv* después de lo cual

wherever /weər'evə(r)/ *adv* (*in whatever place*) dónde (diablos). —*conj* dondequiera que

whet /wet/ *vt* (*pt* **whetted**) afilar; (*fig*) aguzar

whether /'weðə(r)/ *conj* si. **~ you like it or not** que te guste o no te guste. **I don't know ~ she will like it** no sé si le gustará

which /wɪtʃ/ *a* (*in questions*) qué. **~ one** cuál. **~ one of you** cuál de vosotros. —*pron* (*in questions*) cuál; (*relative*) que; (*object*) el cual, la cual, lo cual, los cuales, las cuales

whichever /wɪtʃ'evə(r)/ *a* cualquier. —*pron* cualquiera que, el que, la que

whiff /wɪf/ *n* soplo *m*; (*of smoke*) bocanada *f*; (*smell*) olorcillo *m*

while /waɪl/ *n* rato *m*. —*conj* mientras; (*although*) aunque. —*vt*. **~ away** pasar (*time*)

whilst /waɪlst/ *conj* = **while**

whim /wɪm/ *n* capricho *m*

whimper /'wɪmpə(r)/ *vi* lloriquear. —*n* lloriqueo *m*

whimsical /ˈwɪmzɪkl/ a caprichoso; (odd) extraño

whine /waɪn/ vi gimotear. —n gimoteo m

whip /wɪp/ n látigo m; (pol) oficial m disciplinario. —vt (pt whipped) azotar; (culin) batir; (seize) agarrar. ~-cord n tralla f. ~ped cream n nata f batida. ~ping-boy n /ˈwɪpɪŋbɔɪ/ n cabeza f de turco. ~round n colecta f. ~ up (incite) estimular

whirl /wɜːl/ vt hacer girar rápidamente. —vi girar rápidamente; (swirl) arremolinarse. —n giro m; (swirl) remolino m. ~pool /ˈwɜːlpuːl/ n remolino m. ~wind /ˈwɜːlwɪnd/ n torbellino m

whirr /wɜː(r)/ n zumbido m. —vi zumbar

whisk /wɪsk/ vt (culin) batir. —n (culin) batidor m. ~ away llevarse

whisker /ˈwɪskə(r)/ n pelo m. ~s npl (of man) patillas fpl; (of cat etc) bigotes mpl

whisky /ˈwɪskɪ/ n güisqui m

whisper /ˈwɪspə(r)/ vt decir en voz baja. —vi cuchichear; (leaves etc) susurrar. —n cuchicheo m; (of leaves) susurro m; (rumour) rumor m

whistle /ˈwɪsl/ n silbido m; (instrument) silbato m. —vi silbar. ~-stop n (pol) breve parada f (en gira electoral)

white /waɪt/ a (-er, -est) blanco. go ~ ponerse pálido. —n blanco; (of egg) clara f. ~-bait /ˈwaɪtbeɪt/ n (pl ~bait) chanquetes mpl. ~ coffee n café m con leche. ~ collar worker n empleado m de oficina. ~ elephant n objeto m inútil y costoso

Whitehall /ˈwaɪthɔːl/ n el gobierno m británico

white: ~ horses n cabrillas fpl. ~hot a (metal) candente. ~ lie

n mentirijilla f. ~ness n blancura f. ~wash n jalbegue m; (fig) encubrimiento m. —vt blanquear; (fig) encubrir

whiting /ˈwaɪtɪŋ/ n (pl whiting) (fish) pescadilla f

whitlow /ˈwɪtləʊ/ n panadizo m

Whitsun /ˈwɪtsn/ n Pentecostés m

whittle /ˈwɪtl/ vt. ~ (down) tallar; (fig) reducir

whiz /wɪz/ vi (pt whizzed) silbar; (rush) ir a gran velocidad. ~ past pasar como un rayo. ~-kid n (fam) joven m prometedor, promesa f

who /huː/ pron que, quien; (interrogative) quién; (particular person) el que, la que, los que, las que

whodunit /huːˈdʌnɪt/ n (fam) novela f policíaca

whoever /huːˈevə(r)/ pron quienquiera que; (interrogative) quién (diablos)

whole /həʊl/ a entero; (not broken) intacto. —n todo m, conjunto m; (total) total m. as a ~ en conjunto. on the ~ por regla general. ~-hearted a sincero. ~-meal a integral

wholesale /ˈhəʊlseɪl/ n venta f al por mayor. —a & adv al por mayor. ~-r /-ə(r)/ n comerciante m & f al por mayor

wholesome /ˈhəʊlsəm/ a saludable

wholly /ˈhəʊlɪ/ adv completamente

whom /huːm/ pron que, a quien; (interrogative) a quién

whooping cough /ˈhuːpɪŋkɒf/ n tos f ferina

whore /hɔː(r)/ n puta f

whose /huːz/ pron de quién. —a de quién; (relative) cuyo

...ral/ *adv* por qué. —*int*
...la!

..к /wɪk/ *n* mecha *f*

...cked /'wɪkɪd/ *a* malo; (*mischievous*) travieso; (*very bad,
fam*) malísimo. ~ness *n* maldad
f

wicker /'wɪkə(r)/ *n* mimbre *m* &
f. —*a* de mimbre. ~work *n* artí-
ulos *mpl* de mimbre

wicket /'wɪkɪt/ *a* (*cricket*) rastrillo *m*

wide /waɪd/ *a* (-er, -est) ancho;
(*fully opened*) de par en par; (*far
from target*) lejano; (*knowledge
etc*) amplio. —*adv* lejos. far and
~ por todas partes. ~ awake *a*
completamente despierto; (*fig*)
despabilado. ~ly *adv* extensamente; (*believed*) generalmente; (*different*) muy. ~n *vt*
ensanchar

widespread /'waɪdspred/ *a*
extendido; (*fig*) difundido

widow /'wɪdəʊ/ *n* viuda *f*. ~ed *a*
viudo. ~er *n* viudo *m*. ~hood *n*
viudez *f*

width /wɪdθ/ *n* anchura *f*. in ~
de ancho

wield /wiːld/ *vt* manejar; ejercer
(*power*)

wife /waɪf/ *n* (*pl* wives) mujer *f*,
esposa *f*

wig /wɪg/ *n* peluca *f*

wiggle /'wɪgl/ *vt* menear. —*vi*
menearse

wild /waɪld/ *a* (-er, -est) salvaje;
(*enraged*) furioso; (*idea*) extravagante; (*with joy*) loco; (*random*) al azar. —*adv* en estado
salvaje. run ~ crecer en estado
salvaje. ~s *npl* regiones *fpl*
salvajes

wildcat /'waɪldkæt/ *a*. ~ strike *n*
huelga *f* salvaje

wilderness /'wɪldənɪs/ *n* desierto *m*

wild: ~fire /'waɪldfaɪl(r)/ *n*.
spread like ~fire correr como

un reguero de pólvora. ~goose
chase *n* empresa *f* inútil. ~life
/'waɪldlaɪf/ *n* fauna *f*. ~ly *adv*
violentamente; (*fig*) locamente

wilful /'wɪlfʊl/ *a* intencionado;
(*self-willed*) terco. ~ly *adv* inten-
cionadamente; (*obstinately*)
obstinadamente

will¹ /wɪl/ *v aux*. ~ you have
some wine? ¿quieres vino? he
~ be será. you ~ be back soon,
won't you? volverás pronto,
¿no?

will² /wɪl/ *n* voluntad *f*; (*document*) testamento *m*

willing /'wɪlɪŋ/ *a* complaciente.
~ to dispuesto a. ~ly *adv* de
buena gana. ~ness *n* buena
voluntad *f*

willow /'wɪləʊ/ *n* sauce *m*

will-power /'wɪlpaʊə(r)/ *n*
fuerza *f* de voluntad

willy-nilly /wɪlɪ'nɪlɪ/ *adv*
quieras que no

wilt /wɪlt/ *vi* marchitarse

wily /'waɪlɪ/ *a* (-ier, -iest) astuto

win /wɪn/ *vt* (*pt* won, *pres p* winning) ganar; (*achieve, obtain*)
conseguir. —*vi* ganar. —*n* victoria *f*. ~ back *vt* reconquistar.
~ over *vt* convencer

wince /wɪns/ *vi* hacer una mueca
de dolor. without wincing sin
pestañear. —*n* mueca *f* de dolor

winch /wɪntʃ/ *n* cabrestante
m. —*vt* levantar con el
cabrestante

wind¹ /wɪnd/ *n* viento *m*; (*in
stomach*) flatulencia *f*. get the ~
up (*sl*) asustarse. get ~ of enterarse de. in the ~ en el aire. —*vt*
dejar sin aliento

wind² /waɪnd/ *vt* (*pt* wound)
(*wrap around*) enrollar; dar
cuerda a (*clock etc*). —*vi* (*road
etc*) serpentear. ~ up *vt* dar
cuerda a (*watch, clock*); (*provoke*) agitar, poner nervioso; (*fig*)
terminar, concluir

wind /wɪnd/: ∼**bag** n charlatán m. ∼**cheater** n cazadora f

winder /ˈwaɪndə(r)/ n devanador m; (of clock, watch) llave f

windfall /ˈwɪndfɔːl/ n fruta f caída; (fig) suerte f inesperada

winding /ˈwaɪndɪŋ/ a tortuoso

wind instrument /ˈwɪnd ɪnstrəmənt/ n instrumento m de viento

windmill /ˈwɪndmɪl/ n molino m (de viento)

window /ˈwɪndəʊ/ n ventana f; (in shop) escaparate m; (of vehicle, booking-office) ventanilla f. ∼**box** n jardinera f. ∼**dresser** n escaparatista m & f. ∼**shop** vi mirar los escaparates

windpipe /ˈwɪndpaɪp/ n tráquea f

windscreen /ˈwɪndskriːn/ n, **windshield** n (Amer) parabrisas m invar. ∼ **wiper** n limpiaparabrisas m invar

wind /wɪnd/: ∼**swept** a barrido por el viento. ∼**y** a (-ier, -iest) ventoso, de mucho viento. **it is** ∼**y** hace viento

wine /waɪn/ n vino m. ∼**cellar** n bodega f. ∼**glass** n copa f. ∼**grower** n vinicultor m. ∼**growing** n vinicultura f. —a vinícola. ∼ **list** n lista f de vinos. ∼**tasting** n cata f de vinos

wing /wɪŋ/ n ala f; (auto) aleta f. **under one's** ∼ bajo la protección de uno. ∼**ed** a alado. ∼**er** /-ə(r)/ n (sport) ala m & f. ∼**s** npl (in theatre) bastidores mpl

wink /wɪŋk/ vi guiñar el ojo; (light etc) centellear. —n guiño m. **not to sleep a** ∼ no pegar ojo

winkle /ˈwɪŋkl/ n bígaro m

win: ∼**ner** /-ə(r)/ n ganador m. ∼**ning-post** n poste m de llegada. ∼**ning smile** n sonrisa f encantadora. ∼**nings** npl ganancias fpl

winsome /ˈwɪnsəm/ a atractivo

wint|er /ˈwɪntə(r)/ n invierno m. —vi invernar. ∼**ry** a invernal

wipe /waɪp/ vt limpiar; (dry) secar. —n limpión m. **give sth a** ∼ limpiar algo. ∼ **out** (cancel) cancelar; (destroy) destruir; (obliterate) borrar. ∼ **up** limpiar; (dry) secar

wire /ˈwaɪə(r)/ n alambre m; (elec) cable m; (telegram, fam) telegrama m

wireless /ˈwaɪəlɪs/ n radio f

wire netting /ˈwaɪəˈnetɪŋ/ n alambrera f, tela f metálica

wiring n instalación f eléctrica

wiry /ˈwaɪərɪ/ a (-ier, -iest) (person) delgado

wisdom /ˈwɪzdəm/ n sabiduría f. ∼ **tooth** n muela f del juicio

wise /waɪz/ a (-er, -est) sabio; (sensible) prudente. ∼**crack** /ˈwaɪzkræk/ n (fam) salida f. ∼**ly** adv sabiamente; (sensibly) prudentemente

wish /wɪʃ/ n deseo m; (greeting) saludo m. **with best** ∼**es** (in letters) un fuerte abrazo. —vt desear. ∼ **on** (fam) encajar a. ∼ **s.o. well** desear buena suerte a uno. ∼**bone** n espoleta f (de las aves). ∼**ful** a deseoso. ∼**ful thinking** n ilusiones fpl

wishy-washy /ˈwɪʃɪwɒʃɪ/ a soso; (person) sin convicciones, falto de entereza

wisp /wɪsp/ n manojito m; (of smoke) voluta f; (of hair) mechón m

wisteria /wɪsˈtɪərɪə/ n glicina f

wistful /ˈwɪstfl/ a melancólico

wit /wɪt/ n gracia f; (person) persona f chistosa; (intelligence) ingenio m. **be at one's** ∼**s' end** no saber qué hacer. **live by one's** ∼**s** vivir de expedientes, vivir del cuento

witch /wɪtʃ/ n bruja f. ∼**craft** n brujería f. ∼**doctor** n hechicero m

with /wɪð/ prep con; (cause, having) de. **be ~ it** (fam) estar al día, estar al tanto. **the man ~ the beard** el hombre de la barba

withdraw /wɪð'drɔː/ vt (pt **withdrew**, pp **withdrawn**) retirar. —vi apartarse. **~al** n retirada f. **~n** a (person) introvertido

wither /'wɪðə(r)/ vi marchitarse. —vt (fig) fulminar

withhold /wɪð'həʊld/ vt (pt **withheld**) retener; (conceal) ocultar (**from** a)

within /wɪð'ɪn/ prep dentro de. —adv dentro. **~ sight** a la vista

without /wɪð'aʊt/ prep sin

withstand /wɪð'stænd/ vt (pt **~stood**) resistir a

witness /'wɪtnɪs/ n testigo m; (proof) testimonio m. —vt presenciar; firmar como testigo (document). **~-box** n tribuna f de los testigos

witticism /'wɪtɪsɪzəm/ n ocurrencia f

wittingly /'wɪtɪŋlɪ/ adv a sabiendas

witty /'wɪtɪ/ a (-ier, -iest) gracioso

wives /waɪvz/ see **wife**

wizard /'wɪzəd/ n hechicero m. **~ry** n hechicería f

wizened /'wɪznd/ a arrugado

wobb|le /'wɒbl/ vi tambalearse; (voice, jelly, hand) temblar; (chair etc) balancearse. **~y** a (chair etc) cojo

woe /wəʊ/ n aflicción f, triste. **~begone** /'wəʊbɪgɒn/ a desconsolado

woke, **woken** /wəʊk, 'wəʊkən/ see **wake**¹

wolf /wʊlf/ n (pl **wolves**) lobo m. **~ cry ~** gritar al lobo. —vt zamparse. **~-whistle** n silbido m de admiración

woman /'wʊmən/ n (pl **women**) mujer f. **single ~** soltera f. **~ize** /'wʊmənaɪz/ vi ser mujeriego. **~ly** a femenino

womb /wuːm/ n matriz f

women /'wɪmɪn/ npl see **woman**. **~folk** /'wɪmɪnfəʊk/ npl mujeres fpl. **~'s lib** n movimiento m de liberación de la mujer

won /wʌn/ see **win**

wonder /'wʌndə(r)/ n maravilla f; (bewilderment) asombro m. **no ~** no es de extrañarse (that que). —vi admirarse; (reflect) preguntarse

wonderful /'wʌndəfl/ a maravilloso. **~ly** adv maravillosamente

won't /wəʊnt/ = **will not**

woo /wuː/ vt cortejar

wood /wʊd/ n madera f; (for burning) leña f; (area) bosque m; (in bowls) bola f. **out of the ~** (fig) fuera de peligro. **~cutter** /'wʊdkʌtə(r)/ n leñador m. **~ed** a poblado de árboles, boscoso. **~en** a de madera. **~land** n bosque m

woodlouse /'wʊdlaʊs/ n (pl **-lice**) cochinilla f

woodpecker /'wʊdpekə(r)/ n pájaro m carpintero

woodwind /'wʊdwɪnd/ n instrumentos mpl de viento de madera

woodwork /'wʊdwɜːk/ n carpintería f; (in room etc) maderaje m

woodworm /'wʊdwɜːm/ n carcoma f

woody /'wʊdɪ/ a leñoso

wool /wʊl/ n lana f. **pull the ~ over s.o.'s eyes** engañar a uno. **~len** a de lana. **~lens** npl ropa f de lana. **~ly** a (-ier, -iest) de lana; (fig) confuso. —n jersey m

word /wɜːd/ n palabra f; (news) noticia f. **by ~ of mouth** de palabra. **have ~s with** reñir con. **in one ~** en una palabra. **in other ~s** es decir. —vt expresar.

~ing n expresión f, términos mpl. ~perfect a. be ~perfect saber de memoria. ~ processor n procesador m de textos. ~y a prolijo

wore /wɔː(r)/ see **wear**

work /wɜːk/ n trabajo m; (arts) obra f. —vt hacer trabajar; manejar (machine). —vi trabajar; (machine) funcionar; (student) estudiar; (drug etc) tener efecto; (be successful) tener éxito. ~ in introducir(se). ~ off desahogar. ~ out vt resolver; (calculate) calcular; (plan). —vi (succeed) salir bien; (sport) entrenarse. ~ up vt desarrollar. —vi excitarse. ~able /'wɜːkəbl/ a (project) factible. ~aholic /wɜːkə'hɒlik/ n trabajador m obsesivo. ~ed up a agitado. ~er /'wɜːkə(r)/ n trabajador m; (manual) obrero m

workhouse /'wɜːkhaʊs/ n asilo m de pobres

work: ~ing /'wɜːkɪŋ/ a (day) laborable; (clothes etc) de trabajo. —n (mec) funcionamiento m. in ~ing order en estado de funcionamiento. ~ing class n clase f obrera. ~ing-class a de la clase obrera. ~man /'wɜːkmən/ n (pl -men) obrero m. ~manlike /'wɜːkmənlaɪk/ a concienzudo. ~manship n destreza f. ~s npl (building) fábrica f; (mec) mecanismo m. ~shop /'wɜːkʃɒp/ n taller m. ~-to-rule n huelga f de celo

world /wɜːld/ n mundo m. a ~ of enorme. out of this ~ maravilloso. —a mundial. ~ly a mundano. ~-wide a universal

worm /wɜːm/ n lombriz f; (grub) gusano m. —vi. ~ one's way insinuarse. ~eaten a carcomido

worn /wɔːn/ see **wear**. —a gastado. ~-out a gastado; (person) rendido

worried /'wʌrɪd/ a preocupado. ~ier /-ə(r)/ a aprensivo m. ~y /'wʌrɪ/ vt preocupar; (annoy) molestar. —vi preocuparse. —n preocupación f. ~ying a inquietante

worse /wɜːs/ a peor. —adv peor; (more) más. ~ n lo peor. ~n vt/i empeorar

worship /'wɜːʃɪp/ n culto m; (title) señor, su señoría. —vt (pt worshipped) adorar

worst /wɜːst/ a (el) peor. —adv peor. —n lo peor. get the ~ of it llevar la peor parte

worsted /'wʊstɪd/ n estambre m

worth /wɜːθ/ n valor m. —a. be ~ valer. it is ~ trying vale la pena probarlo. it was ~ my while (me) valió la pena. ~less a sin valor. ~while /'wɜːθwaɪl/ a que vale la pena

worthy /'wɜːðɪ/ a meritorio; (respectable) respetable; (laudable) loable

would /wʊd/ v aux. ~ you come here please? ¿quieres venir aquí? ~ you go? ¿irías tú? he ~ come if he could vendría si pudiese. I ~ come every day (used to) venía todos los días. I ~ do it lo haría yo. ~-be a supuesto

wound[1] /wuːnd/ n herida f. —vt herir

wound[2] /waʊnd/ see **wind**[2]

wove, woven /wəʊv, 'wəʊvn/ see **weave**

wow /waʊ/ int ¡caramba!

wrangle /'ræŋgl/ vi reñir. —n riña f

wrap /ræp/ vt (pt wrapped) envolver. be ~ped up in (fig) estar absorto en. —n bata f; (shawl) chal m. ~per /-ə(r)/ n, ~ping n envoltura f

wrath /rɒθ/ n ira f. **~ful** a iracundo

wreath /riːθ/ n (pl -ths /-ðz/) guirnalda f; (for funeral) corona f

wreck /rek/ n ruina f; (sinking) naufragio m; (remains of ship) buque m naufragado. **be a nervous ~** tener los nervios destrozados. —vt hacer naufragar; (fig) arruinar. **~age** n restos mpl; (of building) escombros mpl

wren /ren/ n troglodito m

wrench /rentʃ/ vt arrancar; (twist) torcer. —n arranque m; (tool) llave f inglesa

wrest /rest/ vt arrancar (from a)

wrestl|e /'resl/ vi luchar. **~er** /-ə(r)/ n luchador m. **~ing** n lucha f

wretch /retʃ/ n desgraciado m; (rascal) tunante m & f. **~ed** a miserable; (weather) horrible, de perros; (dog etc) maldito

wriggle /'rɪgl/ vi culebrear. **~ out of** escaparse de. **~ through** deslizarse por. —n serpenteo m

wring /rɪŋ/ vt (pt **wrung**) retorcer. **~ out of** (obtain from) arrancar. **~ing wet** empapado

wrinkle /'rɪŋkl/ n arruga f. —vt arrugar. —vi arrugarse

wrist /rɪst/ n muñeca f. **~watch** n reloj m de pulsera

writ /rɪt/ n decreto m judicial

write /raɪt/ vt/i (pt **wrote**, pp **written**, pres p **writing**) escribir. **~ down** vt anotar. **~ off** vt cancelar; (fig) dar por perdido. **~ up** vt hacer un reportaje de; (keep up to date) poner al día. **~-off** n pérdida f total. **~r** /-ə(r)/ n escritor m; (author) autor m. **~up** n reportaje m; (review) crítica f

writhe /raɪð/ vi retorcerse

writing /'raɪtɪŋ/ n escribir m; (handwriting) letra f. **in ~** por

escrito. **~s** npl obras fpl. **~-paper** n papel m de escribir

written /'rɪtn/ see **write**

wrong /rɒŋ/ a incorrecto; (not just) injusto; (mistaken) equivocado. **be ~** no tener razón; (be mistaken) equivocarse. —adv mal. **go ~** equivocarse; (plan) salir mal; (car etc) estropearse. —n injusticia f; (evil) mal m. **in the ~** equivocado. **~ of** ser injusto con. **~ful** a injusto. **~ly** adv mal; (unfairly) injustamente

wrote /rəʊt/ see **write**

wrought /rɔːt/ a. **~ iron** n hierro m forjado

wrung /rʌŋ/ see **wring**

wry /raɪ/ a (**wryer**, **wryest**) torcido; (smile) forzado. **~ face** n mueca f

X

xenophobia /zenə'fəʊbɪə/ n xenofobia f

Xerox /'zɪərɒks/ n (P) fotocopiadora f. **xerox** n fotocopia f

Xmas /'krɪsməs/ n abbr (Christmas) Navidad f, Navidades fpl

X-ray /'eksreɪ/ n radiografía f. **~s** npl rayos mpl X. —vt radiografiar

xylophone /'zaɪləfəʊn/ n xilófono m

Y

yacht /jɒt/ n yate m. **~ing** n navegación f a vela

yam /jæm/ n ñame m, batata f

yank /jæŋk/ vt (fam) arrancar violentamente

Yankee /'jæŋkɪ/ n (fam) yanqui m & f

yap /jæp/ vi (pt **yapped**) (dog) ladrar

yard[1] /jɑːd/ n (measurement) yarda f (= 0.9144 metre)

yard[2] /jɑːd/ n (patio m; (Amer, garden) jardín m

yardage /'jɑːdɪdʒ/ n metraje m

yardstick /'jɑːdstɪk/ n (fig) criterio m

yarn /jɑːn/ n hilo m; (tale, fam) cuento m

yashmak /'jæʃmæk/ n velo m

yawn /jɔːn/ vi bostezar. — n bostezo m

year /jɪə(r)/ n año m. **be three ~s old** tener tres años. **~-book** n anuario m. **~ling** /'jɜːlɪŋ/ n primal m. **~ly** a anual. — adv anualmente

yearn /jɜːn/ vi. **~ for** anhelar. **~ing** n ansia f

yeast /jiːst/ n levadura f

yell /jel/ vi gritar. — n grito m

yellow /'jeləʊ/ a & n amarillo (m). **~ish** a amarillento

yelp /jelp/ n gañido m. — vi gañir

yen /jen/ n muchas ganas fpl

yeoman /'jəʊmən/ n (pl **-men**). **Y~ of the Guard** alabardero m de la Casa Real

yes /jes/ adv & n sí (m)

yesterday /'jestədeɪ/ adv & n ayer (m). **the day before ~** anteayer m

yet /jet/ adv todavía, aún; (already) ya. **as ~** hasta ahora. — conj sin embargo

yew /juː/ n tejo m

Yiddish /'jɪdɪʃ/ n judeoalemán m

yield /jiːld/ vt producir. — vi ceder. — n producción f; (com) rendimiento m

yoga /'jəʊgə/ n yoga m

yoghurt /'jɒgət/ n yogur m

yoke /jəʊk/ n yugo m; (of garment) canesú m

yokel /'jəʊkl/ n patán m, palurdo m

yolk /jəʊk/ n yema f (de huevo)

yonder /'jɒndə(r)/ adv a lo lejos

you /juː/ pron (familiar form) tú, vos (Arg), (pl) vosotros, vosotras, ustedes (LAm); (polite form) usted, (pl) ustedes; (familiar, object) te, (pl) os, les (LAm); (polite, object) le, la, (pl) les; (familiar, after prep) ti, (pl) vosotros, vosotras, ustedes (LAm); (polite, after prep) usted, (pl) ustedes. **with ~** (familiar) contigo, (pl) con vosotros, con vosotras, con ustedes (LAm); (polite) con usted, (pl) con ustedes; (polite reflexive) consigo. **I know ~** te conozco, le conozco a usted. **you can't smoke here** aquí no se puede fumar

young /jʌŋ/ a (-er, -est) joven. **~ lady** n señorita f. **~ man** n joven m. **her ~ man** (boyfriend) su novio m. **the ~** npl los jóvenes mpl; (of animals) la cría f. **~ster** /'jʌŋstə(r)/ n joven m

your /jɔː(r)/ a (familiar) tu, (pl) vuestro; (polite) su

yours /jɔːz/ poss pron (el) tuyo, (pl) (el) vuestro, el de ustedes (LAm); (polite) el suyo. **a book of ~** un libro tuyo, un libro suyo. **Y~s faithfully**, **Y~s sincerely** le saluda atentamente

yourself /jɔː'self/ pron (pl **yourselves**) (familiar, subject) tú mismo, tú misma, (pl) vosotros mismos, vosotras mismas, ustedes mismos (LAm), ustedes mismas (LAm); (polite, subject) usted mismo, usted misma, (pl) ustedes mismos, ustedes mismas; (familiar, object) te, (pl) os, se (LAm); (polite, object) se; (familiar, after prep) ti, (pl) vosotros, vosotras, ustedes (LAm); (polite, after prep) sí

youth /ju:θ/ *n* (*pl* **youths** /ju:ðz/)
juventud *f*; (*boy*) joven *m*; (*young
people*) jóvenes *mpl*. ∼**ful**. *a*
joven, juvenil. ∼**hostel** *n* albergue *m* para jóvenes

yowl /jaʊl/ *vi* aullar. —*n* aullido
m

Yugoslav /ˈjuːɡəslɑːv/ *a* & *n* yugoslavo (*m*). ∼**ia** /-ˈslɑːvɪə/ *n* Yugoslavia *f*

yule /juːl/ *n*, **yule-tide** /ˈjuːltaɪd/
n (*old use*) Navidades *fpl*

Z

zany /ˈzeɪnɪ/ *a* (-ier, -iest)
estrafalario

zeal /ziːl/ *n* celo *m*

zealot /ˈzelət/ *n* fanático *m*

zealous /ˈzeləs/ *a* entusiasta. ∼**ly**
/ˈzeləslɪ/ *adv* con entusiasmo

zebra /ˈzebrə/ *n* cebra *f*. ∼ **crossing** *n* paso *m* de cebra

zenith /ˈzenɪθ/ *n* cenit *m*

zero /ˈzɪərəʊ/ *n* (*pl* -os) cero *m*

zest /zest/ *n* gusto *m*; (*peel*) cáscara *f*

zigzag /ˈzɪɡzæɡ/ *n* zigzag *m*. —*vi*
(*pt* **zigzagged**) zigzaguear

zinc /zɪŋk/ *n* cinc *m*

Zionis|m /ˈzaɪənɪzəm/ *n* sionismo
m. ∼**t** *n* sionista *m* & *f*

zip /zɪp/ *n* cremallera *f*. —*vt*. ∼
(**up**) cerrar (la cremallera)

Zip code /ˈzɪpkəʊd/ *n* (*Amer*)
código *m* postal

zip fastener /zɪpˈfɑːsnə(r)/ *n* cremallera *f*

zircon /ˈzɜːkən/ *n* circón *m*

zither /ˈzɪðə(r)/ *n* cítara *f*

zodiac /ˈzəʊdɪæk/ *n* zodiaco *m*

zombie /ˈzɒmbɪ/ *n* (*fam*) autómata *m* & *f*

zone /zəʊn/ *n* zona *f*

zoo /zuː/ *n* (*fam*) zoo *m*, jardín *m*
zoológico. ∼**logical** /zəʊə
ˈlɒdʒɪkl/ *a* zoológico

zoolog|ist /zəʊˈɒlədʒɪst/ *n*
zoólogo *m*. ∼**y** /zəʊˈɒlədʒɪ/ *n*
zoología *f*

zoom /zuːm/ *vi* ir a gran velocidad. ∼ **in** (*photo*) acercarse
rápidamente. ∼ **past** pasar zum-
bando. ∼ **lens** *n* zoom *m*

Zulu /ˈzuːluː/ *n* zulú *m* & *f*

Numbers · Números

zero	0	cero
one (first)	1	uno (primero)
two (second)	2	dos (segundo)
three (third)	3	tres (tercero)
four (fourth)	4	cuatro (cuarto)
five (fifth)	5	cinco (quinto)
six (sixth)	6	seis (sexto)
seven (seventh)	7	siete (séptimo)
eight (eighth)	8	ocho (octavo)
nine (ninth)	9	nueve (noveno)
ten (tenth)	10	diez (décimo)
eleven (eleventh)	11	once (undécimo)
twelve (twelfth)	12	doce (duodécimo)
thirteen (thirteenth)	13	trece (decimotercero)
fourteen (fourteenth)	14	catorce (decimocuarto)
fifteen (fifteenth)	15	quince (decimoquinto)
sixteen (sixteenth)	16	dieciséis (decimosexto)
seventeen (seventeenth)	17	diecisiete (decimoséptimo)
eighteen (eighteenth)	18	dieciocho (decimoctavo)
nineteen (nineteenth)	19	diecinueve (decimonoveno)
twenty (twentieth)	20	veinte (vigésimo)
twenty-one (twenty-first)	21	veintiuno (vigésimo primero)
twenty-two (twenty-second)	22	veintidós (vigésimo segundo)
twenty-three (twenty-third)	23	veintitrés (vigésimo tercero)
twenty-four (twenty-fourth)	24	veinticuatro (vigésimo cuarto)
twenty-five (twenty-fifth)	25	veinticinco (vigésimo quinto)
twenty-six (twenty-sixth)	26	veintiséis (vigésimo sexto)

thirty (thirtieth)	30	treinta (trigésimo)
thirty-one (thirty-first)	31	treinta y uno (trigésimo primero)
forty (fortieth)	40	cuarenta (cuadragésimo)
fifty (fiftieth)	50	cincuenta (quincuagésimo)
sixty (sixtieth)	60	sesenta (sexagésimo)
seventy (seventieth)	70	setenta (septuagésimo)
eighty (eightieth)	80	ochenta (octogésimo)
ninety (ninetieth)	90	noventa (nonagésimo)
a/one hundred (hundredth)	100	cien (centésimo)
a/one hundred and one (hundred and first)	101	ciento uno (centésimo primero)
two hundred (two hundredth)	200	doscientos (ducentésimo)
three hundred (three hundredth)	300	trescientos (tricentésimo)
four hundred (four hundredth)	400	cuatrocientos (cuadringentésimo)
five hundred (five hundredth)	500	quinientos (quingentésimo)
six hundred (six hundredth)	600	seiscientos (sexcentésimo)
seven hundred (seven hundredth)	700	setecientos (septingentésimo)
eight hundred (eight hundredth)	800	ochocientos (octingentésimo)
nine hundred (nine hundredth)	900	novecientos (noningentésimo)
a/one thousand (thousandth)	1000	mil (milésimo)
two thousand (two thousandth)	2000	dos mil (dos milésimo)
a/one million (millionth)	1,000,000	un millón (millonésimo)

Spanish Verbs · Verbos españoles

Regular verbs:
in -ar (*e.g.* **comprar**)
Present; compr|o, ~es, ~a,
~amos, ~áis, ~an
Future: comprar|é, ~ás, ~á,
~emos, ~éis, ~án
Imperfect: compr|aba, ~abas,
~aba, ~ábamos, ~abais,
~aban
Preterite: compr|é, ~aste, ~ó,
~amos, ~asteis, ~aron
Present subjunctive: compr|e,
~es, ~e, ~emos, ~éis, ~en
Imperfect subjunctive: compr|ara,
~aras, ~ara, ~áramos,
~arais, ~aran
compr|ase, ~ases, ~ase,
~ásemos, ~aseis, ~asen
Conditional: comprar|ía, ~ías,
~ía, ~íamos, ~íais, ~ían
Present participle: comprando
Past participle: comprado
Imperative: compra, comprad

in -er (*e.g.* **beber**)
Present: beb|o, ~es, ~e, ~emos,
~éis, ~en
Future: beber|é, ~ás, ~á,
~emos, ~éis, ~án
Imperfect: beb|ía, ~ías, ~ía,
~íamos, ~íais, ~ían
Preterite: beb|í, ~iste, ~ió,
~imos, ~isteis, ~ieron
Present subjunctive: beb|a, ~as,
~a, ~amos, ~áis, ~an
Imperfect subjunctive: beb|iera,
~ieras, ~iera, ~iéramos,
~ierais, ~ieran
beb|iese, ~ieses, ~iese,
~iésemos, ~ieseis, ~iesen
Conditional: beber|ía, ~ías, ~ía,
~íamos, ~íais, ~ían
Present participle: bebiendo
Past participle: bebido
Imperative: bebe, bebed

in -ir (*e.g.* **vivir**)
Present: viv|o, ~es, ~e, ~imos,
~ís, ~en
Future: vivir|é, ~ás, ~á,
~emos, ~éis, ~án
Imperfect: viv|ía, ~ías, ~ía,
~íamos, ~íais, ~ían
Preterite: viv|í, ~iste, ~ió,
~imos, ~isteis, ~ieron
Present subjunctive: viv|a, ~as,
~a, ~amos, ~áis, ~an
Imperfect subjunctive: viv|iera,
~ieras, ~iera, ~iéramos,
~ierais, ~ieran
viv|iese, ~ieses, ~iese,
~iésemos, ~ieseis, ~iesen
Conditional: vivir|ía, ~ías, ~ía,
~íamos, ~íais, ~ían
Present participle: viviendo
Past participle: vivido
Imperative: vive, vivid

Irregular verbs:
[1] **cerrar**
Present: cierro, cierras, cierra,
cerramos, cerráis, cierran
Present subjunctive: cierre,
cierres, cierre, cerremos,
cerréis, cierren
Imperative: cierra, cerrad

[2] **contar, mover**
Present: cuento, cuentas, cuenta,
contamos, contáis, cuentan
muevo, mueves, mueve,
movemos, movéis, mueven
Present subjunctive: cuente,
cuentes, cuente, contemos,
contéis, cuenten
mueva, muevas mueva,
movamos, mováis, muevan
Imperative: cuenta, contad
mueve, moved

[3] jugar

Present: juego, juegas, juega, jugamos, jugáis, juegan
Preterite: jugué, jugaste, jugó, jugamos, jugasteis, jugaron
Present subjunctive: juegue, juegues, juegue, juguemos, juguéis, jueguen

[4] sentir

Present: siento, sientes, siente, sentimos, sentís, sienten
Preterite: sentí, sentiste, sintió, sentimos, sentisteis, sintieron
Present subjunctive: sienta, sientas, sienta, sintamos, sintáis, sientan
Imperfect subjunctive: sint|iera, ~ieras, ~iera, ~iéramos, ~ierais, ~ieran
sint|iese, ~ieses, ~iese, ~iésemos, ~ieseis, ~iesen
Present participle: sintiendo
Imperative: siente, sentid

[5] pedir

Present: pido, pides, pide, pedimos, pedís, piden
Preterite: pedí, pediste, pidió, pedimos, pedisteis, pidieron
Present subjunctive: pid|a, ~as, ~a, ~amos, ~áis, ~an
Imperfect subjunctive: pid|iera, ~ieras, ~iera, ~iéramos, ~ierais, ~ieran
pid|iese, ~ieses, ~iese, ~iésemos, ~ieseis, ~iesen
Present participle: pidiendo
Imperative: pide, pedid

[6] dormir

Present: duermo, duermes, duerme, dormimos, dormís, duermen
Preterite: dormí, dormiste, durmió, dormimos, dormisteis, durmieron

Present subjunctive: duerma, duermas, duerma, durmamos, durmáis, duerman
Imperfect subjunctive: durm|iera, ~ieras, ~iera, ~iéramos, ~ierais, ~ieran
durm|iese, ~ieses, ~iese, ~iésemos, ~ieseis, ~iesen
Present participle: durmiendo
Imperative: duerme, dormid

[7] dedicar

Preterite: dediqué, dedicaste, dedicó, dedicamos, dedicasteis, dedicaron
Present subjunctive: dediqu|e, ~ues, ~e, ~emos, ~éis, ~en

[8] delinquir

Present: delinco, delinques, delinque, delinquimos, delinquís, delinquen
Present subjunctive: delinc|a, ~as, ~a, ~amos, ~áis, ~an

[9] vencer, esparcir

Present: venzo, vences, vence, vencemos, vencéis, vencen
esparzo, esparces, esparce, esparcimos, esparcís, esparcen
Present subjunctive: venz|a, ~as, ~a, ~amos, ~áis, ~an
esparz|a, ~as, ~a, ~amos, ~áis, ~an

[10] rechazar

Preterite: rechacé, rechazaste, rechazó, rechazamos, rechazasteis, rechazaron
Present subjunctive: rechac|e, ~es, ~e, ~emos, ~éis, ~en

[11] conocer, lucir

Present: conozco, conoces, conoce, conocemos, conocéis, conocen
luzco, luces, luce, lucimos, lucís, lucen

Present subjunctive: conozc|a, ~as, ~a, ~amos, ~áis, ~an luzc|a, ~as, ~a, ~amos, ~áis, ~an

[12] pagar
Preterite: pagué, pagaste, pagó, pagamos, pagasteis, pagaron
Present subjunctive: pagu|e, ~es, ~e, ~emos, ~éis, ~en

[13] distinguir
Present: distingo, distingues, distingue, distinguimos, distinguís, distinguen
Present subjunctive: disting|a, ~as, ~a, ~amos, ~áis, ~an

[14] acoger, afligir
Present: acojo, acoges, acoge, acogemos, acogéis, acogen aflijo, afliges, aflige, afligimos, afligís, afligen
Present subjunctive: acoj|a, ~as, ~a, ~amos, ~áis, ~an aflij|a, ~as, ~a, ~amos, ~áis, ~an

[15] averiguar
Preterite: averigüé, averiguaste, averiguó, averiguamos, averiguasteis, averiguaron
Present subjunctive: averigü|e, ~es, ~e, ~emos, ~éis, ~en

[16] agorar
Present: agüero, agüeras, agüera, agoramos, agoráis, agüeran
Present subjunctive: agüere, agüeres, agüere, agoremos, agoréis, agüeren
Imperative: agüera, agorad

[17] huir
Present: huyo, huyes, huye, huimos, huís, huyen
Preterite: huí, huiste, huyó, huimos, huisteis, huyeron

Present subjunctive: huy|a, ~as, ~a, ~amos, ~áis, ~an
Imperfect subjunctive: huy|era, ~eras, ~era, ~éramos, ~erais, ~eran
huy|ese, ~eses, ~ese, ~ésemos, ~eseis, ~esen
Present participle: huyendo

[18] creer
Preterite: creí, creíste, creyó, creímos, creísteis, creyeron
Imperfect subjunctive: crey|era, ~eras, ~era, ~éramos, ~erais, ~eran
crey|ese, ~eses, ~ese, ~ésemos, ~eseis, ~esen
Present participle: creyendo
Past participle: creído

[19] argüir
Present: arguyo, arguyes, arguye, argüimos, argüís, arguyen
Preterite: argüí, argüiste, arguyó, argüimos, argüisteis, arguyeron
Present subjunctive: arguy|a, ~as, ~a, ~amos, ~áis, ~an
Imperfect subjunctive: arguy|era, ~eras, ~era, ~éramos, ~erais, ~eran
arguy|ese, ~eses, ~ese, ~ésemos, ~eseis, ~esen
Present participle: arguyendo
Imperative: arguye, argüid

[20] vaciar
Present: vacío, vacías, vacía, vaciamos, vaciáis, vacían
Present subjunctive: vacíe, vacíes, vacíe, vaciemos, vaciéis, vacíen
Imperative: vacía, vaciad

[21] acentuar
Present: acentúo, acentúas, acentúa, acentuamos, acentuáis, acentúan

Present subjunctive: acentúe,
acentúes, acentúe, acentuemos,
acentuéis, acentúen
Imperative: acentúa, acentuad

[22] ateñer, engullir
Preterite: atañí, ~aste, ~ó,
~amos, ~asteis, ~eron
engullí ~iste, ~ó, ~imos,
~isteis, ~eron
Imperfect subjunctive: atañera,
~eras, ~era, ~éramos,
~erais, ~eran
atañese, ~eses, ~ese,
~ésemos, ~eseis, ~esen
engullera, ~eras, ~era,
~éramos, ~erais, ~eran
engullese, ~eses, ~ese,
~ésemos, ~eseis, ~esen
Present participle: atañendo
engullendo

[23] aislar, aullar
Present: aíslo, aíslas, aísla,
aislamos, aisláis, aíslan
aúllo, aúllas, aúlla, aullamos
aulláis, aúllan
Present subjunctive: aísle, aísles,
aísle, aislemos, aisléis, aíslen
aúlle, aúlles, aúlle, aullemos,
aulléis, aúllen
Imperative: aísla, aislad
aúlla, aullad

[24] abolir, garantir
Present: abolimos, abolís
garantimos, garantís
Present subjunctive: not used
Imperative: abolid
garantid

[25] andar
Preterite: anduve, ~iste, ~o,
~imos, ~isteis, ~ieron
Imperfect subjunctive:
anduviera, ~ieras, ~iera,
~iéramos, ~ierais, ~ieran
anduviese, ~ieses, ~iese,
~iésemos, ~ieseis, ~iesen

[26] dar
Present: doy, das, da, damos, dais,
dan
Preterite: di, diste, dio, dimos
disteis, dieron
Present subjunctive: dé, des, dé,
demos, deis, den
Imperfect subjunctive: diera,
dieras, diera, diéramos, dierais,
dieran
diese, dieses, diese, diésemos,
dieseis, diesen

[27] estar
Present: estoy, estás, está,
estamos, estáis, están
Preterite: estuve, ~iste, ~o,
~imos, ~isteis, ~ieron
Present subjunctive: esté, estés,
esté, estemos, estéis, estén
Imperfect subjunctive: estuviera,
~ieras, ~iera, ~iéramos,
~ierais, ~ieran
estuviese, ~ieses, ~iese,
~iésemos, ~ieseis, ~iesen
Imperative: está, estad

[28] caber
Present: quepo, cabes, cabe,
cabemos, cabéis, caben
Future: cabré, ~ás, ~á, ~emos,
~éis, ~án
Preterite: cupe, ~iste, ~o,
~imos, ~isteis, ~ieron
Present subjunctive: quepa, ~as,
~a, ~amos, ~áis, ~an
Imperfect subjunctive: cupiera,
~ieras, ~iera, ~iéramos,
~ierais, ~ieran
cupiese, ~ieses, ~iese,
~iésemos, ~ieseis, ~iesen
Conditional: cabría, ~ías, ~ía,
~íamos, ~íais, ~ían

[29] caer
Present: caigo, caes, cae, caemos,
caéis, caen
Preterite: caí, caiste, cayó,
caímos, caísteis, cayeron

Present subjunctive: caig|a, ~as, ~a, ~amos, ~áis, ~an
Imperfect subjunctive: cay|era, ~eras, ~era, ~éramos, ~erais, ~eran
cay|ese, ~eses, ~ese, ~ésemos, ~eseis, ~esen
Present participle: cayendo
Past participle: caído

[30] **haber**
Present: he, has, ha, hemos, habéis, han
Future: habr|é ~ás, ~á, ~emos, ~éis, ~án
Preterite: hub|e, ~iste, ~o, ~imos, ~isteis, ~ieron
Present subjunctive: hay|a, ~as, ~a, ~amos, ~áis, ~an
Imperfect subjunctive: hub|iera, ~ieras, ~iera, ~iéramos, ~ierais, ~ieran
hub|iese, ~ieses, ~iese, ~iésemos, ~ieseis, ~iesen
Conditional: habr|ía, ~ías, ~ía, ~íamos, ~íais, ~ían
Imperative: habe, habed

[31] **hacer**
Present: hago, haces, hace, hacemos, hacéis, hacen
Future: har|é, ~ás, ~á, ~emos, ~éis, ~án
Preterite: hice, hiciste, hizo, hicimos, hicisteis, hicieron
Present subjunctive: hag|a, ~as, ~a, ~amos, ~áis, ~an
Imperfect subjunctive: hic|iera, ~ieras, ~iera, ~iéramos, ~ierais, ~ieran
hic|iese, ~ieses, ~iese, ~iésemos, ~ieseis, ~iesen
Conditional: har|ía, ~ías, ~ía, ~íamos, ~íais, ~ían
Past participle: hecho
Imperative: haz, haced

[32] **placer**
Preterite: plació/plugo

Present subjunctive: plazca
Imperfect subjunctive: placiera/pluguiera
placiese/pluguiese

[33] **poder**
Present: puedo, puedes, puede, podemos, podéis, pueden
Future: podr|é, ~ás, ~á, ~emos, ~éis, ~án
Preterite: pud|e, ~iste, ~o, ~imos, ~isteis, ~ieron
Present subjunctive: pueda, puedas, pueda, podamos, podáis, puedan
Imperfect subjunctive: pud|iera, ~ieras, ~iera, ~iéramos, ~ierais, ~ieran
pud|iese, ~ieses, ~iese, ~iésemos, ~ieseis, ~iesen
Conditional: podr|ía, ~ías, ~ía, ~íamos, ~íais, ~ían
Past participle: pudiendo

[34] **poner**
Present: pongo, pones, pone, ponemos, ponéis, ponen
Future: pondr|é, ~ás, ~á, ~emos, ~éis, ~án
Preterite: pus|e, ~iste, ~o, ~imos, ~isteis, ~ieron
Present subjunctive: pong|a, ~as, ~a, ~amos, ~áis, ~an
Imperfect subjunctive: pus|iera, ~ieras, ~iera, ~iéramos, ~ierais, ~ieran
pus|iese, ~ieses, ~iese, ~iésemos, ~ieseis, ~iesen
Conditional: pondr|ía, ~ías, ~ía, ~íamos, ~íais, ~ían
Past participle: puesto
Imperative: pon, poned

[35] **querer**
Present: quiero, quieres, quiere, queremos, queréis, quieren
Future: querr|é, ~ás, ~á, ~emos, ~éis, ~án

Preterite: quis|e, ~iste, ~o,
~imos, ~isteis, ~ieron
Present subjunctive: quiera,
quieras, quiera, queramos,
queráis, quieran
Imperfect subjunctive: quis|iera,
~ieras, ~iera, ~iéramos,
~ierais, ~ieran
quis|iese, ~ieses, ~iese,
~iésemos, ~ieseis, ~iesen
Conditional: querr|ía, ~ías, ~ía,
~íamos, ~íais, ~ían
Imperative: quiere, quered

[36] **raer**
Present: raigo/rayo, raes, rae,
raemos, raéis, raen
Preterite: raí, raíste, rayó, raímos,
raísteis, rayeron
Present subjunctive: raig|a, ~as,
~a, ~amos, ~áis, ~an
ray|a, ~as, ~a, ~amos, ~áis,
~an
Imperfect subjunctive: ray|era,
~eras, ~era, ~éramos,
~erais, ~eran
ray|ese, ~eses, ~ese,
~ésemos, ~eseis, ~esen
Present participle: rayendo
Past participle: raído

[37] **roer**
Present: roo/roigo/royo, roes,
roe, roemos, roéis, roen
Preterite: roí, roíste, royó, roímos,
roísteis, royeron
Present subjunctive:
roa/roiga/roya, roas, roa,
roamos, roáis, roan
Imperfect subjunctive: roy|era,
~eras, ~era, ~éramos,
~erais, ~eran
roy|ese, ~eses, ~ese,
~ésemos, ~eseis, ~esen
Present participle: royendo
Past participle: roído

[38] **saber**
Present: sé, sabes, sabe, sabemos,
sabéis, saben
Future: sabr|é, ~ás, ~á, ~emos,
~éis, ~án
Preterite: sup|e, ~iste, ~o,
~imos, ~isteis, ~ieron
Present subjunctive: sep|a, ~as,
~a, ~amos, ~áis, ~an
Imperfect subjunctive: sup|iera,
~ieras, ~iera, ~iéramos,
~ierais, ~ieran
sup|iese, ~ieses, ~iese,
~iésemos, ~ieseis, ~iesen
Conditional: sabr|ía, ~ías, ~ía,
~íamos, ~íais, ~ían

[39] **ser**
Present: soy, eres, es, somos, sois,
son
Imperfect: era, eras, era, éramos,
erais, eran
Preterite: fui, fuiste, fue, fuimos,
fuisteis, fueron
Present subjunctive: se|a, ~as,
~a, ~amos, ~áis, ~an
Imperfect subjunctive: fu|era,
~eras, ~era, ~éramos,
~erais, ~eran
fu|ese, ~eses, ~ese, ~ésemos,
~eseis, ~esen
Imperative: sé, sed

[40] **tener**
Present: tengo, tienes, tiene,
tenemos, tenéis, tienen
Future: tendr|é, ~ás, ~á,
~emos, ~éis, ~án
Preterite: tuv|e, ~iste, ~o,
~imos, ~isteis, ~ieron
Present subjunctive: teng|a, ~as,
~a, ~amos, ~áis, ~an
Imperfect subjunctive: tuv|iera,
~ieras, ~iera, ~iéramos,
~ierais, ~ieran
tuv|iese, ~ieses, ~iese,
~iésemos, ~ieseis, ~iesen

Conditional: tendría, ~ías, ~ía,
~íamos, ~íais, ~ían
Imperative: ten, tened

[41] traer
Present: traigo, traes, trae,
traemos, traéis, traen
Preterite: traje, ~iste, ~o,
~imos, ~isteis, ~eron
Present subjunctive: traiga, ~as,
~a, ~amos, ~áis, ~an
Imperfect subjunctive: trajera,
~eras, ~era, ~éramos,
~erais, ~eran
trajese, ~eses, ~ese,
~ésemos, ~eseis, ~esen
Present participle: trayendo
Past participle: traído

[42] valer
Present: valgo, vales, vale,
valemos, valéis, valen
Future: valdré, ~ás, ~á,
~emos, ~éis, ~án
Present subjunctive: valga, ~as,
~a, ~amos ~áis, ~an
Conditional: valdría, ~ías, ~ía,
~íamos, ~íais, ~ían
Imperative: val/vale, valed

[43] ver
Present: veo, ves, ve, vemos, véis,
ven
Imperfect: veía, ~ías, ~ía,
~íamos, ~íais, ~ían
Preterite: vi, viste, vio, vimos,
visteis, vieron
Present subjunctive: vea, ~as,
~a, ~amos, ~áis, ~an
Past participle: visto

[44] yacer
Present: yazco/yazgo/yago,
yaces, yave, yacemos, yacéis,
yacen
Present subjunctive:
yazca/yazga/yaga, yazcas,

yazca, yazcamos, yazcáis,
yazcan
Imperative: yace/yaz, yaced

[45] asir
Present: asgo, ases, ase, asimos,
asís, asen
Present subjunctive: asga, ~as,
~a, ~amos, ~áis, ~an

[46] decir
Present: digo, dices, dice,
decimos, decís, dicen
Future: diré, ~ás, ~á, ~emos,
~éis, ~án
Preterite: dije, ~iste, ~o,
~imos, ~isteis, ~eron
Present subjunctive: diga, ~as,
~a, ~amos, ~áis, ~an
Imperfect subjunctive: dijera,
~eras, ~era, ~éramos,
~erais, ~eran
dijese, ~eses, ~ese, ~ésemos,
~eseis, ~esen
Conditional: diría, ~ías, ~ía,
~íamos, ~íais, ~ían
Present participle: dicho
Imperative: di, decid

[47] reducir
Present: reduzco, reduces,
reduce, reducimos, reducís,
reducen
Preterite: reduje, ~iste, ~o,
~imos, ~isteis, ~eron
Present subjunctive: reduzca,
~as, ~a, ~amos, ~áis, ~an
Imperfect subjunctive: redujera,
~eras, ~era, ~éramos,
~erais, ~eran
redujese, ~eses, ~ese,
~ésemos, ~eseis, ~esen

[48] erguir
Present: irgo, irgues, irgue,
erguimos, erguís, irguen
yergo, yergues, yergue,
erguimos, erguís, yerguen

Preterite: erguí, erguiste, irguió, erguimos, erguisteis, irguieron
Present subjunctive: irg|a, ∼as, ∼a, ∼amos, ∼áis, ∼an
yerg|a, ∼as, ∼a, ∼amos, ∼áis, ∼an
Imperfect subjunctive: irgu|iera, ∼ieras, ∼iera, ∼iéramos, ∼ierais, ∼ieran
irgu|iese, ∼ieses, ∼iese, ∼iésemos, ∼ieseis, ∼iesen
Present participle: irguiendo
Imperative: irgue/yergue, erguid

[49] ir

Present: voy, vas, va, vamos, vais, van
Imperfect: iba, ibas, iba, íbamos, ibais, iban
Preterite: fui, fuiste, fue, fuimos, fuisteis, fueron
Present subjunctive: vay|a, ∼as, ∼a, ∼amos, ∼áis, ∼an
Imperfect subjunctive: fu|era, ∼eras, ∼era, ∼éramos, ∼erais, ∼eran
fu|ese, ∼eses, ∼ese, ∼ésemos, ∼eseis, ∼esen
Present participle: yendo
Imperative: ve, id

[50] oír

Present: oigo, oyes, oye, oímos, oís, oyen
Preterite: oí, oíste, oyó, oímos, oísteis, oyeron
Present subjunctive: oig|a, ∼as, ∼a, ∼amos, ∼áis, ∼an
Imperfect subjunctive: oy|era, ∼eras, ∼era, ∼éramos, ∼erais, ∼eran
oy|ese, ∼eses, ∼ese, ∼ésemos, ∼eseis, ∼esen

Present participle: oyendo
Past participle: oído
Imperative: oye, oíd

[51] reír

Present: río, ríes, ríe, reímos, reís, ríen
Preterite: reí, reíste, rió, reímos, reísteis, rieron
Present subjunctive: ría, rías, ría, riamos, riáis, rían
Present participle: riendo
Past participle: reído
Imperative: ríe, reíd

[52] salir

Present: salgo, sales, sale, salimos, salís, salen
Future: saldr|é, ∼ás, ∼á, ∼emos, ∼éis, ∼án
Present subjunctive: salg|a, ∼as, ∼a, ∼amos, ∼áis, ∼an
Conditional: saldr|ía, ∼ías, ∼ía, ∼íamos, ∼íais, ∼ían
Imperative: sal, salid

[53] venir

Present: vengo, vienes, viene, venimos, venís, vienen
Future: vendr|é, ∼ás, ∼á, ∼emos, ∼éis, ∼án
Preterite: vin|e, ∼iste, ∼o, ∼imos, ∼isteis, ∼ieron
Present subjunctive: veng|a, ∼as, ∼a, ∼amos, ∼áis, ∼an
Imperfect subjunctive: vin|iera, ∼ieras, ∼iera, ∼iéramos, ∼ierais, ∼ieran
vin|iese, ∼ieses, ∼iese, ∼iésemos, ∼ieseis, ∼iesen
Conditional: vendr|ía, ∼ías, ∼ía, ∼íamos, ∼íais, ∼ían
Present participle: viniendo
Imperative: ven, venid

Verbos Irregulares Ingleses

Infinitivo	*Pretérito*	*Participio pasado*
arise	arose	arisen
awake	awoke	awoken
be	was	been
bear	bore	borne
beat	beat	beaten
become	became	become
befall	befell	befallen
beget	begot	begotten
begin	began	begun
behold	beheld	beheld
bend	bent	bent
beset	beset	beset
bet	bet, betted	bet, betted
bid	bade, bid	bidden, bid
bind	bound	bound
bite	bit	bitten
bleed	bled	bled
blow	blew	blown
break	broke	broken
breed	bred	bred
bring	brought	brought
broadcast	broadcast(ed)	broadcast
build	built	built
burn	burnt, burned	burnt, burned
burst	burst	burst
buy	bought	bought
cast	cast	cast
catch	caught	caught
choose	chose	chosen
cleave	clove, cleft, cleaved	cloven, cleft, cleaved
cling	clung	clung
clothe	clothed, clad	clothed, clad
come	came	come
cost	cost	cost
creep	crept	crept
crow	crowed, crew	crowed
cut	cut	cut
deal	dealt	dealt
dig	dug	dug
do	did	done
draw	drew	drawn
dream	dreamt, dreamed	dreamt, dreamed
drink	drank	drunk
drive	drove	driven
dwell	dwelt	dwelt

Infinitivo	Pretérito	Participio pasado
eat	ate	eaten
fall	fell	fallen
feed	fed	fed
feel	felt	felt
fight	fought	fought
find	found	found
flee	fled	fled
fling	flung	flung
fly	flew	flown
forbear	forbore	forborne
forbid	forbad(e)	forbidden
forecast	forecast(ed)	forecast(ed)
foresee	foresaw	foreseen
foretell	foretold	foretold
forget	forgot	forgotten
forgive	forgave	forgiven
forsake	forsook	forsaken
freeze	froze	frozen
gainsay	gainsaid	gainsaid
get	got	got
give	gave	given
go	went	gone
grind	ground	ground
grow	grew	grown
hang	hung, hanged	hung, hanged
have	had	had
hear	heard	heard
hew	hewed	hewn, hewed
hide	hid	hidden
hit	hit	hit
hold	held	held
hurt	hurt	hurt
inlay	inlaid	inlaid
keep	kept	kept
kneel	knelt	knelt
knit	knitted, knit	knitted, knit
know	knew	known
lay	laid	laid
lead	led	led
lean	leaned, leant	leaned, leant
leap	leaped, leapt	leaped, leapt
learn	learned, learnt	learned, learnt
leave	left	left
lend	lent	lent
let	let	let
lie	lay	lain
light	lit, lighted	lit, lighted
lose	lost	lost

Infinitivo	*Pretérito*	*Participio pasado*
make	made	made
mean	meant	meant
meet	met	met
mislay	mislaid	mislaid
mislead	misled	misled
misspell	misspelt	misspelt
mistake	mistook	mistaken
misunderstand	misunderstood	misunderstood
mow	mowed	mown
outbid	outbid	outbid
outdo	outdid	outdone
outgrow	outgrew	outgrown
overcome	overcame	overcome
overdo	overdid	overdone
overhang	overhung	overhung
overhear	overheard	overheard
override	overrode	overridden
overrun	overran	overrun
oversee	oversaw	overseen
overshoot	overshot	overshot
oversleep	overslept	overslept
overtake	overtook	overtaken
overthrow	overthrew	overthrown
partake	partook	partaken
pay	paid	paid
prove	proved	proved, proven
put	put	put
quit	quitted, quit	quitted, quit
read /ri:d/	read /red/	read /red/
rebuild	rebuilt	rebuilt
redo	redid	redone
rend	rent	rent
repay	repaid	repaid
rewrite	rewrote	rewritten
rid	rid	rid
ride	rode	ridden
ring	rang	rung
rise	rose	risen
run	ran	run
saw	sawed	sawn, sawed
say	said	said
see	saw	seen
seek	sought	sought
sell	sold	sold
send	sent	sent
set	set	set
sew	sewed	sewn, sewed
shake	shook	shaken

Infinitivo	Pretérito	Participio pasado
shear	sheared	shorn, sheared
shed	shed	shed
shine	shone	shone
shoe	shod	shod
shoot	shot	shot
show	showed	shown, showed
shrink	shrank	shrunk
shut	shut	shut
sing	sang	sung
sink	sank	sunk
sit	sat	sat
slay	slew	slain
sleep	slept	slept
slide	slid	slid
sling	slung	slung
slit	slit	slit
smell	smelt, smelled	smelt, smelled
smite	smote	smitten
sow	sowed	sown, sowed
speak	spoke	spoken
speed	speeded, sped	speeded, sped
spell	spelt, spelled	spelt, spelled
spend	spent	spent
spill	spilt, spilled	spilt, spilled
spin	spun	spun
spit	spat	spat
split	split	split
spoil	spoilt, spoiled	spoilt, spoiled
spread	spread	spread
spring	sprang	sprung
stand	stood	stood
steal	stole	stolen
stick	stuck	stuck
sting	stung	stung
stink	stank, stunk	stunk
strew	strewed	strewn, strewed
stride	strode	stridden
strike	struck	struck
string	strung	strung
strive	strove	striven
swear	swore	sworn
sweep	swept	swept
swell	swelled	swollen, swelled
swim	swam	swum
swing	swung	swung
take	took	taken
teach	taught	taught
tear	tore	torn

Infinitivo	*Pretérito*	*Participio pasado*
tell	told	told
think	thought	thought
thrive	thrived, throve	thrived, thriven
throw	threw	thrown
thrust	thrust	thrust
tread	trod	trodden, trod
unbend	unbent	unbent
undergo	underwent	undergone
understand	understood	understood
undertake	undertook	undertaken
undo	undid	undone
upset	upset	upset
wake	woke, waked	woken, waked
waylay	waylaid	waylaid
wear	wore	worn
weave	wove	woven
weep	wept	wept
win	won	won
wind	wound	wound
withdraw	withdrew	withdrawn
withhold	withheld	withheld
withstand	withstood	withstood
wring	wrung	wrung
write	wrote	written